Lecture Notes in Artificial Intelligence   11908

Subseries of Lecture Notes in Computer Science

Series Editors

Randy Goebel
  University of Alberta, Edmonton, Canada
Yuzuru Tanaka
  Hokkaido University, Sapporo, Japan
Wolfgang Wahlster
  DFKI and Saarland University, Saarbrücken, Germany

Founding Editor

Jörg Siekmann
  DFKI and Saarland University, Saarbrücken, Germany

More information about this series at http://www.springer.com/series/1244

Ulf Brefeld · Elisa Fromont ·
Andreas Hotho · Arno Knobbe ·
Marloes Maathuis · Céline Robardet (Eds.)

Machine Learning and Knowledge Discovery in Databases

European Conference, ECML PKDD 2019
Würzburg, Germany, September 16–20, 2019
Proceedings, Part III

 Springer

Editors
Ulf Brefeld
Leuphana University
Lüneburg, Germany

Elisa Fromont (iD)
IRISA/Inria
Rennes, France

Andreas Hotho (iD)
University of Würzburg
Würzburg, Germany

Arno Knobbe (iD)
Leiden University
Leiden, the Netherlands

Marloes Maathuis (iD)
ETH Zurich
Zurich, Switzerland

Céline Robardet (iD)
Institut National des Sciences Appliquées
Villeurbanne, France

ISSN 0302-9743 ISSN 1611-3349 (electronic)
Lecture Notes in Artificial Intelligence
ISBN 978-3-030-46132-4 ISBN 978-3-030-46133-1 (eBook)
https://doi.org/10.1007/978-3-030-46133-1

LNCS Sublibrary: SL7 – Artificial Intelligence

This Springer imprint is published by the registered company Springer Nature Switzerland AG
The registered company address is: Gewerbestrasse 11, 6330 Cham, Switzerland

Preface

We are delighted to introduce the proceedings of the 2019 edition of the European Conference on Machine Learning and Principles and Practice of Knowledge Discovery in Databases (ECML PKDD 2019). ECML PKDD is an annual conference that provides an international forum for the latest research in all areas related to machine learning and knowledge discovery in databases, including innovative applications. It is the premier European machine learning and data mining conference and builds upon a very successful series of ECML PKDD conferences.

ECML PKDD 2019 was held in Würzburg, Germany, during September 16–20, 2019. The conference attracted over 830 participants from 48 countries. It also received substantial attention from industry, both through sponsorship and participation at the conference.

The main conference program consisted of presentations and posters of 130 accepted papers and 5 keynote talks by the following distinguished speakers: Sumit Gulwani (Microsoft Research), Aude Billard (EPFL), Indrė Žliobaitė (University of Helsinki), Maria Florina Balcan (Carnegie Mellon University), and Tinne Tuytelaars (KU Leuven). In addition, there were 24 workshops, 8 tutorials, and 4 discovery challenges.

Papers were organized in three different tracks:

- Research Track: research or methodology papers from all areas in machine learning, knowledge discovery, and data mining
- Applied Data Science Track: papers on novel applications of machine learning, data mining, and knowledge discovery to solve real-world use cases, thereby bridging the gap between practice and current theory
- Journal Track: papers that were published in special issues of the journals *Machine Learning* and *Data Mining and Knowledge Discovery*

We received a record number of 733 submissions for the Research and Applied Data Science Tracks combined. We accepted 130 (18%) of these: 102 papers in the Research Track and 28 papers in the Applied Data Science Track. In addition, there were 32 papers from the Journal Track. All in all, the high-quality submissions allowed us to put together a very rich and exciting program.

For 60% of accepted Research Track and Applied Data Science Track papers, accompanying software and/or data were made available. These papers are flagged as Reproducible Research (RR) papers in the proceedings. RR flags, in use since 2016 in the ECML PKDD conference series, underline the importance given to RR in our community.

The Awards Committee selected research papers that were considered to be of exceptional quality and worthy of special recognition:

- Data Mining Best Student Paper Award: "FastPoint: Scalable Deep Point Processes" by Ali Caner Türkmen, Yuyang Wang, and Alexander J. Smola

- Machine Learning Best Student Paper Award: "Agnostic feature selection" by Guillaume Doquet and Michèle Sebag
- Test of Time Award for highest impact paper from ECML PKDD 2009: "Classifier Chains for Multi-label Classification" by Jesse Read, Bernhard Pfahringer, Geoff Holmes, and Eibe Frank

Besides the strong scientific program, ECML PKDD 2019 offered many opportunities to socialize and to get to know Würzburg. We mention the opening ceremony at the Neubau Church, the opening reception at the Residence Palace, the boat trip from Veitshöchheim to Würzburg, the gala dinner at the Congress Center, the poster session at the New University, and the poster session at the Residence Palace Wine Cellar. There were also social events for subgroups of participants, such as the PhD Forum, in which PhD students interacted with their peers and received constructive feedback on their research progress, and the Women in Science Lunch, in which junior and senior women met and discussed challenges and opportunities for women in science and technology.

We would like to thank all participants, authors, reviewers, area chairs, and organizers of workshops and tutorials for their contributions that helped make ECML PKDD 2019 a great success. Special thanks go to the University of Würzburg, especially to Lena Hettinger and the student volunteers, who did an amazing job. We would also like to thank the ECML PKDD Steering Committee and all sponsors. Finally, we thank Springer and Microsoft for their continuous support with the proceedings and the conference software.

February 2020

Ulf Brefeld
Elisa Fromont
Andreas Hotho
Arno Knobbe
Marloes Maathuis
Céline Robardet

Organization

General Chairs

Élisa Fromont   University of Rennes 1, France
Arno Knobbe   Leiden University, the Netherlands

Program Chairs

Ulf Brefeld   Leuphana University of Lüneburg, Germany
Andreas Hotho   University of Würzburg, Germany
Marloes Maathuis   ETH Zürich, Switzerland
Céline Robardet   INSA-Lyon, France

Journal Track Chairs

Karsten Borgwardt   ETH Zürich, Switzerland
Po-Ling Loh   University of Wisconsin, USA
Evimaria Terzi   Boston University, USA
Antti Ukkonen   University of Helsinki, Finland

Local Chairs

Lena Hettinger   University of Würzburg, Germany
Andreas Hotho   University of Würzburg, Germany
Kristof Korwisi   University of Würzburg, Germany
Marc Erich Latoschik   University of Würzburg, Germany

Proceedings Chairs

Xin Du   Technische Universiteit Eindhoven, the Netherlands
Wouter Duivesteijn   Technische Universiteit Eindhoven, the Netherlands
Sibylle Hess   Technische Universiteit Eindhoven, the Netherlands

Discovery Challenge Chairs

Sergio Escalera   University of Barcelona, Spain
Isabelle Guyon   Paris-Sud University, France

Workshop and Tutorial Chairs

Peggy Cellier   INSA Rennes, France
Kurt Driessens   Maastricht University, the Netherlands

Demonstration Chairs

Martin Atzmüller	Tilburg University, the Netherlands
Emilie Morvant	University of Saint-Etienne, France

PhD Forum Chairs

Tassadit Bouadi	University of Rennes 1, France
Tias Guns	Vrije Universiteit Bruxelles, Belgium

Production, Publicity and Public Relations Chairs

Parisa Kordjamshidi	Tulane University and Florida IHMC, USA
Albrecht Zimmermann	Université de Caen Normandie, France

Awards Committee

Katharina Morik	TU Dortmund, Germany
Geoff Webb	Monash University, Australia

Sponsorship Chairs

Albert Bifet	Télécom ParisTech, France
Heike Trautmann	University of Münster, Germany

Web Chairs

Florian Lautenschlager	University of Würzburg, Germany
Vanessa Breitenbach	University of Würzburg, Germany

ECML PKDD Steering Committee

Michele Berlingerio	IBM Research, Ireland
Albert Bifet	Télécom ParisTech, France
Hendrik Blockeel	KU Leuven, Belgium
Francesco Bonchi	ISI Foundation, Italy
Michelangelo Ceci	University of Bari Aldo Moro, Italy
Sašo Džeroski	Jožef Stefan Institute, Slovenia
Paolo Frasconi	University of Florence, Italy
Thomas Gärtner	University of Nottinghem, UK
Jaakko Hollmen	Aalto University, Finland
Neil Hurley	University College Dublin, Ireland
Georgiana Ifrim	University College Dublin, Ireland
Katharina Morik	TU Dortmund, Germany
Siegfried Nijssen	Université catholique de Louvain, Belgium
Andrea Passerini	University of Trento, Italy

Céline Robardet	INSA-Lyon, France
Michèle Sebag	Université Paris Sud, France
Arno Siebes	Utrecht University, the Netherlands
Myra Spiliopoulou	Magdeburg University, Germany
Jilles Vreeken	Saarland University, Germany

Program Committees

Guest Editorial Board, Journal Track

Annalisa Appice	University of Bari Aldo Moro, Italy
Marta Arias	Universitat Politècnica de Catalunya, Spain
Martin Atzmueller	Tilburg University, the Netherlands
Albert Bifet	Télécom ParisTech, France
Hendrik Blockeel	KU Leuven, Belgium
Toon Calders	University of Antwerp, Belgium
Michelangelo Ceci	University of Bari Aldo Moro, Italy
Loïc Cerf	Universidade Federal de Minas Gerais, Brazil
Nicolas Courty	Université Bretagne Sud, IRISA, France
Bruno Cremilleux	Université de Caen Normandie, France
Tijl De Bie	Ghent University, Belgium
Krzysztof Dembczyński	Poznan University of Technology, Poland
Yagoubi Djamel Edine	StarClay, France
Tapio Elomaa	Tampere University of Technology, Finland
Rémi Emonet	Université de Lyon à Saint Étienne, France
Stefano Ferilli	University of Bari, Italy
Joao Gama	University of Porto, Portugal
Tias Guns	VUB Brussels, Belgium
Amaury Habrard	Université Jean Monnet, France
Xiao He	NEC Laboratories Europe, Germany
Jaakko Hollmén	Aalto University, Finland
Szymon Jaroszewicz	Polish Academy of Sciences, Poland
Alipio Jorge	University of Porto, Portugal
Ajin Joseph	University of Alberta, Canada
Samuel Kaski	Aalto University, Finland
Kristian Kersting	TU Darmstadt, Germany
Dragi Kocev	Jožef Stefan Institute, Slovenia
Peer Kröger	Ludwig-Maximilians-Universität Munich, Germany
Ondrej Kuzelka	KU Leuven, Belgium
Mark Last	Ben-Gurion University of the Negev, Israel
Matthijs van Leeuwen	Leiden University, the Netherlands
Limin Li	Xi'an Jiaotong University, China
Jessica Lin	George Mason University, USA
Christoph Lippert	Hasso Plattner Institute, Germany
Brian Mac Namee	University College Dublin, Ireland

Area Chairs, Research and Applied Data Science Tracks

Fabrizio Angiulli	DIMES, University of Calabria, Italy
Roberto Bayardo	Google Research, USA
Michael Berthold	Universität Konstanz, Germany
Albert Bifet	Université Paris-Saclay, France
Hendrik Blockeel	KU Leuven, Belgium
Francesco Bonchi	ISI Foundation, Italy
Toon Calders	Universiteit Antwerpen, Belgium
Michelangelo Ceci	University of Bari, Italy
Nicolas Courty	IRISA, France
Bruno Crémilleux	Université de Caen Normandie, France
Philippe Cudre-Mauroux	Exascale Infolab, Switzerland
Jesse Davis	KU Leuven, Belgium
Tijl De Bie	Ghent University, Belgium
Tapio Elomaa	Tampere University, Finland
Amir-massoud Farahmand	Vector Institute, Canada
Paolo Frasconi	Università degli Studi di Firenze, Italy
Johannes Fürnkranz	TU Darmstadt, Germany
Patrick Gallinari	LIP6, France
Joao Gama	INESC TEC, LIAAD, Portugal
Aristides Gionis	Aalto University, Finland
Thomas Gärtner	University of Nottingham, UK
Allan Hanbury	Vienna University of Technology, Austria
Jaakko Hollmén	Aalto University, Finland
Eyke Hüllermeier	University of Paderborn, Germany
Alipio Jorge	INESC, Portugal
Marius Kloft	University of Southern California, USA
Nick Koudas	University of Toronto, Canada
Stefan Kramer	Johannes Gutenberg University Mainz, Germany
Sébastien Lefèvre	Université de Bretagne Sud, IRISA, France
Jörg Lücke	Universität Oldenburg, Germany
Giuseppe Manco	ICAR-CNR, Italy
Pauli Miettinen	Max-Planck Institute for Informatics, Germany
Anna Monreale	University of Pisa, Italy
Katharina Morik	TU Dortmund, Germany
Siegfried Nijssen	Université Catholique de Louvain, Belgium
Andrea Passerini	University of Trento, Italy
Mykola Pechenizkiy	TU Eindhoven, the Netherlands
Francois Petitjean	Monash University, Australia
Elmar Rueckert	University Luebeck, Germany
Tom Schaul	DeepMind, UK
Thomas Seidl	LMU Munich, Germany
Arno Siebes	Universiteit Utrecht, the Netherlands
Myra Spiliopoulou	Otto-von-Guericke-University Magdeburg, Germany
Einoshin Suzuki	Kyushu University, Japan

Marc Tommasi	Lille University, France
Celine Vens	KU Leuven, Belgium
Christel Vrain	University of Orleans, France
Jilles Vreeken	CISPA Helmholtz Center for Information Security, Germany
Min-Ling Zhang	Southeast University, Bangladesh
Herke van Hoof	University of Amsterdam, the Netherlands

Program Committee Members, Research and Applied Data Science Tracks

Ehsan Abbasnejad	The University of Adelaide, Australia
Leman Akoglu	CMU, USA
Tristan Allard	University of Rennes, France
Aijun An	York University, Canada
Ali Anaissi	The University of Sydney, Australia
Annalisa Appice	University of Bari, Italy
Paul Assendorp	Werum, Germany
Ira Assent	University of Aarhus, Denmark
Martin Atzmüller	Tilburg University, the Netherlands
Alexandre Aussem	Université Lyon 1, France
Suyash Awate	Indian Institute of Technology (IIT) Bombay, India
Antonio Bahamonde	Universidad de Oviedo, Spain
Jaume Baixeries	Universitat Politècnica de Catalunya, Spain
Vineeth N. Balasubramanian	Indian Institute of Technology, India
Jose Balcazar	Universitat Politecnica de Catalunya, Spain
Sambaran Bandyopadhyay	IBM Research, India
Zhifeng Bao	RMIT University, Australia
Mitra Baratchi	Leiden University, the Netherlands
Sylvio Barbon	Universidade Estadual de Londrina, Brazil
Gianni Barlacchi	FBK Trento, Italy
Martin Becker	Stanford University, USA
Srikanta Bedathur	IIT Delhi, India
Edward Beeching	Inria, France
Vaishak Belle	University of Edinburgh, UK
Andras Benczur	Hungarian Academy of Sciences, Hungary
Daniel Bengs	DIPF, Germany
Petr Berka	University of Economics, Prague, Czech Republic
Marenglen Biba	University of New York in Tirana, Albania
Chris Biemann	University of Hamburg, Germany
Battista Biggio	University of Cagliari, Italy
Thomas Bonald	Télécom ParisTech, France
Gianluca Bontempi	Université Libre de Bruxelles, Belgium
Henrik Bostrom	KTH Royal Institute of Technology, Sweden
Tassadit Bouadi	Université de Rennes 1, France
Ahcène Boubekki	Leuphana University of Lüneburg, Germany
Zied Bouraoui	Université d'Artois, France

Paula Branco	Dalhousie University, Canada
Pavel Brazdil	University of Porto, Portugal
Dariusz Brzezinski	Poznan University of Technology, Poland
Sebastian Buschjager	TU Dortmund, Germany
Ricardo Campello	University of Newcastle, Australia
Brais Cancela	University of A. Coruña, Spain
Francisco Casacuberta	Universidad Politecnica de Valencia, Spain
Remy Cazabet	University of Lyon, France
Peggy Cellier	IRISA, France
Loic Cerf	UFMG, Brazil
Tania Cerquitelli	Politecnico di Torino, Italy
Ricardo Cerri	Federal University of São Carlos, Brazil
Tanmoy Chakraborty	Indraprastha Institute of Information Technology Delhi (IIIT-D), India
Edward Chang	HTC Research & Healthcare, USA
Xiaojun Chang	Monash University, Australia
Jeremy Charlier	University of Luxembourg, Luxembourg
Abon Chaudhuri	Walmart Labs, USA
Keke Chen	Wright State University, USA
Giovanni Chierchia	ESIEE Paris, France
Silvia Chiusano	Politecnico di Torino, Italy
Sunav Choudhary	Adobe Research, India
Frans Coenen	The University of Liverpool, UK
Mario Cordeiro	Universidade do Porto, Portugal
Robson Cordeiro	University of São Paulo, Brazil
Roberto Corizzo	University of Bari, Italy
Fabrizio Costa	Exeter University, UK
Vitor Santos Costa	Universidade do Porto, Portugal
Adrien Coulet	Loria, France
Bertrand Cuissart	University of Caen, France
Boris Cule	Universiteit Antwerpen, Belgium
Alfredo Cuzzocrea	University of Trieste and ICAR-CNR, Italy
Alexander Dallmann	University of Würzburg, Germany
Claudia d'Amato	University of Bari, Italy
Maria Damiani	University of Milano, Italy
Martine De Cock	University of Washington Tacoma, USA
Tom Decroos	KU Leuven, Belgium
Juan Jose del Coz	University of Oviedo, Spain
Anne Denton	North Dakota State University, USA
Christian Desrosiers	ETS, Italy
Nicola Di Mauro	University of Bari, Italy
Claudia Diamantini	Università Politecnica delle Marche, Italy
Jilles Dibangoye	INSA-Lyon, France
Tom Diethe	University of Bristol, UK
Wei Ding	University of Massachusetts Boston, USA
Stephan Doerfel	Micromata GmbH, Germany

Carlotta Domeniconi	George Mason University, USA
Madalina Drugan	Eindhoven University of Technology, the Netherlands
Stefan Duffner	University of Lyon, France
Wouter Duivesteijn	TU Eindhoven, the Netherlands
Sebastijan Dumancic	KU Leuven, Belgium
Ines Dutra	INESC TEC, Portugal
Mireille El Gheche	EPFL, Switzerland
Jihane Elyahyioui	Monash University, Australia
Dora Erdos	Boston University, USA
Samuel Fadel	University of Campinas, Brazil
Ad Feelders	Universiteit Utrecht, the Netherlands
Jing Feng	TU Darmstadt, Germany
Stefano Ferilli	University of Bari, Italy
Carlos Ferreira	INESC TEC, Portugal
Cesar Ferri	Universitat Politecnica Valencia, Spain
Matthias Fey	TU Dortmund, Germany
Rémi Flamary	Université côte d'Azur, France
Razvan Florian	Romanian Institute of Science and Technology, Romania
Germain Forestier	University of Haute Alsace, France
Eibe Frank	University of Waikato, New Zealand
Fabio Fumarola	Universita degli Studi di Bari Aldo Moro, Italy
Paulo Gabriel	Universidade Federal de Uberlandia, Brazil
Amita Gajewar	Microsoft Corporation, USA
Esther Galbrun	Aalto University, Finland
Dragan Gamberger	Rudjer Boskovic Institute, Croatia
Byron Gao	Texas State University, USA
Junbin Gao	The University of Sydney, Australia
Paolo Garza	Politecnico di Torino, Italy
Konstantinos Georgatzis	QuantumBlack, Singapore
Pierre Geurts	Montefiore Institute, Belgium
Arnaud Giacometti	University of Tours, France
Rémi Gilleron	Lille University, France
Mike Gimelfarb	University of Toronto, Canada
Uwe Glasser	Simon Fraser University, Canada
Dorota Glowacka	University of Helsinki, Finland
Heitor Gomes	Télécom ParisTech, France
Rafael Gomes Mantovani	Federal Technology University of Parana, Brazil
Vicenç Gomez	Universitat Pompeu Fabra, Spain
Vanessa Gomez-Verdejo	Universidad Carlos III de Madrid, Spain
James Goulding	University of Nottingham, UK
Cédric Gouy-Pailler	CEA, France
Josif Grabocka	Universität Hildesheim, Germany
Michael Granitzer	University of Passau, Germany
Derek Greene	Data Analytics, Ireland
Quanquan Gu	University of California, Los Angeles, USA

Riccardo Guidotti	University of Pisa, Italy
Francesco Gullo	UniCredit R&D, Italy
Tias Guns	Vrije Universiteit Brussel, Belgium
Xueying Guo	University of California, Davis, USA
Deepak Gupta	University of Amsterdam, the Netherlands
Thomas Guyet	IRISA, France
Stephan Günnemann	Technical University of Munich, Germany
Maria Halkidi	University of Pireaus, Greece
Barbara Hammer	CITEC, Switzerland
Jiawei Han	UIUC, USA
Tom Hanika	University of Kassel, Germany
Mohammad Hasan	Indiana University and Purdue University Indianapolis, USA
Xiao He	Alibaba Group, China
Denis Helic	TU Graz, Austria
Andreas Henelius	University of Helsinki, Finland
Daniel Hernandez-Lobato	Universidad Autonoma de Madrid, Spain
Jose Hernandez-Orallo	Polytechnic University of Valencia, Spain
Sibylle Hess	TU Eindhoven, the Netherlands
Thanh Lam Hoang	IBM Research, Ireland
Frank Hoeppner	Ostfalia University of Applied Science, Germany
Arjen Hommersom	University of Nijmegen, the Netherlands
Tamas Horvath	University of Bonn and Fraunhofer IAIS, Germany
Homa Hosseinmardi	USC ISI, USA
Chao Huang	University of Notre Dame, USA
David Tse Jung Huang	The University of Auckland, New Zealand
Yuanhua Huang	European Bioinformatics Institute, UK
Neil Hurley	University College Dublin, Ireland
Dino Ienco	Irstea Institute, France
Angelo Impedovo	University of Bari Aldo Moro, Italy
Iñaki Inza	University of the Basque Country, Spain
Tomoki Ito	The University of Tokyo, Japan
Mahdi Jalili	RMIT University, Australia
Szymon Jaroszewicz	Polish Academy of Sciences, Poland
Giuseppe Jurman	Fondazione Bruno Kessler, Italy
Anup Kalia	IBM Research, USA
Toshihiro Kamishima	National Institute of Advanced Industrial Science and Technology, Japan
Michael Kamp	Fraunhofer IAIS, Germany
Bo Kang	Ghent University, Belgium
Pinar Karagoz	METU, Turkey
Konstantinos Karanasos	Microsoft, UK
Sarvnaz Karimi	DATA61, Australia
George Karypis	University of Minnesota, USA
Mehdi Kaytoue	Infologic, France
Mikaela Keller	University of Lille, France

Latifur Khan	The University of Texas at Dallas, USA
Beomjoon Kim	MIT, USA
Daiki Kimura	IBM Research AI, USA
Frank Klawonn	Helmholtz Centre for Infection Research, Germany
Jiri Klema	Czech Technical University, Czech Republic
Tomas Kliegr	University of Economics, Prague, Czech Republic
Dragi Kocev	Jozef Stefan Institute, Slovenia
Levente Kocsis	Hungarian Academy of Science, Hungary
Yun Sing Koh	The University of Auckland, New Zealand
Effrosyni Kokiopoulou	Google AI, Switzerland
Alek Kolcz	Twitter, USA
Wouter Kool	University of Amsterdam, the Netherlands
Irena Koprinska	The University of Sydney, Australia
Frederic Koriche	Université d'Artois, France
Lars Kotthoff	University of Wyoming, USA
Danai Koutra	University of Michigan, USA
Polychronis Koutsakis	Murdoch University, Australia
Tomas Krilavicius	Vytautas Magnus University, Lithuania
Yamuna Krishnamurthy	NYU, USA, and Royal Holloway University of London, UK
Narayanan C. Krishnan	IIT Ropar, India
Matjaz Kukar	University of Ljubljana, Slovenia
Meelis Kull	University of Tartu, Estonia
Gautam Kunapuli	UT Dallas, USA
Vinod Kurmi	IIT Kanpur, India
Ondrej Kuzelka	University of Leuven, Belgium
Nicolas Lachiche	University of Strasbourg, France
Sofiane Lagraa	University of Luxembourg, Luxembourg
Leo Lahti	University of Turku, Estonia
Christine Largeron	LabHC Lyon University, France
Christine Largouet	IRISA, France
Pedro Larranaga	Universidad Politécnica de Madrid, Spain
Niklas Lavesson	Jonkoping University, Sweden
Binh Le	University College Dublin, Ireland
Florian Lemmerich	RWTH Aachen University, Germany
Marie-Jeanne Lesot	LIP6, France
Dagang Li	Peking University, China
Jian Li	Tsinghua University, China
Jiuyong Li	University of South Australia, Australia
Limin Li	Xi'an Jiaotong University, China
Xiangru Lian	University of Rochester, USA
Jefrey Lijffijt	Ghent University, Belgium
Tony Lindgren	Stockholm University, Sweden
Marco Lippi	University of Modena and Reggio Emilia, Italy
Bing Liu	University of Illinois at Chicago, USA
Corrado Loglisci	Universita degli Studi di Bari Aldo Moro, Italy

Peter Lucas	Leiden University, the Netherlands
Sebastian Mair	Leuphana University, Germany
Arun Maiya	Institute for Defense Analyses, USA
Donato Malerba	University of Bari, Italy
Chaitanya Manapragada	Monash University, Australia
Luca Martino	University of Valencia, Spain
Elio Masciari	ICAR-CNR, Italy
Andres Masegosa	University of Almeria, Spain
Florent Masseglia	Inria, France
Antonis Matakos	Aalto University, Finland
Wannes Meert	KU Leuven, Belgium
Corrado Mencar	University of Bari Aldo Moro, Italy
Saayan Mitra	Adobe, USA
Atsushi Miyamoto	Hitachi America Ltd., USA
Dunja Mladenic	Jozef Stefan Institute, Slovenia
Sandy Moens	Universiteit Antwerpen, Belgium
Miguel Molina-Solana	Imperial College London, UK
Nuno Moniz	University of Porto, Portgual
Hankyu Moon	Samsung SDS Research, USA
Joao Moreira	INESC TEC, Portugal
Luis Moreira-Matias	Kreditech Holding SSL, Germany
Emilie Morvant	Université Jean Monnet, France
Andreas Mueller	Columbia Data Science Institute, USA
Asim Munawar	IBM Research, Japan
Pierre-Alexandre Murena	Télécom ParisTech, France
Mohamed Nadif	LIPADE, Université Paris Descartes, France
Jinseok Nam	Amazon, USA
Mirco Nanni	ISTI-CNR Pisa, Italy
Amedeo Napoli	LORIA, France
Sriraam Natarajan	UT Dallas, USA
Fateme Nateghi	KU Leuven, Belgium
Benjamin Negrevergne	Université Paris Dauphine, France
Benjamin Nguyen	INSA-CVL, France
Xia Ning	OSU, USA
Kjetil Norvag	NTNU, Norway
Eirini Ntoutsi	Leibniz Universität Hannover, Germany
Andreas Nurnberger	Magdeburg University, Germany
Luca Oneto	University of Pisa, Italy
Kok-Leong Ong	La Trobe University, Australia
Francesco Orsini	MDOTM S.r.l., Italy
Martijn van Otterlo	Tilburg University, the Netherlands
Nikunj Oza	NASA Ames, USA
Pance Panov	Jozef Stefan Institute, Slovenia
Apostolos Papadopoulos	Aristotle University of Thessaloniki, Greece
Panagiotis Papapetrou	Stockholm University, Sweden
Youngja Park	IBM, USA

Ioannis Partalas	Expedia Group, Switzerland
Charlotte Pelletier	Monash University, Australia
Jaakko Peltonen	University of Tampere, Finland
Lukas Pfahler	TU Dortmund, Germany
Nico Piatkowski	TU Dortmund, Germany
Andrea Pietracaprina	University of Padova, Italy
Gianvito Pio	University of Bari, Italy
Claudia Plant	University of Vienna, Austria
Marc Plantevit	Université de Lyon, France
Pascal Poncelet	Lirmm, France
Miguel Prada	Universidad de León, Spain
Paul Prasse	University of Potsdam, Germany
Philippe Preux	Inria, France
Buyue Qian	Xi'an Jiaotong University, China
Masoume Raeissi	CWI, the Netherlands
Dimitrios Rafailidis	Maastricht University, the Netherlands
Jorg Rahnenführer	TU Dortmund, Germany
Chedy Raissi	Inria, France
Sutharshan Rajasegarar	Deakin University, Australia
Jan Ramon	Inria, France
Santu Rana	Deakin University, Australia
Huzefa Rangwala	George Mason University, USA
Chotirat Ratanamahatana	Chulalongkorn University, Thailand
Jan Rauch	University of Economics, Prague, Czech Republic
Ievgen Redko	Laboratoire Hubert Curien, France
Chiara Renso	ISTI-CNR, Italy
Achim Rettinger	Trier University, Germany
Rita Ribeiro	University of Porto, Portugal
Fabrizio Riguzzi	Università di Ferrara, Italy
Jan van Rijn	Leiden University, the Netherlands
Matteo Riondato	Two Sigma Investments, USA
Pieter Robberechts	KU Leuven, Belgium
Juan Rodriguez	Universidad de Burgos, Spain
Fabrice Rossi	Université Paris 1 Pantheon-Sorbonne, France
Ryan Rossi	Adobe Research, USA
Celine Rouveirol	Université Paris-Nord, France
Yannick Rudolph	Leuphana University, Germany
Stefan Rueping	Fraunhofer IAIS, Germany
Anne Sabourin	Télécom ParisTech, France
Yvan Saeys	Ghent University, Belgium
Amrita Saha	IBM Research, India
Lorenza Saitta	Università del Piemonte Orientale, Italy
Tomoya Sakai	NEC, Japan
Tetsuya Sakurai	University of Tsukuba, Japan
Ansaf Salleb-Aouissi	Columbia University, USA
Somdeb Sarkhel	Adobe, USA

Claudio Sartori	University of Bologna, Italy
Luciano Sbaiz	Google AI, Switzerland
Pierre Schaus	UC Louvain, Belgium
Tobias Scheffer	University of Potsdam, Germany
Ute Schmid	University of Bamberg, Germany
Lars Schmidt-Thieme	University of Hildesheim, Germany
Christoph Schommer	University of Luxembourg, Luxembourg
Matthias Schubert	Ludwig-Maximilians-Universität München, Germany
Rajat Sen	UT Austin and Amazon, USA
Vinay Setty	University of Stavanger, Norway
Mattia Setzu	University of Pisa, Italy
Chao Shang	University of Connecticut, USA
Junming Shao	University of Electronic Science and Technology of China, China
Bernhard Sick	University of Kassel, Germany
Diego Silva	Universidade Federal de São Carlos, Brazil
Jonathan Silva	UFMS, Brazil
Nikola Simidjievski	University of Cambridge, UK
Andrzej Skowron	University of Warsaw, Poland
Dominik Slezak	University of Warsaw, Poland
Daniel V. Smith	DATA61, Australia
Gavin Smith	University of Nottingham, UK
Tomislav Smuc	Institute Ruđer Bošković, Croatia
Arnaud Soulet	University of Tours, France
Mauro Sozio	Institut Mines Télécom, France
Alessandro Sperduti	University of Padova, Italy
Jerzy Stefanowski	Poznan University of Technology, Poland
Bas van Stein	Leiden University, the Netherlands
Giovanni Stilo	University of L'Aquila, Italy
Mahito Sugiyama	National Institute of Informatics, Japan
Mika Sulkava	Natural Resources Institute Finland, Finland
Yizhou Sun	UCLA, USA
Viswanathan Swaminathan	Adobe, USA
Stephen Swift	Brunel University London, UK
Andrea Tagarelli	DIMES - UNICAL, Italy
Domenico Talia	University of Calabria, Italy
Letizia Tanca	Politecnico di Milano, Italy
Jovan Tanevski	Jozef Stefan Institute, Slovenia
Nikolaj Tatti	University of Helsinki, Finland
Maryam Tavakol	TU Dortmund, Germany
Maguelonne Teisseire	Irstea, France
Choon Hui Teo	Amazon, USA
Alexandre Termier	Université Rennes 1, France
Stefano Teso	KU Leuven, Belgium
Ljupco Todorovski	University of Ljubljana, Slovenia
Alexander Tornede	UPB, Germany

Ricardo Torres	IC-Unicamp, Brazil
Volker Tresp	Siemens AG and Ludwig Maximilian University of Munich, Germany
Isaac Triguero	University of Nottingham, UK
Ivor Tsang	University of Technology Sydney, Australia
Vincent Tseng	National Chiao Tung University, Taiwan
Charalampos Tsourakakis	Boston University, USA
Radu Tudoran	Huawei, Germany
Cigdem Turan	TU Darmstadt, Germany
Nikolaos Tziortziotis	Tradelab, France
Theodoros Tzouramanis	University of the Aegean, Greece
Antti Ukkonen	University of Helsinki, Finland
Elia Van Wolputte	KU Leuven, Belgium
Robin Vandaele	Ghent University, Belgium
Iraklis Varlamis	Harokopio University of Athens, Greece
Ranga Vatsavai	North Carolina State University, USA
Julien Velcin	University of Lyon, France
Bruno Veloso	University of Porto, Portugal
Shankar Vembu	University of Toronto, Canada
Deepak Venugopal	University of Memphis, USA
Ricardo Vigario	NOVA University of Lisbon, Portugal
Prashanth Vijayaraghavan	MIT, USA
Herna Viktor	University of Ottawa, Canada
Willem Waegeman	Universiteit Gent, Belgium
Di Wang	Microsoft, USA
Hao Wang	Leiden University, the Netherlands
Jianyong Wang	Tsinghua University, China
Yuyi Wang	ETH Zürich, Switzerland
Jeremy Weiss	Carnegie Mellon University, USA
Marcel Wever	Paderborn University, Germany
Joerg Wicker	The University of Auckland, New Zealand
Marco Wiering	University of Groningen, the Netherlands
Martin Wistuba	IBM Research, Ireland
Christian Wolf	INSA-Lyon, France
Christian Wressnegger	TU Braunschweig, Germany
Gang Wu	Adobe Research, USA
Lina Yao	UNSW, Australia
Philip Yu	University of Illinois at Chicago, USA
Bianca Zadrozny	IBM Research, USA
Gerson Zaverucha	Federal University of Rio de Janeiro, Brazil
Bernard Zenko	Jozef Stefan Institute, Slovenia
Chengkun Zhang	The University of Sydney, Australia
Jianpeng Zhang	TU Eindhoven, the Netherlands
Junping Zhang	Fudan University, China
Shichao Zhang	Guangxi Normal University, China
Yingqian Zhang	Eindhoven University of Technology, the Netherlands

Sichen Zhao	The University of Melbourne, Australia
Ying Zhao	Tsinghua University, China
Shuai Zheng	Hitachi America Ltd., USA
Arthur Zimek	University of Southern Denmark, Denmark
Albrecht Zimmermann	Université de Caen Normandie, France
Indre Zliobaite	University of Helsinki, Finland
Tanja Zseby	TU Wien, Austria

Sponsors

Contents – Part III

Ranking

Applied Data Science: Computer Vision and Explanation

Applied Data Science: Healthcare

Applied Data Science: E-commerce, Finance, and Advertising

Applied Data Science: Rich Data

Applied Data Science: Applications

Demo Track

Reinforcement Learning and Bandits

Deep Ordinal Reinforcement Learning

Alexander Zap, Tobias Joppen[(✉)], and Johannes Fürnkranz

TU Darmstadt, 64289 Darmstadt, Germany
alexander.zap@stud.tu-darmstadt.de, {tjoppen,juffi}@ke.tu-darmstadt.de

Abstract. Reinforcement learning usually makes use of numerical rewards, which have nice properties but also come with drawbacks and difficulties. Using rewards on an ordinal scale (ordinal rewards) is an alternative to numerical rewards that has received more attention in recent years. In this paper, a general approach to adapting reinforcement learning problems to the use of ordinal rewards is presented and motivated. We show how to convert common reinforcement learning algorithms to an ordinal variation by the example of Q-learning and introduce Ordinal Deep Q-Networks, which adapt deep reinforcement learning to ordinal rewards. Additionally, we run evaluations on problems provided by the OpenAI Gym framework, showing that our ordinal variants exhibit a performance that is comparable to the numerical variations for a number of problems. We also give first evidence that our ordinal variant is able to produce better results for problems with less engineered and simpler-to-design reward signals.

Keywords: Reinforcement learning · Ordinal rewards

1 Introduction

Conventional reinforcement learning (RL) algorithms rely on numerical feedback signals. Their main advantages include the ease of aggregation, efficient gradient computation, and many use cases where numerical reward signals come naturally, often representing a quantitative property. However, in some domains numerical rewards are hard to define and are often subject to certain problems. One issue of numerical feedback signals is the difficulty of *reward shaping*, which is the task of creating a reward function. Since RL algorithms use rewards as direct feedback to learn a behavior which optimizes the aggregation of received rewards, the reward function has a significant impact on the behavior that is learned by the algorithm. Manual creation of the reward function is often expensive, non-intuitive and difficult in certain domains and can therefore cause a bias in the optimal behavior that is learned by an algorithm. Since the learned behavior is sensitive to these reward values, the rewards of an environment should not be introduced or shaped arbitrarily if they are not explicitly known or naturally defined. This can also lead to another problem called *reward hacking*, where algorithms are able to exploit a reward function and miss the intended goal of the environment, caused by being

© Springer Nature Switzerland AG 2020
U. Brefeld et al. (Eds.): ECML PKDD 2019, LNAI 11908, pp. 3–18, 2020.
https://doi.org/10.1007/978-3-030-46133-1_1

able to receive better rewards through undesired behavior. The use of numerical rewards furthermore requires *infinite rewards* to model undesired decisions in order to not allow trade-offs for a given state. This can be illustrated by an example in the medical domain, where it is undesirable to be able to compensate one occurrence of *death of patient* with multiple occurrences of *cured patient* to stay at a positive reward in average and therefore artificial feedback signals are used that can not be averaged. These issues have motivated the search for alternatives, such as preference-based feedback signals [13].

In this paper, we investigate the use of rewards on an ordinal scale, where we have information about the relative order of various rewards, but not about the magnitude of the quality differences between different rewards. Our goal is to extend reinforcement learning algorithms so that they can make use of ordinal rewards as an alternative feedback signal type in order to avoid and overcome the problems with numerical rewards.

Reinforcement learning with ordinal rewards has multiple advantages and directly addresses multiple issues of numerical rewards. Firstly, the problem of *reward shaping* is minimized, since the manual creation of the ordinal reward function specifically by the reward ordering often is intuitive and can be done easily without the need of exact specifications for reward values. Even though the creation of ordinal reward values, so-called reward tiers, through the ascending order of feedback signals introduces a naturally defined bias, it omits the largely introduced artificial bias by the manual shaping of reward values. At the same time, ordinal rewards simplify the problem of *reward hacking* because the omission of specific numeric reward values has the effect that any possible exploitation of rewards by an algorithm is only dependent on an incorrect reward order, which can be more easily fixed than the search for correct numerical values. While the use of *infinite rewards* can not be modelled directly, it is still possible to define infinite rewards as highest or lowest ordinal reward tier, and implement policies which completely avoid and encourage certain tiers.

Since the creation of the ordinal reward function is cheap and intuitive, it is especially suitable for newly defined environments since it enables the easy definition of ordinal rewards by ordering the possible outcomes naturally by desirability. Additionally it should be noted that for existing environments with numerical rewards it is possible to extract ordinal rewards from these environments.

The focus of this paper is the technique of using ordinal rewards for reinforcement learning. To this end, we propose an alternative reward aggregation for ordinal rewards, introduce a method for policy determination from ordinal rewards and compare the performance of ordinal reward algorithms to algorithms for numerical rewards. In Sect. 2, we discuss related work and previous approaches. A formal definition of common reinforcement learning terminology can be found in Sect. 3. Section 4 introduce reinforcement learning algorithms which use ordinal reward aggregations instead of numerical rewards, and illustrates the differences to conventional approaches. In Sect. 5 experiments are executed on the framework of OpenAI Gym and common reinforcement learning algorithms are compared to ordinal reinforcement learning.

2   Related Work

The technique of using rewards on an ordinal scale as an alternative to numerical rewards is mainly based on the approach of preference learning (PL) [1]. In contrast to traditional supervised learning, PL follows the core idea of having preferences over states or symbols as labels and predicting these preferences as the output on unseen data instances instead of labelling data with explicit nominal or numerical values.

Recently, there have been several proposals for combining PL with RL, where pairwise preferences over trajectories, states or actions are defined and applied as feedback signals in reinforcement learning algorithms instead of the commonly used numerical rewards. For a survey of such preference-based reinforcement learning algorithms, we refer the reader to [13].

While preference-based RL provides algorithms for learning an agent's behavior from pairwise comparison of trajectories, [12] presents an approach for creating preferences over multiple trajectories in the order of ascending ordinal reward tiers, thereby deviating from the concept of pairwise comparisons over trajectories. Using a tutor as an oracle, this approach approximates a latent numerical reward score from a sequence of received ordinal feedback signals. This alternative reward computation functions as a reward transformation from the ordinal to the numerical scale and is applicable on top of an existing reinforcement learning algorithm.

Contrary to this approach, we do not use a tutor for the comparison of trajectories but can directly use ordinal rewards as a feedback signal. In order to use environments where numerical feedback already exists without the need for acquiring human feedback about the underlying preferences, we automatically extract rewards on an ordinal scale from existing environments with numerical rewards. To this end, we adapt an approach that has been proposed for Monte-Carlo Tree Search [4] to reinforcement learning.

Furthermore, we handle ordinal rewards in a similar manner as previous approaches by directly using aggregated received ordinal rewards for comparing different options. The idea of direct comparison of ordinal rewards builds on the works of [2,4,10,11], which provide criteria for the direct comparison of ordinal reward aggregations. We utilize the approach of [4], which transfers the numerical reward maximization problem into a best-choice maximization problem for an alternative computation of the value function for reinforcement learning from ordinal feedback signals. [4] used this idea for adapting Monte Carlo Tree Search to the use of ordinal rewards.

In summary, we automatically transfer numerical feedback into preference-based feedback and propose a new conceptual idea to utilize ordinal rewards for reinforcement learning, which should not be seen as an alternative for the existing algorithms stated above. Hence, we do not compare the performance of our new approach to any of the algorithms that use additional human feedback, but to common RL techniques that use numerical feedback.

3   Markov Decision Process and Reinforcement Learning

In this section, we briefly recapitulate Markov decision processes and reinforcement learning algorithms. Our notation and terminology is based on [8].

3.1   Value Function and Policy for Markov Decision Process

A *Markov Decision Process* (MDP) is defined as a tuple of (S, A, P, R) with S being a finite set of states, A being a finite set of actions, T being the transition function $S \times A \times S \to \mathbb{R}$ that models the probability of reaching a state s' when action a is performed in state s, and R being the reward function $S \times A \times S \to \mathbb{R}$ which maps a reward r from a subset of possible rewards $r \in \{r_1, ..., r_n\} \subset \mathbb{R}$ to executing action a in state s and reaching s' in the process. For further work we assume that T is deterministic and a transition always has the probability of 0 or 1. Furthermore it is assumed that each action $a \in A$ is executable in any state $s \in S$, hence the transition function is defined for every element in $S \times A \times S$. A policy π is the specification which decision to take based on the environmental state. In a deterministic setting, it is modeled as a mapping $\pi : S \to A$ which directly maps an environmental state s to the decision a which should be taken in this state. The value function $V_\pi(s)$ represents the expected quality of a policy π in state s with respect to the rewards that will be received in the future. Value functions for numerical rewards are computed by the expectation of the discounted sum of rewards $\mathbb{E}[R]$. The value function $V_\pi(s)$ of a policy π in an environmental state s therefore can be computed by

$$V_\pi(s) = \mathbb{E}[R], \quad R = \sum_{t=0}^{\infty} \gamma^t r_t \tag{1}$$

where R is the discounted sum of rewards when following policy π, γ a discount factor, and r_t the direct reward at time step t. The optimal policy π^* in a state s is the policy with the largest $V_\pi(s)$, which complies with the goal of an RL algorithm to maximize expected future reward.

3.2   Reinforcement Learning

Reinforcement learning can be described as the task of learning a policy that maximizes the expected future numerical reward. The agent learns iteratively by updating its current policy π after every action and the corresponding received reward from the environment. Furthermore, the agent may perform multiple training sessions, so-called episodes, in the environment. Using the previously defined formalism, this can be expressed as approximating the optimal policy iteratively with a function $\hat{\pi}$, by repeatedly choosing actions that lead to states s with the highest estimated value function $V_{\hat{\pi}}(s)$. In the following section two common reinforcement learning algorithms are introduced.

Q-learning. The key idea of the Q-learning algorithm [9] is to estimate Q-values $Q(s, a)$, which estimate the expected future sum of rewards $\mathbb{E}[R]$ when choosing an action a in a state s and following the optimal policy π^* afterwards. Hence the Q-value can be seen as a measure of *goodness* for a state-action pair (s, a), and therefore, in a given state s, the optimal policy π^* should select the action a that maximizes this value in comparison to other available actions in that state. The approximated Q-values are stored and iteratively updated in a Q-table. The Q-table is updated after an action a has been performed in a state s and the reward r and the newly reached state s' is observed. The computation of the expected Q-value is done by

$$\hat{Q}(s, a) = r(s, a) + \gamma \max_{a'} Q(s', a') \tag{2}$$

Following this so-called Bellman equation, every previously estimated Q-value is updated with the newly computed expected Q-value with the formula

$$Q(s, a) = Q(s, a) + \alpha[r(s, a) + \gamma \max_{a'} Q(s', a') - Q(s, a)] \tag{3}$$

where α represents a learning rate and γ the discount factor.

Deep Q-Network. The original Q-learning algorithm is limited to very simple problems, because of the explicitly stored Q-table, which essentially memorizes the quality of each possible state-action pair independently. Thus it requires, e.g., that each state-action pair has to be visited a certain number of times in order to make a reasonable prediction for this pair. A natural extension of this method is to replace the Q-table with a learned Q-function, which is able to predict a quality value for a given, possibly previously unseen state-action pair. The key idea behind the Deep Q-Network (DQN) [6,7] is to learn a continuous function $Q^{DQN}(s)$ in the form of a deep neural network with m input nodes, which represent the feature vector of s, and n output nodes, each containing the Q-value of one action a.

Neural networks can be iteratively updated to fit the output nodes to the desired Q-values. The expected Q-value for a state-action pair is calculated in the same manner as defined in (2) with the difference that the Q-values are now predicted by the DQN, with one output node $Q_a^{DQN}(s)$ for each possible action a. Therefore (2) becomes

$$\hat{Q}_a^{DQN}(s) = r(s, a) + \gamma \max_{a'} Q_{a'}^{DQN}(s') \tag{4}$$

where $Q_a^{DQN}(s)$ represents the Q-value node of action a in state s.

In order to optimize the learning procedure, DQN makes use of several optimizations such as *experience replay*, the use of a separate *target and evaluation network*, and *Double Deep Q-Network*. More details on these techniques can be found in the following paragraphs.

Experience Replay. Using a neural network to fit the Q-value of the previously executed state-action pair as described in (4) leads to overfitting to recent experiences because of the high correlation between environmental states across multiple successive time steps, and the property of neural networks to overfit recently seen training data. Instead of only using the previous state-action pair for fitting the DQN, experience replay [5] uses a memory M to store previous experience instances (s, a, r, s') and iteratively reuses a random sample of these experiences to update the network prediction at every time step.

Target and Evaluation Networks. Frequently updating the neural network, which is simultaneously used for the prediction of the expected Q-value, leads to unstable fitting of the network. Therefore these two tasks, firstly the prediction of the target Q-value for network fitting and secondly the prediction of the Q-value which is used for policy computation, allows for a split into two networks. These two networks are the *evaluation network*, which is used for policy computation, and the *target network*, which is used for predicting the target value for continuously fitting the evaluation network. In order to keep the target network up to date, it is replaced by a copy of the evaluation network every c steps.

Double Deep Q-Network. Deep Q-Networks tend to overestimate the prediction of Q-values for some actions, which may result in an unjustified bias towards certain actions. To address this problem, Double Deep Q-Networks [3] additionally use the target and evaluation networks to decouple the action choice and Q-value prediction by letting the evaluation network choose the next action to be played, and letting the target network predict the respective Q-value.

4   Deep Ordinal Reinforcement Learning

In this section, Markov decision processes and reinforcement learning algorithms are adapted to settings with ordinal reward signals. More concretely, we present a method for reward aggregation that fits ordinal rewards and explain how this method can be used in Q-learning and Deep Q-Networks in order to learn to solve environments that return feedback signals on an ordinal scale.

4.1   Ordinal Markov Decision Process

Similar to the standard Markov Decision Process, [10] defines an ordinal version of an MDP as a tuple of (S, A, T, R_o) with the only difference that R_o is the reward function $S \times A \times S \to \mathbb{N}$ is modified to return ordinal rewards instead of numerical ones. Thus, it maps executing action a in state s and reaching state s' to an ordinal reward r_o from a subset of possible ordinal rewards $r_o \in \{1, ..., n\} \subset \mathbb{N}$, with n representing the number of ordinal rewards. Whereas a real-valued reward provides information about the qualitative size of the reward, the ordinal scale breaks rewards down to naturally ordered *reward tiers*. These reward tiers solely represent the rank of desirability of a reward compared to all other possible rewards, which is noted as the ranking position r_o of a reward r in the set of all possible rewards $\{r_1, ..., r_n\}$. Interpreting the reward signals on an ordinal scale still allows us to order and directly compare individual reward signals, but while the numerical scale allows for comparison of rewards by means of the magnitude of their difference, ordinal rewards do not provide this information.

In order to aggregate multiple ordinal rewards, a distribution to store and represent the expected frequency of received rewards on the ordinal scale is constructed. This distribution is represented by a vector $D(s, a)$, in which $d_i(s, a)$ represents the frequency of receiving the ordinal reward r_i by executing a in s. The distribution vector is defined by

$$D(s, a) = \begin{bmatrix} d_1(s, a) \\ ... \\ d_n(s, a) \end{bmatrix} \tag{5}$$

Through normalization of distribution vector D, a probability distribution P can be constructed, which represents the expected probability of receiving a reward. The probability distribution is represented by a probability vector $P(s, a)$, in which $p_i(s, a)$ represents the estimated probability of receiving the ordinal reward r_i by executing a in s. Hence the probability vector can be defined by

$$P(s, a) = \begin{bmatrix} p_1(s, a) \\ ... \\ p_n(s, a) \end{bmatrix} \text{ with } \sum_{i=1}^{n} p_i(s, a) = 1 \text{ and } 0 \leq p_i(s, a) \leq 1 \tag{6}$$

Value Function for Ordinal Rewards. While numerical rewards enable the representation of value function $V_\pi(s)$ by the expected sum of rewards, the value function for environments with ordinal rewards needs to be estimated differently. Since ordinal rewards are aggregated in a distribution of received ordinal rewards, the calculation of value function $V_\pi(s)$ in state s can be done based on $P(s, a)$ for action a that is selected by policy π. Hence the computation of the value function can be modeled by the following formula of

$$V_\pi(s) = F(P(s, a)) \text{ with } a = \pi(s) \tag{7}$$

The computation of the value function from probability distribution $P(s, a)$ through function F is performed by the technique of *measure of statistical superiority* [4]. This measure computes the probability that action a receives a better ordinal reward than a random alternative action a' in the same environmental state s. This probability can be calculated through the sum of all probabilities of a receiving a better ordinal reward o than a'. Hence the probability of an action a performing better than another action a' can be defined as

$$\mathbb{P}(a \succ a') = \sum_{o=1}^{n} p_o(s, a) \cdot \left(p_{o <}(s, a') + \frac{1}{2} p_o(s, a') \right)$$

$$\text{with } p_{o <}(s, a) = \sum_{i=1}^{o-1} p_i(s, a)$$

To deal with ties, additionally half the probability of a receiving the same reward tier as a' is added.

The function of the measure of statistical superiority therefore is computed through the averaged winning probability of a against all other actions a' by

$$F(P(s,a)) = \mathbb{E}[\mathbb{P}(a \succ a')] = \frac{\sum_{a'} \mathbb{P}(a \succ a')}{k-1} \tag{8}$$

for k available actions in state s.

Based on (7), the optimal policy π^* can be determined in the same way as for numerical rewards (1) by maximizing the respective value function $V_\pi(s)$.

4.2   Transformation of Existing Numerical Rewards to Ordinal Rewards

If an environment has pre-defined rewards on a numerical scale, transforming numerical rewards $r \in \{r_1, ..., r_n\} \subset \mathbb{R}$ into ordinal rewards $r_o \in \{1, ..., n\} \subset \mathbb{N}$ can easily be done by translating every numerical reward to its ordinal position within all possible numerical rewards. This way the lowest possible numerical reward is mapped to position 1, and the highest numerical reward is mapped to position n, with n representing the number of possible numerical rewards. This transformation process simply results in removing the metric and semantic of distances of rewards but keeping the order.

4.3   Ordinal Reinforcement Learning

In Sect. 4.1, we have shown how to compute a value function $V_\pi(s)$ and defined the optimal policy π^* for environments with ordinal rewards. This can now be used for adapting common reinforcement learning algorithms to ordinal rewards.

Ordinal Q-learning. For the adaptation of the Q-learning algorithm to ordinal rewards, we do not directly update a Q-value $Q(s,a)$ that represents the quality of a state-action pair (s,a) but update the distribution $D(s,a)$ of received ordinal rewards. The target distribution is computed by adding the received ordinal reward i (represented through unit vector e_i of length n) to the distribution $D(s', \pi^*(s'))$ of taking an action in the new state s' according to the optimal policy π^*. The previous distribution $D(s,a)$ is updated with the target distribution by interpolating both values with learning rate α, which can be seen in the formula

$$D(s,a) = D(s,a) + \alpha[e_i(s,a) + \gamma D(s', \pi^*(s')) - D(s,a)] \tag{9}$$

In this adaptation of Q-learning[1], the expected quality of state-action pair (s,a) is not represented by the Q-value $Q(s,a)$ (3) but by the function $F(P(s,a))$ (8) of the probability distribution $P(s,a)$, which is derived from the iteratively updated distribution $D(s,a)$.

---

[1] This technique of modifying the Q-learning algorithm to deal with rewards on an ordinal scale can analogously be applied to other Q-table based reinforcement learning algorithms like *Sarsa* and *Sarsa-λ* [14].

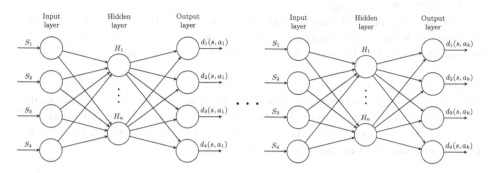

Fig. 1. Example of an array of ordinal deep neural networks for DQN for reward distribution prediction

Ordinal Deep Q-Network. Because ordinal rewards are aggregated by a distribution instead of a numerical value, the neural network is adapted to predict distributions $D(s, a)$ instead of Q-values for every possible action. Hence for one action the network does not predict a 1-dimensional Q-value, but predicts an n-dimensional reward distribution with n being the length of the ordinal scale. Since this distribution has to be computed for each of k actions, the adaptation of the Deep Q-Network algorithm to ordinal rewards requires a differently structured neural network. Contrary to the original Deep Q-Network where one network simultaneously predicts k Q-values for all actions, the structure of the ordinal DQN consists of an array of k neural networks, from which every network computes the expected ordinal reward distribution $D(s, a)$ for one separate action a. In a deep neural network for the prediction of distributions every output node of the network computes one distribution value $d_i(s, a)$. The structure of neural networks used for the prediction of distributions can be seen in Fig. 1.

The prediction of the ordinal reward distributions $D(s, a)$ for all actions can afterwards be normalized to a probability distribution and used in order to compute the value function $V_\pi(s)$ through the measure of statistical superiority as has been previously defined in (7). Once the value function and policy have been evaluated, the ordinal variant of the DQN algorithm follows a similar procedure as ordinal Q-learning and updates the prediction of the reward distribution for (s, a) by fitting $D_a^{DQN}(s)$ to the target reward distribution:

$$\hat{D}_a^{DQN}(s) = e_{r_o}(s, a) + \gamma D_{\pi^*(s')}^{DQN}(s') \tag{10}$$

The main difference in the update step between ordinal Q-learning (9) and ordinal DQN consists of fitting the neural network of action a for input s to the expected reward distribution by backpropagation instead of updating a Q-table entry (s, a). Additional modifications to the ordinal Deep Q-Network in form of experience replay, the split of the target and evaluation network and the usage of a Double DQN are done in a similar fashion as described with the standard DQN algorithm in Sect. 3.2. These modifications can be seen in the following paragraphs.

Experience Replay. A memory M is used to sample multiple saved experience elements (s, a, r_o, s') randomly and replay these previously seen experiences by fitting the ordinal DQN networks to the samples of earlier memory elements.

Target and Evaluation Networks. In order to prevent unstable behavior by using the same networks for the prediction and updating step, we use separate evaluation networks to predict reward distributions for the policy computation, and use target networks to predict the target reward distributions which are used for fitting the evaluation networks continuously.

Double Deep Q-Network. The neural networks of ordinal DQN tend to overestimate the prediction of the reward distributions for some actions, which may result in an unjustified bias towards certain actions. Therefore, in order to determine the next action to be played by π^*, the measure of statistical superiority is computed based on the reward distributions predicted by the evaluation networks. Afterwards the prediction of the reward distribution for this action is computed by the respective target network.

5   Experiments and Results

In the following, the standard reinforcement algorithms described in Sect. 3.2 and the ordinal reinforcement learning algorithms described in Sect. 4.3 are evaluated and compared in a number of testing environments.[2]

5.1   Experimental Setup

The environments which are used for evaluation are provided by OpenAI Gym,[3] which can be viewed as a unified toolbox for our experiments. All environments expect an action input after every time step and return feedback in form of the newly reached environmental state, the direct reward for the executed action, and the information whether the newly reached state is terminal. The environments that the algorithms were tested on were *CartPole* and *Acrobot*.[4]

Policies of the reinforcement learning algorithms were modified to use ϵ-greedy exploration [8], which encourages early exploration of the state space and increases exploitation of the learned policy over time. In the experiments the maximum exploitation is reached after half of the total episodes. In order to directly compare the standard and the ordinal variants of reinforcement learning algorithms, the quality of the learned policy and the computational efficiency are investigated across all environments with varying episode numbers.

---

[2] The source code for the implementation of the experiments can be found in https://github.com/az79nefy/OrdinalRL.

[3] For further information about OpenAI visit https://gym.openai.com.

[4] Further technical details about the environments CartPole and Acrobot from OpenAI can be found in https://gym.openai.com/envs/CartPole-v0/ and https://gym.openai.com/envs/Acrobot-v1/.

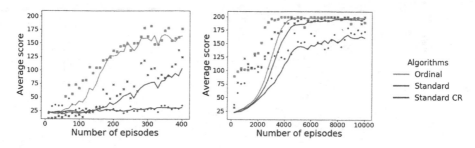

Fig. 2. CartPole scores of standard and ordinal Q-learning for 400 and 10000 episodes (Color figure online)

Information about the quality of the learned policy is derived from the sum of rewards over a whole episode (score) or the win rate while the efficiency is measured by real-time processing time. Additionally to the standard variant with unchanged rewards, the performance of standard Q-learning algorithms is tested with changed rewards in order to simulate the performance on environments where no optimal reward engineering has been performed. It should be noted that the modifications of the rewards is performed under the constraints of remaining existing reward order, therefore not changing the transformation to the ordinal scale. The change of rewards (CR) from the existing numerical rewards $r \in \{r_1, ..., r_n\}$ is performed for all rewards by the calculation of $r_{CR,i} = \frac{r_i - min(r)}{100}$.

The parameter configuration of the Q-learning algorithms is learning rate $\alpha = 0.1$ and discount factor $\gamma = 0.9$. The parameter configuration of the Deep Q-Network algorithm is learning rate $\alpha = 0.0005$ and discount factor $\gamma = 0.9$. As for the network specific parameters, the *Adam* optimizer is used for the network fitting, the target network is getting replaced every 300 fitting updates, the experience memory size is 200000 and the replay batch size is 64.

5.2   Experimental Results

The results of the comparison between numerical and ordinal algorithms for the CartPole- and Acrobot-environment in terms of score, win rate and computational time are shown and investigated in the following. This comparison is performed based on the averaged results from 10 and respectively 5 independent runs of Q-learning and Deep Q-Network on the environments.

Q-learning. In Fig. 2 the scores for the CartPole-environment over the course of 400 and 10000 episodes can be seen which were played by an agent using the ordinal (orange) as well as the standard Q-learning algorithm, with (red) and without (blue) modified rewards. Additionally the individual dots in this figure represent the scores achieved by the respective algorithms by using the optimal policy instead of ϵ-greedy exploration. The evaluation of these scores shows that

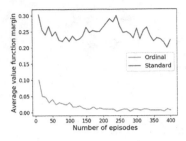 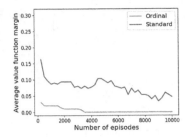

Fig. 3. Comparison of value function margin for best action of standard and ordinal Q-learning for 400 and 10000 episodes of CartPole (Color figure online)

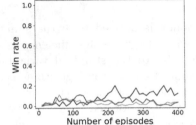 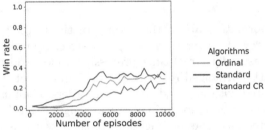

Fig. 4. Acrobot win rates of standard and ordinal Q-learning for 400 and 10000 episodes

the ordinal variant of Q-learning performs better than the standard variant with engineered rewards for 400 episodes and reaches the optimal score of 200 quicker for 10000 episodes. Additionally the use of ordinal rewards significantly outperforms the standard variant with modified rewards for both episode numbers. Therefore it can be seen that ordinal Q-learning is able to learn a good policy better than the standard variants for the CartPole-environment.

In order to explain the difference of learned behavior between the standard and ordinal variant, the average relative difference of Q-values $Q(s, a)$ and respectively measure of statistical superiority functions $F(P(s, a))$ for the two possible actions were plotted and compared in Fig. 3 for standard (blue) and ordinal (orange) Q-learning. It can be seen for both episode numbers that the policy which is learned by ordinal RL through the measure of statistical superiority converges to a difference of 0, meaning that the function $F(P(s, a))$ converges to similar values for both actions. This can be interpreted as the policy learning to play safely and rarely entering any critical states where this function would indicate strong preference towards one action (e.g. in big angles). On the other side it can be seen for 400 episodes that common RL does not converge towards similar Q-values for the actions over time and therefore a policy is learned that enters critical states more often. It should be noted that the Q-value differences for standard Q-learning converges to 0 for evaluations with more episodes and a safe policy is eventually learned as well.

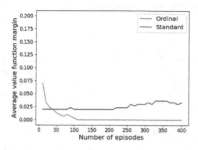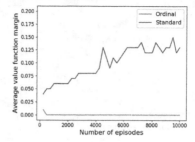

Fig. 5. Comparison of value function margin for best action of standard and ordinal Q-learning for 400 and 10000 episodes of Acrobot

Table 1. Computation time comparison of standard and ordinal Q-learning for varying episode numbers

Number of episodes	CartPole		Acrobot	
	Standard	Ordinal	Standard	Ordinal
400	2.10 s	4.17 s	35.74 s	52.85 s
2000	10.07 s	24.86 s	174.38 s	266.40 s
10000	67.29 s	130.09 s	855.15 s	1258.30 s
50000	354.52 s	667.87 s	4149.78 s	6178.76 s

In Fig. 4 the win rates from the Acrobot-environment were plotted over the course of 400 and 10000 episodes similarly as the scores for the CartPole-environment and it can be seen for low episode numbers that while the policy learned by the standard variant of Q-learning with unchanged rewards performs better than the policy learned by the ordinal variant, changing the numerical values of rewards yields the same performance as the ordinal variant. But for high episode numbers it should be noted that the ordinal variant reaches a similar performance as the standard variant with a win rate of 0.3 after 10000 episodes and clearly outperforms the win rate of the standard Q-learning algorithm with CR.

Similar as for the CartPole-environment, the F- and Q-function margins of the best actions over the course of 400 and 10000 episodes were compared in Fig. 5 and yield different observations for the standard and ordinal variants, and it can be therefore be concluded that the learned policies differ. While the ordinal variant decreases the relative margin of $F(P(s, a))$ of the best action and therefore learns a policy which plays safely, the standard variant learns a policy which maximizes the Q-value margin of the best action and therefore follows a policy which enters critical states more often. While the standard variant learns a good policy quicker, it should be noted that both policies perform comparably after many episodes despite the policy differences.

As can be seen in Table 1, using the ordinal variant results in an additional computational load by a factor between 0.8 and 1.2 for CartPole and 0.5 for Acrobot.

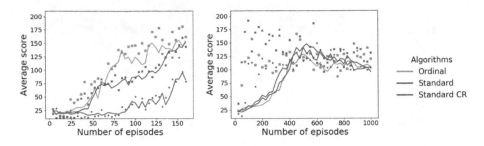

Fig. 6. CartPole scores of standard and ordinal DQN for 160 and 1000 episodes

The additionally required computational capacity is caused by the computation of the measure of statistical superiority which is less efficient than computing the expected sum of rewards. This factor could be reduced by using the iterative update of the function *measure of statistical superiority* described in [4].

Deep Q-Network. In Fig. 6 the scores achieved in the CartPole-environment by the ordinal as well as the standard Deep Q-Network, with and without CR, can be seen over the course of 160 and 1000 episodes. For 160 episodes it can be seen that ordinal DQN as well as the standard variant without CR converge to a good policy reaching an episode score close to 150. Contrary to this performance, modified rewards negatively impact standard Q-learning and therefore its performance is significantly worse, not reaching a score above 100. Additionally for low episode numbers it should be noted that the policy learned by the ordinal variant of Deep Q-Network is able to achieve good scores faster than the standard variant, matching the observation made for the Q-learning algorithms. The evaluation for 1000 episodes shows that the performances of standard, with and without CR, and ordinal DQNs are comparable.

Figure 7 plots the win rate of Deep Q-Network algorithms for the Acrobot-environment over the course of 160 and 1000 episodes. For 160 episodes standard DQN with engineered rewards performs better than the ordinal variant, but loses this quality once the rewards are modified. For high episode numbers it can be seen that the ordinal variant is comparable to the standard algorithm without CR and solves the environment with a win rate of close to 1.0, but clearly outperforms the standard DQN with modified rewards which is only able to achieve a win rate of 0.6. It should be noted that all variants of DQN are able to learn a better policy than their respective Q-learning algorithms, achieving a higher win rate in less than 160 episodes.

Additionally, it should be noted that the use of the ordinal variant of DQN adds an additional computational factor between 0 and 0.5 for the CartPole-environment and 1.0 for the Acrobot-environment, as can be seen in Table 2.

Since the evaluation of the ordinal Deep Q-Network algorithm shows comparable results to the standard DQN with engineered rewards and furthermore outperforms the standard variant with modified rewards, it can be concluded

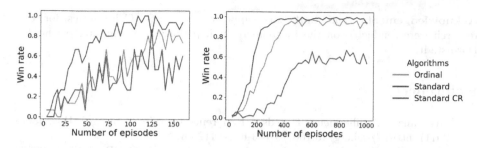

Fig. 7. Acrobot win rates of standard and ordinal DQN for 160 and 1000 episodes

Table 2. Computation time comparison of standard and ordinal DQN

Number of episodes	CartPole		Acrobot	
	Standard	Ordinal	Standard	Ordinal
160	1520.01 s	2232.48 s	3659.44 s	7442.49 s
400	6699.69 s	7001.79 s	9678.80 s	19840.88 s
1000	15428.41 s	15526.84 s	23310.36 s	47755.90 s

that the conversion of the Deep Q-Network algorithm to ordinal rewards is successful. Therefore it has been shown that algorithms of deep reinforcement learning can as well be adapted to the use of ordinal rewards.

6 Conclusion

In this paper we have shown that the use of ordinal rewards for reinforcement learning is able to reach and even improve the quality of standard reinforcement learning algorithms with numerical rewards. We compared RL algorithms for both numerical and ordinal rewards on a number of tested environments and demonstrated that the performance of the ordinal variant is mostly comparable to the learned common RL algorithms that make use of engineered rewards while being able to significantly improve the performance for modified rewards.

Finally, it should be noted that ordinal reinforcement learning enables the learning of a good policy for environments without much effort to manually shape rewards. We hereby lose the possibility of reward shaping to the same degree that numerical rewards would allow, but therefore gain a more simple-to-design reward structure. Hence, our variant of reinforcement learning with ordinal rewards is especially suitable for environments that do not have a natural semantic of numerical rewards or where reward shaping is difficult. Additionally this method enables the usage of new and unexplored environments for RL only with the specification of an order of desirability instead of the needed effort of manually engineering numerical rewards with sensible semantic meaning.

Acknowledgements. This work was supported by DFG. Calculations for this research were conducted on the Lichtenberg high performance computer of the TU Darmstadt.

References

1. Fürnkranz, J., Hüllermeier, E. (eds.): Preference Learning. Springer, Heidelberg (2011). https://doi.org/10.1007/978-3-642-14125-6
2. Gilbert, H., Weng, P.: Quantile reinforcement learning. CoRR abs/1611.00862 (2016)
3. Hasselt, H.V., Guez, A., Silver, D.: Deep reinforcement learning with double Q-learning. In: Proceedings of the Thirtieth AAAI Conference on Artificial Intelligence, AAAI 2016, pp. 2094–2100. AAAI Press (2016)
4. Joppen, T., Fürnkranz, J.: Ordinal Monte Carlo tree search. CoRR abs/1901.04274 (2019)
5. Lin, L.J.: Reinforcement learning for robots using neural networks. Ph.D. thesis, Carnegie Mellon University, Pittsburgh, PA, USA (1992). uMI Order No. GAX93-22750
6. Mnih, V., et al.: Playing atari with deep reinforcement learning. CoRR abs/1312.5602 (2013)
7. Mnih, V., et al.: Human-level control through deep reinforcement learning. Nature **518**(7540), 529–533 (2015)
8. Sutton, R.S., Barto, A.G.: Reinforcement Learning - An Introduction. Adaptive Computation and Machine Learning, 2nd edn. MIT Press, Cambridge (2018)
9. Watkins, C.J., Dayan, P.: Q-learning. Mach. Learn. **8**, 279–292 (1992)
10. Weng, P.: Markov decision processes with ordinal rewards: reference point-based preferences. In: Proceedings of the 21st International Conference on Automated Planning and Scheduling (ICAPS 2011), Freiburg, Germany. AAAI Press (2011)
11. Weng, P.: Ordinal decision models for Markov decision processes. In: Proceedings of the 20th European Conference on Artificial Intelligence (ECAI 2012), pp. 828–833. IOS Press, Montpellier (2012)
12. Weng, P., Busa-Fekete, R., Hüllermeier, E.: Interactive q-learning with ordinal rewards and unreliable tutor. In: Proceedings of the ECML/PKDD-13 Workshop on Reinforcement Learning from Generalized Feedback: Beyond Numeric Rewards (2013)
13. Wirth, C., Akrour, R., Neumann, G., Fürnkranz, J.: A survey of preference-based reinforcement learning methods. J. Mach. Learn. Res. **18**(136), 1–46 (2017)
14. Zap, A.: Ordinal reinforcement learning. Master's thesis, Technische Universität Darmstadt (2019, to appear)

Sample-Efficient Model-Free Reinforcement Learning with Off-Policy Critics

Denis Steckelmacher[1]($\boxtimes$), Hélène Plisnier[1], Diederik M. Roijers[2], and Ann Nowé[1]

[1] Vrije Universiteit Brussel, Pleinlaan 2, 1050 Brussels, Belgium
`dsteckel@ai.vub.ac.be`
[2] VU Amsterdam, De Boelelaan 1105, 1081 HV Amsterdam, The Netherlands

Abstract. Value-based reinforcement-learning algorithms provide state-of-the-art results in model-free discrete-action settings, and tend to outperform actor-critic algorithms. We argue that actor-critic algorithms are limited by their need for an *on-policy* critic. We propose Bootstrapped Dual Policy Iteration (BDPI), a novel model-free reinforcement-learning algorithm for continuous states and discrete actions, with an actor and several *off-policy* critics. Off-policy critics are compatible with experience replay, ensuring high sample-efficiency, without the need for off-policy corrections. The actor, by slowly imitating the average greedy policy of the critics, leads to high-quality and state-specific exploration, which we compare to Thompson sampling. Because the actor and critics are fully decoupled, BDPI is remarkably stable, and unusually robust to its hyper-parameters. BDPI is significantly more sample-efficient than Bootstrapped DQN, PPO, and ACKTR, on discrete, continuous and pixel-based tasks. Source code: https://github.com/vub-ai-lab/bdpi. Appendix: https://arxiv.org/abs/1903.04193.

Keywords: Reinforcement learning · Value iteration · Actor-critic

1 Introduction and Related Work

State-of-the-art stochastic actor-critic algorithms, used with discrete actions, all share a common trait: the critic Q^π they learn directly evaluates the actor [23,26,37,47]. Some algorithms allow the agent to execute a policy different from the actor, which the authors refer to as off-policy, but the critic is still on-policy with regards to the actor [18, for instance]. ACER and the off-policy actor-critic [12,44] use off-policy corrections to learn Q^π from past experiences, DDPG learns its critic with an on-policy SARSA-like algorithm [24], Q-prop [17] uses the actor in the critic learning rule to make it on-policy, and PGQL [28] allows for an off-policy V function, but requires it to be combined with on-policy advantage values. Notable examples of algorithms without an on-policy critic are AlphaGo

© Springer Nature Switzerland AG 2020
U. Brefeld et al. (Eds.): ECML PKDD 2019, LNAI 11908, pp. 19–34, 2020.
https://doi.org/10.1007/978-3-030-46133-1_2

Zero [38], that replaces the critic with a slow-moving target policy learned with tree search, and the Actor-Mimic [31], that minimizes the cross-entropy between an actor and the Softmax policies of critics (see Sect. 4.2). The need of most actor-critic algorithms for an on-policy critic makes them incompatible with state-of-the-art value-based algorithms of the Q-Learning family [3,20], that are all highly sample-efficient but off-policy. In a *discrete-actions* setting, where off-policy value-based methods can be used, this raises two questions:

1. Can we use *off-policy* value-based algorithms in an actor-critic setting?
2. Would the actor bring anything positive to the agent?

In this paper, we provide a positive answer to these two questions. We introduce Bootstrapped Dual Policy Iteration (BDPI), a novel actor-critic algorithm. Our actor learning rule, inspired by Conservative Policy Iteration (see Sects. 2.4 and 3.2), is robust to off-policy critics. Because we lift the requirement for on-policy critics, the full range of value-based methods can now be leveraged by the critic, such as DQN-family algorithms [20], or exploration-focused approaches [3,9]. To better isolate the sample-efficiency and exploration properties arising from our actor-critic approach, we use in this paper a simple DQN-family critic. We learn several Q-Functions, as suggested by [30], with a novel extension of Q-Learning (see Sect. 3.1). Unlike other approaches, that use the critics to compute means and variances [11,27], BDPI uses the information in each individual critic to train the actor. We show that our actor learning rule, combined with several off-policy critics, can be compared to bootstrapped Thompson sampling (Sect. 3.4).

Our experimental results in Sect. 4 show that BDPI significantly outperforms state-of-the-art actor-critic *and* critic-only algorithms, such as PPO, ACKTR and Bootstrapped DQN, on a set of discrete, continuous and 3D-rendered tasks. Our ablative study shows that BDPI's actor significantly contributes to its performance and exploration. To the best of our knowledge, this is the first time that, in a discrete-action setting, the benefit of having an actor can be clearly identified. Finally, and perhaps most importantly, BDPI is highly robust to its hyper-parameters, which mitigates the need for endless tuning (see Sect. 4.5). BDPI's ease of configuration and sample-efficiency are crucial in many real-world settings, where computing power is not the bottleneck, but data collection is.

2   Background

In this section, we introduce and review the various formalisms on which Bootstrapped Dual Policy Iteration builds. We also compare current actor-critic methods with Conservative and Dual Policy Iteration, in Sects. 2.3 and 2.4.

2.1   Markov Decision Processes

A discrete-time Markov Decision Process (MDP) [6] with discrete actions is defined by the tuple $\langle S, A, R, T, \gamma \rangle$: a possibly-infinite set S of states; a finite set

A of actions; a reward function $R(s_t, a_t, s_{t+1}) \in \mathbb{R}$ returning a scalar reward r_{t+1} for each state transition; a transition function $T(s_{t+1}|s_t, a_t) \in [0, 1]$ determining the dynamics of the environment; and the discount factor $0 \leq \gamma < 1$ defining the importance given by the agent to future rewards.

A stochastic stationary policy $\pi(a_t|s_t) \in [0, 1]$ maps each state to a probability distribution over actions. At each time-step, the agent observes s_t, selects $a_t \sim \pi(.|s_t)$, then observes r_{t+1} and s_{t+1}, which produces an $(s_t, a_t, r_{t+1}, s_{t+1})$ *experience* tuple. An optimal policy π^* maximizes the expected cumulative discounted reward $\mathbb{E}_{\pi^*}[\sum_t \gamma^t r_t]$. The goal of the agent is to find π^* based on its experience within the environment, with no *a-priori* knowledge of R and T.

2.2   Q-Learning, Experience Replay and Clipped DQN

Value-based reinforcement learning algorithms, such as Q-Learning [45], use experience tuples and Eq. 1 to learn an action-value function Q^*, also called a *critic*, which estimates the expected return for each action in each state when the optimal policy is followed:

$$Q_{k+1}(s_t, a_t) = Q_k(s_t, a_t) + \alpha \delta_{k+1} \qquad (1)$$
$$\delta_{k+1} = r_{t+1} + \gamma \max_{a'} Q_k(s_{t+1}, a') - Q_k(s_t, a_t)$$

with $0 < \alpha < 1$ a learning rate. At acting time, the agent selects actions having the largest Q-Value, plus some exploration. To improve sample-efficiency, experience tuples are stored in an *experience buffer*, and are periodically re-sampled for further training using Eq. 1 [25]. Before convergence, Q-Learning tends to over-estimate the Q-Values [19], as positive errors are propagated by the max operator of Eq. 1. Clipped DQN [14], that we use as the basis of our critic learning rule (Sect. 3.1), addresses this bias by applying the max operator to the minimum of the predictions of two independent Q-functions, such that positive errors are removed by the minimum operation. Addressing this over-estimation has been shown to increase sample-efficiency and robustness [19].

2.3   Policy Gradient and Actor-Critic Algorithms

Instead of choosing actions according to Q-Values, Policy Gradient methods [40,46] explicitly learn an *actor* $\pi_\theta(a_t|s_t) \in [0, 1]$, parametrized by a weights vector θ, such as the weights of a neural network. The objective of the agent is to maximize the expected cumulative discounted reward $\mathbb{E}_\pi[\sum_t \gamma^t r_t]$, which translates to the minimization of Eq. 2 [40]:

$$\mathcal{L}(\pi_\theta) = -\sum_{t=0}^{T} \left\{ \frac{\mathcal{R}_t}{Q^{\pi_\theta}(s_t, a_t)} \right\} \log(\pi_\theta(a_t|s_t)) \qquad (2)$$

with $a_t \sim \pi_\theta(s_t)$ the action executed at time t, and $\mathcal{R}_t = \sum_{\tau=t}^{T} \gamma^\tau r_\tau$ the Monte-Carlo return from time t onwards. At every training epoch, experiences are used to compute the gradient $\frac{\partial \mathcal{L}}{\partial \theta}$ of Eq. 2, then the weights of the policy are adjusted by a small step in the opposite direction of the gradient. A second gradient update requires fresh experiences [40], which makes Policy Gradient quite sample-inefficient. Three approaches have been proposed to increase the sample-efficiency of Policy Gradient: trust regions, that allow larger gradient steps to be taken [36], surrogate losses, that prevent divergence if several gradient steps are taken [37], and stochastic[1] actor-critic methods [4,23], that replace the Monte-Carlo R_t with an estimation of its expectation, $Q^{\pi_\theta}(s_t, a_t)$, an *on-policy* critic, shown in Eq. 2, bottom.

The use of Q^{π_θ}-Values instead of Monte-Carlo returns leads to a gradient of lower variance, and allows actor-critic methods to obtain impressive results on several challenging tasks [15,26,44]. However, conventional actor-critic algorithms may not provide any benefits over a cleverly-designed critic-only algorithm, see for example [28], Sect. 3.3. Actor-critic algorithms also rely on Q^{π_θ} to be accurate for the current actor, even if the actor itself can be distinct from the actual behavior policy of the agent [12,16,44]. Failing to ensure this accuracy may cause divergence [23,40].

2.4   Conservative and Dual Policy Iteration

Approximate Policy Iteration and Dual Policy Iteration are two approaches to Policy Iteration. API repeatedly evaluates a policy π_k, producing an *on-policy* Q^{π_k}, then trains π_{k+1} to be as close as possible to the greedy policy $\Gamma(Q^{\pi_k})$ [21,35]. Conservative Policy Iteration (CPI) extends API to *slowly* move π towards the greedy policy [33]. Dual Policy Iteration [39] formalizes as CPI several modern reinforcement learning approaches [2,38], by replacing the greedy function with a *slow-moving* target policy π':

$$\Gamma(Q^{\pi_k}) \tag{API}$$
$$\pi_{k+1} \leftarrow (1-\alpha)\pi_k + \alpha\Gamma(Q^{\pi_k}) \tag{CPI}$$
$$(1-\alpha)\pi_k + \alpha\pi'_k \tag{DPI}$$

with $0 < \alpha \le 1$ a learning rate, set to a small value in Conservative Policy Iteration algorithms (0.01 in our experiments). Among CPI algorithms, Safe Policy Iteration [33] dynamically adjusts the learning rate to ensure (with high probability) a monotonic improvement of the policy, while [41] propose the use of statistical tests to decide whether to update the policy.

While theoretically promising, CPI algorithms present two important limitations: their convergence is difficult to obtain with function approximation [7,43]; and their update rule and associated set of bounds and proofs depend on Q^{π_k}, an *on-policy* function that would need to be re-computed before every iteration

---

[1] Deterministic actor-critic methods are slightly different and outside the scope of this paper.

in an on-line setting. As such, CPI algorithms are notoriously difficult to implement, with [33] reporting some of the first empirical results on CPI. Our main contribution, presented in the next section, is inspired by CPI but distinct from it in several key aspects. Our actor learning rule follows the Dual Policy Iteration formalism, with a target policy π' built from off-policy critics (see Sect. 3.2). The fact that the actor gathers the experiences on which the critics are trained can be compared to the *guidance* that π gives to π' in the DPI formalism [39].

3   Bootstrapped Dual Policy Iteration

Our main contribution, Bootstrapped Dual Policy Iteration (BDPI), consists of two original components. In Sect. 3.1, we introduce an aggressive off-policy critic, inspired by Bootstrapped DQN and Clipped DQN [14,30]. In Sects. 3.2 to 3.3, we introduce an actor that leads to high-quality exploration, further enhancing sample-efficiency. We detail BDPI's exploration properties in Sect. 3.4, before empirically validating our results in a diverse set of environments (Sect. 4). Our implementation of BDPI is available on https://github.com/vub-ai-lab/bdpi.

3.1   Aggressive Bootstrapped Clipped DQN

We begin our description of BDPI with the algorithm used to train its critics, Aggressive Bootstrapped Clipped DQN (ABCDQN). Like Bootstrapped DQN [30], ABCDQN consists of $N_c > 1$ critics. Combining ABCDQN with an actor is detailed in Sect. 3.2. When used without an actor, ABCDQN selects actions by randomly sampling a critic for each episode, then following its greedy function.

Each critic of ABCDQN is trained with an aggressive algorithm loosely inspired by Clipped DQN and Double Q-Learning [14,19]. Each critic maintains two Q-functions, Q^A and Q^B. Every *training iteration*, Q^A and Q^B are swapped, then Q^A is trained with Eq. 3 on a set of experiences sampled from an experience buffer, shared by all the critics. Contrary to Clipped DQN, an on-policy algorithm that uses $V(s_{t+1}) \equiv \min_{l=A,B} Q^l(s_{t+1}, \pi(s_{t+1}))$ as target value, ABCDQN removes the reference to $\pi(s_{t+1})$ and instead uses the following formulas:

$$Q^A_{k+1}(s_t, a_t) = Q^A_k(s_t, a_t) + \alpha\big(r_{t+1} + \gamma V(s_{t+1}) - Q^A_k(s_t, a_t)\big) \qquad (3)$$
$$V(s_{t+1}) \equiv \min_{l=A,B} Q^l\big(s_{t+1}, \text{argmax}_{a'}\, Q^A_k(s_{t+1}, a')\big)$$

We increase the aggressiveness of ABCDQN by performing several *training iterations* per *training epoch*. Every *training epoch*, every critic is updated using a different batch of experiences, for $N_t > 1$ *training iteration*. As mentioned above, a training iteration consists of applying Eq. 3 on the critic, which produces Q_{k+1} values, either stored in a tabular critic, or used to optimize the parameters of a parametric critic Q_θ. The parameters minimize $\sum_{(s,a)}(Q_\theta(s, a) - Q_{k+1}(s, a))^2$, using gradient descent for *several* gradient steps.

ABCDQN achieves high sample-efficiency (see Sect. 4), but its purposefully exaggerated aggressiveness makes it prone to overfitting. We now introduce an actor, that alleviates this problem and leads to high-quality exploration, comparable to Thompson sampling (see Sect. 3.4).

3.2   Training the Actor with Off-Policy Critics

To improve exploration, and further increase sample-efficiency, we now complement our ABCDQN critic with the second component of BDPI, its actor. The actor π takes inspiration from Conservative Policy Iteration [33], but replaces on-policy estimates of Q^π with our off-policy ABCDQN critics. Every *training epoch*, after every critic i has been updated on its batch of experiences $E_i \subset B$ uniformly sampled from the experience buffer, the actor is sequentially trained towards the greedy policy of all the critics:

$$\pi(s) \leftarrow (1 - \lambda)\pi(s) + \lambda\Gamma(Q^{A,i}_{k+1}(s, \cdot)) \qquad \forall\, i, \forall\, s \in E_i \qquad (4)$$

with $\lambda = 1 - e^{-\delta}$ the actor learning rate, computed from the maximum allowed KL-divergence δ defining a *trust-region* (see Appendix B), and Γ the greedy function, that returns a policy greedy in $Q^{A,i}$, the Q^A function of the i-th critic. Pseudocode for the complete BDPI algorithm is given in the appendix, and summarized in Algorithm 1.

Contrary to Conservative Policy Iteration algorithms, and because our critics are off-policy, the greedy function is applied on an estimate of Q^*, the optimal Q-function, instead of Q^π. The use of an actor, that slowly imitates approximations of $\Gamma(Q^*) \equiv \pi^*$, leads to an interesting relation between BDPI and Thompson sampling (see Sect. 3.4). While expressed in the tabular form in Eqs. 3 and 4, the BDPI update rules produce Q-Values and probability distributions that can directly be used to train any kind of function approximator, on the mean-squared-error loss, and for as many gradient steps as desired. The Policy Distillation literature [34] suggests that implementing the actor and critics with neural networks, with the actor having a smaller architecture than the critic, may lead to good results. Large critics reduce bias [13], and a small policy has been shown to outperform and generalize better than big policies [34]. In this paper, we use actors and critics of the same size, and leave the evaluation of asymmetric architectures for future work.

---

for *every critic* $i \in [1, N_c]$ **do**
    $E \leftarrow$ N experiences sampled from the buffer;
    for N_t *training iterations* **do**
        Swap $Q^{A,i}$ and $Q^{B,i}$;
        Update $Q^{A,i}$ of critic i on E with Equation 3;
    end
    Update actor on E with Equation 4;
end

Algorithm 1: Learning with Bootstrapped Dual Policy Iteration (summary)

3.3 BDPI and Conservative Policy Iteration

The standard Conservative Policy Iteration update rule (see Sect. 2.4) updates the actor π towards $\Gamma(Q^\pi)$, the greedy function according to the Q-Values arising from π. This slow-moving update, and the inter-dependence between π and Q^π, allows several properties to be proven [21], and the optimal policy learning rate α to be determined from Q^π [33]. Because BDPI learns off-policy critics, that can be arbitrarily different from the on-policy Q^π function, the Approximate Safe Policy Iteration framework [33] would infer an "optimal" learning rate of 0. Fortunately, a non-zero learning rate still allows BDPI to learn efficiently. In Sect. 3.4, we show that the off-policy nature of BDPI's critics makes it approximate Thompson sampling, which CPI's on-policy critics do not do. Our experimental results in Sect. 4 further illustrate how BDPI allows fast and robust learning, even in difficult-to-explore environments.

3.4 BDPI and Thompson Sampling

In a bandit setting, Thompson sampling [42] is regarded as one of the best ways to balance exploration and exploitation [1,10]. Thompson sampling consists of maintaining a posterior belief of how likely any given action is optimal, and drawing actions directly from this probability distribution. In a reinforcement-learning setting, Thompson sampling consists of selecting an action a according to $\pi(a|s) \equiv P(a = \mathrm{argmax}_{a'} Q^*(s, a'))$, with Q^* the optimal Q-function.

BDPI learns off-policy critics, that produce estimates of Q^*. Sampling a critic and updating the actor towards its greedy policy is therefore equivalent to sampling a function $Q \sim P(Q = Q^*)$ [30], then updating the actor towards $\Gamma(Q)$, with $\Gamma(Q)(s, a) = \mathbb{1}[a = \mathrm{argmax}_{a'} Q(s, a')]$, and $\mathbb{1}$ the indicator function. Over several updates, and thanks to a small λ learning rate (see Eq. 4), the actor learns the expected greedy function of the critics, which (intuitively) folds the indicator function into the sampling of Q, leading to an actor that learns $\pi(a|s) = P(a = \mathrm{argmax}_{a'} Q^*(s, a'))$, the Thompson sampling equation for reinforcement learning.

The use of an explicit actor, instead of directly sampling critics and executing actions as Bootstrapped DQN does [30], positively impacts BDPI's performance (see Sect. 4). [27] discuss why Bootstrapped DQN, without an actor, leads to a higher regret than their Information Directed Sampling, and propose to add a Distributional RL [5] component to their agent. [29] presents arguments against the use of Distributional RL, and instead combines Bootstrapped DQN with prior functions. In the next section, we show that BDPI largely outperforms Boostrapped DQN, along with PPO and ACKTR, without relying on Distributional RL nor prior functions. We believe that having an explicit actor changes the way the posterior is computed, which may positively influence exploration compared to actor-less approaches.

4   Experiments

To illustrate the properties of BDPI, we compare it to its ablations and a wide range of reinforcement learning algorithms, in four environments with completely different state-spaces and dynamics. Our results demonstrate the high sample-efficiency and exploration quality of BDPI. Moreover, these results are obtained with the same configuration of critics, experience replay and learning rates across environments, which illustrates the ease of configuration of BDPI. In Sect. 4.5, we carry out further experiments, that demonstrate that BDPI is more robust to its hyper-parameters than other algorithms. This is key to the application of reinforcement learning to real-world settings, where vast hyper-parameter tuning is often infeasible.

4.1   Algorithms

We evaluate the algorithms listed below:

BDPI	*this paper*
ABCDQN, BDPI without an actor	*this paper*
BDPI w/AM, see Sect. 4.2	*this paper*
BDQN, Bootstrapped DQN	[30]
PPO	[37]
ACKTR	[47]

Except on *Hallway*,[2] a 3D environment described in the next section, all algorithms use feed-forward neural networks to represent their actor and critic, with one (2 for PPO and ACKTR) hidden layers of 32 neurons (256 on *LunarLander*). The state is one-hot encoded in *FrozenLake*, and directly fed to the network in the other environments. The neural networks are trained with the Adam optimizer [22], using a learning rate of 0.0001 (0.001 for PPO, ACKTR uses its own optimizer with a varying learning rate). Unless specified otherwise, BDPI uses $N_c = 16$ critics, all updated every time-step on a different 256-experiences batch, sampled from the same shared experience buffer, for 4 applications of our ABCDQN update rule. BDPI trains its neural networks for 20 epochs per training iteration, on the mean-squared-error loss (even for the policy).

Hallway being a 3D environment, the algorithms are configured differently. Changes to BDPI are minimal, as they only consist of using the standard Deep-Mind convolutional layers, a hidden layer of 256 neurons, and optimizing the networks for 1 epoch per training iteration, instead of 20. PPO and ACKTR, however, see much larger changes. They use the DeepMind layers, 16 replicas of the environment (instead of 1), a learning rate of 0.00005, and perform gradient steps every 80 time-steps (per replica, so 1280 time-steps in total). These PPO and ACKTR parameters are recommended by the author of *Hallway*.

---

[2] https://github.com/maximecb/gym-miniworld.

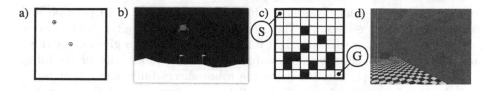

Fig. 1. The four environments. (a) *Table*, a large continuous-state environment with a black circular robot and a blue charging station. (b) *LunarLander*, a continuous-state task based on the Box2D physics simulator. (c) *Frozen Lake*, an 8-by-8 slippery gridworld where black squares represent fatal pits. (d) *Hallway*, a 3D pixel-based navigation task. (Color figure online)

4.2   BDPI with the Actor-Mimic Loss

To the best of our knowledge, the Actor-Mimic [31] is the only actor-critic algorithm, along with BDPI, that learns critics that are off-policy with regards to the actor. The Actor-Mimic is designed for transfer learning tasks. One critic per task is trained, using the off-policy DQN algorithm. Then, the cross-entropy between the actor and the Softmax policies $S(Q_i)$ of all the critics is minimized, using the (simplified) loss of Eq. 5.

$$\mathcal{L}(\pi_\theta) = -\sum_{s \in S, a \in A, i < N} S(Q_i)(a|s) \log(\pi_\theta(a|s)) \tag{5}$$

Applying the Actor-Mimic to a single-task setting is possible. We implemented an agent based on BDPI, that retains its ABCDQN critics, but replaces our actor learning rule of Eq. 4 with the Actor-Mimic loss of Eq. 5. Because we only change how the actor is trained, and still use our aggressive critics, we ensure the fairest comparison between our actor learning rule and the cross-entropy loss of the Actor-Mimic. In our experiments, the Actor-Mimic loss with Softmax policies fails to learn efficiently, even after extensive hyper-parameter tuning, probably because the Softmax prevents the policy from becoming deterministic in states where this is necessary. We therefore replaced the Softmax with the greedy function, which led to the much better results that we present in Sect. 4.4.

4.3   Environments

Our evaluation of BDPI takes place in four environments that challenge the algorithms on different aspects of reinforcement learning: exploration with sparse rewards (*Table*), high-dimensional state-spaces (vector *LunarLander*, pixel-based *Hallway*), and high stochasticity (*FrozenLake*).

Table simulates a tiny robot on a large table that has to locate its charging station and dock (see Fig. 1a). The table is a 1-by-1 square. The goal is located at $(0.5, 0.5)$, and the robot always starts at $(0.1, 0.1)$, facing away from the goal. A fixed initial position makes exploration more challenging, as the robot never spawns close to the goal. The robot observes its current (x, y, θ) position and orientation, with $\theta \in [-\pi, \pi]$. Three actions allow the robot to either move forward 0.005 units, or turn left/right 0.1 rad. A reward of 0 is given every time-step. The episode finishes with a reward of -50 if the robot falls off the table, 0 after 200 time-steps, and 100 when the robot successfully docks, that is, its location is $(0.5 \pm 0.05, 0.5 \pm 0.05, \frac{\pi}{4} \pm 0.3)$. The slow speed of the robot and reward sparsity make *Table* more difficult to explore than most Gym tasks [8].

LunarLander is a high-dimensional continuous-state physics-based simulation of a rocket landing on the moon (see Fig. 1b). The agent observes the location and velocities of various components of the lander, and has access to four actions: doing nothing, firing the left/right side engines for one time-step, and firing the main engine. The reward signal for this task is quite complicated but informative, as it directly maps the distance between the rocket and the landing pad to a reward, on every time-step. The environment is considered solved when a cumulative reward of 200 or more is achieved per episode [8].

FrozenLake is a 8×8 grid composed of slippery cells, holes, and one goal cell (see Fig. 1c). The agent can move in four directions (up, down, left or right), with a probability of $\frac{2}{3}$ of actually performing an action other than intended. The agent starts at the top-left corner of the environment, and has to reach the goal at its bottom-right corner. The episode terminates when the agent reaches the goal, resulting in a reward of $+1$, or falls into a hole, resulting in no reward.

Hallway is a 3D pixel-based environment, that simulates a camera-based robotic task in the real world. *Hallway* consists of a rectangular room with a target red box, and the agent. The size of the room, location of the goal and initial position of the agent are randomly chosen for each episode. Four discrete actions allow the agent to move forward/backward and turn left/right. Movement is slow, and the amount of movement is stochastic for each time-step. The reward signal is sparse: 0 every time-step, and 1 when the goal is reached. The episode ends with a reward of 0 after 500 time-steps. This sparse reward function heavily stresses the ability of a reinforcement-learning algorithm to train deep convolutional neural networks on small amounts of reward data.

4.4 Results

Figure 2 shows the cumulative reward per episode obtained by various agents in our four environments. These results are averaged across 8 runs per agent, with the shaded regions representing the standard error. The plots compare BDPI to the algorithms detailed in Sect. 4.1, and display the effect of varying key hyper-parameters of BDPI.

Algorithms. BDPI is the most sample-efficient of all the algorithms, and also achieves the highest returns (especially on hard-to-explore *Table* and pixel-based *Hallway*). BDPI with the Actor-Mimic loss matches BDPI with our actor learning rule on *Table*, but fails to learn *LunarLander* and *Hallway*. ABCDQN (BDPI without its actor) fails on *Table*, an environment where exploration is key, and is generally inferior to BDPI. These results show that both having an explicit actor,

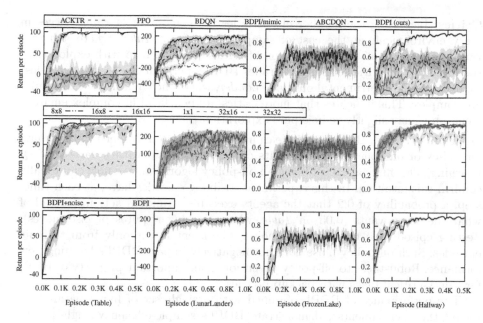

Fig. 2. Results on our four environments. *Top:* BDPI (16 critics, updated for 4 iterations per time-step) outperforms all the other algorithms in every environment. *Middle:* Varying the number of critics and how often they are trained, as long as there are more than one critic, only has minimal impact on BDPI's performance, which demonstrates its robustness. *Bottom:* Adding off-policy noise (see text) does not impact BDPI on any of the environments.

and training it with our update rule of Sect. 3.2, are necessary to achieve top performance. Bootstrapped DQN is highly sample-efficient on *FrozenLake*, but does not explore well enough on the other environments. PPO and ACKTR, after extensive tuning and with several implementations tested, are not as sample-efficient as BDPI and Bootstrapped DQN, two off-policy algorithms using experience replay. Even with per-environment hyper-parameters, PPO and ACKTR need about 5K episodes to learn *FrozenLake*, and 1K episodes on *Table*. BDPI is the only algorithm that, with a single configuration for all the environments, automatically adjusts to the complexity of a task to achieve maximum sample-efficiency.

Interestingly, PPO and ACKTR do perform well on 3D *Hallway*. We tentatively point out that, due to the prevalence of pixel-based environments in the modern reinforcement-learning literature, current algorithms and hyper-parameters may focus more on the representation learning problem than on the reinforcement learning aspect of tasks. Also note that on *Hallway*, PPO and ACKTR use 16 replicas of the environment (instead of 1 for BDPI, and PPO/ACKTR on the other environments). This setting greatly stabilizes the algorithms, but cannot be applied to real-world physical robots.

Critics. Increasing the number of critics leads to smoother learning curves in every environment, at the cost of sample-efficiency in *Table*, where a higher variance in the bootstrap distribution of critics seems to help with exploration. Having only one critic seriously degrades BDPI's performance, and having less than 16 critics is detrimental on *LunarLander*, where the environment dynamics are complex. This indicates that more critics are beneficial in complex environments, but may slightly reduce pure exploration.

Off-Policy Noise. BDPI's actor learning equations do not refer to any behavior policy or on-policy return, and its critics are learned with a variant of Q-Learning. This hints at BDPI being an off-policy algorithm. We now empirically confirm this intuition. In this experiment, training episodes have, at each time-step, a probability of 0.2 that the agents executes a random action, instead of what the actor wants (0.05 on *Table*, where docking requires precise moves). Testing episodes do not have this noise. The agent learns only from training episodes. Such off-policy noise does not negatively impact BDPI's learning performance. Robustness to off-policy execution is an important property of BDPI for safety-critical tasks with backup policies.

The performance of BDPI, obtained with a single set of hyper-parameters for all the environments[3], demonstrate BDPI's sample-efficiency, high-quality exploration, and strong robustness to hyper-parameters, as rigorously detailed in the next section.

4.5 Robustness to Hyper-parameters

Hyper-parameters often need to be tweaked depending on the environment. Therefore, it is highly desirable that an algorithm provides good performance even if not optimally configured, as BDPI does. To objectively measure an algorithm's robustness to its hyper-parameters, we draw inspiration from sensitivity analysis. Thousands of runs of the algorithm are performed on randomly-sampled configurations of hyper-parameters, with each configuration evaluated on the total reward obtained over 800 episodes on *LunarLander*. Then, we compute the average absolute difference of total reward between random pairs of configurations, weighted by their distance in configuration space. This measures how much changing hyper-parameters affects performance. The appendix gives more details, and lists the hyper-parameters we consider for each algorithm.

We evaluated numerous algorithms available in the OpenAI baselines. The algorithms, sorted by ascending sensitivity, are DQN with Prioritized ER (930), BDPI (1167), vanilla DQN (1326), A2C (2369), PPO (2452), then ACKTR (5815). Figure 5 in the appendix shows that the apparent robustness of DQN-family algorithms comes from them performing equally badly for every configuration. 35% of BDPI's configurations outperform the best configuration among all the other algorithms.

---

[3] Only the number of hidden neurons changes between some environments, a trivial change.

5   Conclusion and Future Work

In this paper, we propose Bootstrapped Dual Policy Iteration (BDPI), an algorithm where a bootstrap distribution of aggressively-trained off-policy critics provides an imitation target for an actor. Multiple critics, combined with our actor learning rule, lead to high-quality exploration, comparable to bootstrapped Thompson sampling. Off-policy critics can be learned with any state-of-the-art value-based algorithm, depending on the application domain. BDPI is easy to implement, and remarkably robust to its hyper-parameters. The hyper-parameters we used for the highly-stochastic *FrozenLake* gridworld allowed BDPI to largely outperform the state of the art on three other environments, one of which pixel-based. This, and the availability of BDPI's full source code, makes it one of the first plug-and-play reinforcement-learning algorithm that can easily be applied to new tasks.

While we focus on discrete actions in this paper, the high-quality exploration and robustness to sparse rewards of BDPI lead to encouraging results with discretized continuous action spaces. In Fig. 3, we show that Binary Action Search, an approach that allows precise control of continuous actions, at the cost of increased sparsity in the reward function [32], allows BDPI to outperform the Soft Actor-Critic and TD3, three state-of-the-art continuous-actions algorithms. In future work, we will explore and evaluate various discretization approaches, pursuing the goal of applying BDPI to today's complicated continuous-action tasks.

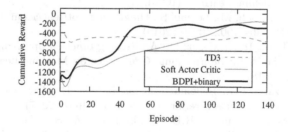

Fig. 3. BDPI adjusted for continuous actions with Binary Action Search [32] is more sample-efficient than TD3 [14, seems to quickly learn to spin] and the Soft Actor-Critic [18] on the Inverted Pendulum task.

Acknowledgments. The first and second authors are funded by the Science Foundation of Flanders (FWO, Belgium), respectively as 1129319N Aspirant, and 1SA6619N Applied Researcher.

References

1. Agrawal, S., Goyal, N.: Analysis of Thompson sampling for the multi-armed bandit problem. In: Conference on Learning Theory (COLT) (2012)
2. Anthony, T., Tian, Z., Barber, D.: Thinking fast and slow with deep learning and tree search. In: Advances in Neural Information Processing Systems (NIPS), pp. 5366–5376 (2017)
3. Arjona-Medina, J.A., Gillhofer, M., Widrich, M., Unterthiner, T., Hochreiter, S.: RUDDER: return decomposition for delayed rewards. arXiv abs/1806.07857 (2018)
4. Barto, A.G., Sutton, R.S., Anderson, C.W.: Neuronlike adaptive elements that can solve difficult learning control problems. IEEE Trans. Syst. Man Cybern. **13**(5), 834–846 (1983)
5. Bellemare, M.G., Dabney, W., Munos, R.: A distributional perspective on reinforcement learning. In: International Conference on Machine Learning (ICML), pp. 449–458 (2017)
6. Bellman, R.: A Markovian decision process. J. Math. Mech. **6**, 679–684 (1957)
7. Böhmer, W., Guo, R., Obermayer, K.: Non-deterministic policy improvement stabilizes approximated reinforcement learning. arXiv abs/1612.07548 (2016)
8. Brockman, G., et al.: OpenAI Gym (2016)
9. Burda, Y., Edwards, H., Storkey, A., Klimov, O.: Exploration by random network distillation. arXiv abs/1810.12894 (2018)
10. Chapelle, O., Li, L.: An empirical evaluation of Thompson sampling. In: Advances in Neural Information Processing Systems (NIPS), pp. 2249–2257 (2011)
11. Chen, R.Y., Sidor, S., Abbeel, P., Schulman, J.: UCB exploration via Q-ensembles. arXiv abs/1706.01502 (2017)
12. Degris, T., White, M., Sutton, R.S.: Linear off-policy actor-critic. In: International Conference on Machine Learning (ICML) (2012)
13. Fu, J., Kumar, A., Soh, M., Levine, S.: Diagnosing bottlenecks in deep Q-learning algorithms. arXiv abs/1902.10250 (2019)
14. Fujimoto, S., Hoof, H.V., Meger, D.: Addressing function approximation error in actor-critic methods. In: International Conference on Machine Learning (ICML), pp. 1582–1591 (2018)
15. Gruslys, A., Azar, M.G., Bellemare, M.G., Munos, R.: The reactor: a sample-efficient actor-critic architecture. arXiv abs/1704.04651 (2017)
16. Gu, S., Lillicrap, T., Turner, R.E., Ghahramani, Z., Schölkopf, B., Levine, S.: Interpolated policy gradient: merging on-policy and off-policy gradient estimation for deep reinforcement learning. In: Advances in Neural Information Processing Systems (NIPS), pp. 3849–3858 (2017)
17. Gu, S., Lillicrap, T., Ghahramani, Z., Turner, R.E., Levine, S.: Q-prop: sample-efficient policy gradient with an off-policy critic. In: International Conference on Learning Representations (ICLR) (2017)
18. Haarnoja, T., Zhou, A., Abbeel, P., Levine, S.: Soft actor-critic: off-policy maximum entropy deep reinforcement learning with a stochastic actor. arXiv abs/1801.01290 (2018)
19. van Hasselt, H.: Double Q-learning. In: Neural Information Processing Systems (NIPS), p. 9 (2010)
20. Hessel, M., et al.: Rainbow: combining improvements in deep reinforcement learning. arXiv abs/1710.02298 (2017)
21. Kakade, S., Langford, J.: Approximately optimal approximate reinforcement learning. In: International Conference on Machine Learning (ICML), pp. 267–274 (2002)

22. Kingma, D., Ba, J.: Adam: a method for stochastic optimization. arXiv preprint arXiv:1412.6980 (2014)
23. Konda, V.R., Borkar, V.S.: Actor-critic-type learning algorithms for Markov decision processes. SIAM J. Control Opt. **38**(1), 94–123 (1999)
24. Lillicrap, T.P., et al.: Continuous control with deep reinforcement learning. arXiv abs/1509.02971 (2015)
25. Lin, L.J.: Self-improving reactive agents based on reinforcement learning, planning and teaching. Mach. Learn. **8**(3–4), 293–321 (1992)
26. Mnih, V., et al.: Asynchronous methods for deep reinforcement learning. In: International Conference on Machine Learning (ICML), p. 10 (2016)
27. Nikolov, N., Kirschner, J., Berkenkamp, F., Andreas, K.: Information-directed exploration for deep reinforcement learning. In: International Conference on Learning Representations (ICLR) (2019, in preparation)
28. O'Donoghue, B., Munos, R., Kavukcuoglu, K., Mnih, V.: PGQ: combining policy gradient and Q-learning. In: International Conference on Learning Representations (ICLR), p. 15 (2017)
29. Osband, I., Aslanides, J., Cassirer, A.: Randomized prior functions for deep reinforcement learning. arXiv abs/1806.03335 (2018)
30. Osband, I., Blundell, C., Pritzel, A., Van Roy, B.: Deep exploration via bootstrapped DQN. In: Advances in Neural Information Processing Systems (NIPS) (2016)
31. Parisotto, E., Ba, J., Salakhutdinov, R.: Actor-mimic: deep multitask and transfer reinforcement learning. In: International Conference on Learning Representations (ICLR) (2016)
32. Pazis, J., Lagoudakis, M.G.: Binary action search for learning continuous-action control policies. In: International Conference on Machine Learning (ICML), pp. 793–800. ACM (2009)
33. Pirotta, M., Restelli, M., Pecorino, A., Calandriello, D.: Safe policy iteration. In: Proceedings of the 30th International Conference on Machine Learning (ICML), pp. 307–315 (2013)
34. Rusu, A.A., et al.: Policy distillation. arXiv abs/1511.06295 (2015)
35. Scherrer, B.: Approximate policy iteration schemes: a comparison. In: Proceedings of the 31th International Conference on Machine Learning (ICML), pp. 1314–1322 (2014)
36. Schulman, J., Levine, S., Abbeel, P., Jordan, M.I., Moritz, P.: Trust region policy optimization. In: International Conference on Machine Learning (ICML) (2015)
37. Schulman, J., Wolski, F., Dhariwal, P., Radford, A., Klimov, O.: Proximal policy optimization algorithms. arXiv abs/1707.06347 (2017)
38. Silver, D., et al.: Mastering the game of go without human knowledge. Nature **550**(7676), 354 (2017)
39. Sun, W., Gordon, G.J., Boots, B., Bagnell, J.A.: Dual policy iteration. arXiv abs/1805.10755 (2018)
40. Sutton, R., McAllester, D., Singh, S., Mansour, Y.: Policy gradient methods for reinforcement learning with function approximation. In: Neural Information Processing Systems (NIPS), p. 7 (2000)
41. Thomas, P.S., Theocharous, G., Ghavamzadeh, M.: High confidence policy improvement. In: International Conference on Machine Learning (ICML), pp. 2380–2388 (2015)
42. Thompson, W.R.: On the likelihood that one unknown probability exceeds another in view of the evidence of two samples. Biometrika **25**(3/4), 285–294 (1933)

43. Wagner, P.: A reinterpretation of the policy oscillation phenomenon in approximate policy iteration. In: Advances in Neural Information Processing Systems (NIPS), pp. 2573–2581 (2011)
44. Wang, Z., et al.: Sample efficient actor-critic with experience replay. Technical report (2016)
45. Watkins, C., Dayan, P.: Q-learning. Mach. Learn. **8**(3–4), 279–292 (1992)
46. Williams, R.J.: Simple statistical gradient-following algorithms for connectionist reinforcement learning. Mach. Learn. **8**(3), 229–256 (1992)
47. Wu, Y., Mansimov, E., Grosse, R.B., Liao, S., Ba, J.: Scalable trust-region method for deep reinforcement learning using Kronecker-factored approximation. In: Advances in Neural Information Processing Systems (NIPS), pp. 5279–5288 (2017)

Learning 3D Navigation Protocols on Touch Interfaces with Cooperative Multi-agent Reinforcement Learning

Quentin Debard[1]([✉]), Jilles Steeve Dibangoye[2], Stéphane Canu[3], and Christian Wolf[4]

[1] Itekube, LIRIS, Caen, France
quentin.debard@itekube.com
[2] Inria, CITI-Lab, INSA-Lyon, Villeurbanne, France
jilles-steeve.dibangoye@insa-lyon.fr
[3] LITIS, INSA-Rouen, Saint-Étienne-du-Rouvray, France
stephane.canu@insa-rouen.fr
[4] LIRIS, Inria, CITI-Lab, INSA-Lyon, Villeurbanne, France
christian.wolf@insa-lyon.fr

Abstract. Using touch devices to navigate in virtual 3D environments such as computer assisted design (CAD) models or geographical information systems (GIS) is inherently difficult for humans, as the 3D operations have to be performed by the user on a 2D touch surface. This ill-posed problem is classically solved with a fixed and handcrafted interaction protocol, which must be learned by the user. We propose to automatically learn a new interaction protocol allowing to map a 2D user input to 3D actions in virtual environments using reinforcement learning (RL). A fundamental problem of RL methods is the vast amount of interactions often required, which are difficult to come by when humans are involved. To overcome this limitation, we make use of two collaborative agents. The first agent models the human by learning to perform the 2D finger trajectories. The second agent acts as the interaction protocol, interpreting and translating to 3D operations the 2D finger trajectories from the first agent. We restrict the learned 2D trajectories to be similar to a training set of collected human gestures by first performing state representation learning, prior to reinforcement learning. This state representation learning is addressed by projecting the gestures into a latent space learned by a variational auto encoder (VAE).

Keywords: Multi-agent · Deep reinforcement learning · H-C interfaces

1 Introduction

The goal in user interface (UI) design is to propose a communication protocol between human users and a given machine that is intuitive, quick, precise, and which minimizes the amount of training required for new users not yet familiar

© Springer Nature Switzerland AG 2020
U. Brefeld et al. (Eds.): ECML PKDD 2019, LNAI 11908, pp. 35–52, 2020.
https://doi.org/10.1007/978-3-030-46133-1_3

with it. Designing such an interface is not trivial, as some of these desired properties are contradictory. Furthermore, some of these objectives are difficult to quantify, such as intuitivity of the interface or, more generally, user satisfaction.

Our work focuses on a specific component of touch user interfaces, which we call the interaction protocol. This protocol defines the rules that allow the computer to interpret 2D user gestures performed on touch tables into actions in the virtual environment. In the literature, this interaction protocol refers to the software side of an interaction technique [14, 21]. In this paper, we address the problem of automatically learning a suitable interaction protocol for graphical user interfaces on touch surfaces, which requires users to manipulate 3D objects, for instance in computer assisted design (CAD) software or in geographic information systems (GIS). In these situations, the problem is particularly ill-posed, as the trajectories produced by a user on the flat touch screen are restricted to a 2D surface, whereas the applications require the user to perform manipulations in a virtual 3D environment. To give a concrete example, inspecting a virtual mechanical product or navigating in a virtual building or city requires the possibility to change the camera viewpoint through rotations, translations, zooming, i.e. to manipulate 6 degrees of freedom (3 for the camera position and 3 for the camera direction) through trajectories of eventually multiple fingers in the 2D plane of the touch table. There is no universally accepted canonical solution for this kind of problem.

Advanced methods approach this mapping from gestures to actions in a 3D environment using several parameters: not only the 2D gesture themselves, but also the position of the camera (view of the user), the state of the 3D environment, etc. [5, 7]. Theoretically, these methods offer more complex manipulation strategies and higher efficiency. However, the challenge here lies in the combination of precision and efficiency on one hand, and ease of use and learnability (by humans) on the other hand.

In this work, we propose to learn these interaction protocols automatically from interactions with humans. The mapping from 2D gestures to actions in the 3D environment is performed by a trainable agent whose policy is learned using reinforcement learning (RL). Such an agent observes user gestures, translates them into actions in the 3D environment and receives a reward, which should be related to user satisfaction in the optimal case. The motivations behind this choice are two-fold:

- to automatically learn complex interactions protocols instead of handcrafting them;
- to create *adaptive* user interfaces, where not only the human users (classically) adapts to the interface, but the computer also adapts to the way the interaction protocol is imagined by the user through online learning during usage.

The main challenge lies in the requirement of massive amounts of interactions, necessary for current RL algorithms, but which are difficult or impossible to come by when humans are involved. Requesting users to provide gestures and feedback on satisfaction at each iteration would be overly complicated and not realistic for any complex application.

In this work, we propose to circumvent this problem by firstly pre-training the RL agent from interaction with a learned user model which is jointly learned with the target agent. The interactions of the user model are statistically constrained to natural interactions collected in a static dataset. Secondly, creating loss/reward signals during this pre-training phase from success measures in standard interaction tasks, e.g. *"go to place X"*.

The paper is organized as follows: Sect. 2 discusses related work in reinforcement learning and HCI. Section 3 presents the exact formulation of the HCI problem as a reinforcement learning problem. Section 4 introduces the main contribution of this work: the formulation as a cooperative multi-agent problem, where the user model is jointly learned with the interaction protocol, restricting simulated interactions to natural ones. Two different experimental sections report evaluations of the approach on two scenarii of increasing complexity. Section 5 describes experiments on a simple 2D environment where users manipulate a 2D object on a 2D surface in a similar fashion to the widely known *"Pinch-To-Zoom"* interface developed for smartphones and tablets. The common solution of this type of environment being known, the objective here is to automatically learn this interaction protocol from interactions instead of handcrafting it. Finally, Sect. 6 describes experiments on the targeted application, namely learning a 2D to 3D interface protocol involving navigation in 3D environments. This application features additional complexities, such as the non-unicity of the solution (discussed in Sect. 4) and the impossibility to analytically define an optimal user.

2   Related Work

Our work stands between two active fields of computer science: human-computer interface (HCI) and machine learning (ML). We will shortly describe relevant work in both areas to paint the background.

Adaptive User Interface—The goal of Adaptive User Interfaces (AUI) is to adapt its visualization and its interactions to fit individual users' intent better. Machine learning, in this case, is traditionally used for user intent modelization. For an overview of state-of-the-art AUI with adaptive visualization, see [1]. To our knowledge, there is no prior work on learning the interaction protocol of an interface with continuous action space.

Reinforcement Learning and UI Design—Reinforcement learning (RL) is a machine learning framework in which a software agent learns to solve an environment by taking actions that maximizes some cumulative reward. RL has seen some specific uses for AUI design, more precisely for user profiling and representation tasks. In [23], an agent learns to detect user preferences implicitly from observing user behavior instead of direct feedback. In [11], an agent uses user feedback to display personalized web pages.

Machine Learning and 3D Interaction Design—3D user interface (UI) design has been studied for about 20 years [6]. In the 3D UI context, a good overview of current state-of-the-art 3D UI methods is given in [21]. While ML has been used in user interface and user experience design for about two decades [16,25], using machine learning for interaction design is to the best of our knowledge an application yet to be explored. In the UI context, ML is classically used to improve the accuracy of an existing interaction protocol: in [24], a gaussian process regression is used to improve touch accuracy. In [8,10,18], supervised deep learning is used to improve the recognition rate of some multi-touch gesture classes.

Reinforcement Learning and Generative Models—Combining the latent representations of generative models with policy learning was explored in some recent work. In [13], the encoding part of a modified VAE is used to build disentangled representations for a RL policy to use in domain adaptation tasks. In [20], a VAE together with an agent are trained for different purposes: synthesize training data from real observations of the policy, embed the observations to provide latent representations to the policy and measure reward signals in the latent space.

Learning from Demonstration—In our paper, we are trying to learn a user model from a small part of all the possible interactions a user can perform. In [22], a model-based agent is built from examples given by a demonstrator that can either be a generative model, open loop excitation or an expert.

3   Learning an Interaction Protocol as a Reinforcement Problem

Our goal is to learn an interaction protocol coupling user trajectories with actions in a 3D application like CAD or GIS while maximizing the user's satisfaction. We cast this as an RL problem, where the agent gets observations in the form of finger trajectories and outputs actions, which correspond to viewpoint changes in a 3D environment. Because user intentions and gestures can have long term dependencies and depend on multiple latent factors, this problem could be modeled as a partially observable Markov decision process (POMDP). Assessing the complexity of such a modelization for a novel application, we prefer in this paper to consider the problem as a fully observed Markov decision process (MDP) by stacking two-time instants. This implies considering that the information given at two following time instants is enough to predict user intent. The problem is then treated as an MDP with continuous observation and action spaces. The agent A observes the state in the form of finger trajectories s and receives a reward r after performing an action a in the application. An agent A learns a policy π such as $a = \pi(s)$ to maximize its expected return, i.e., the expectation of cumulated reward. Figure 1 illustrates this situation.

In the RL nomenclature, the agent interacts with an environment, which, in our case, corresponds to, both, the human user and the application, e.g. a

CAD or GIS software (see Fig. 1). The agent observes a state, i.e. the user's finger trajectories, and then performs actions that change the viewpoint in the 3D software and which lead to a new state (new user gestures). The agent also receives feedback in the form of a reward. It is important to note here that user satisfaction is difficult to measure directly if we do not want the resort to solutions which estimate emotions from facial expressions. In the next sections, we will propose proxy metrics which approximate satisfaction.

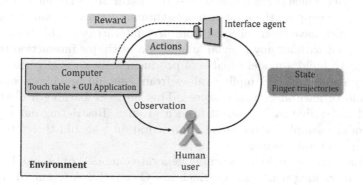

Fig. 1. Learning user interface protocols from interactions with users as an MDP/RL problem.

4   Jointly Learning the Interface Protocol and Human Behavior

Deep networks require large-scale training datasets, and Deep RL is not an exception. More so, RL requires dynamic data in the form of interactions, typically millions or billions when observations are of high dimensions and/or when the regularities are complex. In robotics, where interactions with physical robots are slow (not faster than physical time) and expensive, this leads to the tendency of training from simulations, for instance [2,3] for robot navigation and [26] for grasping, and to the sim-to-real transfer problems [26].

Similar to robotics, learning from human interactions is limited. It is restricted to physical real-time, and the effort required from humans during training is to be taken into account. More so, human time is expensive. For these reasons, we address this by simulating the environment, which in our case also involves simulating the human user. However, while simulating robots through handcrafted solutions is feasible, at least approximately, human behavior is inherently difficult to model. For this reason, we propose a formulation where human behavior is learned jointly with the interface task itself. The next two sub sections describe the two main challenges for this task: (i) restricting the learned user behavior to realistic human gestures (Subsect. 4.1), and (ii) solving the joint learning problem (Subsect. 4.2).

4.1   Learning the Manifold of Natural Human Gestures

Let $x \in \mathcal{X}$ be an observation in the form of natural two-finger trajectories performed by a human user. We define an observation as a N-length sequence of 4-tuples, each 4-tuple consists of a pair of coordinates (x, y), one for each of the two fingers. $\mathcal{X} = \mathbb{R}^{4N}$ is the space of observations of length N. The gesture space $\mathcal{X}$ thus covers all possible pairs of 2D trajectories, including trajectories which are anatomically impossible to perform by human fingers. Our objective is to learn a subspace which corresponds to gestures naturally performed by humans. To this end, we suppose the existence of a training dataset of natural gestures $X = \{x_i\}$, which have been collected from user interactions. This training data can be collected without any manual annotation as simple interaction traces.

We want to build a model capable of producing any natural gesture x from a latent representation z. Sampling values from z should provide us samples of the manifold of natural human gestures. This involves learning a distribution $p(x|z)$ and to be able to evaluate it from a given z. Restricting our simulated user to produce samples of the latent representation z should therefore restrict it to produce natural gestures.

Several approaches exist for learning generative models of probability distributions from training data, among which are Generative Adversarial Networks (GANs) [12] and Variational Auto-Encoders (VAEs) [15]. Our definition of $p(x|z)$ can be related to the generative part of a GAN or the decoder part of a VAE. In this work, we chose VAEs for two reasons: they are simpler to train and less sensitive to hyperparameters; and the latent space is smoother, due to its soft constraint to be close to a multivariate Gaussian.

The VAE is trained on the dataset X, approximating the distribution $p_\theta(x)$ by measuring the reconstruction error on a sample x_i coded by an encoder E into a code z_i, then reconstructed into $\hat{x}_i$ using a decoder D. To describe the problem from a probabilistic point of view, the probability $p_\theta(x)$ of a sample x can be decomposed into a prior and a likelihood as:

$$p_\theta(x) = \int p_\theta(x|z)p_\theta(z)dz \tag{1}$$

where the prior on z is defined as a standard Gaussian distribution $p_\theta(z) = \mathcal{N}(\mathbf{0}, \mathbf{I})$. In our case (continuous values), we can assume that the likelihood is Gaussian distributed:

$$p_\theta(x|z) = \mathcal{N}(x|D(z, \phi_d), \sigma^2 \mathbf{I}) \tag{2}$$

where $D(z, \phi_d)$ is the decoder of the VAE. The integral is difficult to evaluate, but can be approximated by a point estimate $z = q_\phi(x)$ from the variational distribution q:

$$p_\theta(x) \approx \mathcal{N}(x|D(q_\phi(x), \phi_d), \sigma^2 \mathbf{I}) \tag{3}$$

$q_\phi(z|x)$ can be seen as an encoder, noted $E(x, \phi_e)$. In this case, we need to ensure that $q_\phi(z|x)$ is a good estimate of the true posterior $p_\theta(z|x)$. This is done using the Kullback-Leibler divergence, noted D_{KL}. Considering the approximation error for only a sample x_i, the KL divergence becomes $D_{KL}(E(x_i, \phi_e)||p(z))$. As stated earlier, $p_\theta(z) = \mathcal{N}(\mathbf{0}, \mathbf{I})$. If we use the L_2-norm to measure the reconstruction error, the total error can be written as a variation of the evidence lower bound (ELBO):

$$ELBO_i = ||x_i - D(E(x_i, \phi_e), \phi_d)||_2 - \beta \ D_{KL}(E(x_i, \phi_e)||\mathcal{N}(\mathbf{0}, \mathbf{I})) \qquad (4)$$

where β is a parameter allowing us to adjust the tradeoff between the reconstruction precision and the latent space regularity [19]. We can then update ϕ_e and ϕ_d by minimizing this error using back-propagation.

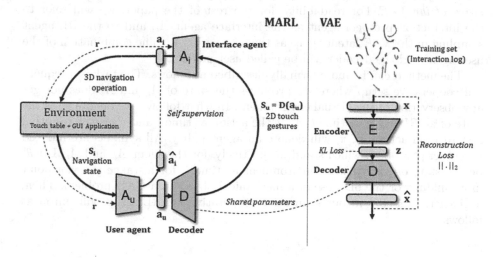

Fig. 2. Cooperative multi-agent RL problem for jointly learning user interface protocol and user behavior. Generative models are blue and RL policies are green (best viewed in color). (Color figure online)

4.2 Cooperative Multi-agent RL

We formulate the task of jointly learning the user interface protocol and human behavior as a cooperative multi-agent reinforcement (MARL) problem, as shown in Fig. 2. Two agents are learned jointly, each with its own policy:

- agent A_i corresponds to the user interface. Learning its policy is the original goal of this work, as this agent is responsible for translating 2D finger gestures into actions in the 3D environment (CAD or GIS software).
- agent A_u corresponds to the simulated user, with which agent A_i interacts. The only purpose of A_u is to replace human users during the costly pre-training phase. In contrast to A_i, A_u is discarded after training.

These two agents are trained to maximize the same objective function, sharing the same reward (detailed in Sect. 4.3), which makes this problem a *cooperative* multi-agent problem. Only A_i directly takes action in the virtual 3D environment, whereas A_u acts indirectly by producing the input of A_i.

Learning both agents by maximizing the joint reward without additional constraints could naturally lead to degenerate solutions, which are efficient (allow to navigate quickly), but where the gestures exchanged between the two agents are artificial and not easily and naturally doable by humans. For this reason, we restrict the exchange between A_i and A_u to a representation z learned by the VAE described in Sect. 4.1. More precisely, after training the VAE, we discard its encoder. The agent A_u learns a policy on an action space which corresponds to the latent representation z. Each action z is then decoded to a natural gesture x through the decoder of the learned VAE, as illustrated in Fig. 2. In other words, *the policy of the user agent learns to produce gestures by navigating the latent space of the VAE.* For readability, for the rest of the paper, we will refer to the interaction protocol agent as the interface agent A_i, and to the RL agent sampling in the VAE latent space as the user agent A_u. The combination of the user agent and the decoder will be called user model U.

The method can be more formally described as follows. The task is a sequential cooperative setup where A_u produces the state of A_i and A_i does not get any observation of the virtual environment. In what follows, we denote s^t as the state of an RL agent at time t, a^t as the action at time t and r^t as the resulting reward from action a^t. π will denote an agent policy. All symbols are indexed by subscripts u or i, which stand, respectively, for the agent A_u and A_i. Let θ^t be the state of the software environment at time t, for instance the viewpoint in a building, or the 6D pose of a mechanical object in a CAD problem. Then, a given time step t in our sequential cooperative MARL setup will unroll as follows:

$$
\begin{aligned}
s_u^t &= \theta^t \\
a_u^t &= D(\pi_u(s_u^t)) \\
s_i^t &= a_u^t \\
a_i^t &= \pi_i(s_i^t) = \Delta\theta^t \\
s_u^{t+1} &= \theta^{t+1} \\
r_u^t &= r_i^t = r(a_i^t, s_u^{t+1})
\end{aligned}
\tag{5}
$$

where $\Delta\theta^t$ is a variation of the parametrization of the object, and $r_u^t = r_i^t$ is the joint reward at time t. We can note that the constraint on A_u actions defined by D is mandatory for our setup to converge to a cooperative setup. Indeed, supposing that we directly have $s_i^t = \pi_u(s_u^t))$, the policy of one of the agents will degenerate to an identity, effectively lowering the complexity of the problem by getting rid of the intermediate representation between the two agents. One agent will end up observing and taking actions directly in the virtual environment, breaking the paradigm of this setup.

4.3   Defining the Reward Function

The goal of this work is to optimize user satisfaction during interactions, which is not easily measurable. We can attempt to empirically break it down to a set of less subjective parts: precision of the interactions, expressiveness, intuitivity and ease of use. The latter two are difficult to measure directly but can be added as learned soft constraints to the agent. In this work, we make the assumption that the latent representation learned by the VAE from interaction logs encodes intuitivity and ease of use, leveraged by restricting the user agent A_u to an action space defined as the latent representation of the VAE.

The former two (precision and expressiveness) are performance metrics related to the environment the agents are trying to solve. If we restrict ourselves to training from situations where the objective of the HCI experiment is known, these measures can be optimized directly by defining an appropriate reward function. As examples we could imagine asking users questions like *"Find Waldo in this building by navigating there"* or *"view the carburator of this V6 engine from above allowing to see inside it"*. The downside to this approach is restricting training to situations with known outcomes and objectives. This still allows learning interfaces in a co-adaptive fashion, in two consecutive stages: a first off-line training stage on a set of "training users", followed by an enrollment training phase, where each user is asked to solve custom scenarii to adapt the system to its own interface behavior. It does *not*, however, allow continuous adaptation during usage with unknown objectives.

We will detail our chosen reward functions in the experimental section. It suffices to say at this point, that they measure a distance to the goal in the given user defined task. However, it is important to remember that our true goal is not for the agents to maximize their rewards, which only partially relate to user satisfaction. Convergence of cumulated reward is a necessary condition for a good solution, but not sufficient. Only humans can assess the true quality of these interaction protocols.

4.4   Stabilizing Learning with Self-supervision

In the standard formulation as described above, during training, the interface agent A_i learns to interpret actions produced by the user agent A_u, while A_u does not get any (unfiltered) information from the interface and as such cannot infer how the interface will interpret a gesture it produces. Furthermore, since the interface policy π_i evolves during training, the target for the user agent A_u is unstable, which makes training difficult.

We stabilize training by forcing A_u to approximate decisions taken by the interface A_i in the form of self-supervision. We add a second predictor head to A_u, which predicts the output of A_i. This predictor shares common layers with the classical predictor of the policy π_u, which ensures that the learned feature representation benefits both predictors. The new predictor is supervised with the real output of the interface agent A_i using the L_2 loss $\mathcal{L}_e = ||a_i - \hat{a}_i||_2$. $\hat{a}_i$ is the interface action predicted by A_u, and a_i is the interface action predicted by

A_i. In practice, this loss only affects the user actor π_u, the critic taking no part in this estimation. This is an external training signal added to the RL signal coming from the critic estimation of the state-action value function Q. As a note, adding a coefficient to the new loss to control its impact did not yield any meaningful improvements.

5 Experiments 1: A Simple Problem—Solving "Pinch-to-Zoom"

As a first proof of concept, we will attempt to solve a well-known continuous HCI, for which a handcrafted solution does exist, the goal being to verify whether learning can discover the existing solution. Our choice here is the well known "Pinch-to-Zoom" interface widely used for smartphones and tablets. The name is a misnomer, since the interface not only allows to zoom, but also to translate and rotate the content of surface through 2D gestures made by two fingers. We suppose that a user performs gestures with exactly two fingers on a touch screen and we investigate the motion between two different time instants. We denote by $l = [l_x \ l_y]^T$ the screen coordinates of a single finger at the first instant and by $l' = [l'_x \ l'_y]^T$ the coordinates at the second instant. If we need to explicitly identify a finger, we will index finger i with a superscript as in l^i or l'^i. The coordinates are normalized between [0 0] (top-left) and [1 1] (bottom-right).

The Known Solution—We will first derive the analytical form of the known solution before describing the experiments learning it. The gestures performed by the user are a combination of translation, rotation and scaling. We suppose that the 2D finger motion on the screen induces the same 2D motion of the manipulated surface, which can be seen as a special case of affine transformation where the shear component is zero. It transforms coordinates l into l' as $l' = Al + t$ where $t = [t_x \ t_y]^T$ is the translation component and the rotation+scaling matrix can be calculated from the rotation angle α and the scaling factor σ as follows:

$$A = \begin{bmatrix} \cos\alpha & -\sin\alpha \\ \sin\alpha & \cos\alpha \end{bmatrix} \begin{bmatrix} \sigma & 0 \\ 0 & \sigma \end{bmatrix} = \begin{bmatrix} \sigma\cos\alpha & -\sigma\sin\alpha \\ \sigma\sin\alpha & \sigma\cos\alpha \end{bmatrix} \tag{6}$$

The 4 parameters of the motion are thus α, σ, t_x, t_y, which we will combine into a parameter vector $\theta = [\sigma\cos\alpha \ \ \sigma\sin\alpha \ \ t_x \ \ t_y]^T$. If we have motion of two different fingers (l^1, l'^1) and (l^2, l'^2), then the following linear relationship between the coordinates and the parameter vector θ holds: $d = D\theta$, where d is a vector containing the target coordinates and D is a matrix containing the source coordinates in a suitable form:

$$\begin{bmatrix} l'^1_x \\ l'^1_y \\ l'^2_x \\ l'^2_y \end{bmatrix} = \begin{bmatrix} l^1_x & -l^1_y & 1 & 0 \\ l^1_y & l^1_x & 0 & 1 \\ l^2_x & -l^2_y & 1 & 0 \\ l^2_y & l^2_x & 0 & 1 \end{bmatrix} \begin{bmatrix} \sigma\cos\alpha \\ \sigma\sin\alpha \\ t_x \\ t_y \end{bmatrix} \tag{7}$$

Because D is always invertible (except for the degenerated case where both fingers are at the origin), this linear equation can be solved easily as $\hat{\theta} = D^{-1}d$.

Learning a Solution—We now let an RL agent learn this protocol. Let the state of the agent be a two-finger motion $s_i = [l_x^1 \ l_y^1 \ l_x^2 \ l_y^2 \ l_x'^1 \ l_y'^1 \ l_x'^2 \ l_y'^2]$ performed by the user, where superscripts index fingers and subscripts indicate x or y coordinates. Agent actions $a_i = [\sigma \cos \alpha \ \ \sigma \sin \alpha \ \ t_x \ \ t_y]^T$ are continuous vectors of size 4, which correspond to the parameters of an affine motion transformation without shear component. Note that while this affine transformation has the same functional form as the one expressed in the analytical solution above, we here describe output motion only (motion the manipulated object will endure) and not input finger motion. In other words, in this RL scenario, we do *NOT* suppose that object motion equals finger motion.

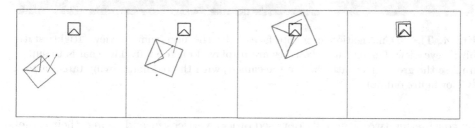

Fig. 3. An example rollout of the interface policy learned for the "Pinch-To-Zoom" problem. The rectangle need to be superimposed, finger trajectories are indicated by arrows. (Color figure online)

The environment is a simple scenario, where a user is required to move a virtual surface containing an object (a red rectangle). The goal is to bring this object to a fixed position by superimposing it on an object which does *not* move with the manipulated surface, i.e. a black rectangle "painted" on the glass of the device. The reward function in this task is the sum of L_1- and L_2-distances the object vertices and the target vertices:

$$r = -\sum_i \left(||o_i - t_i||_1 + ||o_i - t_i||_2 \right) - 0.2 \tag{8}$$

where o_i and t_i are the coordinates of $i-th$ vertice of the respective rectangle. Let us recall that the interface agent does *not* have access to these positions, else it would learn to simply ignore user gestures. The constant -0.2 reward is set to continuously encourage fast solutions. A positive reward of $+25$ is given if the agent successfully finishes an episode. These arbitrary values are chosen so that the expectation of the sum of rewards per episode is close to 0 for an agent close to the optimal solution.

Handcrafted Simulation of the User—For this toy problem, the cooperative multi-agent formulation proposed in Sect. 4 is not necessary. We instead handcraft a solution simulating a user who is aware of the "Pinch-To-Zoom" protocol, i.e. of the known analytical solution. We would like to stress that the agent is of course *not* aware of the solution. The interface solution expressed in Eq. 7 allows us to compute simulated user trajectories: this can simply be done

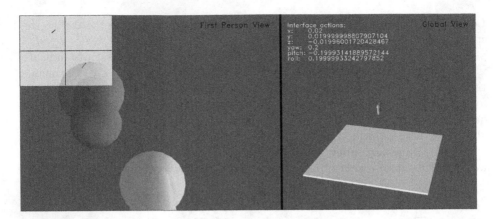

Fig. 4. The 3D navigation user interface. Left: the user/camera view; Right: static bird's eye view. Current user gestures are displayed on top left. The goal is to superimpose the green arrow attached to the camera with the red non moving target arrow. (Color figure online)

by considering two diagonally opposed object vertices v_1 and v_2 and their target position v_1' and v_2'. For a sampling time, we can consider that the user will move the object toward the target while keeping the vertices v_i on the segments $[v_i,\ v_i']$ (which is the optimal way to solve the task). It means we can find intermediate positions of v_i on these segments using the linear combination:

$$v_i^{inter} = (1 - \mu)v_i + \mu v_i', \ \mu = \max(1, \frac{0.5}{||v_i' - v_i||_2}) \tag{9}$$

μ is the user's gesture velocity. A small μ will mean small relative increments toward the target. This definition of μ goes in the sense that a human user will tend to do faster gestures while far from the target and slower, more precise gestures while close to it. Now that we have two points of the wanted intermediate object position, we can solve the Eq. 7 in order to get the transformation of every point of the object to the intermediate position. At last, we can choose two random points p_1 and p_2 on the object, transform them using the computed $\hat{\theta}$ parameters and build the two trajectories $[p_1,\ p_1^{inter}]$ and $[p_2,\ p_2^{inter}]$. The state bs_i of the agent will be the concatenation of these two trajectories, resulting in a vector of size 8.

Results—We compare our trained agent to an optimal solution. This optimal solution is easily modelled as we defined both the analytic solution of a user and of the interface. On an average of 100 episodes, the optimal solution finishes an episode in 40 steps and obtains a reward of +0.5 per episode.

After a training of about 300k steps, the interface agent obtains very similar results: on an average of 100 episodes, it finishes an episode in 41 steps and obtains a reward of +0.4. It is visually impossible to separate the optimal solution from the learned agent. An illustration of a rollout in the environment is given in Fig. 3.

6   Experiments 2: 3D Navigation from 2D Gestures

We now discuss the experiments on the real 3D navigation user interface, for which no optimal solution is known to exist. As described in the introduction, we want to learn an agent to map 2D finger gestures to motion in a 3D environment, an ill-posed problem. To this end, we extended the 2D toy problem to 3D, maintaining the user's goal of moving a (now 3D) content to superimpose an object over a non-moving object, as shown in Fig. 4. As there is no simple handcrafted way to simulate a human user, we use the multi-agent RL setup described in Sect. 4. The 3D affine transformation to be learned by the interface agent can be expressed using homogeneous coordinates in 4 dimensions as a 4×4 matrix ϕ:

$$\phi = \begin{bmatrix} r_{11} & r_{12} & r_{13} & t_1 \\ r_{21} & r_{22} & r_{23} & t_2 \\ r_{31} & r_{32} & r_{33} & t_3 \\ 0 & 0 & 0 & 1 \end{bmatrix}, R = \begin{bmatrix} r_{11} & r_{12} & r_{13} \\ r_{21} & r_{22} & r_{23} \\ r_{31} & r_{32} & r_{33} \end{bmatrix}, t = \begin{bmatrix} t_1 \\ t_2 \\ t_3 \end{bmatrix} \tag{10}$$

As we do not consider scaling (redundant with forward motion), the matrix is totally parametrized by 6 coefficients: $[\tau_x, \tau_y, \tau_z, \rho_x, \rho_y, \rho_z]$, where τ. and ρ. are, respectively, translation coefficients and Euler angles on the 3 axis. We limit the Euler angles to $]-\pi, \pi]$ to ensure their unicity given an axis. Such a vector can define transformations as well as object positions when using a fixed referential in the environment. With this formalization, The user agent A_u gets as observations the camera position vector and learns a policy over actions which are trajectory vectors $[l_x^1 \ l_y^1 \ l_x'^1 \ l_y'^1 \ l_x^2 \ l_y^2 \ l_x'^2 \ l_y'^2]$. The interface agent A_i observes the output of A_u and learns a policy over residual transformation vectors of the camera, i.e. $s_u^{t+1} = s_u^t + a_i$. We define the reward equivalent to the 2D problem in Sect. 5, given in Eq. (8), the difference being that each object has 2 vertices instead of 3, and that vertices are in 3D space.

VAE Training and Architectures—We train the latent 2D gesture representation with a VAE on a dataset of multi-touch interaction gestures, in particular the Itekube-7 Dataset [10]. We used all the two-finger gestures from the translation, pinch and rotation classes. Each gesture of the dataset was sampled using the dynamic sampling described in [10] to fix the length of the gestures to 10 timesteps. The VAE was trained for 50 epochs with $\beta = 0.07$, a batch size of 128, and a learning rate 0.002. The latent code is of size 8. The encoder and the decoder are both recurrent. Encoder: a one-layer GRU [9] with a hidden state of size 256 and ReLU activation. It is recurrent in time and reads inputs of size 4 (two 2D finger positions). Second, two FC layer predict, respectively, the mean and the stddev of the latent code from the last hidden state. The decoder is a two-layer GRU: The first layer has a hidden state of size 128 with ReLU activation, the second layer has a hidden state of size 4 (to reconstruct the position of both fingers at each timestep), no activation. The entire code is fed to it at every timestep, i.e. the number of unrollings of the GRU will determine the number of timesteps of the reconstruction. At training time, this number is set to the

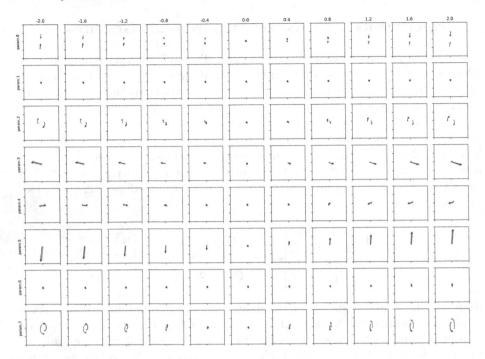

Fig. 5. Navigating the latent space learned by the VAE. Middle column: zero code z. Lines correspond to different modified latent variables (dim $= 8$). Columns correspond to different values.

number of timesteps of the original data (10), but at inference time, this number can be arbitrarily, which allows to produce shorter or longer trajectories from the same latent code.

Figure 5 visualizes the latent representation, and reconstruction examples are given in Fig. 6. The representations from the latent space are satisfying as we can observe some high level features and disentanglement: for instance, dimension 0 expresses pinch, while dimension 2 expresses clockwise rotation.

Multi-agent RL Training—We chose the model-free off-policy actor-critic method Deep Deterministic Policy Gradient (DDPG) [17]. In our setup, an epoch cycle consists of two phases: (i) a rollout phase on an episode, where all quadruplets [state, action, reward, new state] are stored in the replay memory of the agents; (ii) a training phase where quadruplets are randomly sampled from the memory, batched (in sizes of 4096) and used to train the actor and the critic of the agents. We define an epoch as 100 epoch cycles. The training is arbitrarily stopped when no improvement on the metrics is observed. A training session takes about 2 days on a Titan-X Pascal GPU.

Join training of both, A_u and A_i, was not successfull. We suspect the added variance and the moving value of state-action pairs for both agents as a source of the problem. Similar to [4], we chose to train them in an alternating manner:

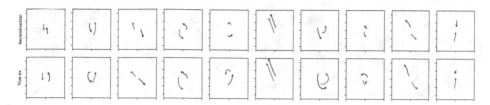

Fig. 6. Reconstruction examples made by the VAE. The first line displays reconstructed gestures while the second displays the corresponding original gestures.

Table 1. Results on the 3D environment. The last line gives theoretical optimal results based on the interface action amplitude, without considering a naturalness constraint. The Mean reward/ep. is the mean cumulated reward per episode obtained in the best performing epoch. The Mean nb. steps/ep. is the mean number of timesteps needed to successfully finish an episode in the best performing epoch. The Nb. training steps is the number of environment steps that was needed to attain the best performing epoch. Stacking improves usability but *NOT* efficiency.

	Mean reward/ep.	Mean #steps/ep.	Nb. training steps
No Stacking	3.6 ± 1.0	53 ± 1	$17.6\,M \pm 0.4\,M$
+ Stacking	0.5 ± 1.5	56 ± 4	$24.6\,M \pm 6.3\,M$
Theoretical Opt.	5.0	40	N/A

during an epoch, only one agent will be trained, while the weights of the other agents are kept fixed.

Stacking Timesteps—We consider two ways for the two agents to communicate. The simplest one is a two-instant communication: the decoder produces a gesture of only two time instants, and the interface produces the corresponding action. It is simple, but leads to non-smooth user gestures difficult to appreciate from a human viewpoint is hard. We also consider stacking time instants: A_u produces a complete gesture of 10 timesteps, and A_i must produce the corresponding sequence of actions (9 if there are 10 timesteps). In this case, a step from the RL perspective will contain 10 update steps of the environment. This decouples the update speed of the agents from the sampling speed of the finger gestures, referred to as "*Stacking*" in Table 1.

Architectures—In what follows, FCX refers to an FC layer with X hidden units, with layer normalization and ReLU activation. The actor of A_u is an MLP with two hidden FC100 layers. The output layer is FC and activated with tanh, predicting a vector of size 8 (the latent code z expanded by the VAE decoder D). Another FC100 layer is plugged to the first hidden layer, with an output layer producing the estimate $\hat{a}_i$. The critic of A_u is an MLP with two hidden FC100 layers. The policy action is concatenated to the first hidden layer. A linear FC layer predicts the value Q.

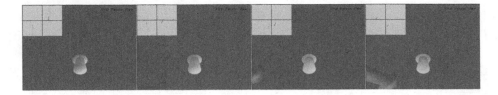

Fig. 7. An example of 4 back to back frames from the MARL setup learning the 3D navigation problem with instant stacking. We want to emphasize on the continuous aspect of user gestures (top-left) and the semantic. We can see that the user agent is currently performing a rotation-like gesture.

The actor of A_i is an MLP with two hidden FC64, and an output layer with tanh activation. The output size is either 6 for the standard solution or $6 \times 9 = 54$ for the stacked solution. The critic of A_i has the same architecture as the critic of A_u, except hidden layers are FC64.

Results—Quantitative results are given in Table 1. Each setup was reproduced with 3 different random seeds. We consider that a run has converged whenever all 100 episodes of an epoch are successful. Once it has converged, it can still improve by solving episodes faster. This is measured as the mean number of steps needed to solve an episode. The mean reward per episode is also correlated to the quality of the interaction protocol, but should be interpreted differently. Indeed, a run with a lower mean step per episode but a higher mean reward per episode is most likely less satisfactory than a run with higher steps but lower reward. This is because the first type of solutions tend to be less continuous with harsher action changes, while the second is technically slower but goes in the direction of the objective more smoothly.

"Stacking" and usability—the interaction protocols must also be observed visually in order to assess their global quality: good interfaces should display distinctive characteristics, such as a similar curvature between 2d trajectories and 3D movements of the camera, or well defined classes for similar actions. While stacking does *NOT* improve efficiency (as shown in Table 1), it makes the protocol usable. The continuous aspect of gestures using instant stacking is illustrated in Fig. 7, videos are provided in the supplementary material.

7   Conclusion

We presented a novel method for automatically learning interaction protocols from natural interactions. While our application for this paper is limited to touch interfaces, this setup can virtually be applied to any technology and any software, as long as a large enough interaction dataset can be collected. We want this work to be a step toward a better co-adaptive relation between the human and a computer, allowing for individually suited interfaces and higher levels of interaction. Future work will model the interaction protocol as a POMDP, which should allow to better represent long term dependencies and tackle more complex regularities. The main remaining problem is to fine-tune the learned models on real human users, which requires large-scale efforts with a large amount of human partners.

References

1. Alvarez-Cortes, V., Zayas, B., Silva, V., Ramirez Uresti, J.: Current trends in adaptive user interfaces: challenges and applications, pp. 312–317 (2007)
2. Beattie, C., et al.: DeepMind Lab. arXiv:1612.03801 (2016)
3. Beeching, E., Wolf, C., Dibangoye, J., Simonin, O.: Deep reinforcement learning on a budget: 3D control and reasoning without a supercomputer. arXiv:1904.01806 (2019)
4. Boutilier, C.: Planning, learning and coordination in multiagent decision processes. In: Theoretical Aspects of Rationality and Knowledge, pp. 195–210 (1996)
5. Bowman, D., et al.: New directions in 3D user interfaces. IJVR **5**, 3–14 (2006)
6. Bowman, D.A., Kruijff, E., LaViola, J.J., Poupyrev, I.: An introduction to 3-D user interface design. Presence: Teleoper. Virtual Environ. **10**, 96–108 (2001)
7. Cashion, J., Wingrave, C., LaViola Jr., J.J.: Dense and dynamic 3D selection for game-based virtual environments. IEEE Trans. Vis. Comput. Graph. **18**, 634–642 (2012)
8. Chen, Z., Anquetil, É., Mouchère, H., Viard-Gaudin, C.: A graph modeling strategy for multi-touch gesture recognition. In: International Conference on Frontiers in Handwriting Recognition (2014)
9. Cho, K., et al.: Learning phrase representations using RNN encoder-decoder for statistical machine translation. In: Conference on Empirical Methods in Natural Language Processing (2014)
10. Debard, Q., Wolf, C., Canu, S., Arné, J.: Learning to recognize touch gestures: recurrent vs. convolutional features and dynamic sampling. In: International Conference on Automatic Face and Gesture Recognition (2018)
11. Ferretti, S., Mirri, S., Prandi, C., Salomoni, P.: Exploiting reinforcement learning to profile users and personalize web pages. In: International Computer Software and Applications Conference Workshops (2014)
12. Goodfellow, I., et al.: Generative adversarial nets. In: NIPS, pp. 2672–2680 (2014)
13. Higgins, I., et al.: DARLA: improving zero-shot transfer in RL. In: ICML (2017)
14. Hinckley, K., Wigdor, D.: The Human-Computer Interaction Handbook: Fundamentals, Evolving Technologies and Emerging Applications. CRC Press, Boca Raton (2012)
15. Kingma, D.P., Welling, M.: Auto-encoding variational bayes. CoRR abs/1312.6114 (2014)
16. Langley, P.: Machine learning for adaptive user interfaces. In: Brewka, G., Habel, C., Nebel, B. (eds.) KI-1997: Advances in Artificial Intelligence, pp. 53–62 (1997)
17. Lillicrap, T.P., et al.: Continuous control with deep reinforcement learning. CoRR abs/1509.02971 (2015)
18. Lü, H., Li, Y.: Gesture coder: a tool for programming multi-touch gestures by demonstration. In: SIGCHI Conference on Human Factors in Computing Systems (2012)
19. Matthey, L., et al.: β-vae: learning basic visual concepts with a constrained variational framework. In: ICLR (2017)

20. Nair, A., Pong, V., Dalal, M., Bahl, S., Lin, S., Levine, S.: Visual reinforcement learning with imagined goals. In: NeurIPS, pp. 9209–9220 (2018)
21. Ortega, F.R., Abyarjoo, F., Barreto, A., Rishe, N., Adjouadi, M.: Interaction Design for 3D User Interfaces: The World of Modern Input Devices for Research, Applications, and Game Development. A. K. Peters, Ltd., Natick (2016)
22. Ross, S., Bagnell, D.: Agnostic system identification for model-based reinforcement learning. In: ICML (2012)
23. Seo, Y.W., Zhang, B.T.: A reinforcement learning agent for personalized information filtering. In: International Conference on Intelligent User Interfaces (2000)
24. Weir, D., Rogers, S., Murray-Smith, R., Löchtefeld, M.: A user-specific machine learning approach for improving touch accuracy on mobile devices. In: ACM Symposium on User Interface Software and Technology, pp. 465–476 (2012)
25. Weld, D.S., et al.: Automatically personalizing user interfaces. In: IJCAI, pp. 1613–1619 (2003)
26. Peng, X.B., Andrychowicz, M., Zaremba, W., Abbeel, P.: Sim-to-real transfer of robotic control with dynamics randomization. In: ICRA (2018)

Safe Policy Improvement with Soft Baseline Bootstrapping

Kimia Nadjahi[1]([⊠]), Romain Laroche[2]([⊠]), and Rémi Tachet des Combes[2]

[1] LTCI, Télécom Paris, Institut Polytechnique de Paris, Palaiseau, France
kimia.nadjahi@telecom-paris.fr
[2] Microsoft Research Montréal, Montreal, Canada
{romain.laroche,remi.tachet}@microsoft.com

Abstract. Batch Reinforcement Learning (Batch RL) consists in training a policy using trajectories collected with another policy, called the
behavioural policy. Safe policy improvement (SPI) provides guarantees
with high probability that the trained policy performs better than the
behavioural policy, also called baseline in this setting. Previous work
shows that the SPI objective improves mean performance as compared
to using the basic RL objective, which boils down to solving the MDP
with maximum likelihood (Laroche et al. 2019). Here, we build on that
work and improve more precisely the SPI with Baseline Bootstrapping
algorithm (SPIBB) by allowing the policy search over a wider set of policies. Instead of binarily classifying the state-action pairs into two sets
(the *uncertain* and the *safe-to-train-on* ones), we adopt a softer strategy
that controls the error in the value estimates by constraining the policy change according to the local model uncertainty. The method can
take more risks on uncertain actions all the while remaining provably-
safe, and is therefore less conservative than the state-of-the-art methods.
We propose two algorithms (one optimal and one approximate) to solve
this constrained optimization problem and empirically show a significant
improvement over existing SPI algorithms both on finite MDPS and on
infinite MDPs with a neural network function approximation.

1 Introduction

In sequential decision-making problems, a common goal is to find a good policy
using a limited number of trajectories generated by another policy, usually called
the behavioral policy. This approach, also known as Batch Reinforcement Learning (Lange et al. 2012), is motivated by the many real-world applications that

---

K. Nadjahi and R. Laroche—Equal contribution.
K. Nadjahi—Work done while interning at Microsoft Research Montréal.
Finite MDPs code available at https://github.com/RomainLaroche/SPIBB.
SPIBB-DQN code available at https://github.com/rems75/SPIBB-DQN.

Electronic supplementary material The online version of this chapter (https://
doi.org/10.1007/978-3-030-46133-1_4) contains supplementary material, which is
available to authorized users.

U. Brefeld et al. (Eds.): ECML PKDD 2019, LNAI 11908, pp. 53–68, 2020.
https://doi.org/10.1007/978-3-030-46133-1_4

naturally fit a setting where data collection and optimization are decoupled (contrary to online learning which integrates the two): *e.g.* dialogue systems (Singh et al. 1999), technical process control (Ernst et al. 2005; Riedmiller 2005), medical applications (Guez et al. 2008).

While most reinforcement learning techniques aim at finding a high-performance policy (Sutton and Barto 1998), the final policy does not necessarily perform well once it is deployed. In this paper, we focus on Safe Policy Improvement (SPI, Thomas 2015; Petrik et al. 2016), where the goal is to train a policy on a batch of data and guarantee with high probability that it performs at least as well as the behavioural policy, called baseline in this SPI setting. The safety guarantee is crucial in real-world applications where bad decisions may lead to harmful consequences.

Among the existing SPI algorithms, a recent computationally efficient and provably-safe methodology is SPI with Baseline Bootstrapping (SPIBB, Laroche et al. 2019; Simão and Spaan 2019). Its principle consists in building the set of state-action pairs that are only encountered a few times in the dataset. This set is called the bootstrapped set. The algorithm then reproduces the baseline policy for all pairs in that set and trains greedily on the rest. It therefore assumes access to the baseline policy, which is a common assumption in the SPI literature (Petrik et al. 2016). Other SPI algorithms use as reference the baseline performance, which is assumed to be known instead (Thomas 2015; Petrik et al. 2016). We believe that the known policy assumption is both more informative and more common, since most Batch RL settings involve datasets that were collected using a previous system based on a previous algorithm (*e.g.* dialogue, robotics, pharmaceutical treatment). While the empirical results show that SPIBB is safe and performs significantly better than the existing algorithms, it remains limited by the binary classification of the bootstrapped set: a pair either belongs to it, and the policy cannot be changed, or it does not, and the policy can be changed entirely.

Our contribution is a reformulation of the SPIBB objective that allows slight policy changes for uncertain state-action pairs while remaining safe. Instead of binarily classifying the state-action pairs into two sets, the uncertain and the safe-to-train-on ones, we adopt a strategy that extends the policy search to soft policy changes, which are constrained by an error bound related to the model uncertainty. The method is allowed to take more risks than SPIBB on uncertain actions, and still has theoretical safety guarantees under some assumptions. As a consequence, the safety constraint is softer: we coin this new SPI methodology *Safe Policy Improvement with Soft Baseline Bootstrapping* (Soft-SPIBB). We develop two algorithms to tackle the Soft-SPIBB problem. The first one solves it exactly, but is computationally expensive. The second one provides an approximate solution but is much more efficient computation-wise. We empirically evaluate the performance and safety of our algorithms on a gridworld task and analyze the reasons behind their significant advantages over the competing Batch RL algorithms. We further demonstrate the tractability of the approach by designing a DQN algorithm enforcing the Soft-SPIBB constrained policy optimization. The empirical results, obtained on a navigation task, show that Soft-SPIBB safely improves the baseline, and again outperforms all competing algorithms.

2   Background

2.1   Markov Decision Processes

We consider problems in which the agent interacts with an environment modeled as a *Markov Decision Process* (MDP): $M^* = \langle \mathcal{X}, \mathcal{A}, P^*, R^*, \gamma \rangle$, where $\mathcal{X}$ is the set of states, $\mathcal{A}$ the set of actions, P^* the unknown transition probability function, R^* the unknown stochastic reward function bounded by $\pm R_{max}$, and $\gamma \in [0, 1)$ the discount factor for future rewards. The goal is to find a policy $\pi : \mathcal{X} \to \Delta_{\mathcal{A}}$, with $\Delta_{\mathcal{A}}$ the set of probability distributions over the set of actions $\mathcal{A}$, that maximizes the expected return of trajectories $\rho(\pi, M^*) = V_{M^*}^\pi(x_0) = \mathbb{E}_{\pi, M^*} \left[\sum_{t \geq 0} \gamma^t R^*(x_t, a_t) \right]$. x_0 is the initial state of the environment and $V_{M^*}^\pi(x)$ is the value of being in state x when following policy π in MDP M^*. We denote by Π the set of stochastic policies. Similarly to $V_{M^*}^\pi(x)$, $Q_{M^*}^\pi(x, a)$ denotes the value of taking action a in state x. $A_M^\pi(x, a) = Q_M^\pi(x, a) - V_M^\pi(x)$ quantifies the advantage (or disadvantage) of action a in state x.

Given a dataset of transitions $\mathcal{D} = \langle x_j, a_j, r_j, x_j' \rangle_{j \in [\![1, |\mathcal{D}|]\!]}$, we denote the state-action pair counts by $N_{\mathcal{D}}(x, a)$, and its Maximum Likelihood Estimator (MLE) MDP by $\widehat{M} = \langle \mathcal{X}, \mathcal{A}, \widehat{P}, \widehat{R}, \gamma \rangle$, with:

$$\widehat{P}(x'|x, a) = \frac{\sum_{\langle x_j = x, a_j = a, r_j, x_j' = x' \rangle \in \mathcal{D}} 1}{N_{\mathcal{D}}(x, a)} \quad \text{and} \quad \widehat{R}(x, a) = \frac{\sum_{\langle x_j = x, a_j = a, r_j, x_j' \rangle \in \mathcal{D}} r_j}{N_{\mathcal{D}}(x, a)}.$$

The difference between an estimated parameter and the true one can be bounded using classic concentration bounds applied to the state-action counts in $\mathcal{D}$ (Petrik et al. 2016; Laroche et al. 2019): for all state-action pairs (x, a), we know with probability at least $1 - \delta$ that,

$$||P^*(\cdot|x, a) - \widehat{P}(\cdot|x, a)||_1 \leq e_P(x, a), \quad |R^*(x, a) - \widehat{R}(x, a)| \leq e_P(x, a) R_{max}, \quad (1)$$

$$\left| Q_{M^*}^{\pi_b}(x, a) - Q_{\widehat{M}}^{\pi_b}(x, a) \right| \leq e_Q(x, a) V_{max}, \quad (2)$$

where $V_{max} \leq \dfrac{R_{max}}{1 - \gamma}$ is the maximum of the value function, and the two error functions may be derived from Hoeffding's inequality (see A.2) as

$$e_P(x, a) := \sqrt{\frac{2}{N_{\mathcal{D}}(x, a)} \log \frac{2|\mathcal{X}||\mathcal{A}|2^{|\mathcal{X}|}}{\delta}} \quad \text{and} \quad e_Q(x, a) := \sqrt{\frac{2}{N_{\mathcal{D}}(x, a)} \log \frac{2|\mathcal{X}||\mathcal{A}|}{\delta}}.$$

We will also use the following definition:

Definition 1. *A policy π is said to be a policy improvement over a baseline policy π_b in an MDP $M = \langle \mathcal{X}, \mathcal{A}, P, R, \gamma \rangle$ if the following inequality holds in every state $x \in \mathcal{X}$:*

$$V_M^\pi(x) \geq V_M^{\pi_b}(x) \quad (3)$$

2.2   Safe Policy Improvement with Baseline Bootstrappping

Our objective is to maximize the expected return of the target policy under the constraint of improving with high probability $1 - \delta$ the baseline policy. This is known to be an NP-hard problem (Petrik et al. 2016) and some approximations are required to make it tractable. This paper builds on the Safe Policy Improvement with Baseline Bootstrapping methodology (SPIBB, Laroche et al. 2019). SPIBB finds an approximate solution to the problem by searching for a policy maximizing the expected return in the MLE MDP $\widehat{M}$, under the constraint that the policy improvement is guaranteed in the set of plausible MDPs Ξ:

$$\operatorname*{argmax}_{\pi} \rho(\pi, \widehat{M}), \text{ s.t. } \forall M \in \Xi, \rho(\pi, M) \geq \rho(\pi_b, M) - \zeta \tag{4}$$

$$\Xi = \left\{ M = \langle \mathcal{X}, \mathcal{A}, R, P, \gamma \rangle \text{ s.t. } \forall x, a, \begin{matrix} ||P(\cdot|x,a) - \widehat{P}(\cdot|x,a)||_1 \leq e_P(x,a), \\ |R(x,a) - \widehat{R}(x,a)| \leq e_P(x,a)R_{max} \end{matrix} \right\} \tag{5}$$

The error function e_P is such that the true MDP M^* has a high probability of at least $1 - \delta$ to belong to Ξ (Iyengar 2005; Nilim and El Ghaoui 2005). In other terms, the objective is to optimize the target performance in $\widehat{M}$ such that its performance is ζ-approximately at least as good as π_b in the admissible MDP set, where ζ is a precision hyper-parameter. Expressed this way, the problem is still intractable. SPIBB is able to find an approximate solution within a tractable amount of time by applying a special processing to state-action pair transitions that were not sampled enough in the batch of data. The methodology consists in building a set of rare thus uncertain state-action pairs in the dataset $\mathcal{D}$, called the bootstrapped set and denoted by $\mathcal{B}$: the bootstrapped set contains all the state-action pairs $(x, a) \in \mathcal{X} \times \mathcal{A}$ whose counts in $\mathcal{D}$ are lower than a hyper-parameter $N_\wedge$. SPIBB algorithms then construct a space of allowed policies, *i.e* policies that are constrained on the bootstrapped set $\mathcal{B}$, and search for the optimal policy in this set by performing policy iteration. For example, Π_b-SPIBB is a provably-safe algorithm that assigns the baseline π_b to the state-action pairs in $\mathcal{B}$ and trains the policy on the rest. $\Pi_{\leq b}$-SPIBB is a variant that does not give more weight than π_b to the uncertain transitions.

SPIBB's principle amounts to search over a policy space constrained such that the policy improvement may be precisely assessed in M^*. Because of the hard definition of the bootstrapped set, SPIBB relies on a binary decision-making and may be too conservative. Our novel method, called Soft-SPIBB, follows the same principle, but relaxes this definition by allowing soft policy changes for the uncertain state-action pairs, and offers more flexibility than SPIBB while remaining safe.

This idea might seem similar to Conservative Policy Iteration (CPI), Trust Region Policy Optimization (TRPO), or Proximal Policy Optimization (PPO) in that it allows changes in the policy under a proximity regularization to the old policy (Kakade and Langford 2002; Schulman et al. 2015, 2017). However, with Soft-SPIBB, the proximity constraint is tightened or relaxed according to the amount of samples supporting the policy change (see Definition 2). Additionally,

CPI, TRPO, and PPO are designed for the online setting. In the batch setting we consider, they would be either too conservative if the proximity regularization is applied with respect to the fixed baseline, or would converge to the fixed point obtained when solving the MLE MDP if the proximity regularization is moving with the last policy update (Corollary 3 of Geist et al. 2019).

2.3 Linear Programming

Linear programming aims at optimizing a linear objective function under a set of linear in-equality constraints. The most common methods for solving such linear programs are the simplex algorithm and interior point methods (IPMs, Dantzig 1963). Even though the worst-case computational complexity of the simplex is exponential in the dimensions of the program being solved (Klee and Minty 1972), this algorithm is efficient in practice: the number of iterations seems polynomial, and sometimes linear in the problem size (Borgwardt 1987; Dantzig and Thapa 2003). Nowadays, these two classes of methods continue to compete with one another: it is hard to predict the winner on a particular class of problems (Gondzio 2012). For instance, the hyper-sparsity of the problem generally seems to favour the simplex algorithm, while IPMs can be much more efficient for large-scale linear programming.

3 Safe Policy Improvement with Soft Baseline Bootstrapping

SPIBB allows to make changes in state-action pairs where the model error does not exceed some threshold ϵ, which may be expressed as a function of $N_\wedge$. This may be seen as a hard condition on the bootstrapping mechanism: a state-action pair policy may either be changed totally, or not at all. In this paper, we propose a softer mechanism where, for a given error function, a local error budget is allocated for policy changes in each state x. Similarly to SPIBB, we search for the optimal policy in the MDP model $\widehat{M}$ estimated from the dataset $\mathcal{D}$, but we reformulate the constraint by using Definitions 2 and 3.

Definition 2. *A policy π is said to be (π_b, e, ϵ)-constrained with respect to a baseline policy π_b, an error function e, and a hyper-parameter ϵ if, for all states $x \in \mathcal{X}$, the following inequality holds:*

$$\sum_{a \in \mathcal{A}} e(x, a) \big| \pi(a|x) - \pi_b(a|x) \big| \le \epsilon.$$

Definition 3. *A policy π is said to be π_b-advantageous in an MDP $M = \langle \mathcal{X}, \mathcal{A}, P, R, \gamma \rangle$ if the following inequality holds in every state $x \in \mathcal{X}$:*

$$\sum_{a \in \mathcal{A}} A_M^{\pi_b}(x, a) \pi(a|x) \ge 0 \tag{6}$$

Remark 1. By the policy improvement theorem, a π_b-advantageous policy is a policy improvement over π_b. The converse is not guaranteed.

3.1   Theoretical Safe Policy Improvement Bounds

We show that constraining π_b-advantageous policies appropriately allows safe policy improvements. Due to space limitation, all proofs have been moved to the appendix, Section A.

Theorem 1. *Any (π_b, e_Q, ϵ)-constrained policy π that is π_b-advantageous in $\widehat{M}$ satisfies the following inequality in every state x with probability at least $1 - \delta$:*

$$V_{M*}^{\pi}(x) - V_{M*}^{\pi_b}(x) \geq -\frac{\epsilon V_{max}}{1 - \gamma}. \tag{7}$$

Constraining the target policy to be advantageous over the baseline is a strong constraint that leads to conservative solutions. To the best of our findings, it is not possible to prove a more general bound on (π_b, e_Q, ϵ)-constrained policy improvements. However, the search over (π_b, e_P, ϵ)-constrained policies, where e_P is an error bound over the probability function P (Eq. 2), allows us to guarantee safety bounds under Assumption 1, which states:

Assumption 1. *There exists a constant $\kappa < \frac{1}{\gamma}$ such that, for all state-action pairs $(x, a) \in \mathcal{X} \times \mathcal{A}$, the following inequality holds:*

$$\sum_{x', a'} e_P(x', a') \pi_b(a'|x') P^*(x'|x, a) \leq \kappa e_P(x, a). \tag{8}$$

Lemma 1, which is essential to prove Theorem 2 below, relies on Assumption 1.

Lemma 1. *Under Assumption 1, any (π_b, e_P, ϵ)-constrained policy π satisfies the following inequality for every state-action pair (x, a) with probability at least $1 - \delta$:*

$$\left| Q_{M*}^{\pi}(x, a) - Q_{\widehat{M}}^{\pi}(x, a) \right| \leq \left(\frac{e_P(x, a)}{1 - \kappa\gamma} + \frac{\gamma\epsilon}{(1 - \gamma)(1 - \kappa\gamma)} \right) V_{max}.$$

Theorem 2. *Under Assumption 1, any (π_b, e_P, ϵ)-constrained policy π satisfies the following inequality in every state x with probability at least $1 - \delta$:*

$$V_{M*}^{\pi}(x) - V_{M*}^{\pi_b}(x) \geq V_{\widehat{M}}^{\pi}(x) - V_{\widehat{M}}^{\pi_b}(x) - 2 \left\| d_{M*}^{\pi_b}(\cdot|x) - d_{\widehat{M}}^{\pi_b}(\cdot|x) \right\|_1 V_{max}$$

$$- \frac{1 + \gamma}{(1 - \gamma)^2 (1 - \kappa\gamma)} \epsilon V_{max}. \tag{9}$$

Remark 2. The theorems hold for any error function e_P verifying 2 w.p. $1 - \delta$.

Remark 3. Π_b-SPIBB (Laroche et al. 2019) is a particular case of Soft-SPIBB where the error function $e_P(x, a)$ equals ∞ if $(x, a) \in \mathcal{B}$ and $\frac{\epsilon}{2}$ otherwise.

Remark 4. Theorem 2 has a cubic dependency in the horizon $\frac{1}{1-\gamma}$, which is weaker than SPIBB's bounds, but allow us to safely search over more policies, when using tighter error functions. We will observe in Sect. 4 that Soft-SPIBB empirically outperforms SPIBB both in mean performance and in safety.

3.2 Algorithms

In this section, we design two safe policy improvement algorithms to tackle the problem defined by the Soft-SPIBB approach. They both rely on the standard policy iteration process described in Pseudo-code 1, where the policy improvement step consists in solving in every state $x \in \mathcal{X}$ the locally constrained optimization problem below:

$$\pi^{(i+1)}(\cdot|x) = \underset{\pi \in \Pi}{\mathrm{argmax}} \sum_{a \in \mathcal{A}} Q^{(i)}_{\widehat{M}}(x,a)\pi(a|x) \tag{10}$$

subject to:

Constraint 1: π being a probability: $\sum_{a \in \mathcal{A}} \pi(a|x) = 1$ and $\forall a,\ \pi(a|x) \geq 0$.

Constraint 2: π being (π_b, e, ϵ)-constrained.

Pseudo-code 1: Policy iteration process for Soft-SPIBB

Input: Baseline policy π_b, MDP model precision level ϵ and dataset $\mathcal{D}$.
Compute the model error concentration bounds $e(x,a)$.
Initialize $i = 0$ and $\pi^{(0)}(\cdot|x) = \pi_b(\cdot|x)$.
while *policy iteration stopping criterion not met* **do**

  Policy evaluation: compute $Q^{(i)}_{\widehat{M}}$ with dynamic programming.
  Policy improvement: set $\pi^{(i+1)}(\cdot|x)$ as the (exact or approximate) solution of the optimization problem defined in Equation 10.
  $i \leftarrow i + 1$
return $\pi^{(i)}$

Exact-Soft-SPIBB: The Exact-Soft-SPIBB algorithm computes the exact solution of the local optimization problem in (10) during the policy improvement step. For that, we express the problem as a Linear Program (LP) and solve it by applying the simplex algorithm. Note that we chose the simplex over IPMs as it turned out to be efficient enough for our experimental settings. For tractability in large action spaces, we reformulate the non-linear Constraint 2 as follows: we introduce $|\mathcal{A}|$ auxiliary variables $\{z(x,a)\}_{(x,a) \in \mathcal{X} \times \mathcal{A}}$, which bound from above each element of the sum. For a given $x \in \mathcal{X}$, Constraint 2 is then replaced by the following $2|\mathcal{A}| + 1$ linear constraints:

$$\forall a \in \mathcal{A}, \qquad\qquad \pi(a|x) - \pi_b(a|x) \leq z(x,a), \tag{11}$$

$$\forall a \in \mathcal{A}, \qquad\qquad -\pi(a|x) + \pi_b(a|x) \leq z(x,a), \tag{12}$$

$$\sum_a e(x,a)z(x,a) \leq \epsilon. \tag{13}$$

Approx-Soft-SPIBB: We also propose a computationally-efficient algorithm, which returns a sub-optimal target policy $\pi_{\sim}^{\odot}$. It relies on the same policy iteration, but computes an approximate solution to the optimization problem. The approach still guarantees to improve the baseline in $\widehat{M}$: $\rho(\pi_{\sim}^{\odot}, \widehat{M}) \geq \rho(\pi_b, \widehat{M})$, and falls under the Theorems 1 and 2 SPI bounds. Approx-Soft-SPIBB's local policy improvement step consists in removing, for each state x, the policy probability mass m^- from the action a^- with the lowest Q-value. Then, m^- is attributed to the action that offers the highest Q-value improvement by unit of error $\partial\epsilon$:

$$a^+ = \operatorname*{argmax}_{a \in \mathcal{A}} \frac{\partial\pi(a|x)}{\partial\epsilon} \left(Q_{\widehat{M}}^{(i)}(x, a) - Q_{\widehat{M}}^{(i)}(x, a^-) \right) \tag{14}$$

$$= \operatorname*{argmax}_{a \in \mathcal{A}} \frac{Q_{\widehat{M}}^{(i)}(x, a) - Q_{\widehat{M}}^{(i)}(x, a^-)}{e(x, a)} \tag{15}$$

Once m^- has been reassigned to another action with higher value, the budget is updated accordingly to the error that has been spent, and the algorithm continues with the next worst action until a stopping criteria is met: the budget is fully spent, or $a^- = a^*$, where a^* is the action with maximal state-action value. The policy improvement step of Approx-Soft-SPIBB is further formalized in Pseudo-code 2, found in the appendix, Section A.8.

Theorem 3. *The policy improvement step of Approx-Soft-SPIBB generates policies that are guaranteed to be (π_b, e, ϵ)-constrained.*

Remark 5. The argmax operator in the result returned by Pseudo-code 2 is a convergence condition. Indeed, the approximate algorithm does not guarantee that the current iteration policy search space includes the previous iteration policy, which can cause divergence: the algorithm may indefinitely cycle between two or more policies. To ensure convergence, we update $\pi^{(i)}$ with $\pi^{(i+1)}$ only if there is a local policy improvement, *i.e.* when $\mathbb{E}_{a \sim \pi^{(i+1)}(\cdot|x)}[Q_{\widehat{M}}^{(i)}(x, a)] \geq \mathbb{E}_{a \sim \pi^{(i)}(\cdot|x)}[Q_{\widehat{M}}^{(i)}(x, a)]$.

Both implementation of the Soft-SPIBB strategy comply to the requirements of Theorem 1 if only one policy iteration is performed. In Sect. 4.1, we empirically evaluate the 1-iteration versions, which are denoted by the '1-step' suffix.

Complexity Analysis: We study the computational complexity of Exact-Soft-SPIBB and Approx-Soft-SPIBB. The error bounds computation and the policy evaluation step are common to both algorithms, and have a complexity of $\mathcal{O}(|\mathcal{D}|)$ and $\mathcal{O}(|\mathcal{X}|^3|\mathcal{A}|^3)$ respectively. The part that differs between them is the policy improvement.

Exact-Soft-SPIBB solves the LP with the simplex algorithm, which, as recalled in Sect. 2.3, is in practice polynomial in the dimensions of the program being solved. In our case, the number of constraints is $3|\mathcal{A}| + 1$.

Theorem 4. *Approx-Soft-SPIBB policy improvement has a complexity of $\mathcal{O}(|\mathcal{X}||\mathcal{A}|^2)$.*

Model-Free Soft-SPIBB: The Soft-SPIBB fixed point may be found in a model-free manner by fitting the Q-function to the target $y^{(i+1)}$ on the transition samples $\mathcal{D} = \langle x_j, a_j, r_j, x'_j \rangle_{j \in [\![1,N]\!]}$:

$$y_j^{(i+1)} = r_j + \gamma \sum_{a' \in \mathcal{A}} \pi^{(i+1)}(a'|x'_j) Q^{(i)}(x'_j, a'), \tag{16}$$

where $\pi^{(i+1)}$ is obtained either exactly or approximately with the policy improvement steps described in Sect. 3.2. Then, the policy evaluation consists in fitting $Q^{(i+1)}(x, a)$ to the set of $y_j^{(i+1)}$ values computed using the samples from $\mathcal{D}$.

Theorem 5. *Considering an MDP with exact counts, the model-based policy iteration of (Exact or Approx)-Soft-SPIBB is identical to the model-free policy iteration of (resp. Exact or Approx)-Soft-SPIBB.*

The model-free versions are less computationally efficient than their respective model-based versions, but are particularly useful since it makes function approximation easily applicable. In our infinite MDP experiment, we consider Approx-Soft-SPIBB-DQN as the DQN algorithm fitted to the model-free Approx-Soft-SPIBB targets. The Exact-Soft-SPIBB counterpart is not considered for tractability reasons. We recall that the computation of the policy improvement step relies on the estimates of an error function e_P, which may, for instance, be indirectly inferred from pseudo-counts $\widetilde{N}_{\mathcal{D}}(x, a)$ (Bellemare et al. 2016; Fox et al. 2018; Burda et al. 2019).

4   Soft-SPIBB Empirical Evaluation

This section intends to empirically validate the advances granted by Soft-SPIBB. We perform the study on two domains: on randomly generated finite MDPs, where the Soft-SPIBB algorithms are compared to several Batch RL competitors: basic RL, High Confidence Policy Improvement (Thomas 2015, HCPI), Reward-Adjusted MDPs (Petrik et al. 2016, RaMDP), Robust MDPs (Iyengar, 2005; Nilim and El Ghaoui 2005), and to Soft-SPIBB natural parents: Π_b-SPIBB and $\Pi_{\leq b}$-SPIBB (Laroche et al. 2019); and on a helicopter navigation task requiring function approximation, where Soft-SPIBB-DQN is compared to basic DQN, RaMDP-DQN, and SPIBB-DQN. All the benchmark algorithms had their hyper-parameters optimized beforehand. Their descriptions and the results of the hyper-parameter search is available in the appendix, Section B.2 for finite MDPs algorithms and Section C.3 for DQN-based algorithms.

In order to assess the safety of an algorithm, we run a large number of times the same experiment with a different random seed. Since the environments and the baselines are stochastic, every experiment generates a different dataset, and the algorithms are evaluated on their mean performance over the experiments, and on their conditional value at risk performance (CVaR), sometimes also called the expected shortfall: $X\%$-CVaR corresponds to the mean performance over the $X\%$ worst runs.

4.1 Random MDPs

In the random MDPs experiment, the MDP and the baseline are themselves randomly generated too. The full experimental process is formalized in Pseudo-code 2 found in the appendix, Section B.1. Because every run involves different MDP and baseline, there is the requirement for a normalized performance. This is further defined as $\bar{\rho}$:

$$\bar{\rho}(\pi, M^*) = \frac{\rho(\pi, M^*) - \rho(\pi_b, M^*)}{\rho(\pi^*, M^*) - \rho(\pi_b, M^*)}. \tag{17}$$

In order to demonstrate that Soft-SPIBB algorithms are safely improving the baselines on most MDPs in practice, we use a random generator of MDPs. All the details may be found in the appendix, Section B.1. The number of states is set to $|\mathcal{X}| = 50$, the number of actions to $|\mathcal{A}| = 4$ and the connectivity of the transition function to 4, *i.e.*, for a given state-action pair (x, a), its transition function $P(x'|x, a)$ is non-zero on four states x' only. The reward function is 0 everywhere except when entering the goal state, which is terminal and where the reward is equal to 1. The goal is chosen in such a way that the optimal value function is minimal.

Random Baseline: For a randomly generated MDP M, baselines are generated according to a predefined level of performance $\eta \in \{0.1, 0.2, 0.3, 0.4, 0.5, 0.6,$ $0.7, 0.8, 0.9\}$: $\rho(\pi_b, M) = \eta\rho(\pi^*, M) + (1 - \eta)\rho(\tilde{\pi}, M)$, where π^* and $\tilde{\pi}$ are respectively the optimal and the uniform policies. The generation of the baseline consists in three steps: optimization, where the optimal Q-value is computed; softening, where a softmax policy is generated; and randomization, where the probability mass is randomly displaced in the baseline. The process is formally and extensively detailed in the appendix, Section B.1.

Dataset Generation: Given a fixed size number of trajectories, a dataset is generated on the following modification of the original MDPs: addition of another goal state (reward is set to 1). Since the original goal state was selected so as to be the hardest to reach, the new one, which is selected uniformly, is necessarily a better goal.

Complexity Empirical Analysis: In Fig. 1, we show an empirical confirmation of the complexity results on the gridworld task. Exact-Soft-SPIBB has a linear dependency in the number of actions. We also notice that Approx-Soft-SPIBB runs much faster: even faster than Π_b-SPIBB, and 2 times slower than basic RL. Note that the policy improvement step is by design

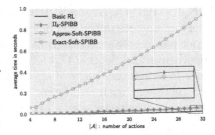

Fig. 1. Average time to convergence.

exactly linearly dependent on the number of states $|\mathcal{X}|$. This is the reason why we do not report experiments on the dependency on $|\mathcal{X}|$. We do not report complexity empirical analysis of the other competitors because we do not pretend to have optimal implementations of them, and the purpose of this analysis is to show that Approx-Soft-SPIBB solves the tractability issues of Exact-Soft-SPIBB. In Theory, Robust MDPs and HCPI are more complex by at least an order of magnitude.

Benchmark Results: Figures 2a and b respectively report the mean and 1%-CVAR performances with a strong baseline ($\eta = 0.9$). Robust MDPs and HCPI perform poorly and are not further discussed. Basic RL and RaMDP win the benchmark in mean, but fail to do it safely, contrary to Soft-SPIBB and SPIBB algorithms. Exact-Soft-SPIBB is slightly better than Approx-Soft-SPIBB in mean, but also slightly worse in safety. Still in comparison to Approx-Soft-SPIBB, Exact-Soft-SPIBB's performance does not justify the computational complexity increase and will not be further discussed. Approx-Soft-SPIBB demonstrates a significant improvement over SPIBB methods, both in mean and in safety. Finally, the comparison of Approx-Soft-SPIBB with Approx-Soft-SPIBB 1-step shows that the safety is not improved in practice, and that the asymptotic optimality is compromised when the dataset becomes larger.

Sensitivity to the Baseline: We continue the analysis with a heatmap representation as a function of the strength of the baseline: Figs. 3a and b display heatmaps of the 0.1%-CVaR performance for RaMDP and Approx-Soft-SPIBB ($\epsilon = 2$) respectively. The colour of a cell indicates the improvement over the baseline normalized with respect to the optimal performance: red, yellow, and green respectively mean below, equal to, and above baseline performance. We observe that RaMDP is unsafe for strong baselines (high η values) and small datasets, while Soft-SPIBB methods become slightly unsafe only with $\eta = 0.9$ and less than 20 trajectories, but are safe everywhere else.

Sensitivity to Hyper-Parameters: We carry on with 1%-CVaR performance heatmaps as a function of the hyper-parameters for RaMDP (Fig. 4a) and Approx-Soft-SPIBB (Fig. 4b) in the hardest scenario ($\eta = 0.9$). The choice of 1%-CVaR instead of 0.1%-CVaR is justified by the fact that the 0.1%-CVaR RaMDP heatmap is almost completely red, which would not allow us to notice the interesting thresholding behaviour: when $\kappa_{adj} \geq 0.0035$, RaMDP becomes over-conservative to the point of not trying to reach the goal anymore. In contrast, Approx-Soft-SPIBB behaves more smoothly with respect to its hyper-parameter, its optimal value being in interval [0.5, 2], depending on the safety/performance trade-off one wants to achieve. In the appendix, Section B.3, the interested reader may find the corresponding heatmaps for all Soft-SPIBB algorithms for mean and 1%-CVaR performances. In particular, we may observe that, despite not having as strong theoretical guarantees as their 1-step versions, the Soft-SPIBB algorithms demonstrate similar CVaR performances.

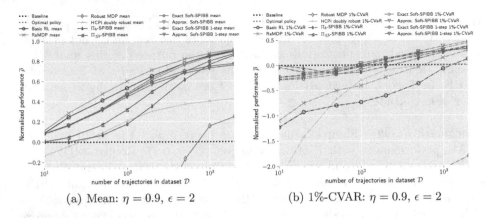

(a) Mean: $\eta = 0.9$, $\epsilon = 2$ (b) 1%-CVAR: $\eta = 0.9$, $\epsilon = 2$

Fig. 2. Benchmark on Random MDPs domain: mean and 1%-CVAR performances for a hard scenario ($\eta = 0.9$) and Soft-SPIBB with $\epsilon = 2$

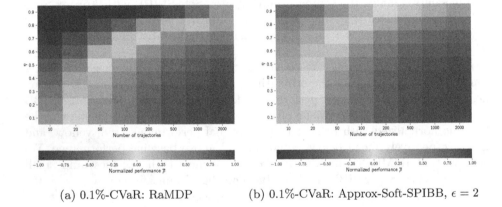

(a) 0.1%-CVaR: RaMDP   (b) 0.1%-CVaR: Approx-Soft-SPIBB, $\epsilon = 2$

Fig. 3. Influence of η on Random MDPs domain: 0.1%-CVaR heatmaps as a function of η

4.2 Helicopter Domain

To assess our algorithms on tasks with more complex state spaces, making the use of function approximation inevitable, we apply them to a helicopter navigation task (Fig. 5(c)). The helicopter's start point is randomly picked in the teal region, its initial velocity is random as well. The agent can choose to apply or not a fixed amount of thrust forward and backward in the two dimensions, resulting in 9 actions total. An episode ends when the agent reaches the boundary of the blue box or has a speed larger than some maximal value. In the first case, it receives a reward based on its position with respect to the top right corner of the box (the exact reward value is chromatically indicated in the figure). In the second, it gets a reward of -1. The dynamics of the helicopter obey Newton's second law

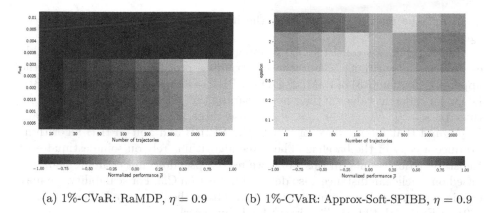

(a) 1%-CVaR: RaMDP, $\eta = 0.9$ (b) 1%-CVaR: Approx-Soft-SPIBB, $\eta = 0.9$

Fig. 4. Sensitivity to hyperparameter on Random MDPs: 1%-CVaR heatmaps for $\eta = 0.9$

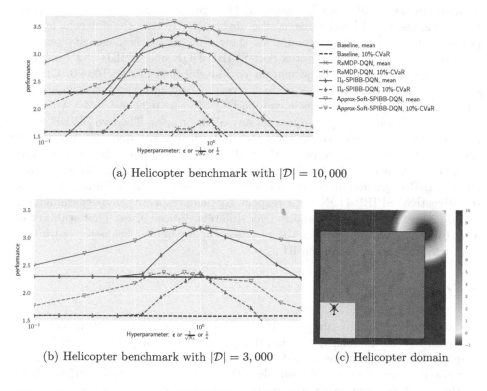

(a) Helicopter benchmark with $|\mathcal{D}| = 10,000$

(b) Helicopter benchmark with $|\mathcal{D}| = 3,000$ (c) Helicopter domain

Fig. 5. Helicopter: mean and 10%-CVaR as a function of the hyper-parameter value

with an additive centered Gaussian noise applied to its position and velocity. We refer the reader to the appendix, Section C.1 for the detailed specifications. We generated a baseline by training online a DQN (Mnih et al. 2015) and applying a softmax on the learnt Q-network. During training, a discount factor of 0.9 is used, but the reported results show the undiscounted return obtained by the agent.

The experiments consist in 300 training runs (necessary to obtain reasonable estimates of algorithms' safety, the full training procedure is described in the appendix, Section C.3) of RaMDP-DQN, SPIBB-DQN and Approx-Soft-SPIBB-DQN, for different values of their hyper-parameters (resp. κ, $N_\wedge$ and ϵ). We note that for $\kappa = 0$, $N_\wedge = 0$ or $\epsilon = +\infty$, those three algorithms become standard DQN, and that for $N_\wedge = \infty$ or $\epsilon = 0$, the SPIBB and Soft-SPIBB algorithms produce a copy of the baseline. The three algorithms rely on some estimates of the state-action counts. In this work, we used a pseudo-count estimate heuristic based on Euclidean distance, also detailed in Section C.3. For scalability, we may consider several pseudo-count methodologies from the literature Bellemare et al. (2016); Fox et al. (2018). This is left for future work.

The results of our evaluation can be found in Fig. 5, where we plot the mean and 10%-CVaR performances of the different algorithms for two sizes of datasets (more results may be found in the appendix, Section C.4). In order to provide meaningful comparisons, the abscissa represents the different hyper-parameters transformed to account for their dimensional homogeneity (except for a scaling factor). Both Approx-Soft-SPIBB-DQN and SPIBB-DQN outperform RaMDP-DQN by a large margin on the datasets of size 10,000. On the smaller datasets, RaMDP-DQN performs very poorly and does not even appear on the graph. For the same reason, vanilla DQN (mean: 0.22 and 10%-CVaR: -1 with $|\mathcal{D}| = 10,000$) does not appear on any of the graphs. The two SPIBB algorithms significantly outperform the baseline both in mean and 10%-CVaR. At their best hyper-parameter value, their 10%-CVaR is actually better than the mean performance of the baseline. Approx-Soft-SPIBB-DQN performs better than SPIBB-DQN both in mean and 10%-CVaR performances. Finally, it is less sensitive than SPIBB-DQN with respect to their respective hyperparameters, and demonstrates a better stability over different dataset sizes. That stability is a useful property as it reduces the requirement for hyper-parameter optimization, which is crucial for Batch RL.

5   Conclusion

We study the problem of safe policy improvement in a Batch RL setting. Building on the SPIBB methodology, we relax the constraints of the policy search to propose a family of algorithms coined Soft-SPIBB. We provide proofs of safety and of computational efficiency for an algorithm called Approx-Soft-SPIBB based on the search of an approximate solution that does not compromise the safety guarantees. We support the theoretical work with an extensive empirical analysis where Approx-Soft-SPIBB shines as the best compromise average performance vs. safety. We further develop Soft-SPIBB in a model-free manner which helps its application to function approximation. Despite the lack of theoretical safety guarantees with function approximation, we observe in our experiments where the function approximation is modelled as a neural network, that Soft-SPIBB allows safe policy improvement in practice and significantly outperforms the competing algorithms both in safety and in performance.

References

Bellemare, M., Srinivasan, S., Ostrovski, G., Schaul, T., Saxton, D., Munos, R.: Unifying count-based exploration and intrinsic motivation. In: Proceedings of the 29th Advances in Neural Information Processing Systems (NIPS) (2016)

Borgwardt, K.H.: The Simplex Method: A Probabilistic Analysis. Springer, Heidelberg (1987). https://doi.org/10.1007/978-3-642-61578-8

Burda, Y., Edwards, H., Storkey, A., Klimov, O.: Exploration by random network distillation. In: Proceedings of the 7th International Conference on Learning Representations (ICLR) (2019)

Dantzig, G.: Linear Programming and Extensions. Rand Corporation Research Study. Princeton Univ. Press, Princeton (1963)

Dantzig, G.B., Thapa, M.N.: Linear Programming 2: Theory and Extensions. Springer, New York (2003). https://doi.org/10.1007/b97283

Ernst, D., Geurts, P., Wehenkel, L.: Tree-based batch mode reinforcement learning. J. Mach. Learn. Res. **6**, 503–556 (2005)

Fox, L., Choshen, L., Loewenstein, Y.: Dora the explorer: directed outreaching reinforcement action-selection. In: Proceedings of the 6th International Conference on Learning Representations (ICLR) (2018)

Geist, M., Scherrer, B., Pietquin, O.: A theory of regularized Markov decision processes. In: Proceedings of the 36th International Conference on Machine Learning (ICML) (2019)

Gondzio, J.: Interior point methods 25 years later. Eur. J. Oper. Res. **218**(3), 587–601 (2012)

Guez, A., Vincent, R.D., Avoli, M., Pineau, J.: Adaptive treatment of epilepsy via batch-mode reinforcement learning. In: Proceedings of the 23rd AAAI Conference on Artificial Intelligence, pp. 1671–1678 (2008)

He, K., Zhang, X., Ren, S., Sun, J.: Delving deep into rectifiers: surpassing human-level performance on imagenet classification. arXiv preprint arXiv:1502.01852 (2015)

Iyengar, G.N.: Robust dynamic programming. Math. Oper. Res. **30**(2), 257–280 (2005)

Kakade, S., Langford, J.: Approximately optimal approximate reinforcement learning. In: Proceedings of the 19th International Conference on Machine Learning (ICML), vol. 2, pp. 267–274 (2002)

Klee, V., Minty, G.J.: How good is the simplex algorithm? In: Shisha, O. (ed.) Inequalities, vol. III, pp. 159–175. Academic Press, New York (1972)

Lange, S., Gabel, T., Riedmiller, M.: Batch reinforcement learning. In: Wiering, M., van Otterlo, M. (eds.) Reinforcement Learning. Adaptation, Learning, and Optimization, vol. 12, pp. 45–73. Springer, Heidelberg (2012). https://doi.org/10.1007/978-3-642-27645-3_2

Laroche, R., Trichelair, P., Tachet des Combes, R.: Safe policy improvement with baseline bootstrapping. In: Proceedings of the 36th International Conference on Machine Learning (ICML) (2019)

Mnih, V., et al.: Human-level control through deep reinforcement learning. Nature **518**(7540), 529 (2015)

Nilim, A., El Ghaoui, L.: Robust control of Markov decision processes with uncertain transition matrices. Oper. Res. **53**(5), 780–798 (2005)

Paszke, A., et al.: Automatic differentiation in PyTorch. In: NIPS-W (2017)

Petrik, M., Ghavamzadeh, M., Chow, Y.: Safe policy improvement by minimizing robust baseline regret. In: Proceedings of the 29th Advances in Neural Information Processing Systems (NIPS) (2016)

Riedmiller, M.: Neural fitted Q iteration – first experiences with a data efficient neural reinforcement learning method. In: Gama, J., Camacho, R., Brazdil, P.B., Jorge, A.M., Torgo, L. (eds.) ECML 2005. LNCS (LNAI), vol. 3720, pp. 317–328. Springer, Heidelberg (2005). https://doi.org/10.1007/11564096_32

Schulman, J., Levine, S., Abbeel, P., Jordan, M., Moritz, P.: Trust region policy optimization. In: Proceedings of the 32nd International Conference on Machine Learning (ICML) (2015)

Schulman, J., Wolski, F., Dhariwal, P., Radford, A., Klimov, O.: Proximal policy optimization algorithms. arXiv preprint arXiv:1707.06347 (2017)

Simão, T.D., Spaan, M.T.J.: Safe policy improvement with baseline bootstrapping in factored environments. In: Proceedings of the 32nd AAAI Conference on Artificial Intelligence (2019)

Singh, S.P., Kearns, M.J., Litman, D.J., Walker, M.A.: Reinforcement learning for spoken dialogue systems. In: Proceedings of the 13th Advances in Neural Information Processing Systems (NIPS), pp. 956–962 (1999)

Sutton, R.S., Barto, A.G.: Reinforcement Learning: An Introduction. The MIT Press, Cambridge (1998)

Thomas, P.S.: Safe reinforcement learning. Ph.D. thesis, Stanford university (2015)

Tieleman, T., Hinton, G.: Lecture 6.5-rmsprop: divide the gradient by a running average of its recent magnitude. COURSERA: Neural Netw. Mach. Learn. 4(2), 26–31 (2012)

van Hasselt, H., Guez, A., Silver, D.: Deep reinforcement learning with double q-learning. CoRR, abs/1509.06461 (2015)

Weissman, T., Ordentlich, E., Seroussi, G., Verdu, S., Weinberger, M.J.: Inequalities for the L1 deviation of the empirical distribution. Hewlett-Packard Labs, Technical report (2003)

Practical Open-Loop Optimistic Planning

Edouard Leurent[1,2]($\boxtimes$) and Odalric-Ambrym Maillard[1]

[1] SequeL Team, INRIA Lille - Nord Europe, Paris, France
{edouard.leurent,odalric.maillard}@inria.fr
[2] Renault Group, Paris, France

Abstract. We consider the problem of online planning in a Markov Decision Process when given only access to a generative model, restricted to open-loop policies - i.e. sequences of actions - and under budget constraint. In this setting, the *Open-Loop Optimistic Planning* (OLOP) algorithm enjoys good theoretical guarantees but is overly conservative in practice, as we show in numerical experiments. We propose a modified version of the algorithm with tighter upper-confidence bounds, KL-OLOP, that leads to better practical performances while retaining the sample complexity bound. Finally, we propose an efficient implementation that significantly improves the time complexity of both algorithms.

Keywords: Planning · Online learning · Tree search

1 Introduction

In a *Markov Decision Process* (MDP), an agent observes its current state s from a state space S and picks an action a from an action space A, before transitioning to a next state s' drawn from a transition kernel $\mathbb{P}(s'|s,a)$ and receiving a bounded reward $r \in [0,1]$ drawn from a reward kernel $\mathbb{P}(r|s,a)$. The agent must act so as to optimise its expected cumulative discounted reward $\mathbb{E}\sum_t \gamma^t r_t$, also called expected *return*, where $\gamma \in [0,1)$ is the discount factor. In *Online Planning* [14], we do not consider that these transition and reward kernels are known as in *Dynamic Programming* [1], but rather only assume access to the MDP through a *generative model* (e.g. a simulator) which yields samples of the next state $s' \sim \mathbb{P}(s'|s,a)$ and reward $r \sim \mathbb{P}(r|s,a)$ when queried. Finally, we consider a *fixed-budget* setting where the generative model can only be called a maximum number of times, called the budget n.

Monte-Carlo Tree Search (MCTS) algorithms were historically motivated by the application of computer Go, and made a first appearance in the CrazyStone software [8]. They were later reformulated in the setting of Multi-Armed Bandits by [12] with their *Upper Confidence bounds applied to Trees* (UCT) algorithm. Despite its popularity [15–17], UCT has been shown to suffer from several limitations: its sample complexity can be at least doubly-exponential for some problems (e.g. when a narrow optimal path is hidden in a suboptimal branch), which is much worse than uniform planning [7]. The Sparse Sampling

© Springer Nature Switzerland AG 2020
U. Brefeld et al. (Eds.): ECML PKDD 2019, LNAI 11908, pp. 69–85, 2020.
https://doi.org/10.1007/978-3-030-46133-1_5

algorithm of [11] achieves better worst-case performance, but it is still non-polynomial and doesn't adapt to the structure of the MDP. In stark contrast, the *Optimistic Planning for Deterministic systems* (OPD) algorithm considered by [10] in the case of deterministic transitions and rewards exploits the structure of the cumulative discounted reward to achieve a problem-dependent polynomial bound on sample complexity. A similar line of work in a deterministic setting is that of SOOP and OPC by [3,4] though they focus on continuous action spaces. OPD was later extended to stochastic systems with the *Open-Loop Optimistic Planning* (OLOP) algorithm introduced by [2] in the open-loop setting: we only consider sequences of actions independently of the states that they lead to. This restriction in the space of policies causes a loss of optimality, but greatly simplifies the planning problem in the cases where the state space is large or infinite. More recent work such as StOp [18] and TrailBlazer [9] focus on the probably approximately correct (PAC) framework: rather than simply recommending an action to maximise the expected rewards, they return an ε-approximation of the value at the root that holds with high probability. This highly demanding framework puts a severe strain on these algorithms that were developed for theoretical analysis only and cannot be applied to real problems.

Contributions. The goal of this paper is to study the practical performances of OLOP when applied to numerical problems. Indeed, OLOP was introduced along with a theoretical sample complexity analysis but no experiment was carried-out. Our contribution is threefold:

- First, we show that in our experiments OLOP is overly pessimistic, especially in the low-budget regime, and we provide an intuitive explanation by casting light on an unintended effect that alters the behaviour of OLOP.
- Second, we circumvent this issue by leveraging modern tools from the bandits literature to design and analyse a modified version with tighter upper-confidence bounds called KL-OLOP. We show that we retain the asymptotic regret bounds of OLOP while improving its performances by an order of magnitude in numerical experiments.
- Third, we provide a time and memory efficient implementation of OLOP and KL-OLOP, bringing an exponential speedup that allows to scale these algorithms to high sample budgets.

The paper is structured as follows: in Sect. 2, we present OLOP, give some intuition on its limitations, and introduce KL-OLOP, whose sample complexity is further analysed in Sect. 3. In Sect. 4, we propose an efficient implementation of the two algorithms. Finally in Sect. 6, we evaluate them in several numerical experiments.

Notations. Throughout the paper, we follow the notations from [2] and use the standard notations over alphabets: a finite word $a \in A^*$ of length h represents a sequence of actions $(a_0, \cdots, a_h) \in A^h$. Its prefix of length $t \leq h$ is denoted $a_{1:t} = (a_0, \cdots, a_t) \in A^t$. A^∞ denotes the set of infinite sequences of actions.

Two finite sequences $a \in A^*$ and $b \in A^*$ can be concatenated as $ab \in A^*$, the set of finite and infinite suffixes of a are respectively $aA^* = \{c \in \mathcal{A}^* : \exists b \in A^*$ such that $c = ab\}$ and aA^∞ defined likewise, and the empty sequence is $\emptyset$.

During the planning process, the agent iteratively selects sequences of actions until it reaches the allowed budget of n actions. More precisely, at time t during the mth sequence, the agent played $a_{1:t}^m = a_1^m \cdots a_t^m \in A^t$ and receives a reward Y_t^m. We denote the probability distribution of this reward as $\nu(a_{1:t}^m) = \mathbb{P}(Y_t^m | s_t, a_t^m) \prod_{k=1}^{t-1} \mathbb{P}(s_{k+1} | s_k, a_k^m)$, and its mean as $\mu(a_{1:t}^m)$, where s_1 is the current state.

After this exploration phase, the agent selects an action $a(n)$ so as to minimise the *simple regret* $r_n = V - V(a(n))$, where $V = V(\emptyset)$ and $V(a)$ refers to the value of a sequence of actions $a \in A^h$, that is, the maximum expected discounted cumulative reward one may obtain after executing a:

$$V(a) = \sup_{b \in aA^\infty} \sum_{t=1}^\infty \gamma^t \mu(b_{1:t}), \tag{1}$$

2   Kullback-Leibler Open-Loop Optimistic Planning

In this section we present KL-OLOP, a combination of the OLOP algorithm of [2] with the tighter Kullback-Leibler upper confidence bounds from [5]. We first frame both algorithms in a common structure before specifying their implementations.

2.1   General Structure

First, following OLOP, the total sample budget n is split in M trajectories of length L in the following way:

M is the largest integer such that $M \lceil \log M / (2 \log 1/\gamma) \rceil \leq n$;
$L = \lceil \log M / (2 \log 1/\gamma) \rceil$.

The look-ahead tree of depth L is denoted $\mathcal{T} = \sum_{h=0}^L A^h$.

Then, we introduce some useful definitions. Consider episode $1 \leq m \leq M$. For any $1 \leq h \leq L$ and $a \in A^h$, let

$$T_a(m) \overset{\text{def}}{=} \sum_{s=1}^m \mathbb{1}\{a_{1:h}^s = a\}$$

be the number of times we played an action sequence starting with a, and $S_a(m)$ the sum of rewards collected at the last transition of the sequence a:

$$S_a(m) \overset{\text{def}}{=} \sum_{s=1}^m Y_h^s \mathbb{1}\{a_{1:h}^s = a\}$$

Algorithm 1: General structure for Open-Loop Optimistic Planning

---

1 **for** *each episode* $m = 1, \cdots, M$ **do**
2   Compute $U_a(m-1)$ from (4) for all $a \in \mathcal{T}$
3   Compute $B_a(m-1)$ from (5) for all $a \in A^L$
4   Sample a sequence with highest B-value: $a^m \in \arg\max_{a \in A^L} B_a(m-1)$

5 **return** the most played sequence $a(n) \in \arg\max_{a \in A^L} T_a(M)$

Table 1. Different implementations of Algorithm 1 in OLOP and KL-OLOP

Algorithm	OLOP	KL-OLOP
Interval I	$\mathbb{R}$	$[0, 1]$
Divergence d	d_{QUAD}	d_{BER}
$f(m)$	$4 \log M$	$2 \log M + 2 \log\log M$

The empirical mean reward of a is $\quad \hat{\mu}_a(m) \stackrel{\text{def}}{=} \dfrac{S_a(m)}{T_a(m)} \quad$ if $T_a(m) > 0$, and $+\infty$ otherwise. Here, we provide a more general form for upper and lower confidence bounds on these empirical means:

$$U_a^\mu(m) \stackrel{\text{def}}{=} \max\left\{ q \in I : T_a(m)d\left(\frac{S_a(m)}{T_a(m)}, q\right) \leq f(m) \right\} \tag{2}$$

$$L_a^\mu(m) \stackrel{\text{def}}{=} \min\left\{ q \in I : T_a(m)d\left(\frac{S_a(m)}{T_a(m)}, q\right) \leq f(m) \right\} \tag{3}$$

where I is an interval, d is a divergence on $I \times I \to \mathbb{R}^+$ and f is a non-decreasing function. They are left unspecified for now and their particular implementations and associated properties will be discussed in the following sections.

These upper-bounds U_a^μ for intermediate rewards finally enable us to define an upper bound U_a for the value $V(a)$ of the entire sequence of actions a:

$$U_a(m) \stackrel{\text{def}}{=} \sum_{t=1}^{h} \gamma^t U_{a_{1:t}}^\mu(m) + \frac{\gamma^{h+1}}{1-\gamma} \tag{4}$$

where $\frac{\gamma^{h+1}}{1-\gamma}$ comes from upper-bounding by one every reward-to-go in the sum (1), for $t \geq h+1$. In [2], there is an extra step to "sharpen the bounds" of sequences $a \in A^L$ by taking:

$$B_a(m) \stackrel{\text{def}}{=} \inf_{1 \leq t \leq L} U_{a_{1:t}}(m) \tag{5}$$

The general algorithm structure is shown in Algorithm 1. We now discuss two specific implementations that differ in their choice of divergence d and non-decreasing function f. They are compared in Table 1.

2.2   OLOP

To recover the original OLOP algorithm of [2] from Algorithm 1, we can use a quadratic divergence d_{QUAD} on $I = \mathbb{R}$ and a constant function f_4 defined as follows:

$$d_{\text{QUAD}}(p, q) \overset{\text{def}}{=} 2(p - q)^2, \qquad f_4(m) \overset{\text{def}}{=} 4 \log M$$

Indeed, in this case $U_a^\mu(m)$ can then be explicitly computed as:

$$U_a^\mu(m) = \max\left\{ q \in \mathbb{R} : 2\Big(\frac{S_a(m)}{T_a(m)} - q\Big)^2 \leq \frac{4 \log M}{T_a(m)} \right\} = \hat{\mu}_a(m) + \sqrt{\frac{2 \log M}{T_a(m)}}$$

which is the Chernoff-Hoeffding bound used originally in Sect. 3.1 of [2].

2.3   An Unintended Behaviour

From the definition of $U_a(m)$ as an upper-bound of the value of the sequence a, we expect increasing sequences $(a_{1:t})_t$ to have non-increasing upper-bounds. Indeed, every new action a_t encountered along the sequence is a potential loss of optimality. However, this property is only true if the upper-bound defined in (2) belongs to the reward interval $[0, 1]$.

Lemma 1. *(Monotony of $U_a(m)$ along a sequence)*

- *If it holds that $U_b^\mu(m) \in [0, 1]$ for all $b \in A^*$, then for any $a \in A^L$ the sequence $(U_{a_{1:h}}(m))_{1 \leq h \leq L}$ is non-increasing, and we simply have $B_a(m) = U_a(m)$.*
- *Conversely, if $U_b^\mu(m) > 1$ for all $b \in A^*$, then for any $a \in A^L$ the sequence $(U_{a_{1:h}}(m))_{1 \leq h \leq L}$ is non-decreasing, and we have $B_a(m) = U_{a_{1:1}}(m)$.*

Proof. We prove the first proposition, and the same reasoning applies to the second. For $a \in A^L$ and $1 \leq h \leq L - 1$, we have by (4):

$$U_{a_{1:h+1}}(m) - U_{a_{1:h}}(m) = \gamma^{h+1} U_{a_{1:h+1}}^\mu(m) + \frac{\gamma^{h+2}}{1 - \gamma} - \frac{\gamma^{h+1}}{1 - \gamma}$$

$$= \gamma^{h+1}(\underbrace{U_{a_{1:h+1}}^\mu(m)}_{\in [0,1]} - 1) \leq 0$$

We can conclude that $(U_{a_{1:h}}(m))_{1 \leq h \leq L}$ is non-increasing and that $B_a(m) = \inf_{1 \leq h \leq L} U_{a_{1:h}}(m) = U_{a_{1:L}}(m) = U_a(m)$. $\qquad\square$

Yet, the Chernoff-Hoeffding bounds used in OLOP start in the $U_a^\mu(m) > 1$ regime – initially $U_a^\mu(m) = \infty$ – and can remain in this regime for a long time especially in the near-optimal branches where $\hat{\mu}_a(m)$ is close to one.

Under these circumstances, the Lemma 1 has a drastic effect on the search behaviour. Indeed, as long as a subtree under the root verifies $U_a^\mu(m) > 1$ for every sequence a, then all these sequences share the same B-value $B_a(m) = U_{a_{1:1}}(m)$. This means that OLOP cannot differentiate them and exploit information from their shared history as intended, and behaves as uniform sampling instead. Once the early depths have been explored sufficiently, OLOP resumes its intended behaviour, but the problem is only shifted to deeper unexplored subtrees.

This consideration motivates us to leverage the recent developments in the Multi-Armed Bandits literature, and modify the upper-confidence bounds for the expected rewards $U_a^\mu(m)$ so that they respect the reward bounds.

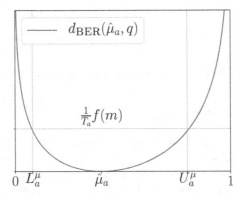

Fig. 1. The Bernoulli Kullback-Leibler divergence d_{BER}, and the corresponding upper and lower confidence bounds U_a^μ and L_a^μ for the empirical average $\hat{\mu}_a$. Lower values of $f(m)$ give tighter confidence bounds that hold with lower probabilities.

2.4   KL-OLOP

We propose a novel implementation of Algorithm 1 where we leverage the analysis of the kl-UCB algorithm from [5] for multi-armed bandits with general bounded rewards. Likewise, we use the Bernoulli Kullback-Leibler divergence defined on the interval $I = [0, 1]$ by:

$$d_{\text{BER}}(p, q) \overset{\text{def}}{=} p \log \frac{p}{q} + (1 - p) \log \frac{1 - p}{1 - q}$$

with, by convention, $0 \log 0 = 0 \log 0/0 = 0$ and $x \log x/0 = +\infty$ for $x > 0$. This divergence and the corresponding bounds are illustrated in Fig. 1.

$U_a^\mu(m)$ and $L_a^\mu(m)$ can be efficiently computed using Newton iterations, as for any $p \in [0, 1]$ the function $q \to d_{\text{BER}}(p, q)$ is strictly convex and increasing (resp. decreasing) on the interval [p, 1] (resp. [0, p]).

Moreover, we use the constant function $f_2 : m \to 2 \log M + 2 \log \log M$. This choice is justified in the end of Sect. 5. Because f_2 is lower than f_4, the Fig. 1 shows that the bounds are tighter and hence less conservative than that of OLOP, which should increase the performance, provided that their associated probability of violation does not invalidate the regret bound of OLOP.

Remark 2 (Upper bounds sharpening). The introduction of the B-values $B_a(m)$ was made necessary in OLOP by the use of Chernoff-Hoeffding confidence bounds which are not guaranteed to belong to $[0, 1]$. On the contrary, we have in KL-OLOP that $U_a^{\mu}(m) \in I = [0, 1]$ by construction. By Lemma 1, the upper bounds sharpening step in line 3 of Algorithm 1 is now superfluous as we trivially have $B_a(m) = U_a(m)$ for all $a \in A^L$.

3   Sample Complexity

We say that $u_n = \widetilde{O}(v_n)$ if there exist $\alpha, \beta > 0$ such that $u_n \leq \alpha \log(v_n)^{\beta} v_n$. Let us denote the proportion of near-optimal nodes κ_2 as:

$$\kappa_2 \overset{\text{def}}{=} \limsup_{h \to \infty} \left| \left\{ a \in a^H : V(a) \geq V - 2\frac{\gamma^{h+1}}{1-\gamma} \right\} \right|^{1/h}$$

Theorem 3 (Sample complexity). *We show that KL-OLOP enjoys the same asymptotic regret bounds as OLOP. More precisely, for any $\kappa' > \kappa_2$, KL-OLOP satisfies:*

$$\mathbb{E}r_n = \begin{cases} \widetilde{O}\left(n^{-\frac{\log 1/\gamma}{\log \kappa'}}\right), & \text{if } \gamma\sqrt{\kappa'} > 1 \\ \widetilde{O}\left(n^{-\frac{1}{2}}\right), & \text{if } \gamma\sqrt{\kappa'} \leq 1 \end{cases}$$

4   Time and Memory Complexity

After having considered the sample efficiency of OLOP and KL-OLOP, we now turn to study their time and memory complexities. We will only mention the case of KL-OLOP for ease of presentation, but all results easily extend to OLOP.

The Algorithm 1 requires, at each episode, to compute and store in memory of the reward upper-bounds and U-values of all nodes in the tree $\mathcal{T} = \sum_{h=0}^{L} A^h$. Hence, its time and memory complexities are

$$C(\text{KL-OLOP}) = O(M|\mathcal{T}|) = O(MK^L). \qquad (6)$$

The curse of dimensionality brought by the branching factor K and horizon L makes it intractable in practice to actually run KL-OLOP in its original form even for small problems. However, most of this computation and memory usage is wasted, as with reasonable sample budgets n the vast majority of the tree $\mathcal{T}$ will not be actually explored and hence does not hold any valuable information.

We propose in Algorithm 2 a lazy version of KL-OLOP which only stores and processes the explored subtree, as shown in Fig. 2, while preserving the inner workings of the original algorithm.

Theorem 4 (Consistency). *The set of sequences returned by Algorithm 2 is the same as the one returned by Algorithm 1. In particular, Algorithm 2 enjoys the same regret bounds as in Theorem 3.*

Property 5 (Time and memory complexity). Algorithm 2 has time and memory complexities of:

$$C(\texttt{Lazy KL-OLOP}) = O(KLM^2)$$

The corresponding complexity gain compared to the original Algorithm 1 is:

$$\frac{C(\texttt{Lazy KL-OLOP})}{C(\texttt{KL-OLOP})} = \frac{n}{K^{L-1}}$$

which highlights that only a subtree corresponding to the sample budget n is processed instead of the search whole tree $\mathcal{T}$.

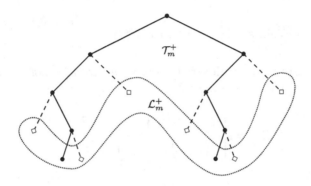

Fig. 2. A representation of the tree $\mathcal{T}_m^+$, with $K = 2$ actions and after episode $m = 2$, when two sequences have been sampled. They are represented with solid lines and dots •, and they constitute the explored subtree $\mathcal{T}_m$. When extending $\mathcal{T}_m$ with the missing children of each node, represented with dashed lines and diamonds ◇, we obtain the full extended subtree $\mathcal{T}_m^+$. The set of its leaves is denoted $\mathcal{L}_m^+$ and shown as a dotted set.

Proof. At episode $m = 1, \cdots, M$, we compute and store in memory the reward upper-bounds and U-values of all nodes in the subtree $\mathcal{T}_m^+$. Moreover, the tree $\mathcal{T}_m^+$ is constructed iteratively by adding K nodes at most L times at each episode from 0 to m. Hence, $|\mathcal{T}_m^+| = O(mKL)$. This yields directly $C(\texttt{Lazy KL-OLOP}) = \sum_{m=1}^{M} O(mKL) = O(M^2KL)$. □

5   Proof of Theorem 3

We follow step-by step the pyramidal proof of [2], and adapt it to the Kullback-Leibler upper confidence bound. The adjustments resulting from the change of confidence bounds are highlighted. The proofs of lemmas which are not significantly altered are listed in the Supplementary Material.

We start by recalling their notations. Let $1 \leq H \leq L$ and $a^* \in A^L$ such that $V(a^*) = V$. Considering sequences of actions of length $1 \leq h \leq H$, we define the

---

Algorithm 2: Lazy Open Loop Optimistic Planning

1 Let M be the largest integer such that $M \log M / (2 \log 1/\gamma) \leq n$
2 Let $L = \log M / (2 \log 1/\gamma)$
3 Let $\mathcal{T}_0^+ = \mathcal{L}_0^+ = \{\emptyset\}$
4 **for** *each episode* $m = 1, \cdots, M$ **do**
5 $\quad$ Compute $U_a(m-1)$ from (4) for all $a \in \mathcal{T}_{m-1}^+$
6 $\quad$ Compute $B_a(m-1)$ from (5) for all $a \in \mathcal{L}_{m-1}^+$
7 $\quad$ Sample a sequence with highest B-value: $a \in \arg\max_{a \in \mathcal{L}_{m-1}^+} B_a(m-1)$
8 $\quad$ Choose an arbitrary continuation $a^m \in aA^{L-|a|}$ $\qquad$ // e.g. uniformly
9 $\quad$ Let $\mathcal{T}_m^+ = \mathcal{T}_{m-1}^+$ and $\mathcal{L}_m^+ = \mathcal{L}_{m-1}^+$
10 $\quad$ **for** $t = 1, \cdots, L$ **do**
11 $\quad\quad$ **if** $a_{1:t}^m \notin \mathcal{T}_m^+$ **then**
12 $\quad\quad\quad$ Add $a_{1:t-1}^m A$ to $\mathcal{T}_m^+$ and $\mathcal{L}_m^+$
13 $\quad\quad\quad$ Remove $a_{1:t-1}^m$ from $\mathcal{L}_m^+$

14 **return** the most played sequence $a(n) \in \arg\max_{a \in \mathcal{L}_m^+} T_a(M)$

---

subset $\mathcal{I}_h$ of near-optimal sequences and the subset $\mathcal{J}$ of sub-optimal sequences that were near-optimal at depth $h-1$:

$$\mathcal{I}_h = \left\{ a \in A^h : V - V(a) \leq 2\frac{\gamma^{h+1}}{1-\gamma} \right\}, \quad \mathcal{J}_h = \left\{ a \in A^h : a_{1:h-1} \in \mathcal{I}_{h-1} \text{and} a \notin \mathcal{I}_h \right\}$$

By convention, $\mathcal{I}_0 = \{\emptyset\}$. From the definition of κ_2, we have that for any $\kappa' > \kappa_2$, there exists a constant C such that for any $h \geq 1$, $|\mathcal{I}_h| \leq C\kappa'^h$ Hence, we also have $|\mathcal{J}_h| \leq K|\mathcal{I}_{h-1}| = O(\kappa'^h)$.

Now, for $1 \leq m \leq M$, $a \in A^t$ with $t \leq h$, $h' < h$, we define the set $\mathcal{P}_{h,h'}^a(m)$ of suffixes of a in $\mathcal{J}_h$ that have been played at least a certain number of times:

$$\mathcal{P}_{h,h'}^a(m) = \left\{ b \in aA^{h-t} \cap \mathcal{J}_h : T_b(m) \geq 2f(m)(h+1)^2\gamma^{2(h'-h+1)} + 1 \right\}$$

and the random variable:

$$\mathcal{T}_{h,h'}^a(m) = \mathbb{1}\{T_a(m-1) < 2f(m)(h+1)^2\gamma^{2(h'-h+1)} + 1 \leq T_a(m)\}$$

Lemma 6 (Regret and sub-optimal pulls). *The following holds true:*

$$r_n \leq \frac{2K\gamma^{H+1}}{1-\gamma} + \frac{3K}{M} \sum_{h=1}^{H} \sum_{a \in \mathcal{J}_h} \frac{\gamma^h}{1-\gamma} T_a(M)$$

The rest of the proof is devoted to the analysis of the term $\mathbb{E} \sum_{a \in \mathcal{J}_h} T_a(M)$. The next lemma describes under which circumstances a suboptimal sequence of actions in $\mathcal{J}_h$ can be selected.

Lemma 7 (Conditions for sub-optimal pull). *Assume that at step $m + 1$ we select a sub-optimal sequence a^{m+1}: there exist $0 \leq h \leq L, a \in \mathcal{J}_h$ such that $a^{m+1} \in aA^*$. Then, it implies that one of the following propositions is true:*

$$U_{a^*}(m) < V, \qquad \text{(UCB violation)}$$

or

$$\sum_{t=1}^{h} \gamma^t L_{a_{1:t}}^{\mu}(m) \geq V(a), \qquad \text{(LCB violation)}$$

or

$$\sum_{t=1}^{h} \gamma^t \left(U_{a_{1:t}}^{\mu}(m) - L_{a_{1:t}}^{\mu}(m) \right) > \frac{\gamma^{h+1}}{1 - \gamma} \qquad \text{(Large CI)}$$

Proof. As $a_{1:h}^{m+1} = a$ and because the U-values are monotonically increasing along sequences of actions (see Remark 2 and Lemma 1), we have $U_a(m) \geq U_{a^{m+1}}(m)$. Moreover, by Algorithm 1, we have $a^{m+1} = \arg\max_{a \in A^L} U_a(m)$ and $a^* \in A^L$, so $U_{a^{m+1}}(m) \geq U_{a^*}(m)$ and finally $U_a(m) \geq U_{a^*}(m)$.

Assume that (UCB violation) is false, then:

$$\sum_{t=1}^{h} \gamma^t U_{a_{1:t}}^{\mu}(m) + \frac{\gamma^{h+1}}{1 - \gamma} = U_a(m) \geq U_{a^*}(m) \geq V \qquad (7)$$

Assume that (LCB violation) is false, then:

$$\sum_{t=1}^{h} \gamma^t L_{a_{1:t}}^{\mu}(m) < V(a), \qquad (8)$$

By taking the difference (7)–(8),

$$\sum_{t=1}^{h} \gamma^t \left(U_{a_{1:t}}^{\mu}(m) - L_{a_{1:t}}^{\mu}(m) \right) + \frac{\gamma^{h+1}}{1 - \gamma} > V - V(a)$$

But $a \in \mathcal{J}_h$, so $V - V(a) \geq \frac{2\gamma^{h+1}}{1-\gamma}$, which yields (Large CI) and concludes the proof. □

In the following lemma, for each episode m we bound the probability of (UCB violation) or (LCB violation) by a desired confidence level δ_m, whose choice we postpone until the end of this proof. For now, we simply assume that we picked a function f that satisfies $f(m)\log(m)e^{-f(m)} = O(\delta_m)$. We also denote $\Delta_M = \sum_{m=1}^{M} \delta_m$.

Lemma 8 (Boundary crossing probability). *The following holds true, for any $1 \leq h \leq L$ and $m \leq M$,*

$$\mathbb{P}\left((\text{UCB violation}) \text{ or } (\text{LCB violation}) \text{ is true}\right) = O((L + h)\delta_m)$$

Proof. Since $V \leq \sum_{t=1}^{h} \gamma^t \mu(a_{1:t}^*) + \frac{\gamma^{h+1}}{1-\gamma}$, we have,

$$\mathbb{P}\left((\text{UCB violation})\right) = \mathbb{P}\left(U_{a^*}(m) \leq V\right)$$

$$= \mathbb{P}\left(\sum_{t=1}^{L} \gamma^t U_{a_{1:t}^*}^{\mu}(m) \leq \sum_{t=1}^{L} \gamma^t \mu(a_{1:t}^*)\right)$$

$$\leq \mathbb{P}\left(\exists 1 \leq t \leq L : U_{a_{1:t}^*}^{\mu}(m) \leq \mu(a_{1:t}^*)\right)$$

$$\leq \sum_{t=1}^{L} \mathbb{P}\left(U_{a_{1:t}^*}^{\mu}(m) \leq \mu(a_{1:t}^*)\right)$$

In order to bound this quantity, we reduce the question to the application of a deviation inequality. For all $1 \leq t \leq L$, we have on the event $\{U_{a_{1:t}^*}^{\mu}(m) \leq \mu(a_{1:t}^*)\}$ that $\hat{\mu}_{a_{1:t}^*}(m) \leq U_{a_{1:t}^*}^{\mu}(m) \leq \mu(a_{1:t}^*) < 1$. Therefore, for all $0 < \delta < 1 - \mu(a_{1:t}^*)$, by definition of $U_{a_{1:t}^*}^{\mu}(m)$:

$$d(\hat{\mu}_{a_{1:t}^*}(m), U_{a_{1:t}^*}^{\mu}(m) + \delta) > \frac{f(m)}{T_{a_{1:t}^*}(m)}$$

As d is continuous on $(0,1) \times [0,1]$, we have by letting $\delta \to 0$ that:

$$d(\hat{\mu}_{a_{1:t}^*}(m), U_{a_{1:t}^*}^{\mu}(m)) \geq \frac{f(m)}{T_{a_{1:t}^*}(m)}$$

Since d is non-decreasing on $[\hat{\mu}_{a_{1:t}^*}(m), \mu(a_{1:t}^*)]$,

$$d(\hat{\mu}_{a_{1:t}^*}(m), \mu(a_{1:t}^*)) \geq d(\hat{\mu}_{a_{1:t}^*}(m), U_{a_{1:t}^*}^{\mu}(m)) \geq \frac{f(m)}{T_{a_{1:t}^*}(m)}$$

We have thus shown the following inclusion:

$$\{U_{a_{1:t}^*}^{\mu}(m) \leq \mu(a_{1:t}^*)\} \subseteq \left\{\mu(a_{1:t}^*) > \hat{\mu}_{a_{1:t}^*}(m) \text{ and } d(\hat{\mu}_{a_{1:t}^*}(m), \mu(a_{1:t}^*)) \geq \frac{f(m)}{T_{a_{1:t}^*}(m)}\right\}$$

Decomposing according to the values of $T_{a_{1:t}^*}(m)$ yields:

$$\{U_{a_{1:t}^*}^{\mu}(m) \leq \mu(a_{1:t}^*)\} \subseteq \bigcup_{n=1}^{m} \left\{\mu(a_{1:t}^*) > \hat{\mu}_{a_{1:t}^*,n} \text{ and } d(\hat{\mu}_{a_{1:t}^*,n}, \mu(a_{1:t}^*)) \geq \frac{f(m)}{n}\right\}$$

We now apply the deviation inequality provided in Lemma 2 of Appendix A in [5]: $\forall \varepsilon > 1$, provided that $0 < \mu(a_{1:t}^*) < 1$,

$$\mathbb{P}\left(\bigcup_{n=1}^{m} \{\mu(a_{1:t}^*) > \hat{\mu}_{a_{1:t}^*,n} \text{ and } nd_{\text{BER}}(\hat{\mu}_{a_{1:t}^*,n}, \mu(a_{1:t}^*)) \geq \varepsilon\}\right) \leq e\lceil \varepsilon \log m\rceil e^{-\varepsilon}.$$

By choosing $\varepsilon = f(m)$, it comes

$$\mathbb{P}\left((\text{UCB violation})\right) \le \sum_{t=1}^{L} e \lceil f(m) \log m \rceil e^{-f(m)} = O(L\delta_m)$$

The same reasoning gives: $\mathbb{P}((\text{LCB violation})) = O(h\delta_m)$.   □

Lemma 9 (Confidence interval length and number of plays). *Let* $1 \le h \le L$, $a \in \mathcal{J}_h$ *and* $0 \le h' < h$. *Then* (Large CI) *is not satisfied if the following propositions are true:*

$$\forall 0 \le t \le h', T_{a_{1:t}}(m) \ge 2f(m)(h+1)^2\gamma^{2(t-h-1)} \tag{9}$$

and

$$T_a(m) \ge 2f(m)(h+1)^2\gamma^{2(h'-h-1)} \tag{10}$$

Proof. We start by providing an explicit upper-bound for the length of the confidence interval $U_{a_{1:t}}^\mu - L_{a_{1:t}}^\mu$. By Pinsker's inequality:

$$d_{\text{BER}}(p,q) > d_{\text{QUAD}}(p,q)$$

Hence for all $C > 0$,

$$d_{\text{BER}}(p,q) \le C \implies 2(q-p)^2 < C \implies p - \sqrt{C/2} < q < p + \sqrt{C/2}$$

And thus, for all $b \in A^*$, by definition of U^μ and L^μ:

$$U_b^\mu(m) - L_b^\mu(m) \le \frac{S_b(m)}{T_b(m)} + \sqrt{\frac{f(m)}{2T_b(m)}} - \left(\frac{S_b(m)}{T_b(m)} - \sqrt{\frac{f(m)}{2T_b(m)}}\right) = \sqrt{\frac{2f(m)}{T_b(m)}}$$

Now, assume that (9) and (10) are true. Then, we clearly have:

$$\sum_{t=1}^{h} \gamma^t \left(U_{a_{1:t}}^\mu(m) - L_{a_{1:t}}^\mu(m)\right) \le \sum_{t=1}^{h'} \gamma^t \sqrt{\frac{2f(m)}{T_{a_{1:t}}(m)}} + \sum_{t=h'+1}^{h} \gamma^t \sqrt{\frac{2f(m)}{T_{a_{1:t}}(m)}}$$

$$\le \frac{1}{(h+1)\gamma^{-h-1}} \sum_{t=1}^{h'} 1 + \frac{1}{(h+1)\gamma^{-h-1}} \sum_{t=h'+1}^{h} \gamma^{t-h'}$$

$$\le \frac{\gamma^{h+1}}{h+1}\left(h' + \frac{\gamma}{1-\gamma}\right) \le \frac{\gamma^{h+1}}{1-\gamma}.$$ □

Lemma 10. *Let* $1 \le h \le L, a \in \mathcal{J}_h$ *and* $0 \le h' < h$. *Then* $T_{h,h'}^a = 1$ *implies that either equation* (UCB violation) *or* (LCB violation) *is satisfied or the following proposition is true:*

$$\exists 1 \le t \le h' : |\mathcal{P}_{h,h'}^{a_{1:t}}(m)| < \gamma^{2(t-h')} \tag{11}$$

Lemma 11. *Let* $1 \leq h \leq L$ *and* $0 \leq h' < h$. *Then the following holds true,*

$$\mathbb{E}|\mathcal{P}_{h,h'}^{\emptyset}(M)| = \tilde{O}\left(\gamma^{-2h'}\mathbb{1}_{h'>0}\sum_{t=0}^{h'}(\gamma^2\kappa')^t + (\kappa')^h\Delta_M\right).$$

Lemma 12. *Let* $1 \leq h \leq L$. *The following holds true,*

$$\mathbb{E}\sum_{a\in\mathcal{J}_h}T_a(M) = \tilde{O}\left(\gamma^{-2h} + (\kappa')^h(1 + M\Delta_M + \Delta_M) + (\kappa'\gamma^{-2})^h\Delta_M\right)$$

Thus by combining Lemma 6 and 12 we obtain:

$$\mathbb{E}r_n = \tilde{O}\left(\gamma^H + \gamma^{-H}M^{-1} + (\kappa'\gamma)^H M^{-1}(1 + M\Delta_M + \Delta_M) + (\kappa')^H\gamma^{-H}M^{-1}\Delta_M\right)$$

Finally,

– if $\kappa'\gamma^2 \leq 1$, we take $H = \lfloor \log M/(2\log 1/\gamma)\rfloor$ to obtain:

$$\mathbb{E}r_n = \tilde{O}\left(M^{-\frac{1}{2}} + M^{-\frac{1}{2}} + M^{-\frac{1}{2}}M^{\frac{\log\kappa'}{2\log 1/\gamma}}\Delta_M\right)$$

For the last term to be of the same order of the others, we need to have $\Delta_M = O(M^{-\frac{\log\kappa'}{2\log 1/\gamma}})$. Since $\kappa'\gamma^2 \leq 1$, we achieve this by taking $\Delta_M = O(M^{-1})$.

– if $\kappa'\gamma^2 > 1$, we take $H = \lfloor\log M/\log\kappa'\rfloor$ to obtain:

$$\mathbb{E}r_n = \tilde{O}\left(M^{\frac{\log\gamma}{\log\kappa'}} + M^{\frac{\log\gamma}{\log\kappa'}}(1 + M\Delta_M + \Delta_M) + M^{\frac{\log 1/\gamma}{\log\kappa'}}\Delta_M\right)$$

Since $\kappa'\gamma^2 > 1$, the dominant term in this sum is $M^{\frac{\log\gamma}{\log\kappa'}}M\Delta_M$. Again, taking $\Delta_M = O(M^{-1})$ yields the claimed bounds.

Thus, the claimed bounds are obtained in both cases as long as we can impose $\Delta_M = O(M^{-1})$, that is, find a sequence $(\delta_m)_{1\leq m\leq M}$ and a function f verifying:

$$\sum_{m=1}^{M}\delta_m = O(M^{-1}) \quad \text{and} \quad f(m)\log(m)e^{-f(m)} = O(\delta_m) \tag{12}$$

By choosing $\delta_m = M^{-2}$ and $f(m) = 2\log M + 2\log\log M$, the corresponding KL-OLOP algorithm does achieve the regret bound claimed in Theorem 3.

6 Experiments

We have performed some numerical experiments to evaluate and compare the following planning algorithms[1]:

---

[1] The source code is available at https://eleurent.github.io/kl-olop/.

- **Random**: returns a random action, we use it as a minimal performance baseline.
- **OPD**: the *Optimistic Planning for Deterministic systems* from [10], used as a baseline of optimal performance. This planner is only suited for deterministic environments, and exploits this property to obtain faster rates. However, it is expected to fail in stochastic environments.
- **OLOP**: as described in Sect. 2.2.[2]
- **KL-OLOP**: as described in Sect. 2.4. (see footnote 2)
- **KL-OLOP(1)**: an aggressive version of **KL-OLOP** where we used $f_1(m) = \log M$ instead of $f_2(m)$. This threshold function makes the upper bounds even tighter, at the cost of an increased probability of violation. Hence, we expect this solution to be more efficient in close-to-deterministic environments. However, since we have no theoretical guarantee concerning its regret as we do with **KL-OLOP**, it might not be conservative enough and converge too early to a suboptimal sequence, especially in highly stochastic environments.

They are evaluated on the following tasks, using a discount factor of $\gamma = 0.8$:

- A highway driving environment [13]: a vehicle is driving on a road randomly populated with other slower drivers, and must make their way as fast as possible while avoiding collisions by choosing on the following actions: **change-lane-left**, **change-lane-right**, **no-op**, **faster**, **slower**.
- A gridworld environment [6]: the agent navigates in a randomly-generated gridworld composed of either empty cells, terminal lava cells, and goal cells where a reward of 1 is collected at the first visit.
- A stochastic version of the gridworld environment with noisy rewards, where the noise is modelled as a Bernoulli distribution with a 15% probability of error, i.e. receiving a reward of 1 in an empty cell or 0 in a goal cell.

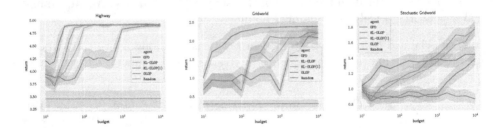

Fig. 3. Numerical experiments: for each environment-agent configuration, we compute the average return over 100 runs—along with its 95% confidence interval—with respect to the available budget n.

The results of our experiments are shown in Fig. 3. The **ODP** algorithm converges very quickly to the optimal return in the two first environments, shown

---

[2] Note that we use the lazy version of **OLOP** and **KL-OLOP** presented in Sect. 4, otherwise the exponential running-time would have been prohibitive.

in Fig. 3a and b, because it exploits their deterministic nature: it needs neither to estimate the rewards through upper-confidence bounds nor to sample whole sequences all the way from the root when expanding a leaf, which provides a significant speedup. It can be seen as an oracle allowing to measure the conservativeness of stochastic planning algorithms. And indeed, even before introducing stochasticity, we can see that OLOP performs quite badly on the two environments, only managing to solve them with a budget in the order of $10^{3.5}$. In stark contrast, KL-OLOP makes a much better use of its samples and reaches the same performance an order of magnitude faster. This is illustrated by the expanded trees shown in Fig. 4: ODP exploits the deterministic setting and produces a sparse tree densely concentrated around the optimal trajectory. Conversely, the tree developed by OLOP is evenly balanced, which suggests that OLOP behaves as uniform planning as hypothesised in Sect. 2.3. KL-OLOP is more efficient and expands a highly unbalanced tree, exploring the same regions as ODP. Furthermore, in the stochastic gridworld environment shown in Fig. 3c, we observe that the deterministic ODP planner's performance saturates as it settles to suboptimal trajectories, as expected. Conversely, the stochastic planners all find better-performing open-loop policies, which justifies the need for this framework. Again, KL-OLOP converges an order of magnitude faster than OLOP. Finally, KL-OLOP(1) enjoys good performance overall and displays the most satisfying trade-off between aggressiveness in deterministic environments and conservativeness in stochastic environments; hence we recommend this tuning for practical use.

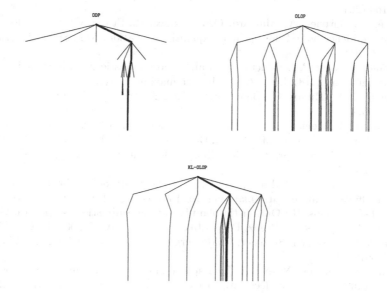

Fig. 4. The look-ahead trees (down to depth 6) expanded by the planning algorithms from the same initial state in the highway environment with the same budget $n = 10^3$. The width of edges represents the nodes visit count $T_a(M)$.

7   Conclusion

We introduced an enhanced version of the OLOP algorithm for open-loop online planning, whose design was motivated by an investigation of the over-conservative search behaviours of OLOP. We analysed its sample complexity and showed that the original regret bounds are preserved, while its empirical performances are increased by an order of magnitude in several numerical experiments. Finally, we proposed an efficient implementation that benefits from a substantial speedup, facilitating its use for real-time planning applications.

Acknowledgments. This work has been supported by CPER Nord-Pas de Calais/FEDER DATA Advanced data science and technologies 2015–2020, the French Ministry of Higher Education and Research, INRIA, and the French Agence Nationale de la Recherche.

References

1. Bellman, R.: Dynamic Programming. Princeton University Press, Princeton (1957)
2. Bubeck, S., Munos, R.: Open loop optimistic planning. In: Proceedings of COLT (2010)
3. Buşoniu, L., Daniels, A., Munos, R., Babuska, R.: Optimistic planning for continuous-action deterministic systems. In: IEEE Symposium on Adaptive Dynamic Programming and Reinforcement Learning, ADPRL (2013)
4. Buşoniu, L., Páll, E., Munos, R.: Continuous-action planning for discounted infinite-horizon nonlinear optimal control with Lipschitz values. Automatica **92**, 100–108 (2018)
5. Cappé, O., Garivier, A., Maillard, O.A., Munos, R., Stoltz, G.: Kullback-Leibler upper confidence bounds for optimal sequential allocation. Ann. Stat. **41**(3), 1516–1541 (2013)
6. Chevalier-Boisvert, M., Willems, L., Pal, S.: Minimalistic gridworld environment for openai gym (2018). https://github.com/maximecb/gym-minigrid
7. Coquelin, P.A., Munos, R.: Bandit algorithms for tree search. In: Proceedings of UAI (2007)
8. Coulom, R.: Efficient selectivity and backup operators in Monte-Carlo tree search. In: van den Herik, H.J., Ciancarini, P., Donkers, H.H.L.M.J. (eds.) CG 2006. LNCS, vol. 4630, pp. 72–83. Springer, Heidelberg (2007). https://doi.org/10.1007/978-3-540-75538-8_7
9. Grill, J.B., Valko, M., Munos, R.: Blazing the trails before beating the path: sample-efficient Monte-Carlo planning. In: Proceedings of NeurIPS (2016)
10. Hren, J.-F., Munos, R.: Optimistic planning of deterministic systems. In: Girgin, S., Loth, M., Munos, R., Preux, P., Ryabko, D. (eds.) EWRL 2008. LNCS (LNAI), vol. 5323, pp. 151–164. Springer, Heidelberg (2008). https://doi.org/10.1007/978-3-540-89722-4_12
11. Kearns, M., Mansour, Y., Ng, A.Y.: A sparse sampling algorithm for near-optimal planning in large Markov decision processes. In: Proceedings of IJCAI (2002)
12. Kocsis, L., Szepesvári, C.: Bandit based Monte-Carlo planning. In: Proceedings of ECML (2006)
13. Leurent, E.: An environment for autonomous driving decision-making (2018). https://github.com/eleurent/highway-env

14. Munos, R.: From Bandits to Monte-Carlo tree search: the optimistic principle applied to optimization. Found. Trends® Mach. Learn. **7**, 1–129 (2014)
15. Silver, D., et al.: Mastering the game of go with deep neural networks and tree search. Nature **529**, 484–503 (2016)
16. Silver, D., et al.: A general reinforcement learning algorithm that masters chess, shogi, and go through self-play. Science **362**(6419), 1140–1144 (2018)
17. Silver, D., et al.: Mastering the game of go without human knowledge. Nature **550**(7676), 354 (2017)
18. Szorenyi, B., Kedenburg, G., Munos, R.: Optimistic planning in Markov decision processes using a generative model. In: Proceedings of NeurIPS (2014)

An Engineered Empirical Bernstein Bound

Mark A. Burgess[1]([✉]), Archie C. Chapman[2], and Paul Scott[1]

[1] College of Engineering and Computer Science, Australian National University,
Canberra, ACT 0200, Australia
markburgess1989@gmail.com, {mark.burgess,paul.scott}@anu.edu.au
[2] School of Electrical and Information Engineering, University of Sydney,
Sydney, NSW 2006, Australia
archie.chapman@sydney.edu.au

Abstract. We derive a tightened *empirical Bernstein bound* (EBB) on
the variation of the sample mean from the population mean, and show
that it improves the performance of *upper confidence bound* (UCB) methods in multi-armed bandit problems. Like other EBBs, our EBB is a
concentration inequality for the variation of the sample mean in terms
of the sample variance. Its derivation uses a combination of probability
unions and Chernoff bounds for the mean of samples and mean of sample
squares. Analysis reveals that our approach can tighten the best existing EBBs by about a third, and thereby halves the distance to a bound
constructed with perfect variance information. We illustrate the practical usefulness of our novel EBB by applying it to a multi-armed bandit
problem as a component of a UCB method. Our method outperforms
existing approaches by producing lower expected regret than variants of
UCB employing several other bounds, including state-of-the-art EBBs.

Keywords: Concentration inequality · Chernoff bounds · Hoeffding's
inequality · Empirical Bernstein bound

1   Introduction

Data-driven processes and decision-making applications typically rely on sample statistics to infer parameters of a population or evaluate decision options.
Depending on the domain, different assumptions can be made about the distribution of the data, which in turn determine which computational routines are used
to compute the required population statistics. These assumptions may be based
on prior information, expert opinion, or determined from the characteristics of
the system under observation.

Within this context, finite-sample *concentration inequalities* are used to place
bounds on the variation of sample statistics around their population values. Such

A great thanks to Sylvie Thiébaux for advice and encouragement.

bounds are applied in a range of data science contexts for a variety of prediction, machine learning and hypothesis testing tasks, including: change detection [11,19] and classification [25] in data streams; outlier analysis in large databases [2]; online optimisation [1,17]; and, of most relevance to this paper, online prediction and learning problems [15,22,23,30], particularly in settings with *bandit feedback* [3,5,31]. In particular, the recently developed *empirical Bernstein bounds* (EBB) are of significant interest [4,22]. These are probability bounds describing the likely difference of a sample mean from the population mean in terms of the *sample* variance, under the assumption that the population data is bounded within an interval of known width. EBBs have been used as a method of generating confidence bounds for the mean, and an outstanding task is to see how much these techniques can be improved.

Given this challenge, in this work, we take inspiration and extend the work of Maurer and Pontil ([22], M&P in the remainder) to develop a new EBB. Our EBB tightens existing bounds by incorporating a combination of bounds on the variation of the sample variance. Specifically, we use two Chernoff bounds, for the sample mean and the mean of sample squares, which are fused using a probability union and variance decomposition, to create a novel probability bound for the sample variance, which is then used to derive our novel EBB.

Evaluations show that our EBB significantly tightens the current state-of-the-art bounds. Specifically, our EBB can shrink the best existing EBBs by about a third. This represents half of the distance between the best existing EBBs and an unattainable Bernstein bound constructed with perfect variance information. Moreover, we demonstrate the use of our novel EBB in an *upper-confidence bound* (UCB) multi-armed bandit (MAB) algorithm. Results from a set of MABs show that using our bound in a UCB algorithm outperforms existing approaches, by producing comparable or lower expected regret than employing other existing bounds, including state-of-the-art EBBs.

The paper is organised as follows. Related work and preliminary concepts are reviewed in Sects. 2 and 3, respectively. Our main results are in Sect. 4, where we derive a novel EBB. In Sect. 5 we evaluate our EBB and show its improvements over existing bounds. In Sect. 6 we apply it to a multi-armed bandit problem as part of a UCB algorithm, which demonstrates how our tighter EBB improves the algorithm's learning performance. Section 7 concludes.

2 Related Work

Concentration inequalities are probabilistic bounds describing how far a random variable is expected to deviate from (or otherwise be concentrated around) a particular value. Most classic concentration inequalities describe the expected deviation of sample statistics, including Chebyshev's inequality [12], the Bernstein's inequalities [10], Hoeffding's inequalities [18] and Bennett's inequalities [7]. Building on these, new analysis has yielded a wide range concentration inequalities and methods of generating them [9,13]. In particular, recent innovations concern the concentration of more-general functions of random variables, such as the Efron-Stein [16] and entropy methods [14], and applications of Talagrand's concentration inequality [28]. Inequalities such as these are used to describe the expected variability of sample statistics, such as the distance of a sample mean from the population mean.

Furthermore, additional sample statistics can be used to tighten such bounds, because these statistics provide extra distributional information that are incorporated as a factor into classical inequalities. EBBs [4,22] are one example of this, where sample variance information is used to tighten a classical Bernstein bound. However, it remains to be seen how far bounds derived by this approach can be tightened.

3   Preliminaries

To begin, we state three lemmas which form the basis for our derivation (proofs in Appendix A.1). The first is an often used result related to union bounds:

Lemma 1 (Probability Union). *For any random variables a, b and c:*

$$\mathbb{P}(a > c) \leq \mathbb{P}(a > b) + \mathbb{P}(b > c)$$

This result is used to bound the probability relationship between two variables via knowledge of the probability relationship between them and a third variable. The second definition relates the value of the sample mean and the value of sample squares to the sample variance. It is expanded here because we will later use these relationships to create bounds for the sample variance from bounds on the sample squares and sample mean.

Lemma 2 (Variance Decomposition). *For n samples x_i, sample mean $\hat{\mu} = \frac{1}{n} \sum_i x_i$, sample variance $\hat{\sigma}^2 = \frac{1}{n-1} \sum_i (x_i - \hat{\mu})^2$, and average of sample squares $\hat{\sigma}_0^2 = \frac{1}{n} \sum_i x_i^2$, the following relationship holds:*

$$\hat{\sigma}_0^2 = \hat{\mu}^2 + \frac{n-1}{n} \hat{\sigma}^2$$

In order to derive our novel bound, we use the next lemma, which encapsulates a range of inequalities called *Chernoff bounds* that give bounds on the mean of random variables:

Lemma 3 (Chernoff Bound). *If $\hat{\mu}$ is sample mean of n independent and identically distributed samples of random variable X then for any $s > 0$ and t:*

$$\mathbb{P}(\hat{\mu} \geq t) \leq \mathbb{E}\left[\exp(sX)\right]^n \exp(-snt)$$

The proof of this statement is straightforward and uses Markov's inequality and the i.i.d of the samples. In the next section, we use these components to derive the bounds on the sample mean and the mean of sample squares, which we then use to create a new EBB.

4   Derivation and Numerical Implementation

In this section, we derive two Chernoff bounds, for the sample mean and the mean of sample squares, (Lemmas 5 and 6, respectively). These are fused using a probability union and variance decomposition, defined above, to derive a bound for the sample variance. This bound is then used to derive our new EBB, as presented in Theorem 7. However, due to its analytic intractability, we complete the derivation by discussing how to numerically implement the bound.

4.1   Derivation

Our first probability bound is a Chernoff bound on the sample mean called *Bennett's inequality*. This bound is not new and was derived by [18] and [7] and has subsequently been a subject of discussion and many further developments [8, 24, 29]; we provide a proof in Appendix A.2.

Theorem 4 (Bennett's inequality). *Let X be a real-valued random variable with a mean of zero and variance σ^2, that is bounded $a \le X \le b$. Then for $t > 0$, the mean $\hat{\mu}$ of n samples of X is probability bounded by:*

$$\mathbb{P}(\hat{\mu} \ge t) \le H_1^n \left(\frac{\sigma^2}{b^2}, \frac{t}{b} \right), \tag{1}$$

where:

$$H_1^n \left(\frac{\sigma^2}{b^2}, \frac{t}{b} \right) = \left(\left(\frac{\frac{\sigma^2}{b^2}}{\frac{\sigma^2}{b^2} + \frac{t}{b}} \right)^{\frac{\sigma^2}{b^2} + \frac{t}{b}} \left(1 - \frac{t}{b} \right)^{\frac{t}{b} - 1} \right)^{\frac{n}{\frac{\sigma^2}{b^2} + 1}}$$

We will also use a double-sided version of this bound:

$$\mathbb{P}(\hat{\mu}^2 \ge r^2) \le H_1^n \left(\frac{\sigma^2}{b^2}, \frac{r}{b} \right) + H_1^n \left(\frac{\sigma^2}{a^2}, \frac{-r}{a} \right) \tag{2}$$

The assumption that the mean is zero can be used without a loss of generality. In this way, Bennett's inequality gives us a probability bound for the difference of the sample mean from the true mean *given the variance*.

However, often in practice the variance is unknown, but can only estimate it via a sample variance statistic. Thus, we derive a bound the difference of the sample variance from the variance as follows (proof in Appendix A.3):

Lemma 5 (Sample square bound). *Let X be a real-valued random variable with a mean of zero and variance σ^2, that is bounded $a \le X \le b$, if $d = \max(b, -a)$ then for $y > 0$, the mean of sample squares $\hat{\sigma}_0^2 = \frac{1}{n} \sum_i x_i^2$ is probability bounded:*

$$\mathbb{P}(\sigma^2 - \hat{\sigma}_0^2 > y) \le H_2^n \left(\frac{\sigma^2}{d^2}, \frac{y}{d^2} \right), \tag{3}$$

where:

$$H_2^n\left(\frac{\sigma^2}{d^2},\frac{y}{d^2}\right) = \left(\left(\frac{1-\frac{\sigma^2}{d^2}}{1+\frac{y}{d^2}-\frac{\sigma^2}{d^2}}\right)^{1+\frac{y}{d^2}-\frac{\sigma^2}{d^2}}\left(\frac{\frac{\sigma^2}{d^2}}{\frac{\sigma^2}{d^2}-\frac{y}{d^2}}\right)^{\frac{\sigma^2}{d^2}-\frac{y}{d^2}}\right)^n$$

It is worth noting that we choose to restrict the use of function H_2^n to cases which are sensible for it to be applied: (i) it is defined for $a < 0 < b$, because otherwise the mean could not be zero), and (ii) $\sigma^2 \leq -ab \leq (b-a)^2/4$ by Popoviciu's inequality [27], as it is not possible for the variance to be larger given the width of the data bounds. It is important that these domain restrictions are conserved with the analysis.

At this point, we have a probability bound on the mean squared (Eq. 2) and a probability bound on the sample squares (Lemma 5). With these in hand, we use lemma 2 to create a bound on the sample variance, as follows.

Lemma 6 (Sample Variance Bound). *For a random variable that is bounded $a \leq X \leq b$ with variance σ^2 and a mean of zero, if $d = \max(b, -a)$ then for $w > 0$, the sample variance $\hat{\sigma}^2$ of n samples is probability bounded by:*

$$\mathbb{P}(\sigma^2 - \hat{\sigma}^2 > w) \leq H_3^n(a, b, w, \sigma^2), \tag{4}$$

where:

$$H_3^n(a,b,w,\sigma^2) = \min_{\phi\in[0,1]}\left\{\begin{array}{l} H_1^n\left(\frac{\sigma^2}{b^2},\frac{\sqrt{\phi(\frac{n-1}{n}w+\frac{1}{n}\sigma^2)}}{b}\right) \\ +H_1^n\left(\frac{\sigma^2}{a^2},\frac{-\sqrt{\phi(\frac{n-1}{n}w+\frac{1}{n}\sigma^2)}}{a}\right) \\ +H_2^n\left(\frac{\sigma^2}{d^2},\frac{(1-\phi)(\frac{n-1}{n}w+\frac{1}{n}\sigma^2)}{d^2}\right) \end{array}\right\}$$

A proof is provided in Appendix A.3. The use of the function H_3^n is subject to the same restrictions on its domain as H_2^n. Thus, in Lemma 4 we have a bound for the sample mean given the variance, and in Lemma 6 we have a probability bound for the difference of the sample variance from the population variance. Next, we outline a method of combining these two to create a bound for the sample mean given the sample variance — and thereby derive a new empirical Bernstein bound. To do this, we now expound a theorem that embodies a process followed by M&P [22].

Before beginning, we introduce some notation. For a function f with ordered inputs, we denote the inverse of f with respect to its ith input (counting from one) as $f^{-(i)}$, assuming it exists. Denote probability bounds on the differences of the sample mean from the mean, and the sample variance from the variance, by $\mathbb{P}(\hat{\mu} - \mu > t) \leq h(\sigma^2, t)$ and $\mathbb{P}(\sigma^2 - \hat{\sigma}^2 > w) \leq f(\sigma^2, w)$, respectively. Note that functions h and f have arguments σ^2 and t, and σ^2 and w, respectively.

Theorem 7 (Essential EBB). *Assume $f^{-(2)}$ and $h^{-(2)}$ both exist, and also if $h^{-(2)}$ is monotonically increasing in its first argument, so that we can define:*

$$z(\sigma^2, w) = \sigma^2 - f^{-(2)}\left(\sigma^2, w\right)$$

If $z^{-(1)}$ exists and is monotonic increasing in its first argument, then for any $x \in [0, y]$, the following relationship holds:

$$\mathbb{P}\left(\hat{\mu} - \mu > h^{-(2)}\left(z^{-(1)}\left(\hat{\sigma}^2, y - x\right), x\right)\right) \leq y$$

Proof. Substituting w for $f^{-2}(\sigma^2, w)$ gives:

$$w \geq \mathbb{P}\left(\sigma^2 - \hat{\sigma}^2 > f^{-(2)}\left(\sigma^2, w\right)\right)$$
$$\geq \mathbb{P}\left(z\left(\sigma^2, w\right) > \hat{\sigma}^2\right)$$
$$\geq \mathbb{P}\left(\sigma^2 > z^{-(1)}\left(\hat{\sigma}^2, w\right)\right)$$
$$\geq \mathbb{P}\left(h^{-2}\left(\sigma^2, t\right) > h^{-(2)}\left(z^{-(1)}\left(\hat{\sigma}^2, w\right), t\right)\right)$$

Substituting t for $h^{-(2)}(\sigma^2, t)$ gives:

$$\mathbb{P}\left(\hat{\mu} - \mu > h^{-(2)}\left(\sigma^2, t\right)\right) \leq t.$$

Applying probability union (Lemma 1) gives:

$$\mathbb{P}\left(\hat{\mu} - \mu > h^{-(2)}\left(z^{-(1)}\left(\hat{\sigma}^2, w\right), t\right)\right) \leq t + w.$$

Letting $y = t + w$ and $x = y - w$ completes the proof. ∎

The result of this Theorem is an EBB, and our novel EBB is completed by substituting $h(\sigma^2, t) = H_1^n\left(\sigma^2/b^2, t/b\right)$ and $f(\sigma^2, w) = H_3^n\left(a, b, w, \sigma^2\right)$ into Theorem 7. Care must be taken in applying this theorem that all the assumptions hold, the inverses exist, and the domains of the functions are propagated through the analysis.

4.2 Numerical Implementation

Analytically solving this new EBB is challenging, however it is possible to evaluate it to arbitrary accuracy using numerical techniques. This section provides a high-level description of a process for calculating our EBB.[1]

This calculation is composed of three primary parts: (i) the computation of function $f(\sigma^2, w) = H_3^n(a, b, y, \sigma^2)$; (ii) verifying that the assumptions of Theorem 7 hold for $h(\sigma^2, t) = H_1$ and $f(\sigma^2, w) = H_3$, and; (iii) calculating the subsequent result of Theorem 7.

First, the function $f(\sigma^2, w) = H_3^n(a, b, w, \sigma^2)$ is the solution to an optimization problem that solves for the minima of an objective function subject to constraint $\phi \in [0, 1]$. Despite its complexity, a solution can be found quickly using a single variable parameter sweep.

---

[1] Sourcecode available at:
https://github.com/Markopolo141/Engineered-Empirical-Bernstein-Bound.

Second, it is necessary to verify the assumptions that $h^{-(2)}$, $f^{-(2)}$ and $z^{-(1)}$ exist and that $z^{-(1)}$ and $f^{-(2)}$ are monotonically increasing in their first argument. It is easy to note that $h(\sigma^2, t) = H_1^n\left(\sigma^2/b^2, t/b\right)$ is a closed-form function that is monotonically decreasing from 1 to 0 on the second argument, so $h^{-(2)}$ exists and is monotonically increasing in its first argument. However the remaining assumptions are more difficult to verify. For any function, the values that the function takes can be plotted as an array of points and the values that the inverse of that function takes can be determined by conducting coordinate swaps on those points. The values of $f(\sigma^2, w) = H_3^n(a, b, w, \sigma^2)$ were computed and were seen to be monotonically decreasing in its second argument confirming that $f^{-(2)}$ exists. The function $z(\sigma^2, w) = \sigma^2 - f^{-(2)}\left(\sigma^2, w\right)$ is then seen to be a manipulation on the coordinate swapped points of $f(\sigma^2, w) = H_3^n(a, b, w, \sigma^2)$. By coordinate swapping again, $z^{-(1)}$ was seen to be a regular function monotonically increasing on its first argument, hence satisfying assumptions.

Third, to numerically calculate the result of Theorem 7 the functions $h^{-(2)}$ and $z^{-(1)}$ were numerically evaluated by direct parameter searches and then composed as: $h^{-(2)}(z^{-(1)}(\hat{\sigma}^2, y - x), x)$ - which is the inner part of the expression of the new EBB parameterised by x explicitly and also a, b implicitly. However we typically don't know the values of a and b, but instead know the mean is somewhere within a finite interval of width $D = b - a$. Given this, we then take the worst case values of a and b consistent with a given D, and then take the best $x \in [0, y]$ subject to all other bounds.

5   Comparison to Existing Bounds

In this section, we make three comparisons of our results to existing concentration bounds, namely (i) Lemma 6 is compared to M&P's entropic bound, then our EBB is compared to (ii) M&P's EBB and (iii) Bennett's inequality with perfect variance information.

First, M&P's entropic bound [22] (originally presented in [21]) is given by:

$$\mathbb{P}(\sigma^2 - \hat{\sigma}^2 > w) \leq \exp\left(\frac{-(n-1)w^2}{2\sigma^2 D^2}\right) \tag{5}$$

The improvement our variance bound (Lemma 6) offers over theirs is given by:

$$Y\left(\frac{\sigma^2}{D^2}, \frac{w}{D^2}, n\right) = \exp\left(\frac{-(n-1)w^2}{2\sigma^2 D^2}\right) - \max_b H_3^n\left(D(1-b), Db, w, \sigma^2\right) \tag{6}$$

where b has a viable range between 0.5 and $0.5 - \sqrt{0.25 - \sigma^2/D^2}$ (via Popoviciu's inequality). Figure 1 plots this improvement against σ^2 and w for $n = 200$, which shows large regions of advantage. However, it is possible to use the minima of several different variance bounds, so in constructing our EBB, we take the minima of our variance bound and the entropic bound.

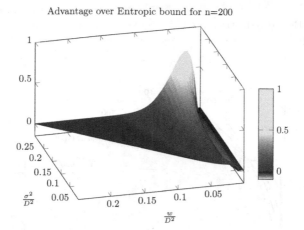

Fig. 1. The strength of our variance bound over Maurer's Entropic bound. The graph of $Y\left(\frac{\sigma^2}{D^2}, \frac{w}{D^2}, n\right)$ from Eq. 6

Second, we compare our EBB directly with M&P's EBB [22], given by:

$$\mathbb{P}\left(\mu - \hat{\mu} > \sqrt{\frac{2\hat{\sigma}^2 \log(2/y)}{n}} + \frac{7D\log(2/y)}{3(n-1)}\right) < y. \tag{7}$$

In order to fairly compare our EBB to M&P's we apply Popoviciu's inequality as a domain restriction, and carry it through their derivation, as we did to our own EBB. Specifically, this is the domain where:

$$\frac{1}{2} > \frac{\sqrt{\hat{\sigma}^2}}{D} + \sqrt{\frac{2\log(2/y)}{n-1}}$$

We plot the improvement our EBB offers in this domain, as shown in Fig. 2. In this plot, a probability 0.5 bound is shown to shrink by approximately one third. More generally, we observe that our refinement of M&P's EBB is be uniformly tighter across a large range of values.

Third, a comparison is made of the further improvement in confidence over our EBB that can be achieved with perfect information about the variance; specifically, Bennett's inequality is used assuming $\hat{\sigma}^2 = \sigma^2$. This improvement is plotted in Fig. 3, which shows that when the variance is small, uncertainty about the variance is the most detrimental to an EBB, such as ours. However, in general, going from our EBB to perfect variance information shrinks the bounds by about another third.

Bound reduction of our EBB over Maurer and Pontil's

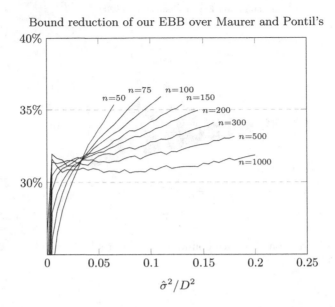

Fig. 2. The percent reduction of the 0.5 probability bound, that going from Maurer and Pontil's EBB to our EBB would achieve, for various n, in the domain valid for their EBB.

Potential bound reduction with $\hat{\sigma}^2 = \sigma^2$ over our EBB

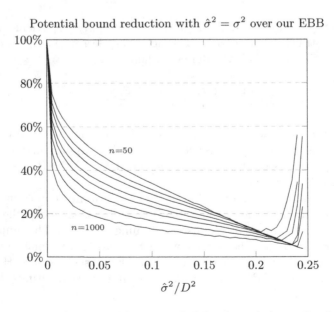

Fig. 3. The percent reduction in the 0.5 probability bound that going from our EBB to using Bennett's inequality (perfect variance information, $\hat{\sigma}^2 = \sigma^2$) achieves, for $n = 50, 75, 100, 150, 200, 300, 500, 1000$.

6   Application: Multi-Armed Bandits

One example use of concentration inequalities is in the context of the *upper-confidence bound* (UCB) method in *multi-armed bandit* (MAB) problems. In this section we consider the performance of UCB employing different concentration inequalities in an example MAB, in order to show the benefit of using our EBB.

6.1   MAB Problem Description

There are several variations of MAB problems, however the classic MAB [26] problem comprises a single bandit machine with K arms, each of which returns rewards that are independently drawn from an unknown distribution when it is pulled. In general, the MAB problem is to design an algorithm for sequentially choosing between the K arms in order to maximise the sum of the (initially unknown) stochastic rewards that each arm yields. Initially, a player must choose exploratory actions to learn about the rewards that each arm returns, before exploiting this information to choose the higher-valued arms. In this way, MABs illustrate finite horizon reinforcement learning dynamics, and is one of the clearest examples of the exploration-exploitation trade-off in machine learning.

Formally, at each time-step, n, a player has to choose which of the arms to pull. However, the player initially has no knowledge of the rewards of each arm, $k \in \mathcal{K}$, so it must learn these values in order to deduce a policy that maximises its sum of rewards. As argued above, in real-world applications, reward values are typically bounded, so we assume that each arm's reward distribution has bounded supports. Denote the mean of this distribution and the width of its support μ_k and D_k, respectively.

Let $A = \{a(1), a(2), \ldots\}$ be a finite sequence of arm pulls, where $a(n)$ is the arm pulled at time-step t, $a(n) \in \mathcal{K}$. Let $R(A)$ be the total return to the player from following the sequence A. The expectation of A is:

$$\mathbb{E}\left[R(A)\right] = \sum_{a(t) \in A} \mu_k$$

An optimal sequence of arm pulls, A^* is one that maximises the expression above, that is:

$$A^* = \arg\max_{A} \mathbb{E}\left[R(A)\right] = \arg\max_{A} \sum_{a(n) \in A} \mu_k$$

However, in order to determine A^*, we have to know the value of μ_k in advance, which we do not. Thus, A^* is a *theoretical* optimum value, which is not achievable in general. Instead, a typical approach to MABs is to define a *loss* or *regret* function, $L(A)$ for an arbitrary algorithm A:

$$L(A) = \mathbb{E}\left[R(A^*)\right] - \mathbb{E}\left[R(A)\right] \tag{8}$$

Using this regret function, the MAB problem is transformed to one of finding a sequence, A, that minimises $L(A)$.

6.2   Upper-Confidence Bound Methods

One well-known and effective strategy for the MAB is UCB [20]. Under UCB, at each iteration, n, the arm with the greatest upper confidence bound on the estimated mean of its reward as inferred from past rewards (at some confidence level) is selected. Specifically, the general form of UCB methods is to define a *confidence interval*, CI on the estimate of the mean:

$$\mathbb{P}\left(\mu - \hat{\mu} \geq CI\right) \leq y$$

where y is a confidence level, and then at each iteration, to select the arm with the greatest upper confidence bound given this confidence interval:

$$a(n) = \arg\max_{k \in \mathcal{K}}\left[\hat{\mu}_k(n) + CI_k(n)\right]$$

where $\hat{\mu}_k(n)$ and $CI_k(n)$ are the mean estimate and confidence interval at time-step n, respectively. In this way, the initial selection of arms is driven by the degree of uncertainty about their rewards, as captured by using the confidence bounds, while over time, the best performing arms are selected more often.

UCB methods can be categorised by the specific type of bandit problem they apply to, and also the method used to infer the confidence interval. One typical UCB method uses Hoeffding's inequality to set the confidence interval [6], where Hoeffding's inequality is given by:

$$\mathbb{P}\left(\mu - \hat{\mu} \geq \sqrt{\frac{D^2 \log(1/y)}{2n}}\right) \leq y. \tag{9}$$

Additionally we consider the EBB type UCB method developed by [4] per their inequality:

$$\mathbb{P}\left(\mu - \hat{\mu} \geq \sqrt{\frac{\hat{\sigma}^2 \log(3/t)}{2n}} + \frac{3D \log(3/t)}{2n}\right) \leq t. \tag{10}$$

We also consider a UCB method with the EBB developed by M&P [22], particularly utilizing the bound of inequality (7) (in Sect. 5). All three are compared to UCB employing our EBB to define the upper confidence bound. Additionally, we also compare to randomly choosing actions, for a naïve baseline. In all cases we selected UCB to minimise a probability 0.5 bound.

We used a confidence level of 0.5 in all cases simply as a representative of a mid-range bound, but note that potentially some different dynamics could occur with the selection of more extreme bounds (i.e. close to 0 or 1).

For the application of our EBB we hand-tuned a function approximating our EBB's numerical probability 0.5 bound:

$$\mathbb{P}\left(\mu - \hat{\mu} \geq \frac{D}{\sqrt{n}} \min\left[\sqrt{2\log 2}, \left(\begin{array}{c}\frac{3}{5}\sqrt{\min\left[1, \frac{\hat{\sigma}^2}{D^2} + \frac{25}{n}\right]} \\ + \ln\left(\max\left[1, n\left(1 - \frac{\hat{\sigma}^2}{D^2}\right)\right]\right)\end{array}\right)^{-4}\right]\right) \lesssim 0.5 \tag{11}$$

The process of creating the above expression involved plotting the numerical data, and manually fitting an approximate symbolic expression. This expression was used *in situ* to simplify the application of our EBB in the bandit context. However the numeric data itself may have been calculated and used directly, at the cost of longer compute times.

6.3   Problem Instances and Results

In the example bandit problems considered here, the number of arms is $K = 8$, each of which yield rewards of between 0 and 1. For each arm k, there is a unique α_k and β_k parameters of its beta distribution over rewards, and for each realization of the problem, these α_k and β_k are drawn uniformly from between 0 and 3. For these problems, we used the different confidence bound approaches, and measured their performance in terms of regret, defined in (8). As noted above, regret is a measure of the performance of bandit algorithms identified by the expected loss of selecting an arm against choosing only the ideal arm. The regret of the different methods of choosing actions was estimated as the average regret obtained across 100,000 instances of this bandit problem. We computed the average regret of these methods over finite arm-pulling budgets, N, in order to assess the algorithm's finite-time performance.

The the performance of the four methods and the naïve baseline are shown in Fig. 4. From this figure, we see that minimizing an upper confidence bound utilizing our inequality (11) results in best performance (lowest regret), except marginally in the region of very small sample budgets.

Expected regret for bandit algorithms with budget N

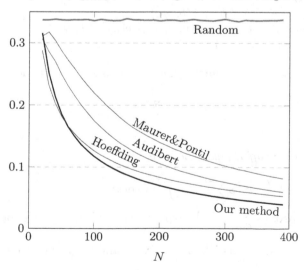

Fig. 4. The expected regret of bandit algorithms and a baseline method in the example bandit problem: UCB method using our bound (11), Hoeffding's, Audibert et al.'s, and Maurer & Pontil's inequalities; and method of uniform randomly choosing an arm.

It is somewhat surprising to see the more complicated EBB methods [4,22] perform worse than the much simpler Hoeffding's inequality. As EBB inequalities are specifically constructed in a way to incorporate the estimate of the variance, then the potential advantage comes when there are sufficiently many samples for reliable variance estimation. However a bound without this construction (such as Hoeffding's inequality) may be tighter and more effective for small/medium sample budgets. As expected, the random method of choosing arms had a constant expected average regret across action budgets, as it does not learn with additional samples of the arms' rewards.

7 Conclusion

In this paper, we have extended existing work on concentration inequalities to derive a new and stronger EBB. Our EBB has many applications, in any setting where a mean value must be estimated with confidence, such as bandit problems. Our EBB was shown to tighten known EBB-based confidence intervals by about a third, thereby improving the value of these types of concentration inequalities. This value was demonstrated in a MAB problem, where using our EBB in a UCB algorithm was shown to improve online learning performance.

A   Proofs

A.1   Small Proofs

Proof (Proof of Probability Union - Lemma 1). For any events A and B
$\mathbb{P}(A \cup B) \leq \mathbb{P}(A) + \mathbb{P}(B)$, hence for events $a > b$ and $b > c$:
$\mathbb{P}((a > b) \cup (b > c)) \leq \mathbb{P}(a > b) + \mathbb{P}(b > c)$
If $a > c$, then $(a > b) \cup (b > c)$ is true irrespective of b, so:
$\mathbb{P}(a > c) \leq \mathbb{P}((a > b) \cup (b > c))$ ∎

Proof (Proof of Variance Decomposition - Lemma 2). By expanding and $\hat{\sigma}^2$:

$$\hat{\sigma}^2 = \frac{1}{n-1} \sum_i \left(x_i - \frac{1}{n} \sum_j x_j \right)^2 = \frac{1}{n-1} \left(\sum_i x_i^2 - \frac{1}{n} \sum_{i,j} x_i x_j \right) = \frac{n}{n-1} \left(\hat{\sigma}_0^2 - \hat{\mu}^2 \right) \quad ∎$$

Proof (Proof of Chernoff Bound - Lemma 3).

$$\mathbb{P}(\hat{\mu} \geq t) = \mathbb{P}\left(\exp\left(s \sum_{i=1}^n x_i \right) \geq \exp(snt) \right)$$
$$\leq \mathbb{E}\left[\exp\left(s \sum_{i=1}^n x_i \right) \right] \exp(-snt) \leq \mathbb{E}\left[\exp\left(sX \right) \right]^n \exp(-snt)$$

using Markov's inequality and the i.i.d of the samples, respectively.   ∎

A.2   A Proof of Bennett's inequality

Theorem 8 (Parabola Fitting). *For $b > 0$, $a < b$ and $z > 0$, there exists an α, β, γ such that: $\alpha x^2 + \beta x + \gamma \geq \exp(x)$ for all $a \leq x \leq b$, and:*

$$z\alpha + \gamma = (z\exp(b) + b^2 \exp(-z/b))(z + b^2)^{-1}.$$

Proof. A example parabola $\alpha x^2 + \beta x + \gamma$ which that satisfies these requirements tangentially touches the exponential curve at one point (at $x = f < b$) and intersects it at another (at $x = b$), as illustrated in Fig. 5. Thus the parabola's intersection at $x = b$ and its tangential intersection at $x = f$ can be written in matrix algebra:

$$\begin{bmatrix} \alpha \\ \beta \\ \gamma \end{bmatrix} = \begin{bmatrix} b^2 & b & 1 \\ f^2 & f & 1 \\ 2f & 1 & 0 \end{bmatrix}^{-1} \begin{bmatrix} \exp(b) \\ \exp(f) \\ \exp(f) \end{bmatrix}$$

This gives our parabola parameters α, β, γ, in terms of f and b, hence:

$$z\alpha + \gamma = (((z + fb - b)(f - b - 1) - b)e^f + (f^2 + z)e^b)(b - f)^{-2}$$

Minimizing with respect to f occurs at $f = \frac{-z}{b}$ and gives the result.   ∎

Proof (Proof of Bennett's inequlity – Lemma 4). As random variable X is bounded $a \leq X \leq b$, for any $s > 0$, by Theorem 8, there exist parameters α, β, γ such that, $\alpha s^2 X^2 + \beta s X + \gamma \geq \exp(sX)$ is always satisfied, hence for these we have:

$$\mathbb{E}\left[\exp(sX)\right] \leq \mathbb{E}[\alpha s^2 X^2 + \beta s X + \gamma] \leq \alpha s^2 \,\mathbb{E}[X^2] + \gamma \leq \alpha s^2 \sigma^2 + \gamma$$
$$\leq (\sigma^2 \exp(sb) + b^2 \exp(-s\sigma^2/b))(\sigma^2 + b^2)^{-1}$$

Hence by application of lemma 3:

$$\mathbb{P}(\hat{\mu} \geq t) \leq (\sigma^2 \exp(sb) + b^2 \exp(-s\sigma^2/b))^n((\sigma^2 + b^2)\exp(st))^{-n}$$

and finding the minimum with respect to s completes the proof.   ∎

A.3   Remaining Proofs

Proof (Proof of Sample Square Bound - Lemma 5). There exist parameters α, γ such for all $a \leq X \leq b$ that $\alpha X^2 + \gamma \geq \exp(-qX^2)$ whence:

$$\mathbb{E}[\exp(-qX^2)] \leq \mathbb{E}[\alpha x^2 + \gamma] \leq \alpha \sigma^2 + \gamma$$

With $d = \max(b, -a)$, we choose (Fig. 6) $\alpha = (\exp(-qd^2) - 1)d^{-2}$ and $\gamma = 1$. Then applying lemma 3 to the mean of the negated sample squares gives:

$$\mathbb{P}(-\hat{\sigma}_0^2 \geq t) \leq \left(\frac{\sigma^2}{d^2}\exp(-qd^2) + 1 - \frac{\sigma^2}{d^2}\right)^n \exp(-qnt)$$

Substituting t for $y - \sigma^2$ and minimizing with q completes the proof.   ∎

Proof (Proof of Sample Variance Bound - Lemma 6). By Lemmas 5 and 2:

$$\mathbb{P}\left(\sigma^2 - \hat{\sigma}^2 > \frac{n}{n-1}\left(\hat{\mu}^2 + y - \frac{1}{n}\sigma^2\right)\right) \leq H_2^n\left(\frac{\sigma^2}{d^2}, \frac{y}{d^2}\right)$$

Also, by manipulating the inner inequality of Eq. 2:

$$\mathbb{P}\left(\frac{n}{n-1}\left(\hat{\mu}^2 + y - \frac{1}{n}\sigma^2\right) \geq \frac{n}{n-1}\left(r^2 + y - \frac{1}{n}\sigma^2\right)\right) \leq H_1^n\left(\frac{\sigma^2}{b^2}, \frac{r}{b}\right) + H_1^n\left(\frac{\sigma^2}{a^2}, \frac{-r}{a}\right)$$

Applying lemma 1 to the above two equations gives:

$$\mathbb{P}\left(\sigma^2 - \hat{\sigma}^2 > \frac{n}{n-1}\left(r^2 + y - \frac{1}{n}\sigma^2\right)\right) \leq H_2^n\left(\frac{\sigma^2}{d^2}, \frac{y}{d^2}\right) + H_1^n\left(\frac{\sigma^2}{b^2}, \frac{r}{b}\right) + H_1^n\left(\frac{\sigma^2}{a^2}, \frac{-r}{a}\right)$$

For $w = \frac{n}{n-1}\left(r^2 + y - '\frac{1}{n}\sigma^2\right)$ there is a range of possible $r, y > 0$ which we parameterise by value ϕ, such that $0 \leq \phi \leq 1$:

$$y(\phi) = (1 - \phi)\left(\frac{n-1}{n}w + \frac{1}{n}\sigma^2\right) \quad \text{and} \quad r(\phi)^2 = \phi\left(\frac{n-1}{n}w + \frac{1}{n}\sigma^2\right)$$

Thus:

$$\mathbb{P}\left(\sigma^2 - \hat{\sigma}^2 > w\right) \leq H_2^n\left(\frac{\sigma^2}{d^2}, \frac{y(\phi)}{d^2}\right) + H_1^n\left(\frac{\sigma^2}{b^2}, \frac{r(\phi)}{b}\right) + H_1^n\left(\frac{\sigma^2}{a^2}, \frac{-r(\phi)}{a}\right)$$

The result of this proof follows by taking the minimum over ϕ.   ■

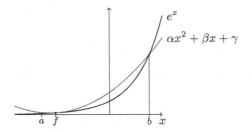

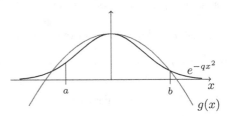

Fig. 5. A parabola parametarised by touching and intercepting points f, b above an exponential curve for all $a \leq x \leq b$

Fig. 6. $g(x) = (e^{-qd^2} - 1)d^{-2}x^2 + 1$ over function $f(x) = e^{-qx^2}$ for all $a \leq x \leq b$ where $d = \max(b, -a)$; in the case $a = -1, b = 1.3, q = 1$

References

1. Agarwal, A., Dekel, O., Xiao, L.: Optimal algorithms for online convex optimization with multi-point bandit feedback. In: 23rd Annual Conference Learning Theory (COLT 2010) (2010)
2. Aggarwal, C.C.: Data Mining: The Textbook, chap. Outlier analysis, pp. 237–263. Springer, Cham (2015). https://doi.org/10.1007/978-3-319-14142-8
3. Audibert, J.Y., Bubeck, S.: Minimax policies for adversarial and stochastic bandits. In: 22nd Annual Conference Learning Theory (COLT 2009) (2009)
4. Audibert, J.-Y., Munos, R., Szepesvári, C.: Tuning bandit algorithms in stochastic environments. In: Hutter, M., Servedio, R.A., Takimoto, E. (eds.) ALT 2007. LNCS (LNAI), vol. 4754, pp. 150–165. Springer, Heidelberg (2007). https://doi.org/10.1007/978-3-540-75225-7_15
5. Auer, P., Cesa-Bianchi, N., Freund, Y., Schapire, R.: The non-stochasticmulti-armed bandit problem. SIAM J. Comput. **31**(1), 48–77 (2003)
6. Auer, P., Cesa-Bianchi, N., Fischer, P.: Finite-time analysis of the multiarmed bandit problem. Mach. Learn. **47**(2), 235–256 (2002)
7. Bennett, G.: Probability inequalities for the sum of independent random variables. J. Am. Stat. Assoc. **57**(297), 33–45 (1962)
8. Bentkus, V., Juškevičius, T.: Bounds for tail probabilities of martingales using skewness and kurtosis. Lith. Math. J. **48**(1), 30–37 (2008)
9. Bercu, B., Delyon, B., Rio, E.: Concentration Inequalities for Sums and Martingales. SM. Springer, Cham (2015). https://doi.org/10.1007/978-3-319-22099-4
10. Bernstein, S.N.: On a modification of Chebyshev's inequality and of the error formula of Laplace. Uchenye Zapiski Nauch. Issled. Kaf. Ukraine Sect. Math. **1**, 38–48 (1924)
11. Bhaduri, M., Zhan, J., Chiu, C., Zhan, F.: A novel online and non-parametric approach for drift detection in big data. IEEE Access **5**, 15883–15892 (2017)
12. Bienaymé, I.J.: Considérations àl'appui de la découverte de Laplace. Comptes Rendus de l'Académie des Sci. **37**, 309–324 (1853)
13. Boucheron, S., Lugosi, G., Bousquet, O.: Concentration inequalities. In: Bousquet, O., von Luxburg, U., Rätsch, G. (eds.) ML -2003. LNCS (LNAI), vol. 3176, pp. 208–240. Springer, Heidelberg (2004). https://doi.org/10.1007/978-3-540-28650-9_9
14. Boucheron, S., Lugosi, G., Massart, P.: Concentration inequalities using the entropy method. Ann. Prob. **31**(3), 1583–1614 (2003)
15. Cesa-Bianchi, N., Lugosi, G.: Prediction, Learning, and Games. Cambridge University Press, Cambridge (2006)
16. Efron, B., Stein, C.: The jackknife estimate of variance. Ann. Stat. **9**(3), 586–596 (1981)
17. Flaxman, A., Kalai, A., McMahan, B.: Online convex optimization in the bandit setting: gradient descent without a gradient. In: Proceedings of 16th Annual ACM-SIAM Symposium on Discrete Algorithms (SODA 2005), pp. 385–394 (2005)
18. Hoeffding, W.: Probability inequalities for sums of bounded random variables. J. Am. Stat. Assoc. **58**(301), 13–30 (1963)
19. Kifer, D., Ben-David, S., Gehrke, J.: Detecting change in data streams. In: Proceedings of 30th International Conference Very Large Data Bases (VLDB 2004), pp. 180–191 (2004)
20. Lai, T., Robbins, H.: Asymptotically efficient adaptive allocation rules. Adv. Appl. Math. **6**(1), 4–22 (1985)

21. Maurer, A.: Concentration inequalities for functions of independent variables. Rand. Struct. Algorithms **29**(2), 121–138 (2006)
22. Maurer, A., Pontil, M.: Empirical Bernstein bounds and sample variance penalization. stat. In: Proceedings of the 22nd Annual Conference Learning Theory (COLT 2009), June 2009
23. Mnih, V., Szepesvári, C., Audibert, J.Y.: Empirical Bernstein stopping. In: Proceedings 25th International Conference Machine Learning (ICML 2008), pp. 672–679 (2008)
24. Pinelis, I.: On the Bennett-Hoeffding inequality. Annales de i'Institut Henri Poincaré - Probabilités et Statistiques **50**(1), 15–27 (2014)
25. Rehman, M.Z., Li, T., Li, T.: Exploiting empirical variance for data stream classification. J. Shanghai Jiaotong Univ. (Sci.) **17**(2), 245–250 (2012)
26. Robbins, H.: Some aspects of the sequential design of experiments. Bull. AMS **55**, 527–535 (1952)
27. Sharma, R., Gupta, M., Kapoor, G.: Some better bounds on the variance with applications. J. Math. Inequalities **4**(3), 355–363 (2010)
28. Talagrand, M.: Concentration of measure and isoperimetric inequalities in product spaces. Publications Mathématiques de l'Institut des Hautes Études Scientifiques **81**(1), 73–205 (1995)
29. Talagrand, M.: The missing factor in Hoeffding's inequalities. Annales de l'Institut Henri Poincare Prob. Stat. **31**(4), 689–702 (1995)
30. Thomas, P.S., Theocharous, G., Ghavamzadeh, M.: High-confidence off-policy evaluation. In: Proceedings of 29th AAAI Conference Artificial Intelligence (AAAI 2015), pp. 3000–3006 (2015)
31. Tran-Thanh, L., Chapman, A.C., Rogers, A., Jennings, N.R.: Knapsack based optimal policies for budget-limited multi-armed bandits. In: Proceedings of 26th AAAI Conference Artificial Intelligence (AAAI 2012), pp. 1134–1140 (2012)

Stochastic Activation Actor Critic Methods

Wenling Shang$^{(\boxtimes)}$ ⓘ, Douwe van der Wal, Herke van Hoof ⓘ,
and Max Welling ⓘ

University of Amsterdam-Bosch-Deltalab, Amsterdam, The Netherlands
{w.shang,h.c.vanhoof,m.welling}@uva.nl

Abstract. Stochastic elements in reinforcement learning (RL) have
shown promise to improve exploration and handling of uncertainty, such
as the utilization of stochastic weights in NoisyNets and stochastic policies in the maximum entropy RL frameworks. Yet effective and general
approaches to include such elements in actor-critic models are still lacking. Inspired by the aforementioned techniques, we propose an effective
way to inject randomness into actor-critic models to improve general
exploratory behavior and reflect environment uncertainty. Specifically,
randomness is added at the level of intermediate activations that feed into
both policy and value functions to achieve better correlated and more
complex perturbations. The proposed framework also features flexibility
and simplicity, which allows straightforward adaptation to a variety of
tasks. We test several actor-critic models enhanced with stochastic activations and demonstrate their effectiveness in a wide range of Atari 2600
games, a continuous control problem and a car racing task. Lastly, in a
qualitative analysis, we present evidence of the proposed model adapting the noise in the policy and value functions to reflect uncertainty and
ambiguity in the environment.

Keywords: Stochastic neural networks · Actor critic methods · Deep
reinforcement learning

1 Introduction

Deep reinforcement learning (DRL)—that is, using deep neural networks (DNNs)
in reinforcement learning—has allowed tremendous progress in areas from game
playing [25] to continuous control [20]. These DNNs generally serve to approximate value functions [38], such as in deep Q-network (DQN) and its variants [25],
or to represent policies [38] such as in policy-gradient methods [35]. Another
family of Deep RL (DRL) methods is the hybrid actor-critic approach, which
employs DNNs to represent value functions as well as policies [24,43] and has
achieved state-of-the-art performances on highly complex RL problems.

Uncertainties play a crucial role in RL, including probabilistic state transitions, noisy reward functions, non-determinisitic action outcomes [11], and

We thank anonymous reviewers for their feedback and NVIDIA for GPU donations.

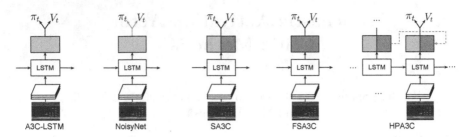

Fig. 1. The baseline **A3C-LSTM** has deterministic latent units and weights only (blue). NoisyNet has stochastic weights (red) over policy and value networks independently. Our proposed methods have stochastic units shared by the two pathway with different configurations:, **SA3C** has half deterministic and half stochastic units in the intermediate layer; **FSA3C** has only stochastic units; **HPA3C** is the same as SA3C but regularized with hierarchical prior from preceding time step during training. (Color figure online)

exploration of infrequently tested actions. Earlier DRL works addressing uncertainty have proposed the use of stochastic neural networks (SNNs). SNNs such as Bayesian Neural Networks (BNNs) and NoisyNets [6,10,32] improve exploration through injecting parametric noise. Nevertheless, parametric noise has not been equally successful in actor-critic methods ([10,32]), which are of particular interest because they have performed at a state-of-the-art level in many environ-ments, including Atari games [5] and continuous robotics control [43]. Similar to other model-free approaches, DRL-based actor-critic methods are also highly sensitive with respect to model architecture and other hyperparameter selections, it is therefore important yet non-trivial to discover means to strengthen actor-critic methods with stochastic modeling components.

We propose to directly sample intermediate latent representations shared by both the policy and value network to propagate more complex, structured perturbations, contrasting parametric noise where the weights for the two networks are jittered independently. Particularly, we contribute to the development of a family of stochastic activation A3C models that effectively incorporate stochastic activations on top of LSTM-Asynchronous Advantage Actor Critic [24, A3C-LSTM], a framework representing the current state-of-the-art in many RL tasks.

An important subsequent contribution of this work is a thorough investigation of the empirical performance of stochastic activation A3C on 7 Atari 2600 benchmark games with stochastic skip frames, where our models generally outperform both the SOTA baseline A3C-LSTM and its NoisyNet variant with stochastic weights. Further examination over these experiments demonstrates the decrease of variance over approximated values from multiple samples of stochastic activations during the course of training, indicating a reduction of model uncertainty. Empirical analysis on the converged value and policy networks also show signs of our proposed models reflecting the intrinsic stochasticity of the environment. We then provide a mathematical link between stochastic activations and a special case of stochastic weights yet highlight their essential practical discrepancies. As an additional contribution, we advance beyond the on-policy A3C-LSTM and incorporate stochastic activations to methods with experience replay and continuous action spaces, namely deep deterministic policy gradients (DDPG) [20] and actor critic with experience replay (ACER) [43]. Pseudocode and full experimental details are in the Appendix; code and video demos are in the Supplementary Materials.

The rest of this paper is organized as follows: first, we discuss related works and preliminaries. Then, we motivate and introduce stochastic activation A3C and our primary model, Stochastic A3C (SA3C), along with two important variants to underline the flexibility of this technique. Next, we present our experimental setup and results, evaluating the overall performance of stochastic units against baselines and stochastic weights. Finally, provide practical advice such as model and hyperparameter selections along with algorithm limitations.

2   Related Work

The treatment of uncertainty has been a long-standing challenge in RL and several lines of research have studied how to address this challenge. Our work is most connected to two general directions, incorporating stochastic components during (1) exploration and (2) inference process.

Epistemic uncertainty, i.e. model uncertainty, reduces as the agents gather more information via exploration. Many exploration mechanisms employ randomized actions instead of always using the best current model (exploitation) to gather more information. These mechanisms include Bayesian methods such as Thompson sampling [13], action-dithering schemes such as ϵ-greedy [38], value randomization such as randomized least-squares value iteration (RLSVI) or with Gaussian Processes [19,30], et cetera. Many of these mechanisms have also been adapted to the context of DRL, such as Thompson sampling via BNNs [6] and deep value randomization [29].

One approach that was developed in the related field of stochastic optimal control (SOC) uses inference techniques for finding the best actions under uncertain dynamics. In order to do so, the return (or related RL objectives) is defined as a factor in a graphical model and probabilistic inference is applied to determine a sequence of actions optimizing this objective [41]. These probabilistic frameworks have inspired DRL algorithms, such as distributive DQN [4] and deep probabilistic inference for learning control (PILCO) [12]. Recently, DRL models built upon the maximum entropy framework [45] by augmenting the standard RL objective with an entropy maximization term to achieve probabilistic inference have gained much attention, thanks to the potential of improving exploration and generalization in the face of uncertainty [14,28]. These works also shed light on our proposed framework in retaining a distributive perspective over values and allowing stochastic policies.

The partially-observable setting explicitly addresses uncertainty about the state that the agent is in. A common strategy compresses the unbounded history of observations into belief states, and then subseuqently applies RL to the belief states [26]. Analytical belief state updates require knowledge of the observation model and transition model – even then is exponential in the number of state variables [26]. DRL-based algorithms that incorporate recurrent modules [24] implicitly maintain analogous internal states. However, these internal states are usually deterministic; in contrast, our model samples its internal states from Gaussian distributions, more similar to belief state approximations in continuous state systems [33].

Our proposed technique fills an important gap in DRL-based actor-critic methods such as A3C-LSTM, where there has been lacking a general yet effective way to include stochastic elements. We apply high-level insights from Bayesian deep learning [17], in particular the use of SNNs, to RL. Applications of SNNs in ML have a long history, [27,39] to list a few. In the regime of RL, SNNs have also shown promising results. For instance, recently, [10] and [32] concurrently proposed to add independent parametric noises to the FC layers for better exploration, resembling BNNs but without the convergence to a posterior. In contrast, our model perturbs (part of) the intermediate activations which are eventually shared by the actor and critic, allowing structured exploration via better correlated randomness on both paths. Similar SNNs have been employed in several hierarchical RL systems to embed complex skills in an abstract form for higher level tasks [9]. [34] leverages a special case, the variational autoencoder [18], to extract latent representations from raw observations for measuring similarities between states. In these works, the SNNs are separately trained. In our work, we directly alter part of the deterministic units within the baseline models to become stochastic and train the model end-to-end. Finally, recent works propose to measure model uncertainty using DNNs with a special type of stochastic units, dropout units, in the context of e.g. better safety [11,16].

3   Preliminaries

We consider the standard discrete time step, discounted RL setup. An agent at time t observes o_t, which is a function of its state s_t, and chooses an action a_t guided by a policy π_t. Its ultimate objective is to maximize the accumulative expected return over time $R = \mathbb{E}_{(s_t,o_t,a_t)\sim\pi_t}[r_t]$, where r_t is the reward at time t. This section focuses on introducing the primary baseline algorithm used in our work, batch A3C-LSTM. To demonstrate the generalizability of our proposed method, we perform additional experiments using actor-critic methods with off-policy replays and the descriptions of these models are introduced later in Sect. 4.2.

Asynchronous advantage actor-critic (A3C) [24] is a model-free, on-policy RL algorithm. Multiple agents are spawned to concurrently interact with the environments with different random seeds and optimize a shared model that approximates both the policy and value functions through asynchronous gradient descent to trade-off bias and variance. A3C models can either be composed of only Convolutional Neural Networks (CNNs) or with an additional recurrent module, usually an LSTM cell. We choose the latter, for it is able to learn more complex state representations to tackle e.g. partially observable environments

Table 1. Results with * and † are cited from [25] and [10]. Due to stochastic frame skipping in our setups which generally yield more difficult environments, our results (last 3 columns) are not precisely comparable to †. Nonetheless we can still clearly conclude the competitiveness of our baseline implementation. The last column presents the results from the optimal stochastic activation models.

Game	Human*	A3C†	NN-A3C†	A3C	NN-A3C	Stochastic Act.
Seaquest	28010	1744 ± 0	943 ± 41	13922 ± 4920	894 ± 313	29656 ± 5317
BeamRider	5775	9214 ± 608	11237 ± 1582	9214 ± 608	6117 ± 1808	13779 ± 3605
MsPacman	15693	2436 ± 249	3401 ± 761	4670 ± 1864	4096 ± 1351	5590 ± 1521
Boxing	4.3	91 ± 1	100 ± 0	99.5 ± 1.0	94 ± 4.4	100 ± 0.0
Breakout	31	$496 pm 56$	347 ± 27	588 ± 180	570 ± 252	621 ± 194
Qbert	13455	18586 ± 574	17896 ± 1522	15333 ± 2462	14352 ± 1335	16045 ± 556
Freeway	29.6	0 ± 0	18 ± 13	23.3 ± 1.2	22.4 ± 0.8	23.9 ± 1.3

with longer time dependencies. Recently, batch A3C-CNN was developed for faster training and efficient utilization of GPUs [1]. We also take advantage of mini-batch training on A3C-LSTM for better stability and apply synchronous descents [1], where backpropagation waits for all agents to finish their actions so as to avoid stale gradients [8]. Some also refer to similar algorithms as A2C [42].

A3C-LSTM (Fig. 1) consists of a CNN to extract features from raw observations, an LSTM cell to compress history, and a value and policy networks. We denote the features extracted by the LSTM as $h_t = f_{\text{LSTM}}(\text{CNN}(o_t), h_{t-1})$. In order to be consistent with models introduced later on, we further add two sets of Fully-Connected (FC) layers on top of h_t, obtaining their concatenation $[f_{\text{FC1}}(h_t), f_{\text{FC2}}(h_t)]$ as inputs to the value and policy networks. This structure allows us to later make either or both of these pathways stochastic. The objective for the value network is to estimate the state value V_t by regressing the estimated t_{max}-step discounted returns with discount rate $\gamma \in (0,1)$ (Eq. 1); the policy network proposes a policy π_t and is guided by advantage-based policy gradients using the generalized advantage estimation $\hat{A}$ (details see [36]), regularized by an entropy term to encourage exploration (Eq. 2).

Value estimation objectvie: $\mathcal{L}_{V_t} = \mathbb{E}_{s_t, o_t, a_t}(\Sigma_{t'=t}^{t_{\text{max}}} \gamma^{t'-t} r_{t'} - V_t)^2,$ (1)

Policy gradient with entropy regularization: $\nabla_\theta \log \pi_t(\hat{A}_t) + \beta \nabla H(\pi_t).$ (2)

Finally, we also compare our proposed method with a sthochastic weight variant of A3C-LSTM, NoisyNet A3C (NN-A3C, Fig. 1). The construction mostly follows [10] and more details are illustrated in the Appendix.

Our architecture and training protocol produce a state-of-the-art level A3C-LSTM, which is an essential component in our work since we aim at developing a technique that is highly competitive, even surpassing the performance of a very powerful baseline. We compare the baseline A3C implementation replicated by us with another mainstream version as well as human players in Table 1.

4 Actor Critic Methods with Stochastic Activation

This section first illustrates how to integrate stochastic activations into A3C-LSTM, arriving at the stochastic activation A3C family of models. We then describe the primary stochastic activation A3C used in our work, along with two additional variants. Finally, we extend the technique of stochastic units to actor-critic methods with off-policy training (DDPG and ACER).

4.1 Stochastic Activation A3C

Inspired by the SNN design from [39] whose intermediate units are half deterministic and half stochastic in order to encode information of different uncertainty levels, we craft an initial version of stochastic activation A3C in a similar manner, termed stochastic A3C (SA3C). Following the output of the LSTM hidden state h_t, the next layer is split into a deterministic channel and a stochastic channel. The deterministic channel $k_t = f_{\mathrm{det}}(h_t)$ is parameterized by a FC layer. The stochastic units follow factored Gaussian distributions. The variance is, for now, set to a fixed value and treated as a hyperparameter, but note that subsequent layers can learn to rely on the deterministic or the stochastic units in any proportion to manage the amount of noise in the value and policy functions. The mean $\mu_t = f_{\mathrm{mean}}(h_t)$ is also parameterized by a FC layer. The pseudocode for SA3C is in Algorithm 1. Fully-Stochastic A3C (FSA3C) is an interesting control setup that replaces the deterministic channel with a stochastic one and attains a fully-stochastic intermediate representation. Hierarchical Prior stochastic activation A3C (HPA3C) is inspired by BNNs that craft their priors to the model parameters in order to achieve certain effects, such as inducing sparsity [21]. Analogously, HPA3C adds a KL-divergence between the stochastic activation distribution and a prior to the objective function. Specifically, the prior for the variance is fixed to a value σ^2, treated as a hyperparameter, and the prior for μ_t is derived from the previous step stochastic latent sample.[1] Our design is also similar in spirit to latent forward modeling [40] where the history predicts and guides the future, but in a more implicit form of prior regularization:

Derivation of $\mu_t^p : z_{t-1} \sim \mathcal{N}(\mu_{t-1}, \sigma^2), \mu_t^p = f^p(z_{t-1})$,

Prior regularization: $\mathrm{KL}\left[\mathcal{N}(\mu_t, \sigma_t^2) \| \mathcal{N}(\mu_t^p, \sigma^2\right] = \log\dfrac{\sigma}{\sigma_t} + \dfrac{\sigma_t^2 + (\mu_t - \mu_t^p)^2}{2(\sigma)^2} - \dfrac{1}{2}$.

We found that a proper prior choice is critical—omitting either the prior on the mean or the variance significantly deteriorates the model performance. The pseudocode for HPA3C is in the Appendix.

Forward propagation through stochastic activation A3C is identical to A3C-LSTM, except that the stochastic activations z_t are sampled from $\mathcal{N}(\mu_t, \sigma_t)$ and then concatenated with the deterministic counterpart k_t as the inputs for the policy and value networks. Backpropagation via the stochastic units is done by the reparametrization trick [18].

---

[1] All operations are element-wise because of the factored Gaussian assumption.

Initialize network parameters θ;
Fix variance σ^2;
for $k = 0, 1, 2, \cdots$ **do**

    Clear gradients $d\theta \leftarrow 0$;

    Simulate under current policy π_{t-1} until $t_{\max}$ steps are obtained, where,

    $h_t = f_{\text{LSTM}}(\text{CNN}(o_t), h_{t-1})$, $\mu_t = f_{\text{mean}}(h_t)$, $k_t = f_{\text{d}}(h_t)$,

    $z_t \sim \mathcal{N}(\mu_t, \sigma_t^2 = \sigma^2)$, $V_t = f_v(z_t, k_t)$, $\pi_t = f_p(z_t, k_t)$, $t = 1, \cdots t_{\max}$;

    $R = \begin{cases} 0, & \text{if terminal} \\ V_{t_{\max}+1}, & \text{otherwise} \end{cases}$;

    for $t = t_{\max}, \cdots 1$ **do**

        $R \leftarrow r_t + \gamma R$;

        $A_t \leftarrow R - V_t$;

        Accumulate gradients from value loss: $d\theta \leftarrow d\theta + \lambda \frac{\partial A_t^2}{\partial \theta}$;

        $\delta_t \leftarrow r_t + \gamma V_{t+1} - V_t$;

        $\hat{A}_t \leftarrow \gamma \tau \hat{A}_{t-1} + \delta_i$;

        Accumulate policy gradients with entropy regularization:

        $d\theta \leftarrow d\theta + \nabla \log \pi_t(a_t) \hat{A}_t + \beta \nabla H(\pi_t)$;

    end

end

Algorithm 1: SA3C

Lastly, it is worth noting that while our models employ Gaussian units thanks to their flexibility and ease to train, the proposed framework can adopt other stochastic units as well. We conduct preliminary experiments with dropout stochastic units in the Appendix and leave further investigation along this direction to future works.

4.2 DDPG and ACER

Deep Deterministic Policy Gradients (DDPG) [20] is an off-policy actor critic method. It explores via injecting action space noise, commonly from the Ornstein-Uhlenbeck process. We equip DDPG with parametric noise [32] (PG-DDPG) or stochastic activation (SDDPG). We do not incorporate an LSTM module to DDPG and its variants. The baseline algorithm thus follows exactly as in [20] and its parametric noise version, PN-DDPG, exactly as in [32] but without randomizing the convolutional layers. Unlike A3C-LSTM, DDPG keeps separate encoders for actor and critic. We only use stochastic activations to the behavior actor network and not to off-policy training.

Actor Critic with Experience Replay (ACER) [43] is a sample-efficient actor-critic algorithm with a hybrid of on/off-policy gradients. We compare amongst ACER and its variants with stochastic units or noisy layer. Augmenting ACER with stochastic activation (SACER) follows the same protocol as augmenting A3C-LSTM with stochastic activation and we also use stochastic activations for off-policy training. As an additional comparison, we construct a NoisyNet version

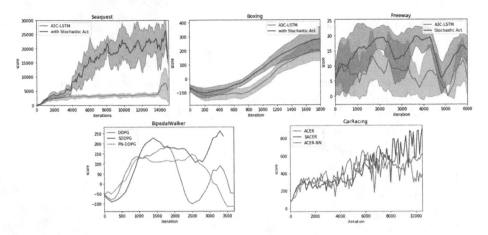

Fig. 2. Training curves over 3 runs (median); vertical: rewards; horizontal: iterations. For Atari games, we plot the curves for the baseline and the best stochastic activation model along with the interquartile range. For the rest, we compare among the baseline, SA3C and then stochastic weights.

of ACER, NN-ACER by similarly randomizing the value and policy networks as in NN-A3C. The pseudocode of our ACER and its stochastic variants are in the Appendix.

5   Experimental Setup and Results

This section first introduces the environments used in our experiments. Extensive ablation studies are done on the Atari games. We then discuss the empirical advantages of stochastic activation A3C over its deterministic baseline and how its design flexibility can adapt well to a variety of environments and tasks. Finally, we present additional results generalizing SA3C to off-policy methods, namely DDPG and ACER, on BipedalWalker2D and CarRacing respectively.

5.1   Environments

Our experiments are primarily done in an on-policy manner on 7 selected classic Atari 2600 games contained in the Arcade Learning Environment [5] and interfaced via OpenAI Gym [7] to cover a diverse range of tasks and exploration types [3]. Full descriptions of these games are in the Appendix. To avoid memorization and impose more randomness, we use the stochastic frame-skipping: each action is repeated for a number, uniformly sampled between 2 and 4, of consecutive frames. Exploration type is categorized by the taxonomy from [3]. The stochasticity of Atari games originates from multiple sources, including frame-skipping, partial observation of some environments, non-stationary policy during training, approximation errors, et cetera. For preprocessing, we crop Atari games to display only the game playing region, subtract estimated mean and divide standard deviation, and rescale to 80×80.

Table 2. We report Atari results following the evaluation protocol in Sect. 5. SA3C outperforms the baselines most of the time. The last column displays the results from the optimal stochastic activation variants for each game which can further boost the testing scores.

Game	A3C-LSTM		SA3C		NoisyNet		Optimal Model		
	Best	Avg.	Best	Avg.	Best	Avg.		Best	Avg.
Seaquest	13922	6785	**28876**	23411	849	1332	HPA3C	**29656**	24992
	±4920	±5050	±4270	±4783	±313	±367		±5317	±3356
BeamRider	9214	8723	**9994**	8966	6117	5838	FSA3C	**13779**	10551
	±608	±627	±3717	±1013	±1808	±287		±3605	±2341
MsPacman	4670	3973	**4960**	4743	4096	3705	FSA3C	**5590**	5382
	±1864	±543	±1639	±220	±1351	±297		±1521	±268
Boxing	**100**	99.7	**100**	99.9	94	11.6	HPA3C	**100.0**	99.6
	±0.0	±0.2	±0.0	±0.0	±4.4	±59.6		±0.0	±0.23
Breakout	588	560	**621**	556	570	551	HPA3C	596	569
	±180	±22	±194	±45	±252	±25		±197	±22
Qbert	15333	14732	**15560**	15365	14352	11231	HPA3C	**16045**	15365
	±2462	±482	±184	±150	±1335	±3348		±556	±150
Freeway	**23.3**	22.8	22.4	21.6	22.4	21.5	HPA3C	**23.9**	23.2
	±1.2	±0.7	±1.1	±0.5	±0.8	±0.6		±1.3	±0.5

DDPG models are tested on a continuous task, BipedalWalker2D, where a robot needs to reach the end of a path within a time limit and positive reward is given for moving forward, totaling ≥300 for reaching the end, while a negative reward of −100 is given for falling. No preprocessing is done for this environment. ACER models are tested with CarRacing, a simple driving simulator whose observations consist of RGB top-view of a race car and a black bar containing other driving information. We only receive the pixel-valued observations and also discretize its action space. More details on the preprocessing of CarRacing is provided in the Appendix.

5.2 Stochastic Activation A3C Results

Hyperparameters and Model Architecture. For Atari, hyperparameters are tuned on Seaquest A3C-LSTM and then transferred to other games. We inherit all common hyperparameters from A3C-LSTM to stochastic activation A3Cs and only tune the additional ones, namely σ^2 for SA3C and FSA3C, HPA3C and the KL term weight for HPA3C. In particular, we would like to emphasize the coefficient for entropy regularization is tuned to perform optimally on the baseline–a higher value in fact deteriorates its performance; in other words, any performance gain via stochastic activations cannot be replaced by increasing the entropy term. For other environments, hyperparameters are tuned on the baseline and then transferred to stochastic weight/activation models.

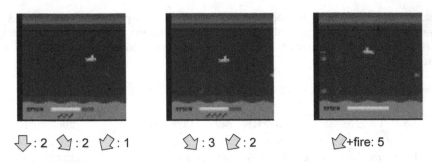

Fig. 3. For SA3C, stochastic activations can result in stochastic policies. The less ambiguous the environment is, the more certain the policies become (left to right). Arrows indicate the direction of movement, followed by the number of times this action being selected (out of 5 samples).

Most games share a common model architecture but we use a slightly slimmer CNN for Boxing, Breakout and Freeway. Since HPA3C needs to learn σ_t, more variance is introduced to the gradients and the resulting stochastic activations require further normalization. After trial-and-error with several techniques such as Batch [15] and Layer [2] Normalization, we pick the most effective option–concatenated ReLU [37]. Full details are given in the Appendix.

Evaluation Protocol. We report Atari results on A3C-LSTM, NN-A3C, SA3C and the best performing stochastic activation A3C variant in Table 2 following the protocol:

1. Train 3 independent runs—a standard DRL practice [31,44].
2. For each run, validate the current model on a non-training random seed, select the best (validated) one after training.
3. Test the selected model for each run on 10 other random seeds not included in training or validation, obtaining $\mu_1 \pm \sigma_1$, $\mu_2 \pm \sigma_2$, $\mu_3 \pm \sigma_3$.
4. Report the best $\mu_i \pm \sigma_i$ under the column "Best".
5. Average across the 3 models, i.e. $\mu \pm \sigma$ over μ_1, μ_2, μ_3, reported under "Avg.".

The proceeding protocol not only showcases how good a policy the algorithm can attain if optimized well but also indicates variances in performance due to policy gradient training. We also plot the training curves composed of average validation scores with the standard deviation bars for Seaquest, Boxing and Freeway in Fig. 2, other games in the Appendix.

Inference and Stochastic Policies. Based on the protocol from [10], NoisyNet is tested by setting the stochastic weights equal to the learned mean. For stochastic activation A3Cs, there are multiple possibilities during evaluation time. One is to only use the mean from the stochastic units, referred to as Maximum A Posteriori (MAP)–borrowing the Bayesian terminology.

Alternatively, we sample the stochastic activations and vote the majority decision, leading to stochastic policies. Figure 3 shows the decisions out of 5 sampled policies for selected states: when there is no clear immediate goal, e.g. no enemy around, decisions tend to diverge, but otherwise they agree. Videos of Seaquest

Table 3. Compare evaluating using μ only (MAP), using a single sampled stochastic activation and averaging over 5 or 50 stochastic activation outcomes. Sampling and averaging 5 activations tend to be optimal.

Seaquest	SA3C	FSA3C	HPA3C
MAP	27695 ± 9096	4387 ± 171	25474 ± 8067
1	27081 ± 6817	**5090 ± 1099**	24475 ± 4765
5	**28876 ± 4270**	4453 ± 592	**29656 ± 5317**
50	28341 ± 9839	4794 ± 523	28341 ± 9839

with deterministic polices from A3C-LSTM versus stochastic policies from SA3C are included in the Supplementary Materials. Table 3 compares different evaluation schemes from Seaquest—for stochastic policies we attempt 1, 5, and 50 samples—and 5 samples give the optimal results for most models. If not mentioned otherwise, all stochastic activation A3C results are obtained by voting among policies from 5 sampled activations.[2]

5.3 Actor-Critic Models with Experience Replay

We further integrate this technique to actor-critic methods with experience replay, namely ACER and DDPG. Complete hyperparameter details are in the Appendix. For DDPG, we plot the median training curves out of 3 independent runs in Fig. 2. We found that DDPG is much less stable in training comparing with A3C-LSTM. Adding stochasticity to DDPG does not improve its training stability, which remains an open question. Nonetheless, SDDPG tends to converge significantly faster than DDPG and DDPG-PN, at iteration 4000, 5900 and 6300 respectively (Table 4). For ACER, we plot the median training curves out of 3 independent runs in 10 K iterations in Fig. 2. However, note that we stop the training once the environment is solved, i.e. average validation score over 10 random runs ≥ 900. Out of the 3 runs (with maximum 10 K iterations), only SACER manage to solve the environment. The median best scores attained by ACER is 891 and NN-ACER 859 (Table 4).

Table 4. Compare various actor-critic baselines with their stochastic-activation/weight variants, tested on BipedalWalker and CarRacing. We report the median iteration of solving the environmen for BipedalWalker and the median best score in 10 K iteration for CarRacing, where 300+ and 900+ are considered solved for each task respectively.

	DDPG	SDDPG	PN-DDPG		ACER	SACER	NN-ACER
BipedalWalker	5900	**3500**	6300	CarRacing	891	**900+**	859

[2] We use 1 sample for Freeway. As it only has 2 actions, voting would strongly diminish policy stochasticity.

Stochastic activations boost the performances of the baselines and outperform parametric space noise. These results confirm the effectiveness of our proposed method when coupled with experience replay.

5.4   Further Analyses of Stochastic Activations

We performed further analyses of stochastic activation networks to investigate the mechanisms behind the observed performance increase. We first inspected the value learning process of SA3C. These results are given below. We investigated several other aspects, including the significance of a shared intermediate stochastic learning, the policy learnign process, and a detailed comparison of to stochastic weights. The results of these experiments are given in the appendix.

Motivated by recent works using dropout units to estimate uncertainty [11,16], we obtain and analyze uncertainty estimations by calculating the sample variance of multiple approximated values over sampled stochastic activations. Concretely, for SA3C models at different training stages, we sample stochastic activations 5 times for each time step, calculate the variances of those resulting values and plot these in Fig. 4 for the first 700 time steps, that is

$$\hat{\sigma_v}^2 = \frac{1}{N-1} \sum_{i=1}^{N} \left(f_V(k_t, z_t)_i - \bar{f}_V \right)^2, \bar{f}_V = \frac{1}{N} \sum_{i=1}^{N} f_V(k_t, z_t)_i, N = 5, t = 1 \cdots 700.$$

The variances tend to go down over training (Fig. 4). This behavior is reminiscent of (Bayesian) models employing distributions over the weights, where these distributions reflect parametric uncertainty. Indeed, there is a connection between stochastic weights and activations that we will discuss more later. Despite the fixed variance of the noise in the stochastic units, the value network is clearly capable of gradually adapting the variance through learning. This can be achieved by shifting focus from stochastic units to deterministic units in downstream computations.

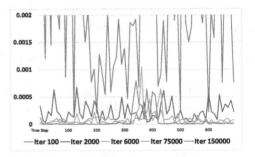

Fig. 4. At different training iterations for SA3C, we sample 5 V_ts via stochastic activations for $t = 1..700$, plot their variances and observe the general trend of variances descends over training.

At convergence time, the value network usually approximates with little variance, reflecting low uncertainty, except for a surge period around step 340 (Fig. 5). This in fact corresponds to a special event where different actions can lead to varying amounts of rewards: the submarine has reached maximum capacity of rescued divers and it can either shoot the upcoming enemy to gain some points or surface to collect a large amount of rewards by releasing the divers— eventually the submarine chooses the latter. Ambiguous situation can increase

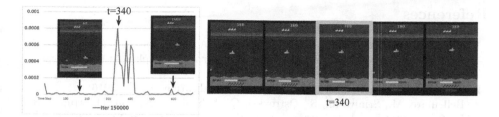

Fig. 5. A zoom-in of the variance plot at convergence (iter 150 K). The variance is generally low except for periods with high unpredictability. Around step 340, the submarine has rescued divers and should surface, but could also shoot the enemy. More details see Sect. 5.4.

the variance comparing to those with a clear target, comparing amongst step 340, 600 and 160. Therefore, we argue that SA3C's adaption to stochastic activations is not merely reducing the influence of the stochastic units, but rather carefully balancing between the deterministic and stochastic signals to implicitly establish a distributional perspective over returns and values, a beneficial trait for RL [23] and a proper reflection of the environment unpredictability.

6 Practical Advice and Algorithm Limitations

Stochastic activation is a general approach to improve A3C but not the panacea to every environment and task. Fully observable environments, such as Breakout, benefit less from stochastic activations. Environments with sparse rewards like Freeway also receive a more limited performance boost. RL problems with sparse rewards and/or more complex logic will require more specialized systems in combination with stochastic units, such as curiosity driven exploration.

The flexibility of stochastic activation A3C allows effective application to a diversity of tasks, but model selection can appear labor-demanding at first glance. From our experiences, SA3C is the go-to model as an initial attempt; if more aggressive exploration seems appropriate, FSA3C is a good candidate; if forecasting the upcoming states is essential in solving the task or rewards are sparse, HPA3C will likely perform better and more stable. One can thus always easily customize the stochastic activation A3C to meet the need of the task.

7 Conclusion

We proposed a flexible and simple to implement technique to improve DRL-based actor-critic methods by adding stochastic activations. The proposed method outperforms existing state-of-the-art baselines on a variety of benchmarks. In future work, we hope to integrate the proposed technique with curiosity-driven exploration to address problems with sparse rewards and experiment with other types of stochastic units such as binary units for feature level count-based exploration [31].

References

1. Adamski, I., Adamski, R., Grel, T., Jedrych, A., Kaczmarek, K., Michalewski, H.: Distributed deep reinforcement learning: learn how to play Atari games in 21 minutes. arXiv (2016)
2. Ba, J.L., Kiros, J.R., Hinton, G.E.: Layer normalization. arXiv (2016)
3. Bellemare, M., Srinivasan, S., Ostrovski, G., Schaul, T., Saxton, D., Munos, R.: Unifying count-based exploration and intrinsic motivation. In: NIPS (2016)
4. Bellemare, M.G., Dabney, W., Munos, R.: A distributional perspective on reinforcement learning. In: ICML (2017)
5. Bellemare, M.G., Naddaf, Y., Veness, J., Bowling, M.: The arcade learning environment: an evaluation platform for general agents. In: IJCAI (2013)
6. Blundell, C., Cornebise, J., Kavukcuoglu, K., Wierstra, D.: Weight uncertainty in neural networks. In: ICML (2015)
7. Brockman, G., et al.: OpenAI Gym (2016)
8. Chen, J., Monga, R., Bengio, S., Jozefowicz, R.: Revisiting distributed synchronous SGD. arXiv (2016)
9. Florensa, C., Duan, Y., Abbeel, P.: Stochastic neural networks for hierarchical reinforcement learning. In: ICLR (2017)
10. Fortunato, M., et al.: Noisy networks for exploration. In: ICLR (2018)
11. Gal, Y., Ghahramani, Z.: Dropout as a Bayesian approximation: representing model uncertainty in deep learning. In: ICML (2016)
12. Gal, Y., McAllister, R., Rasmussen, C.E.: Improving PILCO with bayesian neural network dynamics models. In: ICML Workshop (2016)
13. Ghavamzadeh, M., Mannor, S., Pineau, J., Tamar, A., et al.: Bayesian reinforcement learning: a survey. Found. Trends® Mach. Learn. **8**(5—-6), 359–483 (2015)
14. Haarnoja, T., Zhou, A., Abbeel, P., Levine, S.: Soft actor-critic: off-policy maximum entropy deep reinforcement learning with a stochastic actor. arXiv preprint arXiv:1801.01290 (2018)
15. Ioffe, S., Szegedy, C.: Batch normalization: accelerating deep network training by reducing internal covariate shift. In: ICML (2015)
16. Kahn, G., Villaflor, A., Pang, V., Abbeel, P., Levine, S.: Uncertainty-aware reinforcement learning for collision avoidance. In: arxiv (2016)
17. Kingma, D.P., Salimans, T., Welling, M.: Variational dropout and the local reparameterization trick. In: NIPS (2015)
18. Kingma, D.P., Welling, M.: Auto-encoding variational bayes. In: ICLR (2013)
19. Kuss, M., Rasmussen, C.E.: Gaussian processes in reinforcement learning. In: NIPS (2004)
20. Lillicrap, T.P., et al.: Continuous control with deep reinforcement learning. In: ICLR (2016)
21. Louizos, C., Ullrich, K., Welling, M.: Bayesian compression for deep learning. In: NIPS (2017)
22. Machado, M.C., Bellemare, M.G., Talvitie, E., Veness, J., Hausknecht, M., Bowling, M.: Revisiting the arcade learning environment: evaluation protocols and open problems for general agents. arXiv (2017)
23. Barth-Maron, G., et al.: Distributional policy gradients. In: ICLR (2018)
24. Mnih, V., et al.: Asynchronous methods for deep reinforcement learning. In: ICML (2016)
25. Mnih, V., et al.: Human-level control through deep reinforcement learning. Nature **518**, 529–533 (2015)

26. Murphy, K.P.: A survey of POMDP solution techniques. Technical Report (2000)
27. Neal, R.M.: Learning stochastic feedforward networks. Technical Report (1990)
28. O'Donoghue, B., Munos, R., Kavukcuoglu, K., Mnih, V.: Combining policy gradient and q-learning. arXiv preprint arXiv:1611.01626 (2016)
29. Osband, I., Russo, D., Wen, Z., Van Roy, B.: Deep exploration via randomized value functions. arXiv (2017)
30. Osband, I., Van Roy, B., Wen, Z.: Generalization and exploration via randomized value functions. In: ICML (2016)
31. Ostrovski, G., Bellemare, M.G., Oord, A.V.D., Munos, R.: Count-based exploration with neural density models. In: ICML (2017)
32. Plappert, M., et al.: Parameter space noise for exploration. In: ICLR (2018)
33. Prentice, S., Roy, N.: The belief roadmap: efficient planning in linear pomdps by factoring the covariance (2007)
34. Pritzel, A., et al.: Neural episodic control. In: ICML (2017)
35. Schulman, J., Levine, S., Abbeel, P., Jordan, M., Moritz, P.: Trust region policy optimization. In: ICML (2015)
36. Schulman, J., Moritz, P., Levine, S., Jordan, M., Abbeel, P.: High-dimensional continuous control using generalized advantage estimation. In: ICLR (2016)
37. Shang, W., Sohn, K., Almeida, D., Lee, H.: Understanding and improving convolutional neural networks via concatenated rectified linear units. In: ICML (2016)
38. Sutton, R.S., Barto, A.G.: Reinforcement learning: an introduction. Artificial Intelligence (1998)
39. Tang, Y., Salakhutdinov, R.R.: Learning stochastic feedforward neural networks. In: NIPS (2013)
40. Tian, Y., Gong, Q.: Latent forward model for real-time strategy game planning with incomplete information. In: NIPS Symposium (2017)
41. Todorov, E.: General duality between optimal control and estimation. In: CDC (2008)
42. Wang, J.X., et al.: Learning to reinforcement learn. arXiv (2016)
43. Wang, Z., et al.: Sample efficient actor-critic with experience replay. In: ICLR (2016)
44. Wu, Y., Mansimov, E., Grosse, R.B., Liao, S., Ba, J.: Scalable trust-region method for deep reinforcement learning using kronecker-factored approximation. In: NIPS (2017)
45. Ziebart, B.D., Maas, A.L., Bagnell, J.A., Dey, A.K.: Maximum entropy inverse reinforcement learning (2008)

Policy Prediction Network: Model-Free Behavior Policy with Model-Based Learning in Continuous Action Space

Zac Wellmer[✉] and James T. Kwok

Hong Kong University of Science and Technology, Clear Water Bay, Hong Kong
zac@1984.ai

Abstract. This paper proposes a novel deep reinforcement learning architecture that was inspired by previous tree structured architectures which were only useable in discrete action spaces. Policy Prediction Network offers a way to improve sample complexity and performance on continuous control problems in exchange for extra computation at training time but at no cost in computation at rollout time. Our approach integrates a mix between model-free and model-based reinforcement learning. Policy Prediction Network is the first to introduce implicit model-based learning to Policy Gradient algorithms for continuous action space and is made possible via the empirically justified clipping scheme. Our experiments are focused on the MuJoCo environments so that they can be compared with similar work done in this area.

1 Introduction

Reinforcement learning algorithms can be model-free or model-based. Model-free reinforcement learning attempts to find a policy through interacting with the environment and improving the policy based on previous states and rewards. Model-based reinforcement learning attempts to learn the dynamics of the environment and uses the model to improve the policy through various methods such as planning, exploration, and even training on generated data [5,19]. Though historically, model-based methods capable of predicting near perfect observations [2,10] usually have the benefit of reduced sample complexity, they still struggle to perform as well as model-free methods [8,9,17]. It is therefore appealing to explore achieving the best of both worlds, as collecting the large amount of experience required by model-free methods is oftentimes expensive or infeasible.

Model-based agents traditionally learn a model of the environment that predicts future observations conditioned on previous actions and observations. This approach is sometimes referred to as observation-prediction models [11]. Recreating the original observation is sometimes a questionable objective as the original observation can be dominated by irrelevant information. For example, if the observation is an image and contains a complex background, a large part of the model's capacity can be spent on modeling the background even though it may be irrelevant to information necessary for planning.

© Springer Nature Switzerland AG 2020
U. Brefeld et al. (Eds.): ECML PKDD 2019, LNAI 11908, pp. 118–133, 2020.
https://doi.org/10.1007/978-3-030-46133-1_8

As a response to the issues faced by observation-prediction models, several implicit model-based methods [4,11,18] were introduced and learn an implicit transition module that predicts the value/reward of future states without being subjected to observation reconstruction. Value Prediction Networks (VPN) [11] and TreeQN [4] operate by expanding a tree of predicted reward and value estimates. However, this is feasible only because each branch is linked to a discrete action. ATreeC [4] introduces a policy gradient method but is still not applicable to continuous action spaces because their policy is a multinomial distribution parameterized by the Q-values associated with each branch. Implicit models have seen success in Q-learning approaches, but are not straightforward to apply to policy gradient methods. Many real-world problems, such as robotics or autonomous vehicle applications, lie in continuous action spaces and Q-learning approaches do not naturally extend to continuous action spaces like policy gradient methods.

Policy gradient methods are of primary interest in this paper because of their inherent flexibility in terms of their application to both discrete and continuous action spaces. In particular, we will focus on a model-free policy gradient algorithm called Proximal Policy Optimization (PPO) [17]. PPO is of high interest because of its high performance on popular benchmarks and simplicity.

We propose Policy Prediction Networks (PPN), where the value, reward, policy, and abstract-state are predicted by leveraging a transition model. PPN uses an implicit model-based approach at training time but a model-free approach at rollout time. An implicit model-based approach at training time helps accelerate feature learning via predicting future policies, values, and rewards. All of which encourage the dynamics model to learn features that are well aligned with our objective of finding a policy that maximizes returns. To the best of our knowledge, this is the first work on developing implicit model-based learning for policy gradient methods.

Our contribution is a training procedure that leverages model-based learning for policy gradient algorithms to improve performance and does not trade off computational costs at rollout time. This work introduces implicit transition models for Policy Gradient methods, depth-based objectives, auxiliary reward objectives, and an empirically justified clipping scheme. Furthermore, our work lays down the foundation for future research on using implicit transition models to perform decision-time planning. Empirical results demonstrate the advantage of PPN over the model-free baseline (PPO), which suggests that PPN finds a better state embedding and reduces sample complexity.

2   Background and Related Work

In this section, we will give a brief review of related work on model-based and model-free reinforcement learning. We also introduce terminologies to differentiate between two general approaches in model-based reinforcement learning.

Notations: s_t abstract state, a_t action, r_{t+1} reward from taking a_t at s_t, γ discount, $v_\theta(s_t)$ value of state s_t with respect to parameters θ, A_t advantage, H_t policy entropy, and the subscript t denotes timesteps.

2.1 Policy Gradient Methods

Policy Gradient Methods [21] are a type of reinforcement learning algorithm that directly optimizes policy parameters to maximize expected returns. Policy Gradient methods are more naturally applied to environments with continuous action spaces in comparison to Q-learning approaches. Generally, the policy gradient loss is of the shape:

$$\mathcal{L}_t^\pi = -\log \pi_\theta(a_t|s_t)A_t - H_t,$$

where A_t is an advantage estimate [16, 20, 21], π_θ is the policy with parameter θ, H_t is the policy entropy, s_t is the state at time t, and a_t is the action taken in state s_t.

2.2 Trust Region Policy Optimization

Trust Region Policy Optimization (TRPO) attempts to generate monotonically improving policies following inspiration from conservative policy iteration [7]. However, TRPO contains a few theoretical relaxations that are required to make a practical algorithm. TRPO is left with a hard KL divergence constraint to be less than or equal to δ. This hard constraint can be seen as a trust region on the mean KL divergence.

Let θ' be the old parameters, θ be the new proposed parameters, A_t^{GAE} be the generalized advantage estimate [16]. Which is defined as

$$A_t^{GAE} = \delta_t + (\gamma\lambda)\delta_{t+1} + \cdots + (\gamma\lambda)^{n-t+1}\delta_{n-1}, \tag{1}$$

where λ is a hyperparameter controlling the bias-variance trade-off, and $\delta_t = r_{t+1} + \gamma v_{\theta'}(s_{t+1}) - v_{\theta'}(s_t)$. TRPO's optimization problem is then formulated as:

$$\pi_\theta = \max_{\pi_\theta} L_{\pi_{\theta'}}(\pi_\theta) \ : \ \bar{D}_{KL}(\pi_{\theta'}, \pi_\theta) \leq \delta,$$

where $L_{\pi_{\theta'}}(\pi_\theta) = \frac{\pi_\theta(a|s)}{\pi_{\theta'}(a|s)}A^{GAE}$ is the objective using importance sampling to estimate expected advantage under the new policy, and $\bar{D}_{KL}(\pi_{\theta'}, \pi_\theta)$ is the mean KL divergence between the new and old policy. At this point TRPO offers theoretical inspiration but does not actually offer theoretical guarantees for monotonically improving policies.

2.3 Proximal Policy Optimization

Proximal Policy Optimization (PPO) [17] was introduced as offering similar benefits as TRPO [15], but via a simpler approach. PPO replaces a KL divergence constraint in TRPO via a clipped policy gradient loss:

$$\mathcal{L}_t^\pi = \max(-\text{ratio}_t \cdot A_t^{GAE}, -\text{ratio}_{t,\text{clip}} \cdot A_t^{GAE}), \tag{2}$$

where

$$\text{ratio}_t = \frac{\pi_\theta(a = a_t | s = s_t)}{\pi_{\theta'}(a = a_t | s = s_t)},$$

$$\text{ratio}_{t,\text{clip}} = \text{clip}\left(\frac{\pi_\theta(a = a_t | s = s_t)}{\pi_{\theta'}(a = a_t | s = s_t)}, 1 - \epsilon, 1 + \epsilon\right). \tag{3}$$

Clipping no longer guarantees $\bar{D}_{KL}(\pi_{\theta'}, \pi_\theta) \leq \delta$. Instead, it serves to approximate it (see [6] for further details).

PPO2 [3] is a GPU implementation from OpenAI that offers a key difference from PPO, namely, that the critic is also clipped. More specifically, the critic loss ($\mathcal{L}_t^v$) is now:

$$\mathcal{L}_t^v = \max((v_\theta(s_t) - R_t)^2, (v_{t,\text{clip}} - R_t)^2) \tag{4}$$

where $v_{t,\text{clip}} = \text{clip}(v_\theta(s_t) - v_{\theta'}(s_t), -\epsilon, \epsilon) + v_{\theta'}(s_t)$ is the clipped value estimate, $R_t = \gamma^n v_{\theta'}(s_{t+n}) + \sum_{i=1}^{n} \gamma^{i-1} r_{t+i}$ is the bootstrapped n-step return at time t, and n is the number of steps in the bootstrapped estimate. At this point theoretical guarantees in Conservative Policy Iteration have been dropped to make TRPO a practical algorithm, and the theoretical justifications in TRPO have again been weakened to make the more versatile and empirically superior PPO.

2.4   Model-Based Reinforcement Learning

The essence of model-based reinforcement learning revolves around using a model or learning a model of the environment, and using this to improve a policy. We will be focused on the challenging class of problems where the environment dynamics are unknown and must be learned. In this case, the problem can be broken down further into dynamics models that are learned implicitly and dynamics models that are learned explicitly. It was not until recent years that implicitly learned model-based algorithms received attention [4,11,18].

Explicit Model-Based Methods. Cases of explicit model-based methods involve some form of directly predicting future observations and including this in the loss function, as in:

$$L_t^{model} = \frac{1}{2} \| \hat{x}_t - x_t \|^2,$$

where $\hat{x}_t$ is the predicted observation at time t and x_t is the ground truth observation. Several variations exist that involve learning to predict in an abstract state space [2,5,13,14], and predicting the grounded observation over multiple time steps [10]. This has seen some success and can be useful for learning, planning, and exploration.

These methods are particularly useful when observations contain entirely useful information. However, it can be misleading in the class of problems where parts of the observation do not include useful information. For example, when generating an image frame, a large part of the network's capacity could be dedicated to learning less useful information like the background or objects that are not well aligned with the agent's interest [13].

Implicit Model-Based Methods. Implicit model-based methods are interesting because they are not explicitly tied to reproducing original observations or an encoded observation. Rather, the dynamics model is indirectly learned by finding parameters that allow for an agent to perform optimally. This is done by learning to predict future characteristics such as the value or reward [4,11], but without having a constraint on predicting the ground truth observation. Unfortunately, a downside to implicit approaches is that it is difficult to know what is actually taking place during planning since it is hard to reconstruct the predicted observations.

VPN [11] involve expanding a Q-tree, performing a linear backup along the maximal path, and selecting the maximal backed-up path. At training time, the loss is computed along the tree path followed by rollout actions. The Predictron [18] is similar to VPN except learning is done entirely in an abstract space, whereas VPN is grounded to transitions experienced by the rollout policy. Predictron also offers a meta-objective called consistency which lines up individual estimates with respect to backed-up estimates. We do not explore this in our work, but note that it could serve as an orthogonal improvement. TreeQN and ATreeC [4] introduce a Q learning approach (TreeQN) and a policy gradient approach (ATreeC) that make use of a differentiable tree structure. ATreeC involves expanding a pseudo Q-tree. This is pseudo because the nested value predictions are not directly constrained to represent the value. The backed-up pseudo Q-values are treated as logits and are used to parameterize and sample from a multinomial distribution. These samples are then used as the actions. VPN, ATreeC, and TreeQN are limited to only operating in discrete action spaces. Predictron was used in a continuous action space, the MuJoCo pool environment [22], but was done through discretizing the action space.

3   Policy Prediction Network

Policy Prediction Network uses a combination of model-free and model-based techniques. Actions are made with a model-free approach by the behavior policy at rollout time. However, learning is done with a model-based approach that follows the rollout trajectory. A latent space transition model is embedded into the architecture so that we are able to backpropagate from multiple simulation steps into the future back to a grounded observation. Backpropagation from predictions through the dynamics model, and back to a grounded observation enables the dynamics model to learn features which align with accurate reward predictions, accurate value predictions, and maximizing advantage. This is as opposed to maximizing observation reconstruction as is traditionally done in explicit model-based reinforcement learning.

Our novel contribution is a training scheme that integrates model-free and model-based reinforcement learning to improve sample complexity and performance in exchange for extra computation at training time but at no extra cost in computation at rollout time. Additionally our work offers a foundation for decision-time planning for policy gradient methods and implicit transition models. Our empirical results in Sect. 4 demonstrate the advantage of PPN over model-free baseline (PPO), which suggests that PPN finds a better state embedding and reduces sample complexity.

3.1   Architecture

PPN is comprised of a few components. The components are parameterized by $\theta = \{\theta^{enc}, \theta^v, \theta^r, \theta^{tr}, \theta^\pi\}$ described below. In the following, a hat over variables represents that it is an estimate as opposed to a grounded observation or reward. The superscript represents the forward step predictions. The depth-rollout is expanded to a depth d. For example, $\hat{s}_t^i$ is the predicted state i steps (where $0 \leq i \leq d$) forward in time from t.

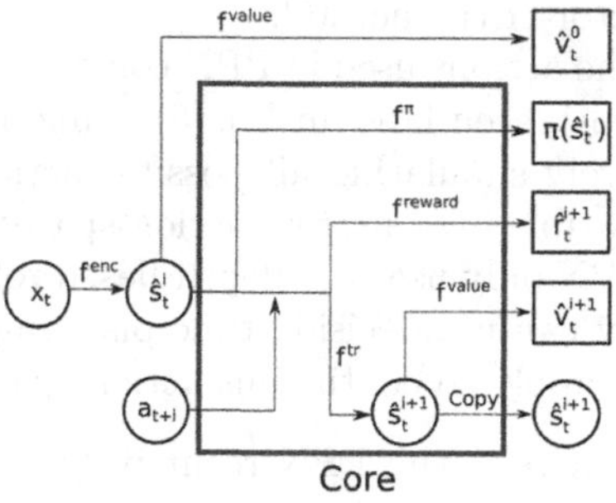

Fig. 1. PPN learns to predict policies, rewards, abstract states, and the value of the abstract states.

Encoding $(f_\theta^{enc}(x_t) = \hat{s}_{t,\theta}^0)$ function embeds the observation (x_t) in an abstract state $(\hat{s}_{t,\theta}^0 \in \mathbb{R}^y)$.

Value $(f_\theta^v(\hat{s}_{t,\theta}^i) = \hat{v}_{t,\theta}^i)$ function estimates the value $(\hat{v}_{t,\theta}^i \in \mathbb{R})$ of the abstract state.

Policy $(\mathcal{N}(f_\theta^\mu(\hat{s}_{t,\theta}^i), f^\Sigma(T)) = \pi_\theta(\hat{s}_{t,\theta}^i))$ function parameterizes a distribution over actions to take given a state $\hat{s}_{t,\theta}^i$. The policy module has two parts. The first (f_θ^μ) producing estimates of the mean $(\mu \in \mathbb{R}^z$ where z is dimensionality of action space) and the second (f^Σ) producing estimates of a diagonal covariance matrix $(\Sigma \in \mathbb{R}^{z \times z})$ to parameterize a normal distribution for the policy (π). This is further described in Sect. 3.2.

Reward $(f_\theta^r(\hat{s}_{t,\theta}^i, a_{t+i}) = \hat{r}_{t,\theta}^{i+1})$ function predicts the reward $(\hat{r}_{t,\theta}^{i+1} \in \mathbb{R})$ for executing the action a_{t+i} at abstract state $\hat{s}_{t,\theta}^i$.

Transition $(f_\theta^{tr}(\hat{s}_{t,\theta}^i, a_{t+i}) = \hat{s}_{t,\theta}^{i+1})$ function transforms the abstract state given an action to the next abstract state $(\hat{s}_{t,\theta}^{i+1} \in \mathbb{R}^y)$ by predicting $\Delta = \hat{s}_{t,\theta}^{i+1} - \hat{s}_{t,\theta}^i$.

We adopt a similar convention from VPN [11] which defines a core module. Figure 1 shows the core module which performs a depth-1 rollout by composing the modules:

$$f_\theta^{enc}(x_t) = \hat{s}_{t,\theta}^0,$$
$$f_\theta^v(\hat{s}_{t,\theta}^0) = \hat{v}_{t,\theta}^0,$$
$$f_\theta^{core}(\hat{s}_{t,\theta}^i, a_{t+i}) = (\pi(\hat{s}_{t,\theta}^i), \hat{r}_{t,\theta}^{i+1}, \hat{v}_{t,\theta}^{i+1}, \hat{s}_{t,\theta}^{i+1}).$$

There are 4 subtle but important differences between PPN depth rollouts and Value Prediction Network depth rollouts.

1. PPN estimates the policy based on the abstract state $(\pi(\hat{s}_{t,\theta}^i))$ at each step of the core module; while in VPN there is no need to predict a policy π because it is a Q-learning method. However, this means it does not naturally apply to continuous action-spaces.
2. PPN produces a value estimate $(\hat{v}_{t,\theta}^0)$ at the base of the depth rollout and uses this as the critic. In VPN, this is not necessary because it is not an actor-critic method.
3. The actions used in PPN come from samples generated by the behavior policy $(\pi_{\theta'})$, seen later in Eq. (5); while in VPN, the actions are chosen by exhaustively simulating all possible actions. Simulating all possible actions is only feasible in a discrete action space.
4. PPN only uses the depth-based rollout at training time. VPN's behavior policy can use decision-time planning [20]. However, this is not straightforward to apply to continuous action spaces and we leave this for future work.

If $d > 1$, the PPN recursively calls the core function (f_θ^{core}) to generate a trajectory of simulated rewards, policies, values, and abstract states conditioned on an initial abstract state $(\hat{s}_{t,\theta}^0)$ and action trajectory $(a_t, \ldots, a_{t+d-1})$. Each recursive call passes on the predicted abstract state $(\hat{s} = \hat{s}')$.

3.2 Planning

Here we introduce our approach to background planning [20] in continuous action spaces performed at training time. PPN has the ability to predict the future abstract states and based on these predicted future abstract states make additional predictions of future rewards, values, and policies. We use a basic planning method which simulates up to a certain depth d collecting reward, value, and policy estimates along the way.

Background planning is done by following the actions performed by the behavior policy and recursively calling f^{core} with the predicted abstract state. Action generation by the rollout policy $(\pi_{\theta'})$ is done by sampling from a normal distribution defined as follows:

$$a_t \sim N(\mu = f_{\theta'}^\mu(\hat{s}_{t,\theta'}^0), \Sigma = f^\Sigma(T)|\hat{s}_{t,\theta'}^0, T). \tag{5}$$

$f^\Sigma(T)$ is a function of the number of samples T seen since the beginning of training, and does not depend on the model parameters. In our experiments the standard deviation used to parameterize a diagonal covariance matrix is exponentially decayed with respect to the number of samples seen, as is done in PPO [17].

Algorithm 1. Policy Prediction Network (PPN), PPO style.

Initialize parameters θ
$\theta' = \theta$
for iteration $= 1, 2, \ldots$ **do**
    Run policy $\pi_{\theta'}$ in environment for n time steps
    Compute advantage estimates $A_1^{GAE}, \ldots, A_n^{GAE}$
    for epoch $= 1, \ldots, K$ **do**
        Shuffle n samples into mini-batches of size $M \leq n$
        for each mini-batch **do**
            T is the set of samples selected for the mini-batch
            $\mathcal{L}_{mb} = \frac{1}{M} \sum_{t \in T} \mathcal{L}_t$
            Optimize $\mathcal{L}_{mb}$ w.r.t. θ
        end for
    end for
    $\theta' = \theta$
end for

3.3 Learning

PPN is trained in a similar manner to typical Policy Gradient algorithms. The novel differences we introduce are depth-based losses, a latent transition model (f^{tr}) embedded into the architecture, auxiliary reward objectives, and a clipping scheme for depth-based losses. Depth-based losses are necessary to train the implicit transition model. The implicit transition model and auxiliary reward help with feature learning via background-planning.

PPN seeks to optimize auxiliary objectives and perform multiple updates on a batch. Trust regions as seen in TRPO can not be directly applied to both cases described above [17] and thus we introduce a clipping approach. Clipping all the network heads is crucial because the parameters of the reward network and value network all share parameters (f^{tr}, f^{enc}) with the policy network. For a visual reference of parameter sharing please see Fig. 1. This means that if any of the networks are updated in an uncontrolled fashion, it can also cause dramatic changes to the policy.

In addition, in Algorithm 1, we show that PPN performs a similar learning algorithm as was done in PPO.

The major differences in training between PPN and PPO come from the loss formulation ($\mathcal{L}$). The behavior policy with parameters (θ') generates an n-step trajectory $(x_1, a_1, x_2, a_2, r_2, \ldots, x_{n+1}, r_{n+1})$. The depth-$i$ predictions are grounded based on the generated n-step action trajectories. The loss at time t accumulates error over the planned trajectory up to a depth d and is defined as:

$$\mathcal{L}_t = \mathcal{L}_t^{\pi} + \alpha_v \mathcal{L}_t^{v} + \alpha_r \mathcal{L}_t^{r}, \tag{6}$$

where minimizing $\mathcal{L}_t^{\pi}$ corresponds to maximizing expected advantage, $\mathcal{L}_t^{v}$ results in an accurate critic, and $\mathcal{L}_t^{r}$ leads to reward predictions that represent the environment's actual reward for a state action pair. α_v, α_r are the penalty coefficients for the value loss and reward loss respectively.

Specifically, we define

$$\mathcal{L}_t^\pi = \frac{1}{d_\pi} \sum_{i=0}^{d_\pi-1} \max(-\text{ratio}_t^i A_{t+i}^{\text{GAE}}, -\text{ratio}_{t,\text{clip}}^i A_{t+i}^{\text{GAE}}) - \alpha_h H, \qquad (7)$$

where $\text{ratio}_t^i = \frac{\pi_\theta(a=a_{t+i}|s=\hat{s}_{t,\theta}^i)}{\pi_{\theta'}(a=a_{t+i}|s=\hat{s}_{t+i,\theta'}^0)}$ is the importance sampling ratio between the new policy and the old policy at depth i, $\text{ratio}_{t,\text{clip}}^i$ is the clipped ratio used to ensure the new parameter's estimate to be near the old parameter's estimate. We offer two possible formulations to clipping in Sect. 3.4. A_t^{GAE} is the generalized advantage estimate defined in (1), and α_h is a hyperparameter for the entropy coefficient.

As for the critic objective, we have the critic loss

$$\mathcal{L}_t^v = \frac{1}{d_v+1} \sum_{i=0}^{d_v} \frac{1}{2} \max((\hat{v}_{t,\theta}^i - R_{t+i})^2, (\hat{v}_{t,\text{clip}}^i - R_{t+i})^2), \qquad (8)$$

which encourages the current value estimate $\hat{v}_{t,\theta}^i$ to be close to the bootstrapped return R_{t+i} at each depth i without moving closer to the target than the clipped estimate $(\hat{v}_{t,\text{clip}}^i)$. The clipped estimate is guaranteed to be near the old parameter's estimate. Notice that $\mathcal{L}_t^v$ is over an extra iteration of the summation. This is because value estimates are made at every state $(\hat{s}_{t,\theta}^0, \ldots, \hat{s}_{t,\theta}^d)$ in the forward plan.

Similarly, the reward loss is

$$\mathcal{L}_t^r = \frac{1}{d_r} \sum_{i=0}^{d_r-1} \frac{1}{2} \max((\hat{r}_{t,\theta}^i - r_{t+i})^2, (\hat{r}_{t,\text{clip}}^i - r_{t+i})^2), \qquad (9)$$

encourages the reward estimate $\hat{r}_{t,\theta}^i$ to be close to the reward r_{t+i} at each depth i without moving closer to the target than the clipped estimate $(\hat{r}_{t,\text{clip}}^i)$.

The maximum in Eqs. (7)–(9) is taken between the unclipped surrogate objective and clipped surrogate objective. In the case of the critic and reward losses ($\mathcal{L}_t^v$ and $\mathcal{L}_t^r$), this means that updates only take place when the estimate from the new parameters (θ) are farther from the target (R_{t+i} in Eq. 8 and r_{t+i} in Eq. 9) than the clipped estimate. When the new parameter's estimate is closer, the max in Eq. 8 and 9 will select the clipped surrogate. The gradient of the clipped surrogate with respect to parameters (θ) will be zero, and thus will not change any parameters. This is desirable because it attempts to prevent destructive updates that push estimates made by θ far from estimates made by θ'.

Remark 1. PPN can be reduced to PPO2 if ($\alpha_r = 0$), $d_\pi = 1$, and $d_v = 0$.

It's possible to use different values of depth for the objectives but unless otherwise noted $d = d_\pi = d_v = d_r$.

3.4   Clipping

We present two approaches to clipping called grounded and ungrounded clipping. In this case, grounded and ungrounded refer to whether we have access to the ground truth observation (x_t). Grounded clipping offers a less strict clipping region, while ungrounded clipping is more aligned with theoretical justifications found in Conservative Policy Iteration [7], TRPO [15], and PPO [17]. Our clipped objectives are advantageous for two reasons. First, they allow for auxiliary reward and depth based updates. Second, they allow us to share parameters between the transition, policy, value, reward, and embedding networks. Both of these are essential to learn the implicit transition model and are helpful with feature learning.

Grounded Clipping. The clipping region is grounded with respect to both the action trajectory $(a_t, \ldots, a_{t+d})$ and the latent state $(\hat{s}^0_{t,\theta'}, \ldots, \hat{s}^0_{t+d+1,\theta'})$. The three grounded clipped estimates are shown in Eqs. (10), (11), and (12):

$$\text{ratio}^i_{t,\text{clip}} = \text{clip}(\text{ratio}^i_t, 1 - \epsilon, 1 + \epsilon), \tag{10}$$

$$\hat{v}^i_{t,\text{clip}} = \text{clip}(\hat{v}^i_{t,\theta} - v^0_{t+i,\theta'}, -\epsilon, \epsilon) + \hat{v}^0_{t+i,\theta'}, \tag{11}$$

$$\hat{r}^i_{t,\text{clip}} = \text{clip}(\hat{r}^i_{t,\theta} - \hat{r}^0_{t+i,\theta'}, -\epsilon, \epsilon) + \hat{r}^0_{t+i,\theta'}. \tag{12}$$

The clipping region is based on the grounded estimates from the old parameters (θ') rather than predicted estimates from old parameters.

Ungrounded Clipping. The clipping region in this case is grounded with respect to only the action trajectory, but ungrounded with respect to the latent state. The ungrounded clipping estimates are defined as:

$$\text{ratio}^i_{t,\text{clip}} = \text{clip}\left(\frac{\pi_\theta(a = a_{t+i}|s = \hat{s}^i_{t\theta})}{\pi_{\theta'}(a = a_{t+i}|s = \hat{s}^i_{t,\theta'})}, 1 - \epsilon, 1 + \epsilon\right)\frac{\pi_{\theta'}(a = a_{t+i}|s = \hat{s}^i_{t,\theta'})}{\pi_{\theta'}(a = a_{t+i}|s = \hat{s}^0_{t+i\theta'})},$$

$$\hat{v}^i_{t,\text{clip}} = \text{clip}(\hat{v}^i_{t,\theta} - v^i_{t,\theta'}, -\epsilon, \epsilon) + \hat{v}^i_{t,\theta'}, \tag{13}$$

$$\hat{r}^i_{t,\text{clip}} = \text{clip}(\hat{r}^i_{t,\theta} - \hat{r}^i_{t,\theta'}, -\epsilon, \epsilon) + \hat{r}^i_{t,\theta'}, \tag{14}$$

and $\text{ratio}^i_t = \frac{\pi_\theta(a = a_{t+i}|s = \hat{s}^i_{t,\theta})}{\pi_{\theta'}(a = a_{t+i}|s = \hat{s}^0_{t+i,\theta'})}$. Notice the change in how $\text{ratio}^i_{t,\text{clip}}$ is defined. We first clip the ratio between new and old ungrounded policies to be no more or less $1 \pm \epsilon$ and then perform importance sampling to account for the advantage being calculated with respect to the rollout policy.

4   Experiments

Our experiments seek to answer the following questions: (1) Is clipping necessary? If so, which type of clipping performs best (Sect. 4.2)? (2) Does PPN outperform model-free baselines (Sect. 4.3)? (3) What effect does depth have on performance (Sect. 4.4)? (4) Is the implicit transition module actually predicting abstract states that are useful to the policy (Sect. 4.5)?

Table 1. Summary of the MuJoCo environments used.

	Observation dimensions	Action dimensions
Hopper-v2	11	3
Walker2d-v2	17	6
Swimmer-v2	8	2
HalfCheetah-v2	17	6
InvertedPendulum-v2	4	1
InvertedDoublePendulum-v2	11	1
Humanoid-v2	376	17
Ant-v2	111	8

4.1 Experimental Setup

Our experiments investigate the comparison of PPN to PPO2 [3] on the OpenAI Gym MuJoCo environments [1, 22]. Preprocessing was done similarly to that of PPO [17]. Both PPO2 and PPN were implemented in Pytorch [12].

The comparison against PPO2 is run over all 8 environments listed in Table 1. Due to returns being subject to high variance, we run tests over 15 seeds (which is 3–5 times more than the related works in [11, 17]).[1] Due to computational constraints in other experiments we run over 5 seeds on the Walker2d-v2 and Ant-v2 environments.

Our PPO2 implementation uses the same hyperparameters as the baselines implementation [3]. The largest difference in our PPO2 implementation is that we do not perform orthogonal initialization. We did not include orthogonal initialization because it was not mentioned in the original PPO and we did not notice any clear performance benefits. For example, our implementation receives roughly double the returns on the HalfCheetah-v2 environment than the results reported by the baselines [3] implementation of PPO2 using orthogonal initialization.

Our PPN implementation uses similar hyperparameters: 2 fully connected layers for the embedding. 2 fully connected residual layers with unit length projections of the abstract-state [4] for the transition module. 1 fully connected layer for the policy mean, value and reward. All hidden layers have 128 hidden units and tanh activations. In practice we use Huber losses instead of L2 losses, as was done in related implicit model based works [11].

4.2 Clipping

We first look into the effect grounded clipping the network heads has on returns gathered by PPN agents. Here we test to see if a strong policy can still be learned if the other network heads (f^r, f^v) are not clipped.

---

[1] Due to computational constraints InvertedDoublePendulum-v2 only uses 5 seeds.

Table 2. Returns using grounded and ungrounded clipping

	Grounded	Ungrounded
Hopper-v2	2172.28	1356.14
Walker2d-v2	2937.20	1717.23
Swimmer-v2	83.22	85.27
HalfCheetah-v2	3509.34	3485.59
InvertedPendulum-v2	996.44	998.47
InvertedDoublePendulum-v2	4336.93	4071.19
Humanoid-v2	574.15	676.31
Ant-v2	1602.15	1566.06

As similarly done by Ilyas *et al.* [6], we fit a normal distribution to the returns achieved by the random seeds. Then we compare points on the cumulative distribution functions (CDF) that correspond to returns of $2, 20, 200, 2000$ for Ant-v2 and $4, 40, 400, 4000$ for Walker2d-v2.

In Fig. 2a and b we can see that clipping all the network heads turns out to be imperative to learn a useful policy. As stated in Sect. 3.3 clipping all the network heads is imperative because they all share parameters (f^{tr}, f^{enc}) with the policy. Additionally, we look into which type of clipping performs best. For the most part Table 2 shows grounded clipping offers the most robust returns. For all other PPN experiments we use the grounded clipping scheme.

4.3   Baseline Comparison

To test our model, we chose to benchmark against PPO2 and use the environments in Table 1. As is done in related works [4], we include depth $d = 1$ and $d = 2$ in our baseline comparison. However, we note that it is possible that larger depth values could be better on other environments.

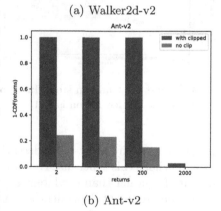

(a) Walker2d-v2

(b) Ant-v2

Fig. 2. Comparison of returns with and without (grounded) clipping of reward and critic.

As can be seen in Fig. 3, we find that PPN finds a better if not comparable policy in all of the environments. We notice that PPN tends to do well in complex

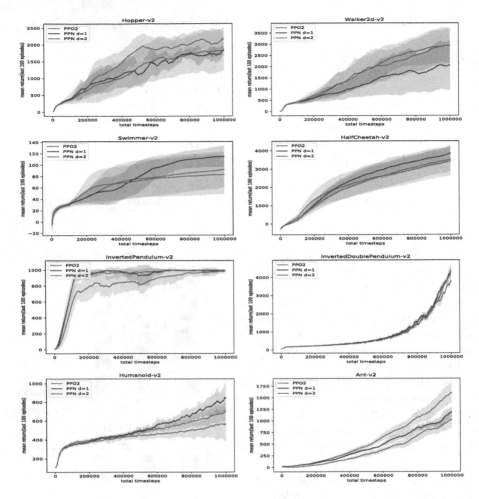

Fig. 3. Results on 1 million step MuJoCo benchmark. Dark lines represent the mean return and the shaded region is a standard deviation above and below the mean.

environments such as Ant-v2. Indeed Humanoid-v2 is an exception to this observation. Perhaps this is because Humanoid-v2's number of observation dimensions (376) are far larger than the latent space (128). Additionally, we notice optimal depth is environment dependent and is further studied in Sect. 4.4.

4.4   Depth

In this section, we explore the effect depth has on returns gathered by PPN agents. Increasing depth forces the agent to learn abstract state which contains information relevant to longer-term environment dynamics.

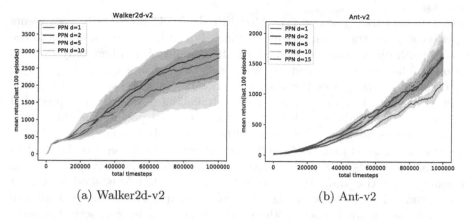

Fig. 4. Returns with respect to d values of 1, 2, 5, and 10.

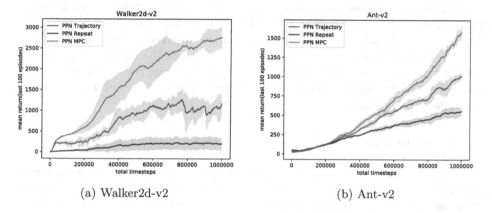

Fig. 5. Returns with respect to three difference action selection approaches.

As seen in Fig. 4 increasing depth (d) offers performance improvements but only up to a certain point. As the depth grows, we become more reliant on having a good transition function and eventually leads to a worse policy.

In Walker2d-v2 (Fig. 4a) we can clearly see a depth of 2 offers performance gains over a depth of 1. However after this point returns decrease as we increase depth. We suspect that optimal depth for Walker2d-v2 may be less than Ant-v2 because the implicit transition module is less accurate. A similar conclusion can be drawn from our observation in Sect. 4.5. Optimal depth is a recurring issue in implicit model-based approaches [4, 11].

4.5 Transition Ablation

We are curious whether the implicit transition module is actually predicting abstract states that resemble reality closely enough to actually be useful to the policy. To test this we perform an ablation study of 3 different types of policy prediction networks. The first type Model Predictive Control (MPC) represents a perfect implicit transition module as the policy in this case has access to the ground truth observation. The standard MPC approach is where only the first action is followed and the rest are replanned. The second type, "trajectory", represents the strength of the transition module. In this case, every d steps a new trajectory is generated by recursively calling f^{core} with the predicted abstract states and the sampled actions the predicted policy. The third type, "repeat", represents a meaningless transition module. In this case, every d steps a new action is generated by the policy and repeated for d steps. If the implicit transition module is bad we expect the returns from trajectory and repeat to be more or less the same. If the implicit transition module is good we expect returns somewhere in between the MPC and repeat curves. Note that all 3 of these approaches are trained in the same manner and have exactly the same parameters.

In Figs. 5a and b we see that the trajectory approach performs much better than repeat but not quite as well as MPC. This is interesting because the trajectory approach only has access to the grounded observation and must simulate d-steps into the future, where as in the MPC approach the action taken at time t always has access to the observation from time t. These results show that the implicit transition module is indeed useful and could be used in future work for decision-time planning.

5   Conclusion

Introduced in this work is a learning scheme for Policy Gradient methods which integrates model-free and model-based learning that reduces sample complexity at no extra cost in computation at rollout time. Additionally, PPN's implicit transition model acts as a first step towards decision-time planning with tree structured architectures in continuous action-spaces. It is interesting to note that while we only explored continuous action spaces in this work it is also possible to extend this to discrete action spaces.

For future work we would like to adapt PPNs to be less sensitive to planning depth and to leverage the transition model for decision-time planning. Decision-time planning is interesting but not straight forward to apply because it changes the behavior policy distribution in ways that are hard to measure.

References

1. Brockman, G., et al.: OpenAI gym. arXiv preprint arXiv:1606.01540 (2016)
2. Chiappa, S., Racaniere, S., Wierstra, D., Mohamed, S.: Recurrent environment simulators. arXiv preprint arXiv:1704.02254 (2017)
3. Dhariwal, P., et al.: OpenAI baselines. https://github.com/openai/baselines (2017)
4. Farquhar, G., Rocktaeschel, T., Igl, M., Whiteson, S.: TreeQN and ATreec: differentiable tree planning for deep reinforcement learning. In: International Conference on Learning Representations (2018). https://openreview.net/forum?id=H1dh6Ax0Z

5. Ha, D., Schmidhuber, J.: Recurrent world models facilitate policy evolution. In: Advances in Neural Information Processing Systems, pp. 2455–2467 (2018)
6. Ilyas, A., et al.: Are deep policy gradient algorithms truly policy gradient algorithms? arXiv preprint arXiv:1811.02553 (2018)
7. Kakade, S., Langford, J.: Approximately optimal approximate reinforcement learning. In: ICML, vol. 2, pp. 267–274 (2002)
8. Mnih, V., et al.: Asynchronous methods for deep reinforcement learning. In: International Conference on Machine Learning, pp. 1928–1937 (2016)
9. Mnih, V., et al.: Human-level control through deep reinforcement learning. Nature **518**(7540), 529 (2015)
10. Oh, J., Guo, X., Lee, H., Lewis, R.L., Singh, S.: Action-conditional video prediction using deep networks in Atari games. In: Advances in Neural Information Processing Systems, pp. 2863–2871 (2015)
11. Oh, J., Singh, S., Lee, H.: Value prediction network. In: Advances in Neural Information Processing Systems, pp. 6118–6128 (2017)
12. Paszke, A., et al.: Automatic differentiation in PyTorch (2017)
13. Pathak, D., Agrawal, P., Efros, A.A., Darrell, T.: Curiosity-driven exploration by self-supervised prediction. In: International Conference on Machine Learning (ICML), vol. 2017 (2017)
14. Schmidhuber, J.: On learning to think: algorithmic information theory for novel combinations of reinforcement learning controllers and recurrent neural world models. arXiv preprint arXiv:1511.09249 (2015)
15. Schulman, J., Levine, S., Abbeel, P., Jordan, M., Moritz, P.: Trust region policy optimization. In: International Conference on Machine Learning, pp. 1889–1897 (2015)
16. Schulman, J., Moritz, P., Levine, S., Jordan, M., Abbeel, P.: High-dimensional continuous control using generalized advantage estimation. In: Proceedings of the International Conference on Learning Representations (ICLR) (2016)
17. Schulman, J., Wolski, F., Dhariwal, P., Radford, A., Klimov, O.: Proximal policy optimization algorithms. CoRR abs/1707.06347 (2017). http://arxiv.org/abs/1707.06347
18. Silver, D., et al.: The predictron: end-to-end learning and planning. In: Proceedings of the 34th International Conference on Machine Learning, ICML 2017, Sydney, NSW, Australia, 6–11 August 2017, pp. 3191–3199 (2017). http://proceedings.mlr.press/v70/silver17a.html
19. Sutton, R.S.: Integrated architectures for learning, planning, and reacting based on approximating dynamic programming. In: Machine Learning Proceedings 1990, pp. 216–224. Elsevier (1990)
20. Sutton, R.S., Barto, A.G.: Reinforcement Learning: An Introduction. MIT Press, Cambridge (2018)
21. Sutton, R.S., McAllester, D.A., Singh, S.P., Mansour, Y.: Policy gradient methods for reinforcement learning with function approximation. In: Advances in Neural Information Processing Systems, pp. 1057–1063 (2000)
22. Todorov, E., Erez, T., Tassa, Y.: MuJoCo: a physics engine for model-based control. In: 2012 IEEE/RSJ International Conference on Intelligent Robots and Systems (IROS), pp. 5026–5033. IEEE (2012)

Attentive Multi-task Deep Reinforcement Learning

Timo Bräm, Gino Brunner$^{(\boxtimes)}$ ⓘ, Oliver Richter$^{(\boxtimes)}$ ⓘ, and Roger Wattenhofer

Department of Information Technology and Electrical Engineering, ETH Zurich,
Zürich, Switzerland
braem.timo@gmail.com,
{brunnegi,richtero,wattenhofer}@ethz.ch

Abstract. Sharing knowledge between tasks is vital for efficient learning in a multi-task setting. However, most research so far has focused on the easier case where knowledge transfer is not harmful, i.e., where knowledge from one task cannot negatively impact the performance on another task. In contrast, we present an approach to multi-task deep reinforcement learning based on attention that does not require any a-priori assumptions about the relationships between tasks. Our attention network automatically groups task knowledge into sub-networks on a state level granularity. It thereby achieves positive knowledge transfer if possible, and avoids negative transfer in cases where tasks interfere. We test our algorithm against two state-of-the-art multi-task/transfer learning approaches and show comparable or superior performance while requiring fewer network parameters.

1 Introduction

Humans are often excellent role models for machines. Unlike machines, humans have been interacting with their environment since time immemorial, and this extensive experience should not be ignored. So how are we humans learning, and what can machines learn from us?

First, humans learn with a limited amount of training data, as we cannot afford to first train for an unreasonably long time before becoming active. Also, we usually do not require labeled training data, but instead rely on experience gained from interactions with our world. This situation is well represented by the reinforcement learning paradigm: We observe the environment and take actions to hopefully maximize our cumulative reward. Second, humans learn many tasks concurrently, not only because there is no time to learn all possible tasks sequentially, but also because tasks are often similar in nature, and useful strategies can be transferred between comparable tasks. This is a fundamental aspect of intelligence known as multi-task learning. Third, our brain would be overwhelmed if it had to focus on all skills acquired over the span of our lives at every point in time. Therefore, we focus our attention to a set of skills useful at the moment.

Authors listed in alphabetical order.

© Springer Nature Switzerland AG 2020
U. Brefeld et al. (Eds.): ECML PKDD 2019, LNAI 11908, pp. 134–149, 2020.
https://doi.org/10.1007/978-3-030-46133-1_9

If we were not able to relate similar tasks and attend to skills based on extrinsic or intrinsic cues, our brain would not be able to learn much. Recent advances in neuroscience [17] also suggest that the attention mechanisms of humans are themselves learned through reinforcement learning.

In this paper, we investigate the combination of these three paradigms, in other words, we study *attentive multi-task deep reinforcement learning*. More specifically, we employ the insight of human attention by developing a simple yet effective architecture for model-free multi-task reinforcement learning. We use a neural network based attention mechanism to focus on sub-networks depending on the current state of the environment and the task to be solved. Most recent work [2,12,15,29] in the multi-task/transfer deep reinforcement learning setting capitalize on some shared property between tasks. In contrast, our approach makes no assumptions about the similarity between tasks. Instead, possible relations are automatically inferred during training.

An additional advantage of using an attention based architecture is that unrelated tasks can effectively be separated and learned in different sub-parts of the architecture. We thereby automatically embrace the *negative transfer* problem (the effect that training one task might actually harm performance on another task) which most related approaches omit in their evaluation. We show that our approach scales economically with an increasing number of tasks as the attention mechanism automatically learns to group related skills in the same part of the architecture. We back our claims by comparing against two state of the art algorithms [26,29] on a large set of grid world tasks with different amounts of transferable knowledge. We show that our method scales better in the number of parameters per task, while achieving comparable or superior performance in terms of steps to convergence. Especially, when the action spaces of the tasks are not aligned we outperform [26,29].[1]

2   Related Work

Transfer learning in classical reinforcement learning [28] is a well established research area. Even though Lin [18] already used neural networks in combination with reinforcement learning, a renewed interest in this combination came with the recent success on Atari (DQN, [21]), followed by an increased interest in developing transfer learning techniques specific to deep learning. Parisotto et al. [22] train a neural network to predict the features and outputs of several expert DQNs and use multi-task network weights as initialization for a target task DQN. Rusu et al. [25] use a single network to match expert DQN policies from different games by policy distillation. Yin et al. [30] improve policy distillation by making the convolutional layers task specific and by using hierarchical experience replay. Schmitt et al. [27] also build on the idea of policy distillation but additionally propose to anneal the teacher signal such that the student

---

[1] To stimulate future research in this area, our source code is available at: https://github.com/braemt/attentive-multi-task-deep-reinforcement-learning.

can surpass the teacher's performance. Further, in [7,11,23] knowledge is transferred from human expert demonstrations, while the algorithm of Aytar et al. [1] learns from YouTube video demonstrations. Gupta et al. [9] transfer knowledge from source to target agent by training matched feature spaces. Closely related to our approach is the work of Rajendran et al. [24] who also incorporate several sub-networks and an attention mechanism to transfer knowledge from an expert network. In contrast to the architecture described in [24] and all related work mentioned so far, our algorithm learns multiple tasks simultaneously from scratch, without guidance from any demonstrations or experts. This makes our approach self-sustained and as such more general than mentioned related work.

Glatt et al. [8] train a DQN on a source task and investigate how the learned weights, which are used as initialization for a target task, alter the performance. In a similar manner, [4,6,10] show that some transfer is possible by simply training one network on multiple tasks. However, since these algorithms do not incorporate any task-specific weights, the best that can be done is to interpolate between conflicting tasks. In contrast, our method allows conflicting tasks to be learned in separate networks.

One interesting line of research [2,3,15,16,31] capitalizes on transferring knowledge based on successor features, i.e., shared environment dynamics. In contrast, our method does not rely on shared environment dynamics nor action alignment across tasks.

Czarnecki et al. [5] use multiple networks similar to our approach. However, their focus is on automated curriculum learning. Therefore they adjust the policy mixing weights through population based training [13] while we learn attention weights conditioned on the task state.

Rusu et al. [26] introduce *Progressive Neural Networks* (PNN), an effective approach for learning in a sequential multi-task setting. In PNN, a new network and lateral connections for each additional task are added in order to enable knowledge transfer, which speeds up the training of subsequent tasks. The additional network parts let the architecture grow super-linearly, while our network scales economically with an increasing number of tasks. Another strong approach is introduced by Teh et al. [29]. Their algorithm, *Distral*, learns multiple tasks at once by sharing knowledge through a distillation process of an additional shared policy network. In contrast to our approach, this requires an aligned action space and a separate network for each task. We compare against Distral and PNN in our experiments.

3   Background

In reinforcement learning, an agent learns through interactions with an environment. The agent repeatedly chooses an action $a_t \in \mathcal{A}$ at step t and observes a reward $r_t \in \mathbb{R}$ and the next state $s_{t+1} \in \mathcal{S}$, where $\mathcal{A}$ and $\mathcal{S}$ denote the sets of possible actions and states, respectively. The agent chooses the actions according

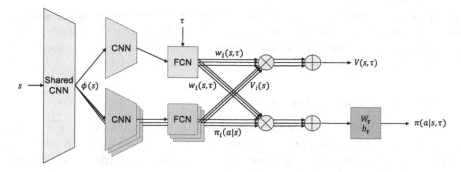

Fig. 1. Our architecture consists of an attention network (blue), which decides the weighting of the sub-network outputs (red) to generate the policy and value function on a task and state basis. The first convolutional layers are shared between the attention network and the sub-networks. The weighted sub-network policies are transformed by a task-specific layer (in green) to account for different numbers of possible actions in different tasks. (Color figure online)

to a policy $\pi(a_t|s_t) : S \times A \rightarrow [0,1]$ which indicates the probability of choosing action a_t in state s_t. The objective is to find a policy that maximizes the expected discounted return, i.e., to find

$$\pi^* = \max_{\pi} \left(\mathbb{E}_\pi \left[\sum_{t'=0}^{\infty} \gamma^{t'} r_{t'} \right] \right)$$

where $\gamma \in [0,1]$ is the discount factor for future rewards.

In this work, we train on this objective using asynchronous advantage actor-critic training (A3C, [20]), a well established policy gradient method that uses multiple asynchronous actors for experience collection. However, our approach is general and can be readily applied to most on- and off-policy deep reinforcement learning algorithms.

In multi-task reinforcement learning, the goal is to solve a set of tasks $\mathcal{T}$ simultaneously by training a policy $\pi(a_t|s_t, \tau)$ and value function $V(s_t, \tau)$, also referred to as critic, for each task $\tau \in \mathcal{T}$. While the objective to maximize the discounted rewards in each of the tasks remains unchanged, an additional goal is to share knowledge between tasks to accelerate training.

4   Architecture

Our network architecture, as shown in Fig. 1, consists of a number of independent sub-networks and an attention module that weights the output of all sub-networks to generate a weighted policy and value function per task. The policies are then used to choose the next action in each of the environments. The attention and sub-networks all operate on top of a shared CNN that extracts high-level features of the environments. The attention network determines whether sub-networks become specialized on certain tasks, or whether they learn features that are shared across a group of tasks. However, we do not explicitly enforce this. Thus, we do not require any a-priori knowledge about the nature of the tasks or about their similarity. In other words, we do not make any assumptions about whether potential for positive or negative transfer exists.

4.1 Shared Feature Extractor

The first stage of our architecture consists of a CNN that outputs a state-embedding $\phi(s)$. The embedding $\phi(s)$ is shared among all following sub-networks as well as the attention network. Thus, $\phi(s)$ will learn general high-level features that are relevant for all subsequent parts of the architecture. Since we do not decrease the dimensionality of the input in these layers, the architecture can in the (worst) case, where no information can be shared, learn an approximate identity mapping from s to $\phi(s)$ and leave the specialization to the sub-networks.

4.2 Attention Network

One could think of several ways how to combine the different sub-network outputs into a policy per task. One way would be to choose in each time step one of the sub-networks directly as policy. However, this sort of hard attention leads to noisy gradients (since a stochastic sampling operation would be added to the computation graph) and no complex interactions of several sub-networks could be learned. Therefore we employ a soft attention mechanism, where the final output is a linear combination of the sub-networks' outputs. Intuitively, this allows all sub-networks that are helpful to contribute to the policy and value function. This can also be seen as an ensemble, where different sub-networks with possibly different specializations vote on the next action, but where the final decision is governed by an attention network.

More concretely, the attention network consists of a CNN that operates on the shared embedding $\phi(s)$. The output of the CNN is fed into a fully connected network (FCN) that projects the output into a latent vector. This vector is then concatenated with a one-hot encoding of the task ID τ from which the input s originates, and processed further in the fully connected network. Finally, a linear layer with softmax activation produces the attention weights $w_i(s, \tau)$, which decide the contribution of the policy and value functions of each sub-network i in state s of task τ.

4.3 Sub-networks

We use N sub-networks that contribute to the final weighted policy and value function. The number of sub-networks can be chosen based on resource requirements and/or availability. In a practical application of our method, one would choose the maximum number of networks for which the entire model still fits into memory. Unused sub-networks can be automatically ignored by the attention network (see Sect. 6.4), and could potentially be pruned to reduce the overall number of parameters. In our experiments we choose a small number of networks to show that we can achieve comparable or superior performance to state of the art methods while requiring substantially fewer parameters. Specifically, we chose the number of sub-networks N depending on the number of tasks. That is, we roughly add one sub-network for four tasks. More precisely we let $N = \lfloor (|\mathcal{T}| + 2)/4 \rfloor + 1$, as we found this scaling to work well in our experiments. The sub-networks can act independently, as in an ensemble, or specialize on certain types of (sub-)tasks. The exact mode of operation depends on the nature of the tasks and is governed by the attention network. In other words, if the attention network decides that specialization is most beneficial, then the sub-networks will be encouraged to specialize, and vice versa.

The sub-networks all have the same architecture and get the embedding $\phi(s)$ as input. First, a CNN learns to extract sub-network specific features from $\phi(s)$ that are then passed to a FCN. From the last hidden representation of the FCN, a linear layer directly outputs the value function estimate $V_i(s)$ for the i-th sub-network. A softmax layer maps the last hidden representation of the FCN to a $|\mathcal{A}_{max}|$-dimensional vector $pi_i(a|s)$, where $|\mathcal{A}_{max}|$ is the largest action space size across all tasks.

4.4   Attentive Multi-task Network

The attention weighted $\pi_i(a|s)$ is in the end fed to a task-specific linear layer that maps it to the action dimension of each task, and a final softmax normalization is applied to generate a valid probability distribution over actions, i.e., a policy. More formally, the sub-network outputs $\pi_i(a|s)$ are combined into the final policy as

$$\pi(a|s, \tau) = \text{softmax} \left(W_\tau \cdot \left(\sum_i^N \pi_i(a|s) w_i(s, \tau) \right) + b_\tau \right)$$

where $W_\tau \in \mathbb{R}^{|\mathcal{A}_\tau| \times |\mathcal{A}_{max}|}$ is a task-specific weight matrix and $b_\tau \in \mathbb{R}^{|\mathcal{A}_\tau|}$ is a task-specific bias. Note that W_τ and b_τ are shared across the sub-networks and only depend on the task.

Putting everything together, we use the attention weights $w_i(s, \tau)$ to also compute the final value function $V(s, \tau)$ from the outputs of the sub-networks as

$$V(s, \tau) = \sum_{i=1}^N w_i(s, \tau) V_i(s)$$

5   Task Environments

To evaluate our approach we create a set of environments which are designed to have the potential for positive as well as negative knowledge transfer. Since we aim at evaluating our approach on a large set of tasks, we opt for simple, easy to generate environments, even though our initial results on the Arcade

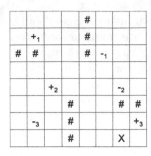

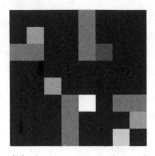

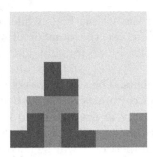

(a) # are walls and X is the target. + (−) denote objects giving positive (negative) rewards. If only one bonus (penalty) object is present, it is located at +₁ (−₁).

(b) A state space of a grid world task. The player is the white square. Walls, the target, three bonus objects and one penalty object are present.

(c) Example state of the connect four task. The agent controls the dark tokens, the random opponent controls the gray tokens.

Fig. 2. (a) Grid world environment template. (b) Example of a concrete grid world instantiation. (c) Example of a concrete connect four state.

Learning Environment [19] (not reported here) were promising as well. We leave the adaption of our methodology to more complex environments to future work as we aim to show the evolution of transfer depending on the number of tasks in this report, which was not feasible on more complex tasks within our resource constraints due to the large amount of networks trained (600 for Fig. 4 alone) and experiments conducted.

5.1 Grid Worlds

The first set of environments contains 20 grid world tasks. The environments of this set consist of 8 × 8 gray-scale images representing the state of the environment. The agent is a single pixel in the grid and the possible actions are moving up, down, left or right. For all tasks, the goal is to reach a target pixel where a positive reward is received and the episode terminates. The environments can also contain additional objects that represent positive/negative rewards, as well as impassable walls. All objects in the environments are at fixed locations, and only the starting location of the player is random. Figure 2a shows the template for all tasks and Fig. 2b shows an example of such an environment as seen by the agent.

In the following we give a detailed description of every variation, each defining a task. In the first task, the goal is to find the target as fast as possible. No walls or additional rewards are put into the environment, just the agent and the target. To encourage speed, the agent is penalized with a small negative reward at every step. In the other tasks there is no such penalty, but if the player leaves the board, a negative reward of −0.5 is observed and the episode is terminated. This is also the only difference between task one and two: The goal of the second task is to reach the target without leaving the board. In the third task, a bonus object is added at location marked $+_1$ in Fig. 2a that yields a positive reward when collected. In the fourth task, additionally to the bonus object of task 3, another bonus object at location $+_2$ and a penalty object at the location marked with $-_1$ are added. The penalty object yields a negative reward when collected. The fifth and sixth task both contain three bonus objects at the locations marked with a + in Fig. 2a, where the sixth task additionally contains another penalty object at location $-_2$. Tasks 7 and 8 are visually indistinguishable from tasks 4 and 5, but we invert the rewards of the bonus and penalty objects in order to test negative transfer. Similar to these two tasks, tasks 9 and 10 consist of three objects looking like penalty objects (at locations marked with $-$) but yielding positive reward. Task 10 additionally contains an object that looks like a bonus object at location $+_1$ (see Fig. 2a) yielding a negative reward. Tasks 11 to 20 are the same as tasks 1 to 10 but additionally contain impassable walls. The maximum achievable reward is set to 1.0 for all tasks, distributed equally among bonus objects and target. For example, if there are three bonus objects, the target and bonus objects yield rewards of 0.25 each. The penalty objects give a negative reward that is equal in magnitude to the bonus objects' positive reward. In addition, walking into a wall yields a reward of -0.5. Furthermore, if the agent does not reach the target after 200 steps, the task terminates without any additional reward.

5.2   Connect Four

To test the behavior of our model on unrelated tasks with little to no potential for knowledge transfer, we generate environments from a completely different domain. We implement a two-player game based on connect four. Each location or token is represented by a single pixel. The agent drops in a token from the top, which then appears on top of the top most token in the column, or in the bottom row if the column was empty. The goal of this task is to have four tokens in a horizontal, vertical or diagonal line. Our connect four tasks consist of 8 rows and 8 columns, and thus looks visually similar to the grid world tasks, but has otherwise no relation to them. The agent has 8 different actions to choose from, indicating in which column the token is to be dropped. An example of this is shown in Fig. 2c. If the agent plays an invalid action, i.e., if the chosen column is already full, the agent loses the game immediately. When the agent wins the game it receives a reward of 1, and -1 if it loses. In case of a tie the reward is 0. The opponent chooses a *valid* action uniformly at random. We additionally implement three variations of this basic connect four task. The goal of the first variation is to connect five tokens instead of four. The second and third variation rotate the state of the connect four and connect five tasks by 90°, such that the players now choose rows and not columns.

Table 1. Architecture details for the policy networks (value output is omitted for readability). The base network is the basic network building block for Distral and PNN, each having one such base network per task. Additionally PNN has lateral connections and Distral has an additional base network for the shared policy. The columns *Shared CNN*, *Sub-networks* and *Attention network* describe our architecture (see Sect. 4 and Fig. 1). The + in the attention network Layer 4 indicates concatenation of the task embedding.

	Base network	Shared CNN	Sub-networks	Attention network
Layer 1	$3 \times 3 \times 16$, stride 2	$3 \times 3 \times 32$, stride 2	–	–
Layer 2	$3 \times 3 \times 16$, stride 1	$3 \times 3 \times 32$, stride 1	–	–
Layer 3	$3 \times 3 \times 16$, stride 1	–	$3 \times 3 \times 16$, stride 1	$3 \times 3 \times 16$, stride 1
Layer 4	FC 256	–	FC 256	FC $N \cdot |\mathcal{T}| + |\mathcal{T}|$
Layer 5	Softmax $|\mathcal{A}_\tau|$	–	Softmax $|\mathcal{A}_{max}|$	FC 256
Layer 6	–	–	Softmax $|\mathcal{A}_\tau|$	Softmax N

6 Experiments and Results

We evaluate the performance of our architecture on the set of grid worlds described before and compare the results to two state of the art architectures: Progressive Neural Networks (PNN) [26] and Distral [29]. PNN learns tasks sequentially by freezing already trained networks and adding an additional network for each new task. The new networks are connected to previous ones to allow knowledge transfer. The order in which the tasks are trained with our PNN implementation is sampled randomly for all experiments. In contrast to PNN, but similar to our approach, Distral learns all tasks simultaneously. Here, a distilled policy $\hat{\pi}_0$ is used for sharing and transferring knowledge, while each task also has its own network to learn task-specific policies $\hat{\pi}_\tau$. We implement the *KL+ent 2col* approach (see [29]). The distilled policy network and the task-specific networks have the same network architecture as the base PNN model which is listed as *Base network* in Table 1. Note that even though our architecture starts with more filters in the shared CNN when compared to the base architecture, this does not give us a parameter advantage, since those filters are shared across all tasks while Distral and PNN get additional CNN parameters for each additional task. For all approaches and all experiments, we use the same hyper parameters which are summarized in Table 2. We chose these hyper parameters based on the performance of all three approaches on multiple grid world tasks such that no approach has an unfair advantage. We use the smallest multiple of $|\mathcal{T}|$ (the number of tasks) which is equal or larger than 24 for the number of parallel workers in the A3C training and distribute tasks equally over the workers. The loss function is minimized with the Adam optimizer [14]. For PNN we had to reduce the number of workers to 16, as the memory consumption for a large number of tasks was too high. For Distral, we set $\alpha = 0.5$ and $\beta = 10^4$ and compute the policy as

$$\hat{\pi}_i(a|s) = \text{softmax}(\alpha h(a|s) + f(a|s))$$

Table 2. Hyper parameters used for the experiments.

Stacked input frames	1	Discount factor γ	0.99
Adam learning rate	1e−4	Rollout length	5
Adam β_1	0.9	Entropy regularization	0.02
Adam β_2	0.999	Distral α	0.5
Adam ϵ	1e−08	Distral β	10^4

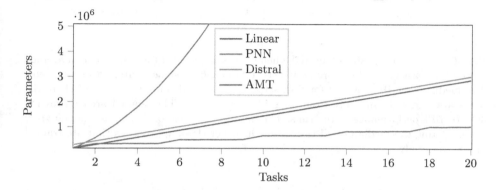

Fig. 3. Number of parameters of the different architecture choices with an increasing number of tasks. *Linear* represents training each task in a separate network of the size of PNNs base model.

where h is the output of the distilled network and f is the β-scaled output of the task-specific network (see Appendix B.2 of [29]).

6.1 Model Size

First, we compare the model sizes of our Attentive Multi-Task (AMT) architecture, PNN, Distral and *Linear*. Linear simply represents training a separate network (same size as the base network) on each task which leads to a linear increase in parameters with each additional task. The results are shown in Fig. 3. In our experiments we add a new sub-network to AMT for every fourth task, thus the number of network parameters grows more slowly with the number of tasks than in the other approaches. Depending on memory requirements we can easily increase or decrease the total number of parameters since we do not assign sub-networks to tasks a-priori; more difficult tasks can automatically be assigned more effective network capacity by the attention network.

Distral uses slightly more parameters than having a separate network for each task due to the additional distilled policy network. The only way to reduce the number of total parameters would be to decrease the size of the task networks. However, unlike our approach, doing so could more strongly affect difficult tasks that require more network capacity to be solved, or tasks that cannot profit from the distilled policy due to a lack of transfer potential. One could tune each task

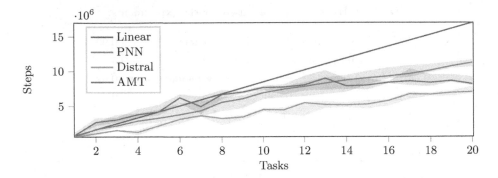

Fig. 4. The number of steps required when trained on a set of tasks to reach an average score of at least 0.9 and a score of at least 0.8 on each task separately over 10^5 steps. The median over 10 runs and for task set sizes between 1 and 20 is shown, where the tasks are sampled randomly from all grid worlds tasks. The shaded area represents 30% to 70% performance of the runs. The number of steps for *Linear* is calculated by extrapolating the median of all runs from the other three approaches that are trained on one task only.

network individually and, e.g., use larger networks for more difficult tasks, but this would require a substantial tuning effort. In contrast, our method assigns effective network capacity automatically, and can thus utilize the available network parameters more efficiently.

PNN also adds a new sub-network for each task and additionally connects all existing sub-networks to the newly added one. Thus, the number of total parameters grows super-linearly in the number of tasks. This parameter explosion causes high memory consumption and high computational costs, which can quickly become a problem when training on an increasing number of tasks with limited hardware.

6.2   Sample Efficiency vs. Number of Tasks

In this section, we compare the performance of AMT to PNN and Distral when trained on an increasing number of tasks. We perform 10 runs for each approach and every number of tasks (from 1 to 20). For each of the 10 runs, the tasks are chosen uniformly at random without replacement from all 20 grid world tasks. The tasks are considered solved if the average score over 10^5 steps is at least 0.9 and each individual task has a score of at least 0.8. The results are shown in Fig. 4. The number of steps required to solve a given number of tasks scales sub-linearly for all three approaches, i.e., training on multiple tasks requires fewer interactions with the environment than training every task separately. This means that knowledge is shared between different tasks in all approaches as expected. For a larger amount of tasks, our approach is faster than PNN and only slightly worse than Distral in terms of steps required to reach the given

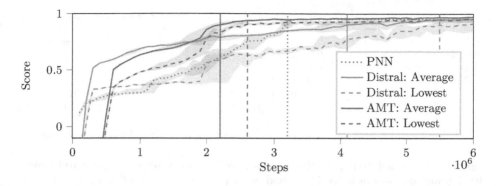

Fig. 5. Median scores over 10 runs. The shaded area represents 30% to 70% performance of the runs. Training is performed on 6 tasks, where we switch the action dimensions for 3 of them. This means that the agent goes to the left instead of the right, to the top instead of the bottom, and vice versa. For AMT and Distral, the solid line represents the average score of all tasks and the dashed line represents the task where the lowest score is observed. For PNN (dotted), a threshold score of 0.95 has to be reached over 10^5 steps before switching to the next task. For each approach, the vertical line is drawn at the first point where the score exceeds 0.9 over 10^5 steps.

performance threshold. Note however that our approach has substantially fewer parameters than the other approaches in this large number of tasks setup.

6.3   Unaligned Action Spaces

To see whether the approaches can handle transfer between domains where the action spaces are not aligned, we take the second, third and fourth grid world task and switch their action dimensions, meaning that the agent goes to the left instead of the right, to the top instead of the bottom, and vice versa. We combine these new tasks with the original grid world tasks 2, 3 and 4 and train the three different approaches to solve these six tasks simultaneously. Figure 5 compares the number of steps required to reach a score of 0.9 on all tasks separately and on average. Our approach clearly outperforms PNN and Distral in the number of steps required the reach the target performance on all tasks. We see two explanations for this: either two of our sub-networks specialize to the two sets of tasks and allow fast transfer as such, or the task specific linear layer (W_τ, b_τ) in our architecture effectively learns to invert the action space of some tasks such that two tasks from the two different sets look similar to a sub-network in our architecture. Most likely, the improvement is due to an entangled combination of both explanations. The results of PNN are comparable to the previous experiment as PNN is also able to deal well with unaligned action spaces. In contrast to multi-task approaches however, PNN is bound to define a threshold for when to freeze the current task's network weights and move on to the next one. Further, a curriculum needs to be specified and tasks learned earlier cannot profit from knowledge discovered during learning later tasks.

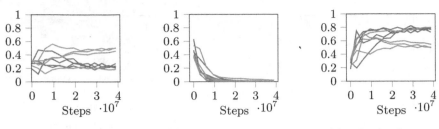

(a) First sub-network.   (b) Second sub-network.   (c) Third sub-network.

Fig. 6. A smoothed average of the attention weights for 8 different grid world tasks. Set 1 (blue) consists of tasks 3 to 6 and set 2 (orange) consists of tasks 7 to 10, for which the reward associated with the collectable objects are inverted. (Color figure online)

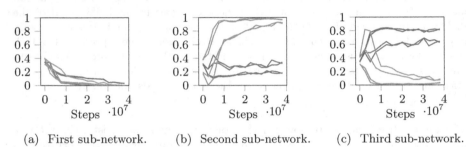

(a) First sub-network.   (b) Second sub-network.   (c) Third sub-network.

Fig. 7. Smoothed average of the attention weights for 8 different tasks of two domains. Grid World (blue) consists of grid world tasks 3 to 6 and Connect Four (orange) consists of the four connect-four/five tasks. The connect-four/five tasks are almost exclusively learned into the second sub-network, while the grid world tasks use mostly the third sub-network. We can see that there is a clear separation between the weights of the tasks of the two domains. (Color figure online)

Therefore PNN ultimately learns slower in this setup than our approach. Distral, an approach that aligns the action space between tasks, requires more steps for these six tasks than for randomly selected six tasks like in the previous experiment, as the distilled policy cannot deal with the three environments and their counterparts at the same time. This underlines our claim that, while other approaches are effective for multi-task learning in a controlled setup, our approach is able to deal with multiple tasks even if the action spaces are not aligned.

6.4   Analyzing the Learned Attention Weights

To give an insight in how tasks are separated into sub-networks we take a subset of the grid world tasks where we expect negative transfer when knowledge is shared. More specifically, we take tasks 3–6 and 7–10. Note that these two sets of tasks are visibly indistinguishable and equivalent apart from the fact that bonus objects yield negative rewards and penalty objects positive rewards in the second set. In Fig. 6 we plot a smoothed average of the attention weights $w_i(s, \tau)$ of each task τ for all sub-networks $i \in \{1, 2, 3\}$. As can be seen in the figure, our architecture discovers that three sub-networks are not needed for these six tasks and learns to discard one of them. Further, one can see a tendency that one set of tasks is learned into one of the sub-networks while the other set of tasks is learned into the other remaining sub-network. Note however, that this distinction is not sharp since there is still a lot of transfer possible between the two sets of tasks, i.e., the agent has to stay on the board and find the target in both sets. This brings us to the interesting question how the distribution of the weights would look like if one uses two sets of tasks from completely unrelated domains. To answer this question, we train our model on connect-four/five and on grid world tasks. Figure 7 shows the weighting of the sub-networks when trained on those tasks. Clearly, the second sub-network learns to specialize on the connect-four/five task. Further, even though the connect-four/five and grid world tasks are unrelated to each other, parts of the "connect-four-knowledge" is used for the grid worlds while the non-overlapping state-action correlations are safely learned in a separate sub-network. Again, one of the sub-networks is left almost unused by all tasks, i.e., the model automatically learned that there are more sub-networks than needed for the two task domains.

7   Conclusion

We present a multi-task deep reinforcement learning algorithm based on the intuition of human attention. We show that knowledge transfer can be achieved by a simple attention architecture that does not require any a-priori knowledge of the relationship between the tasks. We show that our approach achieves transfer comparable to state of the art approaches as the number of tasks increases while using substantially fewer network parameters. Further, our approach clearly outperforms Distral and PNN when the action space between tasks is not aligned, since the task-specific weights and specialized sub-networks can account for this discrepancy. In future work, we plan to apply our approach to more complex tasks by incorporating recent, more resource efficient algorithms like [6, 10].

References

1. Aytar, Y., Pfaff, T., Budden, D., Paine, T.L., Wang, Z., de Freitas, N.: Playing hard exploration games by watching Youtube. CoRR abs/1805.11592 (2018). http://arxiv.org/abs/1805.11592
2. Barreto, A., et al.: Transfer in deep reinforcement learning using successor features and generalised policy improvement. In: Proceedings of the 35th International Conference on Machine Learning, ICML 2018 (2018). http://proceedings.mlr.press/v80/barreto18a.html
3. Barreto, A., et al.: Successor features for transfer in reinforcement learning. In: Advances in Neural Information Processing Systems 30: Annual Conference on Neural Information Processing Systems 2017 (2017). http://papers.nips.cc/paper/6994-successor-features-for-transfer-in-reinforcement-learning

4. Birck, M., Corrêa, U., Ballester, P., Andersson, V., Araujo, R.: Multi-task reinforcement learning: an hybrid A3C domain approach, January 2017
5. Czarnecki, W.M., et al.: Mix&match-agent curricula for reinforcement learning. arXiv preprint arXiv:1806.01780 (2018)
6. Espeholt, L., et al.: IMPALA: scalable distributed deep-RL with importance weighted actor-learner architectures. In: ICML 2018 (2018). http://proceedings.mlr.press/v80/espeholt18a.html
7. Gao, Y., Xu, H., Lin, J., Yu, F., Levine, S., Darrell, T.: Reinforcement learning from imperfect demonstrations. CoRR abs/1802.05313 (2018). http://arxiv.org/abs/1802.05313
8. Glatt, R., da Silva, F.L., Costa, A.H.R.: Towards knowledge transfer in deep reinforcement learning. In: BRACIS 2016 (2016). https://doi.org/10.1109/BRACIS.2016.027
9. Gupta, A., Devin, C., Liu, Y., Abbeel, P., Levine, S.: Learning invariant feature spaces to transfer skills with reinforcement learning. CoRR abs/1703.02949 (2017). http://arxiv.org/abs/1703.02949
10. Hessel, M., Soyer, H., Espeholt, L., Czarnecki, W., Schmitt, S., van Hasselt, H.: Multi-task deep reinforcement learning with PopArt. CoRR abs/1809.04474 (2018). http://arxiv.org/abs/1809.04474
11. Hester, T., et al.: Deep Q-learning from demonstrations. In: AAAI 2018 (2018). https://www.aaai.org/ocs/index.php/AAAI/AAAI18/paper/view/16976
12. Higgins, I., et al.: DARLA: improving zero-shot transfer in reinforcement learning. In: Proceedings of the 34th International Conference on Machine Learning, ICML 2017 (2017). http://proceedings.mlr.press/v70/higgins17a.html
13. Jaderberg, M., et al.: Population based training of neural networks. CoRR abs/1711.09846 (2017). http://arxiv.org/abs/1711.09846
14. Kingma, D.P., Ba, J.: Adam: a method for stochastic optimization. CoRR abs/1412.6980 (2014). http://arxiv.org/abs/1412.6980
15. Laroche, R., Barlier, M.: Transfer reinforcement learning with shared dynamics. In: AAAI 2017 (2017). http://aaai.org/ocs/index.php/AAAI/AAAI17/paper/view/14315
16. Lehnert, L., Littman, M.L.: Successor features support model-based and model-free reinforcement learning. CoRR abs/1901.11437 (2019)
17. Leong, Y.C., Radulescu, A., Daniel, R., DeWoskin, V., Niv, Y.: Dynamic interaction between reinforcement learning and attention in multidimensional environments. Neuron **93**(2), 451–463 (2017)
18. Lin, L.J.: Reinforcement learning for robots using neural networks. Technical report, School of Computer Science, Carnegie-Mellon University, Pittsburgh, PA (1993)
19. Machado, M.C., Bellemare, M.G., Talvitie, E., Veness, J., Hausknecht, M.J., Bowling, M.: Revisiting the arcade learning environment: evaluation protocols and open problems for general agents. CoRR abs/1709.06009 (2017)
20. Mnih, V., et al.: Asynchronous methods for deep reinforcement learning. In: ICML 2016 (2016). http://jmlr.org/proceedings/papers/v48/mniha16.html
21. Mnih, V., et al.: Human-level control through deep reinforcement learning. Nature (2015). https://doi.org/10.1038/nature14236
22. Parisotto, E., Ba, L.J., Salakhutdinov, R.: Actor-mimic: deep multitask and transfer reinforcement learning. CoRR abs/1511.06342 (2015). http://arxiv.org/abs/1511.06342
23. Pohlen, T., et al.: Observe and look further: achieving consistent performance on Atari. CoRR abs/1805.11593 (2018). http://arxiv.org/abs/1805.11593

24. Rajendran, J., Lakshminarayanan, A.S., Khapra, M.M., Prasanna, P., Ravindran, B.: Attend, adapt and transfer: attentive deep architecture for adaptive transfer from multiple sources in the same domain. arXiv preprint arXiv:1510.02879 (2015)
25. Rusu, A.A., et al.: Policy distillation. CoRR abs/1511.06295 (2015). http://arxiv.org/abs/1511.06295
26. Rusu, A.A., et al.: Progressive neural networks. CoRR abs/1606.04671 (2016). http://arxiv.org/abs/1606.04671
27. Schmitt, S., et al.: Kickstarting deep reinforcement learning. CoRR abs/1803.03835 (2018). http://arxiv.org/abs/1803.03835
28. Taylor, M.E., Stone, P.: Transfer learning for reinforcement learning domains: a survey. J. Mach. Learn. Res. **10**, 1633–1685 (2009). https://doi.org/10.1145/1577069.1755839
29. Teh, Y.W., et al.: Distral: robust multitask reinforcement learning. In: Advances in Neural Information Processing Systems 30: Annual Conference on Neural Information Processing Systems 2017 (2017). http://papers.nips.cc/paper/7036-distral-robust-multitask-reinforcement-learning
30. Yin, H., Pan, S.J.: Knowledge transfer for deep reinforcement learning with hierarchical experience replay. In: AAAI 2017 (2017). http://aaai.org/ocs/index.php/AAAI/AAAI17/paper/view/14478
31. Zhang, J., Springenberg, J.T., Boedecker, J., Burgard, W.: Deep reinforcement learning with successor features for navigation across similar environments. In: 2017 IEEE/RSJ International Conference on Intelligent Robots and Systems, IROS 2017 (2017). https://doi.org/10.1109/IROS.2017.8206049

Stochastic One-Sided Full-Information Bandit

Haoyu Zhao[1]([⊠]) and Wei Chen[2]

[1] Institute for Interdisciplinary Information Sciences,
Tsinghua University, Beijing, China
zhaohy16@mails.tsinghua.edu.cn
[2] Microsoft Research, Beijing, China
weic@microsoft.com

Abstract. In this paper, we study the stochastic version of the one-sided full information bandit problem, where we have K arms $[K] = \{1, 2, \ldots, K\}$, and playing arm i would gain reward from an unknown distribution for arm i while obtaining reward feedback for all arms $j \geq i$. One-sided full information bandit can model the online repeated second-price auctions, where the auctioneer could select the reserved price in each round and the bidders only reveal their bids when their bids are higher than the reserved price. In this paper, we present an elimination-based algorithm to solve the problem. Our elimination based algorithm achieves distribution independent regret upper bound $O(\sqrt{T \cdot \log(TK)})$, and distribution dependent bound $O((\log T + \log K)f(\Delta))$, where T is the time horizon, Δ is a vector of gaps between the mean reward of arms and the mean reward of the best arm, and $f(\Delta)$ is a formula depending on the gap vector that we will specify in detail. Our algorithm has the best theoretical regret upper bound so far. We also validate our algorithm empirically against other possible alternatives.

Keywords: Online learning · Multi-armed bandit

1 Introduction

Stochastic multi-armed bandit (MAB) has been extensively studied in machine learning and sequential decision making. The most simple version of this problem consists of K arms, where each arm has an unknown distribution of the reward. The task is to sequentially select one arm at each round so that the total expected reward is as high as possible. In each round, we will gain the reward and only observe the reward of the arm we choose. The trade-off between exploration and exploitation appears extensively in the MAB problem: On the one hand, one might try to play an arm which is played less to explore whether it is good, and on the other hand, one might choose to play the arm with the largest average reward so far to cumulate reward. MAB algorithms are measured by their *regret*, which is the difference in expected cumulative reward between the algorithm and the optimal algorithm that always chooses the best arm.

© Springer Nature Switzerland AG 2020
U. Brefeld et al. (Eds.): ECML PKDD 2019, LNAI 11908, pp. 150–166, 2020.
https://doi.org/10.1007/978-3-030-46133-1_10

A variant of the stochastic MAB problem is the *one-sided full-information bandit*, where there is a set of arms $1, 2, \ldots, K$ and at round t we choose arm I_t, we will gain the reward of I_t at time t and observe the rewards of all arms $i \geq I_t$ at time t (Sect. 2). The adversarial version of the one-sided full-information bandit is first introduced in [7], and in this paper, we study it stochastic version.

One-sided full-information bandit can find applications such as in online auction. Consider for example the second-price auction with a reserve price. In each round, the seller (or auctioneer) sets a reserve price from a finite set of reserve price choices. Each buyer (or bidder) draws a value from its valuation distribution (unknown to the seller), and only submits her value as the bid when her value is at least as high as the reserve price. The seller would observe these bids, give the item to the highest bidder and collect the second highest bid price (including the reserve price) as its reward from the highest bidder. In this case, we can treat each reserve price as an arm. In each round t after the seller announces the reserve price r_t, she will see all bids higher than r_t, and thus she would know the reward she could collect for all reserve prices higher than or equal to r_t, which corresponds to the case of one-sided full-information feedback.[1]

In this paper, we present an elimination-based algorithm for the stochastic one-sided full-information bandit and prove the distribution-independent bound as $O(\sqrt{T(\log T + \log K)})$ and the distribution-dependent bound as $O((\log T + \log K)f(\Delta))$, where T is the time horizon, Δ is a vector of gaps between the mean reward of arms and the mean reward of the best arm, and $f(\Delta)$ is a formula depending on the gap vector that we will specify in Theorem 2 (Sect. 3). We also adopt an existing analysis to show a distribution-independent regret lower bound of $\Omega(\sqrt{T \log K})$ for this case (Sect. 4), which indicates that our algorithm achieves almost matching upper bound. We conduct numerical experiments to show that our algorithm significantly outperforms an existing algorithm designed for the adversarial case (Sect. 5). The empirical results also indicate that a UCB variant has better empirical performance, but it so far has no tight theoretical analysis, and thus our elimination-based algorithm is still the one with the best theoretical guarantee.

1.1   Related Work

Multi-armed Bandit: Multi-armed bandit (MAB) is originally introduced by Robbins [9], and has been extensively studied in the literature (c.f. [4,5]). MAB could be either stochastic, where the rewards of arms are drawn from unknown distributions, or adversarial, where the rewards of arms are determined by an adversary. Our study in this paper belongs to the stochastic MAB category. The classical MAB algorithm includes UCB [2] and Thompson sampling [10] for the stochastic setting and EXP3 [3] for the adversarial setting.

---

[1] Note that the second-price auction is truthful in a single round, but in multi-rounds, it may not be truthful since the bidders may want to lower their bids first so that the seller would learn a lower reserve price. The truthfulness is not the main concern of this paper and its discussion is beyond the scope of this paper.

Multi-armed Bandit with Graph Feedback Structure: One-sided full-information bandit can be viewed as a special case of the MAB problem with graph feedback structure. The arm feedback structure can be represented as a graph (undirected or directed, with or without self-loops), where vertices are arms, and when an arm is played, the rewards of all its neighbors (or out-neighbors) can be observed. The one-sided full-information bandit corresponds to a feedback graph with directed edges pointing from arm i to arm j for all $i \leq j$. The first paper that introduces MAB with graph feedback is [8]. The authors of this paper use the independent number and the clique-partition number to derive the upper and lower bound for the regret. The main results of [8] is the upper and lower bound for the regret for undirected graph feedback MAB problem. Although the bound is tight in the undirected case, there is a gap between the regret upper and lower bounds for directed graphs. When translated to our one-sided full information setting, their regret upper bound is $\tilde{O}(\sqrt{KT})$ but the lower bound is $\tilde{\Omega}(\sqrt{T})$, which are not as tight as we provide in this paper in both upper and lower bounds. In [1], the authors consider the adversarial MAB with general directed feedback graph and close the gap up to some logarithmic factors. However, when applying their results to the one-sided full-information bandit setting, their upper and lower bounds are all worse than ours by a logarithmic factor. Moreover, we provide distribution-dependent bound that only works for the stochastic setting. One-sided full-information bandit is originally proposed in [7], which studies the adversarial setting and proposes a variant of EXP3 algorithm EXP3-RTB to solve this problem in the adversarial setting. Their work focuses on the more general bandit on metric space, and ignores the difference in the logarithmic factors. Stochastic MAB with undirected graph feedback is studied in [6], which proposes a variant of UCB algorithm UCB-N that essentially acts as UCB but updates all observed arms instead of only the played arm in each round. The authors derive a regret upper bound based on the cliques in the feedback graph, but in the one-sided full-information setting the cliques are reduced to singletons and their regret result is reduced to the classical UCB, which is significantly worse than the regret of our algorithm. We include UCB-N in our experiments, which demonstrate good performance of UCB-N, but we cannot provide a better theoretical regret bound for it, and this task is left as a future work item.

2   Model

In this section, we specify a multi-armed bandit model called 'one-sided full information bandit', which is highly related with the online auction problem. Suppose that there are K arms $[K] = \{1, 2, \ldots, K\}$ in total. Each time we play the arm I_t at round t, we will observe the value of arm i, denoted as $X_i^{(t)}$, for all $i \geq I_t$. We study this problem under the stochastic settings, i.e. in each round t, the realized value $X_i^{(t)}$ is drawn from a distribution ν_i, and $X_i^{(t)}$ is independent to $X_i^{(t')}$, for all $t' < t$. The formal definition of the bandit model is given as follow.

Definition 1 (One-sided Full Information Bandit). *There is a set of arms $\{1, 2, \ldots, K\}$, and for each arm $i \in [K]$, it corresponds to an unknown distribution ν_i with support $[0, 1]$, where ν_i is the marginal distribution of ν with support $[0, 1]^K$. In each round t, the environment draws a reward vector $X^{(t)} = (X_1^{(t)}, \ldots, X_K^{(t)})$, where $X^{(t)}$ is drawn from distribution ν. The player then chooses an arm I_t to play, gains the reward $X_{I_t}^{(t)}$ and observes the reward of arms $I_t, I_t + 1, \ldots, K$, i.e. observes $X_i^{(t)}, \forall i \geq I_t$.*

Remark 1. In the definition, we explicitly give the joint distribution ν to describe the value distribution of arms, and denote arm i's reward distribution ν_i as the marginal distribution of ν. This is to emphasize the fact that the distributions corresponding to different arms can be correlated.

The performance of the multi-armed bandit algorithm is measured by regret. In the stochastic bandit scenario, people will use the pseudo-regret to measure the performance more often. The pseudo regret is defined as follow,

Definition 2 (Pseudo-regret). *Let I_t denote the arm that is chosen by algorithm $\mathcal{A}$ to play at round t, then the pseudo-regret of the algorithm $\mathcal{A}$ for T rounds is defined as $\mathbb{E}[\sum_{i=t}^{T}(X_{i*}^{(t)} - X_{I_t}^{(t)})]$, where i^* denotes the best arm in expectation, i.e. $\mathbb{E}[X_{i*}^{(t)}] \geq \mathbb{E}[X_i^{(t)}]$ for all $i \in [K]$.*

In this paper, we only consider pseudo-regret, and henceforth, for convenience, we simply use the term regret to refer to pseudo-regret in the remaining text. For convenience, we will use $\mu_i = \mathbb{E}[X_i^{(t)}]$ to denote the mean of the reward of arm i, and μ_{i*} to denote the mean of the best arm. We will also use $\Delta_i = \mu_{i*} - \mu_i$ to denote the difference of the mean between arm i and the best arm i^*.

3 Algorithm and Regret Analysis

3.1 Elimination Based Algorithm

In this section, we present an elimination-based algorithm to tackle the one-sided full information stochastic bandit problem. We first show an algorithm with known time horizon T. Our algorithm can be generally described as: We maintain a set of arms S_t during the execution of the algorithm. At each round, we will play the arm that has the smallest index in S_t, i.e. $I_t \leftarrow \min_{i \in S_t} i$. At first, $S_1 = [K]$ is the set of all arms, and we will play arm 1 in the first round. At each time t we observe the rewards for the arms $I_t, I_t + 1, \ldots, K$, update the empirical mean of each arm and update the set S_t into S_{t+1}. At each round t, we will delete the arms in S_t whose empirical means are much smaller than the best empirical mean in S_t. More specifically, we have

$$m_t = \operatorname*{argmax}_{i \in S_t} \hat{\mu}_{i,t},$$

Algorithm 1. ELIM: Elimination-based algorithm with known time horizon T

Require: Time horizon T.

1: $S_0 \leftarrow \{1, 2, \ldots, K\}$.

2: $\forall i, \hat{\mu}_{i,0} = 0$.

3: **for** $t = 1, 2, \ldots, T$ **do**

4:     $\rho_t \leftarrow \sqrt{\frac{\ln(KT^2)}{2(t-1)}}$.(The confidence radius ρ_1 at time $t = 1$ is ∞).

5:     $m_{t-1} \leftarrow \text{argmax}_{i \in S_{t-1}} \hat{\mu}_{i,t-1}$.

6:     $S_t \leftarrow \{i \in S_{t-1} \mid \hat{\mu}_{m_{t-1},t-1} - \hat{\mu}_{i,t-1} \leq 2\rho_t\}$.

7:     Play the arm j, where $j \leftarrow \min_{i \in S_t} i$.

8:     Observe the reward $X_i^{(t)}, \forall i \geq j$.

9:     $\forall i \in S_t, \hat{\mu}_{i,t} \leftarrow \hat{\mu}_{i,t-1} \cdot \frac{t-1}{t} + X_i^{(t)} \cdot \frac{1}{t}$.

10: **end for**

---

where $\hat{\mu}_{i,t} = \frac{1}{t} \sum_{s=1}^{t} X_i^{(s)}$ is the empirical mean of arm i after t rounds, and

$$S_t = \{i \in S_{t-1} \mid \hat{\mu}_{m_{t-1},t-1} - \hat{\mu}_{i,t-1} \leq 2\rho_t\},$$

where ρ_t is the *confidence radius* and $\rho_t = \sqrt{\frac{\ln(KT^2)}{2(t-1)}}$ (The confidence radius ρ_1 at around $t = 1$ is ∞). Our whole algorithm is shown in Algorithm 1.

We will show that our algorithm has distribution-independent regret bounded $O(\sqrt{T(\ln K + \ln T)})$, where the best regret bound for one-sided full information bandit till now is $O(\sqrt{T \ln K \ln T})$, which is implied in [7]. Besides the distribution-independent bound, we also give a distribution-dependent bound. The following two theorems show our results, and their proofs will be provided in the next section.

Theorem 1 (Distribution independent regret bound). *Given the time horizon T, the regret of Algorithm 1 is bounded by $4\sqrt{2T \ln(KT^2)} + 3$.*

Theorem 2 (Distribution dependent regret bound). *Let $\{\Delta_{(i)}\}$ be a permutation of $\{\Delta_i \mid i \leq i^*\}$, such that $\Delta_{(1)} \geq \Delta_{(2)} \geq \cdots \geq \Delta_{(i*)} = 0$, and $C = 8 \ln(KT^2)$. Given time horizon T, the regret of Algorithm 1 is bounded by*

$$\Delta_{(1)} + \frac{C}{\Delta_{(1)}} + C \sum_{i=2}^{i^*-1} \left(\frac{1}{\Delta_{(i)}^2} - \frac{1}{\Delta_{(i-1)}^2} \right) \Delta_{(i)} + 2. \tag{1}$$

Note that the standard UCB algorithm will lead to $O(\sum_{i \in [K], \Delta_i > 0} \frac{1}{\Delta_i} \ln T) = O(\sum_{i=1}^{K-1} \frac{1}{\Delta_{(i)}} \ln T)$ distribution dependent regret. In Eq. (1), if we ignore the term $-\frac{1}{\Delta_{(i-1)}^2}$ in the summation, we could obtain the same order regret upper bound. Thus, the regret obtained above is typically better than the UCB regret. To see more clearly the difference, consider the case when the best arm i^* has mean $\mu_{i^*} = \frac{1}{2} + \varepsilon$ and all other arms $i \neq i^*$ have mean $\mu_i = \frac{1}{2}$, the original UCB will lead to $\frac{K-1}{\varepsilon} \ln T$ regret bound, and our algorithm will lead to $\frac{8 \ln(KT^2)}{\varepsilon} + 2 + \varepsilon$ regret bound. Also notice that in the distribution dependent bound, we only add up to i^*, which means that the arms which have indices larger than i^* will not contribute explicitly to the regret upper bound. This directly shows that the location of the best arm matters in our algorithm for one-sided MAB model.

Remark 2. Although the arms with indices larger than that of the best arm do not contribute explicitly to the regret bound, they do contribute to the constant 2 in Eq. (1) of Theorem 2. The contribution comes from a low probability case, which is shown in the proof in the next section.

In Algorithm 1, we assume that we know the time horizon T. Now, we apply the standard 'doubling trick' to get an algorithm with unknown time horizon T, which is shown in Algorithm 2. The distribution independent regret bound is given in Theorem 3.

Algorithm 2. Algorithm with unknown time horizon

1: **for** $i = 0, 1, \ldots$ **do**
2:     In time horizon $2^i, 2^i + 1, \ldots, 2^{i+1} - 1$, run Algorithm 1 with time horizon 2^i.
3: **end for**

Theorem 3. *The regret of Algorithm 2 is bounded by* $20\sqrt{T \ln(KT^2)} + 3\log_2 T + 3$.

3.2 Proof of Theorem 1

Because we want to observe as many arms as possible, we would like to choose an arm with a small index (a small position). In this way, our algorithm maintains a set of arms S_t in each round t, which is the set of arms that are possible to be the best arm. We could let $S_t = [K]$ for each round, then this will lead to large regret, so we would like all arms in S_t have means 'close' to the mean of the best arm, and the best arm i^* is in the set S_t. In this way, we will define "a procedure is nice at round t" in Definition 4 to describe the event that the best arm is in S_t and all of the arms in S_t have means close to that of the best arm. Then we will show in Lemma 2 that the procedure is nice at all rounds $t \leq T$ with high probability. Finally, we will use this lemma to prove Theorem 1. To begin with, we have the following definition and a simple lemma.

Definition 3. *We call the sampling is nice at the beginning of round t if $|\hat{\mu}_{i,t-1} - \mu_i| < \rho_t, \forall i \in S_{t-1}$, where $\rho_t = \sqrt{\frac{\ln(KT^2)}{2(t-1)}}, \forall t \geq 2$ and $\rho_1 = \infty$. Let $\mathcal{N}_t^s$ denote this event.*

Lemma 1. *For each round $t \geq 1$, $Pr\{\neg \mathcal{N}_t^s\} \leq \frac{2}{T^2}$.*

The proof of this lemma is simple with an application of the Hoeffding's Inequality followed by a union bound. For more detail, please see the full version [11]. Then, we have the definition for "procedure is nice at round t" and the main lemma that shows that the procedure is nice happens uniformly at all rounds with high probability. The formal definition is shown in Definition 4 and the lemma is formally stated in Lemma 2.

Definition 4. *We say that the procedure is nice during the algorithm at round t if both of the following are satisfied,*

1. $i^* \in S_t$, where $i^* = \arg\max_{i \in [K]} \mu_i$.
2. $\forall i \in S_t, \mu_{i^*} - \mu_i \leq 4\rho_t$.

Let $\mathcal{N}_t^p$ denote this event.

Lemma 2. *Let $\mathcal{M}_t = \bigcap_{s=1}^t \mathcal{N}_s^p$, then*

$$\forall t \in [T], Pr\{\neg\mathcal{M}_t\} \leq \frac{2}{T}.$$

Proof. We partition the event $\neg\mathcal{M}_t$ into disjoint events, we have

$$\neg\mathcal{M}_t = \neg\mathcal{N}_1^p \cup (\mathcal{M}_1 \cap \neg\mathcal{N}_2^p) \cup \cdots \cup (\mathcal{M}_{t-1} \cap \neg\mathcal{N}_t^p).$$

Note that $\neg\mathcal{M}_t$ is the union of disjoint events, so we have

$$Pr\{\neg\mathcal{M}_t\} = Pr\{\neg\mathcal{N}_1^p\} + \sum_{s=2}^t Pr\{\mathcal{M}_{s-1} \cap \neg\mathcal{N}_s^p\}.$$

First, it is obvious that $Pr\{\neg\mathcal{N}_1^p\} = 0$, since $\mathcal{N}_1^p$ will always happen, then we just need to bound $Pr\{\mathcal{M}_{s-1} \cap \neg\mathcal{N}_s^p\}$ for each $2 \leq s \leq t$. We have

$$Pr\{\mathcal{M}_{s-1} \cap \neg\mathcal{N}_s^p\} = Pr\left\{\left(\bigcap_{r=1}^{s-1} \mathcal{N}_r^p\right) \cap \neg\mathcal{N}_s^p\right\}$$
$$\leq Pr\{\mathcal{N}_{s-1}^p \cap \neg\mathcal{N}_s^p\}.$$

Then we prove that $\mathcal{N}_{s-1}^p \cap \neg\mathcal{N}_s^p \Rightarrow \neg\mathcal{N}^s$. In fact, if $\mathcal{N}_{s-1}^p$ happens, then we have $i^* \in S_{s-1}$, if $i^* \notin S_s$, then let $m_{s-1} = \arg\max_i \hat{\mu}_{i,s-1}$, we have

$$\mu_{i^*} - \hat{\mu}_{i^*,s-1} \geq \mu_{m_{s-1}} - \hat{\mu}_{i^*,s-1}$$
$$\geq \mu_{m_{s-1}} - \hat{\mu}_{m_{s-1},s-1} + 2\rho_s,$$

which leads to $\neg\mathcal{N}_s^s$, since either $\mu_{i^*} - \hat{\mu}_{i^*,s-1} \geq \rho_s$ or $-\mu_{m_{s-1}} + \hat{\mu}_{m_{s-1},s-1} \geq \rho_s$ must happen. If $\mathcal{N}_{s-1}^p$ and $i^* \in S_s$ happens but $\exists i \in S_s, \mu_{i^*} - \mu_i > 4\rho_s$, then

$$\mu_{i^*} - \hat{\mu}_{i^*,s-1} + \hat{\mu}_{i,s-1} - \mu_i$$
$$\geq 4\rho_s - \hat{\mu}_{i^*,s-1} + \hat{\mu}_{i,s-1}$$
$$\geq 4\rho_s - 2\rho_s$$
$$= 2\rho_s,$$

which also leads to $\neg\mathcal{N}_s^s$ by the same argument. So we have $\mathcal{N}_{s-1}^p \cap \neg\mathcal{N}_s^p \Rightarrow \neg\mathcal{N}_s^s$, then we have $Pr\{\mathcal{N}_{s-1}^p \cap \neg\mathcal{N}_s^p\} \leq P(\neg\mathcal{N}_s^s) \leq \frac{2}{T^2}$ from the previous lemma,

$$Pr\{\neg\mathcal{M}_t\} \leq Pr\{\neg\mathcal{N}_1^p\} + \sum_{s=2}^{t} Pr\{\mathcal{M}_{s-1} \cap \neg\mathcal{N}_s^p\}$$
$$\leq 0 + (t-1)\frac{2}{T^2}$$
$$\leq \frac{2}{T}.$$ □

With the result of the previous lemma, we can prove Theorem 1. The proof is just a combination of Lemma 2 and direct calculation. We first partition the regret by an event $\mathcal{M}_T = \bigcap_{j=1}^{T} \mathcal{N}_j^p$, which is defined in Lemma 2, representing the event that for all $t \leq T$, the procedure is nice at round t. From Lemma 2, we know that the event will happen with high probability, and the regret in this case can be bounded easily. Then we just relax the regret in the case that $\mathcal{M}_T$ does not happen to the worst case and we will complete the proof. The proof of the theorem is straight forward, and we put the proof details in the full version.

With Theorem 1, we can prove the regret for Algorithm 2. Direct computation will lead to Theorem 3. The detailed proof is shown in the full version.

3.3   Proof of Theorem 2

The proof of Theorem 2 is based on the following key observation. If arm j has mean value larger than that of arm $j + 1$, i.e. $\mu_j \geq \mu_{j+1}$ and $\Delta_j \leq \Delta_{j+1}$, our algorithm will first play arm j and find that arm $j + 1$ is bad and eliminate arm $j + 1$. Then it will play arm j until arm j is eliminated by the algorithm. However, if we exchange arm j and arm $j + 1$ such that in this case, $\mu_j < \mu_{j+1}$ and $\Delta_j < \Delta_{j+1}$, our algorithm will first play arm j for several times and find that arm j is bad and eliminate j, and then play arm $j + 1$ until arm $j + 1$ is eliminated. The number of total observations of arm j and arm $j+1$ is the same, but the regret of algorithm in the case of $\Delta_j < \Delta_{j+1}$ is worse then the case of $\Delta_j > \Delta_{j+1}$, because we spend more time playing the worse arm j in the first case. Therefore, the best sequence for our algorithms is $\Delta_1 \leq \Delta_2 \leq \cdots \leq \Delta_K$ with no regret, and the worst sequence is $\Delta_1 \geq \Delta_2 \geq \cdots \geq \Delta_K$. Similarly, if i^* is the index of the best arm, when its index is fixed, for any sequence of arms before i^*, we can apply the above idea to do a bubble-sort on Δ_j's to change it into the worst sequence $\Delta_1 \geq \Delta_2 \geq \cdots \geq \Delta_{i^*}$, and then use this worst sequence to bound the regret. In the following proof, we apply this bubble-sort idea to the proof of Lemma 3, which provides an upper bound to the optimal solution of a linear integer program. Then in the proof of Theorem 2, we show that the distribution-dependent regret is upper bounded by the optimal solution of the linear integer program.

Lemma 3. *Let $\{\Delta_{(i)}\}$ be a permutation of $\{\Delta_i \mid i \leq i^*\}$ such that $\Delta_{(1)} \geq \Delta_{(2)} \geq \cdots \geq \Delta_{(i^*)} = 0$, and let C be a constant. Then, let $(a_1, \ldots, a_{i^*}) \in \mathbb{N}^{i^*}$ denote the variables in the following optimization problem, the optimal value of the following optimization problem*

$$\max_{(a_1,\ldots,a_{i*})\in\mathbb{N}^{i*}} \sum_{j=1}^{i^*} a_j \Delta_j$$

$$s.t. \sum_{i=1}^{j} a_i \leq \frac{C}{\Delta_j^2} + 1, \forall j \in \{j' | a_{j'} > 0, j \neq i^*\},$$

is upper bounded by

$$\Delta_{(1)} + \frac{C}{\Delta_{(1)}} + C \sum_{i=2}^{i^*-1} \left(\frac{1}{\Delta_{(i)}^2} - \frac{1}{\Delta_{(i-1)}^2} \right) \Delta_{(i)}.$$

Proof. Let OPT denote the optimal value of the original optimization problem

$$\max_{(a_1,\ldots,a_{i*})\in\mathbb{N}^{i*}} \sum_{j=1}^{i^*} a_j \Delta_j \qquad (2)$$

$$s.t. \sum_{i=1}^{j} a_i \leq \frac{C}{\Delta_j^2} + 1, \forall j \in \{j' | a_{j'} > 0, j \neq i^*\},$$

and OPT' denote the optimal value of the modified optimization problem

$$\max_{(a_1,\ldots,a_{i*})\in\mathbb{N}^{i*}} \sum_{j=1}^{i^*} a_j \Delta_{(j)} \qquad (3)$$

$$s.t. \sum_{i=1}^{j} a_i \leq \frac{C}{\Delta_{(j)}^2} + 1, \forall j \in \{j' | a_{j'} > 0, j \neq i^*\},$$

where $\Delta_{(1)} \geq \Delta_{(2)} \geq \cdots \geq \Delta_{i^*}$ is a permutation of $\{\Delta_i\}_{i \leq i^*}$. We first show that $OPT \leq OPT'$. Suppose $\Delta_{j_0} < \Delta_{j_0+1}$. Let $\bar{\Delta}_{j_0} = \Delta_{j_0+1}, \bar{\Delta}_{j_0+1} = \Delta_{j_0}$, and for all $k \neq j_0, j_0 + 1$, $\bar{\Delta}_k = \Delta_k$, i.e. $\{\bar{\Delta}_j\}$ is obtained by exchanging 2 adjacent elements in $\{\Delta_j\}$. Let $\overline{OPT}$ denote the optimal value of the following optimization problem

$$\max_{(a_1,\ldots,a_{i^*})\in\mathbb{N}^{i^*}} \sum_{j=1}^{i^*} a_j \bar{\Delta}_j \tag{4}$$

$$\text{s.t.} \sum_{i=1}^{j} a_i \leq \frac{C}{\bar{\Delta}_j^2} + 1, \forall j \in \{j' | a_{j'} > 0, j \neq i^*\}.$$

We just have to show that $OPT \leq \overline{OPT}$, then $OPT \leq OPT'$ can be obtained by repeatedly exchanging 2 adjacent elements. To prove $OPT \leq \overline{OPT}$, we just have to show that every feasible solution in the original optimization problem (2) can be transformed into a feasible solution of the optimization problem (4), with the same objective value.

Let $x_1, \ldots, x_{i^*}$ be any feasible solution of the original optimization problem (2). Let $\bar{x}_j = x_j, \forall j \neq j_0, j_0 + 1$, and let $\bar{x}_{j_0} = x_{j_0+1}, \bar{x}_{j_0+1} = x_{j_0}$, and it is obvious that the objective value in the optimization problem (2) and (4) are the same, since we exchange the coefficient and the variable at j_0 and $j_0 + 1$ at the same time. Then we show that $\bar{x}_1, \ldots, \bar{x}_{i^*}$ is also a feasible solution in optimization problem (4).

First for all $j \neq j_0, j_0 + 1$, we have $\sum_{i=1}^{j} \bar{x}_i \leq \frac{C}{\Delta_j^2} + 1$, since it is equivalent to $\sum_{i=1}^{j} x_i \leq \frac{C}{\Delta_j^2} + 1$ and $\bar{x}_j > 0$ is equivalent to $x_j > 0$.

Then we consider the variable $\bar{x}_{j_0} = x_{j_0+1}$. If $x_{j_0+1} > 0$, we have

$$\sum_{i=1}^{j_0} \bar{x}_i \leq \sum_{i=1}^{j_0+1} \bar{x}_i = \sum_{i=1}^{j_0+1} x_i \leq \frac{C}{\Delta_{j_0+1}^2} + 1 = \frac{C}{\Delta_{j_0}^2} + 1.$$

If $x_{j_0+1} = 0$, then $\bar{x}_{j_0} = 0$ and we do not have a constraint for $j = j_0$ in problem (4).

Next we consider the variable $\bar{x}_{j_0+1} = x_{j_0}$. If $x_{j_0+1} > 0$, using $\bar{\Delta}_{j_0+1} < \bar{\Delta}_{j_0}$ we have

$$\sum_{i=1}^{j_0+1} \bar{x}_i = \sum_{i=1}^{j_0+1} x_i \leq \frac{C}{\Delta_{j_0+1}^2} + 1 = \frac{C}{\bar{\Delta}_{j_0}^2} + 1 \leq \frac{C}{\bar{\Delta}_{j_0+1}^2} + 1.$$

If $x_{j_0+1} = 0$ and $x_{j_0} > 0$, we have

$$\sum_{i=1}^{j_0+1} \bar{x}_i = \sum_{i=1}^{j_0+1} x_i = \sum_{i=1}^{j_0} x_i \leq \frac{C}{\Delta_{j_0}^2} + 1 = \frac{C}{\bar{\Delta}_{j_0+1}^2} + 1.$$

If $x_{j_0} = 0$, then $\bar{x}_{j_0+1} = 0$ and we do not need a constraint for $j = j_0 + 1$ in problem (4).

Therefore, after discussing all cases, we know that $(\bar{x}_1, \ldots, \bar{x}_K)$ is a feasible solution of the optimization problem (4). Then with our previous argument, the optimal value OPT' of optimization problem (3) is at least OPT, i.e. $OPT \leq OPT'$.

Then suppose $\{x_{r_i}\}$ is a feasible solution of the modified optimization problem (3), we have

$$
\begin{aligned}
\sum_{i=1}^{i^*} x_{r_i} \Delta_{(i)} &= x_{r_1} \Delta_{(1)} + \sum_{i=2}^{i^*} \left(\sum_{j=1}^{i} x_{r_j} - \sum_{j=1}^{i-1} x_{r_j} \right) \Delta_{(i)} \\
&= \sum_{i=1}^{i^*-1} \left(\Delta_{(i)} - \Delta_{(i+1)} \right) \sum_{j=1}^{i} x_{r_j} + \Delta_{(i^*)} \sum_{j=1}^{i^*} x_{r_j} \\
&\leq \sum_{i=1}^{i^*-1} \left(\Delta_{(i)} - \Delta_{(i+1)} \right) \left(\frac{C}{\Delta_{(i)}^2} + 1 \right) \\
&= \Delta_{(1)} + \frac{C}{\Delta_{(1)}} + C \sum_{i=2}^{i^*-1} \left(\frac{1}{\Delta_{(i)}^2} - \frac{1}{\Delta_{(i-1)}^2} \right) \Delta_{(i)},
\end{aligned}
$$

where we use the fact that $\Delta_{(i^*)} = 0$. So OPT' is also upper bounded, which complete the proof directly.   □

With the conclusion of the lemma, we can prove Theorem 2. The general idea to prove Theorem 2 is the same as proving Theorem 1. We first partition the regret by the event $\mathcal{M}_T$, which is defined in Definition 4. With Lemma 2, $\mathcal{M}_T$ will happen with high probability, and we can just consider the regret when $\mathcal{M}_T$ happens. Then we bound the regret when $\mathcal{M}_T$ happens from the help of Lemma 3.

Proof (Proof of Theorem 2). Similar to the proof of Theorem 1, we have

$$
\mathbb{E}\left[\sum_{t=1}^{T}(\mu_{i^*} - \mu_{I_t})\right] \leq \mathbb{E}\left[\sum_{t=1}^{T}(\mu_{i^*} - \mu_{I_t})|\mathcal{M}_T\right] + \mathbb{E}\left[\sum_{t=1}^{T}(\mu_{i^*} - \mu_{I_t})|\neg\mathcal{M}_T\right] \cdot \Pr\{\neg\mathcal{M}_T\},
$$

and

$$
\mathbb{E}\left[\sum_{t=1}^{T}(\mu_{i^*} - \mu_{I_t})|\neg\mathcal{M}_T\right] \leq T, \Pr\{\neg\mathcal{M}_T\} \leq \frac{2}{T}.
$$

Suppose that the arms $1, 2, \ldots, K$ are played for $a_1, a_2, \ldots, a_K$ times after T rounds and $\mathcal{M}_T$ happens, then the regret is $\sum_{i=1}^{K} a_i \Delta_i$. Then we show that when $\mathcal{M}_T$ happens,

$$
\sum_{i=1}^{K} a_i \Delta_i \leq \Delta_{(1)} + \frac{C}{\Delta_{(1)}} + C \sum_{i=2}^{i^*-1} \left(\frac{1}{\Delta_{(i)}^2} - \frac{1}{\Delta_{(i-1)}^2} \right) \Delta_{(i)}.
$$

First, we only have to consider the arm j with $j < i^*$, since if $\mathcal{M}_T$ happens, our elimination based algorithm (see Algorithm 1) will never choose arm $j > i$ to play, and for arm i^* there is no regret contribution. For arm $j < i^*$, if $a_j \neq 0$, then at the last time the algorithm plays arm j, arm j has been observed for

$\sum_{i=1}^{j} a_j - 1$ times, since we only delete the arms in set S so I_t must be non-decreasing. Then as $\mathcal{M}_T$ happens, we have

$$\Delta_j \leq 4\sqrt{\frac{\ln(KT^2)}{2(\sum_{i=1}^{j} a_i - 1)}},$$

which will lead to

$$\sum_{i=1}^{j} a_i \leq \frac{C}{\Delta_j^2} + 1,$$

where $C = 8\ln(KT^2)$ as defined in Theorem 2. Then we can conclude that when $\mathcal{M}_T$ happens, the regret is bounded by

$$\max_{(a_1,\ldots,a_{i^*})\in\mathbb{N}^{i^*}} \sum_{j=1}^{i^*-1} a_j \Delta_j$$

$$\text{s.t.} \sum_{i=1}^{j} a_i \leq \frac{C}{\Delta_j^2} + 1, \forall j \in \{j'|a_{j'} > 0, j \neq i^*\}.$$

Then from Lemma 3, we know that the optimal value of the above optimization problem is upper bounded, so we have

$$\mathbb{E}[\sum_{t=1}^{T}(\mu_{i^*} - \mu_{I_t})|\mathcal{M}_T] \leq \Delta_{(1)} + \frac{C}{\Delta_{(1)}} + C\sum_{i=2}^{i^*-1}\left(\frac{1}{\Delta_{(i)}^2} - \frac{1}{\Delta_{(i-1)}^2}\right)\Delta_{(i)}$$

Then combine with the previous result, we can finish the proof.   □

Then we have a corollary from this distribution dependent bound.

Corollary 1. *Let $\{\Delta_{(i)}\}$ be a permutation of $\{\Delta_i\}$ such that $\Delta_{(1)} \geq \Delta_{(2)} \geq \cdots \geq \Delta_{(i^*)} = 0$, and $C = 8\ln(KT^2)$ as defined in Theorem 2, then the regret is bounded by $\left(\frac{C}{\Delta_{(i^*-1)}^2} + 1\right)\Delta_{(1)} + 2$.*

4   Lower Bound

The lower bound for multi-armed bandit problems has been extensively studied. However, we notice that there is no regret lower bound for the full-information multi-armed bandit under the stochastic case. In this section, we show that the regret is lower bounded by $\Omega(\sqrt{T\log K})$ in this case, which also implies a regret lower bound of $\Omega(\sqrt{T\log K})$ for the one-sided bandit case. Comparing with the regret upper bound of $O(\sqrt{T(\log K + \log T)})$ of Theorem 1, we can see that our elimination algorithm gives almost a tight regret bound.

In this section, we fix a bandit algorithm. Let I_t denote the choice of the algorithm in round t. Let K denote the total number of arms. For each $j \in [K]$, let $\mathcal{I}_j$ denote the problem instance that $\mu_k = \frac{1}{2}$, for all $k \neq j$, $\mu_j = \frac{1+\varepsilon}{2}$ for some small $\varepsilon > 0$, and each arm is a Bernoulli random variable independent from other arms.

The proof follows from the original proof of lower bound for bandit feedback MAB problem [5], but we need more careful calculation. The original proof for the bandit feedback regret lower bound is $\sqrt{TK}$, and if we directly apply it to the full information feedback case, we would get $\sqrt{T}$ lower bound. With more careful analysis, we could raise this lower bound to $\sqrt{T \log K}$. Following the original analysis, we connect the full information MAB problem with the *bandit-with-prediction* problem, in which the algorithm is given the rewards of all arms in the first T rounds, and it needs to decide which is the best arm. We use y_T to denote the output of an algorithm of the bandit-with-prediction problem in this section. Naturally, we can select the arm with the largest cumulative rewards in the first T rounds as y_T, and this is called Follow-the-Leader strategy. Then we use the reverse Chernoff Bound (Lemma 4) to show the regret lower bound for the Follow-the-Leader strategy, and then we show that Follow-the-Leader strategy has the optimal regret among all the algorithm (up to constants). Finally, we reduce the full information MAB problem to the bandit-with-prediction problem to show its lower bound.

Lemma 4 (Tightness of Chernoff Bound). *Suppose $X_1, X_2, \ldots, X_n$ are i.i.d Bernoulli random variable with $Pr[X_1 = 1] = \frac{1}{2}$, then there exists absolute constants c', d, p such that for all $0 < \varepsilon < d$ such that $\varepsilon^2 \cdot n > p$,*

$$Pr\left\{\frac{1}{n}\sum_{i=1}^{n} X_i > \frac{1}{2} + \varepsilon\right\} > e^{-c'n\varepsilon^2}.$$

The above lemma is a well-known result. For convenience, we put the proof of this lemma in the full version. The following lemma shows that the Follow-the-Leader strategy still could make mistakes on the bandit-with-prediction task.

Lemma 5. *Suppose $\frac{c \ln K}{2\varepsilon^2} \leq T \leq \frac{c \ln K}{\varepsilon^2}$, for a small enough absolute constant c (which is not the constant in the previous lemma) and $0 \leq \varepsilon < d$ (where d is the absolute constant in the previous lemma). Consider the algorithm Follow-the-Leader for the bandits-with-prediction problem. Then for large enough K,*

$$\sum_{j=1}^{K} Pr\{y_T = j | \mathcal{I}_j\} \leq \frac{K}{4}.$$

The next lemma shows that no other algorithms can do much better than the Follow-the-Leader strategy, for the bandit-with-prediction problem.

Lemma 6. *Suppose $\frac{c \ln K}{2\varepsilon^2} \leq T \leq \frac{c \ln K}{\varepsilon^2}$, for a small enough absolute constant c, a large enough K and $0 \leq \varepsilon < d$ where d is the constant in previous lemma. Then for any (deterministic or randomized) algorithm for the bandit-with-prediction problem, there exists at least $\lceil K/3 \rceil$ arms j such that*

$$Pr\{y_T = j | \mathcal{I}_j\} \leq \frac{3}{4}.$$

We can now prove the regret lower bound of the full information bandit problem by utilizing the above result for the bandit-with-prediction problem.

Theorem 4 (Regret lower bound for full information stochastic bandits). *Fix time horizon T and the number of arms K such that $\sqrt{c \ln K / T} < d$, where c, d are the constants in Lemma 6. When K is big enough, then for any bandit algorithm, there exists a problem instance such that $\mathbb{E}[R(T)] \geq \Omega(\sqrt{T \log K})$.*

Please see the full version for the missing proofs.

5   Numerical Experiments

In this section, we show numerical experiments on our elimination based algorithm ELIM together with two other algorithms: (a) EXP3-RTB algorithm introduced in [7], which solves one-sided full information bandit in the adversarial case, and (b) UCB-N algorithm introduced in [6] to solve stochastic multi-armed bandit with side information, and it is essentially UCB but updates any arm when it has an observation, not just the arm played in the round.

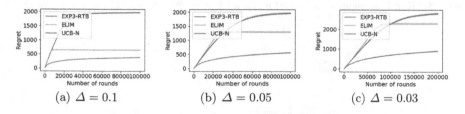

(a) $\Delta = 0.1$ (b) $\Delta = 0.05$ (c) $\Delta = 0.03$

Fig. 1. Uniform-mean suboptimal arms with $K = 20$, $Best = 17$, and varying Δ.

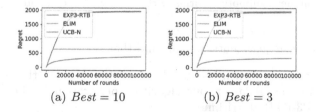

(a) $Best = 10$ (b) $Best = 3$

Fig. 2. Uniform-mean suboptimal arms with $K = 20$, $\Delta = 0.1$, and varying $Best$.

First, we do experiments when all the suboptimal arms have the same mean of 0.6 with a gap Δ towards the best arm, similar to our lower bound analysis setting. We will show results with different Δ setting (Fig. 1) and different best arm position (Fig. 2). For convenience, we let the reward of each arm follows a Bernoulli distribution. Next, we do experiments when the suboptimal arms have means drawn uniformly at random from $(0.2, 0.6)$ except for the mean of the best arm, which is set to $0.6 + \Lambda$ for a parameter Λ. We vary the value of Λ (Fig. 3) and the position of the best arms (Fig. 4).

We use T to denote the total time horizon we choose in the experiments. In most of the experiments, we choose $T = 100000$, but we will choose $T = 200000$ to better distinguish the performance between different algorithms in some cases. We use K to denote the number of arms in our experiments, and we choose $K = 20$ in all of the experiments. We use $Best$ to denote the position of the best arm, which is set to $3, 10, 17$ in different experiments. For each experiment, we run 100 times and draw the 99% confidence interval surrounding the curve (all are very narrow regions surrounding the curve).

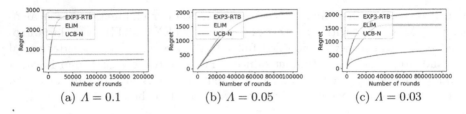

Fig. 3. Random-mean suboptimal arms with $K = 20$, $Best = 17$, and varying Δ.

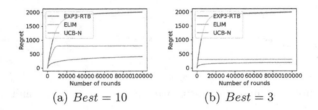

Fig. 4. Uniform-mean suboptimal arms with $K = 20$, $\Delta = 0.1$, and varying $Best$.

From the above experiments, we can find that

1. In both experiments, when the gap between the mean of the best arm and the mean of others is larger, our algorithm performs much better than the existing EXP3-RTB algorithm.
2. In the first experiments, when we change the position of the best arm, the regret line does not change so much. In the second experiments where we add more randomness, if the position of the best arm has small index, then our algorithm will perform better. However, the existing EXP3-RTB algorithm does not have this property.
3. UCB-N consistently outperforms both our algorithm ELIM and the EXP3-RTB algorithm.

Therefore, we can conclude in the stochastic setting, our elimination-based algorithm performs much better than the EXP3-RTB algorithm designed for the same problem but on the adversarial setting, and UCB-N has the best empirical performance. The issue with UCB-N is that we cannot derive a tight theoretical regret bound that also beats or even match ELIM. If we simply use UCB regret bound for UCB-N, it would be too loose and it would be inferior to our elimination based algorithm, as discussed after Theorem 2. The result in [6] on UCB-N cannot be applied here either because it requires mutually observable cliques in the observation graph but for the one-sided full-information case, the only cliques are the trivial singletons, which makes their regret bound reduced to the UCB regret bound. Therefore, our algorithm ELIM is the one that achieves the best theoretical regret bound, significantly outperform the EXP3-RTB algorithm for the adversarial case, while UCB-N has the best empirical performance with an unknown tight theoretical guarantee.

6 Conclusion and Further Work

In this paper, we study the stochastic one-sided full-information bandit and propose an elimination-based algorithm to solve the problem. We provide the upper bounds of the algorithm, and show that it almost matches the lower bound of the problem. Our experiment demonstrates that it performs better than the algorithm designed for the adversarial setting. To the best of our knowledge, our algorithm achieves the best regret bound so far.

One open problem is definitely on the analysis of UCB-N. As we have discussed, its naive regret bound such as the UCB regret bound would be much worse than our elimination algorithm, but its empirical performance shows better results. We are trying to provide a tighter analysis on UCB-N, but it evades several attempts we have made so far, and thus we left it as a future research question. Another direction is to design other algorithms that better utilizes the one-sided full-information feedback structure and achieves both good theoretical and empirical results. Other specific feedback structures corresponding to practical applications are also worth further investigation.

Acknowledgement. Wei Chen is partially supported by the National Natural Science Foundation of China (Grant No. 61433014).

References

1. Alon, N., Cesa-Bianchi, N., Gentile, C., Mansour, Y.: From bandits to experts: a tale of domination and independence. In: Advances in Neural Information Processing Systems, pp. 1610–1618 (2013)
2. Auer, P., Cesa-Bianchi, N., Fischer, P.: Finite-time analysis of the multiarmed bandit problem. Mach. Learn. **47**(2–3), 235–256 (2002)
3. Auer, P., Cesa-Bianchi, N., Freund, Y., Schapire, R.E.: The nonstochastic multiarmed bandit problem. SIAM J. Comput. **32**(1), 48–77 (2002)

4. Berry, D.A., Fristedt, B.: Bandit problems: Sequential Allocation of Experiments. Chapman and Hall, London (1985)
5. Bubeck, S., Cesa-Bianchi, N.: Regret analysis of stochastic and nonstochastic multi-armed bandit problems. Found. Trends Mach. Learn. $5(1)$, 1–122 (2012)
6. Caron, S., Kveton, B., Lelarge, M., Bhagat, S.: Leveraging side observations in stochastic bandits. In: UAI, pp. 142–151 (2012)
7. Cesa-Bianchi, N., Gaillard, P., Gentile, C., Gerchinovitz, S.: Algorithmic chaining and the role of partial feedback in online nonparametric learning. In: Proceedings of the 30th Conference on Learning Theory, pp. 465–481 (2017)
8. Mannor, S., Shamir, O.: From bandits to experts: on the value of side-observations. In: Advances in Neural Information Processing Systems, pp. 684–692 (2011)
9. Robbins, H.: Some aspects of the sequential design of experiments. Bull. Am. Math. Soc. **55**, 527–535 (1952)
10. Thompson, W.R.: On the likelihood that one unknown probability exceeds another in view of the evidence of two samples. Biometrika **25**(3/4), 285–294 (1933)
11. Zhao, H., Chen, W.: Stochastic one-sided full-information bandit. arXiv preprint arXiv:1906.08656 (2019)

BelMan: An Information-Geometric Approach to Stochastic Bandits

Debabrota Basu[1]([✉]), Pierre Senellart[2,3], and Stéphane Bressan[4]

[1] Data Science and AI Division, Chalmers University of Technology,
Göteborg, Sweden
basud@chalmers.se
[2] DI ENS, ENS, CNRS, PSL University, Paris, France
[3] Inria, Paris, France
[4] School of Computing, National University of Singapore, Singapore, Singapore

Abstract. We propose a Bayesian information-geometric approach to the exploration–exploitation trade-off in stochastic multi-armed bandits. The uncertainty on reward generation and belief is represented using the manifold of joint distributions of rewards and beliefs. Accumulated information is summarised by the barycentre of joint distributions, the *pseudobelief-reward*. While the pseudobelief-reward facilitates information accumulation through exploration, another mechanism is needed to increase exploitation by gradually focusing on higher rewards, the *pseudobelief-focal-reward*. Our resulting algorithm, BelMan, alternates between projection of the pseudobelief-focal-reward onto belief-reward distributions to choose the arm to play, and projection of the updated belief-reward distributions onto the pseudobelief-focal-reward. We theoretically prove BelMan to be asymptotically optimal and to incur a sublinear regret growth. We instantiate BelMan to stochastic bandits with Bernoulli and exponential rewards, and to a real-life application of scheduling queueing bandits. Comparative evaluation with the state of the art shows that BelMan is not only competitive for Bernoulli bandits but in many cases also outperforms other approaches for exponential and queueing bandits.

1 Introduction

The *multi-armed bandit* problem [30] is a sequential decision-making problem [11] in which a gambler plays a set of arms to obtain a sequence of rewards. In the *stochastic bandit* problem [7], the rewards are obtained from reward distributions on arms. These reward distributions belong to the same family of distributions but vary in the parameters. These parameters are unknown to the gambler. In the classical setting, the gambler devises a strategy, choosing a sequence of arm draws, that maximises the *expected cumulative reward* [30]. In an equivalent

Electronic supplementary material The online version of this chapter (https://doi.org/10.1007/978-3-030-46133-1_11) contains supplementary material, which is available to authorized users.

formulation, the gambler devises a strategy that minimises the *expected cumulative regret* [26], that is the expected cumulative deficit of reward caused by the gambler not always playing the optimal arm. In order to achieve this goal, the gambler must simultaneously learn the parameters of the reward distributions of arms. Thus, solving the stochastic bandit problem consists in devising strategies that combine both the accumulation of information to reduce the uncertainty of decision making, *exploration*, and the accumulation of rewards, *exploitation* [27]. We refer to the stochastic bandit problem as the *exploration–exploitation bandit* problem to highlight this trade-off. If a strategy relies on independent phases of exploration and exploitation, it necessarily yields a suboptimal regret bound [15]. Gambler has to adaptively balance and intertwine exploration and exploitation [3].

In a variant of the stochastic bandit problem, called the *pure exploration bandit* problem [8], the goal of the gambler is solely to accumulate information about the arms. In another variant of the stochastic bandit problem, the gambler interacts with the bandit in two consecutive phases of pure exploration and exploration–exploitation. The authors of [29] named this variant the *two-phase reinforcement learning* problem.

Although frequentist algorithms with optimism in the face of uncertainty such as UCB [3] and KL-UCB [14] work considerably well for the exploration–exploitation bandit problem, their frequentist nature prevents effective assimilation of a priori knowledge about the reward distributions of the arms [23]. Bayesian algorithms for the exploration–exploitation problem, such as Thompson sampling [34] and Bayes-UCB [21], leverage a prior distribution that summarises a priori knowledge. However, as argued in [22], there is a need for Bayesian algorithms that also cater for pure exploration. Neither Thompson sampling nor Bayes-UCB are able to do so.

Our Contribution. We propose a unified Bayesian approach to address the exploration–exploitation, pure exploration, and two-phase reinforcement learning problems. We address these problems from the perspective of information representation, accumulation, and balanced induction of bias. Here, the uncertainty is two fold. Sampling reward from the reward distributions is inherently stochastic. The other layer is due to the incomplete information about the true paramaters of the reward distributions. Following Bayesian algorithms [34], we maintain a parameterised *belief* distribution for each arm representing the uncertainty on the parameter of its reward distribution. Extending this representation, we use a joint distribution to express the two-fold uncertainty induced by both the belief and the reward distributions of each arm. We refer to these joint distributions as the *belief-reward distributions* of the arms. We set the learning problem in the statistical manifold [2] of the belief-reward distributions, which we call the *belief-reward manifold*. The belief-reward manifold provides a representation for controlling pure exploration and exploration–exploitation, and to design a unifying algorithmic framework.

The authors of [8] proved that, for Bernoulli bandits, if an exploration–exploitation algorithm achieves an upper-bounded regret, it cannot reduce the expected simple regret by more than a fixed lower bound. This drives us to first devise a pure exploration algorithm, which requires a collective representation of the accumulated knowledge about the arm. From an information-geometric point of view [1, 4], the barycentre of the belief-reward distributions in the belief-reward manifolds serves as a succinct summary. We refer to this barycentre as the *pseudobelief-reward*. We prove the pseudobelief-reward to be a unique representation in the manifold. Though pseudobelief-reward facilitates the accumulation of knowledge, it is essential for the exploration-exploitation bandit problem to also incorporate a mechanism that gradually concentrates on higher rewards [27]. We introduce a distribution that induces such an increasing exploitative bias. We refer to this distribution as the *focal distribution*. We incorporate it into the definition of the pseudobelief-reward distribution to construct the *pseudobelief-focal-reward distribution*. This pushes the summarised representation towards the arms having higher expected rewards. We implement the focal distribution using an exponential function of the form $\exp(X/\tau(t))$, where X is the reward, and a parameter $\tau(t)$ dependent on time t and named as *exposure*. Exposure controls the exploration–exploitation trade-off.

In Sect. 2, we apply these information-geometric constructions to develop the BelMan algorithm. BelMan projects the pseudobelief-focal-reward onto belief-rewards to select an arm. As it is played and a reward is collected, BelMan updates the belief-reward distribution of the corresponding arm by projecting of the updated belief-reward distributions onto the pseudobelief-focal-reward. Information geometrically these two projections are studied as information (I-) and reverse information (rI-) projections [10], respectively. BelMan alternates I- and rI-projections between belief-reward distributions of the arms and the pseudobelief-focal-reward distribution for arm selection and information accumulation. We prove the law of convergence of the pseudobelief-focal-reward distribution for BelMan, and that BelMan asymptotically converges to the choice of the optimal arm. BelMan can be tuned, using the exposure, to support a continuum from pure exploration to exploration–exploitation, as well as two-phase reinforcement learning.

We instantiate BelMan for distributions of the exponential family [6]. These distributions lead to analytical forms that allows derivation of well-defined and unique I- and rI-projections as well as to devise an effective and fast computation. In Sect. 3, we empirically evaluate the performance of BelMan on different sets of arms and parameters for Bernoulli and exponential distributions, thus showing its applicability to both discrete and continuous rewards. Experimental results validate that BelMan asymptotically achieves logarithmic regret. We compare BelMan with state-of-the-art algorithms: UCB [3], KL-UCB, KL-UCB-Exp [14], Bayes-UCB [21], Thompson sampling [34], and Gittins index [17], in these different settings. Results demonstrate that BelMan is not only competitive but also outperforms existing algorithms for challenging setups such as those involving many arms and continuous rewards. For the two-phase reinforcement learning, results show that BelMan spontaneously adapts to the explored information, improving the efficiency.

We also instantiate BelMan to the application of queueing bandits [24]. Queueing bandits represent the problem of scheduling jobs in a multi-server queueing system with unknown service rates. The goal of the corresponding scheduling algorithm is to minimise the number of jobs in hold while also learning the service rates. A comparative performance evaluation for queueing systems with Bernoulli service rates show that BelMan performs significantly better than the existing algorithms, such as Q-UCB, Q-ThS, and Thompson sampling.

2   Methodology

Bandit Problem. We consider a finite number $K > 1$ of independent arms. An arm a corresponds to a reward distribution $f_\theta^a(X)$. We assume that the form of the probability distribution $f.(X)$ is known to the algorithm but the parametrisation $\theta \in \Theta$ is unknown. We assume the reward distributions of all arms to be identical in form but to vary over the parametrisation θ. Thus, we refer to $f_\theta^a(X)$ as $f_{\theta_a}(X)$ for specificity. The agent sequentially chooses an arm a_t at each time step t that generates a sequence of rewards $[x_t]_{t=1}^T$, where $T \in \mathbb{N}$ is the time horizon. The algorithm computes a *policy* or strategy that sequentially draws a set of arms depending on her previous actions, observations and intended goal. The algorithm does not know the 'true' parameters of the arms $\{\theta_a^{\text{true}}\}_{a=1}^K$ a priori. Thus, the uncertainty over the estimated parameters $\{\theta_a\}_{a=1}^K$ is represented using a probability distribution $B(\theta_1, \ldots, \theta_K)$. We call $B(\theta_1, \ldots, \theta_K)$ the *belief distribution*. In the Bayesian approach, the algorithm starts with a prior belief distribution $B_0(\theta_1, \ldots, \theta_K)$ [19]. The actions taken and rewards obtained by the algorithm till time t create the history of the bandit process, $\mathcal{H}_t \triangleq [(a_1, x_1), \ldots, (a_{t-1}, x_{t-1})]$. This history $\mathcal{H}_t$ is used to sequentially update the belief distribution over the parameter vector as $B_t(\theta_1, \ldots, \theta_K) \triangleq \mathbb{P}(\theta_1, \ldots, \theta_K \mid \mathcal{H}_t)$. We define the space consisting of all such distributions over $\{\theta_a\}_{a=1}^K$ as the *belief space* $\mathcal{B}$. Following the stochastic bandit literature, we assume the arms to be independent, and perform Bayesian updates of beliefs.

Assumption 1 (Independence of Arms). *The parameters $\{\theta_a\}_{a=1}^K$ are drawn independently from K belief distributions $\{b_t^a(.)\}_{a=1}^K$, such that $B_t(\theta_1, \ldots, \theta_K) = \prod_{a=1}^K b_t^a(\theta_a) \triangleq \prod_{a=1}^K \mathbb{P}(\theta_a \mid \mathcal{H}_t)$.*

Though Assumption 1 is followed throughout this paper, we note it is not essential to develop the framework BelMan relies on, though it makes calculations easier.

Assumption 2 (Bayesian Evolution). *When conditioned over $\{\theta_a\}_{a=1}^K$ and the choice of arm, the sequence of rewards $[x_1, \ldots, x_t]$ is jointly independent. Thus, the Bayesian update at the t-th iteration is given by*

$$b_{t+1}^a(\theta_a) \propto f_{\theta_a}(x_t) \times b_t^a(\theta_a) \tag{1}$$

if $a_t = a$ and a reward x_t is obtained. For all other arms, the belief remains unchanged.

Belief-Reward Manifold. We use the joint distributions $\mathbb{P}(X, \theta)$ on reward X and parameter θ in order to represent the uncertainties of partial information about the reward distributions along with the stochastic nature of reward.

Definition 1 (Belief-reward distribution). *The joint distribution $\mathbb{P}_t^a(X, \theta)$ on reward X and parameter θ_a for the ath arm at the tth iteration is defined as the* belief-reward distribution.

$$\mathbb{P}_t^a(X, \theta) \triangleq \frac{b_t^a(\theta)f_\theta(X)}{\int\limits_{X \in \mathbb{R}} \int\limits_{\theta \in \Theta} b_t^a(\theta)f_\theta(X)\mathrm{d}\theta\mathrm{dx}} = \frac{1}{Z}b_t^a(\theta)f_\theta(X).$$

If $f.(X)$ is a smooth function of θ_a's, the space of all reward distributions constructs a smooth statistical manifold [2], $\mathcal{R}$. We call $\mathcal{R}$ the *reward manifold*. If belief B is a smooth function of its parameters, the belief space $\mathcal{B}$ constructs another statistical manifold. We call $\mathcal{B}$ the *belief manifold* of the multi-armed bandit process. Assumption 1 implies that the belief manifold $\mathcal{B}$ is a product of K manifolds $\mathcal{B}^a \triangleq \{b^a(\theta_a)\}$. Here, $\mathcal{B}^a$ is the statistical manifold of belief distributions for the ath arm. Due to the identical parametrization, the $\mathcal{B}^a$'s can be represented by a single manifold $\mathcal{B}_\theta$.

Lemma 1 (Belief-Reward Manifold). *If the belief-reward distributions $\mathbb{P}(X, \theta)$ have smooth probability density functions, their set defines a manifold $\mathcal{B}_\theta\mathcal{R}$. We refer to it as the* belief-reward manifold. *Belief-reward manifold is the product manifold of the belief manifold and the reward manifold, i.e. $\mathcal{B}_\theta\mathcal{R} = \mathcal{B}_\theta \times \mathcal{R}$.*

The Bayesian belief update after each of the iteration is a movement on the belief manifold from a point b_t^a to another point b_{t+1}^a *with maximum information gain* from the obtained reward. Thus, the belief-reward distributions of the played arms evolve to create a set of trajectories on the belief-reward manifold. The goal of pure exploration is to control such trajectories collectively such that after a long enough time each of the belief-rewards accumulate enough information to resemble the 'true' reward distributions well enough. The goal of exploration–exploitation is to gain enough information about the 'true' reward distributions while increasing the cumulative reward in the path, i.e, by inducing a bias towards playing the arms with higher expected rewards.

Pseudobelief: Summary of Explored Knowledge. In order to control the exploration, the algorithm has to construct a summary of the collective knowledge on the belief-rewards of the arms. Since the belief-reward distribution of each arm is a point on the belief-reward manifold, geometrically their barycentre on the belief-reward manifold represents a valid summarisation of the uncertainty over all the arms [1]. Since the belief-reward manifold is a statistical manifold, we obtain from information geometry that this barycentre is the point on the manifold that minimises the sum of KL-divergences from the belief-rewards of all the arms [2,4]. We refer to this minimising belief-reward distribution as the pseudobelief-reward distribution of all the arms.

Definition 2 (Pseudobelief-reward distribution). *A pseudobelief-reward distribution* $\bar{\mathbb{P}}_t(X, \theta)$ *is a point in the belief-reward manifold that minimises the sum of KL-divergences from the belief-reward distributions* $\mathbb{P}_t^a(X, \theta)$ *of all the arms.*

$$\bar{\mathbb{P}}_t(X, \theta) \triangleq \underset{\mathbb{P} \in \mathcal{B}_\theta \mathcal{R}}{\arg\min} \sum_{a=1} D_{\text{KL}}\left(\mathbb{P}_t^a(X, \theta) \| \mathbb{P}(X, \theta)\right). \tag{2}$$

We prove existence and uniqueness of the pseudobelief-reward for K given belief-reward distributions. This proves the pseudobelief-reward to be an unambiguous representative of collective knowledge. We also prove that the pseudobelief-reward distribution $\bar{\mathbb{P}}_t$ is the projection of the average belief-reward distribution $\hat{\mathbb{P}}_t(X, \theta) = \sum_a \mathbb{P}_t^a(X, \theta)$ on the belief-reward manifold. This result validates the claim of pseudobelief-reward as the summariser of the belief-rewards of all the arms.

Theorem 1. *For given set of belief-reward distributions* $\{\mathbb{P}_t^a\}_{a=1}^K$ *defined on the same support set and having a finite expectation,* $\bar{\mathbb{P}}_t$ *is uniquely defined, and is such that its expectation parameter verifies* $\hat{\mu}_t(\theta) = \frac{1}{K}\sum_{a=1}^K \mu_t^a(\theta)$.

Hereby, we establish as a unique summariser of all the belief–reward distributions. Using this uniqueness proof, we can prove that the pseudobelief–reward distribution $\bar{\mathbb{P}}$ is projection of the average belief–reward distribution $\hat{\mathbb{P}}$ on the belief–reward manifold.

Corollary 1. *The pseudobelief-reward distribution* $\bar{\mathbb{P}}_t(X, \theta)$ *is the unique point on the belief-reward manifold that has minimum KL-divergence from the distribution* $\hat{\mathbb{P}}_t(X, \theta) \triangleq \frac{1}{K}\sum_{a=1}^K \mathbb{P}_t^a(X, \theta)$.

Focal Distribution: Inducing Exploitative Bias. Creating a succinct pseudobelief-reward is essential for both pure exploration and exploration–exploitation but not sufficient for maximising the cumulative reward in case of exploration–exploitation. If a reward distribution having such increasing bias towards higher rewards is amalgamated with the pseudobelief-reward, the resulting belief-reward distribution provides a representation in the belief-reward manifold to balance the exploration–exploitation. Such a reward distribution is called the *focal distribution*. The product of the pseudobelief-reward and the focal distribution jointly represents the summary of explored knowledge and exploitation bias using a single belief-reward distribution. We refer to this as the *pseudobelief-focal-reward distribution-reward distribution* In this paper, we use $\exp\left(\frac{X}{\tau(t)}\right)$ with a time dependent and controllable parameter $\tau(t)$ as the reward distribution inducing increasing exploitation bias.

Definition 3 (Focal Distribution). *A focal distribution is a reward distribution of the form* $L_t(X) \propto \exp\left(\frac{X}{\tau(t)}\right)$, *where* $\tau(t)$ *is a decreasing function of* $t \geqslant 1$. *We term* $\tau(t)$ *the* exposure *of the focal distribution.*

Thus, the pseudobelief-focal-reward distribution-reward distribution is represented as $\bar{\mathbb{Q}}(X, \theta) \triangleq \frac{1}{\bar{Z}_t}\bar{\mathbb{P}}(X, \theta)\exp\left(\frac{X}{\tau(t)}\right)$, where the normalisation factor $\bar{Z}_t = \int_{X \in \mathbb{R}}\int_{\theta \in \Theta}\bar{\mathbb{P}}(X, \theta)\exp\left(\frac{X}{\tau(t)}\right)d\theta dx$. Following Equation (2), we compute the pseudobelief-focal-reward distribution as

$$\bar{\mathbb{Q}}_t(X, \theta) \triangleq \underset{\bar{\mathbb{Q}}}{\arg\min} \sum_{a=1}^{K} D_{\mathrm{KL}}\left(\mathbb{P}_{t-1}^a(X, \theta) \,\|\, \bar{\mathbb{Q}}(X, \theta)\right).$$

The focal distribution gradually concentrates on higher rewards as the exposure $\tau(t)$ decreases with time. Thus, it constrains using KL-divergence to choose distributions with higher rewards and induces the exploitive bias. From Theorem 3, we obtain $\frac{1}{\tau(t)}$ has to grow in the order $\Omega(\frac{1}{\sqrt{t}})$ for exploration–exploitation bandit problem independent of the family of reward distribution. Following the bounds obtained in [14], we set the exposure $\tau(t) = [\log(t) + C \times \log(\log(t))]^{-1}$ for experimental evaluation, where C is a constant (we choose the value $C = 15$ in the experiments) . As the exposure $\tau(t)$ decreases with t, the focal distribution gets more concentrated on higher reward values. For the pure exploration bandits, we set the exposure $\tau(t) = \infty$ to remove any bias towards higher reward values i.e, exploitation.

Algorithm 1. BelMan

1: **Input:** Time horizon T, Number of arms K, Prior on parameters B_0, Reward function f, Exposure $\tau(t)$.
2: **for** $t = 1$ **to** T **do**
3:     /* I-projection */
4:     Draw arm a_t such that

$$a_t = \underset{a}{\arg\min}\, D_{\mathrm{KL}}\left(\mathbb{P}_{t-1}^a(X, \theta) \,\|\, \bar{\mathbb{Q}}_{t-1}(X, \theta)\right).$$

5:     /* Accumulation of observables */
6:     Sample a reward x_t out of $f_{\theta_{a_t}}$.
7:     Update the belief-reward distribution of a_t to $\mathbb{P}_t^a(X, \theta)$ using Bayes' theorem.
8:     /* Reverse I-projection */
9:     Update the pseudobelief-reward distribution to

$$\bar{\mathbb{Q}}_t(X, \theta) = \underset{\bar{\mathbb{Q}} \in \mathcal{B}_\theta \mathcal{R}}{\arg\min} \sum_{a=1}^{K} D_{\mathrm{KL}}\left(\mathbb{P}_t^a(X, \theta) \,\|\, \bar{\mathbb{Q}}(X, \theta)\right).$$

10: **end for**

BelMan: An Alternating Projection Scheme. A bandit algorithm performs three operations in each step– chooses an arm, samples from the reward distribution of the chosen arm and incorporate the sampled reward to update the knowledge-base. BelMan (Algorithm 1) performs the first and the last operations by alternately minimising the KL-divergence $D_{\mathrm{KL}}(. \,\|\, .)$ [25] between the belief-reward distributions of the arms and the pseudobelief-focal-reward distribution-reward distribution. BelMan chooses to play the arm whose belief-reward incurs minimum KL-divergence with respect to the pseudobelief-focal-reward distribution. Following that, BelMan uses the reward collected from the played arm to do Bayesian update of the belief-reward and to update the pseudobelief-focal-reward distribution-reward distribution to the point minimising the sum of KL-divergences from the belief-rewards of all the arms. [10] geometrically formulated such minimisation of KL-divergence with respect to a participating distribution as a projection to the set of the other distributions. For a given t, the belief-reward distributions of all the arms $\mathbb{P}_t^a(X, \boldsymbol{\theta})$ form a set $\mathcal{P} \subset \mathcal{B}_\theta \mathcal{R}$ and the pseudobelief-focal-reward distribution-reward distributions $\bar{\mathbb{Q}}_t(X, \boldsymbol{\theta})$ constitute another set $\mathcal{Q} \subset \mathcal{B}_\theta \mathcal{R}$.

Definition 4 (I-projection). *The* information projection *(or I-projection) of a distribution* $\bar{\mathbb{Q}} \in \mathcal{Q}$ *onto a non-empty, closed, convex set* $\mathcal{P}$ *of probability distributions,* $\mathbb{P}^a$ *'s, defined on a fixed support set is defined by the probability distribution* $\mathbb{P}^{a*} \in \mathcal{P}$ *that has minimum KL-divergence to q:* $\mathbb{P}^{a*} \triangleq \underset{\mathbb{P}^a \in \mathcal{P}}{\arg\min} D_{\mathrm{KL}}(\mathbb{P}^a \| \bar{\mathbb{Q}})$.

BelMan decides which arm to pull by an I-projection of the pseudobelief-focal-reward distribution onto the beliefs-rewards of each of the arms (Lines 3–4). This operation amounts to computing

$$a_t \triangleq \underset{a}{\arg\min} \, D_{\mathrm{KL}}\left(\mathbb{P}_{t-1}^a(X, \theta) \| \bar{\mathbb{Q}}_{t-1}(X, \theta)\right)$$

$$= \underset{a}{\arg\max} \left(\mathbb{E}_{\mathbb{P}_{t-1}^a(X,\theta)}\left[\frac{X}{\tau(t)}\right] - D_{\mathrm{KL}}\left(b_{t-1}^a(\theta) \| b_{\bar{\eta}_{t-1}}(\theta)\right)\right)$$

The first term symbolises the expected reward of arm a. Maximising this term alone is analogous to greedily exploiting the present information about the arms. The second term quantifies the amount of uncertainty that can be decreased if arm a is chosen on the basis of the present pseudobelief. The exposure $\tau(t)$ of the focal distribution keeps a weighted balance between exploration and exploitation. Decreasing $\tau(t)$ decreases the exploration with time which is quite an intended property of an exploration–exploitation algorithm.

Following that (Line 5–7), the agent plays the chosen arm a_t and samples a reward x_t. This observation is incorporated in the belief of the arm using Bayes' rule of Eq. (1).

Definition 5 (rI-projection). *The* reverse information projection *(or rI-projection) of a distribution* $\mathbb{P}^a \in \mathcal{P}$ *onto* $\mathcal{Q}$, *which is also a non-empty, closed, convex set of probability distributions on a fixed support set, is defined by the distribution* $\bar{\mathbb{Q}}^* \in \mathcal{Q}$ *that has minimum KL-divergence from* $\mathbb{P}^a$: $\bar{\mathbb{Q}}^* \triangleq \underset{\bar{\mathbb{Q}} \in \mathcal{Q}}{\arg\min} D_{\mathrm{KL}}(\mathbb{P}^a \| \bar{\mathbb{Q}})$.

Theorem 2 (Central limit theorem). *If* $\tilde{\bar{\mu}}_T \triangleq \frac{1}{K}\sum_{a=1}^K \tilde{\mu}_{t_T^a}^a$ *is estimator of the expectation parameters of the pseudobelief distribution,* $\sqrt{T}(\tilde{\bar{\mu}}_T - \bar{\mu})$ *converges in distribution to a centered normal random vector in* $\mathcal{N}(0, \bar{\Sigma})$. *The covariance matrix* $\bar{\Sigma} = \sum_{a=1}^K \lambda_a \Sigma^a$ *such that* $\frac{T}{K^2 t_T^a}$ *tends to* λ^a *as* $T \to \infty$.

Theorem 2 shows that the parameters of pseudobelief can be constantly esti-mated and their estimation would depend on the accuracy of the estimators of individual arms with a weight on the number of draws on the corresponding arms. Thus, the uncertainty in the estimation of the parameter is more influ-enced by the arm that is least drawn and less influenced by the arm most drawn. In order to decrease the uncertainty corresponding to pseudobelief, we have to draw the arms less explored.

We need an additional assumption before moving into the asymptotic con-sistency claim in Theorem 3.

Assumption 3 (Bounded log-likelihood ratios). *The log-likelihood of the posterior belief distribution at time t with respect to the true posterior belief distribution is bounded such that $\lim_{t \to \infty} \left| \log \frac{\mathbb{P}^a(X,\theta)}{\mathbb{P}^a_t(X,\theta)} \right| \leqslant C < \infty$ for all a.*

This assumption helps to control the convergence of sample KL divergences in to the true KL-divergences as the number of samples grow infinitely. This is a relaxed version of Assumption 2 employed in [18] to bound the regret of Thompson sampling. This is also often used in the statistics literature to control the convergence rate of posterior distributions [33,35].

Theorem 3 (Asymptotic consistency). *Given $\tau(t) = \frac{1}{\log t + c \times \log \log t}$ for any $c \geqslant 0$, BelMan will asymptotically converge to choosing the optimal arm in case of a bandit with bounded reward and finite arms. Mathematically, if there exists $\mu^* \triangleq \max_a \mu(\theta_a)$,*

$$\lim_{T \to \infty} \frac{1}{T} \mathbb{E} \left[\sum_{t=1}^{T} X_{a_t} \right] = \mu^*. \tag{3}$$

We intuitively validate this claim. We can show the KL-divergence between belief-reward of arm a and the pseudobelief-focal-reward is $D_{\mathrm{KL}}(\mathbb{P}^a_t(X,\theta) \parallel \bar{\mathbb{Q}}(X,\theta)) = (1 - \lambda^a)h(b^a_t) - \frac{1}{\tau(t)}\mu^a_t$, for λ^a computed as per Theorem 2. Here, $h(b^a_t)$ denotes the entropy of belief distribution b^a_t of arm a at time t. As $t \to \infty$, the entropy of belief on each arm reduces to a constant dependent on its internal entropy. Thus, when $\frac{1}{\tau(t)}$ exceeds the entropy term for a large t, BelMan greedily chooses the arm with highest expected reward. Hence, BelMan is asymptotically consistent.

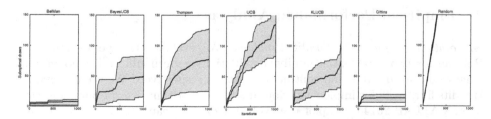

Fig. 1. Evolution of number of suboptimal draws for 2-arm Bernoulli bandit with expected rewards 0.8 and 0.9 for 1000 iterations. The dark black line shows the average over 25 runs. The grey area shows the 75 percentile.

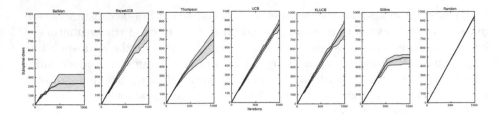

Fig. 2. Evolution of number of suboptimal draws for 20-arm Bernoulli bandit with expected rewards [0.25 0.22 0.2 0.17 0.17 0.2 0.13 0.13 0.1 0.07 0.07 0.05 0.05 0.05 0.02 0.02 0.02 0.01 0.01 0.01] for 1000 iterations.

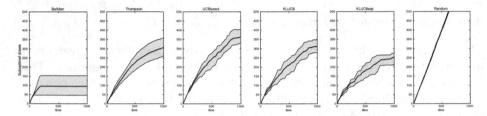

Fig. 3. Evolution of number of suboptimal draws for 5-arm bounded exponential bandit with expected rewards 0.2, 0.25, 0.33, 0.5, and 1.0 for 1000 iterations.

BelMan is applicable to any belief-reward distribution for which KL-divergence is computable and finite. Additionally for reward distributions belonging to the exponential family of distributions, the belief distributions, being conjugate to the reward distributions, also belong to the exponential family [6]. This makes belief-reward distributions flat with respect to KL-divergence. Thus, both I-and rI-projections in BelMan are well-defined and unique for exponential family reward distributions. Furthermore, if we identify the belief-reward distributions with expectation parameters, we obtain the pseudobelief as an affine sum of them. This allows us to compute belief-reward distribution directly instead of computing its dependence on each belief-reward separately. The exponential family includes the majority of the distributions found in the bandit literature such as Bernoulli, beta, Gaussian, Poisson, exponential, and χ^2.

3   Empirical Performance Analysis

Exploration–Exploitation Bandit Problem. We evaluate the performance of BelMan for two exponential family distributions – Bernoulli and exponential. They stand for discrete and continuous rewards respectively. We use the pyma-Bandits library [9] for implementation of all the algorithms except ours, and run it on MATLAB 2014a. We plot the evolution of the mean and the 75 percentile of cumulative regret and number of suboptimal draws. For each instance, we run experiments for 25 runs each consisting of 1000 iterations. We begin with uniform distribution over corresponding parameters as the initial prior distribution for all the Bayesian algorithms.

We compare the performance of BelMan with frequentist methods like UCB [3] and KL-UCB [14], and Bayesian methods like Thompson sampling [34] and Bayes-UCB [21]. For Bernoulli bandits, we also compare with Gittins index [17] which is the optimal algorithm for Markovian finite arm independent bandits with discounted rewards. Though we are not specifically interested in the discounted case, Gittins' algorithm is indeed transferable to the finite horizon setting with slight manipulation. Though it is often computationally intractable, we use it as the optimal baseline for Bernoulli bandits. We also plot performance of the uniform sampling method (*Random*), as a naïve baseline.

From Figs. 1, 2, and 3, we observe that at the very beginning the number of suboptimal draws of BelMan grows linearly and then transitions to a state of slow growth. This initial linear growth of suboptimal draws followed by a logarithmic growth is an intended property of any optimal bandit algorithm as can be seen in the performance of competing algorithms and also pointed out by [16]: an initial phase dominated by exploration and a second phase dominated by exploitation. The phase change indicates the ability of the algorithm to reduce uncertainty by learning after a certain number of iterations, and to find a trade-off between exploration and exploitation. For the 2-arm Bernoulli bandit ($\theta_1 = 0.8, \theta_2 = 0.9$), BelMan performs comparatively well with respect to the contending algorithms, achieving the phase of exploitation faster than others, with significantly less variance. Figure 2 depicts similar features of BelMan for 20-arm Bernoulli bandits (with means 0.25, 0.22, 0.2, 0.17, 0.17, 0.2, 0.13, 0.13, 0.1, 0.07, 0.07, 0.05, 0.05, 0.05, 0.02, 0.02, 0.02, 0.01, 0.01, and 0.01). Since more arms ask for more exploration and more suboptimal draws, all algorithms show higher regret values. On all experiments performed, BelMan outperforms the competing approaches. We also simulated BelMan on exponential bandits: 5 arms with expected rewards $\{0.2, 0.25, 0.33, 0.5, 1.0\}$. Figure 3 shows that

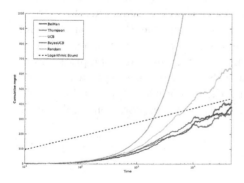
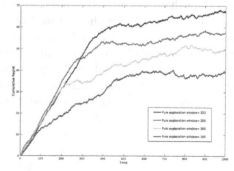

Fig. 4. Evolution of (mean) regret for exploration–exploitation 20-arm Bernoulli bandit setting of Fig. 2 with horizon=50,000.

Fig. 5. Evolution of (mean) cumulative regret for two-phase 20-arm Bernoulli bandits.

BelMan performs more efficiently than state-of-the-art methods for exponential reward distributions- Thompson sampling, UCBtuned [3], KL-UCB, and KL-UCB-exp, a method tailored for exponential distribution of rewards [14]. This demonstrates BelMan's broad applicability and efficient performance in complex scenarios.

We have also run the experiments 50 times with horizon 50 000 for the 20 arm Bernoulli bandit setting of Fig. 2 to verify the asymptotic behaviour of BelMan. Figure 4 shows that BelMan's regret gradually becomes linear with respect to the logarithmic axis. Figure 4 empirically validates BelMan to achieve logarithmic regret like the competitors which are theoretically proven to reach logarithmic regret.

Two-Phase Reinforcement Learning Problem. In this experiment, we simulate a two-phase setup, as in [29]: the agent first does pure exploration for a fixed number of iterations, then move to exploration–exploitation. This is possible since BelMan supports both modes and can transparently switch. The setting is that of the 20-arm Bernoulli bandit in Fig. 2. The two-phase algorithm is exactly BelMan (Algorithm 1) with $\tau(t) = \infty$ for an initial phase of length T_{EXP} followed by the decreasing function of t as indicated previously. Thus, BelMan gives us a single algorithmic framework for three setups of bandit problems- pure exploration, exploration–exploitation, and two-phase learning. We only have to choose a different $\tau(t)$ depending on the problem addressed. This supports BelMan's claim as a generalised, unified framework for stochastic bandit problems.

We observe a sharp phase transition in Fig. 5. While the pure exploration version acts in the designated window length, it explores almost uniformly to gain more information about the reward distributions. We know for such pure exploration the cumulative regret grows linearly with iterations. Following this, the growth of cumulative regret decreases and becomes sublinear. If we also compare it with the initial growth in cumulative regret and suboptimal draws of BelMan in Fig. 2, we observe that the regret for the exploration–exploitation phase is less than that of regular BelMan exploration–exploitation. Also, with increase in the window length the phase transition becomes sharper as the growth in regret becomes very small. In brief, there are three major lessons of this experiment. First, Bayesian methods provide an inherent advantage in leveraging prior knowledge (here, accumulated in the first phase). Second, a pure exploration phase helps in improving the performance during the exploration–exploitation phase. Third, we can leverage the exposure to control the exploration–exploitation trade-off.

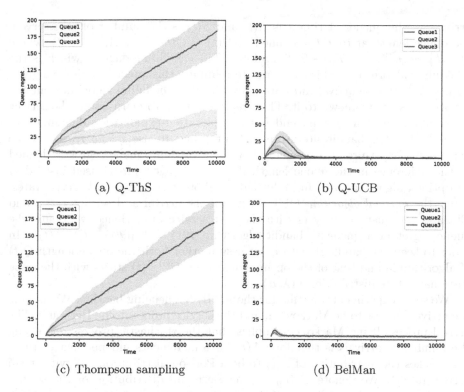

(a) Q-ThS

(b) Q-UCB

(c) Thompson sampling

(d) BelMan

Fig. 6. Queue regret for single queue and 5 server setting with Poisson arrival with arrival rate 0.35 and Bernoulli service distribution with service rates [0.5, 0.33, 0.33, 0.33, 0.25], [0.33, 0.5, 0.25, 0.33, 0.25], and [0.25, 0.33, 0.5, 0.25, 0.25] respectively. Each experiment is performed 50 times for a horizon of 10,000.

4   Application to Queueing Bandits

We instantiate BelMan for the problem of scheduling jobs in a multiple-server multiple-queue system with known arrival rates and unknown service rates. The goal of the agent is to choose such a server for the given system such that the total queue length, i.e. the jobs waiting in the queue, will be as less as possible. This problem is referred as the queueing bandit [24].

We consider a discrete-time queueing system with 1 queue and K servers. The servers are indexed by $a \in \{1, \dots, K\}$. Arrivals to the queue and service offered by the servers are assumed to be independent and identically distributed across time. The mean arrival rate is $\lambda \in \mathbb{R}^+$. The mean service rates are denoted by $\boldsymbol{\mu} \in \{\mu_a\}_{a=1}^K$, where μ_a is the service rate of server a. At a time, a server can serve the jobs coming from a queue only. We assume the queue to be stable i.e, $\lambda < \max_{a \in [K]} \mu_a$. Now, the problem is to choose a server at each time $t \in [T]$ such that the number of jobs waiting in queues is as less as possible. The number of jobs waiting in queues is called the *queue length* of the system. If the number of arrivals to the queues at time t is $A(t)$ and $S(t)$ is the number of jobs served, the queue length at time t is defined as $Q(t) \triangleq Q(t-1) + A(t) - S(t)$, where $Q : [T] \rightarrow \mathbb{R}^{\geqslant 0}$, $A : [T] \rightarrow \mathbb{R}^{\geqslant 0}$, and $S : [T] \rightarrow \mathbb{R}^{\geqslant 0}$. The agent, which is the scheduling algorithm in this case, tries to minimise this queue length for a given horizon $T > 0$. The arrival rates are known to the scheduling algorithm but the service rates are unknown to it. This create the need to learn about the service distributions, and in turn, engenders the exploration-exploitation dilemma.

Following the bandit literature, [24] proposed to use *queue regret* as the performance measure of a queueing bandit algorithm. Queue regret is defined as the difference in the queue length if a bandit algorithm is used instead of an optimal algorithm with full information about the arrival and service rates. Thus, the *optimal algorithm* OPT knows all the arrival and service rates, and allocates the queue to servers with the best service rate. Hence, we define the queue regret of a queueing bandit algorithm $\Psi(t) \triangleq \mathbb{E}\left[Q(t) - Q^{\mathrm{OPT}}(t)\right]$. In order to keep the bandit structure, we assume that both the queue length $Q(t)$ of algorithm $\mathcal{A}$ and that of the optimal algorithm $Q^{\mathrm{OPT}}(t)$ starts with the same stationary state distribution $\nu(\lambda, \mu)$.

We show experimental results for the $M/B/K$ queueing bandits. We assume the arrival process to be Markovian, and the service process to be Bernoulli. The arrival process being Markovian implies that the stochastic process describing the number of arrivals is therefore $A(t)$ have increments independent of time. This makes the distribution of $A(t)$ to be a Poisson distribution [12] with mean arrival rate λ. We denote $B_a(\mu_a)$ is the Bernoulli distribution of the service time of server a. It implies that the server processes a job with probability $\mu_a \in (0, 1)$ and refuses to serve it with probability $1 - \mu_a$. The goal is to perform the scheduling in such a way that the queue regret will be minimised. The experimental results in Fig. 6 depict that BelMan is more stable and efficient than the competing algorithms: Q-UCB, Q-Thompson sampling, and Thompson sampling. We observe that in queues 2 and 3 the average service rates are lower than the corresponding arrival rates. Due to this inherent constraint, the queue 2 and 3 can have unstable queueing systems if the initial exploration of the algorithm does not damp fast enough. Though the randomisation of Thompson sampling is good for exploration but in this case playing the suboptimal servers can induce instability which affects the total performance in future.

5   Related Work

[5] posed the problem of discounted reward bandits with infinite horizon as a single-state Markov decision process [17] and proposed an algorithm for computing deterministic Gittins indices to choose the arm to play. Though Gittins index is proven to be optimal for discounted Bayesian bandits with Bernoulli rewards [17], explicit computation of the indices is not always tractable and does not provide clear insights into what they look like and how they change as sampling proceeds [28]. This motivated researchers to design computationally tractable algorithms [7] that still retain the asymptotic efficiency [26].

These algorithms can be classified into two categories: frequentist and Bayesian. Frequentist algorithms use the history obtained as the number of arm plays and corresponding rewards obtained to compute point estimates of the fitness index to choose an arm. UCB [3], UCB-tuned [3], KL-UCB [14], KL-UCB-Exp [14], KL-UCB$^+$ [20] are examples of frequentist algorithms. These algorithms are designed by the philosophy of optimism in face of uncertainty. This methodology prescribes to act as if the empirically best choice is truly the best choice. Thus, all these algorithms overestimate the expected reward of the corresponding arms in form of frequentist indices.

Bayesian algorithms encode available information on the reward generation process in form of a prior distribution. For stochastic bandits, this prior consists of K belief distributions on the arms. The history obtained by playing the bandit game is used to update the posterior distribution. This posterior distribution is further used to choose the arm to play. Thompson sampling [34], information-directed sampling [32], Bayes-UCB [20], and BelMan are Bayesian algorithms.

In a variant of the stochastic bandit problem, called the *pure exploration bandit* problem [8], the goal of the gambler is solely to accumulate information about the arms. In another variant of the stochastic bandit problem, the gambler interacts with the bandit in two consecutive phases of pure exploration and exploration–exploitation. [29] named this variant the *two-phase reinforcement learning* problem. Two-phase reinforcement learning gives us a middle ground between model-free and model-dependent approaches in decision making which is often the path taken by a practitioner [13]. As frequentist methods are well-tuned for exploration-exploitation bandits, a different set of algorithms need to be developed for pure exploration bandits [8]. [23] pointed out the lack of Bayesian methods to do so. This motivated recent developments of Bayesian algorithms [31] which are modifications of their exploration–exploitation counterparts such as Thompson sampling. BelMan leverages its geometric insight to manage the pure exploration bandits only by turning the exposure to infinity. Thus, it provides a single framework to manage the pure exploration, exploration–exploitation, and two-phase reinforcement learning problems only by tuning the exposure.

6   Conclusion

BelMan implements a generic Bayesian information-geometric approach for stochastic multi-armed bandit problems. It operates in a statistical manifold constructed by the joint distributions of beliefs and rewards. Their barycentre, the pseudobelief-reward, summaries the accumulated information and forms the basis of the exploration component. The algorithm is further extended by composing the pseudobelief-reward distribution with a reward distribution that gradually concentrates on higher rewards by means of a time-dependent function, the exposure. In short, BelMan addresses the issue of the adaptive balance of exploration-exploitation from the perspective of information representation, accumulation, and balanced induction of exploitative bias. Consequently,

BelMan can be uniformly tuned to support pure exploration, exploration–exploitation, and two-phase reinforcement learning problems. BelMan, when instantiated to rewards modelled by any distribution of the exponential family, conveniently leads to analytical forms that allow derivation of a well-defined and unique projection as well as to devise an effective and fast computation. In queueing bandits, the agent tries and minimises the queue length while also learning the unknown service rates of multiple servers. Comparative performance evaluation shows BelMan to be more stable and efficient than existing algorithms in the queueing bandit literature.

We are investigating the analytical asymptotic efficiency and stability of BelMan. We are also investigating how BelMan can be extended to other settings such as dependent arms, non-parametric distributions and continuous arms.

Software

For the code of the queueing bandits, check: https://github.com/Debabrota-Basu/QBelMan.

Acknowledgement. We would like to thank Jonathan Scarlett for valuable discussions. This work is partially supported by WASP-NTU grant, the National University of Singapore Institute for Data Science project WATCHA, and Singapore Ministry of Education project Janus.

References

1. Agueh, M., Carlier, G.: Barycenters in the Wasserstein space. SIAM J. Math. Anal. **43**(2), 904–924 (2011)
2. Amari, S.I., Nagaoka, H.: Methods of Information Geometry Translations of Mathematical Monographs, vol. 191. American Mathematical Society, Providence (2007)
3. Auer, P., Cesa-Bianchi, N., Fischer, P.: Finite-time analysis of the multiarmed bandit problem. Mach. Learn. **47**(2–3), 235–256 (2002)
4. Barbaresco, F.: Information geometry of covariance matrix: cartan-siegel homogeneous bounded domains, mostow/berger fibration and frechet median. In: Nielsen, F., Bhatia, R. (eds.) Matrix Information Geometry, pp. 199–255. Springer, Heidelberg (2013). https://doi.org/10.1007/978-3-642-30232-9_9
5. Bellman, R.: A problem in the sequential design of experiments. Sankhyā Ind. J. Stat. (1933–1960) **16**(3/4), 221–229 (1956)
6. Brown, L.D.: Fundamentals of Statistical Exponential Families: With Applications in Statistical Decision Theory. Institute of Mathematical Statistics (1986)
7. Bubeck, S., Cesa-Bianchi, N., et al.: Regret analysis of stochastic and nonstochastic multi-armed bandit problems. Found. Trends Mach. Learn. **5**(1), 1–122 (2012)
8. Bubeck, S., Munos, R., Stoltz, G.: Pure exploration in multi-armed bandits problems. In: Gavaldà, R., Lugosi, G., Zeugmann, T., Zilles, S. (eds.) ALT 2009. LNCS (LNAI), vol. 5809, pp. 23–37. Springer, Heidelberg (2009). https://doi.org/10.1007/978-3-642-04414-4_7
9. Cappé, O., Garivier, A., Kaufmann, É.: pymaBandits (2012). http://mloss.org/software/view/415/
10. Csiszár, I.: Sanov property, generalized I-projection and a conditional limit theorem. Ann. Probab. **12**(3), 768–793 (1984)

11. DeGroot, M.H.: Optimal Statistical Decisions, Wiley Classics Library, vol. 82. Wiley, Hoboken (2005)
12. Durrett, R.: Probability: Theory and Examples. Cambridge University Press, Cambridge (2010)
13. Faheem, M., Senellart, P.: Adaptive web crawling through structure-based link classification. In: Proceedings ICADL, pp. 39–51. Seoul, December 2015
14. Garivier, A., Cappé, O.: The KL-UCB algorithm for bounded stochastic bandits and beyond. In: COLT. pp. 359–376 (2011)
15. Garivier, A., Lattimore, T., Kaufmann, E.: On explore-then-commit strategies. In: Advances in Neural Information Processing Systems 29, pp. 784–792. Curran Associates, Inc. (2016)
16. Garivier, A., Ménard, P., Stoltz, G.: Explore first, exploit next: the true shape of regret in bandit problems. arXiv preprint arXiv:1602.07182 (2016)
17. Gittins, J.C.: Bandit processes and dynamic allocation indices. J. Roy. Statis. Soc. Ser. B (Methodological) 41(2), 148–177 (1979)
18. Gopalan, A., Mannor, S.: Thompson sampling for learning parameterized Markov decision processes. In: Conference on Learning Theory, pp. 861–898 (2015)
19. Jaynes, E.T.: Prior probabilities. IEEE Trans. Syst. Sci. Cybern. 4, 227–241 (1968)
20. Kaufmann, E.: On bayesian index policies for sequential resource allocation. Ann. Stat. 46(2), 842–865 (2018)
21. Kaufmann, E., Cappé, O., Garivier, A.: On Bayesian upper confidence bounds for bandit problems. In: AISTATS, pp. 592–600 (2012)
22. Kaufmann, E., Kalyanakrishnan, S.: Information complexity in bandit subset selection. In: COLT, pp. 228–251 (2013)
23. Kawale, J., Bui, H.H., Kveton, B., Tran-Thanh, L., Chawla, S.: Efficient Thompson sampling for online matrix-factorization recommendation, In: NIPS. pp. 1297–1305 (2015)
24. Krishnasamy, S., Sen, R., Johari, R., Shakkottai, S.: Regret of queueing bandits. In: Advances in Neural Information Processing Systems. pp. 1669–1677 (2016)
25. Kullback, S.: Information Theory and Statistics. Courier Corporation (1997)
26. Lai, T.L., Robbins, H.: Asymptotically efficient adaptive allocation rules. Adv. Appl. Math. 6(1), 4–22 (1985)
27. Macready, W.G., Wolpert, D.H.: Bandit problems and the exploration/exploitation tradeoff. IEEE Trans. Evol. Comput. 2(1), 2–22 (1998)
28. Nino-Mora, J.: Computing a classic index for finite-horizon bandits. INFORMS J. Comput. 23(2), 254–267 (2011)
29. Putta, S.R., Tulabandhula, T.: Pure exploration in episodic fixed-horizon Markov decision processes. In: AAMAS, pp. 1703–1704 (2017)
30. Robbins, H.: Some aspects of the sequential design of experiments. Bull. Amer. Math. Soc. 58(5), 527–535 (1952)
31. Russo, D.: Simple Bayesian algorithms for best arm identification. In: Conference on Learning Theory, pp. 1417–1418 (2016)
32. Russo, D., Van Roy, B.: An information-theoretic analysis of Thompson sampling. J. Mach. Learn. Res. 17, 1–30 (2014)
33. Shen, X., Wasserman, L., et al.: Rates of convergence of posterior distributions. Ann. Stat. 29(3), 687–714 (2001)
34. Thompson, W.R.: On the likelihood that one unknown probability exceeds another in view of the evidence of two samples. Biometrika 25(3–4), 285 (1933)
35. Wong, W.H., Shen, X.: Probability inequalities for likelihood ratios and convergence rates of sieve MLES. Ann. Stat. 23(2), 339–362 (1995)

Ranking

A Ranking Model Motivated by Nonnegative Matrix Factorization with Applications to Tennis Tournaments

Rui Xia[1](✉), Vincent Y. F. Tan[1,2], Louis Filstroff[3], and Cédric Févotte[3]

[1] Department of Mathematics, National University of Singapore (NUS),
Singapore, Singapore
rui.xia@u.nus.edu, vtan@nus.edu.sg
[2] Department of Electrical and Computer Engineering, NUS, Singapore, Singapore
[3] IRIT, Université de Toulouse, CNRS, Toulouse, France
{louis.filstroff,cedric.fevotte}@irit.fr

Abstract. We propose a novel ranking model that combines the Bradley-Terry-Luce probability model with a nonnegative matrix factorization framework to model and uncover the presence of latent variables that influence the performance of top tennis players. We derive an efficient, provably convergent, and numerically stable majorization-minimization-based algorithm to maximize the likelihood of datasets under the proposed statistical model. The model is tested on datasets involving the outcomes of matches between 20 top male and female tennis players over 14 major tournaments for men (including the Grand Slams and the ATP Masters 1000) and 16 major tournaments for women over the past 10 years. Our model automatically infers that the surface of the court (e.g., clay or hard court) is a key determinant of the performances of male players, but less so for females. Top players on various surfaces over this longitudinal period are also identified in an objective manner.

Keywords: BTL ranking model · Nonnegative matrix factorization · Low-rank approximation · Majorization-minimization · Sports analytics

1 Introduction

The international rankings for both male and female tennis players are based on a rolling 52-week, cumulative system, where ranking points are earned from players' performances at tournaments. However, due to the limited observation window, such a ranking system is not sufficient if one would like to compare dominant players over a long period (say 10 years) as players peak at different times. The ranking points that players accrue depend only on the stage of the

Electronic supplementary material The online version of this chapter (https://doi.org/10.1007/978-3-030-46133-1_12) contains supplementary material, which is available to authorized users.

© Springer Nature Switzerland AG 2020
U. Brefeld et al. (Eds.): ECML PKDD 2019, LNAI 11908, pp. 187–203, 2020.
https://doi.org/10.1007/978-3-030-46133-1_12

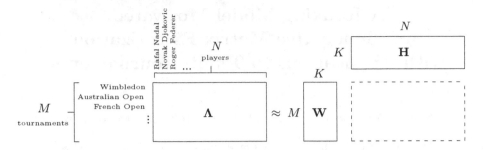

Fig. 1. The BTL-NMF model

tournaments reached by him or her. Unlike the well-studied Elo rating system for chess [1], one opponent's ranking is not taken into account, i.e., one will not be awarded with bonus points by defeating a top player. Furthermore, the current ranking system does not take into account the players' performances under different conditions (e.g., surface type of courts). We propose a statistical model to ameliorate the above-mentioned shortcomings by (i) understanding the relative ranking of players over a longitudinal period and (ii) discovering the existence of any latent variables that influence players' performances.

The statistical model we propose is an amalgamation of two well-studied models in the ranking and dictionary learning literatures, namely, the *Bradley-Terry-Luce* (BTL) model [2,3] for ranking a population of items (in this case, tennis players) based on pairwise comparisons and *nonnegative matrix factorization* (NMF) [4,5]. The BTL model posits that given a pair of players (i, j) from a population of players $\{1, \ldots, N\}$, the probability that the pairwise comparison "i beats j" is true is given by $\Pr(i \text{ beats } j) = \frac{\lambda_i}{\lambda_i + \lambda_j}$. Thus, $\lambda_i \in \mathbb{R}_+ := [0, \infty)$ can be interpreted as the *skill level* of player i and the row vector $\boldsymbol{\lambda} = (\lambda_1, \ldots, \lambda_N)$ parametrizes the BTL model. Other more general ranking models are discussed in [6] but the BTL model suffices as the outcomes of tennis matches are binary.

NMF consists in the following problem. Given a nonnegative matrix $\boldsymbol{\Lambda} \in \mathbb{R}_+^{M \times N}$, one would like to find two matrices $\mathbf{W} \in \mathbb{R}_+^{M \times K}$ and $\mathbf{H} \in \mathbb{R}_+^{K \times N}$ such that their product $\mathbf{WH}$ serves as a good low-rank approximation to $\boldsymbol{\Lambda}$. NMF is a linear dimensionality reduction technique that has seen a surge in popularity since the seminal papers by Lee and Seung [4,7]. Due to the non-subtractive nature of the decomposition, constituent parts of objects can be extracted from complicated datasets. The matrix $\mathbf{W}$, known as the *dictionary matrix*, contains in its columns the parts, and the matrix $\mathbf{H}$, known as the *coefficient matrix*, contains in its rows activation coefficients that encode how much of each part is present in the columns of the data matrix $\boldsymbol{\Lambda}$. NMF has also been used successfully to uncover latent variables with specific interpretations in various applications, including audio signal processing [8], text mining analysis [9], and even analyzing soccer players' playing style [10]. We combine this framework with the BTL model to perform a *sports analytics* task on top tennis players.

1.1   Main Contributions

Model: In this paper, we amalgamate the aforementioned models to rank tennis players and uncover latent factors that influence their performances. We propose a hybrid *BTL-NMF* model (see Fig. 1) in which there are M different skill vectors $\lambda_m, m \in \{1, \ldots, M\}$, each representing players' relative skill levels in various tournaments indexed by m. These row vectors are stacked into an $M \times N$ matrix Λ which is the given input matrix in an NMF model.

Algorithms and Theory: We develop computationally efficient and numerically stable majorization-minimization (MM)-based algorithms [11] to obtain a decomposition of Λ into $\mathbf{W}$ and $\mathbf{H}$ that maximizes the likelihood of the data. Furthermore, by using ideas from [12,13], we prove that not only is the objective function monotonically non-decreasing along iterations, additionally, every limit point of the sequence of iterates of the dictionary and coefficient matrices is a *stationary point* of the objective function.

Experiments: We collected rich datasets of pairwise outcomes of $N = 20$ top male and female players and $M = 14$ (or $M = 16$) top tournaments over 10 years. Our algorithm yielded matrices $\mathbf{W}$ and $\mathbf{H}$ that allowed us to draw interesting conclusions about the existence of latent variable(s) and relative rankings of dominant players over the past 10 years. In particular, we conclude that male players' performances are influenced, to a large extent, by the surface of the court. In other words, the surface turns out to be the pertinent latent variable for male players. This effect is, however, less pronounced for female players. Interestingly, we are also able to validate via our model, datasets, and algorithm that Nadal is undoubtedly the "King of Clay"; Federer, a precise and accurate server, is dominant on grass (a non-clay surface other than hard court) as evidenced by his winning of Wimbledon on multiple occasions; and Djokovic is a more "balanced" top player regardless of surface. Conditioned on playing on a clay court, the probability that Nadal beats Djokovic is larger than $1/2$. Even though the results for the women are less pronounced, our model and longitudinal dataset confirms objectively that S. Williams, Sharapova, and Azarenka (in this order) are consistently the top three players over the past 10 years. Such results (e.g., that Sharapova is so consistent that she is second best) are not directly deducible from official rankings because these rankings are essentially instantaneous as they are based on a 52-week cumulative system.

1.2   Related Work

Most of the works that incorporate latent factors in statistical ranking models (e.g., the BTL model) make use of mixture models. See, for example, [14–16]. While such models are able to take into account the fact that subpopulations within a large population possess different skill sets, it is difficult to make sense of what the underlying latent variable is. In contrast, by merging the BTL model with the NMF framework—the latter encouraging the extraction of *parts* of complex objects—we are able to observe latent features in the learned dictionary matrix $\mathbf{W}$ (see Table 1) and hence to extract the semantic meaning of latent variables. In our particular application, it is the surface type of the court for male tennis players. See Sect. 4.5 where we also show that our solution is more stable and robust (to be made precise) than that of the mixture-BTL model.

The paper most closely related to the present one is [17] in which a topic modelling approach was used for ranking. However, unlike our work in which continuous-valued skill levels in Λ are inferred, *permutations* (i.e., discrete objects) and their corresponding mixture weights were learned. We opine that our model and results provide a more *nuanced* and *quantitative* view of the relative skill levels between players under different latent conditions.

2   Problem Setup, Statistical Model, Likelihood

2.1   Problem Definition and Model

Given N players and M tournaments over a fixed number of years (in our case, this is 10), we consider a dataset $\mathcal{D} := \{b_{ij}^{(m)} \in \{0, 1, 2, \ldots\} : (i, j) \in \mathcal{P}_m\}_{m=1}^{M}$, where $\mathcal{P}_m$ denotes the set of games between pairs of players that have played at least once in tournament m, and $b_{ij}^{(m)}$ is the number of times that player i has beaten player j in tournament m over the fixed number of years.

To model skill levels of each player, we consider a nonnegative matrix Λ of dimensions $M \times N$. The $(m, i)^{\text{th}}$ element $[\Lambda]_{mi}$ represents the skill level of player i in tournament m. We design an algorithm to find a factorization of Λ into two nonnegative matrices $\mathbf{W} \in \mathbb{R}_+^{M \times K}$ and $\mathbf{H} \in \mathbb{R}_+^{K \times N}$ such that the likelihood of $\mathcal{D}$ is maximized. Here $K \le \min\{M, N\}$ is a small integer so the factorization is low-rank. In Sect. 3.3, we discuss different strategies to normalize $\mathbf{W}$ and $\mathbf{H}$ so that they are easily interpretable, e.g., as probabilities. Each column of $\mathbf{W}$ encodes the "likelihood" that a certain tournament m belongs to a certain latent class (e.g., type of surface). Each row of $\mathbf{H}$ encodes the player's skill level in a tournament of a certain latent class.

2.2   Likelihood of the BTL-NMF Model

According to the BTL model and the notations above, the probability that player i beats player j in tournament m is $\Pr(i$ beats j in tournament $m) = [\Lambda]_{mi}/([\Lambda]_{mi} + [\Lambda]_{mj})$. We expect that Λ is close to a low-rank matrix as the number of latent factors governing players' skill levels is small. We would like to exploit the "mutual information" or "correlation" between tournaments of similar characteristics to find a factorization of Λ. If Λ were unstructured, we could solve M independent, tournament-specific problems to learn $(\lambda_1, \ldots, \lambda_M)$. We replace Λ by $\mathbf{WH}$ and the *likelihood* over all games in all tournaments (i.e., of $\mathcal{D}$), assuming conditional independence across tournaments and games, is

$$p(\mathcal{D}|\mathbf{W}, \mathbf{H}) = \prod_{m=1}^{M} \prod_{(i,j) \in \mathcal{P}_m} \left(\frac{[\mathbf{WH}]_{mi}}{[\mathbf{WH}]_{mi} + [\mathbf{WH}]_{mj}} \right)^{b_{ij}^{(m)}}.$$

It is often more tractable to minimize the *negative log-likelihood*. In the sequel, we regard this as our objective function which can be expressed as

$$f(\mathbf{W}, \mathbf{H}) := -\log p(\mathcal{D}|\mathbf{W}, \mathbf{H})$$

$$= \sum_{m=1}^{M} \sum_{(i,j)\in\mathcal{P}_m} b_{ij}^{(m)} \Big[-\log\big([\mathbf{WH}]_{mi}\big) + \log\big([\mathbf{WH}]_{mi} + [\mathbf{WH}]_{mj}\big)\Big]. \quad (1)$$

3 Algorithms and Theoretical Guarantees

In this section, we describe the algorithm to optimize (1), together with accompanying theoretical guarantees. We also discuss how we ameliorate numerical problems while maintaining the desirable guarantees of the algorithm.

3.1 Majorization-Minimization (MM) Algorithm

The MM framework [11] iteratively solves the problem of minimizing a function $f(x)$ and its utility is most evident when the direct of optimization of $f(x)$ is difficult. One proposes an *auxiliary function* or *majorizer* $u(x, x')$ that satisfies the following two properties: (i) $f(x) = u(x, x), \forall x$ and (ii) $f(x) \leq u(x, x'), \forall x, x'$. In addition for a fixed value of x', the minimization of $u(\cdot, x')$ is assumed to be tractable (e.g., there exists a closed-form solution for $x^* = \arg\min_x u(x, x')$). Then we would like to use an iterative approach to find $\{x^{(l)}\}_{l=1}^{\infty}$. It is easy to show that if $x^{(l+1)} = \arg\min_x u(x, x^{(l)})$ then $f(x^{(l+1)}) \leq f(x^{(l)})$ so the sequence of iterates results in a sequence of non-increasing objective values.

Applying MM to our model is more involved as we are trying to find *two* nonnegative matrices $\mathbf{W}$ and $\mathbf{H}$. Borrowing ideas from using MM in NMFs problems (see [18,19]), the procedure first updates $\mathbf{W}$ by keeping $\mathbf{H}$ fixed, then updates $\mathbf{H}$ by keeping $\mathbf{W}$ fixed to its previously updated value. We will describe, in the following, how to optimize the original objective in (1) with respect to $\mathbf{W}$ with fixed $\mathbf{H}$ as the other optimization proceeds in an almost[1] symmetric fashion since $\mathbf{\Lambda}^T = \mathbf{H}^T \mathbf{W}^T$. As mentioned above, the MM algorithm requires us to construct an auxiliary function $u_1(\mathbf{W}, \tilde{\mathbf{W}}|\mathbf{H})$ that majorizes $-\log p(\mathcal{D}|\mathbf{W}, \mathbf{H})$.

The difficulty in optimizing (1) is twofold. The first concerns the coupling of the two terms $[\mathbf{WH}]_{mi}$ and $[\mathbf{WH}]_{mj}$ inside the logarithm. We resolve this using a technique introduced by Hunter in [20]. It is known that for any concave function f, $f(y) \leq f(x) + \nabla f(x)^T (y - x)$. Since the logarithm function is concave, we $\log y \leq \log x + \frac{1}{x}(y - x)$ with equality when $x = y$. These two properties mean that the following is a majorizer of the term $\log([\mathbf{WH}]_{mi} + [\mathbf{WH}]_{mj})$ in (1):

$$\log\big([\mathbf{W}^{(l)}\mathbf{H}]_{mi} + [\mathbf{W}^{(l)}\mathbf{H}]_{mj}\big) + \frac{[\mathbf{WH}]_{mi} + [\mathbf{WH}]_{mj}}{[\mathbf{W}^{(l)}\mathbf{H}]_{mi} + [\mathbf{W}^{(l)}\mathbf{H}]_{mj}} - 1.$$

---

[1] The updates for $\mathbf{W}$ and $\mathbf{H}$ are not symmetric because the data is in the form of a 3-way tensor $\{b_{ij}^{(m)}\}$; this is also apparent in (1) and the updates in (2).

The second difficulty in optimizing (1) concerns $\log([\mathbf{WH}]_{mi}) = \log(\sum_k w_{mk} h_{ki})$. By introducing the terms $\gamma_{mki}^{(l)} := w_{mk}^{(l)} h_{ki}/[\mathbf{W}^{(l)}\mathbf{H}]_{mi}$ for $k \in \{1, ..., K\}$ (which have the property that $\sum_k \gamma_{mki}^{(l)} = 1$) to the sum in $\log(\sum_k w_{mk} h_{ki})$ as was done by Févotte and Idier in [18], and using the convexity of $-\log x$ and Jensen's inequality, we obtain the following majorizer of the term $-\log([\mathbf{WH}]_{mi})$ in (1):

$$-\sum_k \frac{w_{mk}^{(l)} h_{ki}}{[\mathbf{W}^{(l)}\mathbf{H}]_{mi}} \log\left(\frac{w_{mk}}{w_{mk}^{(l)}}[\mathbf{W}^{(l)}\mathbf{H}]_{mi}\right).$$

The same procedure can be applied to find an auxiliary function $u_2(\mathbf{H}, \tilde{\mathbf{H}}|\mathbf{W})$ for the optimization for $\mathbf{H}$. Minimization of the two auxiliary functions with respect to $\mathbf{W}$ and $\mathbf{H}$ leads to the following MM updates:

$$\tilde{w}_{mk}^{(l+1)} \leftarrow \frac{\displaystyle\sum_{(i,j)\in\mathcal{P}_m} b_{ij}^{(m)} \frac{w_{mk}^{(l)} h_{ki}^{(l)}}{[\mathbf{W}^{(l)}\mathbf{H}^{(l)}]_{mi}}}{\displaystyle\sum_{(i,j)\in\mathcal{P}_m} b_{ij}^{(m)} \frac{h_{ki}^{(l)} + h_{kj}^{(l)}}{[\mathbf{W}^{(l)}\mathbf{H}^{(l)}]_{mi} + [\mathbf{W}^{(l)}\mathbf{H}^{(l)}]_{mj}}}, \tag{2a}$$

$$\tilde{h}_{ki}^{(l+1)} \leftarrow \frac{\displaystyle\sum_m \sum_{j\neq i:(i,j)\in\mathcal{P}_m} b_{ij}^{(m)} \frac{w_{mk}^{(l+1)} h_{ki}^{(l)}}{[\mathbf{W}^{(l+1)}\mathbf{H}^{(l)}]_{mi}}}{\displaystyle\sum_m \sum_{j\neq i:(i,j)\in\mathcal{P}_m} (b_{ij}^{(m)} + b_{ji}^{(m)}) \frac{w_{mk}^{(l+1)}}{[\mathbf{W}^{(l+1)}\mathbf{H}^{(l)}]_{mi} + [\mathbf{W}^{(l+1)}\mathbf{H}^{(l)}]_{mj}}}. \tag{2b}$$

3.2   Resolution of Numerical Problems

While the updates in (2) guarantee that the objective function does not decrease, numerical problems may arise in the implementation. Indeed, it is possible that $[\mathbf{WH}]_{mi}$ becomes extremely close to zero for some (m, i). To ameliorate this, our strategy is to add a small number $\epsilon > 0$ to every element of $\mathbf{H}$ in (1). The intuitive explanation that justifies this is that we believe that each player has some default skill level in every type of tournament. By modifying $\mathbf{H}$ to $\mathbf{H} + \epsilon \mathbb{1}$, where $\mathbb{1}$ is the $K \times N$ all-ones matrix, we obtain the objective function:

$$f_\epsilon(\mathbf{W}, \mathbf{H}) := \sum_{m=1}^M \sum_{(i,j)\in\mathcal{P}_m} b_{ij}^{(m)} \Big[-\log\left([\mathbf{W}(\mathbf{H} + \epsilon\mathbb{1})]_{mi}\right)$$
$$+ \log\left([\mathbf{W}(\mathbf{H} + \epsilon\mathbb{1})]_{mi} + [\mathbf{W}(\mathbf{H} + \epsilon\mathbb{1})]_{mj}\right)\Big]. \tag{3}$$

Note that $f_0(\mathbf{W}, \mathbf{H}) = f(\mathbf{W}, \mathbf{H})$, defined in (1). Using the same ideas involving MM to optimize $f(\mathbf{W}, \mathbf{H})$ as in Sect. 3.1, we can find new auxiliary functions, denoted similarly as $u_1(\mathbf{W}, \tilde{\mathbf{W}}|\mathbf{H})$ and $u_2(\mathbf{H}, \tilde{\mathbf{H}}|\mathbf{W})$, leading to following updates

$$\tilde{w}_{mk}^{(l+1)} \leftarrow \frac{\displaystyle\sum_{(i,j)\in\mathcal{P}_m} b_{ij}^{(m)} \frac{w_{mk}^{(l)}(h_{ki}^{(l)}+\epsilon)}{[\mathbf{W}^{(l)}(\mathbf{H}^{(l)}+\epsilon\mathbb{1})]_{mi}}}{\displaystyle\sum_{(i,j)\in\mathcal{P}_m} b_{ij}^{(m)} \frac{h_{ki}^{(l)}+h_{kj}^{(l)}+2\epsilon}{[\mathbf{W}^{(l)}(\mathbf{H}^{(l)}+\epsilon\mathbb{1})]_{mi}+[\mathbf{W}^{(l)}(\mathbf{H}^{(l)}+\epsilon\mathbb{1})]_{mj}}}, \tag{4a}$$

$$\tilde{h}_{ki}^{(l+1)} \leftarrow \frac{\displaystyle\sum_{m}\sum_{j\neq i:(i,j)\in\mathcal{P}_m} b_{ij}^{(m)} \frac{w_{mk}^{(l+1)}(h_{ki}^{(l)}+\epsilon)}{[\mathbf{W}^{(l+1)}(\mathbf{H}^{(l)}+\epsilon\mathbb{1})]_{mi}}}{\displaystyle\sum_{m}\sum_{j\neq i:(i,j)\in\mathcal{P}_m} \frac{(b_{ij}^{(m)}+b_{ji}^{(m)})w_{mk}^{(l+1)}}{[\mathbf{W}^{(l+1)}(\mathbf{H}^{(l)}+\epsilon\mathbb{1})]_{mi}+[\mathbf{W}^{(l+1)}(\mathbf{H}^{(l)}+\epsilon\mathbb{1})]_{mj}}} - \epsilon. \tag{4b}$$

Notice that although this solution successfully prevents division by zero during the iterative process, for the new update of $\mathbf{H}$, it is possible $h_{ki}^{(l+1)}$ becomes negative because of the subtraction by ϵ in (4b). To ensure h_{ki} is nonnegative as required by the nonnegativity of NMF, we set $\tilde{h}_{ki}^{(l+1)} \leftarrow \max\{\tilde{h}_{ki}^{(l+1)}, 0\}$. After this truncation operation, it is, however, unclear whether the likelihood function is non-decreasing, as we have altered the vanilla MM procedure.

We now prove that f_ϵ in (3) is non-increasing as the iteration count increases. Suppose for the $(l+1)^{\text{st}}$ iteration for $\tilde{\mathbf{H}}^{(l+1)}$, truncation to zero only occurs for the $(k,i)^{\text{th}}$ element and and all other elements stay unchanged, meaning $\tilde{h}_{ki}^{(l+1)} = 0$ and $\tilde{h}_{k',i'}^{(l+1)} = \tilde{h}_{k',i'}^{(l)}$ for all $(k',i') \neq (k,i)$. We would like to show that $f_\epsilon(\mathbf{W}, \tilde{\mathbf{H}}^{(l+1)}) \leq f_\epsilon(\mathbf{W}, \tilde{\mathbf{H}}^{(l)})$. It suffices to show $u_2(\tilde{\mathbf{H}}^{(l+1)}, \tilde{\mathbf{H}}^{(l)}|\mathbf{W}) \leq f_\epsilon(\mathbf{W}, \tilde{\mathbf{H}}^{(l)})$, because if this is true, we have the following inequality

$$f_\epsilon(\mathbf{W}, \tilde{\mathbf{H}}^{(l+1)}) \leq u_2(\tilde{\mathbf{H}}^{(l+1)}, \tilde{\mathbf{H}}^{(l)}|\mathbf{W}) \leq f_\epsilon(\mathbf{W}, \tilde{\mathbf{H}}^{(l)}), \tag{5}$$

where the first inequality holds as u_2 is an auxiliary function for $\mathbf{H}$. The truncation is invoked only when the update in (4b) becomes negative, i.e., when

$$\frac{\displaystyle\sum_{m}\sum_{j\neq i:(i,j)\in\mathcal{P}_m} b_{ij}^{(m)} \frac{w_{mk}^{(l+1)}(h_{ki}^{(l)}+\epsilon)}{[\mathbf{W}^{(l+1)}(\mathbf{H}^{(l)}+\epsilon\mathbb{1})]_{mi}}}{\displaystyle\sum_{m}\sum_{j\neq i:(i,j)\in\mathcal{P}_m} \frac{(b_{ij}^{(m)}+b_{ji}^{(m)})w_{mk}^{(l+1)}}{[\mathbf{W}^{(l+1)}(\mathbf{H}^{(l)}+\epsilon\mathbb{1})]_{mi}+[\mathbf{W}^{(l+1)}(\mathbf{H}^{(l)}+\epsilon\mathbb{1})]_{mj}}} \leq \epsilon.$$

Using this inequality and performing some algebra as shown in Sect. S-1 in the supplementary material [21], we can justify the second inequality in (5) as follows

$$f_\epsilon(\mathbf{W}, \tilde{\mathbf{H}}^{(l)}) - u_2(\tilde{\mathbf{H}}^{(l+1)}, \tilde{\mathbf{H}}^{(l)}|\mathbf{W})$$

$$\geq \sum_{m}\sum_{j\neq i:(i,j)\in\mathcal{P}_m} \frac{(b_{ij}^{(m)}+b_{ji}^{(m)})w_{mk}}{[\mathbf{W}(\mathbf{H}^{(l)}+\epsilon\mathbb{1})]_{mi}+[\mathbf{W}(\mathbf{H}^{(l)}+\epsilon\mathbb{1})]_{mj}} \left[h_{ki}^{(l)} - \epsilon\log\left(\frac{h_{ki}^{(l)}+\epsilon}{\epsilon}\right)\right] \geq 0.$$

The last inequality follows because $b_{ij}^{(m)}$, $\mathbf{W}$ and $\mathbf{H}^{(l)}$ are nonnegative, and $h_{ki}^{(l)} - \epsilon \log(\frac{h_{ki}^{(l)}+\epsilon}{\epsilon}) \geq 0$ since $x \geq \log(x+1)$ for all $x \geq 0$ with equality at $x = 0$. Hence, the likelihood is non-decreasing during the MM update even though we included an additional operation that truncates $\tilde{h}_{ki}^{(l+1)} < 0$ to zero.

3.3   Normalization

It is well-known that NMF is not unique in the general case, and it is characterized by a scale and permutation indeterminacies [5]. For the problem at hand, for the learned $\mathbf{W}$ and $\mathbf{H}$ matrices to be interpretable as "skill levels" with respect to different latent variables, it is imperative we consider *normalizing* them appropriately after every MM iteration. However, there are different ways to normalize the entries in the matrices and one has to ensure that after normalization, the likelihood of the model stays unchanged. This is tantamount to keeping the ratio $\frac{[\mathbf{W}(\mathbf{H}+\epsilon\mathbb{1})]_{mi}}{[\mathbf{W}(\mathbf{H}+\epsilon\mathbb{1})]_{mi}+[\mathbf{W}(\mathbf{H}+\epsilon\mathbb{1})]_{mj}}$ unchanged for all (m,i,j). The key observations here are twofold: First, concerning $\mathbf{H}$, since terms indexed by (m,i) and (m,j) appear in the denominator but only (m,i) appears in the numerator, we can normalize over all elements of $\mathbf{H}$ to keep this fraction unchanged. Second, concerning $\mathbf{W}$, since only terms indexed by m appear both in numerator and denominator, we can normalize either rows or columns.

Row Normalization of W and Global Normalization of H
Define the row sums of $\mathbf{W}$ as $r_m := \sum_k \tilde{w}_{mk}$ and let $\alpha := \frac{\sum_{k,i} \tilde{h}_{ki}+KN\epsilon}{1+KN\epsilon}$.
Now consider the following operations: $w_{mk} \leftarrow \frac{\tilde{w}_{mk}}{r_m}$, and $h_{ki} \leftarrow \frac{\tilde{h}_{ki}+(1-\alpha)\epsilon}{\alpha}$. The above update to obtain h_{ki} may result in it being negative; however, the truncation operation ensures that h_{ki} is eventually nonnegative.[2] See also the update to obtain $\tilde{h}_{ki}^{(l+1)}$ in Algorithm 1. The operations above keep the likelihood unchanged and achieve the desired row normalization of $\mathbf{W}$ since

$$\frac{\sum_k \tilde{w}_{mk}(\tilde{h}_{ki}+\epsilon)}{\sum_k \tilde{w}_{mk}(\tilde{h}_{ki}+\epsilon)+\sum_k \tilde{w}_{mk}(\tilde{h}_{kj}+\epsilon)} = \frac{\sum_k \frac{\tilde{w}_{mk}}{r_m}(\tilde{h}_{ki}+\epsilon)}{\sum_k \frac{\tilde{w}_{mk}}{r_m}(\tilde{h}_{ki}+\epsilon)+\sum_k \frac{\tilde{w}_{mk}}{r_m}(\tilde{h}_{kj}+\epsilon)}$$

$$= \frac{\sum_k w_{mk}\frac{(\tilde{h}_{ki}+\epsilon)}{\alpha}}{\sum_k w_{mk}\frac{(\tilde{h}_{ki}+\epsilon)}{\alpha}+\sum_k w_{mk}\frac{(\tilde{h}_{ki}+\epsilon)}{\alpha}} = \frac{\sum_k w_{mk}(h_{ki}+\epsilon)}{\sum_k w_{mk}(h_{ki}+\epsilon)+\sum_k w_{mk}(h_{kj}+\epsilon)}.$$

Column Normalization of W and Global Normalization of H
Define the column sums of $\mathbf{W}$ as $c_k := \sum_m \tilde{w}_{mk}$ and let $\beta := \frac{\sum_{k,i} \hat{h}_{ki}+KN\epsilon}{1+KN\epsilon}$.
Now consider the following operations: $w_{mk} \leftarrow \frac{\tilde{w}_{mk}}{c_k}$, $\hat{h}_{ki} \leftarrow \tilde{h}_{ki}c_k + \epsilon(c_k - 1)$, and $h_{ki} \leftarrow \frac{\hat{h}_{ki}+(1-\beta)\epsilon}{\beta}$. This would keep the likelihood unchanged and achieve the desired column normalization of $\mathbf{W}$ since

---

[2] One might be tempted to normalize $\mathbf{H}+\epsilon\mathbb{1} \in \mathbb{R}_+^{K\times N}$. This, however, does not resolve numerical issues as some entries of $\mathbf{H} + \epsilon\mathbb{1}$ may be zero.

$$\frac{\sum_k \tilde{w}_{mk}(\tilde{h}_{ki} + \epsilon)}{\sum_k \tilde{w}_{mk}(\tilde{h}_{ki} + \epsilon) + \sum_k \tilde{w}_{mk}(\tilde{h}_{kj} + \epsilon)} = \frac{\sum_k \frac{\tilde{w}_{mk}}{c_k}(\tilde{h}_{ki} + \epsilon)c_k}{\sum_k \frac{\tilde{w}_{mk}}{c_k}(\tilde{h}_{ki} + \epsilon)c_k + \sum_k \frac{\tilde{w}_{mk}}{c_k}(\tilde{h}_{kj} + \epsilon)c_k}$$

$$= \frac{\sum_k w_{mk}\frac{(\hat{h}_{ki}+\epsilon)}{\beta}}{\sum_k w_{mk}\frac{(\hat{h}_{ki}+\epsilon)}{\beta} + \sum_k w_{mk}\frac{(\hat{h}_{ki}+\epsilon)}{\beta}} = \frac{\sum_k w_{mk}(h_{ki} + \epsilon)}{\sum_k w_{mk}(h_{ki} + \epsilon) + \sum_k w_{mk}(h_{kj} + \epsilon)}.$$

Using this normalization strategy, it is easy to verify that all entries of $\mathbf{\Lambda}=\mathbf{WH}$ sum to one. This allows us to interpret the entries as "conditional probabilities".

Algorithm 1. MM Alg. for BTL-NMF model with column normalization of $\mathbf{W}$

Input: M tournaments; N players; number of times player i beats player j in tournament m in dataset $\mathcal{D} = \{b_{ij}^{(m)} : i,j \in \{1, ..., N\}, m \in \{1, ..., M\}\}$

Init: Fix $K \in \mathbb{N}$, $\epsilon > 0$, $\tau > 0$ and initialize $\mathbf{W}^{(0)} \in \mathbb{R}_{++}^{M \times K}, \mathbf{H}^{(0)} \in \mathbb{R}_{++}^{K \times N}$.

while diff $\geq \tau > 0$ **do**

(1) **Update** $\forall m \in \{1, ..., M\}, \forall k \in \{1, ..., K\}, \forall i \in \{1, ..., N\}$

$$\tilde{w}_{mk}^{(l+1)} = \frac{\sum_{i,j} b_{ij}^{(m)} \frac{w_{mk}^{(l)}(h_{ki}^{(l)}+\epsilon)}{[\mathbf{W}^{(l)}(\mathbf{H}^{(l)}+\epsilon\mathbf{1})]_{mi}}}{\sum_{i,j} b_{ij}^{(m)} \frac{h_{ki}^{(l)}+h_{kj}^{(l)}+2\epsilon}{[\mathbf{W}^{(l)}(\mathbf{H}^{(l)}+\epsilon\mathbf{1})]_{mi}+[\mathbf{W}^{(l)}(\mathbf{H}^{(l)}+\epsilon\mathbf{1})]_{mj}}}$$

$$\tilde{h}_{ki}^{(l+1)} = \max\left\{ \frac{\sum_m \sum_{j \neq i} b_{ij}^{(m)} \frac{w_{mk}^{(l+1)}(h_{ki}^{(l)}+\epsilon)}{[\mathbf{W}^{(l+1)}(\mathbf{H}^{(l)}+\epsilon\mathbf{1})]_{mi}}}{\sum_m \sum_{j \neq i} \frac{(b_{ij}^{(m)}+b_{ji}^{(m)})w_{mk}^{(l+1)}}{[\mathbf{W}^{(l+1)}(\mathbf{H}^{(l)}+\epsilon\mathbf{1})]_{mi}+[\mathbf{W}^{(l+1)}(\mathbf{H}^{(l)}+\epsilon\mathbf{1})]_{mj}}} - \epsilon, 0 \right\}$$

(2) **Normalize** $\forall m \in \{1, ..., M\}, \forall k \in \{1, ..., K\}, \forall i \in \{1, ..., N\}$

$$w_{mk}^{(l+1)} \leftarrow \frac{\tilde{w}_{mk}^{(l+1)}}{\sum_m \tilde{w}_{mk}^{(l+1)}}; \quad \hat{h}_{ki}^{(l+1)} \leftarrow \tilde{h}_{ki}^{(l+1)} \sum_m \tilde{w}_{mk}^{(l+1)} + \epsilon\left(\sum_m \tilde{w}_{mk}^{(l+1)} - 1\right)$$

Calculate $\beta = \frac{\sum_{k,i} \hat{h}_{ki}^{(l+1)}+KN\epsilon}{1+KN\epsilon}$, $h_{ki}^{(l+1)} \leftarrow \frac{\hat{h}_{ki}^{(l+1)}+(1-\beta)\epsilon}{\beta}$

(3) diff $\leftarrow \max\left\{ \max_{m,k} |w_{mk}^{(l+1)} - w_{mk}^{(l)}|, \max_{k,i} |h_{ki}^{(l+1)} - h_{ki}^{(l)}| \right\}$

end while

return $(\mathbf{W}, \mathbf{H})$ that forms a local maximizer of the likelihood $p(\mathcal{D}|\mathbf{W}, \mathbf{H})$

Algorithm 1 presents pseudo-code for optimizing (3) with columns of $\mathbf{W}$ normalized. The algorithm when the rows of $\mathbf{W}$ are normalized is similar; we replace the normalization step with the procedure outlined above.

3.4 Convergence $\{(\mathbf{W}^{(l)}, \mathbf{H}^{(l)})\}_{l=1}^{\infty}$ to Stationary Points

While we have proved that the sequence of objectives $\{f_\epsilon(\mathbf{W}^{(l)}, \mathbf{H}^{(l)})\}_{l=1}^{\infty}$ is non-increasing (and hence it converges because it is bounded), it is not clear as to whether the sequence of *iterates* generated by the algorithm $\{(\mathbf{W}^{(l)}, \mathbf{H}^{(l)})\}_{l=1}^{\infty}$ converges and if so to what. We define the *marginal functions* $f_{1,\epsilon}(\mathbf{W}|\overline{\mathbf{H}}) := f_\epsilon(\mathbf{W}, \overline{\mathbf{H}})$ and $f_{2,\epsilon}(\mathbf{H}|\overline{\mathbf{W}}) := f_\epsilon(\overline{\mathbf{W}}, \mathbf{H})$. For any function $g : \mathcal{D} \to \mathbb{R}$, we let

$g'(x; d) := \liminf_{\lambda \downarrow 0}(g(x + \lambda d) - g(x))/\lambda$ be the *directional derivative* of g at point x in direction d. We say that $(\overline{\mathbf{W}}, \overline{\mathbf{H}})$ is a *stationary point* of the problem

$$\min_{\mathbf{W} \in \mathbb{R}_+^{M \times K}, \mathbf{H} \in \mathbb{R}_+^{K \times N}} f_\epsilon(\mathbf{W}, \mathbf{H}) \qquad (6)$$

if the following two conditions hold: (i) $f'_{1,\epsilon}(\overline{\mathbf{W}}; \mathbf{W} - \overline{\mathbf{W}}|\overline{\mathbf{H}}) \geq 0$, $\forall \mathbf{W} \in \mathbb{R}_+^{M \times K}$, (ii) $f'_{2,\epsilon}(\overline{\mathbf{H}}; \mathbf{H} - \overline{\mathbf{H}}|\overline{\mathbf{W}}) \geq 0, \forall \mathbf{H} \in \mathbb{R}_+^{K \times N}$. This definition generalizes the usual notion of a stationary point when the function is differentiable and the domain is unconstrained. However, in our NMF setting, the matrices are constrained to be nonnegative, hence the need for this generalized definition.

Theorem 1. *If* $\mathbf{W}$ *and* $\mathbf{H}$ *are initialized to have positive entries (i.e.,* $\mathbf{W}^{(0)} \in \mathbb{R}_{++}^{M \times K} = (0, \infty)^{M \times K}$ *and* $\mathbf{H}^{(0)} \in \mathbb{R}_{++}^{K \times N})$ *and* $\epsilon > 0$, *then every limit point of* $\{(\mathbf{W}^{(l)}, \mathbf{H}^{(l)})\}_{l=1}^{\infty}$ *generated by Algorithm 1 is a stationary point of* (6).

The proof of this theorem, provided in Sect. S-2 of [21], follows along the lines of the main result in Zhao and Tan [12], which itself hinges on the convergence analysis of block successive minimization methods provided by Razaviyayn, Hong, and Luo [13]. We need to verify that $f_{1,\epsilon}$ and $f_{2,\epsilon}$ together with u_1 and u_2 satisfy the five regularity conditions in Definition 3 of [12]. However, there are some important differences vis-à-vis [12] (e.g., analysis of the normalization step in Algorithm 1) which we describe in detail in Remark 1 of [21].

4 Numerical Experiments and Discussion

In this section, we describe how the datasets are collected and provide interesting and insightful interpretations of the numerical results. All datasets and code can be found at the following GitHub repository [21].

4.1 Details on the Datasets Collected

The Association of Tennis Professionals (ATP) is the main governing body for male tennis players. The official ATP website contains records of all matches played. The tournaments of the ATP tour belong to different categories; these include the four Grand Slams, the ATP Masters 1000, etc. The points obtained by the players that determine their ATP rankings and qualification for entry and seeding in following tournaments depend on the categories of tournaments that they participate or win in. We selected the most important $M = 14$ tournaments for men's dataset; these are listed in the first column of Table 1. After determining the tournaments, we selected $N = 20$ players. We wish to have as many matches as possible between each pair of players, so that $\{b_{ij}^{(m)}\}, m \in \{1, \ldots, M\}$ would not be too sparse. We chose players who both have the highest amount of participation in the $M = 14$ tournaments from 2008 to 2017 and also played the most number of matches played in the same period. These players are listed in the first column of Table 2. For each tournament m, we collected an $N \times N$ matrix $\{b_{ij}^{(m)}\}$, where $b_{ij}^{(m)}$ denotes the number of times player i beat player j

in tournament m. A submatrix consisting of the statistics of matches played at the French Open is shown in Table S-1 in [21]. We see that over the 10 years, Nadal beat Djokovic three times and Djokovic beat Nadal once at the French Open.

The governing body for women's tennis is the Women's Tennis Association (WTA) instead of the ATP. As such, we collected data from WTA website. The selection of tournaments and players is similar to that for the men. The tournaments selected include the four Grand Slams, WTA Finals, four WTA Premier Mandatory tournaments, and five Premier 5 tournaments. However, for the first "Premier 5" tournament of the season, the event is either held in Dubai or Doha, and the last tournament was held in Tokyo between 2009 and 2013; this has since been replaced by Wuhan. We decide to treat these two events as four distinct tournaments held in Dubai, Doha, Tokyo and Wuhan. Hence, the number of tournaments chosen for the women is $M = 16$.

After collecting the data, we checked the sparsity level of the dataset $\mathcal{D} = \{b_{ij}^{(m)}\}$. The zeros in $\mathcal{D}$ can be categorized into three different classes.

1. (Zeros on the diagonal) By convention, $b_{ii}^{(m)} = 0$ for all (i, m);
2. (Missing data) By convention, if player i and j have never played with each other in tournament m, then $b_{ij}^{(m)} = b_{ij}^{(m)} = 0$;
3. (True zeros) If player i has played with player j in tournament m but lost every such match, then $b_{ij}^{(m)} = 0$ and $b_{ji}^{(m)} > 0$.

The distributions of the three types of zeros and non-zero entries for male and female players are presented in Table S-2 in [21]. We see that there is more missing data for the women. This is because there has been a small set of dominant male players over the past 10 years but the same is not true for women players. For the women, this means that the matches in the past ten years are played by a more diverse set of players, resulting in the number of matches between the top $N = 20$ players being smaller compared to the top $N = 20$ men.

4.2   Running of the Algorithm

The number of latent variables is expected to be small. We only present results for $K = 2$ in the main paper; the results for $K = 3$ are displayed in Tables S-3 to S-6 in [21]. We also set $\epsilon = 10^{-300}$ which is close to the smallest positive value in Python. The algorithm terminates when the difference of every element of $\mathbf{W}$ and $\mathbf{H}$ between successive iterations is less than $\tau = 10^{-6}$. We checked that the ϵ-modified algorithm in Sect. 3.2 results in non-decreasing likelihoods. See Fig. S-1 in [21]. Since (3) is non-convex, the MM algorithm can be trapped in local minima. Hence, we considered 150 different random initializations for $\mathbf{W}^{(0)}$ and $\mathbf{H}^{(0)}$ and analyzed the result that gave the maximum likelihood among the 150 trials. Histograms of the negative log-likelihoods are shown in Fig. S-2 in [21]. We observe that the optimal value of the log-likelihood for $K = 3$ is higher than that of $K = 2$ since the former model is richer. We also observe that the $\mathbf{W}$'s

Table 1. Learned dictionary matrix **W** for the men's dataset

Tournaments	Row Normalization		Column Normalization	
Australian Open	5.77E-01	4.23E-01	1.15E-01	7.66E-02
Indian Wells Masters	6.52E-01	3.48E-01	1.34E-01	6.50E-02
Miami Open	5.27E-01	4.73E-01	4.95E-02	4.02E-02
Monte-Carlo Masters	1.68E-01	8.32E-01	2.24E-02	1.01E-01
Madrid Open	3.02E-01	6.98E-01	6.43E-02	1.34E-01
Italian Open	0.00E-00	1.00E-00	1.82E-104	1.36E-01
French Open	3.44E-01	6.56E-01	8.66E-02	1.50E-01
Wimbledon	6.43E-01	3.57E-01	6.73E-02	3.38E-02
Canadian Open	1.00E-00	0.00E-00	1.28E-01	1.78E-152
Cincinnati Masters	5.23E-01	4.77E-01	1.13E-01	9.36E-02
US Open	5.07E-01	4.93E-01	4.62E-02	4.06E-02
Shanghai Masters	7.16E-01	2.84E-01	1.13E-01	4.07E-02
Paris Masters	1.68E-01	8.32E-01	1.29E-02	5.76E-02
ATP World Tour Finals	5.72E-01	4.28E-01	4.59E-02	3.11E-02

and **H**'s produced over the 150 runs are roughly the same up to permutation of rows and columns, i.e., our solution is *stable* and *robust* (cf. Theorem 1).

4.3   Results for Men Players

The learned dictionary matrix **W** is shown in Table 1. In the "Tournaments" column, those tournaments whose surface types are known to be clay are highlighted in gray. For ease of visualization, higher values are shaded darker. If the rows of **W** are normalized, we observe that for clay tournaments, the value in the second column is always larger than that in the first, and vice versa. The only exception is the Paris Masters.[3] Since the row sums are equal to 1, we can interpret the values in the first and second columns of a fixed row as the probabilities that a particular tournament is being played on non-clay or clay surface respectively. If the columns of **W** are normalized, it is observed that the tournaments with highest value of the second column are exactly the four tournaments played on clay. From **W**, we learn that surface type—in particular, whether or not a tournament is played on clay—is a germane latent variable that influences the performances of men players.

Table 2 displays the transpose of **H** whose elements sum to one. Thus, if the column $k \in \{1, 2\}$ represents the surface type, we can treat h_{ki} as the skill of

---

[3] This may be attributed to its position in the seasonal calendar. The Paris Masters is the last tournament before ATP World Tour Finals. Top players often choose to skip this tournament to prepare for the more prestigious ATP World Tour Finals. This has led to some surprising results, e.g., Ferrer, a strong clay player, won the Paris Masters in 2012 (even though the Paris Masters is a hard court tournament).

Table 2. Learned transpose $\mathbf{H}^T$ of the coefficient matrix for the men's dataset

Players	matrix $\mathbf{H}^T$		Total Matches
Novak Djokovic	1.20E-01	9.98E-02	283
Rafael Nadal	2.48E-02	1.55E-01	241
Roger Federer	1.15E-01	2.34E-02	229
Andy Murray	7.57E-02	8.43E-03	209
Tomas Berdych	0.00E-00	3.02E-02	154
David Ferrer	6.26E-40	3.27E-02	147
Stan Wawrinka	2.93E-55	4.08E-02	141
Jo-Wilfried Tsonga	3.36E-02	2.71E-03	121
Richard Gasquet	5.49E-03	1.41E-02	102
Juan Martin del Potro	2.90E-02	1.43E-02	101
Marin Cilic	2.12E-02	0.00E-00	100
Fernando Verdasco	1.36E-02	8.79E-03	96
Kei Nishikori	7.07E-03	2.54E-02	94
Gilles Simon	1.32E-02	4.59E-03	83
Milos Raonic	1.45E-02	7.25E-03	78
Philipp Kohlschreiber	2.18E-06	5.35E-03	76
John Isner	2.70E-03	1.43E-02	78
Feliciano Lopez	1.43E-02	3.31E-03	75
Gael Monfils	3.86E-21	1.33E-02	70
Nicolas Almagro	6.48E-03	6.33E-06	60

player i conditioned on him playing on surface type k. We may regard the first and second columns of $\mathbf{H}^T$ as the skill levels of players on non-clay and clay respectively. We observe that Nadal, nicknamed the "King of Clay", is the best player on clay among the $N = 20$ players, and as an individual, he is also much more skilful on clay compared to non-clay. Djokovic, the first man in the "Open era" to hold all four Grand Slams on three different surfaces (hard court, clay and grass) at the same time (between Wimbledon 2015 to the French Open 2016, also known as the Nole Slam), is more of a balanced top player as his skill levels are high in both columns of $\mathbf{H}^T$. Federer won the most titles on tournaments played on grass and, as expected, his skill level in the first column is indeed much higher than the second. As for Murray, the $\mathbf{H}^T$ matrix also reflects his weakness on clay. Wawrinka, a player who is known to favor clay has skill level in the second column being much higher than that in the first. The last column of Table 2 lists the total number of matches that each player participated in (within our dataset). We verified that the skill levels in $\mathbf{H}^T$ for each player are not strongly correlated to how many matches are being considered in the dataset. Although Berdych has data of more matches compared to Ferrer, his

Table 3. Learned transpose $\mathbf{H}^T$ of coefficient matrix for the women's dataset

Players	matrix $\mathbf{H}^T$		Total Matches
Serena Williams	5.93E-02	1.44E-01	130
Agnieszka Radwanska	2.39E-02	2.15E-02	126
Victoria Azarenka	7.04E-02	1.47E-02	121
Caroline Wozniacki	3.03E-02	2.43E-02	115
Maria Sharapova	8.38E-03	8.05E-02	112
Simona Halep	1.50E-02	3.12E-02	107
Petra Kvitova	2.39E-02	3.42E-02	99
Angelique Kerber	6.81E-03	3.02E-02	96
Samantha Stosur	4.15E-04	3.76E-02	95
Ana Ivanovic	9.55E-03	2.60E-02	85
Jelena Jankovic	1.17E-03	2.14E-02	79
Anastasia Pavlyuchenkova	6.91E-03	1.33E-02	79
Carla Suarez Navarro	3.51E-02	5.19E-06	75
Dominika Cibulkova	2.97E-02	1.04E-02	74
Lucie Safarova	0.00E+00	3.16E-02	69
Elina Svitolina	5.03E-03	1.99E-02	59
Sara Errani	7.99E-04	2.69E-02	58
Karolina Pliskova	9.92E-03	2.36E-02	57
Roberta Vinci	4.14E-02	0.00E+00	53
Marion Bartoli	1.45E-02	1.68E-02	39

scores are not higher than that of Ferrer. Thus our algorithm and conclusions are not skewed towards the availability of data.

The learned skill matrix $\mathbf{\Lambda} = \mathbf{WH}$ with column normalization of $\mathbf{W}$ is presented in Tables S-7 and S-8 in the supplementary material [21]. As mentioned in Sect. 2.1, $[\mathbf{\Lambda}]_{mi}$ denotes the skill level of player i in tournament m. We observe that Nadal's skill levels are higher than Djokovic's only for the French Open, Madrid Open, Monte-Carlo Masters, Paris Masters and Italian Open, which are tournaments played on clay except for the Paris Masters. As for Federer, his skill level is highest for Wimbledon, which happens to be the only tournament on grass; here, it is known that he is the player with the best record in the "Open era". Furthermore, if we consider Wawrinka, the five tournaments in which his skill levels are the highest include the four clay tournaments. These observations again show that our model has learned interesting latent variables from $\mathbf{W}$. It has also learned players' skills on different types of surfaces and tournaments from $\mathbf{H}$ and $\mathbf{\Lambda}$ respectively.

4.4 Results for Women Players

We performed the same experiment for the women players except that we now consider $M = 16$ tournaments. The factor matrices $\mathbf{W}$ and $\mathbf{H}$ (in its transpose form) are presented in Tables S-9 in [21] and Table 3 respectively.

It can be seen from $\mathbf{W}$ that, unlike for the men players, the surface type is not a latent variable since there is no correlation between the values in the columns and the surface type. We suspect that the skill levels of women players are not as heavily influenced by the surface type compared to the men. However, the tournaments in Table S-9 are ordered chronologically and we notice that there is a slight correlation between the values in the column and the time of the tournament (first or second half of the year). Any latent variable would naturally be less pronounced, due to the sparser dataset for women players (cf. Table S-2).

By computing the sums of the skill levels for each female player (i.e., row sums of $\mathbf{H}^T$), we see that S. Williams is the most skilful among the 20 players over the past 10 years. She is followed by Sharapova and Azarenka. As a matter of fact, S. Williams and Azarenka have been year-end number one 4 times and once, respectively, over the period 2008 to 2017. Even though Sharapova was never at the top at the end of any season (she was, however, ranked number one several times, most recently in 2012), she had been consistent over this period such that the model and the longitudinal dataset allow us to conclude that she is ranked second. She is known for her unusual longevity being at the top of the women's game. She started her tennis career very young and won her first Grand Slam at the age of 17. Finally, the model groups S. Williams, Sharapova, Stosur together, while Azarenka, Navarro, and Vinci are in another group. There may be some similarities between players who are clustered in the same group. The Λ matrix for women players can be found in Tables S-10 and S-11 in [21].

4.5 Comparison to BTL and Mixture-BTL

Finally, we compared our approach to the BTL and mixture-BTL [14,15] approaches for the male players. To learn these models, we aggregated our dataset $\{b_{ij}^{(m)}\}$ into a single matrix $\{b_{ij} = \sum_m b_{ij}^{(m)}\}$. For the BTL model, we maximized the likelihood to find the optimal parameters. For the mixture-BTL model with $K = 2$ components, we ran an Expectation-Maximization (EM) algorithm [22] to find approximately-optimal values of the parameters and the mixture weights. Note that the BTL model corresponds to a mixture-BTL model with $K = 1$.

The learned skill vectors are shown in Table S-12 in the supplementary material [21]. Since EM is susceptible to being trapped in local optima and is sensitive to initialization, we ran it 100 times and reported the solution with likelihood that is close to the highest one.[4] The solution for mixture-BTL is not stable; other solutions with likelihoods that are close to the maximum one have significantly different parameter values. Two other solutions with similar likelihoods

---

[4] The solution with the highest likelihood is shown in Trial 2 of Table S-13 but it appears that the solution there is degenerate.

are shown in Table S-13 in [21]. As can be seen, some of the solutions are far from representative of the true skill levels of the players (e.g., in Trial 2 of Table S-13, Tsonga has a very high score in the first column and the skills of other players are all very small in comparison) and they are vastly different from one another. This is in stark contrast to our BTL-NMF model and algorithm in which Theorem 1 states that the limit of $\{(\mathbf{W}^{(l)}, \mathbf{H}^{(l)})\}_{l=1}^{\infty}$ is a stationary point of (6). We numerically verified that the BTL-NMF solution is stable, i.e., different runs yield $(\mathbf{W}, \mathbf{H})$ pairs that are approximately equal up to permutation of rows and columns.[5] As seen from Table S-12, for mixture-BTL, neither tournament-specific information nor semantic meanings of latent variables can be gleaned from the parameter vectors. The results of BTL are reasonable and expected but also lack tournament-specific information.

5   Future Work

In the future, we plan to run our algorithm on a larger longitudinal dataset consisting of pairwise comparison data from more years (e.g., the past 50 years) to learn, for example, who is the "best-of-all-time" male or female player. In addition, it would be desirable to understand if there is a natural Bayesian interpretation [19,23] of the ϵ-modified objective function in (3).

Acknowledgements. This work was supported by a Ministry of Education Tier 2 grant (R-263-000-C83-112), an NRF Fellowship (R-263-000-D02-281), and by the European Research Council (ERC FACTORY-CoG-6681839).

References

1. Elo, A.E.: The Rating of Chess Players, Past and Present. Ishi Press International, Bronx (2008)
2. Bradley, R., Terry, M.: Rank analysis of incomplete block designs I: the method of paired comparisons. Biometrika **35**, 324–345 (1952)
3. Luce, R.: Individual Choice Behavior: A Theoretical Analysis. Wiley, New York (1959)
4. Lee, D.D., Seung, H.S.: Learning the parts of objects with nonnegative matrix factorization. Nature **401**, 788–791 (1999)
5. Cichocki, A., Zdunek, R., Phan, A.H., Amari, S.-I.: Nonnegative Matrix and Tensor Factorizations: Applications to Exploratory Multi-Way Data Analysis and Blind Source Separation. John Wiley & Sons Ltd., Chichester (2009)
6. Marden, J.I.: Analyzing and Modeling Rank Data. CRC Press, London (1996)
7. Lee, D.D., Seung, H.S.: Algorithms for nonnegative matrix factorization. In: Neural Information Processing Systems, pp. 535–541 (2000)
8. Févotte, C., Bertin, N., Durrieu, J.L.: Nonnegative matrix factorization with the Itakura-Saito divergence with application to music analysis. Neural Comput. **21**(3), 793–830 (2009)

---

[5] Stationary points are not necessarily equivalent up to permutation or rescaling.

9. Berry, M.W., Browne, M.: Email surveillance using non-negative matrix factorization. Comput. Math. Organ. Theory **11**(3), 249–264 (2005)
10. Geerts, A., Decroos, T., Davis, J.: Characterizing soccer players' playing style from match event streams. In: Machine Learning and Data Mining for Sports Analytics ECML/PKDD 2018 Workshop, pp. 115–126 (2018)
11. Hunter, D.-R., Lange, K.: A tutorial on MM algorithms. Am. Stat. **58**, 30–37 (2004)
12. Zhao, R., Tan, V.Y.F.: A unified convergence analysis of the multiplicative update algorithm for regularized nonnegative matrix factorization. IEEE Trans. Signal Process. **66**(1), 129–138 (2018)
13. Razaviyayn, M., Hong, M., Luo, Z.Q.: A unified convergence analysis of block successive minimization methods for nonsmooth optimization. SIAM J. Optim. **23**(2), 1126–1153 (2013)
14. Oh, S., Shah, D.: Learning mixed multinomial logit model from ordinal data. In: Neural Information Processing Systems, pp. 595–603 (2014)
15. Shah, N.-B., Wainwright, M.-J.: Simple, robust and optimal ranking from pairwise comparisons. J. Mach. Learn. Res. **18**(199), 1–38 (2018)
16. Suh, C., Tan, V.Y.F., Zhao, R.: Adversarial top-K ranking. IEEE Trans. Inf. Theory **63**(4), 2201–2225 (2017)
17. Ding, W., Ishwar, P., Saligrama, V.: A topic modeling approach to ranking. In: Proceedings of the 18th International Conference on Artificial Intelligence and Statistics (AISTATS), pp. 214–222 (2015)
18. Févotte, C., Idier, J.: Algorithms for nonnegative matrix factorization with the β-divergence. Neural Comput. **23**(9), 2421–2456 (2011)
19. Tan, V.Y.F., Févotte, C.: Automatic relevance determination in nonnegative matrix factorization with the β-divergence. IEEE Trans. Pattern Anal. Mach. Intell. **35**(7), 1592–1605 (2013)
20. Hunter, D.R.: MM algorithms for generalized Bradley-Terry models. Ann. Stat. **32**(1), 384–406 (2004)
21. Xia, R., Tan, V.Y.F., Filstroff, L., Févotte, C.: Supplementary material for "A ranking model motivated by nonnegative matrix factorization with applications to tennis tournaments" (2019). https://github.com/XiaRui1996/btl-nmf
22. Dempster, A.P., Laird, N.M., Rubin, D.B.: Maximum likelihood from incomplete data via the EM algorithm. J. R. Stat. Soc. B **39**, 1–38 (1977)
23. Caron, F., Doucet, A.: Efficient Bayesian inference for generalized Bradley-Terry models. J. Comput. Graph. Stat. **21**(1), 174–196 (2012)

A Reduction of Label Ranking
to Multiclass Classification

Klaus Brinker[1]([⊠]) and Eyke Hüllermeier[2]

[1] Hamm-Lippstadt University of Applied Sciences, Hamm, Germany
klaus.brinker@hshl.de
[2] Paderborn University, Paderborn, Germany
eyke@upb.de

Abstract. Label ranking considers the problem of learning a mapping from instances to strict total orders over a predefined set of labels. In this paper, we present a framework for label ranking using a decomposition into a set of *multiclass problems*. Conceptually, our approach can be seen as a generalization of pairwise preference learning. In contrast to the latter, it allows for controlling the granularity of the decomposition, varying between binary preferences and complete rankings as extreme cases. It is specifically motivated by limitations of pairwise learning with regard to the minimization of certain loss functions. We discuss theoretical properties of the proposed method in terms of accuracy, error correction, and computational complexity. Experimental results are promising and indicate that improvements upon the special case of pairwise preference decomposition are indeed possible.

Keywords: Label ranking · Multiclass classification · Structured output prediction · Ensemble learning

1 Introduction

In the recent past, various types of ranking problems emerged in the field of preference learning [12]. A well-known example is "learning to rank" or object ranking [19], where the task is to rank any subset of objects (typically described as feature vectors) from a given domain (e.g. documents). In this paper, our focus is on a related but conceptually different problem called *label ranking* (LR). The task in LR is to learn a mapping from an input space $\mathcal{X}$ to strict total orders over a predefined set $\mathcal{L} = \{\lambda_1, \ldots, \lambda_m\}$ of labels (e.g. political parties, music genres, or social emotions). Like in multiclass classification, these labels are only distinguished by their name but not described in terms of any properties.

Previous approaches to label ranking can be grouped into four main categories with respect to model representation [22]: Algorithms learning real-valued scoring functions for each label [8,15,20], instance-based methods [2,6], tree-based methods [5], and binary decomposition methods [18]. In terms of predictive accuracy, especially the latter turned out to be highly competitive.

Electronic supplementary material The online version of this chapter (https://doi.org/10.1007/978-3-030-46133-1_13) contains supplementary material, which is available to authorized users.

This paper introduces a generalization of binary decomposition in the sense that LR problems are transformed into multiple *multiclass* classification problems. Thus, the atomic elements of our framework are partial rankings of a fixed length k, including pairwise preferences $(k = 2)$ and complete rankings $(k = m)$ as special cases. Encoding rankings over fixed subsets of k labels as (meta-)classes, each such subset gives rise to a multiclass classification problem. At prediction time, the corresponding multiclass classifiers (either all of them or a suitable subset) are queried with a new instance, and their predictions are combined into a ranking on the entire label set $\mathcal{L}$.

Intuitively, a decomposition into partial rankings instead of label pairs increases the degree of overlap between the various subproblems, and thereby the ability to correct individual prediction errors. Formally, it can indeed be shown that, to minimize specific loss functions on rankings, knowledge about binary relationships between labels is principally insufficient; an extreme example is the 0/1-loss, which simply checks whether the entire ranking is correct or not.

Our framework for LR is analyzed from a theoretical perspective with respect to both accuracy, error correcting properties, and computational complexity. More precisely, for the aforementioned 0/1-loss and Kendall's tau rank correlation, we present bounds in terms of the average classification error of the underlying multiclass models on the training data, hence, providing a justification for the general consistency of our approach in the sense that accurate multiclass models imply accurate overall LR predictions on the training data. With respect to error correction, we present a theoretical result on the number of multiclass errors which our framework can compensate while still recovering the correct overall ranking.

Empirically, we also analyze the influence of the decomposition granularity k. Our results are promising and suggest that improvements upon the special case of binary decomposition are indeed possible. In the experiments, we observed a consistent relationship between a suitable choice of k and the overall number of labels m.

Section 2 recalls the problem setting of LR, along with notational conventions. Our novel LR framework is presented in Sect. 3. Sections 4 and 5 analyze theoretical properties in terms of accuracy, error correction, and computational complexity, respectively. Section 6 is devoted to an experimental evaluation of our approach. We conclude with a few remarks and open research directions in Sect. 7.

2   Label Ranking

In label ranking, the goal is to learn a predictive model in the form of a mapping $f : \mathcal{X} \to \mathcal{L}^*$, where $\mathcal{X}$ is an instance space and $\mathcal{L}^*$ the set of all rankings (strict total orders) over a set of labels $\mathcal{L} = \{\lambda_1, \ldots, \lambda_m\}$. Formally, we represent rankings in terms of permutations π of $[m] = \{1, \ldots, m\}$, such that $\pi(i)$ is the (index of the) label at position i. Thus, LR assumes instances $x \in \mathcal{X}$ to be associated with rankings $\pi \in \mathcal{L}^*$. More specifically, we assume this dependency to be probabilistic: Given x as input, there is a certain probability $\mathbf{P}(\pi \mid x)$ to observe the ranking $\pi \in \mathcal{L}^*$ as output.

We suppose training data to be given in the form of a set of observations $\mathcal{D} = \{(x_i, \pi_i)\}_{i=1}^n \subset \mathcal{X} \times \mathcal{L}^*$. Thus, for convenience, we assume the observed rankings to be complete. In practice, this assumption is of course not always fulfilled. Instead, rankings are often incomplete, with some of the labels $\lambda_i \in \mathcal{L}$ being missing. Predictive performance is evaluated in terms of a loss function $\ell : \mathcal{L}^* \times \mathcal{L}^* \rightarrow \mathbb{R}$, which compares observed rankings π with predictions $\hat{\pi}$. Common choices include rank correlation measures such as Kendall's tau and Spearman's rho (which are actually similarity measures).

In the pairwise approach to LR [18], called ranking by pairwise comparison (RPC), one binary model $f_{i,j}$ is trained for each pair of labels (λ_i, λ_j). The task of $f_{i,j}$ is to predict, for a given instance x, whether λ_i precedes or succeeds λ_j in the ranking associated with x. A prediction $\hat{\pi}$ is produced by aggregating the (possibly conflicting) $m(m-1)/2$ pairwise predictions, using techniques such as (weighted) voting.

An important question for any reduction technique is the following: Is it possible to combine the solutions of the individual subproblems into an optimal solution for the original problem? In the case of RPC, this question can be asked more concretely as follows: Is it possible to train and combine the binary predictors $f_{i,j}$ so as to obtain an optimal predictor f for the original LR problem, i.e., a predictor that minimizes the loss ℓ in expectation? Interestingly, this question can be answered affirmatively for several performance measures, including Kendall's tau and Spearman's rho. However, there are also measures for which this is provably impossible. These include the 0/1-loss, the Hamming, the Cayley, and the Ulam distance on rankings, as well as Spearman's footrule [16]. Roughly speaking, for these measures, the loss of information due to projecting the distribution $\mathbf{P}(\cdot \mid x)$ on $\mathcal{L}^*$ to its pairwise marginals $\mathbf{P}_{i,j}(\cdot \mid x)$ is too high. That is, even knowledge about all pairwise marginals does not allow for reconstructing the risk-minimizing prediction $\hat{\pi}$.

Indeed, pairwise relations may easily lead to ambiguities, such as preferential cycles. Knowledge about the distribution of rankings on larger label subsets, such as triplets or quadruples, may then help to disambiguate. This is a key motivation of the approach put forward in this paper, very much in line with the so-called *listwise* approaches to learning-to-rank problems [3]. In this regard, LR is also quite comparable to multi-label classification (MLC): There are loss functions (such as Hamming) that allow for reducing the original MLC problem to binary classification, but also others (such as the subset 0/1-loss) for which reduction techniques cannot produce optimal results, and which require information about the distribution on larger subsets of labels [9].

3   Reduction to Multiclass Classification

In this section, we present a novel framework for solving LR problems using a decomposition into multiple multiclass classification problems. We refer to this approach as LR2MC (Label Ranking to Multiclass Classification).

3.1   Decomposition

For a given $k \in \{2, \ldots, m\}$, consider all label subsets $L \subset \mathcal{L}$ of cardinality k. Each such L gives rise to a label ranking problem on the reduced set of labels. For the special case $k = 2$, the same decomposition into $\binom{m}{2}$ binary classification problems is produced as for RPC.

To illustrate the decomposition process, consider a setting with $m = 4$ labels $\mathcal{L} = \{\lambda_1, \lambda_2, \lambda_3, \lambda_4\}$ and subsets of cardinality $k = 3$. Each of the $\binom{4}{3}$ subsets $\{\lambda_1, \lambda_2, \lambda_3\}$, $\{\lambda_1, \lambda_2, \lambda_4\}$, $\{\lambda_1, \lambda_3, \lambda_4\}$, and $\{\lambda_2, \lambda_3, \lambda_4\}$ gives rise to a separate LR problem. In the following, we denote by $\pi^{(L)}$ the restriction of a ranking $\pi \in \mathcal{L}^*$ to the label subset $L \subset \mathcal{L}$, i.e., $\pi^{(L)} = (\lambda_3, \lambda_4, \lambda_2)$ for $\pi = (\lambda_3, \lambda_4, \lambda_1, \lambda_2)$ and $L = \{\lambda_2, \lambda_3, \lambda_4\}$. For each ranking problem on a label subset L of size 3, there are $3! = 6$ elements in the output space L^*, for example $(\lambda_1, \lambda_2, \lambda_3)$, $(\lambda_1, \lambda_3, \lambda_2)$, $(\lambda_2, \lambda_1, \lambda_3)$, $(\lambda_2, \lambda_3, \lambda_1)$, $(\lambda_3, \lambda_1, \lambda_2)$, $(\lambda_3, \lambda_2, \lambda_1)$ in the case of the label subset $L = \{\lambda_1, \lambda_2, \lambda_3\}$.

In general, for a label ranking problem with $|\mathcal{L}| = m$ labels, we construct a set of $\binom{m}{k}$ ranking problems on label subsets of size $|L| = k$. Each of these problems is then converted into a multiclass problem. To this end, each of the $k!$ rankings $\pi^{(L)} \in L^*$ is associated with a class $c \in C = \{c_1, \ldots, c_{k!}\}$. We denote by f_L the multiclass classifier on subset L. For the sake of simplicity, we assume the decoding of class labels to the associated rankings to be done directly, i.e., f_L is viewed as a mapping $\mathcal{X} \rightarrow L^*$ (instead of a mapping $\mathcal{X} \rightarrow C$), and $f_L(x)$ is the ranking of labels in L predicted for x.

3.2   Aggregation

We will now discuss our approach to combining partial ranking predictions on label subsets into a prediction on the complete label set $\mathcal{L}$. The idea is to find a consensus ranking that disagrees with the minimum number of subset ranking predictions. In Sect. 4, we further elaborate on theoretical properties of this aggregation method.

For a new instance $x \in \mathcal{X}$, we first compute the predicted rankings $\{f_L(x) : L \subset \mathcal{L}, |L| = k\}$ on the $\binom{m}{k}$ label subsets. These predictions are combined into a complete ranking $f(x) \in \mathcal{L}^*$ by minimizing the sum of (p'artial) 0/1-loss values:

$$f(x) \stackrel{\text{def}}{=} \underset{\pi \in \mathcal{L}^*}{\operatorname{argmin}} \sum_{\substack{L \subset \mathcal{L} \\ |L| = k}} \ell_{01}\left(\pi^{(L)}, f_L(x)\right), \tag{1}$$

where

$$\ell_{01}(\rho, \rho') = \begin{cases} 0 & \text{for } \rho = \rho' \\ 1 & \text{for } \rho \neq \rho' \end{cases} \tag{2}$$

for $\rho, \rho' \in L^*$ denotes the 0/1-loss for two label rankings. Ties are broken arbitrarily.

This loss-based aggregation is similar to *Hamming decoding* for computing a multiclass label from binary classifications [1]. Moreover, for $k = 2$, it is identical to the *Slater-optimal* aggregation in pairwise LR [17]. For $k = m$, there is only one label subset $L = \mathcal{L}$. In this case, the risk-minimizing ranking is obviously the multiclass prediction for this set, mapped to the associated label ranking.

3.3   Discussion

What is an optimal choice of k? This question is not easy to answer, and different arguments support different choices:

- Loss of information: The decomposition of a ranking necessarily comes with a loss of information, and the smaller the components, the larger the loss. This argument suggests large values k (close or equal to m).
- Redundancy: The more redundant the predictions, the better mistakes of individual predictors f_L can be corrected. This argument suggests midsize values $k \approx m/2$, for which the number $\binom{m}{k}$ of predictions combined in the aggregation step is largest.
- Simplicity: The difficulty of a multiclass problem increases with the number of classes. This argument suggests small values k, specifically $k = 2$. Practically, it will indeed be difficult to go beyond $k = 4$, since the number of classes $k!$ will otherwise be prohibitive—issues such as class-imbalance and empty classes will then additionally complicate the problem.

As for the last point, also note that for $k > 2$, our reduction to classification comes with a loss of structural information: By mapping partial rankings $\pi^{(L)}$ to class labels c, i.e., replacing the space L^* by the set of classes C, any information about the structure of the former is lost (since C is not equipped with any structure except the discrete metric). This information is only reconsidered in the aggregation step later on. Interestingly, exactly the opposite direction, namely exploiting structure on the label space by turning a multiclass classification into a ranking problem, has recently been considered in [14].

LR2MC is conceptually related to the Rakel method for multilabel classification [21]. Rakel decomposes an MLC problem with m labels into (randomly chosen) MLC problems for subsets of size k, and tackles each of these problems as a multiclass problem with 2^k classes (corresponding to the label subsets). Both approaches share the underlying motivation of taking dependencies between labels and partial rankings, respectively, into account. Moreover, both approaches also resemble error correcting output encodings [10], which aim at improving the overall multiclass classification accuracy by combining multiple binary classifiers and provide a means to distribute the output representation.

4   Theoretical Analysis

In this section, we upper bound the average training 0/1-loss and Kendall's tau rank correlation of LR2MC (as defined in (2)) in terms of the average classification error of the multiclass classifiers $\{f_L\}_{L \subset \mathcal{L}, |L|=k}$ and analyze error correcting properties. Our analysis is similar to [1], where multiclass classification is reduced to learning multiple binary classifiers. In that paper, the authors provide a bound on the empirical multiclass loss in terms of the loss of the binary classifiers and properties and the decomposition scheme.

Theorem 1 (Training loss bound). *Let $\{f_L\}_{L \subset \mathcal{L}, |L|=k}$ with $2 \le k \le m$ denote a set of multiclass models and let ε denote their average classification error on the training sets decomposed from the LR training data $\mathcal{D} = \{(x_i, \pi_i)\}_{i=1}^n$. Then, we can upper bound the average ranking 0/1-loss on the training data as follows:*

$$\frac{1}{n} \sum_{i=1}^n \ell_{01}(\pi_i, f(x_i)) \le \frac{2m(m-1)}{k(k-1)} \cdot \varepsilon$$

Proof. Let $f(x) = \hat{\pi}$ denote the predicted ranking for the training example $(x, \pi) \in \mathcal{D}$. Assume that the predicted and the ground truth rankings disagree, $\pi \ne \hat{\pi}$, hence $\ell_{01}(\pi, \hat{\pi}) = 1$. Moreover, as $\hat{\pi}$ is a minimizer of (1), it holds that

$$\sum_{\substack{L \subset \mathcal{L} \\ |L|=k}} \ell_{01}(\pi^{(L)}, f_L(x)) \ge \sum_{\substack{L \subset \mathcal{L} \\ |L|=k}} \ell_{01}(\hat{\pi}^{(L)}, f_L(x)).$$

Let $S_\Delta \overset{\mathrm{def}}{=} \{L \subset \mathcal{L}^* : |L| = k \wedge \hat{\pi}^{(L)} \ne \pi^{(L)}\}$ denote the label sets of cardinality k, where π and $\hat{\pi}$ disagree. Then,

$$\sum_{L \in S_\Delta} \ell_{01}(\pi^{(L)}, f_L(x)) \ge \sum_{L \in S_\Delta} \ell_{01}(\hat{\pi}^{(L)}, f_L(x)).$$

Therefore,

$$\sum_{\substack{L \subset \mathcal{L} \\ |L|=k}} \ell_{01}(\pi^{(L)}, f_L(x)) \ge \sum_{L \in S_\Delta} \ell_{01}(\pi^{(L)}, f_L(x))$$

$$= \frac{1}{2} \left(\sum_{L \in S_\Delta} (\ell_{01}(\pi^{(L)}, f_L(x)) + \ell_{01}(\pi^{(L)}, f_L(x))) \right)$$

$$\ge \frac{1}{2} \left(\sum_{L \in S_\Delta} \underbrace{(\ell_{01}(\pi^{(L)}, f_L(x)) + \ell_{01}(\hat{\pi}^{(L)}, f_L(x)))}_{\ge 1} \right)$$

$$\ge \frac{1}{2}|S_\Delta| \ge \frac{1}{2}\binom{m-2}{k-2}.$$

The last step follows from the fact that for the non-equal rankings π and $\hat{\pi}$ at least two labels are in reverse order. Hence, all $\binom{m-2}{k-2}$ restrictions to subsets of k labels which contain the inversed label pair are not equal as well, and therefore elements of S_Δ. In summary, a prediction error, i.e., $\ell_{01}(\pi, f(x)) = 1$ implies that

$$\frac{2}{\binom{m-2}{k-2}} \sum_{\substack{L \subset \mathcal{L} \\ |L|=k}} \ell_{01}(\pi^{(L)}, f_L(x)) \ge 1.$$

Moreover, as

$$\frac{2}{\binom{m-2}{k-2}} \sum_{\substack{L \subset \mathcal{L} \\ |L|=k}} \ell_{01}(\pi^{(L)}, f_L(x)) \geq 0$$

for $\ell_{01}(\pi, f(x)) = 0$, it holds for all (x, π) that

$$\ell_{01}(\pi, f(x)) \leq \frac{2}{\binom{m-2}{k-2}} \sum_{\substack{L \subset \mathcal{L} \\ |L|=k}} \ell_{01}(\pi^{(L)}, f_L(x)).$$

Therefore, for the average 0/1-loss, it holds that

$$\frac{1}{n} \sum_{i=1}^{n} \ell_{01}(\pi_i, f(x_i)) \leq \frac{1}{n} \sum_{i=1}^{n} \frac{2}{\binom{m-2}{k-2}} \sum_{\substack{L \subset \mathcal{L} \\ |L|=k}} \ell_{01}(\pi_i^{(L)}, f_L(x_i))$$

$$= \frac{2}{\binom{m-2}{k-2}} \frac{1}{n} \sum_{i=1}^{n} \sum_{\substack{L \subset \mathcal{L} \\ |L|=k}} \ell_{01}(\pi_i^{(L)}, f_L(x_i))$$

$$= \frac{2\binom{m}{k}}{\binom{m-2}{k-2}} \cdot \underbrace{\frac{1}{n\binom{m}{k}} \sum_{i=1}^{n} \sum_{\substack{L \subset \mathcal{L} \\ |L|=k}} \ell_{01}(\pi_i^{(L)}, f_L(x_i))}_{=\varepsilon}$$

$$= \frac{2m(m-1)}{k(k-1)} \cdot \varepsilon$$

For the special case of perfect multiclass models on the training data ($\varepsilon = 0$), the 0/1-loss for LR2MC is zero. Moreover, when entirely ignoring the structure of the output space ($m = k$) and approaching label ranking as a multiclass problem with $m!$ classes, the 0/1-loss for label ranking is bounded by twice the average multiclass error.

Corollary 1 (Error correction). *Let $\{f_L\}_{L \subset \mathcal{L}, |L|=k}$ with $2 \leq k \leq m$ denote a set of multiclass models. For any observation $(x, \pi) \in \mathcal{X} \times \mathcal{L}^*$ with*

$$\sum_{\substack{L \subset \mathcal{L} \\ |L|=k}} \ell_{01}\left(\pi^{(L)}, f_L(x)\right) < \frac{1}{2}\binom{m-2}{k-2}$$

it holds that $f(x) = \pi$.

Proof. As shown in the proof of Theorem 1, $\sum_{\substack{L \subset \mathcal{L} \\ |L|=k}} \ell_{01}(\pi^{(L)}, f_L(x)) \geq \frac{1}{2}\binom{m-2}{k-2}$ for $f(x) \neq \pi$.

Corollary 1 provides some interesting insights into the error correction properties of our framework:

- For $k = 2$, the right-hand side is $\frac{1}{2}$, and hence the inequality is satisfied only if *all* pairwise predictions are correct. Indeed, it is obvious that a single pairwise error may result in an incorrect overall prediction.
- For $k = m$, there exists only a single multiclass model which is mapped to an LR prediction. In this case, a correct overall prediction is guaranteed if this multiclass prediction is correct.
- For $k = \lfloor \frac{m}{2} + 1 \rfloor$ and $k = \lceil \frac{m}{2} + 1 \rceil$, the right-hand side evaluates to the maximum possible value(s) and Corollary 1 indicates that our framework is capable of correcting a substantial number of multiclass errors.

The last point suggests that values $k \approx \frac{m}{2} + 1$ should lead to optimal performance, because the ability to correct errors of individual classifiers is highest for these values. One should keep in mind, however, that the error probability itself, which corresponds to the performance of a $(k!)$-class classifier[1], will (strongly) increase with k. Depending on how quickly this error increases, and whether or not it can be over-compensated through more redundancy, the optimal value of k is supposed to lie somewhere between 2 and $\frac{m}{2} + 1$. This is confirmed by experimental results for a simplified synthetic setting that we present in the supplementary material (Section A.8).

Corollary 2 (Training bound for Kendall's tau). *Rescaling Kendall's τ rank correlation into a loss function by $\frac{1-\tau}{2} \in [0,1]$, it holds under the assumptions of Theorem 1 that*

$$\frac{1}{n} \sum_{i=1}^{n} \frac{1 - \tau(\pi_i, f(x_i))}{2} \leq \frac{2m(m-1)}{k(k-1)} \cdot \varepsilon$$

Proof. Direct consequence of Theorem 1 and the fact that for all rankings π and π' it holds that

$$\frac{1 - \tau(\pi, \pi')}{2} \leq \ell_{01}(\pi, \pi').$$

Corollary 2 shows that the average multiclass error on the training data not only bounds the 0/1-loss but also guarantees a certain level of overall ranking accuracy as measured by Kendall's tau.

5   Computational Complexity

The set of multiclass models is at the core of LR2MC. The training data for each multiclass model consists of the original instances x_i and the appropriate class labels which represent rankings on label subsets. Hence, we need to train and evaluate $\binom{m}{k}$ multiclass models using n training examples with up to $k!$ different class labels.

---

[1] The effective number of classes a classifier is trained on corresponds to the distinct number of permutations of the k labels in the training data, which is normally $< k!$.

Depending on the influence of the number of classes on the complexity of the classification learning algorithm and the choice of k, the computational complexity can increase substantially compared to the pairwise ranking approach, where $\binom{m}{2} = \frac{m(m-1)}{2}$ binary models are required. More precisely, the maximum number of multiclass models for a given m is required for $k = \lfloor \frac{m}{2} \rfloor$ as a consequence of basic properties of binomial coefficients. For this case, it holds that

$$\binom{m}{\lfloor \frac{m}{2} \rfloor} \geq \left(\frac{m}{\lfloor \frac{m}{2} \rfloor} \right)^{\lfloor \frac{m}{2} \rfloor} \geq 2^{\lfloor \frac{m}{2} \rfloor} \geq 2^{\frac{m-1}{2}} = (\sqrt{2})^{m-1}.$$

Hence, the maximum number of multiclass problems is lower bounded by a term which grows exponentially in the number of labels m.

For testing, we need to evaluate all $\binom{m}{k}$ multiclass models and solve the optimization problem (1). Even when ignoring the multiclass model evaluation complexity, the computational complexity for this combinatorial optimization problem increases substantially in m as there are $m!$ possible rankings to be considered. Moreover, as stated above, for $k = 2$, this aggregation method is identical to computing the *Slater-optimal* label ranking which is known to be NP-complete [17].

Overall, even considering that the number of labels m in LR is normally small (mostly < 10, comparable to multiclass classification), computational complexity is clearly an issue for LR2MC. Of course, there are various directions one could think of to improve efficiency. For example, instead of decomposing into all label subsets of size k, one may (randomly) chose only some of them, like in Ra$k$el. Besides, aggregation techniques less expensive than Hamming decoding could be used, such as (generalized) Borda count. While these are interesting directions for future work, the main goal of this paper is to elaborate on the usefulness of the approach in principle, i.e., to answer the question whether or not a generalization from pairwise to multiclass decomposition is worthwhile at all.

6   Experimental Evaluation

6.1   Setup

This section presents an experimental evaluation of the accuracy of LR2MC, which essentially consists of two studies. For the first study, we replicated a setting previously proposed in [4], where a suite of benchmark datasets for label ranking was used[2]; see Table 1 for an overview of the dataset properties. The second study is based on an artificial setting from [13], where the underlying problem is to learn the ranking function induced by an expected utility

---

[2] These are classification and regression datasets from the UCI and Statlog repository, which were turned into label ranking problems. The datasets are publicly available at https://cs.uni-paderborn.de/is/research/research-projects/software/. Due to the computational demands of LR2MC, we restricted our evaluation to datasets with $m \leq 7$ labels.

Table 1. Dataset characteristics

Dataset	Instances	Attributes	Labels
authorship	841	70	4
bodyfat	252	7	7
calhousing	20640	4	4
cpu-small	8192	6	5
fried	40769	9	5
glass	214	9	6
housing	506	6	6
iris	150	4	3
segment	2310	18	7
stock	950	5	5
vehicle	846	18	4
wine	178	13	3

maximizing agent. This setting allows for varying dataset properties, i.e., the number of instances, features, and labels, to study specific aspects of our novel approach in a more controlled setting.

We consider the following evaluation measures: Kendall's tau and Spearman's rho rank correlation coefficients, 0/1 loss, and Hamming distance (number of items for which the predicted rank deviates from the true rank). For coherence, we turn the last two into $[0, 1]$-valued similarity scores: Match is defined as 1 minus 0/1 loss, and Hamming similarity is 1 minus normalized Hamming distance.

For the first study, the empirical results are computed as in [4] using five repetitions of ten-fold cross-validation. In the second study, we averaged the results over 100 repetitions of the synthetic data generation process for each dataset property configuration with separate test sets consisting of 1000 examples.

As base learners, we use the decision tree (J48) and random forest (Random Forest) implementations from the Weka machine learning suite with default parameters [11]. Both methods combine fast training and testing with a natural means of handling multiclass problems without using any further decomposition techniques. This is in contrast to learning methods that make use of reduction techniques themselves (multiclass SVM, for example, uses a decomposition into one-vs-rest or all pairs). By excluding such methods, we try to avoid blending multiclass to binary and label ranking to multiclass decomposition together, which may yield empirical results that are difficult to interpret.

Table 2. Experimental results of the label ranking techniques with decision trees (J48) as base learner in terms of Kendall's tau (in brackets the ranks; best average rank in boldface).

Dataset	RPC	LR2MC-2	LR2MC-3	LR2MC-4	LR2MC-5	LR2MC-6	LR2MC-7
authorship	0.787 (2)	0.789 (1)	0.782 (3)	0.771 (4)			
bodyfat	0.153 (1)	0.143 (2)	0.106 (3)	0.097 (4)	0.073 (5)	0.046 (7)	0.051 (6)
calhousing	0.299 (1)	0.297 (2)	0.206 (3)	0.191 (4)			
cpu-small	0.311 (2)	0.311 (1)	0.265 (3)	0.242 (4)	0.224 (5)		
fried	0.808 (4)	0.814 (3)	0.862 (1)	0.836 (2)	0.749 (5)		
glass	0.801 (5)	0.818 (3)	0.830 (1)	0.826 (2)	0.812 (4)	0.790 (6)	
housing	0.310 (6)	0.333 (4)	0.402 (1)	0.375 (2)	0.341 (3)	0.313 (5)	
iris	0.780 (1)	0.765 (3)	0.777 (2)				
segment	0.830 (7)	0.839 (5)	0.887 (2)	0.888 (1)	0.869 (3)	0.854 (4)	0.832 (6)
stock	0.729 (4)	0.727 (5)	0.781 (1)	0.768 (2)	0.755 (3)		
vehicle	0.815 (2)	0.819 (1)	0.815 (3)	0.795 (4)			
wine	0.862 (2)	0.863 (1)	0.838 (3)				
Average rank	3.08	2.58	**2.17**	2.90	4.00	5.50	6.00

6.2   First Study (Real Data)

Results for the first study are shown in Table 2 for Kendall's tau as performance metric and decision trees as base learner—corresponding results for other metrics and learners can be found in the supplementary material. Note that the rank statistic shown in that table (ranking of methods per dataset, and average ranks per method) is arguably biased, because not all decompositions are applicable to all datasets (for example, LR2MC-5 cannot be used for the 4-label authorship dataset).

Therefore, Table 3 shows average *normalized* ranks, where normalization means that, for each dataset, the ranks are linearly rescaled to have unit sum. As can be seen, none of the approaches consistently outperforms the others. However, a more fine-grained, bipartite analysis of the results demonstrates the dependence of the optimal choice of k on the overall number of labels m (see Corollary 1 and the subsequent theoretical discussion): The pairwise approach outperforms all other methods for datasets with *up to 4 labels* (middle entry in each triplet), while the LR2MC-3 approach outperforms all other methods for datasets with *more than 4 labels* (right entry).

The results for RPC [18] and LR2MC-2 are similar, as expected, since both methods use the same decomposition and only differ in the aggregation step. RPC uses a voting approach that is specifically tailored for Spearman's rho, which in turn bounds Kendall's tau [7]. For these metrics, RPC is indeed very strong.

In agreement with our theoretical arguments, the situation looks different when measuring performance in terms of Match and Hamming. Here, the pairwise approach performs worse, and best results are obtained for LR2MC with

$k = 4$ or $k = 5$. As already explained, pairwise information is not enough to optimize these measures. Theoretically, one may even expect larger values for the optimal k, but practically, classifiers are of course difficult to train on problems with too many classes (and limited data).

6.3   Second Study (Synthetic Data)

In a second study, we carried out a set of experiments using the synthetic setting of [13], which allows for controlling dataset properties. More precisely, in a first scenario, we considered the following setup: $250, 500, 1000, \ldots, 16000$ training instances with 10 features and 7 labels, Match and Hamming as evaluation measures.

Table 3. Experimental results in terms of average *normalized* ranks (best result for each metric/learner combination in boldface) for different combinations of measure (<u>K</u>endall, <u>S</u>pearman, <u>M</u>atch, <u>H</u>amming) and base learner (J48 and <u>R</u>andom <u>F</u>orest): all datasets/datasets with $m \leq 4$ / datasets with $m > 4$.

		RPC	LR2MC-2	LR2MC-3	LR2MC-4	LR2MC-5	LR2MC-6	LR2MC-7
K	J48	.21/**.20**/.21	**.19**/.21/.17	.20/.35/**.09**	.21/.40/.13	.21/—/.21	.23/—/.23	.21/—/.21
K	RF	.20/**.20**/.19	.22/.31/.15	**.17**/.27/**.09**	.20/.37/.13	.23/—/.23	.23/—/.23	.25/—/.25
S	J48	**.15**/**.15**/.16	.22/.27/.18	.19/.35/**.08**	.22/.40/.15	.22/—/.22	.25/—/.25	.23/—/.23
S	RF	**.15**/**.18**/.13	.22/.29/.18	.17/.29/**.07**	.22/.40/.15	.26/—/.26	.24/—/.24	.25/—/.25
M	J48	.31/.33/.29	.28/.35/.23	.20/.24/.18	.11/**.13**/.10	**.10**/—/**.10**	.13/—/.13	.11/—/.11
M	RF	.33/.40/.29	.29/.35/.24	.16/.17/.16	.11/**.13**/.10	**.09**/—/**.09**	.13/—/.13	.17/—/.17
H	J48	.29/.32/.27	.29/.37/.23	.19/.23/.16	**.11**/**.13**/**.09**	.10/—/.10	.16/—/.16	.16/—/.16
H	RF	.29/.32/.27	.32/.40/.27	.19/.22/.17	**.09**/**.10**/**.09**	.10/—/.10	.13/—/.13	.14/—/.14

The experimental results with decision tree base learners are given in Table 4 (detailed results for random forests are available as supplementary material). Here, the ranks are computed *without* normalization in compliance with [4]. Since only the overall number of training examples varies, all considered methods are applicable, for which reason a normalization is not needed.

As expected, the absolute accuracy increases with the number of training examples for all methods. Moreover, the relative performance (ranks) of the methods is identical, regardless of the training set size, except for RPC and LR2MC-2 which achieve very similar results. With decision trees as base learners, LR2MC-4 consistently outperforms all other approaches, including LR2MC-7. This observation again supports the hypothesis that pure classification methods that do not leverage the structure of the output space are more difficult to train. For random forests as base learner, the experimental results are in line with these observations, with the slight difference that LR2MC-3 is the overall winner and a bit better than LR2MC-2 and LR2MC-4, which yield very similar absolute results.

Table 4. Experimental results using decision trees (J48) as base learners in terms of Match (top) and Hamming (bottom), in parentheses the ranks.

Examples	RPC	LR2MC-2	LR2MC-3	LR2MC-4	LR2MC-5	LR2MC-6	LR2MC-7
250	0.128 (4)	0.127 (5)	0.157 (2)	0.165 (1)	0.151 (3)	0.111 (6)	0.081 (7)
500	0.151 (4)	0.149 (5)	0.188 (2)	0.199 (1)	0.178 (3)	0.134 (6)	0.096 (7)
1000	0.176 (4)	0.174 (5)	0.216 (2)	0.231 (1)	0.209 (3)	0.155 (6)	0.111 (7)
2000	0.197 (5)	0.197 (4)	0.246 (2)	0.263 (1)	0.239 (3)	0.178 (6)	0.128 (7)
4000	0.219 (4)	0.216 (5)	0.277 (2)	0.294 (1)	0.269 (3)	0.203 (6)	0.147 (7)
8000	0.243 (5)	0.244 (4)	0.306 (2)	0.323 (1)	0.298 (3)	0.230 (6)	0.166 (7)
16000	0.264 (5)	0.264 (4)	0.337 (2)	0.353 (1)	0.328 (3)	0.256 (6)	0.186 (7)
Average rank	4.43	4.57	2.00	**1.00**	3.00	6.00	7.00
250	0.567 (4)	0.566 (5)	0.595 (2)	0.599 (1)	0.573 (3)	0.514 (6)	0.468 (7)
500	0.591 (5)	0.592 (4)	0.627 (2)	0.629 (1)	0.604 (3)	0.541 (6)	0.492 (7)
1000	0.614 (4)	0.613 (5)	0.652 (2)	0.655 (1)	0.630 (3)	0.568 (6)	0.518 (7)
2000	0.634 (5)	0.635 (4)	0.674 (2)	0.679 (1)	0.653 (3)	0.592 (6)	0.538 (7)
4000	0.655 (5)	0.655 (4)	0.696 (2)	0.700 (1)	0.675 (3)	0.615 (6)	0.560 (7)
8000	0.672 (4)	0.672 (5)	0.715 (2)	0.721 (1)	0.697 (3)	0.635 (6)	0.580 (7)
16000	0.690 (4)	0.689 (5)	0.733 (2)	0.740 (1)	0.717 (3)	0.658 (6)	0.601 (7)
Average rank	4.43	4.57	2.00	**1.00**	3.00	6.00	7.00

In a second scenario, we used the following setting: 2000 training instances with 10 features and $3, 4, \ldots, 7$ labels, Kendall and Spearman as evaluation measures. The experimental results are given in Table 5. This set of experiments completely supports the finding from the first study: For datasets with $m \leq 4$ labels, the pairwise approaches RPC and LR2MC-2 outperform all other decompositions. However, for datasets with $m > 4$ labels, LR2MC-3 consistently achieves the highest accuracy in terms of both Kendall's tau and Spearman's rho.

6.4   Discussion

Our experimental results suggest that the number of labels is an essential property for choosing a suitable decomposition approach in label ranking. More precisely, while standard pairwise decomposition appears to be favorable for datasets with $m \leq 4$ labels, our novel multiclass decomposition with $k = 3$ (LR2MC-3) seems to provide a promising alternative for $m > 4$ labels and rank correlation (Kendall's tau or Spearman's rho) as performance measure. If other measures are used, such as 0/1 loss (Match) or Hamming, higher order decompositions are even more advantageous. Interestingly, in the context of multilabel learning, the experimental conclusions for the conceptually related Rakel method [21] are similar, since label set sizes around $k = 3$ often yield the best accuracy.

As our experimental evaluation suggests that multiclass decomposition with $k = 3$ is a particularly promising alternative to the well-known pairwise label ranking approach, we will add some remarks regarding its computational complexity in terms of the number of classification problems: For a dataset with m

Table 5. Experimental results for the second controlled scenario in terms of *normalized* ranks (best result for each metric/learner combination in boldface) for different combinations of measure (Kendall, Spearman, Match, Hamming) and base learner (J48 and Random Forest): all datasets/datasets with $m \leq 4$/datasets with $m > 4$.

		RPC	LR2MC-2	LR2MC-3	LR2MC-4	LR2MC-5	LR2MC-6	LR2MC-7
K	J48	**.18**/.18	.22/.15	.40/**.05**	.40/.14	—/.23	—/.25	—/.25
K	RF	**.13**/.12	.27/.14	.40/**.05**	.40/.19	—/.25	—/.25	—/.25
S	J48	**.13**/.13	.27/.18	.40/**.05**	.40/.14	—/.25	—/.25	—/.25
S	RF	.22/.08	**.18**/.15	.40/**.07**	.40/.20	—/.25	—/.25	—/.25

labels, pairwise label ranking considers an overall number of $\binom{m}{2}$ binary classification problems, while LR2MC-3 makes use of a decomposition into $\binom{m}{3}$ multiclass problems. Hence, ignoring special cases, there is an increase in the number of classification problems by a factor of $\frac{m-2}{3}$. For example, for $m = 7$ this amounts to roughly 67% more classification problems with the training set size being identical for both approaches. Depending on the application field, the increase in accuracy may justify these computational requirements.

One may hypothesize that the increase in accuracy may be attributed to the increased number of underlying classifiers, and hence may be a straightforward ensemble size consequence. We have conducted some preliminary experiments to further investigate this hypothesis. In these experiments, a maximum number of $\binom{m}{2}$ classifiers was subsampled from the overall set of multiclass classifiers to remove any potential ensemble advantage over the pairwise setting. Interestingly, the experimental results when using the limited number of underlying classifiers are comparable to those of the overall set of classifiers (see supplementary material for some more detailed results), suggesting that ensemble size cannot explain the observed difference in accuracy.

7   Conclusion and Future Research

Accepting pairwise learning as a state-of-the-art approach to label ranking, the major objective of this work was to address the question whether, in principle, going beyond pairwise comparisons and decomposing preference information into partial rankings of length $k > 2$ could be useful. Technically, this question comes down to comparing a reduction to binary classification with a reduction to multiclass classification.

The answer we can give is clearly affirmative: Our method, called LR2MC, tends to be superior to pairwise learning as soon as the number of labels exceeds four. In agreement with our theoretical arguments, this superiority is especially pronounced for performance metrics that are difficult to optimize based on pairwise preference information. Practically, $k = 3$ or $k = 4$ seem to be reasonable choices, which optimally balance various factors responsible for the success of the learning process. Such factors include the inherent loss of information caused by decomposition, the redundancy of the reduction, and the practical difficulty of the individual classification problems created.

While this is an important insight into the nature of label ranking, which paves the way for new methods beyond pairwise preference learning, the increased computational complexity of LR2MC is clearly an issue. In future work, we will therefore elaborate on various ways to reduce complexity and increase efficiency, both in the decomposition and aggregation step. One may think, for example, of incomplete decompositions that do not comprise projections to all label subsets, or mixed decompositions including rankings of different length (instead of using a fixed k). Moreover, the efficiency of the aggregation step could be increased by computationally less complex aggregation techniques, such as the well-known Borda-count. Preliminary experiments suggest that it is indeed possible to substantially reduce the computational complexity for aggregation while still benefit from superior ranking accuracy for datasets with $m > 4$ labels.

Currently, our approach is limited to complete label rankings as training data. Therefore, another direction of future research is to develop a generalization that allows for incorporating partial ranking data. For example, we may generalize LR2MC by inserting a preprocessing step for training examples which are associated with a partial ranking only, and consider all compatible ranking extensions as (weighted) virtual training examples in the decomposition process.

References

1. Allwein, E.L., Schapire, R.E., Singer, Y.: Reducing multiclass to binary: a unifying approach for margin classifiers. J. Mach. Learn. Res. **1**, 113–141 (2000)
2. Brinker, K., Hüllermeier, E.: Case-based label ranking. In: Fürnkranz, J., Scheffer, T., Spiliopoulou, M. (eds.) ECML 2006. LNCS (LNAI), vol. 4212, pp. 566–573. Springer, Heidelberg (2006). https://doi.org/10.1007/11871842_53
3. Cao, Z., Qin, T., Liu, T.Y., Tsai, M.F., Li, H.: Learning to rank: from pairwise approach to listwise approach. In: Proceedings of the 24th International Conference on Machine learning, ICML, pp. 129–136 (2007)
4. Cheng, W., Dembczyński, K., Hüllermeier, E.: Label ranking methods based on the Plackett-Luce model. In: Fürnkranz, J., Joachims, T. (eds.) Proceedings of the 27th International Conference on Machine Learning (ICML-10), Haifa, Israel, pp. 215–222. Omnipress, June 2010
5. Cheng, W., Hühn, J., Hüllermeier, E.: Decision tree and instance-based learning for label ranking. In: Bottou, L., Littman, M. (eds.) Proceedings of the 26th International Conference on Machine Learning (ICML-09), Montreal, Canada, pp. 161–168. Omnipress, June 2009
6. Cheng, W., Hüllermeier, E.: A new instance-based label ranking approach using the mallows model. In: Yu, W., He, H., Zhang, N. (eds.) ISNN 2009. LNCS, vol. 5551, pp. 707–716. Springer, Heidelberg (2009). https://doi.org/10.1007/978-3-642-01507-6_80
7. Coppersmith, D., Fleischer, L.K., Rurda, A.: Ordering by weighted number of wins gives a good ranking for weighted tournaments. ACM Trans. Algorithms **6**(3), 55:1–55:13 (2010)

8. Dekel, O., Manning, C.D., Singer, Y.: Log-linear models for label ranking. In: Thrun, S., Saul, L.K., Schölkopf, B. (eds.) Advances in Neural Information Processing Systems 16 (NIPS 2003), pp. 497–504. MIT Press, Cambridge (2004)
9. Dembczynski, K., Waegeman, W., Cheng, W., Hüllermeier, E.: On label dependence and loss minimization in multi-label classification. Mach. Learn. **88**(1–2), 5–45 (2012)
10. Dietterich, T.G., Bakiri, G.: Solving multiclass learning problems via error-correcting output codes. J. Artif. Intell. Res. **2**, 263–286 (1995)
11. Frank, E., Hall, M.A., Witten, I.H.: The WEKA Workbench. Online Appendix for Data Mining: Practical Machine Learning Tools and Techniques. Morgan Kaufmann, Fourth edn. (2016)
12. Fürnkranz, J., Hüllermeier, E.: Preference learning: an introduction. In: Fürnkranz, J., Hüllermeier, E. (eds.) Preference Learning, pp. 1–18. Springer, Heidelberg (2011). https://doi.org/10.1007/978-3-642-14125-6_1
13. Fürnkranz, J., Hüllermeier, E.: Pairwise preference learning and ranking. In: Lavrač, N., Gamberger, D., Blockeel, H., Todorovski, L. (eds.) ECML 2003. LNCS (LNAI), vol. 2837, pp. 145–156. Springer, Heidelberg (2003). https://doi.org/10.1007/978-3-540-39857-8_15
14. Hamm, J., Belkin, M.: Probabilistic zero-shot classification with semantic rankings. CoRR abs/1502.08039 (2015). http://arxiv.org/abs/1502.08039
15. Har-Peled, S., Roth, D., Zimak, D.: Constraint classification: a new approach to multiclass classification and ranking. In: Advances in Neural Information Processing Systems 15 (NIPS 2002) (2002)
16. Hüllermeier, E., Fürnkranz, J.: On predictive accuracy and risk minimization in pairwise label ranking. J. Comput. Syst. Sci. **76**(1), 49–62 (2010)
17. Hüllermeier, E., Fürnkranz, J.: Comparison of ranking procedures in pairwise preference learning. In: 10th International Conference on Information Processing and Management of Uncertainty in Knowledge-Based Systems (IPMU-04), pp. 535–542 (2004)
18. Hüllermeier, E., Fürnkranz, J., Cheng, W., Brinker, K.: Label ranking by learning pairwise preferences. Artif. Intell. **172**(16–17), 1897–1916 (2008)
19. Liu, T.Y.: Learning to Rank for Information Retrieval. Springer, Heidelberg (2011). https://doi.org/10.1007/978-3-642-14267-3
20. Shalev-Shwartz, S., Singer, Y.: Efficient learning of label ranking by soft projections onto polyhedra. J. Mach. Learn. Res. **7**, 1567–1599 (2006)
21. Tsoumakas, G., Katakis, I., Ioannis, V.: Random k-labelsets for multilabel classification. IEEE Trans. Knowl. Data Eng. **23**(7), 1079–1089 (2011)
22. Zhou, Y., Lui, Y., Yang, J., He, X., Liu, L.: A taxonomy of label ranking algorithms. J. Comput. **9**(3), 557–565 (2014)

Learning to Calibrate and Rerank Multi-label Predictions

Cheng Li[(✉)], Virgil Pavlu, Javed Aslam, Bingyu Wang, and Kechen Qin

Khoury College of Computer Sciences, Northeastern University, Boston, USA
{chengli,vip,jaa,rainicy}@ccs.neu.edu, qin.ke@husky.neu.edu

Abstract. A multi-label classifier assigns a set of labels to each data object. A natural requirement in many end-use applications is that the classifier also provides a well-calibrated confidence (probability) to indicate the likelihood of the predicted set being correct; for example, an application may automate high-confidence predictions while manually verifying low-confidence predictions. The simplest multi-label classifier, called Binary Relevance (BR), applies one binary classifier to each label independently and takes the product of the individual label probabilities as the overall label-set probability (confidence). Despite its many known drawbacks, such as generating suboptimal predictions and poorly calibrated confidence scores, BR is widely used in practice due to its speed and simplicity. We seek in this work to improve both BR's confidence estimation and prediction through a post calibration and reranking procedure. We take the BR predicted set of labels and its product score as features, extract more features from the prediction itself to capture label constraints, and apply Gradient Boosted Trees (GB) as a calibrator to map these features into a calibrated confidence score. GB not only produces well-calibrated scores (*aligned with accuracy* and *sharp*), but also models label interactions, correcting a critical flaw in BR. We further show that reranking label sets by the new calibrated confidence makes accurate set predictions on par with state-of-the-art multi-label classifiers—yet calibrated, simpler, and faster.

Keywords: Multi-label classification · Confidence score calibration · Reranking

1 Introduction

Multi-label classification is an important machine learning task wherein one predicts a subset of labels to associate with a given object. For example, an article can belong to multiple categories; an image can be associated with several tags; in medical billing, a patient report is annotated with multiple diagnosis codes. Formally, in a multi-label classification problem, we are given a set of label candidates $\mathcal{Y} = \{1, 2, \ldots, L\}$. Every data point $x \in \mathbb{R}^D$ matches a subset of labels $\mathbf{y} \subseteq \mathcal{Y}$, which is typically written in the form of a binary vector $\mathbf{y} \in \{0, 1\}^L$, with each bit y_ℓ indicating the presence or absence of the corresponding label.

© Springer Nature Switzerland AG 2020
U. Brefeld et al. (Eds.): ECML PKDD 2019, LNAI 11908, pp. 220–236, 2020.
https://doi.org/10.1007/978-3-030-46133-1_14

The goal of learning is to build a classifier $h : \mathbb{R}^D \to \{0,1\}^L$ which maps an instance to a subset of labels. The predicted label subset can be of arbitrary size.

The simplest approach to multi-label classification is to apply one binary classifier (e.g., binary logistic regression or support vector machine) to predict each label separately. This approach is called binary relevance (BR) [35] and is widely used due to its simplicity and speed. BR's training time grows linearly with the number of labels, which is considerably lower than many methods that seek to model label dependencies, and this makes BR run reasonably fast on commonly used datasets. (Admittedly, BR may still fail to scale to datasets with extremely large number of labels, in which case specially designed multi-label classifiers with sub-linear time complexity should be employed instead. But in this paper, we shall not consider such *extreme* multi-label classification problem).

BR has two well-known drawbacks. First, BR neglects label dependencies and this often leads to prediction errors: some BR predictions are incomplete, such as tagging `cat` but not `animal` for an image, and some are conflicting, such as predicting both the code `Pain in left knee` and the code `Pain in unspecified knee` for a medical note. Second, the confidence score or probability (we shall use "confidence score" and "probability" interchangeably) BR associates to its overall set prediction $\mathbf{y}$ is often misleading, or uncalibrated. BR computes the overall set prediction confidence score as the product of the individual label confidence scores, i.e., $p(\mathbf{y}|x) = \prod_{l=1}^{L} p(y_l|x)$. This overall confidence score often does not reflect reality: among all the set predictions on which BR claims to have roughly 80% confidence, maybe only 60% of them are actually correct (a predicted set is considered "correct" if it matches the ground truth set exactly). Having such uncalibrated prediction confidence makes it hard to integrate BR directly into a decision making pipeline where not only the predictions but also the confidence scores are used in downstream tasks.

In this work, we seek to address these two issues associated with BR. We first improve the BR set prediction confidence scores though a feature-based post calibration procedure to make confidence scores indicative of the true set accuracy (described in Sect. 2). The features considered in calibration capture label dependencies that have otherwise been missing in standard BR. Next we improve BR's set prediction accuracy by reranking BR's prediction candidates using the new calibrated confidence scores (described in Sect. 3). There exist multi-label methods that avoid the label independence assumption from the beginning and perform joint probability estimations [7,9,13,22,23,30]; such methods often require more complex training and inference procedures. In this paper we show that BR base model together with our proposed post calibration/reranking makes accurate set predictions on par with (or better than) these state-of-the-art multi-label methods —yet *calibrated*, *simpler*, and *faster*.

2   Calibrate BR Multi-label Predictions

We first address BR's confidence mis-calibration issue. There are two types of confidence scores in BR: the confidence of an individual label prediction $p(y_l|x)$, and the confidence of the entire predicted set $p(\mathbf{y}|x)$. In this work we take for granted that the individual label scores have already been calibrated, which can be easily done with established univariate calibration procedures such as isotonic regression [31] or Platt scaling [28,39]. We are concerned here with the set confidence calibration; note that calibrating all individual label confidence scores does not automatically calibrate set prediction confidence scores.

2.1 Metrics for Calibration: Alignment Error, Sharpness and MSE

To describe our calibration method, we need the following formal definitions:

- $c(\mathbf{y}) \in [0,1]$ is the confidence score associated with the set prediction $\mathbf{y}$;
- $v(\mathbf{y}) \in \{0,1\}$ is the 0/1 correctness of set prediction $\mathbf{y}$;
- $e(c) = p[v(\mathbf{y}) = 1|c(\mathbf{y}) = c]$ is the average set accuracy among all predictions whose confidence is c. In practice, this is estimated by bucketing predictions based on confidence scores and computing the average accuracy for each bucket.

We use the following standard metrics for calibration [21]:

- Alignment error, defined as $\mathbb{E}_{\mathbf{y}}[e(c(\mathbf{y})) - c(\mathbf{y})]^2$, measures, on average over all predictions, the discrepancy between the claimed confidence and the actual accuracy. The smaller the better.
- Sharpness, defined as $\mathrm{Var}_{\mathbf{y}}[e(c(\mathbf{y}))]$, measures how widely spread the confidence scores are. The bigger the better.
- The mean squared error (MSE, also called Brier Score) defined as $\mathbb{E}_{\mathbf{y}}[(v(\mathbf{y}) - c(\mathbf{y}))^2]$, measures the difference between the confidence and the actual 0/1 correctness. It can be decomposed into alignment error, sharpness and an irreducible constant "uncertainty" due to only classification (not calibration) error [21]:

$$\underbrace{\mathbb{E}_{\mathbf{y}}[(v(\mathbf{y}) - c(\mathbf{y}))^2]}_{MSE} = \underbrace{\mathrm{Var}_{\mathbf{y}}[v(\mathbf{y})]}_{uncertainty} - \underbrace{\mathrm{Var}_{\mathbf{y}}[e(c(\mathbf{y}))]}_{sharpness} + \underbrace{\mathbb{E}_{\mathbf{y}}[(e(c(\mathbf{y})) - c(\mathbf{y}))^2]}_{alignment\ error} \quad (1)$$

Alignment error and sharpness capture two orthogonal aspects of confidence calibration. A small alignment error implies that the confidence score is well aligned with the actual accuracy. However, small alignment error, alone, is not meaningful: the calibration can trivially achieve zero alignment error while being completely uninformative by assigning to all predictions the same confidence score, which is the average accuracy among all predictions on the dataset. A useful calibrator should also separate good predictions from bad ones as much as possible by assigning very different confidence scores to them. In other words, a good calibrator should simultaneously minimize alignment error and maximize sharpness. This can be achieved by minimizing MSE, thus MSE makes a natural objective for calibrator training. Minimizing MSE leads to a standard regression task: one can simply train a regressor c that maps each prediction $\mathbf{y}$ to its binary correctness $v(\mathbf{y})$. Note that training a calibrator by optimizing MSE does not require estimation of $e(c(\mathbf{y}))$, but evaluating its sharpness and alignment error does. Estimating $e(c(\mathbf{y}))$ by bucketing predictions has some subtle issues, as we shall explain later when we present evaluation results in Sect. 2.4.

2.2 Features for Calibration

Besides the training objective, we also need to decide the parametric form of the calibrator and the features to be used. In order to explain the choices we make, we shall use the calibration on WISE dataset[1] as a running example.

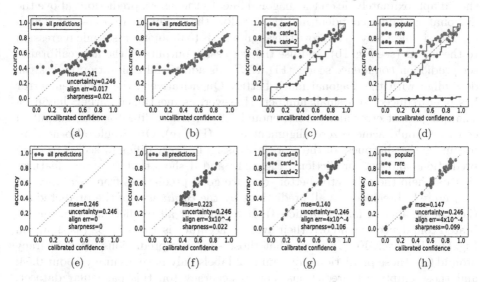

Fig. 1. Multi-label set prediction confidence vs. set prediction accuracy on the WISE dataset. In all sub-figures, each dot represents a group of 100 set predictions with similar confidence scores. The average confidence score in the group is used as x-coordinate, and the average prediction accuracy is used as y-coordinate. (a) BR predictions with the original BR confidence scores. (e) Trivial calibration that gives all predictions the same confidence score which is the overall set accuracy on the dataset. (b) Isotonic regression (the solid line) trained on all predictions. (f) Predictions with isotonic regression calibrated confidence. (c) Break down all predictions by the set cardinality and train a separate isotonic regression (the solid line) for each cardinality. (g) Predictions with confidence calibrated by cardinality-based isotonic regressions. (d) Group all predictions into 3 categories by the popularity of predicted label combination in the training data ground truth (*popular* = the predicted label combination appears at least 100 times; *rare* = the predicted label combination appears less than 100 times; *new* = the predicted label combination does not appear at all in training data), and train a separate isotonic regression (the solid line) for each category. (h) Predictions with confidence calibrated by popularity-based isotonic regressions. To simplify the presentation, all calibrators are trained and evaluated on the same data.

---

[1] https://www.kaggle.com/c/wise-2014/data.

Let us start by visualizing BR's predictions together with its original set prediction confidence calculated as $p(\mathbf{y}|x) = \prod_{l=1}^{L} p(y_l|x)$, in which the individual label probabilities $p(y_l|x)$ have been well-calibrated by standard isotonic regression procedures. We group about every 100 predictions with similar confidence scores into a bucket, and plot those buckets as dots treating the average confidence in the group as the x-coordinate and treating the average prediction accuracy in the group as the y-coordinate[2]. Figure 1a shows that the set confidence scores computed this way are not calibrated even when the individual label confidence scores have been well-calibrated. Well calibrated set predictions should approximately lie on the diagonal line. In the figure, predictions above the diagonal are under-confident and those below the diagonal are over-confident.

The simplest way to improve the alignment is to fit another isotonic regression to these dots (see Fig. 1b), and use the regression outputs as the new calibrated set prediction confidence scores (Fig. 1f). This additional calibration makes the dots align with the diagonal much better. Quantitatively, the alignment error has been reduced to a small number. However, as mentioned earlier, having a small alignment error alone is not enough, as a trivial calibrator that outputs a constant would achieve zero alignment error (Fig. 1e). One would also need to maximize the sharpness of the scores, by assigning very different scores to good predictions and bad predictions. Figure 1c and d show that there are features that can help the calibrator better separate good predictions from bad ones.

Figure 1c breaks down all predictions by the *cardinality* of the predicted set (i.e. the number of labels predicted). If we look at all predictions with uncalibrated confidence around 0.7, their average accuracy is around 0.58 (as shown in Fig. 1b). However, Fig. 1c shows that those singleton predictions have accuracy around 0.8; those predictions containing 2 labels only have accuracy about 0.54; and those empty set predictions have 0 accuracy (on this particular dataset, the ground truth set is always non-empty). Clearly, predictions with different cardinalities require different calibration mappings from the uncalibrated confidence to the actual accuracy. Fitting a separate isotonic regression for each cardinality results in Fig. 1g, which is a clear improvement over the calibration without cardinality (Fig. 1f); thus cardinality feature greatly increases sharpness and reduces MSE. Visually, more points have moved towards left and right ends.

Another useful feature is the *popularity* of predicted label set in the training data (i.e., prior probability). Between two predictions with the same uncalibrated BR confidence, the one that is more popular often has a higher chance of being correct, as shown in Fig. 1d. One can quantize the prior probability into intervals and train separate isotonic regressions for different intervals. Figure 1h shows that this also performs better than having only one isotonic regression.

Both set cardinality and prior probability are features defined on the whole label set, rather than individual labels. Such features capture constraints and dependencies among labels, which were not originally considered by BR.

---

[2] This particular way of bucketing is only for visualization purpose; when we evaluate calibration quantitatively we follow the standard practice of using 10 equal-width buckets.

Therefore these features supplement BR's own prediction score and allow the calibrator to make better overall judgments on the predicted set. There can be other features that help the calibrator better judge set predictions. In order to incorporate arbitrary number of features and avoid manual partitioning of the data and training separate calibrators (which quickly becomes infeasible as the number of features grows), a general multi-variate regressor should be employed. The multi-variate extension of isotonic regression exists [32], but it is not well suited to our problem because some features such as cardinality do not have a monotonic relationship with the calibrated confidence (see Fig. 1c). [21] proposes KNN and regression trees as calibrators for general structured prediction problem.

2.3 Calibrator Model Training

In this work, we choose Gradient Boosted Trees (GB) [11] as the calibrator model. Similar to regression trees, GB as a multi-variate regressor automatically partitions the prediction's feature space into regions and outputs (approximately) the average prediction accuracy in each region as the calibrated confidence score. GB often produces smoother output than trees and generalizes better. GB is also very powerful in modeling complex feature interactions automatically by building many trees on top of the features. To leverage its power we also use the binary representation of the set prediction y itself as features for GB. This way GB can discover additional rules concerning certain label interactions that are not described by the manually designed features (for example, "if two conflicting labels A and B are both predicted, the prediction is never correct, therefore lower the confidence score"). It is also possible to use instance features x during calibration, but we do not find it helpful because BR was already built on x.

There are two commonly used GB variants [11]. The first variant, GB-MSE, uses the tree ensemble score as the output, and MSE as the training objective. The second variant, GB-KL, adds a sigmoid transformation to the ensemble score and uses KL-divergence as the training objective. GB-MSE has the advantage of directly minimizing MSE, which matches the evaluation metric used for calibration (see Sect. 2.1). But it has the disadvantage that its output is not bounded between 0 and 1 and one has to clip its output in order to treat that as a confidence score.

GB-KL has the advantage of providing bounded output, but its training objective does not directly match the evaluation metric used for calibration; note, however, that minimizing KL-divergence also encourages the model output to match the average prediction accuracy, hence achieves the calibration effect. It may appear that one could get the best of both worlds by having sigmoid transformation and MSE training objective at the same time. Unfortunately, adding sigmoid makes MSE a non-convex function of the ensemble scores, thus hard to optimize. In this paper, we choose GB-MSE as our GB calibrator and shall simply call it GB from now on. In supplementary material, we show that GB-KL has very similar performance.

Each BR set prediction is transformed to a feature vector (containing original BR confidence score, set cardinality, set prior probability, and set binary representation) and the binary correctness of the prediction is used as the regression target. Since the goal of GB calibrator is to objectively evaluate BR's prediction accuracy, it is critical that the calibration data to be disjoint from the BR classifier training data. Otherwise, when BR over-fits its training data, the calibrator will see over-optimistic results on the same data and learn to generate over-confident scores. Similarly, it is also necessary to further separate the label calibration data and the set calibration data, since the product of the calibrated label probabilities is used as input to the set calibrator training.

Imposing Partial Monotonicity. Imposing monotonicity is a standard practice in univariate calibration methods such as isotonic regression [31] and Platt scaling [28,39] as it avoids over-fitting and leads to better interpretability. Imposing (partial) monotonicity for a multi-variate calibrator is more challenging. Certain features considered in calibration are expected to be monotonically related to the confidence. For example, the confidence should always increase with the popularity (prior probability) of the predicted set, if all other features of the prediction are unchanged. The same is true for BR score. The rest of the features, including the cardinality of the set and the binary representation of the set, do not have monotonic relations with confidence. Therefore the calibration function is partially monotonic. We have done additional experiments on imposing partial monotonicity for the GB calibrator but did not observe significant improvement (details and experiment results are in supplementary material).

Table 1. Datasets characteristics; label sets = number of label combinations in training set; cardinality = average number of labels per instance; inst/label = the average number of training instances per label. Datasets are obtained from http://mulan. sourceforge.net/datasets-mlc.html, http://cocodataset.org and https://www.kaggle. com/c/wise-2014/data

Dataset	BIBTEX	OHSUMED	RCV1	TMC	WISE	MSCOCO
Domain	bkmark	medical	news	reports	articles	image
Labels	159	23	103	22	203	80
Label sets	2,173	968	622	1,104	2,782	19,597
Features	1,836	12,639	47,236	49,060	301,561	4,096
Instances	7,395	13,929	6,000	28,596	48,643	123,287
Cardinality	2.40	1.68	3.21	2.16	1.45	2.90
Inst/label	89	811	150	2,244	278	3,572

2.4 Calibration Results

We test the proposed GB calibrator for BR set predictions on 6 commonly used multi-label datasets (see Table 1 for details). Each dataset is randomly split into training, calibration, validation and test subsets. BR model with logistic regression base learners is trained on training data; isotonic regression label calibrators and GB set calibrators are trained on (different parts of) calibration data. All hyper parameters in BR and calibrators are tuned on validation data. Calibration results are reported on test data.

For comparison, we consider the following calibrators:

- uncalib: use the uncalibrated BR probability as it is;
- isotonic: calibrate the BR probability with isotonic regression;
- card isotonic: for each label set cardinality, train one isotonic regression;
- tree: use the features considered by GB, train a single regression tree.

To make a fair comparison, for all methods, individual label probabilities have already been calibrated by isotonic regressions. We focus on their abilities to calibrate set predictions. BR prediction is made by thresholding each label's probability (calibrated by isotonic regression) at 0.5. This corresponds to the set with the highest BR score.

The evaluation metrics we use are MSE, sharpness and alignment error, as described in Sect. 2.1. Following the standard practice, we use 10 equal-width buckets to estimate sharpness and alignment error. One issue with evaluation by bucketing is that using different number of buckets leads to different estimations of alignment error and sharpness (but not MSE and uncertainty, whose computations do not depends on bucketing). In fact, increasing the number of buckets will increase both the estimated alignment error and sharpness by the same amount, due to Eq. 1. Using 10 buckets often produces negligible alignment error (relative to MSE), and the comparison effectively focuses on sharpness. This amounts to maximizing sharpness subject to a very small alignment error [14], which is often a reasonable goal in practice. All calibrators are able to achieve small alignment error (on the order of 10^{-3} and contributing to less than 10% of the MSE), so we do not report that. The results are summarized in Table 2. All calibrators improve upon the BR uncalibrated probabilities. Our GB calibrator

Table 2. BR prediction calibration performance in terms of MSE (the smaller the better) and sharpness (the bigger the better). Bolded numbers are the best.

Dataset	Uncertain	Uncalib		Isotonic		Card isotonic		Tree		GB	
		MSE	Sharp	MSE	Sharp	MSE	Sharp	MSE	Sharp	MSE	Sharp
BIBTEX	0.139	0.193	0.007	0.140	0.002	0.109	0.038	0.086	0.065	**0.068**	**0.072**
OHSUMED	0.232	0.226	0.015	0.221	0.013	**0.182**	**0.051**	0.211	0.039	0.189	0.047
RCV1	0.247	0.175	0.077	0.175	0.075	0.159	0.093	0.134	**0.129**	**0.123**	0.126
TMC	0.212	0.192	0.019	0.192	0.020	0.192	0.022	0.194	0.029	**0.180**	**0.032**
WISE	0.249	0.252	0.017	0.234	0.017	0.151	0.098	0.166	0.093	**0.147**	**0.102**
MSCOCO	0.227	0.158	0.075	0.151	0.075	0.150	0.076	0.163	0.070	**0.143**	**0.083**

achieves the overall best MSE and sharpness calibration performance, due to use of additional features extracted from set predictions.

3   Rerank Multi-label Predictions

Now we aim to improve BR's prediction accuracy, by fixing some of the prediction mistakes BR made due to ignoring label dependencies. Our solution is based on the calibrator we just developed. Traditionally, the only role of a calibrator is to map an uncalibrated confidence score to a calibrated confidence score. In that sense the calibrator usually does not affect the classification, only the confidence. In fact, popular univariate calibrators such as isotonic regression and Platt scaling implement monotonic functions, thus preserve the ranking/argmax of predictions. For our multi-variate GB calibrator, however, this is not the case. Even if we constrain the calibrated confidence to be monotonically increasing with the BR prediction scores, there are still other features that may affect the ranking; in particular the argmax predictions before and after calibration might be different **y** sets. If indeed different, the prediction based on calibrated confidence takes into account label dependencies and other constraints (which BR does not), and is more likely to be the correct set (even when the calibrated confidence is not very high in absolute terms). Therefore we can also use GB as a multi-label wrapper on top of BR to rerank its predictions. We name this method as ***BR-rerank***. Figure 2 shows two example images from the MSCOCO datasets on which BR-rerank corrects BR's predictions.

(a)   (b)

Fig. 2. Two example images from the MSCOCO datasets on which BR-rerank corrects BR's predictions. For (a), BR-rerank adds the correct label `baseball glove` to BR's predictions. For (b), BR-rerank removes the incorrect label `toothbrush` from BR's predictions.

To do so, we use a two stage prediction pipeline. For each test instance x, we first list the top K label set candidates **y** by highest BR uncalibrated scores. This can be done efficiently using a dynamic programming procedure which takes advantage of the label independence assumption made in BR, described in [23], and included in the supplementary material of this paper for the sake of completeness. Although the label independence assumption does not hold in practice, we find empirically that when K is reasonably large (e.g., $K = 50$), the correct **y** is often included in the top-K list. The chance that the correct answer is included in the top-K list is commonly called "oracle accuracy", and it is an upper bound of the final prediction accuracy. Empirically, we observe the oracle accuracy to be much higher than the final prediction accuracy, indicating that the candidate generation stage is not a bottleneck of final performance.

Prediction stage two: send the top set candidates with their scores and additional features to the GB calibrator, and select the one with the highest calibrated confidence as the final prediction. The calibrator has to be trained on more than top-1 BR candidates (on a separate calibration dataset) to evaluate correctly prediction candidates, so we train the GB calibrator on top-K candidates. Table 3 shows the two-stage BR-rerank predictions on the two example images in Fig. 2.

Table 3. The two-stage BR-rerank predictions on the two example images in Fig. 2. For each example image, the left column of the table shows the top-5 set prediction candidates generated by BR. The middle column shows the uncalibrated BR confidence score. The right column shows the calibrated BR-rerank confidence score. For Fig. 2a: BR predicts the incorrect set {person,baseball bat} with confidence 0.58. BR-rerank predicts the correct set {person, baseball bat, baseball glove} with confidence 0.17. For Fig. 2b: BR predicts the incorrect set {person, remote, toothbrush} with confidence 0.70. BR-rerank predicts the correct set {person, remote} with confidence 0.18.

Prediction on Fig. 2a		
y candidates	BR score	BR-rerank score
person, baseball bat	0.58*	0.16
person, baseball bat, baseball glove	0.35	0.17*
person, handbag, baseball bat	0.02	0.04
person, sports ball, baseball bat	0.02	0.08
person, handbag, baseball bat, baseball glove	0.01	0.03
Prediction on Fig. 2b		
y candidates	BR score	BR-rerank score
person, remote, toothbrush	0.70*	0.16
person, remote	0.24	0.18*
person, toothbrush	0.03	0.05
person	0.01	0.02
person, tennis racket, remote, toothbrush	0.01	0.01

3.1 Conceptual Comparison with Related Multi-label Classifiers

Although the proposed BR-rerank classifier has a very simple design, it has some advantages over many existing multi-label classifiers. Here we make some conceptual comparisons between BR-rerank and related multi-label classifiers.

BR-rerank can be seen as a stacking method in which a stage-1 model provides initial estimations and a stage-2 model uses these estimations as input and makes the final decision. There are other stacking methods proposed in the literature, and the two most well-known ones are called 2BR [15,34] and DBR [25]. The stage-1 models in 2BR and DBR are also BR models just as in BR-rerank. The stage-2 models in 2BR and DBR work differently. In 2BR, the stage-2 model predicts each label ℓ with a separate binary classifier which takes as input the original instance feature vector x as well as all label probabilities predicted by the stage-1 model. In DBR, the stage-2 model predicts each label ℓ with a separate binary classifier which takes as input the original instance feature vector x as well as the binary absence/presence information of all other labels. The absence/presence of label ℓ itself is not part of the input to avoid learning a trivial mapping. During training, the absence/presence information is obtained from the ground truth; during prediction, it is obtained from the stage-1 model's prediction. Clearly for DBR there is some inconsistency on how stage-2 inputs are obtained. BR-rerank and 2BR do not suffer from such inconsistency. All three stacking methods BR-rerank, 2BR, and DBR try to incorporate label dependencies into final classification. However, both 2BR and DBR have a critical flaw: when their stage-2 models make the final decision for a particular label, they do not really take into account the *final decisions* made for other labels by the stage-2 model; they instead only consider the *initial estimations* on other labels made by the stage-1 model, which can be quite different. As a result, the final set predictions made by 2BR and DBR may not respect the label dependencies/constraints these models have learned. By contrast, the stage-2 model in BR-rerank directly evaluates the final set prediction (based on its binary representation and other extracted features) to make sure that the final set prediction satisfies the desired label dependencies/constraints. For example, in the RCV1 dataset, each instance has at least one label. But DBR predicted the empty set on 6% of the test instances. By contrast, BR-rerank never predicted empty set on this dataset.

Many multi-label methods avoid the label independence assumption made in BR and model the joint distribution $p(\mathbf{y}|x)$ in more principled ways. Examples include Conditional Random Fields (CRF) [13], Conditional Bernoulli Mixtures (CBM) [23], and Probabilistic Classifier Chains (PCC) [7,22,24,30]. Despite the joint estimation formulation, CRF, CBM, and PCC in practice often produce over-confident set prediction confidence scores, due to overfitting. Their prediction confidence must also be post-calibrated.

The pair-wise CRF model [13] captures pairwise label interactions by estimating 4 parameters for each label pair. However, because the model needs to assign dedicated parameters to different label combinations, modeling higher order label dependencies becomes infeasible. The BR-rerank approach we propose relies on boosted trees to automatically build high order interactions as tree learns their splits on the binary representation of the label set – there is no need to allocate parameters in advance. There is another CRF model designed specifically to capture exclusive or hierarchical label relations [9]; this works only when the label dependency graph is *strict* and *a priori* known.

CBM is a latent variable model and represents the joint as a mixture of binary relevance models. However, it is hard to directly control the kinds of dependencies CBM learns, or to enforce constraints in the prediction. For example, CBM often predicts the empty set even on dataset where empty prediction is not allowed. There is no easy way to enforce the cardinality constraint in CBM.

PCC decomposes the joint $p(\mathbf{y}|x)$ into a product of conditional probabilities $p(y_1|x)p(y_2|x, y_1) \cdots p(y_L|x, y_1, \ldots, y_{L-1})$, and reduces a multi-label problem to L binary problems, each of which learns a new label given all previous labels. However, different label chaining orders can lead to different results, and to find the best order is often a challenge. In BR-rerank, all labels are treated as features in the GB calibrator training and they are completely symmetric.

The Structured Prediction Energy Network (SPEN) [1] uses deep neural networks to efficiently encode arbitrary relations between labels, which to large degree avoids parameterization issue associated with pair-wise CRF, but it cannot generate a confidence score for its MAP prediction as computing the normalization constant is intractable. The Predict-and-Constraint method (PC) [2] specifically handles cardinality constraint (but not other label constraints or relations) during learning and prediction. Deep value network (DVN) [18] trains a neural network to evaluate prediction candidates and then uses back-propagation to find the prediction that leads to the maximum score. The idea is similar to our BR-rerank idea. The difference is: DVN could only use the binary encoding of the label set, but not any higher level features extracted from the label set, such as cardinality and prior set probability. That is because its gradient based inference makes it very difficult to directly incorporate such features. There are methods that seek to rank labels [3,12]. Our method differs from theirs in that we rank label sets as opposed to individual labels, and we take into account label dependencies in the label set.

3.2 Classification Results

We test the proposed BR-rerank classifier on 6 popular multi-label datasets (see Table 1 for details). All datasets used in experiments contain at least a few thousands instances. We do not take datasets with only a few hundred instances as their testing performance tends to be quite unstable. We also do not consider datasets with extremely large number of labels as our method is not designed for extreme classification (our method aims to maximize set accuracy but on extreme data it is very unlikely to predict the entire label set correctly due to large label set cardinality and annotation noise). We compare BR-rerank with many other well-known multi-label methods: Binary Relevance (BR) [35], 2BR [15,34], DBR [25], pair-wise Conditional Random Field (CRF) [13], Conditional Bernoulli Mixture (CBM) [23], Probabilistic Classifier Chain (PCC) [30],

Structured Prediction Energy Network (SPEN) [1], PD-Sparse (PDS) [38], Predict-and-Constrain (PC) [2], Deep value network (DVN) [18], Multi-label K-nearest neighbors (KNN) [41], and Random k-label-sets (RAKEL) [36].

Table 4. Prediction performance in terms of set accuracy (top) and instance F1 (bottom). Numbers are shown as percentages. Bold numbers are the best ones on each dataset. "–" means the method could not finish within 24 h on a server with 56 cores and 256G RAM or 4 NVIDIA Tesla V100 GPUs. The ranking indicates for each method, on average over datasets, what position its performance is (lower is better). Our BR-rerank has the best average ranking on both measures. Note also that BR is not the worst as one might naively assume. Hyper parameters for all methods have been tuned on validation set.

Dataset	BR	BR-rerank	2BR	DBR	CBM	CRF	SPEN	PDS	DVN	PC	PCC	RAKEL	KNN
BIBT	16.6	21.5	16.1	20.2	22.9	**23.3**	14.8	16.1	16.2	20.3	21.4	18.3	8.4
OHSU	36.6	**42.0**	37.5	37.6	40.5	40.4	29.1	34.8	18.6	29.5	38.0	39.3	25.4
RCV1	44.5	53.2	42.3	45.8	**55.3**	53.8	27.5	40.8	13.7	39.7	48.7	46.0	46.2
TMC	30.4	**33.3**	32.1	31.7	30.8	28.2	26.7	23.4	20.3	23.0	31.3	27.6	18.9
WISE	52.9	60.5	51.8	55.8	**61.0**	46.4	–	52.4	28.3	–	55.9	3.5	2.4
MSCO	34.7	**35.9**	33.7	32.0	31.1	35.1	34.1	25.0	29.9	31.1	32.1	32.6	29.1
Ranking	6.3	1.8	6.7	5.7	3.3	3.8	10.0	9.8	11.2	10.0	4.5	6.8	11.0
Dataset	BR	BR-rerank	2BR	DBR	CBM	CRF	SPEN	PDS	DVN	PC	PCC	RAKEL	KNN
BIBT	35.9	42.2	36.7	40.1	45.3	46.2	38.6	40.4	47.3	**47.5**	40.9	38.3	23.0
OHSU	62.9	**67.5**	62.9	61.5	67.2	65.6	58.8	66.4	60.0	60.5	61.7	62.3	48.6
RCV1	77.0	78.8	77.5	72.8	**80.3**	75.0	66.5	76.7	36.3	71.7	75.6	76.1	72.3
TMC	65.8	66.8	**67.9**	66.1	65.2	64.4	66.2	64.0	65.5	61.7	64.9	63.6	52.2
WISE	68.3	75.4	69.1	69.9	**76.0**	60.7	–	73.6	62.3	–	69.7	6.2	5.6
MSCO	73.0	73.2	72.6	69.6	70.0	**73.9**	73.2	64.8	72.7	72.7	69.6	71.7	68.2
Ranking	6.3	2.5	5.5	7.3	4.0	5.7	8.3	6.8	7.5	8.8	7.5	8.7	12.0

For evaluation, we report set accuracy and instance F1, defined as:

$$\text{set accuracy} = \frac{1}{N} \sum_{n=1}^{N} \mathbb{I}(\mathbf{y}^{(n)} = \hat{\mathbf{y}}^{(n)}),$$

$$\text{instance F1} = \frac{1}{N} \sum_{n=1}^{N} \frac{2 \sum_{l=1}^{L} y_l^{(n)} \hat{y}_l^{(n)}}{\sum_{l=1}^{L} y_l^{(n)} + \sum_{l=1}^{L} \hat{y}_l^{(n)}},$$

where $\mathbf{y}^{(n)}$ and $\hat{\mathbf{y}}^{(n)}$ are the ground truth and predicted label set for the n-th instance, and $\mathbb{I}(\mathbf{y}^{(n)} = \hat{\mathbf{y}}^{(n)})$ returns 1 when the prediction is perfect and 0 otherwise.

To make a fair comparison, we use logistic regressions as the underlying learners for BR as well as the stage-1 models in BR-rerank, 2BR and DBR. We use gradient boosting as the underlying learners in PCC as well as the stage-2 models in BR-rerank, 2BR and DBR. Each dataset is randomly split into training, validation and test subsets. All classifiers are trained on the training set, with hyper parameters tuned on validation set. Supplementary material contains implementations and hyper parameters tuning details. For BR-rerank and 2BR, since the stage-2 model uses stage-1 model's out-of-sample prediction as input, the stage-1 model and stage-2 model are trained on different parts of the training data. For DBR, since the stage-2 model training only takes the ground truth labels as input, both stage-1 model and stage-2 model are trained on the whole training set.

Test performance is reported in Table 4. As expected, by reranking BR-independent-prediction candidates, BR-rerank outperforms BR significantly. We also observe that generally BR-rerank only needs to rerank the top-10 candidates from BR in order to achieve the best performance (supplementary material shows how its performance changes as K increases). On each dataset, we rank all algorithms by performance, and report each algorithm's average ranking across all datasets. BR-rerank has the best average ranking with both metrics, followed by CBM and CRF. We emphasize that with slightly better performance, BR-rerank is noticeably simpler to use than CBM and CRF. CBM and CRF require implementing dedicated training and prediction procedures, while BR-rerank can be ran by simply combining existing machine learning libraries such as LIBLINEAR [10] for BR and Xgboost [4] for GB. BR-rerank is also much faster than CBM and CRF. Its running time is determined mostly by its stage one, the BR classifier training. See Table 5 for a comparison.

Table 5. Training time of different methods, measured in seconds. All algorithms run multi-threaded on a server with 56 cores.

Dataset	BIBTEX	OHSUMED	RCV1	TMC	WISE	MSCOCO
BR	4	3	7	8	80	1380
BR-rerank	9	6	10	11	88	1393
CBM	64	210	70	224	1320	8520
CRF	353	268	1223	771	16363	14760

4   Other Related Work and Discussion

There are many other approaches to multi-label classification. Some of them focus on exploiting label structures [6,19,27,42]. Several approaches adapt existing machine learning models, such as Bayesian network [40], recurrent neural networks [26,29], and determinantal point process [37].

The idea of first generating prediction candidates and then reranking them using richer features has been considered in several natural language processing tasks, including parsing [8] and machine translation [33]. Here we show that the reranking idea, with properly designed models and features, is well suited for multi-label classification as well. Generative Adversarial Nets (GANs) [16] also employ two models, one for generating samples and one for judging these samples. GANs are usually trained in an unsupervised fashion, and are mainly used for generating new samples. By contrast, our BR-rerank is trained in supervised fashion, and its main goal is to do classification. Also the two models in GANs are trained simultaneously, while the two models in BR-rerank are trained in separate stages.

Besides isotonic regression and Platt scaling, there are also some recent developments on binary, multi-class, and structured prediction calibration methods [5,17,20,21]. Our work instead focuses on how to design the calibrator model and features for the BR multi-label classifier and how to take advantage of the calibrated confidence to get better multi-label predictions.

5   Conclusion

We improve BR's confidence estimation and prediction through a simple post calibration and reranking procedure. We take the BR predicted set of labels and its uncalibrated confidence as features, extract more features from the prediction that capture label constraints, such as the label set cardinality and prior probability, and apply gradient boosted trees (GB) as a calibrator to map the features to a better-calibrated confidence score. GB not only uses these manually designed features but also builds trees on binary label features to automatically model label interactions. This allows the calibrator to better separate good predictions from bad ones, yielding new confidence scores that are not only well aligned with accuracy but also sharp. We further demonstrate that using the new confidence scores we are able to rerank BR's prediction candidates to the point it outperforms state-of-the-art classifiers. Our code and data are available at https://github.com/cheng-li/pyramid.

Acknowledgments. We thank Jeff Woodward for sharing his observation regarding prediction set cardinality, Pavel Metrikov for the helpful discussion on the model design, and reviewers for suggesting related work. This work has been generously supported through a grant from the Massachusetts General Physicians Organization.

References

1. Belanger, D., McCallum, A.: Structured prediction energy networks. In: Proceedings of the International Conference on Machine Learning (2016)
2. Brukhim, N., Globerson, A.: Predict and constrain: modeling cardinality in deep structured prediction. arXiv preprint arXiv:1802.04721 (2018)
3. Bucak, S.S., Mallapragada, P.K., Jin, R., Jain, A.K.: Efficient multi-label ranking for multi-class learning: application to object recognition. In: 2009 IEEE 12th International Conference on Computer Vision, pp. 2098–2105. IEEE (2009)
4. Chen, T., Guestrin, C.: XGBoost: a scalable tree boosting system. In: Proceedings of the 22nd ACM SIGKDD International Conference on Knowledge Discovery and Data Mining, pp. 785–794. ACM (2016)
5. Chen, T., Navrátil, J., Iyengar, V., Shanmugam, K.: Confidence scoring using whitebox meta-models with linear classifier probes. arXiv preprint arXiv:1805.05396 (2018)

6. Chen, Y.N., Lin, H.T.: Feature-aware label space dimension reduction for multi-label classification. In: NIPS, pp. 1529–1537 (2012)
7. Cheng, W., Hüllermeier, E., Dembczynski, K.J.: Bayes optimal multilabel classification via probabilistic classifier chains. In: ICML 2010, pp. 279–286 (2010)
8. Collins, M., Koo, T.: Discriminative reranking for natural language parsing. Comput. Linguist. **31**(1), 25–70 (2005)
9. Deng, J., et al.: Large-scale object classification using label relation graphs. In: Fleet, D., Pajdla, T., Schiele, B., Tuytelaars, T. (eds.) ECCV 2014. LNCS, vol. 8689, pp. 48–64. Springer, Cham (2014). https://doi.org/10.1007/978-3-319-10590-1_4
10. Fan, R.E., Chang, K.W., Hsieh, C.J., Wang, X.R., Lin, C.J.: LIBLINEAR: a library for large linear classification. J. Mach. Learn. Res. **9**(Aug), 1871–1874 (2008)
11. Friedman, J.H.: Greedy function approximation: a gradient boosting machine. Ann. Stat. 1189–1232 (2001)
12. Fürnkranz, J., Hüllermeier, E., Mencía, E.L., Brinker, K.: Multilabel classification via calibrated label ranking. Mach. Learn. **73**(2), 133–153 (2008)
13. Ghamrawi, N., McCallum, A.: Collective multi-label classification. In: Proceedings of the 14th ACM International Conference on Information and Knowledge Management, pp. 195–200. ACM (2005)
14. Gneiting, T., Balabdaoui, F., Raftery, A.E.: Probabilistic forecasts, calibration and sharpness. J. R. Stat. Soc. Ser. B (Stat. Methodol.) **69**(2), 243–268 (2007)
15. Godbole, S., Sarawagi, S.: Discriminative methods for multi-labeled classification. In: Dai, H., Srikant, R., Zhang, C. (eds.) PAKDD 2004. LNCS (LNAI), vol. 3056, pp. 22–30. Springer, Heidelberg (2004). https://doi.org/10.1007/978-3-540-24775-3_5
16. Goodfellow, I., et al.: Generative adversarial nets. In: Advances in Neural Information Processing Systems, pp. 2672–2680 (2014)
17. Guo, C., Pleiss, G., Sun, Y., Weinberger, K.Q.: On calibration of modern neural networks. arXiv preprint arXiv:1706.04599 (2017)
18. Gygli, M., Norouzi, M., Angelova, A.: Deep value networks learn to evaluate and iteratively refine structured outputs. arXiv preprint arXiv:1703.04363 (2017)
19. Hsu, D., Kakade, S., Langford, J., Zhang, T.: Multi-label prediction via compressed sensing. In: NIPS, vol. 22, pp. 772–780 (2009)
20. Kuleshov, V., Fenner, N., Ermon, S.: Accurate uncertainties for deep learning using calibrated regression. arXiv preprint arXiv:1807.00263 (2018)
21. Kuleshov, V., Liang, P.S.: Calibrated structured prediction. In: Advances in Neural Information Processing Systems, pp. 3474–3482 (2015)
22. Kumar, A., Vembu, S., Menon, A.K., Elkan, C.: Learning and inference in probabilistic classifier chains with beam search. In: Flach, P.A., De Bie, T., Cristianini, N. (eds.) ECML PKDD 2012. LNCS (LNAI), vol. 7523, pp. 665–680. Springer, Heidelberg (2012). https://doi.org/10.1007/978-3-642-33460-3_48
23. Li, C., Wang, B., Pavlu, V., Aslam, J.A.: Conditional Bernoulli mixtures for multi-label classification. In: Proceedings of the 33rd International Conference on Machine Learning, pp. 2482–2491 (2016)
24. Liu, W., Tsang, I.: On the optimality of classifier chain for multi-label classification. In: Advances in Neural Information Processing Systems, pp. 712–720 (2015)
25. Montañes, E., Senge, R., Barranquero, J., Quevedo, J.R., del Coz, J.J., Hüllermeier, E.: Dependent binary relevance models for multi-label classification. Pattern Recogn. **47**(3), 1494–1508 (2014)

26. Nam, J., Mencía, E.L., Kim, H.J., Fürnkranz, J.: Maximizing subset accuracy with recurrent neural networks in multi-label classification. In: Advances in Neural Information Processing Systems, pp. 5413–5423 (2017)
27. Park, S.H., Fürnkranz, J.: Multi-label classification with label constraints. In: ECML PKDD 2008 Workshop on Preference Learning, pp. 157–171 (2008)
28. Platt, J., et al.: Probabilistic outputs for support vector machines and comparisons to regularized likelihood methods. Adv. Large Margin Classif. **10**(3), 61–74 (1999)
29. Qin, K., Li, C., Pavlu, V., Aslam, J.: Adapting RNN sequence prediction model to multi-label set prediction. In: Proceedings of the 2019 Conference of the North American Chapter of the Association for Computational Linguistics: Human Language Technologies, (Long and Short Papers), vol. 1, pp. 3181–3190 (2019)
30. Read, J., Pfahringer, B., Holmes, G., Frank, E.: Classifier chains for multi-label classification. Machine. Learn. **85**(3), 333–359 (2011)
31. Robertson, T.: Order restricted statistical inference. Technical report (1988)
32. Sasabuchi, S., Inutsuka, M., Kulatunga, D.: A multivariate version of isotonic regression. Biometrika **70**(2), 465–472 (1983)
33. Shen, L., Sarkar, A., Och, F.J.: Discriminative reranking for machine translation. In: HLT-NAACL 2004 (2004)
34. Tsoumakas, G., Dimou, A., Spyromitros, E., Mezaris, V., Kompatsiaris, I., Vlahavas, I.: Correlation-based pruning of stacked binary relevance models for multi-label learning. In: Proceedings of the 1st International Workshop on Learning from Multi-label Data, pp. 101–116 (2009)
35. Tsoumakas, G., Katakis, I.: Multi-label classification: an overview. Int. J. Data Warehous. Min. **2007**, 1–13 (2007)
36. Tsoumakas, G., Vlahavas, I.: Random k-labelsets: an ensemble method for multilabel classification. In: Kok, J.N., Koronacki, J., Mantaras, R.L., Matwin, S., Mladenič, D., Skowron, A. (eds.) ECML 2007. LNCS (LNAI), vol. 4701, pp. 406–417. Springer, Heidelberg (2007). https://doi.org/10.1007/978-3-540-74958-5_38
37. Xie, P., Salakhutdinov, R., Mou, L., Xing, E.P.: Deep determinantal point process for large-scale multi-label classification. In: ICCV, pp. 473–482 (2017)
38. Yen, I.E., Huang, X., Zhong, K., Ravikumar, P., Dhillon, I.S.: PD-Sparse: a primal and dual sparse approach to extreme multiclass and multilabel classification. In: Proceedings of the 33nd International Conference on Machine Learning (2016)
39. Zadrozny, B., Elkan, C.: Transforming classifier scores into accurate multiclass probability estimates. In: KDD, pp. 694–699. ACM (2002)
40. Zhang, M.L., Zhang, K.: Multi-label learning by exploiting label dependency. In: KDD, pp. 999–1008. ACM (2010)
41. Zhang, M.L., Zhou, Z.H.: ML-KNN: a lazy learning approach to multi-label learning. Pattern Recogn. **40**(7), 2038–2048 (2007)
42. Zhou, T., Tao, D., Wu, X.: Compressed labeling on distilled labelsets for multi-label learning. Mach. Learn. **88**(1–2), 69–126 (2012)

Pairwise Learning to Rank by Neural Networks Revisited: Reconstruction, Theoretical Analysis and Practical Performance

Marius Köppel[1(✉)], Alexander Segner[1], Martin Wagener[1], Lukas Pensel[1], Andreas Karwath[2], and Stefan Kramer[1]

[1] Johannes Gutenberg-Universität Mainz, Saarstraße 21, 55122 Mainz, Germany
makoeppe@students.uni-mainz.de
[2] University of Birmingham, Haworth Building (Y2), Birmingham B15 2TT, UK
a.karwath@bham.ac.uk

Abstract. We present a pairwise learning to rank approach based on a neural net, called DirectRanker, that generalizes the RankNet architecture. We show mathematically that our model is reflexive, antisymmetric, and transitive allowing for simplified training and improved performance. Experimental results on the LETOR MSLR-WEB10K, MQ2007 and MQ2008 datasets show that our model outperforms numerous state-of-the-art methods, while being inherently simpler in structure and using a pairwise approach only.

Keywords: Information retrieval · Machine learning · Learning to rank

1 Introduction

Information retrieval has become one of the most important applications of machine learning techniques in the last years. The vast amount of data in every day life, research and economy makes it necessary to retrieve only relevant data. One of the main problems in information retrieval is the *learning to rank* problem [6,17]. Given a query q and a set of documents $d_1, \ldots, d_n$ one wants to find a *ranking* that gives a (partial) order of the documents according to their relevance relative to q. Documents can in fact be instances from arbitrary sets and do not necessarily need to correspond to queries.

Web search is one of the most obvious applications, however, product recommendation or question answering can be dealt with in a similar fashion. Most

---

M. Köppel, A. Segner and M. Wagener—These authors contributed equally.

Electronic supplementary material The online version of this chapter (https://doi.org/10.1007/978-3-030-46133-1_15) contains supplementary material, which is available to authorized users.

U. Brefeld et al. (Eds.): ECML PKDD 2019, LNAI 11908, pp. 237–252, 2020.
https://doi.org/10.1007/978-3-030-46133-1_15

common machine learning methods have been used in the past to tackle the learning to rank problem [2,7,10,14]. In this paper we use an artificial neural net which, in a pair of documents, finds the more relevant one. This is known as the pairwise ranking approach, which can then be used to sort lists of documents. The chosen architecture of the neural net gives rise to certain properties which significantly enhance the performance compared to other approaches. We note that the structure of our neural net is essentially the same as the one of RankNet [2]. However, we relax some constraints which are used there and use a more modern optimization algorithm. This leads to a significantly enhanced performance and puts our approach head-to-head with state-of-the-art methods. This is especially remarkable given the relatively simple structure of the model and the consequently small training and testing times. Furthermore, we use a different formulation to describe the properties of our model and find that it is inherently reflexive, antisymmetric and transitive. In summary, the contributions of this paper are:

1. We propose a simple and effective scheme for neural network structures for pairwise ranking, called DirectRanker, which is a generalization of RankNet.
2. Theoretical analysis shows which of the components of such network structures give rise to their properties and what the requirements on the training data are to make them work.
3. Keeping the essence of RankNet and optimizing it with modern methods, experiments show that, contrary to general belief, pairwise methods can still be competitive with the more recent and much more complex listwise methods.

The paper is organized as follows: We discuss different models related to our approach in Sect. 2. The model itself and certain theoretical properties are discussed in Sect. 3 before describing the setup for experimental tests in Sect. 4 and their results in Sect. 5. Finally, we conclude our findings in Sect. 6.

2   Related Work

There are a few fundamentally different approaches to the learning to rank problem that have been applied in the past. They mainly differ in the underlying machine learning model and in the number of documents that are combined in the cost during training. Common examples for machine learning models used in ranking are: decision trees [8], support vector machines [4], artificial neural nets [5], boosting [22], and evolutionary methods [12]. During training, a model must rank a list of n documents which can then be used to compute a suitable cost function by comparing it to the ideally sorted list. If $n = 1$ the approach is called *pointwise*. A machine learning model assigns a numerical value to a single document and compares it to the desired relevance label to compute a cost function. This is analogous to a classification of each document. If $n = 2$ the approach is called *pairwise*. A model takes two documents and determines the more relevant one. We implement this concept in our model, the DirectRanker.

If $n > 2$ the approach is called *listwise* and the cost is computed on a whole list of sorted documents. Examples for these different approaches are [6,9,16] for pointwise, [2,4,8] for pairwise and [5,12,23] for listwise models.

Beside our own model the focus of this paper lies mainly on the pairwise approach RankNet [2] and the listwise approach LambdaMART [22]. RankNet is a neural net defining a single output for a pair of documents. For training purposes, a cross entropy cost function is defined on this output.

LambdaMART on the other hand is a boosted tree version of LambdaRank [3] which itself is based on RankNet. Here, listwise evaluation metrics M are optimized by avoiding cost functions and directly defining λ-gradients

$$\lambda_i = \sum_j S_{ij} \left| \Delta M \frac{\partial C_{ij}}{\partial o_{ij}} \right|$$

where ΔM is the difference in the listwise metric when exchanging documents i and j in a query, C is a pairwise cost function, and o_{ij} is a pairwise output of the ranking model. $S_{ij} = \pm 1$ depending on whether document i or j is more relevant.

The main advantages of RankNet and LambdaMART are training time and performance: While RankNet performs well on learning to rank tasks it is usually outperformed by LambdaMART considering listwise metrics which is usually the goal of learning to rank. On the other hand, since for the training of LambdaMART it is necessary to compute a contribution to λ_i for every combination of two documents of a query for all queries of a training set, it is computationally more demanding to train this model compared to the pairwise optimization of RankNet (cf Table 2).

In general, multiple publications (most prominently [5]) suggest that listwise approaches are fundamentally superior to pairwise ones. As the results of the experiments discussed in Sect. 5.1 show, this is not necessarily the case.

Important properties of rankers are their reflexivity, antisymmetry and transitivity. To implement a reasonable order on the documents these properties must be fulfilled. In [20] the need for antisymmetry and a simple method to achieve it in neural nets are discussed. Also [2] touches on the aspect of transitivity. However, to the best of our knowledge, a rigorous proof of these characteristics for a ranking model has not been presented so far. A theoretical analysis along those lines is presented in Sect. 3 of the paper.

3   DirectRanker Approach

Our approach to ranking is of the pairwise kind, i.e. it takes two documents and decides which one is more relevant than the other. This approach comes with some difficulties, as, to achieve a consistent and unique ranking, the model has to define an order. In our approach, we implement a quasiorder $\succeq$ on the feature space $\mathcal{F}$ such that the ranking is unique except for equivalent documents, i.e. documents with the same relevance label. This quasiorder satisfies the following conditions for all $x, y, z \in \mathcal{F}$:

(A) Reflexivity: $x \succeq x$
(B) Totality: $x \not\succeq y \Rightarrow y \succeq x$
(C) Transitivity: $(x \succeq y \wedge y \succeq z) \Rightarrow x \succeq z$

We implement such an order using a ranking function $r : \mathcal{F} \times \mathcal{F} \to \mathbb{R}$ by defining

$$x \succeq y :\Leftrightarrow r(x,y) \geq 0. \tag{1}$$

The conditions (A)–(C) for $\succeq$ can be imposed in form of the following conditions for r:

  (I) Reflexivity: $r(x,x) = 0$
 (II) Antisymmetry: $r(x,y) = -r(y,x)$
(III) Transitivity: $(r(x,y) \geq 0 \wedge r(y,z) \geq 0) \Rightarrow r(x,z) \geq 0$

In our case, r is the output of a neural network with specific structure to fulfill the above requirements. As shown by [20], the antisymmetry can easily be guaranteed in neural network approaches by removing the biases of the neurons and choosing antisymmetric activation functions. Of course, the result will only be antisymmetric, if the features fed into the network are antisymmetric functions of the documents themselves, i.e., if two documents A and B are to be compared by the network, the extracted features of the document pair have to be antisymmetric under exchange of A and B.

This leads to the first difficulty since it is not at all trivial to extract such features containing enough information about the documents. Our model avoids this issue by taking features extracted from each of the documents and optimizing suitable antisymmetric features as a part of the net itself during the training process. This is done by using the structure depicted in Fig. 1.

The corresponding features of two documents are fed into the two subnets nn_1 and nn_2, respectively. These networks can be of arbitrary structure, yet they have to be identical, i.e. share the same structure and parameters like weights, biases, activation, etc. The difference of the subnets' outputs is fed into a third subnet, which further consists only of one ouptut neuron with antisymmetric activation and without a bias, representing the above defined function r. With the following theorem we show that this network satisfies conditions (I) through (III):

Theorem 1. *Let f be the output of an arbitrary neural network taking as input feature vectors $x \in \mathcal{F}$ and returning values $f(x) \in \mathbb{R}^n$. Let o_1 be a single neuron with antisymmetric and sign conserving activation function and without bias taking $\mathbb{R}^n$-valued inputs. The network returning $o_1(f(x) - f(y))$ for $x,y \in \mathcal{F}$ then satisfies (I) through (III).*

Proof. Let the activation function of the output neuron be $\tau : \mathbb{R} \to \mathbb{R}$ with $\tau(-x) = -\tau(x)$ and $\mathrm{sign}(\tau(x)) = \mathrm{sign}(x)$ as required.

  (I) If (II) is fulfilled, then (I) is trivially so because

$$r(x,x) = -r(x,x) \forall x \in \mathcal{F} \Rightarrow r(x,x) \equiv 0.$$

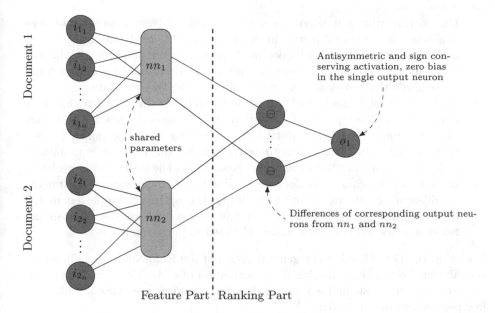

Fig. 1. Schema of the DirectRanker. nn_1 and nn_2 can be arbitrary networks (or other function approximators) as long as they give the same output for the same inputs i_j. The bias of the output neuron o_1 has to be zero and the activation antisymmetric and sign conserving.

(II) The two networks nn_1 and nn_2 are identical (as they share the same parameters). Hence, they implement the same function $f : \mathcal{F} \to \mathbb{R}^n$. The output of the complete network for the two input vectors $x, y \in \mathcal{F}$ is then given by:

$$r(x,y) = \tau[w(f(x) - f(y))] = \tau[wf(x) - wf(y)] =: \tau[g(x) - g(y)], \qquad (2)$$

where w is a weight vector for the output neuron and $g : \mathcal{F} \to \mathbb{R}$. This is antisymmetric for x and y, thus satisfying the second condition (II).

(III) Let $x, y, z \in \mathcal{F}$, $r(x,y) \geq 0, r(y,z) \geq 0$, and let g be defined as in 2. Since τ is required to retain the sign of the input, i.e. $\tau(x) \geq 0 \Leftrightarrow x \geq 0$, $g(x) \geq g(y)$ and $g(y) \geq g(z)$, one finds

$$r(x,z) = \tau[g(x) - g(z)] = \tau\Big[\underbrace{g(x) - g(y)}_{\geq 0} + \underbrace{g(y) - g(z)}_{\geq 0}\Big] \geq 0.$$

Thus, r is transitive and (III) is fulfilled. □

These properties offer some advantages during the training phase of the networks for the distinction of different relevance classes:

(i) Due to antisymmetry, it is sufficient to train the network by always feeding instances with higher relevance in one and instances with lower relevance in the other input, i.e. higher relevance always in i_1 and lower relevance always in i_2 or vice versa.

(ii) Due to transitivity, it is not necessary to compare very relevant and very irrelevant documents directly during training. Provided that every document is trained at least with documents from the corresponding neighbouring relevance classes, the model can implicitly be trained for all combinations, given that all classes are represented in the training data.

(iii) Although it might seem to be sensible to train the model such that it is able to predict the equality of two different documents of the same relevance class, the model is actually restricted when doing so: If the ranker is used to sort a list of documents according to their relevance, there is no natural order of documents within the same class. Hence, the result of the ranker is not relevant for equivalent documents. Furthermore, when only documents of different classes are paired in training, the optimizer employed in the training phase has more freedom to find an optimal solution for ranking relevant cases, potentially boosting the overall performance.

Note that the DirectRanker is a generalization of the RankNet model [2], which is equivalent to the DirectRanker if the activation of o_1 is $\tau(x) = \tanh\left(\frac{x}{2}\right)$, and if a cross entropy cost, and a gradient descent optimizer are chosen, which are free parameters in our model.

For simplicity, we will from now on choose the activation function to be $\tau \equiv \mathrm{id}$. This can be done without loss of generality, since the activation function does not change the order, if τ is sign conserving.

In the following, we try to put the DirectRanker on a more sound basis by analyzing some cases in which the DirectRanker is able to approximate an order (given enough complexity and training samples). More precisely, we present some cases in which the following conditions are guaranteed to be met:

(i) There exists an order $\succeq$ satisfying (A)–(C) on the feature space $\mathcal{F}$.

(ii) A given order $\succeq$ on $\mathcal{F}$ can be represented by the DirectRanker, i.e. there is a continuous function $r : \mathcal{F} \times \mathcal{F} \to \mathbb{R}$ implementing the axioms (I)–(III) and which can be written as $r(x, y) = g(x) - g(y)$ on the whole feature space.

By the universal approximation theorem [11], the second condition implies that r can be approximated to arbitrary precision by the DirectRanker. In the following, we will discuss interesting cases, in which these assumptions are valid:

Theorem 2. *For every countable feature space $\mathcal{F}$ there exists an order $\succeq$ that is reflexive, antisymmetric, and transitive.*

Proof. By definition, for a countable set $\mathcal{F}$, there exists an injective function $g : \mathcal{F} \to \mathbb{N}$. Therefore, choose $x \succeq y :\Leftrightarrow g(x) \geq g(y)$ for $x, y \in \mathcal{F}$. $\square$

In fact, every sorting of the elements of countable sets satisfies (A)–(C), and as we show in the next theorem, it can be approximated by the direct ranker, if the set is uniformly dense:

Theorem 3. *Let $\succeq$ implement (A)–(C) on an uniformly discrete feature space $\mathcal{F}$. Then, the DirectRanker can approximate a function that represents $\succeq$.*

Proof. First, consider $\mathcal{F}$ to be an infinite set. We will use the same notation as above to describe the ranking function r in terms of a continuous function g such that $r(x,y) = g(x) - g(y)$. Since we use neural networks to approximate g, referring to the universal approximation theorem [11], it is sufficient to show that a continuous function $g : \mathbb{R}^n \to \mathbb{R}$ exists such that r has the required properties. We will show that such a function exists by explicit construction. We can iterate through $\mathcal{F}$, since it is discrete and, therefore, countable. Now assign each element $x \in \mathcal{F}$ a value $g(x) \in \mathbb{R}$. Map the first value x_0 to 0, and then iteratively do the following with the i-th element of $\mathcal{F}$:

p1.1 If $\exists j : j < i \wedge x_i \succeq x_j \wedge x_j \succeq x_i$, set $g(x_i) := g(x_j)$ and continue with the next element.

p1.2 If $\forall j$ with $j < i : x_i \succeq x_j$, set $g(x_i) := \max\limits_{j<i} g(x_j) + 1$ and continue with the next element.

p1.3 If $\forall j$ with $j < i : x_j \succeq x_i$, set $g(x_i) := \min\limits_{j<i} g(x_j) - 1$ and continue with the next element. If there are $j, k < i$ with $x_k \succeq x_i \succeq x_j$, choose an arbitrary "largest element smaller than x_i", i.e. an element $x_l \in \mathcal{F}, l < i$ satisfying $x_i \succeq x_l \succeq x \forall x \in \{x_j \in \mathcal{F} | j < i, x_j \not\succeq x_i\}$, and an arbitrary "smallest element larger than x_i", i.e. an element $x_g \in \mathcal{F}, g < i$ such that $x \succeq x_g \succeq x_i \forall x \in \{x_k \in \mathcal{F} | k < i, x_i \not\succeq x_k\}$. Then set $g(x_i) := \frac{g(x_l)+g(x_g)}{2}$ and continue with the next element. This is well-defined since steps 1 through 3 guarantee that every x_l that can be chosen this way is mapped to the same value by g. Analogously for x_g.

One easily sees that this yields a function g for which $g(x) \geq g(y) \Leftrightarrow x \succeq y \, \forall x, y \in \mathcal{F}$ and thus $r(x,y) = g(x) - g(y) \geq 0 \Leftrightarrow x \succeq y$.

Next, we expand g to a continuous function in $\mathbb{R}^n$. Since $\mathcal{F}$ is uniformly discrete, $\exists \delta > 0 \forall i \in \mathbb{N} : B_\delta(x_i) \cap \mathcal{F} = \{x_i\}$, where $B_\delta(x_i) := \{x \in \mathbb{R}^n | \|x - x_i\| < \delta\}$. For every $i \in \mathbb{N}$ define $\tilde{B}_i : \overline{B_{\delta/42}(x_i)} \to \mathbb{R}, x \mapsto 1 - \frac{42\|x-x_i\|}{\delta}$. $\tilde{B}_i$ is obviously continuous on $\overline{B_{\delta/42}(x_i)}$. Expanding this definition to

$$B_i(x) := \begin{cases} \tilde{B}_i(x) & \text{if } x \in \overline{B_{\delta/42}(x_i)} \\ 0 & \text{else} \end{cases}$$

allows us to define a function $g_c : \mathbb{R}^n \to \mathbb{R}, x \mapsto \sum_{i=1}^{\infty} g(x_i) B_i(x)$ which results in the same value as g for all relevant points x_i. This can easily be checked, since $B_n(x_m) = \delta_{mn}$ (using the Kronecker-delta). Thus, it still represents $\succeq$ on $\mathcal{F}$. B_i is continuous since $B_i|_{\overline{B_{\delta/4}}} = \tilde{B}_i$ and $B_i|_{\mathbb{R}^n \setminus B_{\delta/4}} \equiv 0$ are continuous and, therefore, B_i is continuous on the union of these closed sets. We now show that g_c is continuous using the ε-δ-definition:

Let $\varepsilon > 0$ and $x \in \mathbb{R}^n$. If there is no $n \in \mathbb{N}$ such that $x \in \overline{B_{\delta/42}(x_i)}$, we can choose $\tilde{\delta} > 0$ such that $B_{\tilde{\delta}}(x) \cap \overline{B_{\delta/42}(x_i)} = \emptyset \, \forall n \in \mathbb{N}$ since $\mathcal{F}$ is uniformly discrete. Therefore, $g_c|_{B_{\tilde{\delta}}} \equiv 0$ and $|g_c(\tilde{x}) - g_c(x)| = 0 < \varepsilon \forall \tilde{x} \in B_{\tilde{\delta}}(x)$.

If there is such an n, then $B_{\delta/4}(x) \cap \overline{B_{\delta/42}(x_i)}$ is non-empty, if and only if $n = i$. Hence, we can choose $\frac{\delta}{4} > \tilde{\delta} > 0$, such that $|g_c(\tilde{x}) - g_c(x)| < \varepsilon \forall \tilde{x} \in B_{\tilde{\delta}}(x)$

since $g_c|_{B_{\delta/4}(x_i)} = g(x_i) \cdot B_i|_{B_{\delta/4}(x_i)}$ is clearly continuous. Therefore, for every $\varepsilon > 0$ and $x \in \mathbb{R}^n$ we can find $\tilde{\delta} > 0$ such that $|g_c(\tilde{x}) - g_c(x)| < \varepsilon \forall \tilde{x} \in B_{\tilde{\delta}(x)}$, i.e., g_c is continuous.

If $\mathcal{F}$ is finite with N elements, set $g(x_k) = 0$ for $k > N$. Then the proof works analogously as the above. □

Therefore, it theoretically feasible to successfully train the DirectRanker on any finite dataset, and consequently on any real-world dataset. However, the function g might be arbitrarily complex depending on the explicit order. In real-world applications, the desired order is usually not discrete and the task at hand is to predict the order of elements *not* represented in the training data. In the following, we give a reasonably weak condition for which an order $\succeq$ can be approximated by the DirectRanker on more general feature spaces:

Theorem 4. *Let $\succeq$ implement (A)–(C) and $\mathcal{F} \subset \mathbb{R}^n$ be convex and open. For every $x \in \mathcal{F}$ define*

$$\mathcal{P}_x := \{y \in \mathcal{F}|x \nsucceq y\}, \ \mathcal{N}_x := \{y \in \mathcal{F}|y \nsucceq x\}, \ \partial_x := \{y \in \mathcal{F}|x \succeq y \wedge y \succeq x\}.$$

Furthermore, let $(\mathcal{F}/\sim, d)$ be a metric space, where $x \sim y \Leftrightarrow y \in \partial_x$ and $d(\partial_x, \partial_y) = \inf\limits_{x' \in \partial_x, y' \in \partial_y} \|x' - y'\|$. Then, the DirectRanker can approximate $\succeq$ if $\mathcal{P}_x$ and $\mathcal{N}_x$ are open for all $x \in \mathcal{F}$.

Proof (Sketch of the proof). By using the relations (A)–(C), one can show that the function $g : \mathcal{F} \to \mathbb{R}$,

$$g(x) = \begin{cases} d(\partial_{x_0}, \partial_x) & \text{if } x \in \mathcal{P}_{x_0} \\ -d(\partial_{x_0}, \partial_x) & \text{if } x \in \mathcal{N}_{x_0} \quad \forall x \in \mathcal{F} \\ 0 & \text{if } x \in \partial_{x_0} \end{cases}$$

with $g(x_0) = 0$ for some $x_0 \in \mathcal{F}$ satisfies the requirements that g is continuous and implements (A)–(C). This can be done by regarding lines from $x'_0 \in \partial_{x_0}$ to $x \in \mathcal{P}_{x_0}$ and elaborating on the fact that the line has to pass through some $y' \in \partial_y$ if $x \in \mathcal{P}_y$. For more detail, see the supplementary material to this article. □

If there are no two documents with the same features but different relevances, any finite dataset can be extended to $\mathbb{R}^n$ such that the conditions for Theorem 4 are met. In real-world applications, i.e. applications with noisy data, it is in general possible that $\mathcal{P}_x$, $\mathcal{N}_x$, and ∂_x blur out and overlap. In this case, it is of course impossible to find any function that represents $\succeq$. However, the Direct-Ranker still ought to be able to find a "best fit" of a continuous function that maximizes the predictive power on any new documents, even if some documents in the training set are mislabeled. Experiments investigating this are discussed in Sect. 5.2.

4   Experimental Setup

To evaluate the performance of our model and to compare it to other learning to rank approaches, we employ common evaluation metrics and standard datasets (MSLR-WEB10K, MQ2007, MQ2008 [19]). Furthermore we use synthetic data to investigate the dependence of the performance on certain characteristics of the data. Reliable estimates for the performance are gained by averaging over different splits of the dataset using cross-validation on the predefined folds from the original publications and are compared to other models. In all tests, we use the tensorflow library [1] and its implementation of the Adam-Optimizer [15]. In Sect. 4.1 we briefly describe the structure of the LETOR datasets and in Sect. 4.2 how the models are evaluated. In Sect. 4.3 we illustrate how the synthetic datasets are generated and analyzed. For evaluating different models we apply the commonly used metrics NDCG and MAP which are further discussed in the supplemental material.

4.1   The LETOR Datasets

The *Microsoft Learning to Rank Datasets* (LETOR) and especially the MSLR–WEB10K set are standard data sets that are most commonly used to benchmark *learning to rank* models. The dataset consists of 10,000 queries and is a subset of the larger MSLR–WEB30K dataset. Each instance in the dataset corresponds to a query-document pair which is characterized by 136 numerical features. Additionally, relevance labels from 0 (irrelevant) to 4 (perfectly relevant) indicate the relevance of the given document with respect to the query. Ranking documents according to their relevance is often simplified by binarizing the relevance labels using an appropriate threshold, as is done by [12,13]. In our case, we map relevance labels ≥ 2 to 1 and relevance labels ≤ 1 to 0. We use this approach to compare our model to others.

Additionally we evaluate the different algorithms on the much smaller MQ2007 and MQ2008 datasets. These are similar in structure to the MSLR–WEB10K set with some minor differences: The relevance labels range from 0 to 2 and each document consists of 46 features. In this case we binarize the relevance labels by mapping labels ≥ 1 to 1 and relevance labels $= 0$ to 0.

4.2   Grid Search and LETOR Evaluation

We perform grid searches for hyperparameter optimization of our model. The grid searches were performed using the *GridSearchCV* class implemented in the *scitkit-learn* library [18]. One grid search was done to optimize the NDCG@10 and one optimizing the MAP. For each hyperparameter point a 5-fold cross validation (internal) was performed on each training set on each of the 5 predefined folds of the datasets. The models were then again trained using the best hyperparameters using the entire training set before averaging the performance on independent test sets over all 5 folds (external). Before training the model the data was transformed in such a way that the features are following a normal distribution with standard deviation of $1/3$.

For benchmarking the results, the most common *learning to rank* algorithms were also trained and tested with the same method as described above. The implementation of these algorithms are taken from the RankLib library implemented in the Lemur Project [21]. The algorithms are: RankNet [2], AdaRank [23], LambdaMART [22], and ListNet [5].

The used datasets contain queries with only non relevant documents for which the evaluation metrics are not defined. Consequently we exclude those queries from the data.

Furthermore, there are queries with less than 10 documents. For such queries with $k < 10$ documents the NDCG@k is evaluated during the tests.

4.3 Synthetic Data Generation and Evaluation

To study how the DirectRanker performs for differently structured datasets, synthetic data with different characteristics were created and evaluated.

To achieve comparability between the different sets, all datasets have the following properties in common:

(i) The dataset consists of separate training and test sets which are generated independently, but with the same parameters.

(ii) For each relevance class, the features follow a Gaussian distribution in feature space with a constant, but random mean between 0 and 100, and a constant, but random standard deviation between 50 and 100.

(iii) Except for a test in which the performance depending on the size of the dataset is studied, all training sets consist of 10^5 and all test sets consist of 10^4 documents.

(iv) During training, $r(d_i)(1 - o_1(d_i, d_j))^2$ is applied as the cost function as pairs are constructed such that $r(d_i) - r(d_j) = 1$. Here, $r(d)$ is the relevance label of document d.

For the different tests, one parameter describing the dataset is changed and evaluated for different values, keeping all other parameters fixed. These parameters include the size of the training set, the number of relevance classes, the number of features, and noise on the labels. The noise for the labels is generated by assuming a Gaussian for each label with variable standard deviation and rounding to the next integer. This allows for testing larger greater degrees of confusion between more distant relevance classes.

The general procedure for the experiments is the following:

(1) A dataset with the respective parameters is created.

(2) The DirectRanker is trained on the generated training set using our framework.

(3) The trained ranker is tested on the generated test set, again using our framework. For this, 50–150 random samples are drawn from the test set. This subset is then sorted using the trained model and the NDCG@20 is calculated.

The whole test is repeated 50 times and the average value of NDCG@20 over these 50 random subsets is calculated.

(4) These three steps are repeated at least four more times to determine a mean value μ for the NDCG@20, averaged over different datasets with the same characteristics. The standard error is calculated as an uncertainty $\Delta\mu$ of μ.

In the plots showing our test results (Fig. 2a, b, d, c), every data point is the result of applying these four steps for one choice of the dataset parameters. nn_1 and nn_2 consist of a hidden layer with 70 neurons and another one with as many neurons as there are relevance classes. The results of these tests are discussed in Sect. 5.2.

5 Experimental Results

In this section we present the experimental results. First, we compare our model with the commonly used ones (Sect. 5.1). Additionally, we give an outline of the sensitivity on different dataset properties (Sect. 5.2).

5.1 Comparison to Other Rankers

In Table 1 the results of different models on the datasets discussed in Sect. 4.1 are shown. On the MQ2007 and MQ2008 datasets the differences between the models are insignificant (0.54σ difference in the NDCG@10 between the best and worst performing algorithms on the MQ2008 dataset) making the experiments on these sets inconclusive. However, the results on the MSLR–WEB10K set differ significantly. Here LambdaMart outperforms the DirectRanker by 7.2σ on the NDCG@10. On the MAP however, the difference is only 0.2σ. It is important to

Table 1. Performance comparison for different rankers on multiple Letor datasets. The values for ES-Rank, IESR-Rank and IESVM-Rank are taken from [13]. These values are marked with italic. LambdaMart was boosted using the corresponding evaluation metric during training.

Algorithm	MSLR-WEB10K		MQ2008		MQ2007	
	$\langle$NDCG$\rangle$	$\langle$MAP$\rangle$	$\langle$NDCG$\rangle$	$\langle$MAP$\rangle$	$\langle$NDCG$\rangle$	$\langle$MAP$\rangle$
DirectRanker	0.440(4)	0.365(3)	0.720(12)	0.636(11)	0.540(10)	0.534(9)
RankNet	0.157(3)	0.195(2)	0.716(11)	0.642(10)	0.525(11)	0.525(7)
ListNet	0.157(3)	0.192(2)	0.719(10)	0.647(6)	0.526(10)	0.525(9)
LambdaMart	0.476(3)	0.366(3)	0.723(7)	0.624(6)	0.531(12)	0.510(11)
AdaRank	0.400(16)	0.322(10)	0.722(10)	0.653(9)	0.526(10)	0.527(10)
ES-Rank	*0.382*	*0.570*	*0.507*	*0.483*	*0.451*	*0.470*
IESR-Rank	*0.415*	*0.603*	*0.517*	*0.494*	*0.455*	*0.473*
IESVM-Rank	*0.224*	*0.457*	*0.498*	*0.473*	*0.436*	*0.456*

note that for LambdaMart the model was explicitly boosted on NDCG@10 and MAP respectively for the two performance values while the DirectRanker uses a cost function independent of the evaluation metric. On the MSLR–WEB10K set the DirectRanker outperforms all other methods by at least 2.4σ (NDCG@10) or 3.2σ (MAP).

Table 2. Comparing the average run times over the five folds of the MSLR–WEB10K data set in seconds. The values with * were trained on the machine mentioned in the text. The values with † were trained using RankLib. The values with ‡ are taken from [13]. For RankNet two implementations were used. One with Tensorflow and one from RankLib.

Algorithm	Time in seconds
DirectRanker*	151.94(41)
RankNet*	142.27(69)
RankNet*†	2215(351)
AdaRank*†	1261(50)
LambdaMART*†	2664(234)
ListNet*†	3947(481)
ES-Rank‡	1800
IESR-Rank‡	1957
IESVM-Rank‡	34 209

To demonstrate the simplicity of the DirectRanker, we present experiments on the runtime for the model training in Table 2. All tests performed by us have been conducted on an Intel® Core™ i7-6850K CPU @ 3.60 GHz using the above mentioned MSLR–WEB10K dataset averaging over the five given folds. Our model was trained using Tensorflow [1], contrary to the other implementations. This makes the comparison of the run times difficult, however, we also reimplemented RankNet using Tensorflow in the same way as our model. Here it can be seen that the runtime of the DirectRanker and RankNet are of the same order. Thus, we do not boost the training time of the model but only the performance. On the other hand the training time beats all the other models.[1]

5.2 Sensitivity on Dataset Properties

With the following tests we discuss how the DirectRanker performs under different circumstances. The tests were performed as described in Sect. 4.3. The performance of the DirectRanker was tested for different numbers of relevance classes (Fig. 2a), features (Fig. 2b), for variations of noise on the class labels (Fig. 2c), and differently sized training sets (Fig. 2d).

---

[1] For our implementation of the model and the tests see https://github.com/kram erlab/direct-ranker.

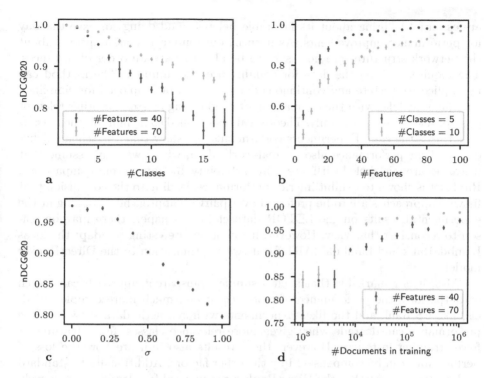

Fig. 2. Plots depicting the sensitivity of the DirectRanker performance on certain data properties, evaluated on the synthetic data (Sect. 4.3). (a) Dependence on the number of relevance classes (10^5 documents in training set). (b) Dependence on the number of features (10^5 documents in training set, five relevance classes). (c) Performance of the DirectRanker with different noise levels on the class labels with 5 classes and 70 features. (d) Dependence on the size of the training set (five relevance classes).

The tests show that, given enough data, our model is able to handle a diverse range of datasets. It especially shows that the DirectRanker can handle many relevance classes as shown in Fig. 2a. As one would expect, the performance decreases with the number of relevance classes. However, this effect can be counteracted by increasing the size of the training set (see Fig. 2d) or the number of features (Fig. 2b). Additionally, Fig. 2c shows the robustness of the DirectRanker against noise on the relevance classes. Up to some small noise (approximately 5% mislabeling, i.e. $\sigma = 0.25$), the performance decreases only marginally, but drops significantly for larger noise. Still, even with 50% of the documents being mislabeled (i.e. $\sigma = 0.75$) the NDCG@20 does not drop below 0.80. This suggests that the theoretical findings in Sect. 3 for ideal data stay valid for real-world data.

6   Discussion and Conclusions

The scheme for network structures proposed and analyzed in this paper is a generalization of RankNet: We show which properties of components of RankNet are essential to bring about its favorable behavior and doing so, pave the way for performance improvements. As it turns out, only a few assumptions about the network structures are necessary to be able to learn an order of instances. The requirements on the data for training are also minimal: The method can be applied to discrete and continuous data, and can be employed for simplified training schedules with the comparison of neighboring classes (or other relevant pairs of relevance classes) only. Theoretical results shed some light on the reasons why this is the case. Experiments confirm this and show that the scheme delivers excellent performance also on real-world data, where we may assume that instances are mislabeled with a certain probability. In many recent comparisons, RankNet is shown to exhibit inferior performance, leading to the conclusion that listwise approaches are to be preferred over pairwise approaches. Looking at the experimental results on the LETOR dataset in this paper, there may be reason to reconsider that view. However, it might be interesting to adapt the ideas LambdaRank and LambdaMART for listwise optimization to the DirectRanker model.

Also, it is remarkable that such a simple, transparent approach can match or outperform the performance of more recent and much more complex models, like ES-Rank and the like. Experiments with synthetic data show how the performance can degrade when given more relevance classes, fewer features or fewer training instances. However, these results also indicate how the loss of performance can be compensated by the other factors. Additionally to standard ranking, we suggest that the DirectRanker can be used for classification as well. First tests showed promising results. A more systematic investigation of this is the subject of future work.

Acknowledgement. We would like to thank Dr. Christian Schmitt for his contributions to the work presented in this paper.

We also thank Luiz Frederic Wagner for proof(read)ing the mathematical aspects of our model.

Parts of this research were conducted using the supercomputer Mogon and/or advisory services offered by Johannes Gutenberg University Mainz (hpc.uni-mainz.de), which is a member of the AHRP (Alliance for High Performance Computing in Rhineland Palatinate, www.ahrp.info) and the Gauss Alliance e.V.

The authors gratefully acknowledge the computing time granted on the supercomputer Mogon at Johannes Gutenberg University Mainz (hpc.uni-mainz.de).

This research was partially funded by the Carl Zeiss Foundation Project: 'Competence Centre for High-Performance-Computing in the Natural Sciences' at the University of Mainz. Furthermore, Andreas Karwath has been co-funded by the MRC grant MR/S003991/1.

References

1. Abadi, M., et al.: TensorFlow: large-scale machine learning on heterogeneous systems (2015). http://tensorflow.org/
2. Burges, C., et al.: Learning to rank using gradient descent. In: Proceedings of the 22nd International Conference on Machine Learning, ICML 2005, pp. 89–96. ACM, New York (2005). http://doi.acm.org/10.1145/1102351.1102363

3. Burges, C., Ragno, R., Le, Q., Burges, C.J.: Learning to rank with non-smooth cost functions. In: Advances in Neural Information Processing Systems 19. MIT Press, Cambridge, January 2007. https://www.microsoft.com/en-us/research/publication/learning-to-rank-with-non-smooth-cost-functions/
4. Cao, Y., Xu, J., Liu, T.Y., Li, H., Huang, Y., Hon, H.W.: Adapting ranking SVM to document retrieval. In: Proceedings of the 29th Annual International ACM SIGIR Conference on Research and Development in Information Retrieval, pp. 186–193. ACM (2006). https://doi.org/10.1145/1148170.1148205
5. Cao, Z., Qin, T., Liu, T.Y., Tsai, M.F., Li, H.: Learning to rank: from pairwise approach to listwise approach, p. 9, April 2007. https://www.microsoft.com/en-us/research/publication/learning-to-rank-from-pairwise-approach-to-listwise-approach/
6. Cooper, W.S., Gey, F.C., Dabney, D.P.: Probabilistic retrieval based on staged logistic regression. In: Proceedings of the 15th Annual International ACM SIGIR Conference on Research and Development in Information Retrieval, pp. 198–210. ACM (1992). http://doi.acm.org/10.1145/133160.133199
7. Freund, Y., Iyer, R., Schapire, R.E., Singer, Y.: An efficient boosting algorithm for combining preferences. J. Mach. Learn. Res. 4(Nov), 933–969 (2003). http://dl.acm.org/citation.cfm?id=945365.964285
8. Friedman, J.H.: Greedy function approximation: a gradient boosting machine. Ann. Stat. 29, 1189–1232 (2000). http://www.jstor.org/stable/2699986
9. Fuhr, N.: Optimum polynomial retrieval functions based on the probability ranking principle. ACM Trans. Inf. Syst. (TOIS) 7(3), 183–204 (1989)
10. Herbrich, R., Graepel, T., Obermayer, K.: Large margin rank boundaries for ordinal regression. In: Advances in Large Margin Classifiers, pp. 115–132 (2000)
11. Hornik, K., Stinchcombe, M., White, H.: Multilayer feedforward networks are universal approximators. Neural Netw. 2(5), 359–366 (1989). https://doi.org/10.1016/0893-6080(89)90020-8
12. Ibrahim, O.A.S., Landa-Silva, D.: ES-Rank: evolution strategy learning to rank approach. In: Proceedings of the Symposium on Applied Computing, pp. 944–950. ACM (2017). https://doi.org/10.1145/3019612.3019696
13. Ibrahim, O.A.S., Landa-Silva, D.: An evolutionary strategy with machine learning for learning to rank in information retrieval. Soft Comput. 22(10), 3171–3185 (2018). https://doi.org/10.1007/s00500-017-2988-6
14. Jiang, L., Li, C., Cai, Z.: Learning decision tree for ranking. Knowl. Inf. Syst. 20(1), 123–135 (2009)
15. Kingma, D.P., Ba, J.: Adam: a method for stochastic optimization. arXiv preprint arXiv:1412.6980 (2014)
16. Li, P., Wu, Q., Burges, C.J.: McRank: learning to rank using multiple classification and gradient boosting. In: Advances in Neural Information Processing Systems, pp. 897–904 (2008)
17. Liu, T.Y.: Learning to rank for information retrieval. Found. Trends Inf. Retr. 3(3), 225–331 (2009). https://doi.org/10.1561/1500000016
18. Pedregosa, F., et al.: Scikit-learn: machine learning in python. J. Mach. Learn. Res. 12, 2825–2830 (2011)
19. Qin, T., Liu, T.: Introducing LETOR 4.0 datasets. CoRR abs/1306.2597 (2013). http://arxiv.org/abs/1306.2597
20. Rigutini, L., Papini, T., Maggini, M., Bianchini, M.: A neural network approach for learning object ranking. In: Kůrková, V., Neruda, R., Koutník, J. (eds.) ICANN 2008. LNCS, vol. 5164, pp. 899–908. Springer, Heidelberg (2008). https://doi.org/10.1007/978-3-540-87559-8_93

21. Croft, W.B., Callan, J.: Lemur toolkit (2001–2012). http://lemurproject.org/contrib.php
22. Wu, Q., Burges, C.J., Svore, K.M., Gao, J.: Adapting boosting for information retrieval measures. Inf. Retr. **13**, 254–270 (2010). https://www.microsoft.com/en-us/research/publication/adapting-boosting-for-information-retrieval-measures/
23. Xu, J., Li, H.: AdaRank: a boosting algorithm for information retrieval. In: Proceedings of the 30th Annual International ACM SIGIR Conference on Research and Development in Information Retrieval, SIGIR 2007, pp. 391–398. ACM, New York (2007). https://doi.org/10.1145/1277741.1277809

Sequential Learning over Implicit Feedback for Robust Large-Scale Recommender Systems

Aleksandra Burashnikova[1,2(✉)], Yury Maximov[1,3], and Massih-Reza Amini[2]

[1] Skolkovo Institute of Science and Technology, Moscow, Russia
{Aleksandra.Burashnikova,y.maximov}@skoltech.ru
[2] Université Grenoble Alpes, Grenoble, France
Massih-Reza.Amini@univ-grenoble-alpes.fr
[3] Theoretical Division T-5 and CNLS, Los Alamos National Laboratory,
Los Alamos, USA
yury@lanl.gov

Abstract. In this paper, we propose a theoretically founded sequential strategy for training large-scale Recommender Systems (RS) over implicit feedback mainly in the form of clicks. The proposed approach consists in minimizing pairwise ranking loss over blocks of consecutive items constituted by a sequence of non-clicked items followed by a clicked one for each user. Parameter updates are discarded if for a given user the number of sequential blocks is below or above some given thresholds estimated over the distribution of the number of blocks in the training set. This is to prevent from updating the parameters for an abnormally high number of clicks over some targeted items, mainly due to bots; or very few user interactions. Both scenarios affect the decision of RS and imply a shift over the distribution of items that are shown to the users. We provide a proof of convergence of the algorithm to the minimizer of the ranking loss, in the case where the latter is convex. Furthermore, experimental results on five large-scale collections demonstrate the efficiency of the proposed algorithm concerning the state-of-the-art approaches, both regarding different ranking measures and computation time.

1 Introduction

With the increasing number of products available online, there is a surge of interest in the design of automatic systems—generally referred to as Recommender Systems (RS)—that provide personalized recommendations to users by adapting to their taste. The study of RS has become an active area of research these past years, especially since the Netflix Prize [1]. One characteristic of online recommendation is the huge unbalance between the available number of products and

Electronic supplementary material The online version of this chapter (https://doi.org/10.1007/978-3-030-46133-1_16) contains supplementary material, which is available to authorized users.

those shown to the users. Another aspect is the existence of bots that interact with the system by providing too many feedback over some targeted items; or many users that do not interact with the system over the items that are shown to them. In this context, the main challenges concern the design of a scalable and an efficient online RS in the presence of noise and unbalanced data. These challenges have evolved in time with the continuous development of data collections released for competitions or issued from e-commerce[1]. New approaches for RS now primarily consider *implicit* feedback, mostly in the form of clicks, that are easier to collect than *explicit* feedback which is in the form of scores. Implicit feedback is more challenging to deal with as they do not depict the preference of a user over items, i.e., (no)click does not necessarily mean (dis)like [9]. For this case, most of the developed approaches are based on the Learning-to-rank paradigm and focus on how to leverage the click information over the unclick one without considering the sequence of users' interactions.

In this paper, we propose a new SequentiAl RecOmmender System for implicit feedback (called SAROS), that updates the model parameters user per user over blocks of items constituted by a sequence of unclicked items followed by a clicked one. The parameter updates are discarded for users who interact very little or a lot with the system. For other users, the update is done by minimizing the average ranking loss of the current model that scores the clicked item below the unclicked ones in a corresponding block. Recently, many other approaches that model the sequences of users feedback have been proposed, but they all suffer from a lack of theoretical analysis formalizing the overall learning strategy. In this work, we analyze the convergence property of the proposed approach and show that in the case where the global ranking loss estimated over all users and items is convex; then the minimizer found by the proposed sequential approach converges to the minimizer of the global ranking loss. Experimental results conducted on five large publicly available datasets show that our approach is highly competitive compared to the state-of-the-art models and, it is significantly faster than both the batch and the online versions of the algorithm.

The rest of this paper is organized as follows. Section 2 relates our work to previously proposed approaches. Section 3 introduces the general ranking learning problem that we address in this study. Then, in Sect. 3.3, we present the SAROS algorithm and provide an analysis of its convergence. Section 4 presents the experimental results that support this approach. Finally, in Sect. 5, we discuss the outcomes of this study and give some pointers to further research.

2   Related Work

Two main approaches have been proposed for recommender systems. The first one, referred to as Content-Based recommendation or cognitive filtering [17], makes use of existing contextual information about the users (e.g., demographic information) or items (e.g., textual description) for the recommendation. The second approach referred to as Collaborative Filtering and undoubtedly the

---

[1] https://www.kaggle.com/c/outbrain-click-prediction.

most popular one [25], relies on past interactions and recommends items to users based on the feedback provided by other similar users. Traditionally, collaborative filtering systems were designed using *explicit* feedback, mostly in the form of rating [11]. However, rating information is non-existent on most e-commerce websites and is challenging to collect, and user interactions are often done sequentially. Recent RS systems focus on learning scoring functions using *implicit* feedback, in order to assign higher scores to clicked items than to unclicked ones rather than to predict the clicks as it is usually the case when we are dealing with explicit feedback [6,18,30]. The idea here is that even a clicked item does not necessarily express the preference of a user for that item, it has much more value than a set of unclicked items for which no action has been made. In most of these approaches, the objective is to rank the clicked item higher than the unclicked ones by finding a suitable representation of users and items in a way that for each user the ordering of the clicked items over unclicked ones is respected by dot product in the joint learned space. One common characteristic of publicly available collections for recommendation systems is the huge unbalance between positive (click) and negative feedback (no-click) in the set of items displayed to the users, making the design of an efficient online RS extremely challenging. Some works propose to weight the impact of positive and negative feedback directly in the objective function [16] to improve the quality. Another approach is to sample the data over a predefined buffer before learning [13], but these approaches do not model the shift over the distribution of positive and negative items, and the system's performance on new test data may be affected. Many new approaches tackle the sequential learning problem for RS by taking into account the temporal aspect of interactions directly in the design of a dedicated model and are mainly based on Markov Models (MM), Reinforcement Learning (RL) and Recurrent Neural Networks (RNN) [2]. Recommender systems based on Markov Models, consider the sequential interaction of users as a stochastic process over discrete random variables related to predefined user behavior. These approaches suffer from some limitations mainly due to the sparsity of the data leading to a poor estimation of the transition matrix [22]. Various strategies have been proposed to leverage the impact of sparse data, for example by considering only the last frequent sequences of items and using finite mixture models [22], or by combining similarity-based methods with high-order Markov Chains [19]. Although it has been shown that in some cases the proposed approaches can capture the temporal aspect of user interactions but these models suffer from high complexity and generally they do not pass the scale. Some other methods consider RS as a Markov decision process (MDP) problem and solve it using reinforcement learning (RL) [15,27]. The size of discrete actions bringing the RL solver to a larger class of problems is also a bottleneck for these approaches. Very recently Recurrent neural networks such as GRU or LSTM, have been proposed for personalized recommendations [7,10,26], where the input of the network is generally the current state of the session, and the output is the predicted preference over items (probabilities for each item to be clicked next). Our proposed strategy differs from other sequential based approaches in the way that the model parameters are updated, at each time a block of unclicked items followed by a clicked one is constituted; and by controlling the number of blocks per user interaction. If for a given user, this number is below or above two prede-fined thresholds found over the distribution of the number of blocks, parameter updates for that particular user are discarded. Ultimately, we provide a proof of convergence of the proposed approach.

3   Framework and Problem Setting

Throughout, we use the following notation. For any positive integer n, $[n]$ denotes the set $[n] \doteq \{1, \ldots, n\}$. We suppose that $\mathcal{I} \doteq [M]$ and $\mathcal{U} \doteq [N]$ are two sets of indexes defined over items and users. Further, we assume that each pair con-stituted by a user u and an item i is identically and independently distributed according to a fixed yet unknown distribution $\mathcal{D}_{\mathcal{U},\mathcal{I}}$.

At the end of his or her session, a user $u \in \mathcal{U}$ has reviewed a subset of items $\mathcal{I}_u \subseteq \mathcal{I}$ that can be decomposed into two sets: the set of preferred and non-preferred items denoted by $\mathcal{I}^+{}_u$ and $\mathcal{I}^-{}_u$, respectively. Hence, for each pair of items $(i, i') \in \mathcal{I}^+{}_u \times \mathcal{I}^-{}_u$, the user u prefers item i over item i'; symbolized by the relation $i \succ_u i'$. From this preference relation a desired output $y_{u,i,i'} \in \{-1, +1\}$ is defined over the pairs $(u, i) \in \mathcal{U} \times \mathcal{I}$ and $(u, i') \in \mathcal{U} \times \mathcal{I}$, such that $y_{u,i,i'} = +1$ if and only if $i \succ_u i'$. We suppose that the indexes of users as well as those of items in the set $\mathcal{I}_u$, shown to the active user $u \in \mathcal{U}$, are ordered by time.

Finally, for each user u, parameter updates are performed over blocks of consec-utive items where a block $\mathcal{B}_u^t = N_u^t \sqcup \varPi_u^t$, corresponds to a time-ordered sequence (w.r.t. the time when the interaction is done) of no-preferred items, N_u^t, and at least one preferred one, $\varPi_u^t$. Hence, $\mathcal{I}^+{}_u = \bigcup_t \varPi_u^t$ and $\mathcal{I}^-{}_u = \bigcup_t N_u^t; \forall u \in \mathcal{U}$.

3.1   Learning Objective

Our objective here is to minimize an expected error penalizing the misordering of all pairs of interacted items i and i' for a user u. Commonly, this objective is given under the Empirical Risk Minimization (ERM) principle, by minimizing the empirical ranking loss estimated over the items and the final set of users who interacted with the system:

$$\hat{\mathcal{L}}_u(\omega) = \frac{1}{|\mathcal{I}^+{}_u||\mathcal{I}^-{}_u|} \sum_{i \in \mathcal{I}^+{}_u} \sum_{i' \in \mathcal{I}^-{}_u} \ell_{u,i,i'}(\omega), \tag{1}$$

and $\mathcal{L}(\omega) = \mathbb{E}_u\left[\hat{\mathcal{L}}_u(\omega)\right]$, where $\mathbb{E}_u$ is the expectation with respect to users cho-sen randomly according to the uniform distribution, and $\hat{\mathcal{L}}_u(\omega)$ is the pairwise ranking loss with respect to user u's interactions. As in other studies, we repre-sent each user u and each item i respectively by vectors $\mathbf{U}_u \in \mathbb{R}^k$ and $\mathbf{V}_i \in \mathbb{R}^k$ in the same latent space of dimension k [12]. The set of weights to be found $\omega = (\mathbf{U}, \mathbf{V})$, are then matrices formed by the vector representations of users $\mathbf{U} = (\mathbf{U}_u)_{u \in [N]} \in \mathbb{R}^{N \times k}$ and items $\mathbf{V} = (\mathbf{V}_i)_{i \in [M]} \in \mathbb{R}^{M \times k}$. The minimization of the ranking loss above in the batch mode with the goal of finding user and item embeddings, such that the dot product between these representations in the latent space reflects the best the preference of users over items, is a common approach. Other strategies have been proposed for the minimization of the empirical loss (1), among which the most popular one is perhaps the Bayesian Personalized Ranking (BPR) model [18]. In this approach, the instantaneous loss, $\ell_{u,i,i'}$, is the surrogate regularized logistic loss for some hyperparameter $\mu \geq 0$:

$$\ell_{u,i,i'}(\boldsymbol{\omega}) = \log\left(1 + e^{-y_{i,u,i'} \mathbf{U}_u^\top (\mathbf{V}_i - \mathbf{V}_{i'})}\right) + \mu(\|\mathbf{U}_u\|_2^2 + \|\mathbf{V}_i\|_2^2 + \|\mathbf{V}_{i'}\|_2^2) \quad (2)$$

The BPR algorithm proceeds by first randomly choosing a user u, and then repeatedly selecting two pairs $(i, i') \in \mathcal{I}_u \times \mathcal{I}_u$.

In the case where one of the chosen items is preferred over the other one (i.e. $y_{u,i,i'} \in \{-1, +1\}$), the algorithm then updates the weights using the stochastic gradient descent method over the instantaneous loss (2). In this case, the expected number of rejected pairs is proportional to $O(|\mathcal{I}_u|^2)$ [21] which may be time-consuming in general. Another drawback is that user preference over items depend mostly on the context where these items are shown to the user. A user may prefer (or not) two items independently one from another, but within a given set of shown items, he or she may completely have a different preference over these items. By sampling items over the whole set of shown items, this effect of local preference is unclear.

3.2 Algorithm SAROS

Another particularity of online recommendation which is not explicitly taken into account by existing approaches is the bot attacks in the form of excessive clicks over some target items. They are made to force the RS to adapt its recommendations toward these target items, or a very few interactions which in both cases introduce biased data for the learning of an efficient RS. In order to tackle these points, our approach updates the parameters whenever the number of constituted blocks per user is lower and upper-bounded (Fig. 1).

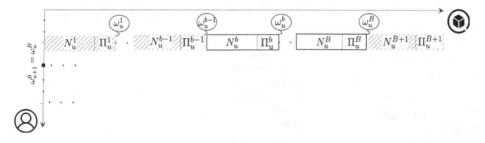

Fig. 1. A pictorial depiction of the sequential updates of weights $(\omega_u^t)_{1 \leq t \leq B}$ for a user $u \in \mathcal{U}$. The horizontal axis represents the sequence of interactions over items ordered by time. Each update of weights $\omega_u^t; t \in \{b, \ldots, B\}$ occurs whenever the corresponding sets of negative interactions, N_u^t, and positive ones, Π_u^t, exist, and that these number of interactions is lower and upper-bounded. For a new user $u+1$, the initial weights $\omega_{u+1}^0 = \omega_u^B$ are the ones obtained from the last update of the previous user's interactions.

In this case, at each time a block $\mathcal{B}_u^t = N_u^t \sqcup \Pi_u^t$ is formed; weights are updated by miniminzing the ranking loss corresponding to this block:

$$\hat{\mathcal{L}}_{\mathcal{B}_u^t}(\boldsymbol{\omega}_u^t) = \frac{1}{|\Pi_u^t||N_u^t|} \sum_{i \in \Pi_u^t} \sum_{i' \in N_u^t} \ell_{u,i,i'}(\boldsymbol{\omega}_u^t). \tag{3}$$

The pseudo-code of SAROS is shown in the following. Starting from initial weights $\boldsymbol{\omega}_1^0$ chosen randomly for the first user. For each current user u, having been shown I_u items, the sequential update rule consists in updating the weights, block by block where after t updates; where the $(t+1)^{th}$ update over the current block $\mathcal{B}_u^t = N_u^t \sqcup \Pi_u^t$ corresponds to one gradient descent step over the ranking loss estimated on these sets and which with the current weights $\boldsymbol{\omega}_u^t$ writes,

$$\boldsymbol{\omega}_u^{t+1} \leftarrow \boldsymbol{\omega}_u^t - \eta \nabla \hat{\mathcal{L}}_{\mathcal{B}_u^t}(\boldsymbol{\omega}_u^t) \tag{4}$$

To prevent from a very few interactions or from bot attacks, two thresholds b and B are fixed over the parameter updates. For a new user $u + 1$, the parameters are initialized as the last updated weights from the previous user's interactions in the case where the corresponding number of updates t was in the interval $[b, B]$; i.e. $\omega_{u+1}^0 = \omega_u^t$. On the contrary case, they are set to the same previous initial parameters; i.e., $\omega_{u+1}^0 = \omega_u^0$.

3.3 Convergence Analysis

We provide proofs of convergence for the SAROS algorithm under the typical hypo-

---

Algorithm SAROS: SequentiAl RecOmmender System

Input: A time-ordered sequence (user and items) $\{(u, (i_1, \ldots, i_{|I_u|}))\}_{u=1}^N$ drawn i.i.d. from $\mathcal{D}_{\mathcal{U}, \mathcal{I}}$
Input: maximal B and minimal b number of blocks allowed per user u
Input: number of epochs E
Input: initial parameters ω_1^0, and (possibly non-convex) surrogate loss function $\ell(\omega)$
for $e \in E$ **do**
    for $u \in \mathcal{U}$ **do**
        Let $N_u^t = \varnothing$, $\Pi_u^t = \varnothing$ be the sets of positive and negative items, counter $t = 0$
        for $i_k \in \mathcal{I}_u$ **do**   ▷ Consider all items displayed to user u
            while $t \leq B$ **do**
                if u provides a negative feedback on item i_k **then**
                    $N_u^t \leftarrow N_u^t \cup \{i_k\}$
                else
                    $\Pi_u^t \leftarrow \Pi_u^t \cup \{i_k\}$
                end if
                if $N_u^t \neq \varnothing$ and $\Pi_u^t \neq \varnothing$ and $t \leq B$ **then**
                    $\omega_u^{t+1} \leftarrow \omega_u^t - \frac{\eta}{|N_u^t||\Pi_u^t|} \sum_{i \in \Pi_u^t} \sum_{i' \in N_u^t} \nabla \ell_{u,i,i'}(\omega_u^t)$
                    $t = t + 1, N_u^t = \varnothing, \Pi_u^t = \varnothing$
                end if
            end while
        end for
        if $t \geq b$ **then**
            $\omega_{u+1}^0 = \omega_u^t$
        else
            $\omega_{u+1}^0 = \omega_u^0$
        end if
    end for
end for
Return: $\bar{\omega}_N = \sum_{u \in \mathcal{U}} \omega_u^0$

thesis that the system is not instantaneously affected by the sequential learning of the weights. This hypothesis stipulates that the generation of items shown to users is independently and identically distributed with respect to some stationary in time underlying distribution $\mathcal{D}_{\mathcal{I}}$, and constitutes the main hypothesis of almost all the existing studies. Furthermore, we make the following technical assumption.

Assumption 1. *Let the loss functions $\ell_{u,i,i'}(\omega)$ and $\mathcal{L}(\omega)$, $\omega \in \mathbb{R}^d$ be such that for some absolute constants $\gamma \geq \beta > 0$ and $\sigma > 0$:*

1. *$\ell_{u,i,i'}(\omega)$ is non-negative for any user u and a pair of items (i, i');*
2. *$\ell_{u,i,i'}(\omega)$ is twice continuously differentiable, and for any user u and a pair of items (i, i') one has $\gamma \|\omega - \omega'\|_2 \geq \|\nabla \ell_{u,i,i'}(\omega) - \nabla \ell_{u,i,i'}(\omega')\|_2$, as well as $\beta \|\omega - \omega'\|_2 \geq \|\nabla \mathcal{L}(\omega) - \nabla \mathcal{L}(\omega')\|_2$,.*
3. *Variance of the empirical loss is bounded $\mathbb{E}_{\mathcal{D}} \left\| \nabla \hat{\mathcal{L}}_u(\omega) - \nabla \mathcal{L}(\omega) \right\|_2^2 \leq \sigma^2$.*

Moreover, there exist some positive lower and upper bounds b and B, such that the number of updates for any u is within the interval $[b, B]$ almost surely.

Our main result is the following theorem which provides a bound over the deviation of the ranking loss with respect to the sequence of weights found by the SAROS algorithm and its minimum in the case where the latter is convex.

Theorem 1. *Let $\ell_{u,i,i'}(\omega)$ and $\mathcal{L}(\omega)$ satisfy Assumption 1. Then for any constant step size η, verifying $0 < \eta \leq \min(\frac{1}{\beta B}, 1/\sqrt{UB(\sigma^2 + 3\gamma^2/b)})$, and any set of users $\mathcal{U} \doteq [U]$; algorithm SAROS iteratively generates a sequence $\{\omega_u^0\}_{u \in \mathcal{U}}$ such that*

$$\frac{1}{\beta} \mathbb{E} \|\nabla \mathcal{L}(\omega_u^0)\|_2^2 \leq \frac{\beta B \Delta_{\mathcal{L}}^2}{u} + 2\Delta_{\mathcal{L}} \sqrt{\frac{B\sigma^2 + 3B\gamma^2/b}{u}},$$

where $\Delta_{\mathcal{L}}^2 = \frac{2}{\beta}(\mathcal{L}(\omega_0) - \mathcal{L}(\omega^*))$, and the expectation is taken with respect to users chosen randomly according to the uniform distribution $p_u = \frac{1}{N}$.

Furthermore, if the ranking loss $\mathcal{L}(\omega)$ is convex, then for the sequence $\{\omega_u^0\}_{u \in \mathcal{U}}$ generated by algorithm SAROS and $\bar{\omega}_u = \sum_{j \leq u} \omega_j^0$ we have

$$\mathcal{L}(\bar{\omega}_u) - \mathcal{L}(\omega_*) \leq \frac{\beta B \Delta_\omega^2}{u} + 2\Delta_\omega \sqrt{\frac{B\sigma^2 + 3B\gamma^2/b}{u}},$$

where $\Delta_\omega = \|\omega_0 - \omega_*\|_2^2$, and $\omega_* = \arg\min_\omega \mathcal{L}(\omega)$.

Proof. *Sketch.* Expectation of the empirical loss taken over a random block $\mathcal{B}_u^t$ for a user u, equals to the expected loss for this user. Then by the law of total expectation one has $\mathbb{E}_{\mathcal{D}_u} \left[k^{-1} \sum_{l=1}^{k} \nabla \hat{\mathcal{L}}_{\mathcal{B}_u^l}(\omega) \right] = \nabla \hat{\mathcal{L}}_u(\omega)$, where $\mathcal{D}_u$ is the conditional distribution of items for a fixed user u. The variance of the gradient estimation over k blocks is bounded by $3\gamma^2/k$, as for any block after the next to $\mathcal{B}_u^t$ and before the previous to $\mathcal{B}_u^t$ are conditionally independent for any fixed $\mathcal{B}_u^t$.

Let g_u^t be a gradient of the loss function taken for user u over block $\mathcal{B}_u^t$:

$$g_u^t = \frac{1}{|N_u^t||\Pi_u^t|} \sum_{i \in N_u^t, i' \in \Pi_u^t} \nabla \ell_{u,i,i'}(\omega_u^{t-1}),$$

According to the notation of Algorithm SAROS let $\delta_u^t = g_u^t - \nabla \mathcal{L}(\omega_u^0)$ and $\omega_u^{t+1} = \omega_u^t - \eta g_u^t$, $\omega_{u+1}^0 = \omega_u^{|\mathcal{B}_u|}$, and $\omega_{u+1}^0 - \omega_u^0 = \eta \sum_{t \in \mathcal{B}_u} g_u^t$, where $\mathcal{B}_u$ is the set of all interacted blocks corresponding to user u. Using the smoothness of the loss function implied by Assumption 1, it comes:

$$\mathcal{L}(\omega_{u+1}^0) = \mathcal{L}(\omega_u^0) - \left(\hat{\eta}_u - \frac{\beta}{2}\hat{\eta}_u^2\right) \|\nabla \mathcal{L}(\omega_u^0)\|_2^2$$

$$- (\hat{\eta}_u - \beta\hat{\eta}_u^2) \sum_{t \in \mathcal{B}_u} \left\langle \nabla \mathcal{L}(\omega_u^0), \frac{\delta_u^t}{|\mathcal{B}_u|} \right\rangle + \frac{\beta}{2}\hat{\eta}_u^2 \sum_{t \in \mathcal{B}_u} \left\| \frac{\delta_u^t}{|\mathcal{B}_u|} \right\|_2^2 \qquad (5)$$

where $\hat{\eta}_u = |\mathcal{B}_u|\eta$. Then by re-arranging and summing up, we get

$$\sum_{u=1}^{N} \left(\hat{\eta}_u - \frac{\beta}{2}\hat{\eta}_u^2\right) \|\nabla \mathcal{L}(\omega_u)\|_2^2 \leq \mathcal{L}(\bar{\omega}_u) - \mathcal{L}(\omega^*)$$

$$- \sum_{u=1}^{N} (\hat{\eta}_u - \beta\hat{\eta}_u^2) \left\langle \nabla \mathcal{L}(\omega_u), \sum_{t \in \mathcal{B}_u} \frac{\delta_u^t}{|\mathcal{B}_u|} \right\rangle + \frac{\beta}{2} \sum_{u=1}^{N} \hat{\eta}_u^2 \left\| \sum_{t \in \mathcal{B}_u} \frac{\delta_u^t}{|\mathcal{B}_u|} \right\|_2^2$$

As the stochastic gradient taken with respect to a block of items gives an unbiased estimate of the gradient, thus

$$\mathbb{E}_{\mathcal{D}_u} \left[\left\langle \nabla \mathcal{L}(\omega_u), \sum_{t \in \mathcal{B}_u} \frac{\delta_u^t}{|\mathcal{B}_u|} \right\rangle \Big| \xi_u \right] = 0, \qquad (6)$$

where ξ_u is a set of users preceding u. As in the conditions of the theorem $b \leq |\mathcal{B}_u|$ almost surely, by the law of total variation, $\mathrm{Var}\,\psi = \mathbb{E}[\mathrm{Var}(\psi|\eta)] + \mathrm{Var}[\mathbb{E}[\psi|\eta]]$:

$$\mathbb{E}_{\mathcal{D}_u} \left\| \sum_{t \in \mathcal{B}_u} \frac{\delta_u^t}{|\mathcal{B}_u|} \right\|_2^2 \leq \sigma^2 + \frac{3\gamma^2}{b} \qquad (7)$$

where the first term on the right-hand side of Eq. (7) comes from Assumption 1, and the second term is due to the variance estimate. Condition $\beta\eta B \leq 1$ implies $\hat{\eta}_u - \beta\hat{\eta}_u^2/2 \geq \hat{\eta}_u/2$, thus

$$\frac{1}{\beta}\mathbb{E}_{\mathcal{D}} \|\nabla \mathcal{L}(\omega)\|_2^2 \leq \frac{1}{\sum_{u=1}^{N} \hat{\eta}_u} \left[\frac{2(\mathcal{L}(\omega_0) - \mathcal{L}(\omega_*))}{\beta} + \left(\sigma^2 + 3\frac{\gamma^2}{b}\right) \sum_{u=1}^{N} \hat{\eta}_u^2 \right]$$

The rest of the proof of the theorem comes along the same lines according to the randomized stochastic gradient descent analysis [3]. □

The full proof is provided in the Supplementary. This result implies that the loss over a sequence of weights $(\omega_u^0)_{u \in \mathcal{U}}$ generated by the algorithm converges to the true minimizer of the ranking loss $\mathcal{L}(\omega)$ with a rate proportional to $O(1/\sqrt{u})$. The stochastic gradient descent strategy implemented in the Bayesian Personalized Ranking model (BPR) [18] also converges to the minimizer of the ranking loss $\mathcal{L}(\omega)$ with the same rate. However, the main difference between BPR and SAROS is their computation time. As stated in Sect. 3.1, the expected number of rejected random pairs sampled by algorithm BPR before making one update is $O(|\mathcal{I}_u|^2)$ while with SAROS, blocks are created sequentially as and when users interact with the system. For each user u, weights are updated whenever a block is created, with the overall complexity of $O(\max_t(|\Pi_u^t| \times |N_u^t|))$, with $\max_t(|\Pi_u^t| \times |N_u^t|) \ll |\mathcal{I}_u|^2$.

4 Experimental Setup and Results

In this section, we provide an empirical evaluation of our optimization strategy on some popular benchmarks proposed for evaluating RS. All subsequently discussed components were implemented in Python3 using the TensorFlow library[2] and computed on Skoltech CDISE HPC cluster "Zhores" [29]. We first proceed with a presentation of the general experimental set-up, including a description of the datasets and the baseline models.

Datasets. We report results obtained on five publicly available datasets, for the task of personalized Top-N recommendation on the following collections:

- ML-1M [5] and NETFLIX [1] consist of user-movie ratings, on a scale of one to five, collected from a movie recommendation service and the Netflix company. The latter was released to support the Netflix Prize competition [1]. For both datasets, we consider ratings greater or equal to 4 as positive feedback, and negative feedback otherwise.
- We extracted a subset out of the OUTBRAIN dataset from of the Kaggle challenge[3] that consisted in the recommendation of news content to users based on the 1,597,426 implicit feedback collected from multiple publisher sites in the United States.
- KASANDR[4] dataset [24] contains 15,844,717 interactions of 2,158,859 users in Germany using Kelkoo's (http://www.kelkoo.fr/) online advertising platform.
- PANDOR[5] is another publicly available dataset for online recommendation [23] provided by Purch (http://www.purch.com/). The dataset records 2,073,379 clicks generated by 177,366 users of one of the Purch's high-tech website over 9,077 ads they have been shown during one month.

---

[2] https://www.tensorflow.org/.
[3] https://www.kaggle.com/c/outbrain-click-prediction.
[4] https://archive.ics.uci.edu/ml/datasets/KASANDR.
[5] https://archive.ics.uci.edu/ml/datasets/PANDOR.

Table 1 presents some detailed statistics about each collection. Among these, we report the average number of positive (click, like) feedback and the average number of negative feedback. As we see from the table, OUTBRAIN, KASANDR, and PANDOR datasets are the most unbalanced ones in regards to the number of preferred and non-preferred items.

Table 1. Statistics on the # of users and items; as well as the sparsity and the average number of + (preferred) and − (non-preferred) items on ML-1M, NETFLIX, OUTBRAIN, KASANDR and PANDOR collections after preprocessing.

Data	$|\mathcal{U}|$	$|\mathcal{I}|$	Sparsity	Avg. # of +	Avg. # of −
ML-1M	6,040	3,706	.9553	95.2767	70.4690
OUTBRAIN	49,615	105,176	.9997	6.1587	26.0377
PANDOR	177,366	9,077	.9987	1.3266	10.3632
NETFLIX	90,137	3,560	.9914	26.1872	20.2765
KASANDR	2,158,859	291,485	.9999	2.4202	51.9384

Table 2. Number of interactions used for train and test on each dataset, and the percentage of positive feedback among these interactions.

Dataset	$|S_{train}|$	$|S_{test}|$	pos_{train}	pos_{test}
ML-1M	797,758	202,451	58.82	52.39
OUTBRAIN	1,261,373	336,053	17.64	24.73
PANDOR	1,579,716	493,663	11.04	12.33
NETFLIX	3,314,621	873,477	56.27	56.70
KASANDR	12,509,509	3,335,208	3.36	8.56

To construct the training and the test sets, we discarded users who did not interact over the shown items and sorted all interactions according to time-based on the existing time-stamps related to each dataset. Furthermore, we considered 80% of each user's first interactions (both positive and negative) for training, and the remaining for the test. Table 2 presents the size of the training and the test sets as well as the percentage of positive feedback (preferred items) for all collections ordered by increasing training size. The percentage of positive feedback is inversely proportional to the size of the training sets, attaining 3% for the largest, KASANDR collection.

We also analyzed the distributions of the number of blocks and their size for different collections. Figure 2 (left) shows boxplots representing the logarithm of the number of blocks through their quartiles for all collections. From these plots, it comes out that the distribution of the number of blocks on PANDOR, NETFLIX and KASANDR are heavy-tailed with more than the half of the users interacting no more than 10 times with the system. Furthermore, we note that on PANDOR the average number of blocks is much smaller than on the two other collections; and that on all three collections the maximum numbers of blocks are 10 times more than the average. These plots suggest that a very small number of users (perhaps bots) have an abnormal interaction with the system generating a huge amount of blocks on these three collections. To have a better understanding, Fig. 2 (right) depicts the number of blocks concerning their size on KASANDR. The distribution of the number of blocks follows a power law distribution and it is the same for the other collections that we did not report for the sake of space. In all collections, the number of blocks having more than 5 items drops drastically. As the SAROS does not sample positive and negative items for updating the weights, these updates are performed on blocks of small size, and are made very often.

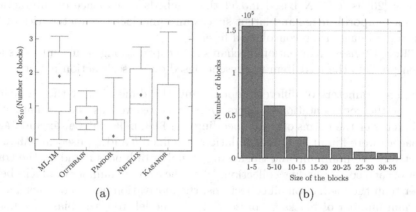

(a)   (b)

Fig. 2. (a) Boxplots depicting the logarithm of the number of blocks through their quartiles for all collections. The median (resp. mean) is represented by the band (resp. diamond) inside the box. The ends of the whiskers represent the minimum and the maximum of the values. (b) Distributions of negative feedback over the blocks in the training set on KASANDR.

Compared Approaches. To validate the sequential approach described earlier, we compared the proposed SAROS algorithm[6] with the following methods:

- MostPop is a non-learning based approach which consists in recommending the same set of popular items to all users.
- Matrix Factorization (MF) [11], is a factor model which decomposes the matrix of user-item interactions into a set of low dimensional vectors in the same latent space, by minimizing a regularized least square error between the actual value of the scores and the dot product over the user and item representations.

---

[6] The code is available on https://github.com/SashaBurashnikova/SAROS.

- BPR [18] corresponds to the model described in the problem statement above (Sect. 3.1), a stochastic gradient-descent algorithm, based on bootstrap sampling of training triplets, and BPR$_b$ the batch version of the model which consists in finding the model parameters $\omega = (\mathbf{U}, \mathbf{V})$ by minimizing the global ranking loss over all the set of triplets simultaneously (Eq. 1).
- Prod2Vec [4], learns the representation of items using a Neural Networks based model, called word2vec [14], and performs next-items recommendation using the similarity between the representations of items.
- GRU4Rec+ [7] is an extended version of GRU4Rec [8] adopted to different loss functions, that applies recurrent neural network with a GRU architecture for session-based recommendation. The approach considers the session as the sequence of clicks of the user that depends on all the previous ones for learning the model parameters by optimizing a regularized approximation of the relative rank of the relevant item which favors the preferred items to be ranked at the top of the list.
- Caser [26] is a CNN based model that embeds a sequence of interactions into a temporal image and latent spaces and find local characteristics of the temporal image using convolution filters.
- SASRec [10] uses an attention mechanism to capture long-term semantics and then predicts the next item to present based on a user's action history.

Hyper-parameters of different models and the dimension of the embedded space for the representation of users and items; as well as the regularisation parameter over the norms of the embeddings for BPR, BPR$_b$, MF, Caser and SAROS approaches were found by cross-validation. We fixed b and B, used in SAROS, to respectively the minimum and the average number of blocks found on the training set of each corresponding collection. With the average number of blocks being greater than the median on all collections, the motivation here is to consider the maximum number of blocks by preserving the model from the bias brought by the too many interactions of the very few number of users. For more details regarding the exact values for the parameters, see the Table 3.

Table 3. Values for the SAROS parameters.

Parameter	ML	OUTBRAIN	PANDOR	NETFLIX	KASANDR
B	78	5	2	22	5
b	1	2	1	1	1
Learning rate	.05	.05	.05	.05	.4

Evaluation Setting and Results. We begin our comparisons by testing BPR$_b$, BPR and SAROS approaches over the logistic ranking loss (Eq. 2) which is used to train them. Results on the test, after training the models 30 min and at convergence are shown in Table 4. BPR$_b$ (resp. SAROS) techniques have the worse (resp. best) test loss on all collections, and the difference between their performance is larger for bigger size datasets.

Table 4. Comparison between BPR, BPR$_b$ and SAROS approaches in terms on test loss after 30 min of training and at convergence.

Dataset	Test Loss, Eq. (1)					
	30 min			At convergence		
	BPR$_b$	BPR	SAROS	BPR$_b$	BPR	SAROS
ML-1M	0.751	0.678	**0.623**	0.744	0.645	**0.608**
OUTBRAIN	0.753	0.650	**0.646**	0.747	0.638	**0.635**
PANDOR	0.715	0.671	**0.658**	0.694	0.661	**0.651**
NETFLIX	0.713	0.668	**0.622**	0.694	0.651	**0.614**
KASANDR	0.663	0.444	**0.224**	0.631	0.393	**0.212**

These results suggest that the local ranking between preferred and no-preferred items present in the blocks of the training set reflects better the preference of users than the ranking of random pairs of items or their global ranking without this contextual information. Furthermore, as in SAROS updates occur after the creation of a block, and that the most of the blocks contain very few items (Fig. 2 - right), weights are updated more often than in BPR or BPR$_b$. This is depicted in Fig. 3 which shows the evolution of the training error over time for BPR$_b$, BPR and SAROS on all collections. As we can see, the training error decreases in all cases, and theoretically, the three approaches converge to the same minimizer of the ranking loss (Eq. 1). However, the speed of convergence is much faster with SAROS.

We also compare the performance of all the approaches on the basis of the common ranking metrics, which are the Mean Average Precision at rank K (MAP@K) over all users defined as MAP@K $= \frac{1}{N} \sum_{u=1}^{N}$ AP@K(u), where AP@K(u) is the average precision of preferred items of user u in the top K ranked ones; and the Normalized Discounted Cumulative Gain at rank K (NDCG@K) that computes the ratio of the obtained ranking to the ideal case and allow to consider not only binary relevance as in Mean Average Precision, NDCG@K $= \frac{1}{N} \sum_{u=1}^{N} \frac{DCG@K(u)}{IDCG@K(u)}$, where DCG@K$(u) = \sum_{i=1}^{K} \frac{2^{rel_i}-1}{\log_2(1+i)}$, rel_i is the graded relevance of the item at position i; and IDCG@K(u) is DCG@K(u) with an ideal ordering equals to $\sum_{i=1}^{K} \frac{1}{\log_2(1+i)}$ for $rel_i \in [0,1]$ [20].

Table 5 presents MAP@5 and MAP@10 (top), and NDCG@5 and NDCG@10 (down) of all approaches over the test sets of the different collections. The non-machine learning method, MostPop, gives results of an order of magnitude lower than the learning based approaches. Moreover, the factorization model MF which predicts clicks by matrix completion is less effective when dealing with implicit feedback than ranking based models especially on large datasets where there are fewer interactions. We also found that embeddings found by ranking based models, in the way that the user preference over the pairs of items is preserved in the embedded space by the dot product, are more robust than the ones found by Prod2Vec. When comparing GRU4Rec+ with BPR that also minimizes the same

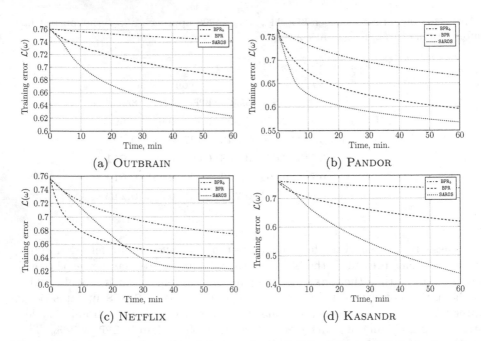

Fig. 3. Evolution of the loss on training sets for both BPR$_b$, BPR and SAROS as a function of time in minutes for all collections.

Table 5. Comparison between MostPop, Prod2Vec, MF, BPR$_b$, BPR, GRU4Rec+, SASRec, Caser and SAROS approaches in terms of MAP@5 and MAP@10 (top), and NDCG@5 and NDCG@10 (down). Best performance is in bold and the second best is underlined.

	MAP@5					MAP@10				
	ML-1M	OUTBRAIN	PANDOR	NETFLIX	KASANDR	ML-1M	OUTBRAIN	PANDOR	NETFLIX	KASANDR
MostPop	.074	.007	.003	.039	.002	.083	.009	.004	.051	.3e-5
Prod2Vec	.793	.228	.063	.669	.012	.772	.228	.063	.690	.012
MF	.733	.531	.266	.793	.170	.718	.522	.267	.778	.176
BPR$_b$	.713	.477	.685	.764	.473	.688	.477	.690	.748	.488
BPR	<u>.826</u>	<u>.573</u>	<u>.734</u>	<u>.855</u>	.507	<u>.797</u>	<u>.563</u>	<u>.760</u>	<u>.835</u>	.521
GRU4Rec+	.777	.513	.673	.774	<u>.719</u>	.750	.509	.677	.757	<u>.720</u>
Caser	.718	.471	.522	.749	.186	.694	.473	.527	.733	.197
SASRec	.776	.542	.682	.819	.480	.751	.534	.687	.799	.495
SAROS	**.837**	**.619**	**.750**	**.866**	**.732**	**.808**	**.607**	**.753**	**.846**	**.747**
	NDCG@5					NDCG@10				
	ML-1M	OUTBRAIN	PANDOR	NETFLIX	KASANDR	ML-1M	OUTBRAIN	PANDOR	NETFLIX	KASANDR
MostPop	.090	.011	.005	.056	.002	.130	.014	.008	.096	.002
Prod2Vec	.758	.232	.078	.712	.012	.842	.232	.080	.770	.012
MF	.684	.612	.300	.795	.197	.805	.684	.303	.834	.219
BPR$_b$	.652	.583	.874	.770	.567	.784	.658	.890	.849	.616
BPR	<u>.776</u>	<u>.671</u>	<u>.889</u>	<u>.854</u>	.603	<u>.863</u>	<u>.724</u>	<u>.905</u>	<u>.903</u>	.650
GRU4Rec+	.721	.633	.843	.777	<u>.760</u>	.833	.680	.862	.854	<u>.782</u>
Caser	.665	.585	.647	.750	.241	.787	.658	.666	.834	.276
SASRec	.721	.645	.852	.819	.569	.832	.704	.873	.883	.625
SAROS	**.788**	**.710**	**.903**	**.865**	**.791**	**.874**	**.755**	**.913**	**.914**	**.815**

surrogate ranking loss, the former outperforms it in case of KASANDR with a huge imbalance between positive and negative interactions. This is mainly because GRU4Rec+ optimizes an approximation of the relative rank that favors interacted items to be in the top of the ranked list while the logistic ranking loss, which is mostly related to the Area under the ROC curve [28], pushes up clicked items for having good ranks in average. However, the minimization of the logistic ranking loss over blocks of very small size pushes the clicked item to be ranked higher than the no-clicked ones in several lists of small size and it has the effect of favoring the clicked item to be at the top of the whole merged lists of items. Moreover, it comes out that SAROS is the most competitive approach, performing better than other approaches over all collections even such as last published Caser and SASRec.

5 Conclusion

The contributions of this paper are twofold. First, we proposed SAROS, a novel learning framework for large-scale Recommender Systems that sequentially updates the weights of a ranking function user by user over blocks of items ordered by time where each block is a sequence of negative items followed by a last positive one. The main hypothesis of the approach is that the preferred and no-preferred items within a local sequence of user interactions express better the user preference than when considering the whole set of preferred and no-preferred items independently one from another. The approach updates the model parameters user per user over blocks of items constituted by a sequence of unclicked items followed by a clicked one. The parameter updates are discarded for users who interact very little or a lot with the system. The second contribution is a theoretical analysis of the proposed approach which bounds the deviation of the ranking loss concerning the sequence of weights found by the algorithm and its minimum in the case where the loss is convex. Empirical results conducted on five real-life implicit feedback datasets support our founding and show that the proposed approach is significantly faster than the common batch and online optimization strategies that consist in updating the parameters over the whole set of users at each epoch, or after sampling random pairs of preferred and no-preferred items. The approach is also shown to be highly competitive concerning state of the art approaches on MAP and NDCG measures.

Acknowledgements. This work at Los Alamos was supported by the U.S. Department of Energy through the Los Alamos National Laboratory as part of LDRD and the DOE Grid Modernization Laboratory Consortium (GMLC). Los Alamos National Laboratory is operated by Triad National Security, LLC, for the National Nuclear Security Administration of U.S. Department of Energy (Contract No. 89233218CNA000001).

References

1. Bennett, J., Lanning, S., et al.: The Netflix prize. In: Proceedings of KDD Cup and Workshop, vol. 2007, p. 35. ACM, New York (2007)
2. Donkers, T., Loepp, B., Ziegler, J.: Sequential user-based recurrent neural network recommendations. In: Proceedings of the Eleventh ACM Conference on Recommender Systems, pp. 152–160 (2017)
3. Ghadimi, S., Lan, G.: Stochastic first-and zeroth-order methods for nonconvex stochastic programming. SIAM J. Optim. **23**(4), 2341–2368 (2013)
4. Grbovic, M., et al.: E-commerce in your inbox: product recommendations at scale. In: Proceedings of SIGKDD, pp. 1809–1818 (2015)
5. Harper, F.M., Konstan, J.A.: The movielens datasets: history and context. ACM Trans. Interact. Intell. Syst. **5**(4), 1–19 (2015)
6. He, X., Zhang, H., Kan, M.-Y., Chua, T.-S.: Fast matrix factorization for online recommendation with implicit feedback. In: SIGIR, pp. 549–558 (2016)
7. Hidasi, B., Karatzoglou, A.: Recurrent neural networks with top-k gains for session-based recommendations. In: Proceedings of CIKM, pp. 843–852 (2018)
8. Hidasi, B., Karatzoglou, A., Baltrunas, L., Tikk, D.: Session-based recommendations with recurrent neural networks. In: ICLR (2016)
9. Hu, Y., Koren, Y., Volinsky, C.: Collaborative filtering for implicit feedback datasets. In: IEEE ICDM, pp. 263–272 (2008)
10. Kang, W., McAuley, J.: Self-attentive sequential recommendation. In: IEEE International Conference on Data Mining, ICDM, pp. 197–206 (2018)
11. Koren, Y.: Factorization meets the neighborhood: a multifaceted collaborative filtering model. In: Proceedings of the 14th ACM SIGKDD International Conference on Knowledge Discovery and Data Mining, pp. 426–434 (2008)
12. Koren, Y., Bell, R., Volinsky, C.: Matrix factorization techniques for recommender systems. Computer **8**, 30–37 (2009)
13. Liu, C.-L., Wu, X.-W.: Large-scale recommender system with compact latent factor model. Expert Syst. Appl. **64**(C), 467–475 (2016)
14. Mikolov, T., Chen, K., Corrado, G., Dean, J.: Efficient estimation of word representations in vector space. CoRR, abs/1301.3781 (2013)
15. Moling, O., Baltrunas, L., Ricci, F.: Optimal radio channel recommendations with explicit and implicit feedback. In: Proceedings of the Sixth ACM Conference on Recommender Systems, RecSys 2012, pp. 75–82. ACM (2012)
16. Pan, R., et al.: One-class collaborative filtering. In: ICDM, pp. 502–511 (2008)
17. Pazzani, M.J., Billsus, D.: Content-based recommendation systems. In: Brusilovsky, P., Kobsa, A., Nejdl, W. (eds.) The Adaptive Web. LNCS, vol. 4321, pp. 325–341. Springer, Heidelberg (2007). https://doi.org/10.1007/978-3-540-72079-9_10
18. Rendle, S., Freudenthaler, C., Gantner, Z., Schmidt-Thieme, L.: BPR: Bayesian personalized ranking from implicit feedback. In: UAI, pp. 452–461 (2009)
19. Ruining, H., Julian, M.: Fusing similarity models with Markov chains for sparse sequential recommendation. In: IEEE ICDM (2016)
20. Schutze, H., Manning, C.D., Raghavan, P.: Introduction to Information Retrieval, vol. 39. Cambridge University Press, Cambridge (2008)
21. Sculley, D.: Large scale learning to rank. In: Workshop on Advances in Ranking, NIPS 2009 (2009)
22. Shani, G., Heckerman, D., Brafman, R.I.: An MDP-based recommender system. J. Mach. Learn. Res. **6**, 1265–1295 (2005)

23. Sidana, S., Laclau, C., Amini, M.R.: Learning to recommend diverse items over implicit feedback on PANDOR. In: Proceedings of the 12th ACM Conference on Recommender Systems, pp. 427–431 (2018)

24. Sidana, S., Laclau, C., Amini, M.R., Vandelle, G., Bois-Crettez, A.: KASANDR: a large-scale dataset with implicit feedback for recommendation. In: Proceedings SIGIR, pp. 1245–1248 (2017)

25. Su, X., Khoshgoftaar, T.M.: A survey of collaborative filtering techniques. Adv. Artif. Intell. (2009)

26. Tang, J., Wang, K.: Personalized top-n sequential recommendation via convolutional sequence embedding. In: ACM International Conference on Web Search and Data Mining (2018)

27. Tavakol, M., Brefeld, U.: Factored MDPs for detecting topics of user sessions. In: Proceedings of the 8th ACM Conference on Recommender Systems, RecSys 2014, pp. 33–40. ACM (2014)

28. Usunier, N., Amini, M.-R., Gallinari, P.: A data-dependent generalisation error bound for the AUC. In: Proceedings of the ICML 2005 Workshop on ROC Analysis in Machine Learning (2005)

29. Zacharov, I., et al.: Zhores - petaflops supercomputer for data-driven modeling, machine learning and artificial intelligence installed in Skolkovo Institute of Science and Technology. CoRR, abs/1902.07490 (2019)

30. Zhang, R., Bao, H., Sun, H., Wang, Y., Liu, X.: Recommender systems based on ranking performance optimization. Front. Comput. Sci. **10**(2), 270–280 (2016). https://doi.org/10.1007/s11704-015-4584-1

Applied Data Science: Computer Vision and Explanation

Automatic Recognition of Student Engagement Using Deep Learning and Facial Expression

Omid Mohamad Nezami[1,2]([✉]), Mark Dras[1], Len Hamey[1], Deborah Richards[1], Stephen Wan[2], and Cécile Paris[2]

[1] Macquarie University, Sydney, NSW, Australia
omid.mohamad-nezami@hdr.mq.edu.au,
{mark.dras,len.hamey,deborah.richards}@mq.edu.au
[2] CSIRO's Data61, Sydney, NSW, Australia
{stephen.wan,cecile.paris}@data61.csiro.au

Abstract. Engagement is a key indicator of the quality of learning experience, and one that plays a major role in developing intelligent educational interfaces. Any such interface requires the ability to recognise the level of engagement in order to respond appropriately; however, there is very little existing data to learn from, and new data is expensive and difficult to acquire. This paper presents a deep learning model to improve engagement recognition from images that overcomes the data sparsity challenge by pre-training on readily available basic facial expression data, before training on specialised engagement data. In the first of two steps, a facial expression recognition model is trained to provide a rich face representation using deep learning. In the second step, we use the model's weights to initialize our deep learning based model to recognize engagement; we term this the engagement model. We train the model on our new engagement recognition dataset with 4627 engaged and disengaged samples. We find that the engagement model outperforms effective deep learning architectures that we apply for the first time to engagement recognition, as well as approaches using histogram of oriented gradients and support vector machines.

Keywords: Engagement · Deep learning · Facial expression

1   Introduction

Engagement is a significant aspect of human-technology interactions and is defined differently for a variety of applications such as search engines, online gaming platforms, and mobile health applications [28]. According to Monkaresi *et al.* [25], most definitions describe engagement as attentional and emotional involvement in a task.

This paper deals with engagement during learning via technology. Investigating engagement is vital for designing intelligent educational interfaces in different learning settings including educational games [14], massively open online courses

© Springer Nature Switzerland AG 2020
U. Brefeld et al. (Eds.): ECML PKDD 2019, LNAI 11908, pp. 273–289, 2020.
https://doi.org/10.1007/978-3-030-46133-1_17

Fig. 1. Engaged (left) and disengaged (right) samples collected in our studies. We blurred the children's eyes for ethical issues, even though we have their parents consent at the time.

(MOOCs) [18], and intelligent tutoring systems (ITSs) [1]. For instance, if students feel frustrated and become disengaged (see disengaged samples in Fig. 1), the system should intervene in order to bring them back to the learning process. However, if students are engaged and enjoying their tasks (see engaged samples in Fig. 1), they should not be interrupted even if they are making some mistakes [19]. In order for the learning system to adapt the learning setting and provide proper responses to students, we first need to automatically measure engagement. This can be done by, for example, using context performance [1], facial expression [35] and heart rate [25] data. Recently, engagement recognition using facial expression data has attracted special attention because of widespread availability of cameras [25].

This paper aims at quantifying and characterizing engagement using facial expressions extracted from images. In this domain, engagement detection models usually use typical facial features which are designed for general purposes, such as Gabor features [35], histogram of oriented gradients [18] and facial action units [4]. To the best of the authors' knowledge, there is no work in the literature investigating the design of specific and high-level features for engagement. Therefore, providing a rich engagement representation model to distinguish engaged and disengaged samples remains an open problem (Challenge 1). Training such a rich model requires a large amount of data which means extensive effort, time, and expense would be required for collecting and annotating data due to the complexities [3] and ambiguities [28] of the engagement concept (Challenge 2).

To address the aforementioned challenges, we design a deep learning model which includes two essential steps: basic facial expression recognition, and engagement recognition. In the first step, a convolutional neural network (CNN) is trained on the dataset of the Facial Expression Recognition Challenge 2013 (FER-2013) to provide a rich facial representation model, achieving state-of-the-art performance. In the next step, the model is applied to initialize our engagement recognition model, designed using a separate CNN, learned on our newly collected dataset in the engagement recognition domain. As a solution to Challenge 1, we train a deep learning-based model that provides our representation model specifically for engagement recognition. As a solution to Challenge 2, we use the FER-2013 dataset, which is around eight times larger than our collected dataset, as external data to pre-train our engagement recognition model and compensate for the shortage of engagement data[1]. The contributions of this work are threefold:

- To the authors' knowledge, the work in this paper is the first time a rich face representation model has been used to capture basic facial expressions and initialize an engagement recognition model, resulting in positive outcomes. This shows the effectiveness of applying basic facial expression data in order to recognize engagement.
- We have collected a new dataset we call the Engagement Recognition (ER) dataset to facilitate research on engagement recognition from images. To handle the complexity and ambiguity of engagement concept, our data is annotated in two steps, separating the behavioral and emotional dimensions of engagement. The final engagement label in the ER dataset is the combination of the two dimensions.
- To the authors' knowledge, this is the first study which models engagement using deep learning techniques. The proposed model outperforms a comprehensive range of baseline approaches on the ER dataset.

2 Related Work

2.1 Facial Expression Recognition

As a form of non-verbal communication, facial expressions convey attitudes, affects, and intentions of people. They are the result of movements of muscles and facial features [11]. Study of facial expressions was started more than a century ago by Charles Darwin [10], leading to a large body of work in recognizing basic facial expressions [11,31]. Much of the work uses a framework of six 'universal' emotions [9]: sadness, happiness, fear, anger, surprise and disgust, with a further neutral category.

Deep learning models have been successful in automatically recognizing facial expressions in images [15,23,24,30,37–39]. They learn hierarchical structures from low- to high-level feature representations thanks to the complex, multi-layered architectures of neural networks. Kahou et al. [17] applied convolutional

---

[1] Our code and trained models are publicly available from https://github.com/omidmnezami/Engagement-Recognition.

neural networks (CNNs) to recognize facial expressions and won the 2013 Emotion Recognition in the Wild (EmotiW) Challenge. Another CNN model, followed by a linear support vector machine, was trained to recognize facial expressions by Tang et al. [34]; this won the 2013 Facial Expression Recognition (FER) challenge [12]. Kahou et al. [16] applied CNNs for extracting visual features accompanied by audio features in a multi-modal data representation. Nezami et al. [27] used a CNN model to recognize facial expressions, where the learned representation is used in an image captioning model; the model embedded the recognized facial expressions to generate more human-like captions for images including human faces. Yu et al. [37] employed a CNN model that was pre-trained on the FER-2013 dataset [12] and fine-tuned on the Static Facial Expression in the Wild (SFEW) dataset [8]. They applied a face detection method to detect faces and remove noise in their target data samples. Mollahosseini et al. [24] trained CNN models across different well-known FER datasets to enhance the generalizablity of recognizing facial expressions. They applied face registration processes, extracting and aligning faces, to achieve better performances. Kim et al. [20] measured the impact of combining registered and unregistered faces in this domain. They used the unregistered faces when the facial landmarks of the faces were not detectable. Zhang et al. [38] applied CNNs to capture spatial information from video frames. The spatial information was combined with temporal information to recognize facial expressions. Pramerdorfer et al. [29] employed a combination of modern deep architectures such as VGGnet [32] on the FER-2013 dataset. They also achieved the state-of-the-art result on the FER-2013 dataset.

2.2 Engagement Recognition

Engagement has been detected in three different time scales: the entire video of a learning session, 10-s video clips and images. In the first category, Grafsgarrd et al. [13] studied the relation between facial action units (AUs) and engagement in learning contexts. They collected videos of web-based sessions between students and tutors. After finishing the sessions, they requested each student to fill out an engagement survey used to annotate the student's engagement level. Then, they used linear regression methods to find the relationship between different levels of engagement and different AUs. However, their approach does not characterize engagement in fine-grained time intervals which are required for making an adaptive educational interface.

As an attempt to solve this issue, Whitehill et al. [35] applied linear support vector machines (SVMs) and Gabor features, as the best approach in this work, to classify four engagement levels: not engaged at all, nominally engaged, engaged in task, and very engaged. In this work, the dataset includes 10-second videos annotated into the four levels of engagement by observers, who are analyzing the videos. Monkaresi et al. [25] used heart rate features in addition to facial features to detect engagement. They used a face tracking engine to extract facial features and WEKA (a classification toolbox) to classify the features into engaged or not engaged classes. They annotated their dataset, including 10-second videos, using self-reported data collected from students during and after their tasks. Bosch *et al.* [4] detected engagement using AUs and Bayesian classifiers. The generalizability of the model was also investigated across different times, days, ethnicities and genders [5]. Furthermore, in interacting with intelligent tutoring systems (ITSs), engagement was investigated based on a personalized model including appearance and context features [1]. Engagement was considered in learning with massively open online courses (MOOCs) as an e-learning environment [7]. In such settings, data are usually annotated by observing video clips or filling self-reports. However, the engagement levels of students can change during 10-s video clips, so assigning a single label to each clip is difficult and sometimes inaccurate.

In the third category, HOG features and SVMs have been applied to classify images using three levels of engagement: not engaged, nominally engaged and very engaged [18]. This work is based on the experimental results of whitehill *et al.* [35] in preparing engagement samples. whitehill *et al.* [35] showed that engagement patterns are mostly recorded in images. Bosch *et al.* [4] also confirmed that video clips could not provide extra information by reporting similar performances using different lengths of video clips in detecting engagement. However, competitive performances are not reported in this category.

We focus on the third category to recognize engagement from images. To do so, we collected a new dataset annotated by Psychology students, who can potentially better recognize the psychological phenomena of engagement, because of the complexity of analyzing student engagement. To assist them with recognition, brief training was provided prior to commencing the task and delivered in a consistent manner via online examples and descriptions. We did not use crowdsourced labels, resulting in less effective outcomes, similar to the work of Kamath *et al.* [18]. Furthermore, we captured more effective labels by following an annotation process to simplify the engagement concept into the behavioral and the emotional dimensions. We requested annotators to label the dimensions for each image and make the overall annotation label by combining these. Our aim is for this dataset to be useful to other researchers interested in detecting engagement from images. Given this dataset, we introduce a novel model to recognize engagement using deep learning. Our model includes two important phases. First, we train a deep model to recognize basic facial expressions. Second, the model is applied to initialize the weights of our engagement recognition model trained using our newly collected dataset.

3 Facial Expression Recognition from Images

3.1 Facial Expression Recognition Dataset

In this section, we use the facial expression recognition 2013 (FER-2013) dataset [12]. The dataset includes images, labeled *happiness, anger, sadness, surprise, fear, disgust,* and *neutral.* It contains 35,887 samples (28,709 for the training set, 3589 for the public test set and 3589 for the private test set), collected by the Google search API. The samples are in grayscale at the size of 48-by-48 pixels (Fig. 2).

Fig. 2. Examples from the FER-2013 dataset [12] including seven basic facial expressions.

We split the training set into two parts after removing 11 completely black samples: 3589 for validating and 25,109 for training our facial expression recognition model. To compare with related work [20,29,37], we do not use the public test set for training or validation, but use the private test set for performance evaluation of our facial expression recognition model.

3.2   Facial Expression Recognition Using Deep Learning

We train the VGG-B model [32], using the FER-2013 dataset, with one less Convolutional (Conv.) block as shown in Fig. 3. This results in eight Conv. and three fully connected layers. We also have a max pooling layer after each Conv. block with stride 2. We normalize each FER-2013 image so that the image has a mean 0.0 and a norm 100.0 [34]. Moreover, for each pixel position, the pixel value is normalized to mean 0.0 and standard-deviation 1.0 using our training part. Our model has a similar performance with the work of Pramerdorfer *et al.* [29] generating the state-of-the-art on FER-2013 dataset. The model's output layer has a softmax function generating the categorical distribution probabilities over seven facial expression classes in FER-2013. We aim to use this model as a part of our engagement recognition model.

4   Engagement Recognition from Images

4.1   Engagement Recognition Dataset

Data Collection. To recognize engagement from face images, we construct a new dataset that we call the Engagement Recognition (ER) dataset. The data samples are extracted from videos of students, who are learning scientific knowledge and research skills using a virtual world named Omosa [14]. Samples are taken at a fixed rate instead of random selections, making our dataset samples representative, spread across both subjects and time. In the interaction with Omosa,

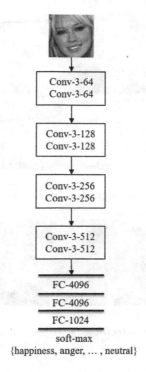

Fig. 3. The architecture of our facial expression recognition model adapted from VGG-B framework [32]. Each rectangle is a Conv. block including two Conv. layers. The max pooling layers are not shown for simplicity.

the goal of students is to determine why a certain animal kind is dying out by talking to characters, observing the animals and collecting relevant information, Fig. 4 (top). After collecting notes and evidence, students are required to complete a workbook, Fig. 4 (bottom).

The videos of students were captured from our studies in two public secondary schools involving twenty students (11 girls and 9 boys) from Years 9 and 10 (aged 14–16), whose parents agreed to their participation in our ethics-approved studies. We collected the videos from twenty individual sessions of students recorded at 20 frames per second (fps), resulting in twenty videos and totalling around 20 h. After extracting video samples, we applied a convolutional neural network (CNN) based face detection algorithm [21] to select samples including detectable faces. The face detection algorithm cannot detect faces in a small number of samples (less than 1%) due to their high face occlusion (Fig. 5). We removed the occluded samples from the ER dataset.

Data Annotation. We designed custom annotation software to request annotators to independently label 100 samples each. The samples are randomly selected from our collected data and are displayed in different orders for different annotators.

Fig. 4. The interactions of a student with Omosa [14], captured in our studies.

Fig. 5. Examples without detectable faces because of high face occlusions.

Each sample is annotated by at least six annotators.[2] Following ethics approval, we recruited undergraduate Psychology students to undertake the annotation task, who received course credit for their participation. Before starting the annotation process, annotators were provided with definitions of behavioral and emotional dimensions of engagement, which are defined in the following paragraphs, inspired by the work of Aslan *et al.* [2].

Behavioral dimension:
- *On-Task*: The student is looking towards the screen or looking down to the keyboard below the screen.
- *Off-Task*: The student is looking everywhere else or eyes completely closed, or head turned away.
- *Can't Decide*: If you cannot decide on the behavioral state.

Emotional dimension:
- *Satisfied*: If the student is not having any emotional problems during the learning task. This can include all positive states of the student from being neutral to being excited during the learning task.
- *Confused*: If the student is getting confused during the learning task. In some cases, this state might include some other negative states such as frustration.

---

[2] The Fleiss' kappa of the six annotators is 0.59, indicating a high inter-coder agreement.

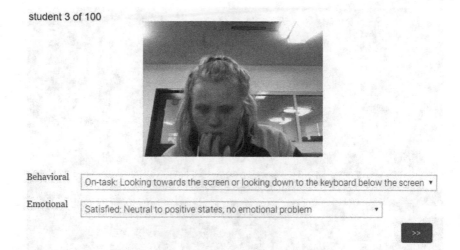

Fig. 6. An example of our annotation software where the annotator is requested to specify the behavioral and emotional dimensions of the displayed sample.

Table 1. The adapted relationship between the behavioral and emotional dimensions from Woolf *et al.* [36] and Aslan *et al.* [2].

Behavioral	Emotional	Engagement
On-task	Satisfied	Engaged
On-task	Confused	Engaged
On-task	Bored	Disengaged
Off-task	Satisfied	Disengaged
Off-task	Confused	Disengaged
Off-task	Bored	Disengaged

- *Bored*: If the student is feeling bored during the learning task.
- *Can't Decide*: If you cannot decide on the emotional state.

During the annotation process, we show each data sample followed by two questions indicating the engagement's dimensions. The behavioral dimension can be chosen among *on-task*, *off-task*, and *can't decide* options and the emotional dimension can be chosen among *satisfied*, *confused*, *bored*, and *can't decide* options. In each annotation phase, annotators have access to the definitions to label each dimension. A sample of the annotation software is shown in Fig. 6. In the next step, each sample is categorized as engaged or disengaged by combining the dimensions' labels using Table 1. For example, if a particular annotator labels an image as *on-task* and *satisfied*, the category for this image from this annotator is *engaged*. Then, for each image we use the majority of the engaged and disengaged labels to specify the final overall annotation. If a sample receives the label of *can't decide* more than twice (either for the emotional or behavioral dimensions)

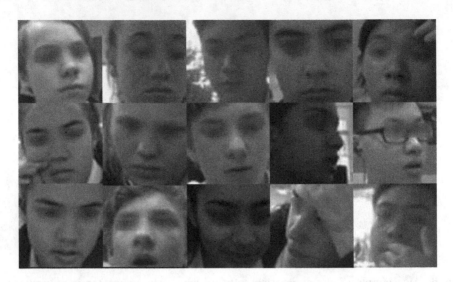

Fig. 7. Randomly selected images of ER dataset including engaged and disengaged.

from different annotators, it is removed from ER dataset. Labeling this kind of samples is a difficult task for annotators, notwithstanding the good level of agreement that was achieved, and finding solutions to reduce the difficulty remains as a future direction of our work. Using this approach, we have created ER dataset consisting of 4627 annotated images including 2290 engaged and 2337 disengaged.

Dataset Preparation. We apply the CNN based face detection algorithm to detect the face of each ER sample. If there is more than one face in a sample, we choose the face with the biggest size. Then, the face is transformed to grayscale and resized into 48-by-48 pixels, which is an effective resolution for engagement detection [35]. Figure 7 shows some examples of the ER dataset. We split the ER dataset into training (3224), validation (715), and testing (688) sets, which are subject-independent (the samples in these three sets are from different subjects). Table 2 demonstrates the statistics of these three sets.

Table 2. The statistics of ER dataset and its partitions.

State	Total	Train	Valid	Test
Engaged	2290	1589	392	309
Disengaged	2337	1635	323	379
Total	4627	3224	715	688

4.2   Engagement Recognition Using Deep Learning

We define two Convolutional Neural Network (CNN) architectures as baselines, one designed architecture and one that is similar in structure to VGGnet [32]. The key model of interest in this paper is a version of the latter baseline that incorporates facial expression recognition. For completeness, we also include another baseline that is not based on deep learning, but rather uses support vector machines (SVMs) with histogram of oriented gradients (HOG) features. For all the models, every sample of the ER dataset is normalized so that it has a zero mean and a norm equal to 100.0. Furthermore, for each pixel location, the pixel values are normalized to mean zero and standard deviation one using all ER training data.

HOG+SVM. We trained a method using the histogram of oriented gradients (HOG) features extracted from ER samples and a linear support vector machine (SVM), which we call the HOG+SVM MODEL. The model is similar to that of Kamath *et al.* [18] for recognizing engagement from images and is used as a baseline model in this work. HOG [6] applies gradient directions or edge orientations to express objects in local regions of images. For example, in facial expression recognition tasks, HOG features can represent the forehead's wrinkling by horizontal edges. A linear SVM is usually used to classify HOG features. In our work, C, determining the misclassification rate of training samples against the objective function of SVM, is fine-tuned, using the validation set of the ER dataset, to the value of 0.1.

Convolutional Neural Network. We use the training and validation sets of the ER dataset to train a Convolutional Neural Networks (CNNs) for this task from scratch (the CNN MODEL); this constitutes another of the baseline models in this paper. The model's architecture is shown in Fig. 8. The model contains two convolutional (Conv.) layers, followed by two max pooling (Max.) layers with stride 2, and two fully connected (FC) layers, respectively. A rectified linear unit (ReLU) activation function [26] is applied after all Conv. and FC layers. The last step of the CNN model includes a softmax layer, followed by a cross-entropy loss, which consists of two neurons indicating engaged and disengaged classes. To overcome model over-fitting, we apply a dropout layer [33] after every Conv. and hidden FC layer. Local response normalization [22] is used after the first Conv. layer. As the optimizer algorithm, stochastic gradient descent with mini-batching and a momentum of 0.9 is used. Using Eq. 1, the learning rate at step t (a_t) is decayed by the rate (r) of 0.8 in the decay step (s) of 500. The total number of iterations from the beginning of the training phase is global step (g).

$$a_t = a_{t-1} \times r^{\frac{g}{s}} \qquad (1)$$

Very Deep Convolutional Neural Network. Using the ER dataset, we train a deep model which has eight Conv. and three FC layers similar to VGG-B architecture [32], but with two fewer Conv. layers. The model is trained using two different scenarios. Under the first scenario, the model is trained from scratch initialized with

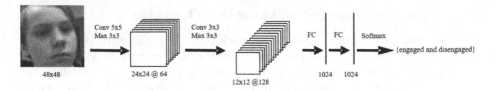

Fig. 8. The architecture of the CNN MODEL. We denote convolutional, max-pooling, and fully-connected layers with "Conv", "Max", and "FC", respectively.

random weights; we call this the VGGNET MODEL (Fig. 9), and this constitutes the second of our deep learning baseline models. Under the second scenario, which uses the same architecture, the model's layers, except the softmax layer, are initialized by the trained model of Sect. 3.2, the goal of which is to recognize basic facial expressions; we call this the ENGAGEMENT MODEL (Fig. 10), and this is the key model of interest in our paper. In this model, all layers' weights are updated and fine-tuned to recognize engaged and disengaged classes in the ER dataset. For both VGGNET and ENGAGEMENT MODELS, after each Conv. block, we have a max pooling layer with stride 2. In the models, the softmax layer has two output units (engaged and disengaged), followed by a cross-entropy loss. Similar to the CNN MODEL, we apply a rectified linear unit (ReLU) activation function [26] and a dropout layer [33] after all Conv. and hidden FC layers. Furthermore, we apply local response normalization after the first Conv. block. We use the same approaches to optimization and learning rate decay as in the CNN MODEL.

5   Experiments

5.1   Evaluation Metrics

In this paper, the performance of all models are reported on the both validation and test splits of the ER dataset. We use three performance metrics including classification accuracy, F1 measure and the area under the ROC (receiver operating characteristics) curve (AUC). In this work, classification accuracy specifies the number of positive (engaged) and negative (disengaged) samples which are correctly classified and are divided by all testing samples (Eq. 2).

$$Accuracy = \frac{TP + TN}{TP + FP + TN + FN} \tag{2}$$

where TP, TN, FP, and FN are true positive, true negative, false positive, and false negative, respectively. F1 measure is calculated using Eq. 3.

$$F1 = 2 \times \frac{p \times r}{p + r} \tag{3}$$

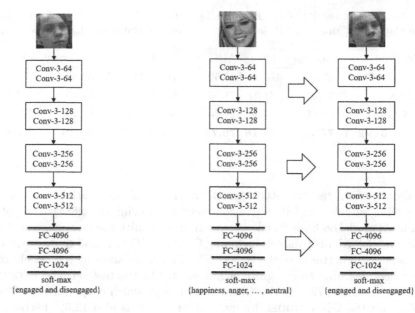

Fig. 9. The architecture of the VGGNET MODEL on ER dataset. "Conv" and "FC" are convolutional and fully connected layers.

Fig. 10. Our facial expression recognition model on FER-2013 dataset (left). The ENGAGEMENT MODEL on ER dataset (right).

where p is precision defined as $\frac{TP}{TP+FP}$ and r is recall defined as $\frac{TP}{TP+FN}$. AUC is a popular metric in engagement recognition task [4,25,35]; it is an unbiased assessment of the area under the ROC curve. An AUC score of 0.5 corresponds to chance performance by the classifier, and AUC 1.0 represents the best possible result.

5.2 Implementation Details

In the training phase, for data augmentation, input images are randomly flipped along their width and cropped to 48-by-48 pixels (after applying zero-padding because the samples were already in this size). Furthermore, they are randomly rotated by a specific max angle. We set learning rate for the VGGNET MODEL to 0.001 and for other models to 0.002. The batch size is set to 32 for the ENGAGEMENT MODEL and 28 for other models. The best model on the validation set is used to estimate the performance on the test partition of the ER dataset for all models in this work.

5.3 Results

Overall Metrics. We summarize the experimental results on the validation set of the ER dataset in Table 3 and on the test set of the ER dataset in Table 4. On the

Table 3. The results of our models (%) on the validation set of ER dataset.

Method	Accuracy	F1	AUC
HOG+SVM	67.69	75.40	65.50
CNN	72.03	74.94	71.56
VGGNET	68.11	70.69	67.85
ENGAGEMENT	**77.76**	**81.18**	**76.77**

Table 4. The results of our models (%) on the test set of ER dataset.

Method	Accuracy	F1	AUC
HOG+SVM	59.88	67.38	62.87
CNN	65.70	71.01	68.27
VGGNET	66.28	70.41	68.41
ENGAGEMENT	**72.38**	**73.90**	**73.74**

validation and test sets, the ENGAGEMENT model substantially outperforms all baseline models using all evaluation metrics, showing the effectiveness of using a trained model on basic facial expression data to initialize an engagement recognition model. All deep models including CNN, VGGNET, and ENGAGEMENT MODELS perform better than the HOG+SVM method, showing the benefit of applying deep learning to recognize engagement. On the test set, the ENGAGEMENT MODEL achieves 72.38% classification accuracy, which outperforms VGGNET by 5%, and the CNN MODEL by more than 6%; it is also 12.5% better than the HOG+SVM method. The ENGAGEMENT MODEL achieved 73.90% F1 measure which is around 3% improvement compared to the deep baseline models and 6% better performance than the HOG+SVM MODEL. Using the AUC metric, as the most popular metric in engagement recognition tasks, the ENGAGEMENT MODEL achieves 73.74% which improves the CNN and VGGNET MODELS by more than 5% and is around 10% better than the HOG+SVM method. There are similar improvements on the validation set.

Confusion Matrices. We show the confusion matrices of the HOG+SVM, CNN, VGGNET, and ENGAGEMENT MODELS on the ER test set in Table 5, Table 6, Table 7 and Table 8, respectively. The tables show the proportions of predicted classes with respect to the actual classes, allowing an examination of precision per class. It is interesting that the effectiveness of deep models comes through their ability to recognize disengaged samples compared to the HOG+SVM MODEL.

Disengaged samples have a wider variety of body postures and facial expressions than engaged sample (e.g. Fig. 1). Due to complex structures, deep learning models are more powerful in capturing these wider variations. The VGGNET MODEL, which has a more complex architecture compared to the CNN MODEL, can also detect disengaged samples with a higher probability. Since we pre-trained the ENGAGEMENT MODEL on basic facial expression data including considerable variations of samples, this model is the most effective approach to recognize disengaged samples achieving 60.42% precision which is around 27% improvement in comparison with the HOG+SVM MODEL

Table 5. Confusion matrix of the HOG+ SVM MODEL (%).

		predicted	
		Engaged	Disengaged
actual	Engaged	92.23	7.77
	Disengaged	66.49	33.51

Table 6. Confusion matrix of the CNN MODEL (%).

		predicted	
		Engaged	Disengaged
actual	Engaged	93.53	6.47
	Disengaged	56.99	43.01

Table 7. Confusion matrix of the VGGNET MODEL (%).

		predicted	
		Engaged	Disengaged
actual	Engaged	89.32	10.68
	Disengaged	52.51	47.49

Table 8. Confusion matrix of the ENGAGEMENT MODEL (%).

		predicted	
		Engaged	Disengaged
actual	Engaged	87.06	12.94
	Disengaged	39.58	60.42

6 Conclusion

Reliable models that can recognize engagement during a learning session, particularly in contexts where there is no instructor present, play a key role in allowing learning systems to intelligently adapt to facilitate the learner. There is a shortage of data for training systems to do this; the first contribution of the paper is a new dataset, labelled by annotators with expertise in psychology, that we hope will facilitate research on engagement recognition from visual data. In this paper, we have used this dataset to train models for the task of automatic engagement recognition, including for the first time deep learning models. The next contribution has been the development of a model, called ENGAGEMENT MODEL, that can address the shortage of engagement data to train a reliable deep learning model. ENGAGEMENT MODEL has two key steps. First, we pre-train the model using basic facial expression data, of which is relatively abundant. Second, we train the model to produce a rich deep learning based representation for engagement, instead of commonly used features and classification methods in this domain. We have evaluated this model with respect to a comprehensive range of baseline models to demonstrate its effectiveness, and have shown that it leads to a considerable improvement against the baseline models using all standard evaluation metrics.

References

1. Alyuz, N., et al.: Semi-supervised model personalization for improved detection of learner's emotional engagement. In: ICMI, pp. 100–107. ACM (2016)
2. Aslan, S., et al.: Human expert labeling process (HELP): towards a reliable higher-order user state labeling process and tool to assess student engagement. Educ. Technol. **57**(1), 53–59 (2017)

3. Bosch, N.: Detecting student engagement: human versus machine. In: UMAP, pp. 317–320. ACM (2016)
4. Bosch, N., et al.: Automatic detection of learning-centered affective states in the wild. In: IUI, pp. 379–388. ACM (2015)
5. Bosch, N., D'mello, S.K., Ocumpaugh, J., Baker, R.S., Shute, V.: Using video to automatically detect learner affect in computer-enabled classrooms. ACM Trans. Interact. Intel. Syst. **6**(2), 17 (2016)
6. Dalal, N., Triggs, B.: Histograms of oriented gradients for human detection. In: CVPR. vol. 1, pp. 886–893. IEEE (2005)
7. D'Cunha, A., Gupta, A., Awasthi, K., Balasubramanian, V.: DAiSEE: Towards user engagement recognition in the wild (2016). arXiv preprint arXiv:1609.01885
8. Dhall, A., Goecke, R., Lucey, S., Gedeon, T.: Static facial expression analysis in tough conditions: data, evaluation protocol and benchmark. In: ICCV, pp. 2106–2112 (2011)
9. Ekman, P.: Basic emotions. In: Dalgleish, T., Power, T. (eds.) The Handbook of Cognition and Emotion, pp. 45–60. John Wiley & Sons, Sussex (1999)
10. Ekman, P.: Darwin and Facial Expression: A Century of Research in Review. ISHK, Los Altos (2006)
11. Fasel, B., Luettin, J.: Automatic facial expression analysis: a survey. Pattern Recogn. **36**(1), 259–275 (2003)
12. Goodfellow, I.J., et al.: Challenges in representation learning: a report on three machine learning contests. In: Lee, M., Hirose, A., Hou, Z.-G., Kil, R.M. (eds.) ICONIP 2013. LNCS, vol. 8228, pp. 117–124. Springer, Heidelberg (2013). https://doi.org/10.1007/978-3-642-42051-1_16
13. Grafsgaard, J., Wiggins, J.B., Boyer, K.E., Wiebe, E.N., Lester, J.: Automatically recognizing facial expression: predicting engagement and frustration. In: Educational Data Mining 2013 (2013)
14. Jacobson, M.J., Taylor, C.E., Richards, D.: Computational scientific inquiry with virtual worlds and agent-based models: new ways of doing science to learn science. Interact. Learn. Environ. **24**(8), 2080–2108 (2016)
15. Jung, H., Lee, S., Yim, J., Park, S., Kim, J.: Joint fine-tuning in deep neural networks for facial expression recognition. In: ICCV, pp. 2983–2991 (2015)
16. Kahou, S.E., et al.: EmoNets: multimodal deep learning approaches for emotion recognition in video. J. Multimodal User Interfaces **10**(2), 99–111 (2016)
17. Kahou, S.E., et al.: Combining modality specific deep neural networks for emotion recognition in video. In: ICMI, pp. 543–550. ACM (2013)
18. Kamath, A., Biswas, A., Balasubramanian, V.: A crowdsourced approach to student engagement recognition in e-learning environments. In: WACV, pp. 1–9. IEEE (2016)
19. Kapoor, A., Mota, S., Picard, R.W., et al.: Towards a learning companion that recognizes affect. In: AAAI Fall symposium, pp. 2–4 (2001)
20. Kim, B.K., Dong, S.Y., Roh, J., Kim, G., Lee, S.Y.: Fusing aligned and non-aligned face information for automatic affect recognition in the wild: a deep learning approach. In: CVPR Workshops, pp. 48–57. IEEE (2016)
21. King, D.E.: Dlib-ml: a machine learning toolkit. J. Mach. Learn. Res. **10**, 1755–1758 (2009)
22. Krizhevsky, A., Sutskever, I., Hinton, G.E.: ImageNet classification with deep convolutional neural networks. In: NIPS, pp. 1097–1105 (2012)
23. Liu, P., Han, S., Meng, Z., Tong, Y.: Facial expression recognition via a boosted deep belief network. In: CVPR, pp. 1805–1812 (2014)

24. Mollahosseini, A., Chan, D., Mahoor, M.H.: Going deeper in facial expression recognition using deep neural networks. In: WACV, pp. 1–10. IEEE (2016)

25. Monkaresi, H., Bosch, N., Calvo, R.A., D'Mello, S.K.: Automated detection of engagement using video-based estimation of facial expressions and heart rate. IEEE Trans. Affect. Comput. **8**(1), 15–28 (2017)

26. Nair, V., Hinton, G.E.: Rectified linear units improve restricted boltzmann machines. In: ICML, pp. 807–814 (2010)

27. Mohamad Nezami, O., Dras, M., Anderson, P., Hamey, L.: Face-cap: image captioning using facial expression analysis. In: Berlingerio, M., Bonchi, F., Gärtner, T., Hurley, N., Ifrim, G. (eds.) ECML PKDD 2018. LNCS (LNAI), vol. 11051, pp. 226–240. Springer, Cham (2019). https://doi.org/10.1007/978-3-030-10925-7_14

28. O'Brien, H.: Theoretical perspectives on user engagement. In: O'Brien, H., Cairns, P. (eds.) Why Engagement Matters, pp. 1–26. Springer, Cham (2016). https://doi.org/10.1007/978-3-319-27446-1_1

29. Pramerdorfer, C., Kampel, M.: Facial expression recognition using convolutional neural networks: state of the art (2016). arXiv preprint arXiv:1612.02903

30. Rodriguez, P., et al.: Deep pain: exploiting long short-term memory networks for facial expression classification. IEEE Trans. Cybern. **99**, 1–11 (2017)

31. Sariyanidi, E., Gunes, H., Cavallaro, A.: Automatic analysis of facial affect: a survey of registration, representation, and recognition. IEEE Trans. Pattern Anal. Mach. Intell. **37**(6), 1113–1133 (2015)

32. Simonyan, K., Zisserman, A.: Very deep convolutional networks for large-scale image recognition(2014). arXiv preprint arXiv:1409.1556

33. Srivastava, N., Hinton, G., Krizhevsky, A., Sutskever, I., Salakhutdinov, R.: Dropout: a simple way to prevent neural networks from overfitting. J. Mach. Learn. Res. **15**(1), 1929–1958 (2014)

34. Tang, Y.: Deep learning using linear support vector machines (2013). arXiv preprint arXiv:1306.0239

35. Whitehill, J., Serpell, Z., Lin, Y.C., Foster, A., Movellan, J.R.: The faces of engagement: automatic recognition of student engagement from facial expressions. IEEE Trans. Affect. Comput. **5**(1), 86–98 (2014)

36. Woolf, B., Burleson, W., Arroyo, I., Dragon, T., Cooper, D., Picard, R.: Affect-aware tutors: recognising and responding to student affect. Int. J. Learn. Technol. **4**(3–4), 129–164 (2009)

37. Yu, Z., Zhang, C.: Image based static facial expression recognition with multiple deep network learning. In: ICMI, pp. 435–442. ACM (2015)

38. Zhang, K., Huang, Y., Du, Y., Wang, L.: Facial expression recognition based on deep evolutional spatial-temporal networks. IEEE Trans. Image Proc. **26**(9), 4193–4203 (2017)

39. Zhang, Z., Luo, P., Loy, C.C., Tang, X.: Learning social relation traits from face images. In: ICCV, pp. 3631–3639 (2015)

Marine Mammal Species Classification Using Convolutional Neural Networks and a Novel Acoustic Representation

Mark Thomas[1](✉), Bruce Martin[2], Katie Kowarski[2], Briand Gaudet[2], and Stan Matwin[1,3]

[1] Faculty of Computer Science, Dalhousie University, Halifax, Canada
`mark.thomas@dal.ca, stan@cs.dal.ca`
[2] JASCO Applied Sciences, Dartmouth, Canada
`{bruce.martin,katie.kowarski,briand.gaudet}@jasco.com`
[3] Institute of Computer Science Polish Academy of Sciences, Warsaw, Poland

Abstract. Research into automated systems for detecting and classifying marine mammals in acoustic recordings is expanding internationally due to the necessity to analyze large collections of data for conservation purposes. In this work, we present a Convolutional Neural Network that is capable of classifying the vocalizations of three species of whales, non-biological sources of noise, and a fifth class pertaining to ambient noise. In this way, the classifier is capable of detecting the presence and absence of whale vocalizations in an acoustic recording. Through transfer learning, we show that the classifier is capable of learning high-level representations and can generalize to additional species. We also propose a novel representation of acoustic signals that builds upon the commonly used spectrogram representation by way of interpolating and stacking multiple spectrograms produced using different Short-time Fourier Transform (STFT) parameters. The proposed representation is particularly effective for the task of marine mammal species classification where the acoustic events we are attempting to classify are sensitive to the parameters of the STFT.

Keywords: Convolutional Neural Networks · Classification · Signal processing · Bioacoustics

1 Introduction

Since their introduction to the area of computer vision, Convolutional Neural Networks (CNNs) have continued to improve upon the state-of-the-art. Recently, a growing collection of research has been brought forward applying CNNs to tasks which are auditory in nature, including: speech recognition [2,7], musical information retrieval [4,14], and acoustic scene classification [21,23].

Stan Matwin's research is supported by the Natural Sciences and Engineering Research Council and by the Canada Research Chairs program.

U. Brefeld et al. (Eds.): ECML PKDD 2019, LNAI 11908, pp. 290–305, 2020.
https://doi.org/10.1007/978-3-030-46133-1_18

Inspired by the compelling results obtained in the previously mentioned domains, researchers in oceanography and marine biology have started to investigate similar solutions to problems in their field. One such problem is the analysis of underwater acoustic data, which is one of the primary methods used to measure the presence, abundance, and migratory patterns of marine mammals [28]. The necessary acoustic data for modelling marine mammal life is often collected using Passive Acoustic Monitoring (PAM) techniques. PAM is non-invasive and reduces the risk of altering the behaviour of a species of interest, unlike GPS tagging. PAM is also less susceptible to harsh weather conditions compared to visual surveys. Acoustic data collected for PAM is often carried out using moored recorders equipped with hydrophones. Stakeholders make use of PAM to adjudicate environmental and governmental policy decisions, for example implementing reduced speed limits on vessels travelling through shipping channels in order to reduce their risk of collision with endangered species of whales [1].

Due to their high cost of deployment, PAM recording devices may be left unattended for months or years at a time before resurfacing, producing very large amounts of data; typically several terabytes per deployment. It is becoming increasingly common for collections of acoustic data to be described at the petabyte scale, making complete human analysis infeasible. As a result, research into automated Detection and Classification Systems (DCS) is widespread and continuing to grow. From a machine learning perspective, a DCS can be interpreted as a hierarchical model containing a binary classifier recognizing whether a signal of interest is present within an acoustic recording, combined with a multiclass classifier for determining the source of the signal. Importantly, marine biologists and oceanographers are typically concerned with the presence or absence of specific species in an acoustic recording. While there have been great advances in the research and development of these systems, many DCS are based on the acoustic properties of a signal of interest and may be specific on a per-dataset basis depending on the equipment that was used or the geographic location of the recordings. Therefore, such systems are often not generalizable and may require being formulated from scratch for a new data set. Moreover, attempts at producing generalizable systems yield high rates of false detections [3].

In this work, we present a deep learning implementation of a DCS composed of a CNN trained on spectrogram representations of acoustic recordings. The main contributions of this work are:

- A CNN capable of classifying three species of marine mammals as well as non-biological sources and ambient noise.
- The classifier makes up an automated DCS that is generalizable and can be adapted to include additional species that produce vocalizations below 1000 Hz.
- A novel visual representation of acoustic data based on interpolating and stacking multiple spectrograms produced using distinct Short-time Fourier Transform parameters.

This work describes a complete application using original data collected for scientific research that could have substantial implications towards environmental policy and conservation efforts. The data was manually selected based on the target species of interest, however, it has not been cleaned and manipulated unlike many research projects in machine learning that use common sets of image data or preprocessed acoustic recordings. Additionally, while the results focused on in this paper are centred on detection and classification of marine mammals, the framework outlined in this paper can be adapted to other tasks such as acoustic scene classification.

The remainder of this paper is organized as follows. In Sect. 2 we review related work on the topic of marine mammal species classification and provide further details on the complexities of the problem. An overview of common representations of acoustic data as well as a novel representation formulated especially for the task of marine mammal species classification is provided in Sect. 3. The data set used in training the CNN and additional information regarding the experimental setup is provided in Sect. 4. The corresponding experimental results are analyzed in Sect. 5. Finally, concluding remarks and future work are presented in Sect. 6.

2   Background and Related Work

CNNs have traditionally been applied to visual recognition tasks on large collections of labelled images. Most notably, CNNs have lead to state-of-the-art performance for classifying commonly used benchmark image data sets and have surpassed human levels of performance [13]. Beyond image classification, CNNs have also been used for object detection [10,12] and in conjunction with Recurrent Neural Networks for natural language processing [15].

Recently, several factors have led researchers to apply CNNs outside of the visual paradigm such as classifying events or patterns found in acoustic recordings. An obvious reason for adapting CNNs to acoustic tasks is the performance levels of the classifiers cited above. A less obvious reason to those not working in the field of acoustics or digital signal processing, is that human analysis of acoustic data is often carried out visually using spectrograms as it is faster to visually identify signals of interest without having to listen to the entire recording. Another reason for using visual representations of acoustic data is that they allow for the analysis and interpretation of sounds outside of the human hearing range. One area, alluded to in Sect. 1, that makes frequent use of visual representations of acoustic data is the detection and classification of marine mammal vocalizations within underwater acoustic recordings (i.e., DCS research).

Research into automated DCS has been a growing topic of interest, in part, as a by-product of the reduced costs in recording equipment which has produced vast amounts of data. Another reason for the growth in DCS research is for conservation purposes, particularly as it relates to endangered species of whales. In developing an automated DCS for marine mammal vocalizations, one hopes to accurately detect and assign a label to an instance of an acoustic recording containing one or more vocalizations produced by a species of interest. However, developing a generalizable DCS presents several distinct challenges.

For one, underwater recordings often have a low signal-to-noise ratio making feature extraction difficult. Another challenge is that ground truth labelled data is difficult to obtain due to the required expertise and training of the labeller. As a result, only a very small fraction of the large collections of acoustic data is suitable for supervised learning. Furthermore, the small numbers of some species coupled with the low rate of occurrence of their vocalizations make for highly unbalanced data.

Traditionally, many of the algorithms used to detect and classify marine mammal vocalizations are derived from the properties of a signal of interest. In general, these approaches can be divided into two categories. The first category of algorithms involves comparing unlabelled data to templates of certain vocalizations. Examples of this approach include *matched filtering*, where a template corresponding to the vocalization of interest is convolved with a signal to produce a detection function that is evaluated using a pre-determined threshold parameter [5]. Another example is *spectrogram correlation*, which first computes a correlation kernel using segments of template spectrograms, following which, the correlation kernel is convolved over a spectrogram of the unlabelled data producing a vector representing the similarity between the spectrogram and the kernel over time. Large similarity values correspond to possible detections. The second category of algorithms involves detecting regions of interest in a spectrogram and extracting features (e.g.: the duration of the detection or the absolute change in frequency) to be used as input vectors for classification. Various detection algorithms are used in the first step of this approach including: neighbourhood search algorithms (e.g., pixel connectivity) in spectrograms that have been filtered, smoothed, and cast to binary representations [3] and contour detectors that operate by continually searching for local maxima within pre-specified frequency bands of normalized spectra over time [19]. These detection algorithms are heavily dependent on the filtering, normalization, and smoothing operations that are performed on each spectrogram. Once the regions of interest are determined, feature vectors are then handed to commonly used classification algorithms such as: linear and quadratic discriminant analysis [3,9], support vector machines [8], and artificial neural networks [8]. Researchers have also likened the task to automatic speech recognition and used Gaussian mixture models and hidden Markov models for classification [22,25].

The algorithms described above involve a large amount of human input–often from experts–which is a limitation to the development of future classifiers for several reasons. In the former category the templates used for detection and classification are largely specific to not only certain species, but also different types of vocalizations produced by the same species. Furthermore, the detection threshold may require fine-tuning depending on the noise characteristics of the data set. For the latter category of algorithms, many of the hyper-parameters provided to the smoothing and noise-removal routines are dependent on the data set. Subsequently, the hand-engineered features are contaminated by these specifications as well as human bias. These limitations yield systems which are not easily generalizable to a broad category of species using data collected at different sampling rates, geographic locations, or using different recording devices.

More recently, researchers have attempted to use deep learning to learn generalizable representations of spectrograms for the purpose of DCS development. In one study, Halkias et al. [11] contrast the performance of a restricted Boltzmann machine and a sparse auto-encoder for classifying five species of baleen whales (*mysticetes*), however, the regions of interest containing the whale calls were assumed to be known. Wang et al. [27] use CNNs to classify spectrograms containing vocalizations of killer whales (*Orcinus orca*) and pilot whales (*Globicephala melas/macrorhynchus*) but similarly do not include non-biological or ambient noise sources. Liu et al. [16] also use CNNs but focus on the classification of call types as opposed to the species that produced them. Finally, Luo et al. [17] train a CNN to detect the high-frequency echolocation clicks of toothed whales (*odontocetes*) using a combination of real audio recordings and synthetic data, however, we are interested in classifying baleen whale vocalizations that occur at a much lower frequency and can be masked by low tonal sounds created by shipping activity.

3   Visual Representations of Acoustic Data

Human analysis of acoustic recordings is performed aurally by listening to an acoustic recording as well as visually using spectrograms. A popular approach for generating spectrograms is through a Short-time Fourier Transform (STFT). The STFT procedure calculates the sinusoidal frequency and phase content of an acoustic signal over time and is most commonly visualized in two dimensions with time on the x-axis, frequency on the y-axis, and intensity expressed by varying colour.

The equation of the discrete-time STFT of a signal $x[n]$ can be expressed as:

$$X(n, \omega) = \sum_{m=-\infty}^{\infty} x[m]w[m - n]e^{-j\omega m} , \qquad (1)$$

where w is a windowing function with a pre-specified length centered at time n. In the equation expressed above, time is discrete and frequency (ω) is continuous, however, in practice both units are discretized and each successive STFT is computed using an implementation of the Fast Fourier Transform (FFT) algorithm (e.g., the Cooley-Tukey algorithm [6]). Equation 1 describes a complex function, therefore, we take the square of the absolute value of $X(n, \omega)$ yielding a spectrogram of the power spectral density. Finally, we convert the intensity from power to a logarithmic scale (i.e., decibels (dB)), as is commonly the case in underwater acoustics.

3.1   Mel-Scaled Spectrograms

A spectrogram computed using the approach formulated above is linear in frequency. Unfortunately, because CNNs are spatially invariant, they are incapable of understanding human perceptions of pitch when frequency is expressed on a linear scale. For example, while the difference between two signals occurring at 1000 Hz and 1500 Hz and two other signals occurring at 10 kHz and 10.5 kHz are numerically equivalent (i.e., equal to 500 Hz), the difference of the lower frequency signals is perceptually much larger to a human listener.

The bandwidth of the data we are attempting to classify is relatively low (i.e., ≤1000 Hz), therefore the CNNs imperception to pitch is not a major concern. However, in order to test this hypothesis, we additionally generate mel-scaled spectrograms whereby frequency is transformed from hertz to mels (from the word melody) using the formula outlined in Eq. 2.

$$\omega_{mel} = 2595 \log_{10} \left(1 + \frac{\omega_{Hz}}{700}\right).$$
(2)

Following this transformation, the resulting frequency scale more closely aligns with the log-like human perception of pitch.

3.2   Novel Representation: Stacked and Interpolated Spectrograms

The majority of the DCS detailed in Sect. 2 were trained using large collections of single channel inputs in the form of spectrograms. During the creation process of said data sets, a decision must be made on the appropriate combination of parameters to pass to the STFT. In practice, when marine biologists analyze acoustic recordings, they will often generate multiple spectrograms using different STFT parameters, for example: changing the length of the FFT window and/or the window overlap. By changing the parameters of the STFT, the time and frequency resolutions of the spectrogram are altered. Using multiple spectrograms with varying resolutions is particularly helpful when annotating underwater acoustic recordings containing marine mammal vocalizations because some species tend to make prolonged low-frequency vocalizations with a small bandwidth (e.g.: blue whale moans), while other species make shorter vocalizations with a larger bandwidth (e.g.: humpback songs). Depending on the set of parameters used to generate the spectrogram, one can easily misclassify a vocalization as a different species or miss the vocalization entirely.

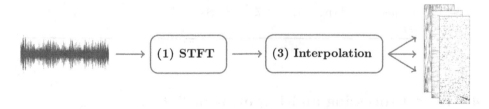

Fig. 1. Simple illustration demonstrating the process of transforming a waveform of an acoustic signal into a multi-channel input via interpolation and stacking.

We propose a novel representation of an acoustic signal that attempts to exploit the strategy used by human experts during the annotation process. First, following Eq. 1, several spectrograms are generated using multiple sets of STFT parameters. Because each of the spectrograms vary in resolution across time and frequency, they are interpolated using a simple linear interpolation spline over a grid proportionate to the smallest time and frequency resolutions. The equation of a linear interpolation spline for some point (n, ω) between (n_i, ω_i) and (n_{i+1}, ω_{i+1}), where n is known, can be expressed as:

$$\omega = \omega_i + \frac{\omega_{i+1} - \omega_i}{n_{i+1} - n_i}(n - n_i) . \tag{3}$$

After interpolation, the dimensions of the matrices corresponding to each spectrogram are the same. The interpolated spectrograms are then stacked to form a multi-channel tensor; imitating the concept of RGB channels in a digital colour image, as depicted in Fig. 1. The details of the algorithm used to produce a single instance of the novel representation described above are outlined in Algorithm 1.

Algorithm 1: Generating an instance of the novel representation

---

Input: The waveform x, function w, and parameters $\Theta = [\theta_1, \theta_2, \ldots, \theta_k]$
Output: A tensor $\mathbf{Z}$ with k channels
1   Initialize the interpolation resolutions ω_0 and n_0 to ∞
2   **for** $i = 1$ *to* k **do**
3   Generate a spectrogram $\mathbf{D}_i = \text{STFT}(x; w, \theta_i)$ (Eqn 1)
4   Maintain a running minimum of ω_0 and n_0
5   **if** $\Delta\omega_i < \omega_0$ **then**
6 | $\omega_0 = \Delta\omega_i$
7   **end**
8   **if** $\Delta n_i < n_0$ **then**
9 | $n_0 = \Delta n_i$
10   **end**
11 **end**
12 **for** $i = 1$ *to* k **do**
13 | Interpolate each spectrogram $\mathbf{S}_i = \text{INTERPOLATE}(\mathbf{D}_i; \omega_0, n_0)$ (Eqn 3)
14 **end**
15 Stack the interpolated spectrograms $\mathbf{Z} = [\mathbf{S}_1, \mathbf{S}_2, \ldots, \mathbf{S}_k]$
16 Return $\mathbf{Z}$

---

4   Data Processing and Experiment Setup

4.1   Recordings of Marine Mammal Vocalizations

The acoustic recordings used to train the classifier were collected by JASCO Applied Sciences using Autonomous Multichannel Acoustic Recorders (AMARs)

during the summer and fall months of 2015 and 2016 in the areas surrounding the Scotian Shelf; along the coast of the Atlantic Canadian provinces (Fig. 2).

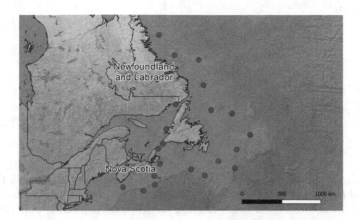

Fig. 2. Map depicting the locations of the recording devices deployed by JASCO Applied Sciences along the Scotian Shelf located off the coast of Atlantic Canada.

The recordings were sampled at both 8 kHz and 250 kHz in order to capture the low frequency vocalizations of baleen whales and high frequency vocalizations of toothed whales, respectively. In this work we focus on the detection and classification of baleen whales. In particular, we are interested in three species: blue whales (*Balaenoptera musculus*), fin whales (*Balaenoptera physalus*), and sei whales (*Balaenoptera borealis*). These species can be particularly challenging to classify as they are each capable of making a similar vocalization known as a down sweep during the summer months. A large collection of baleen whale vocalizations fall below 1000 Hz, therefore, we restrict our set of acoustic recordings to those collected using the 8 kHz sampling rate.

The acoustic recordings were analyzed by marine biology experts producing over 30,000 annotations in the form of bounding boxes around signals pertaining to the three species of whales and other acoustic sources labelled as "non-biological". Other species of whales present in the recording area were also annotated, however, they were not included in this paper. The distribution of annotations is heavily unbalanced in favour of the more vocal fin whales at a 6:1 ratio.

The data sets used for training, validating, and testing each classifier were created in the following fashion. First, the human annotations were centred within an excerpt 30 s long. Four spectrograms depicting typical examples of the 30 s excerpts are provided in Fig. 3; one for each of the possible acoustic sources. Example annotations are drawn using dashed vertical lines. As we can see, not every vocalization that appeared in a spectrogram was labelled. In Fig. 3a for example, there appears to be three blue whale vocalizations occurring consecutively, however, only the second has been annotated.

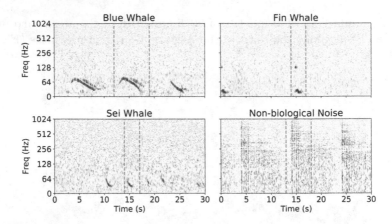

Fig. 3. Example spectrograms displaying frequency in hertz on a log-scale. Examples are provided for each of the three whale species: (a) blue whales, (b) fin whales, (c) sei whales, and (d) non-biological noise. Dashed vertical lines depict the upper and lower bounds of the expert annotations.

For each 30 s excerpt, a smaller ten second long sample (here on referred to as simply a "sample") containing the annotation was randomly selected from the larger excerpt. Due to the partial labelling of the recordings, it is possible that a sample may include more than one vocalization. For example, a sample from time 10 to 20 s in the file used to produce Fig. 3c, would in fact contain three sei whale vocalizations. The set of data containing only ambient noise was produced in a similar fashion, however, they were produced from a large set of files that were known to not contain baleen whale vocalizations. As such, the sampling routine simply selected a ten second sample randomly from the entire file.

A spectrogram of each sample was produced corresponding to the CNN that was being trained and the matrices corresponding to the values of the spectrograms were used as training instances. In total there were five categories of classifiers: three trained on single-channel spectrograms using increasing FFT window lengths (i.e., 256, 2048, and 16,384 samples); one trained on single-channel mel-scaled spectrograms using a window length of 2048 samples and 128 mels; and one trained on a three-channel version of the novel representation described in Sect. 3.2. The three spectrograms used in creating the novel representation used window lengths of 256, 2048, and 16,384 samples respectively and were interpolated to fit within a grid of height 256 and width 128 units. All of the above spectrograms were produced using the Hann window function and used an FFT window overlap of 1/4 the window length. The choice of window lengths were chosen in order to capture short sweeping vocalizations such as whistles (i.e., $256 \approx 1/32$ the sampling rate), a more inclusive group of vocalizations (i.e., $2048 \approx 1/4$ the sampling rate), and long vocalizations that are fairly persistent in frequency (i.e., $16384 \approx 2\times$ the sampling rate). The computed spectrograms were truncated using an upper frequency bound of 1000 Hz and a lower bound of 10 Hz. Apart from the linear interpolant applied in the case of the novel representation, no additional filtering, smoothing, or noise removal was applied to the spectrograms.

In practice, the ten second sampling routine and all subsequent steps including spectrogram generation were executed in parallel on the CPU while the CNN was trained on the GPU. In this way, the sampling routine acted as a quasi-data-augmentation strategy for each training batch. Further details with respect to the CPU, GPU, batch sizes, and other parameters used during training are provided in Sect. 4.2.

Separate training, validation, and test data sets were produced using a random split ratio of 70/15/15, respectively. Table 1 contains the number of files and the corresponding species distributions of each data set.

Table 1. Number of files and the distribution of each acoustic source for the training, validation, and test sets.

Source	Label	Training	Validation	Test
Blue whale	BW	2692 (6.23%)	601 (6.49%)	574 (6.20%)
Sei whale	SW	1701 (3.94%)	332 (3.59%)	383 (4.14%)
Fin whale	FW	15,118 (35.01%)	3244 (35.06%)	3272 (35.36%)
Non-biological	NN	2078 (4.81%)	449 (4.85%)	398 (4.30%)
Ambient	AB	21,589 (50.00%)	4626 (50.00%)	4627 (50.00%)

4.2 Neural Architectures and Training Parameters

We evaluate the performance of two commonly used CNN architectures, namely: ResNet-50 [13] and VGG-19 with batch normalization [24]. The CNNs were implemented in Python using the PyTorch open source deep learning platform [20]. Training was distributed over four NVIDIA P100 Pascal GPUs each equipped with 16 GB of memory. The sampling routine and subsequent data processing was performed in parallel on two 12-core Intel E5-2650 CPUs.

Each CNN–regardless of the FFT window length or number of channels–was trained using the same hyper-parameters apart from the initial learning rate, which was set to 0.001 for the ResNet architecture and 0.01 for the VGG architecture. In both cases, the learning rate decayed exponentially by a factor of 10 using a step schedule of 30 epochs. The batch size of each training step was set to 128 instances. Stochastic Gradient Descent (SGD) with momentum equal to 0.9 and weight decay equal to $1e^{-4}$ was used to optimize a cross-entropy loss function.

The CNNs were each trained for a total of 100 epochs. After each epoch, the validation set was evaluated and the model with the best performance in terms of F-1 Score was saved. An early stopping criteria was not used, however, if the model began to overfit to the training data and the F-1 Score of the validation set did not improve, the best model with respect to the validation set was still maintained. Finally, the training process of each classifier was repeated ten times using different random number generator seeds.

5   Experimental Results

Table 2 contains the mean evaluation metrics and 95% confidence intervals over ten training runs for the ResNet and VGG CNNs.

Table 2. Mean performance and 95% confidence intervals of ten training/testing runs using random number generator seeds for each combination of CNN architecture and STFT parameter set.

	NFFT	Accuracy	Precision	Recall	F-1 score
ResNet-50 performance					
3-channels (Hz)	–	0.953 (±0.016)	0.887 (±0.045)	0.871 (±0.036)	0.878 (±0.031)
1-channel (Hz)	256	0.883 (±0.022)	0.714 (±0.060)	0.641 (±0.037)	0.675 (±0.046)
	2048	0.944 (±0.009)	0.863 (±0.036)	0.838 (±0.039)	0.850 (±0.023)
	16384	0.943 (±0.013)	0.860 (±0.032)	0.847 (±0.058)	0.853 (±0.031)
1-channel (mels)	2048	0.895 (±0.031)	0.762 (±0.067)	0.723 (±0.048)	0.742 (±0.044)
VGG-19 performance					
3-channels (Hz)	–	0.961 (±0.017)	0.906 (±0.044)	0.892 (±0.049)	0.899 (±0.041)
1-channel (Hz)	256	0.914 (±0.024)	0.790 (±0.048)	0.771 (±0.070)	0.780 (±0.053)
	2048	0.959 (±0.019)	0.899 (±0.041)	0.889 (±0.048)	0.894 (±0.039)
	16384	0.951 (±0.017)	0.871 (±0.037)	0.878 (±0.038)	0.875 (±0.028)
1-channel (mels)	2048	0.918 (±0.022)	0.818 (±0.043)	0.784 (±0.036)	0.801 (±0.034)

The classifier trained on the novel representation outperforms the remaining classifiers trained on single-channel inputs. Paired two-sample t-tests indicate that the improvement in performance between the classifier trained on the novel representation is statistically significant in all cases with one exception: the VGG-19 CNN trained on single-channel inputs using a window length of 2048 samples.

Figure 4 contains four confusion matrices: two corresponding to the VGG-19 architecture and two corresponding to the ResNet-50 architecture. In both cases, the best two performing classifiers were those trained on the novel representation and the single-channel linearly scaled spectrogram produced using a window length of 2048 samples.

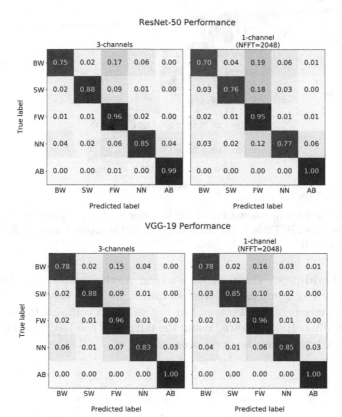

Fig. 4. Normalized confusion matrices of the two best performing classifiers in terms of F-1 Score for the ResNet-50 and VGG-19 CNNs.

5.1 Generalization to Other Acoustic Sources

In order to the demonstrate the ability of the DCS that we have developed to generalize to other acoustic sources below 1000 Hz, we train a new classifier using a transfer learning approach to include humpback whale (*Megaptera novaeangliae*) vocalizations. Specifically, all sixteen convolutional layers in the VGG-19 network trained on the novel representation are frozen. The last three layers of the network are then re-learned on the data set described in Table 1 with an additional 2100 humpback vocalizations. The hyper-parameters and optimization routine used for training the last layers of the network are equivalent to those detailed in Sect. 4.2.

The trained classifier achieves performance levels in terms of accuracy, precision, and recall of 0.948, 0.884, and 0.871, respectively, without the need of re-training the convolutional feature extraction layers of the CNN.

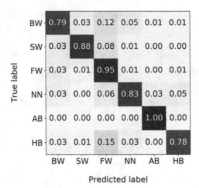

Fig. 5. Normalized confusion matrix of the transfer learning experiment evaluated on the test set described in Table 1 with an additional 450 humpback annotations identified using the label "HB".

t-SNE Embeddings. The transfer learning results exhibit that the CNN is capable of learning complex features contained within a spectrogram. Further proof of this statement can be found in Fig. 6, which contains two-dimensional t-SNE embeddings [18] generated using the output of the last frozen layer of the VGG-19 CNN trained on the novel representation.

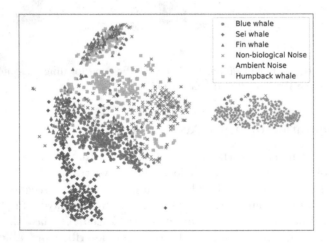

Fig. 6. t-SNE embeddings computed from the output of the last frozen layer of the VGG-19 CNN architecture.

There is a distinct separation between the original five classes of acoustic sources. More importantly, even before learning the last three classifying layers of the VGG-19 CNN, a relatively distinct representation has already been learned for the humpback whale class. This result is significant as it implies additional species with less annotated data can be included in our implementation of a DCS through transfer learning.

6   Conclusion

This paper presents a scientific application focused on detecting and classifying marine mammal vocalizations in acoustic recordings. In particular, we have developed a DCS based on Convolutional Neural Networks that is capable of classifying three species of baleen whales as well as non-biological sources against a background of ambient noise. A novel representation of acoustic signals was introduced and this representation increased the performance of the aforementioned classifier. The DCS was shown to be capable of learning generalizable representations for the purpose of including additional species. The latter note is substantial as it implies that species with very little annotated data–especially those species that are endangered–can be included in the training process of future classifiers through transfer learning.

A well performing and generalizable DCS such as the one that we have developed is of great interest to researchers in the fields of marine biology, bioacoustics, and oceanography as it allows for fast analysis of large acoustic data sets. Such analysis may be used to inform governmental and environmental policy pertaining to conservation efforts of marine mammal life.

6.1   Future Work

The work presented above is part of an ongoing research project focused on developing a DCS to be used in real time on specially developed autonomous hardware (e.g., moored recording devices and/or ocean gliders). With this goal in mind, we must consider time/space complexities and additional research into model compression is necessary. Further research and development is ongoing using data collected from recording devices deployed in various locations around the world. The supplementary data allows for the ability to include a variety of additional species of baleen whales as well as other marine mammals (e.g., pinnipeds). The additional data will also allow for the interpretation of different sources of ambient noise (i.e., soundscapes). Collectively, including additional data from various locations around the world will lead to a more robust DCS of marine mammal vocalizations.

Another option for including additional species of marine mammals for which we have little available data is through data augmentation strategies. In particular, research into using unsupervised or semi-supervised approaches (e.g., Variational Auto-encoders, Generative Adversarial Networks) to increase the size of the training data could be highly beneficial.

Recent work into neural network architectures that operate directly on the waveform of an acoustic signal have shown great promise [26]. While the majority of these results are specific to generative tasks, these architectures–or a suitable alternative–may be used in training a classifier for acoustic recordings such as those described in this paper. In particular, through learning from the waveform directly we avoid any information loss that takes place during a Fourier transform.

Finally, given the promising results of our early experiments reported in Sect. 5.1, we also plan on investigating the use of various transfer learning and meta-learning techniques for the task at hand.

Acknowledgements. Collaboration between researchers at JASCO Applied Sciences and Dalhousie University was made possible through a Natural Sciences and Engineering Research Council Engage Grant. The acoustic recordings described in this paper were collected by JASCO Applied Sciences under a contribution agreement with the Environmental Studies Research Fund.

References

1. Protecting north Atlantic right whales from collisions with ships in the Gulf of St. Lawrence. http://bit.ly/tc_whales
2. Abdel-Hamid, O., Mohamed, A.R., Jiang, H., Deng, L., Penn, G., Yu, D.: Convolutional neural networks for speech recognition. IEEE/ACM Trans. Audio Speech Lang. Process. **22**(10), 1533–1545 (2014)
3. Baumgartner, M.F., Mussoline, S.E.: A generalized baleen whale call detection and classification system. J. Acoust. Soc. Am. **129**(5), 2889–2902 (2011)
4. Choi, K., Fazekas, G., Sandler, M., Cho, K.: Convolutional recurrent neural networks for music classification. In: IEEE International Conference on Acoustics, Speech and Signal Processing (ICASSP), pp. 2392–2396. IEEE (2017)
5. Clark, C.W., Marler, P., Beeman, K.: Quantitative analysis of animal vocal phonology: an application to swamp sparrow song. Ethology **76**(2), 101–115 (1987)
6. Cooley, J.W., Tukey, J.W.: An algorithm for the machine calculation of complex Fourier series. Math. Comput. **19**(90), 297–301 (1965)
7. Deng, L., et al.: Recent advances in deep learning for speech research at Microsoft. In: IEEE International Conference on Acoustics, Speech and Signal Processing (ICASSP), vol. 26, p. 64. IEEE (2013)
8. Dugan, P.J., Rice, A.N., Urazghildiiev, I.R., Clark, C.W.: North Atlantic right whale acoustic signal processing: Part i. comparison of machine learning recognition algorithms. In: IEEE Long Island Systems, Applications and Technology Conference, pp. 1–6. IEEE (2010)
9. Gillespie, D., Caillat, M., Gordon, J., White, P.: Automatic detection and classification of odontocete whistles. J. Acous. Soc. Am. **134**(3), 2427–2437 (2013)
10. Girshick, R.: Fast R-CNN. In: Proceedings of the IEEE International Conference on Computer Vision, pp. 1440–1448 (2015)
11. Halkias, X.C., Paris, S., Glotin, H.: Classification of mysticete sounds using machine learning techniques. J. Acous. Soc. Am. **134**(5), 3496–3505 (2013)
12. He, K., Gkioxari, G., Dollár, P., Girshick, R.: Mask R-CNN. In: Proceedings of the IEEE International Conference on Computer Vision, pp. 2961–2969 (2017)
13. He, K., Zhang, X., Ren, S., Sun, J.: Deep residual learning for image recognition. In: Proceedings of the IEEE Conference on Computer Vision and Pattern Recognition, pp. 770–778 (2016)
14. Humphrey, E.J., Bello, J.P.: Rethinking automatic chord recognition with convolutional neural networks. In: 11th International Conference on Machine Learning and Applications (ICMLA), vol. 2, pp. 357–362. IEEE (2012)
15. Karpathy, A., Fei-Fei, L.: Deep visual-semantic alignments for generating image descriptions. In: Proceedings of the IEEE Conference on Computer Vision and Pattern Recognition, pp. 3128–3137 (2015)

16. Liu, S., Liu, M., Wang, M., Ma, T., Qing, X.: Classification of cetacean whistles based on convolutional neural network. In: 10th International Conference on Wireless Communications and Signal Processing (WCSP), pp. 1–5. IEEE (2018)

17. Luo, W., Yang, W., Zhang, Y.: Convolutional neural network for detecting odontocete echolocation clicks. J. Acous. Soc. Am. **145**(1), EL7–EL12 (2019)

18. van der Maaten, L., Hinton, G.: Visualizing data using t-SNE. J. Mach. Learn. Res. **9**, 2579–2605 (2008)

19. Mellinger, D.K., Martin, S.W., Morrissey, R.P., Thomas, L., Yosco, J.J.: A method for detecting whistles, moans, and other frequency contour sounds. J. Acous. Soc. Am. **129**(6), 4055–4061 (2011)

20. Paszke, A., et al.: Automatic differentiation in PyTorch. In: NIPS-W (2017)

21. Piczak, K.J.: Environmental sound classification with convolutional neural networks. In: IEEE 25th International Workshop on Machine Learning for Signal Processing (MLSP), pp. 1–6. IEEE (2015)

22. Roch, M.A., et al.: Classification of echolocation clicks from odontocetes in the southern California bight. J. Acous. Soc. Am. **129**(1), 467–475 (2011)

23. Salamon, J., Bello, J.P.: Deep convolutional neural networks and data augmentation for environmental sound classification. IEEE Signal Process. Lett. **24**(3), 279–283 (2016)

24. Simonyan, K., Zisserman, A.: Very deep convolutional networks for large-scale image recognition. arXiv preprint arXiv:1409.1556 (2014)

25. Skowronski, M.D., Harris, J.G.: Acoustic detection and classification of microchiroptera using machine learning: lessons learned from automatic speech recognition. J. Acous. Soc. Am. **119**(3), 1817–1833 (2006)

26. van Den Oord, A., et al.: Wavenet: a generative model for raw audio. SSW **125** (2016)

27. Wang, D., Zhang, L., Lu, Z., Xu, K.: Large-scale whale call classification using deep convolutional neural network architectures. In: IEEE International Conference on Signal Processing, Communications and Computing (ICSPCC), pp. 1–5. IEEE (2018)

28. Zimmer, W.M.: Passive Acoustic Monitoring of Cetaceans. Cambridge University Press, New York (2011)

Learning Disentangled Representations
of Satellite Image Time Series

Eduardo H. Sanchez[1,2]([✉]), Mathieu Serrurier[1,2], and Mathias Ortner[1]

[1] IRT Saint Exupéry, Toulouse, France
{eduardo.sanchez,mathias.ortner}@irt-saintexupery.com
[2] IRIT, Université Toulouse III - Paul Sabatier, Toulouse, France
mathieu.serrurier@irit.fr

Abstract. In this paper, we investigate how to learn a suitable representation of satellite image time series in an unsupervised manner by leveraging large amounts of unlabeled data. Additionally, we aim to disentangle the representation of time series into two representations: a shared representation that captures the common information between the images of a time series and an exclusive representation that contains the specific information of each image of the time series. To address these issues, we propose a model that combines a novel component called cross-domain autoencoders with the variational autoencoder (VAE) and generative adversarial network (GAN) methods. In order to learn disentangled representations of time series, our model learns the multimodal image-to-image translation task. We train our model using satellite image time series provided by the Sentinel-2 mission. Several experiments are carried out to evaluate the obtained representations. We show that these disentangled representations can be very useful to perform multiple tasks such as image classification, image retrieval, image segmentation and change detection.

Keywords: Unsupervised learning · Image-to-image translation ·
VAE · GAN · Disentangled representation · Satellite image time series

1 Introduction

Deep learning has demonstrated impressive performance on a variety of tasks such as image classification, object detection, semantic segmentation, among others. Typically, these models create internal abstract representations from raw data in a supervised manner. Nevertheless, supervised learning is a limited approach since it requires large amounts of labeled data. It is not always possible to obtain labeled data since it requires time, effort and resources. As a consequence, semi-supervised or unsupervised algorithms have been developed to reduce the required number of labels. Unsupervised learning is intended to learn useful representations of data easily transferable for further usage. As using smart data representations is important, another desirable property of unsupervised

© Springer Nature Switzerland AG 2020
U. Brefeld et al. (Eds.): ECML PKDD 2019, LNAI 11908, pp. 306–321, 2020.
https://doi.org/10.1007/978-3-030-46133-1_19

methods is to perform dimensionality reduction while keeping the most important characteristics of data. Classical methods are principal component analysis (PCA) or matrix factorization. For the same purpose, autoencoders learn to compress data into a low-dimensional representation and then, to uncompress that representation into the original data. An autoencoder variant is the variational autoencoder (VAE) introduced by Kingma and Welling [13] where the low-dimensional representation is constrained to follow a prior distribution. The VAE provides a way to extract a low-dimensional representation while learning the probability distribution of data. Other unsupervised methods of learning the probability data distribution have been recently proposed using generative models. A generative model of particular interest is generative adversarial networks (GANs) introduced by Goodfellow *et al.* [6,7].

In this work, we present a model that combines the VAE and GAN methods in order to create a useful representation of satellite image time series in an unsupervised manner. To create these representations we propose to learn the image-to-image translation task introduced by Isola *et al.* [11] and Zhu *et al.* [21]. Given two images from a time series, we aim to translate one image into the other one. Since both images are acquired at different times, the model should learn the common information between these images as well as their differences to perform translation. We also aim to create a disentangled representation into a shared representation that captures the common information between the images of a time series and an exclusive representation that contains the specific information of each image. For instance, the common information accross time series could be useful to perform image classification while the knowledge about the specific information of each image could be useful for change detection.

Since we aim to generate any image of the time series from any of its images, we address the problem of multimodal generation, *i.e.* multiple output images can be generated from a single input image. For instance, an image containing harvested fields could be translated into an image containing growing crop fields, harvested fields or a combination of both.

Our approach is inspired by the BicycleGAN model introduced by Zhu *et al.* [22] to address multimodal generation and the model presented by Gonzalez-Garcia *et al.* [5] to address representation disentanglement.

In this work, the following contributions are made. First, we propose a model that combines the cross-domain autoencoder principle proposed by Gonzalez-Garcia *et al.* [5] under the GAN and VAE constraints to address representation disentanglement and multimodal generation. Differences with respect to models [5,22] can be seen in Sect. 2. Our model is adapted to satellite image time series analysis using a simpler architecture (see Sect. 3). Second, we show that our model is capable to process a huge volume of high-dimensional data such as Sentinel-2 image time series in order to create feature representations (see Sect. 4). Third, our model generates a disentangled representation that isolates the common information of the entire time series and the exclusive information of each image. Our experiments suggest that these representations are useful to perform several tasks such as image classification, image retrieval, image segmentation and change detection by outperforming other state-of-the-art methods in some cases (see Sects. 4.2, 4.3, 4.4, 4.5 and 4.6).

2   Related Work

Variational Autoencoder (VAE). In order to estimate the data distribution of a dataset, a common approach is to maximize the log-likelihood function given the samples of the dataset. A lower bound of the log-likelihood is introduced by Kingma and Welling [13]. To learn the data distribution, the authors propose to maximize the lower bound instead of the log-likelihood function which in some cases is intractable. The model is implemented using an autoencoder architecture and trained via a stochastic gradient descent method. It is capable to create a low-dimensional representation where relevant attributes of data are captured.

Generative Adversarial Networks (GANs). Due to its great success in many different domains, GANs [6,7] have become one of the most important research topics. The GAN model can be thought of as a game between two players: the generator and the discriminator. In this setting, the generator aims to produce samples that look like drawn from the same distribution as the training samples. On the other hand, the discriminator receives samples to determine whether they are real (dataset samples) or fake (generated samples). The generator is trained to fool the discriminator by learning a mapping function from a latent space which follows a prior distribution to the data space. However, traditional GANs (DCGAN [18], LSGAN [16], WGAN [1], WGAN-GP [8], EBGAN [20], among others) does not provide a means to learn the inverse mapping from the data space to the latent space. To solve this problem, several models were proposed such us BiGAN [4] or VAE-GAN [14] which include an encoder from the data space to the latent space in the model. The data representation obtained in the latent space via the encoder can be used for other tasks as shown by Donahue *et al.* [4].

Image-to-Image Translation. It is one of the most popular applications using conditional GANs [17]. The image-to-image translation task consists of learning a mapping function between an input image domain and an output image domain. Impressive results have been achieved by the pix2pix [11] and cycleGAN [21] models. Nevertheless, most of these models are monomodal. That is, there is a unique output image for a given input image.

Multimodal Image-to-Image Translation. One of the limitations of previous models is the lack of diversity of generated images. Certain models address this problem by combining the GAN and VAE methods. On the one hand, GANs are used to generate realistic images while VAE is used to provide diversity in the output domain. Recent work that deals with multimodal output is presented by Gonzalez-Garcia *et al.* [5], Zhu *et al.* [22], Huang *et al.* [10] and Ma *et al.* [15]. In particular, to be able to generate an entire time series from a single image, we adopt the principle of the BicycleGAN model proposed by Zhu *et al.* [22] where a low-dimensional latent vector represents the diversity of the output domain.

Since the BicycleGAN model is mainly focused on image generation, the model architecture is not suitable for feature extraction. Instead, we propose a model capable to split the shared information across the time series and the exclusive information of each image that generates the diversity of the output domain.

Disentangled Feature Representation. Recent work is focused on learning disentangled representations by isolating the factors of variation of high-dimensional data in an unsupervised manner. A disentangled representation can be very useful for several tasks that require knowledge of these factors of variation. Chen et al. [3] propose an objective function based on the maximization of the mutual information. Gonzalez-Garcia et al. [5] propose a model based on VAE-GAN image translators and a novel network component called cross-domain autoencoders. This model separates the representation of two image domains into three parts: the shared part which contains common information from both domains and the exclusive parts which only contain factors of variation that are specific to each domain.

In this paper, we propose a model that combines the cross-domain autoencoder component under the VAE and GAN constraints in order to analyze satellite image time series by creating a shared representation that captures the spatial information and an exclusive representation that captures the temporal information. While our method is inspired by the model proposed by Gonzalez-Garcia et al. [5], we would like to highlight some differences: (a) The model [5] considers two image domains whose representation space can be split into two exclusive parts and a shared part. For instance, the authors use a colored MNIST dataset which can be split into: background color (exclusive part), digit color (exclusive part) and digit (shared part). In our case, we consider only a shared part which corresponds to spatial information at a given location on the Earth's surface and an exclusive part which is related to the acquisition time of the images; (b) The model [5] performance is analyzed using simple datasets (colored MNIST, 3D cars and 3D chairs) while running the code provided by the authors to learn their model on Sentinel-2 data fails to converge generating unsatisfactory results as shown in the additional material (see Sect. 1); (c) We use a simpler model architecture composed of 4 networks that implements the exclusive and shared representation encoder, the decoder and the discriminator functions while the model [5] uses 10 networks (2 encoders, 2 decoders, 4 discriminators and 2 GRL decoders) to achieve representation disentanglement which can be difficult to train simultaneously.

3   Method

Let X, Y be two images randomly sampled from a given time series T in a region C. Let $\mathcal{X}$ be the image domain where these images belong to and let $\mathcal{R}$ be the representation domain of these images. The representation domain $\mathcal{R}$ is divided into two subdomains $\mathcal{S}$ and $\mathcal{E}$, then $\mathcal{R} = [\mathcal{S}, \mathcal{E}]$. The subdomain $\mathcal{S}$ contains the common information between images X and Y and the subdomain $\mathcal{E}$ contains the particular information of each image. Since images X and Y belong to the same

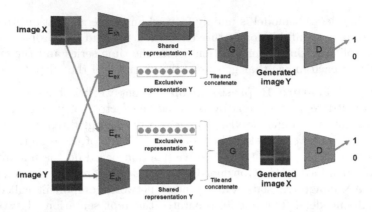

Fig. 1. Model overview. The model goal is to learn both image transitions: $X \to Y$ and $Y \to X$. Both images are passed through the network E_{sh} in order to extract their shared representations. Similarly, the network E_{ex} extracts the exclusive representations corresponding to images X and Y. In order to generate the image Y, the decoder network G takes the shared representation of image X and the exclusive representation of image Y. A similar procedure is performed to generate the image X. Finally, the discriminator D is used to evaluate the generated images.

time series, their shared representations must be identical, $i.e.$ $S_X = S_Y$. On the other hand, as images are acquired at different times, their exclusive representations E_X and E_Y correspond to the specific information of each image.

We propose a model that learns the transition from X to Y as well as the inverse transition from Y to X. In order to accomplish this, an autoencoder-like architecture is used. In Fig. 1, an overview of the model can be observed. Let $E_{sh} : \mathcal{X} \to \mathcal{S}$ be the shared representation encoder and $E_{ex} : \mathcal{X} \to \mathcal{E}$ be the exclusive representation encoder. To generate the image Y, the shared representation of X, $i.e.$ $E_{sh}(X)$, and the exclusive representation of Y, $i.e.$ $E_{ex}(Y)$ are computed. Then both representations are passed through the decoder function $G : \mathcal{R} \to \mathcal{X}$ which generates a reconstructed image $G(E_{sh}(X), E_{ex}(Y))$. A similar process is followed to reconstruct the image X. Then, these images are passed through a discriminator function $D : \mathcal{X} \to [0, 1]$ in order to evaluate the generated images.

The model functions E_{ex}, E_{sh}, G and D are represented by neural networks with parameters $\theta_{E_{ex}}$, $\theta_{E_{sh}}$ and θ_G and θ_D, respectively. The training procedure to learn these parameters is explained below.

3.1   Objective Function

Similarly to Zhu $et\ al.$ [22] and Gonzalez-Garcia $et\ al.$ [5], our objective function is composed of several terms to obtain a disentangled representation.

Concerning the shared representation, images X and Y must have identical shared representations, $i.e.$ $E_{sh}(X) = E_{sh}(Y)$. A simple solution is to minimize the L_1 distance between their shared representations as shown in Eq. 1.

$$L_1^{sh} = \mathbb{E}_{X,Y \sim \mathcal{X}} \left[|E_{sh}(X) - E_{sh}(Y)| \right] \qquad (1)$$

The exclusive representation must only contain the particular information that corresponds to each image. To enforce the disentanglement between shared and exclusive representations, we include a reconstruction loss in the objective function where the shared representations of X and Y are switched. The loss term corresponding to the reconstruction of image X is represented in Eq. 2. Moreover, this loss term can be thought of as the reconstruction loss in the VAE model [13] which maximizes a lower bound of the log-likelihood function. As we enforce representation disentanglement, we minimize the Kullback-Leibler divergence between the data distribution and the generated distribution.

$$L_1^{X,Y} = \mathbb{E}_{X,Y \sim \mathcal{X}} \left[|X - G(E_{sh}(Y), E_{ex}(X))| \right] \qquad (2)$$

On the other hand, the lower bound proposed in the VAE model constraints the feature representation to follow a prior distribution. In our model, we only force the exclusive representation to be distributed as a standard normal distribution $\mathcal{N}(0, I)$ in order to generate multiple outputs by sampling from this space during inference while keeping the shared representation constant. In contrast to Gonzalez-Garcia et al. [5] where a GAN approach is used to constraint the exclusive representation, a simpler and effective solution is to include a Kullback-Leibler divergence term between the distribution of the exclusive representation and the prior $\mathcal{N}(0, I)$. Assuming that the exclusive representation encoder $E_{ex}(X)$ is distributed as a normal distribution $\mathcal{N}(\mu_{E_{ex}(X)}, \sigma_{E_{ex}(X)})$, the Kullback-Leibler divergence can be written as follows,

$$L_{KL}^{X} = -\frac{1}{2} \mathbb{E}_{X \sim \mathcal{X}} \left[1 + \log(\sigma_{E_{ex}(X)}^2) - \mu_{E_{ex}(X)}^2 - \sigma_{E_{ex}(X)}^2 \right] \qquad (3)$$

We include a LSGAN loss [16] in the objective function to encourage the model to generate realistic and diverse images thus improving the learned representations. The discriminator is trained to maximize the probability of assigning the correct label to real images and generated images while the generator is trained to fool the discriminator by classifying generated images as real, i.e. $D(G(E_{sh}(Y), E_{ex}(X))) \rightarrow 1$. The corresponding loss term for image X and its reconstructed version can be seen in Eq. 4 where the discriminator maximizes this term while the generator minimizes it.

$$L_{GAN}^{X} = \mathbb{E}_{X \sim \mathcal{X}} \left[(D(X))^2 \right] + \mathbb{E}_{X,Y \sim \mathcal{X}} \left[(1 - D(G(E_{sh}(Y), E_{ex}(X))))^2 \right] \qquad (4)$$

To summarize, the training procedure can be seen as a minimax game (Eq. 5) where the objective function $\mathcal{L}$ is minimized by the generator functions of the model (E_{ex}, E_{sh}, G) while it is maximized by the discriminator D.

$$\min_{E_{ex},E_{sh},G} \max_{D} \mathcal{L} = L_{GAN}^{X} + L_{GAN}^{Y} + \lambda_{L_1} \left(L_1^{X,Y} + L_1^{Y,X} \right)$$
$$+ \lambda_{L_{KL}} (L_{KL}^{X} + L_{KL}^{Y}) + \lambda_{L_1}^{sh} L_1^{sh} \qquad (5)$$

Where λ_{L_1}, $\lambda_{L_1}^{sh}$ and $\lambda_{L_{KL}}$ are constant coefficients to weight the loss terms.

3.2   Implementation Details

Our model is architectured around four neural networks: the shared representation encoder, the exclusive representation encoder, the decoder and the discriminator. The architecture details are provided in the additional material section. To train our model, we use batches of 64 randomly selected image pairs of size $64 \times 64 \times 4$ from our satellite image time series dataset (see Sect. 4.1). Every network is trained from scratch by using randomly initialized weights as starting point. The learning rate is implemented as a staircase function which starts with an initial value of 0.0002 and decays every 50000 iterations. We use Adam optimizer to update the network weights using a $\beta = 0.5$ during 150000 iterations. Concerning the loss coefficients, we use the following values: $\lambda_{L_1} = 10$, $\lambda_{L_1}^{sh} = 0.5$ and $\lambda_{L_{KL}} = 0.01$ during training. The training algorithm was executed on a NVIDIA Tesla K80 GPU during 3 days to process 100GB of satellite image time series. The training procedure is summarized in Algorithm 1.

Algorithm 1. Training algorithm.

1: Random initialization of model parameters $(\theta_D^{(0)}, \theta_{E_{sh}}^{(0)}, \theta_{E_{ex}}^{(0)}, \theta_G^{(0)})$
2: **for** $k = 1$; $k = k + 1$; $k <$ number of iterations **do**
3:     Sample a batch of m time series $\{T_s^{(1)}, ..., T_s^{(m)}\}$
4:     Sample a batch of m image pairs $\{(X^{(1)}, Y^{(1)}), ..., (X^{(m)}, Y^{(m)})\}$ from $\{T_s^{(i)}\}$
5:     Compute $\mathcal{L}^{(k)}(X^{(i)}, Y^{(i)}, \theta_D^{(k)}, \theta_{E_{sh}}^{(k)}, \theta_{E_{ex}}^{(k)}, \theta_G^{(k)})$

$$
\mathcal{L}^{(k)} = \frac{1}{m} \sum_{i=1}^{m} \left[\left(D(X^{(i)}) \right)^2 + \left(1 - D(G(E_{sh}(Y^{(i)}), E_{ex}(X^{(i)}))) \right)^2 + \left(D(Y^{(i)}) \right)^2 \right.
$$

$$
+ \left(1 - D(G(E_{sh}(X^{(i)}), E_{ex}(Y^{(i)}))) \right)^2 + \lambda_{L_1}^{sh} \left(|E_{sh}(X^{(i)}) - E_{sh}(Y^{(i)})| \right)
$$

$$
+ \lambda_{L_1} \left(|X^{(i)} - G(E_{sh}(Y^{(i)}), E_{ex}(X^{(i)}))| + |Y^{(i)} - G(E_{sh}(X^{(i)}), E_{ex}(Y^{(i)}))| \right)
$$

$$
- \frac{1}{2} \lambda_{L_{KL}} \left(2 + \log(\sigma^2_{E_{ex}(X^{(i)})}) - \mu^2_{E_{ex}(X^{(i)})} - \sigma^2_{E_{ex}(X^{(i)})} + \log(\sigma^2_{E_{ex}(Y^{(i)})}) \right.
$$

$$
\left. \left. - \mu^2_{E_{ex}(Y^{(i)})} - \sigma^2_{E_{ex}(Y^{(i)})} \right) \right]
$$

6:     Update the parameters $\theta_{E_{sh}}^{(k+1)}$, $\theta_{E_{ex}}^{(k+1)}$ and $\theta_G^{(k+1)}$ by gradient descent of $\mathcal{L}^{(k)}$.
7:     Update the parameters $\theta_D^{(k+1)}$ by gradient ascent of $\mathcal{L}^{(k)}$.
8: **end for**

---

4   Experiments

4.1   Sentinel-2

The Sentinel-2 mission is composed of a constellation of 2 satellites that orbit around the Earth providing an entire Earth coverage every 5 days. Both satellites acquire images at 13 spectral bands using different spatial resolutions.

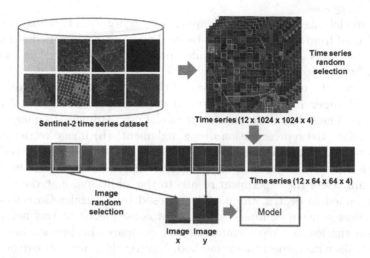

Fig. 2. Training data selection. A batch of smaller time series is randomly sampled from the dataset. At each iteration two images are randomly selected from each time series to be used as input for our model.

In this paper, we use the RGBI bands[1] which correspond to bands at 10 m spatial resolution. Bands are acquired after L-1C processing. In order to organize the data acquired by the mission, Earth surface is divided into square tiles of approximately 100 km on each side. One tile acquired at a particular time is referred to as a granule.

To create our training dataset, we selected 42 tiles containing several regions of interest such as the Amazon rainforest, the Dead Sea, the city of Los Angeles, the Great Sandy Desert, circular fields in Saudi Arabia, among others. The list of tiles is provided in the additional material. As explained by Kempeneers and Soille [12], many of the acquired granules might carry useless information. In our case, the availability of granules for a given tile depends on two factors: the cloud coverage and the image completeness. Therefore, we defined a threshold in order to avoid these kind of problems that affect Earth observation by setting a cloud coverage tolerance of 2% and completeness tolerance of 85%. For each tile, we extracted 12 granules from March 2016 to April 2018 keeping a regular time-step between granules. Then, we selected 25 non-overlapping patches of size 1024×1024 from the center of the tiles to reduce the effect of the satellite orbit view angle. Finally, our training dataset is composed of $42 \times 25 = 1050$ times series each of which is composed of 12 images of size $1024 \times 1024 \times 4$. The training dataset size is around 100 GB. Similarly, we create a test dataset by selecting 6 different tiles whose size is around 14 GB.

In order to analyze the entire time series using smaller patches the following strategy is applied: a batch of time series composed of images of size $64 \times 64 \times 4$ is randomly sampled from the time series of images of size $1024 \times 1024 \times 4$.

---

[1] Red (band 4), Green (band 3), Blue (band 2) and Near infrared (band 8) bands.

Since our model takes two images as input, at each iteration two images are randomly selected from the time series to be used as input for our model. Thus, the whole time series is learned as the training procedure progresses. Data sampling procedure is depicted in Fig. 2.

To evaluate the model performance and the learned representations, we perform several supervised and unsupervised experiments on Sentinel-2 data as suggested by Theis [19]. We evaluate our model on: (a) image-to-image translation to validate the representation disentanglement; (b) image retrieval, image classification and image segmentation to validate the shared representation and (c) change detection to analyze the exclusive representation. We also provide several examples of the experiment results in the additional material section.

As explained in Sect. 2, the model proposed by Gonzalez-Garcia *et al.* [5] fails to converge using Sentinel-2 data. As a consequence, it was not possible to evaluate the learned representations and compare the performance on the proposed tasks with respect to our method. Nevertheless, we compare our model with the BicycleGAN [22] and VAE [13] models and show that our model achieves better results at image classification, image retrieval and change detection.

4.2   Image-to-Image Translation

It seems natural to first test the model performance at image-to-image translation. We sample 9600 time series of size $12 \times 64 \times 64 \times 4$ to evaluate our model. It represents around 20k processed images of size $64 \times 64 \times 4$.

An example of image-to-image translation using our model can be observed in Fig. 3. For instance, let us consider the image in the third row, fifth column. The shared representation is extracted from an image X which corresponds to growing crop fields while the exclusive representation is extracted from another image Y where fields have been harvested. Consequently, the generated image contains harvested fields which is defined by the exclusive representation of image Y. In general, generated images look realistic in both training and test datasets except for small details which are most likely due to the absence of skip connections between the encoders and generator.

We quantify the L_1 distance between generated images $G(E_{sh}(X), E_{ex}(Y))$ and images Y used to extract the exclusive representations. Results can be observed in Table 1 (first column). Pixel values in generated images and real images are in the range of $[-1, 1]$, thus a mean difference of 0.0155 indicates that the model performs well at image-to-image translation. The BicycleGAN model [22] achieves a slightly better result of 0.0136 which is probably due to the use of skip connections. However, our model is mainly focused on representation learning to perform downstream tasks and not on image generation.

A special image-to-image translation case is image autoencoding where the shared and exclusive representations are extracted from the same image. The L_1 distance between images X and autoencoded images $G(E_{sh}(X), E_{ex}(X))$ is computed for comparison purpose in Table 1 (second column). Lower values in terms of L_1 distance are obtained with respect to those of image-to-image translation. We provide the result obtained from the VAE [13] model as a baseline.

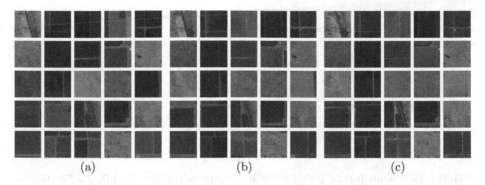

| (a) | (b) | (c) |

Fig. 3. Image translation performed on images of Brawley, California. (a) Images used to extract the shared representations; (b) Images used to extract the exclusive representations; (c) Generated images from the shared representation of (a) and the exclusive representation of (b). More examples are available in the additional material section.

Fig. 4. Multimodal generation. The first row corresponds to a time series sampled from the test dataset. The second row corresponds to a time series where each image is generated by using the same shared representation and only modifying the exclusive representation.

Our model achieves a similar performance generating well-reconstructed images even if this case is not considered during training.

Finally, we perform times series reconstruction in order to show that the exclusive representation encodes the specific information of each image. An image is randomly selected from a time series to extract its shared representation. While keeping the shared representation constant and only modifying the exclusive representation, we reconstruct all the images of the original time series. Results in terms of L_1 distance between the original time series and the reconstructed one are shown in Table 1 (third column). As in the previous cases, the BicycleGAN [22] achieves a slightly better result of 0.0140 with respect to our model performance of 0.0184. An example of time series reconstruction using our model can be seen in Fig. 4. Since the shared representation which represents the spatial location is constant, the experiment suggests that the exclusive representation controls the image information related to the acquisition time.

4.3   Image Retrieval

In this experiment, we want to evaluate whether the shared representation provides information about the geographical location of time series via image

Table 1. Mean and standard deviation values in terms of the L_1 distance for image-to-image translation (first column), image autoencoding (second column) and time series reconstruction (third column).

Method	Image translation	Image autoencoding	Time series reconstruction
VAE [13]	–	0.0086 ± 0.0300	–
BicycleGAN [22]	0.0136 ± 0.0538	0.0045 ± 0.0138	0.0140 ± 0.0503
Ours	0.0155 ± 0.0595	0.0085 ± 0.0318	0.0184 ± 0.0664

retrieval. Given an image patch from a granule acquired at time t_o, we would like to locate it in a granule acquired at time t_f. The procedure is the following: a time series of size $12 \times 1024 \times 1024 \times 4$ is randomly sampled from the dataset. Then, a batch of 64 image patches of size $64 \times 64 \times 4$ is randomly selected as shown in Fig. 5a. The corresponding shared representations are extracted for each image of the batch. The main idea is to use the information provided by the shared representation to locate the image patches in every image of the time series. For each image of the time series, a sliding window of size $64 \times 64 \times 4$ is applied in order to explore the entire image. As the window slides, the shared representations are extracted and compared to those of the images to be retrieved. The nearest image in terms of L_1 distance is selected as the retrieved image at each image of the time series. In our experiment, 150 time series of size $12 \times 1024 \times 1024 \times 4$ are analyzed. It represents around 115k images of size $64 \times 64 \times 4$ to be retrieved and 110M images of size $64 \times 64 \times 4$ to be analyzed.

To illustrate the retrieval algorithm, let us consider an image of agricultural fields. We plot the image patches to be retrieved in Fig. 5a and the retrieved image patches by the algorithm in Fig. 5b. As can be seen, even if some changes have occurred, the algorithm is able to spatially locate most of the patches. In spite of the seasonal changes in the agricultural fields, the algorithm performs correctly since the image retrieval leverages the shared representation which contains common information of the time series. Results in terms of Recall@1 are displayed in Table 2 (last row). We obtain a high value in terms of Recall@1 even if it is not so close to 1. This result can be explained since the dataset contains several time series from the desert, forest and ocean tiles which could be notoriously difficult to retrieve even for humans. For instance, image retrieval performs better in urban scenarios since the city provides details that can be easily identified in contrast to agricultural fields where distinguishing textures can be confusing (see the additional material section).

As a baseline to compare to our method based on the shared representation, we use the raw pixels as feature to find the image location. Our experiments show that using raw pixels yields a poor performance to locate the image patches (see Table 2, third row). We note that even if the retrieved images look similar to the query images, they do not come from the same location. The recommended images using raw pixels are mainly based on the image color. For instance, whenever a harvest fields is used as query image the retrieved images correspond

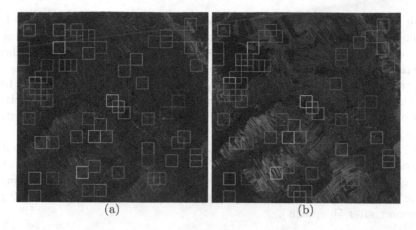

Fig. 5. Image retrieval using shared representation comparison. (a) Selected image from a time series where a batch of 64 image patches (colored boxes) are extracted from; (b) Another image from the same time series is used to locate the selected image patches. The algorithm plots colored boxes corresponding to the nearest image patches in terms of shared representation distance. (Color figure online)

Table 2. Image retrieval results in terms of Recall@1.

Method	Recall@1
VAE [13]	0.4536
BicycleGAN [22]	0.2666
Raw pixels	0.5083
Ours	0.7372

Table 3. Accuracy results in the test dataset.

Model	Accuracy	Epochs
Fully-supervised	62.13%	50
VAE [13]	87.64%	10
BicycleGAN [22]	87.59%	10
Ours	92.38%	10

to harvested fields as well. This is not the case when using shared representations since seasonal changes are ignored in the shared representation. Additionally, we perform the same experiment using the representations extracted from the BicycleGAN [22] and VAE [13] models. As expected, since these models do not disentangle the spatial and temporal information of time series, the performance achieved is considerably poor (see Table 2, first and second rows).

4.4 Image Classification

A common method to evaluate the performance of unsupervised feature representations is to apply them to perform image classification. We test the shared representation extracted by our model using a novel dataset called EuroSAT [9]. It contains 27000 labeled images in 10 classes (residential area, sea, river, highway, etc.). We divide the dataset into a training and test dataset using a 80:20 split keeping a proportional number of examples per class.

We recover the shared representation encoder E_{sh} as feature extractor from our model. We append two fully-connected layers of 64 and 10 units, respectively on top of the feature extractor. We only train these fully-connected layers while keeping frozen the weights of the feature extractor in a supervised manner using the training split of EuroSAT. To provide a comparison, we train a fully-supervised model using the same architecture but randomly initialized weights. Additionally, we use the BicycleGAN [22] and VAE [13] models as feature extractors to train a classifier. Results can be observed in Table 3.

Our classifier achieves an accuracy of 92.38% outperforming the classifiers based on the BicycleGAN [22] and VAE [13] models. Nevertheless, it is important to note that using pretrained weights reduces the training time and allows to achieve better performance with respect to randomly initialized weights (62.13% of accuracy after 50 epochs).

4.5   Image Segmentation

Since the shared representation is related to the location and texture of the image, we perform a qualitative experiment to illustrate its use for image segmentation. An image of size $1024 \times 1024 \times 4$ is randomly selected from a time series. Then, a sliding window of size $64 \times 64 \times 4$ and stride of size 32×32 is used to extract image patches. The shared representations extracted from these image patches are used to perform clustering via k-means. A new sliding window with a stride of 8×8 is used to extract the shared representations from the image. The extracted shared representations are assigned to a cluster. Since several clusters are assigned for each pixel, the cluster is decided by the majority of voted clusters. In Fig. 6, a segmentation map example in Shanghai is displayed. Despite its simplicity, this unsupervised method achieves interesting results. It is able to segment the river, the port area and the residential area, among others. On the other hand, experiments using the raw pixels of the image as feature produce segmentation maps of lower visual quality.

4.6   Change Detection

We perform an experiment to illustrate the use of the exclusive representation for seasonal change detection. Two images of size $1024 \times 1024 \times 4$ are selected from a time series. A sliding window of size $64 \times 64 \times 4$ is used to explore both images using a stride of size 32×32. As the window slides, the exclusive representations are extracted and compared using the L_1 distance. A threshold is defined to determine whether a change has occurred or not. Figure 7 shows an example of change detection maps using the shared and exclusive representations. As can be seen, the exclusive representation is able to identify seasonal changes while the shared representation is not as expected. Our experiments suggest that the low-dimensional exclusive representation captures the factors of variation in time series generating visually coherent change detection maps.

Additionally, we use our learned representations to perform urban change detection on the OSCD dataset [2] which provides 14 training images and 10

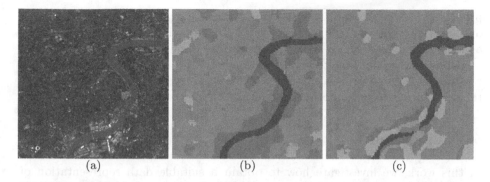

Fig. 6. Image segmentation in Shanghai, China. A sliding window is used to extract the shared representations of the image which in turn are used to perform clustering with 7 classes. (a) Image to be segmented; (b) Segmentation map using shared representations; (c) Segmentation map using raw pixels.

Fig. 7. Seasonal change detection in Brawley, USA. (a) Image X; (b) Image Y; (c) Change detection map using shared representations (d) Change detection map using exclusive representations.

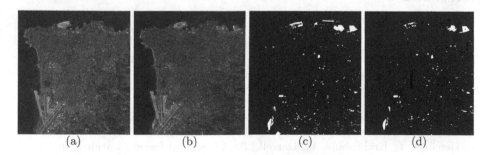

Fig. 8. Urban change detection in Beirut, Lebanon. (a) Image X; (b) Image Y; (c) Ground truth; (d) Change detection map using our model.

test images. Keeping frozen the weights of the encoders, we learn a decoder to create a change detection map of size 64×64. A sliding window is used to generate a complete change detection map. Figure 8 shows an urban change detection example. As the ground truth is not available for test images, the authors [2] provide a website to evaluate them. We obtain an average accuracy of 63.07% outperforming the VAE [13] and BicycleGAN [22] models which achieve an average accuracy of 59.31% and 60.01% respectively. We also train a fully-supervised model using the same architecture of our model but randomly initialized weights which achieves an average accuracy of 60.67%. It suggests that the use of disentangled representations improves the results at image change detection.

5   Conclusion

In this work, we investigate how to obtain a suitable data representation of satellite image time series. We first present a model based on VAE and GAN methods combined with the cross-domain autoencoder principle. This model is able to learn a disentangled representation that consists of a common representation for the images of the same time series and an exclusive representation for each image. We train our model using Sentinel-2 time series which indicates that the model is able to deal with huge amounts of high-dimensional data. Finally, we show experimentally that the disentangled representation can be used to achieved interesting results at multiple tasks such as image classification, image retrieval, image segmentation and change detection. We think the learned representations can be improved by taking into account the time order of images in the model. We leave the development of such algorithm for future work.

Acknowledgments. We would like to thank the projects SYNAPSE and DEEL of the IRT Saint Exupéry for funding and providing computational resources to conduct the experiments.

References

1. Arjovsky, M., Chintala, S., Bottou, L.: Wasserstein generative adversarial networks. In: Proceedings of the 34th International Conference on Machine Learning (2017)
2. Caye Daudt, R., Le Saux, B., Boulch, A., Gousseau, Y.: Urban change detection for multispectral earth observation using convolutional neural networks. In: IEEE International Geoscience and Remote Sensing Symposium (IGARSS) (2018)
3. Chen, X., Duan, Y., Houthooft, R., Schulman, J., Sutskever, I., Abbeel, P.: InfoGAN: interpretable representation learning by information maximizing generative adversarial nets. In: Advances in Neural Information Processing Systems (2016)
4. Donahue, J., Krähenbühl, P., Darrell, T.: Adversarial feature learning. In: International Conference on Learning Representations (2017)
5. Gonzalez-Garcia, A., van de Weijer, J., Bengio, Y.: Image-to-image translation for cross-domain disentanglement. In: Advances in Neural Information Processing Systems (2018)
6. Goodfellow, I., et al.: Generative adversarial nets. In: Advances in Neural Information Processing Systems (2014)
7. Goodfellow, I.J.: NIPS 2016 tutorial: generative adversarial networks (2016). http://arxiv.org/abs/1701.00160

8. Gulrajani, I., Ahmed, F., Arjovsky, M., Dumoulin, V., Courville, A.C.: Improved training of wasserstein GANs. In: Advances in Neural Information Processing Systems (2017)

9. Helber, P., Bischke, B., Dengel, A., Borth, D.: EuroSAT: a novel dataset and deep learning benchmark for land use and land cover classification (2017). http://arxiv.org/abs/1709.00029

10. Huang, X., Liu, M.Y., Belongie, S., Kautz, J.: Multimodal unsupervised image-to-image translation. In: European Conference on Computer Vision (2018)

11. Isola, P., Zhu, J.Y., Zhou, T., Efros, A.A.: Image-to-image translation with conditional adversarial networks. In: Conference on Computer Vision and Pattern Recognition (2017)

12. Kempeneers, P., Soille, P.: Optimizing Sentinel-2 image selection in a big data context. Big Earth Data 1, 145–158 (2017)

13. Kingma, D.P., Welling, M.: Auto-encoding variational Bayes. In: International Conference on Learning Representations (2014)

14. Larsen, A.B.L., Sønderby, S.K., Larochelle, H., Winther, O.: Autoencoding beyond pixels using a learned similarity metric. In: Proceedings of the 33rd International Conference on Machine Learning (2016)

15. Ma, L., Jia, X., Georgoulis, S., Tuytelaars, T., Van Gool, L.: Exemplar guided unsupervised image-to-image translation. In: International Conference on Learning Representations (2019)

16. Mao, X., Li, Q., Xie, H., Lau, R.Y., Wang, Z., Smolley, S.P.: Least squares generative adversarial networks. In: International Conference on Computer Vision (2017)

17. Mirza, M., Osindero, S.: Conditional generative adversarial nets (2014). http://arxiv.org/abs/1411.1784

18. Radford, A., Metz, L., Chintala, S.: Unsupervised representation learning with deep convolutional generative adversarial networks. In: International Conference on Learning Representations (2016)

19. Theis, L., van den Oord, A., Bethge, M.: A note on the evaluation of generative models. In: International Conference on Learning Representations (2016)

20. Zhao, J.J., Mathieu, M., LeCun, Y.: Energy-based generative adversarial network. In: International Conference on Learning Representations (2017)

21. Zhu, J.Y., Park, T., Isola, P., Efros, A.A.: Unpaired image-to-image translation using cycle-consistent adversarial networks. In: International Conference on Computer Vision (2017)

22. Zhu, J.Y., et al.: Toward multimodal image-to-image translation. In: Advances in Neural Information Processing Systems (2017)

Pushing the Limits of Exoplanet Discovery via Direct Imaging with Deep Learning

Kai Hou Yip[1]([⊠]), Nikolaos Nikolaou[1], Piero Coronica[4], Angelos Tsiaras[1],
Billy Edwards[1], Quentin Changeat[1], Mario Morvan[1], Beth Biller[2],
Sasha Hinkley[3], Jeffrey Salmond[4], Matthew Archer[4], Paul Sumption[4],
Elodie Choquet[5], Remi Soummer[6], Laurent Pueyo[6], and Ingo P. Waldmann[1]

[1] Department of Physics and Astronomy, University College London,
Gower Street, London WC1E 6BT, UK
{kai.yip.13,n.nikolaou,angelos.tsiaras.14,billy.edwards.16,
quentin.changeat.18,mario.morvan.18,ingo.star}@ucl.ac.uk
[2] SUPA, Institute for Astronomy, Centre for Exoplanet Science,
University of Edinburgh, Edinburgh, UK
bb@roe.ac.uk
[3] Department of Physics and Astronomy, University of Exeter,
Stocker Road, Exeter EX4 4PY, UK
s.hinkley@exeter.ac.uk
[4] Research Software Engineering, University of Cambridge,
Trinity Lane, Cambridge CB2 1TN, UK
{pc620,js947,ma595,ps459}@cam.ac.uk
[5] Aix Marseille Univ, CNRS, CNES, LAM, Marseille, France
elodie.choquet@lam.fr
[6] STScI, 3700 San Martin Drive, Baltimore, MD 21218, USA
{soummer,pueyo}@stsci.edu

Abstract. Further advances in exoplanet detection and characterisation require sampling a diverse population of extrasolar planets. One technique to detect these distant worlds is through the direct detection of their thermal emission. The so-called direct imaging technique, is suitable for observing young planets far from their star. These are very low signal-to-noise-ratio (SNR) measurements and limited ground truth hinders the use of supervised learning approaches. In this paper, we combine deep generative and discriminative models to bypass the issues arising when directly training on real data. We use a Generative Adversarial Network to obtain a suitable dataset for training Convolutional Neural Network classifiers to detect and locate planets across a wide range of SNRs. Tested on artificial data, our detectors exhibit good predictive performance and robustness across SNRs. To demonstrate the limits of the detectors, we provide maps of the precision and recall of the model per pixel of the input image. On real data, the models can re-confirm bright source detections.

© Springer Nature Switzerland AG 2020
U. Brefeld et al. (Eds.): ECML PKDD 2019, LNAI 11908, pp. 322–338, 2020.
https://doi.org/10.1007/978-3-030-46133-1_20

Keywords: Exoplanet detection · Direct imaging · Computer vision · Generative Adversarial Networks · Convolutional Neural Networks

1 Introduction

In the last 20 years, our understanding of planetary science has undergone what can best be described as a *second Copernican revolution*. With over 4000 discovered[1] exoplanets – planets orbiting stars other than our sun – we now understand that planet formation is an integral part of stellar formation. In other words, every star in our galaxy is likely to host at least one planet [4]. To date, we have only just begun to understand the mechanisms underlying planet formation, evolution and potential habitability and it is only by studying a large population of extrasolar planets that we can begin to place our own solar system in the galactic context. Hence, it is no surprise that the field of extrasolar planets is one of the fastest growing and most dynamic in contemporary astrophysics.

Several exoplanet detection techniques exist. Through their various observational constraints, we find each technique to be sensitive to a specific subset of the planet population. While most detection techniques are indirect in nature and only measure the planet's effect on the received stellar light, we here concern ourselves with the most direct detection method: *direct imaging*. As the name suggests, direct imaging tries to image the planet's thermal emission in-situ by blocking out the light of its host-star to reveal the significantly fainter planetary companion. These directly imaged planets are very young as they still radiate from the heat of their recent formation [2,11,14]. Hence, studying this population gives us a window into early planet formation. To understand the formation and evolution history of our own solar system, it is paramount to study the widest possible range of planetary systems and ages. Therefore, more detections via direct imaging would greatly impact the field.

1.1 The Challenge of Direct Imaging

Detecting a planet via direct imaging poses a significant challenge. Despite significant efforts and technological advances made with this technique, the number of confirmed detections – only 16 exoplanets so far [2] – remains far behind those of other methods. The object of interest is often significantly dimmer than the parent star (best case contrast ratio of $\sim 10^{-5}$). In practice, astronomers increase the planet-flux[2] contrast using a *coronagraph*, a mask blocking the star's light. The resulting image has a reduced contribution from the stellar flux but is still subject to systematic residual flux by the diffracted stellar light inside the instrument optics, resulting in a low *Signal-to-Noise Ratio (SNR)* per image. This systematic noise pattern is known as the '*speckle noise*' and is an instrument specific, quasi-static pattern of light on the detector [16].

---

[1] Paris Observatory Exoplanet Catalogue: http://exoplanet.eu.

[2] The term *flux* refers to the rate of incoming photons.

To first order the quasi-static nature of the speckle noise allows it to be removed by *image subtraction*. This is often performed using *Angular Differential Imaging (ADI)*, where a sequence of images are taken at different roll-angles (i.e. orientations) of the telescope. However for space-based observatories, such as the *Hubble Space Telescope (HST)* or the upcoming *James Web Space Telescope (JWST)*, choices of roll-angles are limited and calibration images are expensive to obtain. Hence we must use other speckle pattern suppression techniques.

The *limited ground truth* (knowledge on whether a given system contains planets or not) has largely restricted any machine learning approaches applied to the problem to *unsupervised learning* techniques. By obtaining a low rank approximation of the data, one can compute the difference of an image and its reconstruction after being projected to this lower dimensional space to remove the dominant components of the speckle pattern. Such methods include, *LOCI* [13], *principal component analysis (PCA)-based algorithms* [1,5,18], and *LLSG* [8] and can be used as a denoising step before *visual inspection*. They cannot classify images as possibly containing planets or not, nor automatically locate planets in images. The latter is achievable by *ANDROMEDA* [3,15] via maximum likelihood estimation on the residual images obtained by pairwise subtraction within the ADI sequence but naturally, it is only applicable to ADI sequence data and hence not applicable to space-based observatories.

The number of *supervised learning* attempts is limited. In [6], the authors use a *Support Vector Machine (SVM)* to classify images as possibly containing planets or not. Here, the authors injected fake planets into real data without establishing the "planet-free" ground-truth first. In [7], the authors used *Singular Value Decomposition (SVD)* of ADI sequence data to remove possible planet signals before planet injection. A *Random Forest* and a *Convolutional LSTM* classifier were then trained on the pre-processed data. Unfortunately, according to the authors, the method did not work on single images but only on sequences of ADI images. For space-based data considered in this paper, this method is therefore not applicable as often only individual images are obtained with space-based telescopes. Moreover, the results reported appear to suggest that their final models produce a very large number of false positive planet detections per frame.

All these methods suffer from class imbalance, i.e. a lack of confirmed planet detections (positive examples) to train on. However, in order to train a supervised model for exoplanet detection, we require a sufficient amount of examples from both classes. Similarly, images without currently known planets should not be used as negative examples. This is because it is possible –in fact, probable– that undiscovered planets are present in the data. For these reasons it is imprudent to train supervised models directly on real data. Simply put, if one assumes 'absence of detection' as 'confirmation of absence' and uses this to train a new model, then (i) the performance of the model is upper bounded by the current state-of-the-art and (ii) the training dataset is biased towards the negative class.

1.2   Overview of the Paper

In this work, we circumvent the aforementioned issues by introducing an intermediate step of generative modelling between the real data and the final discriminative model. By training a *Generative Adversarial Network (GAN)* [9] on real data from the *Near Infrared Camera and Multi-Object Spectrometer (NICMOS)* on the HST, we obtain a generative model of the distribution of the most prominent component of the data: the *speckle noise pattern*, which is the main component of systematic noise in direct imaging. At this stage, any planet signals in the training data are regarded as statistical noise since their occurrence is random and usually buried within the speckle pattern. Our generative model can produce negative class examples (images without planets). We can then create an equal amount of synthetic positive examples (images with planets) by 'injecting' planets on images generated by the GAN.

We use this dataset to train a *Convolutional Neural Network (CNN)* to classify images as positive/negative. By doing so, we avoid the problem of using the real data directly and all the issues that come with it (class imbalance, unknown ground truth, model's performance being upper-bounded by current detection techniques). With the use of *Class Activation Maps (CAM)* [20], we are able to locate injected planets within the images, as a byproduct. Finally, we turn to real data for evaluation and demonstrate that our model can identify *confirmed bright sources*[3] in the dataset. The architecture of our model is shown in Fig. 1.

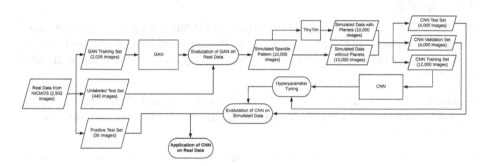

Fig. 1. Flowchart summarising the methodology utilised in this paper.

2   Data and Preprocessing

2.1   The Dataset

The dataset we used consists of single coronagraphic images taken by *Camera 2* on the *HST/NICMOS* instrument during *Cycle 11–16 (Data Delivery 2)*[4].

---

[3] There are no confirmed planet detections on NICMOS filter F110W yet. These *bright sources* are almost certainly background stars. However, detecting these showcases the potential for any bright source –including planets– to be detected.

[4] The original dataset is publicly available at the *HST LAPLACE STScI* archive https://archive.stsci.edu/prepds/laplace/.

All images are from the same wavelength channel, *filter F110W*, and have a dimension of 256 × 256 pixels[5]. The images have already undergone some standard image processing commonly applied to HST data (i.e. *bias calibration, dark calibration & flat calibration*)[6]. *All* images have undergone the *contemp_flats* calibration, where a flat field lamp is used to create a reference image during the process of target acquisition.

This means that the final dataset includes several images of the same observation (raw data) that have undergone different transformations. These transformations can be viewed as a form of *data augmentation* of the raw data. To avoid overfitting, we were careful to include all images of the same target in either only the training set or only the test set. The augmented dataset used consists of 3572 single-channel (F110W filter) images.

2.2 Preprocessing

Image Cropping: The areas of the 256 × 256 images that interest us the most (i.e. those with the highest probability of detecting a planet) are regions in the vicinity of the star, and hence the *speckle pattern*. This occupies only a small portion of the original image so each image was arbitrarily cropped into a 64 × 64 frame. The cropping procedure is carried out by setting [40, 180] as the top-left corner of the 64 × 64 box. As all images are aligned, the position of the speckle pattern stays the same. In Fig. 2, we give an example of an image before and after cropping.

Treatment of Corrupted Images: Out of the initial 3572 images, some were found to contain *overexposed pixels, unexplained bright spots*[7] or *de-focused frames*. After removing these unsuitable frames from the dataset, we are left with 2502 images.

Normalization: The images were normalised linearly so that their pixel intensities are in the range [0, 1] using the maximum and minimum value of each pixel across the entire dataset.

Final Dataset & Train/Test Split: The final dataset of real observations included 2502 single-channel 64 × 64 images with pixel intensities in [0, 1].

We reserved 476 images from this dataset – about 20% of the available datapoints – for evaluation purposes and use the remaining 2026 for training. The training set and the test set contain no targets in common. The test set contains 36 images of stars with confirmed bright sources (3 targets). The final dataset used in the paper is thus split into 3 parts: *Training* (2026 real images w/o

---

[5] The *Field of View (FOV)* of the camera, is 19.2″ × 19.2″ corresponding to images of size 256 × 256 pixels and the *coronagraph* is a circular disk with a radius of 4 pixels.

[6] *Bias calibration* removes unwanted saturated pixels that arise during long exposures. *Dark calibration* corrects for thermal emissions coming from the detector. *Flat calibration* corrects for differences in sensitivity across the CCD detector.

[7] Large bright spots found outside the speckle pattern.

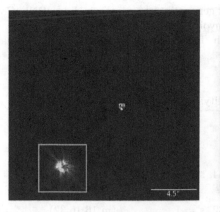 

Fig. 2. Left: Example of a full-sized 256 × 256 image taken by NICMOS. Right: The cropped 64 × 64 image (represented by the yellow square on the left) containing only the vicinity of the stellar speckle pattern. (Color figure online)

confirmed bright sources), *Test (Positive)* (36 real images with confirmed bright sources) & *Test (Unlabeled)* (440 real images w/o confirmed bright sources)[8].

3   A GAN for Modelling the Speckle Pattern Distribution

To train a discriminative model for identifying planets in direct imaging observations we require sufficient data from both classes. Yet positive examples, images containing confirmed exoplanets, are scarce (only 3 targets in our dataset contain confirmed bright sources, amounting to a total of 36 images). Even if there were more, a model trained to only identify planets *detectable* by the current technology would not advance our existing detection capabilities. On the other hand, images without currently known planets cannot be used as negative examples, as they might contain *undiscovered* planets. In fact, we *expect* many of them to do so and the purpose of this paper is to further our ability to discover planets in such images; these examples are *unlabelled*, not negative. Directly using data from real observations to train a discriminative model is therefore unjustified.

Note however, that although we are unaware of the presence of undetected exoplanets in the original data, we know of one component of these images that is present in *all* of them and hinders our ability to detect planets: the *instrument speckle pattern*. Therefore we can instead use the original data to train a generative model of this pattern. This will be the first step towards generating an artificial labelled dataset. Negative examples will consist of instances of this pattern alone and positive examples will consist of the speckle pattern with the introduction of planet signals in the images.

---

[8] Data and code are available at https://github.com/ucl-exoplanets/DI-Project.

Table 1. Architecture of the GAN used for generating the synthetic data. 'BN', 'Conv' & 'FC' denote Batch Normalisation, Convolutional & Fully Connected layers. We denote the # of convolutional filters with 'f', the stride size with 's' & the batch size with 'm'.

Generator		
Layer type	Dimensionality, configuration	Output dimension
Latent space		(m,100)
FC-BN-RELU	2048	(m,4,4,128)
Resize		(m,8,8,128)
Conv-BN-RELU	5 × 5, f = 64, s = 1	(m,8,8,64)
Resize		(m,16,16,64)
Conv-BN-RELU	5 × 5, f = 32, s = 1	(m,16,16,32)
Resize		(m,32,32,32)
Conv-BN-RELU	5 × 5, f = 16, s =1	(m,32,32,16)
Resize		(m,64,64,16)
Conv-BN-RELU	5 × 5, f = 1, s = 1	(m,64,64,1)
Sigmoid		(m,64,64,1)
Discriminator		
Input	64 × 64 × 1	(64,64)
Conv-LeakyRELU	3 × 3, f = 16, s = 1	(m,64,64,16)
MaxPool	2 × 2, s = 2	(m,32,32,16)
Conv-BN-LeakyRELU	3 × 3, f = 32, s = 1	(m,32,32,32)
MaxPool	2 × 2, s = 2	(m,16,16,32)
Conv-BN-LeakyRELU	3 × 3, f = 64, s = 1	(m,16,16,64)
MaxPool	2 × 2, s = 2	(m,8,8,64)
Conv-BN-LeakyRELU	3 × 3, f = 128, s = 1	(m,8,8,128)
FC	256	(m,256)
Sigmoid	2	(m,2)

We train a *Deep Convolutional Generative Adversarial Network (DCGAN)* [17] with a latent space of 100 dimensions to learn a model of the speckle pattern. We have chosen DCGAN as the base due to its stability during training, slightly modifying the architecture to alleviate the *checkerboard effect*[9].

A detailed description of the architecture of the GAN can be found in Table 1. The GAN was trained for 40 epochs using the *ADAM* optimiser with a batch size of 16 and a learning rate of 2×10^{-4}. The remaining hyperparameters were set to default *Keras*[10] values. The hyperparameter optimisation was based on minimising the validation loss on 20% of the training set and was minimal due to

---

[9] The term refers to artifacts caused by the uneven overlap of the deconvolutions of a CNN when the kernel (filter) size is not divisible by the number of strides.

[10] https://keras.io.

the already good performance of the final model. A principled hyperparameter exploration is left for future work.

After training the GAN by minimising the classical cross-entropy-based *adversarial loss* [9] on the training set, we evaluate the performance of the *generator* on the unlabelled test data (440 images w/o confirmed bright sources), based on its ability to reconstruct them. For each of the test examples (real datapoints), we generate 600 samples by the generator (artificial datapoints) and following the approach of [19], we select the one minimising $L_c + \lambda L_p$, where L_c is the *contextual loss* (measuring the difference between observed and generated data using the *pixelwise L1-distance* between the two images), L_p the *perceptual loss* (uses the discriminator to verify the validity of the generated data given the training) and λ, here set to 0.1, controls their trade-off. Comparing the two images gives us an indication of how well the GAN models the real data distribution.

We can assess the quality of the reconstructed images qualitatively, by visual inspection of generated and original images, or quantitatively, by computing their dissimilarity (*pixelwise L1-distance*). Figure 3 shows examples of synthetic images generated by the GAN compared to their real image counterparts and their differences. We show the worst reconstruction produced by the GAN with a dissimilarity score of 6.7×10^{-3} and a more average case with a dissimilarity of 2.0×10^{-3}. Even in the worst case example, we see that the level of similarity between them is sufficient for the GAN to learn a realistic speckle pattern.

We perform image reconstruction on the unlabelled test set (440 images w/o known bright sources). The mean dissimilarity and its standard deviation is $(2.1 \pm 1.3) \times 10^{-3}$ (so the worst case example shown in Fig. 3 is an outlier). Convinced that the GAN can generate adequately realistic imitations of the speckle pattern, we will now use it as a data generator for training a classifier.

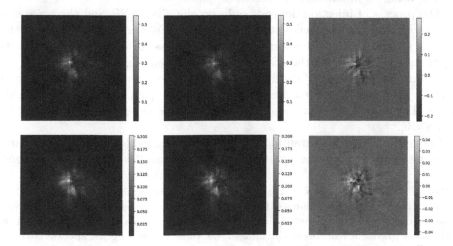

Fig. 3. An original image [left], a reconstruction generated by the GAN [middle] and their difference [right]. Top: Worst reconstruction case in test set (dissimilarity score 6.7×10^{-3}); Bottom: A reconstruction of average quality (dissimilarity score 2.0×10^{-3}).

4   A CNN for Supervised Planet Detection

4.1   Generating Labelled Synthetic Datasets

In order to create synthetic datasets suited to train image classifiers, we generated 10,000 synthetic images using the previously trained GAN model. Although these images are all examples of the negative class, we are able to produce for each of them a duplicate example in the positive class by injecting a planet signal. Because of this *paired samples* approach, a classifier trained on these data is less likely to associate random features of the speckle pattern with the presence of a planet.

The planet signal is introduced by artificially injecting[11] a simulated *Point Spread Function (PSF)*[12] to the image. We used *TinyTim* [12], an instrument-specific PSF simulator for NICMOS, to generate a normalised PSF. Although in real observations the shape of the PSF may differ slightly depending on the position of the light source, in this work we assume this difference to be negligible and thus use the same PSF regardless of the position of the injected planet.

To generate a planet signal with a given SNR, we uniformly sample a pixel $P = (x, y)$ to be its center. We consider a 4×4 window centered[13] at P and we denote by σ the standard deviation of the pixel intensity values in it, so that we can determine the injected signal's brightness. Under the definition of SNR, the total pixel intensity of the signal S_p is computed by

$$S_p = SNR \times \sigma \times (4 \times 4).$$

The intensity of the PSF to be injected in the image is thus determined by S_p and affects the pixels within a 33×33 window centered at P. After the planet PSF injection, each synthetic image is normalised so that its pixel intensities lie in $[0, 1]$ using its minimum and maximum pixel values.

The process of injection depends only on the given SNR and the noise signal surrounding the sampled center. No assumptions were made regarding the planet's separation from the star and its brightness. In order to avoid injecting planets brighter than the star, we impose an additional constraint: if the maximum pixel intensity of the PSF to be injected exceeds that of the original image (speckle pattern), then the signal center is sampled again. In practice this means that certain areas in the center of the image never contain a planet for high SNRs.

Fixing the SNR allows training models at any desired level of 'difficulty' and detecting planet signals over a wide range of brightness levels compared to their

---

[11] We opted not to use a GAN for augmenting the positive examples (i) to fully control the SNR of the injected planets, for evaluation purposes and (ii) because the randomly positioned faint planet signal in positive examples would be easily masked by the most prevalent features of the images, i.e. those comprising the speckle pattern.

[12] The PSF is the response of the telescope optics to incoming light, i.e. it defines the light distribution of a point-source, e.g. a planet, on the detector plane.

[13] The window's top-left corner is $(x - 1, y - 1)$ and bottom-right is $(x + 2, y + 2)$.

Table 2. Architecture of the CNN classifier trained on data with SNR values 1.5 & 1.25. Naming convention follows that of Table 1. For SNR values 1 & 0.75 the only changes where that double convolutional layers were used instead of single ones and the FC layer consisted of 128 neurons.

Layer type	Dimensionality, configuration	Output dimension
Input	$64 \times 4 \times 1$	(64,64)
Conv-RELU-BN	3×3, f = 8, s = 1	(m,64,64,8)
MaxPool	2×2, s = 2	(m,32,32,8)
Conv-RELU-BN	3×3, f = 16, s = 1	(m,32,32,16)
MaxPool	2×2, s = 2	(m,16,16,16)
Conv-RELU-BN	3×3, f = 32, s = 1	(m,16,16,32)
MaxPool	2×2, s = 2	(m,8,8,32)
FC	256	(m,256)
Sigmoid	2	(m,2)

surrounding pixels. It also allows us to assess the limits of a classifier trained to detect objects at a given value of the SNR when deployed on a dataset of a different SNR. To this end, we assembled 4 datasets each obtained by fixing a different SNR level while producing the positive classes. The SNRs considered are 1.5, 1.25, 1 & 0.75.

Before the artificial images are presented to the classifier, the four datasets are split coherently into training (80%, 16000 images) and test (20%, 4000 images) sets. By coherent, we mean the split was applied once on the negative class (which is common among the datasets) and then extended to the positive classes in such a way that paired samples appear in the same set.

4.2   Training the CNN

The four synthetic datasets were used to train and to evaluate various CNN classifiers. The architectures of the CNNs used vary slightly on different SNR levels, as shown in Table 2. All models were trained using the *ADAM* optimiser with default *Keras* values, a learning rate of 10^{-4} and a batch size of 16. Dropout was applied to the final fully connected layers with a rate of 0.35. The maximum number of epochs was 100, but early stopping was applied if the validation loss was not decreasing for 20 epochs. The hyperparameter optimisation was based on minimising the validation loss and was minimal due to the already good performance of the final product. A principled hyperparameter exploration is left for future work.

For each of the 4 different levels of SNR examined (1.5, 1.25, 1 & 0.75), we train a model on the 75% of the corresponding training set (12,000 images) and we use the remaining 25% as a validation set (4,000 images) to monitor the training performance. In the same way as before, this last split is performed coherently, in order to respect the samples' pairing. The training procedure was

Table 3. Test Accuracy (ACC), True Positive Rate (TPR) & True Negative Rate (TNR) of the CNN classifier per training & test SNR combination. We report mean & standard deviation across 5 runs. The SNR applies to Positive examples only, so Negatives are the same for all SNR values on a given run. We see that the lower the SNR on which the CNN is trained, the better its predictive performance across the entire SNR spectrum.

Train SNR		Test SNR			
		1.5	1.25	1	0.75
ACC	1.5	0.972 ± 0.004	0.945 ± 0.006	0.879 ± 0.010	0.752 ± 0.009
TPR		0.943 ± 0.008	0.900 ± 0.012	0.759 ± 0.020	0.503 ± 0.018
TNR		1.000 ± 0.000			
ACC	1.25	0.973 ± 0.004	0.955 ± 0.003	0.900 ± 0.002	0.786 ± 0.010
TPR		0.949 ± 0.007	0.911 ± 0.005	0.803 ± 0.004	0.575 ± 0.021
TNR		0.998 ± 0.003			
ACC	1	0.973 ± 0.003	0.963 ± 0.003	0.938 ± 0.004	0.862 ± 0.006
TPR		0.955 ± 0.011	0.942 ± 0.012	0.897 ± 0.015	0.752 ± 0.024
TNR		0.995 ± 0.004			
ACC	0.75	0.967 ± 0.008	0.957 ± 0.009	0.939 ± 0.011	0.896 ± 0.010
TPR		0.947 ± 0.003	0.927 ± 0.004	0.890 ± 0.010	0.804 ± 0.022
TNR		0.988 ± 0.019			

repeated 5 times for each dataset, applying different train/validation splits and thus producing 5 different models for each SNR considered.

Table 3 shows the performance of the CNNs trained on the same SNR when evaluated on the 4 different test sets (note that the coherency of the splits guarantees that the speckle patterns appearing in the test sets are always unseen data). We observe that the predictive performance is high and the models are robust to deployment on a different SNR than the one they were trained on – especially if the training SNR is lower than the test SNR. This is reasonable, as CNNs trained on lower SNRs (i.e. trained to recognise fainter signals) are expected to perform well at classifying datapoints of higher SNRs (i.e. brighter signals). In light of this, any subsequent results presented are obtained by the CNN trained on SNR = 0.75.

So far, we have assessed the classifiers' capability to detect planets on synthetic data generated from the same distribution as their training set. The fact that models trained at a given SNR can perform well even when the test set SNR is lower is encouraging; it means that the models we train might be able to detect faint planet signals.

5 Locating Planets and Assessing Sensitivity

5.1 Locating Planets

Knowing whether a given image does, or does not, contain a planet does not provide much information on *where* the candidate planet may be located. To answer this question, we visualised the *Class Activation Maps (CAMs)* [20] of the CNN to investigate which regions of the image contribute the most to its predictions. The CAM is obtained by taking the weighted average (w.r.t. their weight to the next layer) of the features in the final convolutional feature map.

As an initial test of our model's ability to locate planets, we applied this technique on its predictions on the synthetic test data (4,000 labelled images not seen by the CNN). Figure 4 shows some examples of True Positives. For each example, we compare the actual location of the planet to the CAM of the CNN, highlighting the regions most inductive to its decision. We see that when the CNN classifies an image as one that contains a planet, it does so because

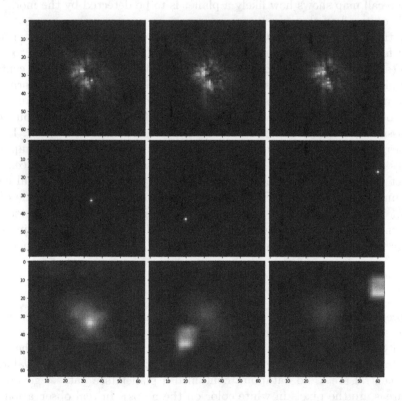

Fig. 4. Locating planets on 3 exemplar synthetic datapoints [Left to Right]. [Top] Input synthetic image containing a planet; [Middle] Actual planet location in the image (contrast enhanced for visualisation); [Bottom] CNN Class Activation Map on the image.

it 'spots' the planet. Thus, the CNN trained to classify images as potentially containing planets can also be used to locate potential planets within the images.

So far the network has performed well on synthetic data generated by the GAN. However, we have yet to answer if it can perform well on actual NICMOS data. Therefore, the next step is to perform the classification on held out images of targets with confirmed bright source detections. Tested on all positive held out real images (36 datapoints of 3 targets: *CQ-Tau*, *DQ-Tau* & *HD10578*) the model can detect the bright source in each image. In Fig. 5, we can see 2 example images with successful detections for each of the 3 targets. The positions of these bright sources (in circle) were independently detected by the ALICE program[14] [10].

5.2   Assessing Sensitivity and Specificity

Finally, in Fig. 6, we visualise the precision and recall capability of the model to locate planets on each pixel of the 64 × 64 images. The precision map shows how likely a planet is to really be centered at a pixel, given the model 'detects' it. The recall map shows how likely a planet is to be detected by the model if it really is centered on that pixel.

For the purposes of this visualisation, we produced an extended synthetic test set for each SNR value, in which, for each of the 64 × 64 pixels, up to 5 test instances (subject to dataset generation restrictions) had a planet PSF centered in that pixel. In Table 3, we were only assessing image classification performance. So, if a model classified a positive example as one that contains a planet, this would count as a True Positive (TP), even if the features most contributing to the classification did not include the center of the planet PSF. Now, for the purposes of assessing planet localisation within the image, such an example will count as a False Positive (FP) for the pixel(s) falsely identified as the center of a planet PSF and a False Negative (FN) for the pixel being the actual center of the undetected planet PSF. We consider it a success (TP) when one of the top 25% pixels activating the model was the center of the injected planet PSF. To assign FPs, we consider the brightest pixel of the CAM (corresponding to 16 pixels in the image) as the predicted planet center. We then calculate per pixel,

$$Precision = \frac{TP}{TP + FP} \quad \text{and} \quad Recall = \frac{TP}{TP + FN}.$$

Both precision and recall are very high in most areas of the image, except for the edges and the center. The edge effects are a result of the convolutions and can easily be avoided by considering larger frames. The blind spot in the center results from the speckle pattern itself and the fact that for high SNR values, in certain central areas, no datapoint contained a planet (see dataset generation; these areas are the pixels in white color on the maps). In real observations the 8 × 8 pixel center of the image is occulted by the coronagraph, so in the innermost region of the speckle pattern it would be impossible to detect any companions.

---

[14] https://archive.stsci.edu/prepds/alice/.

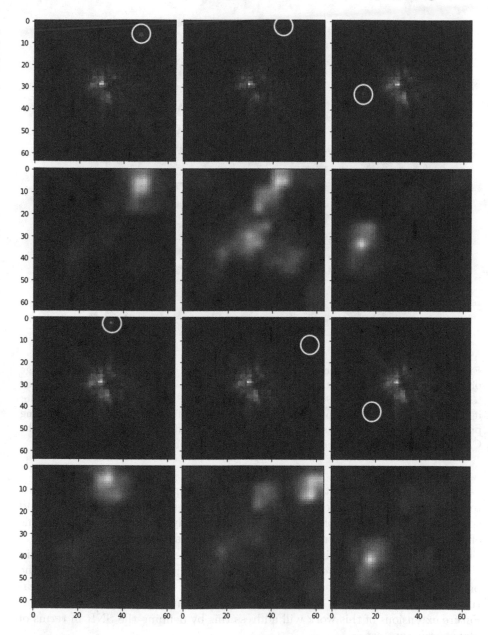

Fig. 5. Original images of CQ-Tau [Left], DQ-Tau [Middle] & HD10578 [Right], each in 2 orientations [1st Row & 3rd Row]. The images contain confirmed bright sources (marked with a circle). [2nd Row & 4th Row]: CNN activation heatmaps of model trained at SNR = 0.75; We see that the model's activation peaks on the bright sources.

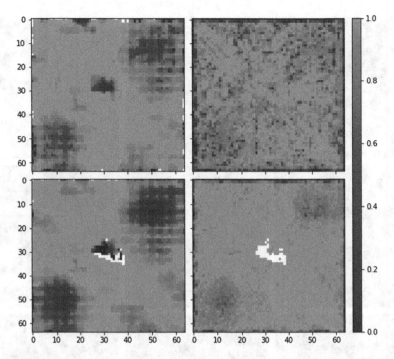

Fig. 6. Precision [Left] & Recall [Right] map of planet localization per input image pixel. We show average results across 5 runs of the CNN trained on SNR = 0.75 when tested on synthetic data of SNR = 0.75 [Top] and SNR = 1.5 [Bottom]. We consider it a True Positive when the planet's PSF center is one of the top 25% most activating pixels of the CAM. To assign False Positives, we consider the brightest pixel of the CAM (corresponding to 16 pixels in the image) as the predicted planet center.

We also see that planets lying on the main components of the speckle pattern (main diagonal & 'cross' centered on the image) are easier to detect and conversely, detections in these areas are more likely to be true planets. This effect appears to be an artifact of the dataset generation: as these are typically the brightest areas on an image, if a planet is to be placed there, to maintain a fixed SNR, it needs to be very bright. When the planet PSF is added to the background image, an already bright area becomes brighter and this is a feature the model picks up as a salient one for predicting the presence of a planet. Future extensions of this work will address this by defining the SNR in terms of planet/star contrast.

6   Conclusions and Future Work

We have demonstrated that deep learning offers a promising direction for taking the field of direct imaging of exoplanets to the next step. By using a generative model of the data and injecting bright sources to generate a labelled synthetic dataset, we bypass the obstacles raised by directly using real data to train a classifier, namely the absence of positive examples and the possible presence of undetected planets in the data.

The supervised CNN classifier trained on the synthetic data can achieve high predictive performance and robustness to not only various levels of SNR, but also to SNR discrepancies between training and testing. Moreover, the model is capable of successfully locating astrophysical point sources within the images with the use of class activation maps. To demonstrate the limits of the model, we provided maps of the precision and recall of the model per pixel of the input image. When evaluated on actual data from NICMOS, the model can reproduce confirmed bright source detections in the data.

Our immediate next step is to apply this methodology to reconfirm the detection of known exoplanetary systems on images from a different filter of *NICMOS*, *FW160*. This will establish its ability to detect exoplanets and open the way for direct application of the method to unlabelled real data to identify new potential planet candidates. The most promising candidates can then be selected based on (i) the calibrated probability estimates of the CNN for each image to contain a planet and then (ii) weighing the heatmaps by the precision maps to pinpoint the most promising location within the images for the planets to be.

There is significant room for further improvement by tuning the architectures and the training hyperparameters of both the GAN used to generate the data and the CNN trained to detect planets. To make the synthetic dataset more realistic, future work will include factoring into the SNR the planet/star contrast, refining the PSF of planets injected at the edges of the image and injecting more than one planet per image at different values of SNR. To improve the planet-detectors themselves, the next steps include leveraging –when available– multiple observations of the same target and combining planet-detectors to obtain an ensemble of predictors covering a wide range of SNR. The models presented here were trained on correctly classifying images as containing injected planets or not. As we saw, this decision was largely based on locating a planet or not, but ultimately, planet localisation was a byproduct of training. Future versions of our system will be trained directly on planet localisation within the images.

Finally, we will move beyond NICMOS and explore direct imaging datasets from different ground and space-based instruments, with a larger number of datapoints, more positive class examples and more observations per target. This will allow us to compare the 'sensitivity' afforded by each instrument, at various levels of SNR and across different regions of an image, to use transfer learning methods and to combine observations from different instruments.

Acknowledgments. This project has received funding from the European Research Council (ERC) under the EU Horizon 2020 research & innovation programme (grant No 758892, ExoAI) and under the EU Seventh Framework Programme (FP7/2007-2013)/ ERC grant No 617119 (ExoLights). Furthermore, we acknowledge funding by the Science & Technology Funding Council (STFC) grants: ST/K502406/1, ST/P000282/1, ST/P002153/1 and ST/S002634/1. We are grateful for the support of the NVIDIA Corporation through the NVIDIA GPU Grant program.

References

1. Amara, A., Quanz, S.P.: PYNPOINT: an image processing package for finding exoplanets. MNRAS **427**, 948–955 (2012)
2. Bowler, B.P.: Imaging extrasolar giant planets. Publ. Astron. Soc. Pac. **128**, 102001 (2016)
3. Cantalloube, F., et al.: Direct exoplanet detection and characterization using the andromeda method: performance on VLT/NaCo data. Astron. Astrophys. **582**, A89 (2015)
4. Cassan, A., et al.: One or more bound planets per Milky Way star from microlensing observations. Nature **481**, 167–169 (2012)
5. Choquet, É., et al.: HD 104860 and HD 192758: two debris disks newly imaged in scattered light with the hubble space telescope. Astrophys. J. **854**(1), 53 (2018)
6. Fergus, R., Hogg, D.W., Oppenheimer, R., Brenner, D., Pueyo, L.: S4: a spatial-spectral model for speckle suppression. Astrophys. J. **794**(2), 161 (2014)
7. Gomez Gonzalez, C.A., Absil, O., Van Droogenbroeck, M.: Supervised detection of exoplanets in high-contrast imaging sequences. Astron. Astrophys. **613**, A71 (2018)
8. Gomez Gonzalez, C.A., et al.: Low-rank plus sparse decomposition for exoplanet detection in direct-imaging ADI sequences. The LLSG algorithm. Astron. Astrophys. **589**, A54 (2016)
9. Goodfellow, I.J., et al.: Generative adversarial networks. ArXiv (2014)
10. Hagan, J.B., Choquet, É., Soummer, R., Vigan, A.: ALICE data release: a reevaluation of HST-NICMOS coronagraphic images. Astron. J. **155**, 179 (2018)
11. Kalas, P., et al.: Optical images of an exosolar planet 25 light-years from earth. Science **322**, 1345 (2008)
12. Krist, J.E., Hook, R.N., Stoehr, F.: 20 years of Hubble Space Telescope optical modeling using Tiny Tim. In: Optical Modeling and Performance Predictions V. Proceedings of the Society of Photo-Optical Instrumentation Engineers, vol. 8127, p. 81270J (2011)
13. Lafrenière, D., Marois, C., Doyon, R., Nadeau, D., Artigau, É.: A new algorithm for point-spread function subtraction in high-contrast imaging: a demonstration with angular differential imaging. Astrophys. J. **660**, 770–780 (2007)
14. Lagrange, A.M., et al.: A giant planet imaged in the disk of the young star β Pictoris. Science **329**, 57 (2010)
15. Mugnier, L.M., et al.: Optimal method for exoplanet detection by angular differential imaging. J. Opt. Soc. Am. A **26**, 1326 (2009)
16. Racine, R., Walker, G.A., Nadeau, D., Doyon, R., Marois, C.: Speckle noise and the detection of faint companions. Publ. Astron. Soc. Pac. **111**(759), 587 (1999)
17. Radford, A., Metz, L., Chintala, S.: Unsupervised representation learning with deep convolutional generative adversarial networks. ArXiv (2015)
18. Soummer, R., Pueyo, L., Larkin, J.: Detection and characterization of exoplanets and disks using projections on Karhunen-Loève eigenimages. Astrophys. J. Lett. **755**, L28 (2012)
19. Yeh, R.A., et al.: Semantic image inpainting with deep generative models. In: CVPR, pp. 5485–5493 (2017)
20. Zhou, B., Khosla, A., Lapedriza, A., Oliva, A., Torralba, A.: Learning deep features for discriminative localization. In: CVPR, pp. 2921–2929 (2016)

J3R: Joint Multi-task Learning of Ratings and Review Summaries for Explainable Recommendation

P. V. S. Avinesh[1(✉)], Yongli Ren[2], Christian M. Meyer[1], Jeffrey Chan[2],
Zhifeng Bao[2], and Mark Sanderson[2]

[1] Research Training Group AIPHES and UKP Lab Computer Science Department,
Technische Universität Darmstadt, Darmstadt, Germany
{avinesh,meyer}@ukp.informatik.tu-darmstadt.de
[2] Computer Science, School of Science, RMIT University, Melbourne, Australia
{yongli.ren,jeffrey.chan,zhifeng.bao,mark.sanderson}@rmit.edu.au
http://www.aiphes.tu-darmstadt.de
http://www.ukp.tu-darmstadt.de

Abstract. We learn user preferences from ratings and reviews by using multi-task learning (MTL) of rating prediction and summarization of item reviews. Reviews of an item tend to describe detailed user preferences (e.g., the cast, genre, or screenplay of a movie). A summary of such a review or a rating describes an overall user experience of the item. Our objective is to learn latent vectors which are shared across rating prediction and review summary generation. Additionally, the learned latent vectors and the generated summary act as explanations for the recommendation. Our MTL-based approach J3R uses a multi-layer perceptron for rating prediction, combined with pointer-generator networks with attention mechanism for the summarization component. We provide empirical evidence for joint learning of rating prediction and summary generation being beneficial for recommendation by conducting experiments on the Yelp dataset and six domains of the Amazon 5-core dataset. Additionally, we provide two ways of explanations visualizing (a) the user vectors on different topics of a domain, computed from our J3R approach and (b) a ten-word review summary of a review and the attention highlights generated on the review based on the user–item vectors.

Keywords: Personalized recommendation · Summarization · Natural Language Processing · Explainable AI

1 Introduction

Product recommender systems have increasingly gained attention in the Information Retrieval and Natural Language Processing communities, both in academia and industry. Most existing recommendation methods are based on collaborative filtering [9,10,21], which primarily learn users' and items' latent factors

© Springer Nature Switzerland AG 2020
U. Brefeld et al. (Eds.): ECML PKDD 2019, LNAI 11908, pp. 339–355, 2020.
https://doi.org/10.1007/978-3-030-46133-1_21

from ratings. Such an approach fails to capture valuable information from actual user experiences, which can be recorded in the form of reviews. This user-generated content is an increasingly important source, useful for both businesses as well as the end user. In this paper, we propose J3R, a novel multi-task learning setup for explainable recommendation based on ratings *and* reviews, which we motivate below.

	User	Aspect Words
⭐⭐⭐⭐⭐ **Better with age.** By T. on March 31, 2017 Verified Purchase Jason seems to be getting better with age. He doesn't have a lot of muscle...natural... he looks good, very fit and knows how to work what he got. Heyyyyy! You talking my language! I can't wait for the next one. So until then, I have one more of Jason to watch...action pack just what the doctor ordered!	T.	Cast: fit, work Genre: action
⭐⭐⭐⭐⭐ **love it** By hairbear2012 on December 27, 2017 Verified Purchase One of the greatness spying movies of all time the action is incredible and the characters storytelling are simple and unquestionably cool	hairbear2012	Genre: Spy, action Screenplay: storytelling
⭐⭐☆☆☆ **Not worth the money** By scooby on January 7, 2018 Verified Purchase As usual it had some decent car chase scenes. Otherwise, it was slow and mundane and just a rehashing of the first 3 films. Again, it left open the possibility of yet another sequel. I hope the 5th is better than the 4th. The first two were really good. This was NOT worth the 13 bucks amazon charged for a 2 year old movie.	scooby	Screenplay: car chase Cost: bucks
⭐☆☆☆☆ **What were they thinking?** By Alex on January 8, 2018 Verified Purchase Wow. Love the other Bourne movies. What were they thinking? Stupid, impossible to believe chase scenes and almost no human interaction. I expected to love this, but very disappointed. I highly recommend the other three however.	Alex	Screenplay: chase scenes, human interaction

Fig. 1. Example ratings, reviews and their summaries for Jason Bourne (2016) on Amazon Movies. Reviews describe detailed personalized opinions and interests of the user w.r.t. the item. The table on the right-hand side shows extracted aspect words from the reviews modeling the users' preferences.

User and Item Profiles for Recommendation. Although recommender systems based on reviews have been previously proposed, [4,16,18,27], they yet do not fully exploit the potential of learning to recommend jointly from both reviews and ratings. Figure 1 shows four reviews on the Jason Bourne (2016) movie, which illustrate the connection between reviews and ratings: Each review consists of a brief summary (e.g., "Better with age" in T.'s review) and the actual review text in addition to the rating (i.e., 1–5 stars). The users focus on multiple different aspects in their reviews. For example, user T. likes Matt Damon's looks, fitness, and the action in the movie. In contrast, Alex and scooby have differing opinions on the use of car chases in the screenplay. The example shown is a typical real-world use case where different users have different interests and opinions about certain aspects of the same item. We aim at exploiting this information from reviews for building user and item profiles. Additionally, we leverage recent advances in deep neural networks to exploit the commonality between the rating and the review summary in a multi-task learning (MTL) approach where rating prediction is the main task and review summary generation is the auxiliary task.

Explainable Recommendation. In a recent review by [7] on European Union regulations on algorithmic decision-making, the authors explain how the Article 22 of the European Union's new General Data Protection Regulation on automated individual decision-making and profiling potentially prohibits a wide range of algorithms currently in use, including recommendation systems, computational advertising, etc. The law effectively states "the right to explanation", where a user could ask for explanations on the decisions made about them by the algorithm. This regulation is only one recent development to strongly encourage the machine-learning-based communities to design algorithms in view of enabling explanations.

Although the primary goal of a recommender system is to produce excellent recommendations, it is a clear advantage if a system provides explanations for its users. Explanations serve multiple purposes, such as building trust, creating transparency, improving efficiency by quicker decision-making, and increasing user satisfaction [24]. There has been a recent surge in methods focusing on explainable recommendation systems [3,4,12,26]. Previous approaches use explicit topics from reviews with users' opinions [26], knowledge graphs [3], tip generation [12] and review ranking [4] for explanations.

In our research, we propose a novel approach to combine explicit topic vectors from reviews with generated review summaries as a way to explain a predicted rating. The final explanations of our J3R system are thus of two types: (a) a histogram of user preferences on different topics of a domain, computed from the updated user vectors learned by our MTL approach and (b) a ten-word review summary of a review and the attention highlights on the review based on the weights learned from the user–item vectors. For the Jason Bourne example from Fig. 1, a user vector for user T. should capture T.'s interest in the cast and the genre based on the user's past reviews. In addition to these histograms, based on the preferences from scooby's vector, the words in Alex's review would be highlighted according to their importance with respect to scooby's profile and the review would be automatically summarized.

Contributions. In this work, (1) we propose a novel combination of multi-layer perceptron and pointer-generator networks for jointly learning the shared users' and items' latent factors using an MTL approach for predicting user ratings and review summary generation – two related tasks that can mutually benefit from each other. (2) Our approach provides a way to explain the predicted ratings with the help of generated summaries and topic histograms, which further enhances the idea of evidence-based recommendation and decision-making. To encourage the research community and to allow for replicating our results, we publish our code as open-source software.[1]

2   Related Work

Previous works address recommendation systems employing (1) content-based filtering, (2) joint models of rating prediction and summary generation, and (3) explainable recommendation.

---

[1] https://github.com/AIPHES/ecml-pkdd-2019-J3R-explainable-recommender.

Content-Based Filtering. Collaborative filtering methods have seen successful for a long time in recommendation systems [9,10,21]. Methods like probabilistic matrix factorization (PMF) [21], non-negative matrix factorization (NMF) [10], singular value decomposition (SVD), and SVD++ [9] have been successfully applied by representing users and items in a shared, low-dimensional space. Vectors in this space represent latent factors of users and items. Using the dot product of two vectors, one can predict a user's rating for a given item. A drawback of these approaches is that the system performance degrades when the rating matrix is sparse, which is often the case for newly developed systems or small communities. Furthermore, the vectors of this latent space have no particular interpretation, which impedes providing an explanation for a recommendation that can be understood by human users.

This propelled researchers towards content-based filtering techniques for recommendation [1,16,18]. Content-based filtering methods typically learn user [16] and item profiles [1] from item descriptions or user reviews. They recommend an item to a user by matching the item's features with that of the user preferences. There are works which identify the importance of aspects for the users by integrating topic models to generate the users' and items' latent factors from review text [18]. Our proposed approach also employs topic models to initialize latent user and item vectors, but we further update them by jointly training for rating prediction and review summary generation.

Joint Models for Rating Prediction and Summary Generation. Multi-task learning approaches have seen significant success in the area of machine learning and natural language processing [19]. The goal of these approaches is to learn two related tasks which can mutually benefit from each other. As rating prediction and review summary generation are two facets of the same user preference of an item, they can be optimized together by sharing the parameters across the model. Although review summary generation has been conducted independently of rating predictions [28], jointly modeling the rating prediction and the review summary generation has as yet only shown first promising results [12,25]. In our work, we go beyond such models by employing pointer-generator neural models and an attention mechanism on user preferences which particularly benefit the auxiliary task of review summary generation.

Explainable Recommendation. Although state-of-the-art methods produce generally good recommendations, they fail to explain the reasons for a particular recommendation. Explanations can serve as a way to understand the algorithms and the models learned. This has led to new research questions for explaining recommendation systems and their output [3,11,12,17]. Some of the promising approaches include topic models as latent factors [17], knowledge graphs [3], and tip generation [11,12]. [17] propose a joint model using reviews and ratings with a Hidden Markov Model and Latent Dirichlet Allocation (LDA). They provide explanations with the help of words from latent word clusters explaining the essential aspects of the user and item pairs. [26] propose explicit factor models for generating explanations by extracting phrases and sentiments from user-written reviews for the items. In our approach, we combine multiple types of explanations and we generate them by jointly learning from reviews and ratings.

The work by [12] first proposes a multi-task learning framework to predict ratings and generate abstractive review summaries, which they extended in [11] by proposing a personalized solution. A major difference between their task and ours is that we generate summaries from the reviews, whereas they generate summaries from user–item latent vectors and the review vocabulary. Thus, the summaries generated in their task tend to be overly general as discussed in their paper. On the contrary, in this paper, our goal is not only to generate summaries but also to use summarization as a method to explain the important content in the reviews based on the user preferences. We leverage recent machine learning advances in pointer-generator networks [22] and attention-based mechanisms [20] which supports the accurate generation of summaries by attending on latent user–item vectors, the users' ratings, and their reviews.

3   Approach

We divide our proposed approach into the three components shown in Fig. 2: (1) First, we build *user and item models* to identify interpretable topic vectors of an item capturing different aspects of the item that users are interested in. (2) Then, we train a *rating prediction model* using these user and item models. (3) Finally, we generate review summaries to explain the recommendations of our system by jointly modeling *rating prediction* and *review summary generation*, using an MTL approach of multi-layer perceptron and pointer-generator networks that utilizes the user and item models. Our final method is called J3R ('**J**oint MTL of **R**atings and **R**eview Summaries for Explainable **R**ecommendation'). We introduce the three components in the following subsections.

3.1   User and Item Models Component

The goal of the first component is to build user and item profiles using the review content. To achieve this goal we first preprocess the data to identify all nouns and noun phrases from the reviews (e.g., 'display', 'battery for a phone') similar to [14]. We collect the nouns in a bag-of-words representation to generate a 1,000-dimensional tf-idf vector, capturing the most frequent nouns describing an item in the given domain. These fixed-size tf-idf vectors are used as input for the LDA [2] topic model to calculate topic vectors. LDA is a probabilistic topic model which aims at finding structures in an unlabeled text collection by identifying different topics based on the word usage. The probability distribution over high probability words gives us an understanding of the contents of the corpus. Thus, reviews grouped into different clusters using LDA can be viewed as random mixtures over latent vectors, where a distribution over the most frequent nouns represents each topic.

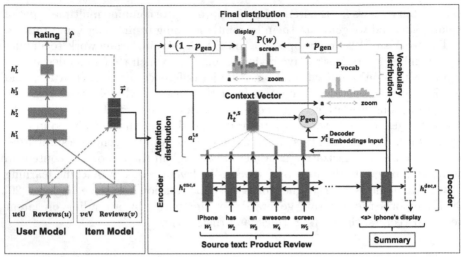

Fig. 2. Model architecture of our joint model for rating prediction and review summarization (J3R). The architecture is divided into three components: (1) user and item models, (2) rating prediction, (3) review summary generation.

Let D be a corpus of M reviews $D_1, D_2, \ldots, D_M$, where each review $D_i = (w_1, w_2, \ldots, w_N)$ is a sequence of N words from a vocabulary $\mathcal{W}$ and k the number of topics. Using LDA, we represent each document D_i as a k-dimensional topic distribution θ_d. Each topic vector, in turn, is an N-dimensional word distribution ϕ_k, which follows a Dirichlet prior β.

There are three steps to LDA: (1) it first draws a k-dimensional topic mixing distribution $\theta_d \sim Dir(\alpha)$ to generate a document d; (2) for each token w_{dn}, it draws a topic assignment z_{dn} from a multinomial distribution $Mult(\phi_{z_{dn}})$; and (3) finally, it draws a word $w_{dn} \in \mathcal{W}$ from $Mult(\phi_{z_{dn}})$ by selecting a topic z_{dn}. To infer these latent variables (ϕ and θ) and hyperparameters (α and β), we compute the probability of the observed corpus:

$$p(D|\alpha, \beta) = \prod_{d=1}^{M} \int p(\theta_d|\alpha) \left(\prod_{n=1}^{N_d} \sum_{z_{dn}} p(z_{dn}|\theta_d)\, p(w_{dn}|z_{dn}, \beta) \right) \mathrm{d}\theta_d \qquad (1)$$

We use all the reviews $Reviews_u$ written by a user u and all reviews $Reviews_v$ of an item v and turn them into N-dimensional tf-idf vectors. To generate topic vector profiles, we input these tf-idf vectors to the learned LDA topic model. The profiles learned using the user and item model are the initial latent vectors $u \in \mathcal{R}^k$ and $v \in \mathcal{R}^k$ for the rating prediction model discussed in the next section and are illustrated in Fig. 2 as *User Model* and *Item Model*.

3.2 Rating Prediction Component

Our rating prediction component is illustrated on the left-hand side of Fig. 2. It uses a traditional recommendation setup where the goal of the recommender is to predict the rating of a given user and item pair. We use a regression function to predict a rating score $\hat{r}$ based on the latent vector representations u and v of the users and items. Typical matrix factorization (MF) approaches do a linear transformation of these vectors as described in Eq. 2, where b is the global bias.

$$\hat{r} = u^{\mathrm{T}} v + b \tag{2}$$

Although these linear transformations achieve state-of-the-art performance in recommendation systems, they cannot capture non-linear interactions between the users' and items' latent factors. Thus, we transfer knowledge from successful non-linear deep learning methods used in natural language processing for our task by concatenating the input vectors u and v as in Eq. 3:

$$h_1^{\mathrm{r}} = relu(W_{h_1}^{\mathrm{r}} (u \oplus v) + b_{h_1}^{\mathrm{r}}) \tag{3}$$

where $W_{h_1}^{\mathrm{r}}$ is the weight matrix of the first hidden layer for the concatenated vector $u \oplus v$, u is the user's latent factors, and v is the item's latent factors. $b_{h_1}^{\mathrm{r}}$ is the bias term and $relu(x) = x^+ = \max(0, x)$ is the non-linear function. The superscript ^{r} represents the parameters and variables for the rating prediction component of our model. To further add non-linearity, we add additional layers of non-linear transformations:

$$h_\ell^{\mathrm{r}} = relu(W_{h_\ell}^{\mathrm{r}} h_{\ell-1}^{\mathrm{r}} + b_{h_\ell}^{\mathrm{r}}) \tag{4}$$

where ℓ is the index of the hidden layer and $W_{h_\ell}^{\mathrm{r}}$ is the corresponding weight matrix. The number of hidden layers is a hyperparameter of our model.

Equation 5 describes the output layer with the weight matrix $W_{h_L}^{\mathrm{r}}$. We use a sigmoid function $\sigma(x) = \frac{1}{1+e^{-x}}$ to output a rating in the range $[0,1]$, which we denormalize to the rating range (e.g., 1–5 stars) during the evaluation.

$$\hat{r} = \sigma(W_{h_L}^{\mathrm{r}} h_L^{\mathrm{r}} + b_{h_L}^{\mathrm{r}}) \tag{5}$$

To optimize the parameters and the latent factors u and v, we define the loss function:

$$\mathcal{L}^{\mathrm{r}} = \frac{1}{|\mathcal{X}|} \sum_{u \in \mathcal{U}, v \in \mathcal{V}} (\hat{r}_{u,v} - r_{u,v})^2 \tag{6}$$

where $\mathcal{X}$ is the training set, $\hat{r}_{u,v}$ is the predicted rating and $r_{u,v}$ is the gold-standard rating assigned by user $u \in \mathcal{U}$ to item $v \in \mathcal{V}$.

3.3 Review Summary Generation Component with Attention on User Preferences

The goal of J3R is to mutually benefit from the available ratings and reviews in two different tasks: (a) rating prediction and (b) review summary generation.

Rating prediction precisely aims at predicting the score for a given user and item pair, whereas the review summary generation component summarizes the review content using a sequence-to-sequence model based on user preferences. The user–item preferences (i.e., the user and item vectors) are shared with the rating prediction component, which are jointly learned using an MTL approach.

Our model is inspired by pointer-generator networks [22] to efficiently summarize the review, by using soft switching between copying words via pointing to the source text and generating words via a fixed vocabulary in a given context. The context in our generation setup consists of the user and item latent vectors $u \in \mathcal{U}$, $v \in \mathcal{V}$, the rating vector r (e.g., if the rating range is [1,5] then a rating vector for 3 stars is $(0, 0, 1, 0, 0)$), and the review D. The tokens of the review text $w_i \in D$ are provided as the input to the encoder one-by-one to produce a sequence of encoder hidden states $h_i^{enc,s}$. At each time step t, the decoder has the decoder states $h_t^{dec,s}$ which receives the word embeddings of the previous word as the input.

An important characteristic of our architecture is the attention distribution $a_i^{t,s}$ that we compute at each time step t with the encoder states $h_i^{enc,s}$, the decoder state $h_t^{dec,s}$, the user vector u, the item vector v, and the rating vector r as shown in Eq. 7–9. It can be viewed as a probability distribution over the source words, user preferences, item factors and rating, which tells the decoder which word to generate.

$$e_i^{t,s} = q^T \tanh(W_h^{enc,s} h_i^{enc,s} + W_h^{dec,s} h_t^{dec,s} + W_r^s(u \oplus v \oplus r) + b_{att}^s) \tag{7}$$

$$a_i^{t,s} = \frac{\exp(e_i^{t,s})}{\sum_{i'=1}^{N} \exp(e_{i'}^{t,s})} \tag{8}$$

where q, $W_h^{enc,s}$, $W_h^{dec,s}$, W_r^s and b_{att}^s are learnable parameters and N is the number of words in the review text. The superscript ^{s} represents the parameters and variables for the review summary generation component of our model.

Using the attention distribution $a_i^{t,s}$, we compute the weighted sum of the encoder hidden states, also known as the context vector $h_t^{*,s}$ as shown in Eq. 9.

$$h_t^{*,s} = \sum_i a_i^{t,s} h_i^{enc,s} \tag{9}$$

To get the vocabulary distribution P_{vocab} at time step t, we concatenate the context vector with the decoder state $h_t^{dec,s}$ and pass it through two linear layers:

$$P_{vocab} = softmax(Q \, (Q' h_t^{dec,s} \oplus h_t^{*,s} + b'^s) + b^s) \tag{10}$$

where Q, Q', b^s and b'^s are learnable parameters.

To finally generate words, we use a pointer-generator network which decides whether to generate the word from the vocabulary P_{vocab} or copy one from the input sequence by sampling from the attention distribution $a^{t,s}$ as shown in Eq. 12. This is done by calculating an additional generation probability p_{gen}^s for time step t, which is calculated from the context vector $h_t^{*,s}$, the decoder state $h_t^{\text{dec},s}$, and the current input to the decoder y_t^s:

$$p_{\text{gen}} = \sigma(W_{h^*}^T h_t^{*,s} + W_{h^{\text{dec}}}^T h_t^{\text{dec},s} + W_y^T y_t^s + b_{\text{gen}}^s) \tag{11}$$

$$P(w) = p_{\text{gen}} P_{\text{vocab}}(w) + (1 - p_{\text{gen}}) \sum_{i=0}^{N} a_i^{t,s} \tag{12}$$

where W_{h^*}, $W_{h^{\text{dec}}}$, W_y, b_{gen}^s are learnable parameters and N is the number of words in the source review. Pointer-generator networks are helpful for handling out-of-vocabulary (OOV) words: if w is an OOV word then $P_{\text{vocab}} = 0$ and the word from the source review text is considered for generation and vice versa.

Finally, we define the loss function for the review summary generation component for the whole sequence as the normalized sum of the negative log likelihood of the target words w_t^*:

$$\mathcal{L}^s = -\frac{1}{T} \sum_{t=0}^{T} \log P(w_t^*) \tag{13}$$

3.4 Multi-task Learning Setup

We use a multi-task learning setup to jointly optimize the rating prediction and the review summary generation components by using a joint loss function $\mathcal{L}^j$:

$$\mathcal{L}^j = \lambda_r \mathcal{L}^r + \lambda_s \mathcal{L}^s + \lambda_o (\|\mathcal{U}\|_2^2 + \|\mathcal{V}\|_2^2 + \|\Omega\|_2^2) \tag{14}$$

where $\mathcal{L}^r$ is the rating regression loss from Eq. 6 and $\mathcal{L}^s$ is the review summary generation loss from Eq. 13. For regularization, we use l_2-norm on the set of neural network parameters Ω, the user latent factors $\mathcal{U}$ and the item latent factors $\mathcal{V}$. λ_r, λ_s, λ_o are hyperparameters.

4 Experiments

Datasets. For our experiments, we use the Amazon 5-core[2] dataset on CDs, Toys, Music, Kindle, Electronics, Movies&TV and the Yelp 2018[3] dataset which are common benchmarks for recommendation systems. To preprocess the datasets, we perform tokenization, part-of-speech tagging and stemming with NLTK.[4] For the summary generation, we represent words using the Google News embeddings for English. Table 1 presents the statistics of the each dataset in terms of the number of reviews, users, items and vocabulary size.

---

[2] http://jmcauley.ucsd.edu/data/amazon.
[3] https://www.yelp.com/dataset/challenge.
[4] https://www.nltk.org/.

Table 1. Basic statistics of evaluation dataset.

Dataset	Reviews	Users	Items	User vocab	Item vocab
CDs	1,097,592	75,258	64,443	363,883	418,414
Toys	167,597	19,412	11,924	56,456	59,414
Music	64,706	5,541	3,568	78,293	83,904
Kindle	982,619	68,223	61,934	184,885	205,915
Electronics	1,685,748	192,403	63,001	256,920	235,408
Movies	1,697,533	123,960	50,052	397,060	495,021
Yelp	3,072,057	199,445	115,798	335,831	340,526

Previous Methods and Baselines. We compare our rating prediction component to the following recommendation algorithms as baselines: Probabilistic Matrix Factorization (PMF) [21] is a Matrix Factorization method using Gaussian distribution to model the users and items latent factors. Non-negative matrix factorization (NMF) [10] factorizes the rating matrix into a user matrix and item matrix to have no negative elements. Singular Value Decomposition (SVD++) [9] is a collaborative filtering method which creates the latent factors considering implicit feedback information. Hidden Factors as Topics (HFT) [16] is a state-of-the-art method that combines latent rating dimensions with latent review topics using exponential transformation function to link the stochastic distributions. Deep Cooperative Neural Networks (DeepCoNN) [27] is a state-of-the-art method that jointly models users and items from textual reviews using two parallel neural networks coupled using a shared output layer. We also utilize the extended version DeepCoNN++, where the shared layer with the Factorization Machine estimator is replaced with a neural prediction layer. The Neural Attentional Regression with Reviews-level Explanation (NAARE) model [4] is a state-of-the-art method that uses a similar neural network architecture as Deep-CoNN++, but additionally uses an attention-based review pooling mechanism to select the reviews for modeling.

Additionally, we compare our review summary generation component to multiple state-of-the-art unsupervised and supervised summarization methods: TF★IDF [15] selects sentences based on their term-frequency-inverse-document-frequency scores. LexRank [5] scores sentences based on PageRank. LSA [23] applies dimensionality reduction to the term-document matrix using singular value decomposition (SVD). KL-Greedy [8] minimizes the Kullback-Leibler (KL) divergence between the word distributions in the document and the summary. ICSI [6] is a global linear optimization method, which extracts a summary by solving a maximum coverage problem of the most frequent bigrams. Seq2Seq-gen [20] is a sequence-to-sequence encoder-decoder model, which encodes the input sequence using a bi-directional LSTM network and decodes using a conditional bi-directional LSTM network with attention. Finally, Pointer-gen denotes the sequence-to-sequence pointer-generator network by [22] using the pointer mechanism to determine a probability function to decide whether to generate the words from the vocabulary or copy from the source.

Experimental Setup. We divide each of the datasets into training, development and testing consisting of 80%, 10%, and 10% of the data respectively, which is a typical split ratio in recommendation evaluation. For all baseline methods (PMF, NMF, SVD++, HFT[5]), we use the Librec toolkit[6] and select the number of latent factors for each domain after fine tuning on the development set. To calculate the topic vectors, we set the tf-idf vectors size to 1,000 and the number of topics k to 10. For our neural network based approach, after hyperparameter fine tuning using random search, we set the latent factors to 32 and the number of hidden layers to 2. For the gradient-based optimization, we use the Adam optimizer.

For review summary generation, we set the beam size to 10 and the maximum summary length to 10 as nearly 80% of the summaries have a maximum of 10 words. We randomly initialize the neural network parameters.

Evaluation Metrics. To evaluate the rating prediction component, we employ two widely used metrics for recommender systems: Mean Absolute Error (MAE) and Root Mean Square Error (RMSE):

$$\text{MAE} = \sum_{u,v} \frac{|r_{u,v} - \hat{r}_{u,v}|}{n}, \qquad \text{RMSE} = \sqrt{\sum_{u,v} \frac{(r_{u,v} - \hat{r}_{u,v})^2}{n}}, \qquad (15)$$

where $r_{u,v}$ is the ground-truth rating, $\hat{r}_{u,v}$ is the predicted rating for a given user u and item v pair, n is the total number of ratings between users and items. To evaluate the review summary generation component, we use ROUGE-1 (R1) and ROUGE-2 (R2) scores [13] between the generated summary and the gold standard summary using the common parameters -c 95 -r 1000 -n 2 -a -m.

5 Results and Analysis

In the following section we analyze the performance of our J3R system in terms of (a) the rating prediction component, (b) the review summary generation component, and (c) its capabilities to explain recommendations.

5.1 Rating Prediction Analysis

Table 2 shows the results of the rating prediction component in comparison to the baselines. It shows that our model J3R consistently outperforms all other methods in terms of MAE and RMSE scores on all datasets. We also observe that the collaborative filtering methods PMF and NMF have low performance scores compared to other baselines. In contrast, SVD++ shows that it is still a strong baseline for recommendation systems as shown in the Netflix Prize 2008.[7]

---

[5] https://github.com/lipiji/HFT.
[6] https://www.librec.net/dokuwiki/doku.php?id=Recommender.
[7] https://www.netflixprize.com/community/topic_1537.html.

SVD++ performs on par or better in comparison to the state-of-the-art neural content-based systems like DeepCoNN, DeepCoNN++, and NARRE on small and medium-sized data. However, the neural approaches perform better on large datasets. Overall, the results show that our J3R-Pointer model performs better in terms of MAE and RMSE scores as compared to the best baseline methods NAARE and SVD++. This shows that review information helps in improving the representation of the user and item latent factors, which is further enhanced with the joint learning of rating prediction and review summary generation. The improvement is consistent and significant across the six datasets, whereas it is slightly lower on the Music dataset (-1.5%) compared to Electronics ($+2.9\%$), Movies&TV ($+2.2\%$), or Yelp ($+4.0\%$). The lower scores for Music is due to fewer reviews available for content-based models, which explains that latent factors of SVD++ also capture better information when there is less training data.

Ablation Analysis. To quantify the impact of each component on the rating prediction task, we do an ablation analysis. We try two different settings contrasting two single-task learning setups with our MTL setup: (a) *MLP*: the rating prediction component (Sect. 3.2), where a multi-layer perceptron based rating prediction model is randomly initialized with user and item vectors, (b) *MLPTopic*: the rating prediction component plus the topic vector component (Sects. 3.1 and 3.2) and (c) two variants of our full setup including all three components and the multi-task learning framework to jointly predict ratings and generate review summaries using user and item topic vectors initialized by the LDA topic vectors: J3R-Pointer is our proposed method using the pointer-generator network. J3R-Seq2Seq is an alternative to [12], where the GRU layers are replaced with LSTM and the rating regression has three hidden layers instead of one.

Table 2. MAE and RMSE scores (lower is better) for our models (lower group) in comparison to the state-of-the-art models (upper group). Best results are bold-faced. Italic and underlined results of J3R-Pointer are significantly better than NAARE, SVD++, and DeepCoNN++ with $p < 0.05$.

Models	CDs		Toys		Music		Kindle		Electronics		Movies		Yelp	
	MAE	RMSE	MAE	RMSE	MAE	RMSE	MAE	RMSE	MAE	RMSE	MAE	RMSE	MAE	RMSE
PMF	.682	.972	.705	.979	.849	.922	.573	.835	.855	1.193	.765	1.083	.967	1.273
NMF	.749	1.082	.693	.999	.700	.997	.651	.956	.952	1.366	.830	1.176	1.024	1.381
SVD++	.667	.956	.636	.907	**.641**	.905	.540	.790	.848	1.163	.750	1.043	.953	1.236
HFT	.746	.979	.645	.892	.665	.911	.664	.869	.846	1.112	.838	1.076	1.028	1.252
DeepCoNN	.695	.944	.669	.912	.672	.901	.565	.791	.866	1.124	.750	1.016	.938	1.186
DeepCoNN++	.682	.933	.652	.900	.659	.894	.553	.783	.824	1.113	.742	1.002	.922	1.202
NARRE	.675	.930	.683	.906	.698	.925	.547	.785	.834	1.107	.736	1.001	.921	1.186
MLP	.751	.995	.695	.967	.710	.990	.627	.857	.875	1.167	.816	1.083	.997	1.324
MLPTopic	.706	.954	.674	.943	.685	.907	.602	.814	.839	1.113	.758	1.059	.967	1.258
J3R-Seq2Seq	.685	.937	.647	.899	.660	.892	.560	.794	.823	1.052	.746	1.008	.919	1.174
J3R-Pointer	*.661*	*.912*	*.634*	*.880*	.656	**.890**	*.538*	*.775*	*.805*	*.995*	*.714*	*.984*	*.881*	*1.009*

Table 2 shows that *MLPTopic* performs better than the simple *MLP* model, which explains that the LDA topic vectors are useful for rating prediction as they capture user–item preferences. Our best performing model J3R-Pointer outperforms the individual components consistently across different domains. This elucidates that multi-task learning of rating prediction with review summary generation initialized with LDA based user and item models capture better user and item latent vectors. Furthermore, J3R-Pointer performs better than J3R-Seq2Seq and shows that the use of pointer network helps in better predictions.

Table 3. ROUGE-1 (R1) and ROUGE-2 (R2) precision scores of the generated summaries. Higher values are better. Best results per dataset are shown in bold.

Models	CDs		Toys		Music		Kindle		Electronics		Movies		Yelp	
	R1	R2	R1	R2	R1	R2	R1	R2	R1	R2	R1	R2	R1	R2
TF⋆IDF	.078	.017	.097	.027	.079	.019	.087	.024	.098	.029	.087	.023	.191	.126
LexRank	.087	.021	.107	.031	**.087**	**.024**	.097	.024	.109	.035	.096	.027	.204	.126
LSA	.068	.012	.077	.018	.068	.013	.070	.015	.081	.020	.074	.016	.122	.061
KL-Greedy	.070	.013	.080	.018	.073	.015	.074	.017	.086	.023	.078	.017	.141	.079
ICSI	.047	.010	.064	.017	.043	.008	.058	.017	.061	.018	.050	.012	.119	.064
Seq2Seq-gen	.108	.025	.114	.026	.053	.005	.139	.035	.177	.065	.134	.040	.219	.131
Pointer-gen	.135	.039	.122	.030	.059	.007	.152	.047	.179	.069	.141	.052	.250	.163
J3R-Seq2Seq	.119	.030	.120	.031	.060	.010	.150	.042	.185	.078	.145	.059	.235	.148
J3R-Pointer	**.156**	**.045**	**.137**	**.040**	.065	.012	**.185**	**.053**	**.190**	**.082**	**.159**	**.065**	**.274**	**.181**

5.2   Review Summary Generation Analysis

Although summarization is our auxiliary task to assist our main task of rating prediction, we separately evaluate the performance of our review summary generation component in this section. Table 3 shows the comparison of the review summary generation of J3R with baseline summarization models.

LexRank is the best-performing method among all the extractive baselines and performs the best on the Music dataset. However, the results show that the generative methods (i.e., Seq2Seq-gen and Pointer-gen) improve in ROUGE-1 and ROUGE-2 when compared to the baseline systems on the other six datasets, whereas for the Music dataset the results are only slightly lower than the best performing system LexRank. Our J3R-Pointer model performs best among all generative methods, exhibiting that the multi-task learning-based method captures user importance during summary generation. For the Music domain, we observe that the generative methods perform worse than the extractive methods due to the small data size available for training. Another reason is that J3R-Pointer's pointer-generator network tends to produce short abstractive summaries, while the extractive baselines produce longer summaries increasing the chances of overlaps with the gold summary. Furthermore, from the data analysis across datasets we observe that about 30% of the dataset have zero ROUGE-1 and ROUGE-2 scores, which explains the overall low ROUGE-1 and ROUGE-2 across various methods.

Table 4. Top five words for each of the top five topics of Movie&TV (left) and Yelp restaurant domain (right) explained with the most representative words.

Director	Genre	DVD	Cast	Cinema
seasons	story	video	actor	scene
episodes	style	collection	role	family
part	horror	quality	performance	love
point	comedy	television	voice	relationship
release	drama	series	dialogue	experience
Food	**Service**	**Cuisine**	**Breakfast**	**Price**
restaurant	server	greek	egg	check
main course	menu	chinese	eat	pay
taste	time	pizza	ppancake	money
experience	owner	rrice	sandwich	stay
soup	stay	ramen	fresh	cost

Fig. 3. (left) Interpretation of the user preferences using an histogram over top five topics from the topic model. (right) Word importance on the source review shows the evidence for the predicted rating.

5.3   Explainability Analysis

Besides performance improvements, an important advantage of our J3R system is the interpretability of the generated recommendations. In this section, we analyze two ways of explanations: (a) illustrating the importance of different topics with respect to a user based on topic vectors and (b) illustrating the word importance in the reviews while summarizing the content for the user.

First, our user model described in Sect. 3.1 illustrates the user's preferences on the important aspects of a domain. Table 4 shows the top five topics with their most representative word and the top five words describing each topic in the Movies&TV and the Yelp restaurant domain. To gain a better interpretation of the topic words, we remove words belonging to multiple topics. Thus, based on the topic distribution θ_d of important words in a domain and the distribution of the words $\phi_{z_{dn}}$ across a topic, a user's preferences are computed from the user vector u created from the reviews written by the user. An example explanation of the preferences of a user who has written 490 reviews in Movies&TV is shown in the histogram on the left-hand side of Fig. 3.

Second, we use the representative words in a review as evidence to explain the rating. We investigate word importance in the review using the attention weights. Figure 3 illustrates an example from the Movie&TV domain on Jason Bourne (2004). In the figure, we describe a scenario where the user decides to buy the DVD of Jason Bourne (2004). The user is overwhelmed by hundreds of reviews before making up the mind about the movie. Our J3R model summarizes each review and illustrates the most representative words of the review using the attention mechanism as described in Sect. 3.3. On the right-hand side of Fig. 3, we highlight the word importance in the source review based on attention weights while generating a review summary. The example shows that phrases like "the spy thriller", "entertaining", "surpasses the original" are highlighted by our model for the generated summary "a good spy thriller". Furthermore, the generated summary and the gold standard summary illustrate the same aspects of a movie (e.g., "genre", "director style").

6   Conclusion and Future Work

We propose a novel explainable recommendation system J3R using an MTL approach to jointly model user rating prediction and review summary generation. Our review summary generation model uses a pointer-generator network with an attention-based framework on user preferences and product attributes extracted from review content and user ratings as context vectors to generate a summary text, which in turn is used as evidence for explaining the predicted rating. Empirical results on benchmark datasets show that J3R achieves better performance than the state-of-the-art models on both rating prediction as well as review summary generation.

In future work, we plan to investigate the cold-start problem, since our model performs well when there is enough information about the users from the review content. However, when there is a new user or a user with less reviews, it is difficult to estimate the user preferences. Thus, a neighborhood model to calculate the similarity of the user to existing users and preference forms can estimate the user preferences with respect to the items. Similarly, for a new product the product attributes similarity can be used to initialize the latent factors for the rating prediction component and the review summary generation component. Furthermore, it would be interesting to explore sentiment analysis as a multi-task approach which is similar to rating prediction.

Acknowledgments. This work has been supported by the German Research Foundation as part of the Research Training Group "Adaptive Preparation of Information from Heterogeneous Sources" (AIPHES) under grant No. GRK 1994/1. Zhifeng Bao and Mark Sanderson are supported by ARC DP170102726.

References

1. Aciar, S., Zhang, D., Simoff, S.J., Debenham, J.K.: Informed recommender: basing recommendations on consumer product reviews. IEEE Intell. Syst. **22**(3), 39–47 (2007)
2. Blei, D.M., Ng, A.Y., Jordan, M.I.: Latent dirichlet allocation. In: Proceedings of NIPS, Vancouver, Canada, pp. 601–608 (2001)
3. Catherine, R., Mazaitis, K., Eskenazi, M., Cohen, W.W.: Explainable entity-based recommendations with knowledge graphs. In: Proceedings of RecSys, Como, Italy (2017)
4. Chen, C., Zhang, M., Liu, Y., Ma, S.: Neural attentional rating regression with review-level explanations. In: Proceedings of WWW, Lyon, France, pp. 1583–1592 (2018)
5. Erkan, G., Radev, D.R.: LexRank: graph-based lexical centrality as salience in text summarization. J. Artif. Intell. Res. **22**, 457–479 (2004)
6. Gillick, D., Favre, B.: A scalable global model for summarization. In: Proceedings of the Workshop on Integer Linear Programming for Natural Language Processing, Boulder, CO, USA, pp. 10–18 (2009)
7. Goodman, B., Flaxman, S.R.: European union regulations on algorithmic decision-making and a "'right to explanation". AI Mag. **38**(3), 50–57 (2017)
8. Haghighi, A., Vanderwende, L.: Exploring content models for multi-document summarization. In: Proceedings of NAACL, Boulder, CO, USA, pp. 362–370 (2009)
9. Koren, Y.: Factorization meets the neighborhood: a multifaceted collaborative filtering model. In: Proceedings of SIGKDD, Las Vegas, NV, USA, pp. 426–434 (2008)
10. Lee, D.D., Seung, H.S.: Algorithms for non-negative matrix factorization. In: Proceedings of NIPS, Denver, CO, USA, pp. 556–562 (2000)
11. Li, P., Wang, Z., Bing, L., Lam, W.: Persona-aware tips generation. In: Proceedings of WWW, San Francisco, CA, USA, pp. 1006–1016 (2019)
12. Li, P., Wang, Z., Ren, Z., Bing, L., Lam, W.: Neural rating regression with abstractive tips generation for recommendation. In: Proceedings of SIGIR, Shinjuku, Tokyo, Japan, pp. 345–354 (2017)
13. Lin, C.Y.: ROUGE: a package for automatic evaluation of summaries. In: Proceedings of the ACL-2004 Workshop on Text Summarization Branches Out, Barcelona, Spain, pp. 74–81 (2004)
14. Liu, B.: Sentiment analysis and subjectivity. In: Indurkhya, N., Damerau, F.J. (eds.) Handbook of Natural Language Processing, 2nd edn, pp. 627–666. CRC Press, Boca Raton (2010)
15. Luhn, H.P.: The automatic creation of literature abstracts. IBM J. Res. Dev. **2**, 159–165 (1958)
16. McAuley, J.J., Leskovec, J.: Hidden factors and hidden topics: understanding rating dimensions with review text. In: Proceedings of RecSys, Hong Kong, China, pp. 165–172 (2013)
17. Mukherjee, S., Popat, K., Weikum, G.: Exploring latent semantic factors to find useful product reviews. In: Proceedings of the 2017 SIAM International Conference on Data Mining, Houston, TX, USA, pp. 480–488 (2017)
18. Musat, C.C., Liang, Y., Faltings, B.: Recommendation using textual opinions. In: Proceedings of IJCAI, Beijing, China, pp. 2684–2690 (2013)
19. Rei, M.: Semi-supervised multitask learning for sequence labeling. In: Proceedings of ACL, Vancouver, Canada, pp. 2121–2130 (2017)

20. Rush, A.M., Chopra, S., Weston, J.: A neural attention model for abstractive sentence summarization. In: Proceedings of EMNLP, Lisbon, Portugal, pp. 379–389 (2015)
21. Salakhutdinov, R., Mnih, A.: Probabilistic matrix factorization. In: Proceedings of NIPS, Vancouver, Canada, pp. 1257–1264 (2007)
22. See, A., Liu, P.J., Manning, C.D.: Get to the point: summarization with pointer-generator networks. In: Proceedings of ACL, Vancouver, Canada, pp. 1073–1083 (2017)
23. Steinberger, J., Jezek, K.: Using latent semantic analysis in text summarization and summary evaluation. In: Proceedings of the 7th ISIM Conference, Rožnov pod Radhoštěm, Czech Republic, pp. 93–100 (2004)
24. Tintarev, N., Masthoff, J.: Designing and evaluating explanations for recommender systems. In: Ricci, F., Rokach, L., Shapira, B., Kantor, P.B. (eds.) Recommender Systems Handbook, pp. 479–510. Springer, Boston, MA (2011). https://doi.org/10.1007/978-0-387-85820-3_15
25. Yu, N., Huang, M., Shi, Y., Zhu, X.: Product review summarization by exploiting phrase properties. In: Proceedings of Coling, Osaka, Japan, pp. 1113–1124 (2016)
26. Zhang, Y., Lai, G., Zhang, M., Zhang, Y., Liu, Y., Ma, S.: Explicit factor models for explainable recommendation based on phrase-level sentiment analysis. In: Proceedings of SIGIR, Gold Coast, Australia, pp. 83–92 (2014)
27. Zheng, L., Noroozi, V., Yu, P.S.: Joint deep modeling of users and items using reviews for recommendation. In: Proceedings of WSDM, Cambridge, UK, pp. 425–434 (2017)
28. Zhou, M., Lapata, M., Wei, F., Dong, L., Huang, S., Xu, K.: Learning to generate product reviews from attributes. In: Proceedings of EACL, Valencia, Spain, pp. 623–632 (2017)

Applied Data Science: Healthcare

Augmenting Semantic Representation of Depressive Language: From Forums to Microblogs

Nawshad Farruque$^{(\boxtimes)}$ ⓘ, Osmar Zaiane ⓘ, and Randy Goebel ⓘ

Department of Computing Science, University of Alberta,
Edmonton, AB T6G 2R3, Canada
{nawshad,zaiane,rgoebel}@ualberta.ca

Abstract. We discuss and analyze the process of creating word embedding feature representations specifically designed for a learning task when annotated data is scarce, like depressive language detection from Tweets. We start from rich word embedding pre-trained from a general dataset, then enhance it with embedding learned from a domain specific but relatively much smaller dataset. Our strengthened representation portrays better the domain of depression we are interested in as it combines the semantics learned from the specific domain and word coverage from the general language. We present a comparative analyses of our word embedding representations with a simple bag-of-words model, a well known sentiment lexicon, a psycholinguistic lexicon, and a general pre-trained word embedding, based on their efficacy in accurately identifying depressive Tweets. We show that our representations achieve a significantly better F1 score than the others when applied to a high quality dataset.

Keywords: Machine learning · Natural language processing · Distributional semantics · Major Depressive Disorder · Social media

1 Introduction

Depression or Major Depressive Disorder (MDD) is regarded as one of the most commonly identified mental health problems among young adults in developed countries, accounting for 75% of all psychiatric admissions [3]. Most people who suffer from depression do not acknowledge it, for various reasons, ranging from social stigma to just ignorance; this means that a vast majority of depressed people remain undiagnosed. Lack of proper diagnosis eventually results in suicide, drug abuse, crime and many other societal problems. For example, depression has been found to be a major cause behind 800,000 deaths committed through suicide each year worldwide[1]. Moreover, the economic burden created by depression is estimated to have been 210 billion USD in 2010 [14] in the USA alone. Hence, detecting, monitoring and treating depression is very important and there

---

[1] https://who.int/mental_health/prevention/suicide/suicideprevent/en/.

© Springer Nature Switzerland AG 2020
U. Brefeld et al. (Eds.): ECML PKDD 2019, LNAI 11908, pp. 359–375, 2020.
https://doi.org/10.1007/978-3-030-46133-1_22

is a huge need for effective, inexpensive and almost real-time interventions. In such a scenario, social media provide the foundation of a remedy. Social media are very popular among young adults where depression is prevalent [15]. In addition, it has been found that people who are otherwise socially aloof (and more prone to having depression) can be very active in the social media platforms [9]. As a consequence, there has been significant depression detection research conducted already, based on various social media components, such as social network size, social media behavior, and language used in social media posts. It is found that, among these multi-modalities, human language alone can be a very good predictor of depression [9]. In the next sections we provide a brief summary of earlier research together with some background supporting our formulation of our proposed methods identifying depression from Tweets.

2   Background and Motivation

Previous studies suggest that the words we use in our daily life can express our mental state, mood and emotion [29]. Therefore analyzing language to identify and monitor human mental health problems has been regarded as an appropriate avenue of mental health modeling. With the advent of social media platforms, researchers have found that social media posts can be used as a good proxy for our day to day language usage [9]. There have been many studies that identify and monitor depression through social media posts in various social media, such as, Twitter [7,9,30], Facebook [24,33] and online forums [39].

Depression detection from social media posts can be specified as a low resource supervised classification task because of the paucity of valid data. Although there is no concrete precise definition of valid data, previous research emphasizes collecting social media posts, which are either validated by annotators as carrying clues of depression, or coming from the people who are clinically diagnosed as depressed, or both. Based on the methods of depression intervention using these data, earlier research can be mostly divided into two general categories: (1) post-specific depression detection (or depressive language detection) [7,16,38], and (2) user-specific depression detection, which considers all the posts made by a depressed user in a specific time window [31,32]. The goal of (1) is to identify depression in a more fine grained level, i.e., in social media posts, which further helps in identifying depression inclination of individuals when analyzed by method (2).

For the post specific depression detection task, previous research concentrate on the extraction of depression specific features used to train machine learning models, e.g., building depression lexicons based on unigrams present in posts from depressed individuals [9], depression symptom related unigrams curated from depression questionnaires [4], metaphors used in depressive language [25], or psycholinguistic features in LIWC [37]. For user specific depression identification, variations of topic modeling have been popular to identify depressive topics and use them as features [31,32]. But recently, some research has used convolutional neural network (CNN) based deep learning models to learn feature representations [28,39]. Most deep learning approaches require a significant volume of labelled data to learn the depression specific embedding from scratch, or from a pre-trained word embedding in a supervised manner. So, in general, both post level and user level depression identification research emphasize the curation of labelled social media posts indicative of depression, which is a very expensive process in terms of time, human effort, and cost. Moreover, previous research showed that a robust post level depression identification system is an important prerequisite for accurately identifying depression at the user level [16]. In addition, most of this earlier research leveraged Twitter posts to identify depression because a huge volume of Twitter posts are publicly available.

Therefore the motivation of our research comes from the need for a better feature representation specific to depressive language, and reduced dependency on a large set of (human annotated) labelled data for depressive Tweet detection task. We proceed as follows:

1. We create a word embedding space that encodes the semantics of depressive language from a small but high quality depression corpus curated from depression related public forums.
2. We use that word embedding to create feature representations for our Tweets and feed them to our machine learning models to identify depressive Tweets; this achieves good accuracy, even with very small amount of labelled Tweets.
3. Furthermore, we adjust a pre-trained Twitter word embedding based on our depression specific word embedding, using a non-linear mapping between the embeddings (motivated by the work of [21] and [35] on bilingual dictionary induction for machine translation), and use it to create feature representation for our Tweets and feed them to our machine learning models. This helps us achieve around 3% higher F1-score than our strongest baseline in depressive Tweets detection.

Accuracy improvements mentioned in points 2 and 3 above are true for a high quality dataset curated through rigorous human annotation, as opposed to the low quality dataset with less rigorous human annotation; this indicates the effectiveness of our proposed feature representations for depressive Tweets detection. To the best of our knowledge, ours is the first effort to build a depression specific word embedding for identifying depressive Tweets, and to formulate a method to gain further improvements on top of it, then to present a comprehensive analysis on the quantitative and qualitative performance of our embeddings. Throughout our paper, we use the phrase "word embedding" as an object that consists of word vectors. So by "word embeddings" we mean multiple instances of that object.

3 Datasets

Here we provide the details of our two datasets that we use for our experiments and their annotation procedure, the corpus they are curated from and their quality comparisons.

3.1   Dataset1

Dataset1 is curated by the ADVanced ANalytics for data SciencE (ADVANSE) research team at the University of Montpellier, France [38]. This dataset contains Tweets having key-phrases generated from the American Psychiatric Association (APA)'s list of risk factors and the American Association of Suicidology (AAS)'s list of warning signs related to suicide. Furthermore, they randomly investigated the authors of these Tweets to identify 60 distressed users who frequently write about depression, suicide and self mutilation. They also randomly collected 60 control users. Finally, they curated a balanced and human annotated dataset of a total of around 500 Tweets, of which 50% Tweets are from distressed and 50% are from control users, with the help of seven annotators and one professional psychologist. The goal of their annotation was to provide a distress score (0–3) for each Tweet. They reported a Cohen's kappa agreement score of 69.1% for their annotation task. Finally, they merged Tweets showing distress level 0, 1 as control Tweets and 2, 3 as distressed Tweets. *Distressed Tweets* carry signs of suicidal ideation, self-harm and depression while control Tweets are about daily life occurrences, such as weekend plans, trips and common distress such as exams, deadlines, etc. We believe this dataset is perfectly suited for our task, and we use their distressed Tweets as our depressive Tweets and their control as our control.

3.2   Dataset2

Dataset2 is collected by a research group at the University of Ottawa [16]. They first filtered depressive Tweets from #BellLetsTalk2015 (a Twitter campaign) based on keywords such as, suffer, attempt, suicide, battle, struggle and first person pronouns. Using topic modeling, they removed Tweets under the topics of public campaign, mental health awareness, and raising money. They further removed Tweets which contain mostly URLs and are very short. Finally, from these Tweets they identified 30 users who self-disclosed their own depression, and 30 control users who did not. They employed two annotators to label Tweets from 10 users as either depressed or non-depressed. They found that their annotators labelled most Tweets as non-depressed. To reduce the number of non-depressive Tweets, they further removed neutral Tweets from their dataset, as they believe neutral Tweets surely do not carry any signs of depression. After that, they annotated Tweets from the remaining 50 users with the help of two annotators with a Cohen's kappa agreement score of 67%. Finally, they labelled a Tweet as depressive if any one of their two annotators agree, to gather more depressive Tweets. This left them with 8,753 Tweets with 706 depressive Tweets.

3.3   Quality of Datasets

Here we present a comparative analysis of our datasets based on the linguistic components present in them relevant to depressive language detection and their curation process as follows:

Analysis Based on Linguistic Components Present in the Datasets: For this analysis, we use Linguistic Inquiry and Word Count (LIWC) [37]. LIWC is a tool widely used in psycholinguistic analysis of language. It extracts the percentage of words in a text, across 93 pre-defined categories, e.g., affect, social process, cognitive processes, etc. To analyse the quality of our datasets, we provide scores of few dimensions of LIWC lexicon relevant for depressive language detection [9,18,26], such as, 1st person pronouns, anger, sadness, negative emotions, etc (see Table 1 for the complete list) for the depressive Tweets present both in our datasets. The bold items in that table shows significant score differences in those dimensions for both datasets and endorses the fact that Dataset1 indeed carries more linguistic clues of depression than Dataset2 (the higher the score, the more is the percentage of words from that dimension is present in the text). Moreover, Tweets labelled as depressive in Dataset2 are mostly about common distress of everyday life unlike those of Dataset1, which are indicative of severe depression. We provide few random samples of Tweets from Dataset1 and Dataset2 depressive Tweets at Table 2 and their corresponding word clouds at Fig. 1 as well.

Table 1. Scores of Dataset1 and Dataset2 in few LIWC dimensions relevant to depressive language detection (bold categories have significant score differences).

LIWC category	Example words	Dataset1 depressive Tweets score	Dataset2 depressive Tweets score
1st person pronouns	I, me, mine	**12.74**	7.06
Negations	No, not, never	**3.94**	2.63
Positive emotion	Love, nice, sweet	**2.79**	2.65
Negative emotion	Hurt, ugly, nasty	**8.59**	6.99
Anxiety	Worried, fearful	0.72	**1.05**
Anger	Hate, kill, annoyed	**2.86**	2.51
Sadness	Crying, grief, sad	**3.29**	1.97
Past focus	Ago, did, talked	2.65	**3**
Death	Suicide, die, overdosed	**1.43**	0.44
Swear	Fuck, damn, shit	**1.97**	1.39

Table 2. Sample Tweets from Dataset1 and Dataset2

Datasets	Depressive Tweets
Dataset1	"I wish I could be normal and be happy and feel things like other people"
	"I feel alone even when I'm not"
	"Yesterday was difficult...and so is today and tomorrow and the days after..."
Dataset2	"Last night was not a good night for sleep... so tired And I have a gig tonight... yawnnn"
	"So tired of my @NetflixCA app not working, I hate Android 5"
	"I have been so bad at reading Twitter lately, I don't know how people keep up, maybe today I'll do better"

Fig. 1. Dataset1 depressive Tweets word cloud (left) and Dataset2 depressive Tweets word cloud (right)

Analysis Based on Data Curation Process: We think Dataset2 is of lower quality compared to Dataset1 for the following reasons: (1) this dataset is collected from the pool of Tweets which is a part of a mental health campaign, and thus compromises the authenticity of the Tweets; (2) the words used for searching depressive Tweets are not validated by any depression or suicide lexicons; (3) although two annotators were employed (none of them are domain experts) to label the Tweets, a Tweet was considered as depressive if at least one annotator labelled it as depressive, which introduced more noise in the data; (4) it is not confirmed how neutral Tweets were identified, since the neutral Tweets may convey depression as well; (5) a person was identified as depressed if s/he disclose their depression, but it was not mentioned how these disclosures were determined. Simple regular expression based methods to identify these self disclosures can introduce a lot of noise in the data. In addition, these self disclosures may not be true.

3.4 Depression Corpus

To build depression specific word embedding we curate our own depression corpus. For this, we collect all the posts from the Reddit depression forum: r/depression[2] from the year 2006 to 2017 and all those from Suicide Forum[3] up through the year 2017 and concatenated to total of 856,897 posts. We choose to use these forums because people who post anonymously in these forums usually suffer from severe depression and share their struggle with depression and its impact in their personal lives [8]. We believe these forums contain useful semantic components indicative of depressive language. Technical and ethical aspects of building word embedding representation on this corpora are presented in Sects. 4.3 and 7 respectively.

4 Feature Extraction Methods

4.1 Bag-of-Words (BOW)

We represent each Tweet as a vector of vocabulary terms and their frequency counts in that Tweet, also known as bag-of-words. The vocabulary terms refer to the most frequent 400 terms existing in the training set. Before creating the vocabulary and the vector representation of the Tweets, we perform the following preprocessing: (1) we make the Tweets all lowercase; (2) tokenize them using NLTK Tweet tokenizer[4]; (3) remove all stop words except the first person pronouns such as, I, me and my (because they are useful for depression detection). The reason for using Tweet tokenizer is to consider Tweet emoticons (:-)), hashtags (#Depression) and mentions (@user) as single tokens.

4.2 Lexicons

We have tried several emotion and sentiment lexicons, such as, LabMT [10], Emolex [23], AFINN [27], LIWC [37], VADER [12], NRC-Hashtag-Sentiment-Lexicon (HSL) [17] and CBET [34]. Among these lexicons we find LIWC and HSL perform the best and hence we report the results of these two lexicons. The following subsections provide a brief description of LIWC, HSL and lexicon-based representation of Tweets.

Linguistic Inquiry and Word Count (LIWC): LIWC is a tool widely used in psycholinguistic analysis of language. It extracts the percentage of words in a text, across 93 pre-defined categories, e.g., affect, social process, cognitive processes, etc. A text input is converted into a 93 length vector representation of that text (in our case Tweets), that are input for our machine learning models. Note that LIWC has been widely used as a good baseline for depressive Tweet detection in earlier research [5,26].

---

[2] https://reddit.com/r/depression/.
[3] https://suicideforum.com/.
[4] www.nltk.org/api/nltk.tokenize.html.

NRC Hashtag Sentiment Lexicon (HSL): This lexicon consists of 54,129 unigrams, each of which has a score that shows the difference between the PMI score of that unigram being associated with positive Tweets and negative Tweets (Tweets having positive/negative hashtags, respectively). The polarity of the score represents the polarity of the sentiment and the magnitude represents the degree of associativity with the sentiments. In our experiments, we tokenize each Tweet as described in Sect. 4.1, then use the lexicon to determine a score for each token in the Tweet, then sum them to provide a single value for each Tweet, which represents the sentiment and magnitude. We use that value as a feature for our machine learning models.

4.3   Distributed Representation of Words

The use of word embedding has been crucial in many downstream NLP tasks; domain specific embedding perform better than generic ones for domain specific tasks [1,2,36], and there have been many attempts till-to-date to make generic embedding useful for particular domain, for example, lexicon based retrofitting [11,40], and supervised retrofitting [28]. Lexicon-based retrofitting algorithms have an inherent problem of limited vocabulary coverage, where supervised retrofitting requires huge amount of labelled data. In contrast, we retrofitted a general pre-trained embedding based on the semantics present in depression specific embedding through a non-linear mapping between them. Our depression-specific embedding is created in an unsupervised manner from depression forum posts. Moreover, through our mapping process we learn a transformation matrix (see Eq. 3), which can be used to predict embedding for Out of Vocabulary (OOV) words, and helps achieve better accuracy.

Word Embedding Representation of Tweets: To represent a Tweet using word embedding, we take the average of the word vectors of the individual words in that Tweet, ignoring the ones that are out of vocabulary (OOV), i.e. absent in the word embedding vocabulary.

General Twitter Word Embedding (GTE): We use a pre-trained skip-gram word embedding having 400 dimensions learned from 400 million Tweets with vocabulary size of $3,039,345$ words [13] as a representative of word embedding learned from general dataset (in our case, Tweets), because we believe this has the most relevant vocabulary for our task. The creator of this word embedding use negative sampling ($k = 5$) with context window size $= 1$ and mincount $= 5$. Since it is pre-trained, we do not have control over the parameters it uses and simply use it as is. We use pre-trained embedding to avoid difficulties arising from creating our own from a huge dataset.

Depression Specific Word Embedding (DSE): We create a 400 dimensional depression specific word embedding (DSE) on our curated depression corpus as mentioned in Subsect. 3.4. First, we identify sentence boundaries in our corpora based on punctuations such as (period, question mark and exclamation). Then we feed each sentence in skip-gram based word2vec implementation in gensim[5]. We use negative sampling ($k = 5$) with the context window size $= 5$ and mincount $= 10$ for the training of this word embedding. DSE has a vocabulary size of 29,930 words. We choose skip-gram for this training because skip-gram learns good embedding from small corpus [20].

Adjusted Twitter Word Embedding (ATE): A Non-linear Mapping Between GTE and DSE: In this step, we find a non-linear mapping between GTE and DSE. The goal of this mapping is to adjust GTE, such that it reflects the semantics of DSE. To do this, we use a Multilayer Perceptron Regressor (MLPR) having a single hidden layer with 400 hidden units and Rectified Linear Unit (ReLU) activations, that tries to minimize the Mean Squared Error (MSE) loss function, $\mathcal{F}(\theta)$ in Eq. 1, using stochastic gradient descent:

$$\mathcal{F}(\theta) = \arg\min_{\theta}(\mathcal{L}(\theta) + \alpha||\theta||_2^2) \tag{1}$$

where

$$\mathcal{L}(\theta) = \frac{1}{m}\sum_{i=1}^{m}\frac{1}{n}\sum_{j=1}^{n}(g_j(x) - y_j)^2 \tag{2}$$

and

$$g(x) = b_1 + (W_1(ReLU(b_2 + W_2x))) \tag{3}$$

here, $g(x)$ is the non-linear mapping function between the embedding x (from GTE) and y (from DSE) of a word $w \in V$, where, V is a common vocabulary between GTE and DSE; W_1 and W_2 are the hidden-to-output and input-to-hidden layer weight matrices respectively, b_1 is the output layer bias vector and b_2 is the hidden layer bias vector (all these weights are indicated as θ in Eq. 1) and α is the $l2$ regularization parameter. In Eq. 2, m and n are respectively the length of V (in our case it is 28,977) and dimension of word vectors (in our case it is 400). Once the MLPR learns the θ that minimizes $\mathcal{F}(\theta)$, it is used to predict the vectors for all the words in GTE. After this step, we finally get adjusted Twitter word embedding representation which encodes the semantics of depression forums as well as word coverage from Tweets, we name it Adjusted Twitter word Embedding (ATE). We use scikit-learn MLPR implementation[6] with default parameter settings for our non-linear mapping, except random state, which is set to 1. This entire process of mapping between embeddings is depicted in Fig. 2.

Conditions for Embedding Mapping/Adjustment: Our non-linear mapping between two embeddings works better given that those two embeddings

---

[5] https://radimrehurek.com/gensim/models/word2vec.html.
[6] https://scikit-learn.org/stable/modules/generated/sklearn.neural_network.
MLPRegressor.html.

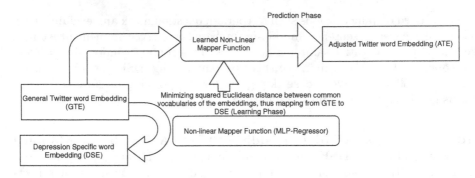

Fig. 2. Non-linear mapping of GTE to DSE (creation of ATE)

are created from the same word embedding creation algorithm (in our case skip-gram) and have same number of dimensions (i.e. 400). We also find that a non-linear mapping between our GTE and DSE produces slightly better ATE than a linear mapping for our task, although the former is a bit slower.

5   Experimental Setup

We report the results of best performing combinations out of all the 24 combinations from six feature extraction methods, such as, BOW, HSL, LIWC, GTE, DSE and ATE (described in Sect. 4) and four machine learning models, including Multinomial Naïve Bayes (MNB), Logistic Regression (LR), Linear Support Vector Machine (LSVM), and Support Vector Machine with radial basis kernel function (RSVM), for both datasets.

We also report the results of two experiments, one by [38] for Dataset1 and another by [16] for Dataset2, where they use their own depression lexicon as a feature representation for their machine learning models. For a single experiment, we split all our data into a disjoint set of training (70% of all the data) and testing (30% of all the data) (see Table 3). We use stratified sampling so that the original distribution of labels is retained in our splits. Furthermore, with the help of 10-fold cross validation in our training set, we learn the best parameter settings for all our model-feature extraction combinations except MNB that requires no such parameter tuning. For the SVMs and LR, we tune the parameter, $C \in \{2^{-9}, 2^{-7}, \ldots, 2^5\}$ and additionally, $\gamma \in \{2^{-11}, 2^{-9}, \ldots, 2^2\}$ for the RSVM. We use min-max feature scaling for all our features. For our imbalanced dataset we use cost sensitive LR and SVMs (as listed above) with class weights inversely proportional to the class frequencies in our input data.

We then find the performance of the best model on our test set. We have run 30 such experiments on 30 random train-test splits. Finally, we report the performance of our model-feature extraction combinations based on the Precision (Prec.), Recall (Rec.) and F1 score averaged over the test sets of those

30 experiments. See Tables 4 and 5 and Fig. 3 depicting the experiment results. We use scikit-learn library[7] for all our experiments.

Table 3. Number of Tweets in the train and test splits for the two datasets. The number of depressive Tweets is in parenthesis.

Datasets	Train	Test
Dataset1	355(178)	152(76)
Dataset2	6127(613)	2626(263)

6 Results Analysis

In this section we report quantitative and qualitative performance analysis of our embeddings in detecting depressive Tweets.

6.1 Quantitative Performance Analysis

In general, Tweet level depression detection is a tough problem and a good F1 score is hard to achieve [16]. Still, our LR-ATE achieves an F1 score of 0.81 which is around 3% better than our strongest baseline (GTE) and 10% better than [38] with F1 score of 0.71 in Dataset1. All the word embedding based models achieve on avg. 0.7926 F1 score which is 8% better than [38]. See Table 4 and Fig. 3.

Table 4. Average Prec., Rec. and F1 scores on Dataset1 best model-feat combination experiments

Category	Model-Feat.	Prec.	Rec.	F1
Baselines	LR-BOW	0.6967	0.8264	0.7548
	LR-HSL	0.6238	**0.9114**	0.7400
	LR-LIWC	0.7409	0.7772	0.7574
	LR-GTE	0.7694	0.7976	0.7822
Our Models	LR-DSE	0.7392	0.8411	0.7852
	LR-ATE	**0.7846**	0.8394	**0.8104**
Prev. Res.	[38]	0.71	0.71	0.71

In Dataset2, which is imbalanced (only 10% samples are depressive Tweets), all the word embedding based models achieve on avg. 0.4284 F1 score which is around 16% better than the best F1 achieved by [16] in the same dataset. However in that dataset, GTE is 4% better than DSE and 0.97% better than ATE, see Table 5 and Fig. 3.

---

[7] https://scikit-learn.org/stable/.

Table 5. Average Prec., Rec. and F1 scores on Dataset2 best model-feat combination experiments

Category	Model-Feat.	Prec.	Rec.	F1
Baselines	RSVM-BOW	0.2374	0.5296	0.3260
	RSVM-HSL	0.1168	0.6513	0.1980
	RSVM-LIWC	0.2635	**0.6750**	0.3778
	RSVM-GTE	0.3485	0.6305	**0.4448**
Our Models	RSVM-DSE	0.3437	0.5198	0.4053
	RSVM-ATE	**0.3497**	0.5821	0.4351
Prev. Res.	[16]	0.1706	0.5939	0.265

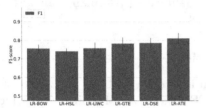 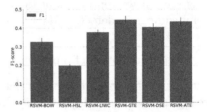

Fig. 3. Error bars for F1 scores on Dataset1 experiments (left) and Dataset2 experiments (right)

In Dataset1, HSL has the best recall, while LIWC has the best recall in Dataset2. In both datasets, HSL has the worst precision, while, LIWC and word embedding based methods have acceptable precision and recall.

6.2 Qualitative Performance Analysis

Here we report correctly predicted Tweets in Table 6 by LR-ATE (our overall best model) and LSVM-ATE (second best model), which are mistakenly predicted as control Tweets (i.e. false negatives) when LR-GTE and LSVM-GTE are used respectively in a test set from Dataset1. The first example from Table 6, *"Tonight may definitely be the night"*, may be indicative of suicidal ideation and should not be taken lightly, also, the second one *"0 days clean"* is the trade mark indication of continued self-harm, although many depression detection models will predict these as normal Tweets.

Additionally, we plot 2-dimensional Principal Component Analysis (PCA) projection of the embedding for LIWC 'POSEMO' and 'NEGEMO' words conveying positive and negative emotions respectively occurred most frequently in our datasets. Also, we use a word *sleepless*, indicating the common sleep problem encountered by many of the depressed people (see Fig. 4). We show that these

Table 6. False negative depressive Tweets when GTE is used, correctly predicted when ATE is used in a test set from Dataset1.

Tweets
"Tonight may definitely be the night"
"0 days clean"
"I'm a failure"
"I understand you're 'busy', but fuck that ... people make time for what they want"
"'Worthless' repeats in her mind as she holds on to what's left of her..."

words clearly form defined clusters, C1 (contains words carrying depressive sentiment) and C2 (contains words carrying non-depressive sentiment) in ATE where in GTE, these clusters overlap. Also, under each of these clusters we notice there are sub-clusters of closely related emotions. Although these sub-clusters are easily identifiable in ATE, they are almost absent in GTE, for example, *fuck* and *hate* are the words mostly used by the depressed people and should belong to C1 but they belong to C2 for GTE, overlapped with *thankful* and *love*. So by adjusting the embedding space of GTE based on DSE, we basically make the clear distinction among the words carrying depressive sentiment and the ones which do not, in their vector space.

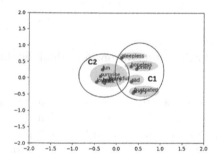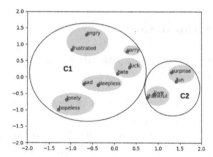

Fig. 4. 2-dimensional PCA projection of emotion carrying words in General Twitter word Embedding (GTE) (left) and Adjusted Twitter word Embedding (ATE) (right)

Overall, in both datasets, word embedding based methods perform much better than BOW and lexicons. The reason is, both GTE and ATE have bigger vocabulary and better feature representation than BOW and lexicons. Among non word embedding methods, BOW and LIWC perform better than HSL, because the former provide better discriminating features than the latter. However, in Dataset1, ATE is better than both GTE and DSE with DSE performing close enough. This confirms that DSE can capture the semantics of depressive language very well. ATE is superior in performance because it leverages both the vocabulary coverage and semantics of a depressive language. In Dataset2, GTE turns out to be better than DSE with ATE performing closely, indicating that Tweet samples in Dataset2 are more about general distress than depression. In this case, the performance is affected mostly by the vocabulary size than the depressive language semantics.

Another important observation is that, in Dataset1 we see the LR classifier performs better where in Dataset2, RSVM works better than all others. We think it is because, both LR and RSVM consider dependency among features unlike feature independence assumption in MNB. LR performing better in Dataset1 confirms that in Dataset1 depressive and non-depressive Tweets are distinct to each other and linearly separable, while Dataset2 Tweets are not and a non-linear classifier such as RSVM is needed.

7   Ethical Concerns

We use *Suicide Forum* posts where users are strictly required to stay anonymous. Moreover, we use Reddit and Twitter *public* posts which incur minimal risk of user privacy violation as established by earlier research [6,19,22] utilizing same kind of data. Our word embeddings are built solely on the text and not on user data of the forums. No user identifiers or user profiles are stored by us as these are not required for our research. Moreover, we have our university research ethics office approval to use datasets released by other organization to us (like our Dataset1 and Dataset2) for conducting our research.

8   Conclusion

In this paper we empirically present the following observations for a high quality dataset:

- For depressive Tweets detection, we can use word embedding trained in an unsupervised manner on a corpus of depression forum posts, which we call Depression Specific word Embedding (DSE) and use it as a feature representation for our machine learning models and can achieve very good accuracy.
- Further, we can use DSE to adjust the general Twitter pre-trained word embedding (available off the shelf) through non-linear mapping between them. This Adjusted Twitter word Embedding (ATE) helps us achieve even better results for our task.
- We need not to depend on human annotated data or labeled data for any of our word embedding representation creation.
- Depression forum posts have specific distributed representation of words and it is different than that of general twitter posts and this is reflected in ATE, see Fig. 4.
- Our DSE and ATE embeddings are publicly available[8].

---

[8] https://doi.org/10.5281/zenodo.3361838.

9   Future Work

In the future we would like to analyze DSE more exhaustively to find any patterns in semantic clusters that specifically identify depressive language. We would also like to use ATE for Twitter depression lexicon induction and discover depressive Tweets. Thus, we can see a lot of promise in its use in creating semi-supervised learning based automated depression data annotation task later on.

Acknowledgements. We thank Natural Sciences and Engineering Research Council of Canada (NSERC) and Alberta Machine Intelligence Institute (AMII) for their generous support to pursue this research. We thank Prof. Greg Kondrak for his valuable advice and Bradley Hauer for his helpful suggestions. We also thank Roberto Vega and Shiva Zamani for their contribution in implementing standard text classification pipeline and initial baseline experiments.

References

1. Asgari, E., Mofrad, M.R.: Continuous distributed representation of biological sequences for deep proteomics and genomics. PLoS ONE **10**(11), e0141287 (2015)
2. Bengio, S., Heigold, G.: Word embeddings for speech recognition. In: Fifteenth Annual Conference of the International Speech Communication Association (2014)
3. Boyd, J.H., Weissman, M.M., Thompson, W.D., Myers, J.K.: Screening for depression in a community sample: understanding the discrepancies between depression symptom and diagnostic scales. Arch. Gen. Psychiatry **39**(10), 1195–1200 (1982)
4. Cheng, P.G.F., et al.: Psychologist in a pocket: lexicon development and content validation of a mobile-based app for depression screening. JMIR mHealth uHealth **4**(3), e88 (2016)
5. Coppersmith, G., Dredze, M., Harman, C.: Quantifying mental health signals in Twitter. In: Proceedings of the Workshop on Computational Linguistics and Clinical Psychology: From Linguistic Signal to Clinical Reality, pp. 51–60 (2014)
6. Coppersmith, G., Dredze, M., Harman, C., Hollingshead, K.: From ADHD to SAD: analyzing the language of mental health on Twitter through self-reported diagnoses. In: Proceedings of the 2nd Workshop on Computational Linguistics and Clinical Psychology: From Linguistic Signal to Clinical Reality, pp. 1–10 (2015)
7. De Choudhury, M.: Role of social media in tackling challenges in mental health. In: Proceedings of the 2nd International Workshop on Socially-Aware Multimedia, pp. 49–52. ACM (2013)
8. De Choudhury, M., De, S.: Mental health discourse on reddit: self-disclosure, social support, and anonymity. In: Eighth International AAAI Conference on Weblogs and Social Media (2014)
9. De Choudhury, M., Gamon, M., Counts, S., Horvitz, E.: Predicting depression via social media. In: Seventh International AAAI Conference on Weblogs and Social Media, p. 2 (2013)
10. Dodds, P.S., Harris, K.D., Kloumann, I.M., Bliss, C.A., Danforth, C.M.: Temporal patterns of happiness and information in a global social network: hedonometrics and Twitter. PLoS ONE **6**(12), e26752 (2011)
11. Faruqui, M., Dodge, J., Jauhar, S.K., Dyer, C., Hovy, E., Smith, N.A.: Retrofitting word vectors to semantic lexicons. In: Proceedings of NAACL (2015)

12. Hutto, C.J., Gilbert, E.: VADER: a parsimonious rule-based model for sentiment analysis of social media text. In: Eighth International AAAI Conference on Weblogs and Social Media (2014)
13. Godin, F., Vandersmissen, B., De Neve, W., Van de Walle, R.: Multimedia lab @ ACL WNUT NER shared task: named entity recognition for Twitter microposts using distributed word representations. In: Proceedings of the Workshop on Noisy User-Generated Text, pp. 146–153 (2015)
14. Greenberg, P.E., Fournier, A.A., Sisitsky, T., Pike, C.T., Kessler, R.C.: The economic burden of adults with major depressive disorder in the United States (2005 and 2010). J. Clin. Psychiatry **76**(2), 155–162 (2015)
15. Gustavson, K., Knudsen, A.K., Nesvåg, R., Knudsen, G.P., Vollset, S.E., Reichborn-Kjennerud, T.: Prevalence and stability of mental disorders among young adults: findings from a longitudinal study. BMC Psychiatry **18**(1), 65 (2018)
16. Jamil, Z., Inkpen, D., Buddhitha, P., White, K.: Monitoring tweets for depression to detect at-risk users. In: Proceedings of the Fourth Workshop on Computational Linguistics and Clinical Psychology-From Linguistic Signal to Clinical Reality, pp. 32–40 (2017)
17. Kiritchenko, S., Zhu, X., Mohammad, S.M.: Sentiment analysis of short informal texts. J. Artif. Intell. Res. **50**, 723–762 (2014)
18. Kuppens, P., Sheeber, L.B., Yap, M.B., Whittle, S., Simmons, J.G., Allen, N.B.: Emotional inertia prospectively predicts the onset of depressive disorder in adolescence. Emotion **12**(2), 283 (2012)
19. Losada, D.E., Crestani, F.: A test collection for research on depression and language use. In: Fuhr, N., et al. (eds.) CLEF 2016. LNCS, vol. 9822, pp. 28–39. Springer, Cham (2016). https://doi.org/10.1007/978-3-319-44564-9_3
20. Mikolov, T., Chen, K., Corrado, G., Dean, J.: Efficient estimation of word representations in vector space. arXiv preprint arXiv:1301.3781 (2013)
21. Mikolov, T., Le, Q.V., Sutskever, I.: Exploiting similarities among languages for machine translation. arXiv preprint arXiv:1309.4168 (2013)
22. Milne, D.N., Pink, G., Hachey, B., Calvo, R.A.: CLPsych 2016 shared task: triaging content in online peer-support forums. In: Proceedings of the Third Workshop on Computational Linguistics and Clinical Psychology, pp. 118–127 (2016)
23. Mohammad, S.M., Turney, P.D.: NRC emotion lexicon. NRC Technical report (2013)
24. Moreno, M.A., et al.: Feeling bad on Facebook: depression disclosures by college students on a social networking site. Depress. Anxiety **28**(6), 447–455 (2011)
25. Neuman, Y., Cohen, Y., Assaf, D., Kedma, G.: Proactive screening for depression through metaphorical and automatic text analysis. Artif. Intell. Med. **56**(1), 19–25 (2012)
26. Nguyen, T., Phung, D., Dao, B., Venkatesh, S., Berk, M.: Affective and content analysis of online depression communities. IEEE Trans. Affect. Comput. **5**(3), 217–226 (2014)
27. Nielsen, F.Å.: A new ANEW: evaluation of a word list for sentiment analysis in microblogs. arXiv preprint arXiv:1103.2903 (2011)
28. Orabi, A.H., Buddhitha, P., Orabi, M.H., Inkpen, D.: Deep learning for depression detection of Twitter users. In: Proceedings of the Fifth Workshop on Computational Linguistics and Clinical Psychology: From Keyboard to Clinic, pp. 88–97 (2018)
29. Pennebaker, J., Mehl, M., Niederhoffer, K.: Psychological aspects of natural language use: our words, our selves. Annu. Rev. Psychol. **54**, 547–577 (2003)

30. Reece, A.G., Reagan, A.J., Lix, K.L., Dodds, P.S., Danforth, C.M., Langer, E.J.: Forecasting the onset and course of mental illness with Twitter data. Sci. Rep. **7**(1), 13006 (2017)
31. Resnik, P., Armstrong, W., Claudino, L., Nguyen, T., Nguyen, V.A., Boyd-Graber, J.: Beyond LDA: exploring supervised topic modeling for depression-related language in Twitter. In: Proceedings of the 2nd Workshop on Computational Linguistics and Clinical Psychology: From Linguistic Signal to Clinical Reality, pp. 99–107 (2015)
32. Resnik, P., Garron, A., Resnik, R.: Using topic modeling to improve prediction of neuroticism and depression. In: Proceedings of the 2013 Conference on Empirical Methods in Natural, pp. 1348–1353. Association for Computational Linguistics (2013)
33. Schwartz, H.A., et al.: Towards assessing changes in degree of depression through Facebook. In: Proceedings of the Workshop on Computational Linguistics and Clinical Psychology: From Linguistic Signal to Clinical Reality, pp. 118–125 (2014)
34. Shahraki, A.G., Zaïane, O.R.: Lexical and learning-based emotion mining from text. In: International Conference on Computational Linguistics and Intelligent Text Processing (CICLing) (2017)
35. Smith, S.L., Turban, D.H., Hamblin, S., Hammerla, N.Y.: Offline bilingual word vectors, orthogonal transformations and the inverted softmax. arXiv preprint arXiv:1702.03859 (2017)
36. Tang, D., Wei, F., Yang, N., Zhou, M., Liu, T., Qin, B.: Learning sentiment-specific word embedding for Twitter sentiment classification. In: Proceedings of the 52nd Annual Meeting of the Association for Computational Linguistics (Volume 1: Long Papers), vol. 1, pp. 1555–1565 (2014)
37. Tausczik, Y.R., Pennebaker, J.W.: The psychological meaning of words: LIWC and computerized text analysis methods. J. Lang. Soc. Psychol. **29**(1), 24–54 (2010)
38. Vioulès, M.J., Moulahi, B., Azé, J., Bringay, S.: Detection of suicide-related posts in Twitter data streams. IBM J. Res. Dev. **62**(1), 7:1–7:12 (2018)
39. Yates, A., Cohan, A., Goharian, N.: Depression and self-harm risk assessment in online forums. arXiv preprint arXiv:1709.01848 (2017)
40. Yu, L.C., Wang, J., Lai, K.R., Zhang, X.: Refining word embeddings using intensity scores for sentiment analysis. IEEE/ACM Trans. Audio Speech Lang. Process. (TASLP) **26**(3), 671–681 (2018)

Augmenting Physiological Time Series Data: A Case Study for Sleep Apnea Detection

Konstantinos Nikolaidis[1]([✉]), Stein Kristiansen[1], Vera Goebel[1],
Thomas Plagemann[1], Knut Liestøl[1], and Mohan Kankanhalli[2]

[1] Department of Informatics, University of Oslo,
Gaustadalleen 23B, 0316 Oslo, Norway
konstan@ifi.uio.no

[2] Department of Computer Science, National University of Singapore,
COM1, 13 Computing Drive, Singapore 117417, Singapore

Abstract. Supervised machine learning applications in the health domain often face the problem of insufficient training datasets. The quantity of labelled data is small due to privacy concerns and the cost of data acquisition and labelling by a medical expert. Furthermore, it is quite common that collected data are unbalanced and getting enough data to personalize models for individuals is very expensive or even infeasible. This paper addresses these problems by (1) designing a recurrent Generative Adversarial Network to generate realistic synthetic data and to augment the original dataset, (2) enabling the generation of balanced datasets based on a heavily unbalanced dataset, and (3) to control the data generation in such a way that the generated data resembles data from specific individuals. We apply these solutions for sleep apnea detection and study in the evaluation the performance of four well-known techniques, i.e., K-Nearest Neighbour, Random Forest, Multi-Layer Perceptron, and Support Vector Machine. All classifiers exhibit in the experiments a consistent increase in sensitivity and a kappa statistic increase by between $0.72 \cdot 10^{-2}$ and $18.2 \cdot 10^{-2}$.

Keywords: Augmentation · GAN · Time series data

1 Introduction

The development of deep learning has led in recent years to a wide range of machine learning (ML) applications targeting different aspects of health [24]. Together with the recent development of consumer electronics and physiological sensors this promises low cost solutions for health monitoring and disease detection for a very broad part of the population at any location and any time. The benefits of automatic disease detection and especially early prognosis and life style support to keep healthy are obvious and result in a healthier society and substantial reduction of health expenses. However, there are high demands on the reliability of any kind of health applications and the applied ML methods must be able to learn reliably and operate with high performance. To achieve this

© Springer Nature Switzerland AG 2020
U. Brefeld et al. (Eds.): ECML PKDD 2019, LNAI 11908, pp. 376–399, 2020.
https://doi.org/10.1007/978-3-030-46133-1_23

with supervised learning, appropriate (labelled) datasets gathered with the physiological sensors that shall be used in a health application are needed for training such that classifiers can learn to sufficiently generalize to new data. However, there are several challenges related to training datasets for health applications including data quantity, class imbalance, and personalization.

In many domains, the quantity of labelled data has increased substantially, like computer vision and natural language processing, but it remains an inherent problem in the health domain [24]. This is due to privacy concerns as well as the costs of data acquisition and data labelling. Medical experts are needed to label data and crowdsourcing is not an option. To enable medical experts to label data, data are typically acquired with two sensor sets. One set with the sensors that should be used in a health application and one sensor set that represents the gold standard for the given task. This problem is magnified by the fact that any new physiological sensor requires new data acquisition and labelling. Furthermore, there is a high probability that the data acquisition results in an unbalanced dataset. Since many health applications aim to detect events that indicate a health issue there should "ideally" be equally many time periods with and without these events. In general, this is unrealistic for a recording from an individual as well as across a larger population that is not selected with prior knowledge of their health issues. For example, in the recent A3 study [30] at the Oslo University Hospital individuals with atrial fibrillation were screened for sleep apnea. In a snapshot from this study with 328 individuals, 62 are classified as normal, 128 with mild apnea, 100 with moderate apnea, and 38 with severe apnea. The severeness of sleep apnea is captured by the Apnea Hypopnea Index (AHI) which measures the average number of apnea events per hour and is classified as follows: $AHI < 15$, (normal), $15 \leq AHI < 30$, (moderate), $AHI \geq 30$, (severe)[1]. It is unrealistic to expect that a sufficiently large dataset for training can be collected from each individual, because it is inconvenient, requires medical experts to label the data, and might be infeasible due to practical reasons for those that develop the application and classifier.

The objectives of this work are to address these problems with insufficient datasets in the health domain: (1) generate synthetic data from a distribution that approximates the true data distribution to enhance the original dataset; (2) use this approximate distribution to generate data in order to rebalance the original dataset; (3) examine the possibility to generate personalized data that correspond to specific individuals; and (4) investigate how these methods can lead to performance improvements for the classification task.

The mentioned problems are relevant for many applications in the health domain. As a proof-of-concept, we focus in our experimental work on the detection of obstructive sleep apnea (OSA). OSA is a condition that is characterized by frequent episodes of upper airway collapse during sleep, and is being recognized as a risk factor for several clinical consequences, including hypertension and cardiovascular disease. The detection and diagnosis is performed via polysomnography (PSG). PSG is a cumbersome, intrusive and expensive procedure with

---

[1] From a ML viewpoint only individuals with severe sleep apnea would produce balanced recordings.

very long waiting times. Traditionally, PSG is performed in a sleep laboratory. It requires the patient to stay overnight and record various physiological signals during sleep, such as the electrocardiogram, electroencephalogram, oxygen saturation, heart rate, and respiration from the abdomen, chest and nose. These signals are manually evaluated by a sleep technician to give a diagnosis. In our earlier work [18], we could show that ML can be used to classify PSG data with good performance, even if only a subset of the signals is used, and that the quality of collected data with commercial-of-the-shelf respiratory sensors approaches the quality of equipment used for clinical diagnosis [19].

In this work, we use different conditional recurrent GAN designs, and four well-known classification techniques, i.e., K-Nearest Neighbor (KNN), Random Forest (RF), Multi-Layer Perceptron (MLP), and Support Vector Machine (SVM) to achieve the aforementioned objectives. Since we want to use datasets that are publicly available and open access, we use the Apnea-ECG and MIT-BIH databases from Physionet [1,2] for our experiments. The reminder of this paper is organized as follows: Sect. 2 presents related works, and Sect. 3 our methods. In Sect. 4 we evaluate these methods through three experiments. Section 5 concludes this paper.

2   Related Work

Although the GAN framework [12] has recently acquired significant attention for its capability to generate realistic looking images [17,23], we are interested in time series generation. The GAN is not as widely used for time series generation as for images or videos, however, works which investigate this approach exist [22]. There are also relevant applications for sequential discrete data [31].

Most works are related to Objective 1 [6,10]. Hyland et al. [10] use a conditional recurrent GAN (based on [21]) to generate realistic looking intensive care unit data, preconditioned on class labels, which have continuous time series form. Among other experiments, they train a classifier to identify a held out set of real data and show the possibility of training exclusively on synthetic data for this task. They also introduce the opposite procedure (train with the real data and test on the synthetic) for distribution evaluation. We use similar methods to synthesize data in the context of OSA, but we expand these techniques by introducing a metric for evaluating the synthetic data quality which is based on their combination. We also investigate methods to give different importance to different recordings. Other works related to medical applications of GANs include [5,16]. Our work is associated with the use of multiple GANs in combination and uses different design and metrics from the above works (both works use designs based on combinations of an auto-encoder and a GAN). Many approaches that include multiple GANs exist such as [9,14].

We note that most of the related work with the exception of [5] focuses individually on the synthetic data generation and evaluation, and not how to use these data to augment the original dataset to potentially improve the generalization capability of other classifiers. To the best of our knowledge only few works [8,20,25] exist that examine the potential application of GANs to produce realistic synthetic data for class rebalancing of a training dataset. Only one of them uses specifically a recurrent GAN architecture. Finally, we did not find any relevant work that depicts the data distribution as a mixture of different recording distributions, with the end-goal of producing more personalized synthetic data.

3   Method

The goal of data augmentation in this work is to train classifiers to successfully detect in physiological time series data health events of interest. In our use case this means to classify every 30 or 60 s window of a sleep recording as apneic (i.e., an apnea event happened) or non-apneic.

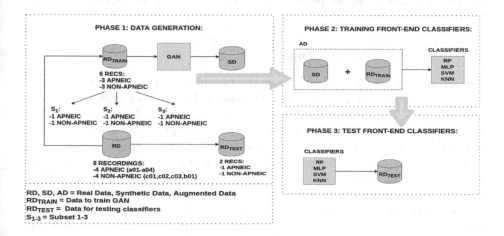

Fig. 1. GAN Augmentation

We use a conditional recurrent GAN to generate a synthetic dataset (SD, see Fig. 1) to augment the original training dataset (RD_{TRAIN}) (Objective 1) and to rebalance an unbalanced RD_{TRAIN} (Objective 2). Furthermore, we extend the single GAN architecture to a multiple GAN architecture to generate more synthetic data that is potentially closer to the test data to enable personalized training (Objective 3). In this section, we introduce the datasets we use, the two GAN architectures, and the metrics used to evaluate the quality of the generated data.

3.1   Data

We focus on the nasal airflow signal (NAF), because it can adequately be used to train a classifier to recognize apneas and yields the best single signal performance [18]. Furthermore, NAF is contained in most recordings (in 12 recordings[2]) in the

---

[2] slp01, slp02a, slp02b, slp03, slp04, slp14, slp16, slp32, slp37, slp48, slp59, slp66, slp67x.

MIT-BIH database. From the Apnea-ECG database we use eight sleep recordings (i.e., a01, a02, a03, a04, c01, c02, c03, b01) that contain the NAF signal with durations 7–10 h. From MIT-BIH we use the 12 recordings that include the NAF signal. Note that MIT-BIH has low data quality (noisy wave-forms, values out of bounds, etc.), especially when compared to Apnea-ECG.

The sampling frequency is 100 Hz for Apnea-ECG and 250 Hz for MIT-BIH and all recordings contain labels for every minute window of breathing for Apnea-ECG and for every 30 s window for MIT-BIH. These labels classify a window as apneic or non-apneic. For Apnea-ECG, there are four severe OSA, apneic recordings(a01–a04) and four normal, non-apneic recordings (c01–c03, b01). AHIs vary from 0 to 77.4. For MIT-BIH, AHIs vary from 0.7 to 100.8. The only pre-processing we perform is rescaling and downsampling of the data to 1 Hz.

3.2   Single GAN Architecture

In order to solve the problems of too small and unbalanced datasets we generate synthetic data and augment the original dataset. Due to its recent successes in generating realistic looking synthetic data, e.g., images and music, we use the GAN framework, in particular, a conditional recurrent GAN. The conditional aspect allows us to control the class of the generated data (apneic, non-apneic). Thus, data from both classes can be generated and the front-end classifiers are able to learn both apneic and non-apneic event types. The generative network G takes as input random sequence from a distribution $p_z(z)$ and returns a sequence that after training should resemble our real data. The discriminator D takes as input the real data with distribution $p_{Data}(x)$ and the synthetic data from G, and outputs the probability of the input being real data. Using cross-entropy error, we obtain the value function [12]:

$$\min_{G} \max_{D} V(D, G) = \mathbb{E}_{x \sim p_{Data}(x)}[\log D(x)] + \mathbb{E}_{z \sim p_Z(z)}[1 - \log D(G(z))] \quad (1)$$

G has the objective to minimize the probability that D correctly identifies the generated data as synthetic (second term of Eq. 1). D has the objective to maximize the probability to correctly classify data as either real or synthetic.

The objective of the generator is to fool the discriminator such that it classifies generated data as real. Through the training the generator learns to produce realistic looking synthetic data. Consequently, the generated data distribution converges to the real data distribution [12]. Inspired by [10], we use a conditional LSTM [15] as G and D, because we are interested in time series generation of sequentially correlated data. LSTMs are able to store information over extended time intervals and avoid the vanishing and exploding gradient issues [11]. G produces a synthetic sequence of values for the nasal airflow and D classifies each individual sample as real or fake based on the history of the sequence.

3.3 Multiple GAN Architecture

The aim for this approach is to ensure that the SD represents in a realistic manner all recordings in RD_{TRAIN}. Each person, depending on various environmental and personal factors has different breathing patterns, but individual characterization is possible.

Such an individualization is often described as bias towards a particular patient [11]. We, in contrast, make the hypothesis that different recording sessions have different data distributions, which together constitute the total apnea/non-apnea distribution of the dataset. In our case different recordings correspond to different individuals. A distinction is made between the recordings and the modes in their distribution since a recording can have more than one mode in its distribution, and different modes in the feature space can be common for different recordings.

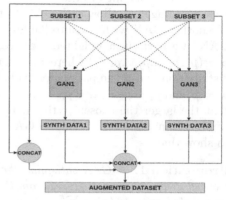

Fig. 2. Three GANs trained separately with a chance to interchange subsets

Since we have insufficient data per recording to successfully perform the experiments of this section, we define disjoint subsets of recordings (hereby called *subsets*), the union of which constitutes the original recording set. Under this hypothesis, the data distribution can be depicted as a mixture of the different recording distributions:

$$p_{Data}(x) = \sum_{i=0}^{k_{rec}} w_{r_i} p_{rec_i}(x) = \sum_{j=0}^{k_{sub}} w_{s_j} p_{sub_j}(x) \tag{2}$$

with:

$$p_{sub_j}(x) = \sum_{l \in sub_j} w_{sb_{lj}} p_{rec_l}(x) \tag{3}$$

where k_{rec} is the total number of recordings, k_{sub} is the total number of subsets, p_{rec_i} is the data distribution of recording i, and $w_{r_i} = 1/k_{rec}$ assuming equal contribution per recording, p_{sub_j} and w_{s_j} is the distribution and weights of subset j, and $w_{sb_{lj}}$ the weights of the recording within each subset.

We restate Eq. 1 to explicitly include the distributions of the subsets by dedicating a pair of G and D to each subset. This allows each GAN to prioritize the data from its respective subset, thus making it less probable to exhibit mode collapse for modes contained in the examined recordings. Each subset contains one apneic and one non-apneic recording (see Sect. 3.1, 4.4).

The goal of this method is to properly represent all recordings in the SD. The potential decrease of collapsing modes due to the use of multiple GANs for different data is an added benefit. There are relevant publications that use similar ensemble techniques to specifically address this issue backed by theoretical or methodological guarantees [14,29].

Since the amount of data per recording is too low to train GAN with only two recordings, we allow each GAN to train with data from the training subset of another GAN with a controllable probability (see Fig. 2). Per iteration, for GANj we perform a weighted dice toss such that $J = (1, 2..., j, ..., k_{sub})$, and $\mathbf{p} = (p_1, p_2, ...p_j, ...p_{k_{sub}})$ where J is a random variable following the multinomial distribution and $\mathbf{p}$ the parameter probability vector of the outcomes. For GANj $p_j = p$, and $p_1 = p_2 = ... = p_{i..} = p_{k_{sub}} = \frac{1-p}{k_{sub}-1} \forall i \neq j$ for a chosen value p. Note that the larger the chosen p, the more pronounced the modes of the recording combination that corresponds to GANi will be. It is relatively straightforward to show that:

Proposition 1. *A GAN satisfying the conditions of Proposition 2 of [12] and trained with a dataset produced from the above method will converge to the mixture distribution:* $p_s(\mathbf{x}) = \sum_i^{k_{sub}} w_i p_{sub_i}(\mathbf{x})$ *where* $w_i = P(J = j)$.

Based on this proposition, this method creates a variation of the original dataset, that gives different predefined importance to the different subsets (see Appendix G for details). The same proposition holds for individual recordings. The value function now for a GAN takes the following form:

$$\min_G \max_D V(D, G) = \mathbb{E}_{x \sim p_s(x)}[\log D(x)] + \mathbb{E}_{z \sim p_Z(z)}[1 - \log D(G(z))] \quad (4)$$

3.4   Metrics

Measuring the quality of data produced by a GAN is a difficult task, since the definition of "realistic" data is inherently vague. However, it is necessary, because the performance of the front-end classifiers is not necessarily a direct measurement of how realistic the synthetic data are. In this subsection we introduce the metrics we use to measure the quality of the synthetic data.

T metric: Hyland et al. [10] introduce two empirical evaluation metrics for data quality: TSTR (Train on Synthetic Test on Real) and TRTS (Train on Real Test on Synthetic). Empirical evaluation indicates that these metrics are useful in our case, however each one has disadvantages. To solve some of these issues we combine them via taking their harmonic mean (in the Appendix F we explain problems with these metrics and reasons to use the harmonic mean):

$$T = \frac{2 * TSTR * TRTS}{TSTR + TRTS} \quad (5)$$

MMD: We chose the Maximum Mean Discrepancy (MMD) [13] measurement since other well-established measurements (e.g., log likelihood) are either not well suited for GAN assessment, because plausible samples do not necessarily imply high log likelihood and vice versa [28], or they are focused on images, like the inception score [26]. There is also a wide variety of alternative approaches [3], however we use the MMD since it is simple to calculate, and is generally in line with our visual assessment of the quality of the generated data.

We follow the method from [27] to optimize the applied MMD via maximizing the ratio between the MMD estimator and the square root of the estimator of the asymptotic variance of the MMD estimator (the t-statistic). Inspired by [10], we further separate parts of the real and synthetic datasets to MMD training and MMD test sets (each contains half real and half synthetic data points). To maximize the estimator of the t-statistic for the training data we run gradient descent to the parameters of our kernel (i.e., Radial Basis Function (RBF) with variance σ as parameter). Then we test the MMD measurement on the MMD test set with the parameters that have been optimized with the training set. In the next section we evaluate the data based on these metrics.

4   Evaluation

To analyze how well we can achieve our objectives with the two GAN architectures, we design three experiments. Before we describe these experiments and their results, we analyze in Sect. 4.1 the quality of the synthetic data with the T-metric, MMD, and visual inspection. In Sects. 4.2–4.4 we present and analyze the experiments. Together with accuracy, specificity, and sensitivity, we use the kappa coefficient [7] as performance metric since it better captures the performance of two-class classification in a single metric than accuracy. For all experiments, the pre-processing of the data is minimal (Sect. 3.1) and we use a wide variety of relatively basic methods as front-end classifiers. This is because we want to focus on investigating the viability of GAN augmentation as a means of performance improvement for a general baseline case. However, the GAN augmentation is applicable to any type of data (e.g., pre-processed apnea data) and is independent of the front-end classifiers. For details about the GAN and the front-end classifiers parameters and design please refer to Appendix A.

4.1   Data Quality Evaluation

To measure the similarity between the synthetic and the real distribution we use the MMD and T-metric (see example in Fig. 3). We execute the tests every 10 epochs during training. Both scores improve as the training procedure progresses, until they stabilize (with minor variation). The T-metric is more unstable with epochs with high score in the initial training phase. However, after epoch 600, the performance of the metric stabilizes around 0.9. Similarly, the majority of MMD variations stop (with few exceptions) around epoch 400.

Another important criterion for recognizing whether the generated data are realistic is the visual inspection of the data. Although not as straightforward as for images, apnea and non-apnea data can be visually distinguished. In Figs. 4

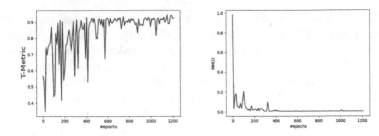

Fig. 3. Mean of T-metric (left) and MMD (right) scores throughout the GAN training

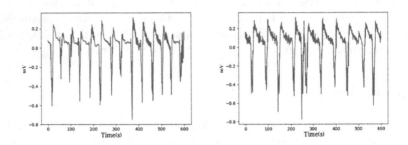

Fig. 4. Real apneic data (left) and good synthetic apneic data (right) for 600 s

and 5 we show examples of real and realistic-looking synthetic data. The generated data are realistic-looking and difficult to distinguish from the real data. For further evaluation of the visual quality and diversity of the real and generated data please refer to the Appendix H.

4.2 Experiment 1: Data Augmentation

In this experiment we investigate whether augmenting RD_{TRAIN} with realistic SD generated from a GAN trained with the same RD_{TRAIN} can have a positive impact on the front-end classifier performance.

Experiment Description: We iterate the experiment 15 times for Apnea-ECG and 10 times for MIT-BIH: We partition RD into RD_{TRAIN} (with 50% of RD data points), RD_{TEST} (25%) and a validation set (25%) via random subsampling. We train the GAN with RD_{TRAIN} . The GAN training is very unstable for the data of the two datasets (especially for MIT-BIH), and a good quality based on our metrics and visual inspection does not necessarily correspond to high performance of the front-end classifiers. For this reason, we use the validation dataset to evaluate the front-end classifier performance. We save the trained GAN model periodically throughout training, generate SD, augment RD_{TRAIN}, and measure the front-end classifier performance on the validation set. The GAN with the maximum validation set performance, and empirically acceptable MMD and T-metric values is chosen to generate SD. To obtain better performance for the MIT-BIH experiments with MLP and KNN, we concatenated data of many good performing models on the validation set, instead of only using the model with the best validation performance.

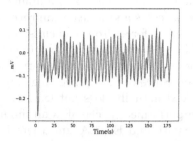 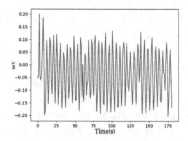

Fig. 5. Real (left) and good synthetic (right) non-apneic data, 175 s

Results: Due to limited space we present in the main text only the kappa statistic for all front-end classifiers (Table 1), and the accuracy, sensitivity, and specificity for the MLP classifier (Table 2) to indicate the general behaviour we observe for all the classifiers. For accuracy, specificity, and sensitivity for KNN, RF and MLP please refer to Appendix B. We use this presentation convention for all experiments (Appendixes C and D for Experiments 2 and 3 respectively).

Table 1. Kappa statistic and standard error for all front-end classifiers for Apnea-ECG and MIT-BIH. All kappa values are multiplied by 100 for legibility.

Kappa statistic ($X \cdot 10^{-2}$) for Apnea-ECG (A), and MIT-BIH (M)			
	MLP	RF	KNN	SVM
A: Baseline	85.89 ± 0.36	90.08 ± 0.26	88.12 ± 0.40	74.75 ± 0.40
A: Exp1:Synth	78.29 ± 0.97	83.88 ± 0.56	85.76 ± 0.49	75.04 ± 0.55
A: Exp1:Augm	86.93 ± 0.45	90.88 ± 0.28	90.12 ± 0.37	76.90 ± 0.57
M: Baseline	25.04 ± 0.88	30.95 ± 1.10	27.15 ± 1.01	0.0 ± 0.0
M: Exp1:Synth	18.35 ± 0.86	21.80 ± 0.95	16.84 ± 1.26	11.02 ± 0.96
M: Exp1:Augm	27.01 ± 0.61	33.01 ± 0.87	29.22 ± 1.01	14.93 ± 1.22

Baseline shows the performance of the front-end classifiers trained only with RD_{TRAIN}. For the synthetic case (*Exp1:Synth*) they are trained only with SD, and for the augmented case (*Exp1:Augm*) with RD_{TRAIN} and SD.

For Apnea-ECG, Exp1:Augm exhibits for all front-end classifiers a statistically significant improvement of the mean of the kappa statistic at $p = 0.05$. The p-value for the one-tailed two sample t-test relative to the Baseline is: p = 0.042 (MLP), p = 0.035 (RF), p = 0.005 (KNN), p = 0.002 (SVM). Notice that SD yields a good performance on its own, and even surpasses the performance of the Baseline for the SVM. We assume that this is due to the better balancing of the synthetic data in relation to the real. In SD, 50% of the generated minutes are apneic and 50% non-apneic, whereas in RD_{TRAIN} approximately 62.2% are non-apneic and 37.8% are apneic depending on the random subsampling.

For MIT-BIH, Expl:Augm shows in most cases a significant improvement of the kappa statistic values relative to the Baseline for all front-end classifiers when we perform the 2-sample one tailed t-test, i.e., p = 0.012 (MLP), p = 0.062 (RF), p = 0.029 (KNN), and p ≃ 0 (SVM). The overall performance is very low, due to the very low data quality for this dataset. Since our pre-processing is minimal this is to be expected. Notice that the SVM actually does not learn at all for the Baseline case. In all the iterations we performed, it classifies all minutes as non-apneic. Interestingly, both for Expl:Synth and Expl:Augm, there is a big improvement for the SVM, since the algorithm successfully learns to a certain extent in these cases. We assume that this is due to the better class balance (more apneas present in the datasets of Expl:Synth and Expl:Augm). Generally, for MIT-BIH the augmentation seems to have a beneficial effect on performance.

Table 2. Accuracy specificity and sensitivity for the MLP classifier

MLP Classifier Apnea-ECG (A), and MIT-BIH (M)			
	Acc.	Spec.	Sens.
A: Baseline	93.19 ± 0.17	94.78 ± 0.19	90.83 ± 0.39
A: Expl:Synth	89.26 ± 0.49	85.48 ± 1.14	95.02 ± 0.94
A: Expl:Augm	93.66 ± 0.20	94.62 ± 0.24	92.28 ± 0.46
M: Baseline	64.6 ± 0.37	75.95 ± 1.16	48.41 ± 1.26
M: Expl:Synth	59.76 ± 0.5	61.6 ± 2.58	57.17 ± 3.16
M: Expl:Augm	64.7 ± 0.25	69.92 ± 0.78	57.08 ± 1.22

From Table 2 we notice that for Expl:Augm, the MLP (both for MIT-BIH and Apnea-ECG) exhibits a clear improvement in sensitivity and a small drop in specificity. This pattern is present for all front-end classifiers. For Expl:Augm there is always a clear improvement in sensitivity, and either a small increase or decrease in specificity. This is an important advantage in a healthcare context since sensitivity reflects the ability of a classifier to recognize pathological events. This observation serves as a motivation for Experiment 2.

Implications for OSA Detection: The goal of this experiment is to reflect a real application scenario in which we have relatively equal amount of data from different patients to train with, and we perform classification for these patients. An example could be mobile OSA detection for patients after monitoring. It serves as an indication that augmentation with synthetic data can yield performance improvements for classifiers that are trained with the goal of OSA detection.

4.3   Experiment 2: Rebalancing Skewed Datasets

To analyze how well the single GAN architecture can be used to rebalance a skewed dataset, we need to create a skewed dataset because Apnea-ECG is nearly balanced with a ratio of 62.2% non-apneic and 37.8% apneic.

Experiment Description: We separate RD into RD_{TRAIN} and RD_{TEST} on a per-recording basis instead of a per event-basis as in the previous experiment. We randomly choose one apneic and one non-apneic recording as RD_{TEST} (i.e., a01 and b01 respectively), and as RD_{TRAIN} we use the remaining six recordings. We choose to evaluate this scenario using Apnea-ECG since it is the dataset for which our front-end classifiers exhibit the better performance.

Fig. 6. Training and Test sets for Experiment 2

To create an unbalanced dataset, one apneic recording (i.e., a04 chosen randomly) is removed from the training dataset RD_{TRAIN} (Fig. 6) resulting in 72.2% non-apneic and 27.8% apneic training data. The augmentation in this experiment rebalances the classes to 50% apneic and 50% non-apneic. This means that we only generate apneic data with the GAN (i.e., SD contains only apneic minutes) and combine them with the original dataset to form AD.

Table 3. Kappa statistic and standard error for all front-end classifiers.

Exp2: Kappa statistic (X $\cdot$ 10^{-2}) a01b01-unbalanced				
	MLP	RF	KNN	SVM
Baseline	88.44 ± 0.54	91.92 ± 0.26	93.16 ± 0.16	74.6 ± 0.2
Exp2:Augm	93.40 ± 0.63	94.56 ± 0.16	94.76 ± 0.45	92.88 ± 0.64

Note that a04 is removed from the training set both for the baseline/augmented training of the front-end classifiers and also for the training of the GAN, i.e., the apneic minute generation relies only on the other two apneic recordings. A validation set is extracted from a01 and b01. Throughout the training of the GAN the validation set is periodically evaluated by the front-end classifiers which are trained each time with AD. We choose the model that generates the SD with which the front-end classifiers perform the best on the validation set. For this experiment we perform five iterations.

Results: The results are shown in Tables 3 and 4. For Exp2:Augm we train the front-end classifiers with AD (i.e., apneic SD and RD_{TRAIN} without a04),

Table 4. Accuracy, specificity and sensitivity for MLP

Exp2: MLP a01b01-unbalanced Acc., Spec., Sens.			
	Acc.	Spec.	Sens.
Baseline	94.22 ± 0.27	99.44 ± 0.09	89.12 ± 0.44
Exp2:Augm	96.70 ± 0.31	98.82 ± 0.24	94.62 ± 0.51

and for the Baseline we train with RD_{TRAIN} without a04. In both cases we evaluate on RD_{TEST}. Compared to Baseline, a performance improvement occurs for Exp2:Augm. This can be noticed in terms of accuracy for the MLP (Table 4, first column) and in terms of kappa for all front-end classifiers (all columns of Table 3). The SVM seems to benefit the most from the rebalancing process. Again, in terms of specificity and sensitivity we notice a similar behaviour as in the previous experiment, i.e., increased sensitivity and stable specifity.

To further evaluate the potential of the proposed technique we compared the results with results when training with the Synthetic Minority Over-sampling Technique (SMOTE) [4]. For all classifiers the proposed method is marginally to significantly superior (i.e.,MLP: $88.7 \pm 0.25 \cdot 10^{-2}$, SVM: $90.9 \pm 0.41 \cdot 10^{-2}$, KNN: $94.54 \pm 0.36 \cdot 10^{-2}$, RF: $93.42 \pm 0.27 \cdot 10^{-2}$).

Implications for OSA Detection: OSA data are generally very unbalanced towards non-apneic events. This experiment implies that GAN augmentation with synthetic data can be used to efficiently rebalance OSA data. This has a positive effect on the detection of apneic events and on the overall classification performance for OSA detection, based on the classifiers we experimented with.

4.4   Experiment 3: Personalization with Multiple GANs

In this experiment, we analyze whether we can improve performance by indirect personalization during GAN training. By *Personalization* we mean that we aim to make the learned distribution of the GAN to approach the specific distribution of the RD_{TEST} for a given proximity metric (MMD). Since we do not use a01 and b01 for the training of the GAN the method we apply is indirect. We use a01 and b01 from Apnea-ECG as RD_{TEST}.

Experiment Description: Based on the discussion in Sect. 3.3, we separate our training recordings into three subsets (Fig. 7). Then we create three GANs (GAN 1, GAN 2, and GAN 3) and we use each subset to train the respective GAN, with a non-zero probability of choosing another subset for the gradient update based on a weighted dice toss (see Sect. 3.3). We set $p = 0.4$ (see Fig. 2), i.e., for one gradient update of GAN 1, the mini-batch is selected with probability 0.4 from Subset1, and probability 0.3 from Subset 2 and 3. We do the same for GAN 2 and 3. The choice of p is made via experimental evaluation.

Proposition 1 implies that through this training, a GAN converges to a mixture of distributions with weights for each subset distribution j equal to $P(J = j)$

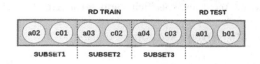

Fig. 7. Training and Test sets for Experiment 3

(see Eq. 4). By controlling $P(J = j)$ we control the weights of the mixture, and thus the degree to which each subset of recordings is represented in SD.

Table 5. Kappa statistic for front-end classifiers

Exp3: Kappa statistic ($X \cdot 10^{-2}$), a01b01 as RD_{TEST}				
	MLP	RF	KNN	SVM
Baseline	92.36 ± 0.37	92.88 ± 0.38	93.12 ± 0.21	88.20 ± 0.37
Exp3:Augm	93.08 ± 0.59	93.6 ± 0.62	94.50 ± 0.39	91.72 ± 0.94
Exp3:AugmP	93.36 ± 0.40	$94.36 \pm .31$	94.58 ± 0.17	93.92 ± 0.23

We use the validation set from a01 and b01 (obtained as in Experiment 2) for two purposes: (1) to evaluate the SD from the three GANs (SD 1, SD 2 and SD 3) and (2) to calculate the MMD between SD 1–3 and this validation set. We examine two cases: In Exp3:Augm, SD 1, SD 2, and SD 3 are combined with RD_{TRAIN} to form AD. SD 1, SD 2, and SD 3 combined have the same size as RD_{TRAIN}. In Exp3:AugmP, we identify the SD that has the lowest MMD in relation to the validation set, and use the corresponding GANi to generate more data until SDi has the size of RD_{TRAIN}. AD is formed by combining RD_{TRAIN} and SDi. In Exp3:AugmP, we perform indirect personalization, since the SDi selected originates from the GAN that best matches the distribution of RD_{TEST} based on the MMD metric. This occurs since the validation set is also extracted from a01 and b01. The experiment is repeated 5 times.

Results: The results are found in Tables 5 and 6. We see that the general behavior is similar to the previous experiments. Again there are improvements for the augmented cases in relation to the Baseline. There are improvements in sensitivity and a small drop in specificity for the MLP cases, which is the case also for the other classifiers (with the exception of RF).

Generally, Exp3:AugmP, exhibits slightly better performance both in terms of kappa and accuracy. SVM and RF seem to gain the most benefits from this approach. Interestingly, in Exp3:AugmP SVM surpasses MLP in terms of kappa.

To further investigate the viability of Exp3:AugmP method we examine in Appendix E different recording combinations as RD_{TEST} (i.e., a02c01, a04b01 and a03b01) and perform Baseline and Exp3:AugmP evaluations for the front-end classifiers. For all cases, for all front-end classifiers we notice improvements for the kappa statistic, that vary from (RF, a02c01):$0.28 \cdot 10^{-2}$ to (MLP, a03b01):

Table 6. Accuracy, specificity and sensitivity for MLP

Exp3: MLP a01b01 Acc., Spec., Sens.			
	Acc.	Spec.	Sens.
Baseline	96.18 ± 0.18	98.92 ± 0.07	93.54 ± 0.25
Exp3:Augm	96.54 ± 0.29	98.4 ± 0.19	94.74 ± 0.51
Exp3:AugmP	96.68 ± 0.20	98.64 ± 0.18	95.2 ± 0.25

$27.12 \cdot 10^{-2}$, especially for low performing cases, e.g., for the (MLP, a03b01) case Baseline kappa is $57.4 \cdot 10^{-2}$ and Exp3:AugmP kappa is $84.5 \cdot 10^{-2}$.

Implications for OSA Detection: This experiment implies that personalization can indeed have a positive impact on classification performance for the detection of OSA. Even the simple indirect approach of Exp3:AugmP exhibits performance advantages for all front-end classifiers in relation to when it is not applied in Exp3:Augm.

5   Conclusion

In this work we examined how dataset augmentation via the use of the GAN framework can improve the classification performance in three scenarios for OSA detection. We notice that for all the cases the augmentation clearly helps the classifiers to generalize better. Even for the simpler classifiers like KNN, we see that augmentation has a beneficial effect on performance. The largest performance improvement is achieved for the SVM for Experiment 2, and in all the cases the metric that increases the most is sensitivity. This leads us to believe that the class balancing that GAN can provide with synthetic data can be useful in situations for which one class is much less represented than others. This is even more pronounced in cases like OSA detection where the vast majority of the data belongs to one of two classes.

As a next step we plan to investigate the viability of creating synthetic datasets that are differentially private. As health data are in many cases withheld from public access, we want to investigate the performance of front-end classifiers when using synthetic datasets that have privacy guarantees and examine how this impacts the performance of the classifiers. Additionally, for the NAF signal, the Apnea-ECG dataset contains only severe apneic or non-apneic patients, and MIT-BIH is generally too noisy. Thus, we want as a next step to investigate different datasets that contain more patients with average AHIs so that the GAN can also map transitional OSA states that are realistic. This could potentially help a classifier to further capture apneic characteristics from a wider range.

Acknowledgement. This work was performed as part of the CESAR project (nr. 250239/O70) funded by The Research Council of Norway.

A   Classifier Parameters

Appendix A summarizes the parameters and details used for the front-end classifiers and GAN.

A.1   Front-End Classifier Parameters

We use SVM, KNN, MLP and RF as our front-end classifiers. The parameters we use are:

- MLP: We use a small feed-forward neural network with one hidden layer with 100 neurons, adam optimizer, relu activation, learning rate equal to 0.001, a batch size of 200, no regularization, and the other parameters set on the default values based on the implementation from https://scikit-learn.org/stable/.
- KNN: K-Nearest Neighbour with five neighbors, euclidean distance, weights based on the distance from the target and the other parameters set on the default values based on the implementation from https://scikit-learn.org/stable/.
- SVM: A Support Vector Machine with an Radial Basis Function kernel, penalty parameter of the error term equal to 1, and the other parameters set on the default values s based on the implementation from https://scikit-learn.org/stable/.
- RF: Random Forest comprised of 50 trees, Gini impurity as function to measure the quality of the split, and the other parameters set on the default values s based on the implementation from https://scikit-learn.org/stable/.

A.2   GAN LSTM

We use TensorFlow and implement two conditional LSTMs one as generator that takes input from a normal distribution with mean=0 and std=1 and outputs sequences of NAF data and a discriminator LSTM that takes as input real and synthetic NAF inputs and outputs $D(x)$ that estimates the chance that the input is real. The inputs, and thus the updates for both nets are per-sample and not per minute. As input for G and D we use an additional conditional vector that maps non-apneas as zero and apneas as one (again per sample). G gradient updates are performed via standard gradient descent with 0.01 learning rate and D via adam optimizer with learning rate 0.01. The mini-batch size is 50, the size (hidden units) of D and G is 300. All these values correspond to the most usual cases, but different configurations have been tested (Tables. 7, 8, 9, 10, 11, 12).

Table 7. Accuracy, specificity, and sensitivity for the RF classifier

RF Classifier Apnea-ECG

	Acc.	Spec.	Sens.
Baseline	95.18 ± 0.12	95.77 ± 0.23	94.32 ± 0.40
Exp1:Synth	92.19 ± 0.27	92.53 ± 0.75	92.46 ± 0.83
Exp1:Augm	95.52 ± 0.13	95.38 ± 0.22	95.74 ± 0.22

RF Classifier MIT-BIH

	Acc.	Spec.	Sens.
Baseline	68.57 ± 0.54	87.43 ± 0.51.9	41.57 ± 0.98
Exp1:Synth	61.97 ± 0.51	66.15 ± 1.65	55.8 ± 2.21
Exp1:Augm	68.02 ± 0.39	76.22 ± 1.61	56.91 ± 2.36

Table 8. Accuracy, specificity, and sensitivity for the KNN classifier

KNN Classifier Apnea-ECG

	Acc.	Spec.	Sens.
Baseline	94.34 ± 0.20	96.88 ± 0.20	90.94 ± 0.39
Exp1:Synth	93.07 ± 0.24	92.27 ± 0.62	94.2 ± 0.56
Exp1:Augm	95.20 ± 0.17	96.01 ± 0.31	94.04 ± 0.51

KNN Classifier MIT-BIH

	Acc.	Spec.	Sens.
Baseline	65.37 ± 0.52	74.43 ± 0.49	53.31 ± 1.22
Exp1:Synth	57.20 ± 0.69	50.78 ± 3.06	66.99 ± 3.82
Exp1:Augm	64.99 ± 0.51	65.26 ± 0.83	64.64 ± 1.24

B   Accuracy, Sensitivity, and Specificity of RF, KNN, and SVM for Exp1

Appendix B complements the results from Experiment 1 presented in the paper with the accuracy, specificity, and sensitivity of RF, KNN, and SVM.

C   Accuracy, Sensitivity, and Specificity of RF, KNN, and SVM for Exp2

Appendix C complements the results from Experiment 2 presented in the paper with accuracy, sensitivity, and specificity of RF, KNN, and SVM.

Table 9. Accuracy, specificity, and sensitivity for the SVM classifier

SVM Classifier Apnea-ECG			
	Acc.	Spec.	Sens.
Baseline	87.38 ± 0.21	81.94 ± 0.43	95.35 ± 0.25
Exp1:Synth	87.48 ± 0.27	80.78 ± 0.40	97.5 ± 0.45
Exp1:Augm	88.40 ± 0.29	82.13 ± 0.61	97.53 ± 0.61
SVM Classifier MIT-BIH			
	Acc.	Spec.	Sens.
Baseline	59.11 ± 0.56	100 ± 0.0	0.0 ± 0.00
Exp1:Synth	57.2 ± 0.69	50.78 ± 3.06	66.99 ± 3.82
Exp1:Augm	57.75 ± 0.63	57.80 ± 1.68	57.62 ± 2.07

Table 10. Accuracy, specificity, and sensitivity for the RF, KNN, and SVM classifiers

RF Classifier Apnea-ECG			
	Acc.	Spec.	Sens.
Baseline	95.96 ± 0.13	99.22 ± 0.11	92.78 ± 0.28
Exp2:Augm	97.28 ± 0.08	98.96 ± 0.20	95.62 ± 0.19
SVM Classifier Apnea-ECG			
	Acc.	Spec.	Sens.
Baseline	87.3 ± 0.11	99.12 ± 0.08	75.74 ± 0.37
Exp2:Augm	96.44 ± 0.32	98.6 ± 0.10	94.28 ± 0.75
KNN Classifier Apnea-ECG			
	Acc.	Spec.	Sens.
Baseline	96.58 ± 0.08	99.28 ± 0.08	92.8 ± 1.15
Exp2:Augm	97.38 ± 0.22	99.06 ± 0.08	95.82 ± 0.31

D Accuracy Sensitivity Specificity of RF,KNN,SVM for Exp3

Appendix D complements the results from Experiment 3 presented in the paper with accuracy, sensitivity, and specificity of RF, KNN, and SVM.

Table 11. Accuracy, specificity, and sensitivity for the RF, KNN and SVM classifiers

RF Classifier Apnea-ECG			
	Acc.	Spec.	Sens.
Baseline	96.44 ± 0.19	96.94 ± 0.33	95.98 ± 0.25
Exp3:Augm	96.8 ± 0.31	98.06 ± 0.51	95.54 ± 0.17
Exp3:AugmP	97.16 ± 0.15	98.98 ± 0.15	95.40 ± 0.17
SVM Classifier Apnea-ECG			
	Acc.	Spec.	Sens.
Baseline	94.12 ± 0.18	98.76 ± 0.06	89.64 ± 0.36
Exp3:Augm	95.86 ± 0.47	97.48 ± 0.73	94.34 ± 0.46
Exp3:AugmP	96.96 ± 0.11	98.40 ± 0.05	95.62 ± 0.21
KNN Classifier Apnea-ECG			
	Acc.	Spec.	Sens.
Baseline	96.56 ± 0.08	99.06 ± 0.08	94.10 ± 0.13
Exp3:Augm	97.29 ± 0.15	99.25 ± 0.16	95.43 ± 0.27
Exp3:AugmP	97.29 ± 0.08	99.11 ± 0.08	95.52 ± 0.13

E   Experiment 3: Results of additional recording combinations for RD_{TEST}

Appendix E supplements the results of Experiment 3 in the paper for kappa with the additional recording combinations a02c01, a03b01,a04b01 for RD_{TEST}.

It is worth to mention that these are all the combinations we examined. No additional combinations were examined.

Table 12. Kappa for different RD_{TEST} combinations a02c01, a03b01, a04b01

Kappa statistic $(X \times 10^{-2})$ combination: a02c01				
	MLP	RF	KNN	SVM
Baseline	80.68 ± 1.0	91.68 ± 0.39	80.83 ± 0.49	87.32 ± 0.50
Exp3:AugmP	86.26 ± 1.39	91.96 ± 0.28	81.72 ± 0.70	92.97 ± 0.35
Kappa statistic $(X \times 10^{-2})$ combination: a04b01				
	MLP	RF	KNN	SVM
Baseline	54.45 ± 0.68	56.46 ± 1.37	71.77 ± 1.08	81.35 ± 0.37
Exp3:AugmP	71.17 ± 3.04	83.19 ± 1.39	83.35 ± 0.49	92.51 ± 0.14
Kappa statistic $(X \times 10^{-2})$ combination: a03b01				
	MLP	RF	KNN	SVM
Baseline	57.41 ± 1.0	59.78 ± 0.79	41.41 ± 0.39	83.57 ± 0.49
Exp3:AugmP	84.57 ± 0.26	78.02 ± 1.9	50.41 ± 4.61	87.34 ± 0.73

F   Reasons for the Design of the T-Metric

Appendix F gives a detailed explanation for our choice of the T-metric. The fundamental observation is that the classifiers have to determine the underlying training set distribution. If the trained classifiers perform well on the test set, then the train and test distributions should be similar.

We follow the evaluation approaches presented in [1] called 'Train on Synthetic-Test on Real' (TSTR), and 'Train on Real-Test on Synthetic' (TRTS). The classifiers are trained on apnea classification with a synthetic dataset and tested on the real training data to perform the TSTR test, and the opposite procedure is performed for the TRTS test. As mentioned in [1], TSTR individually is a potentially better metric for similarity than TRTS, as it is sensitive to mode collapse. If a classifier is trained on synthetic data which have many collapsed modes, the performance on the real training data would be low. However, we argue that individually both metrics can be problematic for distribution comparison in certain cases, such as in binary classification. For example, if the synthetic distribution has a larger difference in variance between the classes, TSTR will not capture this, whereas TRTS will and vice versa. By including both measures in the metric this issue gets mostly solved, since the metric becomes sensitive to this variance. Figure 8 illustrates a concrete example in which the data points from the synthetic distribution are depicted with magenta and cyanic, and from the real with red and blue. In the TSTR test, the classifier learns the magenta separation hyperplane, and in the TRTS the blue separation hyperplane. Here TRTS captures better the dissimilarity between real and synthetic data. The opposite holds if the real and the synthetic distributions are swapped in the example.

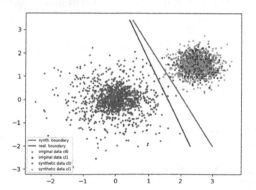

Fig. 8. Example of TSTR and TRTS issues (Color figure online)

The TRTS and TSTR metrics are combined via using the harmonic mean of the two measurements:

$$T = \frac{2 * TSTR * TRTS}{TSTR + TRTS} \tag{1}$$

The harmonic mean was chosen instead of other potential measures (e.g., average) for several reasons. First, the harmonic mean is more punishing to the differences of the scores (for example if TSTR is 0.5 and TRTS is 1, the average would be 0.75, whereas the harmonic mean would be 0.66) . In order to measure similarity, both scores should be high, so this is a desired property. Additionally, if mode collapse occurs, TRTS is expected to have a high performance whereas TSTR is significantly lower. An average would not be able to capture that problem well. Finally, it is worth noting that the T-metric is sensitive to the classifiers' capacity, and this is why all four classifiers are used for the test. Additionally, which metric is used for the TSTR and TRTS tests plays also an important role. We experiment with accuracy and AUROC. A potential problem of this method is that the separation hyperplane criterion could be insensitive to the spread towards unimportant directions for the classification in the feature space.

G   Proposition 1

Appendix G gives a detailed description of Proposition 1. Let X random variable (r.v) such that:

$$
X = \begin{cases} X_0 \sim P_{rec_0} & , if\, A_0 \\ X_1 \sim P_{rec_1} & , if\, A_1 \\ ... & \\ X_N \sim P_{rec_N} & , if\, A_N \end{cases} \tag{2}
$$

where:
A_i: The event that r.v $Z = i$ with $Z \sim$ categorical distribution with $P(A_i) = w_i$
Then:

Theorem 1. $X \sim P_s$ with PDF $p_s(\mathbf{x}) = \sum_i^N w_i p_{rec_i}(\mathbf{x})$ where p_{rec_i} the PDF of $P_{rec_i}, i = ...N$

We have $\forall$ subset S of the feature space D $(S \subseteq D)$, from the Bayes rule:

$$
P(X \in S) = \sum_i P(X \in S|A_i)P(A_i)
$$

$$
= \sum_i P(X_i \in S)P(A_i)
$$

$$
= \sum_i w_i \int_S p_{rec_i}(\mathbf{x})d\mathbf{x} = \int_S \sum_i w_i p_{rec_i}(\mathbf{x})d\mathbf{x} = \int_S p_s(\mathbf{x})d\mathbf{x}
$$

$\forall S \subseteq D$, from Eq. (1), and since A_i disjoint. So $X \sim P_s$.

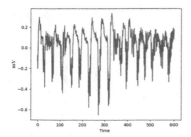 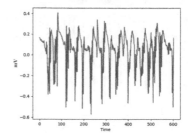

Fig. 9. Noisy real apneic data (left) and good noisy synthetic apneic data (right) for 600sec

We create a dataset $D_x = \{x^{(1)}, x^{(2)}, ..., x^{(m)}\}$, where all of the elements are independently sampled from $X \sim P_s$. From [11], we follow Algorithm (1) with D_x as the real dataset. Under the given conditions, the generator distributions p_g will converge to the real data distribution p_{data}. In our case $p_{data} = p_s$, so from Proposition 2 from [11], p_g converges to p_s. Note that we can control the probabilities w_i which gives us the ability to control the priority of specific recordings in the synthetic dataset.

H   Additional Images of Noisy Real and Synthetic Apneic NAF Data

Appendix H includes additional images of noisy real and synthetic apneic and non-apneic NAF data (Figs. 9, 10, 11, 12). They demonstrate the potential diversity of real apneic events as well as the capability of the proposed system to capture these modalities. Note that the different figures correspond to different runs of the system.

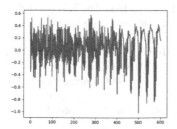 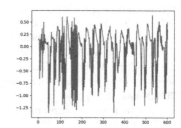

Fig. 10. Additional noisy real apneic data (left) and synthetic apneic data (right) for 600sec

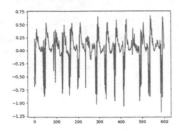 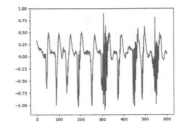

Fig. 11. Additional real apneic data (left) and synthetic apneic data (right) for 600sec

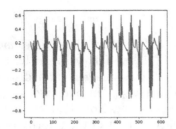 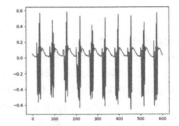

Fig. 12. Additional real apneic data (left) and synthetic apneic data (right) for 600sec. Note that in this case the model distribution potentially has experienced mode collapse.

References

1. https://physionet.org/physiobank/database/apnea-ecg/ (1999). Accessed 26 Mar 2019
2. https://physionet.org/physiobank/database/slpdb/ (1999). Accessed 26 Mar 2019
3. Borji, A.: Pros and cons of gan evaluation measures. Comput. Vis. Image Underst. **179**, 41–65 (2019)
4. Chawla, N.V., Bowyer, K.W., Hall, L.O., Kegelmeyer, W.P.: SMOTE: synthetic minority over-sampling technique. J. Artif. Intell. Res. **16**, 321–357 (2002)
5. Che, Z., Cheng, Y., Zhai, S., Sun, Z., Liu, Y.: Boosting deep learning risk prediction with generative adversarial networks for electronic health records. In: 2017 IEEE International Conference on Data Mining (ICDM), pp. 787–792. IEEE (2017)
6. Choi, E., Biswal, S., Malin, B., Duke, J., Stewart, W.F., Sun, J.: Generating multi-label discrete patient records using generative adversarial networks. arXiv preprint arXiv:1703.06490 (2017)
7. Cohen, J.: A coefficient of agreement for nominal scales. Educ. Psychol. Measur. **20**(1), 37–46 (1960)
8. Douzas, G., Bacao, F.: Effective data generation for imbalanced learning using conditional generative adversarial networks. Expert Syst. Appl. **91**, 464–471 (2018)
9. Durugkar, I., Gemp, I., Mahadevan, S.: Generative multi-adversarial networks. arXiv preprint arXiv:1611.01673 (2016)
10. Esteban, C., Hyland, S.L., Rätsch, G.: Real-valued (medical) time series generation with recurrent conditional gans. arXiv preprint arXiv:1706.02633 (2017)
11. Goodfellow, I., Bengio, Y., Courville, A.: Deep learning. MIT press, Cambridge (2016)

12. Goodfellow, I., et al.: Generative adversarial nets. In: Advances in neural information processing systems, pp. 2672–2680 (2014)
13. Gretton, A., Borgwardt, K., Rasch, M., Schölkopf, B., Smola, A.J.: A kernel method for the two-sample-problem. In: Advances in neural information processing systems, pp. 513–520 (2007)
14. Hoang, Q., Nguyen, T.D., Le, T., Phung, D.: Multi-generator generative adversarial nets. arXiv preprint arXiv:1708.02556 (2017)
15. Hochreiter, S., Schmidhuber, J.: Long short-term memory. Neural Comput. **9**(8), 1735–1780 (1997)
16. Hwang, U., Choi, S., Yoon, S.: Disease prediction from electronic health records using generative adversarial networks. arXiv preprint arXiv:1711.04126 (2017)
17. Isola, P., Zhu, J.Y., Zhou, T., Efros, A.A.: Image-to-image translation with conditional adversarial networks. In: Proceedings of the IEEE conference on computer vision and pattern recognition, pp. 1125–1134 (2017)
18. Kristiansen, S., Hugaas, M.S., Goebel, V., Plagemann, T., Nikolaidis, K., Liestøl, K.: Data mining for patient friendly apnea detection. IEEE Access **6**, 74598–74615 (2018)
19. Løberg, F., Goebel, V., Plagemann, T.: Quantifying the signal quality of low-cost respiratory effort sensors for sleep apnea monitoring. In: Proceedings of the 3rd International Workshop on Multimedia for Personal Health and Health Care, pp. 3–11. ACM (2018)
20. Mariani, G., Scheidegger, F., Istrate, R., Bekas, C., Malossi, C.: Bagan: Data augmentation with balancing gan. arXiv preprint arXiv:1803.09655 (2018)
21. Mirza, M., Osindero, S.: Conditional generative adversarial nets. arXiv preprint arXiv:1411.1784 (2014)
22. Mogren, O.: C-rnn-gan: Continuous recurrent neural networks with adversarial training. arXiv preprint arXiv:1611.09904 (2016)
23. Radford, A., Metz, L., Chintala, S.: Unsupervised representation learning with deep convolutional generative adversarial networks. arXiv preprint arXiv:1511.06434 (2015)
24. Ravì, D., et al.: Deep learning for health informatics. IEEE J. Biomed. Health Inf. **21**(1), 4–21 (2017)
25. Rezaei, M., Yang, H., Meinel, C.: Recurrent generative adversarial network for learning imbalanced medical image semantic segmentation. Multimedia Tools Appl. 1–20 (2019). https://doi.org/10.1007/s11042-019-7305-1
26. Salimans, T., Goodfellow, I., Zaremba, W., Cheung, V., Radford, A., Chen, X.: Improved techniques for training gans. In: Advances in neural information processing systems, pp. 2234–2242 (2016)
27. Sutherland, D.J., et al.:Generative models and model criticism via optimized maximum mean discrepancy. arXiv preprint arXiv:1611.04488 (2016)
28. Theis, L., Oord, A.v.d., Bethge, M.: A note on the evaluation of generative models. arXiv preprint arXiv:1511.01844 (2015)
29. Tolstikhin, I.O., Gelly, S., Bousquet, O., Simon-Gabriel, C.J., Schölkopf, B.: Adagan: Boosting generative models. In: Advances in Neural Information Processing Systems, pp. 5424–5433 (2017)
30. Traaen, G.M., Aakerøy, L., et al.: Treatment of sleep apnea in patients with paroxysmal atrial fibrillation: design and rationale of a randomized controlled trial. Scandinavian Cardiovascular J. **52**(6), 372–377 (2019)
31. Yu, L., Zhang, W., Wang, J., Yu, Y.: SeqGAN: Sequence generative adversarial nets with policy gradient. In: Thirty-First AAAI Conference on Artificial Intelligence (2017)

Wearable-Based Parkinson's Disease Severity Monitoring Using Deep Learning

Jann Goschenhofer[1,2](✉), Franz M. J. Pfister[1,2], Kamer Ali Yuksel[2], Bernd Bischl[1], Urban Fietzek[3,4], and Janek Thomas[1]

[1] Department of Statistics, Ludwig-Maximilians University, Munich, Germany
jann.goschenhofer@stat.uni-muenchen.de
[2] ConnectedLife GmbH, Munich, Germany
[3] Department of Neurology, Ludwig-Maximilians University, Munich, Germany
[4] Department of Neurology and Clinical Neurophysiology, Schoen Clinic Schwabing, Munich, Germany

Abstract. One major challenge in the medication of Parkinson's disease is that the severity of the disease, reflected in the patients' motor state, cannot be measured using accessible biomarkers. Therefore, we develop and examine a variety of statistical models to detect the motor state of such patients based on sensor data from a wearable device. We find that deep learning models consistently outperform a classical machine learning model applied on hand-crafted features in this time series classification task. Furthermore, our results suggest that treating this problem as a regression instead of an ordinal regression or a classification task is most appropriate. For consistent model evaluation and training, we adopt the leave-one-subject-out validation scheme to the training of deep learning models. We also employ a class-weighting scheme to successfully mitigate the problem of high multi-class imbalances in this domain. In addition, we propose a customized performance measure that reflects the requirements of the involved medical staff on the model. To solve the problem of limited availability of high quality training data, we propose a transfer learning technique which helps to improve model performance substantially. Our results suggest that deep learning techniques offer a high potential to autonomously detect motor states of patients with Parkinson's disease.

Keywords: Motor state detection · Sensor data · Time series classification · Deep learning · Personalized medicine · Transfer learning

1 Introduction

Parkinson's disease (PD) is one of the most common diseases of the elderly and the second most common neurodegenerative disease in general after Alzheimer's [38]. Two million Europeans are affected and 1% of the population over the age of 60 in industrial nations are estimated to suffer from PD [1,36]. Fortunately, the disease can be managed by applying the correct personalized dosage

© Springer Nature Switzerland AG 2020
U. Brefeld et al. (Eds.): ECML PKDD 2019, LNAI 11908, pp. 400–415, 2020.
https://doi.org/10.1007/978-3-030-46133-1_24

and schedule of medication, which has to be continuously adapted regarding the progress of this neurodegenerative disease. Crucial for the optimal medication is knowledge about the current latent motor state of the patients, which can not yet be measured effortlessly, autonomously and continuously. The motoric capabilities of the patients are distinguishable into three different motor states which can vary substantially over the course of a day within hours. The most prominent symptom is the tremor but the disease defining symptom is the loss of amplitude and slowness of movement, also referred as bradykinesia [35]. In contrast to bradykinesia, an overpresence of dopaminergic medication can make affected patients execute involuntary excessive movement patterns which may remind an untrained observer of a bizarre dance. This hyperkinetic motor state is termed dyskinesia [40]. In a very basic approximation, people with Parkinson's disease (PwP) can be in three motor states: (1) the bradykinetic state (OFF), (2) a state without appearant symptoms (ON), and (3) the dyskinetic state (DYS) [31]. If the true motor state of PwP was known at all times, the medication dose could be optimized in such a way, that the patient has an improved chance to spend the entirety of his waking day in the ON state. An example for such a closed-loop approach can be found in Diabetes therapy, where the blood sugar level serves as a biomarker for the disease severity. Patients suffering from Diabetes can continuously measure their blood sugar level and apply the individual, correct medication dose of insulin in order to balance the disease. Analogously, an inexpensive, autonomous and precise method to assess the motor state might allow for major improvements in personalized, individual medication of PwP.

Advancements in both wearable devices equipped with motion sensors and statistical modeling tools accelerated the scientific community in researching solutions for motor state detection of PwP since the early 2000s. In 1993, Ghika et al. did pioneering work in this field by proposing a first computer-based system for tremor measurement [14]. A comprehensive overview on the use of machine learning and wearable devices in a variety of PD related problems was recently provided by Ahlrichs et al. [1]. A variety of studies compare machine learning approaches applied on hand-crafted features with deep learning techniques where the latter show the strongest performance [9,20,24–27,38,40,41]. In the present setting, a leave-one-subject-out (LOSO) validation is necessary to yield unbiased performance estimates of the models [37]. Thus, it is surprising that only a subset of the reviewed literature deploys a valid LOSO validation scheme [9,24,25,40,41]. It is noteworthy that one work proposes modeling approaches with a continuous response [26], while the rest of the literature tackles this problem as a classification task to distinguish between the different motor states. Amongst the deep learning approaches, it is surprising that none of the related investigations describe their method to tune the optimal amount of training epochs for the model, which is not a trivial problem as discussed in Sect. 3.3. A strutured overview on the related literature is given in Table 1.

Contributions. This paper closes the main literature gaps in machine learning based monitoring of PD: the optimal problem setting for this task is discussed,

Table 1. Overview on results from the literature on Motor State detection for PwP. In the method column, the MLP refers to a Multi-layer Perceptron, FE to manual feature extraction, SVM to a Support Vector Machine, RF to a Random Forest and LSTM for Long-short-term-memory network. In the label column, the names of the class labels are depicted. From this column, one can infer that only two authors used continuous labels and thus regression models for their task. Generally, a comparison of the reviewed approaches is difficult due to high variation in the data sets, methods and evaluation criteria.

Author	Method	Validation	Subjects	Sensors	Position	Setting	Labels	Results
[25]	FE, SVM	LOSO	19	6	Arist, Ankle	Lab	ON, OFF	Acc.: 90.5%
[41]	CNN	LOSO	30	1	Wrist	Free	OFF, ON, DYS	Acc.: 63.1%
[38]	FE, SVM	Holdout Patients	20	1	Belt	Lab	ON, OFF	Acc.: 94.0%
[24]	LSTM	LOSO	12	1	Ankle	Free	ON, OFF	Acc.: 73.9%
	FE, SVM	LOSO	12	1	Ankle	Free	ON, OFF	Acc.: 65.7%
[9]	CNN	LOSO	10	2	Wrist	Lab	ON, OFF	Acc.: 90.9%
[19]	FE, MLP	Leave-one-day-out	34	2	Wrist	Free	OFF, ON, DYS, Sleep	F1: 55%
[20]	FE, MLP	7-fold CV	34	2	Wrist	Lab	OFF, ON, DYS, Sleep	F1: 76%
[27]	FE, MLP	Train set	23	6	Trunk, wrist, leg	Lab	ON, OFF	F1: 97%
[40]	FE, MLP	LOSO	29	6	Wrist, leg, chest, waist	Lab	DYS Y/N	Acc.: 84.3%
[26]	FE, MLP	80/20 Split	13	6	Trunk, wrist, leg	Free	Continuous	Acc.: 77%
[30]	FE, RF	LOSO	20	1	Wrist	Lab	ON, OFF	AUC: 0.73
	FE, RF	LOSO	20	1	Wrist	Lab	Tremor Y/N	AUC: 0.79
Our approach[a]	CNN	LOSO	28	1	Wrist	Free	Continuous	MAE: 0.77
	CNN	LOSO	28	1	Wrist	Free	9-class	±1 Acc.: 86.95%

[a] Performance measures are detailed in Sect. 5

a customized performance measure is introduced and a valid LOSO validation strategy is applied to compare time series classification (TSC) deep learning and classical machine learning approaches. Furthermore, the application of a transfer learning strategy in this domain is investigated.

This paper is structured as follows: The used data sets are described in Sect. 2. In Sect. 3, peculiarities of the problem as well as the transfer learning strategy are discussed. Furthermore, in Sect. 4 model architectures and problem settings are proposed and their results are discussed in Sect. 5.

2   Data

Data was collected from PwP to model the relation between raw movement sensor data and motor states. The acceleration and rotation of patient's wrists was measured via inertial measurement units (IMUs) integrated in the Microsoft band 2 fitness tracker [32] with a standard frequency of 62.5 Hz. The wrist was chosen as sensor location as it is the most comfortable location for a wearable device to be used in the patients' daily lifes and was shown to be sufficient for the detection of Parkinson-related symptoms [7,30]. The raw sensor data was downsampled to a frequency of 20 Hz as PD related patterns do not exceed this frequency [20]. A standard procedure in human activity recognition is the segmentation of continuous sensor data streams into smaller windows. As the data in this study was annotated by a medical doctor on a minute-level, the window length was set to one minute. To increase the amount of training data, the windows were segmented with an overlap of 80% which is in line with related literature [9,19,44]. To neutralize any direction-specific information, the L_2-norms of the accelerometer and gyroscope measurements are used as model input, leading to two time series per window. Finally, the data was normalized to a $[0,1]$ range via quantile transformation.

We consider the machine learning problem of the feature space $\mathcal{X} \subset \mathbb{R}^p$, with $p = 1200 \cdot 2$, a target space $\mathcal{Y}$ described below and a performance measure $\mathcal{P}$: $\mathcal{Y} \times f(\mathcal{X}) \to \mathbb{R}$ measuring the prediction quality of a model $f : \mathcal{X} \to \mathcal{Y}$, trained on the data set $\mathcal{D} = \{(x^{(1)}, y^{(1)}), ..., (x^{(n)}, y^{(n)})\}$ where a tuple $(x^{(i)}, y^{(i)}) \in \mathcal{X} \times \mathcal{Y}, i = 1, ..., n$ refers to a single labeled one minute window with a frequency of 20 Hz.

The disease severity $\mathcal{Y}$ is measured on a combined version of the UPDRS [16] and the mAIMS scale [29]. The UPDRS scale is based on a diagnostic questionnaire for physicians to rate the severity of the bradykinesia of PwP on a scale with 0 representing the ON state to 4, the severly bradykinetic state. The mAIMS scale is analogue to the UPDRS, but in contrast used for the clinical evaluation of dyskinetic symptoms. Both scales were combined and the UPDRS scale was flipped to cover the whole disease spectrum. The resulting label scale takes values in $\mathcal{Y} = \{-4, ..., 4\}$ where $y^{(i)} = -4$ means a patient is in a severely bradykinetic state, $y^{(i)} = 0$ is assigned to a patient in the ON state and $y^{(i)} = 4$ resembles a severely dyskinetic motor state. The sensor data was labeled by a medical doctor who shadowed the PwP during one day in a free living setting. Thus, the rater monitored each patient, equipped with an IMU, while they performed regular daily activities and the rater clinically evaluated the patients' motor state at each minute. In total, 9356 windows were extracted from the data of 28 PwP. By applying the above described preprocessing steps, the amount of windows was increased to 45944.

3   Challenges

3.1   Class Imbalance

The labeled data set suffers from high label imbalance towards the center of the scale as shown in Fig. 1. Thus, machine learning models will be biased towards predicting the majority classes [21].

A straightforward way of dealing with this problem is to reweight the loss contribution of different training data samples. This way, the algorithm incurs heavier loss for errors on samples from minority classes than for those of majority classes, putting more focus on the minority classes during training. The weights for the classes $j \in \mathcal{Y} = \{-4, ..., 4\}$ are calculated as follows:

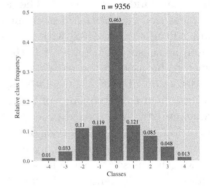

$$c_j = \frac{n}{n_j}; \quad \tilde{c}_j = |\mathcal{Y}| \cdot \frac{c_j}{\sum_{j \in \mathcal{Y}} c_j} \quad (1)$$

Fig. 1. Label distribution of the data which is highly centered around $y = 0$.

where $|\mathcal{Y}|$ describes the amount of classes, n is the total amount of samples, n_j the amount of samples for class j and thus c_j is the inverse relative frequency of class j in the data. Further, the weights $c_j, j \in \mathcal{Y}$ are normalized such that the sum of the weights is equal to the amount of classes. The individual weight of one sample is referred to as $\omega^{(i)}$ which is the normalized weight $\tilde{c}_j$ associated with the label $y^{(i)}$ of this sample i such that $y^{(i)} = j$.

3.2   Custom Performance Measure

It is crucial for the practical application of the final model to select an adequate performance measure which reflects the practical requirements on the model. Based on discussions with involved medical doctors, we found that larger errors should be penalized heavier which implies a quadratic error. Additionally, errors in the wrong direction of the scale, e.g. $\hat{y}^{(i)} = -1, y^{(i)} = 1$, should have a higher negative impact than errors with the same absolute distance in the correct direction, e.g. $\hat{y}^{(i)} = 3, y^{(i)} = 1$. The rationale behind this is that an exaggerated diagnostic evaluation which follows the true pathological scenario harms the patient less than an opposing one. Furthermore, the cost of predicting the wrong pathological direction increases with the severity of the disease: diagnostic errors weigh heavier on patients with strong symptoms compared to patients that are only mildly affected by the disease. In summary, three main requirements on the custom performance measure were identified: non-linearity, asymmetry and not being translation invariant.

Inspired by econometric forecasting [8], the following asymmetric performance measure, which satisfies the first two previous requirements, is introduced:

$$P_\alpha(\mathcal{D}, f) = \frac{1}{|\mathcal{D}|} \sum_{x^{(i)}, y^{(i)} \in \mathcal{D}} \left[\alpha + sign\left(y^{(i)} - f(x^{(i)})\right)\right]^2 \left(f(x^{(i)}) - y^{(i)}\right)^2 \quad (2)$$

where $\alpha \in [-1, 1]$ controls the asymmetry such that:

$$\alpha \begin{cases} \in [-1, 0[, & \text{penalization of underestimation,} \\ = 0, & \text{symmetric loss,} \\ \in]0, 1], & \text{penalization of overestimation.} \end{cases} \quad (3)$$

This performance measure is the squared error multiplied by a factor that depends on the parameter α and on the over- or underestimation of the true label via the *sign* function. As motivated in the third requirement, the asymmetry should depend on the true label values. Therefore, y is connected with α by introducing α^* such that $\alpha = \frac{y^{(i)}}{4}\alpha^*$ where $y^{(i)} \in \mathcal{Y} = \{-4, ..., 4\}$, hence $\alpha^* \in [0, 1]$. The constant denominator 4 is used to link α and α^* in such a way that the sign of α that governs the direction of the asymmetric penalization is controlled by the true labels y. This leads to the formalization:

$$P_{\alpha^*}(\mathcal{D}, \hat{f}) = \frac{1}{|\mathcal{D}|} \sum_{x^{(i)}, y^{(i)} \in \mathcal{D}} \left[\frac{y^{(i)}}{4}\alpha^* + sign\left(y^{(i)} - \hat{f}(x^{(i)})\right)\right]^2 \left(\hat{f}(x^{(i)}) - y^{(i)}\right)^2 \quad (4)$$

The parameter $\alpha^* = 0.25$ was set based on the feedback of the involved medical experts[1]. The model will be heavily penalized for the overestimation of negative labels and for the underestimation of positive labels. For instance, the performance measure for $y^{(i)} = 2$ and prediction $\hat{y}^{(i)} = 1$ is higher (1.265) than for $\hat{y}^{(i)} = 3$ (0.765). The asymmetry of the measure is reciprocally connected to the magnitude of the label y in both, the negative as well as the positive direction, e.g. for $y^{(i)} = 1$ it is more symmetric than for $y^{(i)} = 3$. Furthermore, P_{α^*} collapses to a regular quadratic error for $y^{(i)} = 0$. The behavior of the measure is further illustrated in Fig. 2.

3.3   Leave-One-Subject-Out Validation

Proposed models are expected to perform well on data from patients not seen before. Using regular cross validation (CV) strategies, subject-specific information could be exploited resulting in an overly optimistic estimate of the generalization performance [37]. Consequently, a leave-one-subject-out (LOSO) validation scheme is often applied in settings where much data are gathered from few

---

[1] Feedback was collected by comparing multiple cost matrices as shown in Fig. 3.

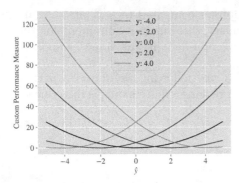

Fig. 2. Behavior of the performance measure $P_{\alpha^*=0.25}$ on the y-axis for different labels y and the corresponding predictions $\hat{y}$ on the x-axis.

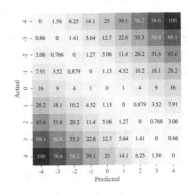

Fig. 3. Cost factors resulting from $P_{\alpha^*=0.25}$ that are associated with each combination of actual and predicted values.

subjects [2, 9, 12]. Thereby, a model is trained on all except one subject and then tested on the left out subject, yielding an unbiased performance estimate. This is repeated for each individual subject and all resulting estimates are averaged.

The usage of early stopping [17] requires the introduction of a tuning step to determine the optimal amount of training epochs e^* in each of the LOSO folds, which in turn requires a second inner split of the data set. In a setting with unlimited computational resources, one would run a proper LOSO validation in the inner folds, determine e^*, train the model on the whole data except the left out subject and evaluate the trained model on that subject. With a total amount of 28 patients, this would result in the training of $28 \cdot 27 = 756$ models for the validation of one specific architecture. As a cheaper solution, the first 80% one minute windows per patient are used for training and the last 20% for early stopping.

3.4 Transfer Learning

One of the most important requirements for the successful training of deep neural networks with strong generalization performance is the availability of a large amount of train data. Next to strong regularization and data set augmentation, one prominent method to fight overfitting and improve the model's generalization performance is transfer learning [43]. A model architecture is first trained on source task $\mathcal{D}_A$. The learned knowledge, manifested in the model's weights, is used to initialize a model that should be trained on the target task $\mathcal{D}_B$. The model is then fine-tuned on $\mathcal{D}_B$ which often leads to faster model convergence and, dependent on the similarity of the tasks, to an improvement in model performance. Though TSC is still an emerging topic in the deep learning community, first investigations into the adoption of transfer learning to time series data have been made [11].

As a source task for the motor state detection, we train the model to classify between one-minute windows that were either gathered from PwP or from healthy patients. Therefore, we use a weakly labeled data set that contains 70175 one-minute windows of sensor data along with the binary target if the corresponding patient suffers from Parkinson's disease or not. Among those patients, 50% were healthy and 50% suffered from PD. The proposed deep learning models were trained on this task and their weights were used for initialization of the models which were then fine-tuned on the actual data as described in Sect. 5.

4 Problem Setting and Models

4.1 Problem Setting

As explained in Sect. 2, the target was measured on a discrete scale $y \in \mathcal{Y} = \{-4, ..., 4\}$ where $y = -4$ represents severe bradykinesia, $y = 0$ the ON state and $y = 4$ severe dyskinesia. This gives rise to the question whether the problem should be modeled as a classification, an ordinal regression or a regression task. The majority of previous research in this domain treats the problem as binary sub-problems with the goal to just detect whether the PwP experience symptoms, regardless of their severity. The granular labeling scheme used here follows an ordinal structure. For instance, a patient with $y = -4$ suffers from more severe bradykinesia than one with $y = -3$. In contrast, simple multi-class classification treats all class labels as if they were unordered. A simple way of including this ordinal information is to treat the labels as if they were on a metric scale and apply standard regression methods. However, this implies a linear relationship between the levels of the labels. For example, a change in the motor state from $y = -4$ to $y = -3$, $\delta_{-4,-3}$, could have a different meaning than $\delta_{-2,-1}$, though they would be equivalent on a metric scale. The formally correct framing of such problems is ordinal regression which takes into account the ordered structure of the target but does not make the strong linearity assumption [18]. This model class is methodologically located at the intersection of classification and metric regression. All three problem settings are compared in Sect. 5.

4.2 Models

Random Forest. A Random Forest [3] was trained on manually extracted features from the raw sensor data, similar to related literature [9,20,24,38]. From each sample window of both signal norms, a total of 34 features such as mean, variance and energy were extracted (a complete list can be found in the digital Appendix). This is a standard procedure in TSC [4,6]. The Random Forest was specifically chosen as a machine learning baseline due to its low dependency on hyperparameter settings and its strong performance in general.

FCN. The Fully Convolutional Net (FCN) was introduced as a strong baseline deep learning architecture for TSC [42]. The implementation resembles that of Wang et al. except that the final layer consists of $|\mathcal{Y}| = 9$ or 1 neuron(s) for classification and regression, respectively.

FCN Inception. Inception modules led to substantial performance increases in computer vision and are motivated by the observation that the kernel size of the convolutional layers are often chosen rather arbitrarily by the deep learning practitioner [39]. The rationale is to give the model the opportunity to choose from different kernel sizes for each convolutional block and distribute the amount of propagated information amongst the different kernels. One inception module consists of branches with with kernel sizes $1, 5, 7$ and 13 respectively and a depth of 64 each, plus one additional max-pooling branch with a kernel size of 3, followed by a convolution block with depth 64 and a kernel size 1. The final FCN Inception architecture essentially follows the original FCN with simple convolutional layers being replaced by 1D inception modules.

FCN ResNet. Similar to the inception modules, the introduction of residual learning has met with great enthusiasm in the deep learning community [22]. The main advantage of such Residual Networks (ResNet) over regular CNNs is the usage of skip-connections between subsequent layers. These allow the information to flow around layers and skip them in case they do not contribute to the model performance, which makes it possible to train much deeper networks. Unlike inception modules, this model class was already adapted for TSC and proven to be a strong competitor for the original FCN [42]. The FCN ResNet was shown to outperform the standard FCN especially in multivariate TSC problems [10]. Others argue that the ResNet is prone to overfitting and thus found it to perform worse than the FCN [42]. For the comparison in Sect. 5, three residual modules are stacked where each of the modules is identical to the standard FCN in order to provide comparability among architectures. The module depths were chosen as proposed by Wang et al. [42].

FCN Broad. Pathologically, the disease severity changes rather slowly over time. Thus, it can be hypothesized that additional input information and a broader view on the data could be beneficial for the model. This model is referred to as FCN Broad and includes the following extension: the raw input data from the previous sample window x_{t-1} and the following sample window x_{t+1} are padded to the initial sample window x_t, which results in a channel depth of 6 for the input layer.

FCN Multioutput. A broad variety of techniques for ordered regression exist [5,13,23,33]. As a neural network based approach for ordered regression is required, a simple architecture is to create a single CNN, which is trained jointly on a variety of binary ranking-based sub-tasks [33]. A key element to allow the network to exploit the ordinal structure in the data is a rank-based transformation of labels. The categorical labels $y \in \mathcal{Y}$ are transformed into $K = |\mathcal{Y}| - 1$ rank-based labels by:

$$y_k^{(i)} = \begin{cases} 1, & \text{if } y^{(i)} > r_k \\ 0, & \text{otherwise,} \end{cases} \tag{5}$$

where r_k is the rank for the k-th sub-problem for $k \in \{1, ..., K\}$. Following this label transformation, a multi-output CNN architecture is proposed where each of the K outputs refers to one binary ranking-based sub-task. These are optimized jointly on a single CNN corpus. Thus, the sub-task k is trained on a binary classification problem minimizing the binary cross entropy loss. The total model output consists of K probability outputs for each input sample. In order to train the CNN jointly on those sub-tasks, the individual losses are combined to one cumulative loss:

$$L^{\text{ranks}}(y^{(i)}, f(x^{(i)})) = \sum_{k=1}^{K} L_k^b(y_k^{(i)}, \hat{y}_k^{(i)}) \tag{6}$$

where L_k^b is the binary cross-entropy loss for sub-task output $\hat{y}_k^{(i)}$. For inference, the K outputs are summed up such that $\hat{y}^{(i)} = \sum_{k=1}^{K} \hat{y}_k^{(i)} - 4$, where the scalar 4 is subtracted from the sum over all probability outputs to map the predictions back to the initial label scale, yielding a continuous output.

FCN Ordinal. A second ordinal regression model was created by training a regular FCN with an additional distance-based weighting factor in the multi-class cross entropy loss L^m:

$$L^{\text{ordinal}}(y^{(i)}, f(x^{(i)})) = \left| y^{(i)} - \hat{y}^{(i)} \right| \cdot L^m(y^{(i)}, \hat{y}^{(i)}) \tag{7}$$

This way, the model is forced to learn the inherent ordinal structure of the data as it is penalized higher for predictions that are very distant to the true labels.

5   Results

The models described in Sect. 4 were implemented in pytorch [34]. Model weights were initialized by Xavier-uniform initialization [15] and ADAM [28] (learning rate $= 0.00005$, $\beta_1 = 0.9$, $\beta_2 = 0.99$) was used for training with a weight decay of 10^{-6}. The performances of the models were compared in a LOSO evaluation as discussed in Sect. 3.3, using the performance measure $P_{\alpha^*=0.25}$ as introduced in Sect. 3.2. Finally, the sequence of motor state predictions is smoothed via a Gaussian filter whose μ and σ parameters were optimized using the same LOSO scheme that was used for model training. The results are summarized in Table 2. An additional majority voting model which constantly predicts $\hat{y} = 0$ is added as a naive baseline.

The FCN was applied in all three problem settings. From Table 2, one can observe that regression performs better than ordered regression and classification. Similar results were obtained for the Random Forest baseline, where regression is superior to classification. It seems that the simple assumption of linearity

Table 2. Results for different models in multiple problem settings, measured using the performance measure introduced in Sect. 3.2 evaluated by LOSO validation. Additional commonly used performance measures are shown for completeness where the MAE is reported in a class-weighted (MAE w.) and a regular version and Acc. ±1 refers to accuracy relaxed by one class level.

Frame	Model	$P_{\alpha^*} = 0.25$	F1	Acc.	Acc. ±1	MAE w.	MAE
Baseline	Majority vote	2.900	0.293	0.702	0.463	0.661	0.960
Classification	FCN	0.800	0.366	0.809	0.340	0.312	0.890
	Random Forest	1.542	0.394	0.802	0.459	0.465	0.802
Ordinal	FCN	0.752	0.321	0.767	0.302	0.311	0.985
	Multioutput FCN	0.922	0.361	0.820	0.352	0.344	0.873
Regression	FCN	**0.635**	0.346	0.843	0.338	0.293	0.836
	FCN Inception	0.726	0.380	0.841	0.370	0.304	0.842
	FCN ResNet	0.841	0.334	0.809	0.309	0.336	0.924
	FCN Broad	0.673	0.347	0.835	0.339	0.294	0.852
	Random Forest	1.310	0.411	0.848	0.436	0.423	0.760

between labels does not have a derogatory effect and a simpler model architecture as well as training process is of larger importance.

The comparison of the deep learning models with the Random Forest offers another interesting finding. For both, regression and classification, all deep learning models outperform the classic machine learning models. This finding justifies the focus on deep learning approaches and is in line with previous research discussed in the Introduction.

Niu et al. [33] claim that the Multioutput CNN architecture outperforms regular regression models in ordinal regression tasks. This can not be supported by the current results as the Multioutput FCN shows weaker performance than each of the deep learning architectures in the regression frame.

Looking at the results from the regression setting, one can observe that the simple FCN manages to outperform all more complex architectures as well as the Random Forest baseline. This could be explained by the increased complexity of these models: the FCN consists of $283,145$ weights, while the FCN Inception contains $514,809$ and the FCN ResNet $512,385$ weights. This problem is aggravated by the limited amount of training data.

As shown in Table 3, the transfer learning approach consistently improved the performance of all tested FCN architectures. This strategy also helped to further push the best achieved performance by the regression FCN, making it the overall best performing model. Transfer learning has the biggest effect on the performance of the Multioutput FCN, which indicates that this model requires a higher amount of training data. This is reasonable as it is arguably the most complex model considered. Further increasing the amount of training data might improve these complex models even more.

Table 3. Performance of the transfer learning approaches compared to their non-pretrained counterparts. Transfer learning consistently improves model performances. Additional commonly used measures are shown for the pretrained models only where the MAE is reported in a class-weighted (MAE w.) and a regular version and ±1 Acc. refers to accuracy relaxed by one class level.

Frame	Model	$P_{\alpha^*=0.25}$		Gain	F1	Acc.	Acc. ±1	MAE w.	MAE
		Regular	Transfer						
Classification	FCN	0.800	0.771	0.029	0.375	0.361	0.813	0.318	0.897
Ordinal	FCN	0.752	0.616	0.136	0.350	0.326	0.802	0.295	0.921
	Multioutput FCN	0.922	0.657	0.265	0.367	0.360	0.829	0.301	0.857
Regression	FCN	0.635	**0.600**	0.035	0.407	0.388	0.870	0.273	0.772

Some resulting predictions[2] from the best performing model are illustrated in Fig. 5 and a confusion matrix of the model predictions is shown in Fig. 4. It is noteworthy that despite the class weighting scheme and the transfer learning efforts, the final model fails in correctly predicting the most extreme class labels.

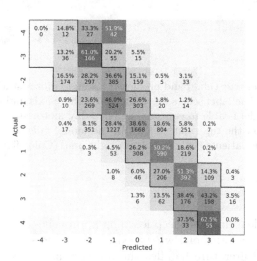

Fig. 4. Row-normalized confusion matrix for predictions from the pretrained regression FCN. Predicted continuous scores were rounded to integers. Allowing for deviations of ±1 (framed diagonal region) yields a relaxed accuracy of 86.96%.

---

[2] Results on all patients can be found here: https://doi.org/10.6084/m9.figshare. 8313149.v1.

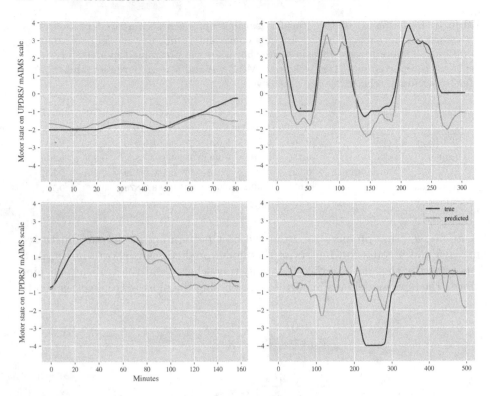

Fig. 5. Comparison of true (blue) and predicted (orange) motor state sequences of four exemplary patients. The label scores are depicted on the y-axis and the minutes on the x-axis. The final model is able to capture the intra-day motor state regime changes of the PwP as shown on the top right plot. Still, the model fails to correctly detect the motor states in some patients e.g. the bottom right one. (Color figure online)

6   Conclusion

Different machine learning and deep learning approaches were evaluated on the task to detect motor states of PwP based on wearable sensor data. While the majority of related literature handles the problem as a classification task, the high quality and resolution of the provided data allows evaluation in different problem settings. Framing the problem as a regression task was shown to result in better performance than ordered regression and classification. Evaluation was done using a leave-one-patient-out validation strategy on 28 PwP using a customized performance measure, developed in cooperation with medical experts in the PD domain. The deep learning approaches outperformed the classic machine learning approach. Furthermore, the comparatively simple FCN offered the most promising results. A possible explanation would be that these intricate models call for more available data for successful training. Since high quality labeled data are scarce and costly in the medical domain, this is not easily achievable.

First investigations into transfer learning approaches were successfully employed and showed model improvements for the deep learning approaches.

There exists a plethora of future work to investigate. Computational limitations made it impossible to evaluate all possible models in all problem settings as well as investigate recurrent neural network approaches. The successful usage of a weakly labeled data set for transfer learning suggests further research on the application of semi-supervised learning strategies. This work clearly shows the difficulty in fairly and accurately comparing existing approaches, as available data, problem setting and evaluation criteria differ widely between publications. The introduced performance measure could be a step into the right direction and can hopefully become a reasonable standard for the comparison of such models. In future work, one could directly use this performance measure as a loss function to train deep neural networks instead of using it for evaluation only.

Acknowledgements. This work was financially supported by ConnectedLife GmbH and we thank the Schoen Klinik Muenchen Schwabing for the invaluable access to medical expert knowledge and the collection of the data set. This work has been partially supported by the German Federal Ministry of Education and Research (BMBF) under Grant No. 01IS18036A, and by an unrestricted grant from the Deutsche Parkinson Vereinigung (DPV) and the Deutsche Stiftung Neurologie.

References

1. Ahlrichs, C., Lawo, M.: Parkinson's disease motor symptoms in machine learning: a review. Health Informatics **2**, (2013)
2. Bao, L., Intille, S.S.: Activity recognition from user-annotated acceleration data. In: Ferscha, A., Mattern, F. (eds.) Pervasive 2004. LNCS, vol. 3001, pp. 1–17. Springer, Heidelberg (2004). https://doi.org/10.1007/978-3-540-24646-6_1
3. Breiman, L.: Random forests. Mach. Learn. **45**(1), 5–32 (2001)
4. Casale, P., Pujol, O., Radeva, P.: Human activity recognition from accelerometer data using a wearable device. In: Vitrià, J., Sanches, J.M., Hernández, M. (eds.) IbPRIA 2011. LNCS, vol. 6669, pp. 289–296. Springer, Heidelberg (2011). https://doi.org/10.1007/978-3-642-21257-4_36
5. Chen, S., Zhang, C., Dong, M., Le, J., Rao, M.: Using ranking-CNN for age estimation. In: The IEEE Conference on Computer Vision and Pattern Recognition (2017)
6. Christ, M., Kempa-Liehr, A.W., Feindt, M.: Distributed and parallel time series feature extraction for industrial big data applications. arXiv preprint arXiv:1610.07717 (2016)
7. Curtze, C., Nutt, J.G., Carlson-Kuhta, P., Mancini, M., Horak, F.B.: Levodopa is a double edged sword for balance and gait in people with parkinson's disease. Mov. Disord. **30**(10), 1361–1370 (2015)
8. Elliott, G., Timmermann, A., Komunjer, I.: Estimation and testing of forecast rationality under flexible loss. Rev. Econ. Stud. **72**(4), 1107–1125 (2005)
9. Eskofier, B.M., et al.: Recent machine learning advancements in sensor-based mobility analysis: deep learning for parkinson's disease assessment. In: Engineering in Medicine and Biology Society, pp. 655–658 (2016)

10. Fawaz, H.I., Forestier, G., Weber, J., Idoumghar, L., Muller, P.A.: Deep learning for time series classification: a review. arXiv preprint arXiv:1809.04356 (2018)
11. Fawaz, H.I., Forestier, G., Weber, J., Idoumghar, L., Muller, P.A.: Transfer learning for time series classification. arXiv preprint arXiv:1811.01533 (2018)
12. Fisher, J.M., Hammerla, N.Y., Ploetz, T., Andras, P., Rochester, L., Walker, R.W.: Unsupervised home monitoring of parkinson's disease motor symptoms using body-worn accelerometers. Parkinsonism Relat. Disord. **33**, 44–50 (2016)
13. Frank, E., Hall, M.: A simple approach to ordinal classification. In: De Raedt, L., Flach, P. (eds.) ECML 2001. LNCS (LNAI), vol. 2167, pp. 145–156. Springer, Heidelberg (2001). https://doi.org/10.1007/3-540-44795-4_13
14. Ghika, J., Wiegner, A.W., Fang, J.J., Davies, L., Young, R.R., Growdon, J.H.: Portable system for quantifying motor abnormalities in parkinson's disease. IEEE Trans. Biomed. Eng. **40**(3), 276–283 (1993)
15. Glorot, X., Bengio, Y.: Understanding the difficulty of training deep feedforward neural networks, pp. 249–256 (2010)
16. Goetz, C.G., et al.: Movement disorder society-sponsored revision of the unified parkinson's disease rating scale (mds-updrs): scale presentation and clinimetric testing results. Mov. Disord. **23**(15), 2129–2170 (2008)
17. Goodfellow, I., Bengio, Y., Courville, A.: Deep learning (2016). http://www.deeplearningbook.org, book in preparation for MIT Press
18. Gutierrez, P.A., Perez-Ortiz, M., Sanchez-Monedero, J., Fernandez-Navarro, F., Hervas-Martinez, C.: Ordinal regression methods: survey and experimental study. IEEE Trans. Knowl. Data Eng. **28**(1), 127–146 (2016)
19. Hammerla, N.Y., Halloran, S., Ploetz, T.: Deep, convolutional, and recurrent models for human activity recognition using wearables. In: Proceedings of the Twenty-Fifth International Joint Conference on Artificial Intelligence (2016)
20. Hammerla, N.Y., Fisher, J., Andras, P., Rochester, L., Walker, R., Plötz, T.: PD disease state assessment in naturalistic environments using deep learning, pp. 1742–1748 (2015)
21. He, H., Garcia, E.A.: Learning from imbalanced data. IEEE Trans. Knowl. Data Eng. **9**, 1263–1284 (2009)
22. He, K., Zhang, X., Ren, S., Sun, J.: Deep residual learning for image recognition. In: Proceedings of the IEEE Conference on Computer Vision and Pattern Recognition (2015)
23. Herbrich, R., Graepel, T., Obermayer, K.: Support vector learning for ordinal regression. In: International Conference on Artificial Neural Networks (1999)
24. Hssayeni, M.D., Burack, M.A., Ghoraani, B.: Automatic assessment of medication states of patients with parkinson's disease using wearable sensors, pp. 6082–6085 (2016)
25. Hssayeni, M.D., Burack, M.A., Jimenez-Shahed, J., Ghoraani, B., et al.: Wearable-based medication state detection in individuals with parkinson's disease. arXiv preprint arXiv:1809.06973 (2018)
26. Keijsers, N.L., Horstink, M.W., Gielen, S.C.: Automatic assessment of levodopa-induced dyskinesias in daily life by neural networks. Mov. Disord. **18**, 70–80 (2003)
27. Keijsers, N.L., Horstink, M.W., Gielen, S.C.: Ambulatory motor assessment in parkinson's disease. Mov. Disord. **21**, 34–44 (2006)
28. Kingma, D.P., Ba, J.: Adam: A method for stochastic optimization (2014). http://arxiv.org/abs/1412.6980
29. Lane, R.D., Glazer, W.M., Hansen, T.E., Berman, W.H., Kramer, S.I.: Assessment of tardive dyskinesia using the abnormal involuntary movement scale. J. Nerv. Ment. Dis. **173**, 353–357 (1985)

30. Lonini, L., et al.: Wearable sensors for parkinson's disease: which data are worth collecting for training symptom detection models. NPJ Digit. Med. **1**, 1–8 (2018)
31. Marsden, C.D., Parkes, J.: "On-off" effects in patients with parkinson's disease on chronic levodopa therapy. Lancet **307**(7954), 292–296 (1976)
32. Microsoft: Microsoft band 2 wearable device (2018). https://www.microsoft.com/en-us/band
33. Niu, Z., Zhou, M., Wang, L., Gao, X., Hua, G.: Ordinal regression with multiple output cnn for age estimation. In: Proceedings of the IEEE Conference on Computer Vision and Pattern Recognition, pp. 4920–4928 (2016)
34. Paszke, A., et al.: Automatic differentiation in pytorch (2017)
35. Postuma, R.B., et al.: MDS clinical diagnostic criteria for parkinson's disease. Mov. Disord. **30**(12), 1591–1601 (2015)
36. Pringsheim, T., Jette, N., Frolkis, A., Steeves, T.D.: The prevalence of parkinson's disease: a systematic review and meta-analysis. Mov. Disord. **29**(13), 1583–1590 (2014)
37. Saeb, S., Lonini, L., Jayaraman, A., Mohr, D.C., Kording, K.P.: The need to approximate the use-case in clinical machine learning. Gigascience **6**(5), 1–9 (2017)
38. Sama, A., et al.: Dyskinesia and motor state detection in parkinson's disease patients with a single movement sensor. In: Annual International Conference of the IEEE Engineering in Medicine and Biology Society, pp. 1194–1197 (2012)
39. Szegedy, C., et al.: Going deeper with convolutions. In: Conference on Computer Vision and Pattern Recognition, pp. 1–9 (2015)
40. Tsipouras, M.G., Tzallas, A.T., Fotiadis, D.I., Konitsiotis, S.: On automated assessment of levodopa-induced dyskinesia in parkinson's disease. In: Engineering in Medicine and Biology Society, pp. 2679–2682 (2011)
41. Um, T.T., et al.: Parkinson's disease assessment from a wrist-worn wearable sensor in free-living conditions: deep ensemble learning and visualization. arXiv preprint arXiv:1808.02870 (2018)
42. Wang, Z., Yan, W., Oates, T.: Time series classification from scratch with deep neural networks: a strong baseline. In: International Joint Conference on Neural Networks, pp. 1578–1585 (2017)
43. Yosinski, J., Clune, J., Bengio, Y., Lipson, H.: How transferable are features in deep neural networks? In: Advances in Neural Information Processing Systems, pp. 3320–3328 (2014)
44. Zeng, M., et al.: Convolutional neural networks for human activity recognition using mobile sensors. In: 2014 6th International Conference on Mobile Computing, Applications and Services (MobiCASE), pp. 197–205 (2014)

Investigating Time Series Classification Techniques for Rapid Pathogen Identification with Single-Cell MALDI-TOF Mass Spectrum Data

Christina Papagiannopoulou[1](✉), René Parchen[2], and Willem Waegeman[1]

[1] Department of Data Analysis and Mathematical Modelling,
Ghent University, Ghent, Belgium
{christina.papagiannopoulou,willem.waegeman}@ugent.be
[2] BiosparQ B.V., Leiden, The Netherlands
parchen@biosparq.nl

Abstract. Matrix-assisted laser desorption/ionization-time-of-flight mass spectrometry (MALDI-TOF-MS) is a well-known technology, widely used in species identification. Specifically, MALDI-TOF-MS is applied on samples that usually include bacterial cells, generating representative signals for the various bacterial species. However, for a reliable identification result, a significant amount of biomass is required. For most samples used for diagnostics of infectious diseases, the sample volume is extremely low to obtain the required amount of biomass. Therefore, amplification of the bacterial load is performed by a culturing phase. If the MALDI process could be applied to individual bacteria, it would be possible to circumvent the need for culturing and isolation, accelerating the whole process. In this paper, we briefly describe an implementation of a MALDI-TOF MS procedure in a setting of individual cells and we demonstrate the use of the produced data for the application of pathogen identification. The identification of pathogens (bacterial species) is performed by using machine learning algorithms on the generated single-cell signals. The high predictive performance of the machine learning models indicates that the produced bacterial signatures constitute an informative representation, helpful in distinguishing the different bacterial species. In addition, we reformulate the bacterial species identification problem as a time series classification task by considering the intensity sequences of a given spectrum as time series values. Experimental results show that algorithms originally introduced for time series analysis are beneficial in modelling observations of single-cell MALDI-TOF MS.

Keywords: MALDI-TOF MS · Single-cell spectrum ·
Single-ionization-event · Classification · Machine learning methods ·
Bacterial species identification · Time series

© Springer Nature Switzerland AG 2020
U. Brefeld et al. (Eds.): ECML PKDD 2019, LNAI 11908, pp. 416–431, 2020.
https://doi.org/10.1007/978-3-030-46133-1_25

1   Introduction

In the diagnostics of infectious diseases, matrix-assisted laser desorption/ionization-time-of-flight mass spectrometry (MALDI-TOF-MS) is used to identify the causative organism of an infection as a first step in establishing an antibiotic therapy. Owing to its ease of use, its reliability and the low cost of ownership, the introduction of MALDI-TOF-MS revolutionized the diagnostics of infectious diseases during the last decade [4]. Specifically, this technology, applied to bacteria, generates a mass spectrum exhibiting peaks of a limited number of (household) proteins (ribosomal proteins) and peptides produced by the organism. Since the extracted structure of these proteins depends on the species, the MALDI mass spectrum is used as a signature enabling identification of microorganisms up to species level.

For a highly reliable classification result, a significant amount of biomass is required in MALDI. However, for most samples used for diagnostics of infectious diseases, the amount of the obtained biomass is often very low. As a consequence, amplification of the bacterial load is required by culturing. Furthermore, since there is almost no part in the human body that does not contain some form of a natural flora consisting of microorganisms, a sample 'harvested' from a patient sample will generally contain a mixture of organisms, optionally including the organism responsible for the infection. Since interpreting samples containing bacterial mixtures is still in an experimental phase [25], for routine diagnostics, isolation of the causative organism is required as well. Thus, even though the time required for a MALDI based identification is extremely short, in terms of seconds or minutes, since it is dominated by the culturing process, the time-to-result is still in the order of multiple hours (over-night culture) to days. Furthermore, for choosing the culture medium/conditions and for choosing the colony(ies) to identify, a-priori knowledge on the cause of the infection is required. If the MALDI process can be applied to individual bacteria, it would be possible to circumvent the need for culturing and isolation, accelerating the whole process.

Separating a patient sample into a stream of individual cells is possible using the technology developed by [26], originally aimed at dispensing individual eukaryotic cells into well plates. In another work, researchers [24] developed an aerosol TOF MS, able to apply MALDI to individual aerosol particles and demonstrated that recognizable spectra could be accumulated from spectra of large numbers of aerosol particles containing pure proteins only. By combining the cell dispensing technology introduced by [26], with the aerosol TOF technology of [24], the desired single-cell capability can be realised. BiosparQ in the Netherlands developed an instrument, called Cirrus D20, together with the appropriate protocols that is able to produce an information rich signature of bacteria based on accumulated spectra. In this paper, we evaluate this single-cell MALDI-TOF MS methodology and we demonstrate the use of the single-particle spectra for the application of pathogen (bacterial species) identification.

The classification of single-cell bacterial fingerprints is not a trivial process even for human annotators. Thus, MALDI-TOF single cell spectrum analysis should be combined with statistical and machine learning methods. Previous studies have focused on the statistical analysis of accumulated spectra (i.e., mass spectra formed by averaging multi-cell mass spectra) [5,11,14,21]. For instance, in the work of [11], machine learning algorithms, such as SVMs [7] and RFs [6], have been exploited for bacterial identification from accumulated MALDI-TOF mass spectra. For species identification, machine learning methods have been also successfully applied on other representations coming from flow cytometry [2,19] and Raman spectroscopy [17,22,23] data. In this work, we focus on the analysis of MALDI-TOF single-cell spectra for rapid species identification using machine learning techniques. Unlike previous studies, e.g., [11,21], instead of only applying general purpose machine learning techniques, we also experimented by framing the problem as a time series classification task. In particular, by mapping mass-over-charge (M/Z) ratios to the time axis, we consider the sequences of the different intensities in a spectrum as time series values. This way, standard time series classification methods [1] can be applied. To the best of our knowledge, this is the first time that machine learning approaches and time series classification methods are being applied on single-cell MALDI-TOF data.

To sum up, the contribution of this paper is two-fold. Based on the implementation of the MALDI-TOF-MS methodology in a single-cell setting described here, we (i) experimentally prove that the single-cell signatures, produced by this MALDI-TOF-MS implementation, are informative in distinguishing different bacterial species by using machine learning data analysis, and (ii) find that algorithms originally introduced for time series analysis are beneficial in modelling observations of single-cell MALDI. As such, we believe that the use of single-cell MALDI-TOF-MS data combined with an accurate modelling approach comprises a solid framework that strives to solve the problem of fast pathogen identification (in terms of minutes or seconds), revolutionizing current state-of-the-art approaches.

2   Materials and Methods

2.1   Bacterial Species

The strains used in this study were provided by the Leiden Centre for Applied Bioscience. They are selected from a group of (opportunistic) pathogens, comprising of *Citrobacter freundii* (*C. freundii*), *Citrobacter koseri* (*C. koseri*), *Enterobacter aerogenes* (*E. aerogenes*), *Klebsiaella oxytoca* (*Kl. oxytoca*), often responsible for common and frequent infections such as urinary tract infections. The identity of these strains is established by evaluation of the cultures on a bioMeriéux Vitek MS MALDI instrument.

2.2   MALDI-TOF Mass Spectrometry

Performing mass spectrometry of larger molecules, such as proteins and peptides, is not evident. Generally, the amount of energy associated with direct ionization of the analyte exceeds the disintegration energy of the analyte molecules. Since, the information content of the resulting molecular debris is low, a soft ionization technique (such as MALDI), that leaves the molecules intact, is essential.

In MALDI, the analyte (proteins and peptides in case of identification of microorganisms), is co-crystalized with an organic substance generally containing an aromatic ring (the so-called MALDI matrix) and illuminated using a pulsed UV laser [10]. Upon absorption of the UV light by the MALDI matrix, part of the MALDI-matrix/analyte mixture is ablated into a plume comprising of analyte molecules, matrix molecules, molecular debris and clusters of molecules. Through a number of, currently still only partly understood, interactions, during this process, protons are transferred to the analyte molecules (see e.g. [15]). That way, charge separation can be achieved with the minimum amount of energy. An electric field accelerates the ions into a field-free drift region. There, the separation of the ions according to their mass-over-charge (M/Z) ratio is achieved.

2.3   Single-Cell MALDI-TOF Mass Spectrometry

Implementation of Single-Cell MALDI. To enable application of MALDI to individual bacteria, three aspects of the conventional MALDI logistics need to be changed. Specifically, (i) instead of preparing a large number of cells on a target plate, individual cells need to be made suitable for applying MALDI, (ii) instead of presenting a large number of cells (on a target plate), individual cells need to be presented to the mass spectrometer, and (iii) instead of classifying an accumulated spectrum resulting from a large number of ionization events (applied on a large number of positions within a spot on the target plate), spectra resulting from a single ionization event (applied on a single cell) need to be classified. For the current application, (i) single cells are prepared using a single-cell dispensing technology developed by [26], and (ii) single cells are presented to the mass spectrometer and ionized using an aerosol TOF (ATOF) technology developed by [24]. The current paper concentrates on the third aspect, classifying spectra resulting from single ionization events applied to individual cells.

MALDI-TOF MS Procedure. In the ATOF mass spectrometer built by BiosparQ BV, each individual particle, which is formed based on a technique described by [26], is illuminated in flight with a pulsed UV laser (337 nm), after which the ions that are produced by the MALDI process are accelerated into the time-of-flight tube. The ions are detected at the end of the time-of-flight tube, using an electron multiplier. For each illuminated particle, the resulting data is recorded as a time series in binary format. The relation between the time-of-flight, and the mass over charge ratio of the ions, M/Z, is given by:

$$M/Z = \left(\frac{T_{TOF} - C_2}{C_1}\right)^2$$

The values of the calibration coefficients C_1 and C_2 are established by calibrating the mass spectrometer using a sample containing a known organism

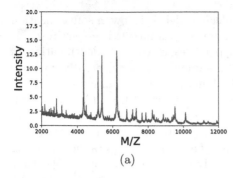 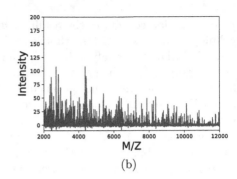

(a)   (b)

Fig. 1. Accumulated and single-cell spectra. (a) Accumulated spectrum of multiple single-ionization-event spectra of the species *Kl. oxytoca*, and (b) single-ionization-event mass spectrum of *Kl. oxytoca*. Note that only the mass range above 2000 Da is considered throughout the analysis. See text for more details.

(E-coli, ATCC 25922) and aligning the resulting spectrum with a reference spectrum of E-coli ATCC 25922 recorded on a Vitek MS MALDI mass spectrometer.

The Structure of Single-Ionization-Event Mass Spectra. Apart from a signature that stems from the analyte molecules, MALDI spectra generally contain signal, or clutter, caused by imperfect ablation of the analyte-MALDI-matrix mixture, leading to (i) charged clusters of molecules and (ii) disintegration of large molecules (and thus leading to charged molecular debris). Note that in single-ionization-event spectra the amplitude of the clutter signal may be of the same order as the analyte signal. However, since the formation of clusters of molecules and molecular debris is a highly stochastic process (while the presence of analyte molecules clearly is not), the expected value of the clutter signal is significantly lower than the one of the analyte signal.

Accumulation of a large number of single-ionization-event spectra will therefore lead to an accumulated spectrum showing high amplitudes at the locations corresponding to the analyte mass molecules and significantly lower amplitudes at intermediate (clutter) locations. By using straightforward baseline correction algorithms, it is possible to remove the clutter contribution from the spectra. However, in single-ionization-event mass spectrum classification, the difference in the clutter and analyte stochastics cannot be used, and a different strategy must be employed. To illustrate the difference between an accumulated signal and a single-cell signal, we depict an accumulated spectrum of the species *Kl. oxytoca* formed by multiple single-ionization-event spectra (Fig. 1a) and a single-ionization-event mass spectrum of *Kl. oxytoca* (Fig. 1b), respectively. From these two figures, it becomes clear that the classification of accumulated spectra is an easier task compared to the classification of single-cell spectra, which is hard even for a human annotator. In our analysis, only the M/Z range above 2000 Da is considered. This is because the well conserved proteins (and peptides)

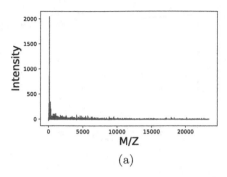
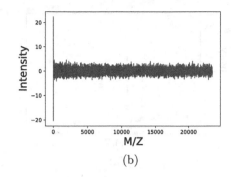

$$\text{(a)} \qquad\qquad\qquad\qquad\qquad\qquad\qquad \text{(b)}$$

Fig. 2. Informative and non-informative data observations. (a) Informative spectrum of a single-ionization-event of a single *C. freundii* particle, and (b) spectrum of an empty particle (non-informative spectrum).

(i.e., not depending strongly on the growth medium and growth circumstances) are located in this part of the signal.

2.4   Data Pre-processing

Using expression (1) and the associated calibration coefficients the single-particle time series are converted into mass spectra. These single-particle spectra are finally normalized using the Root-Mean-Squared (RMS) voltage of the measurement chain noise.

   As a first preprocessing step, we remove particles (observations) that do not contain any information. To do so, we calculate the variance of each particle. If the calculated variance is low, there are no intensities captured by the ionization procedure. In Fig. 2b, an observation of an empty particle is depicted. In this paper, we demonstrate that the single-cell signals, produced by the aforementioned procedure, form a valid signature of the most common bacterial species. To this end, machine learning classifiers are employed to identify bacterial species from single-cell signals. Following the standard practices of machine learning methods, signals of various species should be aligned in a common feature space (i.e., for the same values of M/Z ratios). This is because intensities for the various species may be measured in different M/Z ratios. Therefore, we employ an interpolation technique as a feature construction approach in order to form a common feature representation for all the studied species. The interpolation procedure followed in our experimental study comprises four steps: (i) M/Z values are defined (these values should be in between the maximum and minimum M/Z values existing in the dataset), (ii) a cumulative spectrum of each individual spectrum is formed, (iii) linear interpolation is performed on the cumulative spectrum, (iv) the interpolated values are differentiated and the final signal is produced. The number of M/Z values (bins) defined in step (i) is a tunable parameter that is optimized during the learning process (model training).

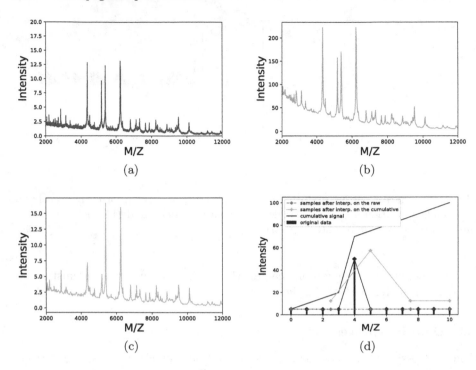

Fig. 3. Comparison of the different interpolation approaches. (a) Original accumulated spectrum of *Kl. oxytoca*, (b) accumulated spectrum after linear interpolation on the cumulative spectra, (c) accumulated spectrum after linear interpolation on the original spectra, and (d) toy example of the two interpolation techniques. The original signal is represented with blue bars, the linear interpolated signal on the original spectrum is represented in red color, and the linear interpolated signal on the cumulative spectrum is colored in green. The corresponding cumulative spectrum is drawn in black color. (Color figure online)

We also experimented by applying the interpolation method directly on the original spectrum values, resulting in low values for the characteristic peaks of the spectra. Figure 3a shows the mean spectrum of *Kl. oxytoca* observations before the interpolation (raw data), Fig. 3b depicts the same mean spectrum after the interpolation procedure on the cumulative spectrum, while Fig. 3c presents the result of the interpolation on the raw spectrum. The number of bins (M/Z values) selected in these examples (Fig. 3b and 3c) is equal to 1000, while the original signal includes intensities for ∼16000 bins. It is observed that the signals in Fig. 3c have been mostly affected by the interpolation, and the peaks of the average spectrum are not well-formed as in the original data (see Fig. 3a). On the other hand, Fig. 3b shows an interpolated signal that is close to the original one (with respect to the high peaks). Although the intensity scale increases due to the cumulative information that each bin captures, by employing interpolation on the cumulative spectrum, the peaks of the original signal are well-preserved. This is important, since these peaks constitute the informative part of a signal.

In Fig. 3d, a toy example of a single-cell spectrum, where a peak is not captured using simple linear interpolation on the original signal, is illustrated. As mentioned above, in single-cell spectra there are no well-shaped peaks (see Fig. 2a for an example) and thus, possible spikes in the signal should be preserved.

2.5 Machine Learning Methods

We conduct an extensive experimental study on the task of species identification from single-cell MALDI-TOF data. In machine learning, species identification can be formulated as a typical classification task. In mathematical notation, an observation in this task is symbolized as a pair $(\mathbf{x}, y)$, where $\mathbf{x}$ is a feature vector of length m, i.e., $(x_1, ..., x_m)$ (m values), and y is a class value. Following this notation, a dataset D, in a classification task, consists of N observations with their associated class labels, i.e., $D = \{\mathbf{X}, \mathbf{y}\} = \{(\mathbf{x}_1, y_1), ..., (\mathbf{x}_N, y_N)\}$. The vector $\mathbf{y}$ represents a discrete class variable with c possible values. In our setting, the observations are the various spectra, the intensities are the values of the m features (bins) and the bacterial species the different class values. We evaluate the results of seven machine learning classifiers, four of them are well-known algorithms that have been broadly applied on MALDI-TOF data, namely random forests (RFs), support vector machines (SVMs), logistic regression (LR), and k-nearest neighbor (KNN). The other three algorithms, originally developed for the task of time series classification (described below), are time series forests (TSF), Bag-of-SFA-Symbols (BOSS) and complexity invariant distance (CID).

The first group of models consists of algorithms that can distinguish non-linearly (e.g., RF) and linearly (e.g, LR) separable data. Some of these algorithms are also able to easily handle high-dimensional data (e.g., RFs), while others are not (e.g., KNN). This is the very first time that a predictive modelling benchmarking is performed on this kind of data and thus, an extensive experimental setup of the most well-known predictive models is necessary to set a strong baseline for future studies. Regarding the various models, the RF [6] is the well-known non-linear ensemble algorithm. The SVMs [7] used in this set-up apply a Gaussian RBF kernel to model non-linear boundaries between the different species. The LR algorithm [9] is a simple method that learns linear boundaries between the classes, while the KNN model [8] serves as an intuitive non-linear baseline algorithm.

The second group of models consists of algorithms that are extensively used in the time series classification task. The aim of a time series classification task is the assignment of a given time series to a particular class. As in other classification problems, a classifier is a function or mapping from the input space to the class values. The only difference from the general classification task, described above, is that the feature vector $\mathbf{x}$ of length m is a time series of the same length. In our setting, the observations of the single-cell MALDI-TOF dataset can be seen as time series, since the ion intensities are consecutive values over the M/Z axis (see Fig. 2a). The class values are again the various bacterial species. To the best of our knowledge, time series classification methods have not yet been investigated on MALDI-TOF data. As such, in the next paragraph, the time series classification methods used in this study are briefly introduced.

Time series classification algorithms enable some automatic feature construction or filtering of the time series values prior or during constructing the classifier. That way, these methods extract high-level representations for the time series or use similarity metrics for measuring the relatedness between the time series [1,13,16]. Time series classification algorithms can be categorized as methods that use: (i) the whole series or the raw data for classification – this family of algorithms mainly consists of one-nearest-neighbour-type (1-NN) classifiers with varying distance measures, (ii) sub-intervals of the raw time series – summary statistics of these sub-intervals are commonly used as discriminative features in this family of classifiers, and (iii) the frequency of the patterns in a given time series – a dictionary of patterns is formed and a histogram for each observation is calculated based on the constructed dictionary by this kind of methods.

In this study, we compare three algorithms, one from each of the aforementioned categories. The complexity invariant distance (CID) [3] algorithm belongs to the first category. This classifier defines the concept of complexity invariance in time series. Intuitively, complex time series are characterized by many peaks and valleys. The distance between pairs of complex time series is frequently greater than the distance between pairs of simple time series (i.e., without many peaks and valleys). A complexity invariant distance measure has been introduced to compensate this phenomenon. Specifically, a distance measure is multiplied by a term that is calculated based on the sum of squares of the first differences of the time series. The Euclidean distance measure has been used as base distance measure from the CID algorithm.

A representative method of the second category is the time series forests (TSF) [12]. This method is similar to the RF model, because it consists of a set of classification trees. Specifically, each tree is trained by using summary statistics (i.e., the mean, standard deviation and slope) of random sub-intervals derived from the times series observations. The calculated summary statistics serve as discriminative features. The classification of a new observation is obtained by majority voting over all trees.

Bag of SFA symbols (BOSS) [20] is an algorithm that belongs to the third category of the methods mentioned above. It starts by creating a dictionary of patterns from the given time series observations. The frequencies of the patterns of this dictionary are used as discriminative features. The different patterns are constructed by using time series sub-intervals in a sliding window setting. Then, the discrete Fourier transform (DFT) is performed on each sub-interval window. Afterwards, the calculated Fourier coefficients are transformed into categorical values (e.g., 'a', 'b', 'c') based on their quantity (i.e., 'high', 'medium', 'low'), and thus, the patterns of the dictionary are formed by the combination of the categorical values of the Fourier coefficients. Finally, each time series observation is represented based on the frequency of the calculated patterns in the time series itself. The classification of a new observation is performed by using an 1-NN-based classifier.

Table 1. Predictive performance on the test set in terms of mean accuracy for the compared predictive models. For each model, the optimal value of the parameter number of bins, which is tuned during the training phase, is also reported.

Model	Number of bins	Mean accuracy
LR	9,000	0.760
RF	9,000	0.727
SVM	500	0.763
KNN	500	0.633
TSF	8,500	**0.832**
CIDNN	500	0.666
BOSS	7,500	0.478

2.6 Experimental Setup

In our experiments, we evaluate the predictive performance of the seven aforementioned classifiers (see Sect. 2.5). Specifically, each classifier is assessed based on its ability to distinguish single-cell spectra of four species, namely *C. koseri*, *C. freundii*, *E. aerogenes* and *Kl. oxytoca*. We use the same train/test splits to obtain a fair comparison between the various tested algorithms. In particular, after the removal of the empty particles (see Sect. 2.4), we keep 1000 examples for each species for training and the 268 examples for test (for each species). Parameter tuning is performed in a separate validation set, which is part of the training set. For all the models, the number of bins is considered as a tunable parameter with a tested range [500, 10000] with steps of 500. For the algorithms LR, RFs, SVMs and KNN, the sklearn [18] python implementation is used, while for the CIDNN, BOSS and TSF the java implementation of [1] is evaluated. For the evaluation procedure we report the mean accuracy for all the species and we present the confusion matrix of the best performing algorithms for further discussion (see Sect. 3).

3 Results and Discussion

In this section, the performance of the classification algorithms is presented. Table 1 shows the predictive performance of the seven classification algorithms in terms of the mean accuracy (over the four classes). The number of bins (features), which is a tunable parameter for each method, is also noted. The first block of algorithms (i.e., LR, RFs, SVMs, and KNN) consists of well-known methods generally-applied in many applications. On the other hand, the second block of methods (i.e., TSF, CIDNN, and BOSS) comprises models that solve time series classification tasks, as discussed in Sect. 2.5.

Overall, the best performing algorithm is the TSF with mean accuracy of 0.832. TSF is considered as a phase dependent classification method. This is due to the fact that it detects the intervals among all observations that are most informative for the classification problem. In our setting, the peaks and valleys, which characterize a bacterial species, are strongly associated with the corresponding M/Z ratios. Therefore, the exact same extracted intervals should be compared across all the observations. This means that comparisons with shifted peaks (or valleys) may lead to incorrect classification results, because spectra of different species may consist of similar signatures (yet not identical). As stated in Sect. 2.5, TSF constructs features from the original time series by calculating summary statistics from arbitrary-sized sub-intervals. This means that it captures information from short-sized intervals till long-sized ones that can even cover entire peaks (and valleys) of the signals. Thus, this combined information (from short and long sub-intervals) comprises a "high-level" representation of the original spectra, imitating the human perception about the spectra. After the feature construction process, TSF selects the features with the maximum discriminative power, by building various weak classifiers (classification trees). This procedure is also combined with majority voting for prediction, ensembling the resulting predictions, a technique that is often beneficial in classification tasks. That way the algorithm is able to explore the discriminative power of more intervals and avoid overfitting.

A high performance (>0.72) is obtained also using other classifiers, such as the SVMs, LR and RFs. These classifiers take combinations of features into account to perform their predictions. This is beneficial in our setting, since combinations of peaks and valleys in the spectra are informative for distinguishing the various bacterial species. Both linear (LR) and non-linear (SVM and RF) models perform similar in this scenario. However, compared to the TSF algorithm, these models are not based on consecutive values (intervals) of a spectrum and thus, are less able to capture information coming from large intervals. On the contrary, TSF encodes the information that the rest of the algorithms do, since it also generates and assesses short intervals (of, e.g., three or four consecutive values). That way, TSF combines information from short and long intervals of the spectrum, and outperforms the other models.

The algorithms that are based on the intuition of the nearest neighbor (NN), i.e., KNN and CIDNN, are outperformed by the aforementioned ones, while the BOSS model gives the worst predictive performance. This result is not surprising, since the NN algorithms are not able to generalize well when the number of features is high (curse of dimensionality). This is the reason why the optimal number of bins is low for these models (i.e., 500) compared to the corresponding number of bins for other models. In addition, the result of the BOSS algorithm is low due to the phase independent features that are extracted during training. As discussed in Sect. 2.5, the BOSS method constructs a dictionary of patterns, and counts the times that these patterns occur in a particular observation. These patterns may occur at any point of the spectrum. Thus, the model counts the presence of the "spectral" patterns by treating them independently from their corresponding M/Z ratios.

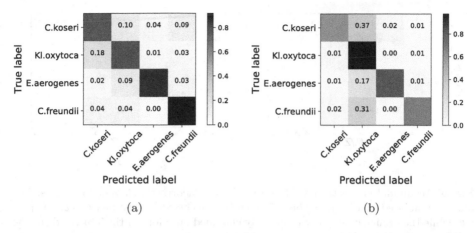

Fig. 4. Normalized confusion matrices for (a) the TSF, and (b) the SVM algorithm.

In Fig. 4, the confusion matrices of the two best performing methods are presented. Specifically, Fig. 4a and b show the accuracy of the TSF and the SVM model per species, respectively. Overall, both models have high discriminative power for all the species. However, the TSF model performs similar for each of the species, while the SVM model performs really high for two species (*Kl. oxytoca* and *E. aerogenes*) and relatively low for the rest of the species (i.e., *C. koseri* and *C. freundii*). In addition, the spectra of the different species are mostly confused with the spectra of *Kl. oxytoca*. This is especially clear for the *C. koseri* species, for which the model gives the lowest accuracy. The confusion with the *Kl. oxytoca* species can be explained by the fact that the spectra of this species includes peaks with low intensities and thus observations with low peaks (from this or other species) are classified as *Kl. oxytoca* observations. Figure 5b confirms this conclusion. The mean spectrum of the misclassified *C. koseri* observations is depicted with orange, while the mean spectrum of the correctly classified observations in blue. Most of the *C. koseri* observations have been confused with the *Kl. oxytoca* observations. More specifically, the misclassified *C. koseri* observations are the ones with low intensity values. Therefore, the clearer the signal peaks (high intensities), the better the result of the species classification task for the SVM classifier. Figure 5a depicts the corresponding misclassified/correctly classified mean of the spectra for the TSF model in orange and blue, respectively. The misclassified observations have higher variance and mean values compared to the correctly classified ones. Differences in variance in these two plots are due to a different number of bins used in the TSF (8500 bins) and the SVMs (500 bins) experiments (tuned in validation set).

Note also that for the classification experiments we assume that the quality of the spectra of different species is similar. However, it is known that even between successive experiments using the same organism there may be a variation in the intensity of peaks (not the position) in the accumulated spectrum, even when exactly the same protocol has been used. Hence, the difference in performance

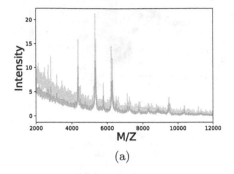
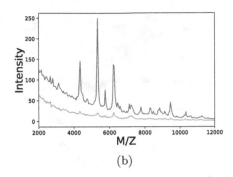

(a)   (b)

Fig. 5. Accumulated spectrum of the correctly and incorrectly classified particles. The blue accumulated spectrum has been formed by the correctly classified *C. koseri* spectra, while the orange one by the incorrectly classified ones for (a) the TSF, and (b) the SVM models. (Color figure online)

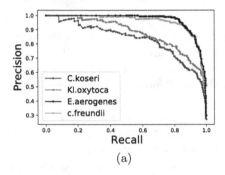
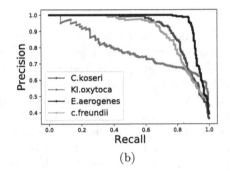

(a)   (b)

Fig. 6. Precision/recall curves for (a) the TSF, and (b) the SVM models.

may be caused by differences in the quality of the spectra. The fact that when using TSF the difference in performance for the different species is less than when using SVN, may indicate that TSF is less sensitive to this type of variation.

From the confusion matrix of Fig. 4b, it seems that the SVM model performs well for the *Kl. oxytoca* species (0.98 accuracy). However, there are many false positive examples that are not taken into account in the calculation of the accuracy metric. The ratio of false positives is incorporated in the estimation of the precision-recall curves, see Fig. 6. Figure 6 shows the precision-recall trade-off for each of the four species for the TSF (Fig. 6a) and the SVM (Fig. 6b) models. The precision-recall curves for each species have been calculated in a one-versus-all fashion. Figure 6a shows that for all the species, the precision is above 0.75 for a recall value of 0.8. This means that 80% of the observations (for each species) is identified correctly with accuracy higher than 75%. On the other hand, Fig. 6b illustrates that for the species *C. koseri*, *E. aerogenes*, and *C. freundii*, the SVM model is able to correctly identify more than 75% of the observations with high precision (more than 80%). However, this is not the case for the *Kl. oxytoca* species, where the precision increases (0.8) only when recall drops to 0.3 (or less). This means that the model misclassifies many examples of the other species (i.e., *C. koseri*, *E. aerogenes* and *C. freundii*), when it comes to predict a high ratio of the *Kl. oxytoca* observations.

4 Conclusion

In this paper, we described an implementation of a MALDI-TOF MS procedure in a setting of single-ionization-event on individual cells. We demonstrated the use of the single-cell MALDI-TOF MS data for the application of bacterial species identification. Specifically, we combined the single-cell spectra produced by the described methodology with machine learning algorithms, and we experimentally proved that these signatures are informative in distinguishing different bacterial species. Finally, we formulated the problem of bacterial species classification as a time series classification task and we found that algorithms originally introduced for time series analysis are beneficial in modelling observations of single-cell MALDI-TOF MS. Our conclusions confirm that the use of single-cell MALDI-TOF-MS data combined with an accurate modelling approach comprises a promising and complete framework that gives the green light for fast species identification. The fast response time, which is in terms of minutes or seconds, revolutionizes current time-consuming approaches (due to the dominant culturing time) in pathogen identification related to human infections.

Acknowledgements. This work is funded by BiosparQ B.V. in the Netherlands. We would like to sincerely thank Dr. Willem van Leeuwen of the Leiden Centre for Applied Bioscience for providing the strains used in this study.

References

1. Bagnall, A., Lines, J., Bostrom, A., Large, J., Keogh, E.: The great time series classification bake off: a review and experimental evaluation of recent algorithmic advances. Data Min. Knowl. Disc. **31**(3), 606–660 (2016). https://doi.org/10.1007/s10618-016-0483-9

2. Bashashati, A., Brinkman, R.R.: A survey of flow cytometry data analysis methods. Adv. Bioinf. **2009**, 19 (2009)

3. Batista, G.E.A.P.A., Keogh, E.J., Tataw, O.M., De Souza, V.M.: CID: an efficient complexity-invariant distance for time series. Data Min. Knowl. Disc. **28**(3), 634–669 (2014)

4. van Belkum, A., Chatellier, S., Girard, V., Pincus, D., Deol, P., Dunne Jr., W.M.: Progress in proteomics for clinical microbiology: MALDI-TOF MS for microbial species identification and more. Expert Rev. Proteomics **12**(6), 595–605 (2015). https://doi.org/10.1586/14789450.2015.1091731

5. van Belkum, A., et al.: Automatic identification of mixed bacterial species fingerprints in a MALDI-TOF mass-spectrum. Bioinformatics **30**(9), 1280–1286 (2014). https://doi.org/10.1093/bioinformatics/btu022

6. Breiman, L.: Random forests. Mach. Learn. **45**(1), 5–32 (2001). https://doi.org/10.1023/A:1010933404324

7. Cortes, C., Vapnik, V.: Support-vector networks. Mach. Learn. **20**(3), 273–297 (1995). https://doi.org/10.1023/A:1022627411411
8. Cover, T., Hart, P.: Nearest neighbor pattern classification. IEEE Trans. Inf. Theory **13**(1), 21–27 (1967). https://doi.org/10.1109/TIT.1967.1053964
9. Cox, D.R.: The regression analysis of binary sequences. J. Roy. Stat. Soc.: Ser. B (Methodol.) **20**(2), 215–232 (1958)
10. Croxatto, A., Prod'hom, G., Greub, G.: Applications of MALDI-TOF mass spectrometry in clinical diagnostic microbiology. FEMS Microbiol. Rev. **36**(2), 380–407 (2012). https://doi.org/10.1111/j.1574-6976.2011.00298.x
11. De Bruyne, K., Slabbinck, B., Waegeman, W., Vauterin, P., De Baets, B., Vandamme, P.: Bacterial species identification from MALDI-TOF mass spectra through data analysis and machine learning. Syst. Appl. Microbiol. **34**(1), 20–29 (2011). https://doi.org/10.1016/j.syapm.2010.11.003
12. Deng, H., Runger, G., Tuv, E., Vladimir, M.: A time series forest for classification and feature extraction. Inf. Sci. **239**, 142–153 (2013)
13. Ding, H., Trajcevski, G., Scheuermann, P., Wang, X., Keogh, E.: Querying and mining of time series data: experimental comparison of representations and distance measures. Proc. VLDB Endowment **1**(2), 1542–1552 (2008)
14. Hsieh, S.Y., et al.: Highly efficient classification and identification of human pathogenic bacteria by MALDI-TOF MS. Mol. Cell. Proteomics **7**(2), 448–456 (2008). https://doi.org/10.1074/mcp.M700339-MCP200
15. Knochenmuss, R.: The coupled chemical and physical dynamics model of MALDI. Ann. Rev. Anal. Chem. **9**(1), 365–385 (2016). https://doi.org/10.1146/annurev-anchem-071015-041750
16. Liao, T.W.: Clustering of time series data - a survey. Pattern Recognit. **38**(11), 1857–1874 (2005). https://doi.org/10.1016/j.patcog.2005.01.025
17. Liu, J., Osadchy, M., Ashton, L., Foster, M., Solomon, C.J., Gibson, S.J.: Deep convolutional neural networks for Raman spectrum recognition: a unified solution. Analyst **142**(21), 4067–4074 (2017)
18. Pedregosa, F., et al.: Scikit-learn: machine learning in Python. J. Mach. Learn. Res. **12**, 2825–2830 (2011)
19. Rubbens, P., Props, R., Boon, N., Waegeman, W.: Flow cytometric single-cell identification of populations in synthetic bacterial communities. Plos One **12**(1), 19 (2017). https://doi.org/10.1371/journal.pone.0169754
20. Schäfer, P.: The BOSS is concerned with time series classification in the presence of noise. Data Min. Knowl. Disc. **29**(6), 1505–1530 (2014). https://doi.org/10.1007/s10618-014-0377-7
21. Schleif, F.M., et al.: Support vector classification of proteomic profile spectra based on feature extraction with the bi-orthogonal discrete wavelet transform. Comput. Vis. Sci. **12**(4), 189–199 (2009). https://doi.org/10.1007/s00791-008-0087-z
22. Schmid, U., Rösch, P., Krause, M., Harz, M., Popp, J., Baumann, K.: Gaussian mixture discriminant analysis for the single-cell differentiation of bacteria using micro-Raman spectroscopy. Chemom. Intell. Lab. Syst. **96**(2), 159–171 (2009). https://doi.org/10.1016/j.chemolab.2009.01.008
23. Sevetlidis, V., Pavlidis, G.: Effective Raman spectra identification with tree-based methods. J. Cult. Heritage (2018)
24. van Wuijckhuijse, A., Stowers, M., Kleefsman, W., van Baar, B., Kientz, C., Marijnissen, J.: Matrix-assisted laser desorption/ionisation aerosol time-of-flight mass spectrometry for the analysis of bioaerosols: development of a fast detector for airborne biological pathogens. J. Aerosol Sci. **36**(5), 677–687 (2005). https://doi.org/10.1016/j.jaerosci.2004.11.003

25. Yang, Y., Lin, Y., Qiao, L.: Direct MALDI-TOF MS identification of bacterial mixtures. Anal. Chem. **90**(17), 10400–10408 (2018). https://doi.org/10.1021/acs. analchem.8b02258
26. Yusof, A., et al.: Inkjet-like printing of single-cells. Lab Chip **11**, 2447–2454 (2011). https://doi.org/10.1039/C1LC20176J

CASTNet: Community-Attentive Spatio-Temporal Networks for Opioid Overdose Forecasting

Ali Mert Ertugrul[1,2], Yu-Ru Lin[1(✉)], and Tugba Taskaya-Temizel[2]

[1] University of Pittsburgh, Pittsburgh, PA, USA
{ertugrul,yurulin}@pitt.edu
[2] Middle East Technical University, Ankara, Turkey
ttemizel@metu.edu.tr

Abstract. Opioid overdose is a growing public health crisis in the United States. This crisis, recognized as "opioid epidemic," has widespread societal consequences including the degradation of health, and the increase in crime rates and family problems. To improve the overdose surveillance and to identify the areas in need of prevention effort, in this work, we focus on forecasting opioid overdose using real-time crime dynamics. Previous work identified various types of links between opioid use and criminal activities, such as financial motives and common causes. Motivated by these observations, we propose a novel spatio-temporal predictive model for opioid overdose forecasting by leveraging the spatio-temporal patterns of crime incidents. Our proposed model incorporates multi-head attentional networks to learn different representation subspaces of features. Such deep learning architecture, called "community-attentive" networks, allows the prediction for a given location to be optimized by a mixture of groups (i.e., *communities*) of regions. In addition, our proposed model allows for interpreting what features, from what communities, have more contributions to predicting local incidents as well as how these communities are captured through forecasting. Our results on two real-world overdose datasets indicate that our model achieves superior forecasting performance and provides meaningful interpretations in terms of spatio-temporal relationships between the dynamics of crime and that of opioid overdose.

Keywords: Forecasting opioid overdose · Spatio-temporal networks · Multi-head attentional networks · Crime dynamics

1 Introduction

Opioid use disorders (OUD) and overdose rates in the United States have increased at an alarming rate since the past decade [21]. Overdose deaths have risen since the 1990s, and the number of heroin overdose deaths has risen sharply since 2010 [17]. The growth rate of opioid overdose together with the number of impacted individuals in the U.S., has led many to classify this as an "opioid epidemic" [13]. Enhanced understanding of the dynamics of the overdose

© Springer Nature Switzerland AG 2020
U. Brefeld et al. (Eds.): ECML PKDD 2019, LNAI 11908, pp. 432–448, 2020.
https://doi.org/10.1007/978-3-030-46133-1_26

epidemic may help policy-makers to develop more effective epidemic prevention mechanisms and control strategies [10].

The opioid epidemic is a complex social phenomenon involving and interacting with various social, spatial and temporal factors [2]. Highlighting the links between opioid use and various factors has drawn significant attention. Studies have identified relationships between opioid use and crime incidences, including cause [1], effect [7] and common causes [19]. Crime occurrences also have non-trivial spatio-temporal characteristics – for example, routine activity theory suggested that crimes may exhibit spatio-temporal lags as the *likely offenders* of one place may reach *suitable targets* in other places. Therefore, how to unveil the complicated relationship between opioid use and crime incidences is challenging. Moreover, detailed assessments of OUD and overdose growth require systematically collected well-resolved spatio-temporal data [6]. Yet, the amount of systematically monitored data either at a regional or local level in the U.S. is limited and there is no common reporting mechanism for incidents. On the other hand, crime data is meticulously collected and stored at finer-grained level. Given the plausible relationship between crime dynamics and opioid use as well as the availability of real-time crime data for various locations, in this study, we explore the capability of forecasting opioid overdose using real-time crime data.

Recent works in predictive modeling have shown significant improvement in spatio-temporal event forecasting and time series prediction [16, 22]. However, these studies suffer from two main concerns. First, most of them overlook the complex interactions between local and global activities across time and space. Only a few have paid attention to this, yet they model the global activities as a single universal representation [3, 4], which is either irrespective of event location or is reweighted based on a pre-defined fixed proximity matrix [14]. None of them learns to differentiate the pairwise activity relationships between a particular event location and other locations. Second, most of the studies mainly focus on performance and lack interpretability to uncover the underlying spatio-temporal characteristics of the activities. Inspired by the idea of multi-head attentional networks [20], we propose a novel deep learning architecture, called "CASTNet," for opioid overdose forecasting using spatio-temporal characteristics of crime incidents, which seeks to address the aforementioned problems. Assuming that different locations could share similar dynamics, our approach aims to learn different representation subspaces of cross-regional dynamics, where each subspace involves a set of locations called "community" sharing similar behaviors. The proposed architecture is "community-attentive" as it allows the prediction for a given location to be individually optimized by the features contributed by a mixture of communities. Specifically, combining the features of the given target location and features from the communities (referred to as local and global dynamics), the model learns to forecast the number of opioid overdoses in the target location. Meanwhile, by leveraging a Lasso regularization [18] and hierarchical attention mechanism, our method allows for interpreting what local and global features are more predictive, what communities contribute more to predicting incidences at a location, and what locations contribute more to each community.

Overall, our contributions include: (1) *A community-attentive spatio-temporal network:* We propose a multi-head attention based architecture that learns different representation subspaces of global dynamics (communities) to effectively forecast the opioid overdoses for different target locations. (2) *Interpretability in hierarchical attention and features:* First, CASTNet incorporates a hierarchical attention mechanism which allows for interpreting community memberships (which locations form the communities), community contributions for forecasting local incidents and informative time steps in both local and global for the prediction. Second, CASTNet incorporates Group Lasso (GL) [18] to select informative features which succinctly captures what activity types at both local- and global-level are more associated with the future opioid overdoses. (3) *Extensive experiments:* We performed extensive experiments using real-world datasets from City of Cincinnati and City of Chicago. The results indicate a significant improvement in forecasting performance with greater interpretability compared to several baselines and state-of-the-art methods.

2   Related Work

The existing works have investigated the links between opioid use and various social phenomena as well as contextual factors including crime and economic stressors. Hammersley et al. [7] stated that opportunities for drug use increase with involvement in criminal behavior. The people dependent on opiates are disproportionately involved in criminal activities [1] especially for the crimes committed for financial gain [15]. Seddon et al. [19] revealed that crime and drug use share common set of causes and they co-occur together. Most of the works studying the relationship between opioid use and social phenomena employed basic statistical analysis, and focused on current situation and trends rather than predicting/forecasting overdose. Moreover, they overlooked the interactions among spatio-temporal dynamics of the locations. Among the studies predicting opioid overdose, [11] have proposed a regression-based approach in state-level. Also, a neural network-based approach has been proposed [4] to forecast heroin overdose from crime data, which identifies the predictive hot-spots. Yet, the effect of these hot-spots on prediction is universal and irrespective of event locations.

Furthermore, there have been studies that utilized spatial and temporal dependencies for event forecasting and time series prediction. Several studies employed neural models to forecast/detect events related to crime [9] and social movements [3]. Additionally, several studies utilized deep neural models for times series prediction. Ghaderi et al. [5] proposed an RNN based model to forecast wind speeds. Qin et al. [16] presented a dual-stage attention-based RNN model to make time series prediction. Similarly, Liang et al. [14] proposed multi-level attention networks for geo-sensory time series prediction. A few of the studies considered the complex relationships between local and global activities, yet they modeled the global activities as a universal representation, which either does not change from event location to location or is adjusted by a pre-defined fixed proximity matrix. Most of these works simply employed a single temporal model to model various local and global spatio-temporal activities, which is insufficient to capture the complex spatio-temporal patterns at both local and global levels. Moreover, existing methods primarily focus on forecasting performance, yet they provide no or limited interpretability capability to unveil the underlying spatio-temporal characteristics of the local and global activities.

3   Method

3.1   Problem Definition

Suppose there are L locations-of-interest (e.g. neighborhoods, districts) and each location l can be represented as a collection of its static and dynamic features. While the static features (e.g. demographics, economical indicators) remain same or change slowly over a longer period of time, the dynamic features are the updates for each time interval t (e.g. day, week). Let X_l^{stat} be the static features of location l, and $X_{t,l}^{dyn}$ the set of dynamic features for location l at time t. We are also given a discrete variable $y_{t^*,l} \in \mathbb{N}$ that indicates the number of opioid overdose incidents (e.g. emergency medical services (EMS) calls, deaths) at location l at future time t^*. The collection of dynamic features from all locations-of-interest within an observing *time window* with size w up to time t can be represented as $\mathcal{X}_{t-w+1:t}^{dyn} = \{\mathcal{X}_{t-w+1}^{dyn}, \ldots, \mathcal{X}_t^{dyn}\}$, where $\mathcal{X}_{t'}^{dyn} = \{X_{t',1}^{dyn}, \ldots, X_{t',L}^{dyn}\}$.

Our goal is to forecast the number of opioid overdose incidents $y_{t^*,l}$ at specific location l at a future time $t^* = t + \tau$, where τ is called the *lead time*. Forecasting is based on the static and dynamic features of the target location itself, as well as the dynamic features in the environment (from all locations-of-interest). Therefore, forecasting problem can be formulated as learning a function $f(X_d^{stat}, \mathcal{X}_{t-w+1:t}^{dyn}) \rightarrow y_{t^*,d}$ that maps the static and dynamic features to the number of opioid overdose incidents at future time t^* at a *target* location d.

To facilitate spatio-temporal interpretation of the forecasting, we seek to develop a model that can differentiate contribution of the features, the locality (local features vs. global features) and the importance of latent communities when contributing to the prediction of other locations. Therefore, we further organize the dynamic features $\mathcal{X}_{t-w+1:t}^{dyn}$ into two sets: the *local* features, $\{X_{t-w+1,d}^{dyn} \ldots, X_{t,d}^{dyn}\}$ represent dynamic features for the target location d, and the *global* features, $\{X_{t-w+1,l}^{dyn} \ldots, X_{t,l}^{dyn}\}$ for $l \in \{1,2,\ldots,L\}$, contain the sequences of dynamic features for all locations of interest.

3.2   Architecture

We propose an interpretable, community-attentive, spatio-temporal predictive model, named CASTNet. Our architecture consists of three primary components, namely local (Fig. 1a), static (Fig. 1b) and global (Fig. 1c) components as follows:

Global Component. This component produces the target location-specific global contribution to forecast the number of incidents at target location d at

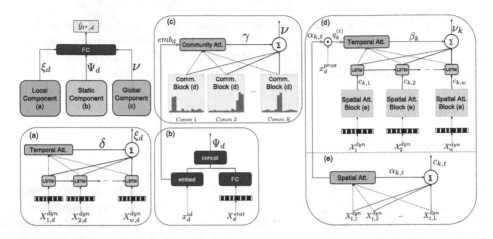

Fig. 1. Overview of CASTNet. Local component (a) models local dynamics of the locations, and static component (b) models the static features. Global component (c) summarizes different representation subspaces (i.e. communities) of global dynamics, learned by community blocks (d), by querying these multi-subspace representations through the embedding of the target location (emb_d). Spatial Att. Block (e) reweights the global dynamics of locations. Checkered rectangles represent GL regularization. Red arrows indicate the queries for the corresponding attentions. "FC": fully-connected layer; "embed": embedding layer.

future time t^*. It consists of K number of community blocks where each community block learns a different representation subspace of the global dynamic features, which is inspired by the idea of multi-head attention [20]. A community block (Fig. 1d) models the global dynamic features through a hierarchical attention network which consists of a spatial attention block (Fig. 1e), a recurrent unit and a temporal attention. For clarity, we explain the internal mechanism of global component in a bottom-up manner in the order (Fig. 1e → 1d → 1c):

Spatial Attention Block is used to reweight the contribution of dynamic features of each location i at time t. The attention weight, $\alpha_{k,t}^{(i)}$, represents the contribution of the location i at time t to the community k. Since higher spatial attention weight for a location indicates the involvement of its dynamic features in this community, we call this community membership. $c_{k,t}$ is the context vector, which summarizes the aggregated contribution of all locations as follows:

$$e_{k,t} = (v_k^{sp})^\top tanh(W_k^{sp} \mathcal{X}_t^{dyn} + b_k^{sp}) \tag{1}$$

$$\alpha_{k,t}^{(i)} = \frac{exp(e_{k,t}^{(i)})}{\sum_{l=1}^{L} exp(e_{k,t}^{(l)})}; \quad c_{k,t} = \sum_{l=1}^{L} \alpha_{k,t}^{(l)} X_{t,l}^{dyn} \tag{2}$$

where $W_k^{sp} \in \mathbb{R}^{n \times n}$, $b_k^{sp} \in \mathbb{R}^n$ and $v_k^{sp} \in \mathbb{R}^n$ are the parameters to be learned, and n is the dynamic feature size of any location. After the context vector $c_{k,t}$ is computed, it is fed to the recurrent unit.

Recurrent unit is used to capture the temporal relationships among the reweighted global dynamic features for the community k as $h_{k,t} = f_k(h_{k,t-1}, c_{k,t})$ where $f_k(.)$ is LSTM [8] for community k, and $h_{k,t}$ is the t-th hidden state of k-th community. We use LSTM in our model (in each community block) since it addresses the vanishing and exploding gradient problems of basic RNNs.

Temporal Attention is applied on top of the LSTM to differentiate the contribution of latent representations of global dynamic features at each time point and for each community. To make the output specific to target location, we incorporate a *query* scheme based on a time-dependent community membership (i.e., contribution of each location to the community) where the membership is further weighted based on the location's spatial proximity to target location (with nearby locations getting larger weights than the further ones). Specifically, let $\beta_k^{(i)}$ denotes the attention weight over the hidden state $h_{k,i}$ of community k at time i. The context vector ν_k, which is aggregate contribution from community k, can be learned through the proximity-based weighting scheme as:

$$q_k^{(i)} = x_d^{prox} \bullet \alpha_{k,i}, \tag{3}$$

$$\beta_k^{(i)} = \frac{exp(q_k^{(i)})}{\sum_{t=1}^{w} exp(q_k^{(t)})}, \quad \nu_k = \sum_{t=1}^{w} \beta_k^{(t)} h_{k,t}, \tag{4}$$

where $x_d^{prox} \in \mathbb{R}^L$ is a vector encoding the proximity of the target location d to all locations. Here, the proximity of two locations is calculated based on the inverse of geographic distance (*haversine*): $prox(l_1, l_2) = \frac{1}{\sqrt{1+dist(l_1, l_2)}}$.

Community Attention aims to produce a global contribution with respect to the target location d by combining different representation subspaces for each of the communities $\{\nu_1, \nu_2, \ldots, \nu_K\}$. A soft-attention approach is then employed to combine the contributions from all K communities. Here, to make the prediction specific to the target location, we use a *query* scheme, which takes each community vector $\{\nu_k\}$ as a *key* and the target location embedding as a *query*:

$$u_k = r^{\mathsf{T}} tanh(V\nu_k + emb_d), \tag{5}$$

$$\gamma^{(i)} = \frac{exp(u_i)}{\sum_{k=1}^{K} exp(u_k)}, \quad \nu = \sum_{k=1}^{K} \gamma^{(k)} \nu_k, \tag{6}$$

where $V \in \mathbb{R}^{m \times m}$, and $r \in \mathbb{R}^m$ are the parameters to be learned, m is the number of hidden units in LSTMs, and ν is the output of the global component.

Local Component. It is designed to model the contribution of local dynamic features for any target location d (Fig. 1a). It includes a recurrent unit and a temporal attention that focuses on the most informative time instants. Dynamic features of target location are fed to the recurrent unit to model local dynamics as $s_t = g(s_{t-1}, X_{t,d}^{dyn})$ where $g(.)$ is LSTM, as in the global component, and s_t is the t-th hidden state of LSTM. Then, we also employ a temporal attention on top of the LSTM in this component, which can select the most informative hidden states (time instants) with respect to the dynamic features of target location d. We only provide the calculation of output vector of the local component to be succinct as: $\xi_d = \sum_{t=1}^{w} \delta^{(t)} s_t$ where $\delta^{(t)}$ is the attention weight for the hidden state at time t, and ξ_d is the output of the local component.

Static Component. It models the static information specific to the target location (Fig. 1b). The input incorporates the static features, X_d^{stat}, and a one-hot encoding vector $x_d^{id} \in \mathbb{R}^L$ that represents the target location. We apply a fully connected layer (FC) to separately learn a latent representation for each of the two types of information. In particular, the one-hot location vector will be converted into an embedding emb_d and will be utilized in the aforementioned query component (see Eq. (5)). Ψ_d is the output of this component, which is concatenation of learned embeddings and latent representation of static features.

Objective Function. The objective function consists of three terms: prediction loss, orthogonality loss and Group Lasso (GL) regularization as follows:

$$\mathcal{L}_{overall} = \mathcal{L}_{predict} + \lambda \mathcal{L}_{ortho} + \eta \mathcal{L}_{GL}, \tag{7}$$

where λ and η are the tuning parameters for the penalty terms, and $\mathcal{L}_{predict} = \frac{1}{N} \sum_{i=1}^{N} (\hat{y}_i - y_i)^2$, is the mean squared error (MSE), $\hat{y}_i$ and y_i are the predicted and actual number of opioid overdose incidents for sample i, respectively. A penalty term, $\mathcal{L}_{ortho}$ is added to avoid learning redundant memberships across communities, i.e., multiple communities may consist of a similar group of locations. To encourage community memberships to be distinguishable, we incorporate $\mathcal{L}_{ortho}$ into the objective function. Let $\bar{\alpha}_k$ be the community membership vector denoting how each location contributes to the community k, averaging over time, and $\Delta = [\bar{\alpha}_1, \bar{\alpha}_2, \ldots, \bar{\alpha}_K] \in \mathbb{R}^{K \times L}$ is a matrix consisting of such membership vectors for all communities, the orthogonality loss is given by:

$$\mathcal{L}_{ortho} = \| \Delta \cdot \Delta^\mathsf{T} - I \|_F^2, \tag{8}$$

where $I \in \mathbb{R}^{K \times K}$ is the identity matrix. This loss term encourages different communities to have non-identical locations as members as much as possible, which helps reduce the redundancy across communities. Lastly, we incorporate GL regularization into objective function, which imposes sparsity on a group level [18]. Our main motivation to employ GL is to select community-level and local-level informative features. It enables us to interpret and differentiate which features are important for opioid overdose incidents. It is defined as:

$$\mathcal{L}_{GL} = \sum_{k=1}^{K} \left(\| Z_k^{glob} \|_{2,1} \right) + \| Z^{local} \|_{2,1} + \| Z^{stat} \|_{2,1}, \tag{9}$$

$$\|Z\|_{2,1} = \sum_{g \in G} \sqrt{|g|}\|g\|_2, \tag{10}$$

where Z_k^{glob} denotes input weight matrix in the kth community block in global component. Z^{local} and Z^{stat} are input weight matrices in the local and static components, respectively. g is vector of outgoing connections (weights) from an input neuron, G denotes a set of input neurons, and $|g|$ is the dimension of g.

3.3   Features

Static features are 9 features from the census data related to economical status (median household income, per capita income, poverty), housing status (housing occupancy and housing tenure), educational level (% of high school graduation and below) and demographics (population, gender and race diversity index).

Dynamic features are to capture the crime dynamics of the locations that may be predictive for opioid overdose. We extract them from public safety data portals of the cities. The crime data gathered from different cities may have different categories. We consider the highest level, "primary crime types" and eliminate rare ones. Crime categories used in this work can be found in Fig. 4. In addition to total number of incidents for each primary crime type, we also use total number of crime and opioid overdose incidents as dynamic features. We extract 14 and 9 crime-related dynamic features for Chicago, and Cincinnati, respectively. Together with the number of opioid overdose incidents, the total number of dynamic features are 15 for Chicago and 10 for Cincinnati.

4   Experiments

4.1   Datasets

We apply our method on two cities, Chicago and Cincinnati. We used "Statistical Neighborhood Approximations" of Cincinnati and "community areas" of Chicago as "neighborhoods". There are 77 and 50 neighborhoods in Chicago and Cincinnati, respectively. While we select 47 neighborhoods from Chicago (where ∼80% of opioid overdose deaths occur), we use all neighborhoods of Cincinnati. Chicago dataset spans (08/03/15 - 08/26/18) and contains 573207 crimes and 1468 opioid overdose deaths. Cincinnati dataset spans (08/01/15 - 06/01/18) and contains 75779 crimes and 5401 EMS responses. We collect the following data:

Crime data: We collect crime incident information (geo-location, time and primary type of the crimes) from the open data portals of the cities. We use Public Safety Crime dataset[1] and Police Data Initiative (PDI) Crime Incidents dataset[2] to extract such information for Chicago and Cincinnati, respectively.

---

[1] https://data.cityofchicago.org/Public-Safety/Crimes-2001-to-present/ijzp-q8t2.

[2] https://data.cincinnati-oh.gov/Safer-Streets/PDI-Police-Data-Initiative-Crime-Incidents/k59e-2pvf.

Opioid overdose data: We collect different types of opioid overdose data for each city since there is no systematic monitoring of drug abuse at either a regional or state level in the U.S. For Chicago, we collect opioid overdose death records (geo-location and time) from Opioid Mapping Initiative Open Datasets[3]. On the other hand, we utilize the EMS response data[4] for heroin overdoses in Cincinnati.
Census data: We use 2010 Census data to extract features about demographics, economical status, housing status and educational status of the neighborhoods.

4.2 Baselines

We compare our model with a number of baselines as follows: **HA**: Historical average, **ARIMA**: a well-known method for predicting future values for time series, **VAR**: a method that captures the linear inter-dependencies among multiple time series and forecasts future values, **SVR**: two variants of Support Vector Regression; SVR_{ind} (trained separate models for each location) and SVR_{all} (trained a single model for all locations), **LSTM**: a network in which dynamic features are fed to LSTM, then the latent representations are concatenated with static features for prediction, **DA-RNN** [16]: a dual-staged attention-based RNN model for spatio-temporal time series prediction, **GeoMAN** [14]: a multi-level attention-based RNN model for spatio-temporal prediction, which shows state-of-the-art performance in the air quality prediction task, **ActAttn** [3]: a hierarchical spatio-temporal predictive framework for social movements.

Furthermore, to evaluate the effectiveness of individual components of our model, we also include its several variants for the comparison: **CASTNet-noGL**: GL regularization is not included in the loss function, **CASTNet-noOrtho**: Orthogonality penalty is not applied so that differentiation of the communities is not encouraged, **CASTNet-noSA**: Spatial attentions are removed from the community blocks. Instead, the feature vectors of all locations are concatenated, **CASTNet-noTA**: The temporal attentions in both local and global components are removed from the architecture, **CASTNet-noCA**: Community attention is removed from the architecture. Instead, the context vectors of the communities are concatenated. **CASTNet-noSC**: The static features are excluded from the architecture, yet the location-ID is still embedded.
Settings: We used 'week' as time unit and 'neighborhood' as location unit. We divided datasets into training, validation and test sets with ratio of 75%, 10% and 15%, respectively. We set $\tau = 1$ to make short-term predictions. For RNN-based methods, hidden unit size of LSTMs was selected from $\{8, 16, 32, 64\}$. The networks were trained using Adam optimizer with a learning rate of 0.001. For each LSTM layer, dropout of 0.1 was applied to prevent overfitting. In our models, the regularization factors λ and η were optimized from the small sets $\{0.001, 0.005, \ldots, 0.05\}$ and $\{0.001, 0.0015, \ldots, 0.01\}$, respectively using grid search. For $ARIMA$ and VAR, the orders of the autoregressive and moving average components were optimized for the time lags between 1 and 11. For RNN-based methods, we performed experiments with different window sizes

---

[3] https://opioidmappinginitiative-opioidepidemic.opendata.arcgis.com/.
[4] https://insights.cincinnati-oh.gov/stories/s/Heroin/dm3s-ep3u/.

$w \in \{5, 10, 15, 20\}$, and shared the results for $w = 10$ (the best setting for all models). Our code and data are available at https://github.com/picsolab/castnet.

Table 1. Performance Results.

	Chicago		Cincinnati	
	MAE	RMSE	MAE	RMSE
HA	0.2329	0.3385	0.5728	0.8727
ARIMA	0.2272	0.3396	0.5717	0.8952
VAR	0.2242	0.3386	0.5606	0.8712
SVR_{ind}	0.2112	0.3321	0.5153	0.8609
SVR_{all}	0.1984	0.3063	0.4886	0.8602
LSTM	0.2024	0.3134	0.5235	0.8267
DA-RNN [16]	0.1726	0.3051	0.4817	0.8225
GeoMAN [14]	0.1679	0.2829	0.5034	0.8453
ActAttn [3]	0.1693	0.2937	0.4827	0.8326
CASTNet-noGL	0.1662	0.3129	0.4703	0.8311
CASTNet-noOrtho	0.1649	0.2948	0.4716	0.8109
CASTNet-noSA	0.1608	0.2893	0.4579	0.8152
CASTNet-noTA	0.1641	0.2876	0.4700	0.8141
CASTNet-noCA	0.1631	0.3069	0.4730	0.8225
CASTNet-noSC	0.1693	0.2980	0.4692	0.8291
CASTNet	**0.1391**	**0.2679**	**0.4516**	**0.8032**

5   Results

5.1   Performance Comparison

Table 1 shows that CASTNet achieves the best performance in terms of both mean absolute error (MAE) and root mean squared error (RMSE) on both datasets. Our model shows 17.2% and 5.3% improvement in terms of MAE and RMSE, respectively, on Chicago dataset compared to state-of-the-art approach GeoMAN. Similarly, CASTNet enhances the performance 6.3% and 2.4% on Cincinnati dataset in terms of MAE and RMSE, respectively, compared to DA-RNN. Furthermore, we observe that mostly spatio-temporal RNN-based models outperform other baselines, which indicates they better learn the complex spatio-temporal relationships between crime and opioid overdose dynamics.

We evaluate the effectiveness of each individual component of CASTNet with an ablation study. As described in Sect. 4.2, each variant is different from the proposed CASTNet by removing one tested component. Table 1 shows that

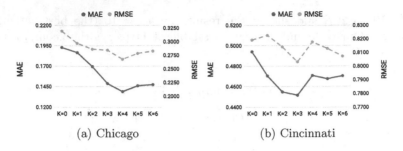

(a) Chicago   (b) Cincinnati

Fig. 2. MAE and RMSE results w.r.t change in the number of communities K.

the removal of GL results in a significantly lower performance compared to the others. In addition, CASTNet-noGL cannot select informative features. Excluding orthogonality term (CASTNet-noOrtho) loses the ability to learn distinguishable communities and reduces the performances. Comparing CASTNet with CASTNet-noCA shows the impact of community attention on the performance, indicating that learning pairwise activity relationships between an event location and communities is crucial. Location-specific static features are informative since their exclusion (CASTNet-noSC) degrades the performance in both cases. Spatial attention provides the least performance gain for both cases, yet, its removal (CASTNet-noSA) results in loss of interpretability. These results reflect that each individual component significantly contributes to the performance.

We further evaluate the performance of CASTNet with respect to the change in number of communities K. We report results for $K \in \{0, 1, \ldots, 6\}$ in Fig. 2. When $K = 0$, the model ignores global contribution, and when $K = 1$, the model yields a single universal representation of global contributions, which is irrespective of event locations. The best performances are obtained when $K = 4$ for Chicago and $K = 3$ for Cincinnati. As K increases until the optimum value, the performance increases, and some communities are decomposed to form new ones. After the optimum value of K, performance starts to decrease slightly or remains stable, and the semantic subspaces of some communities become similar. With this experiment, we indicate that learning different representations of global activities significantly improves the forecasting performance.

5.2   Community Memberships and Community Contributions

We analyze community memberships of the neighborhoods and community contributions on forecasting opioid overdose by answering the following questions. **How do locations contribute to communities?** CASTNet learns different representation subspaces (communities) of global dynamics unlike the previous work [3,14], and each community consists of a group of different members due to orthogonality penalty. We represent the learned communities and their memberships (i.e., the spatial attention weights α in Eq. (2), averaged over time for ease of interpretation) on the left sides of Fig. 3a and b for Chicago and Cincinnati, respectively. Neighborhoods on the left sides of Fig. 3a and Fig. 3b are ordered by the number of crimes. As shown in Fig. 3, most locations have dedicated to one community. For Chicago model (Fig. 3a), *Austin (25)*, which has the highest number of crime incidents and opioid overdose deaths, formed a separate community C_4 by itself. While *North Lawndale (29) and Humboldt Park (23)* together formed the community C_1, *West Garfield Park (26)*, *East Garfield Park (27)* and *North Lawndale (29)* formed C_3. Note that neighborhoods of C_1 and C_3 have the highest opioid overdose death rate after *Austin (25)*. On the other hand, C_2 is formed by the neighborhoods having low crime and overdose death rates including *Fuller Park (37)*, *McKinley Park (59)* and *West Elsdon (62)*. Furthermore, for Cincinnati model (Fig. 3b), *Westwood (49)*, where the highest number of crimes were committed, formed a separate community C_3 by itself similar to *Austin (25)* in Chicago. *East Price Hill (13)*, *West Price Hill (48)*,

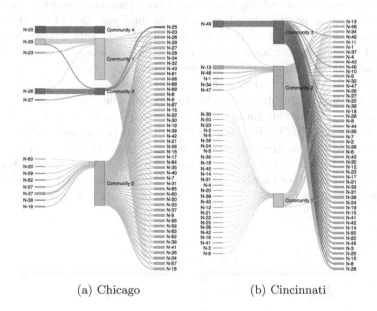

(a) Chicago   (b) Cincinnati

Fig. 3. Community memberships and community contributions on forecasting. For each community, left side represents community memberships (how each location contributes to the community), and right side represents the average community contribution (how the community contribute to predicting a target location). Edge thickness indicates the weight of community membership (left side) and community contribution (right side). Node size denotes overall community membership of a location (left side) and overall community contribution to forecasting overdose (right side) in the target neighborhood. Edge color shows the input and output of a specific community. Node color of a neighborhood indicates the community for which the corresponding neighborhood has the highest membership (left side). Node color of a neighborhood denotes the community from which the neighborhood takes the largest contribution (right side). Edges whose weights are above a certain threshold are shown. (Color figure online)

Avondale (1) and *Over-The-Rhine (34)* formed C_2 where these neighborhoods have the highest crime rate after *Westwood (49)* and the highest opioid overdose rate. C_1 is formed by rest of the neighborhoods (with low and moderate crime rates) and their memberships of that community are almost equal.

How do the communities contribute to forecasting? CASTNet is capable of modeling the pairwise activity relationships between a particular event location and the communities. It allows the target location to attend the communities to select location-specific global contributions. We analyze how these communities contribute to forecasting by visualizing the community attention weights (γ in Eq. (6) averaged over test samples for each neighborhood) in Fig. 3a and Fig. 3b for Chicago and Cincinnati, respectively. The right sides of the figures indicate the average community contributions for the neighborhoods, which are ordered by the number of opioid overdoses on the right sides. For Chicago, C_1 and C_2 have more contributions than others on forecasting overdose. While C_2 contributes more to neighborhoods with low or moderate opioid overdose death rate, C_1 and C_3 contribute more to the neighborhoods with higher death rate meaning that any neighborhood attends more to the community, which is formed by the similar neighborhoods. C_4 does not significantly contribute to any neighborhood although it is formed by a crime hot-spot (*Austin (25)*). For Cincinnati, C_2 is very dominant and makes the largest global contribution to most of the neighborhoods. The neighborhoods that formed C_2 and C_3 (e.g. *East Price Hill (13), West Price Hill (48), Westwood (49)*) are very predictive, and the change in their dynamics have greater impact on forecasting overdoses in the target neighborhoods. On the other hand, C_1 has larger contribution to neighborhoods with the highest overdose rate indicating that crimes committed in the members of C_1 are informative for forecasting overdoses in opioid hot-spots.

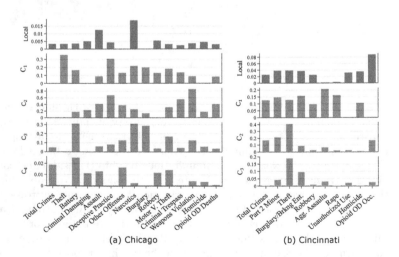

(a) Chicago   (b) Cincinnati

Fig. 4. Importance of dynamic features. Mean absolute values of input weights of local and global components.

5.3 Feature Analysis

We investigate the importance of **dynamic features** by analyzing the mean absolute input weights of local and global components as shown in Fig. 4. For Chicago case, GL selects *Narcotics* and *Assault* as the most important features for future opioid overdose deaths in the same location. Moreover, *Theft, Deceptive Practice, Narcotics, Burglary* and *Motor V. Theft* are the predictive features from C_1 while *Weapons Violation, Deceptive Practice (e.g. Fraud)* and *Criminal Trespass* are significant from C_2. Recall that, C_1 and C_2 are the most contributing communities to forecasting (see Fig. 3a). This shows that property crimes (*e.g. Theft, Burglary, Deceptive Practice*) are more significant predictors than the violent crimes for Chicago. Such crimes previously committed in the members of C_1 and C_2 may be a significant indicator of future opioid overdose deaths in Chicago. On the other hand, *Battery, Narcotics, Burglary, and Motor V. Theft* are predictive features from C_3 while *Battery, Total Crimes* and *Other Offenses (e.g. offenses against family)* are significant from C_4. However, C_3 has larger contribution than other communities for only *Austin (25)*. C_4 does not provide a significant contribution to any neighborhood. For Cincinnati case, *Opioid Overdose Occ.* is the most predictive feature for forecasting future opioid overdose in the same location, which means the local component behaves as an autoregressive module unlike the Chicago case. Furthermore, both violent crimes including *Agg. Assaults, Rape, Homicide, Part 2 Minor (e.g. Menacing)* and property crimes including *Burglary/Breaking Ent., Theft, Part 2 Minor (e.g. Fraud)* are significant features from C_1. On the other hand, *Theft* and *Part 2 Minor* from C_2, and *Theft* and *Burglary* from C_3 are predictive features for future opioid overdose in the target locations. Recall that C_2 and C_3 have more salient contribution on most of the neighborhoods, which implies that commitment of previous property crimes (especially *Theft*) in the members of those communities may be one of the potential indicators of future opioid overdose in the other neighborhoods. Our findings are consistent with the literature that highlighted the connection between crime and drug use, and suggested the property crimes such as theft, burglary might be committed to raise funds to purchase drugs [1].

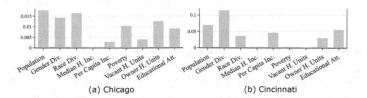

(a) Chicago   (b) Cincinnati

Fig. 5. Importance of static features. Mean absolute values of input weights of FC layer in static component.

We explore the importance of **static features** by analyzing mean absolute input weights of FC in static component (see Fig. 5). For Chicago, demographic features (*Population, Gender Div.* and *Race Div.*) are significant. *Owner Occupied H. units, Poverty* and *Educational Att.* are also informative. For Cincinnati, *Gender Div.* and *Population* are important as well as *Educational Att.* and *Per Capita Income.* Based on the results, the neighborhoods with higher population, and lower or moderate gender diversity may require additional resources to prevent opioid overdose in both cities. Economic status is important for both cities, which is consistent with the previous work suggesting that communities with a higher concentration of economic stressors may be vulnerable to abuse of opioids as a way to manage stress [12]. Among three economic status indicators, GL selects only one, *Poverty* for Chicago and *Per Capita Income* for Cincinnati.

6   Discussion and Future Work

We presented a community-attentive spatio-temporal model to forecast opioid overdose from crime dynamics. We developed a novel deep architecture based on multi-head attentional networks that learns different representation subspaces and allows the target locations to select location-specific community contributions for forecasting local incidents. Meanwhile, it allows for interpreting predictive features in both local-level and community-level, as well as community memberships and community contributions. We showed the strength of our method through extensive experiments. Our method achieved superior forecasting performance on two real-world opioid overdose datasets compared to baselines.

Our results suggest different spatio-temporal crime-overdose potential links. The overdose deaths at a target neighborhood in Chicago appear to be better predicted by crime incidents at neighborhoods in the same community. Also, change in crime incidences in neighborhoods with low crime rates is an important indicator of future overdoses in most of the other neighborhoods. In Cincinnati, the crime incidents occurred in communities comprising those crime hot-spots seem to well predict the overdose events in most of the neighborhoods. Furthermore, the predictive local activities are different in two cases. While the local crime incidents, *Narcotics* and *Assault*, are predictive for local overdose deaths in Chicago, previous overdose occurrences are informative for future overdose incidents in Cincinnati. On the other hand, the global contributions to forecasting local overdose incidents show similar patterns in both cities. Change in property crimes, in particular *Theft, Deceptive Practice, Burglary* and *Weapons Violation* (crime against to society) in Chicago, *Theft* and *Burglary* in Cincinnati, can be significant indicators for future local overdose incidents as well as certain type of violent crimes (*Battery* for Chicago and *Agg. Assault for Cincinnati*). Last but not the least, demographic characteristics, economic status and educational attainment of the neighborhoods in both cities may help forecasting future local incidents. Our findings support the hypothesis that criminal activities and opioid overdose incidents may reveal spatio-temporal lag effects, and are consistent with the literature. As future work, we plan to investigate the link between opioid use and other social phenomena using our method. We also plan to extend our model to consider multi-resolution spatio-temporal dynamics for prediction.

Acknowledgement. This work is part of the research associated with NSF #1637067 and #1739413. Any opinions, findings, and conclusions or recommendations expressed in this material do not necessarily reflect the views of the funding sources.

References

1. Bennett, T., Holloway, K., Farrington, D.: The statistical association between drug misuse and crime: a meta-analysis. Aggress. Violent Behav. **13**(2), 107–118 (2008)
2. Burke, D.S.: Forecasting the opioid epidemic. Science **354**, 529 (2016)
3. Ertugrul, A.M., Lin, Y.-R., Chung, W.-T., Yan, M., Li, A.: Activism via attention: interpretable spatiotemporal learning to forecast protest activities. EPJ Data Sci. **8**(1), 1–26 (2019). https://doi.org/10.1140/epjds/s13688-019-0183-y
4. Ertugrul, A.M., Lin, Y.R., Mair, C., Taskaya Temizel, T.: Forecasting heroin overdose occurrences from crime incidents. In: SBP-BRiMS (2018)
5. Ghaderi, A., Sanandaji, B.M., Ghaderi, F.: Deep forecast: deep learning-based spatio-temporal forecasting. arXiv preprint arXiv:1707.08110 (2017)
6. Gruenewald, P.J.: Geospatial analyses of alcohol and drug problems: empirical needs and theoretical foundations. GeoJournal **78**(3), 443–450 (2013)
7. Hammersley, R., Forsyth, A., Morrison, V., Davies, J.B.: The relationship between crime and opioid use. Addiction **84**(9), 1029–1043 (1989)
8. Hochreiter, S., Schmidhuber, J.: Long short-term memory. Neural Comput. **9**(8), 1735–1780 (1997)
9. Huang, C., Zhang, J., Zheng, Y., Chawla, N.V.: DeepCrime: attentive hierarchical recurrent networks for crime prediction. In: ACM CIKM, pp. 1423–1432 (2018)
10. Jalal, H., Buchanich, J.M., Roberts, M.S., Balmert, L.C., Zhang, K., Burke, D.S.: Changing dynamics of the drug overdose epidemic in the united states from 1979 through 2016. Science **361**(6408), eaau1184 (2018)
11. Kennedy-Hendricks, A., Richey, M., McGinty, E.E., Stuart, E.A., Barry, C.L., Webster, D.W.: Opioid overdose deaths and Florida's crackdown on pill mills. Am. J. Public Health **106**(2), 291–297 (2016)
12. King, N.B., Fraser, V., Boikos, C., Richardson, R., Harper, S.: Determinants of increased opioid-related mortality in the united states and Canada, 1990–2013: a systematic review. Am. J. Public Health **104**(8), e32–e42 (2014)
13. Kolodny, A., Courtwright, D.T., Hwang, C.S., Kreiner, P., Eadie, J.L., Clark, T.W., Alexander, G.C.: The prescription opioid and heroin crisis: a public health approach to an epidemic of addiction. Annu. Rev. Public Health **36**, 559–574 (2015)
14. Liang, Y., Ke, S., Zhang, J., Yi, X., Zheng, Y.: GeoMan: multi-level attention networks for geo-sensory time series prediction. In: IJCAI, pp. 3428–3434 (2018)
15. Pierce, M., et al.: Quantifying crime associated with drug use among a large cohort of sanctioned offenders in England and Wales. Drug Alcohol Depend. **155**, 52–59 (2015)
16. Qin, Y., Song, D., Cheng, H., Cheng, W., Jiang, G., Cottrell, G.W.: A dual-stage attention-based recurrent neural network for time series prediction. In: AAAI, pp. 2627–2633 (2017)
17. Rudd, R.A., Aleshire, N., Zibbell, J.E., Matthew Gladden, R.: Increases in drug and opioid overdose deaths–United States, 2000–2014. Am. J. Transplantat. **16**(4), 1323–1327 (2016)

18. Scardapane, S., Comminiello, D., Hussain, A., Uncini, A.: Group sparse regularization for deep neural networks. Neurocomputing **241**, 81–89 (2017)
19. Seddon, T.: Drugs, crime and social exclusion: social context and social theory in british drugs-crime research. Br. J. Criminol. **46**(4), 680–703 (2005)
20. Vaswani, A., et al.: Attention is all you need. In: NIPS, pp. 5998–6008 (2017)
21. Warner, M., Chen, L.H., Makuc, D.M., Anderson, R.N., Miniño, A.M.: Drug poisoning deaths in the United States, 1980–2008. NCHS Data Brief **81**, 1–8 (2011)
22. Zhao, L., Wang, J., Guo, X.: Distant-supervision of heterogeneous multitask learning for social event forecasting with multilingual indicators. In: AAAI (2018)

Applied Data Science: E-commerce, Finance, and Advertising

Scalable Bid Landscape Forecasting in Real-Time Bidding

Aritra Ghosh[1]([✉]), Saayan Mitra[2], Somdeb Sarkhel[2], Jason Xie[3], Gang Wu[2], and Viswanathan Swaminathan[2]

[1] University of Massachusetts, Amherst, MA, USA
arighosh@cs.umass.edu
[2] Adobe Research, San Jose, CA, USA
{smitra,sarkhel,gawu,vishy}@adobe.com
[3] Adobe Advertising Cloud, Emeryville, CA, USA
jasonxie@adobe.com

Abstract. In programmatic advertising, ad slots are usually sold using second-price (SP) auctions in real-time. The highest bidding advertiser wins but pays only the second highest bid (known as the *winning price*). In SP, for a single item, the dominant strategy of each bidder is to bid the true value from the bidder's perspective. However, in a practical setting, with budget constraints, bidding the true value is a sub-optimal strategy. Hence, to devise an optimal bidding strategy, it is of utmost importance to learn the winning price distribution accurately. Moreover, a demand-side platform (DSP), which bids on behalf of advertisers, observes the winning price if it wins the auction. For losing auctions, DSPs can only treat its bidding price as the lower bound for the unknown winning price. In literature, typically censored regression is used to model such partially observed data. A common assumption in censored regression is that the winning price is drawn from a fixed variance (homoscedastic) uni-modal distribution (most often Gaussian). However, in reality, these assumptions are often violated. We relax these assumptions and propose a heteroscedastic fully parametric censored regression approach, as well as a mixture density censored network. Our approach not only generalizes censored regression but also provides flexibility to model arbitrarily distributed real-world data. Experimental evaluation on the publicly available dataset for winning price estimation demonstrates the effectiveness of our method. Furthermore, we evaluate our algorithm on one of the largest demand-side platform and significant improvement has been achieved in comparison with the baseline solutions.

Keywords: Computational advertising · Real-time bidding · Censored regression · Bid landscape forecasting

---

This work was conducted while the first author was doing an internship at Adobe Research, USA.

U. Brefeld et al. (Eds.): ECML PKDD 2019, LNAI 11908, pp. 451–466, 2020.
https://doi.org/10.1007/978-3-030-46133-1_27

1   Introduction

Real-time Bidding (RTB) has become the dominant mechanism to sell ad slots over the internet in recent times. In RTB, ad display opportunities are auctioned when available from the publishers (sellers) to the advertisers (buyers). When a user sees the ad that won the auction, it is counted as an *ad impression*. An RTB ecosystem consists of supply-side platforms (SSP), demand-side platforms (DSP) and an Ad Exchange. When a user visits a publisher's page, the SSP sends a request to the Ad Exchange for an ad display opportunity which is then rerouted to DSPs in the form of a bid request. DSPs bid on behalf of the advertisers at the Ad Exchange. The winner of the auction places the Ad on the publisher's site. Ad Exchanges usually employ second-price auction (SP) where the winning DSP only has to pay the second highest bidding price [21]. Since this price is the minimum bidding price DSP needs to win, it is known as the *winning price*. When a DSP wins the auction, it knows the actual winning price. However, if the DSP loses the auction, the Ad Exchange does not reveal the winning price. In that case, the bidding price provides a lower bound on the winning price. This mixture of observed and partially-observed (lower bound) data is known as *right censored data*. The data to the *right* of the bidding price is not observed since it is right censored.

For a single *ad impression* under the second price auction scheme, the dominant strategy for an advertiser is to bid the true value of the ad. In this scenario, knowing the bidding prices of other DSPs does not change a bidder's strategy [6]. However, in reality, DSPs have budget constraints with a utility goal (e.g., number of impressions, clicks, conversions). Under budget constraints, with repeated auctions, bidding the true value is no longer the dominant strategy [3]. In this setting, knowledge of the bidding prices of other bidders can allow one to change the bid to improve its expected utility. DSP needs to estimate the cost and utility of an auction to compute the optimal bidding strategy (or bidding price) [23]. To compute the expected cost as well as the expected utility one needs to know the winning price distribution. Therefore, modeling the winning price distribution is an important problem for a DSP [12]. This problem is also referred to as the *Bid landscape forecasting* problem.

Learning the bid landscape from a mix of observed and partially-observed data poses a real challenge. It is not possible for DSPs to know the behavior of the winning price beyond the maximum bidding price. Parametric approaches often assume that the winning price follows some distribution. In the existing literature, Gaussian and Log-Normal distributions are often used for modeling the winning price [5,20]. However, these simple distributions do not always capture all the complexities of real-world data. Moreover, for losing bids, the density of winning price cannot be measured directly, and hence a standard log-likelihood based estimate does not typically work on the censored data. In this scenario, a common parametric method used is *Censored Regression*, which combines the log density and the log probability for winning and losing auctions respectively [13,20]. Another common alternative is to use non-parametric survival based methods using the Kaplan-Meier (KM) estimate for censored data [10]. To improve the performance of the KM estimate, clustering the input is important. Interestingly, in [18], the authors proposed to grow a decision tree based on survival methods. In the absence of distributional assumptions, non-parametric methods (KM) work well. However, efficiently scaling non-parametric methods is also challenging. On the other hand, parametric methods work on strong distributional assumptions. When the assumptions are violated, inconsistency arises. For a general discussion of the censored problem in machine learning, readers are referred to [16].

Learning a distribution is generally more challenging than point estimation. Thus, parametric approaches in previous research often considered point estimation [19,20]. However, to obtain an optimal bidding strategy, one needs the distribution of the winning price. On the other hand, non-parametric approaches like the KM method computes the distribution without any assumptions. However, these methods require clustering the data to improve the accuracy of the model using some heuristics. Clustering based on feature attributes makes these methods sub-optimal impacting generalization ability for dynamic real-world ad data.

In this paper, we close the gap of violated assumptions in parametric approaches on censored data. Censored regression-based approaches assume a unimodal (often Gaussian) distribution on winning price. Additionally, it assumes that the standard deviation of the Gaussian distribution is unknown but fixed. However, in most real-world datasets these assumptions are often violated. For example, in Fig. 1, we present two winning price distributions (learned using the KM estimate) as well as fitted Gaussian distributions[1] on two different partitions of the iPinYou dataset [24]. It is evident from Fig. 1 that the distributions are neither Gaussian (blue line) nor have fixed variance (red line). In this paper, we relax each of these assumptions one by one and propose a general framework to solve the problem of predicting the winning price distribution using partially observed censored data. We first propose an additional parameterization which addresses the fixed variance assumption. Further, the Mixture Density Network is known to approximate any continuous, differentiable function with enough hidden nodes [4]. We propose a Mixture Density Censored Network to learn smooth winning price distribution using the censored data. We refer to it as MCNet in the rest of the paper. Both of our proposed approaches are generalizations of the Censored Regression.

Our main contributions are as follows. The typical deployed system uses Censored regression for point estimation of the winning price. However, we argue that point estimation is not enough for an optimal bidding strategy. We improve upon the parametric Censored Regression model to a general framework under minimal assumptions. We pose Censored Regression as a solution to the winning price distribution estimation problem (instead of a point estimate). To the best of our

---

[1] We fit the unimodal Gaussian minimizing KL divergence with the estimated KM distribution. We would like to point out, although in Fig. 1(b) winning price density is unimodal (within the limit), the probability of winning price beyond the max bid price is high (0.61). Thus the fitted Gaussian has a mean of 350 and std dev of 250 further from the peak at 75.

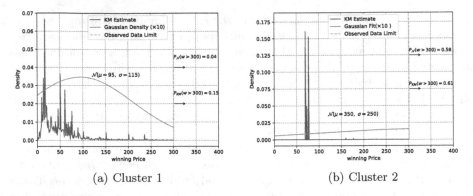

(a) Cluster 1   (b) Cluster 2

Fig. 1. KM Estimate and Gaussian Fit on two clusters of Session-2 date 2013-06-12 on iPinYou [24] (Color figure online)

knowledge, we are the first to apply the mixture density network on censored data for learning the arbitrary distribution of the winning price. Our extensive experiments on a real-world public dataset show that our approach vastly out-performs existing state-of-the-art approaches such as [20]. Evaluation on the historical bid data from Adobe (DSP) shows the efficacy of our scalable solution. While we restricted the analysis to winning price distribution in real-time bidding, MCNet is applicable to any partially observed censored data problem.

2   Background and Related Work

In RTB, a DSP gets bid requests from the Ad exchange. We represent the ith bid request by a feature vector $\mathbf{x}_i$, which captures all the characteristics of the bid request. Most of the elements of $\mathbf{x}_i$'s are categorical (publisher verticals, user's device, etc.). If DSP wins the auction, it pays the second (winning) price. Formally, the winning price is,

$$\mathbf{w}_i = \max\{\mathbf{b}_i^{\text{Pub}}, \mathbf{b}_i^{\text{DSP}_1}, \mathbf{b}_i^{\text{DSP}_2}, \cdots, \mathbf{b}_i^{\text{DSP}_K}\}$$

where $\mathbf{b}_i^{\text{Pub}}$ is the floor price set by the publisher[2] (often 0), and $\mathbf{b}_i^{\text{DSP}_1}, \cdots,$ $\mathbf{b}_i^{\text{DSP}_K}$ are bidding prices from all other participating DSPs. We use $\mathbf{b}_i$ to denote the bidding price from the DSP of our interest. Here we provide an example to illustrate the winning price (in SP auction). Suppose DSPs A, B, C bid $1, $2, $3 respectively for a bid request. DSP C then wins the auction and pays the second-highest price, i.e., $2. For DSP C, the winning price is $2 (observed). For losing DSPs, A, and B, the winning price is $3 (which is unknown to them). In this paper, we define the winning price from the perspective of a single DSP.

---

[2] For simplicity, we view the floor price by the publisher as a bid from an additional DSP.

Learning the landscape of winning price accurately is important for an optimal bidding strategy. A DSP is usually interested in some utility $\mathbf{u}_i$ (e.g., clicks, impressions, conversions) for each bid request $\mathbf{x}_i$ and wants to maximize the overall utility using bidding strategy $\mathcal{A}$ and with budget $\mathcal{B}$. This can be represented by the following optimization problem, $\max_{\mathcal{A}} \sum_i \mathbf{u}_i$ s.t. $\sum_i cost_i \leq \mathcal{B}$, where $cost_i$ is the price the DSP pays, if it wins the auction. Although the variables are unknown beforehand, the expected cost and the utility can be computed using the historical bid information. Thus the problem simplifies to,

$$\max_{\mathcal{A}} \sum_i \mathrm{E}[\mathbf{u}_i|\mathbf{x}_i, \mathbf{b}_i] \text{ s.t. } \sum_i \mathrm{E}[cost_i|\mathbf{x}_i, \mathbf{b}_i] \leq \mathcal{B} \tag{1}$$

Note that, the expected utility $\mathbf{u}_i$ is conditioned on bid request $\mathbf{x}_i$ and the actual bid $\mathbf{b}_i$. For bid request $\mathbf{x}_i$, we represent the winning price distribution as $P_{\mathbf{w}}(\mathbf{W}_i|\mathbf{x}_i)$, and its cumulative distribution function (cdf) as $F_{\mathbf{w}}(\mathbf{W}_i|\mathbf{x}_i)$. If the DSP bids $\mathbf{b}_i$ for $\mathbf{x}_i$, expected cost and expected utility (for SP auction) is,

$$\mathrm{E}[cost_i|\mathbf{x}_i, \mathbf{b}_i] = \int_0^{\mathbf{b}_i} \mathbf{w} P_{\mathbf{w}}(\mathbf{W}_i = \mathbf{w}|\mathbf{x}_i)d\mathbf{w}, \quad \mathrm{E}[\mathbf{u}_i|\mathbf{x}_i, \mathbf{b}_i] = F_{\mathbf{w}}(\mathbf{b}_i|\mathbf{x}_i)\mathrm{E}[\mathbf{u}_i|\mathbf{x}_i]$$

An example of expected utility conditioned on bid request ($\mathrm{E}[\mathbf{u}_i|\mathbf{x}_i]$) is Click-through rate (CTR). CTR prediction is a well-studied problem in academia and the industry [17]. We want to point out that the expected cost ($\mathrm{E}[cost_i|\mathbf{x}_i, \mathbf{b}_i]$) is not the same as the expected winning price ($\mathrm{E}[\mathbf{W}_i|\mathbf{x}_i]$). The former is always lower than the latter and is equal only when $\mathbf{b}_i \to \infty$ (i.e., when the advertiser wins the auction with probability 1 and observe the winning price). Thus predicting the winning price distribution instead of the point estimate is important [15]. Further, for pacing the budget, one requires an estimate of winning price distribution [2]. In [25], the authors proposed an unbiased learning algorithm of click-through rate estimation using the winning price distribution. Earlier parametric methods, considered point estimation of the winning price. The censored regression-based approach assumes a standard unimodal distribution with a fixed but unknown variance to model the winning price [17,20,26]. In another paradigm, non-parametric methods such as the KM estimator has been successful for modeling censored data [10,18].

In the rest of the paper, we use P to denote probability density function (pdf) and Pr to denote the usual probabilities. Next, we describe how Censored Regression is applied to model the winning price.

2.1 Censored Regression

The data available to DSP is right censored by the Ad Exchange, i.e., for losing bids only a lower bound (the bidding price) of the winning price is known. However, a maximum likelihood estimator (MLE) can still work on the censored data with some assumptions.

In [20], the authors assume that the winning price follows a normal distribution with fixed but unknown variance σ. The authors assume a linear relationship between the mean of the normal distribution and the input feature vector.

We use $\mathbf{W}_i$ to represent the random variable of winning price distribution of ith bid request whereas $\mathbf{w}_i$ is the realization of that. Thus $\mathbf{w}_i = \beta^T \mathbf{x}_i + \epsilon_i$ where ϵ_i are independent and identically distributed $(i.i.d)$ from $\mathcal{N}(0, \sigma^2)$ and $\mathbf{W}_i \sim \mathcal{N}(\beta^T \mathbf{x}_i, \sigma^2)$.

One can use any standard distribution in the censored regression approach. In [19], the authors argue that maximal bidding price in the limit (of infinite DSPs) resembles Gumbel distribution. However, for the generality of learning from censored data, we do not constrain on any particular distribution in this paper. Moreover, the linear link function can be replaced with any non-linear function. Thus, $\mathbf{w}_i$ can be parameterized as $\mathbf{w}_i = f(\beta, \mathbf{x}_i) + \epsilon_i$ where f can be any continuous differentiable function. With the success of deep models, in [19], the authors parameterize $f(\beta, \mathbf{x}_i)$ with a deep network for additional flexibility. Since we know the winning price for winning auctions, likelihood is simply the probability density function (pdf) $P(\mathbf{W}_i = \mathbf{w}_i) = \frac{1}{\sigma}\phi(\frac{\mathbf{w}_i - \beta^T \mathbf{x}_i}{\sigma})$ where ϕ is the pdf of standard normal $\mathcal{N}(0, 1)$. Note that, $\mathbf{W}_i$ is the random variable associated with the winning price distribution whereas $\mathbf{w}_i$ is the observed winning price. For losing auctions, as we do not know the winning price, the pdf is unknown to us. However, from the lower bound on the winning price, we can compute the probability that bid $\mathbf{b}_i$ will lose in the auction for bid request $\mathbf{x}_i$, under the estimated distribution of $\mathbf{W}_i$ as $\Pr(\mathbf{W}_i > \mathbf{b}_i) = \Pr(\epsilon_i < \beta^T \mathbf{x}_i - \mathbf{b}_i) = \Phi(\frac{\beta^T \mathbf{x}_i - \mathbf{b}_i}{\sigma})$. Here Φ is the cdf for standard normal distribution. As discussed, ϕ and Φ can be replaced with pdf and cdf of any other distribution (with different parameterization).

Taking $\log$ of the density for winning auctions $\mathcal{W}$ and the log-probability for losing auctions $\mathcal{L}$, we get the following objective function [20],

$$\beta^*, \sigma^* = \arg \max_{\beta, \sigma > 0} \sum_{i \in \mathcal{W}} \log\left(\frac{1}{\sigma}\phi(\frac{\mathbf{w}_i - \beta^T \mathbf{x}_i}{\sigma})\right) + \sum_{i \in \mathcal{L}} \log\left(\Phi(\frac{\beta^T \mathbf{x}_i - \mathbf{b}_i}{\sigma})\right) \quad (2)$$

When the ϵ_i (noise in the winning price model) are i.i.d samples from a fixed variance normal distribution, censored regression is an unbiased and consistent estimator [8, 9].

3   Methodology

In this paper, we build on top of (Gaussian) censored regression-based approach by relaxing some of the assumptions that do not hold in practice. First, we relax the assumption of *homoscedasticity*, i.e., noise (or error) follows a normal distribution with fixed but possibly unknown variance, by modeling it as a fully parametric censored regression. Then we also relax the unimodality assumption by proposing a mixture density censored network. We describe the details of our approaches in the next two subsections.

3.1   Fully Parametric Censored Regression

The censored regression approach assumes that the winning price is normally distributed with a fixed standard deviation. As we discussed, in Fig. 1, the variance of the fitted Gaussian model is not fixed. If the noise ϵ is heteroscedastic or not from a fixed variance normal distribution, the MLE is biased and inconsistent. Using a single σ to model all bid requests, will not fully utilize the predictive power of the censored regression model. Moreover, while the point estimate (mean) of the winning price is not dependent on the estimated variance, the *Bid landscape* changes with σ. We remove the restriction of homoscedasticity in the censored regression model and pose it as a solution to the distribution learning problem.

Specifically, we assume the error term ϵ is coming from a parametric distribution conditioned on the features. This solves the problem of error term coming from fixed variance distribution. We assume the noise term ϵ_i is coming from $\mathcal{N}(0, \sigma_i^2)$ where $\sigma_i = \exp(\alpha^T \mathbf{x}_i)$.

The likelihood for winning the auction is, $P(\mathbf{W}_i = \mathbf{w}_i) = \frac{1}{\exp(\alpha^T \mathbf{x}_i)}$ $\phi(\frac{\mathbf{w}_i - \beta^T \mathbf{x}_i}{\exp(\alpha^T \mathbf{x}_i)})$ where the predicted random variable $\mathbf{W}_i \sim \mathcal{N}(\beta^T \mathbf{x}_i, \exp(\alpha^T \mathbf{x}_i)^2)$ and ϕ is the pdf of $\mathcal{N}(0, 1)$. In fully parametric censored regression, $\epsilon_i \sim \mathcal{N}(0, \exp(\alpha^T \mathbf{x}_i)^2)$ are not *i.i.d* samples. For losing bids, we can similarly compute the probability based on the lower bound (bidding price $\mathbf{b}_i$)

$$\Pr(\mathbf{W}_i > \mathbf{b}_i) = P(\epsilon_i < \beta^T \mathbf{x}_i - \mathbf{b}_i) = \Phi(\frac{\beta^T \mathbf{x}_i - \mathbf{b}_i}{\exp(\alpha^T \mathbf{x}_i)})$$

Under the assumption of normal but varying variance on the noise, we can still get a consistent and unbiased estimator by solving the following problem.

$$\beta^*, \alpha^* = \arg\max_{\beta, \alpha} \sum_{i \in \mathcal{W}} \log\left(\frac{1}{\exp(\alpha^T \mathbf{x}_i)} \phi(\frac{\mathbf{w}_i - \beta^T \mathbf{x}_i}{\exp(\alpha^T \mathbf{x}_i)})\right) + \sum_{i \in \mathcal{L}} \log\left(\Phi(\frac{\beta^T \mathbf{x}_i - \mathbf{b}_i}{\exp(\alpha^T \mathbf{x}_i)})\right)$$

$$(3)$$

3.2   Mixture Density Censored Network (MCNet)

In the previous subsection, we relaxed the fixed variance problem by using a parametric σ. However, no standard distribution can model the multi-modality that we observe in real-world data. For example, in Fig. 1(b), we see mostly unimodal behavior below the max bid price. However, the probability of losing an auction is often high (61% in Fig. 1(b)). Thus even with parametric standard deviation, when we minimize the KL-divergence with a Gaussian, the mean shifts towards the middle. Inspired by the Gaussian Mixture Model (GMM) [4] we propose a Mixture Density Censored Network (MCNet). MCNet resembles a Mixture Density Network while handling partially observed censored data for learning arbitrary continuous distribution.

In a GMM, the estimated random variable $\mathbf{W}_i$ consists of K Gaussian densities and has the following pdf, $P(\mathbf{W}_i = \mathbf{w}_i) = \sum_{k=1}^{K} \frac{\pi_k(\mathbf{x}_i)}{\sigma_k(\mathbf{x}_i)} \phi(\frac{\mathbf{w}_i - \mu_k(\mathbf{x}_i)}{\sigma_k^2(\mathbf{x}_i)})$. Here $\pi_k(\mathbf{x}), \mu_k(\mathbf{x}), \sigma_k(\mathbf{x})$ are the weight, mean and standard deviation for k^{th} mixture density respectively where $k \in \{1, \cdots, K\}$. To model the censored regression problem as a mixture model, a straightforward way is to formulate the mean of the Gaussian distributions with a linear function. Furthermore, to impose positivity of σ, we model the logarithm of the standard deviation as a linear function. We impose a similar positivity constraint on the weight parameters. The parameters of the mixture model are (for $k \in \{1, \cdots, K\}$),

$$\mu_k(\mathbf{x}_i) = \beta_{\mu,k}^T \mathbf{x}_i, \ \ \sigma_k(\mathbf{x}_i) = \exp(\beta_{\sigma,k}^T \mathbf{x}_i), \ \ \pi_k(\mathbf{x}_i) = \frac{\exp(\beta_{\pi,k}^T \mathbf{x}_i)}{\sum_{j=1}^{K} \exp(\beta_{\pi,j}^T \mathbf{x}_i)}$$

We can further generalize this mixture model and define a Mixture Density Network (MDN) by parameterizing $\pi_k(\mathbf{x}_i), \mu_k(\mathbf{x}_i), \sigma_k(\mathbf{x}_i)$ with a deep network. In applications such as speech and image processing and astrophysics, MDNs have been found useful [14,22]. MDN can work with any reasonable choice of base distribution.

MDN combines mixture models with neural networks. The output activation layer, consists of $3K$ nodes ($z_{i,k}$ for $i \in \{\mu, \sigma, \pi\}$ and $k \in \{1, \cdots, K\}$). We use $z_{\mu,k}, z_{\sigma,k}, z_{\pi,k}$ to retrieve the mean, standard deviation and weight parameters of kth density,

$$\mu_k(\mathbf{x}_i) = z_{\mu,k}(\mathbf{x}), \ \ \sigma_k(\mathbf{x}_i) = \exp(z_{\sigma,k}(\mathbf{x})), \ \ \pi_k(\mathbf{x}_i) = \frac{\exp(z_{\pi,k}(\mathbf{x}_i))}{\sum_{j=1}^{K} \exp(z_{\pi,j}(\mathbf{x}_i))} \quad (4)$$

MDN outputs conditional probabilities that are used for learning distribution from fully observed data [4]. For the censored problem, however, we only observe partial data. We can now extend MDN to MCNet on censored data. Instead of conditional output probabilities, MCNet outputs the probability of losing in case auction is lost. Thus, we can compute the log-likelihood function on partially observed data. Taking the likelihood for winning auctions, the corresponding negative log-likelihood for all the winning auctions is given by $\sum_{i \in \mathcal{W}} - \log(\sum_{k=1}^{K} \frac{\pi_k(\mathbf{x}_i)}{\sigma_k(\mathbf{x}_i)} \phi(\frac{\mathbf{w}_i - \mu_k(\mathbf{x}_i)}{\sigma_k(\mathbf{x}_i)}))$ where, ϕ is the pdf of $\mathcal{N}(0,1)$. For losing bids, we can similarly compute the probability of losing based on the lower bound, $\Pr(\mathbf{W}_i > \mathbf{b}_i) = \sum_{k=1}^{K} \pi_k(\mathbf{x}_i) \Phi(\frac{\mu_k(\mathbf{x}_i) - \mathbf{b}_i}{\sigma_k(\mathbf{x}_i)})$

Negative log-probability of all the losing auctions from the mixture density is,

$$\sum_{i \in \mathcal{L}} - \log(\sum_{k=1}^{K} \pi_k(\mathbf{x}_i) \Phi(\frac{\mu_k(\mathbf{x}_i) - \mathbf{b}_i}{\sigma_k(\mathbf{x}_i)})) \quad (5)$$

where, Φ represents the cdf of $\mathcal{N}(0,1)$.

From Fig. 1, recall that the distribution is not unimodal and has multiple peaks. To address the multi-modality of the data we used a mixture of multiple densities. The embedded deep network in the MCNet ($\mathcal{M}$) is trained to learn the mean and standard deviation parameters of each of the constituents of the mixture model as well as the corresponding weights. Combining all the auctions, we get the following optimization function for censored data,

$$
\mathcal{M}^* = \arg\max_{\mathcal{M}} \sum_{i \in \mathcal{L}} \log(\sum_{k=1}^{K} \pi_k(\mathbf{x}_i)\Phi(\frac{\mu_k(\mathbf{x}_i) - \mathbf{b}_i}{\sigma_k(\mathbf{x}_i)}))
$$
$$
+ \sum_{i \in \mathcal{W}} \log(\sum_{k=1}^{K} \frac{\pi_k(\mathbf{x}_i)}{\sigma_k(\mathbf{x}_i)}\phi(\frac{\mathbf{w}_i - \mu_k(\mathbf{x}_i)}{\sigma_k(\mathbf{x}_i)}) \tag{6}
$$

where $\mathcal{M}$ is the neural network (parameters).

3.3 Optimization

It is easy to compute gradients of Eqs. 2, 3 and 6 with respect to all the parameters. We used Adam optimizer for stochastic gradient optimization [11].

4 Experimental Results

In this section, we discuss experimental settings, evaluation measures, and results.

4.1 Experimental Settings

Datasets: We ran experiments on the publicly available iPinYou dataset [24] as well as on a proprietary dataset collected from Adobe Adcloud (a DSP). The iPinYou dataset contains censored winning price information. Further experimentation was done on a sampled week's data from Adobe Adcloud. iPinYou data is grouped into two subsets: session 2 (dates from 2013-06-06 to 2013-06-12), and session 3 (2013-10-19 to 2013-10-27). We experimented with the individual dates within sessions as well. For all the datasets, we allocated 60% for training, 20% for validation and rest 20% for testing. We report the average as well as the standard deviation over five iterations. Similar to previous research on the iPinYou dataset, we remove fields that are not directly related to the winning price at the onset [18,20]. The fields used in our methods are UserAgent, Region, City, AdExchange, Domain, AdSlotId, SlotWidth, SlotHeight, SlotVisibility, SlotFormat, Usertag. Every categorical feature (e.g City), is one-hot encoded, whereas every numerical feature (e.g Ad height) is categorized into bins and subsequently represented as one-hot encoded vectors. This way, each bid request is represented as a high-dimensional sparse vector. Table 1 shows the statistics of sessions in the iPinYou datasets. The number of samples and win rates for individual dates are mentioned in Table 2.

Table 1. Basic statistics of iPinYou sessions

Session	Sample	Feature	Win rate (%)
2	53,289,330	40,664	22.87
3	10,566,743	25,020	29.64

Evaluation Settings: Evaluation on partially observed data is difficult when the winning price is unknown especially for point estimation. In [20], the authors simulated new synthetic data from the original winning auctions. While the added censoring allows validating point estimate, it does not use the whole data (or the true distribution). We evaluate the performance of predicting the winning price distribution rather than the point estimate itself. Thus we use the whole data without generating simulated censoring behavior. This setting is similar to earlier work on the survival tree-based method where the authors evaluated predicting the distribution and used the original data [18].

Parametric Methods: We compared the Censored Regression (CR) approach with our methods: Fully parametric Censored Regression (P-CR) and Mixture Density Censored Network (MCNet). For every method, we added an L2 regularization term for each weight vector to prevent over-fitting. For MCNet, we added an additional hyper-parameter on the number of mixtures. We chose a fully connected hidden layer with 64 nodes with RelU activation function as the architecture. Our framework is general and can be extended to multiple layers. The number of mixture components was varied from 2–4 for individual dates and 2–8 for the experiments on the two sessions. We used Adam optimizer with a learning rate of 10^{-3}. Mini-batch training was employed due to the high volume of the data and we fixed the batch size to 1024 samples. We employed early stopping on the training loss and do not observe the validation loss for early stopping. This way, all the methods are treated similarly. The L2 regularization was varied from 10^{-6} to 10 (in log scale). We implemented the parametric methods in Tensorflow [1]. For the initialization of weight vectors, we sampled randomly from the standard normal distribution in all our experiments.

Recently extending Censored Regression (CR), in [19], the authors proposed to use deep model (DeepCR) to parameterize the mean to provide more flexibility in the point estimation. Additionally, the authors proposed to use Gumbel distribution for point estimation. Note that, MCNet generalizes the DeepCR model when using only one mixture component and Gumbel as the base distribution. We did not see much improvement when using Gumbel to parameterize mixture components with our initial experiments. With enough Gaussian mixture components, MCNet can approximate any smooth distribution. As neural architecture is not the primary motivation for this paper, we do not discuss different architectures or distributions in this paper.

Non-parametric Methods: To the best of our knowledge, parametric methods and non-parametric methods were not compared together for winning price distribution estimation in earlier research. We compared our approaches with non-parametric approaches based on Kaplan-Meier (KM) estimate and the Survival tree (ST) method. The KM and ST based methods produce winning price distributions until the maximum bid price since the winning price behavior above that is unknown. To represent a complete landscape with the probability distribution summing to one, we introduce an extra variable representing the event that the winning price is beyond the maximum bid price. For the Survival tree, we varied the tree height from 1–20.

In the ST method, the Survival tree is built by running an Expectation Maximization (EM) algorithm for each field to cluster similar attributes. If data has F fields and the average number of attributes in each field is K, then for n samples, the EM algorithm takes, $\mathcal{O}(FKln)$ steps to cluster features based on their density for l iterations. With depth d, total complexity becomes $\mathcal{O}(FKlnd)$. Given this runtime, we could not run ST using all attributes of *Domain, SlotId* fields (these fields were removed in previous research [18]). We trimmed the *Domain* and *SlotId* features by combining the attributes that appeared less than 10^3 times. We created *"other domains"* and *"other slot ids"* bins for these less frequent attributes. This improved the time complexity and made the method viable. But for the CR-based methods, we could easily relax this threshold and trimmed both the features where the attributes appeared less than 10 times in the dataset in either session. For a fair comparison, whenever we use the same feature trimming in the parametric methods as ST, we denote using $CR^*, P\text{-}CR^*, MCNet^*$. Note that parametric methods can scale easily whereas the non-parametric ST method cannot.

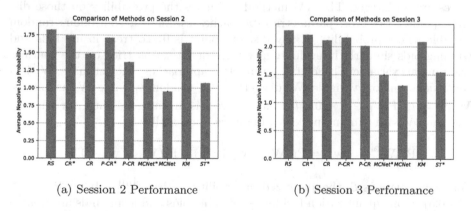

(a) Session 2 Performance   (b) Session 3 Performance

Fig. 2. iPinYou session's *ANLP*. Error bar represents the standard deviation.

Baseline Method: We also propose a simple baseline method and compare it with other methods. The baseline algorithm picks a winning price randomly conditioned on the win rate. We denote this as the Random Strategy (RS).

Formally, let the maximum bid price be z and probability of a win be p. Then, the probability that the winning price is w is given by

$$P(\mathbf{W} = w) = \frac{p}{z} \text{ if } w \in [0, z], \text{ and } 0 \text{ if } w < 0 \text{ and } \int_z^\infty \Pr(\mathbf{W} = w)dw = 1 - p$$

Thus with probability $1 - p$, it predicts the event that winning price is greater than max bid price and with probability p it draws from $\mathcal{U}(0, z)$ where $\mathcal{U}$ is the Uniform distribution.

4.2   Evaluation Measure

Our objective is to learn the distribution of the winning price, rather than the point estimate. Hence, we choose Average Negative Log Probability (*ANLP*) as our evaluation measure similar to [18]. *ANLP* is defined as,

$$ANLP = -\frac{1}{N}\left(\sum_{i \in \mathcal{W}} \log \Pr(\mathbf{W}_i = \mathbf{w}_i) + \sum_{i \in \mathcal{L}} \log \Pr(\mathbf{W}_i \geq \mathbf{b}_i)\right)$$

where $\mathcal{W}$ represents the set of winning auctions, $\mathbf{w}_i$ represents winning price of the ith winning auction, $\mathcal{L}$ is the set of losing auctions, $\mathbf{b}_i$ is the bidding price for the ith losing auction, and $|\mathcal{W}| + |\mathcal{L}| = N$.

Note that, we computed pdf for winning auctions and probability (or the CDF) for losing auctions while optimizing. While the CDF represents the probability of the event, density does not represent probability. Additionally, bid prices are an integer. The KM method estimates the probability on those discrete points. However, parametric approaches estimate a continuous random variable whose probability at any discrete point is 0. To treat losing bids and winning bids similarly in evaluation, we use quantization trick on the continuous random variable [7]. For the parametric approaches, the estimate $\mathbf{W}_i$ is a continuous random variable. We discretized the random variable $\mathbf{W}_i$ as follows, $\mathbf{W}_i^{bin} = l$, if $\mathbf{W}_i \in (l - 0.5, l + 0.5]$ where l is an integer. Thus, for winning auctions $\mathcal{W}$ with winning price $\mathbf{w}_i$, quantized probability is,

$$\Pr(\mathbf{W}_i^{bin} = \mathbf{w}_i) = \Pr(\mathbf{W}_i \leq \mathbf{w}_i + 0.5) - \Pr(\mathbf{W}_i \leq \mathbf{w}_i - 0.5)$$

For losing auctions $\mathcal{L}$, the quantized probability is, $\Pr(\mathbf{W}_i^{bin} \geq \mathbf{b}_i) = \Pr(\mathbf{W}_i \geq \mathbf{b}_i - 0.5)$. Using quantization technique, winning bids and losing bids are treated similarly for all methods.

4.3   Experimental Results

In this section, we discuss quantitative results on iPinYou sessions 2 and 3. In Table 2, we provide average *ANLP* over different dates as well as the standard deviation (std) numbers. In Fig. 2, we mention the result on each session as a whole. Moreover, we plot how number of mixture components as well as tree

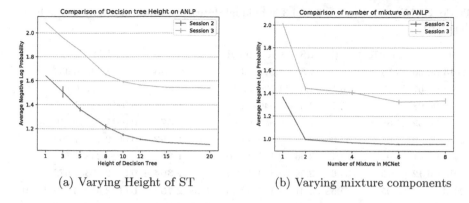

(a) Varying Height of ST　　　　(b) Varying mixture components

Fig. 3. Hyper-parameter effect on *ANLP*

depth affect the result for MCNet and ST respectively in Fig. 3. In sessions 2 and 3 where we include all the dates, we also added the ST method for comparison. As ST did not run with large feature space, we also added CR*, P-CR*, MCNet* for parity (where number of feature was small for all methods).

From Table 2, it is evident, P-CR improves upon CR on most dates (except with low volume dates) asserting the violation of fixed standard deviation assumption. While for P-CR, improvement is around 5%–10%, MCNet improves CR by more than 30% on all dates. Improvement of MCNet re-verify our assumption about the multi-modal nature of the winning price distribution. CR performs better than both RS as well as KM. This is expected as the non-parametric KM estimate does not use any features. However, KM improves RS by around 10% on all dates. ST improves CR and P-CR significantly implying the significance of non-parametric estimators.

In Fig. 2, one can see similar trends over CR, P-CR, and MCNet. With feature trimming, MCNet* performs similarly to ST methods. This is expected as both ST and MCNet can predict arbitrary smooth distributions. Although, when the MCNet approach is restricted to fewer features (MCNet*) on the average it performs similarly to ST, the benefits of parametric methods come from the fact that parametric approaches are scalable to large feature as well as input space. It may be observed that the performance of MCNet improves ST by more than 10% on both sessions. While we used only one hidden layer for MCNet, any deep network can be used to parameterize the mixture density network for potentially improving the MCNet results even further.

In Fig. 3(a), we plot *ANLP* for different depths of the decision trees. It can be observed that for ST, the performance saturates around depth 15. In Fig. 3(b), we also show how the varying number of mixture components impacts *ANLP*. On the larger dataset of Session 2, *ANLP* stabilizes to a low value at 4 mixture components. However, for session 3, *ANLP* starts increasing beyond 6 mixture components, implying over-fitting.

Table 2. *ANLP* on Session 2 and 3 individual dates. We report std only if it is higher than 0.01

Date	≈n(×10⁶)	wr(%)	RS	CR	p-CR	MCNet	KM	ST
2013-06-06	9.58	18.93	1.55	1.212	1.081	**0.756**	1.403	0.956
2013-06-07	11.13	16.16	1.35	1.036	0.913	**0.641** ± 0.02	1.211	0.823
2013-06-08	5.22	31.17	2.37	1.946	1.695	**1.311** ± 0.02	2.131	1.527
2013-06-09	11.88	13.85	1.17	0.887	0.784	**0.574** ± 0.03	1.071	0.710
2013-06-10	5.61	34.06	2.55	2.130	1.809	**1.252** ± 0.06	2.234	1.502
2013-06-11	5.09	34.13	2.56	2.128	1.810	**1.351**	2.248	1.552
2013-06-12	4.75	34.68	2.59	2.189	1.914	**1.364** ± 0.04	2.273	1.572
2013-10-19	0.35	64.58	4.31	4.135	4.285 ± 0.08	**2.791** ± 0.05	3.659	3.056 ± 0.02
2013-10-20	0.32	65.48	4.33	4.167	4.287 ± 0.15	**2.768** ± 0.1	3.737	3.159
2013-10-21	1.54	54.59	3.77	3.466	3.515	**2.338** ± 0.03	3.272	2.529
2013-10-22	1.21	56.00	3.85	3.641	3.569	**2.576** ± 0.03	3.428	2.779
2013-10-23	1.57	14.30	1.22	1.060	1.033	**0.854** ± 0.02	1.157	0.963
2013-10-24	2.18	11.23	0.985	0.831	0.824	**0.618**	0.904	0.698 ± 0.01
2013-10-25	2.23	14.23	1.21	1.015	0.998	**0.771** ± 0.03	1.131	0.888
2013-10-26	0.53	49.90	3.51	3.432	3.433 ± 0.01	**2.577** ± 0.09	3.228	2.931 ± 0.01
2013-10-27	0.59	18.45	1.53	1.367	1.361	**0.937** ± 0.03	1.348	1.104 ± 0.02

Table 3. *ANLP* on Adobe AdCloud Dataset

	CR	P-CR	MCNet	KM	ST
ANLP	0.4744 ± 0.01	0.4722 ± 0.01	**0.3477** ± 0.01	0.4671 ± 0.01	0.4213 ± 0.02

Results on Adobe AdCloud Dataset: We also tested our methods on Adobe Advertising Cloud (DSP) offline dataset. We collected a fraction of logs for one week. The number of samples was $31,772,122$ and the number of features was $33,492$. It had similar categorical as well as real-valued features. We use the same featurization framework and represented each bid request with a sparse vector. In Table 3, we report the *ANLP* results, using the same experimental setup. Note that, MCNet improves CR by 25% while it improves ST by more than 10%. In this dataset, we do see only marginal improvement over using P-CR.

5   Discussion and Future Work

In this paper, we particularly focus on one of the central problems in RTB, the winning price distribution estimation. In practice, DSP depends on the estimated bid landscape to optimize it's bidding strategy. From a revenue perspective, an accurate bid landscape is of utmost importance. While, non-parametric methods can estimate arbitrary distributions, in practice, it is challenging to scale on large datasets. On the other hand, widely used parametric methods, such as Censored

Regression in its original form is highly restrictive. We proposed a novel method based on Mixture Density Networks to form a generic framework for estimating arbitrary distribution under censored data. MCNet generalizes a fully parametric Censored regression approach with the number of mixture components set to one. Additionally, Censored regression is a special case of fully parametric censored regression where the standard deviation is fixed. We provided extensive empirical evidence on public datasets and data from a leading DSP to prove the efficacy of our methods. While the mixture of (enough) Gaussian densities can approximate any smooth distribution, further study is needed on the choice of base distribution. A more subtle point arises when learning with censored data as we do not observe any winning price beyond the maximum bidding price. Without any assumptions on the distribution, it is not provably possible to predict the behavior in the censored region. Non-parametric methods only learn density within the limit of maximum bidding price while under strong assumptions of standard distributions, censored regression predicts the behavior of winning price in the censored region. Although MCNet can approximate any smooth distribution, beyond the maximum bidding price, it leads to non-identifiability similar to the KM estimate. It would be interesting to explore combining MCNet with distributional assumptions where the winning price is never observed.

References

1. Abadi, M., et al.: Tensorflow: a system for large-scale machine learning. In: OSDI, vol. 16, pp. 265–283 (2016)
2. Agarwal, D., Ghosh, S., Wei, K., You, S.: Budget pacing for targeted online advertisements at linkedin. In: Proceedings of the 20th ACM SIGKDD International Conference on Knowledge Discovery and Data Mining, pp. 1613–1619. ACM (2014)
3. Balseiro, S.R., Besbes, O., Weintraub, G.Y.: Repeated auctions with budgets in Ad exchanges: approximations and design. Manage. Sci. **61**(4), 864–884 (2015)
4. Bishop, C.M.: Mixture density networks. Technical report. Citeseer (1994)
5. Cui, Y., Zhang, R., Li, W., Mao, J.: Bid landscape forecasting in online Ad exchange marketplace. In: KDD, pp. 265–273. ACM (2011)
6. Edelman, B., Ostrovsky, M., Schwarz, M.: Internet advertising and the generalized second-price auction: selling billions of dollars worth of keywords. Am. Econ. Rev. **97**(1), 242–259 (2007)
7. Gersho, A., Gray, R.M.: Vector Quantization and Signal Compression, vol. 159. Springer, Boston (2012). https://doi.org/10.1007/978-1-4615-3626-0
8. Greene, W.H.: On the asymptotic bias of the ordinary least squares estimator of the Tobit model. Econometrica J. Econometric Soc. **49**(2), 505–513 (1981)
9. James, I.R., Smith, P.: Consistency results for linear regression with censored data. Ann. Stat. **12**(2), 590–600 (1984)
10. Kaplan, E.L., Meier, P.: Nonparametric estimation from incomplete observations. J. Am. Stat. Assoc. **53**(282), 457–481 (1958)
11. Kingma, D.P., Ba, J.: Adam: a method for stochastic optimization. arXiv preprint arXiv:1412.6980 (2014)
12. Lang, K.J., Moseley, B., Vassilvitskii, S.: Handling forecast errors while bidding for display advertising. In: Proceedings of the 21st International Conference on World Wide Web, pp. 371–380. ACM (2012)

13. Powell, J.L.: Least absolute deviations estimation for the censored regression model. J. Econometrics **25**(3), 303–325 (1984)
14. Salimans, T., Karpathy, A., Chen, X., Kingma, D.P.: PixelCNN++: improving the PixelCNN with discretized logistic mixture likelihood and other modifications. arXiv preprint arXiv:1701.05517 (2017)
15. Wang, J., Zhang, W., Yuan, S.: Display advertising with real-time bidding (RTB) and behavioural targeting. arXiv preprint arXiv:1610.03013 (2016)
16. Wang, P., Li, Y., Reddy, C.K.: Machine learning for survival analysis: a survey. arXiv preprint arXiv:1708.04649 (2017)
17. Wang, R., Fu, B., Fu, G., Wang, M.: Deep & cross network for Ad click predictions. In: Proceedings of the ADKDD 2017, p. 12. ACM (2017)
18. Wang, Y., Ren, K., Zhang, W., Wang, J., Yu, Y.: Functional bid landscape forecasting for display advertising. In: Frasconi, P., Landwehr, N., Manco, G., Vreeken, J. (eds.) ECML PKDD 2016. LNCS (LNAI), vol. 9851, pp. 115–131. Springer, Cham (2016). https://doi.org/10.1007/978-3-319-46128-1_8
19. Wu, W., Yeh, M.Y., Chen, M.S.: Deep censored learning of the winning price in the real time bidding. In: Proceedings of the 24th ACM SIGKDD International Conference on Knowledge Discovery & Data Mining, pp. 2526–2535. ACM (2018)
20. Wu, W.C.H., Yeh, M.Y., Chen, M.S.: Predicting winning price in real time bidding with censored data. In: KDD, pp. 1305–1314. ACM (2015)
21. Yuan, S., Wang, J., Zhao, X.: Real-time bidding for online advertising: measurement and analysis. In: Proceedings of the Seventh International Workshop on Data Mining for Online Advertising, p. 3. ACM (2013)
22. Zen, H., Senior, A.: Deep mixture density networks for acoustic modeling in statistical parametric speech synthesis. In: 2014 IEEE International Conference on Acoustics, Speech and Signal Processing (ICASSP), pp. 3844–3848. IEEE (2014)
23. Zhang, W., Yuan, S., Wang, J.: Optimal real-time bidding for display advertising. In: Proceedings of the 20th ACM SIGKDD International Conference on Knowledge Discovery and Data Mining, pp. 1077–1086. ACM (2014)
24. Zhang, W., Yuan, S., Wang, J., Shen, X.: Real-time bidding benchmarking with iPinYou dataset. arXiv preprint arXiv:1407.7073 (2014)
25. Zhang, W., Zhou, T., Wang, J., Xu, J.: Bid-aware gradient descent for unbiased learning with censored data in display advertising. In: KDD, pp. 665–674. ACM (2016)
26. Zhu, W.Y., Shih, W.Y., Lee, Y.H., Peng, W.C., Huang, J.L.: A gamma-based regression for winning price estimation in real-time bidding advertising. In: 2017 IEEE International Conference on Big Data (Big Data), pp. 1610–1619. IEEE (2017)

A Deep Multi-task Approach
for Residual Value Forecasting

Ahmed Rashed[1]([⊠]), Shayan Jawed[1], Jens Rehberg[2], Josif Grabocka[1],
Lars Schmidt-Thieme[1], and Andre Hintsches[2]

[1] Information Systems and Machine Learning Lab, University of Hildesheim,
Hildesheim, Germany
{ahmedrashed,shayan,josif,schmidt-thieme}@ismll.uni-hildesheim.de
[2] Volkswagen Financial Services AG, Braunschweig, Germany
{Jens.Rehberg,Andre.Hintsches}@vwfs.com

Abstract. Residual value forecasting plays an important role in many
areas, e.g., for vehicles to price leasing contracts. High forecasting accuracy is crucial as any overestimation will lead to lost sales due to customer dissatisfaction, while underestimation will lead to a direct loss in
revenue when reselling the car at the end of the leasing contract. Current
forecasting models mainly rely on the trend analysis of historical sales
records. However, these models require extensive manual steps to filter
and preprocess those records which in term limits the frequency at which
these models can be updated with new data. To automate, improve and
speed up residual value forecasting we propose a multi-task model that
utilizes besides the residual value itself as the main target, the actual
mileage that has been driven as a co-target. While combining off-the-shelf
regression models with careful feature engineering yields already useful
models, we show that for residual values further quantities such as the
actual driven mileage contains further useful information. As this information is not available when contracts are made and the forecast is due,
we model the problem as a multi-task model that uses actual mileage as
a training co-target. Experiments on three Volkswagen car models show
that the proposed model significantly outperforms the straight-forward
modeling as a single-target regression problem.

Keywords: Multi-task learning · Residual value forecasting · Pricing ·
Automotive industry

1 Introduction

Forecasting enables key-decision making in many business applications, including
but not limited to fields of lease, loans and insurance. A leasing system in place,
reduces the initial up-front costs of goods for the clients significantly, for example,
automobile leasing. Globally, there has been a surge in the demand of leased
vehicles, and Germany is leading the market with a very high penetration of
operating leases within Europe [13]. The leasing contracts are designed with

© Springer Nature Switzerland AG 2020
U. Brefeld et al. (Eds.): ECML PKDD 2019, LNAI 11908, pp. 467–482, 2020.
https://doi.org/10.1007/978-3-030-46133-1_28

respect to the residual value of the vehicle at a point in the future. This stands to reason as an overshoot on the estimate would suggest a lower leasing rate leading to diminishing profits if the vehicle is sold at a lower price after the expiration of the leasing contract. Vice versa in the case of undershooting the residual value. Consequently, organizations require a dependable method to forecast residual values as accurately as possible to manage the risk inherent to their business.

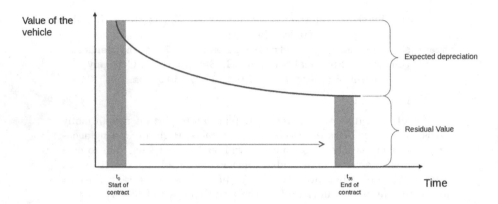

Fig. 1. A sample timeline of depreciation and final residual value of a vehicle.

A residual value forecasting method takes into account various factors such as the initial mileage set for the vehicle, engine configuration, model launch date, list price, etc. On the other hand, there could be factors that are more dynamic in nature as opposed to former which stay static over the leasing period. Actual mileage a vehicle is driven, damages incurred throughout the leasing period are factors that are both unknown at the start of a contract and dynamic. However, it is reasonable to assume that both play an important role in the future residual value of the vehicle. This paper formulates the vehicle residual value forecasting problem as a multi-task learning model by defining other than the primary task of residual value, additional auxiliary tasks of predicting various quantities that are prone to change in the duration of the lease.

Multi-task learning [2] is a mainstay of numerous machine learning applications. The intuition behind learning multiple tasks jointly is to learn a richer shared representation from multiple supervisory tasks than possible from learning a single task. A rich representation as such can then effectively generalize to out of sample test data better. Natural Language Processing [12], Computer Vision [6] and Time Series forecasting [2] domains have benefited from using multi-task learning strategies.

It is worth noting that although forecasting the residual value is of primary importance, we can explore additional auxiliary tasks to model the problem as a multi-task learning problem. These auxiliary tasks solely exist to provide additional supervision. Specifically, we explore four such tasks, the actual mileage the vehicle gets driven, as the initial mileage limit at the time of contract is not set in stone, the cost of damages it can incur, expected days it takes for the vehicle leasing company to resale the vehicle and lastly, the expected date of returning the vehicle as opposed to the initial set date at the time of contract.

This paper foremost tackles the research problem of designing an optimal machine learning model that caters for multiple tasks. Secondly, an exhaustive search procedure is applied to determine the feasibility of incorporating one auxiliary task over another, or possibly multiple together. Third, we validate the results of multi-task learning by comparing to single task learning objective of residual values. Our focus in this paper is on deep neural network architectures to model the task at hand, given that the shared representation between the tasks could be represented by a hidden layer as opposed to more classic machine learning models such as Gradient Boosted Decision Trees [3] and Support Vector Machines [5] where catering for multiple tasks requires considerable alterations.

The rest of the paper is organized as follows. In Sect. 2, we summarize the related work. We discuss the problem formulation of the multi-task residual value forecasting in Sect. 3. In Sect. 4, we present and discuss the technical details of the proposed model. We present the experimental results in Sect. 5. Finally, we conclude with discussing possible future work in Sect. 6.

2   Related Work

This section sketches an overview of prominent methods in automobile residual value forecasting and secondly works that exploit auxiliary tasks in the light of multi-task learning. We note the work from [9], where the authors propose an SVM regression method for automobile residual value forecasting. Model selection for the method was based on an evolution strategy in favor of a grid search procedure. The dataset consisted of more than 100,000 samples for a single vehicle model from an anonymous car manufacturer. Interestingly, the dataset had 176 features without any dimensionality reduction. More closely related to our work is a Neural Network based regression method proposed by [11], which was tested on 5 different however undisclosed vehicle models. Model selection was done via an evolutionary algorithm similar to previously noted work. Lessmann et al. [10] provided a comparative analysis of 19 different regression algorithms applied to a dataset of 450,000 samples of 6 different vehicle models and report that Random Forest [1] based regression achieved the optimal results. Furthermore, the authors noted that some car models were difficult to model than others.

Various approaches have been proposed that fall under the umbrella of multi-task learning. A survey on multi-task learning could be found in [14]. Pioneering work in multi-task learning [2] proposed a neural network regression model that forecast mortality risk. Besides the main target of risk, the authors predicted for various other correlated attributes that lead to a significant gain in accuracy over the main task when compared to single task estimation of the same risk task. Auxiliary tasks have also been explored in but not limited to, Natural language processing [12] and Computer Vision [6]. An unsupervised auxiliary task was defined in [12] that predicted surrounding words together with the main objective of sequence labeling leading to a multi-task learning framework. The authors noted that utilizing the auxiliary task encouraged the framework overall to learn richer features for semantic composition without requiring additional training data and ultimately leading to consistent performance improvements on various sequence modeling benchmarks. Work done by Girshick [6] involved an extensive ablation study that compared the multi-task learning loss of object classification and bounding box regression to single-task object classification. The results established the supremacy of the multi-task learning approach.

In light of the above, we propose a multi-task approach to model the residual value forecasting problem. To the best of our knowledge, our paper is the first to do so. We show that this not only leads to superior performance when compared to a variety of standard baselines but also an equally important result that the proposed method beats the single task learning objective of predicting for the main task.

3   Problem Definition

Residual value forecasting can be formulated as a multi-task regression problem where given some car configuration details $X_c \in \mathbb{R}^m$ and the leasing contract details $X_l \in \mathbb{R}^q$, we need to define a function $\hat{y} : X_c \times X_l \to \mathbb{R}^{|\mathcal{Y}|}$ to predict a set of target values $\mathcal{Y} := \{y_1, y_2, ..., y_{|\mathcal{Y}|}\}$ after the end date of this leasing contract, such as the expected mileage to be driven or the expected damage value. In residual value forecasting, our primary target will be the car's market value (Residual value) y_{mv} after the contract end date while the rest of the targets will act as auxiliary targets $\mathcal{A} := \mathcal{Y}\backslash\{y_{\mathrm{mv}}\}$ that will help in improving the model accuracy and generalization.

4   Proposed Method

Given the car configuration details X_c and the contract details X_l we need to define the multi-target prediction function $\hat{y}$. A good choice for such function will be a multi-layered neural network that has a feature extraction part with hard parameter sharing g and a set of independent prediction heads f_k for every available target k as follows:

$$z = g\left([X_c, X_l]; \theta_g\right) \tag{1}$$

$$\hat{y}_k = f_k\left(z; \theta_{f_k}\right) \tag{2}$$

where z are the extracted latent feature vectors from the contract and car details. g and f are a series of non-linear fully connected layers with network parameters θ_g and θ_f respectively. The full model architecture is shown in Fig. 2.

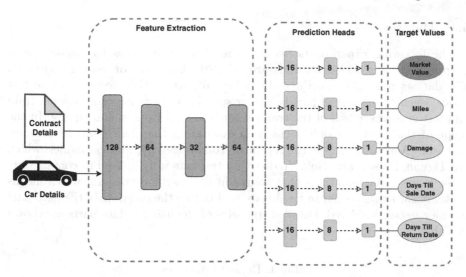

Fig. 2. The proposed multi-layered architecture for residual value forecasting. The first part is a multi-layered neural network for feature extraction with hard parameter sharing and the second part is a set of independent multi-layered prediction heads for every target value to be predicted.

To optimize the proposed model we have to define a separate loss function $\mathcal{L}_{y_k}$ for every prediction head and jointly minimize all of them simultaneously with adding a specific weight for each target loss as follows:

$$\mathcal{L}(\Theta) = \sum_{k=1}^{|\mathcal{Y}|} \alpha_k |y_k - \hat{y}_k| \tag{3}$$

For simplicity, we converted all possible target values to continues values and we used the mean absolute error loss for all targets to avoid any sensitivity with outliers in the training data.

5   Experiments and Results

In this section, multiple experiments were conducted to evaluate and find the best architecture and target values for the proposed model. These experiments aim to answer the following research questions:

RQ1. How many layers of hidden units are needed for the proposed model to learn and predict the target values?

RQ2. What are the best set of co-targets that will improve the residual value forecasting accuracy?

RQ3. How well does the proposed model perform in comparison with the currently employed methodology and other well-known regression models for residual value forecasting?

5.1   Dataset

In the following experiments, we used our VWFS business to business sales propriety dataset which contains around 270k instances of leasing contracts. The dataset was split into three chronological parts with different train to test ratios. Each chronological part is further split into chronologically ordered train and test sets where half of the training set is used for parameter tuning. In the scope of this work, we only focused on evaluating the models on the primary trim line (Anchor model) of the top three Volkswagen popular car models which are Tiguan, Passat, and Golf. To do so, all test sets were filtered to contain only those models. We made sure that train and test parts are disjoint which means that any car instance had to be already sold before the end date of the data part in order to be considered. Detailed statistics of the utilized data parts are shown in Table 1.

Table 1. Datasets statistics

	Train period	Test period	Train #	Test #	Train ratio
Split 1	2002–2014	2015–2019	77980	8702	90.0%
Split 2	2002–2013	2014–2019	54151	22561	75.0%
Split 3	2002–2012	2013–2019	32136	37876	46.0%

5.2   Data Preprocessing

Our first step of data preprocessing was to define the best car configuration and contract features to be used as input. Regarding the car configuration, we used all available configurations that don't contain any personalized data which are shown in Table 2. These features also contain some expert features that might affect the residual value but not part of the car configuration details. For the contract details, we only used the start date, end date, mileage cap per year and contract term in months.

5.3   Exploratory Analysis

Before applying the experiments to answer our research questions, we did some exploratory analysis on the given dataset to have better insights. Firstly we plotted the distributions of all contract types based on their duration term and mileage cap which are shown in Figs. 3(a) and (b). The distributions show that the majority of contracts have duration terms of 36 and 42 months with a mileage cap ranging from 5 km to 100 km per-year. Secondly, the distribution of the top popular car models and their list prices were analyzed. Figure 4(a), shows that the majority of the instance are Passat and Golf while Tiguan has a much lower

Table 2. Car configuration features

Feature name	Type	Expert feature
Brand	Categorical	–
Model description	Categorical	–
Fuel	Categorical	–
Engine	Categorical	–
Engine description	Text	–
Registration date	Date	–
List price	Float	–
Equipements	List	–
Color	Categorical	–
Model's market launch	Date	Yes

frequency. Figure 4(b), shows that there is no significant deviation in the list price between the three models, however, Golf cars have the lowest price range because it falls in the compact cars segment.

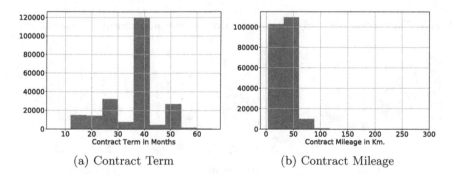

(a) Contract Term   (b) Contract Mileage

Fig. 3. Distribution of contracts' terms and mileage caps

Finally, we analyzed the correlation between the market value and the contracts' term and mileage caps for each car model to identify any anomalies or outliers. Correlation results in Figs. 5 and 6, show that a strong correlation consistently exists between the contract's term, mileage cap, and the future market value. The longer the contract term is, the lower the market value will be. Also, the market value decreases with increasing the contract's mileage cap. The results also show that there is a considerable noise especially in the correlation between the market value and the contract's term, however, a trend is still clearly visible.

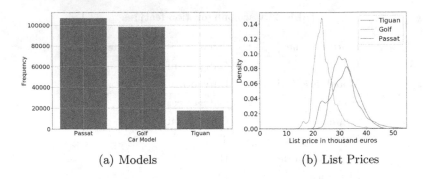

(a) Models   (b) List Prices

Fig. 4. Distributions of car models and their list prices

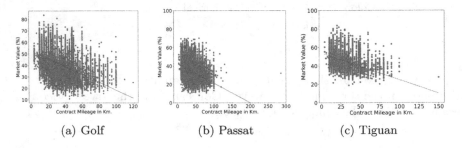

(a) Golf   (b) Passat   (c) Tiguan

Fig. 5. Correlation between the market value percent and contract's mileage cap

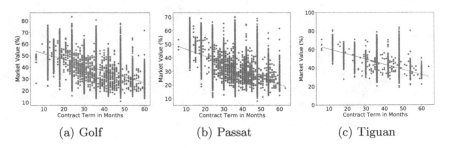

(a) Golf   (b) Passat   (c) Tiguan

Fig. 6. Correlation between the market value percent and contract's term

5.4 Experimental Protocol

For our experimental protocol, we used the last three years of the training part for hyper-parameters tuning using a grid search. We then fully retrain the model again on the complete train part and evaluate on the test part using the mean absolute error metric (MAE). Regarding the grid search, we tested the learn rates of [0.01, 0.001, 0.0001], the batch sizes of [128, 256, 512, 1024, 2048, 2560], the loss weights of [0.1, 0.05, 0.01, 0.005, 0.001, 0.0005, 0.0001, 0.00005, 0.00001] and number of epochs ranging from 50 to 650. The best found hyper-parameters were batch size $= 2048$, Learn rate $= 0.001$, optimizer $=$ ADAM, $\alpha_{mv} = 1.0, \alpha_{miles} = 0.001, \alpha_{damage} = 0.005, \alpha_{saledate} = 0.01$ and $\alpha_{returndate} = 0.01$ for all data splits. Best number of epochs were 350 for the first two data splits and 450 for the third.

5.5   Model Complexity (RQ1)

To tune the model architecture, we applied several experiments on the first data split using different candidate architectures. We started first by increasing the number of shared layers and their width while fixing the prediction heads to one fully connected layer with 16 units. The best candidate shared architecture is then carried over to test a different number of layers for the prediction heads. We used Leaky ReLU activation functions in all of our experiments.

The comparison results in Table 3, shows that the error rate decreases by increasing the number of shared layers until it reaches four layers. Further fine tuning of the prediction heads has a lesser effect on the error rate which decreased from 3.73% to 3.70%.

Table 3. Performance comparison of different candidate architectures

Shared layers	Prediction layers	Mean absolute error (%)
128	16	5.22
64	16	5.32
32	16	5.79
128 × 64	16	6.29
128 × 32	16	6.21
128 × 16	16	7.95
128 × 64 × 32	16	4.0
128 × 64 × 64	16	3.78
128 × 64 × 32 × 16	16	3.74
128 × 64 × 32 × 32	16	3.74
128 × 64 × 32 × 64	16	**3.73**
128 × 64 × 32 × 64	8	3.71
128 × 64 × 32 × 64	32	3.77
128 × 64 × 32 × 64	32 × 16	3.83
128 × 64 × 32 × 64	16 × 8	**3.70**
128 × 64 × 32 × 64	8 × 4	4.01

5.6   Comparison Between Possible Co-targets Values (RQ2)

In this section, an experiment was applied on the first and second data splits to measure the effect of every co-target value. The co-targets are features that are known for the past contracts, however, they are unknown for future contracts.

To illustrate the point, the miles driven (or damage values, etc.) can be known only when a contract ends, while we want to estimate the residual value at the moment a contract being signed. For this reason, those features cannot be utilized as an input in estimating the residual values. As such, we innovate on treating those features which are available only for the training set (i.e. past contracts) as co-target variables.

After filtering all predictor features we managed to identify four possible co-targets to be used for forecasting the market value which are shown in Table 4.

Table 4. Co-targets values

Target name	Description	Type
Miles	The expected actual miles to be driven by the client	Float
Damage value	Expected total damage value	Float
Sale date	Expected sale date after returning the car	Date
Return date	Expected car return date after the contract ends	Date

In order to change all targets into continuous values, we had to change the sale and return dates into a numerical number by using the difference in days between the contract end date and those target dates. A negative number of days for such targets will indicate that the car was returned and sold before the original contract end date.

To have first insights about the candidate co-targets, we plotted their correlation graphs with respect to the market value. Correlation results in Fig. 7, show that there is a strong correlation between the total driven mileage and the market value which means it can be a very good candidate co-target. It also shows that the correlation of all other targets are very noisy however there exist a slight trend that indicates they might be useful as co-targets.

Assigning the correct loss weight α_k to each co-target is a crucial step in fine tuning any multi-task learning models [7,8]. To do so, we conducted a sensitivity analysis using the first data split on the loss weights of each available co-target individually. The best-found weights are then used further in combining multiple co-targets at the same time for the sake of reducing the grid search space over all possible combinations. The sensitivity analysis results in Fig. 8, show that the model is most sensitive to the Miles as a co-target while changing other co-targets weights show no significant effect on the model performance.

Table 5 shows the results for comparing the different co-targets and their effect on the residual value forecasting using the best-found loss weights. Results show that the highest improvement is achieved by adding the expected miles to be driven while the rest of the targets have a negligible effect. Adding the damage along with the miles also has a very small improvement over miles alone, if neglected, we can safely assume the expected miles alone has the most significant effect which is also in line with the results shown in Fig. 8. This can be

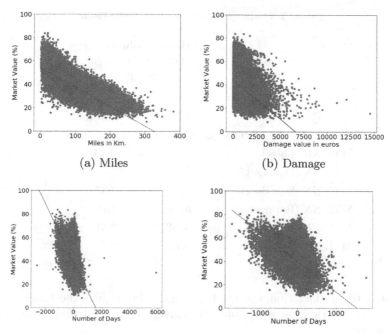

(a) Miles   (b) Damage

(c) Number of days till return date   (d) Number of days till sale date

Fig. 7. Correlation between the market value percent and other co-targets

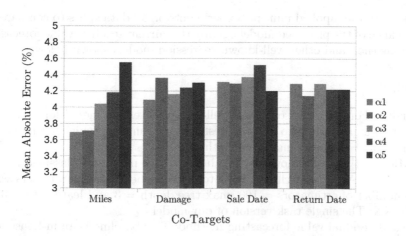

Fig. 8. Comparison between different loss weights for every available co-target. We used $\alpha = [0.001, 0.0005, 0.0001, 0.00005, 0.00001]$ for the miles; $\alpha = [0.01, 0.005, 0.001, 0.0005, 0.0001]$ for the damage; and $\alpha = [0.1, 0.05, 0.01, 0.005, 0.001]$ for the return and sale dates.

Table 5. Co-targets performance comparison

Model	Mean absolute error in market value(%)	
	(2014–2019)	(2015–2019)
Single-task learning		
STL NN	5.57	4.27
Multi-task learning		
MTL NN (Miles)	**3.69**	**3.71**
MTL NN (Damage)	5.64	4.53
MTL NN (Sale date)	5.41	4.37
MTL NN (Return date)	5.49	4.29
MTL NN (Miles + Damage)	**3.68**	**3.70**
MTL NN (All)	3.70	3.74

contributed to the fact that the used damage value is just the total sum and there is no distinction between different damage types and their effect on the market value.

5.7 Comparison with Current Methodology and Baselines Models (RQ3)

In this section we applied multiple experiments on all data splits to compare the performance of the proposed model against the current residual value forecasting manual method and other well-known regression models shown below.

Baselines

1. Random Forest Regressor [1]: A well-known ensemble model for regression. We used a grid search to find the best hyperparameters which are number of estimators = 100 and max tree depth = 3.
2. XGBoost [4]: A well-know gradient boosted tree model for classification and regression. A grid search was used to find the best hyperparameters which are number of estimators = 100, max tree depth = 3 and learn rate = 0.09.
3. STL NN: The single task version of our model
4. Current residual value forecasting method: This baseline is an in-house algorithm designed by the internal residual value management team. It relies mainly on the trend analysis of previous historical sales record after filtering any outliers, adding external factors and market indicators. Figure 9, shows the current workflow of the manual method.

We also compare the results against the Bayes error as we have identical instances that have different market values in the end. This means that the same vehicle type, with the same configuration (including same color, etc.) was sold for different prices at the very same day. Such a variance is dependent on car dealers' selling policies and can not be estimated based on the features we have. This error indicate the best possible accuracy that can be achieved on the given dataset and it was calculated using the average group value as prediction for all identical groups in the test set.

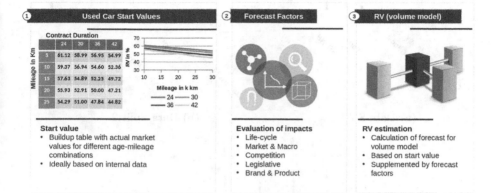

Fig. 9. Workflow of the current manual residual forecasting method. In the first step, regression analysis is done on historical sales record to draw the start value curves for every car model. Secondly, external factors are added to the value curves for adjustment. Finally the residual value is measured by using the adjusted start value curves.

Table 6. Comparison between the multi-task model against other baseline method in terms of mean absolute error percent in market value

Model	Mean absolute error in market value(%)		
	(2013–2019)	(2014–2019)	(2015–2019)
Current method	5.28	6.02	7.78
Random forest	5.26	5.59	4.71
XGBoost	5.26	4.45	3.99
Single-task learning			
STL NN	4.24	5.57	4.27
Multi-task learning			
MTL NN (Miles)	**3.75**	**3.69**	**3.71**
Bayes error			
–	2.12	2.03	2.01

Results. Table 6 shows the comparison results between the multi-task model versus all other models. The results show that the multi-task approach provides

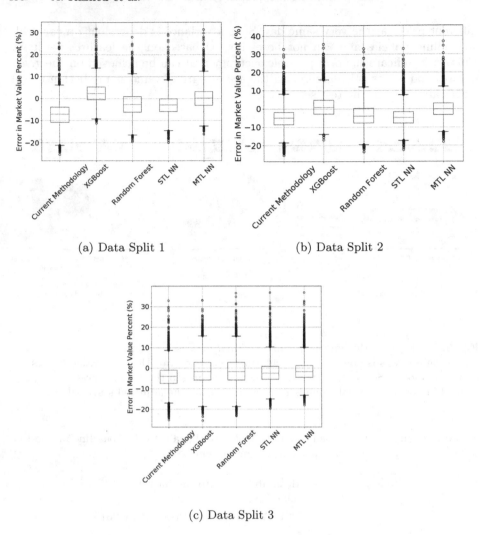

(a) Data Split 1   (b) Data Split 2

(c) Data Split 3

Fig. 10. Distribution of the signed prediction errors

a significant decrease in error compared with the single task version and the improvement over the current forecasting method is ranging from 25% to 50% in terms of error reduction. The results also show that once an adequate number of training instances are available, all baseline machine learning models can provide a competitive accuracy compared with the current manual forecasting method.

It is worth noting that the current manual forecasting method takes around 45 man-days to complete the full process by highly skilled domain experts, while the machine learning models need a couple of minutes to be trained, which is a significant reduction in execution time and effort.

Error plots in Fig. 10, show that the signed prediction errors of the multi-task approach are mostly centered around the zero value with a small standard deviation especially in the first two data splits. All other models have larger deviation and they are shifted further away from the zero value. In the third data split, errors of the multi-task approach are slightly shifted to the negative part, however, the deviation is still small compared to other models. This can be contributed to the fact that the third split has the smaller number of training samples, hence a lower accuracy for all machine learning models.

6 Conclusion and Future Work

In this paper, we proposed a multi-task approach for residual value forecasting that utilizes the expected mileage to be driven as a co-target. The proposed model was then compared against the current manual forecasting method and against well-known off-the-shelf regression models with carefully engineered features. Experimental results on the top three popular Volkswagen car models showed that the multi-task approach significantly outperformed the off-the-shelf models and the current methodology in terms of accuracy and with a significant reduction in execution time compared to the manual method. Results also showed that with the right set of features and enough training instances, the off-the-shelf regression model can provide a competitive accuracy to the current manual methodologies.

In future works, we plan to deploy the model in production to help the residual value management team in decision making and reducing the manual effort. We also plan to apply the model on car models with lesser volume and including extra features that might improve the prediction accuracy such as fuel price indicators and the Ifo business climate index.

Acknowledgments. This work is co-funded by the industry project "Data-driven Mobility Services" of ISMLL and Volkswagen Financial Services (https://www.ismll. uni-hildesheim.de/projekte/dna_en.html).

References

1. Breiman, L.: Random forests. Mach. Learn. **45**(1), 5–32 (2001)
2. Caruana, R.: Multitask learning. Mach. Learn. **28**(1), 41–75 (1997)
3. Chapelle, O., Shivaswamy, P., Vadrevu, S., Weinberger, K., Zhang, Y., Tseng, B.: Boosted multi-task learning. Mach. Learn. **85**(1–2), 149–173 (2011)
4. Chen, T., Guestrin, C.: XGBoost: a scalable tree boosting system. In: Proceedings of the 22nd ACM SIGKDD International Conference on Knowledge Discovery and Data Mining, pp. 785–794. ACM (2016)
5. Evgeniou, T., Micchelli, C.A., Pontil, M.: Learning multiple tasks with kernel methods. J. Mach. Learn. Res. **6**, 615–637 (2005)
6. Girshick, R.: Fast R-CNN. In: Proceedings of the IEEE International Conference on Computer Vision, pp. 1440–1448 (2015)

7. Harutyunyan, H., Khachatrian, H., Kale, D.C., Galstyan, A.: Multitask learning and benchmarking with clinical time series data. arXiv preprint arXiv:1703.07771 (2017)
8. Kendall, A., Gal, Y., Cipolla, R.: Multi-task learning using uncertainty to weigh losses for scene geometry and semantics. In: Proceedings of the IEEE Conference on Computer Vision and Pattern Recognition, pp. 7482–7491 (2018)
9. Lessmann, S., Listiani, M., Voß, S.: Decision support in car leasing: a forecasting model for residual value estimation. In: ICIS, p. 17 (2010)
10. Lessmann, S., Voß, S.: Car resale price forecasting: the impact of regression method, private information, and heterogeneity on forecast accuracy. Int. J. Forecast. **33**(4), 864–877 (2017)
11. Lian, C., Zhao, D., Cheng, J.: A fuzzy logic based evolutionary neural network for automotive residual value forecast. In: Proceedings of International Conference on Information Technology: Research and Education, ITRE 2003, pp. 545–548. IEEE (2003)
12. Rei, M.: Semi-supervised multitask learning for sequence labeling. arXiv preprint arXiv:1704.07156 (2017)
13. Roland: Embracing the Caras-a-Service model – The European leasing and fleet management market, January 2018. https://www.rolandberger.com/publications/publication_pdf/roland_berger_car_as_a_service_final.pdf
14. Ruder, S.: An overview of multi-task learning in deep neural networks. arXiv preprint arXiv:1706.05098 (2017)

Transfer Learning in Credit Risk

Hendra Suryanto[1]([✉]) [iD], Charles Guan[1] [iD], Andrew Voumard[1] [iD],
and Ghassan Beydoun[2] [iD]

[1] Rich Data Corporation, Singapore, Singapore
{info,hendra.suryanto,charles.guan,andrew.voumard}@richdataco.com
[2] University of Technology Sydney, Sydney, Australia
ghassan.beydoun@uts.edu.au
http://www.richdataco.com, http://feit.uts.edu.au

Abstract. In the credit risk domain, lenders frequently face situations where there is no, or limited historical lending outcome data. This generally results in limited or unaffordable credit for some individuals and small businesses. Transfer learning can potentially reduce this limitation, by leveraging knowledge from related domains, with sufficient outcome data. We investigated the potential for applying transfer learning across various credit domains, for example, from the credit card lending and debt consolidation domain into the small business lending domain.

Keywords: Credit risk · Transfer learning · Data science

1 Introduction

We studied a new domain where no or limited historical lending outcomes are available, for example: offering credit to un-banked or under-banked populations or micro to small businesses, where limited historical data is available. Currently, lenders rely mainly on expert rules for credit scoring. Due to high uncertainty in the performance of such scoring models, lenders charge a high fee or simply don't offer credit. Transfer learning from related domains is a potential solution to augment this lack of information and improve financial inclusion. For instance, transferring knowledge from credit card/debt consolidation loans to more risky small business loans or from utility bill payments to loan repayments could potentially deliver a more accurate scoring model.

We investigated the application of transfer learning during the initial stage of a credit risk model implementation, where there was limited historical labelled data available. In the credit risk domain, business priorities are stability and accuracy of model performance, in order to predict the probability of default. We present our approach, that enabled us to combine the outcome of the transferred model from related credit risk domains, with new models based on newly acquired labelled data from new domains. Using this approach, we were able

Supported by Rich Data Corporation.

U. Brefeld et al. (Eds.): ECML PKDD 2019, LNAI 11908, pp. 483–498, 2020.
https://doi.org/10.1007/978-3-030-46133-1_29

to achieve a higher accuracy and maintained stability of the overall model. Experiments on real-world commercial data showed that combining the transferred models and the new models can achieve these goals by using an incrementally transitioned approach. To allow us to publish the results and comply with the privacy requirements of our client's data, we reproduced our experiment using lendingclub.com data, https://www.lendingclub.com/info/download-data.action, which is publicly available.

When a lender expands into new market segments, a new credit risk model is required to assess the credit risk of loan applications. The current approach is based on expert rules, where the credit risk expert builds business rules based on data and available derived data, combined with the expert's experience and knowledge. Lenders initially use an expert model to gather sufficient labelled data, to build a supervised learning model. The expert model is compared against the supervised learning model. If one model performs substantially better than the other, the better model is used. Alternatively, if both models complement each other, they can be combined into an ensemble model. In commercial lending systems, lenders normally charge a higher price or limit credit offerings as there is no (or limited) labelled data to validate the expert models. The result is that many individuals and businesses are excluded from these "formal" lending systems. Organizing data access for a suitable expert to perform analysis on such typically sensitive data may be difficult, for example, when data can only be accessed on site by authorized persons.

We studied two scenarios using a large dataset of existing loan products to enhance the credit risk model for new loan products, which have a much smaller dataset. The first scenario uses Lending Club data to mimic a lender that has existing credit card and debt consolidation data and starts to offer loans to small businesses. The second scenario also uses Lending Club data, to mimic a lender that has an existing credit card loan product and starts to offer car loans.

When we pre-process the Lending Club data, we select 16 variables as inputs and the output to be predicted is the loan status. To simplify the model, we convert the loan status into a binary outcome. 1: for defaulted loans, charged-off loans or late loan payments, 0: for paid-off loans. Any current loans that are not yet due are excluded from this exercise. The pre-processing details are described in Sect. 9.

Credit card and debt consolidation loans are typically unsecured consumer loans. Their scoring model depends mainly on an individual's credit rating, income, expenses and other attributes like stability of their employment and residence. A hive of recent fintech activities in this space (particularly in UK, US and China) accumulated a legacy of historical data and concomitant stable and accurate scoring models, in what is now a crowded and competitive market. Small business lending is a relatively new market for fintechs; it is riskier, more diverse, more challenging to predict the outcomes, and suffers from a scarcity of data. As we can see in the Lending Club data, the quantity of the historical lending outcome for small business loans is far lower, and insufficient to develop a stable and accurate model using traditional supervised learning. With less competition and higher margin for small business lending (compared to consumer lending) it is more valuable for lenders to find ways to predict loan outcomes and serve this market. Furthermore, Micro, Small and Medium Enterprises (MSMEs) are one of the strongest drivers of economic development, innovation and employment. Access to finance is frequently identified as a critical barrier to growth for MSMEs. Creating opportunities for MSMEs in emerging markets is a key way to advance economic development and reduce poverty. 65 million (or 40% of formal MSMEs) in developing countries have unmet financing needs. The MSME finance gap in developing countries is estimated at $5.2 trillion - 1.4 times the current level of MSME lending [5].

2   Related Work

We have seen increasing interest in transferred supervised models - from one domain to another. Most published works in this area cover image processing, for example: Yang proposed transferring parameters on SVM [14], Pan proposed domain adaptation using transfer component analysis [7]. Pan and Yang grouped transfer learning into four approaches: instance-transfer, feature-representation-transfer, parameter-transfer, and relational-knowledge-transfer [8].

Our experimentation combines the reuse of features and derivation of new features from the source (existing) domain. Source domain labels are available; limited target (new) domain labels are available. We also focus on classification. Our experimentation is similar in those ways to Transductive Transfer Learning [7] - one key addition, is to the target classification task optimization. In Transductive Transfer Learning, the source and target tasks must be the same (classification in this case). In our experimentation though, we took a new step in optimizing the target model accuracy, by introducing and experimenting with an extra optimization variable: the level of relative source/target feature data contribution proportions into the target model.

Many papers focus largely on making optimal choices of parameters, features, and source(s), to transfer learning to the target model, as summarized in [12] - which examines homogeneous and even heterogeneous data domains, symmetric and asymmetric feature transformation, for instance-based, feature-based, parameter-based, and relational-based related transfer learning. [3,6,10,13] make specific efforts to minimize 'negative transfer' (a transfer that has a negative impact on the target model). While these approaches help to improve target model results - and can (in some cases) reduce target model build times, our focus was centered on optimizing the target model configuration/composition and design, for the transferred features after they were selected to be inputs to the target model.

3   Credit Risk

Lenders seek to optimize the risk return ratio across their lending portfolios. Accurately and consistently measuring credit risk is the foundation of this optimization. Lenders commonly use the concept of Expected Loss (EL) to measure credit risk. In an unsecured lending scenario, EL is mainly determined by the Probability of Default (PD). Credit scoring models are used to calculate PD. Inputs of a credit scoring model are normally attributes of the loan applicant and their application. In this paper we use a few attributes from lendingclub.com data to illustrate our approach. In credit risk, the most common metrics to assess the quality of credit scoring model are Gini, Kolmogorov-Smirnov statistics (KS), Lift, the Mahalanobis distance and information statistics [9]. In this paper we use Gini for this purpose.

The scoring model output is a score from 0 to 1. It is an estimated probability of default. Usually some part of the data is pre-allocated for calibration of the score. Lenders use a set of decision processes and rules to make an optimal decision with the derived PD and loan application data as inputs. A decision process generally starts with an eligibility test. PD is calculated for the eligible applicants, and then used to group applicants into different decision groups. For instance, the interest rate could vary for different decision groups, as could the loan amount as a percentage of net income.

In this investigation, our focus is credit scoring for unsecured lending. We measure the performance of our credit scoring model using Area Under Receiver Operating Curve (AUC) or $GiniROC$ which is $2AUC - 1$ [4]. GiniROC shares the same concept as Gini, for splitting criteria in CART [2]. Gini and GiniROC, however, have different usages. The metric GiniROC is used to allow the assessment of model quality, based on PD, without needing to convert PD into binary classifications, since the threshold to do those classifications is defined in the credit decisioning.

3.1   Credit Scoring

Credit scoring produces a PD, which is used to predict binary outcomes, loan-paid or loan-defaulted. In real-world scenarios, there are additional outcomes, such as late payment or partial payment. In credit scoring, we need a metric to assess the quality of the model without defining a threshold to convert the PD into a classification. When we have classifications, we can use a metric such as $Fscore$. In credit risk, this decision is deferred to the credit decisioning step, where expert rules are utilized to decide whether the loan is approved or not.

3.2   Credit Decisioning

Credit decisioning consumes PD and produces a decision to approve or decline a loan application. The conversion from PD to a decision is usually driven by a mapping table to map ranges of PD to decisions. The decision is not only to approve or to decline, it may also update the loan amount, interest and term. This model is usually based on expert rules, since the data is usually too sparse and/or the search space is too large for building supervised learning models.

4   Model Development

We developed six example network configurations to empirically assess the effectiveness of our transfer learning algorithm; their detail is explained in Sects. 4.1 and 5. Table 1 shows those configurations in order of increasing Progressive Shift Contribution (PSC) from the source domain to the target domain. The PSC is our novel contribution and is explained in detail in Sect. 5.

Model No 1 is developed by training using source domain data only. The domain contribution in Models No 2 to 5 is progressively shifted from source to target domain. The last model, Model No 6 is trained using target domain data only. The difference in contribution between the source and target domains shows up in the ratio between the number of trained layers using the target domain and the number of trained layers using the source domain. The algorithm can be generalized for any network configuration size. Further details of the algorithm will be discussed in Sect. 5. Source code and data for all experiments is provided, see Sect. 9.

Table 1. Six Network Configurations with PSC

No.	Model name	Source domain contribution	Target domain contribution	Layers trained by source	Layers trained by target	Network configuration
1	$M(v)_e$	100%	0%	4	0	Fig. 2
2	$M(w)_{transfer}$	75%	25%	3	1	Fig. 4
3	$M(wx)_{transfer}$	71%	29%	5	2	Fig. 5
4	$M(wxy)_{transfer}$	60%	40%	6	4	Fig. 6
5	$M(wxyz)_{transfer}$	46%	54%	6	7	Fig. 3
6	$M(u)_n$	0%	100%	0	4	Fig. 1

We discover the optimum network configuration by shifting the PSC from the source to target domain and measure the Gini performance using the target domain test data. The model performance is conceptually influenced by (a) the modelling techniques (e.g. deep learning, gradient boosting machine, generalized linear model), hyper parameters[1], (b) the signal strength in the data and (c) feature engineering; Informally, the relationship between $Gini$ and these factors can be written as follows:

$$Gini = g(test(M_e, s_e)) \tag{1}$$

where s_e is test data from the source domain, M_e is the model trained using training data from the source domain, $test()$ is an activity to test a model on the test data producing the test results and $g()$ is a function to calculate the Gini of the results. M_e is defined as follows:

$$M_e = train(M_0, P_e, t_e, F_e) \tag{2}$$

---

[1] The hyper parameters optimization has been done before this step.

where M_0 is a deep neural network configuration with initial random weights, P_e is a set of hyper parameters to train M_e, t_e is the training data from the source domain, F_e is a set of features derived from t_e, $train()$ is an activity to train a model based on these four factors. The result of $train()$ is a trained model.

To explain how we perform the PSC, we define a function $split()$ to conceptually split M_e into two segments: $Mfix_e$ and $Mfree_e$. $Mfix_e$ is the segment where the layers were trained using t_e and these layers are not retrainable. $Mfree_e$ is the segment where the layers were also trained using t_e, but these layers are trainable using the training data from the target domain t_n.

$$(Mfix_e, Mfree_e) = split(M_e) \tag{3}$$

The inverse function of $split()$ is $c()$, for combining $Mfix_e$ and $Mfree_e$ back into M_e

$$M_e = c(Mfix_e, Mfree_e) \tag{4}$$

To create a mixed model based on both the source and target domain data, we developed a model for the target domain $M_{transfer}$, by transferring the structure and weights of $Mfix_e$ layers and retraining the structure and weights of $Mfree_e$.

$$Mfree_n = train(Mfree_e, P_n, t_n, F_n) \tag{5}$$

Finally, we combined the target model $Mfree_n$ with $Mfix_e$. The result is the transferred model $M_{transfer}$

$$M_{transfer} = c(Mfix_e, Mfree_n) \tag{6}$$

The overall goal is to maximize $Gini_{transfer}$, where s_n is the test data from the target domain:

$$Gini_{transfer} = g(test(M_{transfer}, s_n)) \tag{7}$$

by monitoring $Gini_{transfer}$ as we shift the PSC from the source to target domain data. Finally, we discover the maximum $Gini_{transfer}$ by testing the performance of all six network configurations outlined in Table 1.

4.1   The Base Model

The base models were configured based on network structures. The first is shown in Fig. 1. It has 16 input nodes on the input layer, 3 hidden layers, each layer has 32 nodes and 1 output node on the output layer. This network configuration is selected by using a hyper parameter search to find a near optimum configuration.

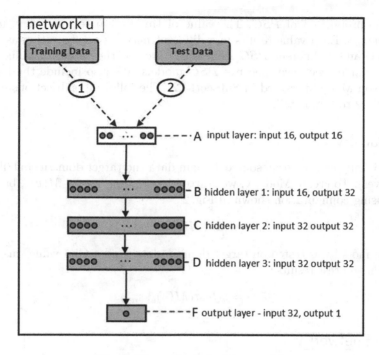

Fig. 1. Network u: the base model

4.2 The Comparison Model (Model U)

The comparison model is based on network configuration u as shown in Fig. 1. This model is trained using the target domain data only (no contribution from source domain data). Similar to Eq. 2, the model built using target domain data, can be defined as follows:

$$M(u)_n = train(M(u)_0, P_n, t_n, F_n) \tag{8}$$

where $M(u)_n$ is a model developed using data from the target domain based on network configuration u, $M(u)_0$ is the initial model based on network configuration u with all weights randomly initialized, P_n, t_n, F_n are parameters, training data and features respectively, used to develop the model $M(u)_n$.

$$Gini = g(test(M(u)_n, s_n)) \tag{9}$$

where s_n is test data from the target domain.

5 Progressive Shift Contribution Models

In Sect. 4, we introduced six models where the Progressive Shift Contribution (PSC) shifts between the source and target domain data. To perform the PSC, we extended the split function defined in Eq. 3 with an additional parameter to define the proportion of *PSC*. The value of this parameter one of: v, w, wx, wxy, or $wxyz$. Each value results in a different network configuration as shown in Table 1, and a different *PSC* from the source to the target domain. Using these five values, we developed five *PSC* models. We also include the baseline Comparison Model discussed in Subsect. 4.2. The following subsections explain models No 2 to 6 in detail.

5.1 Model V

Model v is only created from source domain data (no target domain contribution whatsoever). To create Model v, we started by training model $M(v)_e$, based on Eq. 10, using configuration shown in Fig. 2

$$M(v)_e = train(M(v)_0, P_e, t_e, F_e) \tag{10}$$

Then the model was tested on target domain data, and a Gini value was calculated from the test results.

$$Gini = g(test(M(v)_e, s_n)) \tag{11}$$

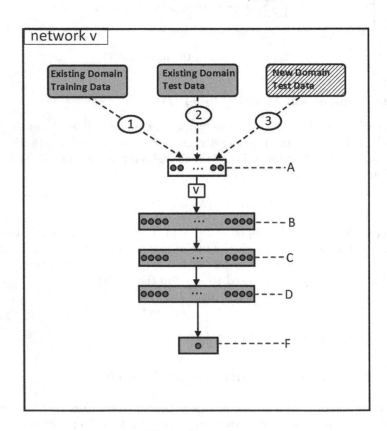

Fig. 2. Network v

5.2 Model Wxyz

This model was created using four parallel networks - each with three hidden layers, connected to the input and output layers. To create this model, we initially copied hidden layers of network v (both the structure and the weights) into networks w, x, y and z. Conceptually, we illustrate the transformation using Eq. 12.

$$M(wxyz)_e = transform(M(v)_e) \qquad (12)$$

Networks w, x, y and z were setup as shown in Fig. 3.

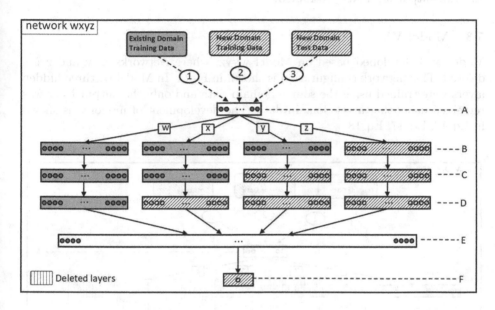

Fig. 3. Network wxyz

After the structure and weights were set (as shown in Fig. 3), we then set the following as trainable, using the target domain data: The 3rd hidden layer of Network x, the 2nd and 3rd hidden layers of Network y, and all hidden layers of Network z. The next three steps are indicated in numbers 1, 2, 3 within ellipses in Fig. 3:

1. Weights for networks w, x, y, z were derived from training using t_e. Some layers in networks x, y, z and w, the output layers are set as trainable, using t_n.
2. Train these layers using t_n.
3. Test the performance of the whole parallel network (w, x, y, z) on s_n, then calculate the Gini value from the test result.

The development of Model wxyz can be summarized by three equations: Eq. 13, Eq. 14, Eq. 15.

$$(Mfix(wxyz)_e, Mfree(wxyz)_e) = split(M(wxyz)_e) \qquad (13)$$

$$Mfree(wxyz)_n = train(Mfree(wxyz)_e, P_n, t_n, F_n) \qquad (14)$$

$$M(wxyz)_{transfer} = c(Mfix(wxyz)_e, Mfree(wxyz)_n) \qquad (15)$$

In Model wxyz, six hidden layers were trained using the source domain data and seven layers were retrained using the target domain data, i.e. six hidden layers and the output layer were retrained.

5.3   Model W

Model w is developed based on Model wxyz, where Networks x, y and z are deleted. This network configuration is shown in Fig. 4. In Model w, three hidden layers were trained using the source domain data and only the output layer was retrained using the target domain data. The development of model w is shown in Eq. 16, Eq. 17, Eq. 18.

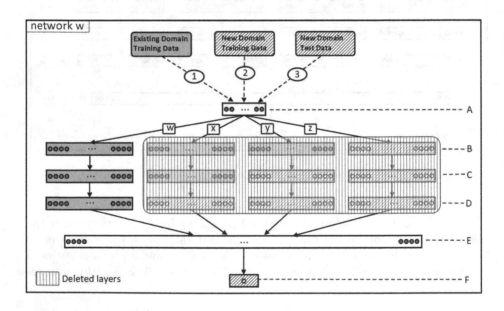

Fig. 4. Network w

$$(Mfix(w)_e, Mfree(w)_e) = split(M(w)_e) \qquad (16)$$

$$Mfree(w)_n = train(Mfree(w)_e, P_n, t_n, F_n) \qquad (17)$$

$$M(w)_{transfer} = c(Mfix(w)_e, Mfree(w)_n) \qquad (18)$$

5.4 Model Wx

Model wx is developed based on Model wxyz, where Networks y and z are deleted. This network configuration shown in Fig. 5. In Model wx, five hidden layers were trained using the source domain data. One hidden layer and the output layer were retrained using the target domain data. The development of model wx is shown in Eq. 19, Eq. 20, Eq. 21.

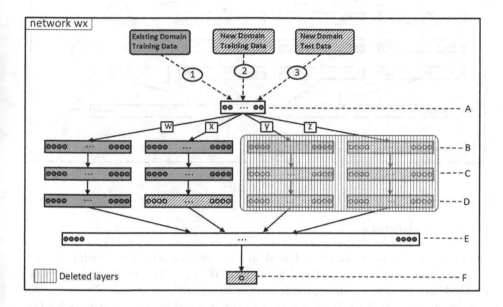

Fig. 5. Network wx

$$(Mfix(wx)_e, Mfree(wx)_e) = split(M(wx)_e) \tag{19}$$

$$Mfree(wx)_n = train(Mfree(wx)_e, P_n, t_n, F_n) \tag{20}$$

$$M(wx)_{transfer} = c(Mfix(wx)_e, Mfree(wx)_n) \tag{21}$$

5.5 Model Wxy

Model wxy is developed based on Model wxyz, where only Network z is deleted. This network configuration is shown in Fig. 6. In Model wxy, six hidden layers were trained using source domain data. Three hidden layers and the output layer were retrained using target domain data. The development of model wxy is shown in Eq. 22, Eq. 23, Eq. 24.

$$(Mfix(wxy)_e, Mfree(wxy)_e) = split(M(wxy)_e) \tag{22}$$

$$Mfree(wxy)_n = train(Mfree(wxy)_e, P_n, t_n, F_n) \tag{23}$$

$$M(wxy)_{transfer} = c(Mfix(wxy)_e, Mfree(wxy)_n) \tag{24}$$

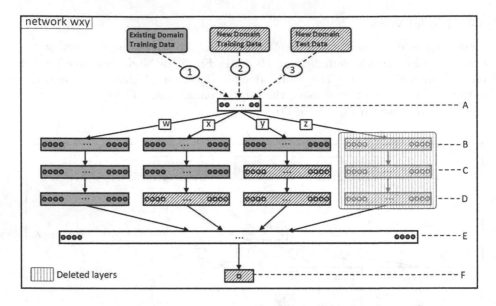

Fig. 6. Network wxy

6   Experiments

In our experiments, we used data based on lendingclub.com data, which is similar to our client's data, with a time range of 2007 to 2018, see Sect. 9. We first created base models - training them from scratch, without transfer learning. We applied a grid search to discover a near optimal set of hyper parameters for the Deep Learning (DL) structure. In these Transfer Learning experiments, we used Credit Card/Debt Consolidation (CD) as the source domain and Small Business (SB) as the target domain. Our goal is to transfer learning from CD to SB, as the data in SB is limited.

Table 2. Performance of Gradient Boosting Machine (GBM) and Deep Learning (DL) on Credit Card and Debt Consolidation (CD) and Small Business Loan (SB) datasets, evaluated using 10 fold cross validation

Name	Sampling	Gini GBM	Gini DL
$CreditCard/DebtConsolidation$	Random	0.43 ± 0.01	0.43 ± 0.01
$SmallBusiness$	Random	0.30 ± 0.05	0.31 ± 0.02

We validated the performance using CD and SB data extracts, by developing comparison models that used Gradient Boosting Machines (GBM). The comparison of performances is shown in Table 2. There is no significant difference between the performance of GBM and DL. The next experiments only focused on DL.

6.1   Experimentation Datasets

We downloaded all datasets from lendingclub.com in mid October 2018. The datasets were filtered based on *purpose* (CD and SB) and *year* (2007 to 2018). 10 datasets were created from the downloaded data. The first extract was dataset $CD4$, time range: 2007 to 2018. The size was 100,000 records, extracted randomly from 940,948 records, where the loan purpose was paying Credit Card and Debt Consolidation. The bad debt rate from this dataset was 21%. Next was dataset $SB4$, time range: 2007 to 2018, the size was 13,794 records where the loan purpose was for investing in Small Business; this type of loan is riskier; the bad debt rate is 30%. No outlier filtering was performed for these two datasets. Datasets $CD1$, $CD2$, $CD3$ are subsets of dataset $CD4$, filtered based on different time ranges. Similarly datasets $SB1$, $SB2$, $SB3$ are subsets of dataset $SB4$. Dataset CCD is also a subset of dataset $CD4$, filtered on Credit Card Loans. Similarly the Car Loan data is extracted from the Lending Club datasets, see Sect. 9.

Table 3. List of datasets for transfer learning experiments, the type column indicates whether the dataset is used as the source or the target of the transfer learning process.

ID	Dataset	Period	Size	Type	Gini
CD1	$CreditCard/DebtConsolidation$	2007–2011	23,813	Source	0.364 ± 0.023
SB1	$SmallBusinessLoan$	2007–2011	1,831	Target	0.272 ± 0.067
CD2	$CreditCard/DebtConsolidation$	2007–2014	100,000	Source	0.417 ± 0.016
SB2	$SmallBusinessLoan$	2007–2014	6,686	Target	0.274 ± 0.040
CD3	$CreditCard/DebtConsolidation$	2007–2016	100,000	Source	0.447 ± 0.013
SB3	$SmallBusinessLoan$	2007–2016	12,114	Target	0.331 ± 0.032
CD4	$CreditCard/DebtConsolidation$	2007–2018	100,000	Source	0.448 ± 0.012
SB4	$SmallBusinessLoan$	2007–2018	13,794	Target	0.351 ± 0.024
CCD	$CreditCard$	2007–2018	100,000	Source	0.463 ± 0.014
CAR	$CarLoan$	2007–2018	12,734	Target	0.436 ± 0.036

All experiments were based on the data in Table 3. They were performed using 10 fold cross validation, repeated 5 times. The base model to be transferred was developed using the dataset $CD1$, $CD2$, $CD3$, $CD4$, CCD and the network configuration u, as shown in Fig. 1 and defined in Eq. 2. One factor that influenced model performance was the strength of signal[2] from the data. Table 3 also shows, the larger the dataset the higher the Gini; as the data is becoming more mature, it represents the real-world better.

Similarly, the Gini for $SB1$, $SB2$, $SB3$, $SB4$ and CAR shown in Table 3 and Table 4 is calculated from the test result of model $M(u)_n$ by applying the function $g()$ on the test results, as defined in Eq. 9.

---

[2] Associated with the outcome being predicted.

6.2 Experimentation Results

The experiment results are summarized in Table 4 where we applied Progressive Shifted Contributions (PSC) from the source to the target domain data. We found that $M(w)_{transfer}$ had the highest Gini of 0.301 a (10.7% improvement compared to $M(u)_n$) for the experiment over source/target:$CD1/SB1$. As the target data became more mature in $CD2/SB2$, $M(w)_{transfer}$ still had the highest Gini of 0.287, however the improvement was only 4.7%. As the target data became more mature in $CD3/SB3$ the contribution shifted toward the target data; model $M(wx)_{transfer}$ had the highest Gini of 0.337. It contributed marginal improvement (1.8%) over $M(u)_n$. Finally, in $CD4/SB4$, the contribution was completely shifted into the target, resulting in $M(u)_n$ having the highest Gini of 0.351.

The experiment on datasets CCD/CAR, $M(w)_{transfer}$ had the highest Gini of 0.447, a small improvement (2.5%) over $M(u)_n$. It shows the Car Loan dataset had similar maturity to the credit card dataset.

The experiments show the contribution was shifted from source to target as the target data matured. The contribution was based on the number of trainable layers using the source and target domain data. All these experiments were performed using 10 fold cross validation, repeated 5 times. That is, each experiment was repeated 50 times; we then record the average of the Gini scores and the standard deviation.

Table 4. Experimentation Results (source: Credit Card/Debt Consolidation, target: Small Business Loan), six models with progressively shifted contribution, built based on source and target datasets described in Table 3, the best performing models are marked with the symbol *.

Model	Source/Target				
	$CD1/SB1$	$CD2/SB2$	$CD3/SB3$	$CD4/SB4$	CCD/CAR
$M(v)_e$	0.157 ± 0.022	0.236 ± 0.051	-0.191 ± 0.260	0.196 ± 0.026	0.262 ± 0.355
$M(w)_{transfer}$	$*0.301 \pm 0.097$	$*0.287 \pm 0.051$	0.334 ± 0.029	0.350 ± 0.029	$*0.447 \pm 0.037$
$M(wx)_{transfer}$	0.292 ± 0.091	0.272 ± 0.054	$*0.337 \pm 0.030$	0.350 ± 0.028	0.434 ± 0.035
$M(wxy)_{transfer}$	0.230 ± 0.087	0.217 ± 0.057	0.300 ± 0.032	0.310 ± 0.030	0.376 ± 0.040
$M(wxyz)_{transfer}$	0.174 ± 0.010	0.172 ± 0.051	0.254 ± 0.029	0.273 ± 0.030	0.310 ± 0.050
$M(u)_n$	0.272 ± 0.067	0.274 ± 0.040	0.331 ± 0.032	$*0.351 \pm 0.024$	0.436 ± 0.036
% improvement	10.7%	4.7%	1.8%	0.0%	2.5%

6.3 Additional Experiments

We investigated the hypothesis that the Gini performance improvement was due to the complexity of the network structure. We conducted experiments as described in Eq. 25 and Eq. 26. The model with network configuration wxyz was trained and retrained on source domain data. The performance of this model was 0.39 ± 0.01, which is lower than the base model Gini 0.43 ± 0.01. It showed that the additional complexity of $M(wxyz)_{transfer}$ did not improve Gini performance. The improvement was instead due to the diversity of the source data, complementing the target data.

$$Mfree(wxyz)_e = train(Mfree(wxyz)_e, P_e, t_e, F_e) \qquad (25)$$

$$M(wxyz)_{retrain} = c(Mfix(wxyz)_e, Mfree(wxyz)_e) \qquad (26)$$

7 Conclusion

We propose an algorithm to progressively shift the contribution from the source to target domains. The *PSC* algorithm lets us evaluate incremental complements of target domain data with source domain data. While we undertook some activities manually, the underlying goal has been to devise a framework that can automatically search for the optimum balance between the source and target domain data, generating the highest Gini score for that combination. Six *PSC* models were built, ranging from Model v (using source domain data only) all the way to Model u (using target domain data only) as described in Table 1.

8 Future Work

The presented research is part of a larger effort to develop transfer learning knowledge based systems. The presented experiment and results are the first of a series of experiments which will be used to discover and formulate a stream of rules. The rules will be incrementally incorporated in a knowledge base, following the Ripple Down Rule framework, specifically geared towards incremental construction of rule-based systems [1,11].

To realise the knowledge based system, an appropriate representation of the transfer context and the transfer recommendations will first be needed, to enable appropriate encoding of rules within the system. To formulate the representation, we will need to identify an adequate set of features for the context transfer, requiring further experiments with additional source data, such as utility payments, taxation, etc. Through these experiments, we will also seek ways to accommodate different *PSC* levels from each data source, and assess target model Gini impact. Further, the representation will need to account for articulating the recommendations output from the rule-based system. We will also require new features to represent the following:

1. Domain adaptation, to adjust the variables/features before performing the transfer learning process.
2. Selection of optimization approaches, by assessing their impact on the target model Gini.

498   H. Suryanto et al.

9   Software and Data

The software and steps to pre-process the data are available at the following Git-lab URL: https://gitlab.com/richdataco/rdc-public/rdc-ic/research/transfer-learning/ecmlpkdd2019.

The datasets for Credit Card, Debt Consolidation, Small Business Loan, Car Loan are available from https://www.lendingclub.com/info/download-data.action.

References

1. Beydoun, G., Hoffmann, A.: Theoretical basis for hierarchical incremental knowledge acquisition. Int. J. Hum. Comput. Stud. **54**(3), 407–452 (2001)
2. Breiman, L.: Some properties of splitting criteria. Mach. Learn. **24**(1), 41–47 (1996)
3. Chattopadhyay, R., Ye, J., Panchanathan, S., Fan, W., Davidson, I.: Multi-source domain adaptation and its application to early detection of fatigue. In: KDD (2011)
4. Flach, P.A.: The geometry of ROC space: understanding machine learning metrics through ROC isometrics. In: Proceedings of the 20th International Conference on Machine Learning (ICML 2003), pp. 194–201 (2003)
5. Forum, S.F.: MSME finance gap, January 2019. https://www.smefinanceforum.org/data-sites/msme-finance-gap/
6. Gao, J., Fan, W., Jiang, J., Han, J.: Knowledge transfer via multiple model local structure mapping. In: KDD (2008)
7. Pan, S.J., Tsang, I.W., Kwok, J.T., Yang, Q.: Domain adaptation via transfer component analysis. IEEE Trans. Neural Netw. **22**(2), 199–210 (2011)
8. Pan, S.J., Yang, Q., et al.: A survey on transfer learning. IEEE Trans. Knowl. Data Eng. **22**(10), 1345–1359 (2010)
9. Řezáč, M., Řezáč, F.: How to measure the quality of credit scoring models. Finance a úvěr Czech J. Econ. Finan. **61**(5), 486–507 (2011)
10. Sun, S., Xu, Z., Yang, M.: Transfer learning with part-based ensembles. In: MCS (2013)
11. Suryanto, H., Compton, P.: Invented predicates to reduce knowledge acquisition. In: Motta, E., Shadbolt, N.R., Stutt, A., Gibbins, N. (eds.) EKAW 2004. LNCS (LNAI), vol. 3257, pp. 293–306. Springer, Heidelberg (2004). https://doi.org/10.1007/978-3-540-30202-5_20
12. Weiss, K., Khoshgoftaar, T.M., Wang, D.D.: A survey of transfer learning. J. Big Data **3**(1), 1–40 (2016). https://doi.org/10.1186/s40537-016-0043-6
13. Xiao, J., Wang, R., Teng, G.E., Hu, Y.: A transfer learning based classifier ensemble model for customer credit scoring. In: 2014 Seventh International Joint Conference on Computational Sciences and Optimization, pp. 64–68 (2014)
14. Yang, J., Yan, R., Hauptmann, A.G.: Cross-domain video concept detection using adaptive SVMS. In: Proceedings of the 15th ACM International Conference on Multimedia, pp. 188–197. ACM (2007)

Cold-Start Recommendation for On-Demand Cinemas

Beibei Li[1,2], Beihong Jin[1,2(✉)], Taofeng Xue[1,2], Kunchi Liu[1,2], Qi Zhang[3],
and Sihua Tian[3]

[1] State Key Laboratory of Computer Sciences, Institute of Software,
Chinese Academy of Sciences, Beijing, China
Beihong@iscas.ac.cn
[2] University of Chinese Academy of Sciences, Beijing, China
[3] Beijing iQIYI Cinema Management Co., Ltd., Beijing, China

Abstract. The on-demand cinemas, which has emerged in recent years, provide offline entertainment venues for individuals and small groups. Because of the limitation of network speed and storage space, it is necessary to recommend movies to cinemas, that is, to suggest cinemas to download the recommended movies in advance. This is particularly true for new cinemas. For the new cinema cold-start recommendation, we build a matrix factorization framework and then fuse location categories of cinemas and co-popular relationship between movies in the framework. Specifically, location categories of cinemas are learned through LDA from the type information of POIs around the cinemas and used to approximate cinema latent representations. Moreover, a SPPMI matrix that reflects co-popular relationship between movies is constructed and factorized collectively with the interaction matrix by sharing the same item latent representations. Extensive experiments on real-world data are conducted. The experimental results show that the proposed approach yields significant improvements over state-of-the-art cold-start recommenders in terms of precision, recall and NDCG.

Keywords: Recommendation system · On-demand cinema ·
Cold-start problem · Matrix factorization · Location category ·
Co-popular relationship

1 Introduction

The on-demand cinemas are a new type of offline entertainment venues for individuals and small groups of audiences. At such a cinema, audiences can choose the favorite movies from local copies of copyrighted movies and watch them. In the recent two years, the number of on-demand cinemas has been increasing rapidly. In China, on-demand cinemas have covered 29 provinces and 92 core cities.

This work was supported by the National Natural Science Foundation of China (No. 61472408) and the joint project with iQIYI (No. LUM18-200032).

© Springer Nature Switzerland AG 2020
U. Brefeld et al. (Eds.): ECML PKDD 2019, LNAI 11908, pp. 499–515, 2020.
https://doi.org/10.1007/978-3-030-46133-1_30

The movies played at on-demand cinemas are ones with ultra-clear HD pictures and HiFi sounds, which usually consume considerable storage space. For example, a Blu-ray HD movie may take up 40–50GB. In order to ensure the watching experience and to avoid the display lag phenomena caused by the network bandwidth limitation, on-demand cinemas usually download movies in advance and store movies locally. However, due to the limited local storage space, on-demand cinemas must choose some potential popular movies from numerous candidates, and then download them for audiences in advance. That is, the local movie libraries of on-demand cinemas will directly influence choices and consumption trends of audiences.

For on-demand cinemas, Xue et al. [19] establish a spatial-temporal recommendation system, which utilizes the history watching records of on-demand cinemas and recommend the movies to the staffs/hosts of on-demand cinemas to download the movies into local movie libraries. However, the above system is only suitable for cinemas that are already in operation and have history watching records. For newly-opened on-demand cinemas, the initial movie libraries will directly affect the operation of the cinemas at the beginning, which further involves the survival of on-demand cinema business. Therefore, it is important to provide an initial movie recommendation list for newly-opened on-demand cinemas.

Recommending movies to new cinemas, i.e., cinema cold-start problem, can be analogous to the user cold-start problem in the traditional recommendation systems. That is, the recommendation objects are on-demand cinemas in our scenarios, and recommendation items are movies.

We notice that in the on-demand cinema scenarios, the surrounding environment of a cinema will affect the composition of audiences. For example, those who live or work around a cinema tend to visit the cinema. Moreover, if the cinema is in the business district, the colleagues are more likely to watch movie together; if the cinema is at living areas, then it is more likely that the family members watch movie together. Therefore, we can explore the point of interest (POI) type information around each new cinema to predict the popularity of each movie in each new cinema. In addition, high-quality movie representations are helpful in dealing with the cinema cold-start problem. Mining the correlation over popularity of two movies is a feasible way.

Based on the above considerations, we establish a basic framework of cold-start model based on matrix factorization, and then fuse side information to serve the cold-start of the on-demand cinemas from two aspects. On the one hand, from the POI type information around the cinemas, we learn location category probability distribution of the cinemas through the latent Dirichlet allocation (LDA), and further apply the linear transformation to the learned distribution to obtain the latent representations of cinemas. On the other hand, we define the movie co-popular relationship and find co-popular contexts of movie pairs, from which we build the shifted positive pointwise mutual information (SPPMI) matrix. Finally, we collectively factorize the SPPMI matrix and the cinema-movie interaction matrix factorization by sharing the latent representations of movies to further improve the quality of movie representations. By conducting extensive experiments on real-world datasets of on-demand cinemas, we demonstrate that our proposed approach yields significant improvement compared with other state-of-art cold-start recommenders in terms of precision, recall, and NDCG.

Our contributions are summarized as follows:

First, we devise a matrix factorization-based model to tackle the cold-start problem of on-demand cinemas, which explores the influence of cinema location category and co-popular relationship between movies. To the best of our knowledge, it is the first work to attempt to solve the on-demand cold-start problem.

Second, extensive experiments performed on real-world datasets demonstrate the effectiveness of our proposed approach. Besides, we evaluate the performance contributions of key components of the proposed approach, including the SPPMI matrix, the location category probability distribution vector learned by LDA and the frequency-based weights.

Third, the proposed approach is also applicable to the warm-start recommendation of on-demand cinemas and the cold-start scenarios of offline stores. Furthermore, the SPPMI matrix component reflecting co-popular relationship between movies can be generalized to any scenario with co-popular relationship between items and serve as a separate module adding to other matrix factorization-based recommendation approaches.

2 Related Work

This work is broadly related to the research in two nonorthogonal categories: cold-start recommendation, embedding techniques.

2.1 Cold-Start Recommendation

The existing methods to solve cold-start recommendation for users can be roughly divided into two categories: interview-based methods and side information based methods [13].

The interview-based methods [13] need to design some representative questions to ask cold-start users and then recommend them based on their feedback. This type of methods consumes a lot of time and manpower, which are not suitable for on-demand cinemas.

Besides directly inquiring cold-start users, side-information including social network information, user profile information or other cross-domain information can be used to solve the problem of cold-start recommendation for users. These methods are called side information based methods. These methods can be further divided into three kinds [9]: similarity based methods, matrix factorization methods, and feature mapping methods.

Recommending based on the similarities between the cold-start user and the other users is the common idea in the similarity based methods. However, the method of calculating the similarity is multifarious. For example, Suvash et al. [15]

measure the similarity between users by using cosine similarity of user side information vectors. Peng et al. [11] construct a parameterized Mahalanobis distance metric using user side information, and learns the parameters of the Mahalanobis distance from the training data, finally, use the learned Mahalanobis distance to measure the similarity between users.

Matrix factorization methods integrate side information on the basis of the interaction matrix factorization. For example, the CMF (Collective Matrix Factorization) model [14] factorizes the interaction matrix and side information jointly by sharing the user hidden vector U and learns the linear mapping function from the user latent representations to the side information. The CTR (Collaborative Topic Regression) model [17] first learns the topic distribution from the content of the article through the LDA [1] model, and then adds Gaussian error to the latent space representations of the articles to solve the cold-start problem of article recommendation.

The core of the feature mapping methods is to learn the transfer function of side information to user hidden space. The main difference between it and collective matrix factorization is that the latter is to learn user latent vector and mapping function simultaneously, while the former has a separate process of learning feature mapping. For example, the BRP-linMap algorithm proposed by Zeno et al. [3] learns a linear feature mapping function from side information to user latent vectors. For a variety of methods to solve the cold-start problem with side information, Sedhain et al. [12] unify them in a linear transformation framework, and propose a low-rank linear regression model LOCO using the side information matrix and the interaction matrix.

2.2 Embedding Techniques

In a recommendation system, the embedding techniques can be used to learn the hidden vectors of users and items, thereby improving the performance of the recommendation results [10, 18, 20].

One way is to express relationships between users or items or otherwise via a graph and then apply graph embedding techniques to learn the latent vectors of users or items. For example, Xie et al. [18] construct four bipartite graphs such as POI-POI, POI-region, POI-time slots and POI-content words for POI recommendation and the learned latent vectors characterize the four effects, i.e., sequential effect, geographical influence, temporal cyclic effect, and semantic effect in POIs. Yu et al. [20] establish a heterogeneous information network based on the potential friend relationships between users and the purchase relationships between user and item to learn the user latent representations. Then, recommendation are made based on the similarity between user latent representations.

Word embedding techniques utilize the contextual information between words to learn the low-dimension representations of words. The techniques have been successful in the field of natural language processing [4] and have recently been introduced into recommendation systems. Grbovic et al. [4] regard the product in a product recommendation system as a word, the product list consumed by a user as a sentence, and propose prov2vec algorithm based on word2vec. Levy et al. [8] demonstrate that the skip-gram negative sampling (SGNS) model for word embedding is equivalent to decomposing the shifted positive pointwise mutual information (SPPMI) matrix. Inspired by this, Liang et al. [10] propose a collective matrix factorization method, which combines the user-item interaction matrix and the SPPMI matrix of the item on the basis of the shared item latent vectors. For calculating the SPPMI matrix, the item lists that have been interacted with by the same user can be regarded as a sentence, each item in the list is regarded as a word, and each item in the list is regarded as context for each other. Subsequently, Cao et al. [2] adopt the similar method to generate the SPPMI matrix. Thus, while the decomposition is being performed, the embeddings of items and lists are simultaneously learned, and the recommendation of item and item list are solved. In addition, for watching video scenarios, Than et al. [16] first define user context, co-like context and co-dislike context, and then obtain the corresponding three SPPMI matrices and perform regularized matrix factorization while fusing with three SPPMI matrices to recommend videos.

Different from the existing work, we combine matrix factorization and item embedding techniques for cold-start recommendation. On the one hand, we utilize location category distribution vectors of cold-start cinemas learned by LDA to obtain the latent representations of cinemas. On the other hand, we exploit co-popular relationship between movies and build the SPPMI matrix. Then, we collectively factorize the SPPMI matrix with the cinema-movie interaction matrix by sharing the latent vectors of the movies.

3   Approach

3.1   Formulation

Recommending movies to startup on-demand cinemas is the user cold-start recommendation problem, where we take a cinema as a user. We split the cinema set S into two disjoint parts: the set of warm-start cinemas S_{tr} whose elements have at least one watching record in the past t timeslots and the set of cold-start cinemas S_{te}, where $S_{tr} \cap S_{te} = \emptyset$. Let $R_{tr} \in \{0,1\}^{|S_{tr}| \times n}$ denote the interaction between warm-start cinemas in S_{tr} and n movies, where $|S_{tr}|$ is the number of warm-start cinemas, and if there is interaction between $i-$th cinema and $j-$th movie, then the element in R_{tr}, i.e., $r_{ij} = 1$. Otherwise $r_{ij} = 0$. Let $X_{tr} \in \mathbb{R}^{|S_{tr}| \times d}$ indicate d-dimension side information of warm-start cinemas and $X_{te} \in \mathbb{R}^{|S_{te}| \times d}$ indicate d-dimension side information of cold-start cinemas. Our goal is to predict the interaction matrix $\hat{R}_{te} \in \mathbb{R}^{|S_{te}| \times n}$ between cinemas in S_{te} and n movies based on R_{tr}, X_{tr} and X_{te}.

3.2   Basic Framework

Matrix factorization is a typical technique for recommendation. Its basic idea is to leverage correlations between users and items with a k-dimension latent space. The interaction matrix $R \in \mathbb{R}^{m \times n}$ between m users and n items is factorized into two low-rank matrices as $U \in \mathbb{R}^{k \times m}$ and $V \in \mathbb{R}^{k \times n}$, which are the latent representations of users and items respectively. The prediction of user-item pairs can be calculated by the inner dot of $U \in \mathbb{R}^{k \times m}$ and $V \in \mathbb{R}^{k \times n}$. Since learning latent representations rely on history interaction data, cold-start problem occurs, which is pervasive in real-world recommendation applications.

Our key point to solve cinema cold-start problem is to learn the cinema latent representations from side information of cinemas. Suppose that there is a function $f(\cdot)$ which can transform the side information of cinemas into their latent representations U_{tr}, which indicates $U_{tr} \approx f(X_{tr})$, then we can replace cinema latent representations U_{tr} by $f(X_{tr})$ in matrix factorization. Since there is side information X_{te} of cold-start cinemas U_{te}, latent representations of cold-start cinemas can be obtained directly with side information matrix X_{te} and transformation function $f(X_{te})$. Further, interaction matrix of cold-start cinemas can be predicted to solve the cold-start problem.

In order to recommending movies to cold-start cinemas, we construct the loss function as following:

$$L = C \odot (R_{tr} - \sigma(f(X_{tr})^T V))^2 + \lambda_f \|\Theta_f\|_F^2 + \lambda_v \|V\|_F^2 \tag{1}$$

Here $\odot$ denotes element-wise matrix multiplication, Θ_f is the parameters of function $f(\cdot)$. λ_f and λ_v are regularization coefficients, σ is sigmoid function, which transforms the prediction values into $(0, 1)$. In Eq. (1), $C \in \mathbb{R}^{m \times n}$ is the confidence coefficient matrix, where larger c_{ij} indicates higher confidence. In on-demand cinema cold-start problem, interaction frequencies of each cinema-movie pair differ a lot from each other. Thus, c_{ij} is set by $c_{ij} = \log(freq_{ij} + 2)$ to reflect how popular movie j is for cinema i, where $freq_{ij}$ is the frequency that movie j is played at cinema i.

As for warm-start cinemas, we assume that their latent representations are close to $f(X_{tr})$ but could diverge from it if they have to, which can be learned from history data. Therefore, we add an offset $\epsilon \sim N(0, \lambda_\epsilon^{-1} I_k)$ on $f(X_{tr})$ as latent representations. That is to say, for a cinema i with side information vector X_i, its latent vector can be calculated as $U_i = f(X_i) + \epsilon_i$, for which the loss function turns into Eq. (2),

$$L = C \odot (R_{tr} - \sigma(U_{tr}^T V))^2 + \lambda_\epsilon \|U_{tr} - f(X_{tr})\|^2 + \lambda_v \|V\|_F^2 + \lambda_f \|\Theta_f\|^2 \tag{2}$$

where λ_ϵ is the hyperparameter for the distribution of the offset.

The optimization objective of the problem is to minimize the loss value in Eq. (2). After solving the objective function, we can obtain the parameters of transforming function $f(\cdot)$, and latent representations of movies V. Furthermore, as for cold-start cinemas, the offsets can be set as the expectation i.e., 0.

Thus, we have $U_{te} = f(X_{te})$. Finally, we use Eq. (3) to predict the interaction matrix, in which the larger value in $\hat{R}_{te}$ is, the higher the watching probability is.

$$\hat{R}_{te} = \sigma(f(X_{te})^T V) \tag{3}$$

During solving the objective function, latent representations of warm-start cinemas and latent representations of movies are learned, which can be used to predict the future interaction matrix of warm-start cinemas by $\hat{R}_{tr} = \sigma(U_{tr}^T V)$.

The above is our basic framework to solve cold-start cinema problem with side information. Its main idea is to learn cinema latent representations from their side information, thereby solving the cold-start problem. Meanwhile, the basic framework can recommend movies to warm-start cinemas, too. In particular, $f(X)$ is a mapping function to transform cinema side information into the latent space, which can be constructed according to actual conditions. The simplest way to construct $f(X)$ is to directly apply linear transformation on the side information matrix.

3.3   Location Categories of Cinemas

In on-demand cinema scenarios, the main audiences of a cinema come from the people who live or work around the cinema, for which the surrounding environment of the cinema and its location category is closely related to the profile of the potential audiences. POI type information around a cinema reflects its location category, so it can be taken as side information of cinemas. Further, we learn a probability distribution vector of cinema location category by LDA algorithm and transform it into the latent space with linear transformation.

Specifically, first, we count the POI types around cinemas. Given a cinema i and its latitude and longitude pair (lat_i, lng_i), we crawl POI information within 1 km of the cinema from the Amap, group it by POI types and count the quantity of each type. Then we get the vector $X_i^{\mathrm{raw}} \in \mathbb{R}^{m \times d}$, where d is the number of different POI types. After processing all cinemas in the same way, we obtain a POI type matrix $X^{\mathrm{raw}} \in \mathbb{R}^{m \times d}$ in which x_{ij}^{raw} is the number of POIs around cinema i belonging to type j. We find that different types of POIs have orders of magnitude differences in quantity. Therefore, we smooth the POI type matrix with logarithmic function and obtain $X^{\mathrm{log}} \in \mathbb{R}^{m \times d}$, where $x_{ij}^{\mathrm{log}} = log_2 x_{ij}^{\mathrm{raw}}$.

As an analogy, we regard a POI type as a word j, POIs around cinema i as a sentence and x_{ij}^{log} in matrix $X^{\mathrm{log}} \in \mathbb{R}^{m \times d}$ as the frequency of occurrence of word j in sentence i. Then, we learn location category distribution of cinemas reflected by POI type vectors via the LDA. We assume the following generative process:

For each cinema $i \in \{1, 2, \ldots, m\}$:

1. Draw the distribution of location category of cinema i, $\theta_i \sim Dirichlet(\alpha)$.
2. Draw the POI type distribution of the location category k, $\phi_k \sim Dirichlet(\beta)$.
3. For each POI around cinema i,i.e., w_{ij}:
    (a) Draw location category $z_{ij} \sim Mult(\theta_i)$.
    (b) Draw POI type $w_{ij} \sim Mult(\phi_{z_{ij}})$.

Based on the above generative process, we obtain the location category probability distribution of cinemas $X^{\text{lda}} \in \mathbb{R}^{m \times l}$, where m is the number of cinemas and l is the number of location category, which is a hyperparameter. The distribution matrix of training cinemas is denoted as X_{tr}^{lda} and the distribution matrix of cold-start cinemas is denoted as X_{te}^{lda}. We transform X_{tr}^{lda} into the cinema latent space with linear function $f(\cdot)$, where f is defined as Eq. (4),

$$f(X) = \Theta_f^T X_{tr}^{\text{lda}} \tag{4}$$

In Eq. (4), $\Theta_f \in \mathbb{R}^{l \times k}$, in which Θ_f is the parameters to learn, k is the dimension of the latent space.

3.4 Co-popular Relationship Between Movies

In matrix factorization based recommendation methods, regularizing with the SPPMI matrix when learning item embeddings can improve performance of the model [10,16]. Inspired by this, we exploit co-popular patterns between two movies and form the corresponding SPPMI matrix. Then we use the SPPMI matrix to learn movie embeddings together with the interaction matrix to improve quality of movie embeddings. After adding SPPMI matrix to the basic framework, the optimization objective is as Eq. (5).

$$\min_{\Theta_f, U_{tr}, V, Y} C \odot \left\| \left\| R_{tr} - \sigma \left(U_{tr}^T V \right) \right\|^2 + \left\| U_{tr} - f \left(X_{tr}^{\text{lda}} \right) \right\|^2 \right.$$
$$+ \alpha \left\| M^{\text{SPPMI}} - V^T Y \right\|^2 + \Omega \left(V, Y, \Theta_f \right) \tag{5}$$

where Y is the context embedding matrix of movies, in which ith column vector denotes the context embedding of movie i. Besides, $\Omega(V, Y, \Theta_f) = \lambda_v \|V\|^2 + \lambda_y \|Y\|^2 + \lambda_f \|\Theta_f\|^2$.

Specifically, during generating the SPPMI matrix, how to define two movies as the context of each other is a key point. We mine the co-popular relationship between two movies from history on-demand data and construct co-popular context among movies.

In detail, the co-popular relationship between movies is mainly considered from two aspects. On the one hand, we observe that the popularity of a movie has time effect. That is to say, audiences may have similar watching behaviors in a certain period, which may be caused by recent hotspot of the society. For example, if a popular cinema movie is released recently, audiences of on-demand cinemas will get more interested in the old movies related to the popular one, such as movies with the same director, in the same series or of the same type, etc. Therefore, related movies are more likely watched in the same period. On the other hand, in a certain period, the closer the frequencies of two movies are watched, the closer the popularities of the two movies are. For example, two movies watched with a similar frequency in the same period may be both hotpot movies in that period. Taking the above two factors into consideration, if two movies A and B are watched with close frequency in the same time window, A and B have co-popular relationship. If movie A and movie B have co-popular relationship and movie A is watched by audiences of a cinema, then we can infer that audiences of the cinema may also like movie B.

In order to get co-popular context of movies and form SPPMI matrix, we sort the different movies that are watched in the same time period in decreasing order according to watching times. In the sorted sequence, the similarly ranked movie pairs form co-popular contexts, from which we build the SPPMI matrix that reflects the movie co-popular relationship. Consider that the movie watched frequency shows a strong periodicity in weeks, we use a week as a time window to generate the frequency sorted sequence. The construction steps of co-popular context is as following, which is also presented in Fig. 1.

1. Split the training data by weeks. Then, count the total watched frequency of each movie in each week and form $Q \in \mathbb{R}^{p \times n}$, where p is the number of weeks of training data, n is the number of movies, q_{ij} is the total watched frequency of movie j in $i - $th week.
2. Sort movies by the total watched frequency in decreasing order and record the corresponding movie number. That is to sort each row in Q decreasingly and form $G \in \mathbb{R}^{p \times n}$, where g_{ij} indicates that movie g_{ij} ranks at jth position in week i, e.g. g_{i1} denotes that movie g_{i1} is watched with most frequency in week i.
3. If we consider the movie as a word, the sorted movie list in week i can be considered as a sentence. The length of the sentence is the number of distinct movies watched in week i, denoted by $a_i = \Sigma_{j=1}^{n} I(q_{ij})$, where if $q_{ij} > 0$ then $I(q_{ij}) = 1$, otherwise $I(q_{ij}) = 0$. After processing data of p weeks in the same way, we form a vector indicating the number of movies watched in each week $a = (a_1, a_2, \ldots, a_p)$.
4. Set the context window size to $2t + 1$, where t is a hyperparameter. As for movie g_{ij} which ranks j in week i, movies ranking within its context window are its co-popular context, which are movies in $(g_{i(j-t)}, \ldots, g_{i(j-1)}, g_{i(j+1)}, \ldots, g_{i(j+t)})$. It is obvious that movies ranking in the first t and last t have less than $2t$ context movies.

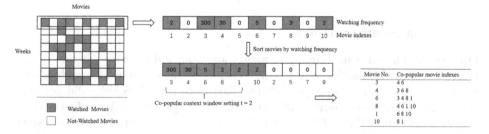

Fig. 1. Illustration of the co-popular relationship among movies, where we assume $t = 2$ and the fixed context window size is $2t + 1 = 5$.

According to the above steps to construct the co-popular context, we can calculate the PMI value between two movies, which is the logarithm of the ratio between their joint probability (the frequency they are co-popular contexts) and their marginal probabilities (the frequency they are watched independently). Then we can form PMI matrix M^{PMI}, where $m_{ij}^{PMI} = \log \frac{\#(i,j)D}{\#(i)\#(j)}$, $\#(i,j)$ is the frequency in which they are co-popular, $\#(i) = \Sigma_j \#(i,j)$ and $\#(j) = \Sigma_i \#(i,j)$, D is the amount of co-popular movie pairs. With PMI, we can obtain SPPMI with Eq. (6).

$$M^{SPPMI}(i,j) = \max\left(M^{PMI}(i,j) - \log(h), 0\right) \tag{6}$$

In Eq. (6), h is is a hyperparameter. The larger h is, the sparser SPPMI matrix is.

Finally, we add the SPPMI matrix obtained into Eq. (5). Then we optimize the objective function with Adam algorithm and finally learn the parameters.

4   Experiments

In this section, we conduct extensive experiments on real-world on-demand data to answer the following five research questions:

RQ1: How does our approach perform compared with other state-of-art cold-start recommenders?

RQ2: Does the SPPMI matrix enhance the perfomance when handling cold-start problem?

RQ3. Do location category distribution vectors learned by LDA outperform log-smoothed POI type vectors?

RQ4. We use frequency-based weights in our loss function. Does it affect the performance?

RQ5. Our approach is also suitable for warm-start applications. So, how does it perform on warm-start applications?

Among the above questions, RQ1 focuses on performance of our model for cold-start problem. RQ2–RQ4 evaluate the contributions of several key components in our model. RQ5 explores performance of our approach for warm-start problem.

4.1   Experimental Settings

Datasets. The data used in experiments are from iQIYI, which is one of the largest online video platforms in China. We collect real-world on-demand records between July 1, 2016 and Sept 1, 2018. There are total 798,886 valid records, covering 6,160 different movies, 207 cinemas and 29 provinces. We split the data by weeks, group the data of 24 weeks to be a dataset and construct three datasets with different periods as shown in Table 1.

For each dataset, data in the first 22 weeks are used to construct training sets while data of the last 2 weeks are used to construct testing sets. The following is the strategy to construct cold-start datasets. Taking the balance of cinema geographical distribution into consideration, we select cold-start cinemas randomly

Table 1. Timespans of datasets

Number	Start time	End time
Dataset 1	4/3/2017	9/17/2017
Dataset 2	9/25/2017	3/18/2018
Dataset 3	3/19/2018	9/2/2018

at each province, where the proportion of cold-start cinemas in each province is not less than 10%. Then we eliminate the on-demand records for these chosen cinemas, thus construct cold-start datasets. For each dataset, we split cinemas into three folds randomly and obtain 9 cold-start training sets and 9 testing sets, respectively. Finally, we collect POI information of cinemas within 1 km.

Experiments for cold-start recommendation are designed to predict the interaction matrix of testing cinemas in the future 2 weeks based on the first 22 weeks of warm-start cinemas and the side information of all cinemas.

To gain insights into the watching records, we perform some statistical analysis. We plot the number of movies with respect to the movie watched frequency in Fig. 2, from which we observe that the movie frequency distribution show a long tail distribution. Further, we find that interactions related to the 20% most popular movies occupy 86.9% of total interactions. This is consistent with most recommendation benchmarks, such as Nexflix [6] and Yelp [5] datasets, which highlights the sparsity challenge faced by recommendation systems. Besides, the watched frequency of a movie reflects its popularity among audiences. Huge differences in the watched frequencies indicate that different movies have huge difference of popularity for the same cinema.

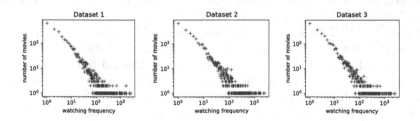

Fig. 2. Long tail distribution of movie watched frequency in each dataset

Metrics. In this paper, we select three common ranking metrics to evaluate our approach. They are precision@k, recall@k and NDCG@k (Normalized Discounted Cumulative Gain), in which k ranges in $[1, 5, 10, 20, 50]$.

Hyperparameter Settings. Default hyperparameter settings are listed influence Table 2.

Table 2. Hyperparameter settings

Hyperparameters	Settings
Initial Learning Rate	0.05
Dimension of Latent Space	50
α	0.5
$\lambda_v, \lambda_y, \lambda_f$	0.0001
h	1

4.2   Performance Evaluation for Cold-Start Recommendation

In this section, to justify the effectiveness of our proposed approach, we compare with the following state-of-art algorithms:

1. Most popular: This is a non-personalized recommendation approach, which selects the top-N movies with the highest watched frequency in the past t timeslots as the recommendation in the next timeslot. This approach generates the same recommendation for all cinemas.
2. Cos-Cos [15]: This is a similarity based method. It obtains K-nearest neighbor cinemas of cold-start cinemas according to the cosine similarity of cinema side information and generates the recommendation with the history data of neighbor cinemas.
3. CMF [14]: This is a matrix factorization based method. It collectively factorizes interaction matrix and the side information matrix by sharing user latent representations. Then the latent representations of cold-start users can be obtained with their side information. In this paper, we improve the original CMF model with frequency-based weights.
4. MetricRec [11]: This is a similarity based method based on Mahalanobis distance. It constructs the parameterized Mahalanobis distance with the cinema side information, whose parameters can be learned from training data. As for cold-start cinemas, we get K-nearest-neighbor users based on learned Mahalanobis distances and generate the recommendation.
5. LOCO [12]: This is a low-rank linear regression method. It regards the interaction matrix as a linear regression of cinema side information, in which the linear transformation matrix is low-rank. Similar to CMF, we improve the originsl LOCO model with frequency-based weights.

Side information inputted into competitors is a log-smoothed POI type matrix $X^{\log}$. Comparison results of precision, recall and NDCG are listed in Table 3. We observe: (1) Our approach significantly outperforms other competitors in all metrics with different hyperparameter k. (2) Although, our approach and CMF are both matrix factorization based model, our approach significantly outperforms CMF. There are mainly two reasons. On the one hand, we jointly factorized the interaction matrix and the co-popular SPPMI matrix by sharing item embeddings, which enhances item embeddings by exploiting co-popular patterns among movies. On the other hand, location category vectors learned by LDA are used to learn user latent representations in our approach, while log-smoothed POI type vectors are used in CMF. The latter is weaker to reflect cinema location categories. (3) As an unexpected finding, Most Popular approach is a very competitive approach in different metrics. It mainly results from the long tail distribution of movie watched frequency, which means only a small number of popular movies meet needs of most audiences. (4) Metric-Rec and Cos-Cos are all similarity based cold-start models. However Metric-Rec learns similarity parameters from training data while Cos-Cos adopts cosine similarity directly, which may be the main reason why Cos-Cos performs worse. This section answers RQ1.

Table 3. Performance comparison for cold-start recommendation

	Most Popular			Cos-Cos			CMF		
	Precision	Recall	NDCG	Precision	Recall	NDCG	Precision	Recall	NDCG
@1	0.401	0.004	0.401	0.123	0.001	0.172	0.492	0.005	0.492
@5	0.518	0.024	0.531	0.288	0.014	0.269	0.472	0.023	0.480
@10	0.541	0.050	0.529	0.267	0.024	0.275	0.443	0.043	0.457
@20	0.523	0.096	0.515	0.239	0.044	0.239	0.403	0.077	0.423
@50	0.449	0.206	0.440	0.254	0.119	0.249	0.342	0.161	0.369
Avg	0.486	0.076	0.483	0.234	0.040	0.241	0.430	0.062	0.444
	MetricRec			LOCO			Ours		
	Precision	Recall	NDCG	Precision	Recall	NDCG	Precision	Recall	NDCG
@1	0.456	0.004	0.456	0.682	0.007	0.682	**0.806**	**0.008**	**0.806**
@5	0.491	0.023	0.487	0.651	0.032	0.656	**0.765**	**0.038**	**0.777**
@10	0.497	0.046	0.492	0.610	0.059	0.624	**0.755**	**0.075**	**0.766**
@20	0.464	0.087	0.47	0.575	0.110	0.594	**0.693**	**0.134**	**0.719**
@50	0.406	0.189	0.425	0.479	0.222	0.514	**0.548**	**0.260**	**0.600**
Avg	0.463	0.070	0.466	0.560	0.086	0.614	**0.713**	**0.103**	**0.734**

4.3   Rationality Evaluation

In this section, we conduct an ablation study to illustrate the design rationalization of our approach, in which we verify contributions to performance of several main components of our approach, including the SPPMI matrix reflecting co-popular patterns among movies, location category probability distribution vectors learned by LDA and the frequency-based weights. This section answers RQ2–RQ4.

Effect of the SPPMI Matrix. We collectively factorize SPPMI matrix formed by co-popular relationship among movies and the interaction matrix to enhance item embeddings. In order to evaluate the effect of SPPMI matrix, we remove

SPPMI matrix but keep other settings the same. The results are shown in Table 4. We observe that the recommendation performance improves a lot with SPPMI matrix, especially in recall, in which recall@10 improves by 31.58%, recall@20 improves by 24.07%. This section answers RQ2.

Table 4. Effect of the SPPMI matrix

	Without SPPMI matrix			With SPPMI matrix			Improvement		
	Precision	Recall	NDCG	Precision	Recall	NDCG	Precision	Recall	NDCG
@1	0.741	0.007	0.741	0.806	0.008	0.806	8.77%	14.29%	8.77%
@5	0.666	0.032	0.680	0.765	0.038	0.777	14.86%	18.75%	14.26%
@10	0.607	0.057	0.633	0.755	0.075	0.766	24.38%	31.58%	21.01%
@20	0.576	0.108	0.602	0.693	0.134	0.719	20.31%	24.07%	19.44%
@50	0.472	0.218	0.513	0.548	0.260	0.600	16.10%	19.27%	16.96%
Avg	0.612	0.084	0.634	0.713	0.103	0.734	16.89%	21.59%	16.09%

Effect of the LDA-Based Location Category Vectors. In our approach, location category probability distribution vectors are learned by LDA. In order to evaluate the contribution of this module, we conduct a control experiment by directly replacing the X^{lda} with X^{log}, where we keep other settings the same. Performance comparison results are listed in Table 5. We observed that X^{lda} performs better than X^{log} in all metrics, which answers RQ3.

Table 5. Effect of the LDA-based location category vectors

	Log-smoothed vectors			LDA-based vectors			Improvement		
	Precision	Recall	NDCG	Precision	Recall	NDCG	Precision	Recall	NDCG
@1	0.680	0.007	0.680	0.806	0.008	0.806	18.53%	14.29%	18.53%
@5	0.679	0.033	0.680	0.765	0.038	0.777	12.67%	15.15%	14.26%
@10	0.673	0.066	0.676	0.755	0.075	0.766	12.18%	13.64%	13.31%
@20	0.616	0.120	0.635	0.693	0.134	0.719	12.50%	11.67%	13.23%
@50	0.498	0.236	0.539	0.548	0.260	0.600	10.04%	10.17%	11.32%
Avg	0.629	0.092	0.642	0.713	0.103	0.734	13.18%	12.98%	14.13%

Effect of the Frequency-Based Weights. In order to evaluate the effect of frequency-based weights, we conduct a control experiment by replacing the frequency-based weights with traditional fixed weights, in which we set $w_2 = 1$ for all movie-cinema pairs with $r_{ij} = 1$ and $w_2 = 0.5$ for all movie-cinema pairs with $r_{ij} = 0$. The hyperparameters are selected via the cross validation to achieve the best performance. Besides, other settings are kept the same with our approach. The comparison results are listed in Table 6. We observe that our performance has improved a lot, in which NDCG and precision are improved by 23.43% on average and recall has improved by 15.33% on average. This section answers RQ4.

Table 6. Effect of the frequency-based weights

	Fixed weight			Frequency weight			Improvement		
	Precision	Recall	NDCG	Precision	Recall	NDCG	Precision	Recall	NDCG
@1	0.617	0.007	0.617	0.806	0.008	0.806	30.63%	14.29%	30.63%
@5	0.649	0.034	0.643	0.765	0.038	0.777	17.87%	11.76%	20.84%
@10	0.628	0.065	0.632	0.755	0.075	0.766	20.22%	15.38%	21.20%
@20	0.567	0.114	0.588	0.693	0.134	0.719	22.22%	17.54%	22.28%
@50	0.448	0.221	0.491	0.548	0.260	0.600	22.32%	17.65%	22.20%
Avg	0.582	0.088	0.594	0.713	0.103	0.734	22.75%	15.33%	23.43%

4.4   Performance Evaluation for Warm-Start Recommendation

Though our approach solves the cinema cold-start problem, it is suitable for warm-start recommendation as well. In order to evaluate the performance for warm-start application, we compare our approach with WMF (Weighted Matrix Factorization) [7], which is a typical approach for warm-start recommendation.

To construct warm-start datasets, we use data of the first 22 weeks from each dataset and side information of corresponding cinemas as the warm-start training sets and form the interaction matrix R. At the same time, we obtain weight matrix W based on movie-cinema interaction frequency. Then, we predict the interaction matrix in the future two-weeks $\hat{R}$ with cinema latent representations U and movie latent representations I learned from training sets and select the top N movies as recommendation. We adopt frequency-based weights for WMF. Average results of three datasets are shown in Table 7.

Table 7. Performance comparison with WMF for warm-start recommendation

	WMF			Our approach			Improvement		
	Precision	Recall	NDCG	Precision	Recall	NDCG	Precision	Recall	NDCG
@1	0.608	0.007	0.608	0.806	0.008	0.806	32.57%	14.29%	32.57%
@5	0.624	0.035	0.628	0.765	0.038	0.777	22.60%	8.57%	23.73%
@10	0.559	0.061	0.581	0.755	0.075	0.766	35.06%	22.95%	31.84%
@20	0.519	0.113	0.546	0.693	0.134	0.719	33.53%	18.58%	31.68%
@50	0.423	0.228	0.467	0.548	0.260	0.600	29.55%	14.04%	28.48%
Avg	0.547	0.089	0.566	0.713	0.103	0.734	30.66%	15.69%	29.66%

We observe that our approach outperforms WMF in all metrics. The results can be explained from two aspects. On the one hand, we model the cinema location category, which reflects the preference of the potential audiences. On the other hand, the SPPMI matrix models co-popular relationship among movies, which enhances movie embeddings and improves the recommendation performance.

5   Conclusion

In order to solve the on-demand cinema cold-start problem, we propose a matrix factorization based approach which fuses location categories of cinemas and co-popular relationship among movies. We collect POI type information within 1 km of the cinema as the cinema side information. Then we learn the location category probability distribution vector by LDA, which is used to approximate cinema latent representations. Besides, we construct the co-popular context of movies and form the SPPMI matrix, which is factorized collectively with the interaction matrix by sharing the same item latent representations. We conduct extensive experiments on real on-demand records. Firstly, we compare with other state-of-art cold-start approaches, which prove our approach has a significant improvement of performance. Secondly, we conduct the ablation study to verify the contributions to performance of several major components. Thirdly, we find that our approach outperforms weighted matrix factorization for warm-start recommendation.

References

1. Blei, D.M., Ng, A.Y., Jordan, M.I.: Latent dirichlet allocation. J. Mach. Learn. Res. **3**, 993–1022 (2003)
2. Cao, D., Nie, L., He, X., Wei, X., Zhu, S., Chua, T.S.: Embedding factorization models for jointly recommending items and user generated lists. In: Proceedings of the 40th International ACM SIGIR Conference on Research and Development in Information Retrieval, pp. 585–594. ACM (2017)
3. Gantner, Z., Drumond, L., Freudenthaler, C., Rendle, S., Schmidt-Thieme, L.: Learning attribute-to-feature mappings for cold-start recommendations. In: 2010 IEEE International Conference on Data Mining, pp. 176–185 (2010)
4. Grbovic, M., et al.: E-commerce in your inbox: product recommendations at scale. In: Proceedings of the 21th ACM SIGKDD International Conference on Knowledge Discovery and Data Mining, pp. 1809–1818. ACM (2015)
5. He, X., Zhang, H., Kan, M.Y., Chua, T.S.: Fast matrix factorization for online recommendation with implicit feedback. In: Proceedings of the 39th International ACM SIGIR conference on Research and Development in Information Retrieval, pp. 549–558. ACM (2016)
6. Koren, Y.: Factorization meets the neighborhood: a multifaceted collaborative filtering model. In: Proceedings of the 14th ACM SIGKDD International Conference on Knowledge Discovery and Data Mining, pp. 426–434. ACM (2008)
7. Koren, Y., Bell, R.M., Volinsky, C.: Matrix factorization techniques for recommender systems. IEEE Comput. **42**(8), 30–37 (2009)
8. Levy, O., Goldberg, Y.: Neural word embedding as implicit matrix factorization. Adv. Neural Inf. Process. Syst. **3**, 2177–2185 (2014)

9. Li, J., Lu, K., Huang, Z., Shen, H.T.: Two birds one stone: on both cold-start and long-tail recommendation. In: ACM on Multimedia Conference (2017)

10. Liang, D., Altosaar, J., Charlin, L., Blei, D.M.: Factorization meets the item embedding: regularizing matrix factorization with item co-occurrence. In: Proceedings of the 10th ACM Conference on Recommender Systems, pp. 59–66. ACM (2016)

11. Peng, F., et al.: MetricRec: metric learning for cold-start recommendations. In: Li, J., Li, X., Wang, S., Li, J., Sheng, Q.Z. (eds.) ADMA 2016. LNCS (LNAI), vol. 10086, pp. 445–458. Springer, Cham (2016). https://doi.org/10.1007/978-3-319-49586-6_30

12. Sedhain, S., Menon, A.K., Sanner, S., Xie, L., Braziunas, D.: Low-rank linear coldstart recommendation from social data. In: AAAI, pp. 1502–1508 (2017)

13. Shi, L., Zhao, W.X., Shen, Y.: Local representative-based matrix factorization for cold-start recommendation. ACM Trans. Inf. Syst. **36**(2), 22 (2017)

14. Singh, A.P., Gordon, G.J.: Relational learning via collective matrix factorization. In: Proceedings of the 14th ACM SIGKDD International Conference on Knowledge Discovery and Data Mining, pp. 650–658 (2008)

15. Suvash, S., Scott, S., Darius, B., Lexing, X., Jordan, C.: Social collaborative filtering for cold-start recommendations. In: Proceedings of the ACM Conference on Recommender Systems, vol. 14, RecSys (2014)

16. Tran, T., Lee, K., Liao, Y., Lee, D.: Regularizing matrix factorization with user and item embeddings for recommendation. In: Proceedings of the 27th ACM International Conference on Information and Knowledge Management, pp. 687–696. ACM (2018)

17. Wang, C., Blei, D.M.: Collaborative topic modeling for recommending scientific articles. In: Proceedings of the 17th ACM SIGKDD International Conference on Knowledge Discovery and Data Mining, pp. 448–456. ACM (2011)

18. Xie, M., Yin, H., Wang, H., Xu, F., Chen, W., Wang, S.: Learning graph-based poi embedding for location-based recommendation. In: Proceedings of the 25th ACM International on Conference on Information and Knowledge Management, pp. 15–24. ACM (2016)

19. Xue, T., Jin, B., Li, B., Liu, K., Zhang, Q., Tian, S.: Spatial-temporal recommendation for on-demand cinemas. In: Li, G., Yang, J., Gama, J., Natwichai, J., Tong, Y. (eds.) DASFAA 2019. LNCS, vol. 11448, pp. 373–377. Springer, Cham (2019). https://doi.org/10.1007/978-3-030-18590-9_48

20. Yu, J., Gao, M., Li, J., Yin, H., Liu, H.: Adaptive implicit friends identification over heterogeneous network for social recommendation. In: Proceedings of the 27th ACM International Conference on Information and Knowledge Management, pp. 357–366. ACM (2018)

Shallow Self-learning for Reject Inference in Credit Scoring

Nikita Kozodoi[1,2(✉)], Panagiotis Katsas[2], Stefan Lessmann[1],
Luis Moreira-Matias[2], and Konstantinos Papakonstantinou[2]

[1] Humboldt University of Berlin, Berlin, Germany
[2] Monedo, Hamburg, Germany
nikita.kozodoi@hu-berlin.de

Abstract. Credit scoring models support loan approval decisions in the financial services industry. Lenders train these models on data from previously granted credit applications, where the borrowers' repayment behavior has been observed. This approach creates sample bias. The scoring model is trained on accepted cases only. Applying the model to screen applications from the population of all borrowers degrades its performance. Reject inference comprises techniques to overcome sampling bias through assigning labels to rejected cases. This paper makes two contributions. First, we propose a self-learning framework for reject inference. The framework is geared toward real-world credit scoring requirements through considering distinct training regimes for labeling and model training. Second, we introduce a new measure to assess the effectiveness of reject inference strategies. Our measure leverages domain knowledge to avoid artificial labeling of rejected cases during evaluation. We demonstrate this approach to offer a robust and operational assessment of reject inference. Experiments on a real-world credit scoring data set confirm the superiority of the suggested self-learning framework over previous reject inference strategies. We also find strong evidence in favor of the proposed evaluation measure assessing reject inference strategies more reliably, raising the performance of the eventual scoring model.

Keywords: Credit scoring · Reject inference · Self-learning · Evaluation

1 Introduction

Financial institutions use supervised learning to guide lending decisions. The resulting credit scoring models, also called scorecards, predict the probability of default (PD) – an applicant's willingness and ability to repay debt [31]. Loan approval decisions are made based on whether the scorecard predicts an applicant to be a repaying borrower (*good* risks) or a likely defaulter (*bad* risks).

Scoring models are trained on data of accepted applicants. Their repayment behavior has been observed, which provides the labels for supervised learning.

© Springer Nature Switzerland AG 2020
U. Brefeld et al. (Eds.): ECML PKDD 2019, LNAI 11908, pp. 516–532, 2020.
https://doi.org/10.1007/978-3-030-46133-1_31

Inevitably, the sample of accepted clients (accepts) differs from the overall population of credit applicants. Accepts have passed the screening of the lender's scorecard, whereas the population also includes clients who have been denied credit by that scorecard (rejects) as well as customers who have not applied for credit. As a result, scoring models suffer from sample bias. Training a classifier only on data from accepts deteriorates the accuracy of PD predictions when the scorecard is out into production for screening incoming credit applications [28].

Reject inference refers to techniques that remedy sampling bias through inferring labels for rejects. Previous research has suggested several approaches including naive strategies (e.g., label all rejects as *bad*) and model-based techniques [28]. However, empirical evidence concerning the value of reject inference and the efficacy of labeling strategies is scarce. Several studies use incomplete data, which only contain accepted cases (e.g. [5,11]), do not have a labeled unbiased sample with both accepts and rejects (e.g., [7]) or use synthetic data (e.g., [16]). In addition, the data sets employed in prior studies are usually low-dimensional (e.g., [21]), which is not representative of the real-world credit scoring data used today [33]. Previous work is also geared toward linear models and support vector machines (SVM) [1,19,21]. Yet, there is much evidence that other algorithms (e.g., tree-based ensembles) outperform these methods in credit scoring [18,34].

The contribution of this paper is two-fold. First, we introduce a novel self-learning framework for reject inference in credit scoring. Our framework includes two different probabilistic classifiers for the training and labeling stages. The training stage benefits from using a strong learner such as gradient boosting. However, we suggest using a shallow (i.e. weaker) learner for the labeling stage and show that it achieves higher calibration with respect to the true PD [23]. As a result, we maximize the precision of our model on the extreme quantiles of its output and minimize the noise introduced on newly labeled rejects.

Second, we introduce a novel measure (denoted as *kickout*) to assess reject inference methods in a reliable and operational manner. Aiming at labeling rejects to raise the scorecard performance, the acid test of a reject inference strategy involves comparing a scorecard without correction for sample bias to a model that has undergone reject-inference based correction on data from an unbiased sample of clients including both accepts and rejects with actual labels for both groups of clients. Such a sample would represent the operating conditions of a scorecard and thus uncover the true merit of reject inference [11]. However, obtaining such a sample is very costly as it requires a financial institution to lend money to a random sample of applicants including high-risk cases that would normally be denied credit. Drawing on domain knowledge, the proposed *kickout* measure avoids dependence on the actual labels of rejects and, as we establish through empirical experimentation, assesses the merit of a reject inference method more accurately than previous evaluation approaches. The data set used in this paper includes an unbiased sample containing both accepts and rejects, giving us a unique opportunity to evaluate a scorecard in its operating conditions.

The paper is organized as follows. Section 2 reviews related literature on reject inference. Section 3 revisits the reject inference problem, presents our self-learning framework and introduces the kickout measure. Section 4 describes our experimental setup and reports empirical results. Section 5 concludes the paper.

2   Literature Review

The credit scoring literature has suggested different model-based and model-free approaches to infer labels of rejected cases. Some model-free techniques rely on external information such as expert knowledge to manually label rejects [22]. Another approach is to label all rejected cases as *bad* risks [28], assuming that the default ratio among the rejects is sufficiently high. One other strategy is to obtain labels by relying on external performance indicators such as credit bureau scores or an applicant's outcome on a previous loan [2,28].

Model-based reject inference techniques rely on a scoring model to infer labels for rejects. Table 1 depicts corresponding techniques, where we sketch the labeling strategy used in a study together with the base classifier that was used for scorecard development. Table 1 reveals that most reject inference techniques have been tested with linear models such as logistic and probit regression.

The literature distinguishes several approaches toward model-based reject inference such as augmentation, extrapolation, bivariate models and others [19]. Extrapolation refers to a set of techniques that use the initial scoring model trained on the accepts to label the rejected cases. For instance, hard cutoff augmentation labels rejects by comparing their model-estimated PDs to a pre-defined threshold [28]. Parceling introduces a random component, separating the rejected cases into segments based on the range (e.g., percentile) of PDs. Instead of assigning labels based on the individual scores of rejects, they are labeled randomly within the identified segments based on the expected default rate for each score range. A drawback of such techniques is their reliance on the performance of the initial scoring model when applied to rejects.

Augmentation (or re-weighting) is based on the fact that applicants with a certain distribution of features appear in the training data disproportionately due to a non-random sample selection [11]. Re-weighting refers to the techniques that train an additional model that separates accepts and rejects and predicts the probability of acceptance. These probabilities are then used to compute sampling weights for a scoring model.

Some scholars suggest using a two-stage bivariate probit model or two-stage logistic regression to perform reject inference [6]. A bivariate model incorporates the Heckman's correction to account for a sample bias within the model, estimating both acceptance and default probability. These models assume linear effects within the logistic or probit regression framework.

Empirical studies have shown little evidence that reject inference techniques described above improve scorecard's performance [3,9,11,32]. Recently suggested alternatives rely on semi-supervised learning. For example, Maldonado et al. have shown that self-learning with SVM outperforms well-known reject inference techniques such as ignoring rejects or labeling all rejects as *bad* risks [21]. Their

Table 1. Model-based reject inference methods

Reference	Inference technique	Base model
Reichert et al. [24]	LDA-based	LDA
Joanes [16]	Reclassification	LR
Hand et al. [15]	Ratio prediction	–
Hand et al. [15]	Rebalancing model	–
Feelders [12]	Mixture modeling	LR, QDA
Banasik et al. [6]	Augmentation	LR, Probit
Smith et al. [29]	Bayesian network	Bayesian
Crook et al. [11]	Reweigthing	LR
Verstraeten et al. [32]	Augmentation	LR
Banasik et al. [3]	Augmentation	LR
Fogarty [13]	Multiple imputation	LR
Montrichard [22]	Fuzzy augmentation	LR
Banasik et al. [4]	Augmentation	LR, Probit
Banasik et al. [4]	Bivariate probit	Probit
Kim et al. [17]	Bivariate probit	–
Banasik et al. [5]	Augmentation	Survival
Maldonado et al. [21]	Self-training	SVM
Maldonado et al. [21]	Co-training	SVM
Maldonado et al. [21]	Semi-supervised SVM	SVM
Chen et al. [10]	Bound and collapse	Bayesian
Bücker et al. [7]	Reweighting	LR
Siddiqi [28]	Define as bad	–
Siddiqi [28]	Soft cutoff augmentation	–
Siddiqi [28]	Hard cutoff augmentation	–
Siddiqi [28]	Parceling	–
Siddiqi [28]	Nearest neighbors	-
Anderson et al. [1]	Mixture modeling	LR
Li et al. [19]	Semi-supervised SVM	SVM

work is continued by [19], who propose a semi-supervised SVM that uses a non-linear kernel to train a scoring model.

We follow recent studies and cast the reject inference problem in a semi-supervised learning framework. Our approach to solve the problem is a variation of self-learning adapted to a credit scoring context by extending the work of [21].

3   Methodology

3.1   Self-learning for Reject Inference

In reject inference, we are given a set of n examples $x_1, ..., x_n \in \mathbb{R}^k$, where k is the number of features. Set X consists of l accepted clients $x_1^a, ..., x_l^a \in X^a$

with corresponding labels $y_1^a, ..., y_l^a \in \{good, bad\}$ and m rejected examples $x_1^r, ..., x_m^r \in X^r$, whose labels are unknown. To overcome sampling bias and eventually raise scorecard accuracy, reject inference aims at assigning labels $y_1^r, ..., y_m^r$ to the rejected examples, which allows using the combined data for training a scoring model.

Standard self-learning starts with training a classifier $f(x)$ on the labeled examples $x_1^a, ..., x_l^a$ and using it to predict the unlabeled examples $x_1^r, ..., x_m^r$. Next, the subset of unlabeled examples $X^* \subset X^r$ with the most confident predictions is selected such that $f(x_i^* \in X^*) > \alpha$ or $f(x_i^* \in X^*) < 1 - \alpha$, where α is a probability threshold corresponding to a specified percentile of $f(x_i^* \in X^r)$. The selected rejects are labeled in accordance with the classifier's predictions. Cases obtained within this process are removed from X^r and appended to X^a to form a new labeled sample X_1^a. Finally, the classifier is retrained on X_1^a and used to score the remaining cases in X^r. The procedure is repeated until all cases from X^r are assigned labels or until certain stopping criteria are fulfilled [25].

Self-learning assumes that labeled and unlabeled examples in X follow the same distribution [25]. In a credit scoring context, X^a and X^r come from two different distributions because the scoring model employed by the financial institution separates accepts and rejects based on their feature values. The difference in distributions has negative consequences for self-learning: since the initial model is trained on a sample that is not fully representative of the unlabeled data, predictions of this model for the rejects are less reliable. The error is propagated through the iterative self-learning framework, which deteriorates the performance of the final model due to the incorrectly assigned labels.

In this section, we describe a novel shallow self-training framework for reject inference that is geared toward reducing the negative effects of sample bias. The proposed framework consists of three stages: filtering, labeling and model training. We summarize the algorithm steps in Algorithm 2.

Within the proposed framework, we suggest to filter and drop some rejected cases before assigning them with labels. The goal of the filtering stage is two-fold. Firstly, we strive to remove rejected cases that come from the most different part of distribution compared to the accepts. Removing these cases would reduce the risk of error propagation, since predictions of the model trained on the accepts become less reliable as the distribution of cases to be predicted becomes more different from the one observed on the training data. Secondly, we remove rejects that are most similar to the accepted cases. Labeling such cases would potentially provide little new information for a scorecard and might even harm performance due to introducing noise. Therefore, the filtering stage is aimed at removing the cases that could have a negative impact of the scorecard performance.

The filtering is performed with isolation forest, which is a novelty detection method that estimates the normality of a specific observation by computing the number of splits required to isolate it from the rest of the data [20]. We train isolation forest on all accepts in X^a and use it to evaluate the similarity of the rejects in X^r. Next, we remove rejects that are found to be the most and least similar to the accepts by dropping cases within the top β_t and bottom β_b percentiles of the similarity scores. Algorithm 1 describes the filtering stage.

1 train isolation forest classifier $g(x)$ using all data in X^a;
2 use $g(x)$ to evaluate similarity scores of all unlabeled examples in X^r;
3 select a subset $X^* \subset X^r$ such that $g(x_i^* \in X^*) \in [\beta_b, \beta_t]$, where β_b and β_t are values of pre-defined percentiles of $g(x_j^r \in X^r)$, $j = 1, ..., m$.

Algorithm 1: Isolation Forest for Filtering Rejected Examples

After filtering, we use self-learning with distinct labeling and training regimes to perform reject inference. While the scoring model is based on a tree-based algorithm (gradient boosting), we propose using a weak learner for labeling rejects because of its ability to produce better-calibrated predictions [23]. In this paper, we rely on L1-regularized logistic regression (L1) to label rejects.

Logistic regression is a parametric learner which assumes a Gaussian distribution of the data. Because of this assumption, predicted probabilities can be output directly by the sigmoid function. In contrast, XG is a non-parametric learner which has more degrees of freedom and a higher potential for inductive bias reduction. Predicted scores produced by XG are not well calibrated [23]. Consider the example score distributions of L1 and extreme gradient boosting (XG) depicted in Fig. 1. Here, adding regularization to logistic regression is important as we are dealing with high-dimensional data with noisy features. Compared to L1, the range of the output probabilities of XG is wider.

Within the proposed framework, we require the labeling model to produce well-calibrated probabilities as we limit the number of selected rejects based on the predicted PD values. Furthermore, by using different base models for application scoring and reject inference, we strive to reduce bias and error propagation. Hence, using a weak learner for reject inference is more promising.

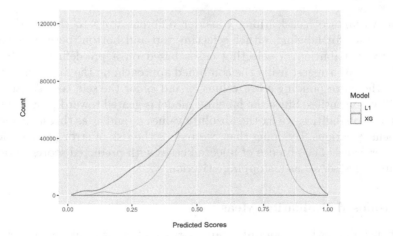

Fig. 1. *Score Densities.* The figure compares the distributions of the scores predicted by two scoring models: L1-regularized logistic regression (red) and extreme gradient boosting (blue). Both models use the same data. (Color figure online)

An important aspect of our framework is to account for a higher default rate among the rejects [21]. Recall that X is partitioned into accepts and rejects based on a scoring model that is currently employed by a financial institution. Assuming that the scoring model in place performs better than a random loan allocation, we expect that the default rate among rejects is higher than among accepts. To address that difference, we introduce the imbalance parameter θ into our self-learning framework. On each labeling iteration, we only select the top $\alpha\%$ of the *good* loans and top $\alpha\theta\%$ of the *bad* loans among rejects for labeling. Keeping only the top-ranked instances ensures that we append rejects with high confidence in the assigned labels, reducing the potential amount of noise. By setting $\theta > 1$ we append more *bad* cases to the training data, accounting for the imbalance. Parameter θ can be optimized at the parameter tuning stage.

1 filter rejected cases in X^r with isolation forest (see Algorithm 1);
2 set $X^* = X^r$;
3 **while** $X^* \neq \emptyset$ **do**
4 | train L1 classifier $f(x)$ with penalty parameter λ on all data in X^a;
5 | use $f(x)$ to predict PD for all unlabeled examples in X^*;
6 | **if** $c_b = \{\}$ *and* $c_g = \{\}$ **then**
7 | | derive c_g: $P(f(x_i^* \in X^*) < c_g) = \alpha$, α is a percentile threshold;
8 | | derive c_b: $P(f(x_i^* \in X^*) > c_b) = \alpha\theta$, θ is the imbalance parameter;
9 | **end**
10 | select $X^* \subset X^r$ such that $f(x_i^* \in X^*) < c_g$ or $f(x_i^* \in X^*) > c_b$;
11 | remove examples in X^* from X^r and append them to X^a;
12 **end**
13 train a scoring model $s(x)$ using XG classifier on all cases in X^a.

Algorithm 2: Shallow Self-Learning for Reject Inference

Different variants of self-learning consider different ways to choose the most confident cases for labeling: either selecting top and bottom percentiles of the probability distribution or selecting cases based on a pre-defined probability threshold [8]. We suggest using the combined approach: on the first iteration, we compute the corresponding score values c_g and c_b for the selected $\alpha\%$ and $\alpha\theta\%$ probability percentiles. Since the labeling model is geared toward providing well-calibrated probabilities, we fix the absolute values c_g and c_b as thresholds for the subsequent iterations. By doing that, we reduce the risk of error propagation on further iterations. The absence of rejected cases with predicted scores above the fixed thresholds serves as a stopping criterion.

3.2 Proposed Evaluation Measure

Performance evaluation is an important part of selecting a suitable reject inference technique. In practice, accurate evaluation of reject inference is challenging. The true labels of rejects are unknown, which prohibits estimating the accuracy directly. Therefore, prior research evaluates the performance of a given technique by comparing the performance of the scorecard before and after appending the labeled rejects to the training data [3,6,19]. The major downside of this approach is that the performance of a scorecard is not evaluated on a representative sample, which should include both accepts and rejects. Since labels of rejects are unknown, the literature suggests to evaluate models on a holdout sample drawn from the accepts which exhibits sample bias (e.g., [21]). Very few empirical studies have access to the data on both accepts and rejects for evaluation [11].

Model selection based on the performance on accepts might lead to selecting a sub-optimal model. Let us illustrate that by comparing the performance of different scoring models validated on the accepts (4-fold stratified cross-validation) and on the unbiased sample consisting of both accepts and rejects. We train a set of scoring models with different meta-parameter values and evaluate their performance in terms of the area under the receiver operating characteristic curve (AUC) [26]. Here, XG is used as a base classifier. Figure 2 depicts the results.

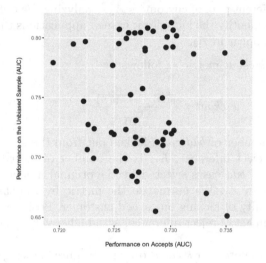

Fig. 2. Comparing AUC on the accepted cases (4-fold stratified cross-validation) and the unbiased sample. The dots indicate scoring models with different meta-parameters.

The rank correlation between AUC values is just 0.0132. Due to the distribution differences between the accepted and rejected cases, the model's performance on the accepted applicants becomes a poor criterion for model selection. This result suggests that there is a need to develop an alternative measure for comparing and evaluating the scoring models in the presence of sample bias.

Without access to an unbiased sample that contains data on a representative set of applicants, the literature suggests performing the evaluation by using synthetic data [16], emulating rejected cases by artificially moving the acceptance threshold [21] or using other criteria based on the applicants' feature values [9]. In this paper, we suggest using *kickout* – a novel evaluation measure based on the known data. We argue that developing such a measure is a valuable contribution since obtaining an unbiased data sample for performance evaluation is costly.

The key idea of *kickout* is to compare a set of applications accepted by a scoring model before and after reject inference. Recall that we have data on the previously accepted X^a and rejected applicants X^r. Here, we partition X^a into two subsets: X^a_{train} and $X^a_{holdout}$. Let $s_1(x)$ be a scoring model trained on X^a_{train}. We use $s_1(x)$ to score cases from $X^a_{holdout}$ and select a pool of customers $A_1 \subset X^a_{holdout}$ that would be accepted by the model using the acceptance rate μ. Thus, A_1 contains the (simulated) accepted applications before reject inference.

The rejected cases in X^r are also split into two subsets: X^r_{train} and $X^r_{holdout}$. The former is labeled with a reject inference technique and appended to the X^a_{train}. Rejected cases in $X^r_{holdout}$ are appended to $X^a_{holdout}$, which now contains labeled accepts and unlabeled rejects, simulating the production-stage environment. Next, we train a new scoring model $s_2(x)$ on the expanded training sample X^a_{train} and use it to score and select customers in $X^a_{holdout}$ using the same acceptance rate μ. Since both training and holdout samples have changed, model $s_2(x)$ would accept a different pool of customers A_2. Analyzing the differences between A_1 and A_2, we can identify the kicked-out cases – applications that were included in A_1 but do not appear in A_2.

We define the *kickout* metric as follows:

$$kickout = \frac{\frac{K_B}{p(B)} - \frac{K_G}{1-p(B)}}{\frac{S_B}{p(B)}} \tag{1}$$

where K_B is the number of *bad* cases kicked out from the set of accepted cases after performing reject inference, K_G is the number of kicked-out *good* cases, S_B is the number of *bad* cases selected by the original model, and $P(B)$ is the share of *bad* cases in A_1. We normalize the metric by the share of *bad* cases to reflect the difficulty of kicking out a *bad* customer. Positive values of *kickout* signal a positive impact of reject inference, with higher values indicating a better performance.

It is important to note that *kickout* does not require knowing the actual labels of the rejected cases that replace previously accepted cases. Instead, the metric focuses on the kicked-out applications. Replacing a *bad* loan with a rejected case may have two possible outcomes. If the newly selected rejected case is also *bad*, we are indifferent between the old and the new scoring model. If the rejected case is *good*, the scoring model improves. Therefore, kicking out a *bad* case has a positive expected value. In contrast, kicking out a *good* case has a negative expected value: we are indifferent between the old and the new scoring model if the new rejected case is *good*, whereas scorecard performance deteriorates if the rejected case is *bad*. Hence, a good reject inference technique should change a scorecard such that it starts to kick out more *bad* and less *good* customers.

The proposed measure relies on two assumptions. First, we assume that all *bad* loans and all *good* loans have the same expected value: that is, replacing one *bad* case with another *bad* case does not have any effect on the model's performance. Given the stable interest rates that determine the return on investment at fixed terms [31] and an uncertain relationship between a loan amount and its PD, we argue that this assumption is reasonable in a credit scoring context. Second, we assume that the *bad* ratio among rejected cases is higher compared to the accepted applications. As we detailed above, this assumption holds if the employed scoring model performs better than random.

4   Experimental Results

4.1   Data Description

The empirical experiments are based on a real-world credit scoring data set on consumer micro-loans provided by Monedo, a Germany-based financial institution. Although the data are not available publicly, it provides a unique opportunity to study reject inference on a high-dimensional data set which includes an unbiased sample with customers who have been granted a loan without scoring.

Table 2. Data summary

Characteristic	Accepts	Rejects	Unbiased
Number of cases	39,579	18,047	1,967
Number of features	2,410	2,410	2,410
Default rate	0.39	Unknown	0.66

The data set contains 2,410 features describing the applicants, their behavior and loan characteristics. The target variable is a binary indicator of whether the customer has repaid the loan. The data consist of 59,593 loan applications, out of which 39,579 were accepted and 18,047 were rejected. The target variable is only observed for the accepts, whereas the repayment status of rejects is unknown. Table 2 summarizes the main characteristics of the data set.

The unbiased sample contains 1,967 customers accepted without scoring. The sample, therefore, includes cases that would normally be rejected by a scorecard. This makes it representative of the through-the-door population of customers who apply for a loan. As noted in Table 2, the default rate in the unbiased sample is 1.7 times higher than on the accepted cases. The unbiased sample allows us to evaluate the performance gains from reject inference on the sample representative of the production environment.

4.2   Experimental Setup

To evaluate the effectiveness of our propositions, we perform two experiments. Experiment 1 benchmarks the proposed self-learning framework against conventional reject inference techniques and standard self-learning. In the second experiment, we illustrate the effectiveness of the new *kickout* measure for model selection. Below, we describe the modeling pipeline for these experiments.

We partition the data into three subsets: accepts, rejects and the unbiased holdout sample. Next, we use 4-fold stratified cross-validation on accepts to perform reject inference. On each iteration, the training folds are used to develop a reject inference technique that is used to infer labels of the rejects. Next, labeled rejects are appended to the training folds, providing a new sample to train a scoring model. Finally, a scoring model after reject inference is evaluated on the remaining fold and on the holdout sample. To ensure robustness, we evaluate performance on 50 bootstraped samples of the holdout set. Performance metrics of the reject inference techniques are then averaged over 4×50 obtained values.

We use XG classifier as a scoring model in both experiments. Meta-parameters of XG are tuned once on a small subset of training data using grid search. Within the experiments, we employ early stopping with 100 rounds while setting the maximum number of trees to 10,000 to fine-tune the model for each fold.

In Experiment I, we compare the suggested self-learning framework to the following benchmarks: ignore rejects, label all rejects as *bad* risks, hard cutoff augmentation, parceling, cross-validation-based voting and standard self-learning. Here, cross-validation-based voting is an adaption of a label noise correction method suggested by [30]. It refers to an extension of hard cutoff augmentation that employs a homogeneous ensemble of classifiers based on different training folds instead of a single scoring model to label the rejects. The labels are only assigned to the cases for which all individual models agree on the label.

We test multiple versions of each reject inference technique with different meta-parameter values using grid search. For shallow self-learning, penalty λ of the labeling model is tuned and optimized once on the first labeling iteration. Table 3 provides the candidate values of meta-parameters.

For performance evaluation, we use three metrics that capture different dimensions of the predictive performance: AUC, Brier Score (BS) and R-Precision (RP). We use AUC as a well-known indicator of the discriminating ability of a model. In contrast, BS measures the calibration of the predicted default probabilities. Last, we use RP as it better reflects the business context. The financial institution that provided data for this study decides on a loan allocation by approving a certain percentage of the least risky customers. RP measures performance only for cases which will indeed be accepted. In our experiments, we compute RP in the top 30% of the applications with the lowest predicted PDs.

In Experiment II, we compare different variants of self-learning using grid search within the cross-validation framework described above. Apart from the three selected performance measures, we also evaluate reject inference in terms of the proposed *kickout* measure. The goal of this experiment is to compare model rankings based on three evaluation strategies: performance on the accepts, performance on the unbiased sample and performance in terms of *kickout*.

4.3   Empirical Results

Experiment I: Assessing the Shallow Self-Learning

Table 4 summarizes the performance of the reject inference techniques on the accepted cases and on the unbiased sample. Recall that the latter serves as a proxy for the production-stage environment for a scoring model, whereas performance on accepts refers to a conventional approach toward evaluation in credit scoring. According to the results, not all methods improve on the benchmark of ignoring rejects: only three out of six techniques achieve higher AUC and lower BS on the unbiased sample, and only one has a higher RP.

Labeling rejects as *bad* performs better than disregarding reject inference on the accepts but does substantially worse on the unbiased sample. In contrast, parceling is outperformed by all other techniques on the accepts but has higher AUC on the unbiased sample. These results support the argument that performance on accepts might be a poor indicator of the production-stage performance.

Regular self-learning outperforms ignoring rejects in terms of AUC and BS but does not improve in terms of RP. The proposed self-learning framework performs best in all three measures on the unbiased sample as well as on the accepted applicants. The best performance is achieved by a self-learning model that includes filtering of rejects ($\beta_b = 1 - \beta_t = 0.02$). Therefore, the suggested modifications help to adjust self-learning for the reject inference problem.

Table 3. Reject inference techniques: parameter grid

Technique	Parameter	Candidate values
Label all as *bad*	–	–
Hard cutoff augmentation	Probability threshold	0.3, 0.4, 0.5
Parceling	Multiplier	1, 2, 3
	No. batches	10
CV-based voting	Probability threshold	0.3
	No. folds	2, 5, 10
Regular self-learning	Labeled percentage α	0.01, 0.02, 0.03
	Max no. iterations	5
Shallow self-learning	Filtered percentage β_b	0, 0.02
	Filtered percentage β_t	1, 0.98
	Penalty parameter λ	$2^{-8}, 2^{-7.5}, ..., 2^{8}$
	Labeled percentage α	0.01, 0.02, 0.03
	Imbalance parameter θ	1, 2
	Max no. iterations	5

Performance gains appear to be modest, supporting the prior findings [15]. We check statistical significance of the differences using Friedman's rank sum test and Nemenyi pairwise test [14]. According to Friedman's test, we reject the null hypothesis that all reject inference techniques perform the same at

Table 4. Comparing performance of reject inference techniques

Method	Accepted cases			Unbiased sample		
	AUC	BS	RP	AUC	BS	RP
Ignore rejects	0.7297	0.1829	0.8436	0.8007	0.2092	0.7936
Label all as bad	0.7332	0.1816	0.8474	0.6797	0.2284	0.7253
Hard cutoff augmentation	0.7295	0.1770	0.8430	0.7994	0.2212	0.7751
Parceling	0.7277	0.1842	0.8430	0.8041	0.1941	0.7851
CV-based voting	0.7293	0.1804	0.8430	0.7167	0.2160	0.7510
Regular self-learning	0.7302	0.1758	0.8434	0.8063	0.1838	0.7929
Shallow self-learning	**0.7362**	**0.1736**	**0.8492**	**0.8070**	**0.1799**	**0.7996**

Table 5. Correlation between evaluation strategies

Evaluation strategy	(1)	(2)	(3)
(1) AUC on the accepted cases	1		
(2) AUC on the unbiased sample	−0.0009	1	
(3) The kickout metric	0.0336	0.4069	1

5% level for AUC ($\chi^2 = 419.82$), RP ($\chi^2 = 326.99$) and BS ($\chi^2 = 485.59$). Nemenyi test indicates that shallow self-learning performs significantly better than all competitors in terms of AUC and RP, whereas differences in BS between standard and shallow self-learning are not statistically significant at 5% level.

Even small differences might have a considerable effect on the costs of the financial institution [27]. Comparing shallow self-learning to ignoring rejects, 0.006 increase in RP translates to 60 less defaulted loans for every 10,000 accepted clients. Considering the average personal loan size of $17,100 and interest rate of 10.36% observed in the US in Q1 2019[1], potential gains from reject inference could amount for up to $1.13 million depending on the recovery rates.

Experiment II: Evaluation Strategy for Model Selection
In the second experiment, we perform model selection on 28 variants of self-learning with different meta-parameter values. Table 5 displays the correlation between model ranks in terms of three evaluation measures: AUC on the accepts, AUC on the unbiased sample and the *kickout* measure.

The absolute value of rank correlations between the performance on the accepts and performance on the unbiased data does not exceed 0.01. In contrast, the rankings based on *kickout* are positively correlated with those on the unbiased sample ($r = 0.41$). Therefore, the common practice to assess reject inference strategies using the model's performance on the accepted cases provides misleading results as there is a very small correlation with the performance

---

[1] Source: https://www.supermoney.com/studies/personal-loans-industry-study/.

on the production stage. In contrast, comparing reject inference techniques using the proposed *kickout* measure is more promising.

Figure 3 illustrates the advantages of using *kickout* instead of the performance on the accepts for model selection. Red points indicate the predictive performance of a scoring model selected by the *kickout* measure, while green

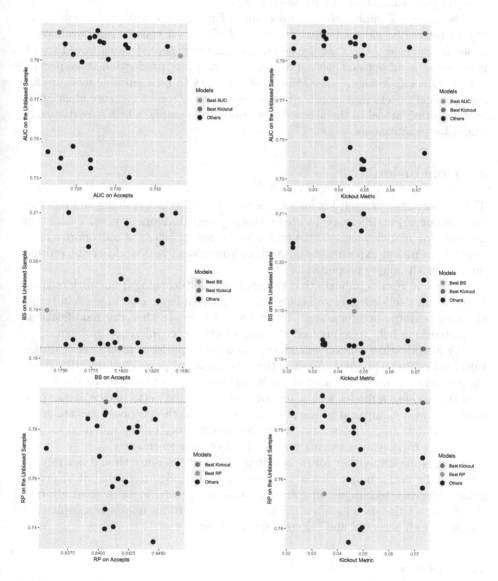

Fig. 3. *Model Selection Results.* Two upper diagrams compare results based on AUC on the accepts (green) and on the kickout metric (red). Two diagrams in the center compare results based on Brier Score on the accepts (green) and kickout (red). Two lower diagrams refer to R-Precision on the accepts (green) and kickout (red). (Color figure online)

dots refer to the best-performing model on the accepts in terms of AUC, BS and RP. As before, we evaluate the selected scoring models on the unbiased sample.

As shown in Fig. 3, using the *kickout* measure results in selecting a better model in terms of all three performance indicators. By relying on *kickout* instead of the performance on the accepts, we are able to identify a scorecard that has a better performance on the unbiased sample.

These results emphasize the importance of using a suitable evaluation strategy to assess the value of reject inference. Relying on conventional evaluation measures such as AUC that are estimated on the accepted cases would result in selecting a suboptimal scoring model in terms of its production-stage performance. Our experiments show that *kickout* proves to be a suitable measure for doing model selection. According to the results, the *kickout* measure identifies a better scoring model in the absence of an unbiased sample, which is particularly useful for practitioners.

5   Conclusion

This paper suggests a self-learning framework with distinct training and labeling regimes for reject inference in credit scoring and develops a novel evaluation measure for model selection. We evaluate the effectiveness of our approach by running empirical experiments on a high-dimensional real-world credit scoring data set with unique properties.

Empirical results indicate that the proposed self-learning framework outperforms regular self-learning and conventional reject inference techniques in terms of three performance measures. These results indicate that the modifications suggested here help to adjust self-learning to the reject inference problem.

We also develop a novel evaluation measure to perform model selection for reject inference techniques. We show that the standard practice of selecting models (or meta-parameters) based on their performance on the accepted cases may lead to choosing a model with a suboptimal predictive performance at the production stage. Compared to the standard approach, the proposed *kickout* measure exhibits a higher correlation with the performance on the unbiased sample and allows to identify a scoring model with better performance.

Our results imply that future research on reject inference should not rely on the model's performance on the accepted cases to judge the value of a certain reject inference technique. The *kickout* measure proves to be a good alternative for practitioners who often do not have access to an unbiased sample that contains both accepted and rejected applications.

References

1. Anderson, B., Hardin, J.M.: Modified logistic regression using the EM algorithm for reject inference. IJDATS 5(4), 359–373 (2013). https://doi.org/10.1504/IJDATS. 2013.058582

2. Ash, D., Meester, S.: Best practices in reject inference. In: Presentation at Credit Risk Modeling and Decision Conference. Wharton Financial Institutions Center, Philadelphia, May 2002
3. Banasik, J., Crook, J.: Credit scoring, augmentation and lean models. J. Oper. Res. Soc. **56**(9), 1072–1081 (2005). https://doi.org/10.1057/palgrave.jors.2602017
4. Banasik, J., Crook, J.: Reject inference, augmentation, and sample selection. Eur. J. Oper. Res. **183**(3), 1582–1594 (2007). https://doi.org/10.1016/j.ejor.2006.06. 072
5. Banasik, J., Crook, J.: Reject inference in survival analysis by augmentation. J. Oper. Res. Soc. **61**(3), 473–485 (2010). https://doi.org/10.1057/jors.2008.180
6. Banasik, J., Crook, J., Thomas, L.: Sample selection bias in credit scoring models. J. Oper. Res. Soc. **54**(8), 822–832 (2003). https://doi.org/10.1057/palgrave.jors. 2601578
7. Bücker, M., van Kampen, M., Krämer, W.: Reject inference in consumer credit scoring with nonignorable missing data. J. Bank. Finance **37**(3), 1040–1045 (2013). https://doi.org/10.1016/j.jbankfin.2012.11.002
8. Chapelle, O., Schölkopf, B., Zien, A.: Semi-Supervised Learning. MIT Press, Cambridge (2006)
9. Chen, G.G., Astebro, T.: The economic value of reject inference in credit scoring. University of Waterloo, Department of Management Science (2001)
10. Chen, G.G., Åstebro, T.: Bound and collapse bayesian reject inference for credit scoring. J. Oper. Res. Soc. **63**(10), 1374–1387 (2012). https://doi.org/10.1057/jors. 2011.149
11. Crook, J., Banasik, J.: Does reject inference really improve the performance of application scoring models? J. Bank. Finance **28**(4), 857–874 (2004). https://doi. org/10.1016/j.jbankfin.2003.10.010
12. Feelders, A.: Credit scoring and reject inference with mixture models. Intell. Syst. Acc. Finance Manage. **9**(1), 1–8 (2000). https://doi.org/10.1002/(SICI)1099-1174(199912)8:4⟨271::AID-ISAF170⟩3.0.CO;2-P
13. Fogarty, D.J.: Multiple imputation as a missing data approach to reject inference on consumer credit scoring. Interstat **41**, 1–41 (2006)
14. García, S., Fernández, A., Luengo, J., Herrera, F.: Advanced nonparametric tests for multiple comparisons in the design of experiments in computational intelligence and data mining: experimental analysis of power. Inf. Sci. **180**(10), 2044–2064 (2010). https://doi.org/10.1016/j.ins.2009.12.010
15. Hand, D.J., Henley, W.E.: Can reject inference ever work? IMA J. Manage. Math. **5**(1), 45–55 (1993). https://doi.org/10.1093/imaman/5.1.45
16. Joanes, D.N.: Reject inference applied to logistic regression for credit scoring. IMA J. Manage. Math. **5**(1), 35–43 (1993). https://doi.org/10.1093/imaman/5.1.35
17. Kim, Y., Sohn, S.: Technology scoring model considering rejected applicants and effect of reject inference. J. Oper. Res. Soc. **58**(10), 1341–1347 (2007). https://doi. org/10.1057/palgrave.jors.2602306
18. Lessmann, S., Baesens, B., Seow, H.V., Thomas, L.C.: Benchmarking state-of-the-art classification algorithms for credit scoring: an update of research. Eur. J. Oper. Res. **247**(1), 124–136 (2015). https://doi.org/10.1016/j.ejor.2015.05.030
19. Li, Z., Tian, Y., Li, K., Zhou, F., Yang, W.: Reject inference in credit scoring using semi-supervised support vector machines. Expert Syst. Appl. **74**, 105–114 (2017). https://doi.org/10.1016/j.eswa.2017.01.011
20. Liu, F.T., Ting, K.M., Zhou, Z.H.: Isolation forest. In: Eighth IEEE International Conference on Data Mining, pp. 413–422. IEEE (2008). https://doi.org/10.1109/ ICDM.2008.17

21. Maldonado, S., Paredes, G.: A semi-supervised approach for reject inference in credit scoring using SVMs. In: Perner, P. (ed.) ICDM 2010. LNCS (LNAI), vol. 6171, pp. 558–571. Springer, Heidelberg (2010). https://doi.org/10.1007/978-3-642-14400-4_43

22. Montrichard, D.: Reject inference methodologies in credit risk modeling. In: The Proceedings of the South-East SAS Users Group (2007)

23. Niculescu-Mizil, A., Caruana, R.: Obtaining calibrated probabilities from boosting. In: UAI, p. 413 (2005)

24. Reichert, A.K., Cho, C.C., Wagner, G.M.: An examination of the conceptual issues involved in developing credit-scoring models. J. Bus. Econ. Stat. 1(2), 101–114 (1983)

25. Rosenberg, C., Hebert, M., Schneiderman, H.: Semi-supervised self-training of object detection models. In: Seventh IEEE Workshops on Applications of Computer Vision, vol. 1, pp. 29–36. IEEE (2005). https://doi.org/10.1109/ACVMOT.2005.107

26. Rosset, S.: Model selection via the AUC. In: Proceedings of the 21st International Conference on Machine Learning, p. 89. ACM (2004). https://doi.org/10.1145/1015330.1015400

27. Schebesch, K.B., Stecking, R.: Using multiple SVM models for unbalanced credit scoring data sets. In: Preisach, C., Burkhardt, H., Schmidt-Thieme, L., Decker, R. (eds.) Data Analysis, Machine Learning and Applications. Studies in Classification, Data Analysis, and Knowledge Organization, pp. 515–522. Springer, Heidelberg (2008). https://doi.org/10.1007/978-3-540-78246-9_61

28. Siddiqi, N.: Credit Risk Scorecards: Developing and Implementing Intelligent Credit Scoring, vol. 3. Wiley, New York (2012)

29. Smith, A., Elkan, C.: A Bayesian network framework for reject inference. In: Proceedings of the Tenth ACM SIGKDD International Conference on Knowledge Discovery and Data Mining, pp. 286–295. ACM (2004). https://doi.org/10.1145/1014052.1014085

30. Verbaeten, S., Van Assche, A.: Ensemble methods for noise elimination in classification problems. In: Windeatt, T., Roli, F. (eds.) MCS 2003. LNCS, vol. 2709, pp. 317–325. Springer, Heidelberg (2003). https://doi.org/10.1007/3-540-44938-8_32

31. Verbraken, T., Bravo, C., Weber, R., Baesens, B.: Development and application of consumer credit scoring models using profit-based classification measures. Eur. J. Oper. Res. 238(2), 505–513 (2014). https://doi.org/10.1016/j.ejor.2014.04.001

32. Verstraeten, G., Van den Poel, D.: The impact of sample bias on consumer credit scoring performance and profitability. J. Oper. Res. Soc. 56(8), 981–992 (2005). https://doi.org/10.1057/palgrave.jors.2601920

33. Wang, D., Zhang, Z., Bai, R., Mao, Y.: A hybrid system with filter approach and multiple population genetic algorithm for feature selection in credit scoring. J. Comput. Appl. Math. 329, 307–321 (2018). https://doi.org/10.1016/j.cam.2017.04.036

34. Wang, G., Hao, J.x., Ma, J., Huang, L.h.: Empirical evaluation of ensemble learning for credit scoring. In: Machine Learning: Concepts, Methodologies, Tools and Applications, pp. 1108–1127. IGI Global (2012). https://doi.org/10.4018/978-1-61520-629-2.ch007

Applied Data Science: Rich Data

LSTM Encoder-Predictor for Short-Term Train Load Forecasting

Kevin Pasini[1,2]([✉]), Mostepha Khouadjia[1], Allou Samé[2], Fabrice Ganansia[3], and Latifa Oukhellou[2]

[1] Université Paris-Est, IFSTTAR, Cosys-Grettia, Champs-sur-Marne, France
[2] IRT SystemX, Saclay, France
Kevin.pasini@irt-systemx.fr
[3] SNCF- Innovation & Recherche, St Denis, France

Abstract. The increase in the amount of data collected in the transport domain can greatly benefit mobility studies and help to create high value-added mobility services for passengers as well as regulation tools for operators. The research detailed in this paper is related to the development of an advanced machine learning approach with the aim of forecasting the passenger load of trains in public transport. Predicting the crowding level on public transport can indeed be useful for enriching the information available to passengers to enable them to better plan their daily trips. Moreover, operators will increasingly need to assess and predict network passenger load to improve train regulation processes and service quality levels. The main issues to address in this forecasting task are the variability in the train load series induced by the train schedule and the influence of several contextual factors, such as calendar information. We propose a neural network LSTM encoder-predictor combined with a contextual representation learning to address this problem. Experiments are conducted on a real dataset provided by the French railway company SNCF and collected over a period of one and a half years. The prediction performance provided by the proposed model are compared to those given by historical models and by traditional machine learning models. The obtained results have demonstrated the potential of the proposed LSTM encoder-predictor to address both one-step-ahead and multi-step forecasting and to outperform other models by maintaining robustness in the quality of the forecasts throughout the time horizon.

Keywords: Machine learning · Time series forecasting · Representation learning · Mobility data · Transport · Train load

1 Introduction

In recent years, the population growth in metropolitan areas has led to overcrowding on trains. Transport operators are working on enriching real-time passenger information systems by providing passengers with train loads in addition to train schedules. This information can allow passengers to better plan their

© Springer Nature Switzerland AG 2020
U. Brefeld et al. (Eds.): ECML PKDD 2019, LNAI 11908, pp. 535–551, 2020.
https://doi.org/10.1007/978-3-030-46133-1_32

daily trips, which can improve overall comfort and avoid overcrowding on trains. Moreover, such forecasting can be used by public transport authorities and transport operators either to enrich public transport route planning or to improve the synchronization of train traffic with passenger flows. Transport operators will increasingly need to assess and predict network passenger load to improve train regulation processes and service quality levels.

The development of smart technologies and the rapid growth in data storage abilities have increased the availability of massive transport data, such as passenger affluence, train load, real-time train schedules and so forth. This increase in data contributes to leveraging the developments in data mining and machine learning approaches for processing such spatio-temporal data to extract valuable information with the aim of providing better services to passengers or to match the transport supply with the demand. This paper addresses the forecasting of train load at a railway station considering a historical dataset that includes two data sources: train load data and automatic vehicle location. The latter source contains all information related to the train operation (delay, time of arrival/departure of vehicles and so on). Most of the prediction problems in this domain address the prediction of passenger affluence at an aggregated level (per 15 min or 30 min time horizon) [1–3]. In contrast to these studies, we focus here on the prediction at the non-aggregated level, taking into account real-time train schedules. This induces variability in the time step of the time series that we should predict. Furthermore, the prediction model has to take contextual factors impacting train load into account, such as calendar information (day, time, holiday and so forth) and train operation.

We address this prediction task as a multi-step short-term forecasting problem on irregularly structured times series influenced by several contextual factors. We work at the station level for each passage of train, which involves a temporal variability, making difficult the application of techniques that usually exploit structure regularity of time series. To handle these specificities, we rely on the abstraction capabilities of neural networks linked to the concept of representation learning [4]. The underlying idea is to build a mobility representation of our known influential factors. The model takes the form of an encoder-predictor neural network architecture associated with representation learning on contextual factors. It aims to predict the train load of the next trains of a station from the values of the last trains and all the contextual features characterizing these trains.

This paper is organized as follows. Section 1.1 is devoted to related work conducted on prediction models dedicated to public transport demand forecasting and on some main works on deep neural networks. In Sect. 2, we detail the case study that we consider and our dataset. Section 3 presents the proposed methodology formulated in a general framework. The evaluation of the proposed model is then conducted in Sect. 4 through different experiments, aiming to compare the performance of the proposed model to those provided by four baseline models on the one hand and to illustrate the learning representation space of the network on the other hand. Section 4.4 concludes the paper.

1.1   Related Work

Numerous studies have addressed the mining of large-scale mobility data for exploration, clustering or prediction purposes. Depending on the available data, on the scale of analysis and on the targeted goal, different types of methodologies can be distinguished. For example, the authors in [5] propose predicting crowding levels from automated fare collection data by using simple techniques based on historic aggregates. Models proposed in [6] take the form of an neural network architecture using feature engineering capturing daily and monthly trends to perform daily passenger demand forecasting. The study conducted in [7] explores the viability of building a fare-recommendation system for public transport to avoid incorrect fares. For this purpose, the authors propose a two-step approach: predicting future travel habits and then matching travel habits to fares.

Extensive research on predictive models in the transport domain has been conducted. Most of the works address the prediction of passenger flows. In [8], the authors propose a deep neural network model to forecast passenger demand related to an on-demand ride service station. The combination of convolutional layers with LSTM layers allows taking spatial, temporal and exogenous dependencies into account. An LSTM recurrent neural network was proposed in [1] to address the short-term forecasting of passenger flows in a transport network. The authors in [9] work on short-term subway ridership prediction by means of a gradient boosting decision tree model. On the basis of smart card data, the authors build a prediction model using both temporal features (time and calendar) and historical data related not only to subway activities but also to bus transfer activities. Following the same line of research, the authors in [10] examine causal relationships between the adjacent flows on a public transport station with transport service features. The proposed methodology, which is based on a dynamic Bayesian network, allows highlighting such causalities and performing the prediction. Recently, the authors in [11] formalized the problem of tram load passenger prediction as a classification task, where the passenger load is labelled into different classes depending on the percentage of occupied seats. Once this labelling is performed, the authors build classical machine learning classifiers, such as k-nearest-neighbours, multi-layer perceptron, grading boosting decision tree and random forest, to predict the level of crowding in the transport. Here, temporal and historical data were used as model inputs.

Advanced machine learning models, particularly deep learning models, have also recently been proposed to address forecasting problems. Recurrent neural networks [12] are potential tools capable of capturing the dynamics of the time series. These models have even been extended to handle regular spatio-temporal data by [13] with a convolutional LSTM for weather prediction. In parallel, early research work has been accomplished by [14]. The authors propose a recurrent neural network encoder-decoder for a statistical machine translation system. This model is capable of capturing both semantic and syntactic structures of phrases. Considering the spatio-temporal dependencies in the forecasting, [3] proposes a dynamical spatio-temporal neural network for forecasting the time series of spatial processes. The idea investigated in this model is to learn both temporal and spatial dependencies between the series to be predicted through a combined use of a latent embedding structured by the temporal dynamics of the series and a decoder mechanism to make the prediction. In [2], the authors work on forecasting the flow of crowds in all regions of a city by means of a deep-learning-based model. Historical trajectory data, weather and events are used to build the model. Residual neural networks and a parametric fusion mechanism are employed to design the forecasting model of crowd traffic.

Focusing on the transport domain, most of the aforementioned research works propose achieving the load/affluence prediction using classical classification or regression machine learning models. These models do not allow fully exploiting the sequential structure of the time series to be predicted. Moreover, they do not consider variability in time steps of the data, as it is the case here. The flexible transportation schedule, the variability in transport demand, and the contextual factors lead to complex dynamics of the series that the model should capture.

To address the structural variability in the passenger load series and influence factors, we rely on the abstraction capabilities of deep neural network models linked to the concept of representation learning [4]. The underlying idea is to learn a meaningful representation of mobility flows taking contextual factors into account. The proposed model takes the form of an RNN encoder-decoder neural network [14] associated with the representation learning of contextual factors. It aims to predict the passenger load of the next trains at a station from measures of the last trains and all the contextual features characterizing all of these trains at the same station. Note that the experiments will be performed on a real dataset collected over a long period (one and a half years), which leads to a robust evaluation of the models. Before detailing the proposed model, the next section will describe the real dataset used in the experiments.

2   Data Description

Our study focuses on a dataset collected from a French railway line that serves approximately fifty stations located in the northern area of suburban Paris. The railway line carries approximately 250,000 passengers daily. The dataset covers a period of 18 months from January 2015 to June 2016 on 40 stations for daytime exploitation from 5 am to 2 am of the next day. It includes both timetable information and count data of passengers boarding and alighting at each station collected by radar sensors on trains (2000000 records covering 86% of trains). These heterogeneous sources of data that have been enriched with calendar information enable us to reconstruct the passenger load on each train departing from a station.

The main goal of this study concerns the forecasting of univariate train load series for each station. To have an idea of the time series to be predicted, Fig. 1 shows an example of weekday and weekend daily train passenger load profiles collected from two stations. The suburb station accounts for approximately 22000 train stops with a particularity low train frequency and few train routes that serve this station. Conversely, the inner-city station accounts for approximately

84000 train stops with an important train frequency and multiple train routes that serve the station. Figure 1 provides insights on the forecasting problem to be solved and highlights the particularities of our dataset, namely:

- A variable sampling period due to the train timetables and railway operation. Each station has its own train frequency evolution.
- A specific temporal behaviour of each time series, which was found to be linked to the spatial location of public transport stations and geographical aspects of the city (population & employment densities, leisure and so forth).
- Train load series are impacted by calendar factors such as the type of day (weekday or weekend), holiday, public holiday and so on.
- Train load series are also impacted by train characteristics that are closely linked to their services (multi-destination line, various train services).

In addition to these contextual factors, public transport demand and therefore train load passengers can also be impacted by events (social, cultural, sport and so forth). The time series forecasting model has to face all the temporal, spatial and exogenous factors listed above. In this paper, a prediction model will be built for each railway station. The next section details the methodology developed to achieve this prediction task.

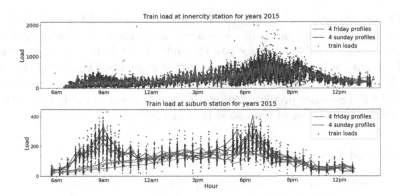

Fig. 1. Train loads in year 2015 per hour on suburb and inner-city stations

3   LSTM Encoder-Predictor

In this section we formalize the application of the recurrent encoder-predictor architecture to our particular structural constraints: a train sequence with variable time steps and heterogeneous attributes. Let $(y_1, .., y_t)$ denote the sequence to be predicted, where y_t corresponds to a passenger train load in the same station, t referring to the trains arrival order. It is assumed that each realization y_t is associated with an observation S_t which includes contextual features e_t and past measures m_t. We have tackled the issue of the variability of the time between consecutive trains by encoding it as a contextual feature associated with specific coefficients in the model. We also use the notation y_I, S_I, e_I and m_I to designate the subsequences $(y_t)_{t \in I}$, $(S_t)_{t \in I}$, $(e_t)_{t \in I}$, $(m_t)_{t \in I}$ with $I \subset [1; T]$. Given a time window $W_i = [i - k, i + k']$ composed of a past horizon $P_i = [i - k, i[$ and a future horizon $F_i = [i, i + k']$, the goal of our multi-step forecasting approach is to infer a realization on the horizon y_{F_i} from information available on S_{W_i} as shown in Fig. 2. Table 1 summarizes the notation used in this article.

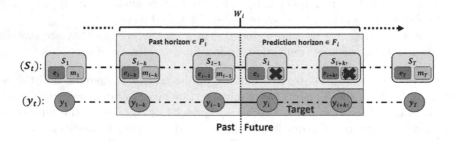

Fig. 2. Illustration of notations used in the forecasting model

This forecasting is particularly challenging because it asks to understand the laws behind realizations (y_t) taking into account the multiple influencing factors. The model must be able to dissociate the influencing factors on a structurally irregular sequence by exploiting the contextual attributes. Following the line of research on the RNN encoder-decoder proposed by [14], we propose a neural network LSTM encoder-predictor for short-term multi-step prediction including a representation learning of the contextual factors.

3.1   Method Description

Given observations on a time window S_{W_i}. It aims to reconstruct the k last realizations $\hat{y}_{P_i}$ and to predict the k' next realizations $\hat{y}_{F_i}$ considering contextual information e_{P_i} and measure information m_{P_i} on past horizon and contextual information e_{F_i} on future horizon. It is a deep neural network that can be decomposed into sub-parts with specific roles. A general illustration of the proposed model is given in Fig. 3. The arrangement of the different components of the LSTM are detailed in Fig. 4. The sub-parts of the proposed architecture are described as follows.

$$LSTM_{EP}(X_i) = LSTM_{EP}(m_{P_i}, e_{P_i}, e_{F_i}) = (\hat{y}_{P_i}, \hat{y}_{F_i}) \tag{1}$$

Table 1. Notation and variable

Notation	
t	A time step $t \in [1, T]$
$y_1, ..., y_T$	(y_t) Realization series
$S_1, ..., S_t$	(S_t) Observation sequences
$e_1, ..., e_T$	(e_t) Sequence of feature contextual vectors
$m_1, ..., m_T$	(m_t) Sequence of feature measure vectors
	Windows
W_i	$[i - k, i + k']$: Window associated to the ith observation
P_i	$[i - k, i[$: Past horizon of window W_i
F_i	$[i, i + k']$: Prediction horizon of window W_i
X_i	$(m_{P_i}, e_{P_i}, e_{F_i})$ Input features from the window W_i
	Latent space (see Subsect. 3.1)
$u_1, ..., u_T$	(u_t) Contextual representation
$h_1, ..., h_T$	(h_t) Latent past dynamic
$r_1, ..., r_T$	(r_t) Latent reconstruction state
$z_1, ..., z_T$	(z_t) Latent prediction state
	Model and sub-part
$LSTM_{EP}$	Neural network model
$Fact$	MLP factoring contextual features
Enc	Recurrent encoder of past observation
Dec	Recurrent decoder of past observation
$Pred$	Recurrent predictor of future observation
$Reconst$	MLP to reconstruct past realizations
$Predict$	MLP to predict future realizations

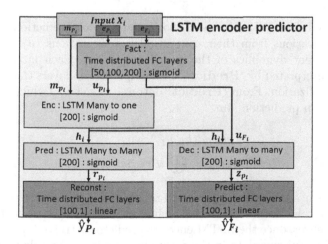

Fig. 3. General architecture of the LSTM encoder-predictor network

Fact: A context factory is dedicated to synthesize contextual features (e_t) as contextual representation (u_t). It is a preprocessing multilayer perceptron applied on each observation to regularize contextual representations.

$$Fact(e_{P_i}, e_{F_i}) = \bigoplus_{t \in (P_i \cup F_i)} Fact(e_t) = \bigoplus_{t \in (P_i \cup F_i)} u_t = (u_{P_i}, u_{F_i}) \qquad (2)$$

Enc: A many-to-one LSTM 'encoder' is dedicated to capture a past latent dynamic (h_i) from the past measures m_{P_i} and the past contextual representations (u_{P_i}).

$$Enc(m_{P_i}, u_{P_i}) = h_i \qquad (3)$$

Dec: A many-to-many LSTM 'decoder' decodes recurrently latent reconstruction states r_{P_i} of past observations from latent dynamics of the past horizon (h_i). Each latent reconstruction state is then interpreted by **'Reconst'**, a linear reconstruction layers that infer past observation realization. From **'Reconst'** outputs we get $\hat{y}_{P_i}$. These outputs are used as an intermediate objective during the training phase to facilitate capture of past latent dynamics.

$$Dec(h_i) = r_{P_i} \qquad (4)$$

$$Reconst(r_{P_i}) = \bigoplus_{t \in P_i} Reconst(r_t) = \hat{y}_{P_i} \qquad (5)$$

Enc and *Dec* form an encoder-decoder structure that synthesizing the dynamics of past observations from theirs contextual and measurement features.

Pred: A many-to-many LSTM 'predictor' infers latent prediction states (z_{F_i}) of future observations from their contextual representations (u_{F_i}) taking into account the latent dynamics of the past horizon (h_i). Each latent prediction state is then interpreted by **'Predict'**, a linear prediction layers that infer future observation realization. From **'Predict'** outputs we get $\hat{y}_{F_i}$ which corresponds to the multi-step prediction aim.

$$Pred(h_i, u_{F_i}) = z_{F_i} \qquad (6)$$

$$Predict(z_{F_i}) = \bigoplus_{t \in F_i} Predict(z_t) = \hat{y}_{F_i} \qquad (7)$$

Note that since the model is designed to address variability in the time step, this makes it straightforward to remove observations of the dataset due to missing data. Moreover, once the LSTM encoder-predictor is trained, predictions can be performed on missing data in the future horizon if we are able to reconstruct contextual information.

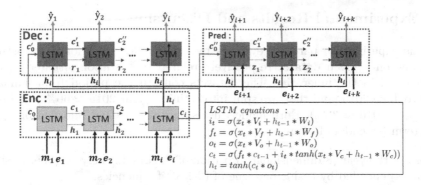

Fig. 4. Details on the layout of the LSTMs

3.2   Optimization

A deep neural network is trained through end-to-end gradient back-propagation by minimizing the following loss function:

$$\mathcal{L}(\theta) = \alpha_p * \sum_{t \in P_i} ||y_t - \hat{y}_t||^2 + \alpha_f * \sum_{t \in F_i} ||y_t - \hat{y}_t||^2,$$

$$With \ \theta = (\theta_{Fact}, \theta_{Enc}, \theta_{Dec}, \theta_{Pred}, \theta_{Reconst}, \theta_{Predict}).$$

(8)

The first term measures the ability of the model to reconstruct the past observations from the latent past dynamics. It is an intermediate objective that facilitates the learning of the past dynamics. The second term measures the prediction ability of the model. Hyper-Parameters α_p and α_f are the weights of the reconstruction and prediction objectives.

For the learning phase, we realize mini-batch optimization thanks to a *Nadam* optimizer [15]. Two gradients (prediction and reconstruction) are propagated from their output layers (Predict and Reconst) to the upstream layers towards the context factory through LSTM layers. The encoder-predictor is implemented based on the *TensorFlow* [16] environment and *Keras* [17] as a library and high-level neural network API.

The parameters have been chosen empirically after several experiments based on model performance and learning convergence. *Fact* is composed of 3 dense layers of size [50, 100, 200] with a sigmoid activation function for a total of 27000 parameters. *Enc*, *Dec*, and *Pred* are 3 LSTM layers of size 200 with a sigmoid activation function for a total of 880000 parameters. *Reconst* and *Predict* are composed of 2 dense layers of size [100, 1] with a linear activation function for a total of 40000 parameters. The whole neural network has approximately 900,000 parameters.

Training is empirically realized on a batch of size 128 on several thousand iterations, which takes few hours on one standard GPU card depending on the dataset and time depth. Further work on the choice of parameters is required to improve the convergence.

4   Experimental Results and Discussion

For the experimental part, we evaluate two models for train load forecasting, each one on a given dataset respectively related to a station situated in the suburb and in the inner city. The datasets concern the period from January 2015 to June 2016, and they are split into training (year $2015 \approx 66\%$) and test sets (year $2016 \approx 33\%$). Both models use several contextual information e_t as long-term (calendar) features:

– Day of the year (8-dimensional): Position of the day in the year (365 possible values) encoded by cosine and sine of (2×4) frequencies.
– Day type (8-dimensional): Position of the day in the week with an additional attribute if the day corresponds to a holiday or not.
– Minutes (8-dimensional): Minute of the day (1440 possible values) encoded by cosine and sine of (2×4) frequencies.
– Train services (8-dimensional): Feature related to the train routes that serve the considered station.

Moreover, we also consider short-term features m_t by considering a lag window that ranges between 1 to 6 past observations:

– Delay (1-dimensional): Difference in minutes between the real and the theoretical schedule of the train at the station.
– Load (6-dimensional): Number of passenger on the train for each of the last 6 passages at the considered station.
– Board (6-dimensional): Numbers of boarded passengers for each of the last 6 train passages at the station.
– Alight (6-dimensional): Numbers of alighted passengers for each of the last 6 train passages at the station.

4.1   Compared Forecasting Models

We compare on both suburb and inner-city stations different classical and machine learning models that serve as baselines for our LSTM EP:

– **Last Value (LV)**: It is the simplest forecasting that consists of forwarding the last observed load on the train to the next one at the same station.
– **Contextual Average (CA)**: It consists of using of the average load of trains that are committed on the same day type and time slice.
– **Gradient Boosting (XGB)** [18]: A regressor model that produces a prediction model in the form of an ensemble of weak decision trees. Two models are proposed depending on the input features:
    • **XGB LT**: Model that is trained based on long-term features e_t.
    • **XGB ST**: Model trained on both long e_t and short-term m_t features.
– **LSTM**: Basic recurrent network using both types of features.
– **LSTM EP**: The proposed RNN trained on context representation using both types of features.

The best parameters of XGB have been selected with a grid search procedure in conjunction with cross validation for $K = 3$ as the number of folds.

We evaluate the performance of models on each time step by root mean square error (RMSE) and weighted absolute percentage error (WAPE) measures:

$$WAPE\ score : \frac{\sum_t \|y_t - \hat{y}_t\|}{\bar{y}} \tag{9}$$

WAPE is a derivative of the MAE that can be interpreted as the percentage of the overall error compared to the average value of the actual observation.

4.2 Forecasting Results

The evaluation of the forecasting models is conducted by making comparisons based on performance metrics. These metrics are expressed in terms of RMSE and WAPE and are given for both the training and the test phases for the suburb and inner-city stations. The five models defined in Sect. 4.1, namely, the basic last value (LV), the contextual average (CA), the gradient boosting (XGB) short term (ST), long term (LT) and the LSTM-EP are compared. The errors obtained for both the training and test sets are given in Table 2.

The results show that advanced models (XGB, LSTM) outperform the LV and CA models. This performance improvement could mainly be explained by the fact that the XGB and LSTM models have better generalisation abilities and are able to fit more complex models than LV and CA, which simply predict by forwarding the last observed value or averaging historical data. The basic LSTM performs less in the inner-city station compared to the suburb station. This can be explained by its difficulties to deal with the heterogeneity in term of train services with that kind of station. Overall, LSTM EP leads to the best results since it is able to capture in better way the underlying dynamics of the temporal irregularity related to the heterogeneity of train services by means of its encoder-decoder component.

Looking at the prediction error of the LSTM EP according to the load to predict (see Fig. 5), we observe that errors are increasing according to the load. The model tends to slightly overestimate weakly loaded trains and greatly underestimate the highly loaded trains. Heavily loaded trains are rare and present contextual information similar to many less loaded trains, which explains the difficulty of the model in predicting large loads. To remedy this problem, provisioning features to distinguish these trains appears to be necessary. One could imagine indicators related to the disturbance of the network and the known presence of events near the station.

As shown in Fig. 6, the model makes errors of the same order of magnitude for weekdays and weekends with different difficulties. The variance of the error over a time slot is correlated to the importance of the load. On weekdays, we observe larger errors in the morning and afternoon peak hour linked to the strong variance and high load. The model makes average errors in the middle of the day and low errors in the morning and evening. On weekends, except in the morning,

Table 2. Model performance on both studied stations

Model	Suburb			Inner city	
	WAPE	RMSE		WAPE	RMSE
LV	17.9	35.8	Train score	41.9	186.7
CA	13.7	28.7		14.2	73.1
XGB LT	8.4	17.2		8.3	44.75
XGB ST	7.5	15.1		8.2	43.5
LSTM	11.5	24.3		8.9	51.5
LSTM EP	10.7	22.1		10.9	57.7
LV	24.1	47.2	Test score	46.9	205.0
CA	19.0	40.0		18.5	96.5
XGB LT	18.8	38.9		13.4	76.0
XGB ST	16.8	35.7		12.7	73.0
LSTM	16.2	34.0		13.7	75.3
LSTM EP	**16.0**	**33.8**		**12.9**	**72.4**

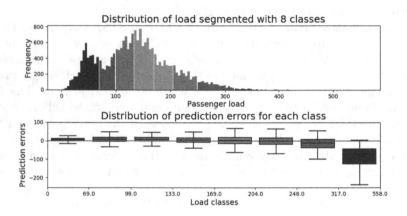

Fig. 5. Prediction errors depend on load class for suburb station

a relatively similar error variance is observed with a maximum at noon and in the middle of the afternoon. We also observe that the model has more trouble predicting weekend evenings than weekday evenings.

When we examine the performance of the models on multi-step temporal prediction, the LSTM EP outperforms XGB and basic LSTM for the next 6 time steps (Table 3 and Table 4). These time steps correspond to the train passages at the station and range between 14 to 182 min for the suburb station, whereas it ranges between 2 to 61 min when considering the inner-city station since the train passages are more frequent.

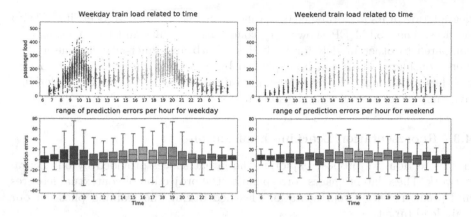

Fig. 6. Prediction errors depend on hour class for suburb station

Table 3. RMSE test score of the suburb station for the multi-step forecasting models

Model	t + 1	t + 2	t + 3	t + 4	t + 5	t + 6
Time interval*	14–32	29–62	44–92	59–122	75–152	90–182
XGB LT	38.9	38.9	38.9	38.9	38.9	38.9
XGB ST	35.7	36.6	36.7	36.7	37.6	38.1
LSTM	34.0	34.4	34.8	35.5	36.3	36.9
LSTM EP	**33.8**	**34.0**	**34.1**	**34.4**	**34.7**	**34.9**

Table 4. RMSE test score on the inner-city station for the multi-step forecasting

Model	t + 1	t + 2	t + 3	t + 4	t + 5	t + 6
Time interval*	2–13	5–23	9–31	12–43	15–53	18–61
XGB LT	76.0	76.0	76.0	76.0	76.0	76.0
XGB ST	73.0	72.8	73.3	73.8	73.4	73.5
LSTM	75.3	75.4	80.2	83.9	90.5	92.9
LSTM EP	**72.4**	**72.1**	**72.1**	**72.2**	**72.6**	**72.8**

*The 5th and 90th percentiles of the time interval in the passage of trains at the time T and T+n

Note that these performances are obtained with a single model that simultaneously predicts the load at all the time steps for both LSTM models. The XGB LT is time-step invariant since it only considers long term features. For XGB ST, we have as many models as the considered time steps. The performance of short-term models are slightly degraded when we move forward in time, excepted for basic LSTM in the case of inner city station, where we can notice a strong degradation of its performance over time steps due to the heterogeneity of train services. The LSTM EP shows very competitive results and better robustness compared to other models for both the suburb and inner-city stations for all steps considered. This can be explained by a better understanding of contextual factors through a latent representation that helps to capture the underlying dynamics of train service at the station.

4.3   Representation Learning Exploration

In this section, we propose exploring the latent spaces provided by our neural network. These latent spaces correspond to the projection of contextual features and predictive state representations learned during the training phase of our train load target.

For this purpose, we first project the learned representation of the penultimate layer of our LSTM EP obtained during the training of the train load at the suburb station. Figure 7 shows the scatter plot of the dimensional reduction of the latent representation. For each sub-plot, the considered representation is projected depending on a given feature (day, hour, month, train load). Each colour block represents a common category of the handled feature. Dimensionality reduction is performed by preserving large pairwise distances between the points with the help of principal component analysis (PCA) to reduce 200-dimensional data into 50 dimensions, followed by a T-distributed stochastic neighbour embedding (tSNE) to reduce the dimensionality from 50 to 2 or 3 dimensions. As shown in Fig. 7, the contextual representation (u_t) is strongly structured according to different levels depending on each contextual feature.

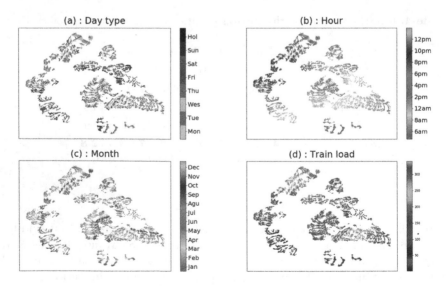

Fig. 7. Latent representation (u_t) according to contextual features obtained after dimensionality reduction (PCA + tSNE)

Each point of the obtained structure reflects a train passage, and depending on the gradient of the underlying structure, we can highlight the profile of train service during weekday and weekend (see Fig. 7a), the frequency of service with a distinction between the rush and off-peak periods (see Fig. 7b), the seasonality (see Fig. 7c) and the load range (see Fig. 7d).

Fig. 8. Predictive latent space (z_t) after applying 3-dimensional reduction

When we reduce the predictive latent space (z_t) to 3 dimensions, we can observe the structure of the manifold as a spiralling band representing the daily evolution of the train load (Fig. 8).

4.4   Conclusion

In this paper, we investigated train load forecasting on both single- and multi-step time horizons. The single step aims to predict the load for the next train at the station, whereas the goal of multi-step is to predict ahead of time the load for further train passages. The forecasting problem is particularly challenging since we have variability in train services and several contextual factors that could have a major impact on the time series to be predicted. For this purpose, we proposed a model called LSTM EP based on an encoder-decoder combined with a representation learning of contextual factors. This network has the particularity of being able to learn a contextual representation from contextual features, to capture the latent past dynamics through the underlying sub-structure of the encoder-decoder, and then forecast the forthcoming dynamics with the help of the predictive layer. The representation learning is a key value for the proposed architecture; it contributes to understanding the features and representation of the underlying dataset, which is essential for selecting the best neural network architecture for this prediction task.

The obtained results have demonstrated the potential of the LSTM encoder-predictor to address the short-term prediction of train load at stations compared to the Gradient Boosting model and basic LSTM. We evaluated the performance of the proposed model on two real datasets related to suburb and inner-city stations for single and multi-step forecasting horizons of the train load. On both configurations, the LSTM EP outperforms the LSTM, XGB and baseline models by maintaining robustness in the quality of the forecasts throughout the time horizon.

Future research should investigate the exploration of the learned representation. In particular, it would be interesting to investigate the ability of the predictive latent space to characterize abnormal situations, such as disturbances and traffic anomalies.

References

1. Toqué, F., Côme, E., El Mahrsi, M.K., Oukhellou, L.: Forecasting dynamic public transport origin-destination matrices with long-short term memory recurrent neural networks. In: IEEE 19th International Conference on Intelligent Transportation Systems (ITSC), pp. 1071–1076 (2016)
2. Zhang, J., Zheng, Y., Qi, D.: Deep spatio-temporal residual networks for citywide crowd flows prediction. In: AAAI Association for the Advancement of Artificial Intelligence, pp. 1655–1661 (2017)
3. Ziat, A., Delasalles, E., Denoyer, L., Gallinari, P.: Spatio-temporal neural networks for space-time series forecasting and relations discovery. In: IEEE International Conference on Data Mining ICDM, pp. 705–714 (2017)
4. Bengio, Y., Courville, A., Vincent, P.: Representation learning: a review and new perspectives. IEEE Trans. Pattern Anal. Mach. Intell. **35**(8), 1798–1828 (2013)
5. Ceapa, I., Smith, C., Capra, L.: Avoiding the crowds: Understanding tube station congestion patterns from trip data. In: ACM SIGKDD International Workshop on Urban Computing, pp. 134–141 (2012)
6. Tsai, T.-H., Lee, C.-K., Wei, C.-H.: Neural network based temporal feature models for short-term railway passenger demand forecasting. Expert Syst. Appl. **36**(2), 3728–3736 (2009)
7. Lathia, N., Capra, L.: Mining mobility data to minimise travellers' spending on public transport. In: 17th ACM SIGKDD International Conference on Knowledge Discovery and Data Mining, pp. 1181–1189 (2011)
8. Ke, J., Zheng, H., Yang, H., Chen, X.M.: Short-term forecasting of passenger demand under on-demand ride services: a spatio-temporal deep learning approach. Transp. Res. Part C Emerg. Technol. **85**, 591–608 (2017)
9. Ding, C., Wang, D., Ma, X., Li, H.: Predicting short-term subway ridership and prioritizing its influential factors using gradient boosting decision trees. Sustainability **8**(11), 1100 (2016)
10. Roos, J., Bonnevay, S., Gavin, G.: Short-term urban rail passenger flow forecasting: a dynamic Bayesian network approach. In: ICMLA International Conference on Machine Learning and Applications, pp. 1034–1039 (2016)
11. Heydenrijk-Ottens, L., Degeler, V., Luo, D., van Oort, N., van Lint, J.: Supervised learning: predicting passenger load in public transport. In: CASPT Conference on Advanced Systems in Public Transport and TransitData (2018)

12. Gers, F.A., Schmidhuber, J., Cummins, F.: Learning to forget: continual prediction with LSTM. ICANN International Conference on Artificial Neural Networks (1999)
13. Xingjian, S., Chen, Z., Wang, H., Yeung, D.-Y., Wong, W.-K., Woo, W.-C.: Convolutional LSTM network: a machine learning approach for precipitation nowcasting. In: NIPS Advances in Neural Information Processing Systems, pp. 802–810 (2015)
14. Cho, K., et al.: Learning phrase representations using RNN encoder-decoder for statistical machine translation. In: EMNLP Empirical Methods in Natural Language Processing, pp. 1724–1734 (2017)
15. Sutskever, I., Martens, J., Dahl, G.E., Hinton, G.E.: On the importance of initialization and momentum in deep learning. In: ICML International Conference on Machine Learning, vol. 28, no. 1139–1147, p. 5 (2013)
16. Abadi, M., et al.: Tensorflow: a system for large-scale machine learning. In: OSDI Symposium on Operating Systems Design and Implementation, pp. 265–283 (2016)
17. Chollet, F., et al.: Keras (2015)
18. Chen, T., Guestrin, C.: Xgboost: a scalable tree boosting system. In: SIGKDD International Conference on Knowledge Discovery and Data mining, pp. 785–794 (2016)

Characterization and Early Detection of Evergreen News Articles

Yiming Liao[1], Shuguang Wang[2], Eui-Hong (Sam) Han[3], Jongwuk Lee[4],
and Dongwon Lee[1]([⊠])

[1] The Pennsylvania State University, State College, USA
{yiming,dongwon}@psu.edu
[2] The Washington Post, District of Columbia, USA
shuguang.wang@washpost.com
[3] Marriott International, Bethesda, USA
mmmshan@gmail.com
[4] Sungkyunkwan University, Seoul, Korea
jongwuklee@skku.edu

Abstract. Although the majority of news articles are only viewed for days or weeks, there are a small fraction of news articles that are read across years, thus named as *evergreen* news articles. Because evergreen articles maintain a timeless quality and are consistently of interests to the public, understanding their characteristics better has huge implications for news outlets and platforms yet there are few studies that have explicitly investigated on evergreen articles. Addressing this gap, in this paper, we first propose a flexible *parameterized* definition of evergreen articles to capture their long-term high traffic patterns. Using a real dataset from the Washington Post, then, we unearth several distinctive characteristics of evergreen articles and build an early prediction model with encouraging results. Although less than 1% of news articles were identified as evergreen, our model achieves 0.961 in ROC AUC and 0.172 in PR AUC in 10-fold cross validation.

Keywords: News articles · Long-term popularity · Evergreen

1 Introduction

Articles that consistently gain traffic over time, named as *evergreen* articles, are of importance to newsrooms because they signal a topic of lasting interests to readers. News outlets and platforms want to continue to serve such articles to new readers over time in many ways–e.g., re-promoting through social media channels or linking next to regular news. Evergreen articles can also provide authoritative and reliable information during recurring events–e.g., solar eclipses or seasonal flu.

This work was finished when Eui-Hong (Sam) Han worked at the Washington Post.

U. Brefeld et al. (Eds.): ECML PKDD 2019, LNAI 11908, pp. 552–568, 2020.
https://doi.org/10.1007/978-3-030-46133-1_33

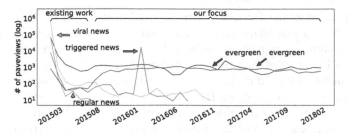

Fig. 1. Examples of news articles' pageview patterns.

Journalists at one of top-10 US daily newspapers by circulations, the **Washington Post** (referred to as *WaPo* in the following), whom we interviewed in 2018, currently rely on their memory for keeping track of evergreen news articles. Some newsroom editors in WaPo manually maintain a short list of evergreen articles for reference while others try to identify evergreens by their traffic history and manual confirmation. While the traffic pattern of evergreen articles needs to be thoroughly understood based on a time series analysis, at present, journalists do not have a good or agreed-upon definition of evergreen articles in terms of time series of traffic performance patterns, nor easy-to-use query tools to explore time series data. Furthermore, even after identifying potential candidate evergreen articles, journalists face a daunting challenge of manually reviewing a large number of candidate articles.

Even though we only interviewed journalists at WaPo for this study, we believe that the utility of evergreen articles and challenges associated with identifying them are universal across different news organizations. We believe that the characterization and automatic identification of evergreen articles, especially at early stages, are important tasks with research challenges and practical benefits.

Prior work includes popularity analysis conducted in various domains, such as news articles [9,16,21], videos [5,12], shared images [7,24] and online series [3]. As illustrated in Fig. 1, we can categorize news articles into different types per their temporal traffic patterns. For example, viral news gain significant attention when publishing, though are only viewed for a few days just like regular news, while triggered news refer to those articles that are revisited due to some occurring events. Because the lifespans of the majority of news articles are found to be short [9,21], existing studies mainly focused on the short-term popularity (i.e., *trending*) prediction. However, some noticed that certain topics of news articles have a longer life cycle [11,17], but inferring the popularity of such long-term popular contents (i.e., *evergreen*) turned out to be very difficult [19]. To our best knowledge, none of prior works have systematically examined on the characteristics of evergreen articles and their automatic identification.

To remedy this gap, this paper starts with the first research question **(RQ1)**: *how can we reliably identify evergreen news articles at a large scale?* Journalists' judgment on evergreen articles currently relies on the manual inspection on the content of articles. Due to the large number of articles being published daily, however, it is infeasible for journalists to qualitatively check the traffic data to select potential candidate articles for further manual review. Therefore, to auto-select quality evergreen candidates for journalists, we propose to define an evergreen in terms of its traffic aligned with journalists' judgment. Having obtained a highly qualified dataset of evergreen news articles using traffic-based definition, then, we investigate on **RQ2:** *what are the characteristics of evergreen news articles?* and explore possible factors correlating their long-term popularity. Instead of taking years to monitor articles' long-term traffic pattern, finally, we move to tackle **RQ3:** *can we identify evergreen news articles at early stages?* and recommend potential evergreen articles published in recent months to journalists.

In answering these research questions, we make the following main contributions:

1. To our best knowledge, this paper is the first work to explicitly study news articles' long-term popularity.
2. We formally propose a parameterized definition of an evergreen article with respect to the article's historical page view data, as validated by journalists.
3. We analyze possible factors correlating news articles' long-term popularity.
4. Based on our analysis, we build machine learning models for the early detection of evergreen news articles and report promising results from empirical experiments as well as real deployment in WaPo.

2   Related Work

Since predicting news articles' popularity has long been considered as an important research area, there are a lot of existing efforts to this problem. However, unlike other online content, such as videos and photos, the life spans of news articles tend to be shorter and their view counts often decrease faster [9,19]. As a consequence, the majority of previous studies lies in the scope of *short-term* news articles' popularity analysis. In this section, we review related works and contrast them to our work under two categories: (1) news articles' popularity prediction; (2) long-term popularity prediction for other online content.

Predicting Popularity of News. As one of the first investigations on the popularity prediction of online content, [19] discovers that news stories exhibit a much shorter lifespan than videos and usually become outdated after hours. Besides inferring future popularity by historical time series, recent works take advantage of news articles' content information in prediction [9,14]. To better understand user participation in news' propagation, researchers are also interested in predicting the number of users' comments [16,21–23], number of votes [10,16,19] and number of tweets [1]. As noted earlier, due to the short lifespan nature of news, almost all of these existing works focus on predicting news articles' popularity within a short time. The most related work to ours is [6], where they define *long shelf life* news articles–i.e., those taking at least 80 h to reach 60% of their total page views in the lifetime. Despite targeting at analyzing long shelf life news articles, however, [6] fails to consider the temporal dynamics of news articles' long-term popularity, thus cannot capture *evergreen* news articles, which consistently attract high traffic over their lifetime across many years. In this paper, taking temporal dynamics into consideration, we propose a reliable measurement to capture long-term popular news articles and perform a systematic analysis on them.

Predicting Long-Term Popularity. Although few works in news domain study long-term popularity prediction, there are some works focusing on long-term popularity prediction of other online content, such as videos [5,20] and paper publications [18]. To model popularity evolution, viewing content propagation as a stochastic process is one of the most common methods. For example, [18] adopts the reinforced Poisson process in paper citation network and [26] models the cascading in social network as a Hawkes process. For complex systems such as video platforms, where content propagation is difficult to model, researchers turn to time series approach and feature driven approach. In time series approaches, often, early popularity series are used for future predictions. For instance, [5] assigns varying weights to videos' historical popularity series via a multiple-linear regression model to predict future popularity. Due to the dependency on the historical popularity, time series approaches usually require an extended period of observations and suffer from the so-called *cold-start* problem. Feature driven approaches are proposed to address such issues. Diverse types of potential features that may impact popularity are incorporated into the prediction, such as text features [4], author features [15] and meta features [12]. Similar to videos, news articles have various traffic sources, including search engine and social media, which makes the propagation also hard to model. Hence, this paper adopts the feature driven approach with historical popularity series to predict news articles' long-term popularity.

Compared with other online content, news stories generally are more time sensitive. Only a very small fraction of published news articles exhibit long-term popularity patterns over many years, which makes the problem more challenging. Understanding why these small number of articles are consistently of interest to the public will benefit both journalists and news sites. To our best knowledge, our work is the first to systematically define evergreen articles, to examine their characteristics, and to predict them at early stages.

3 RQ1: Defining Evergreens with Traffic

This section first introduces the dataset used in the later analysis and experiments. Then, we answer *RQ1: how can we reliably identify evergreen news articles at a large scale?* by proposing a parameterized definition of evergreen news articles in terms of traffic data.

3.1 The Washington Post News Article Dataset

Our dataset contains more than 400,000 news articles published by WaPo from January 2012 to June 2017. For each article, we dumped its monthly page view

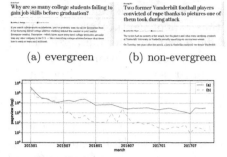

(a) evergreen   (b) non-evergreen

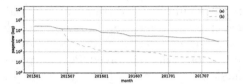

(c) two news articles' monthly page views

Fig. 2. Articles with similar initial traffic data show different long-term popularity pattern. For example, article (a) consistently receives high traffic in long term, while (b)'s monthly page views drop dramatically over time.

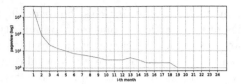

Fig. 3. Median page views of news articles published from January 2012 to December 2015

Fig. 4. Median filtered page views of two example articles from Fig. 2(c).

data from its publication date to March 2018. The *median* page view of each article's i-th month after initial publication is shown in Fig. 3. Because the distribution of news articles' page views in i-th month is highly skewed, where most page views are zero, we present median page views, instead of average page views here. Note that the articles' monthly page views in Fig. 3 drop faster than log-linear and down to around 20 at 3rd month already, which is consistent with previous observation [19] and confirms the short lifespan of news articles.

3.2 Definition of Evergreen Articles

Consulting journalists at WaPo, we set the observation time of each article up to 2 years after its first publication, which is significantly longer than the period studied in prior studies. Specifically, we denote the monthly page view series of an article in its first 24 months after publication as $PV = (pv_1, pv_2, ..., pv_{24})$, where pv_i is the page view number in i_{th} month after its publication. As shown in Fig. 3, the popularity of news articles drops dramatically and down to tens at 3rd month. Since most news articles become outdated after 3rd month, we view the first 3-month traffic data as a news article's *initial traffic* and use it to define trending articles. More specifically,

Definition 1 (Trending Article). *During the observation period, we sort news articles by their total page views in the first 3 months, $\sum_{i=1}^{3} pv_i$, in descending order and consider the first k ranked articles as* **top-k trending** *articles.*

As a motivating example to capture evergreens, in Fig. 2, we present two news articles published in January 2015 and their monthly page views till October 2017. Note that, despite receiving similar page views in the first a few months, these two articles exhibit radically different long-term traffic patterns. Article (a) maintains high traffic long after its publication and receives more than 5,000 page views a year later, while the traffic of article (b) drops dramatically to around 100 after a year. Clearly, article (a) is consistently of more interest to readers, thus fits the definition of an evergreen.

Although most news articles have a short lifespan similar to article (b) in Fig. 2 and exhibit a fast decaying traffic pattern after the initial publication, we still observe occasional peaks long after their publication. Interviewed with domain experts at WaPo, we found out these peaks mainly resulted from (1) journalists at WaPo promoted these articles; (2) these articles were associated with occurring events. These sudden traffic peaks are usually caused by stochastic events[1] and very difficult to predict. Accordingly, to better capture long-term popular news articles, we propose to use *median filters* to remove those sudden peaks. In processing page view series via median filtering with window size γ, each month contain median value in a γ-size window around the corresponding month (e.g. $\hat{pv}_i = median([pv_{i-\frac{\gamma}{2}}, ..., pv_{i+\frac{\gamma}{2}}])$). We denote the smoothed page view series as $\hat{PV} = (\hat{pv}_1, \hat{pv}_2, ..., \hat{pv}_{24})$, and present examples of smoothed traffic pattern in Fig. 4.

In addition, because of news articles' trending nature, initial traffic of news articles generally are significantly higher than the rest, up to several orders of magnitude. Therefore, we ignore the first 3-month traffic when identifying evergreen news articles. Traffic patterns of evergreen articles should not decrease too fast. To get smooth traffic series, we adopt accumulated traffic series and use the following *normalized* metric to measure a traffic pattern,

Definition 2 (Accumulated Traffic Ratio (ATR)). *Denote an article's total page view number from 4th month to i_{th} month after its publication as $N_i = \sum_{j=4}^{i} \hat{pv}_j$, where $4 \le i \le 24$. Then, an article's ATR for i_{th} month is defined as $ATR_i = \frac{N_i}{N_{24}}$, where $4 \le i \le 24$.*

When an article has constant traffic, its ATR starts low but will increase linearly. At the same time, since trending articles' traffic mostly falls in the first a few months, their ATR starts high but increases slowly. If we look at the area under ATR for an evergreen article vs. a trending article, the evergreen article will have smaller area[2]. In addition, to ensure the quality of candidate evergreen articles, journalists at WaPo require a few hundred pageviews per month for each article.

With these observations, we propose the following parameterized operational definition of an evergreen news article.

---

[1] Even though some events occur more regularly than others, such as seasonal festivals and holidays, and thus might be predictable, the impact of events on news articles' long-term popularity is beyond the scope of this paper. We leave it for future study.

[2] Because the median filtering is employed to smooth page view series, occasional traffic peaks are removed and will not affect the area.

Definition 3 ((α,β,γ)-Evergreen Article). *Ignoring the initial first 3-month traffic, we denote the monthly page view time series of an article x during the remaining observation period as $PV = (pv_4, pv_5, ..., pv_{24})$. Then, first, we use: (1) the median filter with a window size γ months to smooth the time series PV as $\hat{PV} = (\hat{pv}_4, \hat{pv}_5, ..., \hat{pv}_{24})$. If the smoothed time series $\hat{PV}$ satisfies (2) average monthly page view at least α such that: $\frac{1}{21}\sum_{i=4}^{24}\hat{pv}_i \geq \alpha$, and (3) normalized area under ATR at most β such that: $\frac{1}{21}\sum_{i=4}^{24} ATR_i \leq \beta$, then, the article x is referred to as an (α, β, γ)-**evergreen** article.*

Note that α guarantees the minimum monthly page views, β controls the decaying rate of an article's page views, and γ is used to remove the sudden page view peaks caused by unpredictable events. Although *median filters* help remove sudden traffic peaks, smoothing page view series will lose some information on series dynamics, and the loss will increase with the increase of γ. With the observation that most sudden traffic peaks only last for 1 or 2 months, a smooth window of 5-month should remove most sudden traffic peaks. As such, empirically, we set $\gamma = 5$ (months), and explore different α and β values in Sect. 3.3.

Table 1. Journalist validation with different α and β

α	250-500	500-1000	>1000
Positive Rate%	3.33%	10.00%	25.00%

(a) β=1.0, γ=5(months)

β	0.0-0.6	0.6-0.7	0.7-1.0
Positive Rate%	18.33%	11.67%	6.67%

(b) α=250, γ=5(months)

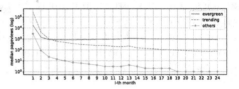

Fig. 5. Median page view comparison between evergreen and trending news articles

3.3   Tuning α and β

To guarantee each article to have at least a 2-year traffic history, we use news articles published from Jan. 2012 to Dec. 2015 for analysis, and reserve the remaining articles published from Jan. 2016 to Jun. 2017 for testing purpose. Ignoring articles with zero first 3-month page views, which are mainly caused by traffic tracking errors, we have 250,642 news articles in the training set.

To further validate the effect of α and β in capturing evergreens, we consulted domain experts at WaPo to manually label a few samples from each criterion[3]. More specifically, we sample 60 articles from each α with β=1.0 and each β with $\alpha \geq 250$, then mix them up for labeling. As expected, Table 1 shows the agreement of journalists on our definition that an article with larger α and lower

---

[3] Labeling details are similar to Newsroom Editor's Evaluation in Sect. 5 E4.

β is more likely to be evergreen. Considering the rarity of evergreen articles, our definition is confirmed to filter out most non-evergreen articles and produce highly qualified evergreen datasets. Weighing both the quality and size of the dataset, we adopt ($\alpha = 500$, $\beta = 0.6$, $\gamma = 5$) as the criterion to finally obtain 1,322 evergreens out of 250,642 new articles in WaPo, a mere 0.5% of all news articles, and use them as the base evergreen articles for further analysis and experiments.

Comparison with Trending Articles. To make a fair comparison, from January 2012 to December 2015, we select the same number of 1,322 trending articles, of which less than 10% are overlapped with evergreen articles. Then, the median page view comparison between evergreen and trending articles is shown in Fig. 5. As expected, trending articles initially attract significantly higher traffic than evergreen articles, but quickly fade away from users' attention. On the contrary, evergreen articles are consistently of interest to the public, and generally obtain almost one order of magnitude higher monthly page views than trending articles after one year of publication.

4   RQ2: Characterizing Evergreens

Having identified evergreen news articles from traffic data, we turn to *RQ2: what are the characteristics of evergreen news articles?* In this section, we focus on characterizing evergreen news articles, and examine on possible factors correlating their long-term popularity.

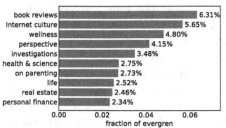

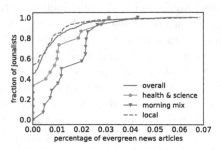

Fig. 6. Top 10 categories with the highest evergreen ratios

Fig. 7. CDF of fraction of evergreens in each journalist's publication.

Category. Previous studies show categories that are manually assigned by journalists play an important role in identifying trending articles, where some categories tend to generate more viral articles than others [9]. Therefore, we investigate here if there exists a similar relationship between categories and evergreens. Excluding categories with less than 100 articles, we sort the remaining 127 categories by their evergreen ratio (i.e., a fraction of evergreen articles over all articles

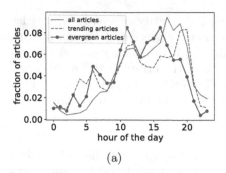 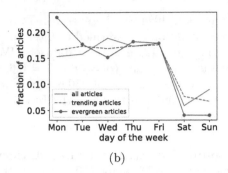

(a)   (b)

Fig. 8. (a) Fraction of articles published in each hour of the day; (b) fraction of articles published on each day of the week.

in a category) and present the top 10 categories in Fig. 6. Unsurprisingly, *book reviews*, *perspective* and *investigations* are less time sensitive and convey higher proportion of evergreen articles. In addition, people pay continuous attention to Internet culture, health and lifestyle related topics. Among categories conveying fewer evergreen articles, besides *politics* and *sports*, *movies* and *music* are less intuitive ones, where only 1 or 2 articles out of thousands meet our criterion. One possible explanation is, though movies and music are less time-sensitive and so do their reviews, they are more likely to be affected by popular culture.

Topic. Although categories are manually assigned by editors and describe the main genres of articles, we found the manually assigned categories are both noisy and coarse-grained. For example, some categories such as *perspective* and *local* are broad and could include articles related to education and real estate, which are more likely to be evergreen than others in the same category. Therefore, to extract more fine-grained topics and better understand articles in terms of content, we utilize topic modeling techniques. More specifically, we train a 1,000-topic noun only topic model using the LightLDA [13,25], and compare topic distributions between evergreen and non-evergreen articles. Based on article contents, *wellness, health, housing, research studies* and *parenting* are the most sustainable and lasting topics, which are consistent with a few top evergreen categories. When digging into other top categories, we discover that articles about history, family and relationship/friend are more likely to be evergreen in *book reviews*, while evergreen articles in *Internet culture* talk more about diseases, research studies, relationship/friend and parenting than non-evergreen. In addition, history, education, parenting and family are among the most evergreen topics in *perspectives*. As expected, article contents go beyond categories and provide more informative topics, indicating that categories are not enough and we should consider article contents in evergreen detection.

Publication Time. Next, we explore the relationship between news articles' long-term popularity and their publication time. Figure 8 shows the fraction of articles published in each hour of the day and on each day of the week. Interestingly, trending articles are more evenly distributed across the hours and days, even well represented at odd times such as those from midnight to 8 am or over weekends. Although most news articles are published in the afternoon, evergreen news articles are mostly published in the middle of the day. More interestingly, few evergreen news articles are published on weekends, while Monday conveys the most evergreen articles. Unlike trending articles, which are time sensitive, evergreen articles are less urgent, so journalists may spend more time on editing or polishing over the weekends and publish them on Monday. Since the distribution of evergreen news articles' publication times does show distinctly different patterns from regular articles, we include publication times of articles as an important feature in learning.

Journalist. "Who writes an article" is another important meta data to consider. In this section, we examine the role of journalists on articles' long-term popularity. There are over 12,000 journalists in total in our dataset. After removing the journalists who have written less than 100 articles, we have 479 journalists who have written a total of 187,769 articles. Consistent with the ratio of the entire dataset, it turns out that 870 articles among 187,769 articles (i.e., 0.5%) are (α, β, γ)-evergreen articles. Around 50% of the journalists who wrote more than 100 articles published at least one evergreen news article. In Fig. 7, we present cumulative distribution function (CDF) of fraction of evergreen news articles in each journalist's publication. For each fraction X, CDF shows the proportion of journalists with the fraction of evergreen publication less than or equal to X. This figure illustrates that, although most journalists have written a small proportion of evergreen news articles, there are indeed a few journalists good at publishing long-term popular news articles. In order to exclude the possible effect of category on journalists' publication, we select a few categories, including *health & science, morning mix* and *local,* and check CDF of fraction of evergreens per journalist in exactly the same category[4]. As shown in Fig. 7, even for articles in the same categories, we still observe similar CDF of percentage of evergreen articles per journalist, indicating that, besides categories, writing styles, such as wordings and article structures, should also matter in evergreen production. As such, journalist information can give some hints on the early detection of evergreens.

5   RQ3: Predicting Evergreens Early

Taking insights from last section, we intend to answer *RQ3: can we predict evergreen articles at an early stage?* and attempt to build an accurate machine learning model to unearth early a small fraction of evergreen articles among many non-evergreen articles. To better validate our learned model, we conduct the following experiments:

---

[4] Although each journalist usually publishes in various categories, here we only consider journalists' articles in each selected category and exclude journalists having < 100 articles in each selected category.

E1. We first show the results of stratified 10-fold cross validation on the training set (Jan. 2012–Dec. 2015).

E2. Using the best setting from 10-fold cross validation, then, we train a model on the training set (Jan. 2012–Dec. 2015) and test the model on the new articles published later (Jan. 2016–Apr. 2016).

E3. In addition to classification measurements, we present temporal page view patterns of predicted evergreen news articles published in subsequent months (Jan. 2016–Dec. 2016).

E4. Finally, we consult newsroom editors in WaPo to manually check and validate the quality of predicted evergreen articles.

Set-Up. For a given news article, after observing its initial traffic in the first three months, we predict whether it will be an evergreen or ephemeral story. Based on the analysis in the last section, we propose to exploit three feature sets in our model as follows:

1. **Traffic features**: As indicated in prior works, the degree of popularity at the early stages are strongly related to that of future popularity. Thus, we extract the traffic features from the first 3-month traffic data, including the number of monthly page views, the difference of page views of two consecutive months, and the decreasing rate between two consecutive months. Note that, when defining evergreen news articles, we ignored their first 3-month page views and labeled articles only by their later popularity patterns.

2. **Content features**: Topic analysis demonstrates that content features, including keywords and topics, are also important clues in detecting evergreens. Therefore, we exploit word embedding and bag-of-words trick to extract content features from news articles. More specifically, we train an unsupervised FastText [2] model on all news articles with 200-dimension feature vectors.

3. **Meta features**: Based on the observations in the last section, we selectively include meta features such as news articles' category, publication time, and journalist information. There are two challenges to encode categories and journalists information as features: (1) both categories and journalists are numerous in our dataset (e.g. our dataset contain more than 120,000 journalists), *one-hot encoding* (i.e., encoding each category or journalist as an isolate feature dimension) will easily cause overfitting; (2) categorical values of category and journalist are not fixed and vary with time, for example, many journalists come and go. To tackle these issues and obtain more compact meta features for each article, we propose a simple but effective approach to encode category and journalist information: use the average FastText embedding of all prior published articles in the same category or by the same journalist as its meta feature. As a result, similar categories are close to each other in our category feature space. For example, *opinion* is close to *postpartisan*, while *lifestyle* is close to *entertainment*. Likewise, journalists with similar writing styles are close to one another. Finally, we include publication hour of the day and day of the week as categorical features.

Evaluation Metrics. As described in the Sect. 3.3, we use ($\alpha = 500$, $\beta = 0.6$, $\gamma = 5$) as the criterion that yields 1,322 articles out of the total 250,642 news articles as evergreen news articles. Note that this is a binary classification problem with a significantly skewed class distribution ratio of 0.5 : 99.5. Because of the highly imbalanced dataset, we choose to compare models with both Area Under Receiver Operating Characteristic Curve (ROC AUC) and Area Under Precision Recall Curve (P-R AUC), where random baselines are 0.5 and 0.005 respectively.

Moreover, in real settings, journalists expect top-K potential evergreen candidates and want to manually review them to determine true evergreens. Therefore, Precision@K is also provided to measure the performance of top-K predictions. Since only 0.5% articles meet our criterion, the perfect results of Precision@K will be 1.0 when K $\leq$ 0.5%. We set K to 0.1%, 0.2%, 0.5% and 1.0%. Considering averagely there are around 5,000 articles per month, these percentages correspond to top 5, 10, 25 and 50 predictions for each month respectively.

We experimented with three learning models–i.e., Logistic Regression, Random Forest, and Gradient Boost Decision Tree (GBDT)–using all features via stratified 10-fold cross validation. As the model learned using LightGBM package [8] consistently performed the best, in the following experiments, we only report the prediction results using the GBDT as the main learning model.

Table 2. 10-fold cross validation

Metric	Initial traffic	Content feature	Traffic + meta	Traffic + content	Content + meta	Traffic + content + meta
Precision@0.1%	0.1240	0.1440	0.2720	0.2840	0.2120	**0.3480**
Precision@0.2%	0.1400	0.1320	0.2560	0.2780	0.1800	**0.2900**
Precision@0.5%	0.1296	0.1040	0.1912	0.2312	0.1304	**0.2360**
Precision@1.0%	0.0940	0.0892	0.1580	0.1868	0.1032	**0.1952**
ROC AUC (0.5000)	0.9302	0.8752	0.9485	0.9601	0.8851	**0.9608**
P-R AUC (~0.005)	0.0763	0.0533	0.1292	0.1606	0.0705	**0.1718**

E1. Cross Validation. The stratified 10-fold cross validation results of different feature combinations are conducted on the exactly same 10 folds and given in Table 2. The results show that first, using only the first 3-month page view series, it is difficult to identify evergreen news articles. However, adding content and meta features gives a significant improvement on all metrics. When utilizing all features, we achieve the best performance, where the P-R AUC improves from 0.0763 to 0.1718 and Precision@0.5% increases from 0.1296 to 0.2360. More interestingly, pre-publication prediction, which only considers content and meta features, achieves very promising results of having 0.1304 accuracy in top-0.5% prediction. Moreover, when adding traffic features, we observe the boosted improvements in P-R AUC and Precision@K, implying that news article's initial traffic and contents contribute to its long-term popularity in different aspects and both of them are indispensable in the early prediction of evergreens. A possible explanation is that news articles with high initial traffic enjoy high visibility, thus evergreen articles in this group are more likely to be shared or archived by users. For evergreen articles with limited initial traffic, though lacking enough visibility to users in the beginning, because of their timeless quality and interesting topics, they still gain high traffic in the long term via other channels like search engine or re-promotion.

Table 3. Time-Split experiment

Prec@0.1%	Prec@0.2%	Prec@0.5%	Prec@1.0%	ROC AUC	P-R AUC
0.2941	0.2464	0.2326	0.1884	0.9399	0.1534

E2. Time-Split Classification. In real applications, early detection models aim to predict evergreen articles from newly published news articles. Therefore, this time-split experiment is designed to examine how general a learned model is across time. Using the best setting from 10-fold cross validation, we *train* a model on the articles published between Jan. 2012 and Dec. 2015 and *test* it on articles published from Jan. 2016 to Apr. 2016. In the test set, 254 articles ($\sim$0.7%) out of 34,509 are identified as *(500, 0.6, 5)-evergreen*. The result is presented in Table 3. Comparable with 10-fold cross-validation, our model with all of traffic, content, and meta features achieves 0.2941 top-0.1% accuracy and 0.1534 P-R AUC. Note that, since data distribution often varies over time, a time-split experiment is a more challenging setting than cross-validation. Even for evergreen news articles, popularity still varies over time. Thus, the performance gap between cross validation and time-split experiment is due to the changes in data distributions.

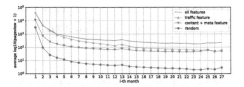

Fig. 9. Page view patterns of top predicted evergreen articles under different feature groups

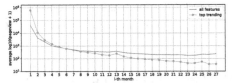

Fig. 10. Page view pattern comparison between top predicted evergreen articles with top trending articles

E3. Time-Split Traffic Evaluation. Because classification measurements are too strict to distinguish news articles with slightly different temporal patterns, we propose to examine temporal page view trajectories of predicted evergreen news articles, which gives more intuition on articles' long-term popularity and serves as more valuable indicators in production. Similar to E2, we train a model on the articles published from Jan. 2012 to Dec. 2015, predict evergreen news articles in each month from Jan. 2016 to Dec. 2016 and monitor their page view trajectories from the publication month till Mar. 2018.

Aimed at comparing different feature groups, we present the traffic patterns of top predicted evergreen articles with different feature groups in Fig. 9. More specifically, for each model, news articles are ranked by the predicted probabilities among their publication month, and we choose the top 100 ranked articles in each month as potential evergreen articles. Consequently, 1,200 articles out of ~100,000 in total are selected in each group. Overall, news articles selected from all feature groups exhibit a long-term popularity pattern, while combining all features obtains the highest monthly page views in the long run. For each month starting from 4th month, we conduct t-test and find that articles predicted with all features attract significantly more page views than other article groups at a p-value < 0.0001. Additionally, although articles predicted with traffic features show dramatically higher initial traffic, they display similar page view trajectories to articles predicted with pre-publication features long after publication.

As shown in Fig. 5, trending news articles, which enjoy significantly higher visibility when just being published, display much higher popularity than most news articles, and thereby should be a strong baseline in long-term popularity prediction. Therefore, in Fig. 10, we present page view pattern comparison between top predicted evergreen articles and top trending articles. Top trending articles consist of the top 100 articles with highest initial traffic in each month. As expected, top trending articles receive much higher traffic in the first few months, while top predicted evergreen articles demonstrate a more stable traffic pattern and consistently gain more page views one year later. For each month starting from 9th month, articles predicted with all features attract significantly more page views than trending articles at a p-value < 0.0001 under t-test.

E4. Newsroom Editor's Evaluation. In order to help newsroom editors at WaPo, we plan to deploy the early detection model and recommend recently published potential evergreen news articles to them. Although we have presented promising performances in classification experiments and indeed observed long-term popularity patterns of predicted evergreens in the time-split evaluation, quality check by journalists themselves is indispensable before actual deployment. Therefore, we include newsroom editors' evaluation in this section, presenting both pre-deployment evaluation and product evaluation.

Identifying evergreen news articles at early stages is challenging to both machines as well as journalists. Predicting whether a news article will be long-term popular requires domain expertise in several areas, including news editing, social media promotion, and search engine optimization (SEO). As only a few domain experts are qualified for this task, we consult an audience development team in WaPo, who is responsible for optimizing news articles and conducting social promotions, to manually check the quality of evergreen predictions in recent months. More specifically, there are three major use cases for evergreen news articles at present in the newsroom:

1. Regularly re-promote evergreens (e.g. parenting guide) on social media.
2. Worth updating. Readers may constantly go over some evergreen news articles (e.g. mass shooting statistics) through web favorites or search engines. To ensure readers get the most recent information, editors should keep updating those articles with new content at times.
3. Embedded as linking URLs to related context (e.g. disease information) and references when editing new articles, which could both motivate readers to be more engaged on the website and serve as SEO purpose.

Based on these three use cases, for each news article in the evaluation, if its value is confirmed in any use case, it will be labeled as a true evergreen.

E4.1. Pre-deployment Evaluation. In the evaluation, for each month from Jan. 2017 to Jun. 2017, we recommended the top 10 potential evergreen news articles predicted by our model to the team at WaPo. Through manually reviewing these 60 news articles, 65% of predictions, 39 in total, were labeled as true evergreens. Considering that only tens of news articles out of thousands published per month could be evergreen articles, 65% top-10 accuracy in monthly prediction is encouraging and indicates that our model is practical enough to be deployed in production.

E4.2. Product Evaluation. Based on the promising results from pre-deployment evaluation, we deployed the evergreen prediction system at WaPo. The system regularly updates evergreen prediction model and sends out weekly recommendations to the newsroom. On every Monday, editors receive the top 5 potential evergreens from articles published during last week and provide feedback in Slack. An example of weekly recommendation is shown in Fig. 11, where 3 out of 5 articles are verified as true evergreens. The system was deployed at WaPo in July 2018 and achieved ~43% accuracy in the weekly recommendation.

More importantly, Both 65% of top-10 accuracy in monthly prediction and 43% of top-5 accuracy in weekly prediction are achieved without any human labels, validating that our parameterized definition of evergreen is reasonable and can produce highly qualified evergreen datasets.

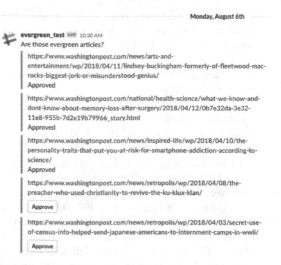

Fig. 11. An example of weekly recommendation

6 Conclusion

This paper presents a study on characterizing and early detecting evergreen news articles. Firstly, taking temporal dynamics into consideration, we proposed a parameterized definition to capture evergreen news articles, which is validated by journalists (**RQ1**). Next, we conducted a quantitative analysis to shed light on evergreen news articles' long-term popularity, and discovered that evergreen articles are closely correlated with several features such as categories, topics, publication time, and journalists (**RQ2**). Finally, based on the insights from our analysis, we built early prediction models on evergreen identification (**RQ3**). Throughout extensive experiments, we have validated that our models gain promising results in early detection of evergreen news articles, and shown that the predicted evergreen news articles indeed exhibit a long-term high traffic pattern. More importantly, verified by journalists, our proposed model achieves encouraging performance in production.

Acknowledgments. We truly appreciate Everdeen Mason, Sophie Ho, Greg Barber and their journalist team at the Washington Post for the valuable feedback and support in both problem formulation and manual evaluation.

References

1. Bandari, R., Asur, S., Huberman, B.A.: The pulse of news in social media: forecasting popularity. In: ICWSM, pp. 26–33 (2012)
2. Bojanowski, P., Grave, E., Joulin, A., Mikolov, T.: Enriching word vectors with subword information. TACL **5**, 135–146 (2017)
3. Chang, B., Zhu, H., Ge, Y., Chen, E., Xiong, H., Tan, C.: Predicting the popularity of online serials with autoregressive models. In: CIKM, pp. 1339–1348. ACM (2014)
4. Cheng, J., Adamic, L., Dow, P.A., Kleinberg, J.M., Leskovec, J.: Can cascades be predicted? In: WWW, pp. 925–936. ACM (2014)
5. Pinto, H., Almeida, J.M., Gonçalves, M.A.: Using early view patterns to predict the popularity of youtube videos. In: WSDM, pp. 365–374. ACM (2013)

6. Elhenfnawy, W., et al.: What differentiates news articles with short and long shelf lives? a case study on news articles at bloomberg. com. In: BDCloud-SocialCom-SustainCom, pp. 131–136. IEEE (2016)
7. Gelli, F., Uricchio, T., Bertini, M., Del Bimbo, A., Chang, S.F.: Image popularity prediction in social media using sentiment and context features. In: MM, pp. 907–910. ACM (2015)
8. Ke, G., et al.: Lightgbm: a highly efficient gradient boosting decision tree. In: NIPS, pp. 3149–3157 (2017)
9. Keneshloo, Y., Wang, S., Han, E.H., Ramakrishnan, N.: Predicting the popularity of news articles. In: SDM, pp. 441–449. SIAM (2016)
10. Lerman, K., Hogg, T.: Using a model of social dynamics to predict popularity of news. In: WWW, pp. 621–630. ACM (2010)
11. Leskovec, J., Backstrom, L., Kleinberg, J.: Meme-tracking and the dynamics of the news cycle. In: SIGKDD, pp. 497–506. ACM (2009)
12. Ma, C., Yan, Z., Chen, C.W.: LARM: a lifetime aware regression model for predicting youtube video popularity. In: CIKM, pp. 467–476. ACM (2017)
13. Martin, F., Johnson, M.: More efficient topic modelling through a noun only approach. In: ALTA Workshop, pp. 111–115 (2015)
14. Marujo, L., Bugalho, M., Neto, J.P.d.S., Gershman, A., Carbonell, J.: Hourly traffic prediction of news stories. arXiv preprint arXiv:1306.4608 (2013)
15. Mishra, S., Rizoiu, M.A., Xie, L.: Feature driven and point process approaches for popularity prediction. In: CIKM, pp. 1069–1078. ACM (2016)
16. Rizos, G., Papadopoulos, S., Kompatsiaris, Y.: Predicting news popularity by mining online discussions. In: WWW, pp. 737–742. ACM (2016)
17. Setty, V., Anand, A., Mishra, A., Anand, A.: Modeling event importance for ranking daily news events. In: WSDM, pp. 231–240. ACM (2017)
18. Shen, H.W., Wang, D., Song, C., Barabási, A.L.: Modeling and predicting popularity dynamics via reinforced poisson processes. In: AAAI, pp. 291–297 (2014)
19. Szabo, G., Huberman, B.A.: Predicting the popularity of online content. Commun. ACM 53(8), 80–88 (2010)
20. Tan, Z., Wang, Y., Zhang, Y., Zhou, J.: A novel time series approach for predicting the long-term popularity of online videos. IEEE Trans. Broadcast. 62(2), 436–445 (2016)
21. Tatar, A., Antoniadis, P., Amorim, M.D., Fdida, S.: From popularity prediction to ranking online news. Soc. Netw. Anal. Min. 4(1), 1–12 (2014). https://doi.org/10.1007/s13278-014-0174-8
22. Tatar, A., Leguay, J., Antoniadis, P., Limbourg, A., de Amorim, M.D., Fdida, S.: Predicting the popularity of online articles based on user comments. In: WIMS, p. 67. ACM (2011)
23. Tsagkias, M., Weerkamp, W., De Rijke, M.: Predicting the volume of comments on online news stories. In: CIKM, pp. 1765–1768. ACM (2009)
24. Wu, B., Mei, T., Cheng, W.H., Zhang, Y., et al.: Unfolding temporal dynamics: predicting social media popularity using multi-scale temporal decomposition. In: AAAI, pp. 272–278 (2016)
25. Yuan, J., et al..: LightLDA: big topic models on modest computer clusters. In: WWW, pp. 1351–1361. ACM (2015)
26. Zhao, Q., Erdogdu, M.A., He, H.Y., Rajaraman, A., Leskovec, J.: SEISMIC: a self-exciting point process model for predicting tweet popularity. In: SIGKDD, pp. 1513–1522. ACM (2015)

Player Vectors: Characterizing Soccer Players' Playing Style from Match Event Streams

Tom Decroos[✉] and Jesse Davis

Department of Computer Science, KU Leuven, Leuven, Belgium
{tom.decroos,jesse.davis}@cs.kuleuven.be

Abstract. Transfer fees for soccer players are at an all-time high. To make the most of their budget, soccer clubs need to understand the type of players they have and the type of players that are on the market. Current insights in the playing style of players are mostly based on the opinions of human soccer experts such as trainers and scouts. Unfortunately, their opinions are inherently subjective and thus prone to faults. In this paper, we characterize the playing style of a player in a more rigorous, objective and data-driven manner. We characterize the playing style of a player using a so-called 'player vector' that can be interpreted both by human experts and machine learning systems. We demonstrate the validity of our approach by retrieving player identities from anonymized event stream data and present a number of use cases related to scouting and monitoring player development in top European competitions.

1 Introduction

Data analysis is becoming increasingly important in many professional sports [19]. Sports clubs are analyzing huge amounts of data in order to gain a competitive advantage over their opposition. Soccer has been a relative late comer to this trend. The classic statistics about a soccer match (e.g., that appear in boxscores or are often reported on television) tend to be raw counts or fractions, such as the ball possession percentage, number of shots on target or pass success percentage. While interesting, these statistics do not give a complete picture of the match. Moreover they can sometimes obscure important information. For example, the raw number of shots a player took does not tell us about the relative difficulty or quality of the attempts. Recently, research has focused on approaches that allow for a deeper and more insightful analysis of soccer players [4]. One well-known example is the expected goals statistic [9], which is now discussed on the popular soccer talk show *Match of the Day* on BBC One.

A reoccurring concept when discussing soccer is a player's style of play. While both Messi and Ronaldo are great players, each one approaches the game in a different way. Fans often form preferences for players based on his perceived style. From a practical point of view, characterizing playing style is important for professional clubs for three following reasons:

© Springer Nature Switzerland AG 2020
U. Brefeld et al. (Eds.): ECML PKDD 2019, LNAI 11908, pp. 569–584, 2020.
https://doi.org/10.1007/978-3-030-46133-1_34

Scouting. Soccer clubs can search the market more intelligently if they know the type of player they are looking for and how well prospective targets match that type. Transfers are expensive, and clubs are always looking for bargains and ways to mitigate risks in player recruitment.

Monitoring Player Development. The coach can inspect the playing style of a player in a human-interpretable player vector. If the player vector matches the expectations of the coach, then the coach can monitor that this player vector remains stable and unchanged. If the player vector does not match the expectations of the coach, then he can give his player some pointers and afterwards monitor how well the player is implementing the advice.

Match Preparation. Understanding the playing style of your opponent can offer certain tactical advantages. The defenders of a team will wish to know what type of attackers they are up against. Similarly, the attackers will be interested in the playing style of the defenders they need to score against.

In this paper, we attempt to characterize a player's playing style in an objective and data-driven manner based on analyzing event stream or play-by-play match data. While playing style is a somewhat subjective concept, our working definition is that a playing style manifests itself as where on the pitch a player tends to perform specific actions with the ball. Our goal is to summarize this playing style in a fixed-length player vector. Characterizing playing style from event stream data is challenging as we have to reason about spatial locations, discrete actions, and a variable number of events. We cope with these challenges by overlaying a grid on the pitch and counting how often each player performs a specific action in a given location. Then, to reduce the dimensionality we perform non-negative matrix factorization. We repeat this for several types of actions. Finally, we concatenate together a player's compressed vectors for each action type to construct his player vector. To evaluate the quality of our player vectors, we propose a retrieval task. Given anonymous event data for a player, we show that we can accurately predict the player's true identify. Moreover, we show how to interpret player vectors and present several qualitative use-cases related to scouting and monitoring player development.

2 Data and Challenges

In this section, we first describe our data set and then highlight a number of data science challenges encountered when analyzing this data.

2.1 Event Stream Data

Event stream data annotates the time and locations of specific events (e.g., passes, shots, dribbles) that occur in a match. This type of data is commercially available from providers such as Opta, WyScout, and STATS. Our data set consists of event stream data from 9155 matches in the five major soccer competitions in Europe: the English Premier League, the German Bundesliga, the Spanish Primera Division, the Italian Serie A and the French Ligue Un. Our data spans almost all matches between the 2012/2013 and 2016/2017 seasons.

Our match event stream data is encoded in the SPADL format [7], which is a format for soccer match event stream data specifically designed to enable automated data analysis. Some of its benefits are that (1) it focuses exclusively on physical on-the-ball actions (e.g., events such as yellow cards and weather changes are ignored), (2) it works with fixed attributes rather than optional information snippets (which are notoriously difficult to deal with in an automated analysis pipeline), and (3) it unifies event stream data from different providers into a common format. Each match is represented as a sequence of roughly 1650 player actions. Each action contains (among others) the following five attributes:

Type: The type of action (e.g., shot, tackle, pass),
Player: The player who performed the action,
Team: The player's team,
StartLoc: The (x,y) location where the action started,
EndLoc: The (x,y) location where the action ended.

2.2 Data Science Challenges

Analyzing event stream data from soccer matches is challenging as soccer is a highly dynamic game with many movements and interactions among players across time and space. Concretely, the challenges include the following:

Challenge 1: Characterizing playing style involves coping with the spatial component of the data, as the location where an action happens is important. However, there is very little exact repetition in event data. That is, the same player rarely performs the same action in the same location. Characterizing playing style therefore requires us to intelligently generalize over the location of actions.
Challenge 2: Actions have both discrete (e.g., Type, Player, Team) and continuous (e.g., StartLoc, EndLoc) attributes. Most machine learning and data mining techniques prefer to work on either discrete or continuous features exclusively and rarely work well on a mix of both.
Challenge 3: Most standard machine learning techniques require fixed-size feature vectors as their input and cannot natively handle a sequence or set of data points of varying size.
Challenge 4: An important aspect of a player's playing style is how he behaves off the ball (e.g., how much does he run and work to regain the ball?). However, this aspect is almost impossible to measure as action sequence data only describes on-the-ball actions.

3 How to Define and Evaluate Playing Style

Characterizing a soccer player's playing style requires reaching a consensus on what constitutes a playing style. While this is an inherently subjective concept, our hypothesis is that a player's playing style arises from the interplay between his skills and the tactics employed by the team. Hence, a style of play will manifest itself in the player's behavior during the game.

Definition 1 (Playing style). *A player's playing style can be characterized by his preferred area(s) on the field to occupy and which actions he tends to perform in each of these locations.*

In our work, we also make the following two assumptions.

Assumption 1: Most players exhibit differences in playing style and can be differentiated on this. While it is possible that two players exhibit such a similar playing style that they cannot be discerned from each other, this is not the case for most pairs of players.

Assumption 2: A player's playing style will not drastically change in a short period of time. That is, in a sequence of consecutive games in a season, each player will exhibit the same playing style. This seems justifiable for two reasons. First, while players' skills and playing style evolve over the course of their career, these changes occur gradually rather than abruptly. Second, while the tenure of managers, who influence tactics, do not tend to be overly long in professional soccer, the majority of teams in a league do not change manager mid season.

Based on this definition and these assumptions, any system that successfully characterizes playing style from match event stream data can be used to retrieve players from anonymized event stream data. This player retrieval task can be more formally defined as follows:

Given: Anonymized event stream data describing actions of player p
Retrieve: The identity of player p

The quality of a system that characterizes playing style can be evaluated by its performance on this player retrieval task, as this task measures how well a system can recognize players and differentiate between them purely based on their actions on the field.

In the next section, we describe our system for solving this task. In addition to characterizing each player's playing style, our system also allows human analysts to interpret our representation of playing style and to automatically compare players' playing style on their similarity.

4   Building Player Vectors

In this section we address the following task:

Given: Event stream data describing actions of player p.
Build: A fixed-size player vector that characterizes player p's playing style and can be interpreted both by human analysts and machine learning systems.

At a high-level, our approach works as follows. First, we select relevant action types for characterizing playing style.

Second, for each player p and relevant action type t, we overlay a grid on the field and count how many times player p performed actions of type t in each grid cell. This transform helps address the first three challenges listed in Sect. 2 because it (1) captures the spatial component, (2) fuses discrete (action type) with continuous (location) features in a unified representation, and (3) converts a variable length set of actions into to a fixed size. We end up with one matrix per player per action type.

Third, we reshape each matrix into a vector and group it together with all other vectors of the same action type to form new, bigger matrices per action type detailing all players' playing style for that specific action type. We then perform non-negative matrix factorization (NMF) to reduce the dimensionality of these matrices. NMF automatically clusters together similar grid cells into a coherent group, which is more informative and intuitive (e.g., for scouting) than looking at individual grid cells where a player operates.

Finally, we construct a player vector for each player by concatenating his compressed vectors of each action type. We also show how to compute the similarity of player vectors (to be used in machine learning algorithms such as clustering and nearest neighbors).

4.1   Selecting Relevant Action Types

Our hypothesis is that the type and location of the actions a player performs are informative of that player's playing style. Our event data contains 19 different types of actions. However, we only consider offensive actions that are performed during open play for two reasons.

First, defense is primarily about positioning, and often this involves picking a position to prevent certain actions from occuring. Hence, by definition, characterizing defensive style requires off-the-ball location data, which we do not have access to. Furthermore, most on-the-ball defensive actions (e.g. tackles, clearances) are usually performed out of necessity rather than because they are indicative of a player's playing style. One effect of this criterion is that all keeper-specific actions are automatically ignored.

Second, the open play criteria means we exclude set piece actions (e.g., free-kicks and throw-ins) from our analysis. Teams typically have set-piece specialists (e.g., for free kicks). Similarly, actions like throw-ins are often performed by a pre-defined position (e.g., fullbacks or wingers), so this is more an artefact of position than style. Moreover, these actions can serve as quasi "primary keys" in the player retrieval task, making the task a less effective proxy for characterizing playing style. While we believe analyzing set pieces is extremely interesting and important, a proper study of these actions would require a different type of analysis than we perform in this paper.

When applying these two criteria, the remaining relevant action types are passes, dribbles, crosses, and shots (Table 1).

Table 1. Each action type must fit two criteria to be considered relevant for characterizing playing style: it must be offensive and it must occur during open play. The relevant action type are passes, dribbles, crosses, and shots.

Action type	Frequency	Offensive	Open play
pass	53.1%	✓	✓
dribble	25.2%	✓	✓
clearance	3.8%		✓
throw_in	2.8%	✓	
interception	2.6%		✓
tackle	2.3%		✓
cross	1.8%	✓	✓
shot	1.5%	✓	✓
bad_touch	1.4%		✓
foul	1.3%		✓
freekick_short	1.3%	✓	
keeper_pick_up	0.8%		✓
keeper_save	0.8%		✓
corner_crossed	0.6%	✓	
freekick_crossed	0.2%	✓	
keeper_claim	0.2%		✓
corner_short	0.1%	✓	
shot_freekick	0.1%	✓	
keeper_punch	0.1%		✓

4.2   Constructing Heatmaps

A heatmap is a summary of the locations where player p performs actions of type t. For each player and action type, we execute the following three steps.

(1) **Counting:** We overlay a grid of size $m \times n$ on the soccer field. Next, we select all of player p's actions of type t in our data set. Per grid cell X_{ij}, we count the number of actions that started in that cell. Hence, we have transformed a variable-size set of actions to a fixed-size matrix $X \in \mathbb{N}^{m \times n}$ containing the raw counts per cell.

(2) **Normalizing:** Two players p_1 and p_2 can have an identical playing style, but if player p_1 played more minutes than player p_2, then player p_1's matrix X will contain higher raw counts than the matrix of player p_2. To combat this, we normalize X such that each cell contains its count if p had played 90 min (1 game). For example, if player p played 1600 min in total in our data set, then we construct the normalized matrix $X' = \frac{90}{1600} X$.

(3) **Smoothing:** We would expect some spatial coherence, or smoothness, in the locations where the actions were performed. However, this coherence can

be disrupted by laying a high granularity grid (i.e., high values for parameters m and n) over the pitch as the boundaries between grid cells are abrupt and somewhat arbitrary. Hence, the counts for nearby cells may exhibit more variance than they should. To promote smoothness in the counts of nearby cells, a Gaussian blur is applied to matrix X'. A Gaussian blur is a standard image processing technique [21] that involves convolving X' with a Gaussian function. Specifically, the value of each cell in X' is replaced by a weighted average of itself and its neighborhood, leading to the blurred matrix $X'' \in \mathbb{R}_+^{m \times n}$.

X'' is the heatmap detailing where player p performs actions of type t (Fig. 1b). For some action types, e.g., passes, we are not just interested in their start locations, but also in their end locations. For these action types, we construct separate heatmaps X''_{start} and X''_{end} using respectively the start and end locations of the actions in the counting step.

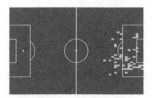 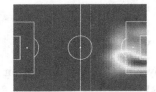 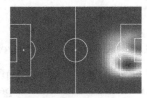

(a) The raw shot heatmap obtained by overlaying a grid and counting shot locations.

(b) The smoothed shot heatmap obtained after normalizing and smoothing the raw shot heatmap.

(c) The same shot heatmap reconstructed from a length-4 feature vector.

Fig. 1. Example of a heatmap detailing the shot playing style of Riyad Mahrez, winger at Leicester City in the 2016/2017 season.

4.3   Compressing Heatmaps to Vectors

The goal is to capture the information available in a heatmap (i.e., the locations where a player p performs actions of type t) in a small vector. We detail our approach for compressing heatmaps to vectors per action type t.

First, we reshape each heatmap X'' to a 1-dimensional vector x of length mn. In the case of action types where we are interested in both the start and end location, we reshape the heatmaps X''_{start} and X''_{end} to vectors x_{start} and x_{end} and concatenate them in a single 1-dimensional vector x of length $2\,mn$. More generally, let $s = 1$ if we are only interested in the start location of an action type and $s = 2$ if we are interested in both the start and end location of an action type. The length of x is then smn.

We then construct the matrix $M = [x_0 x_1 \dots x_l]$ that contains as columns the reshaped heatmaps of all l players in our data set for action type t. Next, we compress matrix M by applying non-negative matrix factorization (NMF), which is a form of principal component analysis where the resulting components contain only positive numbers. This results in two matrices W and H such that:

$$M \approx WH, \tag{1}$$

where $M \in \mathbb{R}_+^{smn \times l}$, $W \in \mathbb{R}_+^{smn \times k}$, and $H \in \mathbb{R}_+^{k \times l}$. Here, k is a user-defined parameter that refers to the number of principal components for action type t.

The columns of W are the principal components that represent basic spatial groups of action type t. These principal components can be visualized as heatmaps (Fig. 2). The rows of H are the small vectors that are the compressed versions of the heatmaps in M. In other words, if the reshaped heatmap x was the i-th column in matrix M, then the i-th row of H is its compressed vector. Each compressed vector can be visualized by multiplying it with the principal component matrix W. The result of this multiplication is a heatmap similar to the original, but reconstructed from only k features (Fig. 1). In addition, each feature in a compressed vector is interpretable in the sense that its numeric value quantifies how often the player executes actions of type t with locations in the spatial group of a specific principal component.

4.4 Assembling Player Vectors

The player vector v of a player p is the concatenation of his compressed vectors for the relevant action types: passes, dribbles, crosses, and shots. The total length of a player vector v is equal to $k_{pass} + k_{dribble} + k_{cross} + k_{shot}$ where k_t is the number of principal components chosen to compress heatmaps of action type t. In this paper, we set k_t as the minimal number of components needed to explain 70% of the variance in the heatmaps of action type t. This parameter setting was empirically found to work well because of the high variability of players' positions in their actions (see Challenge 1 in Sect. 2). Ignoring 30% of the variance allows us to summarize a player's playstyle only by his dominant regions on the field rather than model every position on the field he ever occupied. This design choice lead us to use 4 shot components, 4 cross components, 5 dribble components, and 5 pass components, adding up to form length-18 player vectors.

We can now quantify two players' playing style similarity by computing the Manhattan distance between their player vectors. Manhattan distance works well because the value of each feature in each player vector is a meaningful quantity. The Manhattan distance does not alter this meaning and simply computes the sum of the absolute differences per feature, unlike Euclidean distance which tends to unfairly penalize large differences in a few features. We also empirically confirm that the Manhattan distance works best in Sect. 5.4.

5   Experiments

Evaluating our method is challenging as no objective ground truth exists for characterizing playing style. Therefore our experiments address three main questions: (1) providing intuitions into what information our player vectors capture,

(2) demonstrating how our approach could be used for scouting and monitoring player development by substantiating a number of claims in popular media about professional soccer players, and (3) measuring our performance at the player retrieval task, which we argue in Sect. 3 is an effective proxy for how well our approach characterizes playing style.

5.1   Intuition

Figure 2 illustrates all 18 components (4 shots, 4 crosses, 5 dribbles, 5 passes) corresponding to the weights in our length-18 player vectors. The shot, cross, and dribble components only describe where groups of actions start, while the pass components describe where groups of passes start and end. This is because the end locations of shots, crosses, and dribbles are not informative of a player's playing style. Shots and crosses all end in roughly the same location, while dribbles are usually short and vary in direction such that there is no noticeable difference between their start and end heatmaps.

Figure 3 shows the player vectors of four archetypical players in their 2016/2017 season.

Robert Lewandowski: Striker at Bayern Munich. He shows high weights for three components: *C2: Close shot*, *C13: Center dribble*, and *C14: Center pass*. These are the actions central strikers are expected to focus on.

Jesus Navas: Winger at Manchester City. He shows high weights for three components that are typical of an offensive right winger: *C8: Right backline cross*, *C12: Right flank dribble*, *C18: Right flank pass*.

Kevin De Bruyne: Midfielder at Manchester City. De Bruyne's player vector seems less pronounced than the others at first glance, but is actually very informative. First, we can deduce that De Bruyne plays mostly on the opponent's half due to the non-existent weights for components *C9/C11: Left/Right back dribble* and *C15/C17: Left/Right back to flank pass*. Second, his player vector shows similar values for (almost) all mirroring components (e.g., *C16/C18: Left/Right flank pass*). The exception is shots: his weight for *C4: Right shot* is high, while almost non-existent for *C3: Left shot*. De Bruyne's player vector suggests that he is an offensive central midfielder with no preference towards the left or the right when it comes to passing, dribbling or crossing, but attempts to score only from the right.

Sergio Ramos: Defender at Real Madrid. Two of his components stand out: *C9: Left back dribble* and *C15: Left back to flank pass*. While less notable than his defensive components, Ramos shows an unusually high weight for *C2: Close shot*. This is because Ramos often attempts to head the ball in the goal at corner kicks, as proven by his nine goals in the 2016/2017 season headed in from corner kicks. Ramos is a left-most central defender with a very defensive playing style, except when it comes to corners.

Player vectors can characterize playing style in an intuitive manner that can make sense to domain experts (e.g., scouts and coaches), yet the interpretable components upon which the player vectors are built are constructed in a completely data-driven manner.

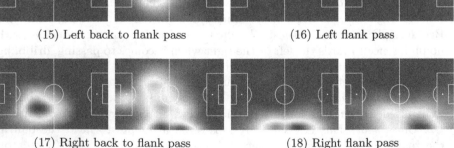

(1) Far shot   (2) Close shot   (3) Left shot   (4) Right shot

(5) L. flank cross   (6) L. backline cross   (7) R. flank cross   (8) R. backline cross

(9) L. back dribble   (10) L. flank dribble   (11) R. back dribble   (12) R. flank dribble

(13) Center dribble   (14) Center pass

(15) Left back to flank pass   (16) Left flank pass

(17) Right back to flank pass   (18) Right flank pass

Fig. 2. The 18 components of our player vectors constructed by compressing heatmaps of shots (1–4), crosses (5–8), dribbles (9–13), and passes (14–18) with non-negative matrix factorization.

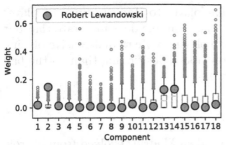

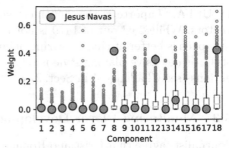

(a) Robert Lewandowski, central striker at Bayern Munich, shows high weights for *C2: Close shot*, *C13: Center dribble*, and *C14: Center pass*.

(b) Jesus Navas, right winger at Manchester City, shows high weights for *C8: Right backline cross*, *C12: Right flank dribble*, and *C18: Right flank pass*.

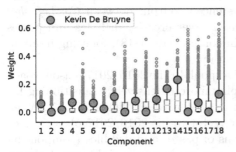

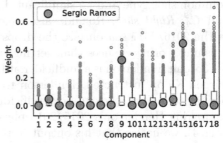

(c) Kevin De Bruyne, central offensive midfielder at Manchester City, shows high weights for all offensive components, favoring neither left nor right.

(d) Sergio Ramos, left-most central defender at Real Madrid, shows high weights for *C9: Left back dribble* and *C15: Left back to flank pass*.

Fig. 3. Visualized player vectors for an archetypical (a) striker, (b) winger, (c) midfielder, and (d) defender in the 2016/2017 season. The boxplots in the background show the distribution of the weights per component.

5.2   Scouting

We investigate three claims in popular media about similar players. We computed and compared player vectors for all 1480 players who played at least 900 min in the 2016/2017 season of the five major soccer competitions in Europe. Lionel Messi is regarded by many as the best soccer player in the world. One player who has been deemed to play similarly to Messi is Paulo Dybala, a fellow Argentinian attacker [13, 23]. When ranked using our player vectors, Dybala is the 2nd most similar player (out of 1479) to Lionel Messi. Idrissa Gueye (midfielder at Everton FC) is often hailed as the new N'golo Kante (midfielder at Chelsea FC) by many journalists [1, 3, 15]. Gueye is the 2nd most similar player to Kante in our data set. Aymeric Laporte is a 24-year-old defender playing for Manchester City FC, who was deemed to be the long-term replacement for 33-year-old Real Madrid defender Sergio Ramos [5, 18], who was named best defender in the world in 2017 by UEFA.[1] Laporte is the 29th most similar player to Ramos using our player vectors. While 29th out of 1479 is not bad, this example does illustrate that our approach is better at characterizing offensive playing style than defensive playing style, as defensive playing style is often more about positioning than on-the-ball actions (see Challenge 4 in Sect. 2).

5.3   Monitoring Player Development

Journalists agree that Cristiano Ronaldo (ex-Real Madrid) evolved from his role as a left winger to a role as a central striker [20, 22]. Our player vectors capture this transition (Fig. 4). Ronaldo's most common shot types in the 2012/2013 season were *C1: Far shot* and *C3: Left shot*. In the 2016/2017 season however, his shot playing style is completely different with *C2: Close shot* as his most common shot type and no significant difference in output between *C3: Left shot* and *C4: Right shot*. Ronaldo also executed fewer crosses, dribbles and passes in the 2016/2017 season (see the drops in components 5–18), focusing more on finishing scoring chances than setting them up.

Jordan Henderson is a midfielder at Liverpool. In the 2016/2017 season, coach Jürgen Klopp instructed Henderson to play more defensively, transitioning his playing style from a box-to-box midfielder to a defensive midfielder [17, 25]. When comparing Henderson's 2015/2016 player vector to his 2016/2017 player vector (Fig. 4), we notice that his output in terms of passes and dribbles (components 9–18) has significantly increased, while his output in terms of shots and crosses has completely disappeared (components 1–8).

5.4   Player Retrieval from Anonymized Match Event Stream Data

Our approach has many parameters: (a) the size of the grid to construct the heatmaps (50×50), (b) the algorithm to smooth the heatmaps (Gaussian blur), (c) the algorithm to compress the heatmaps (non-negative matrix factorization), (d) the number of components to use (4 shots, 4 crosses, 5 dribbles, and 5 passes), and (e) the distance function to compare the player vectors (Manhattan). Normally we would have no experimental way to tune these parameters as playing style is a subjective concept with no ground truth. However, as explained in Sect. 3, we can use player retrieval from anonymized match event stream data as a proxy for characterizing playing style.

We solve the player retrieval task as follows. First, we construct a set of labeled player vectors V using a training event stream data set that has not been anonymized. Second, we obtain a set of anonymous actions performed by a target player p_t and construct a player vector v_t based on these actions. Third, we compare v_t to all $v \in V$ and construct a rank-ordered list of the most similar players to p_t. The quality of this ranking is then the position of the unknown player in the ranking. In other words, if most players appear at the top of their

---

[1] http://www.uefa.com/insideuefa/awards/previous-winners/newsid=2495000.html.

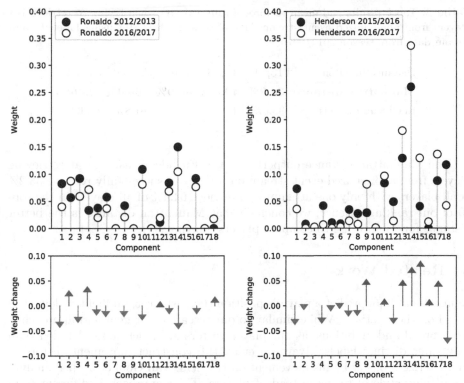

(a) Ronaldo evolved from a left winger in the 2012/2013 season to a central striker in the 2016/2017 season. Note the drop of *C1: Far shot* and *C3: Left shot* and the rise of *C2: Close shot* and *C4: Right shot*.

(b) Henderson transitioned to a more defensive playing style after the 2015/2016 season. Note the almost complete disappearance of shots and crosses (components 1–8) and the rise of passes and dribbles (components 9–18).

Fig. 4. Player vectors illustrating the development of (a) Cristiano Ronaldo, former striker at Real Madrid, and (b) Jordan Henderson, midfielder at Liverpool.

own rankings, then we have successfully characterized playing style. If most players do not appear near the top of their own rankings, then we have failed.

To illustrate this idea, we provide the results of an experiment to test whether Manhattan distance or Euclidean distance is the best distance function for comparing player vectors in Table 2. In our experiment, our training data was labeled event stream data from season 2015/2016 of the five top soccer competitions in Europe and the test data was anonymized event stream data from season 2016/2017 of the same competitions. We only considered players that have played 900 min in the same team in both seasons. This left us with 741 anonymized players in the test data which we de-anonymized using 741 labeled players in the training data.

Table 2. Top-k results and mean reciprocal rank (MRR) when trying to retrieve 741 players from anonymized event stream data of season 2016/2017 using labeled event stream data from season 2015/2016.

Distance function	Top-1	Top-3	Top-5	Top-10	MRR
Manhattan distance	**38.2%**	**49.8%**	**54.9%**	**64.4%**	**0.469**
Euclidean distance	33.0%	47.0%	52.9%	61.8%	0.429

The Manhattan distance outperforms the Euclidean distance at retrieving players from anonymized event stream data. We can successfully retrieve 38.2% of all players with only one attempt and retrieve 64.4% of all players in the top-10 of our rankings. Hence, we conclude that Manhattan distance is the better distance function to use to compare players' playing style.

6   Related Work

Danneels et al. [6] predict a player's position (i.e., attacker, midfielder, defender) based on their actions. While similar to our research, our goal and approach is more broad and ambitious, as our player vectors are much more detailed than only three distinct labels. Gyarmati et al. [14] construct movement vectors to characterize a player by his movement on the field. Van Gool et al. [24] analyze the playing style of teams instead of players. Their approach is different from ours, but their goal is similar as they also try to capture a subjective concept like playing style in a more objective and data-driven way. STATS introduced *STATS Playing Styles* [11], which are eight different styles (e.g., fast tempo, direct play, counter attack) teams use to create shooting opportunities. Fernandez et al. [10] also categorize different styles of play for teams in professional soccer.

Pappalardo et al. [16] and Decroos et al. [7] evaluate a player's quality of performance. Bransen et al. [2] measure players' resilience to mental pressure. The biggest difference between these works and ours is that our paper aims to characterize a player's playing style, with less emphasis on the player's quality of play. One way we could improve our approach is to expand our player vectors with features that capture the tactics a player is involved in (e.g. [8]).

In other sports, Franks et al. [12] used spatial information to categorize shots in professional basketball. In this work, data from the NBA was collected and analyzed using non-negative matrix factorization (NMF). This paper was a huge influence on our work, as our approach on soccer event data is largely inspired by their approach on basketball event data.

7   Conclusion

Objectively characterizing the playing style of professional soccer players has important applications in scouting, player development monitoring, and match preparation. We showed how to construct player vectors by transforming sets of actions from match event stream data to fixed-size players vectors using non-negative matrix factorization. These player vectors offer a complete view of a player's playing style (within the limits of the data source), are constructed in a purely data-driven manner, are human-interpretable and can be used in machine learning systems such as clustering and nearest neighbor analysis.

Acknowledgements. Tom Decroos is supported by the Research Foundation-Flanders (FWO-Vlaanderen). Jesse Davis is partially supported by KU Leuven Research Fund (C14/17/07, C32/17/036), Research Foundation - Flanders (EOS No. 30992574, G0D8819N) and VLAIO-SBO grant HYMOP (150033).

References

1. Adewoye, G.: Everton boss Sam Allardyce compares Idrissa Gueye to N'Golo Kante. http://www.goal.com/en/news/everton-boss-sam-allardyce-compares-idri ssa-gueye-to-ngolo/gddgazktcl3b1ayeadrva1o18
2. Bransen, L., Robberechts, P., Van Haaren, J., Davis, J.: Choke or shine? Quantifying soccer players' abilities to perform under mental pressure. In: MIT Sloan Sports Analytics Conference (2017)
3. Callaghan, S.: Everton boss was spot-on with Idrissa Gueye - N'Golo Kante comparison (2018). http://www.hitc.com/en-gb/2018/04/12/everton-boss-was-spot-on-with-idrissa-gueye-ngolo-kante-comparis/
4. Coles, J.: The Rise of Data Analytics in Football: Expected Goals, Statistics and dam (2016). http://outsideoftheboot.com/2016/07/21/rise-of-data-analytics-in-football/
5. Collins, T.: 4 Possible Replacements Should Real Madrid Sell Sergio Ramos (2015). http://bleacherreport.com/articles/2509541-4-possible-replacements-should-real-madrid-sell-sergio-ramos#slide3
6. Danneels, G., Van Haaren, J., Op De Beéck, T., Davis, J.: Identifying playing styles in professional football. KU Leuven (2014)
7. Decroos, T., Bransen, L., Van Haaren, J., Davis, J.: Actions speak louder than goals: valuing player actions in soccer. arXiv:1802.07127 (2018)
8. Decroos, T., Van Haaren, J., Davis, J.: Automatic discovery of tactics in spatio-temporal soccer match data. In: Proceedings of the 24th ACM SIGKDD International Conference on Knowledge Discovery & Data Mining, pp. 223–232 (2018)
9. Eggels, H.: Expected goals in soccer: explaining match results using predictive analytics, Eindhoven University of Technology (2016)
10. Fernandez-Navarro, J., Fradua, L., Zubillaga, A., Ford, P.R., McRobert, A.P.: Attacking and defensive styles of play in soccer: analysis of Spanish and English elite teams. J. Sports Sci. **34**(24), 2195–2204 (2016)
11. Flynn, M.: STATS Playing Styles - An Introduction (2016). www.stats.com/industry-analysis-articles/stats-playing-styles-introduction

12. Franks, A., Miller, A., Bornn, L., Goldsberry, K.: Characterizing the spatial structure of defensive skill in professional basketball. Ann. Appl. Stat. 2015 **9**(1), 94–121 (2015). arXiv:1405.0231

13. Goal.com: messi admits difficulties in Dybala partnership: he plays like me at Juve. http://www.goal.com/en/news/messi-admits-difficulties-in-dybala-partnership-he-plays-like-me-/1uq96ju5zageb1s1vez93omsi3

14. Gyarmati, L., Hefeeda, M.: Analyzing in-game movements of soccer players at scale. arXiv preprint arXiv:1603.05583 (2016)

15. Kleebauer, A.: Everton's Idrissa Gueye is the new N'Golo Kante - and here are the stats to prove it (2017). https://www.liverpoolecho.co.uk/sport/football/football-news/evertons-idrissa-gueye-new-ngolo-12965076

16. Pappalardo, L., Cintia, P., Ferragina, P., Pedreschi, D., Giannotti, F.: Player-ank: Multi-dimensional and role-aware rating of soccer player performance. arXiv preprint arXiv:1802.04987 (2018)

17. Pierce, J.: Henderson: I'm learning fast in the new midfield role Klopp's given me (2016). https://www.liverpoolecho.co.uk/sport/football/football-news/henderson-im-learning-fast-new-11862193

18. Prenderville, L.: Sergio Ramos 'identifies Aymeric Laporte and Matthijs de Ligt as his long-term replacements' at Real Madrid (2017). https://www.mirror.co.uk/sport/football/transfer-news/sergio-ramos-identifies-aymeric-laporte-11710624

19. Pritchard, S.: Marginal gains: the rise of data analytics in sport (2015). https://www.theguardian.com/sport/2015/jan/22/marginal-gains-the-rise-of-data-analytics-in-sport

20. Romero, A.: Cristiano Ronaldo: the change to a 'number 9' (2016). https://en.as.com/en/2016/12/19/opinion/1482164003_264275.html

21. Shapiro, L., Stockman, G.C.: Computer vision, 2001. Ed: Prentice Hall (2001)

22. Sharma, R.: How Cristiano Ronaldo has been transformed from a winger into a deadly No 9... and why he could really play for Real Madrid into his 40s (2017). http://www.dailymail.co.uk/sport/football/article-4469198/How-Ronaldo-transformed-winger-deadly-No9.html

23. Smith, R.: Is Paulo Dybala the Next Lionel Messi? "He Can Go as High as He Likes" (2017). https://www.nytimes.com/2017/04/10/sports/soccer/paulo-dybala-juventus-lionel-messi-barcelona.html

24. Van Gool, J., Van Haaren, J., Davis, J.: The automatic analysis of the playing style of soccer teams. KU Leuven (2015)

25. Williams, G.: Jordan Henderson is relishing his new role in the Liverpool midfield (2016). https://www.liverpoolecho.co.uk/sport/football/football-news/liverpool-jordan-henderson-jurgen-klopp-12123785

A Semi-supervised and Online Learning Approach for Non-Intrusive Load Monitoring

Hajer Salem[1,2](✉) and Moamar Sayed-Mouchaweh[1]

[1] Department of Computer Science and Automatic Control,
Institut Mines-Télécom Lille Douai, Douai, France
{hajer.salem,moamar.sayed-mouchaweh}@imt-lille-douai.fr
[2] National School of Computer Science ENSI,
Manouba University, Manouba, Tunisia

Abstract. Non-Intrusive Load Monitoring (NILM) approaches aim at identifying the consumption of a single appliance from the total load provided by smart meters. Several research works based on Hidden Markov Models (HMM) were developed for NILM where training is performed offline. However, these approaches suffer from different issues: First, they fail to generalize to unseen appliances with different configurations or brands than the ones used for training. Second, obtaining data about all active states of each appliance requires long time, which is impractical for residents. Third, offline training requires storage of huge amount of data, yielding to share resident consumption data with external servers and causing privacy issues. Therefore, in this paper, a new approach is proposed in order to tackle these issues. This approach is based on the use of a HMM conditioned on discriminant contextual features (e.g., time of usage, duration of usage). The conditional HMM (CHMM) is trained online using data related to a single appliance consumption extracted from aggregated load in order to adapt its parameters to the appliance specificity's (e.g., brand, configuration, etc.). Experiments are performed using real data from publicly available data sets and comparative evaluation are performed on a publicly available NILM framework.

Keywords: Non Intrusive Load Monitoring (NILM) · Load disaggregation · Hidden Markov model · Online learning · Online expectation maximization algorithm

1 Introduction

Non-intrusive load monitoring or power disaggregation refers to the problem of disaggregating single appliance consumption from the total electrical load in a house. NILM has many practical applications in the smart grid development in order to solve many challenges. For instance, it helps to reduce a consumer electricity bill by providing details to consumers about the consumption of each used appliance. Recently, many smart meters have been deployed in Europe.

© Springer Nature Switzerland AG 2020
U. Brefeld et al. (Eds.): ECML PKDD 2019, LNAI 11908, pp. 585–601, 2020.
https://doi.org/10.1007/978-3-030-46133-1_35

However, resident feedback following the smart meter installation in households point out the need to meet protecting privacy requirement. A big issue facing NILM deployment is the privacy loss because residents usually complain about sharing their personal data with utility companies. A potential solution is to perform data processing at the household level where personal data are not shared with external parts. A major advantage of the proposed approach in this paper is to fully protect a consumer privacy. Indeed, the learning and disaggregation modules could both be performed at the level of the smart meter thanks to the low complexity of the proposed approach and on the fly treatment of the data.

Generally NILM systems include three main modules that are data acquisition, model learning and load disaggregation [26]. In this paper, the learning module is enhanced in order to process online. Data is gathered from smart meter installed in households. A low sampling rate of 1/60 Hz (1 min interval) is considered in this paper because it is the real world sampling rate existing in households. Indeed, smart meters with higher sampling rate are expensive for a deployment in residential sector [21].

The NILM framework proposed in this paper is depicted in Fig. 1. The proposed approach is semi-supervised, performs online learning and disaggregation using data gathered from low sampling rate smart meters in order to overcome the discussed challenges in NILM. It pursues the following steps: First data preprocessing is performed and data is analyzed in order to extract discriminating features and prior generic models are created; Second, a method for appropriate edge change detection and a new approach for selecting training windows of a single appliance consumption extracted from the total load is proposed (blocks 2 and 3); Third, a new HMM conditioned on contextual features that we call CHMM for NILM is proposed. Besides, an extended version of an online Expectation Maximization (EM) algorithm for estimating the CHMM parameters is developed (block 4). The algorithm is adapted for NILM and propose a solution to estimate correctly under represented states. Finally, disaggregation is performed using the updated CHMM.

The reminder of this paper is organized as follows: Sect. 2 is a discussion of recent NILM works, their advantages and limits. Section 3 explains data preprocessing performed and the generic models taken as prior. Section 4 develops the edge change detection and training windows selection approach for NILM. The proposed conditional HMM is formalized in Sect. 5. The proposed online parameter estimation approach is developed in Sect. 6. Experiment results are depicted and discussed in Sect. 7. Section 8 concludes the paper and presents future work.

2   Related Work

A common category of NILM approaches assumes that sub-metered ground truth data is available for training prior to performing disaggregation [15,25]. These approaches show promising accuracy results but they violate two requirements of NILM that are generalization and unsupervised disaggregation. Another category of approaches are often based on a signature database of appliances and

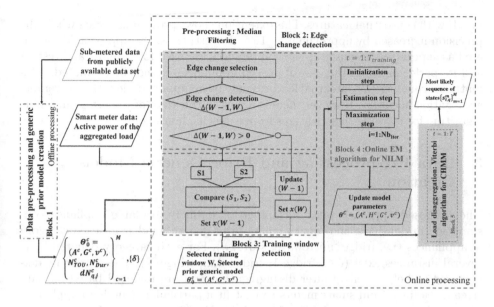

Fig. 1. Proposed approach global diagram

classify appliances according to these signatures [2,23]. However, it is impossible and very expensive to collect all appliances signatures in a database because many instances (specific size, model, etc.) exist for each appliance category.

Several deep learning based approaches [9,13,24] have been proposed for NILM. They showed very promising results regarding generalization to unseen appliances and presented major improvement in terms of complexity. However this performance still prone to: the need to high frequency data which is impractical in residential sector due to return of investment issues; the difficult process of training; and sometimes dependency to labelled data. Unsupervised and semi-supervised HMM based approaches, [14,15], present the best compromise in terms of meeting NILM requirements and disaggregation accuracy [17]. A bench of unsupervised approaches based on variants of Factorial Hidden Markov Models (FHMM) have been proposed [3,8,11,18]. These approaches share almost the same scalability issues. Indeed, these approaches are not applicable for a number of appliances greater than ten [17]. However, integrating non traditional based features seems to alleviate this limitation [18]. Non traditional features refer to contextual based and behavioural based features. Hour of the day, day of the week and duration have been proposed as additional features for FHMM [10] which improved the disaggregation accuracy, at the expense of increasing the model complexity. Furthermore, time of the day and seasonal context-based patterns have been incorporated to a recent NILM approach [7]. A whole year of usage data have been used for training in order to build usage patterns which is impractical for real world application. Power consumption patterns of appliances and user presence have been investigated in [18]. The proposed inference algorithm is an extension to the AFAMAP (Additive Factorial Approximate Maximum a Posteriori) disaggregation algorithm proposed in [11] with contextual features. This extension shows promising results where the precision increased by approximately 15%. Nevertheless, the approach is considered as supervised because the same appliances are used for training and testing and its performance in the case of unseen appliances cannot be evaluated. As a matter of conclusion, contextual features may be an important lever for power disaggregation accuracy. However there is a lack in the state of the art of an online algorithm for learning these features from a specific household.

3   Data Pre-processing and Prior Generic Models Creation

The proposed approach takes advantage of publicly available appliance consumption in databases in order to create prior generic models for each category of appliances (i.e, fridge, microwave, stove,...). For each category denoted by c, several instances exist (e.g., fridge 1, fridge 2,..., fridge N). These prior models are used to help labelling after disaggregation and are updated based on data stream readings from smart meters to best fit a particular household appliance. Mainly, data pre-processing is performed on the data sets and M generic prior models are created. The prior generic model for each appliance, is modeled as a Hidden Markov Model (HMM) with parameters $\theta_0^c = (A_0^c, G_0^c, v_0^c)$.

3.1   Number of States per Appliance and Generic Power Profiles

Clustering analysis have been performed on the publicly available data sets in order to set the number of states Q per appliance and approximate emission distributions. Generic prior emission distributions have been approximated to Gaussian distribution using different instances for each appliance category and setting a prior on the mean of these distributions.

3.2   Generic Contextual Features Distributions

Three additional distributions are considered as additional information that are the distribution of usage duration per state for cooling appliances, the distribution of time of usage per hour of the day for entertainment appliances and some kitchen devices and the difference between state consumption for states within the same appliance. These distributions are obtained as the following:

– **Generic Duration Distribution:** For cooling appliances, the state duration is not related to a user's habits but related to the appliance internal operational behavior. Duration represents an interesting discriminating generalized feature which could be generalized to unseen appliances especially to distinguish between states from different appliances that have similar active power consumption distribution. However, for these appliances, the usage time is not a discriminating feature because cooling appliances consume continuously. Analysis have been performed and showed that state duration of cooling appliances could be generalized to Gaussian density with a Gaussian prior on the mean of these distributions where:

$$Dur_q^m \sim N(\frac{\sum_{i=1}^{N} \mu_{q,i}^c}{N}, \max_{i=1:N} \sigma_{q,i}^c)$$
$$\mu_q^c \sim N(0, \sqrt{\frac{\sum_{j=1:N} (\mu_{q,i}^c - \mu_q^c)^2}{N}})$$

(1)

where $q \in [1 : Q]$ and $i \in [1 : N]$ is the number of instances per appliance category.

- **Generic Usage Time Distribution:** Data have been analyzed in function of usage time. Time of usage have been extracted from the timestamp reported with active power at sampling instant. Data suggest that some appliances such as entertaining appliances (e.g., Laptop, TV, Stereo) are often ON during specific hours of the day. These appliances' times of usage could be generalized over different households because it is concentrated over some hours of the day (after work, in the evening and before sleeping). Generalization over different devices within the same appliance category has been performed in the same manner as for duration.
- **Difference Distribution Between each Appliance Power Profiles:** Difference between power consumption of two different states of the same device has been studied. Difference between two states remains always the same even if further appliances consume simultaneously [11,19]. Using the consumption difference aims at detecting when states of the same appliance are consuming successively in the aggregated load. The consumption difference between two emission probability distributions $X_i \sim N_i$ and $X_j \sim N_j$, $i, j \in \{1, Q\}$ has been approximated to a Gaussian distribution.

3.3 Prior Adaptive Edge Change Thresholds

An adaptive edge change threshold is proposed. Edge change detection consists in detecting if an appliance changes its state from one to another. A naive approach deployed in almost power disaggregation approaches [11,22] is to monitor power consumption readings and to flag an event when the power change deviates beyond a fixed threshold. However, a fixed threshold could be within an appliance variance when it is too small and hence detects false state changes. Besides, choosing a large threshold may lead the system to loop state transitions with small consumption. For this current work, the edge change is detected based on an adaptive threshold δ_W that dynamically changes according to the detected appliance state operating during the last observed window of observations. Several thresholds are proposed and are computed according to the variance of the emission distributions of the generic prior models. Indeed, a clustering is performed on the different variances of appliances states consumption. The minimal variance within each cluster $i \in [1, Nb_{clusters}]$ has been set as an event detection threshold δ_i.

4 Edge Change Detection and Online Training Windows Selection

4.1 Problem Formulation and Complexity

Power consumption readings $\{y_t\}$ arrive in data streams. An edge change $(\Delta_{t,t-1})$ is detected if the active power consumption difference between y_t and y_{t-1} is greater than a threshold δ_i (see Fig. 2). Let W denotes the current dynamic window of observations. Its size is determined by the number of observations received between the two last successive detected edge changes. δ_i is chosen according to the appliance state denoted by x_q^m identified as operating during window $W - 1$. Indeed, for each appliance state identified as operating during $W - 1$, the proposed approach selects a different threshold δ_i where $i \in [1, Nb_{clusters}]$ as explained above in Sect. 3.3 and illustrated in Fig. 2.

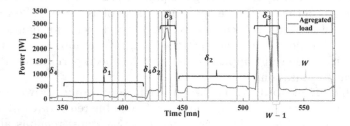

Fig. 2. Event detection example using the adaptive threshold δ_i

The proposed training window selection approach aims at extracting single appliance consumption from the aggregated load to be used as training samples for the HMM parameter estimation. The proposed training module is able to run online and process data on the fly. It succeeds to overcome several shortcomings facing offline training approaches in the state of the art as follows:

- Space Complexity: The proposed approach requires the storage of only data within W. Its space complexity is equal to $O(|W| * D)$ where $|W|$ is the window length and D is the observations dimension; The length of W is usually equal to fzw minutes of consumption data. The spatial complexity of this approach is negligible compared to the spatial complexity of offline training approaches [8,10,11,19] which is equal to $O(T * D)$. Indeed, these approaches require the storage of the full training data (T) which is equal to several days of consumption data.
- Time Complexity: The proposed approach is based on the Kullback Leibler divergence and a posteriori probability estimation that have at the worst case a temporal complexity of $O(1)$. Besides, the proposed online EM algorithm performs on the fly data processing and has a temporal complexity equal to $O(Q^2)$ where Q is the number of an appliance states. This proposed approach has significantly a lower complexity compared to the state of the art

approaches based on the Forward Backward algorithm, which iterates over the full training data T and has a temporal complexity of $O(Q^2T)$ per iteration.

4.2   The Proposed Training Window Selection Method

As mentioned above, only data within the last window W is registered. Besides, the training module memorizes sufficient statistics related to: (i) the consumption distribution denoted by N_{est}, (ii) the difference distribution between $(W, W-1)$ denoted by dN_{est} and (iii) the contextual features (time of the day, duration). In the sequel, we enumerate the different scenarios that might explain an edge change detection and propose a method that evaluates each scenario. The steps of the proposed method are enumerated in block (3) of Fig. 1. Two types of edge changes $\Delta_{W,W-1}$ could be observed: a positive edge change and a negative one.

On the one hand, a negative $\Delta_{W,W-1}$, is interpreted as the appliance state x_i^m, active within $(W-1)$, turns off when $\Delta_{W,W-1}$ is detected. In order to identify x_i^m, the proposed method pursues the following steps: First, the distribution of observations within $(W-1)$ is approximated to a Gaussian distribution N_{est}, with a mean equal to $|\Delta_{W,W-1}|$; Second, N_{est} is compared to all prior generic model emission distributions $\{g_i^m\}_{m=1}^M$ based on Kullback Leibler divergence. A subset of most similar prior generic appliance states are selected and are compared further by computing a posteriori probability of contextual features; A score is computed for each potential active appliance state and the state having the highest score is identified as the state operating during window $(W-1)$. Finally, observations within $W-1$ are fed to the online EM algorithm to update the parameters of the appliance m model.

On the other hand, a positive $\Delta_{W,W-1}$ could be explained by two scenarios as follows:

First Scenario: the edge change corresponds to an appliance state q of appliance m'' that was OFF within $(W-1)$ and turns ON during W. Let's denote by $x_i^{m'}$ the state appliance that was identified active within $W-1$. In this case the mean power consumption of the new activated state $x_q^{m''} \approx \Delta_{W,W-1}$ and its consumption distribution is approximated to $N_{est}(\Delta_{W,W-1}, \sigma_W)$. The proposed evaluation procedure adopted in this scenario consists in comparing the Kullback Leibler divergence between the estimated distribution N_{est} within W and all prior generic models emission distributions of appliances categories. A subset of most similar states is selected. Then a posteriori probability of the observed contextual feature is calculated. The state having the maximal probability is selected as potentially consuming during W.

Second Scenario: The edge change corresponds to the same appliance m that changes its active state (q_1) during $W-1$ to its second active state (q_2) during W. In this case the mean power consumption of x_{q2}^m is approximated to $\mu_{q2}^m \approx \Delta_{W,W-1} + \mu_{q1}^m$ and its consumption distribution is approximated to $N_{est}(\mu_{q2}^m{''}, \sigma_W)$. The difference distribution dN_{est} observed within W is compared to all prior generic difference distributions dx_i^m defined in Sect. 3. Kullback

Leibler divergence is computed between dN_{est} and each prior generic difference distribution. A subset of most similar states is selected. Further comparison is performed based on a posteriori probability of contextual features and a score is computed. The state having the highest score is selected.

The two selected states from each potential scenario are compared according to their mutual scores and the one having the highest score is identified as active. For some observation windows, the proposed approach may not select any appliance state as consuming during W. Indeed, the proposed algorithm only selects a window of observations where it confidently recognize an appliance is operating based on both Kullback Leibler and Maximum a Posterior. Finally, the samples within a selected window are used as training data for the proposed CHMM.

5   Conditional Hidden Markov Model(CHMM)

In this work, we suggest to condition the hidden state on the probability of usage during hours of the day. The likelihood of appliance state q being active during an hour of the day td $p(x = q|t = td)$ follows a Multinomial distribution of probabilities $(h_{1,q}, ..., h_{td,q}, ..., h_{24,q})$ and a number of trials n_h that is the number of observations per hour where $td \in \{1, ..., 24\}$, $\forall q \in \{1, ..., Q\}$ and $\sum_{td=1}^{24} h_{td,q} = 1$. Indeed, as shown in Fig. 3, appliances states have higher probability to be active during some hours of the day than others. For a particular household, the time of usage of appliances encapsulates the user habits and it is interesting to learn these habits online. Therefore, the hidden states X are conditioned on both the transition matrix A and a usage time matrix H.

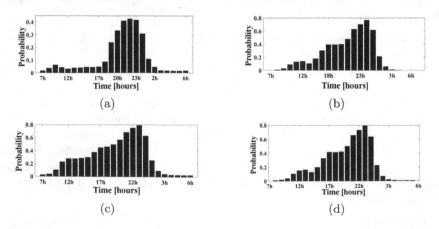

Fig. 3. Histograms of usage time probabilities over hours of the day: (a) Lamp, (b) Television, (c) Stereo, (d) Entertainment

Henceforth, the proposed joint probability distribution over latent variables and observed ones is given by Eq. (2) where $\theta = (v, g, A, H)$:

$$p\left(X_{1:T}, Y_{1:T} | \theta\right) = p(x_1|v)p(y_1|x_1)p(x_1|h_{td}) \prod_{t=2}^{T} \left[p(x_t|x_{t-1}, A)p(x_t|td, H)p(y_t|x_t, g) \right] \tag{2}$$

An example of a washing machine model is represented in Fig. 4(a) and the graphical representation of the CHMM is depicted in Fig. 4(b).

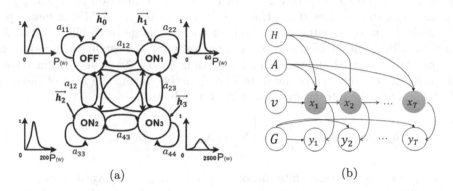

(a)   (b)

Fig. 4. (a): Example of a CHMM modeling a washing machine with four states, (b): Conditional HMM graphical representation

6   Online Parameter Estimation: Online EM for NILM

The EM algorithm is one of the most popular algorithms for parameter inference in HMMs due to its convergence properties and robustness. An online EM algorithm has been proposed by Cappé et al. [4]. The algorithm main objective is to train HMM with continuous observations on data streams. Data are processed just one time and never stored. We opted to adapt this algorithm to NILM and extend it to CHMM. In this work, this algorithm is enriched and modified according to two main points: (1) A new approximate filter $\psi(x)$ and intermediate quantity ρ^h are added to the model in order to estimate recursively the time of usage parameters; (2) A new decreasing sequence γ_n is proposed. This new sequence ensures the learning of parameters related to under represented states in training data. Indeed, some appliances states are rarely observed. A second challenge facing the application of Online EM [4] to NILM, is that this algorithm is designed to train only one HMM from data generated continuously from the same model. This is not the case in NILM. Indeed, data are generated from different models. Observations y_t and y_{t+1} may be generated from different models HMM_i and HMM_j where $i, j \in \{1, M\}$.

6.1   The New Time of Usage Parameter Estimation

The proposed online EM algorithm for CHMM aims at learning a new matrix H of size $24 \times Q$. Each row vector of H denotes the probabilities of each state q to be active during the hour of the day $td \in [1 : 24]$. The sum of each row has to be equal to one. In the online EM considered by [4], the leaned parameter θ is composed of the state transition matrix A and the mean vector and covariance matrix associated with each of the q emission distribution g_q. In such a model, there are two distinct types of EM complete-data sufficient statistics which give rise to two separate forms of the auxiliary function ρ_{n+1}^q and ρ_{n+1}^g and an approximate filter ϕ_{n+1}. However, in the proposed CHMM, a new type of sufficient statistic related to the hour of the day usage probability is added. Therefore, in addition to the two previous forms of the auxiliary function, a new one is introduced and formulated according to Eq. (9) in Algorithm 1 and computes the expectation of the state j being active during the hour of the day td according to the intermediate quantity 4 as follows:

$$\rho_{n+1}^h(j, k, td; \theta) = \frac{1}{n} \mathbb{E}_{v,\theta} \left[\sum_{t=1}^{n} \mathbb{1}\{X_t = j, t = td\} | X_n = k, \right], \qquad (3)$$

Besides, a new approximate filter denoted by ψ_{n+1} and a backward retrospective probability denoted by r_{n+1}^h are defined as formulated respectively in Eqs. (7) and (11) of Algorithm 1. Finally, a new parameter update formula is proposed for the maximization step in order to update h_{θ_n} (Eq. 13, Algorithm 1).

6.2   New Proposed Weights

A well known problem of EM algorithm is the convergence rate. Indeed, the latter depends on the initial parameters θ_0 [6]. Besides, the weights γ_{n+1} in Eqs. (8), (9) and (10) have crucial importance for the rate of convergence. It is usually chosen to form a positive decreasing sequence. A step size of $\gamma_n = n^{-\alpha}$ is used in [4] where $\alpha \in [0.5, 0.8]$. New studies showed that a decreasing sequence equal to $Cn^{-\alpha}$ (C is a constant) reaches better rates of convergences [16]. Still, all these fully decreasing sequences are proposed based on the assumption that observed data are generated from all HMM states continuously which is not the case in NILM. The decreasing sequence adopted in almost EM algorithms applies the same factor (α) regardless of the observations. However, for under represented states (case of unbalanced observations), the left hand side of Eqs. (8), (9) and (10) could be omitted due to a small value of γ and a small number of observations.

In this current work, the decreasing sequence γ_n is considered as an adaptive cooling schedule of a simulated annealing algorithm that could increase. The application of a different cooling rate, that depends on the representation of states, would allow the algorithm to best fit to rare observations. Hence, γ_{n+1} continue to decrease if the consequent observations are generated from a state for which training windows have been selected. We memorize a flag per appliance state to denote if a training window has been found for the considered state or not. In the case of a first training window selected for an appliance state (a HMM latent variable), γ_{n+1} increases in order to give more important weights to the observed data from the new observed state.

6.3   Online EM Algorithm for Conditioned HMM

The auxiliary EM function is defined for the CHMM as follows:

$$Q(\theta, \theta') = \sum_{i=1}^{Q} \sum_{j=1}^{Q} S_n^q(i,j) \log a(i,j) \times S_n^h(j) \log h(td, j) \tag{4}$$

$$- \frac{1}{2} \sum_{i=1}^{K} \left(\frac{S_{n,2}^g(i,\theta)}{v(i)} - \frac{2\mu(i)S_{n,1}^g(i)}{v(i)} + S_{n,0}^g \left(\frac{\mu^2(i)}{v(i)} + \log v(i) \right) \right)$$

The proposed online EM for CHMM applied to NILM is described in Algorithm 1. First prior parameters $\theta_0 = (v_0, G_{\theta_0}, A_{\theta_0}, H_{\theta_0})$ are initialized where A_{θ_0} is the initial transition matrix, H_{θ_0} is the initial hour usage probability matrix. Then both initial values of the approximated filters $\hat{\phi}_0(x)$ and $\hat{\psi}_0(x)$ are initialized [Algorithm 1, line 2]. The auxiliary quantities (8, 9, 10) are initialized to zero. Then for each new observation within a selected training window W, the approximate filters ϕ and ψ are updated as formulated in (6) and (7). A test is performed in order to verify the representation of states. The parameters update formulas of the maximization step are calculated by maximizing Eq. (4) with respect to a_θ, h_θ μ_θ and σ_θ and satisfying the constraints $\sum_j^Q a(i,j) = 1$, $\sum_{td=1}^{24} h(j, td) = 1$ as formulated in (12)–(15).

7   Experimental Evaluation

We implemented the proposed approach using Matlab 2017b on a 64-bit windows 10 PC with core intel(R) i5-3320M CPU processor and 8.00 GB of memory. Experiments have been carried out on Nilm-Eval [5] framework for disaggregation of real-world electricity consumption data. We conducted our experiments using three publicly available data sets for real world electricity consumption. Two European databases named Tracebase [20] and Electricity Consumption and Occupancy (ECO) [1] and an American database named the Reference Energy Disaggregation Data Set (REDD) [12]. All the conducted experiments in this paper are based on low frequency sampling data of $1/60$ Hz (1 min interval) sampling rate. Each obtained result is an average of 10 independent runs of the algorithm. Prior models have been built using both Tracebase and REDD data sets to cover a maximal number of appliance categories. For each appliance category, seven different appliance instances are used to build the prior models. For each instance, the same number of samples (data) are used. We carried out three kinds of experiments in order to test the proposed approach. All the carried experiments are based on data from household 2 of ECO data set because it contains the maximal number of appliances.

Algorithm 1. Online Expectation Maximization (EM)

1: **Initialization**
2: Compute for $x \in X$

$$\phi_0(x) = \frac{v(x)g_{\hat{\theta}_0}(x, y_0)}{\sum_{x' \in X} v(x')g_{\hat{\theta}_0}(x', y_0)}, \quad \psi_0(x, td) = \frac{h_{\theta_0}(td, x)}{\sum_{td' \in [1:24]} h_{\theta_0}(td', x)} \quad (5)$$

3: $\hat{\rho}_0^q(x) = 0$, $\hat{\rho}_0^h(x) = 0$, $\hat{\rho}_0^g(x) = 0$
4: **Recursion**
5: **for** $n \geq 0$ **do**
6:     Compute, for $x \in X$
7:     **Approximate filter Update**

$$\hat{\phi}_{n+1}(x) = \frac{\sum\limits_{x' \in X} \hat{\phi}_n(x')a_{\hat{\theta}_n}(x', x)g_{\hat{\theta}_n}(x, y_{n+1})}{\sum\limits_{x', x'' \in X} \hat{\phi}_n(x')a_{\hat{\theta}_n}(x', x'')g_{\hat{\theta}_n}(x'', y_{n+1})}, \quad (6)$$

$$\hat{\psi}_{n+1}(x, td) = \frac{\sum\limits_{x' \in X} \hat{\psi}_n(x', td_n)h_{\hat{\theta}_n, i}(td, x)}{\sum\limits_{td' \in [1:24]} \sum\limits_{x' \in X} \hat{\psi}_n(x')h_{\hat{\theta}_n, i}(td', x')} \quad (7)$$

8:     **Stochastic Approximation E-step**
9:     **if** flag == true **then**
10:        $\gamma_{n+1} = \gamma_1$
11:    **else**
12:        $\gamma_{n+1} = (n+1)^{-\alpha}$
13:    **end if**

$$\rho_{n+1}^q(i, j, k; \theta) = \gamma_{n+1}\delta(j-k)\hat{r}_{n+1}(i|j) + (1-\gamma_{n+1})\sum_{k'=1}^{Q} \hat{\rho}_n^q(i, j, k')\hat{r}_{n+1}(k'|k), \quad (8)$$

$$\rho_{n+1}^h(j, k, td; \theta) = \gamma_{n+1}\delta(j-k)\delta(t-td)\hat{r}_{n+1}^h(j|td) + (1-\gamma_{n+1})\sum_{k'=1}^{Q} \hat{\rho}_n^h(j, k', td)\hat{r}_{n+1}^h(j|td), \quad (9)$$

$$\rho_{n+1}^g(i, k) = \gamma_{n+1}\delta(i-k)s(Y_{n+1}) + (1-\gamma_{n+1})\sum_{k'=1}^{Q} \hat{\rho}_n^g(i, k', \theta)\hat{r}_{n+1}(k'|k), \quad (10)$$

Where:
$$r_{n+1}(i|j) = \frac{\hat{\phi}_n(i)q_{\hat{\theta}_n}(i, j)}{\sum_{i'=1}^{Q} \hat{\phi}_n(i')q_{\hat{\theta}_n}(i', j)}, \quad r_{n+1}^h(j|td) = \frac{\hat{\psi}_n(j, td)h_{\hat{\theta}_n}(td, j)}{\sum_{td'=1}^{24} \hat{\psi}_n(j, td')h_{\hat{\theta}_n}(td', j)} \quad (11)$$

if $n \geq n_{min}$ **then**   Update the parameters:

$$a_{\theta_n}(i, j) = \frac{S_n^q(i, j)}{\sum_{j=1}^{Q} S_n^q(i, j)} \quad (12)$$

$$h_{\theta_n}(td, i) = \frac{S_n^h(td, i)}{\sum_{j=1}^{Q} S_n^h(td, j)} \quad (13)$$

$$\mu_{\theta_n}(i) = \frac{S_{n,1}^g(i)}{S_{n,0}^g(i)} \quad (14)$$

$$\sigma_{\theta_n}(i) = \mu_{\theta_n}^2(i) + \frac{S_{n,2}^g(i) - S_{n,1}^g(i) \times \mu_{\theta_n}(i)}{S_{n,0}^g(i)} \quad (15)$$

    else   set $\hat{\theta}_{n+1} = \hat{\theta}_n$ **end if**=0

7.1 Evaluation of the Proposed Training Window Selection Approach

The main goal of the first experiment is to evaluate the accuracy of the selected training windows. Evaluations have been carried out in terms of True Positive rate (TPR) and False Positives rate (FPR). True Positive rate measures the proportion of actual appliance activation in the ground truth data (plug level data) identified correctly by the proposed approach. False positive rate measures the proportion of appliance activation identified by the proposed approach and do not exist in the ground truth data. The intended metrics verify that the selected windows for training correspond truly to windows where a state of a specific appliance is active. The obtained results shown in Table 1 highlight that the proposed approach succeeds to find online training windows for all appliances. The evaluation have been performed on data from two weeks of consumption. The approach shows also robustness to noise. For instance, appliances that have never been ON (i.e., the kettle) during the test period, have not been identified as active (FP=0). Unfortunately, the fridge and freezer false positive rates are important. However, this is a common problem because these appliances are consuming continuously and their steady state is frequently confused with states from different appliances. These results also reveal that duration feature considered for cooling appliances is not discriminating enough.

Table 1. Accuracy evaluation of detected training windows

	Fridge	Dishwasher	Laptop	Freezer	TV	Air Exhaust	Lamp	Kettle	Stereo	Tablet	Entertainment	Stove
TPR	0.42	0.38	0.49	0.41	0.43	0.29	0.35	0	0.27	0	0.44	0.56
FPR	0.31	0.06	0.16	0.68	0.02	0.01	0	0	0	0	0.06	0.01

7.2 Evaluation of the Proposed Online EM

The second kind of experiment evaluates the impact of the new proposed weights γ on the accuracy of the parameter estimation. A comparison between the effect of γ used in the online EM algorithm [4] and the one proposed in this work is conducted on the entertainment appliance. Indeed, the entertainment appliance is a typical example of appliances that have imbalanced represented states. Figure 5(c) shows data observed within the two first days of consumption of the appliance in household 2. We can observe that the state ON 2 is under represented compared to the two other states and is rarely active. For the scope of this experiment, we focused on the mean update of the appliance state emission distributions. We can visually distinguish three different states where the OFF state has a mean around 0 W, the ON 1 state has a mean around 160 W and the ON 2 state has a mean around 40 W. Figure 5(a) shows that the online EM algorithm proposed in [4] converges to a mean around 10 W for the case of the state ON2. This is explained by the fact that the algorithm confuses between ON 1 and ON 2 states. However, the adaptive γ sequence proposed in this work

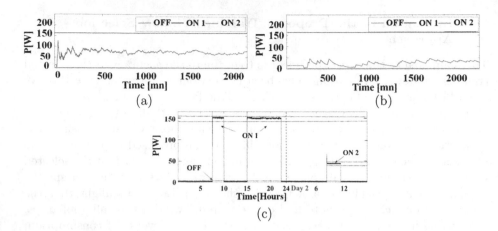

Fig. 5. Result comparison between updated mean of probability emission distribution of the entertainment appliance, (a):Online EM with $\gamma = n^{-\alpha}$, (b):Online EM with proposed γ, (c):Selected training windows

helps the algorithm to converge accurately to the real state mean as shown in Fig. 5(b) because it gives more important weights to observations generated from the new detected state.

7.3   Load Disaggregation Evaluation

The third kind of experiments intend to evaluate the impact of conditioning on the time of usage probabilities on the disaggregation results. Accuracy has been evaluated using the same data from household 2. Evaluation have been performed on 90 days of consumption data. Accuracy reports how much power is being consumed by an appliance compared to its actual consumption and is computed as follows [11]:

$$Acc = 1 - \frac{\sum_{t=1}^{T} |\hat{y}_t^m - y_t^m|}{2\sum_{t=1}^{T} y_t^m}$$

where y_t^m is the real consumption of appliance m and $\hat{y}_t^m$ is the estimated consumption of appliance m during time t.

Three variants of HMM are compared where the first variant is a HMM trained on sub-metered data denoted by "Supervised HMM". The second variant, is a HMM trained using sample data selected online using the method developed in Sect. 4.2 and using the online EM proposed in [4]. This second variant is denoted by "Online HMM". The third variant is the CHMM formalized in Sect. 5, trained on data samples selected using the method developed in Sect. 4.2 and the online EM for CHMM developed in Sect. 6. This third variant is denoted by "Online CHMM". Results are depicted in Table 2. The proposed CHMM outperforms the two other models mainly on the lamp, dishwasher, stereo and laptop

Table 2. Accuracy results using the proposed CHMM trained online, a supervised HMM trained on sub-metered data and a HMM trained online

	Fridge	Freezer	Lamp	Dish-washer	Stereo	Laptop	Tablet	Air Exhaust	Enter-tainment	Kettle	Stove	TV
Supervised HMM	0.46 ± 0.02	0.49 ± 0.04	0.59 ± 0.12	0.56 ± 0.11	0.58 ± 0.08	0.52 ± 0.09	0.49 ± 0.05	0.51 ± 0.08	0.57 ± 0.07	0.55 ± 0.04	0.49 ± 0.07	0.53 ± 0.04
Online HMM	0.47 ± 0.03	0.5 ± 0.03	0.58 ± 0.09	0.55 ± 0.15	0.51 ± 0.08	0.33 ± 0.12	0.49 ± 0.01	0.53 ± 0.09	0.53 ± 0.05	0.54 ± 0.01	0.49 ± 0.03	0.49 ± 0.03
Online CHMM	0.57 ± 0.02	0.52 ± 0.03	0.85 ± 0.02	0.83 ± 0.02	0.64 ±0.03	0.77 ± 0.01	0.5 ± 0.04	0.69 ± 0.04	0.75 ± 0.08	0.68 ± 0.02	0.81 ± 0.03	0.86 ± 0.02

appliances. This improvement highlights that time of usage is an important discriminating feature for the aforementioned appliances. However, accuracy results obtained for cooling appliances are approximately the same for the three models. This could be interpreted as the time of usage has no additional impact on disaggregation for these appliances. Moreover, the results obtained by comparing the first two models "Supervised HMM" and "Online HMM" show that both models give similar accuracy results which confirms that training the model online gives the same results as using sub-metered data.

8   Conclusion

In this paper, a semi-supervised approach performing online learning for Non-intrusive Load Monitoring (NILM) was proposed. The aim is to develop an algorithm that can be embedded in a smart meter in order to alleviate the privacy issues facing NILM. The proposed approach succeeded to extract training samples from the aggregated load online for each appliance. Training using samples selected from the aggregated load gave the same accuracy results as training on sub-metered data. Besides, a new conditional hidden Markov model (CHMM) that condition on usage time was proposed for NILM. An online Expectation Maximization algorithm was developed to learn CHMM parameters. Disaggregation based on the proposed CHMM improved accuracy results especially for appliances such as: the lamp, the dishwasher, the stereo and the laptop.

Future work will consider a conditional factorial hidden Markov model (CFHMM) where the time of usage will be used to block sample for a particular hour of the day on a subset of active appliances. The aim of this blocked sampling is to decrease the computational complexity of inference algorithms in factorial hidden Markov models.

References

1. Beckel, C., Kleiminger, W., Cicchetti, R., Staake, T., Santini, S.: The ECO data set and the performance of non-intrusive load monitoring algorithms. In: Proceedings of the 1st ACM Conference on Embedded Systems for Energy-Efficient Buildings, pp. 80–89. ACM (2014)

2. Berges, M., Goldman, E., Matthews, H.S., Soibelman, L., Anderson, K.: User-centered nonintrusive electricity load monitoring for residential buildings. J. Comput. Civil Eng. **25**(6), 471–480 (2011)
3. Bonfigli, R., Principi, E., Fagiani, M., Severini, M., Squartini, S., Piazza, F.: Nonintrusive load monitoring by using active and reactive power in additive factorial hidden markov models. Appl. Energy **208**, 1590–1607 (2017)
4. Cappé, O.: Online EM algorithm for hidden markov models. J. Comput. Graph. Stat. **20**(3), 728–749 (2011)
5. Cicchetti, R.: NILM-Eval: Disaggregation of real-world electricity consumption data. Master's thesis, ETH Zurich (2014)
6. Dempster, A.P., Laird, N.M., Rubin, D.B.: Maximum likelihood from incomplete data via the EM algorithm. J. Roy. Stat. Soc. Ser. B (Methodological) **39**, 1–38 (1977)
7. Dinesh, C., Makonin, S., Bajic, I.V.: Incorporating time-of-day usage patterns into non-intrusive load monitoring. In: 2017 IEEE Global Conference on Signal and Information Processing (GlobalSIP), pp. 1110–1114. IEEE (2017)
8. Egarter, D., Bhuvana, V.P., Elmenreich, W.: Paldi: Online load disaggregation via particle filtering. IEEE Trans. Instrument. Measure. **64**(2), 467–477 (2015)
9. Kelly, J., Knottenbelt, W.: Neural NILM: deep neural networks applied to energy disaggregation. In: Proceedings of the 2nd ACM International Conference on Embedded Systems for Energy-Efficient Built Environments, pp. 55–64. ACM (2015)
10. Kim, H., Marwah, M., Arlitt, M., Lyon, G., Han, J.: Unsupervised disaggregation of low frequency power measurements. In: Proceedings of the 2011 SIAM International Conference on Data Mining, pp. 747–758. SIAM (2011)
11. Kolter, J.Z., Jaakkola, T.: Approximate inference in additive factorial HMMs with application to energy disaggregation. Artif. intell. Stat. **22**, 1472–1482 (2012)
12. Kolter, J.Z., Johnson, M.J.: Redd: a public data set for energy disaggregation research. In: Workshop on Data Mining Applications in Sustainability (SIGKDD), San Diego, CA. vol. 25, pp. 59–62 (2011)
13. Lange, H., Bergés, M.: The neural energy decoder: energy disaggregation by combining binary subcomponents. In: NILM2016 3rd International Workshop on Non-Intrusive Load Monitoring. nilmworkshop.org Google Scholar (2016)
14. Makonin, S., Bajic, I.V., Popowich, F.: Efficient sparse matrix processing for nonintrusive load monitoring (NILM). In: 2nd International Workshop on Non-Intrusive Load Monitoring (2014)
15. Makonin, S., Popowich, F., Bajić, I.V., Gill, B., Bartram, L.: Exploiting HMM sparsity to perform online real-time nonintrusive load monitoring. IEEE Trans. Smart Grid **7**(6), 2575–2585 (2016)
16. Moulines, E., Bach, F.R.: Non-asymptotic analysis of stochastic approximation algorithms for machine learning. In: Advances in Neural Information Processing Systems, pp. 451–459 (2011)
17. Nalmpantis, C., Vrakas, D.: Machine learning approaches for non-intrusive load monitoring: from qualitative to quantitative comparation. Artif. Intell. Rev. **52**, 1–27 (2018)
18. Paradiso, F., Paganelli, F., Giuli, D., Capobianco, S.: Context-based energy disaggregation in smart homes. Fut. Internet **8**(1), 4 (2016)
19. Parson, O., Ghosh, S., Weal, M., Rogers, A.: Non-intrusive load monitoring using prior models of general appliance types. In: Twenty-Sixth AAAI Conference on Artificial Intelligence (2012)

20. Reinhardt, A., et al.: On the accuracy of appliance identification based on distributed load metering data. In: Sustainable Internet and ICT for Sustainability (SustainIT), 2012, pp. 1–9. IEEE (2012)
21. Salem, H., Sayed-Mouchaweh, M., Hassine, A.B.: A review on machine learning and data mining techniques for residential energy smart management. In: 2016 15th IEEE International Conference on Machine Learning and Applications (ICMLA), pp. 1073–1076. IEEE (2016)
22. Weiss, M., Helfenstein, A., Mattern, F., Staake, T.: Leveraging smart meter data to recognize home appliances. In: 2012 IEEE International Conference on Pervasive Computing and Communications (PerCom), pp. 190–197. IEEE (2012)
23. Welikala, S., Dinesh, C., Ekanayake, M.P.B., Godaliyadda, R.I., Ekanayake, J.: Incorporating appliance usage patterns for non-intrusive load monitoring and load forecasting. IEEE Trans. Smart Grid 10(1), 448–461 (2019)
24. Zhang, C., Zhong, M., Wang, Z., Goddard, N., Sutton, C.: Sequence-to-point learning with neural networks for non-intrusive load monitoring. In: Thirty-Second AAAI Conference on Artificial Intelligence (2018)
25. Zia, T., Bruckner, D., Zaidi, A.: A hidden markov model based procedure for identifying household electric loads. In: IECON 2011–37th Annual Conference on IEEE Industrial Electronics Society, pp. 3218–3223. IEEE (2011)
26. Zoha, A., Gluhak, A., Imran, M.A., Rajasegarar, S.: Non-intrusive load monitoring approaches for disaggregated energy sensing: a survey. Sensors 12(12), 16838–16866 (2012)

Compact Representation of a Multi-dimensional Combustion Manifold Using Deep Neural Networks

Sushrut Bhalla$^{(\boxtimes)}$ [iD], Matthew Yao [iD], Jean-Pierre Hickey [iD], and Mark Crowley [iD]

University of Waterloo, Waterloo, ON N2L 3G1, Canada
{sushrut.bhalla,matthew.yao,j6hickey,mcrowley}@uwaterloo.ca

Abstract. The computational challenges in turbulent combustion simulations stem from the physical complexities and multi-scale nature of the problem which make it intractable to compute scale-resolving simulations. For most engineering applications, the large scale separation between the flame (typically sub-millimeter scale) and the characteristic turbulent flow (typically centimeter or meter scale) allows us to evoke simplifying assumptions–such as done for the flamelet model–to pre-compute all the chemical reactions and map them to a low-order manifold. The resulting manifold is then tabulated and looked-up at run-time. As the physical complexity of combustion simulations increases (including radiation, soot formation, pressure variations etc.) the dimensionality of the resulting manifold grows which impedes an efficient tabulation and look-up. In this paper we present a novel approach to model the multi-dimensional combustion manifold. We approximate the combustion manifold using a neural network function approximator and use it to predict the temperature and composition of the reaction. We present a novel training procedure which is developed to generate a smooth output curve for temperature over the course of a reaction. We then evaluate our work against the current approach of tabulation with linear interpolation in combustion simulations. We also provide an ablation study of our training procedure in the context of over-fitting in our model. The combustion dataset used for the modeling of combustion of H_2 and O_2 in this work is released alongside this paper.

Keywords: Deep learning · Combustion manifold modelling · Flamelet models

1 Introduction

The field of turbulent combustion modeling is concerned with the prediction of complex chemical reactions–and the resulting heat release–coupled with an underlying turbulent flow field. Numerical combustion is a central design tool

© Springer Nature Switzerland AG 2020
U. Brefeld et al. (Eds.): ECML PKDD 2019, LNAI 11908, pp. 602–617, 2020.
https://doi.org/10.1007/978-3-030-46133-1_36

within the fields of energy production, automotive engineering (internal combustion engines), and aerospace engineering (rocket engines, gas turbines). The computational challenges in turbulent combustion simulations stem from the physical complexities and multi-scale nature of the problem which make it intractable to compute scale-resolving simulations, in spite of having a set of equations governing the problem. For most engineering applications, the large scale separation between the flame (typically sub millimeter/microsecond scale) and the characteristic turbulent flow (typically centimeter or meter/minute or hour scale) allows us to evoke simplifying assumptions–such as done for the flamelet model– to pre-compute all the chemical reactions and map them to a low-order manifold; the resulting manifold can then be tabulated and looked-up at run-time. The main benefit of the flamelet model is that is allows a decoupling of the turbulent flow field (and the inherent mixing) and the chemical reactions. The Damköhler number, which represents a ratio of the time scale of the chemical reactions to the transport phenomena, is often used to bound the region of validity of the flamelet model. A simplified illustration of the flamelet model for non-premixed combustion is shown in Fig. 1. With an increasing demand on the physical complexity of combustion simulations (through the inclusion of radiation, soot formation, pressure variations, wall-heat transfer etc.), the dimensionality of the resulting manifold increases and leads to the curse of dimensionality which impedes an efficient tabulation and look-up for engineering simulations. A central question in this field is how to efficiently model high dimensional manifolds necessary to capture the relevant physics of the problem and relating them to the chemical composition, pressures, and other factors computed during simulations. While the underlying governing equations for the physics are available, they are highly expensive computationally and not usable for the vast number of queries needed to run a combustion simulation of a realistic system. The ideal model would represent the well understood physical relationships in a fast, flexible form which could use varying dimensions as needed for a particular simulation or analysis task.

In the majority of the engineering-relevant, non-premixed combustion conditions, there is a large scale separation between the turbulent flow and the flame. This scale separation allows us to assume that a turbulent flame is comprised of a series of locally laminar flames, often called *flamelets*. This very convenient assumption is at the heart of flamelet modeling, one of the most common approaches in combustion modeling. For a given pressure, injection temperature, and fuel and oxidizer composition, all possible laminar flamelets can be uniquely characterized by the local *strain rate*, which is proportional to the velocity difference of the propellants in a counter-flow diffusion flame setup (see Fig. 1 top right). As the laminar combustion only depends on the strain rate (for a given pressure, injector temperature and composition), all the flamelets can be pre-computed, tabulated and queried during run-time, which leads to a great computational advantage for the simulation. In the classical flamelet model, the combustion in any part of the computational domain can be uniquely defined by the local *mixture fraction*, Z (a conserved quantity which varies between 0 for

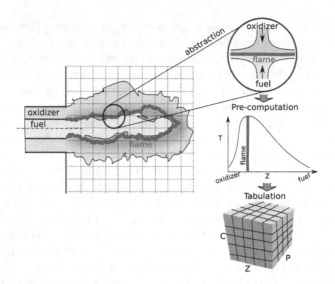

Fig. 1. A turbulent non-premixed flame is illustrated (left). The corrugated turbulent flame is assumed to be made up of locally laminar flames (as illustrated in the top right). The laminar flame (top right) can be computed, *a priori*, for all strain rates and tabulated for lookup at run-time. The tabulation is often done with respect to the known/transported variables from the simulation such as mixture fraction, Z, progress-variable C, variance of mixture fraction Z'', pressure, P (bottom right).

pure oxidizer and 1 for pure fuel), *strain rate*, χ (time scale ratio between the chemical reactions and the flow), and the *mixture fraction variance*, Z'' (which accounts for the turbulent mixing). More recent variations of the flamelet model have replaced the strain rate by a non-conservative *progress variable*, C. This latest model is called the *Flamelet-Progress Variable Approach (FPVA)*. The reader interested in a more comprehensive overview of these combustion modeling paradigms is invited to consult [22].

In recent years, deep learning has been used to achieve state of the art results in image classification [5,26], policy learning [12,18] and natural language processing [25]. Deep learning has the ability to learn compact representations and can naturally handle interpolation of points which are not part of the training data. For the combustion modeling problem, our hypothesis is that deep learning can be used to learn a model of the higher dimension combustion manifold which can be used for simulation. In this paper we present an architecture to test this hypothesis and the techniques, including novel ones, we used to train a discriminative model for combustion. We show that we can reduce the combustion simulation running time and memory requirements compared to the current tabular methods. To examine the relative impact of each model component, we present an ablation study of our regularization methods and training techniques. We also propose an improved over-sampling procedure and a loss function which forces the model to focus on more difficult data points during training.

Significant improvements in modeling for the combustion modeling problem could lead to a revolution in the ability to simulate complex combustion reactions and more efficiently design better engines and power systems. This paper sets the groundwork for such a change by showing how to use deep learning to free modelers from the limits of tabular representations.

2 Related Work

Over the years the classical flamelet methodologies have been extended to tackle increasingly complex reactive flow problems. For example, the slow time-scale of NOx formation has motivated the use of unsteady flamelet [16] and the need to account for radiative heat loss effects due to the sensitivity to temperature of the NO formation has resulted in an FPV framework that includes an additional enthalpy term [7]. Similarly, the strong heat loss at the combustor walls has motivated a wall heat loss model [15,24] which also includes an additional enthalpy term. Many combustion processes, such as liquid rocket combustion, are undertaken under variable pressure conditions which has been integrated into the flamelet framework [17]. Other extensions includes the consideration of multi-fuel systems [3]–which demand the use of two separate mixture fractions– or the inclusion of combustion chemistry that is highly sensitive to molecular diffusion (primarily in partially premixed settings) resulting in the introduction of multidimensional flamelet-generated manifolds (MFM) [20].

There is a growing demand to accurately represent the combustion process in more complex combustion scenarios such as those above. However, this requires a higher-dimensional manifold than the widely used FPVA method which commonly utilizes a three-dimensional tabulation of all the variables of interest, $\phi(Z, \widetilde{Z''^2}, c)$. Not only does the tabulated data occupy a larger portion of the available memory, the searching and retrieval of the pre-tabulated data becomes increasingly expensive in a higher-dimensional space. For example, assuming a standard flamelet table discretization of $(nZ, nZvar, nC) = (200, 100, 50)$ with say 15 tabulated variables, we obtain a pre-computed combustion table of 120 Mb. The addition of a variable such as enthalpy with a very coarse discretization of 20 points, brings the size of the table to 2.4 Gb. Recent consideration of a high-dimensional flamelet generated manifold for stratified-swirled flames with wall heat loss requires a 5D manifold which would be even larger [2]. This could only be achieved by using a very coarse discretization of the flamelet manifold (e.g. only 10 points are used to account for the variance of mixture fraction). One approach to address the large tabulative size has been proposed by using polynomial basis functions [27]; other approaches have looked at the use of Bézier patches [28]. These approaches provide adequate ways to reduce the tabulation size, retrieval time and improve accuracy, but face the inevitable curse of dimensionality. Other approaches seek to use principle component analysis to identify the optimal progress variable for the definition of a low-dimensional manifold [19]. Even if those approaches prove effective, inevitably many multi-physics systems will require a higher-dimensional space to adequately capture the relevant processes.

There has been some previous work on using machine learning for combustion manifold modeling. In 2009, a thorough experimental comparison was carried out by Ihme et al. [8] using a simple *Multi-Layer Perceptron (MLP)* for learning a mapping function to replace the tabular lookup method and thus speed up combustion simulation calculations. They showed that a neural network approach could be more generalizable but they found it had much worse accuracy than the tabular approach. This led to the method not being adopted for combustion simulator evaluations by the community. The approach in [8] was limited to a simple range of MLP variations and focused on the optimization of the network structure relative to a particular metric. They also did not have the benefit of modern deep neural network training techniques or regularization methods and used the classical approach of sigmoid activation functions rather than rectified linear units. In this work we focus on finding an optimal deep neural network training strategy which can achieve results approximately close to the true data curves. We show that our loss function and over sampling methods can achieve better accuracy than [8]. We also demonstrate our approach provides an acceleration over tabular methods for realistic combustion simulator evaluations by leveraging a CUDA enabled GPU. We also implement trained models for the species composition, temperature, source term and heat release.

Recent work [11] has focused on predicting the subgrid scale wrinkling of a flame by using a convolutional neural network. The work focuses on training an autoencoder with a U-Net network structure, which uses the current Direct Numerical Simulation (DNS) snapshot to predict the next DNS snapshot. The training data is a collection of 2 DNS of different flames; a third DNS is used for testing. This is a very simplified model to account for combustion and doesn't make any flamelet-based assumptions. Using a temporally dependent data structure for training limits the work in [11] and it cannot be easily extended to instantaneous combustion evaluations. Their model also requires the flame to be extrapolated to a certain length for the CNN model to be effective, as the autoencoder model they use would fail at the boundary conditions of the flame. In contrast, our model is built with the understanding that there can be multiple flames being simulated at a given instance and they could be running at different resolutions. Resolution in combustion simulations represents the factor by which the flamelet has been discretized based on the precision and accuracy required by the researcher. Thus, our model is built using fully connected layers which map the pressure, mixture fraction and progress variable to the species composition, temperature, source term and heat release.

3 Modeling Methods for High Dimensional Data

In this section we present the techniques we used to train our deep neural network model to predict the composition of the species (H, O_2, O, OH, H_2, H_2O, HO_2, H_2O_2), temperature (T), source term (W) and heat release (HR) of any flamelet given the pressure (P), progress variable (C) and mixture fraction (Z). The training data consists of flamelets for pressure values in the set

$(1, 2, 5, 10, 20, 30, 35, 40, 50)$ bar and the associated progress variable (C) and mixture fraction (Z). We reserve flames at pressure values $(15, 25, 33, 42)$ bar for testing purposes. The validation data set is generated by sampling sections of the flames in the training data set. The data was generated using FlameMaster, a 1D solver for the solution of the laminar, diffusion flamelet equations. The flamelets were generated at varying strain rates, from equilibrium combustion to nearly the quenched solution at varying base pressure levels. For all flamelets, the inflow temperature of the fuel and oxidizer remain constant. At each condition, the flamelets are solved with 1001 grid points with local mesh adaptation.

3.1   Neural Network Design

Table 1. Neural Network design used for prediction. All models use fully connected layers with *Leaky ReLU* as the activation function. Only layers in **bold** are regularized.

Prediction output	Hidden layers
Temperature (T)	**(64,128,512,512,1024,**1024)
Source term (W)	**(64,128,512,512,512,**512)
Heat release (HR)	**(64,128,512,512,1024,2048,**2048)

Four different neural networks are designed for predicting the Species, Heat Release, Temperature and Source Term. The species show a high correlation in combustion time series as the total mass in the systems stays constant. In our experiments for species we predict the fraction of total mass which belongs to each species. In the neural network shown in Fig. 2 the network shares a common model for the first 7 layers and a separate fully connected head of 64 units to predict individual species. This improves the prediction accuracy and also reduces the memory requirements for the model. Note that we also introduce *function generators* (FG) to augment the input data with the function set $(sin, cos, square, exp, log)$ applied over the inputs (Z, C, P). The FG output is concatenated to the input of network. We found that using FGs leads to faster training convergence by providing common transformations right in the training data.

The network design for T and W is similar to the design used for the prediction of species, see Table 1. However, even though T and W are highly correlated, their numerical scales are vastly different, thus, we use separate networks for them. We use *Leaky Rectified Linear Units (ReLu)* as the activation function for all layers in our neural network models unless otherwise specified [4]. All biases are initialized to 0.0 and weights are initialized using *He initialization* [6] with sampling from a normal distribution. All inputs to the network are standardized using Z-score standardization. We follow the same procedure for test set, where we use the mean and variance of the training data set to normalize the inputs. We use the *Adam optimizer* [10] with a learning rate of 0.001 and set the optimizer hyper-parameters to $\beta_1 = 0.9, \beta_2 = 0.999, \epsilon = 1e - 08$.

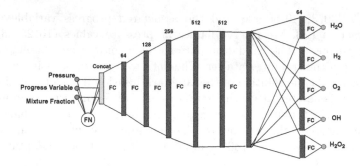

Fig. 2. Deep Neural Network structure used for training of Species. *FC* indicates fully connected layers. *FN* is the function generator.

3.2 Over Sampling Hard Examples

For the remainder of the paper we focus on temperature which is the most essential prediction for combustion simulation. The temperature curve for a single combustion (H_2, O_2) flamelet looks like a parabola as shown in Fig. 3. The temperature curve shown, usually has relatively large gradients in the beginning and end (pure oxidiser or pure fuel). The semi-dome shape at the top of the temperature curve accounts for more than 50% of the input domain and shows the highest variability from flame to flame. When training deep neural networks with uniform sampling, they are easily able to learn the edges of the temperature curve as it shows low variability, however, the model performs poorly in the domain of high variability (the semi-dome). To improve this we employ over-sampling of the *"hard examples"* defined as examples having error larger than median error of the batch:

$$HE(d)_{d \sim D} = \begin{cases} 1 & Error_{epoch_{t-1}}(d) \geq median(\overline{Error_{epoch_{t-1}}(batch_{smpl})}) \\ 0 & otherwise \end{cases} \quad (1)$$

New batches are created by sampling with replacement 75% hard/25% easy examples from the sampling batch $batch_{smpl}$. We arrive at a value of 75% of hard examples through cross validation. A sampling batch refer to a uniformly sampled batch from the training dataset which is at least 2× larger than the training batch size. Using $batch_{smpl}$ for our over-sampling reduces training time and memory requirements when compared to the rank based method employed by online batch selection methods [14].

3.3 Importance Weights Error and Gradient Clipping

Recent techniques for object detection and classification have shown that weighting the loss function separately for hard and easy examples leads to better model predictions [13]. Training of deep neural networks or recurrent networks shows improvements in training stability by performing gradient clipping [21].

We incorporate these techniques in training our model for regression prediction. The gradient clipping clips large gradients in the backpropagation phase of neural network training and thus reduces any damage to our trained model caused by anomalies in our data. Through cross validation, we arrive at a value of 5.0 for gradient clipping. We choose to weight the cost function using a constant value of $\alpha = 0.4$ (in Eq. 2) for all easy data-points $(d{\sim}D)$. The data points with loss in the lower 25 percentile are considered easy. This approach leads to good results in the semi-dome area of the temperature curve because it weighs down the contribution of a large number of easy examples with small gradient updates and allows the training to focus on the data points (d) with higher cost. The approach can also be used as a replacement to over sampling of hard examples. The new loss function is shown in Eq. 2.

$$L_{imp}(d)_{d{\sim}D} = \begin{cases} \alpha \times Cost(T(d), \hat{T}(d)) & loss(d) \leq rank_{25\%}(loss(batch_{smpl})) \\ Cost(T(d), \hat{T}(d)) & otherwise \end{cases}$$

(2)

3.4 Regularization

Over-fitting leads to large oscillation on the training data set which would lead to poor performance in numerical simulators used for modeling combustion. To reduce the chance of oscillation we combine $L1$ and $L2$ regularizers with an $L1L2$ regularized loss function given by the following formula:

$$Loss = Cost(batch) + \lambda_{l1} \times \sum_{i}(|NN_{w_i}|) + \lambda_{l2} \times \sum_{i}(NN_{w_i})^2 \quad (3)$$

Through cross-validation over the accuracy metric and qualitative assessments of the smoothness of the predicted temperature curve, we arrive at the values of $\lambda_{l1} = 0.00015$ and $\lambda_{l2} = 0.000125$. The $L1L2$ cost adds a regularization term to the total loss to be jointly minimized by the optimizer. This forces the network to predict with smaller values of weights which produces smoother predictions of the temperature curve.

We tested other standard regularization techniques including Batch Normalization (BN) [9], Dropout [23] and Layer Normalization (LN) [1] for the regression tasks. BN normalizes the output of a hidden unit based on the mean and variance of training data, this performs poorly when the testing data set is vastly different from the training data. Dropout on the other hand, does not perform well during training. Dropout works by dropping a connection between hidden units with a probability $p = 0.5$ (typical for classification tasks) and optimizing the sub-network. In regression prediction, the scaling factor p used in dropout leads to training predictions lower than the true data and the reverse is true during the testing phase (due to weight scaling). The network with dropout is not able to train well on toy regression problems (for the function $f(x) = x^2$). LN normalizes the input features of the hidden layers on a per data point basis and thus doesn't exhibit the problems from batch normalization. LN seems to be a better fit than batch normalization and dropout for regression tasks, however as we show in the experiments section, the performance with *L1L2* regularization is better.

3.5   Ensemble Model

Many machine learning tasks have shown improved results by using an ensemble of models. In regression, ensembles of models would be highly beneficial as it would reduce the amount of regularization required per model and the accuracy could be improved with careful selection of a set of prediction models. We design an averaging ensemble of trained models. We train five deep neural network models for prediction of the temperature curve. The ensemble model also helps in improving the accuracy of the model. We compute the final prediction by averaging the four best (in terms of deviation from the mean prediction) individual models. This allows us to ignore results from models which didn't perform well on certain data-points and pick the best of all trained models.

4   Results and Discussions

4.1   Quantitative Analysis

Table 2 shows the accuracy and the loss for each prediction variable. A prediction is considered accurate if the model prediction ($\hat{T}(d)$) is within a standard error range E_T, as shown in the formula below for the temperature model:

$$accuracy_{d \sim D} = \begin{cases} 1 & \hat{T}(d) \in \{T(d) - E_T, T(d) + E_T\} \\ 0 & otherwise \end{cases} \tag{4}$$

The value of E_O (where $O \in \{T, W, HR, Species\}$) is computed based on the resolution of the combustion simulator and an expert's opinion. The value of $0.005 \times range$ is used based on the discretization error in typical combustion simulations arising from tabulation method. We detail the values of E_O for each output label in the Table 2. Accuracy is used for model comparison since using the resulting MSE could be misleading. That's because the model could be performing well on easy examples (head and tail of T curves) and poorly on the hard examples (mostly in the semi-dome part of the curve). This would result in a lower loss value but poor accuracy for simulator evaluation purposes.

We focus on the predictions of T and W for our work as their performance is vital for our model to be useful for the combustion community. The mean error results in Table 2 are computed using the formula $ME = \frac{1}{N} \sum_1^N (|y - \hat{y}|)$. For temperature, we see a mean error of 82.44 which is the deviation from the tabulated data on test data set. We show using our simulation tests that this error is sustainable and can be used in combustion simulators. The accuracy of 54.60% represents the number of data points which are predicted within a range of $34.47K$ range of the tabulated data. We see similar accuracy for source term

Table 2. Quantitative analysis of predictions of species composition, temperature (T), source term (W) and Heat release (HR) using the regression model in Fig. 2

	Range $(O_{MAX} - O_{MIN})$	Standard error range (E_O)	Mean error	Training accuracy	Validation accuracy
H	0.0219	0.0001	0.00431	29.23	21.44
O_2	1.0	0.005	0.3419	20.17	12.56
O	0.0665	0.00033	0.00892	55.79	37.43
OH	0.1279	0.00064	0.0345	56.91	43.34
H_2	1.0	0.005	0.2606	38.40	25.41
H_2O	0.8865	0.0044	0.6056	26.19	14.59
HO_2	0.0142	$7.1e - 05$	0.00137	60.36	41.42
H_2O_2	0.0091	$4.5e - 05$	0.00259	55.92	36.05
$HR(J/m^3)$	$93.4e + 81$	$6.4e + 78$	$1.05e + 76$	81.23	81.18
$T(K)$	3295	34.47	82.44	61.97	54.60
W	30	0.149	3.023	71.55	58.144

(W) with a mean error value of 3.023. The R^2 statistic for our model predictions of T and achieve an average value of 0.94 per flamelet predictions. The model is able to capture a large part of the combustion manifold and can be used for evaluation with combustion simulators.

4.2   Ablation Study and Qualitative Analysis

In this section we present an ablation study of our training methodology by varying or removing components and comparing the quantitative results. We also support this with qualitative results where we pick a flamelet from the test data set and analyze the predicted temperature curve generated by our model. The curve used for the qualitative study in this section is for $P = 25\,$bar. As mentioned, the closest pressure values in the training data are at 20 bar and 30 bar. Thus the ablation results also provide us an insight into the interpolation skills of the deep neural network model. The flamelet used for comparison was selected at random and represents an above average performance case of our deep neural network model.

Ablation Study of Regularization Techniques. Figure 3(a) shows the qualitative results for training the neural network with *L1L2* regularization and without any regularization. The *L1L2* regularization forces the weights of the neural network to be closer to 0. This affects the temperature curve generated by our regularized model as seen in Fig. 3(a). The curve shows very little oscillations

Table 3. Quantitative results for regularization of NN on combustion manifold.

	No regularizer	$L1L2$ regularizer	Layer normalization	Batch normalization
Training accuracy	87.59	59.01	44.53	61.68
Testing accuracy	31.44	39.83	23.63	12.28

which is necessary condition for our model to be used in real combustion simulators. Due to the restriction on the weights of the neural network, our model suffers in terms of performance as we get a temperature curve distant from the true data curve. Table 3 summarizes the performance of using different regularization techniques. The value of $\lambda_{L1}, \lambda_{L2}$ is set to $0.00015, 0.000125$ respectively. We see that $L1L2$ regularization performs the best on test data set. We thus use $L1L2$ for all the experiments. BN is also able to train well on the training data set, but performs poorly when the distribution of the data is changed during testing. BN was also not able to scale to larger batch sizes and thus suffered in performance when compared to other methods. LN alleviates the dependence on the training data and normalizes each layer's input features. This results in better performance, and the results of LN are more predictable than batch normalization.

Ablation Study of over Sampling. Next we examine the incremental effect of using over sampling of hard examples from the data set based on the mean square error for each data-point in the previous training epoch. Figure 3(b) shows the comparison of the predicted temperature curves for using over-sampling compared to basic uniform sampling. Both training methods use $L1L2$ regularization with the same hyper-parameters as last subsection. The results clearly show that over sampling is able to better approximate the temperature curve. The over sampling of hard examples allows the network to improve its predictions on semi-dome structure near the top of the temperature curve. The network is able to approximate the beginning and end of the temperature curve as seen with a naive neural network model in Fig. 3(b). The plot shows the temperature (same as previous subsection) curve for a flame at pressure value of 25 bar over the mixture fraction. The mixture fraction denotes the progress of the $3 - D$ combustion flame. Table 4 shows the quantitative improvements in the prediction accuracy of the temperature curves for over-sampling with the same neural network structure and training hyper-parameters used for uniform sampling case. The results show a direct improvement in the qualitative curve structure and the accuracy metric. The fraction of hard examples per batch was set to 0.75 through cross validation.

Ablation Study of Ensemble Model. Next we present an ablation study of the ensemble model used in our work. The Fig. 3(c) shows the comparison

Table 4. Quantitative results for over sampling of NN on combustion manifold.

	Uniform sampling	Over sampling	Ensemble model
Training accuracy	59.01	63.58	61.97
Testing accuracy	39.83	48.87	47.73

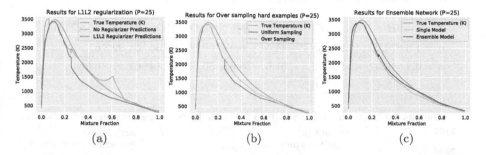

(a)   (b)   (c)

Fig. 3. Ablation study of (a) Regularization techniques, (b) Over Sampling for Neural Network Training and (c) Ensemble models.

of predicted temperature curves for the ensemble method against the best single model temperature curve achieved using over sampling. While regularization reduces the oscillation in the neural network predictions, the over-sampling technique forces the network to shift its weights to focus on the hard examples. This reduces the regularization effect on the network's predictions. Thus, to further reduce the oscillations in the predicted model, we use an ensemble of neural networks. The neural networks differ based on the number of hidden layers, size of hidden layers, weight initialization technique, optimization technique (RMSProp or ADAM optimizer). These variations force each model to converge to a different saddle point in the optimization landscape. The ensemble method achieves better results than the individual model in terms of accuracy and smoothness of the predicted temperature curve. The Fig. 3(c) shows the results for an averaging ensemble network comprised of 4 separately trained neural networks. The Table 4 shows the quantitative comparison of using an ensemble method when compared to the best single deep neural network model.

Ablation Study of Importance Loss Weighting. In this subsection, we present an ablation study for importance weighting the loss of easy and hard data-points. The reduced loss of easy examples, reduces the gradients and thus affects a smaller change in the weights of the neural network. Hard examples, on the other hand, can be highly weighted which leads to large gradients in the neural network and thus the model over-fits to the hard examples. We use cross-validation to arrive at a value of constant error weights of 0.4 for easy examples and 1.0 for hard examples. Table 5 shows the quantitative improvements in the training and test accuracy of the same neural network model with and without importance loss weighting. The importance loss weighting is an important aspect of our training procedure as it can lead to large accuracy improvements in some cases.

Table 5. Comparison of impact on accuracy for differing levels of α in Eq. 2 for hard and easy data. Uses the Mean Square Error cost function.

	H	O_2	O	OH	H_2	H_2O	HO_2	H_2O_2	$T(K)$	W
$\alpha = 1.0$	29.23	18.05	55.79	45.58	38.40	60.56	60.36	55.92	61.97	
$\alpha = 0.4$	46.57	43.6	62.3	51.6	38.51	85.76	62.14	67.41	63.64	

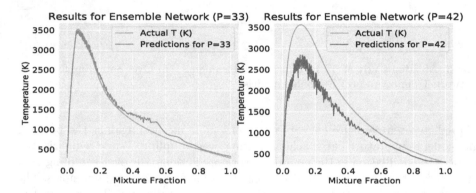

Fig. 4. Study of the consistency of the training data.

4.3   Study of the Consistency of the Training Data

The training data used for our experiments uses pressure values in the set $(1, 2, 5, 10, 20, 30, 35, 40, 50)$ bar. The validation data is generated by reserving 20% of the training data for validation purposes. This approach ensures that the training data and the validation data share the data distribution. The testing data set is comprised of pressure values the neural network has never witnessed before and thus our model must precisely interpolate between the training data-points to generate the accurate temperature curves for the testing data-set. The testing data-set is comprised of pressure values in the set $(15, 25, 33, 42)$. We use our best trained single neural network model to predict the interpolation results for all pressure values in the test set. The model achieve an accuracy of 72.21% and mean error of $68.47K$ for pressure of 33 bar. The model achieve an accuracy of 38.83% and mean error of $661.35K$ for pressure of 42 bar. Figure 4 shows the qualitative comparison for the interpolation results of the neural network model at pressure value of $(33, 42)$ bar. Through experiments on pressure values of 15, 25 bar, we see similar performance. Based on the experimental evaluations, we should be training our model at intervals of 5 bar to achieve better accuracy at interpolated pressure values.

4.4   Model Analysis Using Combustion Simulator

Table 6. Memory requirements and inference time analysis

	Tabulation method	Deep neural networks
Parallel inference time (in ms)	1.2×10^5 ms	13.92
Serial inference time (in s)	10.997 ms	55.27
Memory requirements	184.64 MB	24.158 MB

The efficacy of DNN-based flamelet combustion modelling rests on two important parameters for turbulent combustion simulations. First, the modelling of the high-dimensional manifold should result in a smaller memory footprint compared to traditional tabular approaches. For a three-dimensional manifold, a compact representation takes up about 8 times less memory compared to an adequately resolved table. With increasing dimensionality of the combustion manifold (inclusion of wall heating, NO_x computations etc.) the impact on the DNN model is modest whereas we typically expect a two decade increase in the table size per additional dimension. Second, the query time should be quick for N−dimensional interpolations for simulator evaluations as the size of data and dimensionality increases. Table 6 shows the query time for 50,000 data points performed in serial and batch fashions. The simulator evaluations can be easily parallelized to take advantage of the batched inference time.

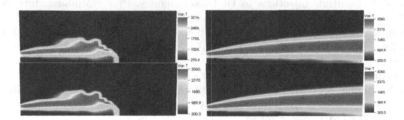

Fig. 5. Comparison of simulation using DNN data (top) and tabulated data (bottom).

As a proof of concept test, a simulation of a piloted hydrogen/oxygen diffusion flame was conducted using OpenFOAM. At a single timestep, the calculated temperature field was replaced using a predicted temperature field obtained via the deep neural net predictions. The solution was then advanced using the newly predicted temperature field. The results are shown in Fig. 5. Although the DNN predicted slightly higher temperature values, both solutions reach the same steady state.

5   Conclusion

In this paper we presented a novel training procedure for approximating high dimensional combustion manifolds for use in combustion simulations using deep neural networks. We propose a novel loss function for regression tasks with examples of varying degree of difficulty. We also propose a fast over sampling methodology based on the cost of each data point. The proposed model achieves sufficient accuracy when compared with tabulated data and runs fast enough to integrate into high dimensional multi-physics simulators of combustion. Our model allows for cheap computation of very complex physics, compared to the traditional tabulation methods which can not scale to high dimensions. We plan to extend this work to focus on dimensionality reduction to understand core aspects of the combustion manifold. Our prediction model for HR does not perform adequately as the output range of HR is large (10^{81}). The drawering technique discussed in [29] can be used to reduce the complexity of learning the range of HR.

References

1. Ba, J.L., Kiros, J.R., Hinton, G.E.: Layer normalization. arXiv preprint arXiv:1607.06450 (2016)
2. Donini, A., Bastiaans, R.J.M., van Oijen, J.A., de Goey, L.P.H.: A 5-D implementation of FGM for the large Eddy simulation of a stratified swirled flame with heat loss in a Gas Turbine combustor. Flow Turbul. Combust. **98**(3), 887–922 (2016). https://doi.org/10.1007/s10494-016-9777-7
3. Felsch, C., Gauding, M., Hasse, C., Vogel, S., Peters, N.: An extended flamelet model for multiple injections in DI Diesel engines. Proc. Combust. Inst. **32 II**, 2775–2783 (2009)
4. Glorot, X., Bordes, A., Bengio, Y.: Deep sparse rectifier neural networks. In: Proceedings of the Fourteenth International Conference on Artificial Intelligence and Statistics, pp. 315–323 (2011)
5. Graham, B.: Fractional max-pooling. arXiv preprint arXiv:1412.6071 (2014)
6. He, K., Zhang, X., Ren, S., Sun, J.: Deep residual learning for image recognition. In: Proceedings of the IEEE Conference on Computer Vision and Pattern Recognition, pp. 770–778 (2016)
7. Ihme, M., Pitsch, H.: Modeling of radiation and nitric oxide formation in turbulent nonpremixed flames using a flamelet/progress variable formulation. Phys. Fluids **20**(5) (2008). https://doi.org/10.1063/1.2911047
8. Ihme, M., Schmitt, C., Pitsch, H.: Optimal artificial neural networks and tabulation methods for chemistry representation in les of a bluff-body swirl-stabilized flame. Proc. Combust. Inst. **32 I**(1), 1527–1535 (2009). https://doi.org/10.1016/j.proci.2008.06.100
9. Ioffe, S., Szegedy, C.: Batch normalization: accelerating deep network training by reducing internal covariate shift. arXiv preprint arXiv:1502.03167 (2015)
10. Kingma, D.P., Ba, J.: Adam: a method for stochastic optimization. arXiv preprint arXiv:1412.6980 (2014)
11. Lapeyre, C., Misdariis, A., Cazard, N., Veynante, D., Poinsot, T.: Training convolutional neural networks to estimate turbulent sub-grid scale reaction rates. arXiv preprint arXiv:1810.03691 (2018)

12. Lillicrap, T.P., et al.: Continuous control with deep reinforcement learning. arXiv preprint arXiv:1509.02971 (2015)
13. Lin, T.Y., Goyal, P., Girshick, R., He, K., Dollár, P.: Focal loss for dense object detection. In: Proceedings of the IEEE International Conference on Computer Vision, pp. 2980–2988 (2017)
14. Loshchilov, I., Hutter, F.: Online batch selection for faster training of neural networks. arXiv preprint arXiv:1511.06343 (2015)
15. Ma, P.C., Wu, H., Ihme, M., Hickey, J.P.: Nonadiabatic flamelet formulation for predicting wall heat transfer in rocket engines. AIAA J. **56**(6), 1–14 (2018). https://doi.org/10.2514/1.J056539
16. Mauss, F., Keller, D., Peters, N.: A lagrangian simulation of flamelet extinction and re-ignition in turbulent jet diffusion flames. Symp. (Intl.) Combust. **23**(1), 693–698 (1991)
17. Mittal, V., Pitsch, H.: A flamelet model for premixed combustion under variable pressure conditions. Proc. Combust. Inst. **34**(2), 2995–3003 (2013)
18. Mnih, V., et al.: Human-level control through deep reinforcement learning. Nature **518**(7540), 529 (2015)
19. Najafi-Yazdi, A., Cuenot, B., Mongeau, L.: Systematic definition of progress variables and Intrinsically Low-Dimensional, Flamelet Generated Manifolds for chemistry tabulation. Combust. Flame **159**(3), 1197–1204 (2012). https://doi.org/10.1016/j.combustflame.2011.10.003
20. Nguyen, P.D., Vervisch, L., Subramanian, V., Domingo, P.: Multidimensional flamelet-generated manifolds for partially premixed combustion. Combust. Flame **157**(1), 43–61 (2010). https://doi.org/10.1016/j.combustflame.2009.07.008
21. Pascanu, R., Mikolov, T., Bengio, Y.: On the difficulty of training recurrent neural networks. In: International Conference on Machine Learning, pp. 1310–1318 (2013)
22. Poinsot, T., Veynante, D.: Theoretical and Numerical Combustion. RT Edwards, Inc., Philadelphia (2005)
23. Srivastava, N., Hinton, G., Krizhevsky, A., Sutskever, I., Salakhutdinov, R.: Dropout: a simple way to prevent neural networks from overfitting. J. Mach. Learn. Res. **15**(1), 1929–1958 (2014)
24. Trisjono, P., Kleinheinz, K., Pitsch, H., Kang, S.: Large eddy simulation of stratified and sheared flames of a premixed turbulent stratified flame burner using a flamelet model with heat loss. Flow Turbul. Combust. **92**(1), 201–235 (2013). https://doi.org/10.1007/s10494-013-9522-4
25. Vaswani, A., et al.: Attention is all you need. In: Advances in Neural Information Processing Systems, pp. 5998–6008 (2017)
26. Wan, L., Zeiler, M., Zhang, S., Le Cun, Y., Fergus, R.: Regularization of neural networks using dropconnect. In: International Conference on Machine Learning, pp. 1058–1066 (2013)
27. Weise, S., Popp, S., Messig, D., Hasse, C.: A computationally efficient implementation of tabulated combustion chemistry based on polynomials and automatic source code generation. Flow Turbul. Combust. **100**(1), 119–146 (2017). https://doi.org/10.1007/s10494-017-9826-x
28. Yao, M., Mortada, M., Devaud, C., Hickey, J.P.: Locally-adaptive tabulation of low-dimensional manifolds using Bezier patch reconstruction. In: Spring Technical Meeting of the Combustion Institute Canadian Section (2017)
29. Żołna, K.: Improving the performance of neural networks in regression tasks using drawering. In: 2017 International Joint Conference on Neural Networks (IJCNN), pp. 2533–2538. IEEE (2017)

Applied Data Science: Applications

Generative Adversarial Networks for Failure Prediction

Shuai Zheng$^{(\boxtimes)}$, Ahmed Farahat, and Chetan Gupta

Industrial AI Lab, Hitachi America Ltd., Santa Clara, CA, USA
{Shuai.Zheng,Ahmed.Farahat,Chetan.Gupta}@hal.hitachi.com

Abstract. Prognostics and Health Management (PHM) is an emerging engineering discipline which is concerned with the analysis and prediction of equipment health and performance. One of the key challenges in PHM is to accurately predict impending failures in the equipment. In recent years, solutions for failure prediction have evolved from building complex physical models to the use of machine learning algorithms that leverage the data generated by the equipment. However, failure prediction problems pose a set of unique challenges that make direct application of traditional classification and prediction algorithms impractical. These challenges include the highly imbalanced training data, the extremely high cost of collecting more failure samples, and the complexity of the failure patterns. Traditional oversampling techniques will not be able to capture such complexity and accordingly result in overfitting the training data. This paper addresses these challenges by proposing a novel algorithm for failure prediction using Generative Adversarial Networks (GAN-FP). GAN-FP first utilizes two GAN networks to simultaneously generate training samples and build an inference network that can be used to predict failures for new samples. GAN-FP first adopts an info-GAN to generate realistic failure and non-failure samples, and initialize the weights of the first few layers of the inference network. The inference network is then tuned by optimizing a weighted loss objective using only real failure and non-failure samples. The inference network is further tuned using a second GAN whose purpose is to guarantee the consistency between the generated samples and corresponding labels. GAN-FP can be used for other imbalanced classification problems as well. Empirical evaluation on several benchmark datasets demonstrates that GAN-FP significantly outperforms existing approaches, including under-sampling, SMOTE, ADASYN, weighted loss, and infoGAN augmented training.

Keywords: Generative Adversarial Networks · Failure Prediction · Imbalanced Classification

1 Introduction

Reliability of industrial systems, products and equipment is critical not only to manufacturers, operating companies, but also to the entire society. For example,

© Springer Nature Switzerland AG 2020
U. Brefeld et al. (Eds.): ECML PKDD 2019, LNAI 11908, pp. 621–637, 2020.
https://doi.org/10.1007/978-3-030-46133-1_37

in 2017, due to electrical fault in a refrigerator, Grenfell Tower fire in London killed 72 people, hospitalized 74 and caused 200 million to 1 billion GBP property damage [1]. Because of the profound impact and extreme costs associated with system failures, methods that can predict and prevent such catastrophes have long been investigated. These methodologies can be grouped under the framework of Prognostics and Health Management (PHM), where prognostics is the process of predicting the future reliability of a product by assessing the extent of deviation or degradation of the product while the product is still working properly; health management is the process of real time measuring and monitoring. The benefits of accurate PHM approaches include: (1) providing advance warning of failures; (2) minimizing unnecessary maintenance, extending maintenance cycles, and maintaining effectiveness through timely repair actions; (3) reducing cost related to inspection and maintenance, reducing cost related to system downtime and inventory by scheduling replacement parts in the right time; and (4) improving the design of future systems [2,3]. Failure prediction is one of the main tasks in PHM.

Failure prediction approaches can be categorized into model-based approaches and data-driven approaches [4]. Model-based approaches use mathematical equations to incorporate a physical understanding of the system, and include both system modeling and physics-of-failure (PoF) modeling. The limitation is that the development of these models requires detailed knowledge of the underlying physical processes that lead to system failure. Furthermore, the physical models are often unable to model environmental interactions. Alternatively, data-driven techniques are gaining popularity. There are several reasons: (1) data-driven methods learn the behavior of the system based on monitored data and can work with incomplete domain knowledge; (2) data-driven methods can learn correlations between parameters and work well in complex systems, such as aircraft engines, HPC systems [5], large manufacturing systems; (3) with the development of IoT systems, large amount of data is being collected in real time, which makes real time monitoring and alerts for PHM possible.

However, data-driven techniques for failure prediction have a set of unique challenges. Firstly, for many systems and components, there is not enough failure examples in the training data. Physical equipment and systems are engineered not to fail and as a result failure data is rare and difficult to collect. Secondly, complex physical systems have multiple failure and degradation modes, often depending upon varying operating conditions. One way to overcome these challenges is to artificially generate failure data such that different failure modes and operating conditions are adequately covered and machine learning models can be learned over this augmented data. Traditionally, oversampling has been used to generate more training samples. However, oversampling cannot capture the complexity of the failure patterns and can easily introduce undesirable noise with overfitting risks due to the limitation of oversampling models. With the successful application of Generative Adversarial Networks (GANs) [6] in other domains, GANs provide a natural way to generate additional data. For example, in computer vision, GANs are used to generate realistic images to improve performance in applications, such as, biomedical imaging [7], person re-identification [8] and image enhancement [9]. In addition, GANs have been used to augment classification problems by using semi-supervised learning [10,11] or domain adaptation [12]. However, GAN methods cannot guarantee the consistency of the generated samples and their corresponding labels. For example, infoGAN is claimed to have 5% error rate in generating MNIST digits [13].

In this work, we propose a novel algorithm that utilizes GANs for Failure Prediction (GAN-FP). Compared to existing work, our contributions are:

1. We propose GAN-FP in which three different modules work collaboratively to train an inference network: (1) In one module, realistic failure and non-failure samples are generated using infoGAN. (2) In another module, the weighted loss objective is adopted to train inference network using real failure and non-failure samples. In our design, this inference network shares the weights of the first few layers with the discriminator network of the infoGAN. (3) In the third module, the inference network is further tuned using a second GAN by enforcing consistency between the output of the first GAN and label generated by the inference network.
2. We design a collaborative mini-batch training scheme for GANs and the inference network.
3. We conduct several experiments that show significant improvement over existing approaches according to different evaluation criteria. Through visualization, we verify that GAN-FP generates realistic sensor data, and captures discriminative features of failure and non-failure samples.
4. Failure prediction is the motivation and typical use case of our design. For broader applications, GAN-FP can be applied to other general imbalanced classification problems as well.

2   Background

2.1   Imbalanced Classification for Failure Prediction

Existing approaches to handle imbalanced data can be categorized into two groups: re-sampling (oversampling/undersampling) and cost-sensitive learning. **Re-sampling** method aims to balance the class priors by undersampling the majority non-failure class or oversampling the minority failure class (or both) [14]. Chawla *et al.* [15] proposed SMOTE oversampling, which generates new synthetic examples from the minority class between the closest neighbors from this class. He *et al.* [16] proposed ADASYN oversampling, which uses a weighted distribution for different minority class examples according to their level of difficulty in learning. Inspired by the success of boosting algorithms and ensemble learning, re-sampling techniques have been integrated into ensemble learning [14]. **Cost-sensitive learning** assigns higher misclassification costs to the failure class than to the non-failure class [17]. Zhang *et al.* [18] proposed an evolutionary cost-sensitive deep belief network for imbalanced classification, which uses adaptive differential evolution to optimize the misclassification costs.

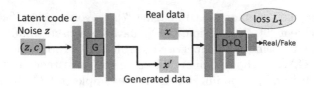

Fig. 1. InfoGAN architecture: latent code **c** and noise vector **z** are combined as input for generator G, $\mathbf{x}' = G(\mathbf{z}, \mathbf{c})$ is generated data, $\mathbf{x}$ is real data, discriminator D tries to distinguish generated data from real data, network Q is used to maximize L_{mutual} (Eq. (2)), loss L_1 is given in Eq. (3).

Using weighted softmax loss function, Jia *et al.* [19] proposed a framework called Deep Normalized CNN for imbalanced fault classification of machinery to overcome data imbalanced distribution. Many hybrid methods combine both re-sampling and cost-sensitive learning [20]. However, limitations exist in both categories. For instance, oversampling can easily introduce undesirable noise with overfitting risks, and undersampling removes valuable information due to data loss. Cost-sensitive learning requires a good insight into the modified learning algorithms and a precise identification of reasons for failure in mining skewed distributions. Data with highly skewed classes also pose a challenge to traditional discriminant algorithms, such as subspace and feature representation learning [21–26]. This makes it further difficult to achieve ideal classification accuracy in failure prediction tasks.

2.2 GAN

Recently, generative models such as Generative Adversarial Networks (GANs) have attracted a lot of interest from researchers and industrial practitioners. Goodfellow *et al.* formulated GAN into a minimax two-player game, where they simultaneously train two models: a generator network G that captures the data distribution, and a discriminator network D that estimates the probability that a sample comes from the true data rather than the generator network G. The goal is to learn the generator distribution $p(\mathbf{x}')$ of G over data $\mathbf{x}'$ that matches the real data distribution $p(\mathbf{x})$. The generator network G generates samples by transforming a noise vector $\mathbf{z} \sim p(\mathbf{z})$ into a generated sample $G(\mathbf{z})$. This generator is trained by playing against the discriminator network D that aims to distinguish between samples from true data distribution $p(\mathbf{x})$ and the generator distribution $p(\mathbf{x}')$. Formally, the minimax game is given by the following expression:

$$\min_{G} \max_{D} V(D, G) = \mathbb{E}_{\mathbf{x} \sim p(\mathbf{x})}[\log D(\mathbf{x})] + \mathbb{E}_{\mathbf{z} \sim p(\mathbf{z})}[\log(1 - D(G(\mathbf{z})))]. \quad (1)$$

InfoGAN [13] is an information-theoretic extension to GAN. InfoGAN decomposes the input noise vector into two parts: incompressible noise vector $\mathbf{z}$ and latent code vector $\mathbf{c}$. The latent code vector $\mathbf{c}$ targets the salient structured

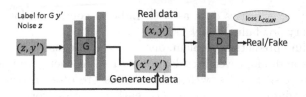

Fig. 2. Conditional GAN (CGAN) architecture: y' and noise vector $\mathbf{z}$ are combined as input for generator G, $\mathbf{x}' = G(\mathbf{z}, y')$ is generated data, $(\mathbf{x}, y)$ is real data-label pair, $(\mathbf{x}', y')$ is generated data-label pair, discriminator D tries to distinguish generated data-label pair from real data-label pair, loss L_{CGAN} is given in Eq. (4).

semantic features of the data distribution and can be further divided into categorical and continuous latent code, where the categorical code controls sample labels and continuous code controls variations. Thus, in infoGAN, the generated sample becomes $G(\mathbf{z}, \mathbf{c})$. InfoGAN introduces a distribution $Q(\mathbf{c} \mid \mathbf{x})$ to approximate $p(\mathbf{c} \mid \mathbf{x})$ and maximizes the variational lower bound, $L_{mutual}(G, Q)$, of the mutual information, $I(\mathbf{c}; G(\mathbf{z}, \mathbf{c}))$:

$$L_{mutual}(G, Q) = \mathbb{E}_{\mathbf{c}\sim p(\mathbf{c}), \mathbf{x}\sim G(\mathbf{z},\mathbf{c})}[\log Q(\mathbf{c} \mid \mathbf{x})] + H(c), \tag{2}$$

where $L_{mutual}(G, Q)$ is easy to approximate with Monte Carlo simulation. In practice, L_{mutual} can be maximized with respect to Q directly and with respect to G via the reparametrization trick. InfoGAN is defined as the following minimax game with a variational regularization of mutual information and a hyperparameter λ_Q:

$$\min_{G,Q} \max_D L_1(D, G, Q) = V(D, G) - \lambda_Q L_{mutual}(G, Q). \tag{3}$$

Figure 1 shows the structure of infoGAN.

Conditional GAN (CGAN) [27] adds extra label information y' to generator G for conditional generation. In discriminator D, both $\mathbf{x}$ and y are presented as inputs and D tries to distinguish if data-label pair is from generated or real data. Figure 2 shows the architecture of CGAN. The objective of CGAN is given as the following minimax game:

$$\min_G \max_D L_{CGAN}(D, G) = \mathbb{E}_{(\mathbf{x},y)\sim p(\mathbf{x},y)}[\log D(\mathbf{x}, y)]$$
$$+ \mathbb{E}_{\mathbf{z}\sim p(\mathbf{z})}[\log(1 - D(G(\mathbf{z}, y'), y'))]. \tag{4}$$

3   GAN-FP: GAN for Failure Prediction

3.1   Motivation

In failure prediction problems, we collect a lot of training data $\mathbf{x}$ and the corresponding labels y. Training data $\mathbf{x}$ usually is sensor data coming from equipment, but can be image, acoustics data as well. Label y contains a lot of non-failure label $0s$ and very few failure label $1s$.

Given a failure prediction problem, one choice is to construct a deep inference neural network and adopt weighted loss objective. As there are not enough real failure samples, test samples with failure labels are often misclassified to the prevalent non-failure class. As mentioned earlier, in this work, we propose the use of GANs to generate realistic failure samples.

To control the class labels of generated samples, we can choose Conditional GAN (CGAN) or infoGAN. CGAN was shown to mainly capture class-level features [13, 28]. In addition to capturing class-level features, infoGAN captures fine variations of features that are continuous in nature using continuous latent code. As mentioned earlier, PHM data has multiple failure modes, and is continuous in nature, hence we use infoGAN as a basic building block in our design.

One problem with simply using infoGAN, is that it cannot guarantee that the generated sample is from a desired class. This means that some generated samples might end up having the wrong label. For example, infoGAN is claimed to have 5% error rate in generating MNIST digits [13]. When we have a 2-class highly imbalanced classification problem like failure prediction, this can have significant negative impact on the usefulness of this approach. In order to alleviate this problem, we propose the use of a second GAN to enforce the consistency of data-label pairs. In the second GAN, we use the inference network P as a label generator.

Once we have generated data, a traditional approach is to use both the generated and real samples to train a classifier. However, since we are sharing layers between the inference network and the discriminator network in the first GAN, and training all three modules simultaneously, we can directly use this inference network to achieve higher inference accuracy.

During building the model, we alternate between the following steps:

1. Update the infoGAN to generate realistic samples for failure and non-failure labels.
2. Update the inference network P using real data. We bootstrap P using the weights of the first few layers of the discriminator of the infoGAN. This is a common approach to save training time and utilize the ability of GAN to extract features.
3. Update inference network P along with the discriminator in the second GAN to make sure that the generated samples and corresponding labels are consistent. This will increase the discriminative power of inference network P.

3.2 GAN-FP Model

Figure 3 shows the design of GAN-FP.

Module 1 adopts an infoGAN to generate class-balanced samples. For the input categorical latent code $\mathbf{c}$, we randomly generate labels $0s$ (non-failure) and $1s$ (failure) with equal probability. The continuous latent code $\mathbf{c}$ and noise vector $\mathbf{z}$ is generated using uniform random process within range $[0, 1]$. Generator

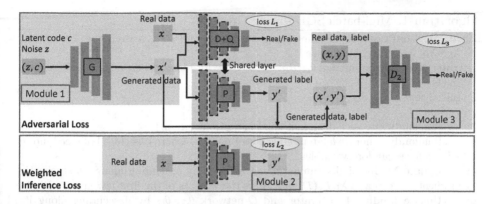

Fig. 3. GAN-FP architecture: there are 3 modules. Module 1 (network G, D and Q) is used to generate failure and non-failure samples using adversarial loss L_1 (Eq. (3)). Module 2 (network P) is an inference module with weighted loss L_2 (Eq. (5)), which trains a deep neural network using real data and label. Module 3 (network P and D_2) is a modified CGAN module with adversarial loss L_3 (Eq. (6)), where network D_2 takes data-label pair as input and tries to distinguish whether the pair comes from real data label $(\mathbf{x}, y)$ or from generated data label $(\mathbf{x}', y')$.

network G is a deep neural network with input $(\mathbf{z}, \mathbf{c})$, and outputs generated sample $\mathbf{x}'$, where $\mathbf{x}'$ has the same size as real data $\mathbf{x}$. Discriminator network D aims to distinguish generated sample $\mathbf{x}'$ from real sample $\mathbf{x}$. Network Q aims to maximize the mutual information between latent code $\mathbf{c}$ and generated sample $\mathbf{x}'$. By jointly training network G, D and Q, module 1 solves the minimax problem denoted in Eq. (3). The first few layers of the discriminative layer $D + Q$ will capture a lot of implicit features about the data. In order to reduce the overall training time, we are going to reuse these weights while training the inference network in the Module 2.

Module 2 consists of a deep neural network P and solves a binary classification problem with weighted loss based on real data and real label. Network P shares the first several layers with D and takes as input real data $\mathbf{x}$ and outputs a probability (denoted as $P(\mathbf{x})$) within range $[0, 1]$ indicating the chance that $\mathbf{x}$ is a failure sample. The real label is denoted as y (0 or 1). In our design, the loss function L_2 for module 2 is cross entropy:

$$\min_P L_2(P) = \mathbb{E}_{(\mathbf{x}, y) \sim p(\mathbf{x}, y)}[-wy \log(P(\mathbf{x})) - (1 - y) \log(1 - P(\mathbf{x}))], \quad (5)$$

where weight $w = \frac{\text{number of non-failure samples}}{\text{number of failure samples}} > 1$. Note at this step, the input for network P is class-imbalanced real data and labels. Loss L_2 is a weighted version which emphasizes more on failure sample prediction. In the training of Module 3, the weights of inference network P will be further tuned using generated data and labels.

Module 3 consists of network P and D_2 and enforces generated data-label pair $(\mathbf{x}', y')$ to look like real data-label pair $(\mathbf{x}, y)$. P serves as the generator

---

Algorithm 1. Mini-batch SGD solving GAN-FP.

Input: Real data and label pairs $\{\mathbf{x}_i, y_i\}$, where $i = 1, 2, ..., n$, hyperparameter λ_G, λ_D, λ_P, λ_{D_2}, λ_{L_2}, batch size b.

Output: Network parameters $\theta_G, \theta_D, \theta_Q, \theta_P, \theta_{D_2}$ for networks G, D, Q, P, D_2 respectively.

 1: Initialize $\theta_G, \theta_D, \theta_Q, \theta_P, \theta_{D_2}$.
 2: **repeat**
 3:      Randomly choose b data and label pairs from $\{\mathbf{x}_i, y_i\}$.
 4:      Randomly generate b latent code $\mathbf{c}$ and noise $\mathbf{z}$, where $\mathbf{c}$ is class-balanced, noise $\mathbf{z}$ is uniform random variables.
 5:      Update Module 1 discriminator network θ_D by ascending along its stochastic gradient w.r.t. $\max_D \lambda_D L_1(D)$ and share the weights of the first few layers with P.
 6:      Update Module 1 generator and Q-network θ_G, θ_Q by descending along its stochastic gradient w.r.t. $\min_{G,Q} \lambda_G L_1(G, Q)$.
 7:      Update inference network θ_P by descending along its stochastic gradient w.r.t. $\min_P \lambda_{L_2} L_2(P)$ and use P as the generator of Module 3.
 8:      Update Module 3 discriminator network θ_{D_2} by ascending along its stochastic gradient w.r.t. $\max_D \lambda_{D_2} L_3(D_2)$.
 9:      Update Module 3 generator network θ_P by descending along its stochastic gradient w.r.t. $\min_P \lambda_P L_3(P)$.
10: **until** Convergence

---

network. Given $\mathbf{x}'$, the generated label $y' = P(\mathbf{x}')$ needs to be as correct as possible. D_2 tries to distinguish the generated data-label pair from real pair. The minimax objective for module 3 is given as:

$$\min_P \max_{D_2} L_3(P, D_2) = \mathbb{E}_{(\mathbf{x},y) \sim p(\mathbf{x},y)}[\log D_2(\mathbf{x}, y)]$$
$$+ \mathbb{E}_{\mathbf{x}' \sim p(\mathbf{x}')}[\log(1 - D_2([\mathbf{x}', P(\mathbf{x}')]))]. \quad (6)$$

While training this module, the weights of the inference network P will be further tuned to increase the discrimination between failure and non-failure labels. The effectiveness of Module 3 to improve inference network P will be validated by comparing the performance of GAN-FP with infoGAN augmented training (denoted as InfoGAN AUG in experiments), where we train the inference network P with generated data without using Module 3.

3.3   Algorithm

Algorithm 1 summarizes the procedure for training GAN-FP. The input data includes real data-label pairs $(\mathbf{x}_i, y_i)$, where $i = 1, 2, ..., n$, and hyperparameter $\lambda_G, \lambda_D, \lambda_P, \lambda_{D_2}, \lambda_{L_2}$, which control the weights of different losses, as in traditional regularization approaches [29,30]. The output of this algorithm is the trained neural network parameters $\theta_G, \theta_D, \theta_Q, \theta_P, \theta_{D_2}$ for network G, D, Q, P, D_2 respectively. Step 1 initializes network parameters. Then we run the minibatch loop until L_1, L_2 and L_3 converge. In each mini-batch loop, Step 3 first randomly chooses a batch of real data-label pairs. Step 4 generates batch size of latent code $\mathbf{c}$ and $\mathbf{z}$. Step 5 to 9 update all 3 modules.

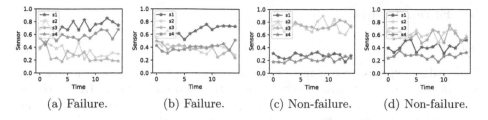

(a) Failure.   (b) Failure.   (c) Non-failure.   (d) Non-failure.

Fig. 4. Real CMAPSS FD001 failure and non-failure samples.

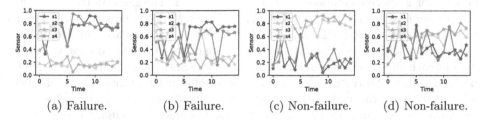

(a) Failure.   (b) Failure.   (c) Non-failure.   (d) Non-failure.

Fig. 5. Generated CMAPSS FD001 failure and non-failure samples.

4   Visualization of Generated Samples

We take CMAPSS FD001 data as an example to visualize the generated samples
and examine if the proposed GAN-FP can generate realistic enough fake samples
for failure prediction task. CMAPSS FD001 data contains failure and non-failure
data for turbofan engines. Each engine sample includes 21 sensors and their
readings are in a continuous time window with 15 time steps. Detailed description
of CMAPSS FD001 is given in Sect. 5.1. Due to space limitations, we chose 4
sensors (s1, s2, s3, s4) and plotted them from real samples and generated samples.
In Fig. 4, we visualize 2 real failure samples and 2 real non-failure samples. As
we can see, for failure samples, sensor s1 has higher values than other sensors,
sensor s2 and s3 have lower values than s1 and s4, especially for time from
6 to 14; for non-failure samples, sensor s4 has lower values, sensor s2 and s3
have higher values than sensor s1 and s4. In Fig. 5, we visualize the same 4
sensors from 2 generated failure samples and 2 generated non-failure samples.
We observe similar visual properties as in Fig. 4: for failure samples, sensor s2
and s3 have lower values than s1 and s4, especially for time from 6 to 14; for
non-failure samples, sensor s2 and s3 have higher values than sensor s1 and s4.
We also observe that noises exist in generated samples. For example, at time
11, sensor s4 in Fig. 5b has a big drop, but at time 12, s4 increases back to a
higher value. Though real sensor data seems more smooth than generated sensor
data, GAN-FP is able to capture the major properties for this failure prediction
task. This shows that GAN-FP can generate very good failure and non-failure
samples and different levels of variations exist in the generated samples.

5 Experiments

5.1 Data

We conduct experiments on one Air Pressure System (APS) data set from trucks [31] and four turbofan engine degradation data sets from NASA CMAPSS (Commercial Modular Aero-Propulsion System Simulation) [32]. For APS data, air pressure system generates pressured air that are utilized in various functions in a truck, such as braking and gear changes. The failure class consists of component failures for a specific component of the APS system. The non-failure class consists of samples not related to APS failures. The CMAPSS data consists of four subsets: FD001, FD002, FD003, and FD004. Data attributes are summarized in Table 1. In each subset, the data records a snapshot of turbofan engine sensor data at each time cycle, which includes 26 columns: 1st column represents engine ID, 2nd column represents the current operational cycle number, 3–5 columns are the three operational settings that have a substantial effect on engine performance, 6–26 columns represent the 21 sensor values. The engine is operating normally at the start of each time series, and develops a fault at some point in time. The fault grows in magnitude until a system failure. The four CMAPSS data sets have different number of operating conditions and fault conditions. For example, FD001 data has one operating condition and one fault condition, and FD002 has six operating conditions and one fault condition. CMAPSS data set is considered benchmark for predictive maintenance [33].

5.2 Experimental Setup and Evaluation Criteria

We use fully connected layers for all the networks. Table 2 shows the network structures for both APS and CMAPSS data. For example, G network for APS data consists of 3 layers, with the first layer 64 nodes, second layer 64 nodes and last layer 170 nodes. For APS data, network Q and P share the first two layers with network D. For CMAPSS data, network Q and P share the first four layers with network D. For both APS and CMAPSS data, the noise vector $\mathbf{z}$ is a 60-dimensional vector with uniform random values within $[0, 1]$. Latent code $\mathbf{c}$ includes 1-dimensional categorical code and 3-dimensional continuous code with uniform random values within $[0, 1]$. The activation function is rectified linear unit by default.

Table 1. Data sets.

Name	Dimension	Failure sample #	Non-failure sample #	Operating condition #	Fault condition #
APS	170	1,000	59,000	N/A	N/A
CMAPSS FD001	315	2,000	12,031	1	1
CMAPSS FD002	315	5,200	31,399	6	1
CMAPSS FD003	315	2,000	16,210	1	2
CMAPSS FD004	315	4,980	39,835	6	2

Table 2. Network structures.

Network	APS	CMAPSS
G	$64, 64, 170$	$64, 256, 500, 500, 315$
D	$170, 64, 1$	$315, 500, 500, 256, 1$
Q	$170, 64, 64, 1$	$315, 500, 500, 256, 64, 1$
P	$170, 64, 64, 1$	$315, 500, 500, 256, 64, 1$
D_2	$171, 64, 1$	$316, 500, 500, 256, 1$

For evaluation, we use AUC (Area Under Curve), (precision, recall, F1) with macro average, micro average, and for the failure class only. All compared methods output the probability that a sample is a failure sample. We then compute the precision and recall curve and calculate AUC. We then can compute both failure and non-failure class precision, recall and F1. Larger values indicate better performance in all these metrics. More about these metrics can be found in [34].

We compare GAN-FP with 17 other methods. For the first 16 methods, we conduct experiments using 4 classifiers in 4 different sampling settings. The 4 classifiers are DNN, SVM (Support Vector Machines), RF (Random Forests) and DT (Decision Trees). The 4 sampling settings are: undersampling, weighted loss, SMOTE oversampling and ADASYN oversampling. The structure of DNN is the same as network P in GAN-FP. Parameters of SVM, RF and DT are tuned to achieve the best accuracy. For undersampling, we fix the failure samples and randomly draw equal size number of non-failure samples for training. For each experiment, we perform 10 times random undersampling. For weighted loss objective, we assign the same class weights as used in Eq. (5). Lastly, we compare with infoGAN augmented DNN (denoted as InfoGAN AUG), which uses infoGAN to generate more failure samples to make the class distribution balanced and then train a DNN for classification. InfoGAN AUG is used to validate the effectiveness of Module 3. Experiments were performed in a 5-fold cross-validation fashion.

5.3   Algorithm Convergence

To examine the training convergence, we take CMAPSS FD001 data as an example and plot the loss changes along the training process. From Eq. (3), we know that Module 1 loss consists of three parts: discriminator (D) loss $\min_D -V(D)$, generator (G) loss $\min_G V(G)$ and mutual information (Q) loss $\min_{G,Q} -L_{mutual}(G, Q)$. Figure 6a shows that D loss and G loss converge along the training. Mutual information (Q) loss is minimized and converged after about 2,000 batches. Advanced accelerating algorithm can reduce training time furthermore [35]. Figure 6b shows that L_2 loss Eq. (5) is decreasing from 0 to 3,000 batches. Figure 6c shows that D2 loss and generator P loss of Module 3 converge along the training. Overall, this shows the effectiveness of Algorithm 1.

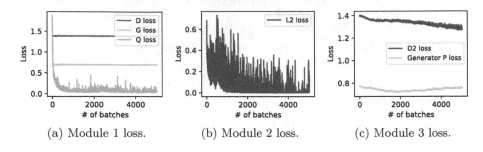

(a) Module 1 loss.　　　(b) Module 2 loss.　　　(c) Module 3 loss.

Fig. 6. Loss.

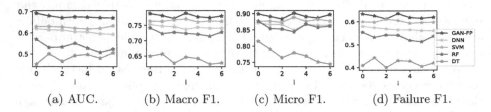

(a) AUC.　　　(b) Macro F1.　　　(c) Micro F1.　　　(d) Failure F1.

Fig. 7. CMAPSS FD001 class imbalance effect using GAN-FP and classifiers with SMOTE: in each figure, the x-axis i indicates $(1000 * i)$ non-failure samples are randomly removed from the training data, we do not remove failure samples. The testing samples are fixed for all experiments.

Table 3. APS result.

		AUC	Macro			Micro			Failure		
			Precision	Recall	F1	Precision	Recall	F1	Precision	Recall	F1
DNN	Undersampling	0.5751	0.7393	0.8118	0.7705	0.9827	0.9827	0.9827	0.4847	0.6350	0.5498
	Weighted loss	0.6131	0.8027	0.8042	0.8034	0.9871	0.9871	0.9871	0.6119	0.6150	0.6135
	SMOTE	0.7077	0.8434	0.8350	0.8391	0.9896	0.9896	0.9896	0.6923	0.6750	0.6835
	ADASYN	0.6971	0.8040	0.8561	0.8279	0.9878	0.9878	0.9878	0.6128	0.7200	0.6621
SVM	Undersampling	0.3130	0.6995	0.7706	0.7293	0.9791	0.9791	0.9791	0.4066	0.5550	0.4693
	Weighted loss	0.3004	0.6829	0.7623	0.7151	0.9773	0.9773	0.9773	0.3737	0.5400	0.4417
	SMOTE	0.5673	0.7432	0.8169	0.7749	0.9830	0.9830	0.9830	0.4924	0.6450	0.5584
	ADASYN	0.5188	0.7225	0.8158	0.7606	0.9810	0.9810	0.9810	0.4510	0.6450	0.5309
RF	Undersampling	0.4274	0.6449	0.8813	0.7052	0.9647	0.9647	0.9647	0.2934	0.7950	0.4286
	Weighted loss	0.3750	0.6838	0.7333	0.7054	0.9781	0.9781	0.9781	0.3765	0.4800	0.4220
	SMOTE	0.4137	0.6602	0.7414	0.6919	0.9747	0.9747	0.9747	0.3289	0.5000	0.3968
	ADASYN	0.3387	0.6302	0.8360	0.6832	0.9626	0.9626	0.9626	0.2655	0.7050	0.3858
DT	Undersampling	0.5614	0.5928	**0.9330**	0.6376	0.9311	0.9311	0.9311	0.1868	**0.9350**	0.3114
	Weighted loss	0.6310	0.8194	0.8022	0.8106	0.9879	0.9879	0.9879	0.6455	0.6100	0.6272
	SMOTE	0.6471	0.7751	0.8625	0.8125	0.9858	0.9858	0.9858	0.5547	0.7350	0.6323
	ADASYN	0.6094	0.7567	0.8420	0.7930	0.9842	0.9842	0.9842	0.5187	0.6950	0.5940
InfoGAN AUG		0.7343	0.8335	0.8744	0.8527	0.9898	0.9898	0.9898	0.6711	0.7550	0.7106
GAN-FP		**0.8085**	**0.8662**	0.8955	**0.8803**	**0.9918**	**0.9918**	**0.9918**	**0.7358**	0.7959	**0.7647**

5.4   Effect of Class Imbalance

We compare the classification performance of different approaches when the number of majority non-failure samples is decreased. Figure 7 shows that, for CMAPSS FD001, there is no significant performance loss when the number of majority non-failure samples is decreased. Among all experiments, GAN-FP gives the best performance in terms of the four metrics.

5.5   Comparison with Other Methods

Table 3 shows the result for APS data. Table 4, 5, 6 and 7 show the results for CMAPSS. The best performing methods in each column is in bold. Note that CMAPSS data sets have different levels of difficulty since they have different number of operating conditions and fault conditions. Overall, GAN-FP shows better results in terms of AUC and F1 score compared to its counterparts. The fact that GAN-FP outperforms InfoGAN AUG shows the effectiveness of Module 3.

Table 4. CMAPSS FD001.

		AUC	Macro			Micro			Failure		
			Precision	Recall	F1	Precision	Recall	F1	Precision	Recall	F1
DNN	Undersampling	0.6381	0.7525	0.7895	0.7687	0.8785	0.8785	0.8785	0.5624	0.6650	0.6094
	Weighted loss	0.6030	0.7327	0.7614	0.7455	0.8678	0.8678	0.8678	0.5315	0.6125	0.5691
	SMOTE	0.6196	0.7397	0.7678	0.7524	0.8717	0.8717	0.8717	0.5437	0.6225	0.5804
	ADASYN	0.6185	0.7473	0.7559	0.7515	0.8764	0.8764	0.8764	0.5635	0.5875	0.5753
SVM	Undersampling	0.6331	0.7592	0.7720	0.7653	0.8824	0.8824	0.8824	0.5825	0.6175	0.5995
	Weighted loss	0.6498	0.7485	**0.7972**	0.7689	0.8757	0.8757	0.8757	0.5511	0.6875	0.6118
	SMOTE	0.6295	0.7491	0.7822	0.7638	0.8767	0.8767	0.8767	0.5579	0.6500	0.6005
	ADASYN	0.6224	0.7461	0.7893	0.7646	0.8746	0.8746	0.8746	0.5492	0.6700	0.6036
RF	Undersampling	0.5531	0.7046	0.7466	0.7218	0.8497	0.8497	0.8497	0.4782	0.6025	0.5332
	Weighted loss	0.5378	0.7067	0.7504	0.7245	0.8507	0.8507	0.8507	0.4813	0.6100	0.5380
	SMOTE	0.5701	0.7486	0.7355	0.7418	0.8771	0.8771	0.8771	0.5733	0.5375	0.5548
	ADASYN	0.5238	0.7322	0.7134	0.7221	0.8696	0.8696	0.8696	0.5470	0.4950	0.5197
DT	Undersampling	0.5279	0.6096	0.7109	0.5977	0.6901	0.6901	0.6901	0.2787	**0.7400**	0.4049
	Weighted loss	0.4699	0.6631	0.6695	0.6662	0.8336	0.8336	0.8336	0.4200	0.4400	0.4298
	SMOTE	0.4521	0.6406	0.6629	0.6500	0.8151	0.8151	0.8151	0.3758	0.4500	0.4096
	ADASYN	0.4471	0.6373	0.6596	0.6466	0.8130	0.8130	0.8130	0.3701	0.4450	0.4041
InfoGAN AUG		0.6128	0.7256	0.7716	0.7446	0.8621	0.8621	0.8621	0.5129	0.6450	0.5714
GAN-FP		**0.6927**	**0.8021**	0.7759	**0.7881**	**0.8992**	**0.8992**	**0.8992**	0.6707	0.6022	**0.6346**

Table 5. CMAPSS FD002.

		AUC	Macro			Micro			Failure		
			Precision	Recall	F1	Precision	Recall	F1	Precision	Recall	F1
DNN	Undersampling	0.5503	0.6996	0.7501	0.7193	0.8452	0.8452	0.8452	0.4662	0.6173	0.5312
	Weighted loss	0.5431	0.7014	0.7549	0.7219	0.8458	0.8458	0.8458	0.4681	0.6279	0.5363
	SMOTE	0.5383	0.6920	**0.7675**	0.7166	0.8331	0.8331	0.8331	0.4427	0.6760	0.5350
	ADASYN	0.5377	0.6910	0.7666	0.7156	0.8322	0.8322	0.8322	0.4410	0.6750	0.5334
SVM	Undersampling	0.5212	0.6888	0.7057	0.6965	0.8454	0.8454	0.8454	0.4601	0.5106	0.4840
	Weighted loss	0.5199	0.6869	0.7021	0.6939	0.8447	0.8447	0.8447	0.4576	0.5029	0.4792
	SMOTE	0.5438	0.6844	0.7435	0.7055	0.8324	0.8324	0.8324	0.4366	0.6192	0.5121
	ADASYN	0.5444	0.6917	0.7334	0.7085	0.8419	0.8419	0.8419	0.4559	0.5817	0.5112
RF	Undersampling	0.4610	0.6649	0.7293	0.6853	0.8149	0.8149	0.8149	0.4005	0.6096	0.4834
	Weighted loss	0.4836	0.6675	0.7234	0.6868	0.8206	0.8206	0.8206	0.4087	0.5875	0.4821
	SMOTE	0.4368	0.6519	0.7225	0.6714	0.7999	0.7999	0.7999	0.3752	0.6144	0.4659
	ADASYN	0.4409	0.6524	0.7204	0.6718	0.8018	0.8018	0.8018	0.3772	0.6067	0.4652
DT	Undersampling	0.4956	0.5892	0.6753	0.5668	0.6583	0.6583	0.6583	0.2494	**0.6990**	0.3676
	Weighted loss	0.4149	0.6306	0.6338	0.6322	0.8184	0.8184	0.8184	0.3651	0.3760	0.3704
	SMOTE	0.3949	0.5848	0.6221	0.5929	0.7549	0.7549	0.7549	0.2732	0.4365	0.3360
	ADASYN	0.4244	0.5999	0.6451	0.6104	0.7641	0.7641	0.7641	0.2959	0.4788	0.3658
InfoGAN AUG		0.5484	0.6945	0.7658	0.7187	0.8363	0.8363	0.8363	0.4489	0.6673	0.5367
GAN-FP		**0.5666**	**0.7081**	0.7488	**0.7249**	**0.8521**	**0.8521**	**0.8521**	0.4847	0.6043	**0.5379**

Table 6. CMAPSS FD003.

		AUC	Macro			Micro			Failure		
			Precision	Recall	F1	Precision	Recall	F1	Precision	Recall	F1
DNN	Undersampling	0.6211	0.7423	0.7998	0.7663	0.8971	0.8971	0.8971	0.5263	0.6750	0.5915
	Weighted loss	0.6035	**0.7654**	0.7654	0.7654	**0.9078**	**0.9078**	**0.9078**	**0.5825**	0.5825	0.5825
	SMOTE	0.6207	0.7376	0.8142	0.7674	0.8935	0.8935	0.8935	0.5126	0.7125	0.5962
	ADASYN	0.6199	0.7451	0.7964	0.7670	0.8987	0.8987	0.8987	0.5331	0.6650	0.5918
SVM	Undersampling	0.5718	0.7469	0.7666	0.7562	0.9004	0.9004	0.9004	0.5446	0.5950	0.5687
	Weighted loss	0.6338	0.7449	0.8123	0.7722	0.8979	0.8979	0.8979	0.5282	0.7025	0.6030
	SMOTE	0.6166	0.7356	0.7967	0.7606	0.8935	0.8935	0.8935	0.5134	0.6725	0.5823
	ADASYN	0.6113	0.7480	0.7799	0.7625	0.9007	0.9007	0.9007	0.5435	0.6250	0.5814
RF	Undersampling	0.5152	0.7223	0.7778	0.7452	0.8871	0.8871	0.8871	0.4913	0.6375	0.5550
	Weighted loss	0.5693	0.7520	0.7602	0.7560	0.9026	0.9026	0.9026	0.5566	0.5775	0.5669
	SMOTE	0.5266	0.7164	0.7933	0.7454	0.8816	0.8816	0.8816	0.4747	0.6800	0.5591
	ADASYN	0.5276	0.7120	0.7866	0.7402	0.8794	0.8794	0.8794	0.4676	0.6675	0.5499
DT	Undersampling	0.5460	0.6206	0.7671	0.6229	0.7453	0.7453	0.7453	0.2744	0.7950	0.4080
	Weighted loss	0.4309	0.6625	0.6607	0.6616	0.8678	0.8678	0.8678	0.4000	0.3950	0.3975
	SMOTE	0.4751	0.6604	0.7052	0.6780	0.8554	0.8554	0.8554	0.3839	0.5125	0.4390
	ADASYN	0.4364	0.6408	0.6782	0.6555	0.8463	0.8463	0.8463	0.3510	0.4625	0.3991
InfoGAN AUG		0.6167	0.7620	0.7768	0.7691	0.9067	0.9067	0.9067	0.5728	0.6100	0.5908
GAN-FP		**0.7093**	0.7584	**0.8635**	**0.7970**	0.9040	0.9040	0.9040	0.5416	**0.8117**	**0.6497**

Table 7. CMAPSS FD004.

		AUC	Macro			Micro			Failure		
			Precision	Recall	F1	Precision	Recall	F1	Precision	Recall	F1
DNN	Undersampling	0.4826	0.7038	0.7719	0.7297	0.8748	0.8748	0.8748	0.4550	0.6396	0.5317
	Weighted loss	0.5065	0.7197	0.7788	0.7436	0.8847	0.8847	0.8847	0.4860	0.6426	0.5534
	SMOTE	0.5360	0.7107	**0.7802**	0.7374	0.8786	0.8786	0.8786	0.4670	0.6536	0.5448
	ADASYN	0.5398	0.7192	0.7711	0.7408	0.8852	0.8852	0.8852	0.4871	0.6245	0.5473
SVM	Undersampling	0.4588	0.6770	0.7760	0.7070	0.8501	0.8501	0.8501	0.3979	0.6807	0.5022
	Weighted loss	0.4553	0.6749	0.7756	0.7048	0.8478	0.8478	0.8478	0.3935	0.6827	0.4993
	SMOTE	0.4983	0.6986	0.7767	0.7268	0.8700	0.8700	0.8700	0.4428	0.6566	0.5289
	ADASYN	0.4978	0.6979	0.7708	0.7248	0.8706	0.8706	0.8706	0.4432	0.6426	0.5246
RF	Undersampling	0.4748	0.6914	0.7335	0.7090	0.8721	0.8721	0.8721	0.4403	0.5552	0.4911
	Weighted loss	0.4685	0.6836	0.7421	0.7060	0.8648	0.8648	0.8648	0.4217	0.5843	0.4899
	SMOTE	0.4227	0.6730	0.7612	0.7010	0.8503	0.8503	0.8503	0.3941	0.6466	0.4897
	ADASYN	0.4035	0.6618	0.7493	0.6882	0.8417	0.8417	0.8417	0.3740	0.6305	0.4695
DT	Undersampling	0.4947	0.5996	0.7195	0.5957	0.7263	0.7263	0.7263	0.2464	**0.7108**	0.3660
	Weighted loss	0.4026	0.6450	0.6437	0.6443	0.8601	0.8601	0.8601	0.3692	0.3655	0.3673
	SMOTE	0.4243	0.6118	0.6746	0.6285	0.8097	0.8097	0.8097	0.2922	0.5010	0.3691
	ADASYN	0.4195	0.6097	0.6709	0.6259	0.8085	0.8085	0.8085	0.2887	0.4940	0.3644
InfoGAN AUG		0.5581	0.7209	0.7784	0.7443	0.8855	0.8855	0.8855	0.4885	0.6406	0.5543
GAN-FP		**0.5638**	**0.7260**	0.7773	**0.7475**	**0.8890**	**0.8890**	**0.8890**	0.4992	0.6338	**0.5585**

6   Conclusion

In conclusion, we proposed a novel model GAN-FP for imbalanced classification and failure prediction, and experimented it on industrial data. This novel design not only improves modeling performance, but also can have significant potential economical and social values.

References

1. Monaghan, A.: Hotpoint tells customers to check fridge-freezers after grenfell tower fire. The Guardian (2017)
2. Vichare, N.M., Pecht, M.G.: Prognostics and health management of electronics. IEEE Trans. Compon. Packag. Technol. **29**(1), 222–229 (2006)
3. Mosallam, A., Medjaher, K., Zerhouni, N.: Data-driven prognostic method based on bayesian approaches for direct remaining useful life prediction. J. Intell. Manuf. **27**(5), 1037–1048 (2016)
4. Pecht, M.G.: A prognostics and health management roadmap for information and electronics-rich systems. IEICE ESS Fundam. Rev. **3**(4), 4_25–4_32 (2010)
5. Zheng, S., Shae, Z.-Y., Zhang, X., Jamjoom, H., Fong, L.: Analysis and modeling of social influence in high performance computing workloads. In: Jeannot, E., Namyst, R., Roman, J. (eds.) Euro-Par 2011. LNCS, vol. 6852, pp. 193–204. Springer, Heidelberg (2011). https://doi.org/10.1007/978-3-642-23400-2_19
6. Goodfellow, I., et al.: Generative adversarial nets. In: Advances in Neural Information Processing Systems, pp. 2672–2680 (2014)
7. Calimeri, F., Marzullo, A., Stamile, C., Terracina, G.: Biomedical data augmentation using generative adversarial neural networks. In: Lintas, A., Rovetta, S., Verschure, P.F.M.J., Villa, A.E.P. (eds.) ICANN 2017. LNCS, vol. 10614, pp. 626–634. Springer, Cham (2017). https://doi.org/10.1007/978-3-319-68612-7_71

8. Zhong, Z., Zheng, L., Zheng, Z., Li, S., Yang, Y.: Camera style adaptation for person re-identification. In: Proceedings of the IEEE Conference on Computer Vision and Pattern Recognition, pp. 5157–5166 (2018)
9. Yun, K., Bustos, J., Lu, T.: Predicting rapid fire growth (flashover) using conditional generative adversarial networks. Electron. Imaging **2018**(9), 1–4 (2018)
10. Dai, Z., Yang, Z., Yang, F., Cohen, W.W., Salakhutdinov, R.R.: Good semi-supervised learning that requires a bad GAN. In: Advances in Neural Information Processing Systems, pp. 6510–6520 (2017)
11. Tran, T., Pham, T., Carneiro, G., Palmer, L., Reid, I.: A Bayesian data augmentation approach for learning deep models. In: Advances in Neural Information Processing Systems, pp. 2797–2806 (2017)
12. Bousmalis, K., Silberman, N., Dohan, D., Erhan, D., Krishnan, D.: Unsupervised pixel-level domain adaptation with generative adversarial networks. In: The IEEE Conference on Computer Vision and Pattern Recognition (CVPR), vol. 1, p. 7 (2017)
13. Chen, X., Duan, Y., Houthooft, R., Schulman, J., Sutskever, I., Abbeel, P.: InfoGAN: interpretable representation learning by information maximizing generative adversarial nets. In: Advances in Neural Information Processing Systems, pp. 2172–2180 (2016)
14. Nejatian, S., Parvin, H., Faraji, E.: Using sub-sampling and ensemble clustering techniques to improve performance of imbalanced classification. Neurocomputing **276**, 55–66 (2018)
15. Chawla, N.V., Bowyer, K.W., Hall, L.O., Kegelmeyer, W.P.: SMOTE: synthetic minority over-sampling technique. J. Artif. Intell. Res. **16**, 321–357 (2002)
16. He, H., Bai, Y., Garcia, E.A., Li, S.: ADASYN: adaptive synthetic sampling approach for imbalanced learning. In: 2008 IEEE International Joint Conference on Neural Networks (IEEE World Congress on Computational Intelligence), pp. 1322–1328. IEEE (2008)
17. Shen, W., Wang, X., Wang, Y., Bai, X., Zhang, Z.: DeepContour: a deep convolutional feature learned by positive-sharing loss for contour detection. In: Proceedings of the IEEE Conference on Computer Vision and Pattern Recognition, pp. 3982–3991 (2015)
18. Zhang, C., Tan, K.C., Li, H., Hong, G.S.: A cost-sensitive deep belief network for imbalanced classification. IEEE Trans. Neural Netw. Learn. Syst. **30**, 109–122 (2018)
19. Jia, F., Lei, Y., Lu, N., Xing, S.: Deep normalized convolutional neural network for imbalanced fault classification of machinery and its understanding via visualization. Mech. Syst. Signal Process. **110**, 349–367 (2018)
20. Tang, Y., Zhang, Y.Q., Chawla, N.V., Krasser, S.: SVMs modeling for highly imbalanced classification. IEEE Trans. Syst. Man Cybern. B (Cybern.) **39**(1), 281–288 (2009)
21. Zheng, S., Ding, C.: Kernel alignment inspired linear discriminant analysis. In: Calders, T., Esposito, F., Hüllermeier, E., Meo, R. (eds.) ECML PKDD 2014. LNCS (LNAI), vol. 8726, pp. 401–416. Springer, Heidelberg (2014). https://doi.org/10.1007/978-3-662-44845-8_26
22. Zheng, S., Cai, X., Ding, C.H., Nie, F., Huang, H.: A closed form solution to multi-view low-rank regression. In: AAAI, pp. 1973–1979 (2015)
23. Zheng, S., Nie, F., Ding, C., Huang, H.: A harmonic mean linear discriminant analysis for robust image classification. In: 2016 IEEE 28th International Conference on Tools with Artificial Intelligence (ICTAI), pp. 402–409. IEEE (2016)

24. Zheng, S.: Machine learning: several advances in linear discriminant analysis, multi-view regression and support vector machine. Ph.D. thesis, The University of Texas at Arlington (2017)

25. Zheng, S., Ding, C., Nie, F., Huang, H.: Harmonic mean linear discriminant analysis. IEEE Trans. Knowl. Data Eng. (2018). https://doi.org/10.1109/TKDE.2018.2861858

26. Zheng, S., Ding, C.: Sparse classification using group matching pursuit. Neurocomputing **338**, 83–91 (2019). https://doi.org/10.1016/j.neucom.2019.02.001

27. Mirza, M., Osindero, S.: Conditional generative adversarial nets. arXiv preprint arXiv:1411.1784 (2014)

28. Lee, M., Seok, J.: Controllable generative adversarial network. arXiv preprint arXiv:1708.00598 (2017)

29. Zheng, S., Ding, C., Nie, F.: Regularized singular value decomposition and application to recommender system. arXiv preprint arXiv:1804.05090 (2018)

30. Zheng, S., Ding, C.: Minimal support vector machine. arXiv preprint arXiv:1804.02370 (2018)

31. Dua, D., Karra Taniskidou, E.: UCI machine learning repository (2017). http://archive.ics.uci.edu/ml

32. Saxena, A., Goebel, K., Simon, D., Eklund, N.: Damage propagation modeling for aircraft engine run-to-failure simulation. In: 2008 International Conference on Prognostics and Health Management, pp. 1–9. IEEE (2008)

33. Zheng, S., Ristovski, K., Farahat, A., Gupta, C.: Long short-term memory network for remaining useful life estimation. In: 2017 IEEE International Conference on Prognostics and Health Management (ICPHM), pp. 88–95. IEEE (2017)

34. Han, J., Pei, J., Kamber, M.: Data Mining: Concepts and Techniques. Elsevier, Waltham (2011)

35. Zheng, S., Vishnu, A., Ding, C.: Accelerating deep learning with shrinkage and recall. In: 2016 IEEE 22nd International Conference on Parallel and Distributed Systems (ICPADS), pp. 963–970. IEEE (2016)

Interpreting Atypical Conditions in Systems with Deep Conditional Autoencoders: The Case of Electrical Consumption

Antoine Marot[1(✉)], Antoine Rosin[1], Laure Crochepierre[1,2], Benjamin Donnot[1],
Pierre Pinson[3], and Lydia Boudjeloud-Assala[2]

[1] Reseau Transport Electricite R&D, Paris, France
`antoine-marot@live.fr`
[2] Universite de Lorraine, CNRS, LORIA, 57000 Metz, France
[3] DTU Technical University of Denmark, Kongens Lyngby, Denmark

Abstract. In this paper, we propose a new method to iteratively and interactively characterize new feature conditions for signals of daily French electrical consumption from our historical database, relying on Conditional Variational Autoencoders. An autoencoder first learn a compressed similarity-based representation of the signals in a latent space, in which one can select and extract well-represented expert features. Then, we successfully condition the model over the set of extracted features, as opposed to simple target label previously, to learn conditionally independent new residual latent representations. Unknown, or previously unselected factors such as atypical conditions now appear well-represented to be detected and further interpreted by experts. By applying it, we recover the appropriate known expert features and eventually discover, through adapted representations, atypical known and unknown conditions such as holidays, fuzzy non working days and weather events, which were actually related to important events that influenced consumption.

Keywords: Interpretability · Autoencoder · Representation

1 Introduction

1.1 Context

Well-established power systems such as the French power grid are experiencing a mutation with a steep rise in complexity. This is due to many factors, such as new consumer habits in the digital era with new usages relying on more controllable, individual and numerous appliances, as well as a necessary energy transition towards a greater share of renewable energy in the mix and better energy efficiencies to reduce our carbon footprint in climate change. This makes it harder to maintain the proper balance between production and consumption at

© Springer Nature Switzerland AG 2020
U. Brefeld et al. (Eds.): ECML PKDD 2019, LNAI 11908, pp. 638–654, 2020.
https://doi.org/10.1007/978-3-030-46133-1_38

all time, which is a necessary condition for power grid stability to avoid dramatic blackouts. More advanced predictive tools become necessary.

Classical load forecasting methods [1] previously heavily relied on seasonal and deterministic behaviors, modeled through expert features, but hardly grasped atypical and dynamical behaviors. Load analysis and forecasting, whether it is at individual level or a national level, is nevertheless a very dynamic field within the current energy transition era to eventually make smart grids happen, trying to overcome some remaining challenges with recent methods, as reviewed by Wang et al. [2]. Better understanding the new causal factors and the profiles of load consumption, handling their related uncertainties through probabilistic load forecasting [3], as well as dealing with bad and missing data for online predictions in real-time data streams [4], are three of the main research directions in this field. Our work will focus along the first research avenue of electrical consumption characterization, in interaction with experts, especially for new or atypical conditions that are under-represented in a dataset and have been hard to characterize until now, even when some instances were detected.

1.2 Industrial Challenge

Bank holidays, to which we will refer as "holidays" for short in this paper, have been known historical examples of such atypical conditions for electrical consumption, especially in France. A recent data challenge[1] organized by RTE was designed to address this issue of prediction under atypical conditions, with half of the test days being holidays. Machine learning models relying on xgboost or deep neural nets actually showed to perform better than RTE models overall on those atypical days. But they still each had some extreme errors on certain days and best models were different for each day tested. In addition, they were still merely black boxes, not giving many insights to the operators in charge, on the relevant factors for prediction and their effects, insights they could use to adjust the forecast with any new additional information. Eventually operators did not trust those new models on which RTE gave up for now. Trust and interpretability in models and applications are in fact prerequisites for operators responsible of a system in challenging situations: they will be asked for explanations if anything goes unexpected. More generally, beyond automatic method only, this highlights the need we will address here for renewed interpretability in models [9], through causal understanding, modeling and inference, which are essential for operators and humans to properly intervene and control any system [10].

In practice, expert operators spend a lot of time trying to identify the most similar holidays in the past to characterize and predict the consumption of a new holiday, while leaving the forecasting models predict more automatically over the typical days. Even doing so, the day-ahead forecasting error is still approximately of 1.5% Mean Absolute Percentage Error (MAPE) for holidays,

---

[1] RTE Data Challenge: https://dataanalyticspost.com/wp-content/uploads/2017/06/Challenge-RTE-Prevision-de-Consommation.pdf.

reaching sometimes 3%, compare to below 1% MAPE for typical days. Predicting holidays is time-consuming because they do not have tools that give them adapted representations to study collectively those under-represented atypical signals. In addition, because new modes of consumption are appearing, atypical conditions, beyond holidays only, will be of greater importance to well predict. New tools to study and interpret them more efficiently with adapted representations are hence necessary.

1.3   Proposal

In data analysis and knowledge discovery, feature importance [5] and anomaly [7] or outlier [6] detection methods are often helpful to assist human experts. They have helped characterize and label some events for bike sharing systems [8] for instance, while limited in its depth of discovery beyond extreme events. However, they can be complemented with representation learning methods: besides looking at data statistically or individually, similarity-based representations let one investigate signal instances still collectively but also specifically and contextually. In that sense, our paper aims at highlighting the importance of learning adapted representations to let experts efficiently interpret underlying conditions in signals, even with simple feature importance and anomaly detection modules.

While deep learning methods have shown real promises in terms of predictive power, being successfully applied to power flow predictions in power systems for instance [11], they also have a potential to foster interpretability, beyond the black box effect, as illustrated by [12] in which they produce interesting clusters over representations learnt by a neural network. Indeed, deep learning can also be regarded as representation learning [13]. Word2Vec [14], and later Interligua [15], have been major illustrations of such interpretability power since in their latent representation, similarities and generic semantic relations (such as masculine and feminine or translations) between words were recovered. More generally, generative models, deep variational autoencoders in particular, are one family of representation learning models with recent interesting developments [16].

By compressing data signals in a latent representation, autoencoders (AE) implicitly capture the most salient features [17], with possible non-linear and mutual dependencies. To explicitly extract those features for interpretation, score to measure importance of existing expert features can be defined. To integrate and leverage those selected expert feature to discover deeper knowledge, we further consider Conditional Variational Autoencoders (CVAE) [18] which we review later in the method section to learn successive conditional representations. Whereas previous CVAE models mostly used as conditions simple target labels for anomaly detection, signal correction or inpainting [19,20], one major technical contribution of our paper is, for the first time as far as we know of, to effectively learn a full conditional network module over a set of extracted features, to let expert discover new conditions in the residual latent representation.

The paper is organized as follows. First, we give an overview of the characteristics of electrical consumption with a specific focus on holidays. We then present our method based on CVAE to learn adapted representations. We define scores over features and instances to qualify those representations and extract knowledge from them. Finally, successive experiments demonstrate our ability to effectively learn such models and qualify the relevance of the representations to let expert interpret signals under unknown atypical conditions, and label them.

2 French Electrical Consumption: Characteristics and Data

National electrical consumption has been studied and its forecasting improved over the last few decades for power system operators to anticipate the required amount of energy production at every moment to match the demand in the system. Over the years, France has relied more heavily on electricity, given the development of big nuclear power plants which represent up to 75% of the total production, and incentives for electrical heating increased significantly the thermal dependency of electrical consumption. Weekday habits and temperature influence have been among commonly shared expert knowledge to predict electrical consumption. In addition, holidays have been known as atypical events within a year, shifting habits that are still hard to predict.

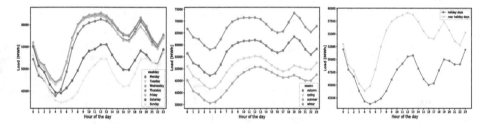

Fig. 1. From left to right, averaged daily load profiles at 30 min resolution highlighting weekdays and seasonal patterns, and holiday atypical profile.

Common Existing Factors for Daily Electrical Consumption and Associated Expert Knowledge. As shown on Fig. 1, over the course of a day, the electrical consumption usually varies according to human activities, lowest in the middle of the night at 4 am and higher during the day, with a peak either at noon or 7 pm depending on the season. Within a week, the consumption is lower during the weekend, because of reduced working activities. Over the 5 weekdays, the profiles look similar but some differences can be noticed:

- The average load is less important on Monday than other week days on morning (from midnight to 2 pm). It is due to the *activity recovery effect*: after the weekend there is some inertia to retrieve a nominal activity level.

- The opposite is observed on Friday afternoon. The average load is less important than in the other weekdays (from 2 pm to midnight), as the activity tends to decrease before the weekend.

Weather, temperature in particular, are important factors as well for electrical consumption in France, with a thermal gradient of approximately 3% more consumption per 1 °C less in winter. Nebulosity, wind, snow, humidity could also influence the consumption but their effect have been harder to characterize and are not yet considered in today's models. These factors are summarized on Fig. 2 through a graphical model, a commonly used representation in the field of causality [10]. It sketches for a quick overview the main relations of dependence and independence between known factors, which we will actually recover through our first experiments to validate the proper learning of our CVAEs. While other methods can recover [21] those causal relationship between common factors when attributes are available in databases, we are mostly interested in events with unknown underlying conditions that might not be yet in any database and which will need additional human interpretation to be defined. These event relations are highlighted in dark, with specific characteristics that can influence the consumption differently.

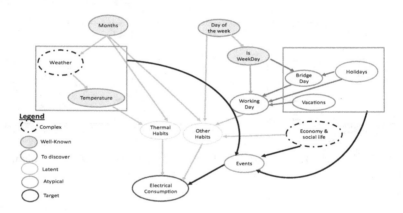

Fig. 2. Simplified graphical model. Well-known factors to integrate as expert knowledge appear as plain green, links to fuzzy atypical conditions we try to interpret appear darker, latent conditions we are also interested in are in blue. (Color figure online)

Atypical Events. One such event category which is well-known are holidays which will serve as a baseline for atypical condition discovery in our experiments. In France, there are 11 holiday days per year which sum to 55, or 3% of the data points in our dataset. They all have in common to be non-working days overall, but can differ in some ways as either days for national or religious celebration and commemorations. Most of them usually appear on fixed dates but not fixed weekdays, and some appear on fixed weekdays but with variable date spread over a month. This hence makes habits different for each holidays compared to a previous year which is even more challenging. When a holiday happens before a weekend, the behavior of consumers usually are more similar to a Saturday. On the following Saturday, the behaviors tend to be similar to a Sunday. For a holiday that happens at the beginning of the week on the contrary, it tends to have Sunday patterns. Often when a holiday happens on a Tuesday or Thursday, many people do not work on the Monday or Friday as well, but it is a fuzzier behavior that is not measured. Those are known as bridge days. Overall, those days look most similar to typical non-working day such as weekends, and some gives an opportunity for a short break, shifting the habits of a typical week.

Other events due to weather or social events can also affect the consumption. As we are looking to characterize a daily profile, weather events happening over a day or longer are likely to be influential and recovered. However, punctual social events often have shorter duration of only few hours and are less likely to affect the consumption over an entire day. Therefore, we will focus on first recovering holiday-like events, then on discovering weather-related events but we will let aside socio-economical events for now over this daily timescale.

Data. The dataset covers the years 2013 to 2017 at a 30-min resolution and was used for the RTE challenge in 2017. This sums up to 1830 daily data points. The temperature profile represents a weighted average over France computed by RTE. Table 1 gathers all the variables, binary, discrete as well as continuous, that will be used in our experiments. Daily Electrical Consumption Profile is our target variable of study. Temperature profile, day of the week, month of the years and holidays are possible features to characterize our electrical consumption. No missing data is reported, apart from the hour change event at the end of winter, which results in a fictitious additional hour with no data. The data at national level is considered clean since it has been used in production for many years with data quality processes, and was further used for the challenge.

Table 1. Summary table of variables in our dataset used in cvae. Categorical variables are One Hot (OH) encoded.

Description	Dimensions	Type	Formula
Daily Consumption Profile	48	Quantitative	$L_i, i = 1, \dots, 48$
Daily Temperature Profile	48	Quantitative	$T_i, i = 1, \dots, 48$
Day of the week indicator (OH)	7	Categorical	$W_i, i = 1, \dots, 7$
Month indicator (OH)	12	Categorical	$M_i, i = 1, \dots, 12$
Holiday indicator (OH)	1	Binary Unbalanced	$H_i, i = 0, 1$

In the next two sections, we present our method to first learn dense representations with autoencoder models, and their conditional extension over extracted features, and later assess the quality of those representations with scores we define to retrieve expert features and extract new ones.

3   CVAE to Learn Conditional Similarities over Features

In this section we explain and motivate the choice of the model we use throughout the experiments performed in the last section. All these experiments share a common objective: representing the input data x, daily consumption profile, by a more compact vector $z = z(x)$. Especially, we want the representation z to reflect a notion of proximity: if two different days x_1 and x_2 are encoded by respectively z_1 and z_2, and that z_1 and z_2 are close together, in the sense of the l_2 norm, then we expect that the days represented by x_1 and x_2 share some common features. Several methods can perform this transformation in the first place but not necessarily as deep by iteratively considering extracted features and adapting the representation. We choose to focus on Variational Autoencoder (VAE), first introduced in [27] and further on their Conditional extension to learn new specific representations z given some conditions c that we denote by $z_{|c}$.

Autoencoders. An Autoencoder is a relatively simple model introduced in [22]. It consists of two parts, one call "encoder" Q (and parametrized by parameters θ) that will transform input x into its latent representation $z = Q_\theta(x)$. It can be learned jointly in a completely unsupervised way with a decoder P (parametrized by vector ϕ) which takes the representation z and who's aim is to transform it back into the original representation x. If we denote by $\hat{x}$ the output of the decoder, i.e. $\hat{x} = P_\phi(z) = P_\phi(Q_\theta(x))$, then the model is trained by minimizing the "reconstruction loss", which is a similarity measure between $\hat{x}$ and x. Most of the time Q and P are represented by deep neural networks. The Autoencoder has some drawbacks: no constraints are set on the latent representation z, the only guarantee is that it can be decoded into the original signal x. Thus it is not always relevant to deduce some properties from the distance between two projections z_1 and z_2. This problem is partially solved by the VAE.

Variational Autoencoders. VAEs aim at learning a parametric latent variable model by maximizing the marginal log-likelihood of the training data $\{x(i)\}_{1 \leq i \leq N}$. Compared to the Autoencoder, it introduces a penalty on the latent space. This latent space z is seen as probabilistic distribution, and must be close to a given prior distribution. It is part of the "variational" literature and is nowadays mostly used to generate data. In this paper, we are interested in the property of the latent space z and will not use the generating capabilities of VAE. Adding this constraint on the latent space has the beneficial effect of regularizing it. In this framework the encoder Q_θ and decoder P_ϕ are better seen as probabilistic distribution, and we will note: $Q_\theta(z|x_i)$ the distribution of variable z given input data x_i. $P_\phi(x_i|z)$ will be the distribution of the reconstructed vector $\hat{x}_i$ from its latent representation z by the decoder P. Training this network is then equivalent to adjust parameters θ and ϕ under the loss:

$$\mathcal{L}_{\lambda-VAE} = \underbrace{\mathcal{L}_{recon}}_{\text{reconstruction loss}} + \lambda \cdot \underbrace{\mathcal{L}_{KL}}_{\text{divergence loss}} \tag{1}$$

$$= -E[\log P_\phi(x_i|z)] + \lambda \cdot \mathcal{D}_{KL}(Q_\theta(z|x_i)\|P(z)) \tag{2}$$

The reconstruction loss measure how well the reconstructed vector $\hat{x}_i$ is close to the original representation x_i, as in the vanilla Autoencoder. The divergence loss minimizes the KL-divergence between $Q_\theta(z|x_i)$, *i.e.* the distance between the latent distribution and its target distribution (the normal distribution usually).

CVAEs. Lastly, we also want to learn adapted representations given existing knowledge. Conditional Variational Autoencoders (CVAE) [18] are an extension that enable to bypass the latent space with some conditional information, such as previously extracted features in our case, to be used for signal reconstruction, freeing the encoder from encoding such information while still achieving proper reconstruction. Figure 3 shows a schematic of this model. The adapted loss function used for the training is:

$$\mathcal{L}_{\lambda-cVAE} = -E[\log P_\phi(x_i|z_{|c},c)] + \lambda \cdot \mathcal{D}_{KL}(Q_\theta(z_{|c}|x_i,c)\|P(z_{|c})) \tag{3}$$

Note that in this case, the conditioning variables represented by vector c is given as input to both the encoder Q_θ and the decoder P_ϕ. It is an architecture that is used to here explicitly disentangle known factors c from other latent residual factors in $z_{|c}$. We will later assess if they factorize properly. In supplementary materials, we explain how we were eventually able to learn properly CVAEs, which are notoriously hard to train [23–25], more especially in our case where we consider training a full conditional network module over extracted features, and not solely inputting a conditional vector over simple target labels.

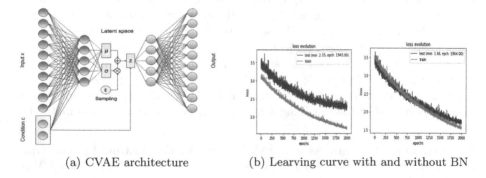

(a) CVAE architecture   (b) Learving curve with and without BN

Fig. 3. Example of CVAE with 2 hidden layers: the architecture is similar to a VAE, except for the additional conditional embedding vector c. Adding a batch normalization (BN) layer unlock the proper learning of the network module for feature conditional embedding to avoid overfitting, as explained in annex.

4   Scores to Recover and Discover Knowledge

We here define scores to assess quantitatively the nature of the representations.

Scores to Assess Feature Importance in Latent Space z. The goal of our method is to extract and further discover some knowledge embedded in the latent space representation we learnt. To assess knowledge recovery of known expert features in the latent space, we can assign them a prediction score to figure out if those features were implicitly selected when compressing information. All the scores are based on a local knn predictor model, either classifier for categorical and binary variables or regressor for continuous variables, using standard euclidean distance metric and a default 5 nearest neighbors. In more details, here is the list of scores used in our experiments for our features of interest apriori:

- F_W and F_M, the scores for day of the week W and months M which are simply the fraction of correctly predicted samples for balanced categories.
- F_{is_w}, the score for *is_weekday* variable is the fraction of properly predicted samples but reweighted, since this is an imbalanced variable (5 weekdays compare to 2 weekend days in a given week). This score is known as an F1 score in the literature, as also defined in sklearn library.
- F_H the score for holidays. Since it is an atypical event variable, we are mostly interested for the instances it occurs. Our score is hence the fraction of true positive holidays only.
- $F_{T_{mean}}$ the score for temperature. For temperature daily profile feature T, we first consider a proxy variable T_{mean} of the average temperature over a day. We then learn a knn regressor for it and use the R2 score over it.

The highest possible value for each score is 1. Scores close to 1 are always a good indicator of a strong dependency of the latent space with the feature associated to the score, hence of its importance. On the contrary, scores of a random projection, give a lower bound for the score to be expected from a feature that is independent from the latent projection, hence insignificant in the encoding.

This feature importance approach could be further extended to be used in automatic feature selection [5]. The goal of our work however here is rather to assess how informative and interpretable a learnt conditional representation is for an expert, rather than defining a new automatic feature selection method.

Score to Detect Event as a Local Outlier in the Latent Space. Once we decided which knowledge to extract and integrate as conditions in the CVAE model, we can train our network in order to obtain a disentangled latent representation of our data. Because of its independence towards the selected feature conditions, this representation also allows us to look for abnormal samples with respect to those conditional features, to guide our exploration in discovering new knowledge. For instance, when conditioning by the day of the week W and the holiday H variables, we expect our representation to be strongly guided by other unselected variables like temperature. What we want to do now is to look for events that are not well represented by these conditions: in other words, outliers or atypical conditions in our representation. To do so, similarly to [4], we decided to use for now a k_{th} nearest-neighbour based outlier score as defined in [28,29]. For the sake of simplicity we use here the 1-nn as our first goal is not to identify systematically outliers but rather study and interpret the representation. Once detected, we want to understand their context and eventually detect if ensemble of atypical events, explained by common factors, are close in the latent space.

5   Experiments to Learn Adapted Representations

Our goal in the following experiments will be to demonstrate our ability to learn successively more specific representations between signals in our dataset with AEs that help reveal some new knowledge to experts. While recovering expert knowledge, we further want to integrate it to enable a more comprehensive exploration than previously possible of other latent features through a similarity space, especially atypical conditions. In our first experiment, we aim at recovering common expert features while highlighting the difficulty at first of learning relevant representations for known atypical signals during holidays. In a second experiment, we show that we can actually learn specific residual representations after conditioning over full sets of extracted features with CVAEs, one main technical contribution of our paper compared to previous CVAEs conditioning on simple target labels. In the third experiment, we focus on the representation most adapted to holidays and explore it to recover some knowledge about them and discover other unexpected similar atypical days. Finally, we explore in a fourth experiment unknown weather atypical conditions, after learning a new representation given previous knowledge over daily features, taking into account atypical conditions from the third experiment. Supplementary materials, code, data and interactive representations are available on GitHub[2]. We explain in the annex our choice of parameters, we never tuned, and hyperparameters, λ and number of training epochs, that we explored and selected.

Experiment 1: Embedding and Expert Features Recovery. In this first experiment, we study 2 models, a classic PCA and a simple VAE, and compare them to a random baseline to measure their respective abilities to learn similarity-based representations and recover common features and dependencies that are described in Table 1: day of the week, weekday or weekend, month of the year, temperature and holidays. First we figured out that most of the variance in the dataset is retrieved on the first 3 dimensions in the case of PCA. 3 dimensions are actually significant as well in the VAE latent space. When learning with more than 3 dimensions, the other dimensions are pruned out with L1-norm in reconstruction Loss. We eventually select a dimension of 4 for our

---

[2] GitHub for paper, annex, data, code and interactive visualizations: https://github.com/marota/Autoencoder_Embedding_Expert_Caracteristion_.

(a) PCA 3D visualizations & features   (b) VAE 3D visualizations & features

Fig. 4. Similarity-based representations with day of the week label on the left, and max daily temperature label on the right over a spherized projection in tensorboard. Data points are more homogeneously spread in VAE representation which makes it easier to navigate into similar or outliers examples.

VAE latent spaces in all our experiments to leave it some more freedom during training. Qualitatively, the VAE projection looks easier to study interactively for a human expert since it is more homogeneously spread, given the gaussian prior, as illustrated on Fig. 4 and better visualized on GitHub. We could expect a human expert to better navigate and study similarities through examples.

Figure 5 summarizes the results of the first experiment. Quantitatively, both models gives very similar scores. As F_{is_w} and F_{Tmean} scores are equally close to 1 for PCA and VAE, they are both able to recover the most salient features to represent daily profiles: temperature and *is_weekday*. Month of the year and day of the week variables also appear as significant features, but they seem less expressive as their scores F_M and F_W are close to 0.5. While weekday and weekend have quite different consumption patterns as illustrated by F_{is_w} score, weekdays have a lot in common which explains the score for day of the week F_W. In the same way, consumption patterns are rather dependent on seasons than individual month, and successive months hence share common consumption patterns decreasing its score.

Eventually, even if holiday score F_H is greater than random, which can suggest some dependency of the consumption over this feature, it is lower than any other features. When looking manually at the representation of holidays in the latent space, we still recover that holidays look more like weekends (in between Saturdays and Sundays) than weekdays. But no holiday appear similar to one another. It is hard yet to ascertain the existence of a condition. The representations created by the two models in Experience 1 hence do not seem appropriate to the analysis of the influence factors of consumption on holidays. To study them properly and independently of common influent factors, it is thus necessary to learn a new specific representation, as we present in Experiment 2.

Experiment 2: Conditioning over Existing Knowledge to Learn New Representations to Be Explored. In this second experiment, we analyze how CVAE models can create more specific and selective representations when conditioning over features we do not want to be influenced by in our exploration. To first assess the quality of the learnt representation, we try in the first place to recover the knowledge described in Fig. 2. In a second step, we will show how we are able to learn a representation more relevant to the analysis of holidays.

Figure 5 summarizes the results of learning different conditional models over known causal factors, either day of the week W, month M and/or temperature T. For all models, residual latent spaces effectively appear to be quite independent of conditional factors, as shown by scores highlighted in green, which are getting close to random. For instance in $CVAE_{|\{T\}}$ model, we condition over temperature T and the corresponding F_T score is near random, highlighting the latent representation independence over temperature. As another result, we see that day of the week condition does not affect the dependency over month M and temperature T in the latent space in model $CVAE_{|\{W\}}$ and conversely in $CVAE_{|\{M,T\}}$. We thus retrieve as a sanity check the natural independence of those factors like previously described in Fig. 2. In addition, we see a simultaneous arising independence of the latent space from $is\_weekday$ variable and W in $CVAE_{|\{W\}}$. This highlights the obvious dependency of $is\_weekday$ over day of the week W. We observe the same but little obvious dependency between M and T. This suggests that beside temperature effects, there might not be strong shift in daily consumer habits from one month to another.

Finally, our known atypical feature, holidays, is eventually well-represented with a high F_H score in the latent spaces of $CVAE_{|\{W\}}$ and $CVAE_{|\{W,M,T\}}$, when conditioning over day of the week W, since they have competing dependencies in common. As a matter of fact, holiday happening on a weekday shifts usual weekday habits to non-working day habits most similar to weekend. Holidays hence appear to be very atypical from the expected consumption prototype on a given weekday. This gives us a new residual latent space in which to study holidays that are well-represented to eventually validate this atypical condition as a relevant feature.

Model Type	Conditions	Conditional layer size before embedding	Feature Scores				
			F_{is_w}	F_W	F_M	F_H	F_{Tmean}
Experiment 1							
random	{}	[]	0.5±0,01	0.14±0,01	0.08±0,01	0.04±0,01	-0,4±0,03
PCA	{}	[]	0.96±0,01	0.51±0,01	0.56±0,01	0.23±0,01	0.91±0,01
VAE	{}	[]	0.96±0,02	0.50±0,02	0.56±0,02	0.27±0,03	0.90±0,02
Experiments 2 & 3							
CVAE	{T}	$Dims_T$=[48,12,4]	0.96±0,02	0.56±0,02	0.19±0,03	0.56±0,03	-0.09±0,1
CVAE	{M}	$Dims_M$=[12,6,3]	0.95±0,02	0.45±0,04	0.12±0,02	0.13±0,03	-0.10±0,1
CVAE	{M, T}	[$Dims_M$, $Dims_T$]	0.96±0,02	0.57±0,02	0.13±0,02	0.22±0,03	-0.31±0,07
CVAE	{W, M, T}	[$Dims_W$,$Dims_M$, $Dims_T$]	0.57±0,02	0.18±0,02	0.12±0,02	0.79±0,02	-0.23±0,07
Experiment 4							
CVAE	{W}	$Dims_W$=[7,5,3]	0.54±0,02	0.18±0,02	0.48±0,03	0.75±0,02	0.89±0,02
CVAE	{W, H}	[$Dims_W$, [1,2]]	0.55±0,02	0.15±0,02	0.45±0,03	0.10±0,02	0.87±0,02
CVAE	{W, H+}	[$Dims_W$, [1,2]]	0.57±0,02	0.16±0,02	0.50±0,03	0.06±0,01	0.89±0,02

Fig. 5. Table of feature scores given several models with different conditions. Experiment 2 highlights that conditioning is properly learnt (green). Holidays appear as a new important feature (blue) when conditioning over weekdays (Color figure online).

Experiment 3: Exploring Similar Holidays and Discovering Additional Weekday Events. After demonstrating proper conditional learning over extracted features, we will now focus on $CVAE_{|\{W,M,T\}}$ to deepen our knowledge over holidays. Since our goal is to recover consumption behaviors specific to these peculiar days, we not only conditioned on weekdays, but also on month and temperature, to focus on unknown specific factors beyond existing knowledge.

In this conditional representation, we reach a feature importance score F_{is_w} of 0.79 for holidays, which is a lot higher than for previous unconditioned representations. Theses results indicate that this CVAE model is suitable to study the peculiarity of most holidays. However, some holidays are not well predicted and we first need to understand why. When analyzing them, most are actually occurring on weekends. This result is interpretable since weekends are already non-working days, hence not really shifting consumer behaviors and thus not atypical: this is a well-known fact we recover. Without integrating expert knowledge over weekdays, this fact could not be recovered in the first unconditioned VAE representation or in $CVAE_{|\{T\}}$, $CVAE_{|\{M\}}$ and $CVAE_{|\{M,T\}}$. The only exception to this statement is a Christmas day happening on a Saturday which actually appears as different from a typical Saturday. This is understandable for this very particular day with huge celebrations. For the remaining 2 holidays not well predicted and happening during weekdays (2015-05-08 and 2016-11-11), they are actually similar to non-working days surrounding holidays as we explain in the following paragraph. We here explained all the instances that were supposedly not well-predicted, highlighting the power of such a representation to study instances collectively in context rather than some model limitation.

Figure 6 shows the conditional latent representation, which confirms that holidays appear more similar to one another than to other days, as they are clustered in the latent space. We then used a manual semi-expert exploration step with Tensorboard Embedding Projector [30] to create new categories of days. In turquoise, we discover 27 days at once in a similar location of the representation which happened during Christmas weeks and during which the great majority of people take vacations: we quickly identified a shared underlying phenomenon as a new condition. As they are also non-working days, this makes them similar to holidays. In green, we discover and label 17 "bridge" days, which are days happening between a holiday and a weekend. Bridge days are often non-working days, with the opportunity for people to take a 4-day break. However, it is not always the case for everyone and every company, leading to a fuzzy mix of working and non-working day behaviors which are hardly measured otherwise. Finally, an exception is the 6th May of 2016, which was actually a bridge day and is not labeled yet. We will see later in the last experiment that it is due to a conjunction of conditions, and not an error in learning this representation. Defining all these new labels interactively and efficiently, 44 in totals related to holidays, demonstrate how informative this representation is for semi-experts to study the characteristics of atypical conditions like holidays, and of days with similar characteristics as well.

In a last step, we looked at the 10 most atypical days based on our outlier score. 4 days were already identified as non-working days previously. The 6 others can actually be interpreted as weather events: 2017-01-21, 2017-01-28, 2013-03-04, 2013-03-13, 2013-03-11 which were all important snowy days in France and 2013-04-14 which was equivalent to a punctual summer day with high temperature gradients from the day before and after. However, this representation is better suited to discover daily events similar to holidays than weather ones. To study further atypical weather conditions independent of daily behaviors, we will explore a last conditional representation over weekdays W and over those new labels related to holidays $H+$, deepening our knowledge by building on it.

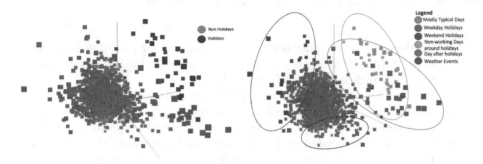

Fig. 6. Latent representation from $CVAE_{|\{W,M,T\}}$, before and after expert labelling. Holidays during weekdays are identified as similar and other non-working days are also discovered. In addition, first weather events are discovered. (Color figure online)

Experiment 4: Discovering New Weather Events. In this last experiment, we want to explore how weather-related events can be represented in a more suited latent space. We first learnt the $CVAE_{|\{W\}}$ model to remove the weekday effect as illustrated in Fig. 7 but this representation only highlighted holidays not yet integrated. As a result, we decided to condition, not only on weekdays W but also on the knowledge of the holidays H. In this representation, non-working days could still be predicted and we decided to include all the labels of Experiment 3 to even more properly condition our latent representation over daily effects. The only remaining working days still predicted were during the Christmas week of 2015, and it is understandable for a weather perspective since it was the hottest Christmas week in French history, hence sharing an additional atypical condition. The resulting weather representation is shown in Fig. 7 (middle).

After creating a representation which qualitatively makes sense to explore the temperature factor, we tried to locate in it the previously detected weather-related events. From Experiment 3, we observed that some previous weather events were actually clustered in this new latent space. We discovered that 2017-01-21 and 2017-01-28 were part of a cold snap starting mid-January and lasting until the end of the month rather than just punctual snowy days: by reusing some previous discovery from a previous representation we here confirmed the

Fig. 7. Left, latent representation from $CVAE_{|\{W\}}$. Holidays are recovered as an important feature here as well and hide the temperature dependency. When conditioning additionally over non-working days with $CVAE_{|\{W,H+\}}$, a smooth 3D V-shape appears, similar to a scatter plot consumption vs temperature.

underlying condition and strengthen our knowledge. As for the other snowy days mentioned in Experiment 3, they were all surrounded by other snowy days at different times, which let us identify new labels.

In order to discover other weather-related atypical events, we looked for the top-100 outliers. As we could expect, some of them had already been manually identified as snowy days. Bridge day 6th of May 2016 also appears as a strong outlier here, indeed associated with a rare dry wind event from the Sahara over France increasing consumption, explaining why it was not strongly detected as a non-working day before with a lower expected consumption. Finally we also discovered recurring hot periods in August accounting for almost a quarter of the top-100 outliers. In this CVAE model, almost all August days between the 7th and 28th of August (except for the 15th, a bank holiday) appeared as atypical. We believe it is due to another underlying feature of interest, not taken into account yet in our data: the significant proportion of employees taking a two-week vacation in August. A new representation, conditioned on temperature additionally, might be interesting to explore in the future to study remaining monthly characteristics.

Across all these experiments, we have explored how these conditional representations could help an expert improve its intuitions on the influent factors for consumption in an interpretable and iterative process, building and strengthening knowledge iteration after iteration. We have first recovered existing expert knowledge, which can be seen as a functionally-grounded evaluation in the taxonomy of [9]: a first level of interpretability. We further showed that we could explore specific representations to discover new events and interpret them as non-working days and weather characteristics. Such experiments can be used in the future for a human-grounded evaluation, the second level of interpretability.

6   Conclusion

We showed how CVAEs could actually be used to recover existing expert knowledge and further learn specific representations for atypical conditions discovery in electrical consumption. This helped study those peculiar situations collectively to eventually interpret quickly some latent additional conditions to augment expert knowledge. In particular, we recovered holidays and their characteristics and discovered similar non-working days as daily events. We eventually detected unknown influential weather events and interpreted them in the appropriate representation. New time scales could be explored and our method improved with more specific architectures such as temporal convolution or attention-based ones. New scores for atypical condition detection could also be used for an even deeper exploration. More generally, given the ability of neural nets to deal with many kinds of data, we believe our approach could be applied more generically to other systems. It could finally be integrated in new iterative and interactive tools for experts [26], to help them explore, interpret and label more exhaustively specific cases of interest within relevant representations of their data.

References

1. Singh, A.K., Ibraheem, I., Khatoon, S., Muazzam, M., Chaturvedi, D.K.: Load forecasting techniques and methodologies: a review. In: Power, Control and Embedded Systems Conference (ICPCES) (2012)
2. Wang, Y., Chen, Q., Hong, T., Kang, C.: Review of smart meter data analytics: applications, methodologies, and challenges. J. IEEE Trans. Smart Grid **10**, 3125–3148 (2018)
3. Hong, T., Pinson, P., Fan, S., Zareipour, H., Troccoli, A., Hyndman, R.J.: Probabilistic energy forecasting: Global Energy Forecasting Competition 2014 and beyond. Int. J. Forecast. **32**(3), 896–913 (2016)
4. Corizzo, R., et al.: Anomaly detection and repair for accurate predictions in geo-distributed Big Data. Big Data Res. **16**, 18–35 (2019)
5. Li, J., Cheng, K., et al.: Feature selection: a data perspective. ACM Comput. Surv. **9**(4), 45 (2010). Article 39
6. Kriegel, H., Kröger, P., Zimek, A.: Outlier detection techniques. In: Tutorial 665 KDD 2010 (2010)
7. Chandola, V., Banerjee, A., Kumar, V.: Anomaly detection: a survey. ACM Comput. Surv. **41**(3), 1–58 (2009)
8. Fanaee-T, H., Gama, J.: Event labeling combining ensemble detectors and background knowledge. Prog. Artif. Intell. **2**, 113–127 (2013). https://doi.org/10.1007/s13748-013-0040-3
9. Doshi-Velez, F., Kim, B.: Towards a rigorous science of interpretable machine learning. http://arxiv.org/abs/1702.08608 (2017)
10. Pearl, J.: Causality. Cambridge University Press, Cambridge (2009)
11. Guyon, I., Donnot, B., Marot, A., et al.: Introducing machine learning for power system operation support. In: IEEE IREP Conference (2017)
12. Xie, J., Girshick, R., Farhadi, A.: Unsupervised deep embedding for clustering analysis. In: ICML (2016)
13. Goodfellow, I., Bengio, Y., Courville, A.: Deep Learning. MIT Press, Cambridge (2016)
14. Mikolov, T., Sutskever, I., Chen, K., Corrado, G., Dean, J.: Distributed Representations of Words and Phrases and their Compositionality. In: NIPS (2013)

15. Johnson, M., Schuster, M., et al.: Google's multilingual neural machine translation system: enabling zero-shot translation. CoRR, abs/1611.04558 (2016)
16. Tschannen, M., Zurich, E., et al.: Recent advances in autoencoder-based representation learning. In: Workshop on Bayesian Deep Learning NeurIPS (2018)
17. Hinton, G., Salakhutdinov, R.: Reducing the dimensionality of data with 675 neural networks. Science **313**(5786), 504–507 (2006)
18. Kingma, D.P., Mohamed, S., Rezende, D.J., Welling, M.: Semi-supervised learning with deep generative models. In: NIPS (2014)
19. Fan, C., Xiao, F., et al.: Analytical investigation of autoencoder-based methods for unsupervised anomaly detection, in building energy data. Appl. Energy **211**, 1123–1135 (2018)
20. Lopez-Martin, M., Carro, B., Sanchez-Esguevillas, A., Lloret, J.: Conditional variational autoencoder for prediction and feature recovery applied to intrusion detection in IoT. Sensors **17**(9), 1967 (2017)
21. Esposito, F., Malerba, D., Ripa, V., Semeraro, G.: Discovering causal rules in relational databases. In: Cybernetics and Systems Studies (1996)
22. Liou, C.-Y., Huang, J.-C., Yang, W.-C.: Modeling word perception using the Elman network. J. Neurocomput. **71**, 3150–3157 (2008)
23. Dieng, A.B., Kim, Y., Rush, A.M., Blei, D.M.: Avoiding latent variable collapse with generative skip models. In: AISTATS (2019)
24. Burgess, C.P., et al.: Understanding disentangling in beta-VAE. In: NIPS (2017)
25. Yeung, S., Kannan, A., Dauphin, Y., Fei-Fei, L.: Tackling over-pruning in variational autoencoders. In: ICML Workshop on Principled Approaches to Deep Learning (2017)
26. Boudjeloud-Assala, L., Pinheiro, P., Blansch, A., Tamisier, T., Otjacques, B.: Interactive and iterative visual clustering. Inf. Vis. **15**(3), 181–197 (2016)
27. Kingma, D.P., Welling, M.: Auto-encoding variational Bayes (2013)
28. Upadhyaya, S., Singh, K.: Nearest neighbour based outlier detection techniques. Int. J. Comput. Trends Technol. **3**(2), 299–303 (2012)
29. Ramaswamy, S., Rastogi, R., Shim, K.: Efficient algorithms for mining outliers from large data sets. In: ACM SIGMOD Record, vol. 29, no. 2. ACM (2000)
30. Smilkov, D., et al.: Embedding projector: interactive visualization and interpretation of embeddings. arXiv preprint arXiv:1611.05469 (2016)

Manufacturing Dispatching Using Reinforcement and Transfer Learning

Shuai Zheng[✉], Chetan Gupta, and Susumu Serita

Industrial AI Lab, Hitachi America Ltd., Santa Clara, CA, USA
{Shuai.Zheng,Chetan.Gupta,Susumu.Serita}@hal.hitachi.com

Abstract. Efficient dispatching rule in manufacturing industry is key to ensure product on-time delivery and minimum past-due and inventory cost. Manufacturing, especially in the developed world, is moving towards on-demand manufacturing meaning a high mix, low volume product mix. This requires efficient dispatching that can work in dynamic and stochastic environments, meaning it allows for quick response to new orders received and can work over a disparate set of shop floor settings. In this paper we address this problem of dispatching in manufacturing. Using reinforcement learning (RL), we propose a new design to formulate the shop floor state as a 2-D matrix, incorporate job slack time into state representation, and design lateness and tardiness rewards function for dispatching purpose. However, maintaining a separate RL model for each production line on a manufacturing shop floor is costly and often infeasible. To address this, we enhance our deep RL model with an approach for dispatching policy transfer. This increases policy generalization and saves time and cost for model training and data collection. Experiments show that: (1) our approach performs the best in terms of total discounted reward and average lateness, tardiness, (2) the proposed policy transfer approach reduces training time and increases policy generalization.

Keywords: Reinforcement learning · Transfer learning · Dispatching

1 Introduction

In a manufacturing process, a production order moves through a sequence of job processing steps to arrive at a final product. The problem of dispatching is the assigning the next job to be processed for a given machine. Inefficient scheduling and dispatching can cause past-due cost (past-due cost is the cost when a job cannot be delivered on time) as well as inventory cost (inventory cost is the storage cost when the job is finished before due time) to go up. It is obvious that all manufacturing managers want on-time delivery and minimum past-due and inventory cost. However, achieving these goals requires efficient production scheduling that minimizes these costs. Furthermore, manufacturing is moving towards a high mix low volume product mix, which makes this even more challenging, due to an ever-evolving product mix, causing larger variations in job types and job arrival rates.

© Springer Nature Switzerland AG 2020
U. Brefeld et al. (Eds.): ECML PKDD 2019, LNAI 11908, pp. 655–671, 2020.
https://doi.org/10.1007/978-3-030-46133-1_39

Production scheduling problems can be categorized by shop configurations and scheduling objectives. Depending on the number of processing machines, there can be single-machine environment [1] and parallel-machine environment [2]. Depending on the number of operations (or stages, steps) of each job, there are single-operation and multi-operation environment [3]. Depending on the objective of scheduling, there are completion time based scheduling [4] (trying to increase machine efficiency) and due date based scheduling [5] (trying to be close to promised delivery dates). Multi-operation parallel-machine problems can be solved through multi-agent algorithms or can be decomposed into solving several single-operation problems [6]. In this work, we focus on dynamic dispatching for due date based objective, which has broader generalization and can be used in different shop floor settings. Dynamic dispatching is also critical for predictive maintenance tasks [7,8], which schedule machine maintenance using data-driven and model-based approaches. Furthermore, dispatching only schedules the imminent job with the highest priority and is particularly suitable for dynamic/stochastic environments due to its low computational time in deployment/testing stage.

Traditionally to address the problem of dispatching, a lot of hyper-heuristics have been proposed and shown to be effective and reusable in different shop conditions [6]. Even though some exact solutions for deterministic scheduling problems are available, manufacturing shop floor depends on heuristics. This is because exact solutions are computationally expensive (and hence infeasible) in deployment stage and cannot solve problems for dynamic and stochastic environments. Since heuristics are very problem-specific and usually achieved by trial and error, hyper-heuristics [6] which automate the design of heuristics attract a lot of interest and have been shown effective in manufacturing as well as other industries such as: bin packing [9], vehicle routing [10], project scheduling [11]. Many hyper-heuristics are based on machine learning approaches, such as neural networks, logistic regression, decision trees, Support Vector Machines, genetic algorithms, genetic programming, reinforcement learning.

Recently, existing works have used deep reinforcement learning for scheduling problems [12,13]. For dispatching purpose, we propose a new design to formulate the shop floor state as a 2-D matrix, incorporate job slack time into state representation. We also design lateness and tardiness rewards function for reinforcement learning. In a manufacturing shop, there are many similar production lines, where designing and maintaining a separate reinforcement learning model for each line is not feasible. To address this, we propose a transfer approach for dispatching policy using manifold alignment. Unlike discriminant subspace learning [14–16] and sparse enforced learning [17–19] where the purpose is to separate classes, manifold alignment [20] learns a subspace by matching the local geometry and preserving the neighborhood relationship within each space. In summary, the contributions of this work are:

1. The reinforcement learning module uses deep learning and policy gradient to minimize job due related cost. Compared to existing work, the novelty is that we formulate the shop floor state as a 2-D matrix, incorporate job slack time

into state representation, and design lateness and tardiness rewards function for dispatching purpose.

2. The transfer learning module transfers dispatching policy between shop floors using manifold alignment. Compared to existing work, the novelty is that our approach formulates shop floor states transfer using manifold alignment, and we design a method to recover actions from sequence of states.

To test our approach, we build a simulator to simulate dynamic factory settings, where we can change factory configurations and job characteristics, such as job queue length, machine processing capacity, job arrival distribution. A simulator is needed since it is very difficult to run live experiments on an actual production line. Another option is to somehow use actual data in a shop floor, however this is a challenge: the data collected on the shop floor is mainly state and scheduling decision record data which is static in nature and cannot provide feedback on the scheduling decisions. These data can be used for hyper-heuristics rules extraction, but not for *dynamic* environment [6]. Furthermore, corporations are reluctant to share real data, because these data include trade secrets and sensitive financial information. In fact, most published works for *dynamic* production scheduling are based on simulators [6]. Using simulator to pre-train model and then deploying it into real factories can further reduce data collection and training effort.

2 Related Work

2.1 Production Scheduling

Hyper-heuristics are promising to handle dynamic and stochastic scheduling problems and have recently emerged as a powerful approach to automate the design of heuristics for production scheduling [6]. The basic idea of hyper-heuristics is to learn scheduling rules from a set of very good training scheduling instances. These training instances are considered optimal or perfect. Hyper-heuristics can then replicate these scheduling instances as closely as possible. Depending on the learning method, hyper-heuristics can be classified into supervised learning and unsupervised learning. Examples of supervised learning hyper-heuristics include neural networks [21], logistic regression [22], decision trees [23], Support Vector Machines [24], etc. Genetic algorithms (GA) and Genetic Programming (GP) are evolutionary computation methods and have been used for dynamic job shop scheduling problems. Reinforcement learning is an efficient algorithm to learn optimal behaviors through reward feedback information from dynamic environments [13]. $TD(\lambda)$ based reinforcement learning was used for manufacturing job shop scheduling to improve resource utilization [25]. Resource scheduling for computer clusters is also very related, such as Tetris [26] and resource scheduling in HPC [27]. RL-Mao [12] uses policy gradient reinforcement learning to reduce computer job slowdown. The difference of our work and RL-Mao lies in that our work integrates manufacturing job slack time into state representation and the objective functions using lateness and tardiness are specifically designed for manufacturing dispatching.

2.2   Reinforcement Learning Background

In reinforcement learning, an agent interacts with an environment $\mathcal{E}$ over many discrete time steps [28]. The state space of $\mathcal{E}$ is defined within $\mathcal{S}$. At each time step t, the agent receives a state $s_t \in \mathcal{S}$ and performs an action $a_t \in \mathcal{A}$ following a policy π, where $\mathcal{A}$ defines the action space of this agent. The agent receives a reward r_t for this action and a new state s_{t+1} is then presented to the agent. The policy π is a mapping function from states s_t to a_t, denoted by $\pi(a_t|s_t)$, which gives the probability of taking action a_t. This process continues until the agent reaches a termination state or time t exceeds a maximum threshold. The cumulative discounted reward starting from time t is defined as:

$$R_t = \sum_{k=0}^{\infty} \gamma^k r_{t+k}, \tag{1}$$

where $\gamma \in (0,1]$ is a discounted factor. The goal of a reinforcement agent is to obtain a policy which maximizes the expected total discounted reward starting from time $t = 0$:

$$J(\pi) = \mathbb{E}[R_0|\pi]. \tag{2}$$

In policy-based model-free reinforcement learning, policy is directly parameterized as a function from states to actions, $\pi(a|s;\theta)$, where parameter θ is updated using gradient ascent on $\mathbb{E}[R_t|\pi]$. One example of this category is the REINFORCE algorithm [29,30]. Using the policy gradient theorem [29], the gradient with respect to θ can be given as $\nabla_\theta \log \pi(a_t|s_t;\theta)R_t$, which is an unbiased estimate of $\nabla_\theta \mathbb{E}[R_t|\pi]$. In order to reduce the variance of this estimate, we can subtract a baseline from the return, where baseline $b_t(s_t)$ is a learned function of state. The resulting gradient is thus given as

$$\nabla_\theta \log \pi(a_t|s_t;\theta)(R_t - b_t). \tag{3}$$

The term $R_t - b_t$ is used to scale the policy gradient and can be seen as the advantage of action a_t in state s_t.

3   Dispatching with Reinforcement Learning

3.1   Problem Description

Objective. Dispatching performance can be evaluated in terms of lateness L and tardiness TA. The objective of this problem is to minimize the average lateness and tardiness of all jobs. For one single job, let the completion time be c. Lateness is the absolute difference between job due time and job completion time:

$$L = |c - d|, \tag{4}$$

Fig. 1. Overall design of Deep Manufacturing Dispatching (DMD).

where $L \in [0, +\infty)$. Thus lateness considers both inventory and past-due cost. Tardiness only considers the lateness when the job is late. Tardiness TA is defined as:

$$TA = max(c - d, 0), \tag{5}$$

where $TA \in [0, +\infty)$. Tardiness focuses on past-due cost, but not inventory cost.

Constraints. Since this is a single-operation environment, there is no precedence constraint between jobs/operations. Disjunctive constraint is enforced in this problem, so that no two jobs can be processed at the same time. If the job is being processed, it cannot be paused. All jobs are equally important.

3.2 Design

Figure 1 shows the overall design of proposed Deep Manufacturing Dispatching (DMD). The environment includes job queue and processing machine. At each time step, reinforcement learning agent observes a state s, which includes job queue state and machine state (schedule of next T time steps), then outputs a probability vector with respect to each action using a deep learning model as function approximator. The agent will then perform action a with the highest probability and receive a reward r from the environment.

There are n job slots and m backlog slots. Each job has a processing time (job length) p and a due time d. At each time step, the probability of arriving a new job is $\lambda \in (0, 1)$. When a job arrives, it will be placed on one of the n job slots randomly. If job slots are full, the job will be placed on backlog slots. For jobs placed on backlog slots, only job count can be seen and those jobs cannot be selected by dispatcher. As the backlog design for computer jobs in [12], it is reasonable that the reinforcement agent only considers jobs in job slots, not those on backlog slots, because jobs in job slots arrive earlier and get higher priority. Let t_{curr} indicate current time. Slack time $slack$ of a job is defined as:

$$slack = d - t_{curr} - p. \tag{6}$$

If $slack > 0$, it means that if this job is started now, it will be completed before its due time; if $slack < 0$, it means that it will be completed after its due time. We now explain the design details of DMD elements: state space, action space, reward, training.

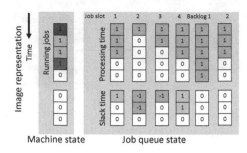

Fig. 2. State representation: this state looks $T = 5$ time steps ahead of current time and slack time array length is $Z = 3$; there are $n = 4$ job slots and $m = 10$ backlog slots. The machine state (schedule of next T time steps) tells that the next 4 time steps have been scheduled. For the job in job slot 1, $p = 3$, $slack = 1$; for the job in job slot 3, $p = 2$, $slack = -1$. There are 8 jobs waiting in backlog. Different colors in machine state represent different jobs.

State Space. State space includes both states of the machine and job queue. At any time step, we consider the states T time steps ahead and we use a Z length array to represent the slack time. We use a 2-D matrix to represent machine state (schedule of next T time steps) and job queue state. One example is shown in Fig. 2. Value 1 in machine state means that the machine at that time step has been allocated, and value 0 means that the machine will be idle. As time proceeds one time step, the T-length array shifts up by one unit and a new 0 value is appended to the bottom. Job queue state consists of n job slots and m backlog. Different colors in machine state indicate different jobs.

Each job slot is represented using two arrays: processing time and slack time. The processing time array is represented using a T length array, with the number of 1s indicating job length p. The slack time is represented using a Z length array, where 1 means positive $slack$ and -1 means negative $slack$. The sum of slack time array represents job $slack$.

Backlog state is represented by several T length array, with a total of m slots, where each slot represents a job. In Fig. 2, backlog is represented using 2 5-length array and there are 8 jobs in backlog. The 0s under machine state and backlog do not represent slack time and are padded to make the state as a complete 2-D matrix. There are 2 benefits using this 2-D representation: (1) 2-D representation can capture the relationship between job characteristics and machine status, and we can use deep learning method to discover hidden patterns from 2-D representations; (2) we can represent schedule in T time steps ahead of time.

Action Space. At each time step, the dispatcher performs multiple actions to select a subset of jobs from n job slots until an invalid or void action is selected. The action a is a subset of $\{\emptyset, 1, ..., n\}$, where $\emptyset$ is a void action and no job slot is selected. Void action allows dispatcher to save more resources for larger jobs.

We let the dispatcher make a decision at each time step, instead of only when the machine is idle. This is because jobs are scheduled T time steps ahead. The decision of the dispatcher is to decide which job to allocate within the next T time step, not for which job to run next immediately, so we do not consider the machine is idle or not. Instead, we consider the schedule T time steps ahead.

Reward. We design the reward at each time step with respect to lateness and tardiness as:

$$r_L = -\sum_{j \in \mathbb{P}} \frac{L_j}{p_j}, \tag{7}$$

$$r_{TA} = -\sum_{j \in \mathbb{P}} \frac{TA_j}{p_j}, \tag{8}$$

where $\mathbb{P}$ is set of jobs that are currently being processed by the machine. Summation of r_L and r_{TA} over all time steps for the running jobs equals to the total lateness and tardiness.

Training. We run the simulator multiple times to get a batch of trajectories. At each time t, we record the state s_t, action a_t and reward r_t. The discounted reward R_t at time t can then be computed using Eq. (1). b_t is a baseline function, which can be the average reward at time t of multiple trajectories.

3.3 Scalability and Generalization

The complexity comes from training and deployment/testing stage. In training stage, the computational time mainly depends on the training of reinforcement learning agent. From Figs. 3 and 4, we found that the objective function converges fast. Pre-training with simulated data, transfer learning and other accelerated computing [31] can further reduce training time. In deployment/testing stage, the computational time is very fast and the same as testing time of a deep neural network. This ensures the quick response to different shop floor conditions.

4   Dispatching Policy Transfer

In reinforcement learning area, some approaches using manifold learning for cross-domain transfer learning [32–34] have been applied in games and apprentice learning, where control of games, such as Cart Pole and Simple Mass, shares similar control mechanism to balance an object. However, for dispatching problems, due to the complexity of manufacturing settings, it is not straightforward to transfer dispatching rules among factories or product lines. In our proposed Deep Manufacturing Dispatching (DMD) framework, the following features of the training data will affect the data distribution: 1. factory setting parameters, which are used to describe job queue states and machine states, including length of processing time array T, length of slack time array Z, number of job

---

Algorithm 1. Policy transfer learning.

Input: Source environment $\mathcal{E}_x$, target environment $\mathcal{E}_y$, source optimal policy π^{x*}.
Output: Target optimal policy π^{y*}.
 1: Find state projection $\chi: \mathcal{S}^x \to \mathcal{S}^y$ using Algorithm 2.
 2: Following optimal policy π^{x*}, generate source state trajectories, $\{s_{00}^x, s_{01}^x, ...\}$, $\{s_{10}^x, s_{11}^x, ...\}$, ...
 3: Compute target state trajectories in $\mathcal{S}^y$, $\{s_{00}^y, s_{01}^y, ...\}$, $\{s_{10}^y, s_{11}^y, ...\}$,..., using Eq. 9.
 4: Recover policy π^y using Algorithm 3.
 5: Fine-tune policy π^y and get optimal policy π^{y*}.

---

slots n, number of backlog slots m, etc.; 2. job characteristics parameters, such as job length distribution, job arrival speed, job due time distribution. To apply a trained policy in a new factory setting or when job characteristics changes, knowledge transfer would greatly improve the performance of learning by avoiding expensive data collection process and reducing training time.

Given source environment $\mathcal{E}_x$ with state space $\mathcal{S}^x$ and action space $\mathcal{A}^x$, target environment $\mathcal{E}_y$ with state space $\mathcal{S}^y$ and action space $\mathcal{A}^y$, source optimal policy $\pi^{x*}(a|s)$ is already learned. Transfer learning can be used to learn target optimal policy $\pi^{y*}(a|s)$. There are two types of policy transfer: (1) same-environment transfer, where factory setting parameters are not changed, but job characteristics parameters are changed; (2) cross-environment transfer, where factory setting parameters are changed. For cross-environment transfer, the job queue and machine states are changed, and input dimension of source policy is different from the input dimension of target policy, so source policy cannot be applied directly in new environment. To successfully and effectively transfer π^{x*} to π^{y*}, we propose the following transfer strategy as shown in Algorithms 1.

In step 1, we want to find a state projection χ, so that for any source state $s^x \in \mathcal{S}^x$, a corresponding target state is given as:

$$s^y = \chi s^x. \tag{9}$$

We will introduce how to find this projection χ in Algorithm 2. Using computed target environment trajectories from step 3, step 4 recovers policy π^y using Algorithm 3.

Find Projection χ. Manifold alignment [20] learns a subspace by matching the local geometry within source space and target space. Given some random source states $s_0^x, s_1^x, ...$, random target states $s_0^y, s_1^y, ...$, manifold alignment looks for two projections α and β to minimize cost function:

$$C(\alpha, \beta) = \mu \sum_{i,j} (\alpha^T s_i^x - \beta^T s_j^y)^2 W^{i,j} + 0.5 \sum_{i,j} (\alpha^T s_i^x - \alpha^T s_j^x)^2 W_x^{i,j}$$
$$+ 0.5 \sum_{i,j} (\beta^T s_i^y - \beta^T s_j^y)^2 W_y^{i,j}, \tag{10}$$

where α and β project source states and target states into a space of dimension d_{share}. This is also similar to the idea in [35,36], where different views of images

Algorithm 2. Find projection χ using manifold alignment.

Input: Random source states $s_0^x, s_1^x, ...$, random target states $s_0^y, s_1^y, ...$
Output: Projection χ for state transfer $\mathcal{S}^x \to \mathcal{S}^y$.
1: Compute W_x, W_y, W using Eqs. (11, 13)
2: Compute L_x, L_y using Eq. (21).
3: Compute Ω_1, Ω_2, Ω_3, Ω_4 using Eq. (23).
4: Formulate matrix L and Z using Eq. (20).
5: Solve Eq. (19).
6: Compute χ using Eq. (24).

---

use a shared regression coefficient. $(\alpha^T s_i^x - \alpha^T s_j^x)^2 W_x^{i,j}$ minimizes the difference of s_i^x and s_j^x with weight $W_x^{i,j}$. $W_x^{i,j}$ can be computed using the kernel function in Euclidean space:

$$W_x^{i,j} = \exp(-\|s_i^x - s_j^x\|). \tag{11}$$

Similarly, $(\beta^T s_i^y - \beta^T s_j^y)^2 W_y^{i,j}$ minimizes the difference of s_i^y and s_j^y with weight $W_y^{i,j}$, which can be computed using Eq. (11) similarly.

$(\alpha^T s_i^x - \beta^T s_j^y)^2 W^{i,j}$ minimizes the difference of s_i^x and s_j^y in the shared space with weight $W^{i,j}$. To compute $W^{i,j}$, we can compare their knn local geometry matrix. Knn local geometry matrix $R_{s_i^x}$ is defined as a $(k+1) \times (k+1)$ matrix, with the (k_1, k_2)-th element as:

$$R_{s_i^x}(k_1, k_2) = \|z_{k_1} - z_{k_2}\|, \tag{12}$$

where $z = \{s_i^x, z_1, z_2, ..., z_k\}$, z_{k_1} and z_{k_2} are the k_1-th and k_2-th nearest neighbors, $\|z_{k_1} - z_{k_2}\|$ is Euclidean distance of z_{k_1} and z_{k_2}. $R_{s_j^y}$ can be computed similarly using Eq. (12). $W^{i,j}$ can then be given as:

$$W^{i,j} = \exp(-dist(R_{s_i^x}, R_{s_j^y})), \tag{13}$$

$$dist(R_{s_i^x}, R_{s_j^y}) = \min_{1 \le h \le k!} min(dist_1(h), dist_2(h)), \tag{14}$$

where $dist(R_{s_i^x}, R_{s_j^y})$ is the minimum distance of $k!$ possible permutations of the k neighbors of s_i^x and s_i^y. The distances of h-th permutation $dist_1(h)$ and $dist_2(h)$ is given as:

$$dist_1(h) = \|\{R_{s_j^y}\}_h - w_1 R_{s_i^x}\|_F, \tag{15}$$

$$dist_2(h) = \|R_{s_i^x} - w_2 \{R_{s_j^y}\}_h\|_F, \tag{16}$$

$$w_1 = \operatorname{Tr} R_{s_i^x}^T \{R_{s_j^y}\}_h / \operatorname{Tr} R_{s_i^x}^T R_{s_i^x}, \tag{17}$$

$$w_2 = \operatorname{Tr}\{R_{s_j^y}\}_h^T R_{s_i^x} / \operatorname{Tr}\{R_{s_j^y}\}_h^T \{R_{s_j^y}\}_h, \tag{18}$$

where Tr is matrix trace operator, w_1 and w_2 are two weights terms.

Minimizing cost function Eq. (10) can be formulated as:

$$C(\phi) = \phi^T Z L Z^T \phi, \tag{19}$$

Algorithm 3. Recover policy π^y.

Input: State trajectories $\{s_{00}^y, s_{01}^y, ...\}$, $\{s_{10}^y, s_{11}^y, ...\}$,...
Output: Policy π^y.
1: Compute action trajectories in $\mathcal{A}^y$, $\{a_{00}^y, a_{01}^y, ...\}$, $\{a_{10}^y, a_{11}^y, ...\}$, ..., using Eq. (25).
2: Train π^y with a deep model by using state trajectories as input feature, action trajectories as output class labels.

---

where

$$\phi = \begin{pmatrix} \alpha \\ \beta \end{pmatrix}, Z = \begin{pmatrix} X & 0 \\ 0 & Y \end{pmatrix}, L = \begin{pmatrix} L_x + \mu\Omega_1 & -\mu\Omega_2 \\ -\mu\Omega_3 & L_y + \mu\Omega_4 \end{pmatrix}. \tag{20}$$

Columns of X are vector representations of state of $s_0^x, s_1^x, ...$; columns of Y are vector representations of state of $s_0^y, s_1^y, ...$; L_x and L_y are given as:

$$L_x = D_x - W_x, \ L_y = D_y - W_y, \tag{21}$$

where D_x and D_y are diagonal matrix:

$$D_x^{ii} = \sum_j W_x^{ij}, \ D_y^{ii} = \sum_j W_y^{ij}. \tag{22}$$

Ω_1 and Ω_4 are diagonal matrices. Ω_2 is the same as W, Ω_3 is the same as the transpose of W. Ω_1, Ω_2, Ω_3 and Ω_4 are given as:

$$\Omega_1^{ii} = \sum_j W^{ij}, \ \Omega_2^{ij} = W^{ij}, \ \Omega_3^{ij} = W^{ji}, \ \Omega_4^{ii} = \sum_j W^{ji}. \tag{23}$$

d_{share} is a tuning parameter indicating the size of the shared space. Finally, χ is given as:

$$\chi = \beta^{T\dagger}\alpha^T, \tag{24}$$

where $\dagger$ is matrix pseudo inverse.

Recover Policy π^y. Algorithm 3 shows how to recover policy π^y given state trajectory $\{s_{00}^y, s_{01}^y, ...\}$, $\{s_{10}^y, s_{11}^y, ...\}$, ... We know that when at state $s_{0(t-1)}^y$, an action $a_{0(t-1)}^y \in \mathcal{A}^y$ was taken and then the state evolved from $s_{0(t-1)}^y$ to s_{0t}^y. However, we cannot directly get the action $a_{0(t-1)}^y$ by comparing $s_{0(t-1)}^y$ and s_{0t}^y. Our approach is to try all possible actions in $\mathcal{A}^y$ and record the states $\widetilde{s_{0t}^y}(a)$ after taking each action, then compare states $\widetilde{s_{0t}^y}(a)$ with s_{0t}^y. To compute $\widetilde{s_{0t}^y}(a)$, when action a is taken, we remove the a-th job in job queue and set it to be 0s in matrix $s_{0(t-1)}^y$. We use the following equation to find the $a_{0(t-1)}^y$:

$$a_{0(t-1)}^y = \underset{a \in \mathcal{A}^y}{\arg\min} \|\widetilde{s_{0t}^y}(a) - s_{0t}^y\|, \tag{25}$$

where $\|\widetilde{s_{0t}^y}(a) - s_{0t}^y\|$ is distance between states $\widetilde{s_{0t}^y}(a)$ and s_{0t}^y.

Using Eq. (25), we can find action trajectories $\{a_{00}^y, a_{01}^y, ...\}$, $\{a_{10}^y, a_{11}^y, ...\}$, ... We initialize the target policy π^y using a deep model, such as DNN or Deep CNN, and train policy π^y as a classifier from s^y to a corresponding a^y.

5 Experiments

5.1 Experiment Setup and Evaluation Metrics

Experiment Settings. Unless otherwise noted, the default setting is given as below: the machine looks $T = 15$ time steps ahead, length of slack time array is $Z = 5$, number of job slots is $n = 10$, number of backlog slots is $m = 60$. We test a set of different values for the following job characteristics parameters:

1. **Job arrival speed** $\lambda \in (0, 1)$ is the probability of arriving a new job at each time step, with default $\lambda = 0.5$.
2. **Small job probability** p_{small} indicates the probability that the new job length is short, with default $p_{small} = 0.8$. The short job length distribution is a random number in $[1, 2]$; the long job length distribution is a random number in $[6, 10]$.
3. **Urgent job probability** p_{urgent} indicates probability of the job slack time is very short, with default $p_{urgent} = 0.5$. When the job arrives, the urgent job slack time distribution is a random number in $[1, 5]$; the non-urgent job slack time distribution is a random number in $[5, 10]$.

At any time step, if the job queue is full, the new job will be dropped, a penalty -10 will be added to reward r_t. We use Deep Neural Network (DNN) to model policy $\pi_{a|s;\theta}$. The input is state representation from Fig. 2. The output is a probability vector of length same as action space $\mathcal{A}$. The activation function in hidden layer is rectified linear unit and the activation function in the last layer is Softmax. The DNN network structure we use is 2 hidden layers with 128 and 64 neurons respectively.

Training and Testing Data. For each experiment, we use the same setting to generate 10 random trajectories for training and testing respectively. Then we train each comparing method on the same training data and test it on the same testing data.

Evaluation Metrics. To evaluate the performance and business impact, we use total discounted reward (Eq. (2)) and average lateness (Eq. (4)), tardiness (Eq. (5)). Total discounted reward includes the penalty when a job was dropped if the job queue is full. Average lateness and tardiness only consider those jobs that are successfully finished, which are straightforward and valuable to business users. The reported results are the average values over 10 random testing trajectories.

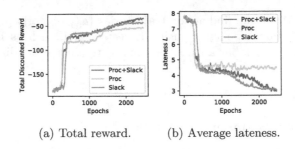

(a) Total reward.   (b) Average lateness.

Fig. 3. Effectiveness of state presentation. "Proc+Slack": using both Processing time and Slack time of Job queue in Fig. 2. "Proc": using only Processing time. "Proc": using only Slack time.

Table 1. Total discounted reward using different objective and trajectory length.

Trajectory length	Lateness objective				Tardiness objective			
	50	100	150	200	50	100	150	200
EDF	−65.05	−116.06	−215.65	−513.53	−57.03	−95.67	−192.64	−493.14
LST	−77.11	−144.45	−260.93	−624.76	−69.09	−130.97	−247.45	−611.28
Random Forest	−65.05	−115.47	−211.37	−433.40	−57.03	−92.46	−195.20	−410.39
SVM	−65.05	−115.47	−212.48	−348.01	−57.03	−92.46	−185.50	−324.99
Neural Network	−65.05	−115.47	−164.58	−238.31	−57.03	−92.46	−137.60	−199.19
Tetris	−21.65	−89.37	−73.66	−154.15	−8.93	−16.67	−24.46	−102.53
RL-Mao	−7.00	−57.39	−250.51	−212.32	−38.86	−118.54	−223.05	−370.97
DMD	**−0.51**	**−34.47**	**−63.30**	**−133.14**	**−0.22**	**−4.09**	**−9.43**	**−14.55**

5.2 Effectiveness of State Presentation Fig. 2

Figure 3 shows the effectiveness of combining processing time and slack time information in state presentation (Fig. 2). Combining both processing and slack time gives the highest total discounted lateness reward and lowest average lateness. Different to computer job resource management [12], slack time is important for manufacturing dispatching.

5.3 Comparison with Existing Algorithms

We compare the proposed Deep Manufacturing Dispatching (DMD) with 7 other dispatching policies: 2 due time related manual designed rules (EDF for Earliest-Due-First, LST for Least-Slack-Time), 3 hyper-heuristics using machine learning (random forest, SVM, and neural network with 2 hidden layers), and reinforcement learning based RL-Mao [12] and Tetris [26]. For hyper-heuristics, under each experiment setting, we choose the best heuristic rule in terms of average lateness or tardiness as ground truth rule.

Tables 1 and 2 show DMD gets the highest reward and lowest average lateness and tardiness. Unless other noted, the default trajectory length is 100 time steps.

Table 2. Average lateness and tardiness using different objective and trajectory length.

Trajectory length	Average lateness				Average tardiness			
	50	100	150	200	50	100	150	200
EDF	5.29	4.44	7.02	11.68	5.77	5.38	8.71	13.89
LST	6.71	5.48	8.26	13.80	7.07	6.21	9.31	15.35
Random Forest	5.29	4.38	5.89	9.03	5.77	5.40	6.69	10.66
SVM	5.29	4.38	5.48	7.32	5.77	5.40	6.72	8.70
Neural Network	5.29	4.38	4.37	5.23	5.77	5.40	5.29	7.33
Tetris	6.13	8.08	5.73	8.20	8.25	14.17	6.20	10.07
RL-Mao	5.29	6.39	7.35	8.06	7.78	9.10	9.21	10.43
DMD	**2.11**	**3.16**	**3.60**	**5.01**	**1.51**	**2.24**	**3.68**	**4.14**

Table 3. Total discounted lateness reward with various job characteristics.

	Job arrival speed λ					Small job p_{small}			Urgent job p_{urgent}		
	0.1	0.3	0.5	0.7	0.9	0.2	0.5	0.8	0.1	0.5	0.9
EDF	−31.12	−96.99	−116.06	−317.59	−415.87	−305.49	−246.97	−116.06	−71.92	−116.06	−115.08
LST	−31.12	−126.23	−144.45	−378.46	−422.32	−316.67	−278.47	−144.45	−75.77	−144.45	−120.12
Random Forest	−31.12	−78.22	−115.47	−205.24	−246.33	−106.16	−106.33	−115.47	−71.15	−115.47	−111.95
SVM	−31.12	−78.66	−115.47	−208.10	−131.94	−154.18	−124.25	−115.47	−71.15	−115.47	−111.95
Neural Network	−31.12	−78.66	−115.47	−219.09	−260.66	−111.56	−150.48	−115.47	−71.15	−115.47	−111.95
Tetris	−28.39	−83.46	−89.37	**−53.08**	−107.22	−70.08	−48.26	−89.37	−68.74	−89.37	−69.85
RL-Mao	−13.79	−58.95	−57.39	−136.36	−178.74	−99.27	−74.24	−57.39	−49.70	−57.39	−48.11
DMD	**−11.12**	**−14.48**	**−34.47**	−62.37	**−106.70**	**−56.33**	**−43.26**	**−34.47**	**−38.45**	**−34.47**	**−36.86**

In manufacturing scheduling, where job frequency is not as high as computer jobs, this trajectory length is reasonable. We can see from Table 1 that as the length of trajectory increases, the total discounted reward decreases overall. Tables 3 and 4 show total discounted reward and average lateness with different settings of λ, p_{small} and p_{urgent}. Overall, for 19 settings (8 settings in Tables 1 and 2 and 11 settings in Tables 3 and 4), DMD gets best results for 18 settings on total discounted reward and 16 settings on average lateness and tardiness. Best performing methods in each column are in bold.

5.4 Dispatching Policy Transfer

In step 1 of Algorithm 1, we generate 2000 random states from source environment and target environment respectively for each transfer setting. The following four transfer learning settings are considered: (1) Same-environment: Source $\lambda = 0.5$; Target $\lambda = 0.7$. (2) Same-environment: Source $\lambda = 0.5$, $p_{small} = 0.8$; Target $\lambda = 0.7$, $p_{small} = 0.5$. (3). Cross-environment: Source $n = 10$; Target $n = 15$. (4). Cross-environment: Source $n = 10$, $m = 60$; Target $n = 15$,

Table 4. Average lateness with various job characteristics.

	Job arrival speed λ					Small job p_{small}			Urgent job p_{urgent}		
	0.1	0.3	0.5	0.7	0.9	0.2	0.5	0.8	0.1	0.5	0.9
EDF	5.33	5.00	4.44	16.29	19.41	21.05	12.83	4.44	3.26	4.44	4.67
LST	5.33	6.28	5.48	20.89	22.54	21.18	15.00	5.48	4.00	5.48	4.94
Random Forest	5.33	4.00	4.38	8.21	12.73	8.11	5.42	4.38	**2.88**	4.38	4.32
SVM	5.33	4.16	4.38	8.21	**4.02**	9.47	5.68	4.38	**2.88**	4.38	4.32
Neural Network	5.33	4.16	4.38	10.30	15.43	**7.61**	6.36	4.38	**2.88**	4.38	4.32
Tetris	5.33	7.67	8.08	6.58	12.78	7.75	6.30	8.08	7.68	8.08	6.26
RL-Mao	4.50	6.65	6.39	9.35	10.87	11.62	8.19	6.39	5.15	6.39	5.83
DMD	**3.45**	**3.21**	**3.16**	**4.51**	9.74	7.70	**4.32**	**3.16**	4.55	**3.16**	**4.03**

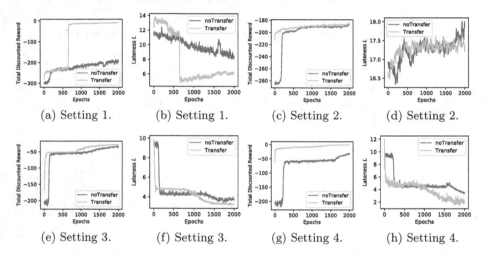

(a) Setting 1.   (b) Setting 1.   (c) Setting 2.   (d) Setting 2.

(e) Setting 3.   (f) Setting 3.   (g) Setting 4.   (h) Setting 4.

Fig. 4. Policy transfer evaluation using Deep Manufacturing Dispatching (DMD).

$m = 30$. In all figures, *noTransfer* curve is trained from scratch under target setting, *Transfer* curve is initialized using the output of Algorithm 3 under source setting, then trained under target setting. Figure 4 shows total discounted reward and average lateness of the 4 transfer settings using DMD. We find that policy transferring reduces training time and gives larger total discounted reward and smaller average lateness compared to training from scratch. Table 5 shows the results using 3 hyper-heuristics. Best results are highlighted for each transfer setting. Note that, as mentioned in Sect. 5.1, dropped job penalty is considered in total discounted reward, but not in average lateness. We find that policy transfer gives competitive or better results than training from scratch using hyper-heuristics. This shows the effectiveness of Algorithm 1.

Table 5. Policy transfer evaluation for hyper-heuristics.

Transfer setting		noTransfer				Transfer			
		1	2	3	4	1	2	3	4
Total discounted lateness	Random Forest	−205.24	−216.44	−120.22	−120.22	−140.02	−205.97	−115.47	−115.47
	SVM	−208.10	−189.27	−115.47	−115.47	−128.26	−213.40	−115.47	−115.47
	Neural Network	−219.09	−229.46	−114.15	−121.65	−174.52	−204.55	−115.47	−115.47
Average lateness	Random Forest	8.21	14.05	4.63	4.63	**5.08**	**10.63**	**4.38**	**4.38**
	SVM	8.21	13.05	**4.38**	**4.38**	**5.13**	**10.96**	**4.38**	**4.38**
	Neural Network	10.30	16.74	**4.38**	4.72	**7.00**	**13.40**	**4.38**	**4.38**

6 Conclusion

Dispatching is a difficult yet important problem. It is not straightforward due to the complexity of manufacturing settings. We showed the promising application of combining reinforcement learning and transfer learning in manufacturing industry. The transfer learning module increases the generalization of learned dispatching rules and saves cost and time for data collection and model training.

References

1. Park, J., Nguyen, S., Zhang, M., Johnston, M.: Genetic programming for order acceptance and scheduling. In: 2013 IEEE Congress on Evolutionary Computation (CEC), pp. 1005–1012. IEEE (2013)
2. Jakobović, D., Jelenković, L., Budin, L.: Genetic programming heuristics for multiple machine scheduling. In: Ebner, M., O'Neill, M., Ekárt, A., Vanneschi, L., Esparcia-Alcázar, A.I. (eds.) EuroGP 2007. LNCS, vol. 4445, pp. 321–330. Springer, Heidelberg (2007). https://doi.org/10.1007/978-3-540-71605-1_30
3. Garey, M.R., Johnson, D.S., Sethi, R.: The complexity of flowshop and jobshop scheduling. Math. Oper. Res. **1**(2), 117–129 (1976)
4. Vazquez-Rodriguez, J.A., Ochoa, G.: On the automatic discovery of variants of the neh procedure for flow shop scheduling using genetic programming. J. Oper. Res. Soc. **62**(2), 381–396 (2011)
5. Mascia, F., López-Ibáñez, M., Dubois-Lacoste, J., Stützle, T.: From grammars to parameters: automatic iterated greedy design for the permutation flow-shop problem with weighted tardiness. In: Nicosia, G., Pardalos, P. (eds.) LION 2013. LNCS, vol. 7997, pp. 321–334. Springer, Heidelberg (2013). https://doi.org/10.1007/978-3-642-44973-4_36
6. Branke, J., Nguyen, S., Pickardt, C.W., Zhang, M.: Automated design of production scheduling heuristics: a review. IEEE Trans. Evol. Comput. **20**(1), 110–124 (2016)
7. Mobley, R.K.: An Introduction to Predictive Maintenance. Elsevier, Amsterdam (2002)
8. Zheng, S., Ristovski, K., Farahat, A., Gupta, C.: Long short-term memory network for remaining useful life estimation. In: 2017 IEEE International Conference on Prognostics and Health Management (ICPHM), pp. 88–95. IEEE (2017)

9. Özcan, E., Parkes, A.J.: Policy matrix evolution for generation of heuristics. In: Proceedings of the 13th Annual Conference on Genetic and Evolutionary Computation. ACM (2011)

10. Vonolfen, S., Beham, A., Kommenda, M., Affenzeller, M.: Structural synthesis of dispatching rules for dynamic dial-a-ride problems. In: Moreno-Díaz, R., Pichler, F., Quesada-Arencibia, A. (eds.) EUROCAST 2013. LNCS, vol. 8111, pp. 276–283. Springer, Heidelberg (2013). https://doi.org/10.1007/978-3-642-53856-8_35

11. Frankola, T., Golub, M., Jakobovic, D.: Evolutionary algorithms for the resource constrained scheduling problem. In: 30th International Conference on Information Technology Interfaces, ITI 2008, pp. 715–722. IEEE (2008)

12. Mao, H., Alizadeh, M., Menache, I., Kandula, S.: Resource management with deep reinforcement learning. In: Proceedings of the 15th ACM Workshop on Hot Topics in Networks, pp. 50–56. ACM (2016)

13. Chen, X., Hao, X., Lin, H.W., Murata, T.: Rule driven multi objective dynamic scheduling by data envelopment analysis and reinforcement learning. In: 2010 IEEE International Conference on Automation and Logistics (ICAL), pp. 396–401. IEEE (2010)

14. Zheng, S., Ding, C.: Kernel alignment inspired linear discriminant analysis. In: Calders, T., Esposito, F., Hüllermeier, E., Meo, R. (eds.) ECML PKDD 2014. LNCS (LNAI), vol. 8726, pp. 401–416. Springer, Heidelberg (2014). https://doi.org/10.1007/978-3-662-44845-8_26

15. Zheng, S., Nie, F., Ding, C., Huang, H.: A harmonic mean linear discriminant analysis for robust image classification. In: 2016 IEEE 28th International Conference on Tools with Artificial Intelligence (ICTAI), pp. 402–409. IEEE (2016)

16. Zheng, S., Ding, C., Nie, F., Huang, H.: Harmonic mean linear discriminant analysis. IEEE Trans. Knowl. Data Eng. (2018). https://doi.org/10.1109/TKDE.2018.2861858

17. Zheng, S., Ding, C.: Sparse classification using group matching pursuit. Neurocomputing **338**, 83–91 (2019). https://doi.org/10.1016/j.neucom.2019.02.001

18. Zheng, S., Ding, C.: Minimal support vector machine. arXiv preprint arXiv:1804.02370 (2018)

19. Zheng, S., Ding, C., Nie, F.: Regularized singular value decomposition and application to recommender system. arXiv preprint arXiv:1804.05090 (2018)

20. Wang, C., Mahadevan, S.: Manifold alignment without correspondence. In: IJCAI, vol. 2, p. 3 (2009)

21. Weckman, G.R., Ganduri, C.V., Koonce, D.A.: A neural network job-shop scheduler. J. Intell. Manuf. **19**(2), 191–201 (2008)

22. Ingimundardottir, H., Runarsson, T.P.: Supervised learning linear priority dispatch rules for job-shop scheduling. In: Coello, C.A.C. (ed.) LION 2011. LNCS, vol. 6683, pp. 263–277. Springer, Heidelberg (2011). https://doi.org/10.1007/978-3-642-25566-3_20

23. Li, X., Olafsson, S.: Discovering dispatching rules using data mining. J. Sched. **8**(6), 515–527 (2005). https://doi.org/10.1007/s10951-005-4781-0

24. Shiue, Y.R.: Data-mining-based dynamic dispatching rule selection mechanism for shop floor control systems using a support vector machine approach. Int. J. Prod. Res. **47**(13), 3669–3690 (2009)

25. Zhang, W., Dietterich, T.G.: A reinforcement learning approach to job-shop scheduling. In: IJCAI, vol. 95, pp. 1114–1120. Citeseer (1995)

26. Grandl, R., Ananthanarayanan, G., Kandula, S., Rao, S., Akella, A.: Multi-resource packing for cluster schedulers. ACM SIGCOMM Comput. Commun. Rev. **44**(4), 455–466 (2015)

27. Zheng, S., Shae, Z.-Y., Zhang, X., Jamjoom, H., Fong, L.: Analysis and modeling of social influence in high performance computing workloads. In: Jeannot, E., Namyst, R., Roman, J. (eds.) Euro-Par 2011. LNCS, vol. 6852, pp. 193–204. Springer, Heidelberg (2011). https://doi.org/10.1007/978-3-642-23400-2_19
28. Sutton, R.S., Barto, A.G., et al.: Reinforcement Learning: An Introduction. MIT Press, Cambridge (1998)
29. Williams, R.J.: Simple statistical gradient-following algorithms for connectionist reinforcement learning. Mach. Learn. 8(3–4), 229–256 (1992)
30. Sutton, R.S., McAllester, D.A., Singh, S.P., Mansour, Y.: Policy gradient methods for reinforcement learning with function approximation. In: Advances in Neural Information Processing Systems, pp. 1057–1063 (2000)
31. Zheng, S., Vishnu, A., Ding, C.: Accelerating deep learning with shrinkage and recall. In: 2016 IEEE 22nd International Conference on Parallel and Distributed Systems (ICPADS), pp. 963–970. IEEE (2016)
32. Ammar, H.B., Eaton, E., Ruvolo, P., Taylor, M.E.: Unsupervised cross-domain transfer in policy gradient reinforcement learning via manifold alignment. In: Proceedings of AAAI (2015)
33. Joshi, G., Chowdhary, G.: Cross-domain transfer in reinforcement learning using target apprentice. arXiv preprint arXiv:1801.06920 (2018)
34. Pan, S.J., Yang, Q., et al.: A survey on transfer learning. IEEE Trans. Knowl. Data Eng. 22(10), 1345–1359 (2010)
35. Zheng, S., Cai, X., Ding, C., Nie, F., Huang, H.: A closed form solution to multiview low-rank regression. In: AAAI, pp. 1973–1979 (2015)
36. Zheng, S.: Machine learning: several advances in linear discriminant analysis, multiview regression and support vector machine. Ph.D. thesis, The University of Texas at Arlington (2017)

An Aggregate Learning Approach for Interpretable Semi-supervised Population Prediction and Disaggregation Using Ancillary Data

Guillaume Derval[1]([✉])(ID), Frédéric Docquier[2], and Pierre Schaus[1](ID)

[1] ICTEAM, UCLouvain, Louvain-la-Neuve, Belgium
{guillaume.derval,pierre.schaus}@uclouvain.be
[2] IRES, UCLouvain, Louvain-la-Neuve, Belgium
frederic.docquier@uclouvain.be

Abstract. Census data provide detailed information about population characteristics at a coarse resolution. Nevertheless, fine-grained, high-resolution mappings of population counts are increasingly needed to characterize population dynamics and to assess the consequences of climate shocks, natural disasters, investments in infrastructure, development policies, etc. Disaggregating these census is a complex machine learning, and multiple solutions have been proposed in past research. We propose in this paper to view the problem in the context of the aggregate learning paradigm, where the output value for all training points is not known, but where it is only known for aggregates of the points (i.e. in this context, for regions of pixels where a census is available). We demonstrate with a very simple and interpretable model that this method is on par, and even outperforms on some metrics, the state-of-the-art, despite its simplicity.

Keywords: Disaggregation · Aggregate learning · GIS

1 Introduction

Most countries periodically organize rounds of censuses of their population at a granularity that differs from country to country. The level of disaggregation is often governed by the administrative division of the country. Although census data are usually considered as accurate in terms of population counts and characteristics, the spatial granularity, that is sometimes in the order of hundreds of square kilometers, is too coarse for evaluating local policy reforms or for making informed decisions about health and well-being of people, economic and environmental interventions, security, etc. (see [23]). For example, fine-grained, high-resolution mappings of the distribution of the population are required to assess the number of people living at or near sea level, near hospitals, in the

---

Electronic supplementary material The online version of this chapter (https://doi.org/10.1007/978-3-030-46133-1_40) contains supplementary material, which is available to authorized users.

U. Brefeld et al. (Eds.): ECML PKDD 2019, LNAI 11908, pp. 672–687, 2020.
https://doi.org/10.1007/978-3-030-46133-1_40

vicinity or airports and highways, in conflict areas, etc. They are also needed to understand how population movements react to various types of shocks such as natural disasters, conflicts, plant creation and closures, etc.

Multiple methods can be used to produce gridded data sets (also called rasters), with pixels of a relatively small scale compared to the administrative units of the countries. Notably, the Gridded Population of the World (GPW) [3] provides a gridded dataset of the whole world, with a resolution of 30 arcseconds (i.e. pixels of approximately $1 \, km^2$ at the equator). The method used in GPW assumes that population is uniformly distributed within each administrative unit. With minor adjustments for boundaries and water bodies, the density of the population in a pixel is identical to the density of the population of the administrative unit in the underlying census.

More advanced and successful models rely on ancillary and remotely sensed data, and are trained using machine learning techniques (see [6, 18, 20]). These data can include information sensed by satellite (nighttime light intensities, temperature, etc.) or data provided by NGOs and governments (on health facilities, road infrastructure, etc.). These models are used to *disaggregate* coarse census data into a grid of small pixels, using ancillary data to predict the population distribution within the census unit. The level of resolution is either imposed by the method or decided by the user. As an example, such models predict that people concentrate near the road infrastructure rather than in cultivation fields; or that the density of the population in highly elevated regions is smaller than near the sea level.

These models show various degrees of usability and accuracy. Among the methods cited above, RF [20] (for Random Forest, the family of algorithms on which the method is based) gives the best results using remotely sensed and ancillary data. However, the results of RF are seemingly artificial. The right panel of Fig. 1 shows a fine-grained population mapping of Cambodia generated with the RF model from [20]. Geometrical shapes clearly emerge from the population disaggregation. On the contrary, as depicted on the left panel of Fig. 1, our PCD (for Pure Census Disaggregation) method generates maps with a natural distribution aspect.

All methods in the literature are converted into standard supervised regression learning tasks. Supervised regression learning aims to predict an output value associated with a particular input vector. In its standard form, the training set contains an individual output value for each input vector. Unfortunately, the disaggregation problem does not directly fit into this supervised regression learning framework since the prediction function is not directly available for input vectors. In a disaggregation problem, the input consists of a partition of the training set (the pixels of each unit) and for each partition, the sum of the output values is constrained by the census count. This framework is exactly the one introduced as the aggregated output learning problem by [16]. Our PCD method conceives the formulation of the disaggregation problem as an aggregated output learning problem. PCD is able to train the model based on a much larger training set composed of pixels. This approach is parameterized by the error function that the user seeks to minimize.

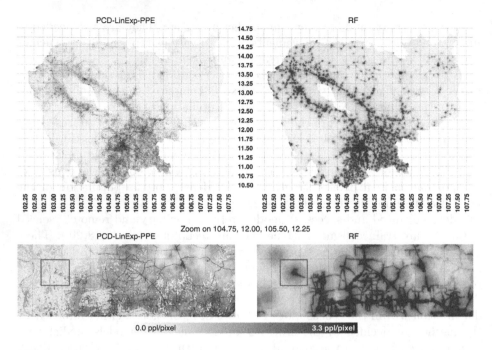

Fig. 1. Cambodian population maps obtained by PCD-LinExp-PPE (a specialization of PCD using the PCD-LinExp model type, introduced in a later section) and RF. The bottom maps are a zoom of a specific, moderately populated region of Cambodia. The red box highlights a region where RF produces seemingly artificial results: it creates a circle around a (non-displayed) hospital, and saturates near the road network.

PCD can be used with a large variety of model types. In this paper, we consider a specific model, arguably simplistic, that is called PCD-LinExp. The PCD-LinExp model can be written as:

$$f_{\theta=(a,b,c)}(\boldsymbol{D}_{p_x,p_y}) = \max(0, \exp(\boldsymbol{a}^T \boldsymbol{D}_{p_x,p_y} + b) + c),$$

where f is the predicted population count, the vector $\boldsymbol{a}$ and scalars b and c are parameters to estimate, and $\boldsymbol{D}_{p_x,p_y}$ is a set of sensed/ancillary covariates of a given pixel located at p_x, p_y.

PCD-LinExp is arguably simplistic. This is by design, for two reasons. First, it is interpretable: each available remotely sensed covariate is associated to a single parameter in the vector $\boldsymbol{a}$. Second, the aim of this paper is to show that the aggregate learning approach is particularly suitable and gives good results on this particular problem. Future research will focus on more complex models. Despite its simplicity, we actually show in the result section that, due to its comparatively small unadjusted error compared to other methods, PCD-LinExp can be used to predict population counts when census data are not available, something that is not possible with existing methods.

As a case study, we experiment it on Cambodia using various sets of remotely sensed/ancillary data. While this is not the main focus of this paper, we shortly interpret the result of our method on Cambodia. Our main result, the disaggregated map of Cambodia, is depicted on the left panel of Fig. 1. This paper also discusses methodological issues raised by existing approaches. In particular, we demonstrate that the previously used error metrics are biased when available census data involves administrative units with highly heterogeneous surfaces and population densities. We propose alternative metrics that better reflect the accuracy properties that should be fulfilled by a sound disaggregation approach. We then present the results for Cambodia and compare methods using various error metrics, providing statistical evidence that PCD-LinExp generates the most accurate results.

1.1 Notations and Definitions

A country is divided into administrative units (abbreviated as AUs), that are part of various administrative levels and form a hierarchy. For example, in Cambodia, the AUs at the finest level of the AU hierarchy are called *communes*, which are grouped into *districts*. In most countries, the census is conducted at the finest possible level of the AU hierarchy. For simplicity, throughout this paper, we refer to an AU at the finest administrative level as *units*, and use the term *superunit* for an AU at the coarser level.

Definition 1 (Units, Superunits). *Let $\mathcal{U}$ be the set of units and $\mathcal{S}$ the set of superunits. Let us denote by* $\mathrm{units}(s) = \{u \mid u \in s\}$ *the set of units in a superunit s. The set of pixels in a unit is* $\mathrm{pixels}(u) = \{p \mid p \in u\}$ *and by extension the set of pixels in a superunit is* $\mathrm{pixels}(s) = \bigcup_{u \in \mathrm{units}(s)} \mathrm{pixels}(u)$. *A pixel p is a triple (p_x, p_y, p_w), where (p_x, p_y) is the position of the pixel and p_w the weight of the pixel in the unit, which is the area of the pixel covered by the unit;* $\mathrm{surface}(u) = \sum_{p \in \mathrm{pixels}(u)} p_w$ *is the total surface of the unit u;* $\mathrm{surface}(s)$ *for superunits is defined similarly. We further define* $\mathrm{census}(u)$ *as the population count of unit u and* $\mathrm{census}(s) = \sum_{u \in \mathrm{units}(s)} \mathrm{census}(u)$ *as the population count of superunit s.*

An example illustrating the definitions is provided in Fig. 2.

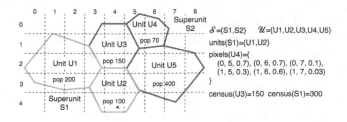

Fig. 2. Notation example.

1.2   Existing Methods for Disaggregation

None of the existing approaches use the aggregate learning framework [16]. They use standard supervised learning approaches where the training set contains an individual output value for each input vector. The input data available for the disaggregation problem does not directly fit into this framework since the prediction value for each pixel is not available; an aggregate form is available, however (the census count for a unit). Existing disaggregation methods first transform the data to make them fit into the standard regression problem. Existing approaches are differentiated by their transformation method, by the error metric used to evaluate the quality of the learned function, and by the family of machine learning algorithm used to train the model.

Areal weighting [8,10] is a straightforward method to redistribute the census data to a grid of pixels. The population predicted for each pixel is the sum of the contribution of each unit that contains the pixel. The contribution of a unit to a pixel p is defined as $\text{prediction}_u(p) := \frac{p_w}{\sum_{p' \in \text{pixels}(u)} p'_w} \cdot \text{census}(u)$. The Gridded Population of the World (GPW) dataset [3] provides a raster (grid) of the population density/count at a fine resolution for the whole world. After census data is gathered, it is converted into a grid using an additional dataset on water bodies only. It is then a direct application of areal weighting, where each pixel weight p_w is adjusted for the ratio of water bodies inside the pixel.

Dasymetric modeling is an extension of areal weighting using ancillary data [7,14,24]. A weight is inferred from this ancillary data, which redistribute the population according to these weights. Land use/cover are often used as ancillary data [5,15,21]. Methods used to select the weights vary from purely heuristic choice of weights [5] to use of Expectation-Maximization or Logit regression [9], and other linear regression models [2]. The methods below can all be seen as members of the Dasymetric modeling family, with the specificity that they all use more complex machine learning algorithm to predicts the weights accorded to each ancillary data type. They are also (mostly) agnostic on the type of the data and can handle multiple types at the same time, in a generic way, which is not the case for the methods presented above.

Random Forest (RF) method: pixel aggregation. The methodology followed by [20] solves a regression problem in order to predict, for any pixel on a grid, the logarithm of the population count in this pixel. It is based on nonparametric machine learning techniques (RF) and uses observable covariates such as presence of hospitals, road networks, nightlight intensities, etc. Each covariate is mapped/projected on a grid of pixels (also denoted raster) spreading over the selected country. The resolution of this grid is decided by the user. In [20], it is set at $8.33e^{-4}$ degrees, which approximately corresponds to 100 m sided square pixels at the equator. A key contribution of [20] is the methodology to extract a training set used by the RF [1] machine learning algorithm.

One data point is produced for each unit in the original training set. Each data point is a vector, containing a value (binary or floating point) for each covariate. These values are resulting from the pixel aggregation step, which varies with the type of covariate: for continuous covariates, the result of the aggregation of pixels is the mean of the covariate values of these pixels. For binary covariates, the mode (class majority) of the pixel's covariate values is taken as a summary for the unit. We thus obtain $|U|$ data points (remember that $|U| \ll$ the number of pixels), having each a fixed size, suitable for standard supervised machine learning techniques, such as random forests, neural networks, or SVMs. The training set is then used to learn a RF regression model.

Let us denote the training data as $\boldsymbol{D}$, a tensor in three dimensions, such that $\boldsymbol{D}_{x,y,f}$ gives the value of the covariate f at position x, y. $\boldsymbol{D}_{x,y}$ gives the vector of all the covariate values at position x, y. The regression $RF(\boldsymbol{D}_{x,y})$ is thus able to predict a population density for a pixel with covariates values $\boldsymbol{D}_{x,y}$.

Corrected output of linear regression model (dasymetric redistribution). The method used by [20] does not directly consider the output of $RF(\boldsymbol{D}_{x,y})$ as the predictor for the population density. Instead, it considers the output of the RF for each pixel as a weighting layer used for subsequent dasymetric redistribution (also called pycnophylactic redistribution [22]).

For each unit u, a correcting factor $w(u)$ is computed as

$$w(u) = \frac{\text{census}(u)}{\sum_{p \in \text{pixels}(u)} p_w \cdot RF(\boldsymbol{D}_{p_x,p_y})}.$$

The predicted density estimator for the pixel p lying in unit u is then

$$\text{prediction}(p) = RF(\boldsymbol{D}_{p_x,p_y}) \cdot w(u).$$

During the training of the model, this would, of course, lead to an error of zero. Therefore, the dasymetric redistribution is only applied on superunits. This part of the method obviously limits the usage of the method to situations where the census data is available, at least at a coarse resolution. We call the error *adjusted* if it is dasymetrically redistributed, and *unadjusted* otherwise.

Learning from heuristic, using satellite images and deep neural networks [18] relax the problem in a different way; they use an external census grid, produced in a heuristic way [4], as ground truth. More precisely, they train their model based on a grid made from the 2000 US census, and validate it by measuring the prediction accuracy on the 2010 US census. This "relaxation" of the initial problem allows using standard supervised machine learning techniques. As these census grids are extrapolated from the official census, they suffer from higher errors, making the dataset noisier. However, compared to the Pixel Aggregation relaxation, it creates a much larger dataset, with one data point per pixel rather than one point per unit. In their paper, Robinson et al. do not use ancillary data. They use satellite images in the visible and invisible spectrum. They use a

Convolutionnal Neural Network model (abbreviated CNN, see [13]), which is a modified VGG-A neural net [19]. The neural net is given a window of pixels of size 74 × 74 (each pixel being approximately 15 m × 15 m), and predicts a (single) class for this set of pixels. It is a classification task, each class representing a given population range, obtained after binning the US censuses. The method uses a different type of data, among which some are not available in most countries (census grids). Hence, the interest in comparing this method with others is limited, and is thus not included here. Another method, LL [6] use the same preprocessing method (using a nearest neighbor method to produce the heuristic grid). LL is a prediction method that converts all covariates into a grid with pixels of size 250 m × 250 m (approx. 0.0625 km^2), and then assigns a ground truth for the population count of each pixel. The latter is proxied with the mean population density of the *unit* they belong to. As for the previous method, we do not compare our method to LL. The data types are different (they only rely on satellite images) and the results are too coarse (both RF and our method uses pixels that are 6.25 times smaller in surface). In the original paper [6], the LL method produces good results but only after applying the dasymetric redistribution (as with RF).

2   Data Preparation

In order to compare our PCD-LinExp method with existing ones, various data sets have been collected for Cambodia. These include both data sensed by satellites, and data provided by the Cambodian administration and by NGOs. The description of the dataset, along with the preprocessing done, is available in the additional resources of this paper. Both the data and the preprocessing are similar to the ones in the article describing the RF method [20].

In our experiments, we select a resolution of $8.33e^{-4}$ degrees, which approximately corresponds to squares of 100 m sides at the equator. We then obtain a stack of rasters, which can be represented as a tensor in three dimensions. We call this tensor D, with $D_{x,y,f}$ being the pixel of the feature f at position x, y. In the case of Cambodia, the dimension of this tensor is 6617 × 5468 × 42. We use $D_{x,y}$ as notation for the vector of all the covariates at position x, y. One difference between our method to prepare data and the one in [20] is that our data are standardized. In order to reduce numerical errors and make covariates equally important at the beginning of the computation, each feature is centered (resulting covariates have their mean equal to zero) and transformed such that they have a unit variance.

3   Evaluation

3.1   Error Metrics

Assuming the finest ground truth we have is the administrative unit of the census, all errors metrics are in the form $e(\text{census}, \text{prediction}, \text{surface}, \mathcal{U})$, where census, prediction and surface are functions $\mathcal{U} \to \mathbb{R}^+$ that give the effective and predicted population of a unit and its surface, respectively.

Existing methods [6,18,20] mostly use the RMSE criterion and its variants to estimate the prediction error. In our context, the RMSE is defined as:

$$e_{RMSE} = \sqrt{\frac{\sum_{u \in \mathcal{U}} \left(\text{prediction}(u) - \text{census}(u)\right)^2}{|\mathcal{U}|}}.$$

RMSE is biased towards highly populated, low-surface administrative units. An analysis of the data on Cambodia shows that there are smaller-surface units than high-surface ones, and that the small ones tend to be more populated. In most countries, the division of the country in administrative units is such that the number of inhabitants in each unit is not too large.

Since there are more small regions than large ones, methods that better predict these regions have better scores. Said differently, e_{RMSE} overemphasizes errors on small, highly populated regions. We are aware that this is not always a desirable property. Users might be more interested in accurately disaggregating high-surface administrative units than smaller units with already more precise population count.

Figure 3 provides an example of two sets of units, with the same population, but with different predictions. Both of them have $e_{RMSE} = 700$. As can be seen, the example on the left panel makes very important errors on units U3 (error = 496) and U2 (272), where actual population counts are relatively small. However, these errors do not contribute a lot to the RMSE and are instead absorbed by the error of unit U1 (1000), which is relatively small compared to its population, but large in absolute value. On the contrary, the example on the right panel of Fig. 3 gives a more balanced error distribution. In absolute value the error is greater in U1. However, compared to the actual population counts, they are smaller in each administrative unit.

Fig. 3. Example of administrative units with equal RMSE. In this diagram, for simplicity, *pop* and *pred* are respectively abbreviations for census and prediction.

We postulate that a sound error metric for the disaggregation problem should be expressed in per-pixel units, therefore being independent of the surface of each unit and be based on relative population deviations rather than on absolute population counts.

We introduce the Per-Pixel-Error (PPE):

$$e_{PPE} = \frac{1}{\sum_{u \in \mathcal{U}} \text{surface}(u)} \sum_{u \in \mathcal{U}} \text{surface}(u) \cdot \frac{|\text{prediction}(u) - \text{census}(u)|}{\text{census}(u)},$$

which is a surface-weighted average of relative deviations from the effective population (i.e. a Weighted Mean Absolute Percentage error, with surfaces as weights). PPE is thus independent from the size of the unit. Moreover, the use of relative deviations allows to effectively compare less-populated units to more-populated ones. In the examples from Fig. 3, considering that all units have the same surface, the left example has a PPE of 86.5% while the right one has a PPE of 10%. Remember that they have exactly the same RMSE (700).

A squared variant of PPE, the Per-Pixel Squared Error (PPSE), is defined as:

$$e_{PPSE} = \frac{1}{\sum_{u \in \mathcal{U}} \text{surface}(u)} \sum_{u \in \mathcal{U}} \text{surface}(u) \cdot \frac{(\text{prediction}(u) - \text{census}(u))^2}{\text{census}(u)},$$

(which is a Weighted Root Mean Squared Error metric weighed by surface) which overweights greater error ratios.

In the quantitative analysis below, we conduct our experiments using PPE and PPSE as error metrics. We also use RMSE so as to compare our results with previous works. MAE was used in previous works, but it suffers from the same shortcomings as RMSE and does not provide additional relevant information, and as such is omitted in our experiments.

3.2   Comment on Dasymetric Redistribution

As discussed previously, dasymetric redistribution is a commonly used processing method to rescale (ex-post) the population in a given surface using a weight map. This method is used by RF [20]. The main argument justifying the use of dasymetric redistribution is the full exploitation of the available information included in the population census. If a disaggregation method predicts that there are 3,500 people in a given AU, and that the census reports an actual population of 4,500, dasymetric redistribution consists of multiplying all pixels within the AU by $\frac{4500}{3500}$, thus reducing the visible error.

While the method seems intuitive and duly justified, it actually increases the prediction error in some cases. This is not only due to the fact that the population census is, like all types of databases, subject to errors and various noises. It is also due to the fact that large local errors in a given region are *transferred* to the whole region.

As an example, let us consider the case where we have two units composed each of one pixel. These units are grouped into a single superunit. Table 1 shows (on the left) the actual and predicted population counts of these units, along with the adjusted prediction after dasymetric redistribution on the superunit. The total population of the superunit is 200, but the predicted population is 160.

The correcting factor to be applied is $\frac{200}{160} = 1.25$. The right part of Table 1 shows the error metrics applied before and after the dasymetric redistribution. In our example, both metrics increase after the redistribution. The reason is the error made originally on unit B. The low prediction forces the redistribution to increase the global count, dramatically increasing the error on unit A.

Table 1. Example for dasymetric redistribution

Unit	Real pop.	Pred. pop.	Adj. pop.
A	100	120	150
B	100	40	50

Metric	Unadjusted	Adjusted
RMSE	$\sqrt{2000}$	$\sqrt{2500}$
PPE	40%	50%

Another drawback of dasymetric redistribution is that it breaks the dichotomy between inputs and outputs in the validation stage. Indeed, the dasymetric redistribution is applied to superunits (it would lead to an error of zero if applied to units). This implies that part of the prediction truth values are used to correct the output, before prediction errors are computed. We leave as an open question the relevance of using dasymetric redistribution. In practice, we notice that it sometimes increases the error in our experiments. Dasymetric redistribution also tends to make comparisons between methods difficult, as it *squeezes* the original errors. To allow comparison with previous works, we produce both the unadjusted and adjusted (by dasymetric redistribution) results in our experiments.

4 Pure Census Disaggregation (PCD)

Existing methods require preprocessing the data before estimating the model. We propose to formalize the disaggregation problem in the context of aggregated output learning [16]. We call this formulation PCD. Aggregated output learning is a family of methods where the response information (the value to be predicted) about each data point is unknown. However, for specific subsets of data points, the sum of their responses is known. The disaggregation problem can be converted into an aggregated output learning problem: each pixel is a data point, and the subsets of data points for which we have the sum of the responses are AUs' pixels (the aggregated responses are the census counts).

In our context, solving the disaggregation problem consists of learning a function f that, when applied and aggregated over all pixels of an AU, predicts the census count of this AU with accuracy. More precisely, we attempt to find the parameters θ of a model f_θ such that a given error metric (e_{PPE}, e_{PPSE}, e_{RMSE}, etc.) is minimized:

$$\arg\min_{\theta} error(\text{census}, \text{prediction}_{\theta,D}, \text{surface}, \mathcal{U}),$$

where prediction$_{\theta,D}$ is a function $\mathcal{U} \to \Re^+$ in the following form:

$$\text{prediction}_{\theta,D}(u) = \sum_{p \in \text{pixels}(u)} p_w \cdot f_\theta(\boldsymbol{D}_{p_x,p_y}).$$

Unlike the alternative techniques discussed previously, the error function is plugged into the PCD problem being globally minimized by gradient descent, in order to find $\boldsymbol{\theta}$. Other techniques are applicable to solve aggregated output learning problems [16] and can be applied to PCD. The prediction function for a unit is not based on a summary; it is composed of individual and unsupervised predictions for all pixels.

The method is semi-supervised: while information is given to the method about administrative units of the census, no indication about the population is available at the individual pixel level. We use the name PCD-LinExp to indicate the usage of LinExp in the PCD framework.

An Interpretable Model. We decide to focus on a regression model that we call LinExp. By design, it is easily interpretable. Remember the model can be written as:

$$f_{(a,b,c)}(\boldsymbol{D}_{p_x,p_y}) = \max(0, \exp(\boldsymbol{a}^T \boldsymbol{D}_{p_x,p_y} + b) + c),$$

where $\boldsymbol{a}$ is a vector containing one parameter for each covariate, whose scalar product with the vector of covariate at position (p_x, p_y) is given to the exp function; b and c are two scalars allowing correcting the output. The output is then passed into a function $\max(0, \bullet)$ (a ReLU [11], here used outside its traditional scope) to ensure the output is positive. The presence of the exp function is motivated by the distribution of the census.

As the covariates in the tensor $\boldsymbol{D}$ have been standardized (they are centered and have unit variance), the vector $\boldsymbol{a}$ is directly interpretable as the importance of each covariate:

- a high absolute value indicates that the covariate contributes highly to the prediction, while a low absolute value indicates its contribution is small;
- positive values indicate that each increase of the covariate increases the predicted population, while negative values do the opposite.

The model is convex; however, when plugged into an error function such as e_{RMSE} or e_{PPE}, it becomes non-convex, mainly due to the sum of absolute (or squared) values of exponentials. Using a (sub-)gradient descent algorithm minimizing the error function on the training set is then a simple yet effective choice to find good values for parameters a, b, c.

The function to be optimized for PCD-LinExp, given that e_{PPE} is used, is

$$\underset{a,b,c}{\arg\min} \ \frac{1}{\sum_{u \in \mathcal{U}} \operatorname{surface}(u)} \sum_{u \in \mathcal{U}}$$

$$\left(\operatorname{surface}(u) \cdot \frac{|(\sum_{p \in \operatorname{pixels}(u)} p_w \cdot \max(0, \exp(a^T D_{p_x, p_y} + b) + c)) - \operatorname{census}(u)|}{\operatorname{census}(u)} \right).$$

Optimization. Due to the presence of the exp function in the model, it is quite sensitive to sudden erroneous increases in the vector a, which can make the output explode and even overflow. Hence, relatively small learning rates are used, and we choose to avoid the use of stochastic gradient descent (SGD): the whole dataset is computed at each iteration. This is allowed by the relatively small size of our dataset; bigger datasets (not fitting entirely in memory) would require using SGD.

Optimization is done using the Adam algorithm [12]. Adam, for *Ada*ptive *m*oment estimation, is a variation of the standard Stochastic Gradient Descent algorithm; it uses on first-order gradients and estimations of the first and second moments of these gradients to regularize learning steps.

We use learning rates of 0.01 for vectors a and b, and of 0.001 for vector c. These values result from manual tuning. We run 1000 iterations of Adam before finishing and returning the results. Experiments show that convergence is most of the time reached before ~500 iterations.

Initialization. Concerning initialization, we attempt to have at the first iterations a small value for $a^T x + b$, as a large value may produce very important gradients, which is not desired. Experiments have shown that having $a = 0$ and a negative value for b (we chose -4) works well in practice. Indeed, it greatly underestimates the population during the first few iterations of the gradient descent.

Experimental Setup. In order to evaluate correctly the different methods (PCD-LinExp, RF) presented earlier, we implemented a common test framework in Python. The PyTorch library [17] was chosen to create the PCD-LinExp models. The RF implementation relies on the library provided in the first publication of the method (i.e. the `randomforests` library of the R language). The new RF implementation has been tested in similar conditions than in the original paper and gives similar results (in fact, we obtain better results, which is probably due to small differences in the data).

We used standard 10-fold cross-validation to test methods. Cambodia is divided into 193 districts, which are themselves divided into 1621 communes. As we have to test the dasymetric redistribution, we need to keep communes inside the same district into the same fold. We thus obtain folds with 19 districts (three folds have 20 districts). As far as the cross-validation works is concerned, a fold is used as test set, and the other nine folds are used as training set.

The fold used to test the models is then changed. We then obtain 10 measures of the generalization of the methods, from which we take the mean. The measures chosen are the Per-Pixel-Error (PPE), the Per-Pixel-Squared-Error (PPSE), and the Root Mean Square Error (RMSE).

RF-Adj. In order to produce more accurate comparisons between the different methods, we introduce a small variation of the RF method, that we call RF-adjusted (abbreviated as RF-adj). The motivation behind RF-Adj is that RF tends to over-predict population by a fair margin, as it is not constructed to run on unadjusted errors (it was originally described with dasymetric redistribution included in the method [20]).

RF-Adj is a simple adjustment that minimizes the error on the training set. Given a trained RF function, the RF_{ajd} function is defined as $RF_{adj}(\boldsymbol{D}_{p_x,p_y}) = c \cdot RF(\boldsymbol{D}_{p_x,p_y})$, where c is the mean factor of error for each unit in the training set:

$$c = \frac{\sum_{u \in \mathcal{U}_{\text{training}}} \frac{\text{prediction}_{\text{RF}}(u)}{\text{census}(u)}}{|\mathcal{U}_{\text{training}}|}.$$

Experiments show that RF-Adj generates smaller *unadjusted* errors than RF.

5   Results and Discussion

Figure 1 (at the beginning of the paper) compares the population maps generated by the PCD-LinExp-PPE and RF methods, before dasymetric redistribution. Results obtained by PCD-LinExp-RMSE and RF-Adj are not included as there are visually similar to PCD-LinExp-PPE and RF, respectively. The two methods identify similar regions of high population density, notably near the capital Phnom Penh (at the south-east of the country) and around the lake Tonlé Sap, in the center of the country. Visually, PCD-LinExp-PPE produces a seemingly more detailed map than RF, with less "saturation". On the one hand, PCD-LinExp-PPE highlights the role of the road infrastructure. On the other hand, RF produces circles of high population density around hospitals and roads.

Table 2 shows the error metrics of the methods described in our experimental setup. Box plots containing the data of the individual folds are depicted in Fig. 4. Running a paired t-test (null hypothesis mean(A-B) = 0, and a p-value limit of 0.05) on the fold errors reveals that LinExp-PPE and LinExp-RMSE significantly less PPE/PPSE than RF and RF-Adj on unadjusted metrics. LinExp-RMSE is significantly better than all the other methods on unadjusted RMSE. On adjusted metrics, no method is significantly better than another, but LinExp-PPE that is dominated by all method on the adjusted RMSE metric.

PCD-LinExp-PPE and PCD-LinExp-RMSE better perform when using the unadjusted PPE/PPSE metric; PCD-LinExp-RMSE generates better results for the unadjusted RMSE metric. The PCD-LinExp unadjusted outcomes are comparable to the adjusted outcomes obtained after dasymetric redistribution, which strengthens our claim that PCD-LinExp can be used to predict the population where census data are not available.

Figure 5 shows the unadjusted PPE error obtained for each unit as a function of the surface of the unit. PCD-LinExp-PPE and PCD-LinExp-RMSE generate smaller errors. The errors obtained under PCD-LinExp-PPE are globally independent of the unit surface. This is because the PPE metric reduces the influence of the surface. As expected, other methods that do not account for the surface generate greater errors for less-populated, high-surface units. Smaller errors are obtained for highly populated, small-surface units as this would greatly impact the RMSE.

Table 2. Error metrics

Method	Unadjusted			Adjusted		
	PPE	PPSE	RMSE	PPE	PPSE	RMSE
Areal weighting	N/A	N/A	N/A	87.90%	215.46%	6777.71
PCD-LinExp-PPE	45.43%	45.46%	6202.23	39.75%	34.19%	4407.64
PCD-LinExp-RMSE	54.20%	78.35%	3889.35	39.84%	34.45%	3335.68
RF	178.07%	914.97%	6584.09	39.74%	32.44%	3175.68
RF-Adj	127.50%	512.72%	4742.39	39.68%	32.24%	3199.69

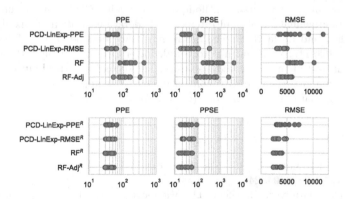

Fig. 4. Scatter plot of the error metrics for each model and for each fold. While it is difficult to compare results for the redistributed errors, PCD-LinExp-PPE and PCD-LinExp-RMSE give the best result on unadjusted errors. The methods PCD-LinExp-PPE^R, PCD-LinExp-$RMSE^R$, RF^R and RF-Adj^R are redistributed counterparts of the original methods.

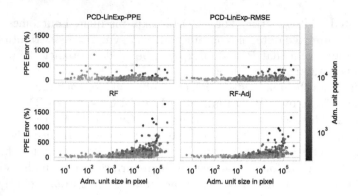

Fig. 5. Error for each unit for all models.

Overall, all results presented in this section indicate that PCD-LinExp-PPE and PCD-LinExp-RMSE generate better results than RF and RF-Adj, at least for predicting the population (i.e. on unadjusted errors). The comparison for population disaggregation (using adjusted errors) is more difficult, as all experiments indicate ties. We explained previously that using dasymetric redistribution breaks the training set/test set dichotomy, and thus should be avoided. However, this demonstrates that using the aggregate learning framework with a very simple model in this problem outperforms/is on par (depending on the metric) with more complex models not using aggregate learning.

Acknowledgments. Computational resources have been provided by the supercomputing facilities of the Université catholique de Louvain (CISM/UCL) and the Consortium des Équipements de Calcul Intensif en Fédération Wallonie Bruxelles (CÉCI) funded by the Fond de la Recherche Scientifique de Belgique (F.R.S.-FNRS) under convention 2.5020.11. We would like to thank Pavel Demin and the CP3 group that shared with us part of their reserved resources. The second and third authors acknowledge financial support from the ARC convention on "New approaches to understanding and modeling global migration trends" (convention 18/23-091).

References

1. Breiman, L.: Random forests. Mach. Learn. **45**(1), 5–32 (2001). https://doi.org/10.1023/A:1010933404324
2. Briggs, D.J., Gulliver, J., Fecht, D., Vienneau, D.M.: Dasymetric modelling of small-area population distribution using land cover and light emissions data. Remote Sens. Environ. **108**(4), 451–466 (2007). https://doi.org/10.1016/j.rse.2006.11.020
3. Center for International Earth Science Information Network - CIESIN - Columbia University: Gridded population of the world, Version 4 (GPWv4): Population density, Revision 10, 11 July 2018 (2017). https://doi.org/10.7927/H4DZ068D
4. Center for International Earth Science Information Network - CIESIN - Columbia University: U.S. census grids 2010 (Summary file 1), 19 July 2018 (2017). https://doi.org/10.7927/H40Z716C

5. Dmowska, A., Stepinski, T.F.: High resolution dasymetric model of U.S. demographics with application to spatial distribution of racial diversity. Appl. Geogr. **53**, 417–426 (2014). https://doi.org/10.1016/j.apgeog.2014.07.003
6. Doupe, P., Bruzelius, E., Faghmous, J., Ruchman, S.G.: Equitable development through deep learning: the case of sub-national population density estimation. In: Proceedings of the 7th Annual Symposium on Computing for Development, DEV 2016, pp. 6:1–6:10. ACM, New York (2016). https://doi.org/10.1145/3001913.3001921
7. Eicher, C.L., Brewer, C.A.: Dasymetric mapping and areal interpolation: implementation and evaluation. Cartogr. Geogr. Inf. Sci. **28**(2), 125–138 (2001)
8. Flowerdew, R., Green, M.: Developments in areal interpolation methods and GIS. In: Fischer, M.M., Nijkamp, P. (eds.) Geographic Information Systems, Spatial Modelling and Policy Evaluation, pp. 73–84. Springer, Heidelberg (1993). https://doi.org/10.1007/978-3-642-77500-0_5
9. Gallego, F.J.: A population density grid of the European union. Popul. Environ. **31**(6), 460–473 (2010). https://doi.org/10.1007/s11111-010-0108-y
10. Goodchild, M.F., Anselin, L., Deichmann, U.: A framework for the areal interpolation of socioeconomic data. Environ. Plan. A **25**(3), 383–397 (1993)
11. Hahnloser, R.H., Sarpeshkar, R., Mahowald, M.A., Douglas, R.J., Seung, H.S.: Digital selection and analogue amplification coexist in a cortex-inspired silicon circuit. Nature **405**(6789), 947 (2000)
12. Kingma, D.P., Ba, J.: Adam: a method for stochastic optimization. CoRR abs/1412.6980 (2014). http://arxiv.org/abs/1412.6980
13. LeCun, Y., Bottou, L., Bengio, Y., Haffner, P.: Gradient-based learning applied to document recognition. Proc. IEEE **86**(11), 2278–2324 (1998)
14. Mennis, J.: Generating surface models of population using dasymetric mapping. Prof. Geogr. **55**(1), 31–42 (2003)
15. Monmonier, M.S., Schnell, G.A.: Land use and land cover data and the mapping of population density. Int. Yearb. Cartogr. **24**(115), e121 (1984)
16. Musicant, D.R., Christensen, J.M., Olson, J.F.: Supervised learning by training on aggregate outputs. In: Seventh IEEE International Conference on Data Mining (ICDM 2007), pp. 252–261. IEEE (2007)
17. Paszke, A., et al.: Automatic differentiation in PyTorch (2017)
18. Robinson, C., Hohman, F., Dilkina, B.: A deep learning approach for population estimation from satellite imagery. In: Proceedings of the 1st ACM SIGSPATIAL Workshop on Geospatial Humanities, pp. 47–54. ACM (2017)
19. Simonyan, K., Zisserman, A.: Very deep convolutional networks for large-scale image recognition. arXiv preprint arXiv:1409.1556 (2014)
20. Stevens, F.R., Gaughan, A.E., Linard, C., Tatem, A.J.: Disaggregating census data for population mapping using random forests with remotely-sensed and ancillary data. Plos One **10**(2), 1–22 (2015). https://doi.org/10.1371/journal.pone.0107042
21. Tian, Y., Yue, T., Zhu, L., Clinton, N.: Modeling population density using land cover data. Ecol. Model. **189**(1–2), 72–88 (2005)
22. Tobler, W.R.: Smooth pycnophylactic interpolation for geographical regions. J. Am. Stat. Assoc. **74**(367), 519–530 (1979)
23. UN Economic and Social Council: Resolution adopted by the economic and social council on 10 June 2015 (2020 world population and housing census programme), August 2015. http://www.un.org/ga/search/view_doc.asp?symbol=E/RES/2015/10
24. Wright, J.K.: A method of mapping densities of population: with cape cod as an example. Geogr. Rev. **26**(1), 103–110 (1936)

Optimizing Neural Networks for Patent Classification

Louay Abdelgawad[1(✉)], Peter Kluegl[1], Erdan Genc[1], Stefan Falkner[2], and Frank Hutter[2]

[1] Averbis GmbH, Freiburg, Germany
{louay.abdelgawad,peter.kluegl,erdan.genc}@averbis.com
[2] Machine Learning Institute, Albert-Ludwigs University of Freiburg, Freiburg im Breisgau, Germany
sfalkner@informatik.uni-freiburg.de, fh@cs.uni-freiburg.de

Abstract. A great number of patents is filed everyday to the patent offices worldwide. Each of these patents has to be labeled by domain experts with one or many of thousands of categories. This process is not only extremely expensive but also overwhelming for the experts, due to the considerable increase of filed patents over the years and the increasing complexity of the hierarchical categorization structure. Therefore, it is critical to automate the manual classification process using a classification model. In this paper, the automation of the task is carried out based on recent advances in deep learning for NLP and compared to customized approaches. Moreover, an extensive optimization analysis grants insights about hyperparameter importance. Our optimized convolutional neural network achieves a new state-of-the-art performance of 55.02% accuracy on the public **Wipo-Alpha** dataset.

Keywords: Text classification · Deep learning · Patent classification · Hyperparameter optimization

1 Introduction

A patent is a document issued by a governmental office in order to protect the rights of an invention from being produced, used, or sold, without the permission of the inventor. For an invention to be patented, it has to fulfill three characteristics; it has to be novel, it has to provide an improvement step of something already available, and it has to be implementable by the industry.[1]

According to the Patent Technology Monitoring Team[2], the number of patents filed every year has increased from $417,508$ to $629,647$ between the years 2005 to 2015. It is important to assign each patent to its corresponding category in order to be later reviewed by the suitable domain examiner, who can

---

[1] https://www.epo.org/applying/basics.html (accessed June 20, 2019).

[2] https://www.uspto.gov/web/offices/ac/ido/oeip/taf/us_stat.htm (accessed June 20, 2019).

© Springer Nature Switzerland AG 2020
U. Brefeld et al. (Eds.): ECML PKDD 2019, LNAI 11908, pp. 688–703, 2020.
https://doi.org/10.1007/978-3-030-46133-1_41

decide whether the patent should be granted or not. However, automating this process is complicated for different reasons.

As the focus of research changes over time, the patent categories change as well. Some categories are merged into one category, new categories are added, or even the definition of a category changes [11]. Furthermore, the label distribution is highly imbalanced as patents tend to follow a Pareto-like distribution; i.e. 80% of the patents fall into 20% of the categories [1,9].

Another issue is the distribution of words in the patents [11]. Unique words may be decisive in the patent classification process, but due to their rarity they are often discarded at the preprocessing step. Moreover, patents usually contain many scientific terms and to avoid plagiarism or to obfuscate relatedness the statements are often described in a complicated manner. In conclusion, patents are manifold, well-structured and long documents. The patent classification categories are large, complex, time-variant, and non-uniformly distributed hierarchies. Therefore, unlike other types of content which allows an easier categorization, patent classification is an ambitious and challenging task.

There exist several publications about automatic hierarchical classification of patents, mainly based on classical machine learning approaches like SVMs. In combination with elaborate feature engineering they achieved state-of-the-art results [11].

In recent years, the NLP community experienced major improvements in text classification driven by the rise of neural network models like recurrent neural nets (RNN) and convolutional neural nets (CNN). Yet, these models are mainly applied on short text passages, e.g. sentiment analysis or question type classification, not on large documents like patents [17].

This work compares recent approaches for text classification applied on the patent classification task. We investigate the boundaries on how much a neural network can be improved with a variety of different word embeddings and hyperparameter optimization. A detailed report of our optimization findings is provided to guide other researchers.

The experimental results are based on two different datasets, a non-disclosed collection of patents and a freely available dataset for comparison to previous approaches and reproducibility [8]. Our optimized convolutional neural network model achieves a new state-of-the-art performance improvement from 49.02% [24] to 55.02% accuracy on the freely available dataset. Likewise, the CNN model outperforms our baseline, a hierarchical SVM (cf. Sect. 3.4), from 58.72% to 65.43% accuracy.

The rest of the paper is structured as follows. Section 2 provides related work for patent classification and text classification based on neural networks. Section 3 describes the general task and the approach applied in this work. An empirical study that illustrates our results is presented in Sect. 4. Section 5 concludes with a summary.

2   Related Work

Text classification, or document classification more specifically, are typical Natural Language Processing (NLP) tasks which deal with the automated assignment of one or multiple pre-defined labels to a given text or document respectively. Over the years, document classification has been applied to many different areas to overcome error-prone and cumbersome manual labeling. Patent classification is the task of assigning hierarchical single or multi-labels to patent documents.

There exist different classification hierarchies depending on the patent office in which the patent is filed [11]. This work focuses on classification based on International Patent Classification (IPC) and the Cooperative Patent Classification (CPC) hierarchies, which are further described in Sect. 3.1.

The task has already been discussed and evaluated with most approved document classification approaches in several publications. Gomez et al. [11] conducted a comprehensive survey which highlights the challenges of the task and summarizes previous results. In the following, the focus will be shifted towards more recent advances in the field, which are driven by the advent of deep neural nets. In the scope of this work, a hierarchical Support Vector Machine, a customized approach that has been performing very well on the task [10], will serve as a baseline (cf. Sect. 3.4).

Early improvements in text classification with deep learning started with the Dynamic Convolutional Neural Networks (DCNN) method [17]. The authors first adopted Convolutional Neural Networks (CNNs), a model well-received in the computer vision domain, to the field of NLP. Following this work, Yoon Kim created another CNN architecture [18]. The main improvement was to embed the input words using pre-trained word embeddings [21] before passing them into the neural network. Moreover, Kim's CNN, as the author named it, uses a single stage of wide parallel convolutions instead of several stacked convolutions on top of each other.

Zhang created a network which works on character-level instead of word-level [30]. Therefore, it does not require any pre-knowledge of the words. Following the success of very deep networks in the field of computer vision such as ResNet [26] and DenseNet [14], one character is read at a time and then fed to convolution and max-pooling layers. Shortly after, Conneau et al. suggested a network to further increase the depth [5] by introducing shortcut links, another idea introduced in ResNet [26].

Many researchers discovered that the combination of CNN and RNN architecture is beneficial, leading to better results. This is due to the different advantages of CNNs and RNNs [27]. The convolutional network has the advantage of extracting higher-level features that are invariant to local translation. On the other hand, a recurrent network is able to capture long-term dependencies. Xiao et al. created an architecture named ConvRec [27], which extends Kim's CNN with a BiLSTM between the convolutional layers and the classification layer.

Kowsari et al. introduced an architecture, consisting of two networks, which is able to use hierarchical features of labels [19]. One network predicts the first level of the label and passes it on to the second network which predicts the full label.

Yang et al. applied attention mechanisms on document classification [28]. The idea is that the contribution or importance of word in a text can vary based on the context. As a consequence, when classifying text, not all words should be weighted the same. Therefore, an attention layer is built on top of a bi-directional gated recurrent unit (GRU) [3] in order to highlight words at positions with high impact on the label.

Howard et al. created ULMFiT [13], which employs transfer learning. Instead of using word embeddings, a language model is used to represent words. Afterwards, the model is finetuned and the output layers are adjusted to fit the need of the classification task.

Recent trends employing pre-trained language models and context awareness include ELMo [23] and BERT [6]. Bidirectional Encoder Representations from Transformers (BERT) achieves state-of-the-art performance on eleven natural language processing tasks by adding an output layer on top of the pre-trained language model. The language model is trained by masking words in sentences and learning to predict these masked words from their context.

There are only few publications discussing patent classification using deep learning especially with freely available methods or datasets for comparison. Risch et al. solve the same task using an RNN and self-trained word embeddings in RNN-patent [24]. Likewise, Grawe et al. use LSTM with Word2Vec embeddings to classify patents [12]. However, in their work they only consider 50 different categories.

3   Patent Classification

3.1   Patents and Codes

Patents can be understood as rights granted to inventors that allow them to take legal actions against anyone using their invention without permission. According to Gomez et al. [11], patents are usually organized in the following structure:

- **Title:** Patent's name.
- **Bibliographical data:** Contains the ID number of the patent, the names of the inventor and the applicant, and the citations to other patents and documents.
- **Abstract:** A brief overview or description of the patent.
- **Description:** A more in-depth explanation of the invention.
- **Claims:** Legal distinction of the patent and its application fields.

A patent classification system is a hierarchical system used for categorizing patents into different classes, in which patents discussing similar topics are grouped together under the same label.

There exist several patent classification schemes that patent offices abide by. Two popular schemes are the International Patent Classification scheme (IPC) and the Cooperative Patent Classification scheme (CPC) which are used in this paper. The classification hierarchy is divided into sections, then classes, sub-classes, main groups and finally subgroups. Table 1 shows how the hierarchical structure of the G06K9/6296 label is broken down.

One patent may have more than one label assigned to it, as it can cover different topics at the same time. However, in the scope of this work, the classification is treated as single label task, i.e. only the most important CPC code is considered.

Table 1. Breakdown of the G06K9/6296 label using the CPC scheme.

Structure	Label	Description
Section	G	Physics
Class	G06	Computing; Calculating; Counting
Subclass	G06K	Recognition of data; Presentation of data; Record careers
Main group	G06K9/62	Methods or arrangements for recognition using electronic means
Subgroup	G06K9/6296	Graphical models, e.g. Bayesian networks

3.2 Preprocessing

This subsection describes the applied preprocessing steps for all the experiments. Firstly, the patent title, abstract, description, and claims are concatenated together into a single text. As the types of CNNs used in this work require a constant sized input length, the texts are truncated to 1500 words. This maximum sequence length was identified empirically in previous evaluations. Shorter sequences are padded using white spaces. Furthermore, the text is normalized by lower-casing, removing all non-alphabetic characters and reducing all multi-spaces to a single white space. To split the text into words, the default Keras tokenizer[3] is used. Finally, only the 20,000 most frequent words are considered.

3.3 Word Embeddings

A word embedding describes a mapping that translates single words or phrases taken from a vocabulary into an n-dimensional real-valued vector space. It is usually the rationale to find a representation which preserves syntactic and semantic attributes and can be passed on to a machine learning algorithm.

The choice of an effective word embedding depends on a large variety of parameters, e.g. the model itself, embedding size, the corpora used for training or the action taken for unknown words. Many standardized and well-described word embeddings, trained on different corpora, can be found online. Among these, the three most popular models (GloVe [22], Word2Vec [21] and FastText [2]) are tested based on different embedding sizes.

---

[3] https://keras.io/preprocessing/text/ (accessed June 20, 2019).

3.4   Applied Methods

In the experiments of this work, we compare several approaches ranging from classical SVM to very recently published neural networks. Two methods are described in more detail in the following. We apply a hierarchical SVM model as a strong baseline and Kim's CNN as a neural network for further optimization.

Hierarchical SVM. These models proved to be successful in production environments. They provide a good trade-off between training speed, prediction speed, accuracy, and memory footprint. The hierarchical structure, in form of a tree, is aligned to the CPC scheme. Each node of the tree consists of a single-label classifier implemented by several one-vs-all linear SVMs. In order to avoid some ambiguities in the CPC codes and to improve the accuracy, the first two levels have been merged, i.e. the first node in the hierarchical model classifies labels like G06 (cf. Table 1). The final prediction of the model is determined using a greedy search on the product of the softmax confidences of each node in the tree path. The features of the single SVMs consist of a bag-of-stems of the first 2000 characters of each section. The features are weighted using logarithmic frequencies with redundancy [20] and L2-normalized. Overall, hSVM scales considerably better in terms of amount of labels compared to non-hierarchical SVMs and is therefore applied especially for the large dataset (cf. Sect. 4.1).

Yoon Kim's CNN. A recap of Kim's CNN is presented in this section as it is the most used method in this work. The preprocessed text is fed to Kim's CNN through an embedding lookup, which converts word IDs to vectors represented in a highdimensional vector space. Afterwards, one or more 1-D convolutional layers are applied on top of the embedding layer. These convolutional layers may have different sizes and the convolutional filters are typically named regions. Furthermore, each of these regions have filters with different weights. A max-over-time pooling is then applied to the output of the convolutional layers. Thereafter, the output of all the layers is concatenated and fed to a softmax in order to obtain a probability distribution over the label classes.

3.5   Optimization and Assumptions

Hyperparameter Optimization. Neural network parameters can be divided into two types, the normal and the hyperparameters. Normal parameters, such as weights and biases, are changed during training. Hyperparameters, such as learning rate and batch size, are set before the training begins. Hyperparameter optimization describes the process of tuning these parameters by running different configurations in order to choose the optimal one. Hyperparameter optimization techniques range from simple random search to more sophisticated, efficient methods such as Bayesian Optimization (BO). In this work, BOHB, a state-of-the-art hyperparameter optimization technique by Falkner et al. [7], is used to tune the parameters. It combines the best of two worlds leveraging the strong performance of BO while maintaining the speed of hyperband (HB).

Assumptions. Three main assumptions are set up to limit the computing time to a feasible maximum when comparing different models with different parameter configurations.

First, all default hyperparameters are comparable, i.e. if model x is better than model y based on the default settings, x will remain better than y, when tuning the parameters of both models.

Second, if model x performs better than model y on a subset, then x will remain better than y on the whole dataset.

Third, improvements made on a subset have the same effect on the whole dataset, i.e., if for example a parameter is tuned on a subset, then this change will reflect on the whole dataset as well.

We note that in practice these assumptions only hold approximately, but they do motivate the choices made in our algorithm.

4   Experimental Results

4.1   Datasets

Two collections of datasets are utilized in this work. The first dataset called `Pat` consists of a non-disclosed collection of 1.05 million English patents that have been filed to a patent office. The patents contain complete sections like title, abstract, claims and description with 2500 words on average and are labeled according to the CPC scheme. This dataset represents the main task of routing new patent applications to the correct expert examiner. Each patent is assigned to a range of CPC codes, grouped by the starting code of the range. These ranges represent the area of expertise of the examiner groups. Considering these ranges as target labels leads to a single-label classification task with an overall amount of 1382 classes. Due to its real world nature the dataset is highly imbalanced. The most frequent class includes around 30100 instances, while around 30% of the classes include less than 100. The average number of documents per class on each CPC level decreases considerably from $151,296$ examples on the 1st level to 31 examples on the 5th level. For testing the models on this dataset, a separate set of $118,177$ patents with the same class-distribution is utilized.

A subset of `Pat` called `Pat16` contains $250,017$ patents filed in 2016 and applies a reduced set of 8 classes corresponding to the first level of the CPC code. This reduced and simplified dataset is used in different variations of optimization for performance reasons. As a separate test set for `Pat16`, $115,795$ patents filed in 2017 are utilized.

For comparable results, a second, freely available, dataset is used. Among other `Wipo` datasets[4] and the CLEF-IP dataset[5], `Wipo-Alpha` was chosen as it

---

[4] https://www.wipo.int/classifications/ipc/en/ITsupport/Categorization/dataset/index.html (accessed May 4, 2019).

[5] http://www.ifs.tuwien.ac.at/~clef-ip/download/2011/index.shtml (accessed May 4, 2019).

provides text for all sections and a distinguished single CPC/IPC class for the single-label classification.

Wipo-Alpha contains $75K$ English patents with overall 451 classes. The separate test set consists of $28,926$ patents. It was used in previous evaluations and shares most characteristics with the main dataset.

4.2   Model Selection

Several previously published models with good results are evaluated on both datasets Pat16 and Wipo-Alpha, in order to pick a reasonable model for further optimization. The default hyperparameters mentioned in the publications of each model are used for the preliminary comparison, except for BERT [6] for which learning rate, input sequence length, and batch size were optimized using random search.

As shown in Table 2, ULMFiT [13] and BERT achieve the highest accuracy on both experiments. However, it takes 68 h to train ULMFiT on Pat16 (around 20% of Pat), which is considerably slower compared to the other methods that take only a couple of hours (ranging from 3 to 9 h)[6]. The reason is that building a language model from a very large corpus requires a lot of computing time. In addition, training Bi-LSTMs is generally slower than training CNNs.

The results of BERT are only provided for Wipo-Alpha as an initial comparison. It is not investigated further in this work because it was not yet available when the main part of this work was done. The language model is applied for classification using the commonly used approach[7].

Table 2. Accuracy (%) of previously published methods for the reduced subset Pat16 and a freely available dataset Wipo-Alpha.

Method	Pat16	Wipo-Alpha
Linear SVM [25]	68.8	41.0
NB [29]	65.5	33.0
FastText [16]	74.4	29.6
HAN [28]	79.7	49.3
Yoon Kim's CNN [18]	80.5	49.5
VDCNN [5]	76.1	41.3
ULMFiT [13]	**82.8**	49.7
BERT [6]	–	**53.4**

---

[6] Specifications of the used machine: OS: CentOS Linux 7.5, RAM: 32 GB Kingston HyperX Fury DDR4, CPU: Intel Core i7-7700, GPU: MSI GeForce GTX 1080 Ti Gaming X 11G.

[7] https://github.com/google-research/bert#sentence-and-sentence-pair-classification-tasks (accessed June 24, 2019).

Therefore, the next best model, Kim's CNN [18], is used for further experiments. 20 epochs can be trained within 3 h on the Pat16 subset. It is important to choose a model which can be trained relatively quickly, in order to further optimize it using hyperparameter optimization tools and apply other experiments and improvements.

4.3 Model Optimization

Word Embeddings. First, the impact of different word embeddings on the accuracy is investigated. The three popular models, i.e. GloVe [22], Word2Vec [21] and FastText [2] are tested based on the different embedding sizes available online. Furthermore, custom Word2Vec and FastText embeddings are trained on Pat containing 1.05 million patents.

Word2Vec and FastText utilize the skip-gram or CBOW algorithm to generate embeddings. Yet, FastText additionally considers n-gram sub-words as input instead of whole words as atomic units. Apart from the increased training time, it enables the model to embed unseen words. The word "Propene", for example, is unseen in the training corpus, yet FastText can assign a vector near the vector of the seen word "Propylene" which can be advantageous in domains with complex language like patents. Word2Vec lacks this ability and only offers the option to assign a random or zero-valued vector to unseen words.

There are many hyperparameters that can be optimized during the training of a custom word embedding [4]. In this work, only the default values are employed in order to ensure transferability. For testing the embeddings, a CNN was trained and evaluated on the Pat16 subset for each embedding. Thereby, the embeddings were allowed to adapt during training time. The results of the evaluation are shown in Table 3. The accuracy on the first level of the patent hierarchy is used as evaluation metric.

The FastText embeddings trained on the in-domain corpus surpasses all other approaches. Yet, given sufficient embedding size (300) and training corpus the out-of-the-box embeddings reach satisfying results.

The same behaviour can be observed regarding the Wipo-Alpha dataset. Using custom FastText embeddings increases the accuracy from 49.45% to 52.26% with respect to the best pre-trained embeddings (GloVe, 300 dimensions, 1.9M words).

Hyperparameter Optimization. In this section, the results of applying Hyperparameter Optimization by using BOHB [7] are investigated. In total, 30 runs of BOHB were executed on both the Pat and Wipo-Alpha dataset. The hyperparameters are optimized using only the training set of the respective dataset.

In the case of the Pat dataset, it is possible to completely randomize training and evaluation set in order to mitigate overfitting due to its size. Therefore before each iteration two disjoint, stratified subsets containing 20% of the complete dataset are sampled for training and validation.

Table 3. Results of different word embedding variations. The size of the vocabulary is given by the predefined embedding models.

Model	Dimensions	Corpus size	Vocab size	Acc. %
GloVe	500	840B	2.2M	80.05
GloVe	300	42B	1.9M	80.27
GloVe	300	6B	400K	79.77
GloVe	200	6B	400K	79.60
GloVe	100	6B	400K	78.85
GloVe	50	6B	400K	77.50
FastText (skip-gram)	300	600B	2.5M	80.50
Word2Vec (skip-gram, custom)	300	2.5B	350K	80.81
FastText (skip-gram, custom)	300	2.5B	350K	81.35

As for `Wipo-Alpha`, a random 20% of the training set is used for validation in each evaluation.

Table 4. Hyperparameters ranges.

Parameter	Range
Learning rate	$[1e^{-5}, 9e^{-3}]$
Batch size	$[16, 256]$
Dropout rate	$[0.1, 0.6]$
Number of words	$[10000, 60000]$
Regions size	$[1, 15]$
Number of filters	$[500, 3000]$
Sequence length	$[300, 2500]$

The examined hyperparameter ranges are illustrated in Table 4. Furthermore, Table 5 shows the best found parameters and their importance with respect to the prediction accuracy calculated by the fANOVA tool [15].

It can be seen that the importance of the parameters is similar in both datasets, except for Learning Rate, Dropout Rate, and Regions Size. It is hypothesized that the importance of these parameters differ between the two datasets mainly because of the differences in number of classes $(1,382/451)$ and their size $(250,000/75,000)$.

Table 6 shows that applying BOHB increases the accuracy by 1.59% on the 20% subset of `Pat` and by 2.76% on `Wipo-Alpha`.

Table 5. Optimal hyperparameters.

Parameter	Pat	Importance (%)	Wipo-Alpha	Importance (%)
Learning rate	0.0002	21.9	0.0011	63.5
Batch size	64	1.3	128	0.1
Dropout rate	0.75	26.2	0.26	7.5
Number of words	17567	6.7	23140	3.9
Regions size	[4, 5, 6]	12.9	[6]	0.1
Number of filters	2097	4.3	2426	7.9
Sequence length	984	3.1	1431	5.5

Table 6. Hyperparameter optimization results.

Dataset	Before BOHB	After BOHB
Pat (20%)	60.84	62.43
Wipo-Alpha	52.26	55.02

Results. The results after optimizing the CNN applied on the whole dataset are shown in Table 7. The optimized CNN (CNNopt) yields 6% higher accuracy than RNN-patent [24] achieving the current state-of-the-art results on Wipo-Alpha. Additionally, the results surpass a neural network based on BERT (cf. Table 2). The default CNN uses an upstream embedding (GloVe 300) and achieves an accuracy of 49.45%. The difference to the results before applying BOHB in Table 6 is caused by the usage of the custom FastText embeddings. Regarding Pat, optimizing the CNN increases accuracy from 62.01% to 65.43%, yielding a 6.71% improvement compared to the hSVM the baseline.

Table 7. Optimized results compared to base lines. Only available baseline results and published results for the datasets are given. Previously published methods of Table 2 are neglected due to runtime performance.

Method	Pat	Wipo-Alpha
SVM	–	41.00
RNN-patent	–	49.00
hSVM	58.72	–
CNN	62.01	49.45
CNNopt	**65.43**	**55.02**

4.4 Discussion and Error Analysis

Figure 1 shows the accuracy on each level for both models, hSVM and CNNopt. CNNopt outperforms hSVM on all levels by a small delta although CNNopt is not a hierarchical method like the applied SVM.

The top-k results of CNNopt can be seen in Fig. 2 providing an overview of the accuracy of each prediction. The accuracy reaches 95% when considering the top-6 predictions for all 1382 classes.

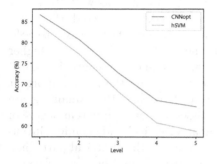

Fig. 1. Accuracy on each level for hSVM and CNNopt on Pat.

Fig. 2. Accuracy for top-k predictions of CNNopt on Pat.

Hierarchical Results. As an experiment to present the hierarchical structure of CNNopt, the accuracy is calculated at each level regardless of the other levels. For example, if there are 100 examples in total, and in the first level 80 of them are classified correctly, then the first level accuracy is 80%. Afterwards, if 65 of those 80 are classified correctly in the second level, then the second level accuracy is 81.25% (65 out of 80 correct). This procedure is continued for all levels. Table 8 shows the results for hSVM and CNNopt, which indicate that CNNopt follows a hierarchical classification structure. Although the given labels are independent of one another and have no structure, its results are slightly better than hSVM at each level. Furthermore, a hierarchical CNN was implemented and evaluated but without considerable improvements, which is on par with the findings in this section.

Table 8. Level independent accuracy on Pat for investigating the dependence on the hierarchical structure.

Accuracy %	hSVM	CNNopt
First level	84.1	86.6
Second level	91.7	93.0
Third level	88.4	90.2
Fourth level	89.0	90.9
Fifth level	96.8	97.7

Confusion Matrix. The optimized network CNNopt achieves an accuracy of 80.5% on Pat16 and 90.3% on Pat when considering only the first level. Initially, it was assumed that the data imbalance lowers the accuracy. However, the confusion matrix in Fig. 3 highlights the main reason which is the similarity of classes. For example, the model shows the highest error rates between the two categories "Electricity" and "Physics" which share common characteristics. The second highest error rate classes are the "Human Necessities" (health, hygiene, tobacco, food additives) and "Chemistry", which are similar as well. To ascertain this hypothesis, the top-2 accuracy was considered. As expected, the result improved from 80.5% to 95.5% on Pat16, while improving from 90.3% to 98% on Pat. Another hypothesis behind the reason the top-2 accuracy is much higher than the top-1 accuracy is that these patents are originally classified by multi-labels not only one label. In the single label dataset, only the most important class selected by some hidden heuristics is considered and the remaining are ignored. A patent may belong to different classes but with different levels of concentration (e.g. a patent may be discussing an electrical and chemical invention at the same time, but if it is concentrating more on the electrical part, then the leading class would be Electricity, while Chemistry would be a sub-class).

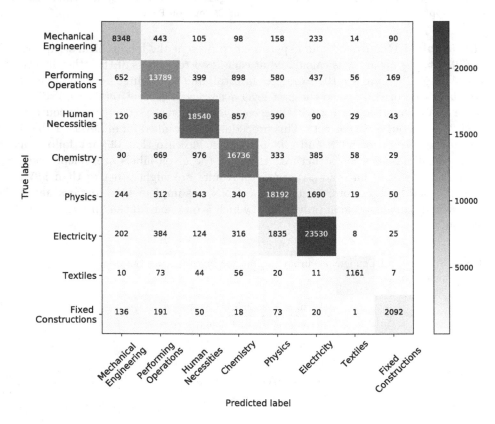

Fig. 3. Confusion matrix for the predictions of CNNopt restricted to the first level.

Error Analysis. After inspecting and analyzing a sample of the common errors, three main types of errors can be identified:

1. Labels are classified correctly up to a certain level.
2. Labels are wrongly classified, but actually related.
3. Labels are wrongly classified.

Table 9. Different types of errors with labels description.

	Label	Description
Predicted	A61K31/00	Medicinal preparations containing organic active ingredients
Truth	A61K9/00	Medicinal preparations characterised by special physical form
Predicted	G06F21/00	Security arrangements for protecting computers, components thereof, programs or data against unauthorized activity
Truth	H04L29/00	Arrangements for network security (security arrangements for protecting computers or computer systems against unauthorized activity)
Predicted	B65H1/00	Supports or magazines for piles from which articles are to be separated
Truth	G07D1/00	Coin dispensers

Table 9 shows examples of the three types of errors and the description of the labels. The most frequent types of errors are the first and second ones. Using top-k predictions would mitigate these errors. However, this would lead to a multi-label classification problem, which would require modifications in the final layer of the network.

5   Conclusion

The task of automated classification of patents is far from being solved but with the growth of new patents filed from year to year it becomes more important every day. In this work we have studied the performance of several recent neural network models on the automated patent classification problem. It was shown that CNNs are a suitable choice in terms of accuracy and training/inference speed. We applied state-of-the-art hyperparameter optimization techniques to the problem and presented its effects on the accuracy. Furthermore, the results indicate that a complex hierarchical network may not be needed as the CNN learns the hierarchy of the labels by itself. The code for reproducing the experimental results is released as open source.[8]

---

[8] https://github.com/lo2aayy/patent-classification.

References

1. Benzineb, K., Guyot, J.: Automated patent classification. In: Lupu, M., Mayer, K., Tait, J., Trippe, A. (eds.) Current Challenges in Patent Information Retrieval, pp. 239–261. Springer, Heidelberg (2011). https://doi.org/10.1007/978-3-642-19231-9_12
2. Bojanowski, P., Grave, E., Joulin, A., Mikolov, T.: Enriching word vectors with subword information. Trans. Assoc. Comput. Ling. **5**, 135–146 (2017)
3. Chung, J., Gulcehre, C., Cho, K., Bengio, Y.: Empirical evaluation of gated recurrent neural networks on sequence modeling. In: NIPS 2014 Workshop on Deep Learning (2014)
4. Caselles-Dupré, H., Lesaint, F., Royo-Letelier, J.: Word2Vec applied to recommendation: hyperparameters matter. In: Proceedings of the 12th ACM Conference on Recommender Systems, pp. 352–356. ACM (2016)
5. Conneau, A., Schwenk, H., Barrault, L., Lecun, Y.: Very deep convolutional networks for text classification. In: Proceedings of the 15th Conference of the European Chapter of the Association for Computational Linguistics, vol. 1, pp. 1107–1116. ACL (2017)
6. Devlin, J., Chang, M.W., Lee, K., Toutanova, K.: BERT: pre-training of deep bidirectional transformers for language understanding. In: Proceedings of the 2019 Conference of the North American Chapter of the Association for Computational Linguistics: Human Language Technologies, vol. 1, pp. 4171–4186. ACL (2018)
7. Falkner, S., Klein, A., Hutter, F.: BOHB: robust and efficient hyperparameter optimization at scale. In: Proceedings of the 35th International Conference on Machine Learning, PMLR, vol. 80, pp. 1437–1446 (2018)
8. Fall, C.J., Törcsvári, A., Benzineb, K., Karetka, G.: Automated categorization in the international patent classification. In: SIGIR Forum, vol. 1, pp. 10–25. ACM (2003)
9. Fall, C.J., Benzineb, K.: Literature survey: issues to be considered in the automatic classification of patents. In: World Intellectual Property Organization, vol. 29 (2002)
10. Fernández-Delgado, M., Cernadas, E., Barro, S., Amorim, D.: Do we need hundreds of classifiers to solve real world classification problems? J. Mach. Learn. Res. **15**, 3133–3181 (2014)
11. Gomez, J.C., Moens, M.-F.: A survey of automated hierarchical classification of patents. In: Paltoglou, G., Loizides, F., Hansen, P. (eds.) Professional Search in the Modern World. LNCS, vol. 8830, pp. 215–249. Springer, Cham (2014). https://doi.org/10.1007/978-3-319-12511-4_11
12. Grawe, M.F., Martins, C.A., Bonfante, A.G.: Automated patent classification using word embedding. In: 16th IEEE International Conference on Machine Learning and Applications (ICMLA), pp. 408–411. IEEE (2017)
13. Howard, J., Ruder, S.: Universal language model fine-tuning for text classification. In: Proceedings of the 56th Annual Meeting of the Association for Computational Linguistics, ACL, vol. 1, pp. 328–339 (2018)
14. Huang, G., Liu, Z., Van Der Maaten, L., Weinberger, K.Q.: Densely connected convolutional networks. In: 30th IEEE Conference on Computer Vision and Pattern Recognition, pp. 2261–2269. IEEE (2017)
15. Hutter, F., Hoos, H.H., Leyton-Brown, K.: An efficient approach for assessing hyperparameter importance. In: ICML, JMLR Workshop and Conference Proceedings, PMLR, vol. 32, pp. 754–762 (2014)

16. Joulin, A., Grave, E., Bojanowski, P., Mikolov, T.: Bag of tricks for efficient text classification. In: Proceedings of the 15th Conference of the European Chapter of the Association for Computational Linguistics, vol. 2, pp. 427–431. ACL (2017)
17. Kalchbrenner, N., Grefenstette, E., Blunsom, P.: A convolutional neural network for modelling sentences. In: Proceedings of the 52nd Annual Meeting of the Association for Computational Linguistics, vol. 1, pp. 655–665. ACL (2014)
18. Kim, Y.: Convolutional neural networks for sentence classification. In: Proceedings of the 2014 Conference on Empirical Methods in Natural Language Processing, pp. 1746–1751. ACL (2014)
19. Kowsari, K., Brown, D.E., Heidarysafa, M., Meimandi, K.J., Gerber, M.S., Barnes, L.E.: HDLTex: hierarchical deep learning for text classification. In: 16th IEEE International Conference on Machine Learning and Applications, pp. 364–371. IEEE (2017)
20. Leopold, E., Kindermann, J.: Text categorization with support vector machines. How to represent texts in input space? Mach. Learn. **46**, 423–444 (2002). https://doi.org/10.1023/A:1012491419635
21. Mikolov, T., Chen, K., Corrado, G., Dean, J.: Efficient estimation of word representations in vector space. In: CoPR (2013)
22. Pennington, J., Socher, R., Manning, C.: GloVe: global vectors for word representation. In: Proceedings of the 2014 Conference on Empirical Methods in Natural Language Processing, pp. 1532–1543. ACL (2014)
23. Peters, M.E., Neumann, M., Iyyer, M., Gardner, M., Clark, C., Lee, K., Zettlemoyer, L.: Deep contextualized word representations. In: Proceedings of the 2018 Conference of the North American Chapter of the Association for Computational Linguistics: Human Language Technologies, pp. 2227–2237. ACL (2018)
24. Risch, J., Krestel, R.: Domain-specific word embeddings for patent classification. In: Data Technologies and Applications, vol. 53, pp. 108–122. Emerald Publishing Limited (2019)
25. Steinwart, I., Christmann, A.: Support Vector Machines, 1st edn. Springer, New York (2008). https://doi.org/10.1007/978-0-387-77242-4
26. Wu, S., Zhong, S., Liu, Y.: Deep residual learning for image steganalysis. Multimedia Tools Appl. **77**(9), 10437–10453 (2017). https://doi.org/10.1007/s11042-017-4440-4
27. Xiao, Y., Cho, K.: Efficient character-level document classification by combining convolution and recurrent layers. preprint arXiv:1602.00367 (2016)
28. Yang, Z., Yang, D., Dyer, C., He, X., Smola, A., Hovy, E.: Hierarchical attention networks for document classification. In: Proceedings of the 2016 Conference of the North American Chapter of the Association for Computational Linguistics: Human Language Technologies, pp. 1480–1489. ACL (2016)
29. Zhang, H., Li, D.: Naïve bayes text classifier. In: 2007 IEEE International Conference on Granular Computing (GRC 2007), pp. 708–708. IEEE (2007)
30. Zhang, X., Zhao, J., LeCun, Y.: Character-level convolutional networks for text classification. In: Proceedings of the 28th International Conference on Neural Information Processing Systems, vol. 1, pp. 649–657. MIT Press (2015)

The Search for Equations – Learning to Identify Similarities Between Mathematical Expressions

Lukas Pfahler[✉], Jonathan Schill, and Katharina Morik

TU Dortmund University, Dortmund, Germany
{lukas.pfahler,jonathan.schill,katharina.morik}@tu-dortmund.de

Abstract. On your search for scientific articles relevant to your research question, you judge the relevance of a mathematical expression that you stumble upon using extensive background knowledge about the domain, its problems and its notations. We wonder if machine learning can support this process and work toward implementing a search engine for mathematical expressions in scientific publications. Thousands of scientific publication with millions of mathematical expressions or equations are accessible at arXiv.org. We want to use this data to learn about equations, their distribution and their relations in order to find similar equations. To this end we propose an embedding model based on convolutional neural networks that maps bitmap images of equations into a low-dimensional vector-space where similarity is evaluated via dot-product. However, no annotated similarity data is available to train this mapping. We mitigate this by proposing a number of different unsupervised proxy tasks that use available features as weak labels. We evaluate our system using a number of metrics, including results on a small hand-labeled subset of equations. In addition, we show and discuss a number of result-sets for some sample queries. The results show that we are able to automatically identify related mathematical expressions. Our dataset is published at https://whadup.github.io/EquationLearning/ and we invite the community to use it.

Keywords: Applied data science track · Data science · Preference learning and ranking · Deep learning

1 Motivation

Finding relevant scientific publications to your own research question with the tools currently available is a tedious and at times frustrating endeavor. Every day, huge amounts of new scientific manuscripts are published. On the pre-print

---

Electronic supplementary material The online version of this chapter (https://doi.org/10.1007/978-3-030-46133-1_42) contains supplementary material, which is available to authorized users.

U. Brefeld et al. (Eds.): ECML PKDD 2019, LNAI 11908, pp. 704–718, 2020.
https://doi.org/10.1007/978-3-030-46133-1_42

service arXiv.org alone, more than 140,000 papers where uploaded in 2018[1]. This flood of scientific manuscripts is impossible to filter, index and organize manually. Hence scientists rely heavily on existing search engines like Google Scholar or Mendeley to find relevant content, mainly by using keyword search. Keyword search has limitations, because similar concepts are referred to using different terminology between disciplines or even between subfields. For instance in machine learning we talk about features and labels, whereas statisticians might refer to the same concepts as independent and dependent variables.

However, once an interesting candidate paper is identified, it is usually not immediately read thoroughly from beginning to end. Instead, the scientist might briefly scan the pages for clues that indicate if the paper is indeed relevant. The most useful clues for disciplines like computer science or physics are arguably the equations used to describe the main ideas. A trained reader can easily match patterns of concepts in equations, generalize between different notations and use extensive background-knowledge to estimate the relevance of a paper to their own research questions. We wonder whether machine learning can help automatize this process.

The service arXiv.org grants access to thousands of publications, many containing mathematical expressions. We process a sample of publications and derive a dataset of equations in a standardized format. While this dataset is not manually annotated in any form – particularly similarities are not labeled – it still contains valuable information on equations and their relations. Ultimately the goal is to exploit this information and provide a search-engine that allows users to find equations related to their own research.

To this end we train embedding models based on convolutional neural networks. These networks take an equation represented as a fixed-size bitmap image and embed it in a low-dimensional vector space. Similarities can then be evaluated by dot-product in a low-dimensional space. Since ground-truth similarities are not available, we propose a number of unsupervised proxy tasks that take the available information and use it to define weak labels that guide the training of the embedding model. We evaluate their usefulness in an empirical study. For evaluation purposes we have hand-labeled a small set of equation into categories. This way we can show that our embedding model is capable of grouping related equations into clusters.

The rest of this paper is structured as follows: After discussing related work and orthogonal approaches, we present the dataset we created in greater detail. In Sect. 4 we present the unsupervised learning tasks that we design to train embedding models as well as the convolutional neural networks we use to tackle the tasks. Particular emphasis is put into choosing suitable loss functions. Section 5 presents our empirical study; after presenting our validation dataset and the metrics used to measure our success, we do a quantitative and qualitative analysis of our models. Finally we summarize our contribution and present directions of future work.

---

[1] https://arxiv.org/stats/monthly_submissions.

2   Related Work

The idea to implement a search engine for mathematical expressions is not new, see for instance [6,8,20,21,28,33,34]. Most of these systems work on the level of symbols and use inverted index structures designed for text to retrieve formulas. Zannibi et al. distinguish between text-based and tree-based approaches [34] and propose a similarity measure based on the number of matching subtrees in a symbol layout tree derived from the LaTex source. Kamali and Tompa apply tree-edit-distance to retrieve similar equations [8]. NGuyen et al. use a tree-representation of the equation and derive features that are used in a tf-idf vector space [20].

To the best of our knowledge we propose the first system that represents mathematical expressions as bitmap images and uses machine learning to detect similarities. This way we can build on a rich set of works on similarity learning between images. The current boom of deep networks, and in particular convolutional neural networks, has heavily impacted computer vision. One important task is detecting similar images or similar objects in images or videos and a popular architecture for learning these similarities are Siamese networks, i.e. convolutional neural networks that are used to encode two images into a shared vector space where the similarity is measured. Examples of this application include identifying products in different product photos on e-commerce websites [27], person re-identification in photos [4,35], detection of models of vehicles [13].

Because we do not have labels for learning similarities, we proceed to view the problem as an embedding learning problem. Since Mikolov et al. proposed word2vec [17], these models have become increasingly popular for unsupervised learning of similarities. The underlying hypothesis of word embeddings is that words that appear together frequently share semantic similarities. This principle has been extended to other domains, including textual documents [12] or users in social networks [22]. We can view a whole publication as the context and compute embeddings of the equations that capture regularities in their distribution. We can construct a similar analogy to collaborative filtering [9,29], where we want to learn to recommend items to users based on the logged interactions of all users and items. Two items that are consumed by the same user may be similar. This problem is often formulated as a matrix factorization problem where items and users are mapped to low-dimensional embeddings such that their dot-product models the logged interactions. Now instead of the dichotomy of users and items, we have equations and documents, still we want to learn to identify similarities between equations. The major difference between our approach and both word embeddings and collaborative filtering is that we do not view equations as atomic units, which would be counterproductive as almost no equation appears identically in two documents, but as examples with features, in our case the grayscale information of a bitmap image.

Many machine learning tasks evolve around the use of LaTeX documents. There is plenty of research on converting images of equations back to valid LaTeX source [2,11]. We believe our data set might be a welcome addition to the available datasets of this branch of research. Even more challenging than parsing to LaTeX is parsing to a representation of the equation in a symbolic math description [23]. This could allow us to apply powerful solvers like Maple or Mathematica to judge similarities.

$$\min_{w} \frac{1}{n} \sum_{i=1}^{n} \ell(y_i, w^\top x_i) + \lambda\|w\|^2 \qquad \boxed{\min_{w} \frac{1}{n} \sum_{i=1}^{n} \ell(y_i, w^\top x_i) + \lambda\|w\|^2} \qquad (1)$$

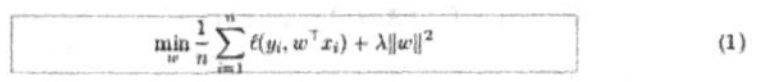

Fig. 1. Example equation (left) with corresponding bitmap graphic (right), the orange box marks the center rectangle used for learning. Note the decrease in visual clarity due to converting to a low-resolution bitmap. (Color figure online)

3   The Dataset

The popular pre-print service arXiv.org hosts thousands of scientific publications; for the majority of these publications LaTex sources are available. This allows us to easily extract the mathematical expressions and represent them as images. Each publication has a unique arXiv-id. For this study, we only work on a small subset of publications, a combination of two publicly available crawls of arXiv-ids at Kaggle.com[2] and at Andrej Karpathy's page[3]. The publications in these crawls are mainly from machine-learning related subdomains of computer science. For each publication in these crawls, we try to download and extract the source files, obtaining more than 44 k publications.

From these sources we extract snippets that describe mathematical equations as well as snippets that define new commands or macros. With these snippets, we are able to compile more than 600,000 equations; the major cause for failed compilation being more complicated user-defined LaTeX macros or the use of non-standard LaTeX packages. We have decided to work with bitmap images of equations rather than working with a text based representation like LaTex. This representation is invariant to the authors' LaTeX programming style, use of macros, etc. Additionally the LaTeX sources of a scientific publication are often unavailable, particularly on platforms other than arXiv, but images of equations may be identified and cropped from digital documents automatically in future projects. The images we create are 531×106 pixels in size, however for more efficient learning we only use the center rectangle of size 333×32 pixels for training. This decrease in height does not affect single-line equations, the decrease in width does not affect equations that fit into a single column in a two-column layout, longer equations will miss beginning and end. See Fig. 1 for an example equation and the corresponding bitmap.

In addition to the image data, for each equation we know the arXiv-id of the corresponding publication. For each publication we know the title as well as the abstract, additional meta-data could be obtained via this identifier at a later point.

---

[2] https://www.kaggle.com/neelshah18/arxivdataset.
[3] https://cs.stanford.edu/people/karpathy/arxiv_10K_export.zip.

We have applied only rudimentary data-cleaning on the images. Most notably, we omit images that are mostly white background and have only few black foreground pixels. The majority of these images are artifacts of failed LaTeX compilation.

Our dataset is published at https://whadup.github.io/EquationLearning/ and we invite the community to use it.

4   Unsupervised Training

Usually similarities between objects are learned in a supervised manner, where a dataset of labeled pairs is available. Since we do not have labeled data, we propose a number of unsupervised proxy training tasks for learning embeddings. All our proposed embedding models are based on the same encoder architecture that embeds a bitmap equation x into a low-dimensional vector space. We denote this operation by $f(x) : \mathbb{R}^{333 \times 32} \to \mathbb{R}^d$. These embeddings can then be used for computing similarities between equations. We compute the similarity between two equations by taking the dot-product of the embeddings

$$s(x_1, x_2) = \langle f(x_1), f(x_2) \rangle.$$

This allows us to store all embeddings in an efficient index structure, e.g. a navigable small-network graph [15], and efficiently perform similarity search by embedding the query. Depending on the particular proxy task, we try various loss functions for optimizing our models.

4.1   Equation-Encoder

Our equation-encoder is a standard convolutional neural network. We try two different networks, a small and a large one. The small model is comprised of three convolution layers with 32 channels, each followed by a MaxPooling layer, followed by a final fully connected linear layer, as depicted in Fig. 2. The larger model uses 6 convolution layers with 64 channels each, every other layer followed by a MaxPooling layer. Then the embedding is computed by a two fully connected layers. We apply batch normalization between the fully connected layers for more stable optimization, but freeze that layer in later epochs of training. Both models map into a space of dimensionality $d = 64$. All non-linearities are rectifying linear units (ReLU). In total, the small model has 45,504 parameters, while the number of parameters in the large model is 255,040.

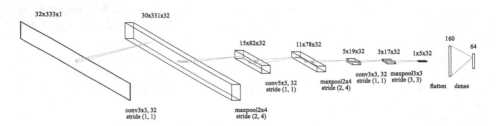

Fig. 2. Equation encoder architecture (small)

4.2 Learning Tasks and Loss Functions

We want to learn an encoder that embeds two equations into a low dimensional vector space, such that the dot product between two embeddings is large if and only if the corresponding equations are similar. Unfortunately, in our application we do not have gold-standard labels for similar and dissimilar pairs available. We design a number of unsupervised proxy tasks that use the available features as weak labels and argue why they are related to the real task.

Latex-Symbols as Labels. The first proxy task we propose is to treat expressions in the available LaTeX-code as labels. We train a network based on our equation encoder, that has to decide if a given equation contains a selected symbol. This way the convolutional equation encoder has to learn to identify letters, numbers or symbols in an equation, a task loosely related to optical character recognition.

Abstract-Keywords as Labels. The second task uses the abstract that is available for each publication to derive labels. We automatically extract keywords from those abstracts using RAKE [24] and label equations with those keywords. This task tries to link equations to background knowledge about research domains, particularly the objects of investigation. Prominent keywords include 'deep learning', 'optimization', 'classification', etc. This task is very similar to a weak-label task proposed by Denton et al. who train to label images on social media platforms by the hashtags used to describe the images [3].

Both of these tasks are multi-label classification tasks with a large number of classes. We choose a negative-sampling approach for training [16]: For each possible label y we have a weight vector $w_y \in \mathbb{R}^d$. We jointly learn the encoder and these weights, such that the dot-product of $\langle f(x), w_y \rangle$ is large when y is in the set of labels of x and small otherwise. To train, we randomly generate pairs of equations and labels; with probability 0.5 we create a pair with a correct label, otherwise we choose an incorrect label uniformly at random. This process generates data (x, y, z) where $z \in \{0, 1\}$ describes whether the label y fits the data x or not. Treating this as a binary classification problem with two inputs, we train by minimizing the cross entropy loss of the logistic function $\sigma(a) = 1/(1 + \exp(-a))$ applied to the scalar product

$$\ell_{log}(x, y, z) = -z \ln(\sigma(\langle f(x), w_y \rangle)) - (1 - z) \ln(1 - \sigma(\langle f(x), w_y \rangle)). \quad (1)$$

Document-Context as Labels. Finally, we propose a proxy similarity learning task by choosing weak labels for pairs of examples. We say that two equations are similar if they appear in the same publication. This task is reminiscent of the word2vec embedding model by Mikolov et al. [17] popular in natural language processing, where two words are similar if they appear in the same context in a document. While it appears plausible that two equations in a publication are somehow related, the inverse is not necessarily true: Two equations can be related if they are from different documents. In fact it is our goal to identify those related documents. Like Mikolov et al., we use negative sampling to address this:

We create artificial pairs of dissimilar equations by sampling equations from our collection uniformly and proclaiming them as dissimilar. We conjecture that the probability of accidentally sampling a similar pair is sufficiently small. Hence the labels should have a level of noise that still allows learning [10].

We explore two different types loss functions for this task. The first one works on annotated pairs of equations. Mobahi et al. [19] propose the *Siamese loss*: Given a margin Δ, the dot product of the embeddings should be larger than Δ for a similar pair and less than $-\Delta$ otherwise. We use $y = \pm 1$ to encode the similarity and define

$$\ell_{siam}(x_1, x_2, y) = \max(0, \Delta - y\langle f(x_1), f(x_2)\rangle). \tag{2}$$

The equation encoder is used twice to calculate the loss, motivating the term 'Siamese' network, because we can also view this as two convolutional networks that share all their weights (twins) and that are connected by the loss function.

The second loss works on triples of equations, so that the encoder is used three times per training example: Given an equation x, the so-called anchor, a similar equation x_+ and a dissimilar equation x_-, we want the encoder to judge the similar pair as more similar then the dissimilar pair. Balntas et al. propose to formulate this as a margin loss as well [1]. Furthermore they propose to swap the roles of anchor example and the positive example if this yields a larger loss value to obtain a more strict loss:

$$\ell_{tri}(x, x_+, x_-) = \max \begin{cases} 0 \\ \Delta - \langle f(x), f(x_+)\rangle + \langle f(x), & f(x_-)\rangle \\ \Delta - \langle f(x_+), f(x)\rangle + \langle f(x_+), & f(x_-)\rangle \end{cases} \tag{3}$$

Margin losses require that the magnitude of embeddings is controlled either by applying regularization or normalization. Otherwise arbitrary absolute margins can be satisfied by scaling the output by a large enough values. We choose to normalize our embeddings to unit length $\bar{f}(x) = f(x)/(\|f(x)\|_2 + \epsilon)$ where a small, constant $\epsilon > 0$ is added for numerical stability. This choice avoids the introduction of yet another hyperparameter that controls regularization.

Following Janocha and Czarnecki [7] we use squared hinge losses ℓ^2_{siam} and ℓ^2_{tri} instead of hinge losses for faster convergence.

4.3   Training Procedure

We train our models using the ADAM optimizer, a variant of stochastic gradient descent. We initialize the learning rate at 0.00025 and reduce it by a factor of 0.1 every 10 epochs of training. We train using minibatches of size 100 and run training for 30 epochs.

All of our training tasks involve negative sampling; the triples task sample an additional positive point. For every gradient step, we sample new negative/positive samples. This way we hope to avoid overfitting to the particular choices of pairs/triples used for training.

The margin losses use a margin $\Delta = 1$, the constant used for normalizing the encoder output is $\epsilon = 10^{-5}$. The filters of the convolutional neural layers are initialized uniformly in $(-k^{-1/2}, k^{-1/2})$ where k is the number of weights per filter. The weights of the linear layers are initialized uniformly in $(-m^{-1/2}, m^{-1/2})$ where m is the input dimensionality of the layer.

5 Evaluation

In this section we experimentally evaluate the models we proposed in the previous section. First we try to establish quantitative metrics for measuring the quality of our embeddings. To this end, we curate a small evaluation dataset with hand-labeled equations. Second, we do a qualitative evaluation and inspect a few queries and discuss the results.

5.1 Gold-Label Evaluation Data

Quantitative evaluation is difficult whenever we cannot compare to a ground truth. This problem arises in many unsupervised learning applications, including clustering [14] and embedding learning [5,18,26]. Word Embedding models are often evaluated by computing measures using a small, manually labeled set of word pairs. Following their experimental protocol, we hand-labeled about 100 equations into 13 categories of equations that we have identified as prominent in machine learning literature. These include equations describing the empirical risk minimization principle, the k-means objective, the dual formulation of the kernelized support vector machine, but also concentration inequalities and Rademacher averages used in the theoretical analysis of machine learning algorithms. Under our embedding model, equations that belong to the same category should have higher similarity than inter-category pairs. Thus quantitative measure of embedding quality are possible. Note that this labeled dataset is used exclusively for evaluation purposes and never for learning.

5.2 Metrics

To get a detailed picture of the quality of our embeddings, we evaluate a number of different metrics.

Margin Losses on Eval Data. We can evaluate the Siamese ℓ_{siam} and Triplet losses ℓ_{tri} on all triples in the evaluation data. In contrast to the training phase, now the similarity is measured with respect to the hand-annotated labels and not with respect to the weak-label based on the arXiv-id.

Hard Ranking on Eval Data. In addition to the triplet margin loss, we can also evaluate a discrete ranking loss, that is 0, if the anchor example is more similar to the positive example than the negative example and 1 otherwise. We can evaluate this over all triples derived from the evaluation dataset and measure how many triples are ranked wrong.

Nearest-Neighbor Accuracy on Eval Data. We compute leave-one-out estimates of the accuracy for 1-nearest-neighbor classification for the hand-labeled evaluation data. This metric measures how many nearest-neighbor pairs share the same category.

Loss on Hold-Out Data. We evaluate the margin losses and the hard ranking loss on hold-out data. This allows us to assess whether we are overfitting to the training data. For comparability between models we use the weak label based on the document context for all models.

5.3   Quantitative Results

We investigate a total of 12 different models, using 6 small architectures and 6 large architectures. The first four models of both architectures are trained using the different proxy tasks, namely predicting latex symbols (SYMBOLS), predicting keywords in the abstracts (ABSTRACT), training using the document context with triples loss (TRIPLES) and Siamese loss (SIAMESE). In addition we try a transfer learning approach where we initialize the network with the weights trained using the symbol-task (SYMBOLS+TRIPLES) or the abstract-task (ABSTRACT+TRIPLES) and then proceed to train the network on the triples-task. This way we hope to combine the benefits of both weak labels.

Table 1. Performance metrics for small models. Best scores in bold letters.

	SYMBOLS	ABSTRACT	TRIPLES	SIAMESE	SYMBOLS+TRIPLES	ABSTRACT+TRIPLES
Eval Accuracy	0.4712	0.5096	**0.6827**	0.5385	0.5385	0.6058
Eval Ranking	0.3762	**0.2355**	0.3675	0.4637	0.4408	0.3259
Eval Triples	0.8885	0.9033	0.8091	0.9208	0.8918	**0.7633**
Eval Siamese	0.9088	0.9437	0.8403	0.8777	0.8789	**0.8132**
Hold-Out Ranking	0.5520	0.4540	0.3341	0.3642	0.3353	**0.3331**
Hold-Out Triples	1.0342	0.9819	0.8015	0.8120	0.8040	**0.8010**
Hold-Out Siamese	0.9578	0.9739	0.8458	**0.8392**	0.8469	0.8439

Table 2. Performance metrics for large models. Best scores in bold letters.

	SYMBOLS	ABSTRACT	TRIPLES	SIAMESE	SYMBOLS+TRIPLES	ABSTRACT+TRIPLES
Eval Accuracy	0.4135	0.4808	**0.6827**	**0.6827**	0.5385	0.5673
Eval Ranking	0.3568	**0.2485**	0.2812	0.3598	0.3409	0.2848
Eval Triples	0.8736	0.7936	0.6921	0.7867	0.7555	**0.6715**
Eval Siamese	0.8886	0.8852	0.7680	0.8168	0.7861	**0.7530**
Hold-Out Ranking	0.5474	0.5186	**0.2942**	0.3048	0.3181	0.3098
Hold-Out Triples	1.0382	0.4851	**0.7245**	0.7314	0.7861	0.7397
Hold-Out Siamese	0.9480	0.9592	0.7972	0.7970	0.7916	**0.7897**

We have summarized our results for the small architecture in Table 1 and for the large architecture in Table 2. First of all, we note that a larger model size is beneficial for the problem at hand. It allows us to obtain larger margins on both hold-out and evaluation data. Furthermore we note that pretraining has a negative effect on the nearest neighbor accuracy, but has advantages for the Siamese and Triples loss. Overall, the pure Triples-model or the Triples model with abstract pretraining seem to perform best. A notable exception is that the ABSTRACT model has the best ranking performance on the eval dataset. This is probably due to the manual labeling process for curating the evaluation dataset. We used keyword search in the abstract to identify candidate papers for a given category of equations, the same information was used to train the model, while all other models did not have access to the abstract information.

We visually inspect the performance of the large TRIPLES-embedding in a hierarchical clustering of our labeled evaluation data. The clustering is done using agglomerative clustering with the complete-linkage strategy and dot-product similarity. In Fig. 3 we see that on the lower levels of the hierarchy many clusters belong to a unique category of equations and that the computed similarities are high. On the right side of the plot, we see that categories mix, but do so in a plausible manner: the connection from sgd (stochastic gradient descent) and convex (equations describing properties like convexity or Lipschitz continuity) is apparent, as articles analyzing the convergence of optimization algorithms rely heavily on these definitions. The connection between Rademacher complexities and concentration inequalities cannot be denied as well.

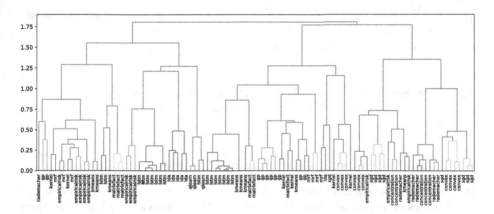

Fig. 3. A dendrogram showing a hierarchical clustering of our evaluation dataset according to our embedding model, colored according to hand-annotated labels, gray for non-pure clusters.

(q) $c_i^t = v^T \tanh(W_h h_i + W_s s_t + b_{\text{attn}} + W_c cov_t)$

$B[p_o] = \dfrac{T(\sigma, w_1^n) + 1}{n + |\Sigma|}$

(1) $h_0 = f(W_{bh} h_{-1} + W_{he} c_0 + W_{hs} s + W_{hv} v)$

(2) $h_0 = f(W_{hh} h_{-1} + W_{he} c_0 + W_{hs} s)$

$B[p_o] = \dfrac{T(\sigma, w_1^n) + \alpha m_o}{n + \alpha |\Sigma|}$

$A_d(\kappa) = \dfrac{I_{d/2}(\kappa)}{I_{d/2-1}(\kappa)}$

(3) $y_t = \text{softmax}(W_o f(W_{dec} s_t + V_{dec} d_t))$

$C_M'(\kappa) = -C_M(\kappa) \cdot \dfrac{I_{s+1}(\kappa)}{I_s(\kappa)}$

(4) $\beta_{tj} = v^T \tanh(W s_{t-1} + U x_j + V h_j)$,

$R(\pi) = \dfrac{|G(\pi) \cap S_{pair}|}{|G(\pi)|}$,

(5) $h_0 = f(W_{bh} h_{-1} + W_{he} c_0 + W_{vh} v)$

$Q(k, a) = C_k \cdot \prod_{i=1}^{a} \dfrac{C_{ia,k}}{C_k}$

(a)   (b)

Fig. 4. Sample Queries and Results: The first line shows queries, the remaining lines show the top-5 results. Shows center rectangle only.

(q) $V^\pi(s) = \sum_{s' \in S} \mu(\pi(s), s, s')\big(r(\pi(s), s, s') + V^\pi(s')\big)$

$\mathcal{L}_r = \dfrac{1}{r} \sum^{L} \log p(Y, z^{(\ell)}) - D[q(z|X) \| p(z)]$

(1) $\hat{Q}(s, a) \leftarrow R(s, a) + \gamma \sum_{s' \in S} \gamma P(s, a, s') \bigotimes_{a'} \hat{Q}(s', a')$.

$(\theta_x^*, \theta_y^*) = \arg \max_{(\theta_x, \theta_y)} \text{corr}(f_x(X; \theta_x), f_y(Y; \theta_y))$.

(2) $b_{t+1}(\theta') = \eta \Pr(s', r | s, a, \theta') \displaystyle\int_{S, \Theta} \Pr(s', \theta' | s, a, \theta) b_t(\theta) ds d\theta$.

$\hat{w}(Y, \theta) \approx p(Y|\theta) = \int p(X, Y|\theta) \, dX$.

(3) $\dfrac{1}{q(\tilde{a}|s)}(\hat{Q}_w^\pi(s, a) - \hat{r} - \gamma \hat{Q}_w^\pi(\tilde{s}, \mu(\tilde{s}))^2$.

$p(z_t^k; X_t, L_{y_t^k}) \sim \mathcal{N}(L_{z_t^k} \ominus X_t, R)$

(4) $g_x(s'|s) = \sum_{a^1, a^2} \pi^1(a^1|s) \pi^2(a^2|s) p(s'|s, a^1, a^2)$.

$\theta = \arg\min_\eta \mathbb{E}_{P_{trg}(x) P(y|x)}[-\log \hat{P}(Y|X)] + \lambda \|\theta\|_2^2$.

(5) $Q^A(s, a) = Q^A(s, a) + \alpha_t(s, a)(y - Q^A(s, a))$
$\quad\;\; Q^B(s, a) = Q^B(s, a) + \alpha_t(s, a)(y - Q^B(s, a))$.

$\dfrac{\partial}{\partial ...} \log p(y|\hat{X}(\omega), \theta)$

(a)   (b)

Fig. 5. More Sample Queries and Results: The first line shows queries, the remaining lines show the top-5 results. Shows center rectangle only. The results for these queries are more diverse.

5.4   A Qualitative Analysis of Example Queries

We choose to evaluate the large model without pretraining, because it beats the model pretrained with abstract keywords on 4 of 7 metrics. In Fig. 4 we want to show some example queries with their respective top results[4]. In the first column we query an equation that describes a modified variant of an LSTM recurrent neural network. The system returns equations that seem to describe other recurrent network architectures or parts of recurrent units like the output part in row (3). In the second column the system does not work as well: The first result is relevant, however it is from the same publication as the query. That is (a) not very useful for the user, and (b) not difficult for the system

---

[4] In the supplementary material you can find a table of the corresponding works.

to identify, as the query-answer-pairs were used during training. The remaining answers seem to have no semantic similarity. However they are at least visually similar: Short equation where an uppercase character function equals a term with a fraction. This difference in quality between the two columns is also expressed in the computed similarities. While the most relevant equation on the left has a similarity of 0.99, the most relevant equation on the right that is not from the same paper, has a similarity of only 0.91.

In Fig. 5 we see more examples: On the left we query a definition of the value function, an expression related to reinforcement learning. And indeed all results are related to reinforcement learning. Even (2), which looks the most dissimilar, is taken from a survey on reinforcement learning[5]. On the right, the equations appear more diverse, but all involve probabilistic modeling. The computed similarities range between 0.93 and 0.90, which again is substantially lower than on the left.

Overall the quality of the results is convincing, the results contain useful and related equations in most cases. It seems that our system has learned to group equations that belong to a subfield of machine learning together in a latent space. Using a visual representation helps comparing the coarse structure of expressions.

6   Conclusion and Outlook

This work has worked towards the development of a search engine for mathematical expressions in scientific publications. We have created a dataset of equations that we used to learn to detect similarities between equations based on unsupervised training tasks. Our models work on bitmap image representations of equations and we use standard convolutional neural networks to compute low-dimensional embeddings of those equations[6]. In order to evaluate our system, we have hand-labeled real equations into categories. This way we tested how informative our embeddings are for grouping equations into categories and retrieving equations of the same category. A qualitative analysis revealed that or system is indeed capable of retrieving related equations.

We see many opportunities to further improve our system. First we believe it is crucial to refine the process we use to generate weak labels. Using the whole document context may be to broad and does not recognize that scientific publications have a sequential nature. We want to look into generating better weak labels by including the text in the paragraphs surrounding an equation. Furthermore we want to use the citation network to generate positive labels between two different documents. Generating better labels for learning also includes generating better negative labels. Currently our system generates negative examples

---

[5] Mohammad Ghavamzadeh, Shie Mannor, Joelle Pineau, Aviv Tamar. *Bayesian Reinforcement Learning: A Survey*, 2016.

[6] We made both our code for computing embeddings and our dataset available at https://github.com/Whadup/EquationLearning/.

by sampling uniformly at random, but more advanced sampling routines are possible.

In the future we want to generate training data not only based on weak labels, but also on simulations and symbolic math-solvers like SymPy or Maple. This way we hope to generate pairs of equations that not only share a semantic context, but that are actually equivalent pairs. We can also think about other forms of relations other than equivalence, e.g. lower- or upper-bounds. Preliminary experiments with a very simple grammar that allowed us to randomly generate pairs of equivalent equations showed a stark mismatch between the space of equations we encounter in real scientific publications and the space of synthetically generated equations. More advanced methods for synthetic generation of labeled data are necessary, maybe using advances in generative models or generative adversarial models [32].

Another point of attack for further improvements is the family of models used for embedding the bitmap equations into a vector space. A plain feed-forward convolutional neural network may very well be inferior to a more task-specifically designed model. Currently a lot of research investigates models that can solve simple mathematical problems [25,30]. Innovation from that area of research could inspire new models that can detect more advanced connections between pairs of equations.

Ultimately the goal is to have a running search system, which offers new exciting research possibilities in learning from logged interactions and hopefully provides the community a new tool for efficient literature search.

Acknowledgment. Parts of this work are based on the results of an undergraduate group project, we thank its participants Abdullah, Jan, Jonas, Lars, Marc, Marcel, Omar, Oskar, Sven and Xiazhe for contributing to building a prototype. Part of the work on this paper has been supported by Deutsche Forschungsgemeinschaft (DFG) within the Collaborative Research Center SFB 876 "Providing Information by Resource-Constrained Analysis", project A1. This research has been funded by the Federal Ministry of Education and Research of Germany as part of the competence center for machine learning ML2R (01|S18038A).

References

1. Balntas, V., Riba, E., Ponsa, D., Mikolajczyk, K.: Learning local feature descriptors with triplets and shallow convolutional neural networks. In: Wilson, R.C., Hancock, E.R., Smith, W.A.P. (eds.) Proceedings of the British Machine Vision Conference (BMVC), pp. 119.1–119.11. BMVA Press (2016)
2. Deng, Y., Kanervisto, A., Ling, J., Rush, A.M.: Image-to-markup generation with coarse-to-fine attention (2017)
3. Denton, E., Weston, J., Fergus, R.: User conditional hashtag prediction for images. In: Proceedings of the 21th ACM SIGKDD International Conference on Knowledge Discovery and Data Mining, pp. 1731–1740 (2015)
4. Ding, S., Lin, L., Wang, G., Chao, H.: Deep feature learning with relative distance comparison for person re-identification. Technical report (2015)

5. Gladkova, A., Drozd, A.: Intrinsic evaluations of word embeddings: what can we do better? In: Proceedings of the 1st Workshop on Evaluating Vector Space Representations for NLP, pp. 36–42 (2016)
6. Hu, X., Gao, L., Lin, X., Tang, Z., Lin, X., Baker, J.B.: WikiMirs: a mathematical information retrieval system for Wikipedia. In: Proceedings of the 13th ACM/IEEE-CS Joint Conference on Digital Libraries, JCDL 2013, pp. 11–20. ACM, New York (2013). https://doi.org/10.1145/2467696.2467699. http://doi.acm.org/10.1145/2467696.2467699
7. Janocha, K., Czarnecki, W.M.: On loss functions for deep neural networks in classification. Schedae Informaticae **25**, 1–10 (2017). https://doi.org/10.4467/20838476SI.16.004.6185. http://arxiv.org/abs/1702.05659
8. Kamali, S., Tompa, F.W.: Retrieving documents with mathematical content. In: Proceedings of the 36th International ACM SIGIR Conference on Research and Development in Information Retrieval, pp. 353–362. ACM (2013)
9. Koren, Y., Bell, R., Volinsky, C.: Matrix factorization techniques for recommender systems. Computer **42**(8), 30–37 (2009). https://doi.org/10.1109/MC.2009.263. http://www2.research.att.com/~volinsky/papers/ieeecomputer.pdf
10. Krishna, A., Brendan, M., Natarajan, N.: Learning from binary labels with instance-dependent noise. Mach. Learn. **107**(8), 1561–1595 (2018). https://doi.org/10.1007/s10994-018-5715-3
11. Le, A.D., Nakagawa, M.: Training an end-to-end system for handwritten mathematical expression recognition by generated patterns. In: 2017 14th IAPR International Conference on Document Analysis and Recognition (ICDAR), vol. 1, pp. 1056–1061. IEEE (2017)
12. Le, Q., Mikolov, T.: Distributed representations of sentences and documents. In: International Conference on Machine Learning - ICML 2014, vol. 32, pp. 1188–1196 (2014). https://doi.org/10.1145/2740908.2742760
13. Liu, H., Tian, Y., Wang, Y., Pang, L., Huang, T.: Deep relative distance learning: tell the difference between similar vehicles. In: 2016 IEEE Conference on Computer Vision and Pattern Recognition (CVPR), pp. 2167–2175 (2016)
14. von Luxburg, U., Williamson, R.C., Guyon, I.: Clustering: science or art? In: JMLR Workshop and Conference Proceedings, vol. 27, pp. 65–79 (2012)
15. Malkov, Y., Ponomarenko, A., Logvinov, A., Krylov, V.: Approximate nearest neighbor algorithm based on navigable small world graphs. Inf. Syst. **45**, 61–68 (2014). https://doi.org/10.1016/j.is.2013.10.006. http://www.sciencedirect.com/science/article/pii/S0306437913001300
16. Mikolov, T., Chen, K., Corrado, G., Dean, J., Chen, K., Dean, J.: Efficient estimation of word representations in vector space. CoRR abs/1301.3, pp. 1–12 (2013). http://arxiv.org/pdf/1301.3781.pdf
17. Mikolov, T., et al.: Distributed representations of words and phrases and their compositionality. In: Advances in Neural Information Processing Systems, vol. abs/1310.4, pp. 1–9 (2013)
18. Mikolov, T., Yih, W.T., Zweig, G.: Linguistic regularities in continuous space word representations. In: Proceedings of the Human Language Technologies: Conference of the North American Chapter of the Association of Computational Linguistics, Westin Peachtree Plaza Hotel, Atlanta, Georgia, USA, 9–14 June 2013, pp. 746–751 (2013)
19. Mobahi, H., Collobert, R., Weston, J.: Deep learning from temporal coherence in video. In: Proceedings of the 26th Annual International Conference on Machine Learning (ICML), pp. 737–744 (2009)

20. Nguyen, T.T., Chang, K., Hui, S.C.: A math-aware search engine for math question answering system, pp. 724–733, August 2012
21. Nguyen, T.T., Hui, S.C., Chang, K.: A lattice-based approach for mathematical search using formal concept analysis. Expert Syst. Appl. **39**(5), 5820–5828 (2012). https://doi.org/10.1016/j.eswa.2011.11.085. http://www.sciencedirect.com/science/article/pii/S0957417411016319
22. Perozzi, B., Al-Rfou, R., Skiena, S.: DeepWalk: online learning of social representations. In: KDD, pp. 701–710 (2014). https://doi.org/10.1145/2623330.2623732
23. Raja, A., Rayner, M., Sexton, A., Sorge, V.: Towards a parser for mathematical formula recognition. In: Borwein, J.M., Farmer, W.M. (eds.) MKM 2006. LNCS (LNAI), vol. 4108, pp. 139–151. Springer, Heidelberg (2006). https://doi.org/10.1007/11812289_12
24. Rose, S., Engel, D., Cramer, N., Cowley, W.: Automatic keyword extraction from individual documents. In: Text Mining: Applications and Theory, pp. 1–20 (2010). https://doi.org/10.1002/9780470689646.ch1
25. Saxton, D., Grefenstette, E., Hill, F., Kohli, P.: Analysing mathematical reasoning abilities of neural models, pp. 1–17 (2019)
26. Schnabel, T., Labutov, I., Mimno, D., Joachims, T.: Evaluation methods for unsupervised word embeddings. In: Proceedings of the 2015 Conference on Empirical Methods in Natural Language Processing, pp. 298–307, September 2015
27. Shankar, D., Narumanchi, S., Ananya, H.A., Kompalli, P., Chaudhury, K.: Deep learning based large scale visual recommendation and search for e-commerce (2017)
28. Stalnaker, D., Zanibbi, R.: Math expression retrieval using an inverted index over symbol pairs. In: Document Recognition and Retrieval XXII, vol. 9402, February 2015. https://doi.org/10.1117/12.2074084
29. Verstrepen, K.: Collaborative filtering with binary, positive-only data. Ph.D. thesis, Universiteit Antwerpen (2015)
30. Wang, L., Wang, Y., Cai, D., Zhang, D., Liu, X.: Translating math word problem to expression tree. In: Proceedings of the 2018 Conference on Empirical Methods in Natural Language Processing, Brussels, Belgium, 31 October–4 November 2018, pp. 1064–1069 (2018). https://aclanthology.info/papers/D18-1132/d18-1132
31. Wu, F., Wang, Z., Zhang, Z., Yang, Y., Luo, J.: Weakly semi-supervised deep learning for multi-label image annotation. IEEE Trans. Big Data **1**(3), 109–122 (2015). https://doi.org/10.1109/TBDATA.2015.2497270
32. Yu, L., Zhang, W., Wang, J., Yu, Y.: SeqGAN: sequence generative adversarial nets with policy gradient. In: Thirty-First AAAI Conference on Artificial Intelligence (2017)
33. Zanibbi, R., Davila, K., Kane, A., Tompa, F.W.: Multi-stage math formula search: using appearance-based similarity metrics at scale. In: Proceedings of the 39th International ACM SIGIR Conference on Research and Development in Information Retrieval, SIGIR 2016, pp. 145–154. ACM, New York (2016). https://doi.org/10.1145/2911451.2911512. http://doi.acm.org/10.1145/2911451.2911512
34. Zanibbi, R., Tompa, F.W.: The Tangent Search Engine : Improved Similarity Metrics and Scalability for Math Formula Search (Section 6)
35. Zhang, R., Lin, L., Zhang, R., Zuo, W., Zhang, L.: Bit-scalable deep hashing with regularized similarity learning for image retrieval and person re-identification. IEEE Trans. Image Process. **24**(12), 4766–4779 (2015). https://doi.org/10.1109/TIP.2015.2467315

Data-Driven Policy on Feasibility Determination for the Train Shunting Problem

Paulo Roberto de Oliveira da Costa[1]([✉]), Jason Rhuggenaath[1],
Yingqian Zhang[1], Alp Akcay[1], Wan-Jui Lee[2], and Uzay Kaymak[1]

[1] Eindhoven University of Technology, 5612, AZ Eindhoven, The Netherlands
{p.r.d.oliveira.da.costa,j.s.rhuggenaath,yqzhang,
a.e.akcay,u.kaymak}@tue.nl
[2] Dutch Railways, 3511 CA Utrecht, The Netherlands
wan-jui.lee@ns.nl

Abstract. Parking, matching, scheduling, and routing are common problems in train maintenance. In particular, train units are commonly maintained and cleaned at dedicated shunting yards. The planning problem that results from such situations is referred to as the Train Unit Shunting Problem (TUSP). This problem involves matching arriving train units to service tasks and determining the schedule for departing trains. The TUSP is an important problem as it is used to determine the capacity of shunting yards and arises as a sub-problem of more general scheduling and planning problems. In this paper, we consider the case of the Dutch Railways (NS) TUSP. As the TUSP is complex, NS currently uses a local search (LS) heuristic to determine if an instance of the TUSP has a feasible solution. Given the number of shunting yards and the size of the planning problems, improving the evaluation speed of the LS brings significant computational gain. In this work, we use a machine learning approach that complements the LS and accelerates the search process. We use a Deep Graph Convolutional Neural Network (DGCNN) model to predict the feasibility of solutions obtained during the run of the LS heuristic. We use this model to decide whether to continue or abort the search process. In this way, the computation time is used more efficiently as it is spent on instances that are more likely to be feasible. Using simulations based on real-life instances of the TUSP, we show how our approach improves upon the previous method on prediction accuracy and leads to computational gains for the decision-making process.

Keywords: Planning and scheduling · Graph classification · Local search · Train shunting

1 Introduction

Parking, matching, scheduling of service tasks and *routing* problems are common in railway networks and arise when trains are not in operation. In such cases, train units are maintained and cleaned at dedicated shunting yards (Fig. 1). The planning problem that arises from such situations is referred to as the Train Unit

© Springer Nature Switzerland AG 2020
U. Brefeld et al. (Eds.): ECML PKDD 2019, LNAI 11908, pp. 719–734, 2020.
https://doi.org/10.1007/978-3-030-46133-1_43

Shunting Problem (TUSP). The problem involves matching train units to arriving and departing train services as well as assigning the selected compositions to appropriate shunting yard tracks for maintenance. To assess the capacity of each of its shunting yards, the Dutch Railways (NS) has developed an internal simulator. This simulator is used to both determine the capacity of shunting yards as well as analyse different planning scenarios. Currently, a Local Search heuristic (LS) applying a simulated annealing algorithm [5] is used to find feasible solutions. The LS requires an initial solution as a starting point, and at the end of a run, the LS either returns a feasible or infeasible plan. The LS is more computationally efficient than the previously formulated mathematical optimisation model [14]. However, given the number of shunting yards and scenarios, the capability of improving the evaluation speed of the LS can bring significant computational gain to NS.

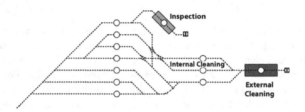

Fig. 1. "Kleine Binckhorst" in The Hague. Shunting yard with specific tracks for inspection and cleaning tasks [1]

In recent years, many studies have investigated using machine learning models to accelerate the search for optimal solutions when solving combinatorial optimisation problems [11,15,22]. In the context of train shunting, the authors of [19] consider the parking of trains as a complete (reinforcement) learning problem. In [6,21], machine learning methods are used to learn the relationship between initial solutions an a feasibility output from the LS heuristic.

In this paper, we use graph encoding [5] to represent each intermediate solution as an activity graph of maintenance activities. Activity graphs allow us to use a graph representation of the solution space and search for local discriminative features of shunting plans. We then use a Deep Graph Convolutional Neural Network (DGCNN) [23] as a feature extractor to train a model that predicts the future feasibility of each precedence graph. We formalise the approach of [21] by including a sequence of seen shunting plans during an LS run as training examples. We show how to combine the predictions with the LS to derive a policy that decides to terminate the LS run based on the sequence of intermediate solutions seen so far. This way, the train shunting simulator can decide on whether or not it should invest time in a set of solutions alongside the LS, and can determine the feasibility of given instances with higher confidence. We present a schematic view of our approach in Fig. 2, and summarise or main contributions as follows:

- We demonstrate that encoding both activity graphs of (intermediate) solutions and important domain knowledge such as time-related information

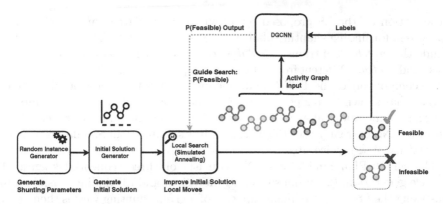

Fig. 2. Diagram depicting the proposed methodology

(see Sect. 3.2) leads to better predictions on feasibility determination of planning instances.

- We develop a learning policy that can be used along with local search on determining feasibility of a given planning instance. We show that taking into account the sequence of intermediate solutions in the search increases the prediction accuracy.

The rest of our paper is organised as follows. In Sect. 2, we describe the background information and related work. In Sect. 3, we present the proposed algorithm and show how we learn the LS outputs using the proposed DGCNN. In Sect. 4, we describe the experimental setup and the main results in comparison to the previously proposed method.

2   Background and Related Work

2.1   Train Unit Shunting Problem

Shunting yards have some specific characteristics that make the shunting problem complex and interconnected. For example, routing movements can only happen over tracks, which imposes restrictions of possible movements and turns. Furthermore, some tracks can be approached from both ends while others can only be approached from one side of a track. Also, multiple trains can be parked on the same one-end track; therefore, trains have to be parked in the order they must leave as overtaking is not possible, while specific tracks exist for cleaning and inspecting. Coupling and decoupling of train units are also important. Train units can be combined to form longer compositions, units can be of different types, but only train units with the same type can be combined. Lastly, trains have to leave at specific times to meet the transportation demands and ideally should not be delayed as this impacts the train network.

The TUSP has been shown to be an NP-complete problem [7,8]. Several works have attempted to solve variations of the TUSP, including mixed integer programming (MIP), dynamic programming and column generation methods [9]. We focus our attention on the LS proposed by [5] where a simulated annealing heuristic is proposed for finding shunting plans with service activities. The shunting plans include the *matching* of trains, *scheduling* of service tasks, assignment to *parking* tracks and *routing*. Different from other exact approaches, the algorithm integrates all the components of the TUSP simultaneously rather than sequentially. The LS heuristic has shown better performance on real-world instances when compared to a MIP formulation [5] as well as being able to handle larger instances. More important, NS currently uses this heuristic in its Shunt Plan Simulator to define the capacity of its service sites.

The Shunt Plan Simulator at NS consists of three sequential stages: (1) instance generation, (2) initial solution generation, and (3) finding feasible solutions using the LS. The maximum capacity of a given shunting yard is then determined by repeatedly running the local search heuristic with different instances and scenarios. After a number of runs, the simulation converges towards a number of train units for which the heuristic can solve at least 95% of the instances. The capacity of a shunting yard is defined as the number of train units it can serve during a 24-h period.

The instance generator derives instances for the TUSP automatically. Instances can be generated for each shunting yard individually based on a day schedule. Examples of parameters are number of train units, arrival/departure distributions and service tasks. The output of the instance generator is a set of arriving trains (AT), a set of departing trains (DT) and a set of service tasks (ST) for each train unit. For both AT and DT, train compositions, train units and arrival/departure time are specified. For each train unit, a list of ST is specified for the time they are present on the service site. Trains can be composed of one or more train units of the same type, which are a set of carriages that form a self-propelling vehicle. The same unit type can have multiple sub-types, where the sub-type indicates the number of carriages.

The output of the instance generator serves as input for the initial solution generator. The algorithm of Hopcroft-Karp [10] is used to produce a matching between arriving and departing train units. Next, a service task schedule is greedily constructed to form an initial solution. Note that, in general, initial solutions are not feasible, as they may violate temporal or routing constraints. After the initial solution is found, the LS applies 11 local search operators to move through the search space. Intermediate random restarts are used if no improvement can be found for a specified running time. The LS ends when a feasible solution has been found or when a maximum running time is reached. A detailed explanation of the heuristic can be found in [5].

2.2   Graph Classification

A shunting plan can be modelled as an *activity graph*. An activity graph contains all the activities that have to be completed during a plan. Moreover, it represents the dependencies and activity order via a directed graph. Figure 3 depicts an activity graph of a shunting plan. The activities nodes, including Arrival (A), Service (S), Parking (P), Movement (M) and Departure (D), are connected by edges indicating the precedence relationships. Corresponding train units are assigned to activities nodes representing the complete shunting plan. Given the graph structure that arises from shunting plans, we relate our problem setup to that of graph classification.

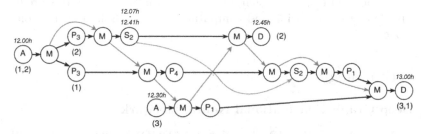

Fig. 3. The activity graph of a shunting plan. A train unit number is encoded in brackets. Activity nodes are encoded with starting and ending times. Black edges represent the order of operations of train units. Blue edges represent the order of the movements and green edges indicate which service task is completed first. Activity nodes encode specific service tasks and parking tracks as a subscript [21] (Color figure online)

Previously proposed methods in graph classification can be subdivided into graph kernel methods and topological methods. Graph kernels measure the similarity between graphs by directly comparing substructures within graphs. For example, [20] presented a family of graphs kernels using the Weisfeiler-Lehman (WL) test of isomophormism to extract graph features. Results show that the features can capture node and topological information and are competitive in comparison to other graph classification methods. On the other hand, topological methods extract features directly from graphs. Such features can represent either local (e.g. node degrees) or global (e.g. number of nodes) information about an input graph. The extracted features can be combined to create a multidimensional input vector to a machine learning algorithm [2–4]. More recently, methods that can extract useful features directly from graph representations without computing graph kernels or topological features have been proposed. Current state-of-the-art results have been achieved using Convolutional Neural Networks (CNN) tailored to extract graphs features automatically. Such methods showed competitive performance against other graph kernel algorithms [13,17,23].

For the TUSP, a topological method [6] has been proposed to extract local and global features from initial solutions. The features are then used to predict the feasibility of an initial solution using several machine learning algorithms. Results show that time-related features are the most import for prediction accuracy in the tested data. Later, [21] uses a DGCNN [23] to extract graph features (node classes) directly from the activity graphs of initial solutions without incurring in manual feature engineering. The results show that the DGCNN can achieve similar performance when compared to [6], suggesting that the DGCNN model is able to extract useful features from shunting plans.

Our work builds upon the work of [21] as to generalise the feasibility prediction to an arbitrary graph during the LS run. We improve on the original model and use the DGCNN to extract node and time features (see Sect. 3.2) from the shunting plans. Lastly, we provide a generalisation of the algorithm and show that we can use it to predict the feasibility of a given plan in a local search run at each iteration. This modification allows for more saved time as a prediction can be made at each iteration and computation can be halted on unpromising search space.

3 Methodology

3.1 Deep Graph Convolutional Neural Network

A Deep Graph Convolutional Neural Network (DGCNN) [23] accepts graphs of arbitrary structure as inputs. It aims at extracting useful deep features characterising the information encoded in a graph and determining how to sequentially read a graph in a meaningful and consistent order. Graph convolution layers are used to extract local substructure features and define a consistent node ordering. The convolution layers mimic the behaviour of the Weisfeiler-Lehman Subtree Kernel [20] and the Propagation Kernel [16] which are commonly used to extract graph features in classification tasks. To sequentially read graphs in a consistent order, a *SortPooling* layer sorts the nodes under a predefined order and unifies input sizes. The layer achieves a fixed length representation of a graph that is later combined with traditional convolutional and dense layers to map the inputs to an output class. Empirical results have shown that the DGCNN achieved state-of-the-art performance on several graphs classification tasks. In our work, we use a slightly modified version of the DGCNN to extract features from shunting plans.

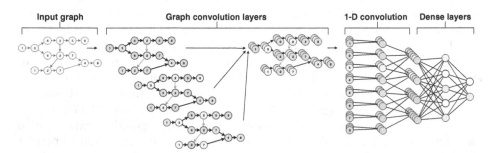

Fig. 4. The DGCNN architecture for shunting plans adapted from [23]. An input graph of arbitrary structure is first passed through multiple graph convolution layers where node labels are propagated between neighbours, visualised as different colours. Node features are then passed to traditional CNN structures [21]

3.2   Graph Convolution of Shunting Plans

We denote a graph representation of a shunting plan as a graph G represented by $G = (V, E)$ where V represents the set of nodes and E represents the set of edges on the graph. We use n to determine the total number of nodes in a graph. Moreover, our nodes encode eight different activities in a shunting plan, these activities are represented as node labels. The original representation is modified to include more information about the graphs. We include specific types of activities to effectively exploit the second localized graph convolution of the DGCNN which involves appending node labels of neighbouring nodes.

Our shunting plans contain, among others, Parking (P) and Service (S) activity nodes. Similar to [21], we encode information on P and S activities by appending extra information to the nodes. The specific parking and services tracks are appended to the respective nodes to encode more information about the moves. In the topological model of [6], temporal features are deemed important to extract useful information from scheduling plans. In particular, the time between train arrivals and service tasks are the most important features to predict feasibility, as shown in [6]. Therefore, to aggregate more temporal information from time features for each activity node in a plan, we also encode the following time-related features:

- $x_s \in \mathbb{R}^n$: *time between the current activity and the start of the plan.*
- $x_e \in \mathbb{R}^n$: *time between the current activity and the end of the plan.*
- $x_d \in \mathbb{R}^n$: *activity duration.*
- $x_a \in \mathbb{R}^n$: *average time between an activity and all its adjacent activity nodes.*

We denote a 0/1 symmetric adjacency matrix of a graph as A. We use $X \in \mathbb{R}^{n \times c}$ to denote a graph's node information matrix with each row representing a node and a c-dimensional feature vector. Our features correspond to both node labels and to time features. As proposed by [23] we stack multiple graph convolutions of the form:

$$Z^{t+1} = f(\tilde{D}^{-1}\tilde{A}Z^t W^t) \tag{1}$$

where $Z^0 = X$, $\tilde{A} = A + I$ is the adjacency matrix of the graph with self-loops, $\tilde{D}$ is its diagonal degree matrix with $\tilde{D}_{ii} = \sum_j \tilde{A}_{ij}$, $W^t \in \mathbb{R}^{c_t \times c_{t+1}}$ is a matrix of trainable convolution parameters and c_t are the convolution channels. f is a nonlinear activation function, $Z^t \in \mathbb{R}^{n \times c_t}$ is the output activation matrix and t represents the t-th convolution layer. After multiple graph convolution layers (Eq. 1), the outputs are combined to generate multiple feature channels for a given shunting plan graph. We concatenate the output of h graph convolution layers horizontally to form a concatenated output, written as $Z^{1:h} \in \mathbb{R}^{n \times \sum_1^h c_t}$. Unlike [23] we do not implement the *SortPooling* layer as our graphs already represent an ordered shunting plan. However, we unify the output tensor in the first dimension from n to k. After, several 1-D convolution and MaxPooling layers are concatenated to a dense layer and an output layer to form the output. A chart view of the graph convolutions is shown in Fig. 4.

3.3   Learning Feasibility Using Local Search

To learn the future feasibility of a given shunting plan, we generate instances with a number of trains τ, and run the LS procedure for each instance for a predefined maximum running time r. We denote as L the total number of runs of the LS procedure where l represents the l-th LS run for $l = 1, ..., L$. Thus, L is a parameter of the LS and has to be selected depending on the problem instance. For each LS run, we generate graphs G_i where $i = 0, .., N_l$, where N_l is the total number of graphs for the l-th LS run and G_0 is the initial solution.

For each run of the LS an associated class can be retrieved at the end of the procedure representing either a feasible (1) or infeasible solution (0). Moreover, each graph G_i can have its corresponding class $y_i \in \{0, 1\}$ according to the number of look-ahead iterations W considered. That is, after each LS run, a graph G_i in the sequence of solutions of the LS will have y_i defined by the feasibility of the solution $G_{min\{N_l, W+i\}}$. The parameter W is a hyper-parameter of the proposed method, and when $W \geq N_l$ all the graphs in a run will have as output class the feasibility of the final solution of the LS.

Algorithm 1: General Graph Feasibility Classification

Output: Feasibility Prediction $\hat{y}_{test}$
Input: Local Search (LS), Look-ahead Window (W), r, L, DGCNN, e, b
for $l \leftarrow 1$ **to** L **do**
    Generate G_0, $i \leftarrow 0$;
    while *running time* $\leq r$ **do**
        if G_i *is feasible* **then stop**;
        $G_{i+1} \leftarrow$ LS(G_i);
        $i \leftarrow i + 1$;
    end
    $N_l \leftarrow i$
    for $i \leftarrow 0$ **to** N_l **do**
        $X_i \leftarrow$ ExtractFeatures(G_i);
        if $G_{min\{N_l, W+i\}}$ *is feasible* **then** $y_i \leftarrow 1$;
        else $y_i \leftarrow 0$;
    end
    $X_l, y_l \leftarrow$ Concatenate($X_0, ..., X_{N_l}$; $y_0, ..., y_{N_l}$);
end
$\{X_{train}, y_{train}\}_{j=1}^{m}, \{X_{test}, y_{test}\}_{j=1}^{m'} \leftarrow$ Balance($X_1, ..., X_L$; $y_1, ..., y_L$);
while *number of epochs* $\leq e$ **do**
    for $j \leftarrow 0$ **to** $\lfloor m/b \rfloor$ **do**
        $\tilde{X}, \tilde{y} \leftarrow$ SelectBatch(X_{train}, y_{train});
        TrainDGCNN($\tilde{X}, \tilde{y}$);
    end
end
$\hat{y}_{test} \leftarrow$ PredictDGCNN(X_{test});

We denote the number of nodes in a graph G_i as n_i, and extract c node labels and temporal features from each graph G_i to form an input matrix $X_i \in \mathbb{R}^{n_i \times c}$. Then, we collect $N_l + 1$ (including the initial solution) matrices X_i, to form tensors $\boldsymbol{X}_l$ where each row is a matrix X_i. Similarly, we collect classes y_i to form $\boldsymbol{y}_l \in \mathbb{Z}_2^{(N_l+1) \times 1}$. Then, we run L Local Search procedures and concatenate instances $\boldsymbol{X}_l$ and $\boldsymbol{y}_l$ to form $\boldsymbol{X}$ with $N_L = \sum_{l=1}^{L} N_l + 1$ matrices X_i, and $\boldsymbol{y}$ with N_L rows, each containing a binary class. Next, we separate the data between training $\{\boldsymbol{X}_{train}, \boldsymbol{y}_{train}\}_{j=1}^{m}$ and testing examples, $\{\boldsymbol{X}_{test}, \boldsymbol{y}_{test}\}_{j=1}^{m'}$. However, to avoid biasing the DGCNN towards any given instance, we randomly select the same number of graphs from any given instance (LS run) l. We proceed to undersample the majority class until we get m training and m' testing examples. During training, we randomly select b training examples X_i and y_i, in mini-batches of data and pass as inputs to the modified DGCNN algorithm. Finally, we train the network to classify between feasible and infeasible solutions until we observe a total number of epochs e. The proposed feasibility classification algorithm is shown in Algorithm 1.

4   Results

In this section, we first present the experimental setups and the data used in the evaluations. We then evaluate the performance of the proposed method in predicting the feasibility of an initial solution. Next, we generalise the model to consider an arbitrary graph in the local search solution sequence. Also, we show that the proposed method can be used in combination with the local search to escape unpromising search areas. Finally, we estimate the difference in running time with and without the DGCNN predictions.

4.1   Setup of Experiments

Data Generation. We generate data instances from the instance generator in the shunt plan simulator. The instance generator can be specified according to a set of input parameters based on the day-to-day schedule at the given service site. The most important parameters include: (1) number of train units, (2) different train unit types and sub-types, (3) probability distributions of arrivals per unit type, and (4) set of service tasks including duration. We generated 1,489 instances for training purposes and 1,143 instances for testing purposes, i.e. 2,632 instances in total, with varying initial random seeds. We ran the shunting plan simulator for the same amount of time (three days) to generate both training and testing instances, with the difference in numbers being the difficulty of solving the instances and machine running time. All instances were generated with 21 train units based on the "average" service site "Kleine Binckhorst" operated by NS. The amount of train units $\tau = 21$ has been purposely chosen as an increasing number of train units increases the difficulty in finding feasible solutions. As seen in previous works [6,21], 21 trains yields a balanced yet challenging feasibility problem. Initial solutions were created for all instances and the LS procedure was applied to search for feasible solutions. The maximum running time allowed for LS is set to $r = 300$ s. We selected the remaining input parameters under "normal operation" conditions, that is: two types of train units, two different sub-types (6 and 4 units), three service tasks (technical maintenance A/B and internal cleaning) and arrival/departure distributions matching real-world scenarios.

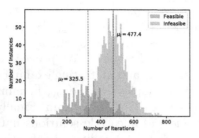

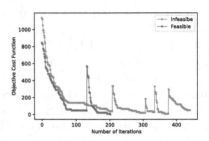

Fig. 5. Distribution and mean values of number iterations for feasible and infeasible solutions

Fig. 6. Objective function of the LS versus number of iterations for one feasible and infeasible example

Among generated instances for training, 1,081 (72%) are infeasible at the end of the LS run, while 408 (28%) are considered feasible. In Fig. 5, we show the distribution of the number of iterations of the local search for feasible and infeasible instances. As can be noted from the distributions, our experimental setup is very challenging (imbalanced), i.e. it is hard for the LS to find feasible solutions in the maximum allowed running time. The main reasons for the difficulty in our dataset are related to the increased number of conflicts considered in the problem instance. Therefore, our model is faced with a much harder problem then previous classification tasks for the same number of train units [6,21]. Moreover, the LS also performs random moves as internal restarts when it cannot move to a better solution within a determined time limit (30 s). A typical plot of the cost function over time for a feasible and infeasible solution is shown in Fig. 6. This stochastic behaviour of the search procedure makes it specially challenging to predict feasibility even when solution are "close" to feasibility.

Experimental Settings. To accommodate for the imbalance between the classes, we undersample the majority class until we achieve a 50% of the examples for each class. We perform 5-fold cross validation (4 folds for training and 1 fold for cross-validation) using one training fold for manual hyperparameter search. We report the results on the testing graphs (1,143 instances). Moreover, the DGCNN is implemented with graph convolutions with channels: $32 \times 32 \times 32 \times 1$; unifying nodes in graph k: 0.6; learning rate: 1e−5; number of training epochs: 200 and batch size: 50. The remaining layers consist of two 1-D convolutional and MaxPooling layers and one dense layer implemented as described in the original paper. The dense layer has 128 hidden units followed by a *softmax* layer as output. A dropout rate of 0.5 is used after the dense layer. The hyperbolic tangent function ($tanh$) is used in graph convolution layers, and rectified linear units ($ReLU$) in the remaining layers. Stochastic Gradient Descent (SGD) with the Adam updating rule [12] were used for optimisation.

All our experiments were conducted on an Intel(R) Core(TM) i5-7200U 2.50 GHz CPU, 8 GB RAM and Nvidia GTX 1070 GPU. Implementation was done in C# for the LS procedure and in Python (3.7.1). The PyTorch [18] library (0.2.2) and a modified implementation of the DGCNN [23] were used for training the neural network architecture.

4.2   Initial Solution Classification Performance

In this section, we evaluate the classification performance of the graph classification models (Algorithm 1) trained under different settings. We consider the following settings:

- DGCNN-IS: A DGCNN using only node labels and initial solutions during training [21] (X_0 *with only node labels*).
- DGCNN-IS-T: A DGCNN with additional temporal features using only the initial solutions for training (X_0 *with additional temporal features*).
- DGCNN-MS-T: A DGCNN with additional node temporal features using the first 10% of the graphs in each instance of a LS run for training. (X_0-$X_{\lfloor 0.1 \cdot N_l \rfloor}$ *in* X_{train}, X_i *with additional temporal features*).

All models consider as class labels y_i the final feasibility status at the end of an LS run ($W = N_l$). We perform inference on the initial solutions G_0 on the test dataset. The classification results, including *accuracy* (ACC), *true positive rate* (TPR) and *true negative rate* (TNR) for the prediction models trained under different settings are displayed in Table 1. All results displayed are calculated on balanced test instances.

Table 1. Comparison between the proposed models. Adding time features improves performance by 10%.

Method	DGCNN-IS [21]	DGCNN-IS-T	DGCNN-MS-T
ACC(%)	54.10 ± 2.37	$\mathbf{60.01 \pm 1.67}$	59.96 ± 1.68
TPR(%)	52.93 ± 11.47	58.25 ± 9.10	$\mathbf{82.08 \pm 2.53}$
TNR(%)	55.28 ± 10.27	$\mathbf{60.38 \pm 7.37}$	37.86 ± 4.99

Results show that temporal features add important information for the classification of feasible instances. The model without time features (DGCNN-IS) shows a drop in performance in comparison to the results presented in [21]. This is due to more complicated instances being used, disallowing certain moves in the shunting yard. The DGCNN-IS-T achieves an improved performance of approximately 10% when compared to the DGCNN-IS model. Lastly, the DGCNN-MS-T also shows similar accuracy performance with the model trained only on the initial solution. However, it has a much higher TPR than the other models, showing that the model is biased towards predicting positive (feasible) classes, but worse at capturing infeasible instances (TNR). These results motivate us to consider a variant of the prediction model that can be used alongside the local search procedure.

4.3   Evaluation in Combination with Local Search

In this section we consider a variant of the prediction model of the previous subsection. We generalise the training of the DGCNN and show how to combine the prediction with the LS in to improve decision-making.

In the models of Subsect. 4.2, the feasibility label at the end of a LS run was used for training the DGCNN. This can be generalised by using the concept of *time-window look-ahead*: instead of looking at the label at the very end of a LS run, we look at the label of the graph that is W solutions ahead of the current one. We refer to this specification as DGCNN-MS-T-W (DGCNN using multiple solutions including temporal features looking ahead W graphs). The intuition behind this specification is to predict or score whether the graph W iterations in the future is similar to graphs that are within W iterations of being feasible. Here W controls how eager the decision-maker is to learn about feasibility (by looking ahead during a run of the LS).

It is interesting to look at the predictions of the DGCNN-MS-T-W model over various runs of the LS. For each iteration i in a run of LS, the associated graph G_i can be fed to DGCNN-MS-T-W and results in a predicted score $\phi(G_i)$. We note that the values of $\phi(G_i)$ can vary according to the problem instance considered (e.g. varying τ). Figure 7 shows the averaged (moving average over the last 10 iterations) scores $\phi(G_i)$ over the cross-validation runs of the LS for both feasible and infeasible instances. From Fig. 7 we observe the following patterns: the feasibility scores are lower for infeasible solutions when compared to feasible solutions. Moreover, scores decay over time for observed infeasible solutions, showing that the model is capturing the look-ahead prediction function. In the figure, there is no clear constant threshold value that could be derived for all iterations. Therefore, we need to look at other metrics to define an appropriate value.

The observed patterns can be used to design a simple policy that combines a trained DGCNN-MS-T-W model with the LS. For example, given an instance of TUSP, one can use the following threshold policy:

1. Start the LS with the initial solution and run it for K iterations.
2. For each iteration i where $0 \leq i \leq K$, we pass the current solution G_i to DGCNN-MS-T-W to get a feasibility score $\phi(G_i)$.
3. If an arbitrary function g of the feasibility scores $\phi(G_i)$ seen up to iteration K falls below some threshold $0 < \alpha_{IF} < 1$, we stop the LS and classify the instance as infeasible.

Algorithm 2: Threshold Policy for the TUSP Local Search

Output: Feasibility of l
Input: Local Search (LS), Trained DGCNN-MS-T-W, r, Instance: l
Generate G_0, $i \longleftarrow 0$;
while *running time* $\leq r$ **do**
    if G_i *is feasible* **then**
        $l \longleftarrow$ feasible;
        stop;
    end
    if $i \leq K$ **then**
        $\phi(G_i) \longleftarrow$ PredictDGCNN-MS-T-W(G_i);
        if $g(\phi(G_0), ..., \phi(G_i)) \leq \alpha_{IF}$ **then**
            $l \longleftarrow$ infeasible;
            stop;
        end
    end
    else
        $G_{i+1} \longleftarrow$ LS(G_i);
        $i \longleftarrow i + 1$;
    end
end

We show the general form of the policy in Algorithm 2.

The values of α_{IF} can, for example, be obtained from the analysis of Fig. 7 and can vary for different difficulties of the TUSP. While the value K can be estimated empirically using the available training data. For example, we could select K by considering the expected *number of iterations* until feasibility or based on the expected *running time* until a certain iteration. The main motivation for considering such a procedure is the expected reduction in computation time. If we have a reasonable prediction model, then computational resources are used more efficiently because we only continue the LS procedure if we are highly uncertain about (in-)feasibility.

Performance Gains in Combination with LS. To quantify the added value of a procedure like the threshold policy, we consider the following performance indicators: (1) Classification metrics such as accuracy, false positive rate, false negative rate, true positive rate and true negative rate. These metrics are important as they show how often the threshold policy comes to the same conclusion as LS. (2) Saved computational time. In those cases that the threshold policy and the LS come to the same conclusion, we can look at the running time that is saved by the threshold policy. We define the constants $K = 200$ iterations since at that point the LS has spent on average 80 s (26% of the total running time) looking for a solution. For the purpose of more stability in the predictions, we define g to be the average score between iterations 0 an K. That is, we consider as a decision point iteration K. However, other functions are possible,

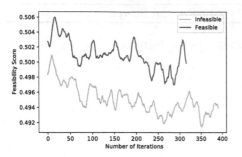

Fig. 7. Moving average over the last 10 iterations of the feasibility scores $\phi(G_i)$ averaged over cross-validation runs of the LS procedure

Table 2. Confusion matrix of one of the folds for the final classification of DGCNN-MS-T-W, with $W = 150$

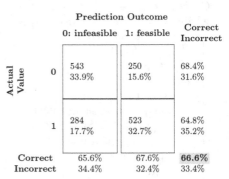

| | | Prediction Outcome | | Correct Incorrect |
		0: infeasible	1: feasible	
Actual Value	0	543 33.9%	250 15.6%	68.4% 31.6%
	1	284 17.7%	523 32.7%	64.8% 35.2%
	Correct Incorrect	65.6% 34.4%	67.6% 32.4%	**66.6%** 33.4%

for example, one could consider each $\phi(G_i)$, $0 \le i \le K$ as a decision point. In our tests, using each $\phi(G_i)$ resulted in too many disagreements between predictions and feasibility, leading to wasted computational time. Moreover, since we expect that feasible solutions will be found on average in 325 iterations, we define our look ahead window $W = 150$ to accommodate that interval with $K + W$.

In Table 2, we show the results of the confusion matrix coming from one of the folds in our experiments. The DGCNN-MS-T-W model achieves the best accuracy of all attempted models with accuracy: $64.0\% \pm 1.07$ over all 5-folds. However, this result would not be beneficial if the policy to halt the LS does not lead to saved computational time. To maintain consistency with our previous models, we define a threshold $\alpha_{IF} = 0.5$ to calculate the new running times considering the new policy. We compute the difference between the expected running time of the LS before and after the policy based on the DGCNN. We use the confusion matrix percentages from Table 2, the average running times (feasible: 157 s, infeasible: 300 s) weighted by the original imbalanced data to compute estimates based on a Markov chain. Such Markov chain arises as even after stopping the LS, we are still uncertain about the feasibility of the next time we run the LS for the same instance.

After computing the running times, we achieve a 8% reduction for a single instance, which can account for roughly 20 h in total real time. We point out that the proposed policy does not halt the LS when it is "certain" about feasibility. A change in the policy to consider such cases, can yield gains up to 30% in running times with the counterpart of losing some feasibility certainty. Lastly, we point out that the extra burden to calculate the scores $\phi(G_i)$ for the solutions only adds little computational time as it only requires scoring a small number of graphs ($K = 200$) during each LS run.

5   Discussion and Conclusion

We studied the Train Unit Shunting Problem that is faced by NS. This problem involves matching arriving train units to service tasks and determining the schedule for departing trains. The TUSP is an important problem as it is used to determine the capacity of shunting yards and arises as a sub-problem of more general scheduling and planning problems. As the TUSP is a complex problem, NS currently uses a local search (LS) heuristic to determine if an instance of TUSP has a feasible solution. In the LS, solutions are represented as an activity graph and the LS takes as input an initial solution produced by an initial solution generator.

We showed how a machine learning approach can be used in combination with a local search heuristic to improve decision-making. First, we focused on predicting feasibility of an instance of TUSP at the start of a run of the LS. A Deep Graph Convolutional Neural Network is used as a prediction model to determine feasibility of a shunting plan. We employed different training strategies such as (i) training on the initial solution; (ii) training on the initial solution including temporal features; (iii) training on multiple solutions and including temporal features. We showed that training based on (ii) achieved an accuracy of 60%, a 10% relative improvement over the baseline (i). Our second contribution expands the original models to account for arbitrary graphs during an LS run. We control the eagerness to find a feasible solution by setting the labels over a number of iterations ahead. We show that the best model achieves the accuracy of 64%. We also study how such model can be used in combination with the LS. We evaluate the effect of a policy using the proposed models and show that it can lead to reduced running times.

An interesting direction for future work is to consider other aspects in addition to feasibility in a multi-task learning approach. For example, shunting plans with a low number of crossings are generally preferred by decision-makers. Moreover, in our current work we only decide whether to keep running the LS or to stop its execution. Another direction is to design machine learning algorithms that interact directly with the LS operators and can select the most suitable operators given a certain plan.

Acknowledgements. The work is partially supported by the NWO funded project Real-time data-driven maintenance logistics (project number: 628.009.012).

References

1. Sporenplanonline. http://www.sporenplan.nl/. Accessed 20 Mar 2019
2. Aggarwal, C., Subbian, K.: Evolutionary network analysis: a survey. ACM Comput. Surv. (CSUR) **47**(1), 10 (2014)
3. Akoglu, L., Tong, H., Koutra, D.: Graph based anomaly detection and description: a survey. Data Min. Knowl. Disc. **29**(3), 626–688 (2014). https://doi.org/10.1007/s10618-014-0365-y

4. Bonner, S., Brennan, J., Theodoropoulos, G., Kureshi, I., McGough, A.S.: Deep topology classification: a new approach for massive graph classification. In: 2016 IEEE International Conference on Big Data (Big Data), pp. 3290–3297 (2016)
5. van den Broek, R.: Train Shunting and Service Scheduling: an integrated local search approach. Master's thesis, Utrecht University (2016)
6. Dai, L.: A machine learning approach for optimization in railway planning. Master's thesis, Delft University of Technology, March 2018
7. Freling, R., Lentink, R.M., Kroon, L.G., Huisman, D.: Shunting of passenger train units in a railway station. Transp. Sci. **39**(2), 261–272 (2005)
8. Haahr, J., Lusby, R.M.: Integrating rolling stock scheduling with train unit shunting. Eur. J. Oper. Res. **259**(2), 452–468 (2017)
9. Haahr, J.T., Lusby, R.M., Wagenaar, J.C.: Optimization methods for the train unit shunting problem. Eur. J. Oper. Res. **262**(3), 981–995 (2017)
10. Hopcroft, J.E., Karp, R.M.: An $n^{5/2}$ algorithm for maximum matchings in bipartite graphs. SIAM J. Comput. **2**(4), 225–231 (1973)
11. Khalil, E., Dai, H., Zhang, Y., Dilkina, B., Song, L.: Learning combinatorial optimization algorithms over graphs. In: Advances in Neural Information Processing Systems, pp. 6348–6358 (2017)
12. Kingma, D.P., Ba, J.: Adam: a method for stochastic optimization. arXiv preprint arXiv:1412.6980 (2014)
13. Kipf, T., Welling, M.: Semi-supervised classification with graph convolutional networks. CoRR (2016)
14. Kroon, L.G., Lentink, R.M., Schrijver, A.: Shunting of passenger train units: an integrated approach. Transp. Sci. **42**(4), 436–449 (2008)
15. Lombardi, M., Milano, M.: Boosting combinatorial problem modeling with machine learning. In: IJCAI 18, pp. 5472–5478 (2018)
16. Neumann, M., Garnett, R., Bauckhage, C., Kersting, K.: Propagation kernels: efficient graph kernels from propagated information. Mach. Learn. **102**(2), 209–245 (2015). https://doi.org/10.1007/s10994-015-5517-9
17. Niepert, M., Ahmed, M., Kutzkov, K.: Learning convolutional neural networks for graphs. CoRR (2016)
18. Paszke, A., et al.: Automatic differentiation in pytorch (2017)
19. Peer, E., Menkovski, V., Zhang, Y., Lee, W.J.: Shunting trains with deep reinforcement learning. In: 2018 IEEE International Conference on Systems, Man, and Cybernetics (SMC), pp. 3063–3068. IEEE (2018)
20. Shervashidze, N., Schweitzer, P., Leeuwen, E.J.V., Mehlhorn, K., Borgwardt, K.M.: Weisfeiler-Lehman graph kernels. J. Mach. Learn. Res. **12**, 2539–2561 (2011)
21. van de Ven, A., Zhang, Y., Lee, W., Eshuis, R., Wilbik, A.: Determining capacity of shunting yards by combining graph classification with local search. In: ICAART - Volume 2, pp. 285–293 (2019)
22. Verwer, S., Zhang, Y., Ye, Q.C.: Auction optimization using regression trees and linear models as integer programs. Artif. Intell. **244**, 368–395 (2017)
23. Zhang, M., Cui, Z., Neumann, M., Chen, Y.: An end-to-end deep learning architecture for graph classification. In: AAAI 18, pp. 4438–4445 (2018)

Automated Data Transformation with Inductive Programming and Dynamic Background Knowledge

Lidia Contreras-Ochando[1(✉)], Cèsar Ferri[1], José Hernández-Orallo[1],
Fernando Martínez-Plumed[1], María José Ramírez-Quintana[1],
and Susumu Katayama[2]

[1] Valencian Research Institute for Artificial Intelligence (vrAIn),
Universitat Politècnica de València, Valencia, Spain
{liconoc,jorallo,mjramirez}@upv.es, {cferri,fmartinez}@dsic.upv.es
[2] University of Miyazaki, Miyazaki, Japan
skata@cs.miyazaki-u.ac.jp

Abstract. Data quality is essential for database integration, machine learning and data science in general. Despite the increasing number of tools for data preparation, the most tedious tasks of data wrangling –and feature manipulation in particular– still resist automation partly because the problem strongly depends on domain information. For instance, if the strings "17th of August of 2017" and "2017-08-17" are to be formatted into "08/17/2017" to be properly recognised by a data analytics tool, humans usually process this in two steps: (1) they recognise that this is about dates and (2) they apply conversions that are specific to the date domain. However, the mechanisms to manipulate dates are very different from those to manipulate addresses. This requires huge amounts of background knowledge, which usually becomes a bottleneck as the diversity of domains and formats increases. In this paper we help alleviate this problem by using inductive programming (IP) with a dynamic background knowledge (BK) fuelled by a machine learning meta-model that selects the domain, the primitives (or both) from several descriptive features of the data wrangling problem. We illustrate these new alternatives for the automation of data format transformation, which we evaluate on an integrated benchmark and code for data wrangling, which we share publicly for the community.

Keywords: Inductive programming · Data wrangling automation · Declarative programming languages · Dynamic background knowledge

This research was supported by the EU (FEDER) and the Spanish MINECO RTI2018-094403-B-C32, and the Generalitat Valenciana PROMETEO/2019/098. L. Contreras-Ochando was also supported by the Spanish MECD (FPU15/03219). J. Hernández-Orallo is also funded by FLI (RFP2-152). F. Martínez-Plumed was also supported by INCIBE (Ayudas para la excelencia de los equipos de investigación avanzada en ciberseguridad), the European Commission (JRC) HUMAINT project (CT-EX2018D335821-101), and UPV (Primeros Proyectos de Investigación PAID-06-18).

© Springer Nature Switzerland AG 2020
U. Brefeld et al. (Eds.): ECML PKDD 2019, LNAI 11908, pp. 735–751, 2020.
https://doi.org/10.1007/978-3-030-46133-1_44

1   Introduction

Data science must integrate data from very different data sources (e.g., databases, repositories, webs, spreadsheets, documents, etc.). Rarely does this data come in a clean, consistent and well-structured way. Data wrangling, or data munging, is a process that usually involves data manipulation tasks that are repetitive, tedious and very time-consuming, such as transforming data into another format that can be properly processed and that makes the whole process more reliable [14]. Table 1 shows some data gathered in different formats, depending on the user's geographical region. Note that converting the (non-standardised) data from each column into a unified format needs a non-negligible manual effort.

Table 1. Example of personal data in different standard formats.

Name	Address	Phone	Date & Time
Alejandro Pala C.	C/Jose Todos, 22	+34 465 698	03/04/17 19:39
Clau Bopper	Rua bolog, 136	1195546	27/06/2017 22 h 56
Srta. Maria Garcia	Av. Del Mar 14, piso 6, 12	659332	4 octubre 2017 10:20
Dr Lauren Smith	Flat 5, Royal Court, Coventy	748526	30 October 2017 9:45
Sabrina Bunha P.	Rua Beni, 365, Alegre	+55 51 987	27/11/2017 07 h 05
Mr David Bozz	88 Lane of trees, Texas 77925	8259744	10/2/2018 12:30 PM
Lara Alsi	Av. Grande 2325 7p	54-12-3652	25/2/2018 17.00

Recently, some tools have shown powerful skills in automating data wrangling tasks. Concretely, Inductive Programming (IP) [7,10] has been successfully applied to data wrangling problems. IP learns programs from a few examples possibly using declarative background knowledge (BK). From a machine learning (ML) point of view, the BK can be seen as a kind of bias, which is usually composed of a set of auxiliary primitives or concepts that can be combined to find a hypothesis that covers the data. But if this set of primitives becomes too large then the search for a suitable combination becomes huge. As usual, bias makes learning of some hypotheses easier (or possible) at the cost of other hypotheses. In general terms, *every problem becomes easy with appropriate background knowledge*. As a consequence, *the solution lies in finding this background knowledge*.

Consider Table 2. The difficulty of this problem lies in the different date formats, where the day can be the first, second or third number, and these numbers can be delimited by different symbols. A system based only on basic string transformations may never find the right solution using only one example since it does not know what the real problem is: extracting the first number? The first two digits? Or everything before any symbol? We must know how dates work, their constraints and how they are usually represented. We need BK.

Table 2. Example of a dataset with an input column composed of dates under very different formats and the output where the day of the month is extracted.

Id	Input	Output	Id	Input	Output
1	25-03-74	25	4	06 30 1975	30
2	03/29/86	29	5	25-08-95	25
3	1998/12/25	25	6	...	...

In order to automate this process, the system (1) must recognise that it is handling names, dates or any other domain and (2) must have a sufficiently rich set of functions to deal with that particular domain. This size of the BK (the number of primitives) is known as *breadth* (b), while the minimum number of such primitives that have to be combined in the solution is known as *depth* (d). If we only provide very general primitives, d would increase considerably. However, as more kinds of domains are required, the library would become very large, and hence b. Clearly, both depth and breadth highly influence the hardness of the problem, jointly with the number of examples, n. Actually, for theory-driven induction, this hardness strongly depends on d and b, in a way that is usually exponential, $O(b^d)$ [6,12], with n being mostly irrelevant (indeed, most problems are solved from just one example). How can we keep both, and especially b, at very low levels?

In this paper, we propose to control the depth and breadth of the inductive inference problem by using *dynamic background knowledge* for each problem. We do this in three different ways. First, we structure the BK into specific subsets (domains) and select the most appropriate one. Second, we build a ranker that selects the most appropriate primitives depending on the problem. In both cases we use off-the-shelf ML techniques applied to a set of meta-characteristics based on the syntax of the inputs to be processed. Finally, we perform a combination of both approaches. As we will see, these approaches find a good trade-off between knowledge breadth and the solution depth. As a result, we solve effectively and efficiently a wide range of data wrangling manipulation problems, with the user just providing one example. For assessing the approaches, we introduce a new data wrangling benchmark consisting of a number of data transformation examples from the literature and others new problems.

This paper presents general ideas that go well beyond the particular use of IP to data science or other data manipulation applications. Overall, this paper contains four main contributions: (1) we show that the required breadth and depth for a particular theory-driven inductive inference problem can be minimised through the appropriate selection of primitives in the BK; (2) we propose several strategies to *dynamically* select or construct this appropriate BK automatically following the idea of detecting the best specialised functions according to the context of the particular problem to solve; (3) we develop and apply this schema to the important problem of data wrangling, which take a relevant portion of many data science applications; (4) we provide an open benchmark for further progress, replicability and comparison in this area. The paper is organised as follows. Section 2 summarises relevant related work. Section 3 addresses the problem of automating data wrangling with an IP system. Section 4 describes our approach for handling the BK. The experimental evaluation is included in Sect. 5. Finally, Sect. 6 closes the paper with the conclusions and future work.

2   Related Work

Data wrangling is one scenario, among many others in data science and elsewhere, where learning must be done from very few examples. In these cases, the transfer or use of previous knowledge must impose a strong bias to make the problem solvable. In particular, the term 'inductive bias' refers to the assumptions a learning system does to prioritise some hypotheses over others [19]. In approaches where the hypothesis combines primitives or concepts, the inductive bias has the aim of adapting the depth –how many primitives or elements are needed– and breadth –how many choices there are in the librariy of components– of the learning process. Thus, with no alteration of the search procedure, the BK can be used to produce a bias on learning. However, as the BK grows to reduce the depth d for more and more problems, the search becomes intractable because of the growth of the breadth b. This problem has been analysed in incremental and lifelong learning scenarios [6,18,20]. The general idea is to combine the hypothesis generation process with a forgetting mechanism to limit the amount of BK that must take part in learning. The results shown in [25] suggest the usefulness of a measure of relevance on the BK to guide the search over programs relying on expert knowledge. In a recent work [17], the idea of ranking the functions according to some text features is presented. However, in this work the authors are based on the fact that input and output strings are related. For instance, the output is a substring of the input.

As said in the introduction, IP is an important paradigm in ML that is typically (but not always) theory-driven. IP is concerned with the problem of learning programs (typically recursive) from incomplete specifications such as input/output examples [10] and BK. The use of BK facilitates some problems but suffers from the general intractability issues when it gets large. Still, the great advantage of IP is that it can infer a solution for one or a few examples. In this regard, data wrangling and data transformation is one of the applications where IP has been shown very successful (see [4,26]), because the training data is generated online by the user, and we can only have a small number of examples (the benefit of automation disappears if the user has to provide many examples). IP has been so successful for data wrangling [10] that Microsoft included some of these tools in Excel, such as *FlashFill* [8]. One of the reasons of the success of these systems is the use of domain-specific languages (DSLs) [9], which are ad-hoc for data wrangling and data manipulation situations, and reduce the search space considerably.

With the goal of automatically transforming data within a spreadsheet format, Trifacta *Wrangler* [13] generates a ranked list of suggested transformations also inferred automatically from user input, the data type and some heuristics using programming-by-demonstration techniques. More recently, Neural Program Induction has been presented as an alternative for learning string transformations. In [21] the authors introduce a system that uses Neuro-Symbolic Program Synthesis to learn programs in a DSL by incrementally expanding partial programs. They perform experiments with I/O data wrangling examples having common substrings. Although the system is able to solve many of these examples it still has some limitations. On the one hand, the use of a DSL with many expressions implies a combinatorial explosion problem when a large number of programs have to be learned. On the other hand, due to their use of common substrings, the aforementioned example about date transformation, again, is impossible to solve. As another relevant work, in [22] the authors propose NPBE (Neural Programming by Example), a Programming by Example model based on deep neural networks. NPBE induces string manipulation programs based on simple I/O pairs by inferring the right functions and arguments. For assessing the validity of the induced programs, the authors create 1000 random examples using the *same* syntax structure, which is something that does not hold in general, as we see in Table 1.

Although the use of DSL systems for data wrangling automation seems prominent, it also brings further disadvantages: (1) using DSLs implies the use of languages that are specifically defined for a particular type of data processing. (2) Whenever a new application or domain is required, a new DSL has to be created, and the inductive engine recoded for it. (3) These systems work using a basic set of transformations, normally working with unique input-output pairs but not with an entirely table, and assuming the inputs of the same domain to be in a unique format. (4) DSL-based systems usually have 'program aliasing' problems (many different programs satisfying the examples) in such a way that more examples are needed to distinguishing the right hypothesis, affecting their performance [5].

Finally, the most recent work dealing with automatic data transformation is *TDE* (Transform Data by Example) [11]. In this work a search engine for Excel that indexes program snippets from different sources in order to find relevant functions for solving problems related to data transformation using two or more examples. Even when their results are better than other existing tools, the system uses more than 50k functions and their results tend to have many different solutions that the user has to select from. As we will show in Sect. 5, this dependency on the user's manual effort results in worse results when the domain of the problem is not easy to detect.

3   Automating Data Wrangling with a General-Purpose IP System

Instead of using DSLs for each particular context (e.g., dates, addresses, etc.), we propose to use a general-purpose IP system provided with a suitable domain (set of primitives) as BK. Hence, in our approach, the automation of data manipulation tasks is done as follows: (1) we take one example which is used to select the appropriate set of primitives that form the BK; (2) one or more examples are sent to an IP system, such as a first few rows in Table 2, which are the ones a user could complete to trigger the process; (3) using the selected BK and the examples, the IP system learns a function f that correctly transforms the input of the examples to the given outputs; and (4) the function f is applied to the rest of the inputs, obtaining the new values for the output column automatically.

For the purpose of this work we have used *MagicHaskeller* [15] as the general-purpose IP system. The reasons for that choice are that *MagicHaskeller* exploits the power of the underlying language Haskell for very compact representations of the hypotheses, and it is able to solve many problems using only one example from the data. Despite this choice, the setting and the new techniques for dynamic knowledge allocation that we introduce in the next section could be replicated using other IP learning systems.

In a nutshell, *MagicHaskeller* receives an input example (x) and the expected result (y), and returns a list of functions (f) that make the values of the expressions f x and y be equal, which in Haskell notation is expressed as the Boolean predicate f x == y. *MagicHaskeller* looks for combinations of one or more functions (primitives) from its library to work like the f above. The solution (if exists) is a combination of d functions (where $d \leq d_{max}$). Trying to reduce d, we may be tempted to add a great number of powerful functions to the library. But, if so, *MagicHaskeller* will have many primitives to choose from (the breadth value b), suffering from a combinatorial explosion.

MagicHaskeller comes with 189 predefined primitives, the *default* BK, but they are insufficient for complex or very specific problems. In order to overcome this limitation, we have extended the generic BK including common string operators and nomenclature used in popular data manipulation tools (RapidMiner[1] and Trifacta[2]):

- **Constants:** Symbols, numbers, words or list of words.
- **Map:** Boolean functions for checking string structures.
- **Transform:** Functions that return the string transformed using one or more of the following operations:
  - **Add:** Appending elements to a string, adding them at the beginning, ending or a fixed position.
  - **Split:** Splitting the string into two or more strings by positions, constants or a given parameter.
  - **Concatenate:** Joining strings, elements of an array, constants or given parameters with or without adding other parameters or constants between them.
  - **Replace:** Changing one or more string elements by some other given element. This operation includes converting a string to uppercase and lowercase.

---

[1] RapidMiner Studio - Feature List: https://goo.gl/oYypMh.
[2] Trifacta Wrangler - Wrangle Language: https://goo.gl/pJHSFw.

- **Exchange:** Swapping elements inside strings.
- **Delete/Drop/Reduce:** Deleting one or more string elements by some other given parameter, a position, size or mapping some parameter or constant.
- **Extraction:** Get one or more string elements.

In total, we have added 108 functions, what we call the *freetext* BK. However, as we have seen with the example in Table 2, these functions may not be enough to solve specific tasks in some domains that would require more precise functions.

With this set of functions in the system's library, we are able to solve many common string manipulation problems. However, when data belong to a particular domain and the problem at hand ends up being a very exclusive task pertaining to that domain, more precise functions are needed in order to get correct results considering the context. We have explored the domains that are common in data wrangling problems (Excel[3] and Trifacta[4]) and we have created different Domain-Specific BKs (DSBK) according to them. We have modified *MagicHaskeller* so that a different DSBK can be used each time, as if it were selected by the user. All the DSBKs include specific functions for the domain and some *freetext* and *default* functions that can be useful for the specific problems of each domain as well. This is the final list of DSBKs [2]:

- *Dates* (23 domain-specific functions + 139 default/freetext functions): Extracting days from a substring, extending to a 4-digit full format, etc.
- *Emails* (23 domain-specific functions + 139 default/freetext functions): Getting all after the '@' symbol, append the '@' symbol, etc.
- *Names* (9 domain-specific functions + 93 default/freetext functions): Getting the initials of a name, creating a user login, etc.
- *Phones* (12 domain-specific functions + 104 default/freetext functions): Setting the prefix by country, detecting a phone in a text, etc.
- *Times* (5 domain-specific functions + 124 default/freetext functions): Change between 24/12 h format, changing time zone, etc.
- *Units* (24 domain-specific functions + 124 default/freetext functions): Convert units of length, mass, time, temperature, etc.

We use the term *global* for the set of all primitives, including *default*, *freetext* and all the domain functions above mentioned (374 unique primitives). Of course, using this massive BK the system would not work, so one simple idea is to have the user choosing the appropriate domain in order to use the DSBK associated with the domain, an idea already explored in the literature to reduce the size of the BK [16]. However, in the long term, this is giving too much responsibility to the user. In the next section, we explore a new approach for automatically selecting a dynamic set of primitives for the BK.

---

[3] Excel - Data types in Data Models: https://goo.gl/uWnbZh.

[4] Trifacta Documentation - Supported Data Types: https://goo.gl/pVlowi.

4   Dynamic Background Knowledge

If we want to automatically detect the domain of a problem as humans do, we need a way to identify the characteristics that distinguish the domains. For instance, we can see that the '@' symbol is very distinctive for emails, while dates in numeric format usually come with some specific punctuation for separating days, months and years. Following this idea, we have defined some descriptive *meta-features* that can be extracted automatically and describe different characteristics of the inputs, such as how the string starts (e.g., *start_upper*, *start_digit*, etc.), how it ends (i.e. *end_lower*, *end_digit*, etc.), which kind of symbols it contains (e.g., *has_numbers*, *has_dots*, etc.) and what structure they have (e.g., *is_onlyNumeric*, *is_onlyPunctuation*, etc.). We defined $n = 54$ meta-features in total, extracted by using regular expressions. Figure 1 shows an example of some of these characteristics extracted from dates and emails.

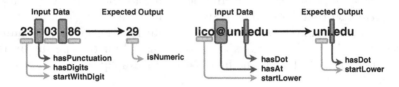

Fig. 1. An example of meta-features that can be extracted from the examples of different domains (dates and emails in the figure).

The idea of identifying domains was inspired by what a user would do to organise a large library of functions. But do we really need the notion of domain? Can we just do the selection of primitives by a ranking approach over the whole BK? As explained in the following paragraphs and illustrated in Fig. 2, the information extracted from the input examples is going to be used in different ways:

1. **Domain identification for the appropriate DSBK** (*Inferred Domain*). As we want to automate the process, the domain can no longer be provided by the user, so we need to find a way to select the right domain for each problem. To do this, we train a *domain classifier* from a dataset composed of meta-features of m examples with correctly labelled domains. So, we have $n + 1$ columns (meta-features and domain) and m rows. The classifier is learned off-line with a pool of examples.
2. **Building dynamic BK by ranking the primitives from *global*** (*Ranking*). For this, we use the descriptive features for each example as input variables and the primitives that are used in the solution of the example as labels. We generate a *primitive estimator*, with the probability that a primitive may be needed for a particular problem. Since *global* has many primitives (374 primitives), we actually have a set of binary classifiers, one for each primitive, determining whether the primitives are required or not.

3. **Building dynamic BK by ranking the primitives from the identified domain** (*Inferred Domain + Ranking*). We also explore a combination of the two previous approaches. Namely, given a new problem, we first use the *domain classifier* to identify the most convenient domain according to the extracted features. Then we rank all primitives using the *primitive estimator* but, in this case, only the functions included in the DSBK identified are taken into account. Finally, only the $k = 12$ best functions are used as BK.[5]

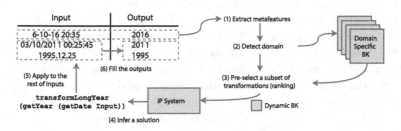

Fig. 2. Automating data wrangling with IP: process example. The first row (Input and Output) is used as an input example for the IP system. The function returned is applied to the rest of the instances to obtain the outputs.

5 Experiments

Unfortunately, at the beginning of this research there were no general benchmark or public repository to analyse the quality of new data wrangling tools [3]. In order to overcome this issue and for the experimental evaluation in this and future papers,[6] we collected most of the examples previously presented in the literature [1,8,23,24]. In addition, we generated new examples based on the problems that appear in these papers. In total, we gathered 95 datasets (with 6 instances each) with different data wrangling problems including names, phones, emails, times and unit transformations. All the datasets are published as the first *data wrangling dataset repository*, openly available at http://dmip.webs.upv.es/ datawrangling/index.html and are summarised in Table 3.

In this section, we present a summary of the results obtained by applying our system and other related systems on this repository. The complete results of these experiments can be found in [2], and the code is available at: https:// github.com/liconoc/DataWrangling-DSI.

---

[5] We observed that the maximum number of functions needed to solve the most complex problem collected in our benchmark is $k = 12$.

[6] An application example of our system can be seen on: https://www.youtube.com/ watch?v=wxFhXYyonOw.

Table 3. Datasets included in the new data wrangling repository offered for the research community.

Id	Description	Expected output
1, 2	Add punctuation	The date split by a punctuation sign
3 . . . 5	Change format	The date in one particular format
6, 7	Change Punctuation	The date in one particular format
8 . . . 10	Get Day	The day in numeric format
11, 12	Get Day Ordinal	The day in numeric ordinal format
13, 14	Get Month Name	The name of the month
15, 16	Get Week Day	The name of the weekday
17, 18	Reduce Month Name	The name of the month reduced to three letters
19, 20	Set Format	The date split in DMY format
21 . . . 23	Generate Email	An email created with name and domain
24 . . . 27	Get After At	Everything after the at symbol
28, 29	Get Domain	The domain before the dot
30	Before At	Everything before the at symbol
31, 32	Add Title	The name with a title
33, 34	Get Title	The title attached to the name, if exists
35, 36	Generate Login	A login generated using the name
37 . . . 45	Reduce name	The name reduced before the surname (s)
46 . . . 50	Add Prefix by Country	Phone numbers with the prefix of the countries
51, 52	Delete Parentheses	The list of phone numbers without parentheses
53, 54	Get Number	A phone number presented in the string, if exists
55 . . . 59	Set Prefix	The list of phone numbers with the prefix
60, 61	Set Punctuation	A phone number split by a punctuation sign
62, 63	Add Time	The time increasing the hour by the integer
64, 65	Append o'clock Time	The time appending an o'clock time
66, 67	Append Time	The time appending the integer as new component
68, 69	Convert Time	The time formatted to 24 h format
70, 71	Convert Time	The time formatted to a given format
72, 73	Convert Time	The time formatted to 12 h format
74 . . . 77	Convert Time	The time changed using time zone
78, 79	Delete Time	The time deleting the last component
80, 81	Get Hour	The hour component
82, 83	Get Minutes	The minutes component
84, 85	Get Time	A time presented in the string
86 . . . 89	Convert Units	The value transformed to a different magnitude
90, 91	Get System	The system represented by the magnitude
92, 93	Get Units	The units of the system
94, 95	Get Value	The numeric value without any magnitude

5.1   Strategies of Employing BK Functions

First, we want to determine which is the best strategy for selecting the BK to be used in data wrangling problems in such a way that the overall system is accurate and fast at the same time.

To build the *domain classifier* and the *primitive estimator*, we used the 54 descriptive meta-features and one off-the-shelf machine learning method: random forest (the learning method that obtained the best results [2]). We applied a leave-one-out cross validation approach using the 95 datasets, such that, for each fold, 94 datasets are used for training both classifiers and the remaining dataset is used for testing. As evaluation metrics we used accuracy for the domain classifier, and AUC (the Area under the ROC curve which is a standard metric for ranking performance) for the primitive estimator. The results obtained for the *domain classifier* showed that the descriptive meta-features are useful to express the information about the domain since the classifier is able to predict the domain correctly 88.6% of the times (see Table 4). Analogously, the experiments performed with the *primitive estimator* (see [2] for details) obtained an average $AUC = 0.97$, showing that it can predict accurately the functions needed to solve the problems.

Table 4. Results for the domain detection using the meta-features with different machine learning methods. The best results are highlighted in bold.

Method	Acc.	Kappa
C5.0 Tree	0.822	0.786
Neural Network	0.741	0.689
Naïve Bayes	0.458	0.350
Random Forest	**0.886**	**0.847**

The different strategies to configure the BK we experimentally analysed are:

1. *Default*: We use the default BK included in MagicHaskeller.
2. *Freetext*: We use the freetext BK (basic string transformation functions).
3. *Global*: We provide a BK composed by all the functions.
4. *User Domain*: We know (or the user gives) the correct domain (DSBK) for the problem.
5. *Inferred Domain*: We identify the domain of the problem automatically using the *domain classifier* and we select its associated DSBK.
6. *Ranking*: We rank all the functions of the global BK using the *primitive estimator*.
7. *Inferred Domain + Ranking*: We apply the *primitive estimator* to obtain the ranking of functions in the BK identified by the *domain classifier*.

We consider strategies 1, 2 and 3 as baselines since they do not constitute any improvement in the handling of the BK. Strategy 4 is included just as a human-assisted (semi-automated) reference, since it requires the manual recommendation of the appropriate DSBK. The experiments try to show whether our proposals (strategies 5, 6 and 7 introduced in Sect. 4) are able to improve the performance over the baselines, in time and accuracy. We also applied a leave-one-out cross validation using the 95 datasets, such that, for each fold from the six examples that contains the test dataset, only one random example is given to the IP system which, jointly with the *domain classifier* and the *primitive estimator*, infers a pattern that is applied to the five remaining examples. Accuracy is computed as the ratio of correctly covered examples by the induced pattern.

Table 5. Average time (in seconds) and the average accuracy for the seven strategies. The best accuracy is highlighted in bold.

	Strategy	Time	acc
1	Default	48.14 ± 28.46	0.09 ± 0.21
2	Freetext	78.77 ± 44.00	0.14 ± 0.25
3	Global	136.18 ± 67.97	0.06 ± 0.17
4	User Domain	74.23 ± 43.45	0.92 ± 0.20
5	Inferred Domain	75.45 ± 44.38	0.91 ± 0.24
6	Ranking	46.81 ± 25.51	**0.96 ± 0.12**
7	Inferred Domain + ranking	46.37 ± 26.89	0.94 ± 0.18

Table 5 shows the average time and accuracy for the seven strategies. The average times include the duration of the whole process: from the extraction of the first example to the automatic transformation of the rest of the outputs (as described in Fig. 2). Concretely, we have measured: (1) time for detecting the domain (strategies 5 and 7); (2) time for ranking the functions (strategies 6 and 7); and (3) time of running the IP system (all strategies). In each execution we have used a $d_{max} = 12$ in *MagicHaskeller*, which means that the solution will have 12 functions at most (which is the number of functions selected by the ranking estimator as explained in Sect. 4). Considering the running times of Table 5, we conclude that the proposed strategies are able to speed up the whole process, especially those using the ranking of primitives.

If we consider accuracy, the baseline approaches are poor since they do not have the appropriate functions in the BK (*default* and *freetext* strategies), or there are too many functions to explore (*global* strategy). Strategies 6 and 7 are even able to outperform strategy 4, which requires a human. Only strategy 5 remains below this human-assisted reference. One of the reasons of these results is the misclassification of the emails domain, which means that strategy 5 is using an incorrect domain and the right solution is not obtained in this case.

5.2   Comparison with Related Systems

We have also compared the performance of our Dynamic BK selection approach using the ranking strategy with other data wrangling tools, specifically *FlashFill*, *Trifacta Wrangler* and *TDE (Transform Data by Example)*.

FlashFill works in a similar way as our approach, namely, it uses one, two or more input instances to try to infer a potential solution which is then applied to the rest of examples. *TDE* also works similarly except that it needs at least two instances for learning. However, *Trifacta Wrangler* works in a slightly different fashion: it tries to discover patterns and perform actions in the entire dataset. Each of these actions can involve one change (e.g., merge two columns) and they are saved in a final *recipe*. As we have used a d_{max} value equal to 12 in Magic-Haskeller, in order to make a fair comparison with *Trifacta Wrangler*, we limit the maximum number of actions in each Wrangler recipe to 12. Additionally, although some tools are able to generate more than one solution, if they exist (as *TDE* and *MagicHaskeller* do), for the experiments we have only considered the first solution offered by the systems.

Due to space limitations, Table 6 shows some illustrative outcomes obtained by the analysed systems for some datasets (one dataset per each domain described in Sect. 3) as well as their accuracy values. The first instance (in italics) for each dataset (*input* column) is the one used for inferring the solution (except for *TDE* that, as mentioned above, needs the two first instances for learning). The complete results of this comparison between systems can be found in [2].

Flashfill works well with emails and some basic string transformations, but it fails when it has to deal with people's names, problems related to phones or times, and dates in different formats. Something similar is observed in the *TDE* results: inconsistent data formats cause *TDE* finds incorrect solutions because it is not able to detect the domain or the problem at hand. On the other hand, *Trifacta Wrangler* is able to detect some data types or domains, for instance: 'url', 'time', 'phone' since it has some predefined formats for each domain. In this way the tool is capable of solving very domain-specific problems (e.g., getting the month or the day in a date, detect an email or extract the hour of a time stamp), although with some limitations (e.g., it cannot deal with inconsistent or different formats in the same set of input data). The last problem of *Trifacta Wrangler* is that the user needs to know the language behind the tool or some regular expressions in order to solve more complex examples. On the contrary our system is able to solve most of the problems using only one example given by the user in the same way one can fill data in a spreadsheet, having into account that the user does not need to know any technical knowledge related to the system or the language behind it.

The authors of *TDE* have also created a benchmark of stackoverflow-related questions[7] that can also be used in order to test data transformation systems. We have tested our system with the 225 datasets of this benchmark in the same conditions as our system, i.e., using the first instance of each dataset as the

---

[7] TDE Benchmark: https://github.com/Yeye-He/Transform-Data-by-Example.

Table 6. Results obtained by *FlashFill, Trifacta Wrangler, TDE* and our approach (Dynamic BK with ranking strategy), on a sample of datasets of six different domains. *Output* is the expected output. The first row of each dataset is the example given to *FlashFill, MagicHaskeller* and *Trifacta Wrangler* to generate the solution. For *TDE* the two first examples are used. Green colour means correct result; Red colour means incorrect result.

Input	Output	FlashFill	Wrangler	TDE	DBK
03/29/86	*29*				
74-03-31	31	03	03	*31*	31
99/12/13	13	12	12	/1	13
11.02.96	11	02		/1	11
31/05/17	31	05	05	31	31
25-08-85	25	08	08	25	25
Accuracy:		0	0	0.5	1
Dr. Eran Yahav	*Yahav, E.*				
Prof. Kath S. Fish	Fish, K	Fish, Kath S.	S, K.	*Fish, K.*	Fish, K.
Bill Gates, Sr	Gates, B	Sr., G.	Sr, G.	Sr.	Gates, B.
George Ciprian Nec	Nec, G	Nec, C.	Nec, C.	Nec	Nec, G.
Ken McMillan, II	McMillan, K	II, M.	II, M.	II	McMillan, K.
Mr. David Jones	Jones, D	Jones, D.	Jones, D.	Jones, D.	Jones, D.
Accuracy:		0.2	0.2	0.25	1
1:34:00 PM CST	*1:34:00*				
01:55	01:55	01:55	01:55	*01:55*	01:55
3:40 AM	3:40	3:40	3:40	h3:40 A:00	3:40
07:05:59	07:05:59	07:05:59	07:05:59	h7:05:5:59	07:05:59
08:40 UTC	08:40	08:40	08:40	r8:40 U	08:40
16:15:12	16:15:12	16:15:12	16:15:12	h6:15:1:12	16:15:12
Accuracy:		1	1	0	1
1441.8 mg → *g*	*1.4418001*				
84 kg → *g*	84000.0	8.4418001		*84000.0*	84000.0
14300 ms → *s*	8700000.0	1.4418001		s	14.3
87 s → *ns*	8700000.0	8.4418001		ns	8700000.0
12.20 dg → *mg*	1220.0	1.4418001		mg	1220.0
1854 dam → *dm*	185400.0	1.4418001		dm	185400.0
Accuracy:		0	0	0	1

input example for our system. In this way, our system solves 35.1% of these datasets, using the functions that we have defined. We have to consider that this benchmarck includes domains not defined in our system and some specific problems that need ad-hoc functions in order to be solved. Having in mind the examples not solved, we can include new functions in our system, for instance, new unit conversions or the extraction of plain text from languages such as HTML.

Finally, we can also compare our system with the Neuro-Symbolic Program Synthesis system of [21], at least conceptually, as it cannot be applied directly to the data wrangling repository. As we already discussed in the related work section, Parisotto et al. describe some problems that their system is not able to solve since they require four or more *Concat* operations. One of these problems is transforming phone numbers into a consistent format. For instance, given the input "(425) 221 6767" the expected output would be "425-221-6767", and given the input "206.225.1298" the expected output would be "206-225-1298". In this case, our system is able to solve this problem by using three basic primitives of the *freetext* domain. Besides this example, our system is able to solve some other examples that this kind of system does not solve since input and output have nothing in common. For instance, given the input "2pm" the expected output would be "14:00". This example implies knowledge of times and, in this case, our system is also able to solve the problem.

The comparisons above may look non-systematic, but all these approaches use different settings and additional data, apart from a very different number of examples, which makes the results not really comparable. This is one of the reasons why the presented benchmark and the minimum requirements of our method can be set as a baseline to beat by future variants of these and other approaches.

6   Conclusions

Most data science applications require the manipulation of data that is in different formats. One key issue that humans rely on is their domain knowledge, which allows them to use primitives that are specific to the domain, when coding transformations. However, if a large number of primitives is included in the background knowledge to cover a variety of situations we get an intractable problem, as we have too many to choose from. In this paper, we have proposed different strategies that try to reduce the size of the background knowledge, based on an automated selection of the domain and/or a ranking of primitives to build the BK dynamically for each example. We have illustrated all this in the real problem of formatting data of very different domains from just one example.

To properly evaluate our system (and other existing and future data wrangling systems), We have introduced a new repository of 95 data wrangling datasets, which we make available for the community. We have performed experiments over this benchmark to illustrate the several strategies to the dynamic selection or construction of background knowledge, showing that they greatly improve accuracy and reduce time, especially strategy 6, the ranking approach.

Summing up, we have presented a data wrangling system that (1) uses off-the-shelf (and open) IP and ML techniques, (2) learns from one example, (3) is automated and does not require the user's input for the domain selection, and (4) covers a wide range of string manipulation problems, with results well above other approaches.

As future work, we plan to study the proposed strategies for other IP systems and domains to improve the system. We also want to consider other ways to solve the ranking of functions to avoid a fixed value of k, for instance, using a threshold based on the probabilities returned by the *primitive estimator*.

References

1. Bhupatiraju, S., Singh, R., Mohamed, A.r., Kohli, P.: Deep API programmer: learning to program with APIs. arXiv preprint arXiv:1704.04327 (2017)
2. Contreras-Ochando, L.: DataWrangling-DSI: BETA - Extended Results (2019). https://doi.org/10.5281/zenodo.2557385
3. Contreras-Ochando, L., Ferri, C., Hernández-Orallo, J., Martínez-Plumed, F., Ramírez-Quintana, M.J., Katayama, S.: General-purpose declarative inductive programming with domain-specific background knowledge for data wrangling automation. arXiv preprint arXiv:1809.10054 (2018)
4. Cropper, A., Tamaddoni-Nezhad, A., Muggleton, S.H.: Meta-interpretive learning of data transformation programs. In: Inoue, K., Ohwada, H., Yamamoto, A. (eds.) ILP 2015. LNCS (LNAI), vol. 9575, pp. 46–59. Springer, Cham (2016). https://doi.org/10.1007/978-3-319-40566-7_4
5. Devlin, J., Bunel, R.R., Singh, R., Hausknecht, M., Kohli, P.: Neural program meta-induction. In: NIPS, pp. 2077–2085 (2017)
6. Ferri-Ramírez, C., Hernández-Orallo, J., Ramírez-Quintana, M.J.: Incremental learning of functional logic programs. In: Kuchen, H., Ueda, K. (eds.) FLOPS 2001. LNCS, vol. 2024, pp. 233–247. Springer, Heidelberg (2001). https://doi.org/10.1007/3-540-44716-4_15
7. Flener, P., Schmid, U.: An introduction to inductive programming. Artif. Intell. Rev. **29**(1), 45–62 (2008)
8. Gulwani, S.: Automating string processing in spreadsheets using input-output examples. In: Proceedings of the 38th Principles of Programming Languages, pp. 317–330 (2011)
9. Gulwani, S., Harris, W.R., Singh, R.: Spreadsheet data manipulation using examples. Commun. ACM **55**(8), 97–105 (2012)
10. Gulwani, S., Hernandez-Orallo, J., Kitzelmann, E., Muggleton, S.H., Schmid, U., Zorn, B.: Inductive programming meets the real world. Commun. ACM **58**(11), 90–99 (2015)
11. He, Y., Chu, X., Ganjam, K., Zheng, Y., Narasayya, V., Chaudhuri, S.: Transform-data-by-example (TDE): an extensible search engine for data transformations. Proc. VLDB Endow. **11**(10), 1165–1177 (2018)
12. Henderson, R.: Incremental learning in inductive programming. In: Schmid, U., Kitzelmann, E., Plasmeijer, R. (eds.) AAIP 2009. LNCS, vol. 5812, pp. 74–92. Springer, Heidelberg (2010). https://doi.org/10.1007/978-3-642-11931-6_4
13. Kandel, S., Paepcke, A., Hellerstein, J., Heer, J.: Wrangler: interactive visual specification of data transformation scripts. In: Proceedings of the SIGCHI Conference on Human Factors in Computing Systems, pp. 3363–3372. ACM (2011)
14. Kandel, S., et al.: Research directions in data wrangling: visualizations and transformations for usable and credible data. Inf. Vis. **10**(4), 271–288 (2011)
15. Katayama, S.: An analytical inductive functional programming system that avoids unintended programs. In: Proceedings of the ACM SIGPLAN 2012 Workshop on Partial Evaluation and Program Manipulation PEPM, pp. 43–52. ACM (2012)
16. Kietz, J.U., Wrobel, S.: Controlling the complexity of learning in logic through syntactic and task-oriented models. In: Inductive Logic Programming. Citeseer (1992)

17. Menon, A., Tamuz, O., Gulwani, S., Lampson, B., Kalai, A.: A machine learning framework for programming by example. In: ICML, pp. 187–195 (2013)
18. Mitchell, T., et al.: Never-ending learning. Commun. ACM **61**(5), 103–115 (2018)
19. Mitchell, T.M.: The need for biases in learning generalizations. Rutgers Univ., New Jersey (1980)
20. Mitchell, T.M., et al.: Theo: a framework for self-improving systems. In: Architectures for Intelligence: The Twenty-Second Carnegie Mellon Symposium on Congnition, pp. 323–355 (1991)
21. Parisotto, E., Mohamed, A.r., Singh, R., Li, L., Zhou, D., Kohli, P.: Neuro-symbolic program synthesis. arXiv preprint arXiv:1611.01855 (2016)
22. Shu, C., Zhang, H.: Neural programming by example. In: AAAI, pp. 1539–1545 (2017)
23. Singh, R., Gulwani, S.: Predicting a correct program in programming by example. In: Kroening, D., Păsăreanu, C.S. (eds.) CAV 2015. LNCS, vol. 9206, pp. 398–414. Springer, Cham (2015). https://doi.org/10.1007/978-3-319-21690-4_23
24. Singh, R., Gulwani, S.: Transforming spreadsheet data types using examples. In: Proceedings of the 43rd Principles of Programming Languages, pp. 343–356 (2016)
25. Srinivasan, A., King, R.D., Bain, M.E.: An empirical study of the use of relevance information in inductive logic programming. JMLR **4**, 369–383 (2003)
26. Wu, B., Szekely, P., Knoblock, C.A.: Learning data transformation rules through examples: preliminary results. In: Information Integration on the Web, p. 8 (2012)

Demo Track

BK-ADAPT: Dynamic Background Knowledge for Automating Data Transformation

Lidia Contreras-Ochando[1]([✉]), César Ferri[1], José Hernández-Orallo[1],
Fernando Martínez-Plumed[1], María José Ramírez-Quintana[1],
and Susumu Katayama[2]

[1] Valencian Research Institute for Artificial Intelligence (vrAIn), Universitat
Politècnica de València, Valencia, Spain
{liconoc,jorallo,mjramirez}@upv.es, {cferri,fmartinez}@dsic.upv.es
[2] University of Miyazaki, Miyazaki, Japan
skata@cs.miyazaki-u.ac.jp

Abstract. An enormous effort is usually devoted to data wrangling, the tedious process of cleaning, transforming and combining data, such that it is ready for modelling, visualisation or aggregation. Data transformation and formatting is one common task in data wrangling, which is performed by humans in two steps: (1) they recognise the specific domain of data (dates, phones, addresses, etc.) and (2) they apply conversions that are specific to that domain. However, the mechanisms to manipulate one specific domain can be unique and highly different from other domains. In this paper we present **BK-ADAPT**, a system that uses inductive programming (IP) with a dynamic background knowledge (BK) generated by a machine learning meta-model that selects the domain and/or the primitives from several descriptive features of the data wrangling problem. To show the performance of our method, we have created a web-based tool that allows users to provide a set of inputs and one or more examples of outputs, in such a way that the rest of examples are automatically transformed by the tool.

Keywords: Data science automation · Data wrangling · Data transformation · Dynamic background knowledge

1 Introduction

Data science in general, and machine learning in particular, usually integrates data from very different data sources. Data usually comes messy, diverse,

This research was supported by the EU (FEDER) and the Spanish MINECO RTI2018-094403-B-C32, and the Generalitat Valenciana PROMETEO/2019/098. L. Contreras-Ochando was also supported by the Spanish MECD (FPU15/03219). J. Hernández-Orallo is also funded by FLI (RFP2-152). F. Martínez-Plumed was also supported by INCIBE, the European Commission (JRC) HUMAINT project (CT-EX2018D335821-101), and UPV (PAID-06-18).

© Springer Nature Switzerland AG 2020
U. Brefeld et al. (Eds.): ECML PKDD 2019, LNAI 11908, pp. 755–759, 2020.
https://doi.org/10.1007/978-3-030-46133-1_45

unstructured and incomplete. Data wrangling represents a daunting amount of work involving tasks such as data transformation, cleaning, parsing, etc. Despite many tasks being highly repetitive, tedious and time-consuming, they resist full automation to this day. This happens especially because the problem strongly depends on having specific domain information (that is, knowing if the data is about dates, phones, etc. and how these domains work), which requires huge amounts of background knowledge. In this paper, we tackle this problem with the aid of Inductive Programming [3], using only one example transformed by the user as input information. This input will be used to control the size of the background knowledge in two different ways. First, selecting the most appropriate domain. Second, building a ranker that selects the most appropriate primitives depending on the problem. In both cases we use off-the-shelf machine learning techniques applied to a set of descriptive syntax-based meta-characteristics from the inputs to be processed.

In order to automate data transformation process, the system (1) must recognise that it is handling one particular domain and (2) must have a sufficiently rich set of functions to deal with that particular domain. A system based only on basic string transformations may never find the right solution, firstly because they assume all the data is coming with the same structure and format, and second because when the problem at hand ends up being a very exclusive task pertaining to one domain, more precise functions are needed in order to get correct results considering the context. This particular limitation can be seen in tools such as *Flashfill* [2], for instance, when it is not able to extract the day from two dates if they are in different date formats. Another problem with tools such as *Trifacta* [4] is that they have fixed formats for each domain of data, so when a different format is presented they are not able to recognise the example belonging to the domain nor transform it into another format. Besides, *Trifacta* requires that the user knows its *Wrangle* language (a specific DSL[1]) in order to solve more complex problems that cannot be solved automatically. Finally, some systems such as [6] need examples having some common sub-strings in order to transform them, at least two output examples or they produce a list of solutions that the user has to choose from, making the whole process just partially automated.

In this paper we present a system that automates data transformations independently of their format and domain, using only one output example and with minimum user effort: the functions are applied automatically to the inputs.

2   System Overview

As humans do in the first step involving data transformation, we need a way to identify the characteristics that distinguish the domain. For instance, we can see that the '@' symbol is very distinctive for emails, while dates in numeric format usually come with some specific punctuation for separating days, months and years. To do this, we propose to use a general-purpose IP system provided with

---

[1] Wrangle language: https://docs.trifacta.com/display/SS/Wrangle+Language.

a suitable domain set of primitives as BK and descriptive *meta-features* that are extracted automatically from the examples such that they can be mapped with the domain or the primitives that are more appropriate for the example.

2.1 System Functionality

BK-ADAPT uses MagicHaskeller [5] as the underlying IP system. BK-ADAPT works as follows: (1) one output example is filled and used to select the appropriate set of primitives that form the dynamic BK; (2) using the selected BK and the example, MagicHaskeller learns a function f that correctly transforms the input of the example to the given output; and (3) the function f is applied to the rest of the inputs, obtaining the new values for the output column automatically.

The BK is composed of *basic string manipulation functions* and functions that can be useful for the specific problems of each domain as well. The list of domains for this demo is: dates, emails, names, phones, times and units. However, this list can be increased and/or include different domains. More concretely, the BK to be used for MagicHaskeller to solve one given example is dynamically generated in two different ways: (1 *Inferred Domain*) The domain is automatically detected and the correct BK is used; (2 *Dynamic BK by primitive ranking*). The BK is formed by those primitives that are more likely to be needed for solving the example. To this end, the BK-ADAPT system uses two learning modules trained using the descriptive meta-features previously extracted from the examples: a domain classifier, that predicts the domain an example belongs to, and a *primitive estimator* that estimates the probability of each primitive to be used for solving the example[2,3].

2.2 System Architecture and User Interface

BK-ADAPT has been developed as a web application which main interface simulates a spreadsheet or table with input/output text fields. In this interface, the input field is used as a way to provide the original value for the attribute we want to transform, and the output field is the result the user wants to obtain. The goal of the system is, given just one input/output example, try to fill the outputs of the rest of instances whose output fields have not been filled. The transformation process is completely automatic and transparent for the user.[4]

3 Target Users and Demonstration

As we have seen at Sect. 1, data wrangling is widely reported as an intense manual process for data scientists which manual involvement affects the time needed to finish a project or data analysis. BK-ADAPT allows the user to use the time

---

[2] The complete description of the approach can be found at: [1].

[3] The code is available at: https://github.com/liconoc/DataWrangling-DSI.

[4] A demo can be seen on: https://www.youtube.com/watch?v=wxFhXYyonOw.

in other and more important tasks. In this demo we will show some examples of data transformation from different domains that can be automatically transformed without great manually effort. An example of the problem can be seen at Table 1. The table shows data with different standards (depending on the country) that have to be adapted to a unique format.

Table 1. Example of personal data in different standard formats.

Name	Address	Phone	Date & Time
Alejandro Pala C.	C/Jose Todos, 22	+34 465 698	03/04/17 19:39
Clau Bopper	Rua bolog, 136	1195546	27/06/2017 22h56
Srta. Maria Garcia	Av. Del Mar 14, piso 6, 12	659332	4 octubre 2017 10:20
Sabrina Bunha P.	Rua Beni, 365, Alegre	+55 51 987	27/11/2017 07h05
Mr David Bozz	88 Lane of trees, Texas 77925	8259744	10/2/2018 12:30 PM

4   Conclusions

In this paper we present an inductive system to deal with the automation of data transformation tasks using only one example from the user. Different strategies have been introduced aiming at reducing the size of the BK, based on an automated selection of the domain or a ranking of primitives to build the BK dynamically for each example. A new repository of 95 data wrangling datasets has been released to the community available at http://dmip.webs.upv.es/datawrangling/, which have been used to test BK-ADAPT, illustrating how the the dynamic selection of background knowledge works. Finally, we provide a user-friendly web application to enhance BK-ADAPT usability, an thus the automation of this kind of task in the data wrangling process.

References

1. Contreras-Ochando, L., Ferri, C., Hernández-Orallo, J., Martínez-Plumed, F., Ramírez-Quintana, M.J., Katayama, S.: Automated data transformation with inductive programming and dynamic background knowledge. In: Proceedings of the European Conference on Machine Learning and Knowledge Discovery in Databases, ECML PKDD 2019 (2019, to appear)
2. Gulwani, S.: Automating string processing in spreadsheets using input-output examples. In: Proceedings of 38th Principles of Programming Languages, pp. 317–330 (2011)
3. Gulwani, S., Hernandez-Orallo, J., Kitzelmann, E., Muggleton, S.H., Schmid, U., Zorn, B.: Inductive programming meets the real world. Commun. ACM **58**(11), 90–99 (2015)
4. Kandel, S., Paepcke, A., Hellerstein, J., Heer, J.: Wrangler: interactive visual specification of data transformation scripts. In: Proceedings of the SIGCHI Conference on Human Factors in Computing Systems, pp. 3363–3372. ACM (2011)

5. Katayama, S.: An analytical inductive functional programming system that avoids unintended programs. In: Proceedings of PEPM, pp. 43–52. ACM (2012)
6. Shu, C., Zhang, H.: Neural programming by example. In: AAAI, pp. 1539–1545 (2017)

A Tool for Researchers: Querying Big Scholarly Data Through Graph Databases

Fabio Mercorio[1,2]($\boxtimes$), Mario Mezzanzanica[1,2], Vincenzo Moscato[3], Antonio Picariello[3], and Giancarlo Sperlì[3]

[1] Department of Statistics and Quantitative Methods,
University of Milano-Bicocca, Milan, Italy
fabio.mercorio@unimib.it
[2] CRISP Research Centre, University of Milano-Bicocca, Milan, Italy
[3] Department of Electrical Engineering and Information Technology,
University of Naples Federico II, Naples, Italy

Abstract. We demonstrate GraphDBLP, a tool to allow researchers for querying the DBLP bibliography as a graph. The DBLP source data were enriched with semantic similarity relationships computed using word-embeddings. A user can interact with the system either via a Web-based GUI or using a shell-interface, both provided with three parametric and pre-defined queries. GraphDBLP would represent a first graph-database instance of the computer scientist network, that can be improved through new relationships and properties on nodes at any time, and this is the main purpose of the tool, that is freely available on Github. To date, GraphDBLP contains 5+ million nodes and 24+ million relationships.

Keywords: Graph databases · Big Scholarly Data · Word embeddings

1 Introduction and Motivation

Nowadays, the number of scientific publications is increasing apace, making the network of collaborations, topics, papers, and venues more complex than ever. Not surprisingly, the term *Big Scholarly Data* has been recently coined to refer to the rapidly growing of scholarly source of information (e.g., large collections of scholarly data with million authors, papers, citations, figures, tables, as well as massive scale related data such as scholarly networks) [8]. The analysis of such data and network is useful for researchers to identify colleagues working on similar topics, to make a profile of a researcher for understanding its research interests on the basis of its academic records and scores, as well as to identify experts on a specific research area. The idea behind GraphDBLP - firstly presented in [4] - is to build-up a model of DBLP as a graph, exploiting word-embeddings to discover similarities between researchers that, in turn, can be included as relationships within the graph (see Fig. 1a).

There is a growing interest in studying and understanding network of researchers - as in the case of computer scientists - to perform influence analysis [1]; community mining [7]; recommend research experts [6]; and recently to

© Springer Nature Switzerland AG 2020
U. Brefeld et al. (Eds.): ECML PKDD 2019, LNAI 11908, pp. 760–763, 2020.
https://doi.org/10.1007/978-3-030-46133-1_46

browse scholarly data as a graph [3], just to name a few recent works. To date, GraphDBLP is the first tool that models the DBLP data as a graph database exploiting vector-space models to derive semantic similarities between publications. GraphDBLP has been deployed on top of the Neo4j graph-database, acting as a tool that anyone can query and improve over time.

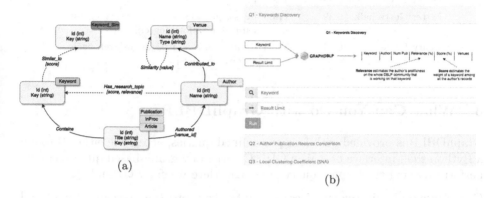

(a)

(b)

Fig. 1. (a) The DBLP Graph Model. Solid lines are relationships extracted from the DBLP XML file. Dotted lines are derived through Cypher queries on the graph. (b) Snapshot of the GraphDBLP Web-app.

2   Approach

GraphDBLP is modelled as a multigraph to allow for multiple edges to exist between two nodes. It contains 5+ million nodes and 24.7+ million relationships, enabling users to browse 3.3+ million publications authored by 1.7 million researchers on more than 5 thousand publication venues. Thanks to the use of word-embeddings, more than 7.5 thousand keywords and related similarity values were collected. The GraphDBLP data model is shown in Fig. 1a. The SIMILARITY relation estimates the similarity between two venues based on the network of authors that publish on specific venues (i.e., the CONTRIBUTED_TO relation of Fig. 1a). Then, the Jaccard index is used to compute similarities between two venues v_1 and v_2 on the basis of the authors that they have in common. Since DBLP does not explicitly provide neither topics nor abstracts of the stored publications, we decided to exploit publication titles to extract research keywords. Keywords from the Faceted-DBLP project were used as ground-truth, as it uses GrowBag graphs for identifying computer-science specific keywords [2]. Then, for each title, we computed a list of top-k most similar keywords through word2vec, using [5] to learn a sequence of 4-grams to identify SIMILAR_TO relations.

The HAS_RESEARCH_TOPIC relation was computed using the Cypher query language on the graph, computing the number of matches of the tripartite subgraph (authors)-[authored]-(publications)-[contains]-(keywords). Further details are in [4].

Table 1. Output of query Q1 - Knowledge Discovery for the keyword *knowledge_management* (top-5 items returned). Values are shown in %

Author	Relevance	Score	Venues (DBLP id)
Murray E. Jennex	0.63	46.15	[ijkm, isf, ijiscram, joeuc, amcis, hicss]
Stefan Smolnik	0.42	15.84	[hicss, wm, icis]
David T. Croasdell	0.39	41.67	[hicss]
Petter Gottschalk	0.39	17.86	[hicss, jilt, kbs, es, ijitm, eswa, eg, isf, irmj, jkm, informingscij]
Henry Linger	0.34	38.24	[ijkm, sjis, ajis, itp, jds, isdevel, pacis, amcis, icis, ecis]

3   What Can You Do with GraphDBLP?

GraphDBLP is provided with four pre-defined queries, accessible either through a Python shell interface or a Web GUI. Clearly, any graph-based queries can be performed using the Cypher query language. Here we show Q1 and Q2.

Q1: Keyword Discovery takes as input a keyword (i.e., research topic) and returns a list of authors working on that topic, along with venues where they have published their research (see Table 1). The *relevance* estimates the prolificacy of the author within the whole DBLP community that has been working on that topic, while the *score* estimates the weight of that keyword among all the author's publication records. This query is useful to perform expert finding on a given research topic and similar research fields.

Q2: Researcher Profiling takes as input the name of a researcher for extracting all the topics on which she/he has been working along her/his career (Table 2). This query is useful to profile researchers, and to discover other researchers working on similar or related topics. To this end, a list of keyword similarities is returned for each topic with the similarity value.

Scalability. A performance test was executed on a GraphDBLP instance[1] measuring the running time for Q1 and Q2. Our tests selected a random set of $k \in [10, 100, 1000, 5000]$ keywords for Q1, and authors for Q2. Results showed that the running time is acceptable even in worst cases, as GraphDBLP averagely requires 0.01 (7.9) s for executing Q1 (Q2) while it never needed more than 0.33 (32.1) s for completing Q1 (Q2).

4   Limitation and Future Work

Though we are continuously working to upgrade GraphDBLP, it already includes a range of features that motivate us to share our work with the community. With this work, we seek to encourage other researchers to use our tool, with the aim to build a shared and freely accessible network of computer scientists as a graph.

---

[1] Intel i-7 Linux Machine with 64 Gb RAM.

Table 2. Output of Q2 - Researcher Profiling for *Fabio Mercorio* (top-3 keywords and researchers). Values in %

Suggested Author			Fabio Mercorio		Keyword	Keyword Similarities
Name	Rel	Score	Rel	Score		(value) ≥ 0.6
Subbarao Kambhampati	0.64	26.85	0.05	18.52	planning	motion planning (0.6), optimal planning (0.6), planner (0.65), planning control (0.63), path planning (0.63)
Eva Onaindia	0.41	52.11				
Dana S. Nau	0.37	27.42				
Ismael Caballero	3.41	40.51	0.42	14.81	data quality	software quality (0.74), information quality (0.84), service quality (0.73), public health (0.72), data privacy (0.71), business intelligence (0.71)
Mario Piattini	2.98	4.28				
Angelica Caro	2.45	69.7				
Edmund Clarke	1.33	17.11	0.11	11.1	model checking	safety properties (0.77), state machines (0.8), abstraction refinement (0.83), reachability analysis (0.79), runtime verification (0.79), abstract interpretation (0.78), timed automata (0.78), formal verification (0.78), model checker (0.85)
Moshe Vardi	1.16	10.99				
E. Allen Emerson	0.95	29.63				

To date, GraphDBLP does not take into account citations and research abstracts. We are currently working to improve the similarity relationships by using citations and texts from the AMiner project. We are also working to provide GraphDBLP as a service through REST-APIs.

DEMO. The Demo video is accessible at https://youtu.be/eoDX-782Z8M while the source code is on Github.[2]

References

1. Chikhaoui, B., Chiazzaro, M., Wang, S.: A new granger causal model for influence evolution in dynamic social networks: the case of DBLP. In: AAAI (2015)
2. Diederich, J., Balke, W.T., Thaden, U.: Demonstrating the semantic GrowBag: automatically creating topic facets for FacetedDBLP. In: ACM/IEEE-CS Joint Conference on Digital Libraries, p. 505. ACM (2007)
3. Durand, G.C., et al.: Exploring large scholarly networks with Hermes. In: EDBT (2018)
4. Mezzanzanica, M., Mercorio, F., Cesarini, M., Moscato, V., Picariello, A.: GraphDBLP: a system for analysing networks of computer scientists through graph databases. Multimedia Tools Appl. **77**(14), 18657–18688 (2018). https://doi.org/10.1007/s11042-017-5503-2
5. Mikolov, T., Sutskever, I., Chen, K., Corrado, G.S., Dean, J.: Distributed representations of words and phrases and their compositionality. In: Advances in Neural Information Processing Systems, pp. 3111–3119 (2013)
6. Moreira, C., Calado, P., Martins, B.: Learning to rank academic experts in the DBLP dataset. Expert Syst. **32**(4), 477–493 (2015)
7. Mercorio, F., Mezzanzanica, M., Moscato, V., Picariello, A., Sperli, G.: DICO: a graph-db framework for community detection on big scholarly data. IEEE Trans. Emerg. Top. Comput. (2019). https://doi.org/10.1109/TETC.2019.2952765
8. Xia, F., Wang, W., Bekele, T.M., Liu, H.: Big scholarly data: a survey. IEEE Trans. Big Data **3**(1), 18–35 (2017)

---

[2] https://github.com/fabiomercorio/GraphDBLP.

OCADaMi: One-Class Anomaly Detection and Data Mining Toolbox

Andreas Theissler[✉][iD], Stephan Frey, and Jens Ehlert

Aalen University of Applied Sciences, Aalen, Germany
andreas_theissler@web.de

Abstract. This paper introduces the modular anomaly detection toolbox OCADaMi that incorporates machine learning and visual analytics. The case often encountered in practice where no or only a non-representative number of anomalies exist beforehand is addressed, which is solved using one-class classification. Target users are developers, engineers, test engineers and operators of technical systems. The users can interactively analyse data and define workflows for the detection of anomalies and visualisation. There is a variety of application-domains, e.g. manufacturing or testing of automotive systems. The functioning of the system is shown for fault detection in real-world automotive data from road trials. A video is available: https://youtu.be/DylKkpLyfMk.

Keywords: Anomaly detection · Machine learning · Framework · Visual analytics · Demo

1 Introduction

This paper introduces the modular toolbox OCADaMi for one-class anomaly detection. Anomaly detection (AD) refers to reporting data points that have unexpected behaviour w.r.t. a training set, user experience or pre-defined thresholds. In this work machine learning-based approaches are used. Target users are developers, engineers, test engineers, and operators of technical systems. The application-domain is manifold, e.g. manufacturing or automotive systems.

In practice, a representative set of anomalies can often not be obtained. An example is fault detection, where a representative training set would mean to know all potential faults and to have corresponding labelled data. In contrast, normal data can easily be obtained from a system in normal operation mode. As opposed to using a two-class approach, an alternative is to use a training set of normal data and classify deviations as anomalies referred to as one-class classification [5]. OCADaMi can be used for:

We thank IT-Designers GmbH and STZ Softwaretechnik for funding this research and many former associates and students for their contributions.

U. Brefeld et al. (Eds.): ECML PKDD 2019, LNAI 11908, pp. 764–768, 2020.
https://doi.org/10.1007/978-3-030-46133-1_47

1. interactive data analysis using visual analytics
2. the creation of AD-workflows that can be run, optimized and exported
3. AD using the toolbox or by integrating the workflow in own applications
4. moving towards a supervised scenario, since during operation anomalies are detected gradually improving knowledge about the previously unknown or non-representative anomaly class.

1.1 Related Work

The application of AD on automotive data was shown in [3], in sensor networks in [1] and for intrusion detection systems in [4]. The authors have previously used OCADaMi for fault detection in automotive time series [9] and for the analysis of automotive after sales data [7].

In terms of alternative tools, Dd_tools by David Tax [6] has inspired the development of OCADaMi. While [6] is a feature-rich Matlab toolbox requiring the user to program, OCADaMi offers a configurable, user-centric framework with tightly integrated visualizations. In contrast to existing applications like KNIME or Rapid Miner, OCADaMi focusses on the specific problem of anomaly detection based on a training set of normal data and is not meant to be a generic data mining toolbox.

2   The Anomaly Detection Toolbox OCADaMi

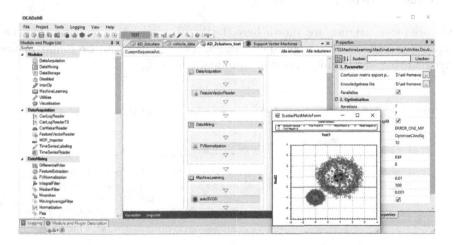

Fig. 1. Workflow with data acquisition, feature scaling and SVDD. Results are shown in the two-dimensional feature space.

OCADaMi is implemented as a modular, extensible framework in .NET, in specific in C#. The UI is implemented with Workflow foundation, Windows Presentation Foundation and WinForms and enables users to create sequential workflows by chaining the desired plug-ins to fit their custom analysis needs (see Fig. 1). OCADaMi provides techniques for supporting the user in managing the workflows and in easily reproducing the results. Detailed reports are exported with results, in- and output of plug-in, generated visualisations, and knowledgebases. Advanced visualisation plug-ins are provided. As OCADaMi is implemented as a plug-in architecture, it is easily extensible by own plug-ins. The toolbox can interop with the R environments and exchange data. The toolbox is described following the steps of CRISP-DM [10]:

Data understanding: Using advanced interactive visualisations, value ranges, outliers, and correlations in feature space can be inspected.

Data preparation: As a form of user-centric machine learning, the application allows to incorporate expert knowledge to compensate the lack of a representative and labelled two-class training set. Visual analytics enables the user to filter the data, e.g. to remove measurement errors. Different pre-processing steps like scaling, time series filtering or resampling can be applied and time series data can be transformed to alternative representations.

Modelling: Users can select from a range of one-class models like a thresholded variant of k-NN as described in [8], LOF [2], and the one-class SVM support vector data description (SVDD) [5].

Evaluation: Results can be evaluated visually or on the basis of metrics.

Deployment: The toolbox can be used or the workflow can be integrated into own applications.

3   Case Studies

Two brief case studies are shown here, both using one-class classification, i.e. exclusively training on normal data points. More details can be found in the accompanying video and in previous publications [8,9].

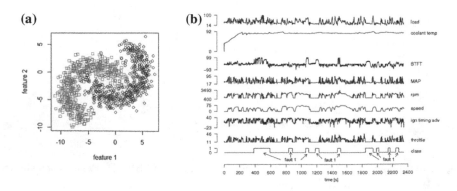

Fig. 2. Test sets of the case studies with normal data points and anomalies. (a) Case study 1: Artificial data set with banana-shaped clusters where the right cluster is the normal class. (b) Case study 2: Multivariate time series showing a recording from a vehicle road trial. Anomalies are depicted by the class label on the bottom.

3.1   Case Study 1: Two Banana Shaped Clusters

To show the functionality of OCADaMi, an artificial two-dimensional data set is used with two banana-shaped clusters with Gaussian noise. The test set is shown in Fig. 2(a) where the right cluster corresponds to the normal class that was used to train the one-class classifier. This data set simulates the typical situation where anomalies are data points outside the normal value range in one or more features.

A thresholded variant of k-NN, as described in [8], is used for anomaly detection. Classification results on the blind test set are $TPR = 96.3\%$ and $TNR = 98.0\%$, where anomalies correspond to the negative class.

3.2   Case Study 2: Real-World Data from Automotive Tests

Anomaly detection in automotive systems is highly relevant due to the increasing complexity of modern vehicles, e.g. induced by safety or comfort systems. The training data consists of recordings from test drives in normal operation mode recorded during overland drives. The recordings are multivariate time series with 8 signals, like engine load, vehicle speed, and rpm. An example of one road trial in the test set is shown in Fig. 2(b).

The focus is the detection of intermittent faults which manifest themselves in anomalies in the correlation of the signals. This is an imbalanced classification problem with a training set consisting of multiple normal multivariate time series with a total 24604 s at a sample rate of time point per second. The test set holds 12076 data points, with about 18% anomalies.

The data is first scaled, then SVDD with an RBF kernel is used. The toolbox offers autoSVDD, which autonomously determines the hyperparameters C and σ from the training set using recursive grid-search with repeated 7-fold cross validation. The determined hyperparameters are $C = 0.7778$ and $\sigma = 0.6968$. For more details the reader is referred to [8].

In a post-processing step subsequences are formed grouping together adjacent classified data points of the input time series. Since faults in the recordings can be of arbitrary length, variable-length subsequences are formed. Results on the blind test set from overland drives are $TPR = 78.7\%$ and $TNR = 73.8\%$. These results can be improved by building ensembles of multiple one- and two-class classifiers [9].

4   Conclusion

It was shown how one-class anomaly detection can be achieved using OCADaMi. Usage is easy and customizable due to its modular structure and the out-of-the-box implementations. Large data sets can be processed by transmitting the workflow queue to another computing node. Case studies showed AD on (1) artificial data sets and for (2) real-world data from automotive test drives.

References

1. Bosman, H.H., Iacca, G., Tejada, A., Wörtche, H.J., Liotta, A.: Ensembles of incremental learners to detect anomalies in ad hoc sensor networks. Ad Hoc Netw. **35**(C), 14–36 (2015)
2. Breunig, M.M., Kriegel, H.P., Ng, R.T., Sander, J.: LOF: identifying density-based local outliers. In: SIGMOD Conference, pp. 93–104 (2000)
3. Prytz, R., Nowaczyk, S., Roegnvaldsson, T.S., Byttner, S.: Predicting the need for vehicle compressor repairs using maintenance records and logged vehicle data. Eng. Appl. Artif. Intell. **41**, 139–150 (2015)
4. Soudi, A., Khreich, W., Hamou-Lhadj, A.: An anomaly detection system based on ensemble of detectors with effective pruning techniques. In: IEEE International Conference on Software Quality, Reliability and Security, pp. 109–118. IEEE Computer Society (2015)
5. Tax, D., Duin, R.: Support vector data description. Mach. Learn. **54**(1), 45–66 (2004)
6. Tax, D.: Ddtools, the data description toolbox for matlab, January 2018. Version 2.1.3
7. Theissler, A.: Multi-class novelty detection in diagnostic trouble codes from repair shops. In: 2017 IEEE 15th International Conference on Industrial Informatics (INDIN), pp. 1043–1049, July 2017. https://doi.org/10.1109/INDIN.2017.8104917
8. Theissler, A.: Detecting anomalies in multivariate time series from automotive systems. Ph.D. thesis, Brunel University London (2013)
9. Theissler, A.: Detecting known and unknown faults in automotive systems using ensemble-based anomaly detection. Knowl. Based Syst. **123**(1), 163–173 (2017). https://doi.org/10.1016/j.knosys.2017.02.023
10. Wirth, R.: CRISP-DM: Towards a standard process model for data mining. In: Proceedings of the Fourth International Conference on the Practical Application of Knowledge Discovery and Data Mining, pp. 29–39 (2000)

MatrixCalculus.org – Computing Derivatives of Matrix and Tensor Expressions

Sören Laue[1,2]($\boxtimes$), Matthias Mitterreiter[1], and Joachim Giesen[1]

[1] Friedrich-Schiller-Universität Jena, Jena, Germany
{soeren.laue,matthias.mitterreiter,joachim.giesen}@uni-jena.de
[2] Data Assessment Solutions GmbH, Hannover, Germany

Abstract. Computing derivatives of matrix and tensor expressions is an integral part of developing and implementing optimization algorithms in machine learning. However, it is a time-consuming and error-prone task when done by hand. Here, we present the first system that performs matrix and tensor calculus automatically.

Keywords: Matrix/tensor calculus · Higher order derivatives · Automatic differentiation

1 Introduction

The importance of computing derivatives of matrix and tensor expressions in machine learning can be illustrated on the classical logistic regression problem for linear, binary classification. In this problem, a data matrix $X \in \mathbb{R}^{m \times n}$ is given along with a binary label vector $y \in \{-1, +1\}^m$, and the goal is to find a hyperplane that separates the positive from the negative points as well as possible. Since linear, binary classification is a fundamental task, there are numerous highly efficient solvers available for the logistic regression problem [4]. Almost all of these solvers are based on first order methods. However, for problems involving only up to a thousand features, Newton-type solvers can be even faster. This can be relevant, if one has to solve many of these small problems. For Newton-type solvers, one has to compute the gradient and the Hessian of the logistic regression objective function $f(w) = \sum \log(\exp(-y \odot Xw) + 1)$. This is typically done by hand, a time consuming and error-prone task. Surprisingly, up until very recently, there was no algorithm known for computing derivatives of matrix and tensor expressions like $f(w)$. So far, matrix calculus was considered more of an art than a science.

Recently, Laue et al. [3] derived the first algorithm for computing matrix and tensor derivatives. The resulting derivatives are again a matrix or tensor expression. This is especially important when the derivatives are again a vector or matrix expressions, because such expressions can be mapped directly onto highly tuned BLAS (basic linear algebra subroutines) implementations. Here, we present the first system that implements this algorithm. We also provide

© Springer Nature Switzerland AG 2020
U. Brefeld et al. (Eds.): ECML PKDD 2019, LNAI 11908, pp. 769–772, 2020.
https://doi.org/10.1007/978-3-030-46133-1_48

some use cases and comparisons to other frameworks. The system is available at http://www.MatrixCalculus.org. This website has attracted more than 30,000 users in the year 2018.

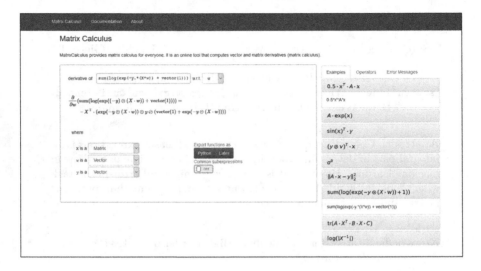

Fig. 1. Screenshot of the www.MatrixCalculus.org website.

2   System Description

Our system implements the algorithm for computing derivatives of matrix and tensor expressions that has been presented in [3]. After computing the derivative, the system performs a number of expression simplifications, like for instance, constant folding, removal of zero and identity tensors for better readability and faster evaluation.

A screenshot of the matrix calculus website is shown in Fig. 1. Once the user has entered his/her matrix expression, the derivative is computed and displayed instantly. A feature that has been proven to be very useful for many users is exporting the expressions and their derivatives as Python code. Since many users asked for a correctness proof of the derivative, the Python code also contains a numerical check that approximates derivatives by finite symmetric differences.

3   Target Audience and Use Cases

The target audience of the matrix calculus website are a machine learning researchers who want to implement optimization algorithms for new machine learning problems. We illustrate a typical use case with the following example.

Suppose one would like to implement a solver for embedding data points into low-dimensional space. A classic algorithm for this problem is multidimensional scaling (MDS). For a given distance matrix $D \in \mathbb{R}^{n \times n}$ a set of points

$X \in \mathbb{R}^{n \times d}$ in d-dimensional Euclidean space has to be computed such that their Euclidean distances closely approximate the distance matrix. There are a number of solvers for this problem. However, if the data has some hierarchical structure, like for instance in social networks, then it is known that embedding into low-dimensional Euclidean space will incur large distortions. This is different when emebdding into hyperbolic space [9]. Hence, hyperbolic embedding has recently attracted interest in the machine learning community [6,8]. However, there does not yet exist a general solver that can solve the hyperbolic embedding problem that is given as

$$\min_{X} \quad \|D - \log(XGX^{\top})\|_{\mathrm{Fro}}^2$$
$$\text{s.t.} \quad \mathrm{diag}(XGX^{\top}) = 1,$$

where $\|.\|_{\mathrm{Fro}}$ is the Frobenius norm and $G = \mathrm{diag}(-1, 1, \ldots, 1) \in \mathbb{R}^d$ is a diagonal matrix. Any gradient based solver for this problem needs the derivative of the objective function with respect to X. Computing this derivative is a non-trivial task and so far the researcher would have to do it by hand. www.MatrixCalculus. org solves this problem immediately. Knowing that D and G are symmetric matrices, the result is $\frac{\partial f}{\partial X} = -4 \cdot (D - \log(X \cdot G \cdot X^{\top})) \oslash (X \cdot G \cdot X^{\top}) \cdot X \cdot G$, where $\oslash$ is the element-wise division. The advantage of having a matrix calculus algorithm is even more pronounced for second order methods that need the Hessian of the objective function. Computing the Hessian by hand is basically infeasible.

4 Comparison to Other Systems

Here, we present the first system for automatically computing derivatives of matrix and tensor expressions. Surprisingly, there exists no other system for this fundamental task. Even the classic computer algebra systems like Mathematica, Maple, or Sage cannot perform matrix calculus. The same holds true for the classic automatic differentiation frameworks like ADOL-C [10] or TAPENADE [2]. While the direct integration of matrix and tensor operators into automatic differentiation frameworks like TensorFlow [1], PyTorch [7] or autograd [5] is under active development, so far their output functions still have to be scalar. Hence, Hessians or Jacobians cannot be computed directly by these frameworks that compute these derivatives entrywise. For instance, the expression graph computed by TensorFlow for the Hessian of the simple quadratic function $x^{\top}Ax$ with a square matrix $A \in \mathbb{R}^{n \times n}$ has more than one million nodes for $n = 1000$. This should be compared to the compact expression $A + A^{\top}$ for the Hessian that is computed by matrix calculus. Figure 2 shows the running times for evaluating the Hessian produced by different systems for this quadratic function. Since our system is the only system that can compute the derivative in matrix form, it can map the derivate directly to efficient BLAS calls. As a result, evaluating the derivative is two orders of magnitude faster on a CPU and three orders of magnitude faster on a GPU than the expressions that are produced by the other systems. The situation is similar for other functions.

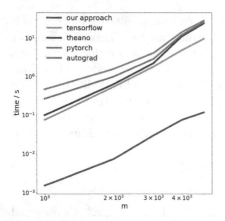 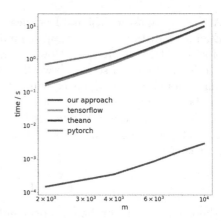

Fig. 2. Log-log plot of the running times for evaluating the Hessian of the quadratic function on a CPU (left) and on a GPU (right).

Acknowledgements. Sören Laue has been funded by Deutsche Forschungsgemeinschaft (DFG) under grant LA 2971/1-1.

References

1. Abadi, M., et al.: Tensorflow: a system for large-scale machine learning. In: US ENIX Conference on Operating Systems Design and Implementation (OSDI), pp. 265–283. USENIX Association (2016)
2. Hascoët, L., Pascual, V.: The Tapenade automatic differentiation tool: principles, model, and specification. ACM Trans. Math. Softw. **39**(3), 20:1–20:43 (2013)
3. Laue, S., Mitterreiter, M., Giesen, J.: Computing higher order derivatives of matrix and tensor expressions. In: Advances in Neural Information Processing Systems (NeurIPS) (2018)
4. Laue, S., Mitterreiter, M., Giesen, J.: GENO - GENeric optimization for classical machine learning. In: Advances in Neural Information Processing Systems (NeurIPS) (2019)
5. Maclaurin, D., Duvenaud, D., Adams, R.P.: Autograd: effortless gradients in numpy. In: ICML AutoML Workshop (2015)
6. Nickel, M., Kiela, D.: Poincaré embeddings for learning hierarchical representations. In: Advances in Neural Information Processing Systems (NIPS), pp. 6338–6347 (2017)
7. Paszke, A., et al.: Automatic differentiation in pytorch. In: NIPS Autodiff Workshop (2017)
8. Sala, F., De Sa, C., Gu, A., Ré, C.: Representation tradeoffs for hyperbolic embeddings. In: International Conference on Machine Learning (ICML) (2018)
9. Stai, E., Karyotis, V., Papavassiliou, S.: A hyperbolic space analytics framework for big network data and their applications. IEEE Netw. **30**(1), 11–17 (2016)
10. Walther, A., Griewank, A.: Getting started with adol-c. In: Combinatorial Scientific Computing, pp. 181–202. Chapman-Hall CRC Computational Science (2012)

Towards a Predictive Patent Analytics and Evaluation Platform

Nebula Alam[(⊠)], Khoi-Nguyen Tran, Sue Ann Chen, John Wagner,
Josh Andres, and Mukesh Mohania

IBM Research Australia, Southbank, VIC 3006, Australia
{anebula,khndtran,sachen,john.wagner,josh.andres,mukeshm}@au1.ibm.com

Abstract. The importance of patents is well recognised across many regions of the world. Many patent mining systems have been proposed, but with limited predictive capabilities. In this demo, we showcase how predictive algorithms leveraging the state-of-the-art machine learning and deep learning techniques can be used to improve understanding of patents for inventors, patent evaluators, and business analysts alike. Our demo video is available at http://ibm.biz/ecml2019-demo-patent-analytics.

Keywords: USPTO · Patents · Data mining · Machine learning · Patent mining · Patent information retrieval

1 Introduction

Patents detail the innovations of individuals, organisations, and countries and represent the competitive landscape of ideas important to a society. Over the past decade, there has been a steady growth of intellectual property (IP) filing activity globally, averaging around 8% per year [9]. The main contributors of global growth in IP filings are China, USA, and Japan, contributing over 70% of patents out of 3.17 million that are filed worldwide in 2017 [8]. By the end of 2018, more than 10 million patents have been issued by the United States Patent and Trademark Office (USPTO) [10]. The importance of patents is well recognised across many regions of the world and many patent mining systems have been proposed [12], but with limited predictive capabilities.

In this demo, we showcase how predictive algorithms using state-of-the-art machine learning and deep learning techniques can improve evaluation of patents for inventors, patent evaluators, and business analysts. Currently, we have completed the engineering groundwork, summary statistics for inventors and for organisations, and a predictive algorithm of when filed patents will be issued by the patent office. This algorithm learns from the text of issued (i.e. granted) patents and estimates when published patents (i.e. in application stage) will be granted. In future demos and a technical publication, we will show how representational methods for patent text can significantly improve comparisons for search, modifying phrasing of ideas to shorten grant time, and identifying gaps in

© Springer Nature Switzerland AG 2020
U. Brefeld et al. (Eds.): ECML PKDD 2019, LNAI 11908, pp. 773–776, 2020.
https://doi.org/10.1007/978-3-030-46133-1_49

the knowledge coverage of patents and generating patent ideas from those gaps. Our patent data source is from the USPTO from 2005 to 2019 and a future technical publication will detail the data and algorithms used in this demo.

1.1 Related Work

Patent Systems. There is a variety of existing proprietary and free online patent search systems with various capabilities. Intellectual property offices (IPOs) around the world provide basic search capabilities on keywords, publication number, authors and date ranges[1,2,3], as well as basic analytics tools and machine readable data. Private patent search systems such as TotalPatent[4] build on this data to provide confidential capabilities (including search) for inventors and organisations. Public patent search systems such as lens.org[5] and Google Patents[6] also make use of this data to provide additional commercial services or integration with other data sources to serve different market needs.

Patent Mining. A variety of patent mining techniques have been proposed as seen from a survey as reviewed by Zhang et al. [12] and semantic methods based on text by Bonino et al. [3]. These techniques serve to extract information about technological innovations for businesses to make strategic investment [7] and to resolve problems inherent within the patent data for search and analysis. Research based methods generally enrich the patent data, such as with metadata [1], the classification taxonomy from the patent office [11], derived data from the patent text and text summarisations [4], informative data from patent citations and academic citations [6], patent domains [5], relationship with other patents [2], and a combination of methods for forecasting technologies [7].

2 System Architecture

Figure 1 shows the high level architecture of the system. A **Data Extractor** module is responsible for extraction-transformation-loading (ETL) of issued and published patents from the **USPTO Bulk Data store**. This data is then processed to extract features to train models, where the best model is stored for deployment. The models are trained in the **ML Training Module** using `Scikit-learn`[7] and Tensorflow[8] libraries. To create features from the patent text, we use a combination of manually engineered features, derived features, and representational features (e.g. `word2vec`[9], `fastText`[10]). The prediction task

---

[1] Espacenet: https://www.epo.org/searching-for-patents/technical/espacenet.html.
[2] Patent Full-Text and Image Search: https://www.uspto.gov/patent.
[3] PatentScope: https://patentscope.wipo.int/search/en/search.jsf.
[4] https://www.lexisnexis.com/totalpatent/.
[5] https://www.lens.org/.
[6] https://patents.google.com.
[7] https://scikit-learn.org/stable/.
[8] https://github.com/tensorflow/tensorflow.
[9] https://www.tensorflow.org/tutorials/representation/word2vec.
[10] https://fasttext.cc/.

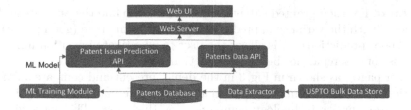

Fig. 1. System architecture overview

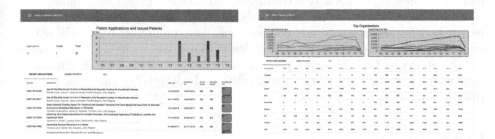

Fig. 2. Inventor's patent page.   **Fig. 3.** Organisation patent summary page.

in this demo is to estimate number of days until a patent will be issued, which includes a confidence score for each prediction made. A **Patent Issue Prediction API** is built around this model, exposing the predictive capability through a RESTful API, allowing end-users to estimate how soon their filed patents may be issued. Users can then examine other characteristics, such as the topic and domain of patents to determine factors affecting the estimated issued time. We provide a **Patent Data API** that encapsulates logic for querying the database, and provides end points for easy retrieval of selective and aggregated data, allowing direct access to the data for further analysis. A **Web User Interface** presents the analytics and prediction to the end-users, which is the front-end to our demo.

3 Target Users and Demo

Our system aims to target inventors, business analysts (and managers), invention evaluators, and patent attorneys. Currently, we have completed the engineering work and UIs catering for inventors and business analysts. We differentiate from current offerings such as Google Patents by focusing on predictive approaches based on machine and deep learning, but can be integrated into existing systems.

Inventors find a page summarising their inventions and applications at the USPTO, as shown in Fig. 2. Our technical contribution here is the underlying machine learning algorithm that predicts, with a prediction confidence score, when a patent application will be granted using features extracted from the patent text. For their granted patents, the user will also find the estimate and the confidence with the variance in prediction coloured from green (good prediction) to red (poor prediction). This allows the user to investigate invention filing time and cause of descrepancies between prediction and results.

Other pages, as shown in Fig. 3 in the demo, present and compare summary statistics of filed patents at targeted organisations. We manually disambiguated over a dozen major technology companies for this work. This view gives an overview of significant inventors within organisations and their output inventions. Similarly, users can perform additional data mining for organisations to find their emerging technology investments and themes of their inventions.

Our future versions showcase underlying deep learning representations of patent text for fast retrieval and comparisons. These representations will allow evaluating patent ideas from short text descriptions (e.g. verifying ideas), clustering patents to find infringing patents and emerging areas (this is currently done via topic modelling and citation graphs), and potentially generating patent titles to seed ideas for inventors.

References

1. Agatonovic, M., et al.: Large-scale, parallel automatic patent annotation. In: Proceedings of the 1st ACM Workshop on Patent Information Retrieval (PaIR) (2008)
2. Bergeaud, A., Potiron, Y., Raimbault, J.: Classifying patents based on their semantic content. PLoS ONE **12**(4), e0176310 (2017)
3. Bonino, D., Ciaramella, A., Corno, F.: State-of-the-art and forecoming evolutions in intelligent patent informatics. World Patent Inf. **32**(1), 30–38 (2010)
4. Brügmann, S., et al.: Towards content-oriented patent document processing: intelligent patent analysis and summarization. World Patent Inf. **40**, 30–42 (2015)
5. Guo, Y., Gomes, C.: Ranking structured documents: a large margin based approach for patent prior art search. In: Proceedings of the 21st International Joint Conference on Artificial Intelligence (IJCAI) (2009)
6. Julie, C., Joris, G., Bart, V.L.: Delineating the scientific footprint in technology: identifying scientific publications within non-patent references. Scientometrics **91**(2), 383–398 (2012)
7. Kyebambe, M.N., Cheng, G., Huang, Y., He, C., Zhang, Z.: Forecasting emerging technologies: a supervised learning approach through patent analysis. Technol. Forecast. Soc. Change **125**, 236–244 (2017)
8. Organization, W.I.P.: WIPO IP facts and figures 2018. Technical report, World Intellectual Property Organization (2018)
9. Organization, W.I.P.: World intellectual property indicators 2018. Technical report, World Intellectual Property Organization (2018)
10. Patent, U.S., Office, T.: Fy 2018: Performance and accountability report. Technical report, United States Patent and Trademark Office (2018)
11. Xiao, T., et al.: KNN and re-ranking models for English patent mining at NTCIR-7. In: Proceedings of NTCIR-7 Workshop Meeting (2008)
12. Zhang, L., Li, L., Li, T.: Patent mining: a survey. ACM SIGKDD Explor. Newsl. **16**(2), 1–19 (2014)

A Virtualized Video Surveillance System for Public Transportation

Talmaj Marinč[1]([✉]), Serhan Gül[1], Cornelius Hellge[1], Peter Schüßler[2],
Thomas Riegel[3], and Peter Amon[3]

[1] Fraunhofer Heinrich Hertz Institute, Einsteinufer 37, 10587 Berlin, Germany
{talmaj.marinc,serhan.guel,cornelius.hellge}@hhi.fraunhofer.de
[2] DResearch Fahrzeugelektronik GmbH,
Otto-Schmirgal-Straße 3, 10319 Berlin, Germany
schuessler@dresearch-fe.de
[3] Siemens Corporate Technology, Otto-Hahn-Ring 6, 81739 München, Germany
{thomas.riegel,p.amon}@siemens.com

Abstract. Modern surveillance systems have recently started to employ computer vision algorithms for advanced analysis of the captured video content. Public transportation is one of the domains that may highly benefit from the advances in video analysis. This paper presents a video-based surveillance system that uses a deep neural network based face verification algorithm to accurately and robustly re-identify a subject person. Our implementation is highly scalable due to its container-based architecture and is easily deployable on a cloud platform to support larger processing loads. During the demo, the users will be able to interactively select a target person from pre-recorded surveillance videos and inspect the results on our web-based visualization platform.

Keywords: Video-based security · Surveillance · Face verification

1 Introduction

Intelligent surveillance systems are increasingly playing an important role in the identification of potential security threats in private and public spaces. The new generation of multimedia surveillance systems collects, stores, and analyzes information from various sensors, and implement advanced mechanisms for event notification and sharing. Computer vision based systems are rapidly gaining importance due to various reasons including the increased quality of the capture devices, increased processing capabilities enabled by the developments in graphics processing technologies, and the availability of public and private clouds providing massive amounts of computation power [4].

Several intelligent surveillance systems have been proposed in recent years, and some real-world deployments have also been reported [6]. Camps et al. [1] deployed a person re-identification system at a busy airport in the USA. Their

---

This research has received funding from the German Federal Ministry for Economic Affairs and Energy under the VIRTUOSE-DE project.

U. Brefeld et al. (Eds.): ECML PKDD 2019, LNAI 11908, pp. 777–780, 2020.
https://doi.org/10.1007/978-3-030-46133-1_50

system integrates various computer vision algorithms such as foreground detection, pedestrian detection as well as person tracking, and operates using the airport's network infrastructure in real time. Zhang et al. [7] present a real-time distributed wireless surveillance system for surveillance in enterprise campuses. Their system intelligently partitions the computing among the local device, different edge computing nodes, and the cloud. In this paper, we introduce a video-based security system for public transportation (PT), specifically for surveillance in public buses. Our system utilizes the surveillance cameras installed in a bus and enables the re-identification of a suspect when (s)he switches to another vehicle within a pre-defined region of interest (RoI). The proposed system can be used by various stakeholders such as fleet management system (FMS) providers, technology providers (infrastructure as a service, IaaS) as well as governments and public authorities. Our system is *modular* in the sense that it contains easily exchangeable software components that communicate over a simple REST API. This enables easy upgrade of the video analysis components (e.g., neural network) when better performing algorithms become available. Secondly, our system is highly *scalable* due to its architecture that uses Docker containers for component-level virtualization. Thus, it is possible to easily start multiple instances of a processing block as well as efficiently manage several search processes through an orchestration software located in a cloud server. Finally, our system is capable of providing more advanced analysis compared to motion detection and background subtraction based systems, due to its advanced face verification module based on a pre-trained DNN.

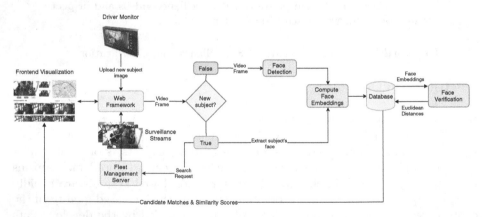

Fig. 1. System architecture and workflow of the proposed video surveillance system for public transportation.

2 System Overview

The proposed system comprises the following components which are displayed in Fig. 1. Each component runs in its own Docker container enabling easy horizontal scalability of the processing blocks.

Web Framework. The backend logic is developed in Django, a web framework written in Python. For serving the static files we employ a more efficient Nginx server with a reverse proxy to the Django backend.

For spawning concurrent tasks, we use the task manager Celery. A spawned task is terminated after a pre-defined timeout or may be killed directly through a post request.

Video Source. The public buses used in our setup are equipped with multiple IP cameras delivering resolutions up to 1080p and certified for usage in vehicles (on-board). The video streams from the cameras (H.264/AVC) are fetched by the Mobile Digital Video Recorder (MDVR, HydraIP MR4410) which provides the integrated 3G/4G/WLAN communication modules for mobile ground communication from vehicle to the cloud and/or back office application.

Fleet Management System (FMS). FMS is a web-based, multi-user back office application for centralized alarm management, diagnostic, and maintenance purposes of the on-board systems. The application allows controlling video streams from the video recorders of an entire bus fleet and includes features such as location management, map view, and management of vehicle metadata.

Face Detection. In order to detect the faces that serve as comparison images in the face verification process, we use the Single Shot Detector (SSD) [3] implemented in OpenCV. SSD relies on a pre-trained DNN for detection and the OpenCV implementation employs a ResNet [2] base network which provides high detection accuracy with very low false positive rates.

Face Verification. Faces are compared through the embeddings computed by a pre-trained Facenet [5] model from Dlib. It projects each face image onto a 128-dimensional vector space, in which the faces belonging to the same person are close to each other in terms of their Euclidean distances. Our system allows visual confirmation of the face verification output by a human operator in order to eliminate potential false positives before alarming the security personnel.

Message Queues and Database. We use the in-memory database Redis for queuing of the images that are to be processed by the face detection and face verification components. These processing components asynchronously pull and process the data. Since the algorithms are constantly loaded in memory, they are ready to immediately process any data that appear in the queues.

In order to store the relevant data, we use the database PostgreSQL. PostgreSQL allows saving the face embeddings, which are used for face verification, as arrays. Thus, the expensive operation of computing face embeddings is performed only once for each face image. Since the computation of Euclidean distance between embeddings is cheap, this setup enables fast comparison between any two subjects stored in the database.

Visualization. Although intelligent computer-based surveillance systems have reached amazing capabilities, humans are still necessary for approving further actions, especially if those concern fundamental rights. To support such a decision, a browser-based dashboard has been implemented, which allows a human operator in the control center to approve incoming notifications, trigger a search request, inspect retrieved results, accept one of the proposed matches, and terminate the search, or alternatively, reject the matches and continue the search.

3   Proof-of-Concept Setup

In this demonstration, we show how the system components work together to re-identify a searched subject in a surveillance network. For this, we use pre-recorded video streams from multiple cameras in two buses containing 11 different subjects. During the recording session, the subjects went in and out of the field-of-views of different cameras within a bus, and also changed from one bus to another. We use the video streams from Bus 1 to simulate a touchscreen where the user (in the role of the bus driver) can interactively choose the suspect to be searched. The video streams from Bus 2 simulate the surveillance streams uploaded by FMS that are used to re-identify the subject.

Our demo setup consists of two screens: one shows the video streams on which the simulation if performed, and the other shows the results on a web browser on our visualization dashboard. We show the initial subject selection, the detected faces on the surveillance videos and the candidate matches provided by the face verification model. Users may interact and select the search subject in the provided set of surveillance videos. Demo video is available at: https://datacloud.hhi.fraunhofer.de/nextcloud/s/dX8ZLi7PRQ22YTA.

References

1. Camps, O., et al.: From the lab to the real world: re-identification in an airport camera network. IEEE Trans. Circuits Syst. Video Technol. **27**(3), 540–553 (2017)
2. He, K., Zhang, X., Ren, S., Sun, J.: Deep residual learning for image recognition. In: Proceedings of the IEEE Conference on Computer Vision and Pattern Recognition, pp. 770–778 (2016)
3. Liu, W., et al.: SSD: single shot multibox detector. In: Leibe, B., Matas, J., Sebe, N., Welling, M. (eds.) ECCV 2016. LNCS, vol. 9905, pp. 21–37. Springer, Cham (2016). https://doi.org/10.1007/978-3-319-46448-0_2
4. Neal, D., Rahman, S.: Video surveillance in the cloud? arXiv preprint arXiv:1512.00070 (2015)
5. Schroff, F., Kalenichenko, D., Philbin, J.: Facenet: A unified embedding for face recognition and clustering. In: Proceedings of the IEEE Conference on Computer Vision and Pattern Recognition, pp. 815–823 (2015)
6. Ye, Y., Ci, S., Katsaggelos, A.K., Liu, Y., Qian, Y.: Wireless video surveillance: a survey. IEEE Access **1**, 646–660 (2013)
7. Zhang, T., Chowdhery, A., Bahl, P.V., Jamieson, K., Banerjee, S.: The design and implementation of a wireless video surveillance system. In: Proceedings of the 21st Annual International Conference on Mobile Computing and Networking, pp. 426–438. ACM (2015)

Distributed Algorithms to Find Similar Time Series

Oleksandra Levchenko[1]([✉]), Boyan Kolev[1], Djamel-Edine Yagoubi[1],
Dennis Shasha[1,2], Themis Palpanas[3], Patrick Valduriez[1], Reza Akbarinia[1],
and Florent Masseglia[1]

[1] Inria & LIRMM, Univ. Montpellier, Montpellier, France
{oleksandra.levchenko,boyan.kolev,djamel-edine.yagoubi,patrick.valduriez,
reza.akbarinia,florent.masseglia}@inria.fr
[2] Department of Computer Science, New York University, New York, USA
shasha@cs.nyu.edu
[3] University of Paris, Paris, France
themis@mi.parisdescartes.fr

Abstract. As sensors improve in both bandwidth and quantity over
time, the need for high performance sensor fusion increases. This
requires both better (quasi-linear time if possible) algorithms and paral-
lelism. This demonstration uses financial and seismic data to show how
two state-of-the-art algorithms construct indexes and answer similarity
queries using Spark. Demo visitors will be able to choose query time
series, see how each algorithm approximates nearest neighbors and compare times in a parallel environment.

Keywords: Time series · Indexing · Similarity search · Distributed
data processing · Spark

1 Introduction

As hardware technology improves for sensors, the need for efficient and scalable
algorithms increases to fuse the resulting time series. Sensors produce thousands
and up to billions of time series, so the first step in fusion is often to find similar
time series. Applications include statistical arbitrage strategies in finance and
the detection of earthquakes in seismic data.

To handle such large numbers of time series, algorithms require high performance indexing. Creating an index over billions of time series by using traditional
centralized approaches is highly time consuming.

An appealing opportunity for improving performance of the index construction and similarity search on such massive sets of time series, therefore, is to
take advantage of the computing power of distributed systems and parallel

The research leading to these results has received funds from the European Union's
Horizon 2020 Framework Programme for Research and Innovation, under grant agreement No. 732051.

U. Brefeld et al. (Eds.): ECML PKDD 2019, LNAI 11908, pp. 781–785, 2020.
https://doi.org/10.1007/978-3-030-46133-1_51

frameworks. However, a naive parallel implementation of existing techniques would under-exploit the available computing power. We have implemented parallel algorithms for two state-of-the-art approaches to construct indexes and to provide similarity search on large sets of time series by carefully distributing the work load. Our solution takes advantage of the computing power of distributed systems by using parallel frameworks, in this case Spark.

2 Parallel Similarity Search Methods

This section reviews similarity search methods with specific attention to parallel index construction both to increase speed and improve quality.

2.1 parSketch

parSketch [3] is a parallel implementation of the sketch/random projection-based method, both for index construction and querying. The basic idea is to multiply each time series in a database (or in a sliding window context, each window of a time series) with a set of random vectors, yielding a dot product. The vector of those dot products is a "sketch" for each time series. Then two time series can be compared by comparing sketches with approximation guarantees [1] that improve the more random vectors there are.

In our implementation of this idea, given a length m time series or a window of a time series, $\mathbf{t} \in R^m$, we compute its dot product with N -1/+1 random vectors $\mathbf{r}_i \in \{1, -1\}^m$. This results in N inner products (dot products) called the *sketch* (or random projection) of t_i. Specifically, $sketch(t_i) = (\mathbf{t_i} \bullet \mathbf{r_1}, \mathbf{t_i} \bullet \mathbf{r_2}, ..., \mathbf{t_i} \bullet \mathbf{r_N})$. We compute sketches for $t_1, ..., t_b$ using the same random vectors $r_1, ..., r_N$. By the Johnson-Lindenstrauss lemma [1], the distance $\|\mathbf{sketch(t_i)} - \mathbf{sketch(t_j)}\|$ is a good approximation of $\|\mathbf{t_i} - \mathbf{t_j}\|$. Specifically, if $\|\mathbf{sketch(t_i)} - \mathbf{sketch(t_j)}\| < \|\mathbf{sketch(t_k)} - \mathbf{sketch(t_m)}\|$, then it's very likely that $\|\mathbf{t_i} - \mathbf{t_j}\| < \|\mathbf{t_k} - \mathbf{t_m}\|$. Our index is a set of grid structures to hold the time series sketches. Each grid maintains the sketch values corresponding to a specific set of random vectors over all time series.

Our implementation of the sketch-based approach *parSketch* parallelizes every step of algorithm: the computation of sketches, the creation of multiple grid structures, and the computation of pairwise similarity, thus exploiting each available core and taking full advantage of parallel data processing

2.2 DPiSAX

DPiSAX [4] is a parallel solution to construct the state-of-the-art iSAX-based index [2]. The iSAX representation is based on the PAA representation which allows for dimensionality reduction while providing the important lower bounding property. The idea of PAA is to have a fixed segment size, and minimize dimensionality by using the mean values of each segment.

The SAX representation takes as input the reduced time series obtained using PAA. It discretizes this representation into a predefined set of symbols, with a given cardinality, where a symbol is a binary number. The iSAX representation uses a variable cardinality for each symbol of SAX representation, each symbol is accompanied by a number that denotes its cardinality.

Our parallel partitioned version of iSAX algorithm is based on a sampling phase that allows anticipating the distribution of time series among the computing nodes. *DPiSAX* splits the full dataset for distribution into partitions using the partition table constructed at the sampling stage. Then each worker builds an independent iSAX index on its partition.

3 Experimental Evaluation

In order to provide an unbiased comparison, (i) all methods were implemented using the same tools, (ii) all the experiments were run in the same pre-deployed computing environment, and (iii) on the same datasets. Applications were implemented with Scala and Apache Spark. A distributed relational storage, set up as a number of PostgreSQL instances, is used for *parSketch* to store indexed data (grids). The implementation makes use of indexes to achieve efficient query processing. The *DPiSAX* implementation uses an HDFS cluster to keep index data in distributed files, so that partitions of the index are stored and retrieved in parallel.

Experiments were conducted on a cluster[1] of 16 compute nodes with two 8 cores Intel Xeon E5-2630 v3 CPUs, 128 GB RAM, 2 x 558 GB capacity storage per node. The cluster is running under Hadoop version 2.7, Spark v. 2.4 and PostgreSQL v. 9.4 as a relational database system.

Search methods were evaluated over two real datasets and two synthetic ones. The real datasets are: Seismic that contains 40 million time series, and Finance with 72 million time series. For the purpose of experimentation, we generated synthetic Random Walk input datasets, whose sizes/volumes vary between 50M to 500M time series size of 256 points. At each time point, a random walk generator cumulatively adds to the value of the previous time point a random number drawn from a Gaussian distribution N(0,1). Another synthetic dataset is Random, containing 200M series, each of which is a close approximation to "white noise".

4 Demonstration

The user can observe and compare search method performances on a range of input datasets. The demonstration GUI enables the user to use drop-downs to choose the input dataset and set of queries, to vary specific parameters for methods: grid cell size (affects only the output of *parSketch*), Search type (only for *DPiSAX*) and then to observe the difference in performance (Fig. 1).

---

[1] http://www.grid5000.fr.

A bar chart compares 3 methods in terms of time performance per batch of queries. We use three quality metrics: (i) Quality Ratio is defined to be correlation of the 10th time series found by a particular method divided by the 10th closest time series found by direct computation of correlation. (ii) Recall is calculated as a fraction of relevant items in the top 10 time series found by particular method over the top 10 time series found by direct correlations. (iii) Mean Average Precision which considers the order of top 10 time series found by particular search method over ranked sequence of time series returned by direct correlations.

Line charts on the right side of the screen depict the top 10 time series found for the given input. The scroll bar allows the user to examine each query in the batch using visual plots and the quality ratio, for the different search methods.

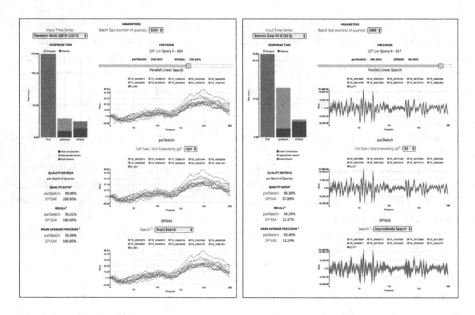

Fig. 1. Users can select input dataset and number of queries to execute, and can examine individual queries and answers, as well as quality and execution time of searches. The demonstration GUI and video are available at: http://imitates.gforge.inria.fr/

References

1. Achlioptas, D.: Database-friendly random projections: Johnson-Lindenstrauss with binary coins. J. Comput. Syst. Sci. **66**(4), 671–687 (2003)
2. Camerra, A., Shieh, J., Palpanas, T., Rakthanmanon, T., Keogh, E.: Beyond one billion time series: indexing and mining very large time series collections with iSAX2+. Knowl. Inf. Syst. **39**(1), 123–151 (2013). https://doi.org/10.1007/s10115-012-0606-6

3. Yagoubi, D.E., et al.: ParCorr: efficient parallel methods to identify similar time series pairs across sliding windows. DMKD **32**(5), 1481–1507 (2018)
4. Yagoubi, D.E., Akbarinia, R., Masseglia, F., Palpanas, T.: Dpisax: Massively distributed partitioned isax. In: International Conference on Data Mining (ICDM) (2017)

UnFOOT: Unsupervised Football Analytics Tool

José Carlos Coutinho[1,2](✉), João Mendes Moreira[2], and Cláudio Rebelo de Sá[1]

[1] University of Twente, Enschede, The Netherlands
j.c.milheirosoarescoutinho@student.utwente.nl,
c.f.pinhorebelodesa@utwente.nl
[2] University of Porto, Porto, Portugal
jmoreira@fe.up.pt

Abstract. Labelled football (soccer) data is hard to acquire and it usually needs humans to annotate the match events. This process makes it more expensive to be obtained by smaller clubs. UnFOOT (Unsupervised Football Analytics Tool) combines data mining techniques and basic statistics to measure the performance of players and teams from positional data. The capabilities of the tool involve preprocessing the match data, extraction of features, visualization of player and team performance. It also has built-in data mining techniques, such as association rule mining, subgroup discovery and a proposed approach to look for frequent distributions.

Keywords: Sports analytics · Association rules · Subgroup discovery · Data visualization

1 Introduction

There already exist tools that given the positional and event-labeled data can extract useful knowledge from the teams and players (Bialkowski *et al.* [1], Gudmundsson *et al.* [2]). However, these tools require event-labeled data, which can be more expensive to obtain than positional data.

UnFOOT[1] uses positional data from players in a football match and extracts different statistics as well as performance indicators of players and teams. This and other information can be explored in more detail in the data analysis section of the tool.

2 UnFOOT Tool

UnFOOT offers a simple and intuitive GUI for analyzing football matches only from spatiotemporal data of players[2]. The pipeline involves 3 stages: Processing of the data, Representation and Data Mining.

---

[1] This work was financed by the project *Kids First*, project number 68639.
[2] A demonstration can be watched at https://youtu.be/x86tg48qEs4.

© Springer Nature Switzerland AG 2020
U. Brefeld et al. (Eds.): ECML PKDD 2019, LNAI 11908, pp. 786–789, 2020.
https://doi.org/10.1007/978-3-030-46133-1_52

Table 1. Example of the records in the input dataset. *Period* corresponds to the period of the match (1 for the first half and 2 for the second half). *Timestamp* is the time elapsed since the beginning of the period. x and y correspond to the coordinates of the player which are relative to the center of the football field.

ID	Player_id	Period	Timestamp	x	y
1	2	1	15	−37	−45
2	2	1	16	−35	−49

Processing. UnFOOT loads the players' positional data, which should come in 6 columns with the format shown in Table 1. In these experiments, the measurement's frequency was 0.1 s (i.e. 10 record per second) and the $x = 0$ and $y = 0$ correspond to center of the field.

After loading the data, the tool makes one pass on the data and outputs a new dataset with extracted features. These features include the distance covered, the speed and the acceleration of the players. The dataset is divided into time windows of the same size. For each window, several internal modules extract different performance indicators and statistics from the positional data. One of the metrics, *pressure* uses a clustering technique (DBSCAN), from the python package *scikit-learn*[3]. With the clusters, we are able to identify moments of higher pressure of the players during the match. In the end of the analysis, the overall and detailed results are stored into a csv file to enable further analysis outside of the tool.

From these performance indicators UnFOOT produces an overall player score which is the mean of the indicators. These player scores are also added together to obtain the score of each team.

Representation and Structure. The GUI is divided in 4 different tabs: *Player, Team, Data Analysis* and *Settings. Player*, evaluates and compares players according to their overall score or specific performance indicators. (Fig. 1(a)); *Team*, displays and compares different team scores and shows the best players.; *Data Analysis*, allows the user to use an interface to execute data mining algorithms on the match data. (Fig. 1(b)); and *Settings*, lets the user load the dataset and define some basic settings before starting the analysis.

Data Mining. The UnFOOT tool has an interface with several data mining techniques to explore the features extracted. One module uses association rules mining to find relationships of performance indicators between consecutive time windows for a selected player. The last method uses subgroup discovery to find subgroups with unusual behaviour relatively to an user defined target. For the association rules mining module, we used *mlxtend*[4], and for the subgroup discovery module we used *pysubgroup*[5].

---

[3] https://scikit-learn.org/stable/modules/clustering.html.
[4] http://rasbt.github.io/mlxtend/.
[5] https://pypi.org/project/pysubgroup/.

Besides, we also propose a method to look for frequent distributions. This distributions can represent speed or distance covered by players. It is similar to frequent pattern mining, except that the items are distributions. For that, we use the Kolmogorov-Smirnov (KS) to verify if the distribution of one player is significantly different from the other players. In the positive case, the distribution is considered a new *item* and stored in a buffer. Then, UnFOOT counts how many times each distinct distribution is observed during the match to obtain the support (frequency) per player. Distributions which have less than 1% of support are discarded. The users can decide the minimum distance between the distributions to filter very similar distributions.

(a) Illustration of the player analysis interface

(b) Illustration of the data analysis interface

Fig. 1. Player and data analysis interfaces

Use Cases. UnFOOT is targeted to football trainers, data analysts and data scientists. Trainers can use UnFOOT to support their analysis of players, teams and matches. This includes comparing different player's performance indicators, but also observing the variation of those indicators along the course of the match.

3   Results

Six real football games were analysed with the tool. Due to privacy issues, we are not able to provide more details about the match, such as the name of the best player per match or the names of the teams. According to some metrics obtained (Table 2), the best player of the match are usually found on the tool's top three players of the winning team. In two cases, they even had the best score overall. Even though the overall score was not originally designed to predict the best player of the match, we use it to validate the scoring function. However, this scoring function can only reasonably assess the quality of players, which are not goalkeepers. This is seen in Game 5, where the best player was actually a goalkeeper. We can also observe that the sum of the team players' individual performance may not be enough to evaluate the performance of the team, since in only half of the cases the highest team score corresponds to the winning team.

Let us now consider the association rules found with the Match 2 data using the association rules mining module. One of the best rules indicated that one striker of Team B was subject to a lot of pressure during the match. During 13% of the match, this player had an intermediate pressure score, which was followed by a high pressure score in 81% of the time. (Rule: Pressure $= 6 \rightarrow$ Pressure $= 9$ support $= 13\%$, confidence $= 81\%$) Also, the subgroup discovery module discovered two interesting subgroups. One indicates that the players playing on the attack with a high speed score tend to have high agility score. The other group indicates that when players have non-intermediate stamina score (high or low) they tend to have a high speed score.

Table 2. Results obtained with UnFOOT.

Match	Winner	Team A score	Team B score	Rank of best player of the match
1	A	758	778	3rd of Team A
2	A	814	811	1st overall
3	A	795	805	3rd of Team A
4	B	832	855	3rd of Team B
5	A	813	796	Last overall
6	A	816	819	1st overall

4   Conclusion

We proposed UnFOOT, a tool which allows a good understanding of players performance during a match or a training. Data analysts and data scientists can easily use the integrated data mining modules to perform more powerful data analysis. They can also modify the parameters of the algorithms, visualize the results and export the extracted features into a csv.

All results given by the tool were obtained only with player positional data, which presents an advantage over other methods. It also allows an easy extension to other invasion-based team sports since it is independent of the event data, which differs between sports. As future work, we would like to extend the tool to detect other events of the match.

References

1. Bialkowski, A., Lucey, P., Carr, P., Yue, Y., Sridharan, S., Matthews, I.: Identifying team style in soccer using formations learned from spatiotemporal tracking data. In: 2014 IEEE International Conference on Data Mining Workshop, pp. 9–14, December 2014. https://doi.org/10.1109/ICDMW.2014.167
2. Gudmundsson, J., Wolle, T.: Football analysis using spatio-temporal tools. Comput. Environ. Urban Syst. **47**, 16–27 (2014). https://doi.org/10.1016/j.compenvurbsys.2013.09.004

ISETS: Incremental Shapelet Extraction from Time Series Stream

Jingwei Zuo[1,2(✉)], Karine Zeitouni[1,2(✉)], and Yehia Taher[1,2(✉)]

[1] DAVID Lab, University of Versailles, Versailles, France
{jingwei.zuo,karine.zeitouni,yehia.taher}@uvsq.fr
[2] Université Paris-Saclay, Saint-Aubin, France

Abstract. In recent years, Time Series (TS) analysis has attracted widespread attention in the community of Data Mining due to its special data format and broad application scenarios. An important aspect in TS analysis is Time Series Classification (TSC), which has been applied in medical diagnosis, human activity recognition, industrial troubleshooting, etc. Typically, all TSC work trains a stable model from an off-line TS dataset, without considering potential Concept Drift in streaming context. Conventional data stream is considered as independent examples (e.g., row data) coming in real-time, but rarely considers Time Series with real-valued data coming in a sequential order, called Time Series Stream. Processing such type of data, requires combining techniques in both communities of Time Series (TS) and Data Streams. To facilitate the users' understanding of this combination, we propose *ISETS*, a web-based application which allows users to monitor the evolution of interpretable features in Time Series Stream.

1 Introduction

Time Series (*TS*) is a sequence of real-valued data, which can be collected from various sources, such as ECG data in medicine, IoT data in smart cities, light-curves in astronomy, etc. In this work, we study the problem of Streaming Time Series Classification (*STSC*): given a Streaming *TS* source, we aim at learning incrementally the concept allowing to predict the class of new input *TS* unit, and catching the concept drift in the data flow.

Concept [1] refers to the target variable, which the learning model is trying to predict. Existing work in data streams is mostly based on the assumption that data instances are independently and identically distributed (i.i.d) within a particular concept. Most *TSC* approaches are biased towards learning a stable concept from an off-line Time Series dataset, but not adaptable to streaming concept-drifting context, where a gradual change of the concept happens along with the input of TS streams. Lazy classifiers such as Nearest Neighbor (1-NN) [5] and dictionary based approaches [4] are applicable for *STSC*. However, every input instance will be considered to adjust the inner concept, which requires potentially a large buffer space and will bring a huge computation cost.

© Springer Nature Switzerland AG 2020
U. Brefeld et al. (Eds.): ECML PKDD 2019, LNAI 11908, pp. 790–793, 2020.
https://doi.org/10.1007/978-3-030-46133-1_53

Our proposal, namely ISETS: **I**ncremental **S**hapelet **E**xtraction from **T**ime **S**eries Stream, is capable of building the gap between Time Series Classification and Data Streams processing. Based on Shapelets [6], interpretable shapes considered as features in Time Series, the web-based application allows users to capture an adaptive concept for new incoming TS with a small memory buffer and a minimal computation cost. Besides, ISETS possesses a highlighted interpretability, as well as scalability in Big Data context. All implementation code, testing datasets and video tutorial are available online[1].

2 System Structure

As shown in Fig. 1, the system is composed by two blocks, namely Shapelet Extraction and Concept Drift Detection. By applying recent extracted Shapelets on new incoming TS streams, we can decide whether or not to cache TS instances into memory according to the Concept Drift Detection. From newly cached TS instances, Shapelet Extraction Block will make use of historical computations and update Shapelet Ranking at a minimal cost.

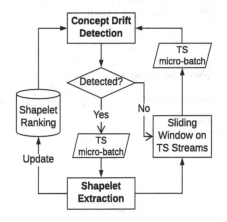

Fig. 1. Main system structure

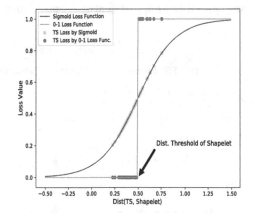

Fig. 2. Loss measure of TS by Sigmoid Function and 0–1 Loss Function

Concept Drift Detection: To detect the concept drift, a simple test can be done by comparing the average loss of the current TS micro-batch and that of all historical TS. Page-Hinkley test [3] is applied here as well for an advanced detection. The classical Shapelet-based approach [6] assumes that a Time Series T can be classified by the inclusion of a class-specified Shapelet $\hat{s}$. (i.e. if $dist(T, \hat{s}) < \hat{s}.dist_{thresh}$, then $T.class = \hat{s}.class$). However, two Time Series with similar distances to a Shapelet may be assigned to different classes by this strategy. A loss measured by a crisp *0–1 Loss Function* is then ill-adapted.

---

[1] https://github.com/JingweiZuo/ISETS.

To this end, we propose a loss measure based on Sigmoid function, to convert the inclusion problem to the possibility that a TS contains the Shapelet. The loss distribution is shown in Fig. 2. Every loss under 0.5 represents a relative acceptable classification result. Intuitively, the cumulative loss represents the adaptability of extracted Shapelets to the current TS micro-batch. Moreover, a forgetting mechanism is proposed when the most recent data are deemed more important. To this end, we apply an exponential moving sum to the loss.

Incremental Shapelet Extraction: The Shapelet Extraction is based on SE4TeC proposed in [7], but with the consideration of streaming data context, where we can observe a Concept Drift, and should deal with evolving features. Therefore, the set of Shapelets will be updated once a Concept Drift is detected, which means only the Time Series beyond the current concept will be taken into account by the computation. Each Shapelet will be given a score for its discriminative power between the classes.

3 About the Demonstration

Through this demonstration, attendees will have the opportunity to explore interpretable Shapelet features and Concept Drift in the context of Time Series

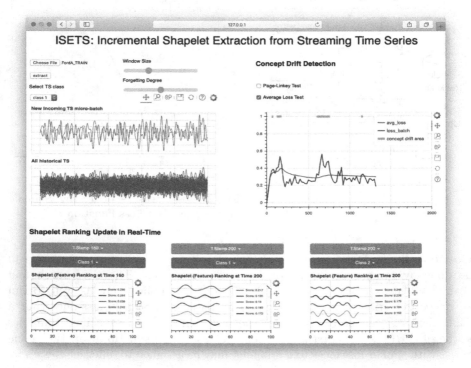

Fig. 3. GUI of ISETS web application

Stream. A web application with GUI shown in Fig. 3 allows an interactive use of the system. For the operations, users can adjust the sliding Window to set the size of input TS micro-batch. By changing system's forgetting degree, users can control the importance of recent coming data on current concept. As the result, our system allows monitoring the occurrence of Concept Drift and the evolution of Shapelet Ranking of each class at different time points. We show in Fig. 3 the intermediate results of the test on FordA dataset [2], which contains 3601 labelled Time Series with a fixed length of 500. The concept drift time periods are marked, where the new incoming TS micro-batches are considered by Shapelet Extraction Block to update the Shapelet Ranking. We can easily capture the Shapelets from different classes and time points.

The Shapelet Extraction process can be either conducted at local or on a remote Spark cluster. We provide also an 1-click cluster based on Docker, to facilitate the replay of the distributed test offline by the user[2].

4 Conclusion

In this paper, we have presented a novel approach, namely ISETS, to bridge the gap between Time Series Classification and Data Streams analysis. A web application is provided to facilitate attendees to interact with the system. ISETS allows users to detect the Concept Drift within Time Series Stream, and monitor the evolution of TS features (i.e., Shapelet) in an interpretable way.

Acknowledgements. This research was supported by DATAIA convergence institute as part of the *Programme d'Investissement d'Avenir*, (ANR-17-CONV-0003) operated by DAVID Lab, University of Versailles Saint-Quentin, and MASTER project that has received funding from the European Union's Horizon 2020 research and innovation programme under the Marie-Slodowska Curie grant agreement N. 777695.

References

1. Bifet, A., Holmes, G., Kirkby, R., Pfahringer, B.: MOA: Massive Online Analysis. Technical report (2010)
2. Dau, H.A., et al.: The UCR time series classification archive (2018). https://arxiv.org/pdf/1810.07758.pdf
3. Gama, J., Zliobait, E.I., Bifet, A., Pechenizkiy, M., Bouchachia, A.: A survey on concept drift adaptation. ACM Comput. Surv. **1**, 1 (2013). Article 1
4. Lin, J., Khade, R., Li, Y.: Rotation-invariant similarity in time series using bag-of-patterns representation. J. Intell. Inf. Syst. **39**(2), 287–315 (2012). https://doi.org/10.1007/s10844-012-0196-5
5. Ueno, K., Xi, A., Keogh, E., Lee, D.J.: Anytime classification using the nearest neighbor algorithm with applications to stream mining. In: Proceedings of the ICDM 2006 (2006)
6. Ye, L., Keogh, E.: Time series shapelets: a new primitive for data mining. In: Proceedings of the KDD 2009, p. 947 (2009)
7. Zuo, J., Zeitouni, K., Taher, Y.: Exploring interpretable features for large time series with SE4TeC. In: Proceedings of the EDBT 2019, pp. 606–609 (2019)

---

[2] https://github.com/JingweiZuo/ISETS/tree/master/Spark_Cluster_Docker.

Industrial Event Log Analyzer - Self-service Data Mining for Domain Experts

Reuben Borrison[(✉)], Benjamin Klöpper, and Sunil Saini

ABB Corporate Research Center, Ladenburg, Germany
`reuben.borrison@de.abb.com`

Abstract. Industrial applications of machine learning rely heavily on deep domain knowledge that data scientist and machine learning expert usually do not have. Iterative and time-consuming communication between machine learning expert and domain expert are the consequence. In this demo, we introduce a semi-functional mock-up that demonstrates how a system can guide domain users through a machine learning process if the scope of problem and data type are narrowed done.

Keywords: Data mining tools · Domain experts · Industrial use case

1 Introduction

The idea to make machine learning or accessible for non-experts is not new. There is an increasing number of data mining or machine learning tools with graphical user interfaces (e.g. [2]). The users of these tools might not require strong programming skills (although they are often very useful) but a very good understanding of general concepts of data mining and machine learning and the available operators. The idea of automated machine learning and AutoML tool (e.g. [1] also address more the phase of model training and selection of hyper-parameter and are thus mainly tools for data scientist and do not help with preparing the data and transforming the data into a format suitable for machine learning algorithms. The challenges with machine learning for industrial application lies not mainly in programming and hyper-parameter tuning. For data types common in industrial problem settings like machine generated data signal data or event data, the data pre-processing and feature engineering are often more complicated, requiring sound programming skills and experience in data engineering and machine learning. Furthermore, industrial machine learning problems can seldom rely on labeled data and thus resort to unsupervised learning problems. The evaluation of the results again require deep understanding of the application domain and the data.

With the demo of the Industrial Event Log Analyzer we want to show that it is possible to provide a software system that enables domain experts without programming capabilities to prepare their data for machine learning algorithms

© Springer Nature Switzerland AG 2020
U. Brefeld et al. (Eds.): ECML PKDD 2019, LNAI 11908, pp. 794–798, 2020.
https://doi.org/10.1007/978-3-030-46133-1_54

by providing detailed and domain affine description of the algorithms and guiding them through the data preparation process. This becomes possible by restricting the scope of the tool to a specific type of data and matching class of specific algorithms.

2   Event Log Analyzer

This section introduces the event log analyzer. A semi-functional mock-up (functions implemented for specific user walkthroughs) and we plan to use to test the user experience of our machine learning self-service concept before developing a fully functional and scalable solution. The key requirements and concepts we want to test are: (1) algorithms developer specify the required input format of the data and (2) provide guidance on how data should be pre-processed to match the required format, (3) are able to relate the output of the machine learning model to the original data the domain expert provided, (4) can flexible add new pre-processing and algorithmic functionality without changes in the framework and especially the UI and finally (5) data scientist are easily capable to implement functionality for this framework.

2.1   Data Flow and Model

Data types are crucial to provide guidance to the domain expert what he can and should do with his data. For this reason, we decided to manage the data in Pandas Dataframes. Figure 1 illustrate the data flow through the application. First, a number of pre-processing steps are applied on the original Dataframe each creating a new Dataframe for further processing. A key requirement is that the pre-processing steps maintain the index of the original Dataframe. The might delete rows in the Dataframe but they do not merge rows or change the index of the rows. In this way, there exist a 1:1 mapping between the raw data and the prepared data frame in the algorithms target format. When the data is in the target format, the algorithm class can generate samples from the prepared Dataframe. It is the responsibility of the algorithm developer to provide a mapping between the index of the sample Dataframe and the index of the target Dataframe. By providing this mapping, the algorithm developer is free to define an n:n (in most cases 1:n) relationship between the rows in the prepared Dataframe and the sample Dataframe - one sample is composed from several rows prepared by the domain expert. Because the target Dataframe index matches the index of the original Dataframe, the samples can be linked to the original Data.

Fig. 1. Data flow

2.2 Software Architecture

Figure 2 show the major two interactions in the tool as sequence diagrams. The framework interacts with pre-processing classes to manipulate the Dataframe. The pre-processing class provides information if it is applicable, what manipulation it will perform and which parameter it requires. It also provides information how the Dataframe could be manipulated to be applicable. It uses the information about the Dataframes datatypes to provide this information The framework will use the parameters - encapsulated in JSON document along with options and help information - to render dynamically a UI for the user to provide the require input. The framework will call the pre-processors run method and receive a manipulated Dataframe. The interaction with the Algorithm class is very similar. The algorithm also uses the datatype information to provide help and hints how to manipulate the Dataframe to reach the target format required by the algorithm. The framework calls three methods implemented by the algorithm sample (produces the training and test samples and the mapping to the index of the input Dataframe), the train method, and the scoring method. Both pre-processor and algorithms need to be derived from an abstract class to be integrated into the framework. Regarding the algorithms, the developer is free to use the framework of his choice, as long as he manages the transformation of the Dataframe input into the required format of his framework of choice.

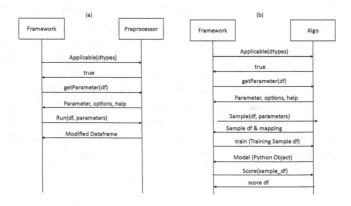

Fig. 2. Sequence diagrams (a) Pre-processor and (b) Algorithm

2.3   Demo Workflow

The tool provides domain expert with an interface to upload the data. Once the data is imported into the system, domain expert can select from a number of algorithms, based on the information provided. After selecting the algorithm, the pre-processing page is shown to the user (Fig. 3), where all the pre-processing options relevant for the selected algorithm are shown. Domain expert can conveniently choose and apply the pre-processing functions on the data. Once the data is prepared according the target format of the selected algorithm, it can be sent for processing by the algorithm. Once the algorithms returns the results, a validation page is shown to the user. The validation step helps building a confusion matrix based on domain expert feedback - particular useful in unsupervised learning problems. The user is required to give labels against the score given by the algorithm. Currently, this only helps building a confusion matrix, in the future active-learning [5] and semi-supervised learning [6] can be incorporated to improve the algorithm performance.

Fig. 3. Pre-processing page

In case of a new problem type Domain expert may ask the data scientist/algorithm developer to develop an algorithm and their pre-processing functions for a specific problem. Data scientists can develop the algorithm according to the specification of the tool and then send the code in a zipped format to the expert or upload the code through the interface provided to them.

3   Conclusion and Future Functionality

With the functional mock-up of the industrial log file we hope to be able to test if domain expert without knowledge about machine learning and data mining can be enabled to execute a machine learning workflow independently and avoid time-intensive interaction with data scientist. The idea is not to remove the interaction entirely, but help the domain expert to create a good base for discussion and fine-tuning by the data scientist. Once questions around the usability are successful answered, future work will deal with scalability of the system (leveraging for instance [4]), the integration of AutoML, Active Learning, semi-supervised learning, and crowd sourcing concepts for labeling and evaluation [3].

References

1. Feurer, M., Klein, A., Eggensperger, K., Springenberg, J., Blum, M., Hutter, F.: Efficient and robust automated machine learning. In: Advances in Neural Information Processing Systems 28, pp. 2962–2970. Curran Associates, Inc. (2015)
2. Hofmann, M., Klinkenberg, R.: RapidMiner: Data Mining Use Cases and Business Analytics Applications. CRC Press, Boca Raton (2013)
3. Karger, D.R., Oh, S., Shah, D.: Efficient crowdsourcing for multi-class labeling. ACM SIGMETRICS Perform. Eval. Rev. **41**(1), 81–92 (2013)
4. Rocklin, M.: Dask: parallel computation with blocked algorithms and task scheduling. In: Proceedings of the 14th Python in Science Conference (2015)
5. Sun, S.: A survey of multi-view machine learning. Neural Comput. Appl. **23**, 2031–2038 (2013). https://doi.org/10.1007/s00521-013-1362-6
6. Zhu, X., Goldberg, A.B.: Introduction to semi-supervised learning. Synth. Lect. Artif. Intell. Mach. Learn. **3**(1), 1–130 (2009)

Author Index

Printed in the United States
By Bookmasters